W. B. YEATS

A Classified Bibliography of Criticism

W. B. YEATS

A Classified Bibliography of Criticism

Second edition, revised and enlarged

K. P. S. JOCHUM

UNIVERSITY OF ILLINOIS PRESS
Urbana and Chicago

Manufactured in the United States of America
C 5 4 3 2 1

This book is printed on acid-free paper.

Library of Congress Cataloging-in-Publication Data

Jochum, K. P. S.
W. B. Yeats : a classified bibliography of criticism / K.P.S. Jochum.—2nd ed., rev. and enl.
p. cm.
Includes bibliographical references.
ISBN 0-252-01762-5 (alk. paper)
1. Yeats, W. B. (William Butler), 1865-1939—Criticism and interpretation—Bibliography. I. Title.
Z8982.J59 1990
[PR5906]
016.821'8—dc20

90-10981
CIP

For R.E.G.M.J.H.J. and A.J.,
the bibliographer's wife and daughter

Contents

Poetry costs money.
—*Joe Gargery*

Preface and Acknowledgments

This bibliography is the second revised edition of a book first published in 1978 under a somewhat different title. Apart from correcting mistakes, the second edition extends the coverage of material until 1986 and includes many items from 1987 and 1988. It also adds numerous items that should have been included in the first edition but had somehow escaped my notice. The year 1986 has a special significance. With it, one hundred years of Yeats criticism can be accounted for, the first recorded example being Katharine Tynan's enthusiastic review of *Mosada* in the *Irish Monthly* of March 1887 (see item G1).

One hundred years (and a little more) of Yeats criticism means 10,152 entries in this bibliography. The number of actual publications is considerably higher because many entries cover several items (a thesis that became a book, articles published prior to their collection in book form, reviews of books on Yeats). All in all I should think this book lists some 12,000 bits of Yeats criticism. My bibliography aims at completeness, not at critical selection.

There are other differences between the first and second editions. The additions to Allan Wade's *Bibliography of the Writings of W. B. Yeats* (formerly section AB) have been eliminated because a revised fourth edition, edited by Colin Smythe, is expected to be published soon. Sections CC, DC, and EC have been restructured. The four sections G, K, L, and M in my first edition ("Books by Yeats Containing Critical and Introductory Material" and studies of the Irish literary and dramatic revival) have been discarded; substantial discussions of Yeats, however, were retained and are now included in other sections, some of them in section EF on Yeats's theatrical activities (as distinct from play criticism).

These changes have necessitated a complete renumbering and some rearranging. The new classification is reflected in the contents. Entries are now numbered consecutively in each of the forty-seven sections; they are referred to in a letter and number combination (e.g., AC45, EE120) to avoid confusion with the first edition.

There are now seven instead of eight indexes; I have dropped the Index of Provenance and the Index of Asterisked Items, the latter identifying books that I thought particularly valuable. In fact, I have dispensed with the asterisks altogether. I have greatly expanded the subject index (from a former seven-and-a-half to sixteen-and-a-half pages) and I have added an Index of Chronology. Although I believe that a classified bibliography is a more valuable research tool, I felt that a chronological arrangement also has its merits. For this reason, index IG lists almost all entries in chronological order by year of publication; the exceptions being the entries in section HC (Musical Renderings), many of which are undated, and the reviews of books on Yeats.

In the interest of greater usefulness several important collections of Yeats criticism, such as the *Dolmen Press Yeats Centenary Papers* or *In Excited Reverie,* have been analyzed so that the individual articles appear in appropriate sections. I have also analyzed a number of important monographs and indexed all the substantial interpretations of individual texts (poems, plays, prose) that they contain. For explanations see the headnotes to sections DD, EE, FA, and FC.

As noted above, the bibliography aims at completeness; its scope is international. It includes all the relevant material contained in its predecessors (listed in section AB). The annual checklists contributed to *Yeats,* numbers 1-5, as well as those for 1986-87 and 1987-88 (to be published in numbers 6 and 7, respectively) have been incorporated in this bibliography. Of the 1988-89 listing (to be published in *Yeats,* number 8), only a small part found its way into this book. My cut-off date is 1988; there are no publications of 1989 or later. This means that I had to leave out the volumes of the new collected edition and many other publications that appeared as the result of the fiftieth anniversary of Yeats's death. I intend to contribute further checklists to *Yeats* and thereby continue my work on an annual basis for some time to come.

Omissions are possible in several areas and for a number of reasons. For some countries, notably France, Spain, and Italy but also Eastern European countries before 1945, there are no adequate bibliographies of articles in periodicals. My coverage of newspapers is not as thorough as I had wished. The Henderson, Holloway, and Horniman collections of press cuttings (listed in section AE) are invaluable but somewhat irritating. Important dates are frequently missing, illegible, or misleading. As a matter of fact, I do not think it necessary to trace every item in these collections because the energy put into the search often exceeds the actual value of the results. I have tried to locate at least one review of first performances of the plays, particularly in the Dublin papers. I have also included some but not all newspaper reviews of books by and about Yeats. I have cited at least one report or summary of important Yeats lectures or speeches, particularly of those mentioned by Karin Strand (BA18) and Donald T. Torchiana (CA118). Other possible omissions are noted in the headnotes to the respective sections.

There are, however, some deliberate omissions. Routine articles in encyclopedias are not included, whereas more extended discussions are. The dividing line here and elsewhere is of course hard to draw. Perfunctory treatments in histories of literature are not mentioned; the same applies to anthologies. I have excluded short reviews, such as the notices in *Library Journal* and *Kirkus*. I have cited only those reviews of books by and on Yeats that I have seen and that are substantially concerned with Yeats. Background material with little or no references to Yeats has been left out. With a few exceptions, no M.A. and B.A. theses have been listed. I include some Arabic, Japanese, and Korean items, but I have made no systematic search in these and other non-European languages. Most of the Japanese Yeats criticism published until 1965 is listed in Shotaro Oshima's *W. B. Yeats and Japan* (CD139). I saw no point in copying Professor Oshima's list, so I restricted myself to include only those items that are written in English and were available to me. I know that a considerable amount of Yeats studies has been published in Japan (also in Korea), but because of the general inaccessibility of these publications and my inability to read them I will have to leave it to somebody else to collect and describe them.

To save space, I have tried to avoid multiple listings as much as possible. Theses and articles that were worked into or became part of books are referred to in the book entry only. In book publications I have cited the latest edition or reprint that I have seen; the date of the first edition is added in square brackets. Different publishers for American or British or Irish editions of the same book are not noted unless the book was issued under different titles. I am aware of the possibility that I may not have traced several articles and reviews (particularly those published anonymously) to their final book publications.

Doctoral theses written at universities in Great Britain, Ireland, the United States, Canada, Germany, Austria, Switzerland, and France are included. They are listed in the sections to which they belong, not separately.

Access to the material is provided through the bibliography's classification scheme, the cross-references appended to most sections, and the indexes, especially the subject index. In the four major parts, B (Biographies), C (The Works), D (The Poetry), and E (The Plays), monographs exclusively on Yeats and of a general nature are listed in sections BA, CA, DA, and EA. General articles in books and periodicals follow next in sections BB, CB, DB, and EB. In parts C, D, and E more specialized studies, including books exclusively on Yeats, will be found in sections CC, DC, and EC (Themes and Types). Readers looking for individual works are advised to check sections DD (Single Poems), EE (Single Plays), FA (Prose Works), and FC (studies of *Per Amica Silentia Lunae* and *A Vision*). I trust that the contents and the indexes will explain themselves sufficiently to direct the reader to the proper material, as will the headnotes prefixed to several sections.

Many items are annotated. Annotations indicate, as a rule, the contents, main argument, subject(s), or approach of the item concerned (often in form of an appropriate quotation). The note (*see index*) refers to the index of that particular book. Sometimes I have taken the liberty to make value judgments. I do not annotate items with self-explanatory titles; publications of a general, introductory, or survey character; or short notes. Because of the sheer mass of the material handled in this bibliography, a little patience in using it may be necessary.

Almost all the items listed in this book were inspected personally; exceptions are marked °. In multiple-title entries the sign precedes that part of the entry that I have not seen. Books are cited as follows:

AUTHOR: *Title.* Place: Publisher, Date [Date of first publication]. Pages. (Series. No.).

Theses appear thus:

AUTHOR: "Title," Degree, University, Date. Pages. (Abstract).

Articles appear thus:

AUTHOR: "Title," *Periodical,* Volume or Year: Issue (Date), Pages. (Most daily and weekly papers are cited by date and pages only. For places of publication see index IF.)

Certain periodicals are quoted by abbreviations. They are mostly those used by the MLA and are also explained in index IF; generally, Journal, Quarterly, Review, and University appear as J, Q, R, and U. UP stands for University Press.

Three primary texts are cited by short titles throughout, namely *The Collected Letters* (see BA22), *The Letters* (BA21), and *Uncollected Prose* (FA35). Wade or W stands for Allan Wade's *Bibliography of the Writings of W. B. Yeats,* third edition of 1968 (AA15).

Needless to say I have used the Roman alphabet; but it should be noted that umlauts ä, ö, and ü are given as if spelt ae, oe, and ue when the word or name is German, and a, o, and u in all other languages. German ß is printed as ss. Several diacritical signs had to be inserted by hand because my word processor could not handle them. Cyrillic characters are transliterated according to the Library of Congress system, and all other non-Roman characters according to the system used in my sources. Mac, Mc, and M' are uniformly treated as Mac.

I have no uniform policy in the handling of pseudonyms and gaelicized names, but I try to be consistent with respect to individuals. Thus Frank O'Connor, John Eglinton, and Andrew E. Malone appear under these names rather than under Michael O'Donovan, William Kirkpatrick Magee, and Lawrence P. Byrne, whereas AE (or A. E. or Y. O.) is always listed under Russell. I have retained the maiden names of Maud Gonne and Katharine Tynan; Ford Madox Hueffer appears under Ford; there are separate entries, however, for that unique phenomenon Fiona Macleod / William Sharp. A reader in doubt about where to look for a certain author is referred to the index of names (index IA).

Anonymous books or books without an apparent editor are listed under the title, unless an author or editor could be ascertained from reliable sources. Anonymous articles in periodicals are listed under Anon., unless an author could be identified (generally from reprints, published catalogs, or other printed references). In three cases I have had access to marked copies. The *Athenaeum* file, now in the Library of the City University of London, identifies some but not all authors; use of the file was made possible through the kind permission of M. M. Hancock, Sub-librarian of the City University. The *Spectator* file was checked for me by its librarian, Charles Seaton, who also gave me permission to use the information; again, not all the authors have been identified. I have also been able to see the marked copies of the *Times Literary Supplement* in the archives of Times Newspapers (the file is, however, not quite complete); the authors are identified with the kind permission of the authors themselves and Jeremy Treglown, editor, and Alan Hollinghurst, deputy editor of the *TLS*. I would also like to thank Anne Dickson of News International for helping me with the identifications.

Some of the material in this bibliography has had previous publication. For permission to use and reprint the entries in the checklists contained in *Yeats: An Annual of Critical and Textual Studies,* volumes 1-3, I would like to thank the publisher, Cornell University Press, and the editor, Richard J. Finneran. Material from the checklists contained in volumes 4 and 5 of this annual is reprinted by permission of UMI Research Press, Ann Arbor, Michigan. Material from the checklists in volumes 6-8 is reprinted by permission of the University of Michigan Press. I would also like to thank Macmillan Press and Warwick Gould for permission to use material published in *Yeats Annual*.

Although this bibliography is essentially the product of one man's labors, from collecting to printing the camera-ready copy, the final result would be much poorer without the help of many individuals and institutions. I am particularly grateful to George Bornstein, the late Alan M. Cohn, Richard J. Finneran, John P. Frayne, Warwick Gould, John S. Kelly, and Colin Smythe for their ready support. For various kindnesses I would like to thank James Lovic Allen, Brian Arkins, Csilla Bertha, Birgit Bramsbäck, David Burnett, Juliet Clutton-Brock, Seamus Deane, Karin Dolling, Denis Donoghue, Eleonore Engelhardt, Willi Erzgräber, Peter Green, Jane Grigson, Diana Hobby, Graham Hough, Werner Huber, A. Norman Jeffares, B. J. Kirkpatrick, Sebastian Köppl, Yuri V. Kovalev, Barbara Krettek, Edward Lense, Zofia Lomnicka, Colin McDowell, Derwent May, Bruce D. Morris, Charles Osborne, Gerd Schmidt, Ronald Schuchard, John and Jean Smith, Frauke Vrba, Stanley Weintraub, Hugh Witemeyer, and, of course, S. A. L.

Many libraries and librarians have been extraordinarily helpful in answering my queries or granting me reader's privileges. Lack of space forbids mentioning them all; nevertheless a special note of thanks is due to the University Libraries in Bamberg, Freiburg, and Göttingen, as well as to the British Library, the University of London Library, the National Library of Ireland, Trinity College Library in Dublin, the Library of Congress, the New York Public Library, the Yeats Archives at SUNY, Stony Brook, and the University of Illinois Library.

I would also like to thank the University of Bamberg for allocating research funds and the German Academic Exchange Service (DAAD) for inviting me to some of its conferences in Great Britain, Ireland, and the United States, thus enabling me to visit important research libraries.

Finally, I want to tell my long-suffering office staff and my former and present student assistants, especially Ingeborg Peñalba, Elisabeth Burkhard, Susanne Heindel, Sibylle Just, Barbara Klein, Ursula Lindner, Susanne Mannmeusel, Barbara Spangel, and Elke Walthes that, thanks to their dedicated work, the book is really and truly finished.

W. B. YEATS

A Classified Bibliography of Criticism

A BIBLIOGRAPHIES, CATALOGS, AND CONCORDANCES

AA Bibliographies of Yeats's Writings

1. ABBOTT, CRAIG S.: "The Case of Sharmel Iris," *PBSA*, 77:1 (First Quarter 1983), 15-34.
Yeats's preface to Iris's *Bread Out of Stone* (Wade 288A) is probably spurious.

2. ANON.: "Bibliographies of Modern Authors: William Butler Yeats," *LMerc*, 2:8 (June 1920), 220-21.

3. BALLIET, CONRAD A.: "Yeats Materials Needed," *Library J*, 111:10 (1 June 1986), 14.
For a projected guide to the manuscripts of Yeats.

4. JOCHUM, K. P. S.: "Additions to the Yeats Bibliography," *BB*, 28:4 (Oct-Dec 1971), 129-35.
Additions to Wade, 3rd edition; will be included in the 4th edition.

5. Ó HAODHA, MICHEÁL: "Unrecorded Yeats Contributions to Periodicals," *IrB*, 2:3/4 (Autumn 1963), 129.
Will be included in Wade, 4th edition.

6. ———: "When Was Yeats First Published?" *IrT*, 5 June 1965, 10.
A sonnet, "I saw a shepherd youth. . . ," signed "Y.," published in *Hibernia*, 1 April 1882, is presumed to be by Yeats.

7. ———: "When Was Yeats First Published?" *Eire*, 2:2 (Summer 1967), 67-71.
Eleven poems, published in *Hibernia* between Apr 1882 and June 1883 over the initial "Y," may have been written by Yeats. See Wade, 4th edition.

8. O'HEGARTY, P. S.: "Notes on the Bibliography of W. B. Yeats," *DM*, 14:4 (Oct-Dec 1939), 61-65; 15:1 (Jan-Mar 1940), 37-42.

9. ROTH, WILLIAM MATSON: *A Catalogue of English and American First Editions of William Butler Yeats*. Prepared for an exhibition of his works held in the Yale University Library beginning May 15, 1939. New Haven, 1939. 104 pp.

10. SAUL, GEORGE BRANDON: *Prolegomena to the Study of Yeats's Poems*. Philadelphia: U of Pennsylvania Press, 1957. 196 pp.
Reprinted °NY: Octagon Books, 1971. The book "purports to give an accurate commentary on the divisions of the relatively definitive . . . *Collected Poems* . . . ; and for individual poems (1) a full record of publication and of title changes . . . , (2) a statement of recorded dates and other significant facts of composition, and (3) an attempted resolution of else unclarified obscurities . . . as well as indication of parallel or closely related passages and recording of available important references and glosses" (p. 7). The book is now largely out of date. See also AA12 and CC202.
Reviews:
- Denis Donoghue, *Studies*, 48:[ ] (Spring 1959), 106-8.
- Thomas Parkinson: "The Respect of Monuments," *SR*, 68:1 (Jan-Mar 1960), 143-49.

- T. J. B. Spencer, *MLR*, 53:4 (Oct 1958), 626-27.
- Peter Ure, *RES*, 11:41 (Feb 1960), 113-14.

11. ———: *Prolegomena to the Study of Yeats's Plays*. Philadelphia: U of Pennsylvania Press, 1958. 106 pp.

Reprinted °NY: Octagon Books, 1971. Organized along the lines of the preceding item; see also AA12 and CC202.

Reviews:
- William C. Burto, *ETJ*, 12:3 (Oct 1960), 233-34.
- Austin Clarke: "Mood of Disillusion," *IrT*, 27&28 Mar 1959, 6.
- [J. M. Hone]: "Yeats's Drama," *TLS*, 24 Apr 1959, 239.
- Thomas Parkinson: "The Respect of Monuments," *SR*, 68:1 (Jan-Mar 1960), 143-49.

12. ———: "W. B. Yeats: Corrigenda," *N&Q*, os 205 / ns 7:8 (Aug 1960), 302-3.

Corrections in the two preceding items.

13. SMYTHE, COLIN: "Allan Wade's *Bibliography of the Writings of W. B. Yeats:* Some *Errata* and *Addenda*," *Long Room*, 8 (Autumn/Winter 1973), 41-42.

Will be incorporated in the 4th edition.

14. SYMONS, ALPHONSE JAMES ALBERT: *A Bibliography of the First Editions of Books by William Butler Yeats*. London: First Edition Club, 1924. viii, 46 pp.

Review: [Richard Jennings], *TLS*, 28 Aug 1924, 526.

15. WADE, ALLAN: *A Bibliography of the Writings of W. B. Yeats*. 3rd edition, revised and edited by Russell K. Alspach. London: Hart-Davis, 1968 [1951]. 514 pp. (Soho Bibliographies. 1.)

Based on a compilation made in 1908 (see HC334). Incorporates Alspach's "Additions to Allan Wade's Bibliography of W. B. Yeats," *IrB*, 2:3/4 (Autumn 1963), 91-114. Includes "The Cuala Press, First Called the Dun Emer Press," 451-57 (a list of publications); "Some Books about Yeats and His Work," 458-66.

George Whalley: "Yeats and Broadcasting," 467-77, an annotated list of broadcasts in which Yeats participated and of some broadcasts concerning Yeats made between 1939 and 1957; this has been updated by Jeremy Silver (BB222-223).

Reviews:
- Anon., *BC*, 1:1 (Spring 1952), 62-63.
- John Hayward, *Library*, series 5 / 7:1 (Mar 1952), 66-68.
- T. R. Henn: "Towards the Study of Yeats," *NSt*, 12 Jan 1952, 43.
- [J. M. Hone]: "Yeats in Youth and Maturity," *TLS*, 7 Mar 1958, 126.
- W. P. M., *DM*, 27:2 (Apr-June 1952), 38-40.
- Donagh MacDonagh: "Two Hundred Books by W. B. Yeats," *IrP*, 8 Jan 1952, 6.
- Gerald D. McDonald, *PBSA*, 52:4 (1958), 322-26.
- [P. S. O'Hegarty]: "The Writings of W. B. Yeats," *TLS*, 25 Jan 1952, 84. Correspondence by Marion Witt, 11 Apr 1952, 251.
- Horace Reynolds: "'To Follow Yeats down All the Diverse Paths,'" *CSM*, 12 June 1952, 13.

See also AB8, CA57, 97, CC210, CD139, EE130, FA21, HC334.

AB Bibliographies of Yeats Criticism

1. CROSS, KENNETH GUSTAV WALTER, and RONALD T. DUNLOP: *A Bibliography of Yeats Criticism, 1887-1965*. With a foreword by A. Norman Jeffares. London: Macmillan, 1971. xxvi, 341 pp.

See also George Monteiro: "Addenda to Cross and Dunlop's *Yeats Criticism 1887-1965*," *PBSA*, 70:2 (Apr-June 1976), 278; lists criticism published in the *Ethical Record*.

Reviews:

- Staffan Bergsten, *Samlaren*, 93 (1972), 280.
- John Bryson: "Yeatsiana," *Books and Bookmen*, 17:199 (Apr 1972), 24.
- [Austin Clarke]: "Yeats as an Adolescent Dreamer," *TLS*, 17 Mar 1972, 311.
- Richard J. Finneran: "Progress Report on the Yeats Industry," *JML*, 3:1 (Feb 1973), 129-33.
- Edwin S. Gleaves, *ARBA*, 4 (1973), 522.
- John Kelly: "Yeats Industry Booming," *THES*, 21 Jan 1972, 17.
- Robert Kent, *Eire*, 7:4 (Winter 1972), 145-46.

2. GERSTENBERGER, DONNA: "Yeats and the Theater: A Selected Bibliography," *MD*, 6:1 (Summer 1963), 64-71.

3. GOULD, WARWICK, and OLYMPIA SITWELL: "'Gasping on the Strand': A Yeats Bibliography, 1981-1983," *YeA*, 3 (1985), 304-23.

4. ———: "A Recent Yeats Bibliography, 1983-84," *YeA*, 4 (1986), 323-35.

5. GOULD, WARWICK: "A Recent Yeats Bibliography, 1984-85," *YeA*, 5 (1987), 320-40.

6. GUHA, NARESH: "W. B. Yeats and Japan (A Select Bibliography)," *JJCL*, 18-19 (1980-81), 125-29.

Very select.

7. JOCHUM, K. P. S.: *W. B. Yeats's Plays: An Annotated Checklist of Criticism*. Saarbrücken: Anglistisches Institut der Universität des Saarlandes, 1966. 180 pp.

8. ———: *W. B. Yeats: A Classified Bibliography of Criticism Including Additions to Allan Wade's "Bibliography of the Writings of W. B. Yeats" and a Section on the Irish Literary and Dramatic Revival*. Urbana: U of Illinois Press, 1978. xiv, 802 pp.

The first edition of the present bibliography; incorporates AA4.

Reviews:

- James Lovic Allen, *IUR*, 8:2 (Autumn 1978), 265-66.
- Richard J. Finneran: "W. B. Yeats: Some Recent Bibliographical and Editorial Work," *Review*, 1 (1979), 233-48.
- René Fréchet, *EA*, 32:4 (Oct-Dec 1979), 492-93.
- Warwick Gould: "Fighting the Waves," *Antiquarian Book Monthly R*, 5:8 (Aug 1978), 341-42.
- Jörg Hoesch, *Zeitschrift für Bibliothekswesen und Bibliographie*, 26:1 (Jan-Feb 1979), 32-35.
- R[obert] H[ogan], *JIL*, 7:2 (May 1978), 187.
- John Kelly, *N&Q*, os 224 / ns 26:6 (Dec 1979), 599.
- Dorothy E. Litt, *ARBA*, 10 (1979), 619-20.
- F. S. L. Lyons: "The Yeats Mountain," *TLS*, 6 Oct 1978, 1114.
- Wesley McCann, *Irish Booklore*, 4:2 (1980), 157-59.
- Andrew Parkin, *CJIS*, 5:1 (June 1979), 127-29.

- Marjorie G. Perloff, *YES,* 11 (1981), 342-43.
- Patrick Rafroidi, *EI,* 3 (Dec 1978), 114-17.
- Götz Schmitz, *Anglia,* 101:1/2 (1983), 286-88.

9. ———: "A Yeats Bibliography for 1981," *Yeats,* 1 (1983), 155-73.

10. ———: "A Yeats Bibliography for 1982," *Yeats,* 2 (1984), 233-57.

11. ———: "A Yeats Bibliography for 1983," *Yeats,* 3 (1985), 175-205.

12. ———: "A Yeats Bibliography for 1984," *Yeats,* 4 (1986), 143-76.

13. ———: "A Yeats Bibliography for 1985/1986," *Yeats,* 5 (1987), 151-97.

To be continued in future issues.

14. STOLL, JOHN E. *The Great Deluge: A Yeats Bibliography*. Troy, N.Y.: Whitston, 1971. vii, 100 pp.

A checklist of criticism, containing about a thousand items. No index, no annotations, no cross references, riddled with errors and mistakes. Reviewed by Richard J. Finneran: "Progress Report on the Yeats Industry," *JML,* 3:1 (Feb 1973), 129-33.

See also CA32, 36, 71, 97, 146, 163-70, CC210, 228, CD24, 139, DD67, 677, EC1.

AC Bibliographies Concerning Yeats in Part and Bibliographies of Anglo-Irish Literature

The listing in this section is highly selective. I do not include the standard bibliographies relevant to English literature in general, such as the *MLA Bibliography* or the *Annual Bibliography of English Language and Literature*.

1. 'ABDUL-HAI, MUḤAMMAD: "A Bibliography of Arabic Translations of English and American Poetry (1830-1970)," *J of Arabic Literature,* 7 (1976), 120-50.

See pp. 147, 150.

2. ADELMAN, IRVING, and RITA DWORKIN: *Modern Drama: A Checklist of Critical Literature on 20th Century Plays*. Metuchen: Scarecrow Press, 1967. 370 pp.

Selective listing of titles in English; see pp. 332-40.

3. ALEXANDER, HARRIET SEMMES: *American and British Poetry: A Guide to Criticism 1925-1978*. Athens, Ohio: Swallow Press, 1984. xii, 486 pp.

See pp. 459-72 for about 700 items of English-language criticism of individual poems by Yeats.

4. ALTIERI, CHARLES F.: *Modern Poetry*. Arlington Heights, Ill.: AHM Publishing Corporation, 1979. xi, 129 pp. (Goldentree Bibliographies.)

"William Butler Yeats," 110-15; 95 items.

5. AMERICAN COMMITTEE FOR IRISH STUDIES: *ACIS Newsletter*. Various places of publication, 1965-1970; 1 (1971)--. Current; numbering irregular.

Contains news, notes, checklists, and reviews.

6. ANDERSON, DAVID L., GEORGIA S. MAAS, and DIANE-MARIE SAVOYE: *Symbolism: A Bibliography of Symbolism as an International and Multi-Disciplinary Movement*. NY: New York UP, 1975. xxiii, 160 pp.
See pp. 131-34 (95 entries).

7. AYLING, RONALD, and MICHAEL J. DURKAN: *Sean O'Casey: A Bibliography*. London: Macmillan, 1978. xxiv, 411 pp.

8. BAKER, BLANCH MERRITT: *Theatre and Allied Arts: A Guide to Books Dealing with the History, Criticism, and Technic of the Drama and Theatre and Related Arts and Crafts*. NY: Wilson, 1952. xiv, 536 pp.
See pp. 118-20.

9. BREED, PAUL F., and FLORENCE M. SNIDERMAN: *Dramatic Criticism Index: A Bibliography of Commentaries on Playwrights from Ibsen to the Avant-Garde*. Detroit: Gale Research Company, 1972. ix, 1022 pp.
See pp. 762-76; lists only criticism in English and omits many standard monographs.

10. BROWN, CHRISTOPHER C., and WILLIAM B. THESING: *English Prose and Criticism, 1900-1950: A Guide to Information Sources*. Detroit: Gale, 1983. xxi, 553 pp. (American Literature, English Literature, and World Literatures in English: An Information Guide Series. 42.)
"W. B. Yeats (1865-1939)," 488-506; about 90 items of criticism of his non-fictional prose.

11. BROWN, STEPHEN JAMES (ed): *A Guide to Books on Ireland*. Part 1: Prose literature, poetry, music, and plays. Dublin: Hodges Figgis / London: Longmans Green, 1912. xviii, 371 pp.
No more published; see index.

12. BUSHRUI, SUHAIL BADI (ed): *IASAIL: International Association for the Study of Anglo-Irish Literature: Fourth Triennial Conference Maynooth, Ireland, July 9-13, 1979. Anglo-Irish Literature in Lebanon and the Arab World: Combined Third and Fourth Triennial Reports 1973-76 and 1976-79*. Beirut: Librairie du Liban, [1979]. 50 unnumbered leaves.
Contains abstracts of theses, a bibliography of actual and forthcoming publications, extracts from Mary Haskell's journal (see BG92), and a pencil drawing of Yeats by Kahlil Gibran, made in Oct 1911.

13. CARPENTER, CHARLES A.: *Modern British Drama*. Arlington Heights, Ill.: AHM Publishing Company, 1979. x, 120 pp. (Goldentree Bibliographies.)
See pp. 20-24 and 99-106 (about 170 items).

14. ———: *Modern Drama Scholarship and Criticism 1966-1980: An International Bibliography*. Toronto: U of Toronto Press, 1986. xxxv, 587 pp.
Yeats, pp. 147-50 (ca. 250 items); continued in *Modern Drama*.

15. CARTY, JAMES: *Bibliography of Irish History, 1912-1921*. Dublin: Stationery Office for Department of Education, 1936. xxxix, 177 pp.

16. ———: *Bibliography of Irish History, 1870-1911*. Dublin: Stationery Office, 1940. xviii, 319 pp.

17. CHICOREL, MARIETTA (ed): *Chicorel Index to Poetry in Anthologies and Collections: Retrospective*. NY: Chicorel, 1975. (Chicorel In-

dex Series. 6. 6A. 6B. 6C.)
See 6C:1819-26.

18. CLINE, GLORIA STARK, and JEFFREY A. BAKER: *An Index to Criticisms of British and American Poetry*. Metuchen: Scarecrow Press, 1972. x, 307 pp.
See pp. 145-48; highly selective.

19. COLEMAN, ARTHUR, and GARY R. TYLER: *Drama Criticism*. Volume 1: A checklist of interpretation since 1940 of English and American plays. Denver: Swallow, 1966. 457 pp.
See pp. 232-35; selective.

20. CONNOR, JOHN M., and BILLIE M. CONNOR: *Ottemiller's Index to Plays in Collections: An Author and Title Index to Plays Appearing in Collections Published between 1900 and Early 1975*. Sixth edition, revised and enlarged. Metuchen: Scarecrow Press, 1976. xiii, 523 pp.
See p. 202.

21. CORSE, LARRY B., and SANDRA CORSE: *Articles on American and British Literature: An Index to Selected Periodicals, 1950-1977*. Chicago: Swallow Press / Ohio UP, 1981. xii, 413 pp.
See pp. 407-10; about 170 items.

22. *Cumulated Dramatic Index 1909-1949*. A cumulation of the F. W. Faxon Company's *Dramatic Index* [etc.]. Boston: Hall, 1965. 2 vols.

23. *Cumulated Magazine Subject Index 1907-1949*. Boston: Hall, 1964. 2 vols.

24. CUTLER, BRADLEY DWYANE, and VILLA STILES: *Modern British Authors: Their First Editions*. NY: Greenberg, 1930. xi, 171 pp.
"William Butler Yeats," 164-67.

25. DAVIES, ALISTAIR: *An Annotated Critical Bibliography of Modernism*. Brighton: Harvester Press / Totowa, N.J.: Barnes & Noble, 1982. xiii, 261 pp. (Harvester Annotated Critical Bibliographies. 1.)
"William Butler Yeats," 69-111 (about 100 entries); see also the indexes for further references.

26. DEALE, EDGAR MARTIN: *A Catalogue of Contemporary Irish Composers*. Second edition. Dublin: Music Association of Ireland, 1973. 108 pp.
See headnote to section HC.

27. DEMING, ROBERT H.: *A Bibliography of James Joyce Studies*. Second edition, revised and enlarged. Boston: Hall, 1977. xii, 264 pp.
Continued by Alan M. Cohn in *James Joyce Quarterly*.

28. DOWLING, LINDA C.: *Aestheticism and Decadence: A Selective Annotated Bibliography*. NY: Garland, 1977. xxviii, 140 pp.
Yeats is mentioned in the "Introduction," vii-xxv. For bibliographical references see the index (not always reliable).

29. DYSON, ANTHONY EDWARD (ed): *English Poetry: Select Bibliographical Guides*. London: Oxford UP, 1971. xi, 378 pp.
Jon Stallworthy: "Yeats," 345-59; a rather selective review of research and list of 89 entries.

30. EAGER, ALAN ROBERT: *A Guide to Irish Bibliographical Material: A Bibliography of Irish Bibliographies and Sources of Information*. Second revised and enlarged edition. Westport, Ct.: Greenwood Press, 1980 [1964]. xv, 502 pp.

31. EDWARDS, JOHN: *The Irish Language: An Annotated Bibliography of Sociolinguistic Publications 1772-1982*. NY: Garland, 1983. xviii, 274 pp. (Garland Reference Library of the Humanities. 300.)
Several references to Yeats (see index).

32. ÉTUDES IRLANDAISES: "The Year's Work in Anglo-Irish Literature," *EI*, 3 (Nov 1974), 41-56.
A select bibliography, continued in subsequent issues; compiled by Patrick Rafroidi (1974-82) and Marie-Jocelyne Deboulonne (since 1983).

33. FABIAN, BERNHARD: *Von Chaucer bis Pinter: Ausgewählte Autorenbibliographien zur englischen Literatur*. Königstein: Athenäum, 1980. x, 206 pp. (Athenäum Taschenbücher. 2154.)
"William Butler Yeats (1865-1939)," 189-94.

34. FRENCH, FRANCES-JANE: *The Abbey Theatre Series of Plays: A Bibliography*. Dublin: Dolmen Press, 1969. 53 pp.

35. GOETHE INSTITUTE DUBLIN: *German Studies in Anglo-Irish Literature 1972-1982*. An exhibition presented by the Goethe Institute Dublin in association with the National Library 1983. With a bibliographical checklist by Heinz Kosok. [Dublin: Goethe Institute, 1983]. 39 pp.

36. GOOCH, BRYAN N. S., and DAVID S. THATCHER: *Musical Settings of Late Victorian and Modern British Literature: A Catalogue*. NY: Garland, 1976. xxv, 1112 pp. (Garland Reference Library of the Humanities. 31.)
See pp. 831-74 (367 items) and headnote to section HC.

37. GROVE, SIR GEORGE: *Grove's Dictionary of Music and Musicians*. Fifth edition, edited by Eric Blom. London: Macmillan, 1954-61. 10 vols.
See 9:381 and headnote to section HC. N.B.: There is no Yeats entry in the *New Grove Dictionary of Music and Musicians* (1980).

38. HARMON, MAURICE: *Modern Irish Literature 1800-1967: A Reader's Guide*. Dublin: Dolmen Press, 1967. 71 pp.

39. ———: *Select Bibliography for the Study of Anglo-Irish Literature and Its Backgrounds: An Irish Studies Handbook*. Portmarnock: Wolfhound Press, 1977. 187 pp.

40. HAYES, RICHARD JAMES (ed): *Manuscript Sources for the History of Irish Civilization*. Boston: Hall, 1965. 11 vols.
See 4:926-29. First supplement 1965-1975, compiled in the National Library of Ireland. Boston: Hall, 1979. 3 vols. (see 1:795-98).

41. ———: *Sources for the History of Irish Civilization: Articles in Irish Periodicals*. Boston: Hall, 1970. 9 vols.
Vols. 1-5: Persons; vols. 6-8: Subjects; vol. 9: Places and Dates.

42. HOFFMAN, HERBERT H., and RITA LUDWIG HOFFMAN (comps): *International Index to Recorded Poetry*. NY: Wilson, 1983. xlvi, 529 pp.

See pp. 257-59 for recordings of Yeats's poetry.

43. HOFFMAN, HERBERT H. (comp): *Recorded Plays: Indexes to Dramatists, Plays, and Actors*. Chicago: American Library Association, 1985. ix, 141 pp.
See pp. 87-88 for a list of recorded Yeats plays.

44. HOWARD, PATSY C.: *Theses in English Literature, 1894-1970*. Ann Arbor: Pierian Press, 1973. xix, 387 pp.
Lists only M.A. and B.A. theses; on Yeats, nos. 8939-9000 (incomplete, authors A-N only).

45. IASAIL (INTERNATIONAL ASSOCIATION FOR THE STUDY OF ANGLO-IRISH LITERATURE): *IASAIL Newsletter*. Dublin, etc., 1971--.
Began publication with no. 1 (Spring/Summer 1971), current. Contains checklists of recent publications and news and notes.

46. ———: "Bibliography Bulletin," *IUR*, 2:1 (Spring 1972), 79-110.
Selective list of publications in various countries through 1970; continued in subsequent issues of *IUR*.

47. JUCHHOFF, RUDOLF, and HILDEGARD FÖHL: *Sammelkatalog der biographischen und literarkritischen Werke zu englischen Schriftstellern des 19. und 20. Jahrhunderts (1830-1958): Verzeichnis der Bestände in deutschen Bibliotheken*. Krefeld: Scherpe, [1959]. 272 pp.
See pp. 267-72; lists books and theses and analyzes collections.

48. KAIN, RICHARD M.: "The Irish Collection: A Personal Account," *Library R* [U of Louisville], 31 (May 1981), 2-48.

49. KERSNOWSKI, FRANK L., C. W. SPINKS, and LAIRD LOOMIS: *A Bibliography of Modern Irish Literature*. San Antonio: Trinity UP, 1976. xv, 157 pp.
See pp. 145-56 (primary and secondary sources, unsatisfactory).

50. KOCZTUR, GIZELLA: *Irish Literature in Hungarian Translation*. A bibliography compiled and published for the Golden Jubilee Congress of International P.E.N. to be held in Dublin in September 1971. Budapest: Hungarian PEN Club, 1971. 65 pp.
See pp. 44-64.

51. KOPPER, EDWARD A.: *John Millington Synge: A Reference Guide*. Boston: Hall, 1979. xxix, 199 pp.

52. KOVALEV, I͡URI VITALEVICH, and ANNA FUKSON: *Current Soviet Bibliography of Studies in Anglo-Irish Literature, 1972-1975*. [Dublin: U of Dublin, Department of Russian, 1981]. 20 pp.

53. KRAWITZ, HENRY: *A Post-Symbolist Bibliography*. Metuchen: Scarecrow Press, 1973. 284 pp.
"Yeats," 234-48. See also "Comparative Studies," 51-95 (not indexed).

54. KUNTZ, JOSEPH MARSHALL, and NANCY CONRAD MARTINEZ: *Poetry Explication: A Checklist of Interpretation since 1925 of British and American Poems Past and Present*. Boston: Hall, 1980 [1950]. xi, 570 pp.
"Yeats," 527-51.

54a. LANGENFELD, ROBERT: *George Moore: An Annotated Secondary*

Bibliography of Writings about Him. NY: AMS Press, 1987. xii, 531 pp. (AMS Studies in Modern Literature. 13.)

55. LEVITT, PAUL M.: *John Millington Synge: A Bibliography of Published Criticism*. Dublin: Irish UP, 1974. ix, 224 pp.

56. MCKENNA, BRIAN: *Irish Literature, 1800-1875: A Guide to Information Sources*. Detroit: Gale, 1978. xvii, 388 pp. (American Literature, English Literature, and World Literatures in English: Information Guide Series. 13.)

57. MCNAMEE, LAWRENCE F.: *Dissertations in English and American Literature: Theses Accepted by American, British and German Universities, 1865-1964*. NY: Bowker, 1968. xi, 1124 pp.

Supplement one, 1964-1968. 1969. x, 450 pp. Supplement two, 1969-1973. 1974. ix, 690 pp.

58. MANLY, JOHN MATTHEWS, and EDITH RICKERT: *Contemporary British Literature: A Critical Survey and 232 Author-Bibliographies*. Revised by Fred B. Millett. NY: Harcourt Brace, 1935 [1921]. xi, 556 pp.

See pp. 518-22. The 1928 edition contains a list of periodical articles on Yeats (p. 318; omitted from the 1935 edition).

59. MIKHAIL, EDWARD HALIM: *Dissertations on Anglo-Irish Drama: A Bibliography of Studies, 1870-1970*. London: Macmillan, 1973. x, 73 pp.

Contains a number of printing mistakes in the Yeats section. Not annotated, incomplete.

60. ———: *J. M. Synge: A Bibliography of Criticism*. Foreword by Robin Skelton. London: Macmillan, 1975. xiii, 214 pp.

Completeness attempted until 1971.

61. ———: *English Drama, 1900-1950: A Guide to Information Sources*. Detroit: Gale, 1977. xiii, 328 pp. (American Literature, English Literature, and World Literatures in English: Information Guide Series. 11.)

See index.

62. ———: *A Research Guide to Modern Irish Dramatists*. Troy, N.Y.: Whitston, 1979. xi, 104 pp.

See pp. 89-93 (35 items only).

63. ———: *An Annotated Bibliography of Modern Anglo-Irish Drama*. Troy, N.Y.: Whitston, 1981. ix, 300 pp.

An enlarged version of *A Bibliography of Modern Irish Drama, 1899-1970* (1972). Not exhaustive; the annotations are often less than helpful.

64. ———: *Lady Gregory: An Annotated Bibliography of Criticism*. Troy, N.Y.: Whitston, 1982. xi, 258 pp.

65. ———: *Sean O'Casey and His Critics: An Annotated Bibliography 1916-1982*. Metuchen: Scarecrow, 1985. x, 348 pp. (Scarecrow Author Bibliographies. 67.)

66. *The New Cambridge Bibliography of English Literature*. Edited by George Watson. Cambridge: UP, 1969-77. 5 vols.

D[avid] H. G[reene]: "Anglo-Irish Literature," 3:1885-1948 (on

Yeats, pp. 1915-34). Includes material through 1965.
In *The Cambridge Bibliography of English Literature*, edited by F. W. Bateson (1940, 1957), the Yeats material was compiled by Sean O'Faolain, Peter Allt, and T. R. Henn (see 3:1059-62; 700-704).

67. NORTON, CLARA MULLIKEN, and others (comps): *Modern Drama and Opera: A Reading List*. Boston: Boston Book Company, 1911-15. 2 vols. (Useful Reference Series. 4. 13.)
Alice Thurston McGirr: "Yeats," 2:148-54; a revision of "Reading List on William Butler Yeats," *BB*, 7:4 (Jan 1913), 82-83.

68. O'DONOGHUE, DAVID JAMES: *The Poets of Ireland: A Biographical and Bibliographical Dictionary of Irish Writers of English Verse*. Dublin: Hodges Figgis / London: Oxford UP, 1912 [1892-93]. iv, 504 pp.
See p. 492.

69. ØKSNEVAD, REIDAR: *Det Britiske Samvelde og Eire i norsk litteratur: En bibliografi / The British Commonwealth of Nations and Eire in Norwegian Literature: A Bibliography*. Oslo: Gyldendal, 1949. 187 pp.
See pp. 74-75.

70. O'NEILL, JAMES J.: *A Bibliographical Account of Irish Theatrical Literature*. Part 1: General theatrical history, players, and theatrical periodicals. Dublin: Falconer, 1920. Pp. 57-88. (Publications of the Bibliographical Society of Ireland. 1:6.)
No more published.

71. PALMER, HELEN H.: *European Drama Criticism 1900-1975*. Second edition. Hamden, Ct.: Shoe String Press / Folkestone: Dawson, 1977 [1968-74]. vii, 653 pp.
"William Butler Yeats," 568-76; selective.

72. POWNALL, DAVID E.: *Articles on Twentieth Century Literature: An Annotated Bibliography 1954 to 1970*. NY: Kraus-Thomson, 1973-80. 7 vols.
"Yeats, William Butler," 7:4825-4950; 596 items.

73. ROYAL IRISH ACADEMY. COMMITTEE FOR THE STUDY OF ANGLO-IRISH LANGUAGE AND LITERATURE: *Handlist*. [Dublin, 1969--].
A list of work in progress. The following installments have been published: 1 (June 1969); 2 (July 1971); Supplement to 2 (n.d.); 3 (Aug 1973); 4 (Sept 1974); 5 (Sept 1975); 6 (Sept 1976); 7 (Dec 1977); 8 (Dec 1978); 9 (Dec 1979); 10 (Dec 1980); 11 (1983).

74. ———: *Handlist of Theses Completed but Not Published*. [Dublin, 1973-77]. 3 vols.

75. SADER, MARION (ed): *Comprehensive Index to English-Language Little Magazines 1890-1970*. Series one. Millwood, N.Y.: Kraus-Thomson, 1976. 8 vols.
See 8:5011-20.

76. SAUL, GEORGE BRANDON: *Stephens, Yeats, and Other Irish Concerns*. NY: New York Public Library, 1954. 45 pp.
"An Introductory Bibliography in Anglo-Irish Literature," 12-18; reprinted from *BNYPL*, 58:9 (Sept 1954), 429-35.
"Thread to a Labyrinth: A Selective Bibliography in Yeats," 19-22; reprinted from *BNYPL*, 58:7 (July 1954), 344-47.

"The Winged Image: A Note on Birds in Yeats's Poems," 23-29; reprinted from *BNYPL*, 58:6 (June 1954), 267-73; reprinted in DC334.

77. SCHLÖSSER, ANSELM: *Die englische Literatur in Deutschland von 1895 bis 1934 mit einer vollständigen Bibliographie der deutschen Übersetzungen und der im deutschen Sprachgebiet erschienenen englischen Ausgaben*. Jena: Biedermann, 1937. vii, 535 pp. (Forschungen zur englischen Philologie. 5.)

Scattered notes on the German Yeats reception (see index), including a list of translations in anthologies.

78. SCHWARTZ, JACOB: *1100 Obscure Points: The Bibliographies of 25 English and 21 American Authors*. London: Ulysses Bookshop, 1931. xiii, 95 pp.

See pp. 41-42. The listing of Yeats items is best described in the foreword: "This is the first bibliography ever written in which the author will not make any apologies for missing items therein" (p. vii).

79. TEMPLEMAN, WILLIAM DARBY (ed): *Bibliographies of Studies in Victorian Literature for the Thirteen Years 1932-44*. Urbana: U of Illinois Press, 1945. ix, 450 pp.

Continued by Austin Wright (ed): *Bibliographies of Studies in Victorian Literature for the Ten Years 1945-1954*. Urbana: U of Illinois Press, 1956. vii, 310 pp.

Robert C. Slack (ed): *Bibliographies of Studies in Victorian Literature for the Ten Years 1955-1964*. Urbana: U of Illinois Press, 1967. xvii, 461 pp.

Ronald E. Freeman (ed): *Bibliographies of Studies in Victorian Literature for the Ten Years 1965-1974*. NY: AMS Press, 1981. xlvii, 876 pp.

Current installments in *Victorian Studies*.

80. THOMPSON, RICHARD J.: "'The Books of My Numberless Dreams': A Basic Booklist in Irish Studies," *Choice*, 15:10 (Dec 1978), 1317-18, 1320-22, 1324-26, 1328-30, 1332-33.

81. ULLRICH, KURT: *Who Wrote about Whom: A Bibliography of Books on Contemporary British Authors*. Berlin: Collignon, 1932. 60 pp.

See index; lists only books published between 1920 and 1931.

82. WEINER, ALAN R., and SPENCER MEANS: *Literary Criticism Index*. Metuchen, N.J.: Scarecrow Press, 1984. xvii, 686 pp.

An index to selected bibliographies. See pp. 675-80.

83. WEITENKAMPF, FRANK: "The Irish Literary Revival: A Contribution to Literary Bibliography," *Lamp*, [series 3] / 29:3 (Oct 1904), 238-40.

Lists and comments upon 29 items.

84. WELLS, STANLEY (ed): *English Drama (Excluding Shakespeare): Select Bibliographical Guides*. London: Oxford UP, 1975. ix, 303 pp.

Ann Saddlemyer: "The Irish School," 248-67; a review of research and a bibliography.

See also DC25.

AD Reviews of Research and Extended Review Articles

It should be noted that the items listed in section AD are not analyzed in this bibliography.

1. ADAMS, HAZARD: "Yeats Scholarship and Criticism: A Review of Research," *TSLL,* 3:4 (Winter 1962), 439-51.

2. ———: "Scholarship and the Idea of Criticism: Recent Writing on Yeats," *GaR,* 26:3 (Fall 1972), 249-78.

3. BEACHAM, WALTON (ed): *Research Guide to Biography and Criticism.* Washington, D.C.: Research Publishing, 1985. 2 vols.
Joseph M. Hassett on Yeats, 2:1315-19.

4. BERGSTEN, STAFFAN: "Nyare Yeatslitteratur," *Samlaren,* 90 (1969), 198-201.

5. BINNI, FRANCESCO: "Yeats e i critici," *Letteratura,* 31 / ns 15: 88-90 (July-Dec 1967), 305-8.

6. CROSS, K. G. W.: "The Fascination of What's Difficult: A Survey of Yeats Criticism and Research," in Jeffares and Cross: *In Excited Reverie* (1965, CA48), 315-37.

7. DAICHES, DAVID: *English Literature.* Englewood Cliffs: Prentice-Hall, 1964. xv, 174 pp.
See pp. 10-18 for comments on American Yeats scholarship with particular condemnation of Delmore Schwartz (CB426).

8. FINNERAN, RICHARD J. (ed): *Anglo-Irish Literature: A Review of Research.* NY: Modern Language Association of America, 1976. vii, 596 pp.
Continued in next item. See R. J. Finneran: "W. B. Yeats," 216-314 (exhaustive survey of the major criticism in English), and the index for further references in the other contributions.

9. ———: *Recent Research on Anglo-Irish Writers: A Supplement to "Anglo-Irish Literature: A Review of Research."* NY: Modern Language Association of America, 1983. xvi, 361 pp.
R. J. Finneran: "W. B. Yeats," 85-153; see also the index.

10. FLETCHER, IAN: "The Present State of Yeats Criticism," *LHY,* 2:2 (July 1961), 22-26.

11. HARPER, GEORGE MILLS: "'All the Instruments Agree': Some Observations on Recent Yeats Criticism," *SR,* 74:3 (July-Sept 1966), 739-54.

12. ———: "'Sing Whatever Is Well Made': Recent Books about Yeats," *CEA,* 33:3 (Mar 1971), 29-35.

13. JEFFARES, A. NORMAN: "An Account of Recent Yeatsiana," *Hermathena,* 72 (Nov 1948), 21-43.

14. ———: "The Last Twelve Years' Yeatsiana," *Levende talen,* 149 (Apr 1949), 109-13.

15. JOCHUM, K. P. S.: "W. B. Yeats: A Survey of Book Publications, 1966-1972," *Anglia,* 92:1/2 (1974), 143-71.

16. *K problemam romantizma i realizma v zarubezhnoi literature kontsa XIX-XX vekov: Sbornik trudov*. Volume 2. Moskva: Moskovskii oblastnoi pedagogicheskii institut imeni N. K. Krupskoi, 1975. 161 pp.
I. K. Eremina: "U. B. Eits v kritike," 92-100.

17. KAIN, RICHARD M.: "W. B. Yeats: Centenary Studies and Tributes," *SoR*, 3:3 (July 1967), 742-56.

18. ———: "The Status of Yeats Scholarship," *Eire*, 2:3 (Autumn 1967), 102-10.

19. KIRSCHNER, ALLEN ROGER: "The Critical Reputation of William Butler Yeats, 1889-1928," M.A. thesis, New York U, 1955. ii, 90 pp.

20. LEARY, LEWIS (ed): *Contemporary Literary Scholarship: A Critical Review*. NY: Appleton-Century-Crofts, 1958. x, 474 pp.
See index for notes on American Yeats scholarship.

21. LIGHTCAP, JANE STREATOR: "William Butler Yeats' Reputation in Selected American Periodicals: 1895-1940," M.A. thesis, U of Florida, 1964. iii, 129 pp.
The periodicals are *Atlantic Monthly, Bookman, Dial, Nation, New Republic,* and *Poetry*.

22. ORACKI, TADEUSZ: "Twórczość W. B. Yeatsa w Polsce," *Kultura*, 23 Feb 1969, 9.
Yeats's work in Poland and in Polish.

23. PARKINSON, THOMAS: "Some Recent Work on Yeats: From Great Modern Poet to Canonical Classic," *SoR*, 15:3 (Summer 1979), 742-52.

24. PATTINSON, JOHN PATRICK: "A Study of British Poetic Criticism between 1930 and 1965 as Exemplified in the Critics of Yeats, Pound, and Eliot," Ph.D. thesis, New York U, 1968. iv, 261 pp. (*DAI*, 30:10 [Apr 1970], 4460A-61A)
"Yeats's British Critics," 48-129.

25. [QUINN, JOHN (comp)]: *Some Critical Appreciations of William Butler Yeats as Poet, Orator, and Dramatist*. S.l., [1903?]. 23 pp.

26. RAFROIDI, PATRICK: "Yeats and Co.," *LanM*, 61:2 (Mar-Apr 1967), 196-206.

27. SANO, TETSURO: [In Japanese] "Recent Yeats Studies," *SELit*, 56:1 (Sept 1979), 147-54.

28. SIDNELL, MICHAEL: "Yeats: Editions and Commentaries," *UTQ*, 41:3 (Spring 1972), 263-74.

29. STALLWORTHY, JON: "A Short Guide to Yeats Studies," *Critical Survey*, 3:1 (Winter 1966), 17-22.

30. STAMM, RUDOLF: *Englische Literatur*. Bern: Francke, 1957. 422 pp. (Wissenschaftliche Forschungsberichte: Geisteswissenschaftliche Reihe. 11.)
See pp. 386-88.

31. TIMM, EITEL: *W. B. Yeats*. Darmstadt: Wissenschaftliche Buchgesellschaft, 1987. x, 178 pp. (Erträge der Forschung. 251.)
In German. An extended review of research; not as useful as it

might have been because of a great number of serious omissions.

32. VALLETTE, JACQUES: "La marque de Yeats," *MercF*, 322:1096 (1 Dec 1954), 705-9.

33. *Voprosy istorii literaturnoĭ kritiki*. Tiumen': Tiumenskiĭ gosudarstvennyĭ universitet, 1977. 157 pp. (Nauchnye trudy. 53.)
V. Khorol'skiĭ: "Poeziia U. B. Ietsa v sovetskoĭ i zarubezhnoĭ kritike," 56-71 ("Y's poetry in Soviet and foreign criticism").

34. WATSON, THOMAS L.: "The French Reputation of W. B. Yeats," *CL*, 12:3 (Summer 1960), 256-62.

35. WITT, MARION: "Yeats: 1865-1939," *PMLA*, 80:4 (Sept 1965), 311-20.
On the present state of Yeats editions and texts, collected and uncollected.

See also AC29, 84, CA29, 89, 97, 123, CB280, CC228, CD38a, 89, 139, 1125, DA8, DD42, 47, 67, 90, 494, FC119, FD1.

AE Catalogs and Collections

This section is most certainly incomplete in its listing of sales catalogs. Various antiquarian booksellers and auction houses are known to have issued catalogs containing Yeats material; however, a systematic search proved to be impossible.

1. The Abbey Theatre: A collection of newscuttings, letters, and other material. 5 vols.
Relating to the theatrical career of the brothers Fay, including letters to Yeats. In the National Library of Ireland, shelfmark IR 3919.n.3.

2. ABBOTT, CHERYL, and J. FRASER COCKS: *James Augustine Healey Collection of Nineteenth and Twentieth Century Irish Literature*. Waterville, Maine: Colby College, 1978. vi, 38 pp.
See especially pp. 35-37.

3. ADAMS, HAZARD: "The William Butler Yeats Collection at Texas," *LCUT*, 6:1 (Spring 1957), 33-38.
For more information about this collection see ibid., 5:4 (Spring 1956), 49, and 6:3 (Spring 1959), 34.

4. ALLEN, JAMES LOVIC: "The Yeats Tapes," *ILS*, 2:2 (Oct 1983), 17, 19.
The microfilms of the Yeats papers at SUNY Stony Brook and in the National Library of Ireland. See Alison Armstrong and Robert G. Lowery: "Focus: Stony Brook," *ILS*, 2:1 (Spring 1983), 20.

5. ANON.: "Emory Buys Yeats Collection," *American Libraries*, 10:9 (Oct 1979), 562.
MSS., letters, and books from the library of Lady Gregory at Emory U Library, Atlanta, Ga. See also AE87.

6. ANON.: "Exhibitions in Retrospect: The Indomitable Irishry," *Gazette of the Grolier Club*, ns 2 (Oct 1966), 4-37.
An exhibition held from October through December 1962.

7. ANON.: "The Charles Riker Collection of William Butler Yeats,"

Kenyon College Library, Gambier, Ohio: Acquisitions Bulletin, 83 (Feb 1959), 1-6; 109 (Nov 1961), 1-4.

8. ASH, LEE: *Subject Collections: A Guide to Special Book Collections and Subject Emphases as Reported by University, College, Public, and Special Libraries and Museums in the United States and Canada.* Fifth edition, revised and enlarged. NY: Bowker, 1978. xi, 1184 pp.
See under Abbey Theatre (p. 1), Ireland, Irish Language and Literature, Irish Literary Renaissance (pp. 519-22), and Yeats (pp. 1176-77).

9. BAKER, PAMELA M., and HELEN M. YOUNG: "W. B. Yeats Material in the University of London Library," *YeA,* 4 (1986), 175-80.
Especially in the Thomas Sturge Moore Collection.

10. BANDLER, SAMUEL WYLLIS: *Selections from the Library of the Late Dr. Samuel Wyllis Bandler of New York City.* NY: Boesen, [194-]. 4 vols.
Lists 64 letters to T. Fisher Unwin and three other pieces, 4:61-62.

11. BATTERSBY & COMPANY (Auctioneers and Valuers): *A Catalogue of a Valuable Collection of Antiquarian and Modern Books.* Sale of 11 October 1966. Dublin: Battersby, 1966.
A mimeographed list; includes some books by Yeats (lots 82, 161-71, 194-96), and five letters, one to an unnamed correspondent, four to J. H. Pollock (dated 12 July, 21 Sept, 25 July 1934, 27 Nov 1934), also a letter from Mrs. Yeats to Pollock (lots 185-90).
See Jonathan Fisher: "Unpublished Letters of W. B. Yeats for Auction," *IrT,* 10 Oct 1966, 8.

12. BIBLIOTHÈQUE NATIONALE: *Gordon Craig et le renouvellement du théâtre.* Paris: Bibliothèque nationale, 1962. 101 pp.
Catalog of an exhibition; a list of items concerning Craig and Yeats appears on pp. 59-61.

13. BLACK, HESTER MARY: *William Butler Yeats: A Catalog of an Exhibition from the P. S. O'Hegarty Collection in the University of Kansas Library.* Lawrence, 1958. 41 pp.
Review: [John Carter]: "American Libraries," *TLS,* 13 Mar 1959, 152; see also AE60, 61, and 72.

14. BLAKE-HILL, PHILIP V.: "The Macmillan Archive," *British Museum Q,* 36:3-4 (Autumn 1972), 74-80.
Includes letters from Yeats. The archives are now in the British Library; a printed index to the microfilm edition published by Chadwyck-Healey is promised for 1988.

15. BOWEN, ZACK: *Annotated Catalogue and Bibliography for the Colum Collection of the Library at State University of New York at Binghamton.* Binghamton: State U of New York, 1970. iv, 45 pp.
Includes material on Yeats in items 53, 55, 56, 78, 81, 91, 160.

16. BRITISH BROADCASTING CORPORATION: *BBC TV Drama Catalogue 1936-1975.* Cambridge: Chadwick-Healey, 1977. 63 microfiches.
See "Authors," fiche 13.

17. ———: *BBC Radio Drama Catalogue 1923-1975.* Cambridge: Chadwyck-Healey, 1977. 125 microfiches.
See "Authors," fiche 33.

18. [BRITISH MUSEUM. DEPARTMENT OF PRINTED BOOKS. KING'S LIBRARY]: *Yeats and His Contemporaries.* [London, 1965]. 10 pp.
Mimeographed guide to the Yeats centenary exhibition at the British Museum. See also "Yeats and His Contemporaries," *British Museum Q,* 28:3-4 (Oct 1964), News Supplement, 1.

19. BROWN, P. A. H.: *Modern British and American Private Presses (1850-1965): Holdings of the British Library.* London: British Museum Publications for the British Library, 1976. iii, 211 pp.
Entries reproduced from the BL catalog. See pp. 37-41 for the Cuala Press, and the index under Yeats.

20. BUSHEE, RALPH: "Morris Library Houses Extensive Yeats Collection," *Daily Egyptian,* 12 Feb 1966, 3.
The Morris Library of Southern Illinois U at Carbondale. See [Thomas J. Jackson]: *The Irish Collection: Rare Book Room / Morris Library.* Carbondale: Southern Illinois U, [1970]. i, 11 pp.

21. CHRISTIE'S: *Important Literary and Musical Manuscripts and Autograph Letters.* Sale of 5 July 1978. London: Christie's, 1978.
Lots 48-54, pp. 28-34 comprise the following Yeats material: Letters from WBY and Mrs. Yeats to Edith Shackleton Heald; a letter from Mrs. Yeats to WBY; letters from Allan Wade to Miss Heald concerning Yeats's letters; a letter from WBY to Herbert [?] Gorman; MS. versions of *Last Poems;* an unpublished poem of four lines beginning "What is the explanation of it all?" (see also DD724); photographs and other items.

22. ———: *Valuable Autograph Letters, Historical Documents and Music Manuscripts.* Sale of 29 Apr 1981. London: Christie's, 1981.
Lists an undated letter to an unnamed correspondent, p. 70.

23. ———: *Valuable Autograph Letters & Historical Documents.* Sale of 20 July 1983. London: Christie's, 1983.
The Douglas Hyde archive, item 366, pp. 45-46, includes a letter from Yeats. The Yeats-Wellesley correspondence, item 396, pp. 56-58, includes unpublished material, among others two letters from T. S. Eliot to Yeats. Item 397, p. 59, lists twelve letters from Hyde to Yeats. See also Geraldine Norman: "£ 18,360 for Yeats's Mail to a Lady," *Times,* 21 July 1983, 2; and AE99.

24. CHRISTIE, MANSON & WOODS INTERNATIONAL: *Modern Literature from the Library of James Gilvarry.* Sale of 7 February 1986. NY: Christie's, 1986.
For Yeats material see items 321-23, 339, 348, 350, 351 (postcard from Lionel Johnson to Yeats, reproduced), 370, 393 (Joyce's copy of *John Sherman and Dhoya*), 403 (a comment by Valery Larbaud on Yeats), 418, 462 (pen and ink drawing of WBY by his brother Jack), 463-565 (first editions with and without inscriptions, letters to May Whitty, Mrs. F. R. Benson, D. J. O'Donoghue, John O'Leary, Ernest Rhys, Violet Hunt, Wilfrid Scawen Blunt, "Michael Field," John Butler Yeats, Arthur Symons, Karel Musek, Ellen Duncan, Lady Gregory, Herman Radin, Joseph M. Hone, Frank Harris, Patrick McCartan, Alice Milligan, John Cournos, A. K. Coomaraswamy, the Duchess of Sutherland, and others, and other material). See report by H. R. Woudhuysen: "Sale of Books and MSS," *TLS,* 14 Feb 1986, 175.

25. CONNOLLY, CYRIL: *Cyril Connolly's One Hundred Modern Books* *from England, France and America 1880-1950*. Catalog by Mary Hirth with an introduction by Cyril Connolly. An exhibition March-December 1971. Austin: Humanities Research Center, U of Texas at Austin, 1971. 120 pp.

See index for Yeats items.

26. COX, E. M. H.: *The Library of Edmund Gosse, Being a Descriptive and Bibliographical Catalogue of a Portion of His Collection*. With an introductory essay by Mr. Gosse. London: Dulau, 1924. 300 pp.

Yeats, pp. 297-99. See also *A Catalogue of the Gosse Correspondence in the Brotherton Collection, Consisting Mainly of Letters Written to Sir Edmund Gosse from 1867 to 1928*. Leeds: U of Leeds, 1950. xiv, 80 pp. (Library Publications. 3.), which lists 25 letters from Yeats to Gosse on p. 80.

27. DOUGAN, ROBERT ORMES (comp): *W. B. Yeats: Manuscripts and Printed Books Exhibited in the Library of Trinity College, Dublin, 1956. Catalogue*. Dublin: Colm O Lochlainn at the Sign of the Three Candles for the Friends of the Library of Trinity College, Dublin, [1956]. 50 pp.

Reprinted: [Darby, Pa.]: Folcroft Press, 1970. Review: [J. M. Hone]: "Books and Manuscripts of W. B. Yeats," *TLS*, 4 May 1956, 276.

28. DURKAN, MICHAEL J.: *William Butler Yeats, 1865-1965*. A catalogue of his works and associated items in Olin Library, Wesleyan University, together with an essay by David R. Clark. Middletown, Ct. [i.e., Dublin: Dolmen Press], 1965. 92 pp.

Wyman W. Parker: "Preface," 7-9; David R. Clark: "Key Attitudes in Yeats," 11-21 (Irish nationalism, religion, mysticism, the aristocratic); catalog, 23-92.

29. EDRICH, I. D.: *W. B. Yeats: A Catalogue*. London: Edrich, 1983. 25 pp.

Sales catalog, 547 items; supplement, 120 items.

30. FLETCHER, IAN (ed): *The Archives of Elkin Mathews 1811-1938*. Bishops Stortford: Chadwyck-Healey, 1973. Microfilm, 1 reel.

The archives are at the U of Reading, a copy of the film is in the British Library. Contains six letters from Yeats, none of them in *Letters* (the one letter there does not seem to be part of the archives).

31. FOX, PETER (ed): *Treasures of the Library: Trinity College Dublin*. Dublin: Royal Irish Academy for Trinity College Dublin, 1986. xiii, 258 pp.

Nicholas Grene: "Modern Irish Literary Manuscripts," 230-38; contains a note on the Yeats MSS.

32. [FRENCH, HANNAH DUSTIN]: "William Butler Yeats at Wellesley," *Friends of the Wellesley College Library Bulletin*, 10 (July 1952), 3-19.

A description of the Yeats collection at Wellesley and memories of Yeats's visits. See also BF95.

33. GALLUP, DONALD: "Ezra Pound (1885-1972): The Catalogue of an Exhibition in the Beinecke Library, 30 October--31 December 1975, Commemorating His Ninetieth Birthday," *YULG*, 50:3 (Jan 1976), 135-63.

"Pound & Yeats," 136-38.

34. GORDAN, JOHN DOZIER: *First Fruits: An Exhibition of First Editions of First Books by English Authors in the Henry W. and Albert A. Berg Collection*. NY: New York Public Library, 1949. 36 pp.
See pp. 35-36 on *Mosada* (W1).

35. ———: "New in the Berg Collection: 1952-1956," *BNYPL*, 61:7 (July 1957), 353-63.
Continued in *BNYPL*, 63:3 (Mar 1959), 134-47; :4 (Apr 1959), 205-15. Includes Yeats material.

36. GORDON, DONALD JAMES, IAN FLETCHER, and FRANK KERMODE: *I, the Poet William Yeats: A Descriptive Guide*. The exhibition was assembled by D. J. Gordon and designed by Margaret Fuller. 21 May--7 June 1957. [Reading: U of Reading, 1957]. i, 31 pp.
A mimeographed guide; see also next item.
Reviews:
- G. S. F[raser]: "Yeats Exhibition at Reading University," *NSt*, 1 June 1957, 706.
- [G. S. Fraser]: "Visual Aids," *TLS*, 7 June 1957, 349.

37. [GORDON, DONALD JAMES, and IAN FLETCHER]: *W. B. Yeats: Images of a Poet. My Permanent or Impermanent Images. Exhibition Catalogue*. [Manchester: U of Manchester, 1961]. 151 pp.
The exhibition was held in Manchester (3 May--3 June 1961) and Dublin (17 June--1 July 1961) and was based on the Reading exhibition (see AE36). Contents: "The Image of the Poet," "Persons and Places" (Thoor Ballylee, Coole Park, Lady Gregory, Robert Gregory, Lionel Johnson, Synge, George Pollexfen, Maud Gonne, John O'Leary, John Butler Yeats, Eva Gore-Booth, Constance Markievicz, Sligo), "The Poet and the Theatre," "Byzantium," "Symbolic Art and Visionary Landscape," "The Dancer" (by Frank Kermode), and "Books and Manuscripts" (by Robin Skelton).
Reviews:
- Anon.: "Important Exhibition of Yeatsiana," *IrT*, 20 June 1961, 9. Correspondence by J. de Courcy, 22 June 1961, 7.
- Richard Ellmann: "Heard and Seen," *NSt*, 8 Dec 1961, 887-88.
- [G. S. Fraser]: "Images of a Poet," *TLS*, 12 May 1961, 293. Correspondence by Frank Kermode, 19 May 1961, 309.
- G. S. Fraser: "Images of Yeats," *NSt*, 19 May 1961, 763.
- Robin Skelton: "Images of a Poet: W. B. Yeats," *IrB*, 1:4 (Spring 1962), 89-97.
- W. L. Webb: "Images of a Poet," *Guardian*, 3 May 1961, 7.
- Margaret Willy, *English*, 14:79 (Spring 1962), 29-30.

38. [GRAY, JOHN ?]: *William McCready of Whiteabbey 1909-1982: Diarist and Book Collector*. Belfast: Linen Hall Library, 1983. iv, 35 pp.
Pamphlet accompanying an exhibition, includes references to two letters by Yeats, pp. 8, 35.

39. GROVER, RACHEL: "De Lury Collection," *Four Decades*, 2:3 (Jan 1979), 174-78.
The Alfred De Lury collection at the U of Toronto Library, which is strong on Yeats and Anglo-Irish literature.

40. HART-DAVIS, RUPERT: *A Catalogue of the Caricatures of Max Beerbohm*. London: Macmillan, 1972. 258 pp.
For Yeats caricatures see nos. 144, 616, 748, 1046, 1650, 1825-29.

41. HASTINGS, HENRY C.: *Spoken Poetry on Records and Tapes: An Index of Currently Available Recordings*. Chicago: Association of College and Reference Libraries, 1957. iv, 52 pp. (ACRL Monographs. 18.)
See p. 32.

42. HECHLER, DAVID: "Opening Yeats Trove to Academe," *NYT*, 19 Jan 1986, section 21, 10.
The cataloging of the Yeats Archives at SUNY Stony Brook.

43. HENDERSON, WILLIAM ARTHUR: Newspaper cuttings, programmes, and photographs relating to the Irish Literary Theatre, 1899-1901, with manuscript notes and an index. 1 vol.
In the National Library of Ireland, MS. 1729.

44. ———: The Irish national theatre movement: Three years' work at the Abbey Theatre told in press cuttings. With manuscript notes and indexes. 1904-7. 1 vol.
In the National Library of Ireland, MS. 1730.

45. ———: The Irish national theatre movement: A year's work at the Abbey Theatre told in press cuttings; also programmes, photographs, and letters. With manuscript notes and indexes. 1908-11. 4 vols.
In the National Library of Ireland, MSS. 1731-34.

46. ———: Press cuttings and theatre programmes relating to literary movements in Ireland. 1909-10. 1 vol.
In the National Library of Ireland, MS. 1736. P.S.: A 1987 prospectus announces the following publication: *The W. A. Henderson Scrapbooks, 1899-1911, from the National Library in Ireland, Dublin*. Brighton: Harvester, to be published 1988/89. Positive microfilm. (Manuscripts of the Irish Literary Renaissance. Series 2: The Abbey Theatre and Cultural Life. Part 1.)

47. HODGES, FIGGIS AND CO., LTD.: *William Butler Yeats: 13 June 1865--13 June 1965*. Dublin: Dolmen Press for Hodges Figgis, 1965. viii pp.
Annotated catalog of an exhibition.

48. HOLLOWAY, JOSEPH: A Collection of 57 copy-books containing newscuttings relating to the Irish Literary Theatre, the Irish National Theatre Society and the Abbey Theatre. Arranged chronologically, 1899-1916.
In the National Library of Ireland, MS. 4374-4430.

49. ———: Newscuttings, relating mainly to the Irish theatre, 1920-1934. 1 vol.
In the National Library of Ireland, MS. 4433.

50. HORNIMAN, ANNIE ELIZABETH FREDERICKA: A collection of newspaper cuttings, etc., concerning the Abbey Theatre, Dublin, 1903-20. 10 vols.
In the John Rylands Library, Manchester, shelfmark R.44272. After 1913 the collection seems to have been made by somebody else. Nevertheless, it is noteworthy that Miss Horniman retained her interest in Abbey affairs after she had severed her connection with the Irish National Theatre. The cuttings were collected by herself, sent by friends, or supplied by a press cutting agency, Woolgar & Roberts, telegram address "Mutilating London."

51. HOUGHTON LIBRARY. HARVARD UNIVERSITY: *Catalogue of Manuscripts in the Houghton Library, Harvard University*. Cambridge: Chadwyck-Healey, 1986. 6 vols.

See 8:436-38 for a list of MSS. and letters by and referring to Yeats, also items relating to the Yeats family.

52. HUNTINGTON LIBRARY: *Guide to Literary Manuscripts in the Huntington Library*. San Marino: Huntington Library, 1979. ix, 539 pp.

See pp. 521-22.

53. IBADAN. UNIVERSITY OF IBADAN. DEPARTMENT OF ENGLISH AND UNIVERSITY LIBRARY: *William Butler Yeats 1865-1965*. Centenary exhibition illustrating some aspects of the life and work of W. B. Yeats, May-June 1965. Ibadan, [1965]. 20 pp.

Mimeographed guide.

54. *Index of Authors and Titles of Kegan Paul, Trench, Trübner & Henry S. King 1858-1912*. Cambridge: Chadwyck-Healey, 1974. Unpaged.

Printed index to the microfilm edition of the archives; contains several references to the publication of *The Wanderings of Oisin* (W2). The film was made in 1973; there is a copy in the British Library.

55. *Index of Manuscripts in the British Library*. Cambridge: Chadwyck-Healey, 1984-86. 10 vols.

See 10:545 for the Yeats MSS.

56. *Index to the Archives of Swan Sonnenschein & Co. 1878-1911*. Cambridge: Chadwyck-Healey, 1975. Unpaged.

Printed index to the microfilm edition of the archives; lists two letters to Yeats. The film was made in 1973; there is a copy in the British Library.

57. INGRAM, ALISON: *Index to the Archives of Grant Richards 1897-1948*. Cambridge: Chadwyck-Healey, 1981. Unpaged.

Printed index to the microfilm of the archives; contains Yeats items. The film was made in 1979; there is a copy in the British Library.

58. JAMES, ELIZABETH INGLI: "The University of Reading Collections," *YeA*, 3 (1985), 167-72.

Of Yeatsiana and related material.

59. KAIN, RICHARD M.: "The Curran Library," *Eire*, 7:4 (Winter 1972), 135-36.

Short description of the Curran collection at University College, Dublin, which includes some Yeats letters.

60. KANSAS UNIVERSITY LIBRARIES. DEPARTMENT OF SPECIAL COLLECTIONS: *A Guide to the Collection*. Lawrence: U of Kansas Libraries, 1964. iv, 31 pp.

"The W. B. Yeats Collection," 11-12. See also AE13, 61, and 72.

61. KANSAS UNIVERSITY LIBRARIES. P. S. O'HEGARTY COLLECTION: *A Catalog of Books in the Library of P. S. O'Hegarty*. Baile Átha Cliath: Teach na hÁrdpháirce, 1958. 4 vols.

Yeats is listed passim, especially 1:1-5 (manuscript material) and 4:76. See Harold Orel: "Playbills of the Abbey Theatre, 1904-1941," *Books and Libraries at the U of Kansas*, 17 (Feb

1958), 11-15 (part of the collection), and AE13, 60, and 72.

62. KISSANE, NOEL: *The National Library of Ireland.* Dublin: Eason, 1984. [24 pp. and printed covers]. (Irish Heritage Series. 42.)
Contains a few references to the Yeats collection.

63. LIBRARY OF CONGRESS CATALOGS: *National Union Catalog of Manuscript Collections.* Washington, D. C.: Library of Congress, 1959--. In progress.
See indexes for Yeats material.

63a. *Location Register of Twentieth-Century English Literary Manuscripts and Letters: A Union List of Papers of Modern English, Irish, Scottish and Welsh Authors in the British Isles.* London: British Library, 1988. 2 vols.
"Yeats, W. B.," 2:1035-45, about 400 entries, including MSS. and letters from and to Yeats.

64. MACKENZIE, NORMAN H.: "Anglo-Irish Literature and the Douglas Library," *Douglas Library Notes,* 18:2 (Winter 1970), 2-7.
The collection in the Douglas Library of Queen's U, Kingston, Ont.

65. ———: "Anglo-Irish Enrichments to Queen's University Libraries," *CJIS,* 11:1 (June 1985), 49-52.
Queen's U, Kingston, Ont.; the collection includes Yeats items.

66. MARCUS, PHILLIP: "Catalogue of Manuscripts in the Olin Library, Cornell University," in O'Driscoll and Reynolds: *Yeats and the Theatre* (1975, CA81), 282-84.
25 letters, of which 18 are not in Wade's edition.

67. MASIN, ANTON C.: *Catalogue of an Exhibit of Selections on William Butler Yeats (1886-1939), Poet of the Gael; and the Yeats Family Contribution to Literature and the Art of the Book: May-September 1980.* Compiled by Anton C. Masin with a preface on Yeats at Notre Dame by William Rufus Rauch. Notre Dame, Ind.: Memorial Library, U of Notre Dame, 1980. xvii, 44 pp.
"Preface: Yeats at Notre Dame and St. Mary's," ix-xii; memories of Yeats's visits in Jan 1904 and 1933.
"Introduction," xiii-xvii; a sketch of Yeats's life and works and a description of the exhibition.
The exhibition included archival material related to Yeats's visits (interviews, newspaper reports, most of them not covered by Strand [BA18], and a somewhat unfavorable personal impression [p. 9]), a letter written by Yeats to his host, and some first editions.

68. MATTSON, FRANCIS O.: "The John Quinn Memorial Collection: An Inventory and Index," *BNYPL,* 78:2 (Winter 1975), 145-230.
Lists letters to and from Yeats and other members of the Yeats family.

69. MILLER, LIAM (ed): *Dolmen XXV: An Illustrated Bibliography of the Dolmen Press 1951-1976.* Dublin: Dolmen Press, 1976. 96 pp. (Dolmen Editions. 25.)

70. NATIONAL GALLERY OF IRELAND: *W. B. Yeats: A Centenary Exhibition.* Dublin: Dolmen Press, 1965. 102 pp.
Contents: Yeats the man; the heritage; the early years; the

family; pictures as inspiration; the poet as painter; the Abbey Theatre; the public life.

71. NATIONAL LIBRARY OF IRELAND: *Partial List of Manuscripts in the Collection of Senator Michael B. Yeats*. [Dublin: National Library of Ireland, 1981?]. 100 pp.
Mimeographed list, unpublished, "compiled June 1978 and July 1981," contains manuscripts, notebooks, letters to and from Yeats, collections of newspaper clippings, and other material.

72. NELICK, FRANK C.: "Yeats, Bullen, and the Irish Drama," *MD*, 1:3 (Dec 1958), 196-202.
Partial description of the P. S. O'Hegarty collection at Kansas U Libraries, which includes letters to A. H. Bullen. See also AE13, 60, 61.

73. NEVILLE, MAURICE F.: *Modern Irish and Anglo-Irish Literature*. Santa Barbara: Maurice F. Neville Rare Books, [1980?]
Sales catalog no. 5. See items 859-1002 and 1037-47; they include letters to Lady Gregory and Margaret Gough.
See also catalog no. 6: *Literary Autographs, Letters and Manuscripts*. [1980?]. Items 506-10 contain further letters.

74. NEW YORK PUBLIC LIBRARY: *Dictionary Catalog of the Albert A. and Henry W. Berg Collection of English and American Literature*. Boston: Hall, 1969. 5 vols.
Includes printed and manuscript material as well as letters. See under Abbey Theatre, 1:1-4; Yeats, 4:469-503 and 5:411-18.

75. ———. LINCOLN CENTER FOR THE PERFORMING ARTS LIBRARY. THEATRE COLLECTION: Collection of clippings, reviews, etc., concerning W. B. Yeats.
Shelfmark MWEZ / + / N.C. / 20,030. Very brittle material.

76. NEWCASTLE-UPON-TYNE. UNIVERSITY LIBRARY: *William Butler Yeats, 1865-1939: Catalogue of an Exhibition, 13th--22nd May 1965*. [Newcastle-upon-Tyne, 1965. 18 pp.]

77. NILAND, NORA: "The Yeats Memorial Museum, Sligo," *IrB*, 2:3/4 (Autumn 1963), 122-26.
Description of the Yeats collection and related material. See also AE89.

78. O'SHEA, EDWARD: *A Descriptive Catalog of W. B. Yeats's Library*. NY: Garland, 1985. xxiii, 390 pp. (Garland Reference Library of the Humanities. 470.)
Reproduces annotations and inscriptions; includes a subject index and an autograph index.
Reviews:
- George Bornstein, *Yeats*, 4 (1986), 219-21.
- Richard J. Finneran: "W. B. Yeats: Early Letters and His Library," *Review*, 9 (1987), 205-14.
- Sarah E. How, *ARBA*, 17 (1986), 466-67.
- Robert E. Ward, *Eire*, 20:4 (Winter 1985), 154-56.

79. ———: "The 1920s Catalogue of W. B. Yeats's Library," *YeA*, 4 (1986), 279-90.
A catalog made after 1920 by an unknown compiler; O'Shea lists the 521 (out of 1159) items that have disappeared.

80. PARKE-BERNET GALLERIES, INC.: *The Important Collection of First Editions of William Butler Yeats*. Property of C. Walter Buhler, Westport, Conn., sold by his order. NY: Parke-Bernet Galleries, 1941. iv, 56 pp. (Sale Number 281.)

The Yeats items appear on pp. 21-33 (nos. 121-82); they include first editions, manuscripts, and letters.

81. ———: *Important Scientific Historical and Musical MSS and Autographs*. Sale of 10 Apr 1962. NY: Parke-Bernet, 1962.

Letter from Yeats to G. B. Shaw, postmarked 1-2 May 1905, item 250.

82. PRINCETON UNIVERSITY LIBRARY. THEATER COLLECTION: Irish theater. 6 vols.

Six scrapbooks containing clippings from daily and weekly papers, most of them from New York, concerning the Abbey Theatre performances in the United States; also book reviews, interviews, sketches, and similar material.

83. QUINN, JOHN: *Complete Catalogue of the Library of John Quinn, Sold by Auction in Five Parts. (With Printed Prices)*. NY: Anderson Galleries, 1924. 2 vols.

Yeats, 2:1128-60, 1204-5 (items 11338-610, 12082-94).

84. RIGGS, SUSAN F., and OSWALDA M. DEVA (comps): *The Healy Collection of Irish Literature in the Department of Special Collections, Stanford University Libraries*. Stanford: Stanford U Libraries, 1978. ix, 216 pp. in two parts (mimeographed).

Part 1 lists letters and manuscripts, including Yeats material. There is also a folder containing clippings from auction catalogs offering Yeats books, manuscripts, and letters. Part 2 lists Dun Emer and Cuala Press books and broadsides with their inscriptions transcribed at length and other printed material. There are many inscriptions by Yeats for a variety of writers and friends.

85. RONDEL, AUGUSTE: Inventaire de la collection théâtrale Auguste Rondel: Théâtre irlandais.

A collection of press cuttings in the Bibliothèque de l'Arsenal, Paris, shelfmark Re. 10.993-11.061.

86. SCHOLES, ROBERT EDWARD: *The Cornell Joyce Collection: A Catalogue*. Ithaca: Cornell UP, 1961. xvii, 225 pp.

See index for letters from, and concerning, Yeats.

87. SCHUCHARD, RONALD: "The Lady Gregory--Yeats Collection at Emory University," *YeA*, 3 (1985), 153-66.

88. SIMMONDS, HARVEY: "John Quinn: An Exhibition to Mark the Gift of the John Quinn Memorial Collection," *BNYPL*, 72:9 (Nov 1968), 569-83.

Includes numerous Yeats items.

89. SLIGO COUNTY LIBRARY AND MUSEUM: *Jack B. Yeats and His Family: An Exhibition of the Works of Jack B. Yeats and His Family at the Sligo County Library and Museum, Sligo, 29th October to 29th December 1971*. Dublin: Irish Printers, [1971]. 91 pp.

Includes Roger McHugh: "Introduction to W. B. Yeats," 47-48, and a list of WBY items. See also AE77.

90. SLIGO COUNTY MUSEUM AND ART GALLERY: *Yeats Exhibition*. Mitsukoshi Department Store, Tokyo, October 1979. [Sligo, 1979]. ca. 80 pp.
A mimeographed list of some 250 items together with supplements.

91. SMYTHE, COLIN: "Collecting Yeats and Publishing Lady Gregory," *PrL*, series 2 / 4:1 (Spring 1971), 4-24.

92. SOTHEBY & CO.: *Catalogue of Printed Books Formerly in the Library at Coole: The Property of the Lady Gregory Estate*. Sale of 20 & 21 Mar 1972. London: Sotheby, 1972.
Facsimile of Yeats's note (dated 1901) on Jacob Bryant's *A New System or an Analysis of Ancient Mythology* (1775), p. 16. See Colin Smythe: "Coole Library," *PrL*, series 2 / 6:2 (Summer 1973), 74-82.

93. SOTHEBY PARKE BERNET & CO.: *Catalogue of Valuable Autograph Letters, Literary Manuscripts and Historical Documents Including . . . a Magnificent Collection of Poetical and Prose Manuscripts, Letters and Books Chiefly by William Butler Yeats from the Library of Lady Gregory*. Sale of 23 and 24 July 1979. London: Sotheby, 1979.
See pp. 240-305. The Yeats material includes a drawing of WBY by his father (reproduced), autograph manuscripts and drafts (many of them reproduced), letters to Lady Gregory, proof corrections, inscriptions, etc. See also p. 141, where a Yeats letter to John Freeman is listed as part of a lot.

94. ———: *Catalogue of Valuable Autograph Letters, Literary Manuscripts, and Historical Documents Including . . . a Collection of Poeti[c]al and Prose Manuscripts, Letters and Books Chiefly by William Butler Yeats from the Library of Lady Gregory*. Sale of 17 Dec 1979. London: Sotheby, 1979.
See pp. 196-236. The Yeats material includes letters to Stephen Gwynn and to Lady Gregory, autograph manuscripts and drafts, inscriptions, etc. See also p. 104 for letters from Sean O'Casey to Augustus John, referring to Yeats.

95. ———: *Valuable Autograph Letters, Literary Manuscripts and Historical Documents*. Sale of 15 Dec 1980. London: Sotheby, 1980.
See pp. 190-203 for 32 letters from Yeats to Elizabeth Radcliffe (Lady Gorell), 1913-17.

96. ———: *Valuable Autograph Letters, Literary Manuscripts and Historical Documents*. Sale of 17 Dec 1981. London: Sotheby, 1981.
See pp. 156-57 (items 293-94): four letters about Iseult Gonne to Dr. Solomons, 4-6 Aug 1920; one letter about the the performance of *The Countess Cathleen* to Mrs. Langridge, [May 1899].

97. ———: *Valuable Autograph Letters, Literary Manuscripts, and Historical Documents Including Sections of Continental and Music Manuscripts*. Sale of 29 and 30 June 1982. London: Sotheby, 1982.
Lists several letters from Yeats to various correspondents and the Lennox Robinson papers (which include Yeats material). See index under Robinson and Yeats.

98. ———: *English Literature Comprising Printed Books, Autograph Letters, and Manuscripts*. Sale of 15 Dec 1982. London: Sotheby, 1982.
Lists letters from and to Yeats, including a letter from Henry James (25 Aug 1915), an autograph draft of "His Dream," letters to Sean O'Casey, some letters about Swift, and several letters to Oliver Edwards.

99. ———: *English Literature Comprising Printed Books, Autograph Letters, and Manuscripts*. Sale of 21 and 22 July 1983. London: Sotheby, 1983.

See items 566-634 (pp. 203-20) for Yeats letters, a pastel drawing, and first editions. Report of this sale and Christie's sale of 20 July (AE23) by Sarah Bradford: "Sales of Books and MSS," *TLS*, 5 Aug 1983, 843-44.

100. ———: *English Literature and English History: Comprising Printed Books, Autograph Letters, and Manuscripts*. Sale of 16-17 July 1984. London: Sotheby, 1984.

See items 118 (acting copy of *The Land of Heart's Desire*, used by Dorothy Paget), 223 (letters to the Stage Society, including four by Yeats, among them one to Harley Granville-Barker and one to Lady Gregory), 252-57 (letters to Sean O'Casey and Margaret Gregory, Lady Gregory's daughter-in-law).

101. ———: *English Literature and History Comprising Books, Autograph Letters and Manuscripts*. Sale of 22 & 23 July 1985. London: Sotheby, 1985.

See items 351 (Broadsides) and 352 (the Great Vellum Notebook, with a two-page description and three reproductions). Press notices by Michael Foley: "£ 275,000 for Yeats Notes," *IrT*, 23 July 1985, 1; Warwick Gould: "Yeats's Great Vellum Notebook," *TLS*, 26 July 1985, 824.

102. ———: *English Literature and History Comprising Printed Books, Autograph Letters and Manuscripts*. Sale of 18 December 1985. London: Sotheby, 1985.

Includes an unpublished essay by Basil Bunting on Yeats (written in 1930) as well as letters by Yeats to Stopford Brooke, William Stevens, Richard Le Gallienne, Lady Genary, D. J. O'Donoghue, one Miss Murphy, John Drinkwater, and John Lane; also the corrected galley proofs for *The King's Threshold*. See also next item.

103. ———: *English Literature and History Comprising Printed Books, Autograph Letters and Manuscripts*. Sale of 10-11 July 1986. London: Sotheby, 1986.

Includes letters to Gwen John and the James F. Gallagher collection of Yeatsiana (i.e., autograph MSS., first editions as well as items from the previous sale: the O'Donoghue, Drinkwater, Murphy, and Le Gallienne letters and the galley proofs).

104. SOTHEBY'S: *English Literature and History, Comprising Printed Books, Autograph Letters and Manuscripts*. Sale of 23 and 24 July 1987. London: Sotheby's, 1987.

Item 127, the vellum manuscript book given by Yeats to Maud Gonne, contains seven poems and the titles of eleven further poems, some of them unpublished. Item 206 includes letters to A. P. Watt.

See also the anonymous note: "To Maud. . . ," *Times*, 2 July 1987, 12; Maurice Chittenden: "For Sale: Lost Love Poems of Yeats," *SunT*, 28 June 1987, 3 (correspondence by Ivo Jarosy: "Accursed Verse," 5 July 1987, 31); Warwick Gould: "'The Flame of the Spirit': A Love Tribute from W. B. Yeats," *TLS*, 17 July 1987, 770; Geraldine Norman: "High Prize for Love Poems," *Times*, 24 July 1987, 14.

104a. ———: *English Literature and History, Comprising Printed*

Books, Autograph Letters and Manuscripts. Sale of 21 and 22 July 1988. London: Sotheby's, 1988.

Includes three letters to Francis Bickley (item 238), two letters to Dorothy Paget (items 266, 268) and four letters to Florence Farr (items 267, 269, 271, 272). Item 271 contains "Upon a Dying Lady" with substantive variants.

105. STRATFORD, JENNY: *The Arts Council Collection of Modern Literary Manuscripts 1963-1972: A Catalogue*. With a preface by Philip Larkin. London: Turret Books, 1974. xxiii, 168 pp.

See pp. xxi, 89, 146, 147.

106. SUTTON, DAVID C.: "Location Register of Twentieth-Century Literary Manuscripts and Letters: Current Yeats Listings," *YeA*, 3 (1985), 295-303.

107. ———: "Location Register of Twentieth-Century Literary Manuscripts and Letters: A Supplementary Listing of Yeats Holdings," *YeA*, 4 (1986), 291-96.

108. ———: "Location Register of Twentieth-Century English Literary Manuscripts and Letters: A Cumulative Yeats Listing (to Autumn, 1985)," *YeA*, 5 (1987), 289-319.

109. SZLADITS, LOLA L.: "New in the Berg Collection, 1962-64," *BNYPL*, 73:4 (Apr 1969), 227-52.

"Lady Gregory and W. B. Yeats," 243-52.

110. ———: "New in the Berg Collection, 1965-1969," *BNYPL*, 75:1 (Jan 1971), 9-29.

"Ireland," 18-24; includes among the Yeats material the typescript of a poem, "Hills of Mourne," attributed to him, and a letter to Sara Allgood, 5 Oct 1935.

111. TRIESCH, MANFRED: "Some Unpublished J. M. Synge Papers," *ELN*, 4:1 (Sept 1966), 49-51.

In the U of Texas Library, among them four letters from Yeats to Maire O'Neill.

112. WHITTINGTON, JENNIFER: *Literary Recordings: A Checklist of the Archive of Recorded Poetry and Literature in the Library of Congress*. Revised, enlarged edition. Washington, D.C.: Library of Congress, 1981 [1966]. vi, 299 pp.

See index, p. 299, for recordings of Yeats's works by Yeats and others (among them George Barker, Padraic Colum, and Theodore Roethke).

113. WILLIAMS, MOELWYN I. (ed): *A Directory of Rare Books and Special Collections in the United Kingdom and the Republic of Ireland*. London: Library Association, 1985. xiii, 664 pp.

See index for a few references to Yeats.

114. YEATS, W. B.: Two albums of cuttings of reviews and articles referring to W. B. Yeats, ca. 1897-1904 and 1904-9.

In the National Library of Ireland, MSS. 12145-46. According to a note I found in these albums, Yeats seems to have subscribed to a press cutting agency (General Press Cutting Association, Ltd., Lennox House, Norfolk Street, London, W.C.).

115. YEATS SOCIETY OF JAPAN: [In Japanese] *Catalogue of the Cente-*

nary Exhibition of the Birth of William Butler Yeats, 19 May--21 May 1966. Edited by the Library of Waseda University and the Yeats Society of Japan. Tokyo: Waseda U, 1966. 32 pp.

See also AA9, AC40, 48, BA1, BB222, 223, CA50, 81, 102, CB343, CC238, CD630, 852, 1038, 1082, 1350, CF35, DD395, FA1, FC34, 41.

AF Concordances

1. CONNER, LESTER IRVIN: "A Yeats Dictionary: Names of the Persons and Places in the Poetry of W. B. Yeats," Ph.D. thesis, Columbia U, 1964. iv, 210 pp. (*DAI*, 28:4 [Oct 1967], 1429A)
An annotated list with only a few attempts at interpretation.

2. COPELAND, TOM W.: "The Proper Names in William Butler Yeats's Non-Dramatic Poetry: An Annotated Index," Ph.D. thesis, Texas Tech, 1957. xxii, 786 pp.

3. DOMVILLE, ERIC: *A Concordance to the Plays of W. B. Yeats*. Based on *The Variorum Edition of the Plays of W. B. Yeats* edited by Russell K. Alspach. Ithaca: Cornell UP, 1972. xxi, 1559 pp. in 2 vols.
Reviews:
- Carl Behm, *ARBA*, 4 (1973), 522-23.
- Daniel J. Casey, *EngR*, 23:1 (Fall 1972), 73-74.
- R. D[erolez], *ES*, 54:4 (Aug 1973), 405.
- T. H. Howard-Hill, *UTQ*, 42:4 (Summer 1973), 425-27.
- David Mann: "Yeats Concordance," *Computers and the Humanities*, 7:6 (Sept-Nov 1973), 449-50.
- M. J. Sidnell, *QQ*, 80:2 (Summer 1973), 298-99.
- Donald T. Torchiana, *MP*, 77:1 (Aug 1979), 112-13.

4. PARISH, STEPHEN MAXFIELD (ed): *A Concordance to the Poems of W. B. Yeats*. Programmed by James Allan Painter. Ithaca: Cornell UP, 1963. xxxix, 967 pp.
"Editor's Preface," v-xxvii, contains some remarks on Yeats's poetic vocabulary. "Programmer's Preface," xxix-xxxvii, explains the technical process of feeding poetry into computers. See also DC6.
Reviews:
- Robert B. Davis, *MP*, 63:1 (Aug 1965), 87-88.
- T. R. Henn, *MLR*, 59:2 (Apr 1964), 285-86.
- Josephine Miles, *VS*, 8:3 (Mar 1965), 290-92.
- [Simon Nowell-Smith]: "Computer and Concordancer," *TLS*, 23 Jan 1964, 69.
- Peter Ure, *RES*, 16:62 (Apr 1965), 221-22.

See also AA10, 11, CC202, 287, FC107.

B BIOGRAPHIES AND BIOGRAPHICAL MATERIAL

BA Books and Pamphlets Exclusively on Yeats

1. BUSHRUI, SUHEIL BADI, and JOHN MURCHISON MUNRO (eds): *Images and Memories: A Pictorial Record of the Life and Work of W. B. Yeats*. Designed by Z. N. Khuri. Beirut: Dar el-Mashreq, 1970. xvi, 164 pp.

Based on an exhibition held in the Jafet Memorial Library of the American U of Beirut, 6-20 Jan 1969.

2. CLARK, DAVID RIDGLEY, and NOEL KAVANAGH (comp): *Yeats and Sandymount*. Dublin: Yeats Association, 1966. 16 pp.

Compiled from previously published material.

3. ELLMANN, RICHARD: *Yeats: The Man and the Masks*. With a new preface. Oxford: Oxford UP, 1979 [1948]. xxxi, 331 pp.

Based on "William Butler Yeats: The Fountain Years," B.Litt. thesis, Trinity College, Dublin, 1947. ii, 107 pp.; and on "Triton among the Streams: A Study of the Life and Writings of William Butler Yeats," Ph.D. thesis, Yale U, 1947. v, 404 pp.

Incorporates: "W. B. Yeats: The End of Youth," *Furioso*, 3:3 (Spring 1948), 25-31; "Robartes and Aherne: Two Sides of a Penny," *KR*, 10:2 (Spring 1948), 177-86; "W. B. Yeats, Magician," *Western R*, 12:4 (Summer 1948), 232-40. The "Preface to the 1979 Edition," xi-xxxii, was first published as "At the Yeatses," *NYRB*, 17 May 1979, 22-25, and reprinted in CB148a. It discusses Mrs. Yeats, her life with WBY, Maud Gonne, and John Butler Yeats.

A classic study of the development of Yeats's mind and work in biographical progression with special reference to the influence of his father. Analyzed in sections DD, EE, FA, FC.

Reviews:

- Anon., *List*, 19 Jan 1950, 124, 126. Correspondence by Joseph Hone, 9 Mar 1950, 435.
- A. W. J. Becker: "In Search of Yeats," *Isis*, 19 May 1949, 16.
- Thomas Bodkin: "Yeats Interpreted," *Birmingham Post*, 15 Nov 1949, 2.
- H[ayden] C[arruth]: "Cherchez l'homme," *Poetry*, 74:4 (July 1949), 244-45.
- [Austin Clarke]: "The Dream and the Analyst," *TLS*, 4 Nov 1949, 716.
- Austin Clarke: "Oedipus and Philomel," *IrT*, 10 Dec 1949, 6.
- Mary M. Colum, *Tomorrow*, 8:6 (Feb 1949), 58-59.
- John Cournos, *Commonweal*, 31 Dec 1948, 308.
- David Daiches, *MLN*, 65:4 (Apr 1950), 267-69.
- Babette Deutsch: "No Longer a Matter of Literature," *NewRep*, 21 Mar 1949, 22-23.
- St. John Ervine: "Unmasking Yeats," *Spect*, 11 Nov 1949, 640, 642. See Van Wyck Brooks: "John Butler Yeats," *Spect*, 9 Dec 1949, 814, who defends JBY against the charges made by Ervine.
- Horace Gregory: "Paradoxical Destiny of Yeats as Poet and Man: Scholarly, Tactful, Intelligent Study of His Personality, Sources, and Crucial Years of Development," *NYHTB*, 14 Nov 1948, 5.
- James Hall: "Essence and Accidents," *VQR*, 25:3 (Summer 1949), 456-58.
- Lawrence Haward: "Ruskin and Yeats," *MGuard Weekly*, 5 Jan

1950, 11.
- J. V. Healy: "On Understanding Yeats," *Western R,* 13:3 (Spring 1949), 182-84.
- F. W. van Heerikhuizen: "Gedreven door angst," *Litterair paspoort,* 7:53 (Jan 1952), 10-11.
- Douglas Hewitt, *N&Q,* os 224 / ns 26:5 (Oct 1979), 386-87.
- Joseph Hone, *CambR,* 72:1752 (2 Dec 1950), 212.
- Brian Inglis: "'I, the Poet. . . ,'" *Spect,* 30 June 1961, 956.
- Leo Kennedy: "Behind Yeat[s]'s Many Masks," *Chicago Sun-Times,* 29 Nov 1948, 56.
- A. M. Klein: "The Masked Yeats," *Northern R,* 3:5 (June-July 1950), 43-45. Reprinted on pp. 282-84 of Klein's *Literary Essays and Reviews.* Edited by Usher Caplan and M. W. Steinberg. Toronto: U of Toronto Press, 1987. xxix, 424 pp.
- R[oger] McH[ugh], *Studies,* 39:155 (Sept 1950), 345-46.
- Seán O'Faoláin: "Yeats Divested," *Britain To-day,* 165 (Jan 1950), 38-39.
- John Pick: "Irishman without Priest," *America,* 22 Jan 1949, 437.
- M. A. R.: "American Professor's Study of Yeats and His Work," *IrI,* 31 Dec 1949, 4.
- Kathleen Raine: "Yeats's Gazebo," *NSt,* 10 Dec 1949, 700, 702.
- Horace Reynolds: "Clearing Mist & Haze from a Shy Man," *SatR,* 13 Nov 1948, 11-12.
- ———: "Reflections on a Poet and His World," *CSM,* 16 Dec 1948, 15.
- Lorna Reynolds, *DM,* 26:4 (Oct-Dec 1951), 58-60.
- A. Rivoallan, *EA,* 5:1 (Feb 1952), 80-81.
- Peter Russell: "Yeats," *Time and Tide,* 3 June 1950, 560.
- Cecil ffrench Salkeld: "Hooded Hawk," *IrW,* 10 (Jan 1950), 72-74.
- Elizabeth Schneider: "Two Studies of Yeats," *Nation,* 29 July 1950, 112-13.
- Donald A. Stauffer: "Artist Shining through His Vehicles," *KR,* 11:2 (Spring 1949), 330, 332-34, 336.
- James Johnson Sweeney: "The Development of the Poet Yeats," *NYTBR,* 19 Dec 1948, 5.
- William Troy: "Poet and Mystifier," *PR,* 16:2 (Feb 1949), 196-98.
- Jacques Vallette: "Un mot sur Yeats," *MercF,* 310:1047 (1 Nov 1950), 566-68.
- Charles Weir, *Furioso,* 4:2 (Spring 1949), 61-63.
- George Whalley: "Yeats's Mind," *YR,* 39:1 (Sept 1949), 165-67.
- Margaret Willy, *English,* 8:43 (Spring 1950), 37-38.
- Edmund Wilson: "New Light on W. B. Yeats," *New Yorker,* 18 Dec 1948, 103-7.

4. GIBBON, MONK: *The Masterpiece and the Man: Yeats as I Knew Him.* London: Hart-Davis, 1959. 226 pp.

An unorthodox book. Gibbon is a distant relation of the Yeats family and describes his encounters with, and opinions of, WBY, occasionally with somewhat less than reverence. At the same time, he is fully appreciative of Yeats's work, especially his poetry. Includes two poems, "Yeats's Earlier Poems" (p. 146) and "On Rereading Yeats" (pp. 221-22), reprinted in HD58-59. Contains some notes on the Yeats-Hopkins, Yeats-Moore, and Yeats-AE relationships, and quotes several letters from Yeats.

Reviews:
- Anon.: "I, the Poet William Yeats," *IrP,* 18 Apr 1959, 4.
- Anon.: "Yeats: Portrait by a Critical Cousin," *Scotsman,* 25

Apr 1959, 13.
- Anon.: "Farewell to Irish Fairies but Not to Playboys," *Times*, 4 June 1959, 15.
- Anon.: "A Partial View," *TLS*, 8 May 1959, 274.
- A[erol] A[rnold], *Personalist*, 42:2 (Spring 1961), 254-55.
- Thomas Bodkin: "Yeats: An Unfriendly Poet," *Birmingham Post*, 5 May 1959, 3.
- Padraic Colum: "Portrait of W. B. Y.," *IrT*, 4 Apr 1959, 6.
- Donald Davie: "Maker and Breaker," *NSt*, 16 May 1959, 695.
- Richard Ellman[n]: "Out of Date Objections to W. B. Yeats," *Chicago Sunday Tribune*, 13 Mar 1960, part 4, 2.
- DeLancey Ferguson: "Memories of Yeats," *NYHTB*, 4 Sept 1960, 6.
- Eric Forbes-Boyd: "Listening to Mr. Gibbon," *CSM*, 23 July 1959, 11.
- René Fréchet: "L'étude de Yeats: Textes, jugements et éclairissements," *EA*, 14:1 (Jan-Mar 1961), 36-47.
- Eric Gillett: "Some Uncommon People," *National and English R*, 152:916 (June 1959), 231-35.
- Vivienne Koch: "Three Lives," *Poetry*, 98:1 (Apr 1961), 59-62.
- Louis MacNeice, *LMag*, 7:8 (Aug 1960), 70-73.
- Donat O'Donnell [i.e., Conor Cruise O'Brien]: "The Great Conger," *Spect*, 22 May 1959, 736. Reprinted in O'Brien: *Writers and Politics*. NY: Pantheon Books, 1965. xxii, 259 pp. (pp. 119-20).
- Frank O'Connor: "A Man with a Grievance," *Nation*, 27 Feb 1960, 190-91.
- Ulick O'Connor: "Ripe Dublin Talk," *Sunday Independent*, 5 July 1959, 10.
- Risteárd Ó Glaisne, *Focus*, 2:6 (June 1959), 27.
- P. P.: "The Man Yeats," *IrI*, 16 May 1959, 8.
- Charles Poore: "Books of the Times," *NYT*, 23 Feb 1960, 29.
- W. R. Rodgers: "Seeing Yeats Plain," *SunT*, 3 May 1959, 17.
- John Unterecker: "In Yeats' Shadow," *NYTBR*, 17 Apr 1960, 20.
- Jacques Vallette: "Vous que j'aimais éperdument," *MercF*, 338: 1160 (Apr 1960), 738-39.
- W. L. Webb: "Flattening Young Men," *MGuard*, 22 May 1959, 4.

5. GOGARTY, OLIVER ST. JOHN: *William Butler Yeats: A Memoir*. With a preface by Myles Dillon. Dublin: Dolmen Press, 1963. 27 pp.

Many of the anecdotes contained in this memoir appear in other books and articles by Gogarty (see BB80-88).

Reviews:
- R[ivers] C[arew], *Dubliner*, 3:1 (Spring 1964), 82-83.
- Richard Ellmann: "Deadly Merits," *NSt*, 20 Mar 1964, 461.
- Stephen Fanning, *Kilkenny Magazine*, 10 (Autumn-Winter 1963), 127, 129, 131.
- Robert Greacen, *List*, 23 Jan 1964, 162.
- T. R. Henn, *MLR*, 59:4 (Oct 1964), 655.

6. HANLEY, MARY: *Thoor Ballylee--Home of William Butler Yeats*. Edited by Liam Miller from a paper given to the Kiltartan Society in 1961. With a foreword by T. R. Henn. Dublin: Dolmen Press, 1965. 32 pp.

An illustrated history of Yeats's tower which was restored in 1963-1965. Reviewed by Giorgio Melchiori, *N&Q*, os 211 / ns 13:11 (Nov 1966), 430-31. There was a second edition in 1977, reprinted in 1984.

7. HARPER, GEORGE MILLS: *"Go Back to Where You Belong": Yeats's Return from Exile*. Dublin: Dolmen Press, 1973. 43 pp. (New Yeats Papers. 6.)

Discusses Yeats's "life-long odyssey" and his views on exile.
Reviews:
- Graham Hough: "Yeats and the Magic of Power," *TLS*, 14 Feb 1975, 160.
- Elizabeth Mackenzie, *N&Q*, os 221 / ns 23:7 (July 1976), 314-15.

8. HONE, JOSEPH: *W. B. Yeats, 1865-1939*. London: Macmillan, 1962 [1942, i.e., 1943]. ix, 504 pp.
The "official" biography, authorized by Mrs. Yeats. Although this is a pleasant book to read, and in some respects still indispensable until the projected new biography appears (see BB59), it is far from perfect. Since Hone wrote close after Yeats's death, many names and incidents had to be omitted; there is also little critical distance to the man and his work. Hone simplifies Yeats's complex personality; he is also not very enlightening on the poetic work. Finally, the documentation is singularly poor. See also CA153 and FB22.
Reviews:
- Peter Allt, *Hermathena*, 62 (Nov 1943), 115-17.
- Anon., *DUJ*, os 35 / ns 4:3 (June 1953), 102-4.
- Anon., *List*, 15 Apr 1943, 457.
- Anon.: "W. B. Yeats and Symbolism," *Poetry R*, 34:2 (Mar-Apr 1943), 126-28. Makes the curious statement that Yeats's "life outside his poetry was not particularly interesting."
- Anon.: "1865-1939," *Time*, 8 Feb 1943, 88, 91.
- Joan Bennett, *RES*, 20:77 (Jan 1944), 90-91.
- Thomas Bodkin: "Poet and Autocrat," *Birmingham Post*, 16 Feb 1943, 2.
- Louise Bogan: "Yeats and His Ireland," *PR*, 10:2 (Mar-Apr 1943), 198-201.
- Elizabeth Bowen: "With Silent Friends," *Tatler and Bystander*, 24 Feb 1943, 246, 248.
- Ernest A. Boyd: "Romantic Ireland's Dead and Gone," *New Leader*, 6 Mar 1943, 3.
- W. Bardsley Brash, *London Q and Holborn R*, 168 / series 6, 12:3 (July 1943), 273-74.
- Paul Vincent Carroll: "Democracy Hater, He Fanned Revolution," *Daily Record and Mail*, 8 Mar 1943, 2.
- Sydney W. Carroll: "The Theatre as a Poet's Workshop," *Daily Sketch*, 11 Feb 1943, 6.
- S. C. Chew: "A Biography of Yeats," *CSM*, 6 Mar 1943, Weekly Magazine section, 11.
- [Harold Child]: "William Butler Yeats: The Dual Anglo-Irish Heritage," *TLS*, 13 Feb 1943, 78.
- A. Choudhuri, *VQ*, 27:3&4 (1961/62), 285-87.
- Richard Church: "A Poet's Design for Living," *FortnR*, os 159 / ns 153:916 (Apr 1943), 258-62.
- Mary M. Colum: "Yeats: He Lived a Full Life," *NYTBR*, 7 Feb 1943, 1, 22.
- Cyril Connolly: "The Last of the Magi," *Obs*, 14 Feb 1943, 3.
- Malcolm Cowley: "The Hosting of the Shee," *NewRep*, 8 Feb 1943, 185-86.
- Gustav Cross: "Yeats: Angry Old Poet," *Sydney Morning Herald*, 17 Nov 1962, 16.
- M. D., *DM*, 18:2 (Apr-June 1943), 60-63.
- Howell Daniels, *AWR*, 13:31 (1962), 94-96.
- J[ames] D[elehanty], *Kilkenny Magazine*, 8 (Autumn-Winter 1962), 56-58.
- Babette Deutsch: "W. B. Yeats, the Greatest Poet of Our Time,"

NYHTB, 7 Feb 1943, 1; 28 Feb 1943, 26.
- Myles Dillon, *JEGP*, 42:4 (Oct 1943), 610-14.
- Clifton Fadiman: "The Magician," *New Yorker*, 6 Feb 1943, 53-55.
- H[ugh] I'A[nson] F[ausset]: "A Poet's Life," *MGuard*, 17 Mar 1943, 3.
- P. J. Gannon, *Studies*, 32:125 (Mar 1943), 130-31.
- Oliver St. John Gogarty: "Ireland's Great Poet," *Gazette*, 24 Apr 1943, 9.
- Horace Gregory: "Yeats as Dublin Saw Him," *YR*, 32:3 (Mar 1943), 599-602.
- ———, *Chimera*, 1:4 (Spring 1943), 45-46, 48.
- Joseph P. Hackett: "Shaw and Yeats," *Studies*, 32:127 (Sept 1943), 369-78. Involves a Shaw-Yeats comparison.
- J. V. Healy: "Ancient Lineaments," *Poetry*, 62:4 (July 1943), 223-28.
- Richard Jennings: "Poetry and Occultism," *Nineteenth Century*, 133:794 (Apr 1943), 180-81.
- F. J. K.: "A Yeats Biography," *IrI*, 29 Mar 1943, 2.
- Patrick Kavanagh: "W. B. Yeats," *Standard*, 26 Feb 1943, 2.
- Charlotte Kohler: "A Faithful Chronicle," *VQR*, 19:3 (Summer 1943), 472-75.
- Lewis Leary: "An Authorized Biography of W. B. Yeats," *SAQ*, 42:3 (July 1943), 303-4.
- T. McAlindon, *CritQ*, 5:2 (Summer 1963), 183-85.
- Desmond MacCarthy: "A Life of Yeats," *SunT*, 14 Feb 1943, 3.
- M. J. MacM[anus]: "Mr. Joseph Hone's Life of Yeats," *IrP*, 9 Mar 1943, 2.
- Samuel Mathai, *Cultural Forum*, 5:2 (Dec 1962 / Jan 1963), 103-4.
- M[argaret] M[eagher], *CathW*, 157:937 (Apr 1943), 99-100.
- E. H. W. Meyerstein: "The Music of Death and Change," *English*, 4:23 (Summer 1943), 161-63.
- John Montague: "Responsibilities," *Guardian*, 22 June 1962, 7. Correspondence by Lovatt Dickson, 2 July, 8; John Montague and Geoffrey de C. Parmiter, 6 July, 10; Ronald Dunlop, 13 July, 10; Lovatt Dickson, 17 July, 8.
- Raymond Mortimer: "Books in General," *NSt*, 13 Feb 1943, 111-12.
- Kate O'Brien, *LLT*, 39:1 (Oct 1943), 59-60, 62.
- Hermann Peschmann: "W. B. Yeats (1865-1939)," *New English Weekly*, 20 May 1943, 41-43.
- Una Pope-Hennessy, *Dublin R*, 213:427 (Dec 1943), 180-82.
- James Reaney: "Yeats Unconquered," *Canadian Forum*, 42:504 (Jan 1963), 235-36.
- Cecil Roberts: "The Majesty of Yeats," *SatR*, 13 Feb 1943, 5. Correspondence by Mary M. Colum, 20 Feb 1943, 15.
- R. A. Scott-James: "The Life of Yeats," *Britain To-day*, 84 (Apr 1943), 23-24.
- Edward Shanks: "W. B. Yeats--Poet and Practical Man," *Daily Dispatch*, 13 Feb 1943, 2.
- Naomi Royde Smith: "W. B. Yeats," *Time and Tide*, 13 Mar 1943, 201-2.
- Robert Speaight: "Light on the Celtic Twilight," *Tablet*, 17 Apr 1943, 188-89.
- Theodore Spencer: "Our Greatest Poet-Statesman," *Atlantic Monthly*, 171:3 (Mar 1943), 148.
- Sir John Squire: "A Great Poet of the English-Speaking World," *ILN*, 6 Mar 1943, 258.
- L. A. G. Strong: "The Eagle Mind of Yeats," *John o' London's*

Weekly, 26 Mar 1943, 241-42.
- P. C. T., *Irish Book Lover,* 29:2 (Mar 1944), 47-48.
- Geoffrey Taylor, *Bell,* 6:1 (Apr 1943), 59-62.
- W. J. Turner: "Poet and Patriot," *Spect,* 19 Feb 1943, 176.
- Lee Varley: "Not the Last Word on Yeats: Big Biography by Hone Taps Rich New Source," *Springfield Union / Springfield Sunday Republican,* 21 Feb 1943, E7.
- Richard Weber, *Dubliner,* 5 (Sept-Oct 1962), 54-56.
- E. V. R. Wyatt: "The Dail and the Druids," *Commonweal,* 16 Apr 1943, 637-40.
- Morton Dauwen Zabel: "Yeats: The Image and the Book," *Nation,* 6 Mar 1943, 348-50. A revised version of this review is included in CA36.

9. MACLIAMMÓIR, MICHEÁL, and EAVAN BOLAND: *W. B. Yeats and His World.* London: Thames & Hudson, 1971. 144 pp.

About 140 pictures and an undistinguished text.

Reviews:
- Peter Ansorge, *Books and Bookmen,* 17:195 (Dec 1971), 20-22.
- [Austin Clarke]: "Poet in Pictures," *TLS,* 19 Nov 1971, 1438.
- Peter Faulkner, *DUJ,* os 65 / ns 34:1 (Dec 1972), 122.
- Brian H. Finney: "Yeats Gallery," *IrP,* 27 Nov 1971, 12.
- Geoffrey Grigson: "Vision, Faith, and Murder," *Country Life,* 28 Oct 1971, 1168.
- Michael Hartnett: "Yeats, Warts and All," *IrT,* 30 Oct 1971, 10.
- John Jordan: "Presenting Yeats," *IrI,* 16 Oct 1971, 8.
- Mary Lappin: "Yeats Surveyed," *Hibernia,* 5 Nov 1971, 16.
- George Mayhew, *BA,* 47:1 (Winter 1973), 153.
- D[iane] R[oman], *JIL,* 1:3 (Sept 1972), 95.

10. MACMANUS, FRANCIS (ed): *The Yeats We Knew.* Memoirs by Pádraic Colum, Francis Stuart, Monk Gibbon, Earnán de Blaghd [i.e., Ernest Blythe], and Austin Clarke. Cork: Mercier Press, 1965. 94 pp. (Thomas Davis Lectures.)

Colum's recollections are largely concerned with Yeats's theatrical career (pp. 13-24); Stuart (27-40) found Yeats's presence a strain and thinks that his "life and his poetry never merged" and that the poetry "lacks an inherent unifying vision of man"; Gibbon (43-57) "never penetrated--as others claim to have done--behind the poetic mask to the human individual"; Blythe (61-75) recollects Abbey Theatre business and comments on Yeats's involvement in politics; and Clarke (79-94) tells of three occasions on which he saw Yeats, at the Abbey, at the Thomas Davis Centenary, and at Coole. Parts of the contributions by Stuart, Gibbon, Clarke, and Blythe are reprinted in BA13, 2:364-95.

Reviews:
- Anon.: "Aghaidh fidil," *Comhar,* 24:7 (July 1965), 23, 25.
- W. R. Grey, *Focus,* 8:8 (Aug 1965), 187.

11. MARTIN, AUGUSTINE: *W. B. Yeats.* Dublin: Gill & Macmillan, 1983. viii, 146 pp. (Gill's Irish Lives.)

A readable popular biography, with emphasis on the poetry rather than on the other works.

Reviews:
- Terence Brown: "Apocalyptic Four," *IrP,* 26 Nov 1983, 9.
- Terence Diggory, *Yeats,* 3 (1985), 244-49.
- Aidan Mathews: "Gill's Irish Lives Series," *ILS,* 3:2 (Fall 1984), 42.

12. MASEFIELD, JOHN: *Some Memories of W. B. Yeats.* NY: Macmillan,

1940. vi, 31 pp.

Reprinted °Folcroft, Pa.: Folcroft Library Editions, 1977; °Norwood, Pa.: Norwood Editions, 1978. Also published Dublin: Cuala Press, 1940; reprinted Shannon: Irish UP, 1971. Includes three poems on Yeats.

Reviews:

- [Austin Clarke]: "Mr. Masefield on Yeats," *TLS,* 8 Feb 1941, 68.
- R. O'F. [Robert Farren], *Bell,* 2:1 (Apr 1941), 96.
- G[arland] G[reever]: "Puzzle-Map Reminiscences," *Personalist,* 22:3 (Summer 1941), 310-11.
- Louis MacNeice: "Through Stained Glass," *Spect,* 7 Feb 1941, 152.
- Horace Reynolds: "Yeats as Portrayed by Masefield," *CSM,* 28 Dec 1940, Weekly Magazine section, 10.
- Winfield Townley Scott: "The Foolish Passionate Man," *Accent,* 1:4 (Summer 1941), 247-50.
- William Soutar: "William Butler Yeats," *Adelphi,* 17:12 (Sept 1941), 425-27.

13. MIKHAIL, EDWARD HALIM (ed): *W. B. Yeats: Interviews and Recollections.* With a foreword by A. Norman Jeffares. London: Macmillan, 1976. xvii, 1-197; xi, 199-426 pp. in 2 vols.

Reprints, completely or in part, about 100 items; references to most of the reprints are made in the relevant entries of this bibliography. The annotations contain numerous errors; even the day and date of Yeats's death are wrong (p. 256).

Reviews:

- Peter Brigg, *ESC,* 5:2 (Summer 1979), 231-35.
- Richard J. Finneran: "W. B. Yeats: Some Recent Bibliographical and Editorial Work," *Review,* 1 (1979), 233-48.
- Warwick Gould: "The Biocritical Heritage," *English,* 26:126 (Autumn 1977), 240-54.
- Nicholas Grene, *N&Q,* os 223 / ns 25:4 (Aug 1978), 379-80.
- [Robert Hogan], *JIL,* 7:2 (May 1978), 185-87.
- Eileen Kennedy, *Eire,* 14:2 (Summer 1979), 150-51.
- F. S. L. Lyons: "The Better Side of Yeats," *TLS,* 17 June 1977, 734.
- Robert M. Snukal, *Ariel,* 9:1 (Jan 1978), 102-4.
- Weldon Thornton, *YES,* 10 (1980), 340-41.
- George Woodcock: "The Irish Renaissance," *QQ,* 84:4 (Winter 1977), 639-45.
- Georges-Denis Zimmermann, *ES,* 60:4 (Aug 1979), 526-28.

14. MOORE, VIRGINIA: *The Unicorn: William Butler Yeats' Search for Reality.* NY: Macmillan, 1954. xxi, 519 pp.

Reprinted NY: Octagon Books, 1973. Based on "Religion and William Butler Yeats," °Ph.D. thesis, Columbia U, 1952. 619 pp. (*DAI,* 12:4 [1952], 427).

Author's summary of what this book tries to give: "1. Some new [biographical] light from talks with George Yeats, Maud Gonne, Ezra Pound, and others. 2. Heretofore unused . . . material from unpublished manuscripts, including the rituals of the Irish 'mysteries' . . . ; also epistolary evidence which alters the accepted view of his relation to Maud Gonne; also . . . the 'Seven Propositions' of 1937 which set forth . . . his mature philosophy. 3. Full biographical and doctrinal use . . . of the ritual and teachings of the 'Christian-cabalistic' secret Order to which Yeats belonged for more than twenty-five years. 4. A detailed study . . . of Yeats' doctrinal sources: Hermetism, Druidism, Cabalism, Neoplatonism, Gnosticism, Rosicrucianism, Blake, and so forth. . . . 5. A painstaking study . . . of Yeats' long pursuit of philosophy, both Western and Eastern. . . . 6. A re-evaluation of . . . *A Vision*. 7. A reassessment of Yeats' relation to Christianity" (p. xvi). Discusses the influence of Plotinus and Berkeley and Yeats's relationship with MacGregor Mathers, Aleister Crowley, and T. Sturge Moore. The book has been criticized for its lack of organization and its gossipy and vulgar style; on the other hand, many scholars have found it quite useful.

Reviews:
- Hazard Adams: "Where All Ladders Start," *Western R*, 19:3 (Winter 1955), 229-34.
- Anon.: "Yeats's Religious Beliefs," *Nation*, 31 July 1954, 96-97.
- S. Appleton, *Thought*, 29:115 (Winter 1954/55), 615-16.
- Mary P. Brody, *CathW*, 179:1072 (July 1954), 317-18.
- Reuben A. Brower: "The Incarnation of Yeats," *YR*, 44:2 (Dec 1954), 290-92.
- Babette Deutsch: "Yeats, with Many Footnotes," *NYHTB*, 18 July 1954, 5.
- René Fréchet, *EA*, 12:4 (Oct-Dec 1959), 365-66.
- Horace Gregory: "Yeats' Golden Dawn," *NYTBR*, 30 May 1954, 6.
- Hugh Kenner: "Unpurged Images," *HudR*, 8:4 (Winter 1956), 609-17.
- Russell Krauss, *Educational Forum*, 19:2, part 1 (Jan 1955), 250-51.
- Irving David Suss, *SAQ*, 54:1 (Jan 1955), 151-53.
- W. D. T[empleman], *Personalist*, 36:4 (Autumn 1955), 424-25.
- Charles Child Walcutt, *ArQ*, 11:2 (Summer 1955), 170-73.
- George Whalley, *QQ*, 62:4 (Winter 1956), 617-21.

15. MURPHY, WILLIAM MICHAEL: *Prodigal Father: The Life of John Butler Yeats (1839-1922)*. Ithaca: Cornell UP, 1978. 683 pp.

The definitive biography of JBY in which his son WBY figures prominently, although not always favorably. Uses a wealth of unpublished material and includes several sketches and drawings which JBY made of WBY.

See also Murphy's "John Butler Yeats" in Jeffrey Meyers (ed): *The Craft of Literary Biography*. London: Macmillan, 1985. x, 253 pp. (pp. 33-54), in which he comments on the genesis of his book.

Reviews:
- Anon.: "Father of the Man," *Economist*, 12 Aug 1978, 91-92.
- Guy Davenport: "Sweet Talker," *Inquiry*, 11 Dec 1978, 18-20.
- Denis Donoghue: "A Distinguished 'Failure,'" *Hibernia*, 24 Aug 1978, 12.
- Terry Eagleton: "Jack [sic] Yeats: In a Son's Shadow," *Books and Bookmen*, 24:2 (Nov 1978), 41.
- Richard Ellmann: "Progenitor of Genius," *NYTBR*, 9 July 1978, 1, 35.
- James W. Flannery, *TJ*, 31:4 (Dec 1979), 558-60.
- Harry Goldgar: "Father of Poet Yeats Has Own Claim to Fame," *Times-Picayune*, 2 July 1978, section III, 4.
- F[rancis] G[olffing], *PRR*, 3:2 (May 1980), 132-34.
- Bryan Guinness: "Portrait Painter and Philosopher," *Apollo*, 109:208 (June 1979), 486-88.
- George M. Harper, *ACIS Newsletter*, 8:3 (Oct 1978), 4.
- John V. Kelleher: "Books Considered," *NewRep*, 19 Aug 1978, 31-33.
- Robert Kirsch: "J. B. Yeats in Search of 'The Perfect Quar-

ry,'" *LA Times*, 25 June 1978, Book Review, 1, 13.
- F. S. L. Lyons: "Poor Painter, Poor Ghost," *TLS*, 22 Sept 1978, 1038-40.
- Derek Mahon: "The Wanderings of JBY," *NSt*, 18 Aug 1978, 217-18.
- Raymond Mortimer: "Yeats: The Poet's Father," *SunT*, 20 Aug 1978, 38.
- Peter Quartermain, *CJIS*, 5:2 (Dec 1979), 71-77.
- Michael Sidnell: "John Butler Yeats," *UTQ*, 49:2 (Winter 1979/80), 180-83.
- Margaret Stanley, *EI*, 3 (Dec 1978), 111-14.
- John Unterecker, *Biography*, 2:2 (Spring 1979), 175-81.
- Helen Vendler: "J. B. Y.," *New Yorker*, 8 Jan 1979, 66-77. See also BD16.
- A. N. Wilson: "Free Spirit," *Spect*, 16 Feb 1980, 21-22. Correspondence by Mary Campbell, 8 Mar 1980, 15.
- Terence Winch: "The Youngest Mind in Dublin," *WashP*, 27 Aug 1978, section E (Book World), 1, 4.

16. O'CONNOR, FRANK: *A Gambler's Throw: Memories of W. B. Yeats*. Edinburgh: Tragara Press, 1975. [17 pp.]

Text of a radio talk given on 13 Feb 1966.

17. ———: *W. B. Yeats: A Reminiscence*. Edinburgh: Tragara Press, 1982. 19 pp.

Text of a radio talk given on 4 May 1947; see also BB172.

18. STRAND, KARIN MARGARET: "W. B. Yeats' American Lecture Tours," Ph.D. thesis, Northwestern U, 1978. iv, 383 pp. (*DAI*, 39:8 [Feb 1979], 4941A)

Charts Yeats's five visits to the U.S. as completely as possible, summarizes lectures and interviews, and reprints several of them. Quotes from unpublished typescripts and letters. Valuable; see also AE67 and the headnotes to sections BE and BF.

19. STRONG, LEONARD ALFRED GEORGE: *A Letter to W. B. Yeats*. London: Hogarth Press, 1932. 31 pp. (Hogarth Letters. 6.)

Some rather adulatory reminiscences. Includes a parody of Mrs. Leo Hunter's "Ode to an Expiring Frog," done in Yeats's style (p. 18).

20. TUOHY, FRANK: *Yeats*. London: Macmillan, 1976. 232 pp.

A non-academic, readable biography, profusely illustrated. Analyzed in sections DD, EE, FA.

Reviews:
- Peter Ackroyd: "Flummery," *Spect*, 23 Oct 1976, 27-28.
- Anon.: "Poetic Postures," *Economist*, 13 Nov 1976, 142.
- Malcolm Brown: "Take Down This Book," *Hibernia*, 5 Nov 1976, 17.
- Connolly Cole: "Enigma in the Epic," *BooksI*, 14 (June 1977), 122.
- Denis Donoghue: "The Hard Case of Yeats," *NYRB*, 26 May 1977, 3-4, 6, 8.
- Helen af Enehjelm: "Angloirländaren W. B. Yeats, drömmare och nationalpoet," *Hufvudstadsbladet*, 17 Mar 1977, 3.
- Edward Engelberg: "Perspectives on Yeats," *New Boston R*, 3:2 (Fall 1977), 14-15.
- Roy Foster: "By Mask and by Magic," *TLS*, 29 Oct 1976, 1358.
- J. F. Hopkins, *Quartet*, 8:57/58 (Winter/Spring 1977), 60-61.
- Parkman Howe: "Vivid Characters in Yeats Volume," *CSM*, 26

Jan 1977, 23.
- Richard G. Hubler: "Yeats: A Poet Who Surpassed Adulation," *LA Times*, 2 Jan 1977, Book Review, 4.
- D. P. King, *WLT*, 51:4 (Autumn 1977), 626.
- James McNally: "Browning Traces in Tuohy's *Yeats*," *Studies in Browning and His Circle*, 5:1 (Spring 1977), 23-26; a list of Browning echoes in Yeats quotations as they appear in Tuohy's book.
- Derek Mahon: "King of the Cats," *NSt*, 5 Nov 1976, 639-40.
- John Mole: "Ballyphallus," *List*, 28 Oct 1976, 544.
- Julian Moynahan: "The Poet, His Love, and His Plays," *NYTBR*, 27 Feb 1977, 8, 10.
- John O'Riordan: "A Fanatic Heart," *Library R*, 25:8 (Winter 1976/77), 340.
- P[amela] van Schaik, *UES*, 15:2 (Sept 1977), 99-100.
- F. X. Shea, *AR*, 35:2-3 (Spring-Summer 1977), 317-18.
- Peter Sheal, *Four Decades*, 1:4 (July 1977), 307-10.
- A. G. Stock, *IUR*, 7:1 (Spring 1977), 131-33.
- Molly Tibbs: "An Introduction to Yeats," *ContempR*, 230:1332 (Jan 1977), 55.
- John Wain: "Horseman, Pass By," *Obs*, 24 Oct 1976, 31.
- David Wright: "A Terrible Beauty," *TES*, 3 Dec 1976, 41.

21. YEATS, W. B.: *The Letters*. Edited by Allan Wade. London: Hart-Davis, 1954. 938 pp.

Reprinted °NY: Octagon Books, 1980. Incorporates *Some Letters from W. B. Yeats to John O'Leary and His Sister from Originals in the Berg Collection*. Edited by Allan Wade. NY: New York Public Library, 1953. 25 pp. (Introduction, pp. 3-5, notes, pp. 19-25). Reprinted from *BNYPL*, 57:1 (Jan 1953), 11-22; :2 (Feb 1953), 76-87.

Wade's introduction to the six parts of the book and the notes provide a good, short biography. This edition will be superseded by the *Collected Letters* (see next item). For reviews see G967-1007.

22. ———: *The Collected Letters of W. B. Yeats*. General editor John Kelly. Oxford: Clarendon Press, 1986--. 12 vols. projected.

Volume One: 1865-1895. Edited by John Kelly, associate editor Eric Domville. 1986. xlii, 548 pp.

Contains a chronological table, a general introduction, and a biographical and historical appendix (extended notes on the most important persons and places), as well as copious annotations. The major recipients in this volume are Douglas Hyde, John O'Leary, Ernest Rhys, Father Matthew Russell, Katharine Tynan, T. Fisher Unwin, and Lily (Susan Mary) Yeats. Includes a poem by Thomas Hutchinson: "To W. B. Yeats: 13/6/94" (p. 390). For reviews see G1604-1652.

See also AE37, CA6, 31, 35, 41, 47, 63, CC172, CD1459, 1465, FC121.

BB Substantial Articles and Parts of Books

1. ALDINGTON, RICHARD: *Life for Life's Sake: A Book of Reminiscences*. London: Cassell, 1968 [1941]. 374 pp.

Reminiscences of Yeats, pp. 95, 97-99, 306-7 (Tagore "hit Yeats bang in the Blavatsky").

2. ANON.: "World-Wide Greetings: Mr. Yeats's Birthday Mail. Plans

for the Future," *IrT,* 15 June 1935, 6.
See also M. C.: "Congratulations to 'W. B. Y.,'" 7.

3. ANON.: "Yeats, 70, Is Feted by Irish Notables: 200 at Dublin Dinner in First Public Tribute Ever Paid to Him in Own Country," *NYT,* 28 June 1935, 19.

4. ANON.: "All Fresh and Wide-Eyed," *New Yorker,* 2 Nov 1963, 40-41.
Interview with Anne Yeats reminiscing about her father.

5. ANON.: "Mr. W. B. Yeats's Estate," *Times,* 23 Oct 1939, 11.
Yeats left a personal estate valued at £ 8,329.

6. ANON.: "W. B. Yeats at School: Interesting Reminiscences of the Irish Poet's Schooldays by a Classmate," *T.P.'s Weekly,* 7 June 1912, 709.
Reprinted in BA13, 1:1-3; see also BB27.

7. ANTHEIL, GEORGE: *Bad Boy of Music.* Garden City: Doubleday, Doran, 1945. vi, 378 pp.
Reminiscences of Yeats, for whose *Fighting the Waves* he wrote the incidental music, pp. 228-29. Says that Yeats, Eliot, Pound, and others corrected the MS. of his detective story *Death in the Dark* (published under the pseudonym Stacey Bishop). See CD148.

8. ATKINSON, F. G.: "W. B. Yeats: A Biographical Note," *N&Q,* os 216 / ns 18:3 (Mar 1971), 106-9.
Accompanies three letters to Arthur Quiller-Couch (1898-1900).

9. Balliett [i.e., BALLIET], CONRAD A.: "The Lives--and Lies--of Maud Gonne," *Eire,* 14:3 (Fall 1979), 17-44.
Corrigenda in 15:1 (Spring 1980), 156. Corrects errors in Maud Gonne's autobiography (BB93) and offers information supplementary to Cardozo (CD478) and Levenson (CD482).

10. ———: "Maud Gonne MacBride: Violent Pacifist," *IRA,* 3 (1982), 93-105.

11. BANGS, FRANCIS H.: "Julia Ellsworth Ford: An Appreciation," *YULG,* 26:4 (Apr 1952), 153-92.
On Mrs. Ford's contacts with Yeats during his first American lecture tour, pp. 153-57.

12. BARKER, DUDLEY: *Prominent Edwardians.* NY: Atheneum, 1969. iii, 257 pp.
"An Episode in the Life of William Butler Yeats," 100-36; retells Yeats's biography from his first meeting with Maud Gonne until her marriage.

13. BARNES, GEORGE: "George Barnes's 'W. B. Yeats and Broadcasting' 1940." Introductory note by Jeremy Silver, *YeA,* 5 (1987), 189-94.

14. BEARDSLEY, AUBREY: *The Letters.* Edited by Henry Maas, J. L. Duncan, and W. G. Wood. Rutherford, N.J.: Fairleigh Dickinson UP, 1970. ix, 472 pp.
Yeats is referred to passim (see index). Incorporates *Letters from Aubrey Beardsley to Leonard Smithers.* Edited with introduction and notes by R. A. Walker. London: First Edition Club, 1937. xvi, 240 pp.

15. BECKSON, KARL E.: "The Rhymers' Club," Ph.D. thesis, Columbia U, 1959. vi, 200 pp. (*DAI,* 20:3 [Sept 1959], 1021-22)
On Yeats and the Rhymers' Club, passim; on his poetry, pp. 148-55; on the Irish Literary Society, whose foundation gave the fatal blow to the Rhymers' Club, pp. 165-85.

16. BEDDINGTON, FRANCES ETHEL: *All That I Have Met.* By Mrs. Claude Beddington. London: Cassell, 1929, xiii, 287 pp.
"Yeats and Shaw," 178-82. She met Yeats in 1916; includes a letter from him, dated 82 Merrion Sq., 9 Feb 1924.

17. BEERBOHM, SIR MAX: *Mainly on the Air.* Enlarged edition. London: Heinemann, 1957 [1946]. x, 192 pp.
"First Meetings with W. B. Yeats," 95-101 (not in 1946 edition). Written in 1914, broadcast on 26 Dec 1954, B.B.C. third programme. Reprinted from *List,* 6 Jan 1955, 15-16, and from *Atlantic Monthly,* 200:3 (Sept 1957), 70-72. Also in John Morris (ed): *From the Third Programme: A Ten Years' Anthology.* London: Nonesuch Press, 1956. x, 339 pp. (pp. 154-61). Extract reprinted in BA13, 1:27-30.
Reviews of the broadcast:
- Anon.: "W. B. Yeats, by Max," *Times,* 28 Dec 1954, 9.
- Martin Armstrong: "The Spoken Word: The Detached Observer," *List,* 6 Jan 1955, 39.

18. BLUNT, WILFRID SCAWEN: *My Diaries: Being a Personal Narrative of Events, 1888-1914.* London: Secker, [1921]. 2 vols.
Yeats visits Blunt on 1 Apr 1898 and experiments magically with him: "The performance was very imperfect, not to say null" (1:290-91). Further meetings with Yeats on 26 Apr 1902 (2:22); 10 and 15 June 1902 (2:28); 2 May 1903 (2:53): Blunt attends a performance of *The Hour-Glass* and finds it a "terrible infliction"; 10 May 1904 (2:100): Blunt detects a trace of the charlatan in Yeats. See also BB76 and 89.

19. BOOTH, JOHN R.: "Yeats as Reviewer," *List,* 18 Aug 1938, 352.
Reminiscences of Yeats when he was a reviewer for the Dublin *Daily Express.*

20. BOSE, ABINASH CHANDRA: "W. B. Yeats: His Last Indian Visitor," *Shakti,* 3:6 (June 1966), 6-11.
A fuller account than the one given in CD1357. Correspondence by Richard Ellmann and Bose, :11 (Nov 1966), 40.

21. BOWRA, SIR CECIL MAURICE: *Memoirs, 1898-1939.* Cambridge, Mass.: Harvard UP, 1967 [1966]. xii, 369 pp.
"W. B. Yeats," 230-42. Reminiscences and an appreciation of Yeats's work, also two letters and a poem by Yeats entitled "To Maurice Bowra" and addressed to him by way of apology when he missed an appointment with Bowra.

22. BOYD, ERNEST: *Portraits Real and Imaginary: Being Memories and Impressions of Friends and Contemporaries, with Appreciations of Divers Singularities and Characteristics of Certain Phases of Life and Letters among the North Americans as Seen, Heard and Divined.* London: Cape, 1924. 265 pp.
"William Butler Yeats," 236-45.

23. BRADFORD, CURTIS B.: "George Yeats: Poet's Wife," *SR,* 77:3 (July-Sept 1969), 385-404.

24. BRENNAN, DIARMUID: "As Yeats Was Going Down Grafton Street," *List,* 6 Feb 1964, 236-38.
Recalls a meeting in the 1930s. Reprinted in BA13, 2:218-24.

25. BROOKE, RUPERT: *The Letters.* Chosen and edited by Geoffrey Keynes. London: Faber & Faber, 1968. xv, 709 pp.
Several references to Yeats (see index), whose work, especially *Deirdre,* Brooke seems to have liked very much. He met Yeats in Mar 1913.

26. BROOKS, SEAN: "The Ties with Sligo," *IrT,* 10 June 1965, vi.

27. BROOKS, SYDNEY: "Entre Nous," *Dublin Figaro,* 24 Sept 1892, 501-2.
Contains reminiscences of Yeats at the High School. It seems, however, that the sections on Yeats were written by Thomas Stuart, not by Brooks; see *Collected Letters,* 1:318. For a revised version see BB6.

28. BROOKS, VAN WYCK: *Emerson and Others.* London: Cape, [1927]. vi, 250 pp.
"John Butler Yeats," 109-20; a memoir referring to WBY passim. See also *A Chilmark Miscellany.* NY: Dutton, 1948. ix, 315 pp. (pp. 273-81).

29. ———: *Opinions of Oliver Allston.* NY: Dutton, 1941. 309 pp.
Contains a few references to WBY (see index).

30. ———: *An Autobiography.* Foreword by John Hall Wheelock, introduction by Malcolm Cowley. NY: Dutton, 1965. xxxvi, 667 pp.
Includes *Scenes and Portraits* (1954), which contains a memoir of John Butler Yeats, "Yeats at Petitpas'," 173-92.

31. BUCKLEY, TOM: "Yeats's Son Finds Poetry Leaves Him Cold," *NYT,* 28 Oct 1972, 33.
Michael Yeats reminisces about his father.

32. BUNTING, BASIL: "Yeats Recollected," *Agenda,* 12:2 (Summer 1974), 36-47.
Reminiscences and some comments on Yeats's works.

33. D., D. [BURCH, VACHER ?]: "Talking with Yeats, the Poet: A Memorable First Meeting," *MGuard,* 2 Feb 1939, 18.
Long letter to the editor about an undated meeting "in a Midland town" (Liverpool?). Says that Yeats refers to him in his autobiography as "my learned man." I assume that this is the man "learned in East Mediterranean antiquities," who supplied Yeats with the annotations to the archer vision in the notes to *Autobiographies.* See R. F. Rattray: "Yeats and Vacher Burch," *TLS,* 23 Sept 1955, 557.

34. CARY, RICHARD: "William Butler Yeats at Colby College," *CLQ,* 6:8 (Dec 1963), 360-69.
Yeats's visit and lecture in Oct 1932.

35. CHETTUR, GOVINDA KRISHNA: *The Last Enchantment: Recollections of Oxford.* Mangalore: B. M. Bookshop, 1934. xiv, 200 pp.
"W. B. Yeats," 33-45, reprinted from °*Madras Mail.* Meetings in 1919-21. See also pp. 30-32.

36. CHRISTY, M. A.: "Yeats's Teacher," *TLS*, 20 May 1965, 397.
Quotes from a letter written by John McNeill, Yeats's teacher at the High School, Dublin.

37. CHUTE, DESMOND: "Poets in Paradise: Recollections of W. B. Yeats and Ezra Pound in Rapallo," *List*, 5 Jan 1956, 14-15.
A shorter and slightly different version was published as "In Commemoration: Poet's Paradise. A Memoir," *Pound Newsletter*, 8 (Oct 1955), 12-14.

38. CLARKE, AUSTIN: *First Visit to England and Other Memories*. Dublin: Bridge Press / London: Williams & Norgate, 1945. 82 pp.
"First Visit to the Abbey Theatre," 37-40; "The Seven Woods," 49-53, a visit with Yeats ca. 1924.

39. ———: *A Penny in the Clouds: More Memories of Ireland and England*. London: Routledge & Kegan Paul, 1968. vii, 216 pp.
Incorporates "Glimpses of W. B. Yeats," *Shenandoah*, 16:4 (Summer 1965), 25-36 (also in CB280); and "Some Memories of W. B. Yeats," *Guardian*, 12 June 1965, 7.

40. CLINTON-BADDELEY, V. C.: "Reciting the Poems," *IrT*, 10 June 1965, iv.
Reminiscences of the broadcasts that Yeats made for the B.B.C.

41. COCKERELL, SYDNEY CARLYLE: *Friends of a Lifetime: Letters to Sydney Carlyle Cockerell*. Edited by Viola Meynell. London: Cape, 1940. 384 pp.
See pp. 268-73. Not all the letters in this collection are reprinted in Wade's edition, and vice versa.

42. COLUM, MARY MAGUIRE: *Life and the Dream*. Dublin: Dolmen Press, 1966 [1947]. vii, 378 pp.
Incorporates "Memories of Yeats," *SatR*, 25 Feb 1939, 3-4, 14 (reprinted in BA13, 2:241-46); "The Yeats I Knew," *Tomorrow*, 4:8 (Apr 1945), 38-43. For reminiscences of Yeats see especially pp. 78-80, 83-102, and 110-23.

43. COLUM, PADRAIC: *Ourselves Alone! The Story of Arthur Griffith and the Origin of the Irish Free State*. NY: Crown, 1959. xvi, 400 pp.
Also published as °*Arthur Griffith*. Dublin: Browne & Nolan, 1959. On Yeats, passim (see index).

44. ———: "Reminiscences of Yeats," *TriQ*, 4 [Fall 1965], 71-76.
Includes Colum's poem on Yeats, here entitled "The Arch Poet: William Butler Yeats." See also CB99 and HD38.

45. COULTER, JOHN: "Farewell to an Irish Poet," *Star Weekly*, 18 Feb 1939, Magazine section, 2, 7.
Reminiscences.

46. ———: *In My Day: Memoirs*. Willowdale, Ont.: Hounslow Press, 1980. vii, 371 pp.
A coil-bound book in "semi-print form," only 93 copies were printed. Reminiscences of Yeats in Dublin, pp. 45, 57-58. For extracts from the book, including the Yeats material, see "All That Bright Cluster," *IrT*, 17 Jan 1981, 9; 24 Jan 1981, 11.

47. COUSINS, JAMES HENRY, and MARGARET E. COUSINS: *We Two Together*. Madras: Ganesh, 1950. xvii, 784 pp.

Recounts a visit to Les Mouettes to see Maud Gonne and Yeats, whom Cousins overheard "composing" poetry (pp. 158-63).

48. CRONIN, COLM: "Ria Mooney Tells of That 'Likeable Person' W. B. Yeats in an Interview with Colm Cronin," *IrP,* 12 June 1965, 10.
For more reminiscences by Ria Mooney see BB154.

49. CROWLEY, ALEISTER: *The Spirit of Solitude: An Autohagiography Subsequently Re-Antichristened The Confessions of Aleister Crowley.* London: Mandrake Press, 1929. 2 vols.
Records a visit to Yeats ca. 1899 to show him some poems. They did not like each other very much (1:232). Mentions Yeats in connection with an account of the Golden Dawn (1:251, 283): "a lank dishevelled Demonologist who might have taken more pains with his personal appearance without incurring the reproach of Dandyism." Identifies Yeats as one of the characters in his short story "At the Fork of the Roads" (1:259; see HE7).
A new edition was published as *The Confessions of Aleister Crowley: An Autohagiography.* Edited by John Symonds and Kenneth Grant. London: Routledge & Kegan Paul, 1979. 960 pp.

50. CURRAN, CONSTANTINE PETER: *Under the Receding Wave.* Dublin: Gill & Macmillan, 1970. 149 pp.
Recollections of Yeats, pp. 93-94; "University College and *The Countess Cathleen*," 96-110 (on the circumstances of the first performance and on the *Playboy* riots). See letter by C. C. S. O'Mahony: "High Days at the Abbey Theatre," *TLS,* 11 Sept 1970, 999, on the *Countess Cathleen* performance.

51. DARROCH, SANDRA JOBSON: *Ottoline: The Life of Lady Ottoline Morrell.* London: Chatto & Windus, 1976. 317 pp.
Several references to Yeats (see index). For Lady Ottoline's photographs see BB157.

52. DAUTHENDEY, MAX: *Gesammelte Werke.* München: Langen, 1925. 6 vols.
"Gedankengut aus meinen Wanderjahren" reports Dauthendey's meeting with Yeats (1:584-86) in spring 1894 where Yeats tried to explain his theory of spirits. Dauthendey attended the first performance of *The Land of Heart's Desire,* but did not understand it and slept soundly. He does not record the meeting in a Paris café that Yeats notes in *Autobiographies.* See also CD359.

52a. DAVID, HUGH: *The Fitzrovians: A Portrait of a Bohemian Society 1900-55.* London: Joseph, 1988. xii, 276 pp.
See index.

53. DE BLACAM, AODH: "Memories of the Mighty," *Irish Bookman,* 1:6 (Jan 1947), 15-18.

54. DENSON, ALAN: *John Hughes Sculptor 1865-1941: A Documentary Biography.* Kendal: Denson, 1969. 516 pp.
See index for references to Yeats.

55. DEVAS, NICOLETTE: *Two Flamboyant Fathers.* London: Collins, 1966. 287 pp.
See pp. 126-31.

56. DICKINSON, PAGE LAWRENCE: *The Dublin of Yesterday.* London: Methuen, 1929. xi, 206 pp.

Memories of Yeats at the Arts Club (ca. 1906), pp. 49-55; of the early days of the Abbey Theatre, pp. 82-98.

57. *The Dictionary of National Biography, 1931-1940.* Edited by L. G. Wickham Legg. London: Oxford UP, 1949. xvi, 968 pp.
Joseph Hone: Yeats, pp. 928-32.

58. DODDS, ERIC ROBERTSON: *Missing Persons: An Autobiography.* Oxford: Clarendon Press, 1977. x, 202 pp.
See index for reminiscences of Yeats (with whom Dodds shared an interest in the occult).

59. DONOGHUE, DENIS: "Viewpoint," *TLS,* 16 Feb 1973, 178.
Donoghue's reasons for abandoning the project of writing the new authorized Yeats biography which had been announced in *TLS,* 17 Dec 1971, 1578. Correspondence by Michael Yeats, 23 Feb 1973, 211; G. S. Fraser and John Whitehead, 2 Mar 1973, 240. See also Donoghue's letter and comment by the Oxford University Press, 9 Feb 1973, 152. The biography was then entrusted to F. S. L. Lyons (see "Commentary," 11 Jan 1974, 33), who died before completion. It will now be written by Roy Foster. Ann Saddlemyer is to write the authorized biography of Mrs. Yeats.

59a. DONOVAN, STEWART: "Remembering Yeats: An Interview with Francis Stuart," *AntigR,* 71-72 (Autumn-Winter 1988), 57-62.

60. DRINKWATER, JOHN: *Discovery: Being the Second Volume of an Autobiography, 1897-1913.* London: Benn, 1932. 235 pp.
Impressions of Yeats, an account of the Pilgrim Players' production of *The King's Threshold,* and Yeats's opinion of it, pp. 170-78.

61. DRUMMOND, ANN: "Florence Farr Emery," *Discourse,* 4:2 (Spring 1961), 97-100.

62. DUFAU-LABEYRIE, FRANCIS: "Notes in Memory of the Dublin Visit," *Poetry Wales,* 12:4 (Spring 1977), 78-83.
Vernon Watkins's visit to Yeats (see also BB255).

63. DULAC, EDMUND: "Yeats, as I Knew Him," *IrW,* 8 (July 1949), 77-87.
Discusses Yeats's occult interests.

64. EAGLE, DOROTHY, and HILARY CARNELL: *The Oxford Literary Guide to the British Isles.* Oxford: Clarendon Press, 1977. xiii, 447 pp.
See index, p. 413, for Yeats references.

65. ——— (eds): *The Oxford Illustrated Literary Guide to Great Britain and Ireland.* Oxford: Oxford UP, 1981. xi, 335 pp.
Based on the preceding item. See index, p. 312.

66. EBERHART, RICHARD: *Of Poetry and Poets.* Urbana: U of Illinois Press, 1979. xiii, 312 pp.
"Poetry as Creative Principle," 8-18; especially p. 8. "Memory of Meeting Yeats, AE, Gogarty, James Stephens," 148-52; reprinted from *LitR,* 1:1 (Autumn 1957), 51-56. Saw Yeats in Oct 1928 and heard him discuss politics. Extract reprinted in BA13, 1:193-96.

67. EGLINTON, JOHN: "Dublin Letter," *Dial,* 72:3 (Mar 1922), 298-301.
Reminiscences.

68. ———: "Yeats at the High School," *Erasmian,* ns 30:1 (June 1939), 11-12.
Reprinted in BA13, 1:3-4.

69. ———: "Early Memories of Yeats," *DM,* 29 [i.e., 28]:3 (July-Sept 1953), 22-26.
Reprinted in BA13, 1:30-34.

70. ELLMANN, RICHARD: "Black Magic against White: Aleister Crowley versus W. B. Yeats," *PR,* 15:9 (Sept 1948), 1049-51.
The Crowley--Althea Gyles--Yeats triangle, as told by Crowley to Ellmann. See also HE7.

71. ERVINE, ST. JOHN GREER: *Some Impressions of My Elders.* NY: Macmillan, 1922. vii, 305 pp.
"William Butler Yeats," 264-305; reprinted from *NAR,* 211:771 (Feb 1920), 225-37, and :772 (Mar 1920), 402-10. Reprinted in BA13, 1:99-117.

72. ———: "Edwardian Authors--III: Portrait of W. B. Yeats," *List,* 1 Sept 1955, 331-32.
Correspondence by C. S. Lewis, 15 Sept 1955, 427.

73. ———: *Bernard Shaw: His Life, Work, and Friends.* London: Constable, 1956. xii, 628 pp.
Contains some not very flattering remarks on Yeats (see index).

74. FALLON, GABRIEL: "Profiles of a Poet," *MD,* 7:3 (Dec 1964), 329-44.
Reprinted in BA13, 1:173-88.

75. FIELD, MICHAEL [i.e., Katherine Harris Bradley and Edith Emma Cooper]: *Works and Days: From the Journals of Michael Field.* Edited by T. and D. C. Sturge Moore. London: Murray, 1933. xxii, 338 pp.
Edith Cooper's recollection of a Yeats visit ca. 1901, pp. 261-63.

76. FINCH, EDITH: *Wilfrid Scawen Blunt: 1840-1922.* London: Cape, 1938. 415 pp.
On Yeats and Blunt, passim (see index). See also BB18 and 89.

77. FROST, ROBERT: *Selected Letters.* Edited by Lawrance Thompson. NY: Holt, Rinehart & Winston, 1964. lxiv, 645 pp.
Some notes containing Frost's impression of Yeats and favorable comments on his poetry, passim (see index). See also BB241.

78. GARRETT, EILEEN J.: *Many Voices: The Autobiography of a Medium.* With an introduction by Allan Angoff. London: Allen & Unwin, 1969. 254 pp.
Reminiscences of Yeats, pp. 20, 27-28, 32, 60-61.

79. GOGARTY, OLIVER D.: "My Brother Willie Was Your Father's Friend," *Bibliotheca Bucnellensis,* ns 7 (1969), 1-13.
Reminiscences of Yeats by Oliver St. John Gogarty's son; includes four letters from Yeats to Gogarty and one from Mrs. Yeats to Gogarty.

80. GOGARTY, OLIVER ST. JOHN: *As I Was Going Down Sackville Street: A Fantasy in Fact.* NY: Reynal & Hitchcock, 1937. x, 342 pp.
Memories of Yeats at Rathfarnham, pp. 105-14; of Yeats and the ghost at Renvyle House, 179-89 (see also Gogarty's "Laying a

Galway Ghost," *Irish Digest*, 2:3 [Jan 1939], 102-4); of the Abbey Theatre, 287-301. It might be useful to heed Gogarty's warning: "The names in this book are real, the characters fictitious." See also BA5.

81. ———: "Yeats--By Gogarty," *Evening Standard*, 30 Jan 1939, 3.
The same page contains the following note: "What must be one of Mr. Yeats's last letters was written on Friday afternoon [27 Jan] to Mr. John Gawsworth, the English poet. It supports a proposal which Mr. Gawsworth is making to the Prime Minister on behalf of the widow of a writer who was a mutual friend."

82. ———: *Going Native*. London: Constable, 1941. ix, 294 pp.
"How Ouseley Came to the Island of Friday-to-Tuesday," 3-22; a more or less fictitious account of a Yeats-Gogarty meeting (Ouseley being Gogarty).

83. ———: *Mourning Became Mrs. Spendlove and Other Portraits, Grave and Gay*. NY: Creative Age Press, 1948. v, 250 pp.
"Reminiscences of Yeats," 209-24; reprinted from *Tomorrow*, 7 [i.e., 6]:9 (May 1947), 16-20. Reprinted in BA13, 2:305-12.

84. ———: *Intimations*. NY: Abelard Press, 1950. vi, 271 pp.
"George Moore's Blackbird," 18-24; the anecdote of a blackbird in Ely Place and Yeats's comments on it. "American Patrons and Irish Poets," 253-68; on Yeats and his American patrons John Quinn and Patrick McCartan.

85. ———: *Rolling Down the Lea*. London: Constable, 1950. vii, 278 pp.
Contains an anecdote about Yeats and Seumas O'Sullivan, pp. 108-11; also some deprecating remarks about the "Abbey Theatre coterie," 210-14.

86. ———: *It Isn't This Time of Year at All! An Unpremeditated Autobiography*. Garden City: Doubleday, 1954. 256 pp.
Recollections of Yeats, passim, especially pp. 154-56 on Yeats and Moore and 242-47 on a private performance of *At the Hawk's Well*.

87. ———: *Start from Somewhere Else: An Exposition of Wit and Humor Polite and Perilous*. Garden City: Doubleday, 1955. 189 pp.
"Augustus John and Yeats," 121-27.

88. ———: *Many Lines to Thee: Letters to G. K. A. Bell from the Martello Tower at Sandycove, Rutland Square and Trinity College Dublin, 1904-1907*. Edited with a commentary by James F. Carens. Dublin: Dolmen Press, 1971. vii, 168 pp. (Dolmen Editions. 14.)
Yeats is mentioned passim in the letters; notes on the Yeats-Gogarty relationship in the commentaries.

89. GOING, WILLIAM T.: "A Peacock Dinner: The Homage of Pound and Yeats to Wilfrid Scawen Blunt," *JML*, 1:3 (Mar 1971), 303-10.
See also BB18 and 76 and BF110.

90. GOLDRING, DOUGLAS: *Odd Man Out: The Autobiography of a "Propaganda Novelist."* London: Chapman & Hall, 1935. xii, 342 pp.
Scattered references to Yeats (see index).

91. ———: *South Lodge: Reminiscences of Violet Hunt, Ford Madox*

Ford and the English Review Circle. London: Constable, 1943. xix, 240 pp.
Yeats is mentioned on pp. xvii, 48-49, 55, 123-24, 125, 160.

92. ———: *The Nineteen Twenties: A General Survey and Some Personal Memories*. London: Nicholson & Watson, 1945. xxiii, 266 pp.
Memories of Yeats, pp. 115-18.

93. GONNE MACBRIDE, MAUD: *A Servant of the Queen: Reminiscences*. London: Gollancz, 1938. 350 pp.
Reprinted Woodbridge, Suffolk: Boydell Press, 1983. Yeats is mentioned on pp. 90, 92-93, 98, 125, 147-48, 170, 172, 176-78, 250, 254-60 (concerning the Golden Dawn), 274-76, 282, 284, 308, 317-18, 328-35 (one of his marriage proposals), 339. The general impression is that Yeats seems to have thought more about Maud Gonne than she about him; most of the above references are not very important. The autobiography ends in 1903 with Maud Gonne's marriage. See also BB9.

94. GOODWIN, K. L.: "Some Corrections to Standard Biographies of Yeats," *N&Q*, os 210 / ns 12:7 (July 1965), 260-62.
Anent Yeats's relations with Pound.

95. GREGG, FREDERICK JAMES: "Going to School with the Poet Yeats," *NY Herald*, 2 Dec 1923, section 9 (Magazine Section), 3.
Yeats at the Anglican High School, Harcourt Street.

96. GREGORY, ANNE: *Me and Nu: Childhood at Coole*. Illustrated by Joyce Dennys with a prefatory note by Maurice Collis. Gerrards Cross: Smythe, 1971. 128 pp.
Written by Lady Gregory's granddaughter; reminiscences of Yeats from a juvenile perspective, pp. 29-33, 89-90, 117, 128.

97. GREGORY, LADY ISABELLA AUGUSTA: *Coole*. Churchtown, Dundrum: Cuala Press, 1931. iv, 51 pp.
Yeats is mentioned on pp. 24, 30, 32, 36-37 (with reference to "The Wild Swans at Coole"), 38, 42, 44-46.

Republished as *Coole*. Completed from the manuscript and edited by Colin Smythe. With a foreword by Edward Malins. Dublin: Dolmen Press, 1971. 107 pp. (Dolmen Editions. 10.). The foreword comments on the Yeats-Lady Gregory relationship (pp. 7-14).

98. ———: *Lady Gregory's Journals*. Edited by Daniel J. Murphy. Gerrards Cross: Smythe / NY: Oxford UP, 1978-87. 2 vols. (Coole Edition of the Works of Lady Gregory. 14. 15.)
A shorter edition was published as *Lady Gregory's Journals 1916-1930*. Edited by Lennox Robinson. London: Putnam, 1946. 344 pp. See also CB337.

Volume one: *Books One to Twenty-Nine: 10 October 1916--24 February 1925*. 1978. xvi, 707 pp. Numerous references to Yeats, his theatrical activities, his efforts to obtain the Hugh Lane pictures, his plays, poems, and other works.

Volume two: *Books Thirty to Forty-Four: 21 February 1925--9 May 1932*. 1987. viii, 748 pp. Numerous references to Yeats; includes his unpublished "The Death of Lady Gregory," pp. 633-38. There is also an "Afterword" by Colin Smythe, pp. 639-60, discussing the troublesome relationship between Yeats and Margaret Gregory (later Gough), Lady Gregory's daughter-in-law, and his role in the publication plans for Lady Gregory's autobiographical writings.

99. ———: "Letters from Lady Gregory and James Stephens." Edited by James F. Carens, *Bibliotheca Bucnellensis,* ns 8 (1970), 1-9.
Letters to Oliver St. John Gogarty; several references to Yeats.

100. ———: *Seventy Years: Being the Autobiography of Lady Gregory.* Edited and with a foreword by Colin Smythe. Gerrards Cross: Smythe, 1974. xvi, 583 pp. (Coole Edition of the Works of Lady Gregory. 13.)
First edition of Lady Gregory's long lost autobiography; includes numerous references to Yeats (see index). See the review by Richard Ellmann, *NYTBR,* 7 March 1976, 6-7, with comments on the Yeats-Lady Gregory relationship.

101. GRIFFIN, GERALD: *The Wild Geese: Pen Portraits of Famous Irish Exiles.* London: Jarrolds, [1938]. 288 pp.
"William Butler Yeats," 151-63; reminiscences and notes on the poetry.

102. GUINNESS, BRYAN: *Potpourri from the Thirties.* Burford, Oxfordshire: Cygnet Press, 1982. xi, 174 pp.
Lord Moyne's reminiscences of Yeats, pp. 30, 33-35, 64-65.

103. GWYNN, FREDERICK LANDIS: *Sturge Moore and the Life of Art.* Lawrence: U of Kansas Press, 1951. xii, 159 pp.
Numerous references to Yeats (see index) with occasional comparisons of Yeats's and Sturge Moore's poetry.

104. GWYNN, STEPHEN: *Garden Wisdom or From One Generation to Another.* Dublin: Talbot Press / London: Unwin, 1921. x, 149 pp.
"The Ageing of a Poet," 1-19; recollections of Yeats and of the first performance of *Cathleen ni Houlihan,* as well as comments on *Responsibilities.*

105. ———: *Experiences of a Literary Man.* NY: Holt, 1927 [1926]. 312 pp.
Some reminiscences of Yeats (see index) and of the beginnings of the Irish literary revival (see especially "Dublin of the 'Eighties," 55-75).

106. ———: "W. B. Yeats: A Great Personality. The Man and His Measure," *Obs,* 5 Feb 1939, 8.

107. ———: "The Passing of W. B. Yeats," *FortnR,* os 151 / ns 145: 867 (Mar 1939), 347-49.

108. HACKETT, FRANCIS: *The Invisible Censor.* NY: Huebsch, 1921. vii, 167 pp.
"William Butler Yeats," 114-18; reprint of F. H.: "Books and Things," *NewRep,* 24 Nov 1917, 100. Recalls a meeting with Yeats in Pennsylvania Railroad Station. Reprinted in BA13, 1:131-35, where the author is not identified.

109. HASSETT, JOSEPH M.: "Yeats and the Chief Consolation of Genius," *Yeats,* 4 (1986), 55-67.
Yeats's relations with Dorothy Wellesley, Margot Ruddock, Ethel Mannin, and Edith Shackleton Heald, and their reflections in his poetry.

110. HELD, GEORGE M. C.: "The Second Book of the Rhymers' Club," *JRUL*, 28:2 (June 1965), 15-21.

111. ———: "1. The Rhymers' Club, 1891-1894 [. . .]," Ph.D. thesis, Rutgers U, 1967. vi, 170 pp. (*DAI*, 28:10 [Apr 1968], 4176A-77A)
"The Rhymers' Club," 1-69.

112. HIND, CHARLES LEWIS: *Authors and I*. London: Lane, 1921. 336 pp.
"W. B. Yeats," 318-24.

113. HINKSON, PAMELA: "Letters from W. B. Yeats," *YR*, 29:2 (Dec 1939), 307-20.
Letters to Katharine Tynan and reminiscences.

114. ———: "The Friendship of Yeats and Katharine Tynan," *FortnR*, os 180 / ns 174:1032 (Oct 1953), 253-64; :1033 (Nov 1953), 323-36.

115. HOLLOWAY, JOSEPH: *Joseph Holloway's Abbey Theatre: A Selection from His Unpublished Journal "Impressions of a Dublin Playgoer."* Edited by Robert Hogan and Michael J. O'Neill, with a preface by Harry T. Moore. Carbondale: Southern Illinois UP, 1967. xxiii, 296 pp.
See also °Michael Joseph O'Neill: "The Diaries of a Dublin Playgoer as a Mirror of the Irish Literary Revival," Ph.D. thesis, University College, Dublin, 1952; and next item.
The excerpts from the diary are concerned mainly with the years 1899-1926; they include reminiscences of Yeats and notes on his plays and lectures. Holloway's diaries are advertised for publication on microfilm, Brighton: Harvester, 1987. 4 parts. (Manuscripts of the Irish Literary Renaissance. Series 1.)

116. ———: *Joseph Holloway's Irish Theatre*. Edited by Robert Hogan and Michael J. O'Neill. Dixon, Calif.: Proscenium Press, 1968-70. 3 vols. (88, 85, 110 pp.)
A sequel to the preceding item; covers the periods 1926-31, 1932-37, 1938-44. Reminiscences of and anecdotes about Yeats appear passim (see index). Contains a parody of "September 1913" by John Burke, entitled "September ?," 3:78-79.

117. HONE, JOSEPH: "A Scattered Fair: From a Diary in a Neutral Country," *Wind and the Rain*, 3:3 (Autumn 1946), 110-15.
Quotes from a diary kept by Elizabeth Corbet Yeats in 1888-89; also reminiscences of Yeats and Maud Gonne.

118. [———]: "W. B. Yeats--A Bio-Bibliography: A Succinct Table of Events and Works," *Irish Library Bulletin*, 9:[10] (Oct 1948), 167-72.

119. HORGAN, JOHN: "May Craig Recalls the Abbey Days in an Interview with John Horgan," *IrT*, 10 June 1965, viii.
Reprinted in BA13, 2:288-90.

120. HYDE, H. MONTGOMERY: "Yeats and Gogarty," *YeA*, 5 (1987), 154-60.
Reminiscences.

121. JAFFE, GRACE MARY SPURWAY: *Years of Grace*. Sunspot, N.M.: Iroquois House, 1979. xi, 203 pp.
The autobiography of Mrs. Yeats's cousin. For reminiscences of Yeats and Mrs. Yeats see pp. 34-37, 55-56, and 163-64. See also

next item.

122. ———: "Vignettes," *YeA*, 5 (1987), 139-53.
An amplification of the preceding item; contains memories of Mrs. Yeats and, marginally, of WBY.

123. JEFFARES, A. NORMAN: "Yeats's Birthplace," *YeA*, 3 (1985), 175-78.
The house was re-numbered several times and is now George's Ville No. 1, 5 Sandymount Avenue.

124. JEFFERSON, GEORGE: *Edward Garnett: A Life in Literature*. London: Cape, 1982. x, 350 pp.
See pp. 18, 28-29, 45-46.

125. JOHNSTON, CHARLES: "Personal Impressions of W. B. Yeats," *Harper's Weekly*, 20 Feb 1904, 291.
Yeats's early interest in science and in Darwin. Reprinted in BA13, 1:13-15.

126. ———: "Yeats in the Making," *Poet Lore*, 17:2 (Summer 1906), 102-12.
Reminiscences and an appreciation of the early work. Extract reprinted in BA13, 1:6-13.

127. JUSSIM, ESTELLE: *Slave to Beauty: The Eccentric Life and Controversial Career of F. Holland Day, Photographer, Publisher, Aesthete*. Boston: Godine, 1981. ix, 310 pp.
On Yeats, pp. 48-51, and passim (see index).

128. KELLER, T. G.: "The Irish Theatre Movement--Some Early Memories," *Sunday Independent*, 6 Jan 1929, 7.
Continued, 13 Jan 1929, 7; 20 Jan 1929, 7. Reminiscences of Yeats, the Irish theater, and a Yeats lecture on Nietzsche.

129. KELLNER, L[EON]: "Yeats," *Nation* [Berlin], 8 Aug 1903, 713-15.
Describes a meeting with Yeats and discusses him as an "otherworldly poet."

130. KELLY, JOHN S.: "Books and Numberless Dreams: Yeats's Relations with His Early Publishers," in Jeffares: *Yeats, Sligo and Ireland* (1980, CA51), 232-53.
The relations with Charles Kegan Paul, who published *The Wanderings of Oisin and Other Poems*, and T. Fisher Unwin, who published several editions of *Poems*.

131. KIERNAN, T. J.: "Lady Gregory and W. B. Yeats," *Southerly*, 14:4 (1953), 239-51.
Reprinted in *DR*, 38:3 (Autumn 1958), 295-306.

132. KINGSMILL, HUGH: *The Best of Hugh Kingsmill*. Selections from his writings edited and introduced by Michael Holroyd. London: Gollancz, 1970. 399 pp.
"Meetings with W. B. Yeats," 273-76. Reprinted from *NSt*, 4 Jan 1941, 10-11, and *The Progress of a Biographer*, London: Methuen, 1949. viii, 194 pp. (pp. 91-94). Reprinted in BA13, 2:294-96. One meeting took place in 1912 and produced the *Hearth and Home* interview (see BE61), the others in 1924.

133. KRITZWISER, KAY: "Yeats Keeps an Eye on Yeats: Living in the

Shade of a Famous Father," *Globe & Mail* [Toronto], 11 Feb 1978, 37.
Interview with Anne Yeats.

134. Tante, Dilly [i.e., KUNITZ, STANLEY JASSPON] (ed): *Living Authors: A Book of Biographies*. NY: Wilson, 1931. vii, 466 pp.
"William Butler Yeats," 451-54.

135. KUNITZ, STANLEY JASSPON, and HOWARD HAYCRAFT (eds): *Twentieth Century Authors: A Biographical Dictionary of Modern Literature*. Complete in one volume with 1,850 biographies and 1,700 portraits. NY: Wilson, 1942. vii, 1577 pp.
See pp. 1560-62.

136. LEGGE, SYLVIA: *Affectionate Cousins: T. Sturge Moore and Marie Appia*. Oxford: Oxford UP, 1980. xiv, 274 pp.
Contains numerous references to Yeats (see index). Reviewed by Ronald Schuchard, *YeA*, 2 (1983), 141-43.

137. LEWIS, CLIVE STAPLES: *Letters*. Edited with a memoir by W. H. Lewis. London: Bles, 1966. v, 308 pp.
Met Yeats in Oxford in 1921, pp. 56-58. See also CD751-753.

138. LEWIS, ROSELLE M.: "William Butler Yeats: With His Medium under a Spell in America's Cult Country," *LA Times*, 17 Jan 1982, Book Review section, 3.
On Yeats's lecture on 2 Apr 1920 at the Friday Morning Club, Los Angeles (see BF147), and on Mrs. Yeats's talking in her sleep while in a train "somewhere in Southern California" (cf. *A Vision*, B, Introduction, § III).

139. LEWIS, WYNDHAM: *The Letters*. Edited by W. K. Rose. London: Methuen, 1963. xxxi, 580 pp.
Yeats is mentioned passim (see index). Includes two letters from Lewis to Yeats, pp. 181-83.

140. LOCK, STEPHEN: "'O That I Were Young Again': Yeats and the Steinach Operation," *British Medical J*, 287:6409 (24-31 Dec 1983), 1964-68.

141. MACDIARMID, HUGH: *The Company I've Kept*. Berkeley: U of California Press, 1967. 288 pp.
Passim (see index). See also CD764.

142. MCGARRY, JAMES P.: *The Castle of Heroes*. Boyle: Roscommon Herald, 1965. vi, 41 pp.
Carraig Mhic Diarmada on Loch Key near Boyle, the Castle of Heroes, of which Yeats and Maud Gonne dreamed and talked.

143. MCGRATH, JOHN: "W. B. Yeats and Ireland," *Westminster R*, 176:1 (July 1911), 1-11.
Reminiscences and on Yeats's concern with Irish literature.

144. MACGREEVY, THOMAS: "Uileachân dubh O," *Capuchin Annual*, 21 (1952), 211-45.
A tour of the Yeats country, County Sligo, and some reminiscences, pp. 220-30, 236-39 (in English).

145. ———: "W. B. Yeats--A Generation Later," *UR*, 3:8 [1966?], 3-14.
Mostly reminiscences. Reprinted in BA13, 2:404-15.

146. MCGUINNESS, NORAH: "Young Painter and Elderly Genius," *IrT*, 10 June 1965, vi.

Reminiscences. Miss McGuinness made masks and costumes for a performance of *The Only Jealousy of Emer* and played the part of the Woman of the Sidhe.

147. MACKEN, MARY M.: "W. B. Yeats, John O'Leary and the Contemporary Club," *Studies*, 28:109 (Mar 1939), 136-42.

148. MACLIAMMÓIR, MICHEÁL: *All for Hecuba: An Irish Theatrical Autobiography*. Boston: Branden Press, 1967 [1946]. viii, 367 pp.

Includes "Yeats, Lady Gregory, Denis Johnston," *Bell*, 6:1 (Apr 1943), 33-42. Reminiscences of Yeats, pp. 68-71 and passim.

149. MANNIN, ETHEL: *Privileged Spectator: A Sequel to "Confessions and Impressions."* Revised edition. London: Jarrolds, [1948] [1939]. 256 pp.

Reminiscences of Yeats, pp. 60-65: Ethel Mannin and Ernst Toller tried to enlist Yeats's support of Ossietzky's nomination for the Nobel Peace Prize (Yeats refused); Yeats declared that setting his poems to music was an outrage (he was played a record of Peter Warlock's music for "He Reproves the Curlew" and thought it was terrible and ridiculous; for Warlock's score see HC305).

150. ———: *Young in the Twenties: A Chapter of Autobiography*. London: Hutchinson, 1971. 192 pp.

Note on Yeats, pp. 67-68. See also BG173.

151. MARTYN, EDWARD: "A Plea for the Revival of the Irish Literary Theatre," *Irish R*, 4:38 (Apr 1914), 79-84.

Martyn's characterization of Yeats is interesting: "A fine poet and subtle literary critic, he has, above all[,] a weird appearance, which is triumphant with middle-aged masculine women, and a dictatorial manner which is irresistible with the considerable bevy of female and male mediocritics interested in intellectual things. In this way he practically dictates to the critics who reproduce his opinions."

152. MEDLEY, ROBERT: *Drawn from the Life: A Memoir*. London: Faber & Faber, 1983. 251 pp.

See pp. 139, 151-54 for reminiscences of Yeats, including a quotation from a letter to Rupert Doone. Some of this material was published as "The Group Theatre 1932-39: Rupert Doone and Wystan Auden," *LMag*, 20:10 (Jan 1981), 47-60.

153. MONROE, HARRIET: *A Poet's Life: Seventy Years in a Changing World*. NY: AMS Press, 1969 [1938]. xi, 488 pp.

"A Banquet: Yeats and Lindsay," 329-39 (incorporates "Poetry's Banquet," *Poetry*, 4:1 [Apr 1914], 25-29), and passim (see index). The *Poetry* version includes an untitled poem by Arthur Davison Ficke, introducing Yeats. See also BE79.

154. MOONEY, RIA: "Players and Painted Stage: The Autobiography of Ria Mooney." Edited by Val Mulkerns and with an introduction by the late Micheál MacLiammóir, *George Spelvin's Theatre Book*, 1:2 (Summer 1978), 3-120; 1:3 (Fall 1978), 65-121.

Reminiscences of Yeats passim, including a letter to Miss Mooney (part 2, p. 109). See also BB48.

155. MOORE, GEORGE: *Hail and Farewell: Ave, Salve, Vale*. Edited by

Richard Allen Cave. Revised edition. Gerrards Cross: Smythe / Washington, D.C.: Catholic U of America Press, 1985 [1976]. 774 pp.

First published in three volumes, 1911-14. Part of vol. 3, section vii, was published as "Yeats, Lady Gregory, and Synge," *English R,* 16:2 (Jan 1914), 167-80; :3 (Feb 1914), 350-64. The editor has provided an introduction with comments on the Moore-Yeats relationship, notes and an index.

George Moore's none-too-objective autobiographical reminiscences of the early years of the Irish literary revival, in the form of a loosely organized novelistic first-person narrative.

Selective contents: Volume 1, section i: Early meetings with WBY, his early works and interest in Blake, and his involvement in the Golden Dawn (here called Golden Door).
1, ii: Rehearsal and first performance of *The Countess Cathleen.*
1, iii: Further meetings with WBY, notes on the Irish Literary Theatre, and the reception of *The Countess Cathleen.*
1, ix: GM revises an early version of *The Shadowy Waters.*
1, x: WBY at Lady Gregory's.
1, xi: How WBY treated Edward Martyn; on *The Shadowy Waters.*
1, xiv-xv and 2, vi: The writing of *Diarmuid and Grania.*
2, vii: The first performance of *Cathleen ni Houlihan.*
3, vii: WBY ridiculed by GM for denouncing the middle classes; on Lady Gregory's collaboration with WBY; also on Synge's being persuaded by WBY to go to Aran.
3, x: Further reminiscences of WBY.

Reviews:

- Denis Donoghue: "A Passing Dog," *Spect,* 1 Jan 1977, 33. Correspondence by Robert Becker, 15 Jan 1977, 17.
- F. S. L. Lyons: "Goodbye to Dublin," *TLS,* 4 Feb 1977, 122.
- Frank Tuohy: "Acts of the Apostles," *Hibernia,* 21 Jan 1977, 16.

156. ———: *Letters of George Moore.* With an introduction by John Eglinton, to whom they were written. Bournemouth: Sydenham, 1942. 88 pp.

Yeats is referred to on pp. 35, 51, 52, 53, 59, 60, 64, 68.

157. MORRELL, LADY OTTOLINE: *Lady Ottoline's Album.* Snapshots and portraits of her famous contemporaries (and of herself), photographed for the most part by Lady Ottoline Morrell. Edited by Carolyn G. Heilbrun. NY: Knopf, 1976. vii, 118 pp.

Several photographs of, and notes on, Yeats (see index). See also BB51.

158. MOSES, MONTROSE J.: "With William Butler Yeats," *TAM,* 8:6 (June 1924), 382-88.

Reminiscences and an interview. Reprinted in BA13, 1:126-31.

159. MOYNIHAN, MAURICE: *Currency and Central Banking in Ireland 1922-1960.* Dublin: Gill & Macmillan / Central Bank of Ireland, 1975. xv, 581 pp.

See pp. 28-35 for Yeats's work on the coinage committee.

160. MOYNIHAN, MICHAEL: "A Poet and His Daughter," *SunT,* 14 Aug 1966, 32.

Reprinted in *Irish Digest,* 87:4 (Oct 1966), 29-32. Anne Yeats's recollections of her father.

161. NEVINSON, HENRY WOODD: *Changes and Chances.* London: Nisbet, 1923. xv, 360 pp.

See pp. 209, 301-3.

162. ———: *More Changes More Chances*. London: Nisbet, 1925. xvii, 427 pp.
See p. 30.

163. ———: *Last Changes, Last Chances*. NY: Harcourt, Brace, 1929. xvii, 361 pp.
Visited Yeats on 30 Oct 1916 and heard him talk about spiritism, pp. 122-23.

164. ———: *Fire of Life*. London: Nisbet/Gollancz, 1935. 448 pp.
Extracts from the preceding three books; see pp. 90-91, 122-23, 340-41.

165. ———: *Visions and Memories*. Collected and arranged by Evelyn Sharp. London: Oxford UP, 1944. viii, 199 pp.
"W. B. Yeats: Poet of Vision," 52-60; reprinted from *LMerc*, 39: 233 (Mar 1939), 485-91. Rambling reminiscences and some general remarks on the early poetry.

166. NEWBOLT, SIR HENRY: *My World as in My Time: Memoirs, 1862-1932*. London: Faber & Faber, 1932. xvi, 321 pp.
Yeats and Newbolt visit Bridges in 1897, pp. 189, 192-94.

167. ———: *The Later Life and Letters*. Edited by his wife, Margaret Newbolt. London: Faber & Faber, 1942. xi, 426 pp.
Reminiscences of Yeats, pp. 4-6, 166-68 (Yeats and Newbolt present Hardy with a medal).

168. NICHOLLS, HARRY: "Memories of the Contemporary Club," *IrT*, 20 Dec 1965, 10; 21 Dec 1965, 8.

169. NOWELL-SMITH, SIMON (ed): *Letters to Macmillan*. London: Macmillan, 1967. 384 pp.
Passim (see index).

170. O'CASEY, SEAN: *Autobiographies*. London: Macmillan, 1981 [1939-54]. 2 vols.
The second edition includes a chronology and an unreliable index by J. C. Trewin, 2:668-80. The following chapters contain important references to Yeats:

"At the Sign of the Pick and Shovel," 1:405-22; defends Yeats against charges made by Irish nationalists.

"Song of a Shift," 1:506-20; the *Playboy* riots.

"Blessed Bridget O'Coole," 2:102-13; first Abbey experiences and a visit to Lady Gregory.

"Where Wild Swans Nest," 2:114-25; the visit continued.

"The Temple Entered," 2:139-57; further Abbey experiences with *The Plough and the Stars*.

"Dublin's Gods and Half-Gods," 2:157-66; a visit to Yeats.

"Dublin's Glittering Guy," 2:167-86; AE and Yeats.

"Inishfallen, Fare Thee Well," 2:231-47; more Abbey experiences and a note on *At the Hawk's Well*.

"London Apprentice," 2:251-68; Yeats's theories of literature.

"The Silver Tassie," 2:268-80.

"The Friggin Frogs," 2:281-91; a visit to Yeats and later relations with the Abbey.

"Feathering His Nest," 2:291-310; more comments on Yeats.

"Black Oxen Passing By," 2:334-47; another visit to Yeats where they talked about communism.

171. O'CONNOR, FRANK: "The Old Age of a Poet," *Bell,* 1:5 (Feb 1941), 7-18.

172. ————: "What Made Yeats a Great Poet?" *List,* 15 May 1947, 761-62.
Rambling reminiscences; does not attempt to answer his own question. See also "Yeats--the Man and the Poet. Condensed from a B.B.C. Broadcast," *Irish Digest,* 28:2 (Sept 1947), 19-23; "Listening to Yeats. Condensed from a Broadcast," *Literary Digest,* 3:4 (Winter 1948), 27-30; and BA17.

173. ————: *Leinster, Munster and Connaught.* London: Hale, [1950]. 296 pp.
Recollections of Yeats, pp. 256-61 and passim (see index).

174. ————: "Quarreling with Yeats: A Friendly Recollection," *Esquire,* 62:6 (Dec 1964), 157, 221, 224-25, 232.
About Abbey Theatre politics and the production of *The Herne's Egg.* Reprinted in BA13, 2:339-45.

175. ————: "The Scholar," *KR,* 27:2 (Spring 1965), 336-43.
Osborn Bergin and what he thought of Yeats.

176. ————: *My Father's Son.* London: Macmillan, 1968. 200 pp.
The second part of O'Connor's autobiography; contains numerous stories about Yeats, partly contained in the preceding five items. See also [Elizabeth Coxhead]: "Up from Cork," *TLS,* 17 Oct 1968, 1173 ("Yeats's death seemed the end of the world; for O'Connor it was, in fact, a release").

177. O'DRISCOLL, ROBERT: "Letters and Lectures of W. B. Yeats," *UR,* 3:8 [1966?], 29-55.
Reprints BF62, 69, 156, CB17, and material on the *Playboy* controversy from *FrJ,* 5 Feb 1907 (see CD1321).

178. OLDEN, ANTHONY: "A Storm in a Chalice," *Library R,* 25:7 (Autumn 1976), 265-69.
The opposition to the periodical *Tomorrow* (1924).

179. PALMER, VANCE: *Louis Esson and the Australian Theatre.* Melbourne: Meanjin Press, 1948. viii, 114 pp.
Esson's reminiscences of Yeats, pp. 3-4, 25-28, and passim (see index). See also BG80-81.

180. PATMORE, BRIGIT: *My Friends When Young.* Edited with an introduction by Derek Patmore. London: Heinemann, 1968. xii, 159 pp.
Incorporates "Some Memories of W. B. Yeats," *Texas Q,* 8:4 (Winter 1965), 152-59. See especially pp. 92-93, 100-1, 109-19.

181. PATMORE, DEREK: "Memories of W. B. Yeats," *IrT,* 21 Dec 1968, 12.

182. PAYNE, BEN IDEN: *A Life in a Wooden O: Memoirs of the Theatre.* New Haven: Yale UP, 1977. xvii, 205 pp.
See index for reminiscences of Yeats and the Abbey Theatre.

183. PEARCE, DONALD: "Dublin's 'National Literary Society,' 1892," *N&Q,* 196:10 (12 May 1951), 213-14.
Edward Leamy's and Yeats's share in the founding of the society.

184. PIPER, DAVID: *The Image of the Poet: British Poets and Their Portraits.* Oxford: Clarendon Press, 1982. xxi, 219 pp.
See pp. 184-91.

185. POUND, EZRA: *The Letters, 1907-1941.* Edited by D. D. Paige. London: Faber & Faber, 1951. 464 pp.
Yeats is mentioned passim (see index); no letter to him is included.

186. POWER, ARTHUR [RICHARD]: "A Contact with Yeats," *Irish Tatler and Sketch,* 74:3 (Dec 1964), 34, 61.
Reprinted in BA13, 1:189-92.

187. ———: "W. B. Yeats: A Memoir," *IrP,* 28 Dec 1974, 8.

188. PRITCHETT, VICTOR SAWDON: "Encounters with Yeats," *NSt,* 4 June 1965, 879-80.
Reprinted in BA13, 2:346-49.

189. ———: *Dublin: A Portrait.* Photographs by Evelyn Hofer. NY: Harper & Row, 1967. 99 pp.
See pp. 13-18.

190. ———: *Midnight Oil.* NY: Random House, 1972. ix, 273 pp.
See pp. 130-33.

191. PRUITT, VIRGINIA D.: "Yeats and the Steinach Operation," *AI,* 34:3 (Fall 1977), 287-96.

192. ———, and RAYMOND D. PRUITT, M.D.: "Yeats and the Steinach Operation: A Further Analysis," *Yeats,* 1 (1983), 104-24.

193. PYLE, HILARY: *Jack B. Yeats: A Biography.* London: Routledge & Kegan Paul, 1970. xii, 228 pp.
Notes on WBY, passim (see index).

194. PYPER, STANTON: "Chosen Vues," *DM,* 1:6 (Jan 1924), 520-26.

195. QUINN, JOHN: "Lady Gregory and the Abbey Theatre," *Outlook,* 16 Dec 1911, 916-19.
Includes reminiscences of Yeats.

196. RASCOE, BURTON: "Contemporary Reminiscences: Notes on [. . .] W. B. Yeates [sic], the Nobel Prize Winner," *Arts & Decoration,* 21:1 (May 1924), 31, 62, 68.

197. ———: *A Bookman's Daybook.* Edited with an introduction by C. Hartley Grattan. NY: Liveright, 1929. xx, 305 pp.
"Two Meetings with W. B. Yeats," 233-35.

198. RATTRAY, ROBERT FLEMING: *Poets in the Flesh: Tagore, Yeats, Dunsany, Stephens, Drinkwater.* Cambridge: Golden Head Press, 1961. v, 13 pp.
"A Day with Yeats," 5-8; in Leicester in 1922. Reprinted in BA13, 1:156-58.

199. REID, BENJAMIN LAWRENCE: *The Man from New York: John Quinn and His Friends.* NY: Oxford UP, 1968. xviii, 708 pp.
On Yeats passim (see index), including quotations of letters to and from him.

200. RHYS, ERNEST: *Everyman Remembers.* London: Dent, 1931. xi, 320 pp.
See pp. 105-14 on the Rhymers' Club; pp. 251-57 on a poetry reading in which Yeats took part; and passim (see index).

201. ———: "W. B. Yeats: Early Recollections," *FortnR,* os 144 / ns 138:823 (July 1935), 52-57.
Yeats at the Rhymers' Club and at Madame Blavatsky's. Reprinted in BA13, 1:34-40.

202. ———: *Letters from Limbo.* London: Dent, 1936. xvii, 289 pp.
See pp. 155-59.

203. ———: *Wales England Wed: An Autobiography.* London: Dent, 1940. ix, 295 pp.
Memories of Yeats, passim, especially pp. 91-93, 104-7 (Yeats and Madame Blavatsky), 172-75 (Yeats and Maud Gonne).

204. RICHARDSON, DOROTHY MILLER: "Yeats of Bloomsbury," *LLT,* 21:20 (Apr 1939), 60-66.
A meeting with Yeats on a street in Bloomsbury and the view from the apartment opposite Yeats's in Woburn Buildings. Reprinted as "Yeats and Bloomsbury," *St. Pancras J,* 12:5 (Oct 1958), 67-70, together with a note on the plaque that marks the house in which Yeats lived. For a slightly fictionalized account of the meeting see the novel *The Trap,* included in *Pilgrimage III.* London: Dent, 1967. 509 pp. (pp. 437-39, 502). See also BB225 and CD1102.

205. RICKETTS, CHARLES: *Self-Portrait Taken from the Letters & Journals.* Collected and compiled by T. Sturge Moore, edited by Cecil Lewis. London: Davies, 1939. xix, 442 pp.
On Yeats, passim (see index). Includes two letters from Ricketts to Yeats, pp. 341-43; a more accurate version of the first of the letters is in BC1 (p. 430). BC1 contains three letters from Ricketts not in BB205.

206. ROBINSON, LENNOX, TOM ROBINSON, and NORA DORMAN: *Three Homes.* London: Joseph, 1938. 261 pp.
Lennox Robinson's reminiscences of Yeats and the Abbey Theatre, pp. 218-34.

207. ROBINSON, LENNOX: *Curtain Up: An Autobiography.* London: Joseph, 1942. 224 pp.
Reminiscences of Yeats and the Abbey Theatre, passim. Part of the material on Yeats's plays (especially pp. 44-72) is also contained in CA35.

208. ———: "William Butler Yeats: Personality," in Jeffares and Cross: *In Excited Reverie* (1965, CA48), 14-23.
Reminiscences and a character sketch.

209. RODGERS, WILLIAM ROBERT: *Irish Literary Portraits [. . .]: W. R. Rodgers's Broadcast Conversations with Those Who Knew Them.* London: British Broadcasting Corporation, 1972. xix, 236 pp.
"W. B. Yeats," 1-21 (broadcast June 1949); reprint of "W. B. Yeats: A Dublin Portrait," in Jeffares and Cross: *In Excited Reverie* (1965, CA48), 1-13. First published in Lawrence Gilliam (ed): *B.B.C. Features.* London: Evans, 1950. 208 pp. (pp. 176-86); also in *Books and Bookmen,* 10:9 (June 1965), 16, 18-20.

Yeats is also mentioned in the programs on Joyce, Moore, Synge, Shaw, Gogarty, Higgins, and AE.
Reviews:
- Anon.: "Literary Lore," *TLS*, 29 Sept 1972, 1148.
- Nona Balakian: "The Charmed Circle: The Irish Writers," *NYT*, 28 Apr 1973, 31; reprinted in *Critical Encounters: Literary Views and Reviews, 1953-1977*. Indianapolis: Bobbs-Merrill, 1978. 250 pp. (pp. 219-22).

210. ROSE, MARILYN GADDIS: "A Visit with Anne Yeats," *MD*, 7:3 (Dec 1964), 299-307.
Anne Yeats talks about her father.

211. ROTHENSTEIN, SIR WILLIAM: *Men and Memories: Recollections*. London: Faber & Faber, 1931-39. 3 vols.
Volume 3 bears the title *Since Fifty*. Memories of Yeats passim (see index), including notes on his revisions of Tagore's *Gitanjali*, his views of Berkeley, Swift, sexual intercourse, and folk song.

212. ———: *Imperfect Encounter: Letters of William Rothenstein and Rabindranath Tagore, 1911-1941*. Edited with an introduction and notes by Mary M. Lago. Cambridge, Mass.: Harvard UP, 1972. xx, 402 pp.
Numerous references to Yeats (see index).

213. RUDDOCK, MARGOT: *The Lemon Tree*. With an introduction by W. B. Yeats. London: Dent, 1938. xiv, 29 pp.
"Almost I Tasted Ecstasy," 1-9, contains her account of her meeting with Yeats. Reprinted in CD1140.

214. [RUSSELL, GEORGE WILLIAM]: *Letters from AE*. Selected and edited by Alan Denson with a foreword by Monk Gibbon. NY: Abelard-Schuman, 1961. xliii, 288 pp.
Reprints some of the letters from BC11. Gibbon's preface, pp. vii-xvi, compares Yeats and AE. Numerous letters are addressed to Yeats, who is also mentioned passim (see index). Extended comments on *The Hour-Glass* in a letter of [2 Mar 1903 (?)], pp. 44-45; reprinted in CA50, pp. 130-31.

215. [———]: "Unpublished Letters from AE to John Eglinton." Edited by H[enry] Summerfield, *Malahat R*, 14 (Apr 1970), 84-107.
Yeats is mentioned passim.

216. RUTENBERG, DANIEL: "A New Date for the Rhymers' Club," *ELT*, 12:3 (1969), 155-57.
See also Karl Beckson, 13:1 (1970), 37-38; R. K. R. Thornton, 14:1 (1971), 49-53.

217. RYAN, MARK FRANCIS: *Fenian Memories*. Edited with an introduction by T. F. O'Sullivan. Dublin: Gill, 1945. xxiv, 226 pp.
"'98 Centenary--Mr. W. B. Yeats a Prominent Figure in the Celebrations," 184-89. See also BF9.

218. SADDLEMYER, ANN: "Synge and Some Companions, with a Note Concerning a Walk through Connemara with Jack Yeats," *YeSt*, 2 (Bealtaine 1972), 18-34.
The companions are WBY, Stephen MacKenna, Masefield, and Jack Yeats.

219. SANDULESCU, CONSTANTIN-GEORGE, and CLIVE HART (eds): *As-*

sessing the 1984 "Ulysses." Gerrards Cross: Smythe / Totowa, N.J.: Barnes & Noble, 1986. xxiv, 247 pp. (Princess Grace Irish Library. 1.)

Richard M. Kain: "Dublin 1904," 92–110, 226–27. What some of the celebrities of the Irish literary scene (including Yeats) did in this memorable year.

220. SHARE, BERNARD: *Irish Lives: Biographies of Fifty Famous Irish Men and Women*. Dublin: Figgis, 1971. Unpaged.

Contains a short biography of Yeats.

221. SHARP, ELIZABETH AMELIA: *William Sharp (Fiona Macleod): A Memoir*. London: Heinemann, 1910. vii, 433 pp.

Contains several letters from Yeats to Sharp and to Fiona Macleod and vice versa; also some reminiscences (see index).

222. SILVER, JEREMY: "W. B. Yeats and the BBC: A Reassessment," *YeA*, 5 (1987), 181–85.

Expands greatly on Whalley's note on "Yeats and Broadcasting" (AA15) and includes a list of radio and television performances of Yeats material, 1926–1938.

See Marie Slocombe: "Cultural Documents," *TLS*, 16 July 1970, 774 (letter to the editor, refers to the recordings Yeats made for the BBC).

223. ———: "Yeats Material in the Radio Telefis Eireann Archives," *YeA*, 5 (1987), 186–88.

A checklist, mostly of reminiscences broadcast by various of Yeats's friends and acquaintances.

224. SIME, GEORGINA, and FRANK NICHOLSON: *Brave Spirits*. [London]: Privately Printed, [1952]. vii, 165 pp.

"A Triple View of W. B. Yeats," 59–83. Recollections of Yeats in Chiswick, where he talked about Madame Blavatsky and tried psychic experiments (see BF3), and of two Yeats lectures in Montreal (see BF38, 112, and 136).

225. SINCLAIR, FREDERICK: "A Poet's World in Woburn Walk," *St. Pancras J*, 2:7 (Dec 1948), 124–27.

See also BB204.

226. SITWELL, EDITH: *Selected Letters*. Edited by John Lehmann and Derek Parker. London: Macmillan, 1970. 264 pp.

See index for some references to Yeats.

227. SPEAIGHT, ROBERT: "William Butler Yeats," *Commonweal*, 31 Mar 1939, 623–24.

228. ———: *William Rothenstein: The Portrait of an Artist in His Time*. London: Eyre & Spottiswoode, 1962. xv, 443 pp.

Yeats is mentioned passim (see index).

229. ———: "W. B. Yeats and Some Later Friendships," *Greyfriar*, 8 (1965), 14–32.

Yeats's friendships with W. J. Turner, Lady Ottoline Morrell, L. A. G. Strong, Wyndham Lewis, Olivia Shakespear, Margot Ruddock, and Dorothy Wellesley; also some personal reminiscences.

230. ———: *The Property Basket: Recollections of a Divided Life*. London: Collins & Harvill Press, 1970. 416 pp.

See index for a few references to Yeats.

231. SPEAKMAN, HAROLD: *Here's Ireland.* NY: McBride, 1931 [1925]. xiii, 353 pp.
"Mr. Yeats and Others," 302-17 (see pp. 302-8).

232. SPENDER, STEPHEN: *World within World: The Autobiography.* London: Hamilton, 1964 [1951]. ix, 349 pp.
Reminiscences of Yeats, pp. 163-66.

233. STARKIE, WALTER: "Poet Immortalized Celtic Lore: Tributes to the Late Dr. W. B. Yeats," *IrI,* 30 Jan 1939, 9.
See also the anonymous obituary on p. 10.

234. ———: "Yeats and Company," *NYTBR,* 14 Nov 1965, 90-92.

235. STRONG, LEONARD ALFRED GEORGE: "Yeats," *Time and Tide,* 4 Feb 1939, 130-31.

236. [———]: "A Memory of Yeats," *List,* 20 Dec 1945, 725.

237. ———: "Reminiscences of Yeats," *List,* 22 Apr 1954, 689-90.
Extracts reprinted in BA13, 1:142-47.

238. ———: "Yeats at His Ease," *LMag,* 2:3 (Mar 1955), 56-65.
Yeats in his Oxford years. Reprinted in BA13, 1:147-55.

239. ———: *Green Memory.* London: Methuen, 1961. 313 pp.
"Memories of Yeats from 1919 to 1924: The conversations were always recorded the morning after they took place and are as nearly accurate as a faithful ear could make them," 242-63. See also pp. 303-6.

240. STURM, FRANK PEARCE: *His Life, Letters, and Collected Works.* Edited and with an introductory essay by Richard Taylor. Urbana: U of Illinois Press, 1969. viii, 382 pp.
On the Yeats-Sturm relationship (mutual influences and biographical connections), passim (see index). Prints the entire Yeats-Sturm correspondence, which is mainly concerned with *A Vision,* pp. 73-110. See also CE422.

241. THOMPSON, LAWRANCE: *Robert Frost: The Early Years, 1874-1915.* London: Cape, 1967. xvii, 641 pp.
Frost meets Yeats, pp. 412-14, and some other references (see index). See also BB77.

242. TOBIN, RICHARD MONTGOMERY: "Personal Memoirs of William Butler Yeats," *Oriel R,* 1:[1 (1943)], 72-76.

243. TURNER, W. J.: "The Yeats I Knew," *List,* 3 Oct 1946, 443-44.

244. TYLER, DOROTHY: "Carl Milles, Yeats, and the Irish Coinage," *MQR,* 22:4 (Autumn 1963), 273-80.
Describes two meetings between Milles and Yeats in London and Detroit. It seems that Yeats encouraged Milles, the Swedish sculptor and one of the artists in the coinage competition, to such an extent that Milles regarded the invitation to participate as an order. Hence his disappointment when somebody else's designs were chosen. On Milles see also BG1.

245. T[YNAN], K[ATHARINE]: "William Butler Yeats," *Sketch,* 29 Nov 1893, 256.
A visit and an interview.

246. ———: *Twenty-five Years: Reminiscences.* London: Smith, Elder, 1913. viii, 355 pp.
The first volume of KT's autobiography. See index for references to Yeats.

247. ———: *The Middle Years.* London: Constable, 1916. viii, 415 pp.
The second volume of KT's autobiography.

248. ———: "Personal Memories of John Butler Yeats," *Double Dealer,* 4:19 (July 1922), 8-15.

249. TYNAN, KATHERINE [sic]: "Letters: 1884-5," *Apex One,* 1 (Sept 1973), 1-27.
Letters to Mrs. James Pritchard of London. KT notes her first meeting with WBY in the letter of 30 June 1885 (p. 23).

250. UNTERECKER, JOHN: "An Interview with Anne Yeats," *Shenandoah,* 16:4 (Summer 1965), 7-20.
Contains some reminiscences of her father, also notes on her designs for *Purgatory.*

251. VALOIS, NINETTE DE: *Come Dance with Me: A Memoir, 1898-1956.* London: Hamilton, 1957. xvi, 234 pp.
Reminiscences of Yeats and the Abbey, pp. 88-98.

252. WALSH, CAROLINE: *The Homes of Irish Writers.* Dublin: Anvil Books, 1982. 192 pp.
"William Butler Yeats 1865-1939," 162-75 (illustrated), and passim (see index).

253. W[ALSH], E. R.: "Reminiscences of 'W. B.': South Frederick Street Days," *IrT,* 10 Feb 1940, 13.
In 1907. Reprinted in BA13, 2:276-80.

254. WATKINS, GEOFFREY M.: "Yeats and Mr. Watkins' Bookshop," in Harper: *Yeats and the Occult* (1975, FC40), 307-10.
John M. Watkins's bookshop as a meeting place of various spiritualists, among them Yeats.

255. WATKINS, VERNON: "Visit to Yeats in Dublin, Spring, 1938," *Poetry Wales,* 12:4 (Spring 1977), 66-77.
Watkins's notes made after the visit, which resulted in the poem "Yeats in Dublin" (HD190). See also BB62.

256. WELLESLEY, DOROTHY: *Far Have I Travelled.* London: Barrie, 1952. 240 pp.
See pp. 162-70.

257. WEYGANDT, CORNELIUS: *Tuesdays at Ten: A Garnering from the Talks of Thirty Years on Poets, Dramatists, and Essayists.* Philadelphia: U of Pennsylvania Press, 1928. 325 pp.
"With Yeats in the Woods of Coole," 176-85; reprinted from *Lippincott's Magazine,* 73:436 (Apr 1904), 484-87; reprinted in BA13, 1:15-19. See index for further notes on Yeats.

258. ———: *On the Edge of Evening: The Autobiography of a Teacher and Writer Who Holds to the Old Ways*. NY: Putnam's, 1946. xi, 217 pp.
Reminiscences of Yeats, passim (see index).

259. WHITTINGTON-EGAN, RICHARD, and GEOFFREY SMERDON: *The Quest of the Golden Boy: The Life and Letters of Richard Le Gallienne*. London: Unicorn Press, 1960. xxiii, 580 pp.
The activities of the Rhymers' Club, pp. 167-76.

260. WILKINSON, MARGUERITE: "A Talk with John Butler Yeats about His Son, William Butler Yeats," *Touchstone*, 6:1 (Oct 1919), 10-17. (Illustrated)

261. YEATS, ANNE: "Faces of My Father," *IrT*, 1 Dec 1976, 10.

262. YEATS, W. B.: "Letters to Matthew Russell, S.J." Edited by Roger McHugh, *IrM*, 82 [i.e., 81]:954 (Feb 1953), 60-63; :955 (Mar 1953), 111-15; :956 (Apr 1953), 148-51.

263. ———: "An Unpublished Letter." Edited by C. G. Martin, *N&Q*, os 203 / ns 5:6 (June 1958), 260-61.
Yeats's answer to an admirer (dated 20 Mar 1906) who had asked for a book on prosody.

264. YOUNG, ELLA: *Flowering Dusk: Things Remembered Accurately and Inaccurately*. NY: Longmans Green, 1945. xvi, 356 pp.
Memories of Yeats, pp. 63-65, 90-93 and passim (see index).

See also AE32, 51, 67, 70, BF126, CA74, 109, 153, CB77, 145, 158, 160, 198, 280, 339, 353, 403, 404, 428, 464, 479, 501, 544, 546, CC50, 91, 219, 295, 354, CD7, 63, 106, 139, 212a, 214, 217, 306, 313, 434, 472a, 477-78, 480, 482-84, 520, 576, 608, 724, 753, 763, 770, 803, 805, 810, 810a, 856, 889, 1024a, 1031, 1042, 1048-48b, 1050, 1052, 1058, 1066, 1104, 1140, 1144, 1154, 1159, 1160, 1171-72, 1198a, 1203, 1206, 1233, 1243, 1245, 1259, 1274, 1277, 1309, 1316, 1321, 1343, 1349, 1350, 1357, 1363, 1396, 1399, 1410, 1418, 1426, 1428, 1442, 1452-53, 1460, 1466, 1467, CE327, DB5, DD679, EC110, EE130, 537, EF1-106, FA57, FC39, 43, 54, FD57, G1042, 1063, 1604-52, HA2, 10, HB2, 7, 11, HD63.

BC Letters to Yeats

1. FINNERAN, RICHARD J., GEORGE MILLS HARPER, WILLIAM M. MURPHY, and ALAN B. HIMBER (eds): *Letters to W. B. Yeats*. London: Macmillan, 1977. xvii, 1-302, xiii, 303-628 pp. in 2 vols.
About 500 letters from more than 4,000 extant. The following correspondents are of special interest: Sara Allgood, Austin Clarke, Padraic Colum, Gordon Craig, Edmund Dulac, St. John Ervine, Florence Farr, Frank J. and William G. Fay, Everard Feilding, Eva Fowler, Oliver St. John Gogarty, Maud Gonne, Miss Horniman, W. T. Horton, Douglas Hyde, Wyndham Lewis, Ethel Mannin, Edward Martyn, John Masefield, Mrs. MacGregor Mathers, Harriet Monroe, George Moore, Gilbert Murray, Standish O'Grady, Shri Purohit Swami, John Quinn, Charles Ricketts, Laura Riding, Lennox Robinson, Mario M. Rossi, William Rothenstein, G. W. Russell (AE), Olivia Shakespear, Elizabeth A. and William Sharp, G. B. Shaw, W. F. Stead, Christina Mary Stoddart, Frank Pearce Sturm, Rabindranath Tagore, Agnes Tobin,

Katharine Tynan, John B. Yeats, Lily Yeats.
Reviews:
- Brian Andrews: "Wade not Balanced," *Honest Ulsterman,* 63 (July-Oct 1979), 80-84.
- Anon.: "Irish Letters," *Economist,* 17 Dec 1977, 134.
- Denis Donoghue: "Such Friends," *Hibernia,* 20 Jan 1978, 23.
- Warwick Gould: "The Poet at the Breakfast Table," *English,* 27:128-129 (Summer-Autumn 1978), 222-39.
- Will C. Jumper, *Poet and Critic,* 12:2 (1980), 47-48.
- Wanda Krajewska, *KN,* 26:2 (1979), 282-84 (in Polish).
- F. S. L. Lyons: "Turning around Ireland's Pivot," *TLS,* 3 Feb 1978, 114.
- Lowry Nelson: "Now That It's Past Let's Call It Modernism," *YR,* 68:2 (Dec 1978), 266-70.
- William H. Pritchard: "Yeats and His Father," *List,* 12 Jan 1978, 60-61.
- Kathleen Raine: "The Sub-Plot to Life's Comedy," *Times,* 23 Jan 1978, 9.
- Lynn Thiesmeyer: "The Greening of the Yeats Industry," *EIC,* 30:3 (July 1980), 256-64.
- John Unterecker, *Biography,* 2:2 (Spring 1979), 175-81.
- Thomas R. Whitaker, *SAQ,* 78:2 (Spring 1979), 260-61.
- Phyllis Zagano: "Writing to Willie," *Book Forum,* 4:3 (1979), 509-10.

2. FOX, MICHAEL, and T. J. BRENNAN: "The New York Gaelic Society Denounce 'The Play Boy,'" *Irish World and American Industrial Liberator,* 21 Oct 1911, 7.
Letter addressed to Yeats. More denunciations of Yeats and of Synge's plays can be found in preceding and subsequent issues.

3. JOHNSON, LIONEL: "Some Letters." Edited by Raymond Roseliep. Editor's Ph.D. thesis, U of Notre Dame, 1954. 221 pp. (*DAI,* 15:3 [1955], 418)
Contains three letters to Yeats: 26 Oct 1892 (pp. 127-28), 8 May 1894 (p. 147), 23 Oct 1894 (pp. 154-57).

4. JOYCE, JAMES: *Letters.* Edited by Stuart Gilbert and Richard Ellmann. NY: Viking Press, 1957-66. 3 vols.
Contains several letters and numerous references to Yeats (see indexes in vols. 1 and 3).

5. LAWRENCE, THOMAS EDWARD: *The Letters.* Edited by David Garnett. London: Cape, 1938. 896 pp.
See pp. 743-44 for the letter, signed T. E. Shaw, in which Lawrence rejects his nomination to the Irish Academy of Letters.

6. MOORE, GEORGE: "The Letters of George Moore to Edmund Gosse, W. B. Yeats, R. I. Best, Miss Nancy Cunard, and Mrs. Mary Hutchinson." Edited by Charles Joseph Burkhart. Editor's Ph.D. thesis, U of Maryland, 1958. xxvi, 410 pp. (*DAI,* 19:1 [July 1958], 131)
Moore's letters to Yeats (1897-1901) are on pp. 254-74. They are mostly concerned with work on *Diarmuid and Grania,* also with *The Countess Cathleen* and *Where There Is Nothing*. Other references to Yeats, passim (see index), particularly p. 196, where Moore condemns *Four Plays for Dancers* as "nonsense."

7. MORRIS, BRUCE: "Arthur Symons's Letters to W. B. Yeats: 1892-1902," *YeA,* 5 (1987), 46-61.
An annotated edition of 12 letters.

8. POUND, EZRA: "Two Incidents," *Shenandoah*, 4:2/3 (Summer-Autumn 1953), 112-16.

Three letters to Yeats, 1931-32.

9. ———: "Letters to William Butler Yeats." Edited with comments by C. F. Terrell, *Antaeus*, 21/22 (Spring/Summer 1976), 34-49.

Nine letters from Pound to Yeats, a short note from Yeats to Pound, and four letters from Pound to Mrs. Yeats.

10. QUINN, JOHN: *The Letters of John Quinn to William Butler Yeats*. Edited by Alan Himber with the assistance of George Mills Harper. Ann Arbor: UMI Research Press, 1983. xiii, 302 pp. (Studies in Modern Literature. 28.)

Based on Himber's Ph.D. thesis, Florida State U, 1977. xi, 479 pp. (*DAI*, 38:5 [Nov 1977], 2753A). The "Introduction," 1-38, chronicles the Yeats-Quinn relationship; the book contains 91 letters and telegrams to Yeats.

Reviews:

- Susan Fisher Miller: "Yeats between the Letters," *ILS*, 4:1 (Spring 1985), 33.
- William M. Murphy, *Yeats*, 3 (1985), 238-44.
- James Pethica, *YeA*, 4 (1986), 252-54.

11. [RUSSELL, GEORGE WILLIAM]: *Some Passages from the Letters of AE to W. B. Yeats*. Dublin: Cuala Press, 1936. iii, 64 pp.

Reprinted °Shannon: Irish UP, 1971. Some of the letters appear, newly transcribed, in BB214.

Reviews:

- Anon.: "AE. [sic] and Mr. W. B. Yeats: Letters of Thirty-Five Years," *IrT*, 31 Oct 1936, 7.
- J. M. Hone: "An Irish Idealist," *Spect*, 25 Sept 1936, 508.

12. SHAW, GEORGE BERNARD: *Collected Letters, 1898-1910*. Edited by Dan H. Laurence. London: Reinhardt, 1972. xxiv, 1017 pp.

A letter to Yeats, pp. 452, 859-61, who is also mentioned passim (see index).

13. ———: *Collected Letters 1911-1925*. Edited by Dan H. Laurence. London: Reinhardt, 1985. xxiv, 989 pp.

Contains a letter to Yeats, pp. 190-91, reprinted from *The Times*, 15 July 1913. Yeats is also referred to on p. 234.

13a. ———: *Collected Letters 1926-1950*. Edited by Dan H. Laurence. London: Reinhardt, 1988. xxvii, 946 pp.

Letter to Yeats re Irish Academy of Letters, reprinted from BC1, pp. 308-9; two letters to Yeats about the suppression of *The Adventures of the Black Girl*, pp. 339-40 and 352-53 (see also p. 348); another letter, pp. 360-61; Shaw's assessment of his relationship with Yeats, pp. 576-77.

14. STEPHENS, JAMES: *Letters of James Stephens*. With an appendix listing Stephens's published writings. Edited by Richard J. Finneran. London: Macmillan, 1974. xxiv, 481 pp.

Includes two letters to Yeats (pp. 387-88) and numerous references to him; see also pp. 30-34 for Stephens's letter answering a review of *The Land of Heart's Desire* (see G309).

15. STEVENSON, ROBERT LOUIS: *The Letters to His Family and Friends*. Selected and edited with notes and introduction by Sidney Colvin. NY: Scribner's, 1899. 2 vols.

Letter to Yeats from Vailima, Samoa, dated 14 Apr 1894, praising "Lake Isle of Innisfrae" [sic], 2:387-88. Reprinted in CA50, pp. 85-86.

16. WELLESLEY, DOROTHY: *Beyond the Grave: Letters on Poetry to W. B. Yeats from Dorothy Wellesley*. Tunbridge Wells: Baldwin, [1949?]. 63 pp.

Letters written to Yeats after his death. Very often they are only marginally concerned with his life and work. See CA170.

17. WILDE, OSCAR: *The Letters*. Edited by Rupert Hart-Davis. London: Hart-Davis, 1962. xxv, 958 pp.

Contains a letter to Yeats [Aug-Sept 1894] re Yeats's *A Book of Irish Verse* (p. 365), also scattered references to Yeats (see index).

18. YEATS, JOHN BUTLER: *Passages from the Letters of John Butler Yeats*. Selected by Ezra Pound. Churchtown, Dundrum: Cuala Press, 1917. viii, 61 pp.

Reprinted °Shannon: Irish UP, 1971. Extracts from letters written to WBY, 1911-16.

Continued as *Further Letters of John Butler Yeats*. Selected by Lennox Robinson. Churchtown, Dundrum: Cuala Press, 1920. v, 83 pp. Reprinted °Shannon: Irish UP, 1971. Extracts from letters written to WBY, 1916-20.

19. ————: *Letters to His Son W. B. Yeats and Others, 1869-1922*. Edited with a memoir by Joseph Hone and a preface by Oliver Elton. NY: Dutton, 1946 [1944]. 304 pp.

Includes an appendix with extracts from Elizabeth C. Yeats's diary, 1888-89, about family life at Bedford Park. Reprinted without any new editorial matter London: Secker & Warburg in association with the Arts Council of Great Britain, 1983. 296 pp.

Reviews of the first edition:

- Anon., *List*, 16 Mar 1944, 305.
- Anon.: "Memorabilia," *N&Q*, 189:11 (1 Dec 1945), 221-22.
- Jacob Bean: "Engaging Contradiction," *Commonweal*, 8 Nov 1946, 96-97.
- Thomas Bodkin: "Father of W. B. Yeats," *Birmingham Post*, 22 Feb 1944, 2.
- E. C., *Connoisseur*, 113:492 (June 1944), 131-32.
- [Harold Child]: "Father and Son: Letters of J. B. to W. B. Yeats," *TLS*, 25 Mar 1944, 152.
- Mary M. Colum: "W. B. [i.e., J. B.?] Yeats' Limberness and Grace," *SatR*, 9 Nov 1946, 16-17.
- Padraic Colum: "Good Conversation in the Form of Letters," *NYHTB*, 13 Oct 1946, 3.
- Babette Deutsch: "Personality," *Poetry*, 69:5 (Feb 1947), 291-95.
- Oliver St. John Gogarty: "From Father to Son," *NYTBR*, 20 Oct 1946, 34.
- David Grene, *ChiR*, 2:1 (Winter 1947), 36-37.
- F. W. van Heerikhuizen: "Brieven van een beminnelijk man," *Litterair paspoort*, 1:2 (Mar 1946), 6-7.
- Robert Hillyer, *Atlantic Monthly*, 178:6 (Dec 1946), 182.
- Helen Landreth, *CathW*, 164:981 (Dec 1946), 276-77.
- [Seumas O'Sullivan?], *DM*, 19:2 (Apr-June 1944), 59-61.
- Horace Reynolds: "He Offered His Son the Poetry of Life," *NYTBR*, 18 June 1944, 25.

- ———: "The Successful Mr. Yeats: John Butler Yeats Was a Success as a Thinker, a Talker, a Letter Writer," *CSM,* 30 Nov 1946, Weekly Magazine, 6.
- T. C. Worsley: "A Poet's Father," *NSt,* 1 Apr 1944, 229-30.

Reviews of the reprint:

- Patrick Skene Catling: "Yeats the Elder," *Spect,* 18 June 1983, 24-25.
- Brian Fallon: "The Old Man in the New World," *IrT,* 28 May 1983, 14.
- Roy Foster: "Companionabilities," *TLS,* 1 July 1983, 691.
- Geoffrey Grigson: "Gloss on History," *Country Life,* 23 June 1983, 1737-38.
- Desirée Hirst: "Inspiring Father, Astonishing Clan," *Tablet,* 20 Aug 1983, 801.
- John Jordan: "Gates of Knowledge," *IrP,* 2 July 1983, 9.
- Nicholas Leonard: "Yeats Postscript on the 'Island of Sinners,'" *IrI,* 4 June 1983, 5.
- Robert Nye: "The Fruits of Ancestor Worship," *Scotsman,* 4 June 1983, Weekend Scotsman, 5.
- Christopher Ricks: "Speaking Well," *LRB,* 18-31 Aug 1983, 3, 5-6.

20. ———: "Death Exultant: A Poem by John B. Yeats." Commentary by Oliver Edwards, *Rann,* 13 (Oct 1951), 8-10.

A letter from JBY to WBY, which contains the poem.

See also AE1, 21, 23, 24, 56, 63a, 68, 71, 98, BB139, 199, 205, 214, 221, BD24, BF104, CD293, 294, 309, 348, 388, 456, 576, 724, 855, 868a, 930, 1082, 1140, 1154, 1184, 1188, 1274, 1283, 1349, 1428, EB156, EF39, 46, 54, 97.

BD The Yeats Family

For the purpose of this bibliography, the Yeats family is defined by its most famous members, John Butler Yeats (JBY), WBY, and Jack Yeats, and by WBY's sisters Elizabeth Corbet ("Lolly") and Susan Mary ("Lily") Yeats. I also include material on WBY's ancestors, his wife, and his children. The listing is highly selective. Only those items are listed that have some bearing on WBY; hence discussions concerned with, e.g., Jack Yeats's paintings are excluded. The standard biography of JBY is that by W. M. Murphy (see BA15).

1. ALLEN, JAMES LOVIC: "All in the Family: Artistic Interaction between W. B. Yeats and His Siblings," *YER,* 5:1 (1978), 32-43.

On WBY, Jack, Lolly, and Lily Yeats; describes a development "from a close and harmonious integration of the Yeats siblings' artistic activities and accomplishments in childhood, youth, and young adulthood to an increasing separation, alienation, and deterioriation of genuine aesthetic interaction in middle years and old age."

2. ANON.: "Where W. B. Yeats Will Lie [. . .]: Associations of Drumcliffe," *IrT,* 6 Feb 1939, 8.

On WBY's ancestors.

3. ARCHIBALD, DOUGLAS N.: *John Butler Yeats.* Lewisburg: Bucknell UP, 1974. 103 pp.

Contains a few notes on the JBY-WBY relationship.

4. ARNOLD, BRUCE: *A Concise History of Irish Art.* London: Thames & Hudson, 1969. 216 pp.

Some notes on JBY and WBY, extended remarks on Jack Yeats (see index).

5. COLUM, PADRAIC: "John Butler Yeats," *Atlantic Monthly,* 172:1 (July 1943), 81-85.

6. ———: "My Memories of John Butler Yeats," *DM,* 32:4 (Oct-Dec 1957), 8-16.

7. GILL, W. W.: "Pollexfen in W. B. Yeats' Ancestry," *N&Q,* 187:14 (30 Dec 1944), 294-95.

8. GORDON, ROBERT: *John Butler Yeats and John Sloan: The Records of a Friendship.* Dublin: Dolmen Press, 1978. 32 pp. (New Yeats Papers. 14.)

First published in a somewhat different form as "John Sloan and John Butler Yeats," *Art J,* 32:3 (Spring 1973), 289-96.

9. GREHAN, IDA: "Miss Yeats, and the Problem of Living in a Poet's Shadow," *Daily Telegraph,* 15 Jan 1971, 15.

10. KENNY ART GALLERY, GALWAY: *An Exhibition of Paintings and Drawings by Jack B. Yeats.* Official opening on Friday 23rd of April [1971] by Anne Yeats. [Galway: Kenny, 1971]. 13 pp.

See pp. 1-3 for Anne Yeats's reminiscences of her uncle.

11. LANDOW, GEORGE P. (ed): *Approaches to Victorian Autobiography.* Athens: Ohio UP, 1979. xlvi, 359 pp.

George Bornstein: "The Antinomial Structure of John Butler Yeats' *Early Memories: Some Chapters of Autobiography* ," 200-11.

12. MCHUGH, ROGER (ed): *Jack B. Yeats: A Centenary Gathering.* Dublin: Dolmen Press, 1971. 114 pp. (Tower Series of Anglo-Irish Studies. 3.)

References to WBY appear passim.

13. MURPHY, WILLIAM M.: "The Ancestry of William Butler Yeats," *YeSt,* 1 (Bealtaine 1971), 1-19.

14. ———: *The Yeats Family and the Pollexfens of Sligo.* With drawings by John Butler Yeats. Dublin: Dolmen Press, 1971. 88 pp. (New Yeats Papers. 1.)

A short biography of the Pollexfen family from about the middle of the 19th century down to WBY (whose mother was born Susan Mary Pollexfen). Includes a genealogical table and 14 drawings by JBY.

Reviews:

- Richard Ellmann, *N&Q,* os 220 / ns 22:5 (May 1975), 226-27.
- Mary Lappin: "J. B., Jack B., W. B.," *IrP,* 19 Feb 1972, 12.
- Eilean Ni Chuilleanain: "Yeats, Gogarty and Others," *IrT,* 29 Jan 1972, 10.

15. ———: "Psychic Daughter, Mystic Son, Sceptic Father," in Harper: *Yeats and the Occult* (1975, FC40), 11-26.

The occult experiences of Lily Yeats, WBY, and their father JBY.

16. ———: "Home Life among the Yeatses," in Jeffares: *Yeats, Sligo and Ireland* (1980, CA51), 170-88.

Answers Helen Vendler's criticism of Murphy's *Prodigal Father* (BA15).

17. PACHTER, MARC, and FRANCES STEVENSON WEIN (eds): *Abroad in America: Visitors to the New Nation 1776-1914.* Washington, D.C.: National Portrait Gallery, Smithsonian Institute / Reading, Mass.: Addison-Wesley, 1975. xix, 347 pp.

Denis Donoghue: "John Butler Yeats 1839-1922," 260-69.

18. RASCOE, BURTON: *Before I Forget.* Garden City: Doubleday, Doran, 1937. xix, 442 pp.

"John Butler Yeats on His Son and on Various Matters," 413-14.

19. SHEEHY, JEANNE: "John Butler Yeats," *Hibernia,* 17 Nov 1972, 18.

20. SKELTON, ROBIN: "'Unarrangeable Reality': The Paintings and Writings of Jack B. Yeats," in Skelton and Saddlemyer: *The World of W. B. Yeats* (1967, CA102), 220-31.

21. SLOAN, JOHN: *John Sloan's New York Scene: From the Diaries, Notes, and Correspondence 1906-1913.* Edited by Bruce St. John. NY: Harper & Row, 1965. xxvi, 658 pp.

Many references to JBY and some remarks on WBY (see index).

22. TYNAN, KATHARINE: *Memories.* London: Nash & Grayson, 1924. v, 432 pp.

"Artist and Philosopher--John Butler Yeats," 273-87.

23. WHITE, JAMES: *John Butler Yeats and the Irish Renaissance.* With pictures from the collection of Michael Butler Yeats and from the National Gallery of Ireland. Dublin: Dolmen Press, 1972. 72 pp. (New Yeats Papers. 5.)

An appreciation of JBY as a portrait painter; with reproductions of 32 paintings (black and white), including some of leading figures of the Irish literary revival; and a catalog of the anniversary exhibition in the National Gallery of Ireland.

24. YEATS, JOHN BUTLER: *Letters from Bedford Park.* A selection from the correspondence (1890-1901) of John Butler Yeats, edited with introduction and notes by William M. Murphy. Dublin: Cuala Press, 1972. x, 79 pp.

Contains some letters to WBY (pp. 6-7, 49, 53-58, 63, 66-68), who is also mentioned passim.

See also AE24, 37, 51, 67, 68, 70, 89, BA3, 15, BB4, 23, 28, 30, 31, 117, 121, 122, 160, 193, 210, 248, 250, 260, 261, BC1, 18-20, BG98, CA4, 47, CB13, 16, 280, 371, 404, 443, CD255, 377, 1035, 1058, 1082, 1231, 1459-67, CF1-35, DD265, HA2, HB11.

BE Interviews with Yeats and Statements to the Press

Items in this and the following section BF are not listed alphabetically but chronologically. The reason for this deviation from my general policy is that interviews and reported lectures can almost be considered primary material. Moreover, nothing is gained by accumulating the material under many ANON.s; most interviewers and reporters are unknown. In all these cases, I merely give the headlines or titles without an added ANON.

Both sections are incomplete; I did not have the time and opportunity to go systematically through the newspapers of all the places Yeats visited in his life. Many items reflect Yeats's American lecture tours and are cited or reprinted in Karin Strand's thesis (BA18). Yeats made five tours: 5 Dec 1903--9 Mar 1904; 21 Sept--18 Oct 1911; 6 Feb--2 Apr 1914; 24 Jan--29 May 1920; 26 Oct 1932--22 Jan 1933 (see Strand, pp. 239-48, for the itineraries). These items, most of which I have not seen, are cited on Ms. Strand's authority and are identified accordingly. I also identify items reprinted by Mikhail (BA13). For places of publication of newspapers see index IF.

1. D[UNLOP], D. N.: "Interview with Mr. W. B. Yeats," *Irish Theosophist,* 2:2 (15 Nov 1893), 147-49 [i.e., 15-17].
Reprinted and misdated as 15 Oct 1893 in *Uncollected Prose,* 1:298-302; and in BA13, 1:19-23. See also BG220.

2. "The New Irish Literary Movement," *Daily Mail,* 26 Apr 1901, 3.
Interview in which Yeats expresses the optimistic opinion that Ireland will be bilingual in 50 years. See Yeats's letter to the *Irish Daily Independent and Daily Nation,* 2 May 1901, 6; not in *Letters* and *Uncollected Prose.*

3. "Mr. W. B. Yeats and the Irish Revival," *Free Lance,* 20 July 1901, 363.
Yeats predicts a dominant role for the Irish language among the intelligent and maintains that the average Irishman is more intelligent than the average Englishman. See Yeats's disclaimer in *Daily Express,* 5 Aug 1901, 5; the interviewer's letter, *Free Lance,* 31 Aug 1901, 508; Yeats's answer and the interviewer's comment, 21 Sept 1901, 578-79. Yeats's disclaimer and answer and the reviewer's comment are reprinted in *Uncollected Prose,* 2:252-54. See also CE247.

4. A., P.: "Views and Interviews: Mr. Yeats Talks about the Gaelic Movement and the Parliamentary Party," *Echo,* 25 Apr 1902, 1.
Reprinted in *Uncollected Prose,* 2:286-90; see also CE247.

5. "A Poet's Discovery: Speaking to the Psaltery. Mr. Yeats Interviewed," *Irish Daily Independent and Daily Nation,* 31 Oct 1902, 5.
A short report of Yeats's speech appears as "Celtic Literary Society: Speaking to Musical Notes," 3 Nov 1902, 2.

6. °"Irish Poet Here," *NY Daily Tribune,* 12 Nov 1903, 4. (Strand)

7. °"Ireland's Newest Poet Here," *NY Sun,* 12 Nov 1903, 7. (Strand)

8. °"Mr. Yeats to Visit Philadelphia," *Old Penn Weekly R,* 14 Nov 1903, 1-2. (Strand)

9. °"W. B. Yeats, Irish Poet," *NY Daily Tribune,* 15 Nov 1903, section II, 7.
Interview, reprinted in Strand, pp. 253-57.

10. °"A Poet's View of the Drama," *NY Sun,* 15 Nov 1903, section III, 7.
Interview, reprinted in Strand, pp. 250-53.

11. °"William Butler Yeats," *Pennsylvanian,* 21 Nov 1903, 1. (Strand)

12. CAREW, KATE: "'I Find New York like Paris, the Buoyancy--the Grace--the Atmosphere!' Says William Butler Yeats, the Irish Poet,"

World, 22 Nov 1903, Magazine section, M3.
The illustrations are reprinted in *Uncollected Prose*, 2:between pp. 160-61. See also next item.

13. "Irish Poet Comes Here to Lecture: William Butler Yeats, Long-legged and Slender, Says Irishmen Are Like the Greeks. Are Not Reading People," *Evening Bulletin*, 23 Nov 1903, 1.
Based on the preceding interview. Its accuracy was questioned by Yeats; see his letter to this newspaper, 24 Nov 1903, 2 (reprinted in Strand, p. 20; not in Wade).

14. °"Poet Yeats and Wellesley Girls," *Boston Daily Advertiser*, 1 Dec 1903, 5. (Strand)

15. °"William Butler Yeats Lectures," *Irish World and American Industrial Liberator*, 19 Dec 1903, 4. (Strand)

16. °"W. B. Yeats Honored," *Irish World and American Industrial Liberator*, 26 Dec 1903, 10. (Strand)
At a dinner in New York, quotes from the speech by Bourke Cockran and from Yeats's reply.

17. °CLANAHAN, WILLIS LEONARD: "William Butler Yeats, Irish Poet, Talks of the Gaelic Revival and Forecasts Its Effect," *St. Louis Post-Dispatch*, 10 Jan 1904, section I, 11. (Strand)

18. °"Yeats Praises Dramatic Club," *Daily Maroon*, 15 Jan 1904, 1. (Strand)
The Dramatic Club of the U of Chicago which performed *The Land of Heart's Desire*. See also °"Editorial," *Daily Maroon*, 19 Jan 1904, 2. (Strand)

19. °"America's Interest in Celtic Revival," *Chicago Evening Post*, 16 Jan 1904, 1. (Strand)

20. °"Chicago Industrialism a Factor in Future Literature," *Inter-Ocean*, 17 Jan 1904, Magazine, 3.
Interview, reprinted in Strand, pp. 258-61.

21. °"Yeats at Indianapolis," *Gaelic American*, 23 Jan 1904, 2. (Strand)

22. °MACDONOUGH, P. J.: "Ireland's Poet and Dramatist Visits Notre Dame," *Notre Dame Scholastic*, 23 Jan 1904, 276. (Strand)

23. °STEVENS, ASHTON: "The Poet Yeats Talks Drama with Ashton Stevens," *SF Examiner*, 30 Jan 1904, 43.
Interview, reprinted in Strand, pp. 261-67. See also p. 7 of the same issue, "Poet Yeats Tells of New Young Ireland," a summary of the lecture on "The Intellectual Revival in Ireland."

24. "Did Not Find Barbarians: William Butler Yeats, Leaving America, Expresses Astonishment," *NYT*, 10 Mar 1904, 1.

24a. "A Poet's Mission: Mr. W. B. Yeats on His Visit to America," *Daily Chronicle*, 18 Mar 1904, 3.

25. "A Poet's Lecture Tour: Mr. W. B. Yeats on America's 'Intellectual Curiosity,'" *Pall Mall Gazette*, 25 Mar 1904, 6.
An interview on American literature.

26. M., R.: "The National Theatre Society: Its Work and Ambitions. A Chat with Mr. W. B. Yeats," *Dublin Evening Mail,* 31 Dec 1904, 4.

27. "*Kincora:* Lady Gregory's Play, Tonight: Interview with Mr. W. B. Yeats," *FrJ,* 25 Mar 1905, 6.
Interview on a school of Irish drama.

28. "Mr. Yeats Interviewed," *Cambridge Daily News,* 25 Nov 1905, [3].
Yeats's views of the theater. The same page carries a review of a performance of *On Baile's Strand.*

29. "Art and Agriculture: The Academy Report. Views of Mr. W. B. Yeats: 'Committees Make Bad Galleries,'" *Evening Telegraph,* 8 Dec 1906, 5.
Yeats's views on the proposal that the Hibernian Academy be administered by the Agricultural and Technical Department.

30. "Abbey Theatre Scene: Interview with Mr. W. B. Yeats," *Evening Telegraph,* 29 Jan 1907, 3-4.
Re Synge's *Playboy;* reprinted in BA13, 1:54-58. See also p. 2, containing W. G. Fay's speech, and the preceding and following issues of this and other papers; e.g., interview in *IrI,* 30 Jan 1907, 5; in *Dublin Evening Mail,* 1 Feb 1907, 5; in *Evening Herald,* 1 Feb 1907, 5 (reprinted in BA13, 1:61-62); in *Evening Telegraph,* 2 Feb 1907, 5. Court procedures are reported in *Evening Herald,* 30 Jan 1907, 1-2 (reprinted in BA13, 1:58-61), and elsewhere.

31. "Interview with Mr. W. B. Yeats," *FrJ,* 30 Jan 1907, 7.
On the *Playboy* (reprinted in CD1321). The correspondence on the same page comments on Yeats's views; the reports are continued in the following issues. See also "The Abbey Theatre: Audience Overawed by Police. Interview with Mr. Yeats," 4 Feb 1907, 4 (reprinted in BA13, 1:62-64).

32. "Death of Mr. Synge," *Evening Herald,* 24 Mar 1909, 1-2.
Includes a short interview with Yeats.

33. "Fighting the Censor: Mr. Yeats on Audiences," *IrI,* 25 Aug 1909, 5.
Interview on the *Blanco Posnet* affair. See also "Mr. Shaw's Play," *Times,* 25 Aug 1909, 5, where Yeats's defense of Shaw's play is quoted in "the course of a conversation to-day."

33a. °"Irish National Drama: Five Years of Progress," *Cambridge Daily News,* 25 May 1910, 2.
Extract reprinted in EF69a, pp. 98-100.

34. UA FHLOINN, RIOBÁRD: Interview with Yeats on politics and the drama, *Irish Nation,* 11 June 1910, 5.

35. "Irish Drama. Interview with Mr. W. B. Yeats: Politics and Plays. £ 5000 Wanted," *Obs,* 19 June 1910, 10.

36. "Abbey Theatre: New System of Stage Scenery Invented by Famous Theatrical Manager to Be Tried on Thursday. Interesting Interview with Mr. Yeats," *Evening Telegraph,* 9 Jan 1911, 3.
The Craig screens; reprinted in *Uncollected Prose,* 2:393-94. A review of the performance of the *The Hour-Glass* by M. M. O'H. appears in the issue of 12 Jan 1911, 3-4.

37. "Mr. W. B. Yeats on the Art of the Minstrel," *IrT*, 6 Feb 1911, 7.

38. "The Irish National Theatre: A Chat with Mr. W. B. Yeats," *Pall Mall Gazette*, 9 June 1911, 5.
See also Yeats's letter, 10 June 1911, 7 (not in Wade), in which he corrects the statement that he had "acquired" Gordon Craig's stage sets.

39. "The Abbey Theatre. Mr. Yeats Interviewed: A Successful Year," *Evening Telegraph*, 10 June 1911, 5.
Yeats on realistic drama.

40. "The Abbey Theatre: Message from Mr. Yeats Regarding Statement in *Evening Telegraph*," *Evening Telegraph*, 28 June 1911, 3.
Yeats reacts to a review of performances of the Abbey Players at the Court Theatre, London, and denies that the auditorium was decorated by Union Jacks and cardbords with prayers for "Our Gracious King."

41. °"Irish Players on Steamer *Zeeland*," *Boston Globe*, 21 Sept 1911, Evening edition, 1. (Strand)
Statement to the press.

42. °"News of the Theatre," *BET*, 22 Sept 1911, 13. (Strand)
An interview.

43. °"Great Intellectual Revival in Ireland, Says William B. Yeats," *Boston Herald*, 22 Sept 1911, 10. (Strand)

44. °TANNER, VIRGINIA: "Poet Yeats Tells of Irish Drama's Growth," *Boston J*, 22 Sept 1911, 12. (Strand)

45. °"Ireland's New Native Drama," *Boston Globe*, 23 Sept 1911, Morning edition, 4.
Interview, reprinted in Strand, pp. 280-82.

46. °"Opened with the New Irish Drama," *Boston Globe*, 24 Sept 1911, 9. (Strand)
An interview.

47. °HALE, PHILIP: "Boston's New Theatre Opens," *Boston Sunday Herald*, 24 Sept 1911, 4.
Yeats's curtain speech on the origin, growth, and artistic purposes of the Abbey Theatre, reprinted in part in Strand, pp. 282-84.

48. °"Plymouth Theatre," *Boston Daily Advertiser*, 26 Sept 1911, 5. (Strand)
Statement to the press. See also *Boston Evening Record*, 26 Sept 1911, 6; reprinted in BA13, 1:68-70.

49. °"Comes to Direct Irish Players," *Boston Globe*, 30 Sept 1911, Morning edition, 4. (Strand)
Interview with Lady Gregory and Yeats.

50. °"Yeats Replies to His Critics; Defends Irish Plays Being Produced Here," *Boston Post*, 5 Oct 1911, 8. (Strand)
Reprinted in BA13, 1:70-72.

51. °"A Lively Discussion over the 'Irish Plays,'" *Sunday Post*, 8

Oct 1911, 37. (Strand)
Interview, reprinted in BA13, 1:73-75.

52. °"Yeats on Theatre Freedom," *NY Sun*, 12 Oct 1911, 9.
Interview, reprinted in Strand, pp. 294-99. Substantially the same interview appeared in *NYT*, *NY Daily Tribune*, *NY Herald*, all for 12 Oct. See also "Yeats Defends the *Playboy*," *Boston Herald*, 12 Oct 1911, 8 (reprinted in BA13, 1:76-77); "Mr. Yeats Explains," *BET*, 13 Oct 1911, 14 (also in BA13, 1:77-78); and "The Irish Plays," *Outlook*, 21 Oct 1911, 397-98.

53. °"Synge's Aran Island Host," *NY Sun*, 21 Oct 1911, 13. (Strand)
Interview on Synge.

54. "The New Ireland Analyzed by W. Butler Yeats," *NYT*, 22 Oct 1911, section V, 8.
A long interview, subtitled "She prospers, but 'we are hoping for a wider culture, a larger tolerance.'--Ireland's chief trouble is that 'England has taught her to hate, and hate is a sterile passion.'"

55. "The *Playboy* Again [. . .]: Abbey Company in America. Interview with Mr. W. B. Yeats," *IrT*, 31 Oct 1911, 4.

56. "Boston's Culture Impressed Yeats: Irish Poet, Now Back in London, Tells of His Experiences in America," *NYT*, 26 Nov 1911, section III, 3.

57. "*The Playboy* [. . .]: Players Arrested. Interview with Mr. W. B. Yeats. His Opinion of Irish-America: 'Twenty Years behind Ireland,'" *Evening Telegraph*, 19 Jan 1912, 3.
Reprinted in BA13, 1:80-82. See also correspondence in issue of 20 Jan, p. 3, and "Interview with Mr. W. B. Yeats," *FrJ*, 19 Jan 1912, 7.

58. "Meaning of *The Playboy*: Mr. W. B. Yeats Interviewed," *IrI*, 20 Jan 1912, 5.
Reprinted in BA13, 1:82-84.

59. "Irish Players in America: Company Arrested. Publicans and Morality," *IrT*, 20 Jan 1912, 8.
Includes "Statement by Mr. W. B. Yeats." See also the editorial, p. 6.

60. "Abbey Players in America: Some Reflections on the Visit," *IrT*, 16 Mar 1912, 7.
An interview with Yeats and Lennox Robinson.

61. Lunn, Hugh [later KINGSMILL, HUGH]: "An Interview with Mr. W. B. Yeats," *Hearth and Home*, 28 Nov 1912, Christmas Number, 229.
Yeats on Shaw, Synge, and Irish politics; see also BB132. Reprinted in BA13, 1:88-91 (where the author is not identified).

62. B., M. M.: "The Poet and Modern Life: Mr. W. B. Yeats in Praise of the Medieval," *Daily News and Leader*, 3 Jan 1913, 12.
Interview on the function of poetry and art in general. Reprinted in *FrJ*, 4 Jan 1913, 8, and *REL*, 4:4 (July 1963), 12-13.

63. "The Gordon Craig Exhibition in Dublin: An Interview with Mr. Yeats," *IrT*, 8 Mar 1913, 7-8.

64. O'B., F. C.: "Stage Setting: Mr. G. Craig's Exhibition," *FrJ,* 19 Mar 1913, 8.

65. BRISTOWE, SYBIL: "Mr. W. B. Yeats: Poet and Mystic. An Interview," *T.P.'s Weekly,* 4 Apr 1913, 421.
Correspondence by Raymond Crompton Rhodes and F. Sheehy Skeffington: "The Irish National Theatre," 18 Apr 1913, 504, and 2 May 1913, 566. The interview was reprinted, together with an introductory note by G[regor] Sarrazin, in *NS,* 21:4 (July 1913), 242-47. The interview is also in BA13, 1:91-95.

66. "The Abbey Players: End of Successful London Season," *Dublin Evening Mail,* 14 July 1913, 2.
An interview.

67. MARSHALL, MARGUERITE MOOERS: "Reaction from the 'Sugar-Candy' Drama, Says Poet Yeats, Has Produced the Vice Play. Great Drama of the Future, He Predicts, Will Come from This Country and Not England, Where a Few Stale Themes Are in Control," *Evening World,* 7 Feb 1914, 3.

68. °"Declares Rich Are Handicap to the Theater," *Detroit Times,* 19 Feb 1914, 6:00 p.m. edition, 1, 9. (Strand)
Interview, includes comments on Irish politics.

69. °"Poet Finds America Literary Desert and Says So Right Out," *Detroit News,* 19 Feb 1914, 1.
Interview, reprinted in Strand, pp. 299-301.

70. "'American Literature Still in Victorian Era'--Yeats. Irish Poet and Dramatist Says Our Pet Phrase, 'Moral Uplift,' Proves This, and Laments That Erin, While It Is Now Turning Out a Big Crop of Tragedies, Is Producing No Comedies," *NYT,* 22 Feb 1914, section V, 10.

71. °"Yeats, in City, Says Despise Not Humble," *Chicago Daily News,* 23 Feb 1914, 3. (Strand)

72. °"Declares Great Poets Are Never Emotional," *Chicago Tribune,* 24 Feb 1914, 10. (Strand)

73. °SYNON, MARY: "Poet and Prophet of Anglo-Irish Here," *Chicago J,* 25 Feb 1914, 3. (Strand)

74. °BENNETT, JAMES O'DONNELL: "The Irish in Moonshine and Fun," *Chicago Record-Herald,* 26 Feb 1914, 6. (Strand)
An interview, and a report of a performance of *The King's Threshold.*

75. °"Interest Aroused in Yeats' Visit," *Evanston Daily News,* 26 Feb 1914, 1 (Strand)

76. °"Yeats Holds Carson Acts as Traitor," *Chicago J,* 27 Feb 1914, section 2, 1. (Strand)

77. °TINEE, MAE: "A Word or Two with the Irish Poet," *Chicago Tribune,* 27 Feb 1914 (?), section VIII, 2.
Interview quoted in Strand, date not given.

78. °WEIL, ELSIE F.: "William Butler Yeats and the New Ireland," *Inter-Ocean,* 1 Mar 1914, Magazine, 1.

Interview, partly reprinted in Strand, pp. 301-6.

79. °"Chicago Poets Honor Bard from Old Erin," *Inter-Ocean,* 2 Mar 1914, 5. (Strand)
See also BB153.

80. °"Irish," *Cincinnati Enquirer,* 6 Mar 1914, 9. (Strand)
Yeats's appearance at a dinner party.

81. °"Luncheon for Mr. Yeats," *NY Herald,* 24 Mar 1914, 10. (Strand)

82. °"Yeats for Home Rule 'as a Step,'" *Philadelphia Inquirer,* 27 Mar 1914, 5. (Strand)

83. NOGUCHI, YONE: "A Japanese Poet on W. B. Yeats," *BmNY,* 43:4 (June 1916), 431-33.

84. "Dispute about a Picture Gallery: Sir Hugh Lane's Unsigned Codicil. England or Ireland? Appeal to the National Gallery. Interview with Mr. W. B. Yeats," *Obs,* 10 Dec 1916, 6.
Reprinted in CD724. See also "Sir Hugh Lane's Pictures: Mr. W. B. Yeats's Reply," 17 Dec 1916, 12 (another interview); correspondence by Lady Gregory and Yeats, 24 Dec 1916, 12; by Robert C. Witt, D. S. MacColl, and Charles Aitken, 31 Dec 1916, 14; by D. S. MacColl, 14 Jan 1917, 14; by Yeats, 21 Jan 1917, 12. There are also other letters during this period not directly concerned with Yeats's position.

84a. °CLARK, BARRETT H.: "In London with William Butler Yeats," *NY Sun,* 25 Aug 1918, 4.
Cited in AC54a.

85. "Irish Poet Tells of Storms at Home: William Butler Yeats Says Self-Government to Suit the People Must Come. Is Opposed to Coercion," *NYT,* 25 Jan 1920, section II, 3.
Interview, reprinted in Strand, pp. 313-14.

86. °"Ireland Suffers from a Fever," *Montreal Daily Star,* 3 Feb 1920, 3. (Strand)

87. °"Cause of Ireland's Woes," *Toronto Evening Telegram,* 3 Feb 1920, no page given.
Interview on Irish-English political problems, reprinted in Strand, pp. 314-17.

88. "Mr. Yeats on Suppressed Ireland," *IrI,* 10 Feb 1920, 6.
Short statement to the press, made on the arrival in New York on 24 Jan 1920.

89. °"Chicago Women Lead the World Says Poet Yeats," *Chicago Evening Post,* 1 Mar 1920, 1. (Strand)

90. °"Yeats Mum on City's Culture," *Chicago J,* 1 Mar 1920, 4.
Interview, reprinted in Strand, pp. 317-18.

91. °"Poet Yeats Finds No Beer Is H--L, Old Dear," *Chicago Tribune,* 1 Mar 1920, section II, 1. (Strand)

92. °"'Dry Humor' for Irish Poet," *Chicago J,* 2 Mar 1920, 13. (Strand)

93. °"Magic Handbag Yields Pierian Nectar to Yeats," *Chicago Tribune,* 2 Mar 1920, 5. (Strand)

94. °"Lots of Women, Song, at Poet's Fete for Yeats," *Chicago Evening Post,* 4 Mar 1920, 2. (Strand)
See also °"Poet Yeats' Rhythm Lures Kitten, But Casino Hirelings Banish It," *Chicago Tribune,* 4 Mar 1920, 15.

95. °"Mr. Yeats' Visit," *Chicago Evening Post,* 5 Mar 1920, 9. (Strand)

96. °"Irish Poet Will Lecture Tonight," *Salt Lake Tribune,* 15 Mar 1920, no page given. (Strand)

97. °"Author Will Speak," *LA Times,* 21 Mar 1920, section III, 38. (Strand)

98. °"Author Yeats in S.F.; Says It's Like Erin," *SF Call and Post,* 25 Mar 1920, 1. (Strand)

99. °"Yeats Pleads for Palestine Home Restoration," *SF Call and Post,* 26 Mar 1920, 24. (Strand)
See also °"Yeats' Pen Aids S.F. Drive for Palestine Fund," *SF Chronicle,* 27 Mar 1920, 6.

100. °"Irish Poet on Visit, Shuns Hotel Crowd," *SF Chronicle,* 26 Mar 1920, 7. (Strand)
An interview.

101. °"Yeats to Lecture," *LA Times,* 28 Mar 1920, 16. (Strand)

102. °"Irish Poet Here Hits at Violence in Erin," *LA Times,* 30 Mar 1920, 4. (Strand)
An interview.

103. °"School of Expression Alumni Hold Banquet," *Boston Globe,* 7 May 1920, Morning edition, 5. (Strand)
See also *BET,* 8 May 1920, section I, 9.

104. WILKINSON, MARGUERITE: "Irish Literature Discussed by William Butler Yeats in an Interview," *Touchstone,* 8:2 (Nov 1920), 81-85.
Reprinted in BA13, 1:120-25.

105. "The Pillar: Question of Its Removal. Various Viewpoints," *Evening Telegraph,* 25 Aug 1923, 4.
Part of an interview with Yeats, who is in favor of removal for aesthetic reasons.

106. "Irish Poet Honoured: Nobel Prize Awarded Senator Yeats. Tribute to Synge," *FrJ,* 15 Nov 1923, 5.
An interview. On the same page: "Inspired in Sligo: Senator Yeats Tells of Early Impressions" (report of a lecture). See also the editorial on p. 4: "Poet and Patriot."

107. "Irish Poet Honoured: Nobel Prize for Mr. Yeats. Our Special Interview," *IrT,* 15 Nov 1923, 7.
An interview on the Irish literary revival. See also the editorial on p. 6: "The Poet's Crown."

108. "Tva Nobelpristagare anlända till Stockholm: En liten pratstund med William Butler Yeats," *Stockholms dagblad,* 9 Dec 1923, page number not available.

"Two Nobel Prize winners arrive in Stockholm: A little conversation with WBY"; interview, includes a photograph of WBY and Mrs. Yeats. See also Gustaf Uddgren: "Yeats som Swedenborgare och andebesvärjare" (Yeats as Swedenborgian and spiritist), 10 Dec 1923 (on Yeats's interest in Swedenborg and Blake); and Per Hallström: "Nobelprisen ha blivit fredspris, bryggor mellan splittrade folk," 11 Dec 1923 (Nobel Prize becomes peace prize, bridges between quarreling nations). See also CD1260.

109. CUMBERLAND, GERALD: *Written in Friendship: A Book of Reminiscences.* NY: Brentano's, 1924. 308 pp.

An interview with Yeats in Maud Gonne's drawing room, pp. 15-18.

110. "How to Restore the Arts: Mr. Yeats's Views," *IrT,* 26 Jan 1924, 7.

On the possibility of appointing a fine arts committee by the state.

111. "From Democracy to Authority: Paul Claudel and Mussolini--A New School of Thought," *IrT,* 16 Feb 1924, 9.

112. PYPER, NANCY: "Four O'Clock Tea with W. B. Yeats," *Musical Life and Arts,* 1:6 (1 Dec 1924), 161-62, 165.

Reprinted in BA13, 1:158-64.

112a. °"George Moore and W. B. Yeats," *Literary R,* 16 Apr 1927, 16.

Apparently an interview with Yeats by Elizabeth Robins Pennell; cited in AC54a.

113. "Censorship in Ireland. The Free State Bill: Senator W. B. Yeats's Views," *MGuard,* 22 Aug 1928, 5.

See also the comment in *IrI,* 23 Aug 1928, 5: "Censorship Bill: Mr. Yeats's Peculiar Views. Sneers at 'Zealots.'"

114. "Mr. Yeats on Irish Censorship: Driving Intellect into Exile. New Bill 'Full of Danger,'" *SunT,* 21 Oct 1928, 21.

115. "As a Bee--Not as a Wasp: Senator Yeats in His Old Age," *IrI,* 22 Oct 1928, 6.

Part of an interview published in the *Observer* (which I have been unable to find).

116. MORGAN, LOUISE: *Writers at Work.* London: Chatto & Windus, 1931. viii, 71 pp. (Dolphin Books. 11.)

"W. B. Yeats," 1-9; based on an interview: "How Writers Work: W. B. Yeats on the Future of Poetry," *Everyman,* 25 June 1931, 683-84. Reprinted in BA13, 2:199-204.

117. "A Poet Broadcasts: W. B. Yeats in Belfast. His First Experience in Front of a Microphone. An Interview on the Drama," *Belfast News-Letter,* 9 Sept 1931, 6.

See also the photograph on p. 7.

118. "Greek Play over Radio: Abbey Players in Belfast. Mr. Yeats Explains the Broadcast," *IrT,* 9 Sept 1931, 4.

The Greek play was Yeats's version of *King Oedipus.*

119. "Yeats's 'Hello to Everybody!' Famous Irish Poet 'on the Air' for the First Time," *Northern Whig and Belfast Post,* 9 Sept 1931, 3.
An interview and a photograph.

120. "'No Question of Disloyalty': Mr. Yeats on Objection to the Oath," *Times,* 4 Apr 1932, 14.
Statement made to a press representative, referring to the Oath of Allegiance.

121. °"Yeats Arrives on *Europa* for Play Opening," *NYHT,* 27 Oct 1932, 3.
Interview on the Irish Academy of Letters, partly reprinted in Strand, pp. 328-30.

122. "Joyce Rejects Bid of Irish Academy," *NYT,* 28 Oct 1932, 17.
The same page carries a note that Yeats was elected an honorary member of the New York Authors Club.

123. SUGRUE, THOMAS: "Irish Writers Ignorant Lot, Yeats Asserts. Only Read Dante, Homer, Shakespeare and Such, Playwright-Poet Says. Evades Politics Deftly. Expects U.S. to Believe O'Neill Is Its Best Writer," *NYHT,* 28 Oct 1932, 19.
Reprinted in Strand, pp. 330-32.

124. °"Irish Politics and Players Both Interest Poet Yeats," *Detroit Free Press,* 12 Nov 1932, 8. (Strand)

125. °"Irish Poet Here, Talks on Affairs of His Nation," *Detroit News,* 12 Nov 1932, 19. (Strand)

126. GILBERT, DOUGLAS: "Yeats, Who Once Spun Erin's Gossamer Dreams, Now Grows Eloquent on Irish Taxation Problem. At 67, Poet and Mystic Dismisses the Past, Discusses Economics and Politics--Calls Machine Age 'a Period of Terror' for the Artist," *NY World-Telegram,* 12 Nov 1932, 4.

127. °"Abbey Players Coming to Detroit around Xmas," *Detroit Times,* 13 Nov 1932, section III, 6-7. (Strand)
An interview.

128. WOOLF, S. J.: "Yeats Foresees an Ireland of Reality: The Poet Describes the Turning of the Country from Romance to the Stern Task of Building," *NYT,* 13 Nov 1932, section VI, 7, 19.

129. °KELLY, RALPH: "Says U.S. Should Subsidize Theater," *Cleveland Plain Dealer,* 15 Nov 1932, 11. (Strand)

130. °"Belfast Events Are Discussed by W. B. Yeats, in Cincinnati," *Cincinnati Enquirer,* 17 Nov 1932, 2. (Strand)
Interview on Irish politics.

131. °"Nobel Poet to Speak," *Cincinnati Enquirer,* 19 Nov 1932, 8. (Strand)

132. °"William Butler Yeats Addresses Students," *Colgate Maroon,* 2 Dec 1932, no page given. (Strand)

133. °SCHRIFTGIESSER, KARL: "W. B. Yeats, in Boston, Sees No End to Irish Censorship in Near Future," *BET,* 9 Dec 1932, 20.
Interview, reprinted in Strand, pp. 335-37.

134. GIBBONS, JOHN W.: "Poet Doesn't Know Name of Own Book," *South Bend Tribune,* 10 Jan 1933, 1, 5.
Interview (accompanied by photograph) and report of a lecture; Yeats comments on Irish politics and G. B. Shaw.

135. "Yeats, Sailing, Pays Tribute to Moore: Praises Realistic Force and Courage of the Writing of the Late Irish Novelist," *NYT,* 23 Jan 1933, 11.

136. "Prizes for Young Authors: Dr. Yeats Outlines Aims of New Academy," *IrP,* 31 Jan 1933, 2.

137. "Abbey Theatre Changes: Proposed Advisory Committee. Interview with Dr. W. B. Yeats," *IrT,* 23 Feb 1935, 5.
Correspondence by Frank O'Connor and Sean O'Faolain, 26 Feb 1935, 4; further correspondence in subsequent issues.

138. "W. B. Yeats Looks Back: Poet Celebrates His Seventieth Birthday," *IrP,* 14 June 1935, 7.
Reprinted in BA13, 2:226-29.

139. "W. B. Yeats Looks Back: Ireland in the Early Days of the Abbey Theatre," *IrP,* 14 Oct 1935, 9.
Reprinted in BA13, 2:230-31.

140. G., H.: "Mr. W. B. Yeats in London: His Seventieth Birthday. Celebration at the Little Theatre," *Obs,* 27 Oct 1935, 15.
Interview, mostly on his own plays.

See also AE67, BA13, BB158, 245, BF47, 55, 179, BG191, CB270, CD139, 1321, 1357, EE323, 424, 449, 476, HB11.

BF Reports and Summaries of Speeches and Lectures

See the headnote to BE for an explanation of the structure and contents of this section. According to Strand (pp. 2-3), the topics for Yeats's American lectures were the following:

1903-4: The Intellectual Revival in Ireland; The Heroic Literature of Ireland; Poetry in the Old Time and in the New; The Theatre and What It Might Be; Emmet the Apostle of Irish Liberty.

1911: The Theatre of Beauty; The Twentieth-Century Revival of Irish Poetry and Drama.

1914: The Theatre and Beauty; John Synge and the Ireland of His Time; Contemporary Lyric Poets.

1920: A Theatre of the People; The Friends of My Youth; The Younger Generation of Poets; Readings.

1932-33: The New Ireland; My Own Poetry; The Irish National Theatre.

1. "Mr. W. B. Yeats on 'Nationality and Literature,'" *United Ireland,* 23 Jan 1892, 3.

2. "The National Literary Society: Meeting in the Rotunda," *United Ireland,* 18 June 1892, 2.
Several speeches in support of the foundation of a National Literary Society, one by Yeats. See also Yeats's letter "A Proposed National Literary Society," *Daily Express,* 2 June 1892, 6 (reprinted in *Collected Letters,* 1:299-300), and the commentary in the same issue, p. 4.

3. "Chiswick," *West London Observer,* 22 July 1893, 6.
Lecture at the Chiswick Lodge of the Theosophical Society on "The Nature of Art and Poetry in Relation to Mysticism." See BB224.

4. "The Young Ireland League: Lecture by Mr. W. B. Yeats," *United Ireland,* 4 Nov 1893, 3.
A lecture on "Irish Fairy Tales."

5. "Belfast Naturalists' Field Club: Lecture by Mr. W. B. Yeats," *Irish News and Belfast Morning News,* 22 Nov 1893, 8.
A lecture on "Irish Fairy Lore." See also "Mr. W. B. Yeats in Belfast--Irish Fairy Lore," *United Ireland,* 2 Dec 1893, 3; and the report in *Annual Report and Proceedings of the Belfast Naturalists' Field Club,* year 31, series 2, part 1, vol. 4 (1893-94), 46-48.

6. R[YAN], W. P.: "With the Irish in Great Britain," *New Ireland R,* 4:4 (Dec 1895), 224-30.
Summarizes and criticizes a Yeats speech on Irish history and reviews *Poems* (W15/16).

7. "The Delegates Dinner," *Irish Homestead,* 6 Nov 1897, 741-42.
Summary of a lecture on the new Irish literature.

8. "The Celtic Movement," *Pall Mall Gazette,* 7 Dec 1897, 12.
On a Yeats lecture and generally on Yeats's "Celtic" interests. See F. Hugh O'Donnell: "'The Celtic Movement' at the London Irish Literary Society," *United Ireland,* 11 Dec 1897, 5: "Mr. Yeats illustrated his weirdly witching theories by several apposite readings from soulful bards. . . . [He] did not often transgress into the region of facts." A more objective report can be found on p. 2 of the same issue ("The Celtic Movement: Interesting Lecture by Mr. Yeats").

9. "The Laying of the Foundation Stone," *FrJ,* 16 Aug 1898, 7.
The '98 and Wolfe Tone celebrations, including a summary of a short speech by Yeats. See also BB217.

10. "Meeting at Gort," *Irish Homestead,* 24 Sept 1898, 804.
Horace Plunkett speaking to co-operative societies, Yeats in the audience commenting on the co-operative movement.

11. "National Literary Society 'at Home,'" *Daily Express,* 10 Jan 1899, 6.
Résumé of a speech on the inauguration of the Irish Literary Theatre. See also a commentary on p. 5; Yeats's letter "Irish Literary Theatre," 12 Jan 1899, 5; a commentary on this letter, p. 4; and Yeats's article "The Irish Literary Theatre," 14 Jan 1899, 3. Yeats's letter and article are reprinted in *Uncollected Prose,* 2:137-42.

12. "Dramatic Ideals and the Irish Literary Theatre," *FrJ,* 8 May 1899, 6.
See "Ideal of Irish Drama: An Interesting Lecture. Mr. W. B. Yeats and His Critics," *Irish Daily Independent,* 8 May 1899, 8.

13. "Irish Literary Theatre: Dinner at the Shelbourne Hotel," *Daily Express,* 12 May 1899, 5-6.
Long article on Yeats's and Martyn's efforts to establish the

Irish Literary Theatre; also summaries of speeches by Yeats, Max Beerbohm, and George Moore.

14. "Trinity College and the Literary Theatre: Speech of Mr. W. B. Yeats," *Daily Express,* 1 June 1899, 5.
A debate on the subject "That any attempt to further an Irish Literary Movement would result in Provincialism."

15. Summary of Yeats's lecture on the Irish literary movement, *Claidheamh Soluis,* 10 June 1899, 200.
See also letter in defense of Yeats by Thomas C. Murray, 24 June 1899, 229, and the editorial, 233; leaders, 1 July 1899, 248-49, and 8 July 1899, 264-65; Murray's answer, 15 July 1899, 277-78; further letters, 12 Aug 1899, 344-45; 19 Aug 1899, 362; 16 Sept 1899, 422-23.

16. "Dr. Douglas Hyde on the Irish Language Movement: Speech by Mr. W. B. Yeats," *Daily Express,* 31 July 1899, 6.
A speech on Hyde and the Gaelic League.

17. "Galway," *Irish Homestead,* 28 Oct 1899, 732.
Yeats, attending a meeting of co-operative societies, makes a speech on the "usefulness of village libraries in spreading a knowledge of the Irish language."

18. "National Literary Society's 'At Home,'" *Irish Daily Independent,* 19 Feb 1900, 6.
A Yeats lecture on "The Irish Literary Theatre."

19. "Irish Literary Theatre: Yesterday's Luncheon. Mr. George Moore on the Celtic Revival," *Daily Express,* 23 Feb 1900, 6.
Speeches by Hyde, Moore, Yeats, and others; editorial in the same issue, p. 4. See also "The Irish Literary Theatre: Speech by Mr. George Moore," *FrJ,* 23 Feb 1900, 6.

20. "Central Branch Sgoruigheacht: Address by Mr. W. B. Yeats," *Claidheamh Soluis,* 27 Oct 1900, 516-17.
A speech on the Irish language.

21. "Pan-Celtic Congress," *FrJ,* 24 Aug 1901, 6.
Includes a report of an address by Yeats on the revival of ancient Irish literature. The discussion, in which Yeats took part, is reported in the issue of 23 Aug, p. 5.

22. O'NEILL, EAMONN: "An Interesting Meeting," *Claidheamh Soluis,* 9 Nov 1901, 555.
Summary of a speech on the "nationalisation of art" and comment.

23. "The Irish Fairy Kingdom: Lecture by Mr. W. B. Yeats," *South Wales Daily News,* 20 Feb 1903, 6.

24. "Irish Plays in the Molesworth Hall: Lecture by Mr. W. B. Yeats," *FrJ,* 16 Mar 1903, 6.
On "The Reform of the Theatre."

25. "Clifford's Inn-Hall," *Times,* 7 May 1903, 15.
A lecture on the art of "chanting."

25a. [NEVINSON, H. W.]: Report of a lecture on heroic and folk literature at Clifford's Inn, *Daily Chronicle,* 13 May 1903, 7.

26. °"Lecture by Mr. W. B. Yeats," *Yale Daily News,* 17 Nov 1903, 1. (Strand)
"The Intellectual Revival in Ireland."

27. °"His Second Lecture," *New Haven Morning J and Courier,* 18 Nov 1903, 3. (Strand)
"The Heroic Literature of Ireland."

28. °"Mr. Yeats's Lecture," *Hartford Daily Courant,* 21 Nov 1903, 14. (Strand)
"The Heroic Literature of Ireland."

29. °"Mr. Yeats' Lecture," *Student* [Amherst College], 21 Nov 1903, no page number given. (Strand)
"The Theatre and What It Might Be."

30. °"Yeats Makes a Few Intellectual Knocks," *North American,* 24 Nov 1903, 3. (Strand)
"The Intellectual Revival in Ireland." For a comment on this report see °"Gaelic Notes," *Irish World and American Industrial Liberator,* 5 Dec 1903, 8. See also °"A Masterful Address," *Pennsylvanian,* 24 Nov 1903, 1; °"National Theatre Needed in Ireland," *Philadelphia Inquirer,* 24 Nov 1903, 2; °"Mr. Yeats' Lecture," *Old Penn Weekly R,* 28 Nov 1903, 2; °"Mr. Yeats' Houston Hall Lecture," *Alumni Register* [U of Pennsylvania], 8 (Dec 1903), 97-102. (Strand, the last item reprinted on pp. 276-80)

31. °"America Near to Ireland," *NY Daily Tribune,* 26 Nov 1903, 6. (Strand)
"The Intellectual Revival in Ireland."

32. °"Mr. Yeats and the Boston Authors' Club," *BET,* 30 Nov 1903, 16. (Strand)
"The Intellectual Revival in Ireland." See also °*Boston Sunday Globe,* 29 Nov 1903, 4. (Strand)

33. °"College Notes," *Mount Holyoke,* 13 (Dec 1903), 221. (Strand)
"The Theatre and What It Might Be."

34. °"Lecture by Mr. Yeats," *Smith College Monthly,* 11 (Dec 1903), 195. (Strand)
"The Heroic Literature of Ireland."

35. °"Modern Theater for Rich and Stupid," *Boston J,* 2 Dec 1903, 8. (Strand)
"Poetry in the Old Time and in the New."

36. °"Yeats on Gaelic Ireland," *Irish World and American Industrial Liberator,* 12 Dec 1903, 12. (Strand)
"The Intellectual Revival in Ireland." See also °"Mr. Yeats's Answer," ibid., p. 4.

37. °"Personal," *NY Dramatic Mirror,* 19 Dec 1903, 67. (Strand)
"The Theatre and What It Might Be."

38. °"Old Time Irish Tales and Songs," *Montreal Daily Star,* 19 Dec 1903, 13.
"The Heroic Literature of Ireland," reprinted in Strand, pp. 270-

72. See also BB224.

39. "An Irish Poet Speaks," *NYT,* 4 Jan 1904, 16.
"The Intellectual Revival in Ireland."

40. °"Poet Yeats Addresses Wednesday Club on Theater," *St. Louis Globe-Democrat,* 7 Jan 1904, 12.
"The Theatre and What It Might Be." See also °"Poet Descries Public Taste," *St. Louis Post-Dispatch,* 7 Jan 1904, 20. (Strand)

41. °"The Irish Literary Revival," *Gaelic American,* 9 Jan 1904, 5. (Strand)
"The Intellectual Revival in Ireland," with an introductory speech by Bourke Cockran. See also °"Guest of the Press Club," ibid., 3 (report of a reception in Yeats's honor).

42. °"Modern Drama Not Delicate Nor True," *Indianapolis News,* 11 Jan 1904, 6.
"The Theatre and What It Might Be," reprinted in Strand, pp. 268-70. For a reminiscence of this lecture see °Joseph Smith: "My Monday Monologue," *Boston Herald,* 16 Oct 1911, 6. (Strand)

43. °"Yeats Talks on Ireland," *Chicago Tribune,* 14 Jan 1904, 7. (Strand)
"The Intellectual Revival in Ireland."

44. °"America, Says W. B. Yeats, Is Land of Aristocracy," *Chicago Tribune,* 15 Jan 1904, 7.
"Poetry in the Old Time and the New."

45. °"Revive Irish Poetry," *St. Paul Pioneer Press,* 22 Jan 1904, 3. (Strand)
"The Intellectual Revival in Ireland."

46. °"Irish Poet and Scholar Tells of Degeneration of Stage," *Daily Californian,* 28 Jan 1904, 1. (Strand)
"The Theatre and What It Might Be."

47. °"Ireland's Poet Makes Address," *SF Chronicle,* 28 Jan 1904, 12.
"The Intellectual Revival in Ireland." See also °"Alhambra Crowded with an Audience of Representative People" and °"William Butler Yeats Tells of the Success of the New Intellectual Movement in Ireland" (including an interview), *SF Examiner,* 28 Jan 1904, 3; °"Yeats Captures California," *Gaelic American,* 13 Feb 1904, 3. (Strand)

48. °"Yeats Talks of Ireland's Poetry," *SF Chronicle,* 31 Jan 1904, 33. (Strand)
"The Theatre and What It Might Be." See °"Folk-Lore and Its Place in Irish Drama," *SF Examiner,* 31 Jan 1904, 29. (Strand)

49. °"Yeats Delivers a Lecture," *Daily Palo Alto,* 1 Feb 1904, 1. (Strand)
"The Heroic Literature of Ireland."

50. °"Poet Yeats Delights a Large Audience," *Evening Bee,* 4 Feb 1904, 2. (Strand)
"The Intellectual Revival in Ireland."

51. °"Theater of Today Has Degenerated," *Daily Cardinal,* 10 Feb

1904, 1. (Strand)
"The Theatre and What It Might Be."

52. °"Talks on Heroic Literature," *Daily Cardinal,* 11 Feb 1904, 1. (Strand)
"The Heroic Literature of Ireland."

53. °"The Old Culture Lost," *Globe,* 15 Feb 1904, 10. (Strand)
"Poetry in the Old Time and in the New." See also °"Renaissance of Irish Literature," *Mail and Empire,* 15 Feb 1904, 7 (reprinted in Strand, pp. 273-76); °"Culture, Ancient and Modern," *Globe,* 16 Feb 1904, 6; °"Mr. William Butler Yeats," *Queen's UJ,* 16 Feb 1904, 36; *Varsity* [U of Toronto], 17 Feb 1904, 263. (Strand)

54. °"Heroic Irish Literature," *Brooklyn Daily Eagle,* 19 Feb 1904, 5. (Strand)
"The Heroic Literature of Ireland."

55. °"Poet Delights His Audience," *Newark Evening News,* 25 Feb 1904, 8. (Strand)
"The Intellectual Revival in Ireland"; includes an interview.

56. °"Emmet the Apostle of Irish Liberty," *Gaelic American,* 5 March 1904, 1, 5. (Strand)
Reprinted in *Uncollected Prose,* 2:311-27.

57. °"Lecture by Mr. William Butler Yeats," *Catholic U Bulletin,* 10 (Apr 1904), 301.
"The Intellectual Revival in Ireland."

58. "Plays and Players: Irish National Theatre [. . .]. Speech of Mr. W. B. Yeats," *FrJ,* 2 Feb 1905, 6.

59. "The New School of Literature and Drama in Ireland," *FrJ,* 11 Apr 1905, 6.
A meeting of the Literary and Historical Society of University College Dublin with a lecture by F. Cruise O'Brien on "The New School of Literature and Drama in Ireland," which refers to Yeats's symbolism. Reply by Yeats, who comments on his own works and on Synge's plays.

60. [PEARSE, P. H.]: "About Literature," *Claidheamh Soluis,* 22 Apr 1905, 7.
On a Yeats speech about "Nationality in Literature."

61. ANNETTE: "W. B. Yeats in Dundee: The Man and His Lecture," *Courier and Argus,* 12 Jan 1906, 7.
"Literature and the Living Voice."

62. "Mr. W. B. Yeats in Aberdeen: Interesting Lecture," *Aberdeen Daily J,* 13 Jan 1906, 3.
"Literature and the Living Voice." See also °*Alma Mater,* 17 Jan 1906, 136 (reprinted in BB177).

63. "The Watts Pictures: Lecture by Mr. W. B. Yeats," *Daily Express,* 26 Jan 1906, 7.
A lecture on "The Ideal in Art."

64. "The Irish Peasantry and the Stage: Paper by Dr. Sigerson," *FrJ,* 6 Feb 1906, 8.

Includes statements by J. B. Yeats on Synge and W. B. Yeats on artistic freedom in Ireland.

65. "Voice and Verse: New Art of Musical Recitation. Mr. W. B. Yeats and a Novel Experience," *Leeds and Yorkshire Mercury,* 15 Mar 1906, 6.

A lecture on "Literature and the Living Voice" and a recital by Florence Farr. See also "A New Vocal Art: Dual Lecture at the University," *Liverpool Daily Post and Liverpool Mercury,* 16 Mar 1906, 8.

66. "National Theatre Society [. . .]: Mr. Yeats and the Training of the Actors," *Daily Express,* 15 Oct 1906, 7.

67. "The Abbey Theatre: Opening of the Season. Address by Mr. Yeats," *FrJ,* 16 Oct 1906, 5.

On the difficulties of creating a national theater.

68. "National Drama: Lecture by Mr. Colm. Interesting Discussion: Views of Mr. W. B. Yeats," *FrJ,* 12 Dec 1906, 5.

Yeats on the possibilities of a national theater. Mr. Colm is actually Padraic Colum.

69. "Mr. W. B. Yeats in Aberdeen. Lecture to Franco Scottish Society: 'The Heroic Poetry of Ireland,'" *Aberdeen Free Press,* 26 Jan 1907, 3.

See also "The Celtic Renaissance," *Bon Accord,* 41:5 (31 Jan 1907), 20 (these two items are reprinted in BB177); "Visit of Mr. W. B. Yeats," *Aberdeen Daily J,* 24 Jan 1907, 4; and "Resumé of a Lecture Given by Mr. W. B. Yeats on Friday, 25th January 1907," *Transactions of the Franco-Scottish Society,* 5:1 (1909), 12-14.

70. "*Playboy:* Abbey Theatre Debate. Some Vigorous Views Expressed by Citizens. Mr. W. B. Yeats on His Defence," *IrI,* 5 Feb 1907, 5-6.

For more material on the *Playboy* affair see index IE (s.v. *Playboy* riots). Yeats's various speeches are also summarized in *Evening Telegraph,* 30 Jan 1907, 2-3; 5 Feb 1907, 2 (where J. B. Yeats's sneer "An island of plaster saints" is quoted); and in other papers.

71. "Mr. Yeats Unbosoms Himself on Literature & the Stage. 'The Living Voice' Poetry in the Aran Isles. Poetic Drama Impossible. Taste of the People Debased [. . .]. Scarcely Any Intellect in Ireland," *Evening Telegraph,* 14 Feb 1907, 2.

The same page carries a report of a discussion on the topic "That decadence is the prevailing characteristic of the modern stage" at the College Historical Society, Trinity College, over which Yeats presided.

72. "Mr. W. B. Yeats on Art. Remarkable Speech: 'The Immoral Irish Bourgeoisie,'" *IrT,* 11 Feb 1908, 7.

Yeats's attack on the bourgeoisie and his views of art for art's sake. Correspondence by A. Lloyd and R. B. A., 12 Feb 1908, 5. See "Mr. Yeats and the Irish Bourgeoisie," *FrJ,* 11 Feb 1908, 9.

73. "Mr. W. B. Yeats and *The Piper,*" *Daily Express,* 17 Feb 1908, 9.

Yeats's speech on Norreys Connell's play. See also the report in *Dublin Evening Mail,* 17 Feb 1908, 2; and CD339-40.

74. "The Abbey Theatre: Mrs. Patrick Campbell as 'Deirdre,'" *FrJ,*

10 Nov 1908, 10.
Includes a short statement by Yeats.

75. [PEARSE, P. H.]: "The Gael in Trinity," *Claidheamh Soluis,* 28 Nov 1908, 9.
The inaugural meeting of the Dublin University Gaelic Society with speeches by Eoin MacNeill, Yeats, Sigerson, and J. P. Mahaffy (!) on "A Plea for Irish Studies."

76. "Feis Ceoil Association: Address by Mr. W. B. Yeats," *IrT,* 10 Feb 1909, 5.

77. "The Tragic Theatre: Lecture by Mr. W. B. Yeats," *IrT,* 9 Feb 1910, 5.

77a. "Ireland and the Arts: Lecture by Mr. W. B. Yeats," *Sinn Féin,* 19 Feb 1910, 5.
A lecture to the Students' National Literary Society. See also a commentary, "Ireland over All," ibid., p. 4; "Mr. Yeats, Propagandist," 26 Feb 1910, 1; correspondence by E. B. and P. McCartan, ibid., p. 4; Alastair Maguire: "Mr. Yeats and His Critic," 5 Mar 1910, 1; "Ireland and the Theatre," "Mr. Yeats' Discovery," "The Greatest Poet," "The False Yeats," 12 Mar 1910, 1.
There is also a caricature of Yeats by "Maolmuaidhe" in the issue of 29 Jan 1910, 1.
Some of the anonymous items may have been written by Arthur Griffith; see Conor Maguire: "Yeats and a Controversy," *IrT,* 19 July 1966, 8 (reminiscences of this lecture and of the reactions by various members of the audience).

78. "The Theatre in Ireland: Views of Mr. W. B. Yeats. The Business of Art. 'The Exposition of Human Nature.' A Connacht Story. Mr. Yeats on Newspapers and Politics. English Influence in Gaelic," *Evening Telegraph,* 4 Mar 1910, 2.
The Connacht story is about Colonel Martin, whose wife was unfaithful to him (see the poem "Colonel Martin"). Also reported as "Lecture by Mr. W. B. Yeats: English Influence in Gaelic," *FrJ,* 4 Mar 1910, 10; "The Theatre and Ireland: Lecture by Mr. W. B. Yeats," *IrT,* 4 Mar 1910, 9, and editorial, 5 Mar 1910, 6.

79. "Poetry and Insanity: Does the Poet's Career Usually End in Misery?" *Daily Chronicle,* 12 Mar 1910, 5.
A lecture on "Contemporary Poets."

80. "Ireland and the Theatre: Mr. W. B. Yeats at the Ard Chraobh of the Gaelic League," *Irish Nation,* 12 Mar 1910, 8.

81. "Mr. W. B. Yeats: Address on Contemporary Poetry," *MGuard,* 1 Nov 1910, 8.

82. "Mr. W. B. Yeats on the Theatre: The Limitations of Realism," *MGuard,* 8 Nov 1910, 6.

83. "Mr. W. B. Yeats on Irish Literature: The Art of J. M. Synge," *MGuard,* 15 Nov 1910, 6.

84. "Lady Gregory 'at Home' at the Abbey Theatre," *IrT,* 22 Nov 1910, 8.
Includes a report of a Yeats speech on the Irish theater.

85. "The People's Vision: Mr. W. B. Yeats on Peasant Culture and the New Drama," *Irish Nation,* 26 Nov 1910, 2.
An address to the Liverpool Playgoer's Society on 15 Nov 1910.

86. O'DRISCOLL, ROBERT: "Yeats on Personality: Three Unpublished Lectures," in O'Driscoll and Reynolds: *Yeats and the Theatre* (1975, CA81), 4-59.
An edition of the lectures held in 1910 on "The Theatre," "Friends of My Youth," and "Contemporary Irish Theatre"; also comments by Edmund Gosse and G. B. Shaw. See next item.

87. RONSLEY, JOSEPH: "Yeats's Lecture Notes for 'Friends of My Youth,'" in O'Driscoll and Reynolds: *Yeats and the Theatre* (1975, CA81), 60-81.
An edition of three drafts for the second lecture in the preceding item.

88. "Tragic Recitation: Mr. Yeats on Lunacy at Evening Parties," *Daily Chronicle,* 17 Feb 1911, 5.
A lecture on "Ireland and the Arts of Speech." See also "Spoken Literature," *Times,* 17 Feb 1911, 10.

89. "Mr. Yeats on the Abbey Theatre," *IrT,* 9 Sept 1911, 8.
Curtain speech at the Abbey.

90. "Yeats upon Irish Drama: His Speech before the Drama League," *BET,* 29 Sept 1911, 14.
See also °"Tells Story of Irish Stage," *Boston Herald,* 29 Sept 1911, 3 (Strand).

91. °"The Abbey Theatre," *BET,* 3 Oct 1911, 14. (Strand)
Another lecture on the Irish theater.

92. "The Theatre of Beauty: Mr. Yeats Talks on Stage Scenery," *BET,* 6 Oct 1911, 14.
Includes comments on the Craig screens; reprinted in Strand, pp. 289-94. See also °"Mr. Yeats to Lecture at 4," *Harvard Crimson,* 5 Oct 1911, 1; °"The Theatre of Beauty," *Harvard Crimson,* 6 Oct 1911, 1. (Strand)

93. °"Luncheon in Honor of Yeats," *Boston Globe,* 7 Oct 1911, Morning edition, 12.
See also °"O'Reilly Club Yeats's Host," *Boston Herald,* 7 Oct 1911, 10. Yeats lectured on the Irish literary revival. (Strand)

94. °"Denies Charge of Paganism," *Boston Globe,* 8 Oct 1911, 11. (Strand)
A lecture on the Irish dramatic movement.

95. °"Yeats Guest at Wellesley," *Boston J,* 10 Oct 1911, 5. (Strand)
Lecture on the Irish theater; see also AE32.

96. °"Irish Poet Talks on New Type of Drama," *North American,* 13 Oct 1911, 2.
See also °"Let's Be Realistic, Says Poet Yeats," *Evening Bulletin,* 13 Oct 1911, 9. (Strand)

97. "Abbey Theatre: Pupils' Performance. Address by Mr. W. B. Yeats," *Evening Telegraph,* 17 Nov 1911, 5.
Reprinted in BA13, 1:78-80. See also "Aims of the Irish Theatre:

W. B. Yeats Talks of It in Its Educational Aspect," *Sun* [NY], 18 Nov 1911, 12.

98. "A New Theory of Apparitions: Lecture by Mr. W. B. Yeats," *IrT*, 13 Jan 1912, 9; and editorial on p. 6.

99. "Dinner to Mr. Rabindra Nath Tagore," *Times*, 13 July 1912, 5.
Quotes extensively from Yeats's speech. See also CD1357.

100. "Home Rule and Religion: A 'Protest Meeting.' Mr. Yeats and Persecution," *IrT*, 25 Jan 1913, 9.
Reprinted in *REL*, 4:3 (July 1963), 23.

101. "'The Theatre and Beauty': Lecture by Mr. W. B. Yeats," *IrT*, 19 Mar 1913, 5.

102. "Mr. Yeats's Ideals: Why He Left Politics. An Indian Parallel," *FrJ*, 24 Mar 1913, 2.
A lecture on "The Poetry of Rabindranath Tagore." See "The Poetry of Rabindranath Tagore: Lecture by Mr. W. B. Yeats," *IrT*, 24 Mar 1913, 11.

103. "Municipal Art Gallery [. . .]: Mr. Yeats and the 'Audience of the Unborn,'" *IrT*, 10 May 1913, 7-8.
See also the editorial on p. 6.

104. "Mr. G. B. Shaw and the Cup Finals: One Way to Get a Shakspere Theatre. A Letter Read at a Performance of *Blanco Posnet*," *MGuard*, 15 July 1913, 10.
A letter from GBS to WBY and a summary of Yeats's speech. Reprinted in *REL*, 4:3 (July 1963), 34-35.

105. "Poet and the Crisis: Characteristic Views of Mr. W. B. Yeats. 'Fanaticism of Dublin,'" *Evening Herald*, 28 Oct 1913, 5.
A speech at a "peace meeting" in the Mansion House occasioned by the 1913 Dublin lockout and strike. "All he would say was this: some day they would have to reckon with those who had fomented fanaticism in Dublin to break up the organization of the workers (applause)."

106. "Ghosts and Dreams: Lecture by Mr. W. B. Yeats," *IrT*, 1 Nov 1913, 7.
A lecture at the Dublin branch of the Psychical Research Society. See also the editorial in the same issue, p. 6; Yeats's letter: "Mr. W. B. Yeats and Ghosts," 3 Nov 1913, 6 (reprinted in *Uncollected Prose*, 2:407-8); "Psychic Phenomena: Strange Experiences. Lecture by Mr. W. B. Yeats," *Daily Express*, 1 Nov 1913, 8; "Mr. W. B. Yeats a Spiritualist," *Light*, 15 Nov 1913, 549.

107. "Yeats Believes in Ghosts: Poet Tells of Conversations with the Dead in Five Languages," *NYT*, 16 Nov 1913, section III, 4.

108. "Award of the Polignac Prize," *Times*, 29 Nov 1913, 11.
A summary of Yeats's laudatio of James Stephens. See also Wade 308 and reprint in CD1245.

109. "Mr. Yeats on the New Drama," *Times*, 9 Jan 1914, 8.
A lecture on "The Tragic Theatre," in which Yeats favors an aristocratic theater of suggestion that is superior to the democratic drama of realism.

110. ALDINGTON, RICHARD: "Presentation to Mr. W. S. Blunt," *Egoist*, 1:3 (2 Feb 1914), 56-57.

Blunt was given a Gaudier Brzeska sculpture and made a speech in which he criticized Yeats's assumption that plays must be written in blank verse. Part of Yeats's reply follows. See Ezra Pound: "Homage to Wilfrid Blunt," *Poetry*, 3:6 (Mar 1914), 220-23, BB89, and CD284.

111. °"Yeats Lectures Here," *Sun* [NY], 10 Feb 1914, 6. (Strand)

On "The Theatre and Beauty."

112. °"Poetic Drama Is Coming into Its Own, Says Yeats," *Montreal Daily Star*, 14 Feb 1914, 11.

"The Theatre and Beauty." See °"W. B. Yeats, Irish Poet, Lectures on Theatre," *Globe*, 14 Feb 1914, 2; °"Irish Poet Talks on Modern Drama," *Mail and Empire*, 14 Feb 1914, 5 (Strand; the last item reprinted on pp. 311-13). See also BB224.

113. °"William Butler Yeats," *Buffalo Express*, 17 Feb 1914, 8. (Strand)

A lecture on "Contemporary Lyric Poets."

114. °TAYLOR, DOROTHY: "An Impression of Yeats," *NY Dramatic Mirror*, 18 Feb 1914, 10. (Strand)

A lecture on "John Synge and the Ireland of His Time."

115. °"Reality, Actor's Duty, Says Yeats," *Detroit Free Press*, 20 Feb 1914, 3.

"The Theatre and Beauty"; see also °"Yeats Lectures at Twentieth Century Club," *Detroit Tribune*, 22 Feb 1914, Society section, 11. (Strand)

116. "Says America Will Produce Great Poets and Artists," *Chicago Daily Tribune*, 24 Feb 1914, 10.

See °"Sex Plays Reaction, Asserts Poet Yeats," *Inter-Ocean*, 24 Feb 1914, 12 (Strand). A lecture on "The Theatre and Beauty."

117. °"Irish Poet Here," *Evanston Press*, 7 Mar 1914, 6. (Strand)

"John Synge and the Ireland of His Time."

118. °"Beauty and Theatre Theme of Irish Poet," *Kenyon Collegian*, 11 Mar 1914, 1. (Strand)

119. °"Yeats Praises *Play Boy*," *WashP*, 11 Mar 1914, 7.

"The Theatre and Beauty." (Strand)

120. °"William B. Yeats Speaks in College Hall on 'John Synge and the Ireland of His Time,'" *Springfield Daily Republican*, 14 Mar 1914, 18.

See also °"William Butler Yeats on the Irish Drama," *Student* [Amherst College], 16 Mar 1914, page number not given (reprinted in Strand, pp. 309-11).

121. °"Modern Trend of Poetry," *Springfield Daily Republican*, 17 Mar 1914, page number not given. (Strand)

"Contemporary Lyric Poets."

122. °"Yeats Gives His Idea of Plays," *New Haven Journal-Courier*, 18 Mar 1914, 3. (Strand)

"John Synge and the Ireland of His Time."

123. °"William Butler Yeats," *Stamford Advocate*, 19 Mar 1914, page number not given.

"Contemporary Lyric Poets," reprinted in Strand, pp. 306-8. See also °"Modern Trend of Art Second Yeats Lecture," *Student* [Amherst College], 19 Mar 1914, page number not given. (Strand)

124. °"Theater of Beauty Returns, Says Yeats," *Memphis Commercial Appeal*, 21 Mar 1914, 7.

See also °"Irish Poet Heard," same page; on "The Theatre and Beauty." (Strand)

125. °"W. B. Yeats Talks on Irish Plays and Poetry," *Daily Pennsylvanian*, 27 Mar 1914, 1. (Strand)

"John Synge and the Ireland of His Time."

126. "Mr. Yeats on Ghosts and Dreams: The Pros and Cons of Spiritism," *Times*, 24 Apr 1914, 13.

See also "Ghosts and Dreams: Lecture by Mr. W. B. Yeats," *Christian Commonwealth*, 29 Apr 1914, 527; "Ghosts and Dreams," *Light*, 2 May 1914, 211-13; 9 May 1914, 223. An address delivered to the London Spiritualist Alliance. An anonymous commentary, "Mr. Yeats on Ghosts and Dreams," appeared in *Light*, 9 May 1914, 222.

See also Peter Kuch: "'Laying the Ghosts'?--W. B. Yeats's Lecture on Ghosts and Dreams," *YeA*, 5 (1987), 114-35, which reprints the material published in *Light*.

127. "Thomas Davis Centenary: Address by Mr. W. B. Yeats," *IrT*, 21 Nov 1914, 9.

See Yeats's *Tribute to Thomas Davis* (1947, Wade 208) and Austin Clarke's reminiscences in CB443.

128. "The Irish Theatre," *Times*, 7 Dec 1915, 5.

A lecture chaired by Sir Thomas Beecham. Yeats obviously believed even at that time that the Irish theater movement would produce a "real national culture."

129. "William Blake and His School: Lecture by Mr. W. B. Yeats," *IrT*, 15 Apr 1918, 3.

Also on Calvert and Palmer.

130. "Psychical Phenomena: Mr. W. B. Yeats and Spiritualism. Advice to the Church and the Press," *IrT*, 27 Jan 1919, 6.

The advice was to stop treating the subject with derision.

131. "College Historical Society: Socialism and the War," *IrT*, 30 Jan 1919, 5-6.

Includes a report of a Yeats speech on p. 6.

132. "Psychical Research: Debate at the Abbey Theatre," *IrT*, 3 Feb 1919, 6.

133. "Abbey Theatre: Mr. W. B. Yeats and Mr. Lennox Robinson Discuss Its Policy," *FrJ*, 26 Apr 1919, 3.

Verbatim (?) report of a conversation between Yeats and Robinson.

134. °"Yeats Speaks on the Theatre," *Globe*, 3 Feb 1920, 9. (Strand)

"The Theatre and Beauty."

135. °"Providing Plays for the People," *Mail and Empire*, 3 Feb 1920, 7.
"A Theatre of the People." See also °"William Butler Yeats Tells of New School of Dramatic Art Embodied in People's Theatre," *Varsity*, 4 Feb 1920, 1, 4. (Strand)

136. °"Audience Charmed by Irish Poet," *Montreal Daily Star*, 4 Feb 1920, 5.
Yeats reading his own poetry, reprinted in Strand, pp. 323-26. See also BB224.

137. °"William Butler Yeats at the Academy of Music," *Daily Hampshire Gazette*, 14 Feb 1920, no page number given. (Strand)
"A Theatre of the People."

138. °"Poet Defends Sinn Feiners," *New Haven Journal-Courier*, 19 Feb 1920, 1.
"The Younger Generation of Poets," reprinted in Strand, p. 319.

139. °"Discusses Younger Poets," *Washington Evening Star*, 20 Feb 1920, 7.
"The Younger Generation of Poets." See also °"Lecture by Irish Poet," *WashP*, 20 Feb 1920, 9. (Strand)

140. °"Poet-Dramatist Delivers Lecture on Irish Theater," *Oberlin R*, 27 Feb 1920, 1, 3.
"A Theatre of the People," reprinted in Strand, pp. 326-28.

141. °BROWNE, LOUISE: "Yeats at Mandel Hall," *Chicago Evening Post*, 3 Mar 1920, 6.
"The Friends of My Youth," reprinted in Strand, pp. 321-23. See also °"Greatest Art of World Arises Out of Ecstasy," *Daily Maroon*, 3 Mar 1920, 1. (Strand)

142. °"W. B. Yeats Lecture Best of Season," *White and Blue* [Brigham Young U], 15 Mar 1920 or later.
"A Theatre of the People," delivered on 13 Mar 1920. (Strand, who does not cite the date of publication)

143. °"Irish Poet Tells of Erin's Ideals," *Salt Lake Tribune*, 16 Mar 1920, no page number given. (Strand)
"A Theatre of the People."

144. °"William Butler Yeats Delights Audience," *Morning Oregonian*, 20 Mar 1920, 6. (Strand)
"A Theatre of the People."

145. °"Irish Poet Tells Aims, Success on Dublin Stage," *SF Call and Post*, 26 Mar 1920, 8. (Strand)
"A Theatre of the People."

146. °NYE, MYRA: "Women's Works, Women's Clubs," *LA Times*, 1 Apr 1920, section II, 2.
"The Younger Generation of Poets," reprinted in Strand, pp. 320-21.

147. °"Friday Morning Club," *LA Times*, 3 April 1920, 5. (Strand)
A poetry reading. See BB138.

148. °"Irish Author Has Lecture on Poets," *Times-Picayune*, 13 Apr

1920, 11. (Strand)
"The Friends of My Youth."

149. °"Plays Should Picture Life of All, Says Irish Poet," *San Antonio Express,* 15 Apr 1920, 4. (Strand)
"A Theatre of the People."

150. °"1000 Persons Hear Irish Poet Talk," *Statesman* [Austin, Texas], 16 Apr 1920, 5. (Strand)
"The Friends of My Youth."

151. °"Irish Dramatist Gives Lecture in Kirksville," *Kirksville Daily Express,* 24 Apr 1920, 1. (Strand)
"A Theatre of the People."

152. °"Yeats Avoids Irish Question," *Boston Herald,* 7 May 1920, 18. (Strand)
"The Younger Generation of Poets."

153. "Last Night's Union Debate: An Irish Night. Mr. W. B. Yeats on Reprisals," *Oxford Chronicle,* 18 Feb 1921, 20.
A speech before the Oxford Union, supporting the motion "That this House would welcome complete Self-Government and condemn reprisals." See also "Reprisals Condemned," *FrJ,* 19 Feb 1921, 5.

154. "The Abbey Theatre: Lecture by Mr. Yeats," *IrT,* 6 May 1921, 5.
A lecture in aid of the Abbey, delivered at J. B. Fagan's residence in Chelsea. See also "Mr. Yeats's Stories of the Abbey Theatre," *Times,* 6 May 1921, 8.

155. WHELDON, F. W.: "Maddermarket Theatre: Norwich Players in *As You Like It.* A Distinguished Guest," *Eastern Daily Press,* 27 Sept 1921, 7.
The guest was Yeats, who made a speech comparing Shakespearean and modern theater.

156. "A Fine Poet," *Sheffield Daily Telegraph,* 23 Nov 1922, 8.
Yeats discussing his own poetry; reprinted in BB177, which contains a note that there is also a report in the *Sheffield Daily Independent,* 23 Nov 1922. See DE128.

157. "Mr. W. B. Yeats in Edinburgh," *Scotsman,* 16 May 1923, 8.
Lecture on "My Own Poetry." See also "Senator Yeats on His Poetry," *IrI,* 17 May 1923, 6.

158. "Mr. W. B. Yeats's Secrets: How His Poems Were Inspired," *IrT,* 30 June 1923, 8.

159. "Major Cooper's Candidature," *IrT,* 25 Aug 1923, 7-8.
Including Yeats's speech of endorsement.

160. "The Modern Novel: An Irish Author Discussed. Mr. Yeats Admires Good Breeding," *IrT,* 9 Nov 1923, 9.
In Jane Austen and Henry James; but does not find it in Dickens. Admires Joyce.

161. "'The Supernatural': Mr. Yeats and His Poems," *IrT,* 15 Nov 1923, 7.
A lecture, "Reading and Comments," at the Central Catholic Library. "The audience consisted for the greater part of ladies."

162. "Abbey's Growth: Senator Yeats Speaks on Irish Drama. Lady Gregory's Art," *FrJ,* 17 Nov 1923, 8.

163. "A Poet's Memoirs: Senator Yeats' Advice to Those in Love. Patriotism Defined," *FrJ,* 26 Jan 1924, 10.
A lecture on his own poetry, especially the love poetry. See also "My Own Poetry: Mr. Yeats' Reading," *IrT,* 26 Jan 1924, 6.

164. "The Old House: Magnificent Building Worthy of Great Country," *IrI,* 5 Mar 1924, 7.

165. "World-Famed Men at the Banquet [. . .]. A Victor at Last. Independent Nation," *IrI,* 4 Aug 1924, 4.
Yeats's speech at the Aonach Tailteann Council Banquet.

166. "Laurel Crowns: Tailteann Honours for Irish Men of Letters," *FrJ,* 11 Aug 1924, 6.

167. "Abbey Theatre: A Government Grant. Act of Intelligent Generosity," *IrT,* 10 Aug 1925, 5.
Summary of Yeats's speech in which he thanked the government. See editorial, "The Irish Drama," 4; "The Abbey Theatre: W. B. Yeats on Decline of Modern Oratory," *Times,* 10 Aug 1925, 12; and CE25a.

168. "Civilization: Mr. W. B. Yeats and France," *IrT,* 12 Nov 1925, 8.
A debate at the College Historical Society, "That civilization has progressed since this society first met." Yeats talks about morals and divorce with reference to Ireland and France.

169. "The Sphere of Woman: Influence in Literature and Politics. Mr. Yeats on Writing a Masterpiece," *IrT,* 17 Nov 1925, 8.

170. "Abbey Theatre Scene," *IrT,* 12 Feb 1926, 7-8.
Yeats's speech in defense of O'Casey's *The Plough and the Stars.* See the editorial, "Cant and Fact," 13 Feb 1926, 6, and "Abbey Theatre Uproar: Impassioned Speech by Mr. Yeats. Audience in Panic. Actors Fight with Republicans," *MGuard,* 13 Feb 1926, 11.

171. "National Theatre: Senator Yeats Defends Abbey," *IrI,* 24 Feb 1926, 8.
In answer to the criticism of Norman Reddin. See also "What Is a National Theatre. Mr. Reddin and the Abbey. Mr. Yeats on Drama and the Artist," *IrT,* 24 Feb 1926, 7-8.

172. "My Own Poetry: Mr. Yeats Talks and Recites," *IrT,* 25 Feb 1926, 6.

173. "The Lane Pictures: Free State Senate Demands Their Return [. . .]. Mr. W. B. Yeats and the King," *IrT,* 15 July 1926, 7.
Yeats's speech in the Senate. See also the editorial on p. 6, deploring Yeats's "attempt . . . to drag the King into this controversy"; and "The Lane Pictures," *Times,* 16 July 1926, 16.

174. "Irish Literature's Position: Senator Yeats on the Bad Past," *IrT,* 9 Nov 1926, 6.

175. "Irish Authors: An Academy of Belles Lettres," *IrI,* 19 Sept 1932, 10.
Yeats's speech at the founding of the Irish Academy of Letters.

176. °"Yeats Traces History of Modern Irish Art," *Ann Arbor Daily News,* 11 Nov 1932, 4. (Strand)
Lecture on "The New Ireland."

177. "°Yeats, Famous Irish Poet, Relates Poetic Experience in Lecture Tuesday Evening," *Kent Stater,* 17 Nov 1932, 1. (Strand)
Lecture on "My Own Poetry."

178. °"W. B. Yeats at Eaton Auditorium Gives Lecture on Irish Drama," *Varsity* [U of Toronto], 24 Nov 1932, 4.
"The Irish National Theatre." See also °"Irish Realism Now Explained by Yeats," *Globe,* 24 Nov 1932, 10. (Strand)

179. °"De Valera's Position Explained by Yeats," *Montreal Daily Star,* 28 Nov 1932, 11.
Lecture on "The New Ireland"; includes an interview. See "Irish Literary Eras and Politics," *Montreal Daily Star,* 29 Nov 1932, 18 (Strand); Richard H. Haviland: "Ireland's Bard Comes: Minstrel from Emerald Isle Has Been Honored by Many Well Qualified to Judge," *Montreal Daily Star,* 26 Nov 1932, 9 (not in Strand).

180. "Irish Movement Leaders Sketched: Rise of National Drama and Literature Traced by Poet and Playwright," *Gazette,* 29 Nov 1932, 9.
There is also a report on p. 2: "Irish Poet Never Heard of Buckley" (both items not in Strand).

181. °"William Butler Yeats Talks on Irish Letters," *Dartmouth,* 30 Nov 1932, 1. (Strand)
"The New Ireland."

182. °"William Butler Yeats Speaks at Bryn Mawr," *College News,* 14 Dec 1932, 1, 3.
"The New Ireland," reprinted in Strand, pp. 332-35.

183. "W. B. Yeats Lectures Here on the Irish Renaissance," *Notre Dame Scholastic,* 13 Jan 1933, 14.

184. °"King Oedipus," *NYHT,* 16 Jan 1933, 8. (Strand)
Curtain speech after the performance of the play.

185. "New Cultural Bond Links Us to Ireland, Says Yeats at Dinner to Irish Notables," *NYT,* 17 Jan 1933, 17.
Short speech on the Irish Academy of Letters. See °"W. B. Yeats and Others Honored at Dinner," *NYHT,* 17 Jan 1933, 5. (Strand)

186. "Modern Irish Literature: Four Epochs of Development. Mr. Yeats's Lecture at Ballsbridge," *IrT,* 18 Feb 1933, 8.

187. "Future of the Theatre: Mr. Yeats Denounces Stage Propaganda," *Times,* 16 Oct 1934, 12.
Summary of Yeats's speech at the Volta assembly (see Wade 181).

188. "Homage to Dr. Yeats: P.E.N. Club's Dinner. Tribute by John Masefield," *IrT,* 28 June 1935, 7-8.
Includes a summary of a speech made by Yeats himself.

189. PATMORE, DEREK: *Private History: An Autobiography.* London: Cape, 1960. 294 pp.
Yeats reading his own poetry in Oxford in 1935, pp. 214-18.

190. "New Demand for Art Treasures. Government to Press British for Lane Pictures," *IrI,* 18 Aug 1937, 10.

Yeats's speech at a dinner given in honor of Patrick McCartan. See also "Dinner to Dr. MacCartan: His Service to Irish Letters. Mr. Yeats to Write a Poem," *IrT,* 18 Aug 1937, 7-8. The poem is "The Municipal Gallery Revisited."

See also AE67, BB11, 34, 115, 128, BE5, 23, 106, 134, BG92, 125, 126, 195, 200, CB12, 443, CD509, 761, 936, 1062, 1321, 1357, EE91, 92, 342, 402, 521, 561, EF13, 24, FA1, FF2, 3, FG8, 31.

BG Less Substantial Material and Obituaries

1. ABEL, ULF: *Carl Milles--Form, idê, medaljkonst.* Stockholm: Proprius, 1980. 146 pp.

"Milles förslag till irländska mynt," 105-9, 126-27; on Milles's designs for the Irish coinage, including remarks on Yeats. See also BB244.

2. ADLARD, JOHN: *Stenbock, Yeats and the Nineties.* London: Woolf, 1969. xi, 113 pp.

Incorporates "Yeats's Stenbock," *Aylesford R,* 8:1 (Summer 1966), 37-41. The title of the book is a misnomer; the only important passage on Yeats is the following: "It must have been through [Lionel] Johnson that Eric [Stenbock] met Yeats and invited him to at least one supper. But here I am frustrated. I have been told that 'in an unpublished notebook of the 'twenties' Yeats left an account of a meeting with Eric. But Mrs. Yeats declined to allow my informant to send me this extract" (p. 60). Yeats mentions Stenbock in the preface to the *Oxford Book of Modern Verse,* in *Autobiographies,* and in *Memoirs.*

3. ANDREWS, IRENE DWEN: "A Glimpse of Yeats," *Reading and Collecting,* 2:3 (Feb-Mar 1938), 8-9.

In Gogarty's house sometime in the thirties.

4. ANON.: Obituary, *Annual Register,* 181 (1939), 425-26.

5. ANON.: "William Butler Yeats, Poet and Patriot," *Christian Century,* 15 Feb 1939, 205.

6. ANON.: "William Butler Yeats," *Church of Ireland Gazette,* 3 Feb 1939, 72-73.

7. ANON.: "Death of W. B. Yeats in France: Famous Irish Poet and Playwright," *Cork Examiner,* 30 Jan 1939, 6.

See also the editorial on the same page.

8. ANON.: "Scoffed at Fairies, But They Made His Living: Wrote 'Innisfree.' Won £ 7,000 Price," *Daily Express,* 30 Jan 1939, 5.

The penny press obituary: "Yeats . . . made a fortune out of fairies. His poems and plays were about places existing only in his mind."

9. ANON.: "W. B. Yeats: Poet, Playwright and Politician. Death at Mentone," *Daily Telegraph,* 30 Jan 1939, 13.

10. ANON.: "William Butler Yeats," *Deutsche Rundschau,* year 65 / 258:3 (Mar 1939), 210-11.

11. ANON.: "W. B. Yeats," *Evening Mail,* 30 Jan 1939, 4.

12. ANON.: "A Poet at Home: A Pen Portrait of Mr. Yeats," *Gael,* 20:1 (Jan 1901), 27.
Yeats at Woburn Place.

13. ANON.: "A Pen Picture of Dr. Douglas Hyde and Mr. Yeats," *Gael,* 21:12 (Dec 1902), 378-79.
An interview with Hyde, who was pestered by a nervous Yeats.

14. ANON.: "Mr. William Butler Yeats to Lecture in the United States This Autumn," *Gael,* 22:11 (Nov 1903), 387.

15. ANON.: "W. B. Yeats Dead in Mentone," *IrP,* 30 Jan 1939, 1, 7.
With an unknown photograph of Yeats in a rose garden. See also editorial: "A Great Poet Passes," 8.

16. ANON.: "De mortuis. . . ," *Irish Rosary,* 43:3 (Mar 1939), 161-65.
Yeats does not express the "truth" (because he was not Catholic), only "the effulgence of the fanciful and the fantastic."

17. ANON.: "Death of Mr. Yeats: Poet of European Reputation," *IrT,* 30 Jan 1939, 7-8.
See also editorial, p. 6; "Burial of W. B. Yeats," 31 Jan 1939, 7; Desmond Fitzgerald: "W. B. Yeats: An Appreciation," 1 Feb 1939, 5; Kitty Clive: "Echoes of the Town: W. B. Yeats' Last Letter," 3 Feb 1939, 4 (to T. J. Kiernan).

18. ANON.: "Home-Coming," *IrT,* 17 Sept 1948, 5.
The burial in Drumcliffe Churchyard. See also "Irish Sailors Bring Body of W. B. Yeats aboard the *Macha,*" 11 Sept 1948, 1; "Yeats Rests under Ben Bulben," 18 Sept 1948, 1, 3; Kees van Hoek: "The Way of the World," 18 Sept 1948, 5; Pro-Quidnunc: "An Irishman's Diary," 18 Sept 1948, 7.

19. ANON.: "Talking to H. O. White," *IrT,* 7 Apr 1962, 8.
Includes some reminiscences.

20. ANON.: "The Burial of Poet Yeats," *Life,* 25 Oct 1948, 146-50.

21. ANON.: "William Butler Yeats," *List,* 2 Feb 1939, 247.
Text of a broadcast in the B.B.C. News Bulletin.

22. ANON.: "W. B. Yeats"; "W. B. Yeats: A Great Figure in Letters"; "Death of W. B. Yeats: A Great Irish Poet and Dramatist," *MGuard,* 30 Jan 1939, 8, 9, 13.

23. ANON.: "William Butler Yeats, 73, Dies; Led Irish Literary Renaissance," *NYHT,* 30 Jan 1939, 8.

24. ANON.: "The Early Days of the Irish National Theatre. With Personal Recollections of Synge, Yeats, Moore, Lady Gregory, and Others. An Interview with P. J. Kelly," *NYT,* 1 June 1919, section IV, 2.
Reprinted in BA13, 1:97-98.

25. ANON.: "W. B. Yeats Dead: Famous Irish Poet," *NYT,* 30 Jan 1939, 13.
See also the editorial: "William Butler Yeats," 31 Jan 1939, 20; and a report: "Yeats Is Mourned All Over Ireland," 21.

26. ANON.: "W. B. Yeats--Veliki engleski pjesnik" [WBY--A great English poet], *Nova riječ,* 4:116 (1939), 6.

27. ANON.: "William Butler Yeats," *Publishers' Weekly,* 4 Feb 1939, 597.

28. ANON.: "William Butler Yeats," *Round Table,* 29:115 (June 1939), 597.

29. ANON.: "W. B. Yeats," *Saturday Night,* 4 Feb 1939, 1.

30. ANON.: "William Butler Yeats: Famous Irish Poet Dies on Riviera," *Scotsman,* 30 Jan 1939, 11.

31. ANON.: "The Late Mr. W. B. Yeats: His Wonderful Love for Sligo and Its Surroundings," *Sligo Champion,* 4 Feb 1939, 5.
See also "The Late Mr. W. B. Yeats: Grave Selected in Drumcliffe Cemetery," 11 Feb 1939, 5.

32. ANON.: "Brought Fame to Sligo: The Passing of Mr. W. B. Yeats," *Sligo Independent and West of Ireland Telegraph,* 4 Feb 1939, 2.
See also "Great Irish Poet to Be Buried in Sligo," 5; and another note under the same heading, 11 Feb 1939, 5.

33. ANON.: Obituary, *TAM,* 23:3 (Mar 1939), 160-61.

34. ANON.: "Mr. W. B. Yeats: A Great Irish Poet and Dramatist," *Times,* 30 Jan 1939, 14.

35. ANON.: "In Drumcliffe Churchyard Yeats Is Laid. . . ," *Times Pictorial,* 25 Sept 1948, 1.

36. ANON.: "W. B. Yeats in America," *T.P.'s Weekly,* 12 Apr 1907, 452.
Negligible anecdotes.

37. BAX, CLIFFORD: *Inland Far: A Book of Thoughts and Impressions.* London: Heinemann, 1925. 332 pp.
Yeats at Woburn Place, pp. 36-38; reprinted in BA13, 1:43-44.

38. BEHAN, BRENDAN: *Brendan Behan's Island: An Irish Sketchbook.* With drawings by Paul Hogarth. [NY]: Geis, 1962, 192 pp.
Behan's mother was maid in Maud Gonne's house and observed Yeats mistaking parsnips for pudding. Behan told the story to an American professor who asked for Yeats's attitude to Stephen's greens (pp. 27-28).

39. BEN BULBIN: "Sligo Snaps," *Western People,* 11 Feb 1939, 12.
A long obituary.

40. B[ENÉT], W[ILLIAM] R[OSE]: "William Butler Yeats 1865-1939," *SatR,* 4 Feb 1939, 8.

41. BENSON, SIR FRANK: *My Memoirs.* London: Benn, 1930. ix, 322 pp.
Recollects a performance of *Diarmuid and Grania,* pp. 310-11.

42. BERRIDGE, VIRGINIA, and GRIFFITH EDWARDS: *Opium and the People: Opiate Use in Nineteenth-Century England.* London: Lane, 1981. xxx, 370 pp.
Yeats is said to have smoked hashish while in Paris (p. 215).

43. [BERRYMAN, JOHN]: Obituary, *Nation,* 4 Feb 1939, 135.

44. BIRNBAUM, MARTIN: *The Last Romantic: The Story of More than Half a Century in the World of Art.* NY: Twayne, 1960. 262 pp.
See pp. 76-77 for a Yeats reminiscence. Birnbaum was given permission to perform *At the Hawk's Well* at the Greenwich Village Theatre, NY, shortly before the first London performance. I do not know whether this performance actually took place.

45. B[ODKIN], T[HOMAS]: "Obituary: Mr. W. B. Yeats," *Birmingham Post,* 30 Jan 1939, 14.

46. BOLSTERLI, MARGARET JONES: *The Early Community at Bedford Park: "Corporate Happiness" in the First Garden Suburb.* London: Routledge & Kegan Paul, 1977. xii, 136 pp.
Contains a few references to Yeats (see index).

47. BOUGHTON, ALICE: *Photographing the Famous.* With a foreword by James L. Ford. NY: Avondale Press, 1928. ix, 111 pp.
John Butler Yeats, pp. 46-47; W. B. Yeats, pp. 70-71.

48. BOWEN, ZACK: "Ninety Years in Retrospect: Excerpts from Interviews with Padraic Colum," *JIL,* 2:1 (Jan 1973), 14-34.
Colum reminisces about Yeats.

49. BOYLAN, HENRY: *A Dictionary of Irish Biography.* Dublin: Gill & Macmillan, 1978. xi, 385 pp.
See pp. 376-78.

50. BROWNE, MAURICE: *Too Late to Lament: An Autobiography.* London: Gollancz, 1955. 403 pp.
Reminiscences of Yeats meeting Vachel Lindsay, pp. 138-39.

51. *Burke's Irish Family Records.* London: Burke's Peerage, 1976. xxxii, 1237 pp.
See pp. 1233-34.

52. CALVERTON, V. F.: Obituary, *Current History,* 50:292 (Mar 1939), 46.

53. CANNELL, KATHLEEN: "A Yankee Poet in Yeat[s]'s Court: Two Aesthetes Meet in a London Lair," *CSM,* 6 Mar 1973, B12.
Ezra Pound and the author went to see Yeats in London in 1913.

54. CAZAMIAN, M.-L.: "William Butler Yeats 1865-1939," *EA,* 3:2 (Apr-June 1939), 127-31.

55. CHAKRAVARTY, AMIYA: "William Butler Yeats," *Modern R,* 65:387 (Mar 1939), 326-29.

56. CHAUVIRÉ, ROGER: "Yeats: Avec Yeats a disparu un grand poète," *Journal des débats,* 9 Apr 1939, 4.

57. CLARKE, LIA: "W. B. Yeats," *Leader,* 11 Feb 1939, 592.
Reminiscences.

58. CLAUSEN, CHRISTOPHER: "Did You Once See Willy Plain?" *VQR,* 58:2 (Spring 1982), 327-32.
Describes an encounter with an old man in 1965, who said that he had had Yeats as a lodger in Hampstead.

59. CLEMENS, CYRIL: "The Passing of W. B. Yeats," *Canadian Bookman,* 22 [i.e., 21]:2 (June/July 1939), 21-25.

60. COBURN, ALVIN LANGDON: *Men of Mark.* London: Duckworth / NY: Kennerley, 1913. 30 pp. plus 33 plates.
Note on taking Yeats's photograph (plate 19), pp. 24-25. The same material appears in *Alvin Langdon Coburn, Photographer: An Autobiography.* Edited by Helmut and Alison Gernsheim. London: Faber & Faber, 1966. 144 pp. (see pp. 33, 70, 72).

61. COLLIS, MAURICE: *The Journey Up: Reminiscences, 1934-1968.* London: Faber & Faber, 1970. 222 pp.
Louis MacNeice insisted that the wrong body was interred in Drumcliffe Churchyard, pp. 83-85.

62. COLUM, PADRAIC: "The Greatness of W. B. Yeats: With His Passing Goes the Foremost Poet of His Time," *NYTBR,* 12 Feb 1939, 1, 17.

63. ————: "A Poet Is Brought Home," *Commonweal,* 22 Oct 1948, 33-36.

64. CONNELY, WILLARD: "Two Irish Poets," *John o' London's Weekly,* 5 Feb 1954, 113-14.
Meetings with Yeats and AE.

65. ————: *Adventures in Biography: A Chronicle of Encounters and Findings.* London: Laurie, 1956. 198 pp.
"Poets in Ireland," 39-51, a railway journey with Yeats ca. 1929.

66. COPPARD, ALFRED EDGAR: *It's Me, O Lord! An Abstract & Brief Chronicle of Some of the Life with Some of the Opinions of A. E. Coppard Written by Himself.* London: Methuen, 1957. 252 pp.
Two short reminiscences of Yeats in Oxford, pp. 154, 188.

67. COUSINS, J. H.: "Yeats--the Immortal," *Madras Mail,* 5 Feb 1939, 6.

68. COWELL, JOHN: *Where They Lived in Dublin.* Photographs of buildings: George Gmelch. Dublin: O'Brien Press, 1980. 160 pp.
"William Butler Yeats (1865-1939): 82 Merrion Square, 2," 104-5.

69. [COWLEY, MALCOLM]: "Yeats," *NewRep,* 8 Feb 1939, 4.

70. [CRONE, JOHN S.]: "Editor's Gossip," *Irish Book Lover,* 7:11&12 (June & July 1916), 181-84.
A short Yeats reminiscence is found on p. 184.

71. ————: "Willie Yeats and John O'Leary," *Irish Book Lover,* 27:5 (Nov 1940), 245-49.
Yeats's letters to O'Leary, reprinted more accurately in *Collected Letters.*

72. CZIRA, SYDNEY GIFFORD: *The Years Flew By: The Recollections of Madame Sydney Czira.* With a conclusion by Jack White. Dublin: Gifford & Craven, 1974. viii, 108 pp.
Includes short reminiscences of Yeats (see index).

73. DOLMETSCH, MABEL: *Personal Recollections of Arnold Dolmetsch.* London: Routledge & Kegan Paul, 1957 [i.e., 1958]. viii, 198 pp.
Records a meeting in 1914, at which occasion Yeats "lilted" some

of his poems. Dolmetsch, however, thought that "he was really only droning it on one note" (pp. 110-11).

74. DREUX, ROBERT: "W. B. Yeats, prix Nobel de littérature, est mort: Ecrivain de langue anglaise, il avait l'inspiration strictement irlandaise," *Ordre,* 31 Jan 1939, 5.

75. DYBOSKI, ROMAN: "W. B. Yeats," *Wiadomości literackie,* 19 Mar 1939, 2.

76. EGERTON, GEORGE: *A Leaf from the Yellow Book: The Correspondence of George Egerton.* Edited by Terence de Vere White. London: Richards Press, 1958. 184 pp.

Two undated letters from Yeats, pp. 34-35; reminiscences, pp. 165-66. George Egerton did not like "fat Willy" (p. 146).

77. ELTON, OLIVER: *Frederick York Powell: A Life and a Selection from His Letters and Occasional Writings.* Oxford: Clarendon Press, 1906. 2 vols.

Some references to Yeats (see index).

78. EMERSON, DOROTHY: "Poetry Corner: William Butler Yeats," *Scholastic,* 34:5 (4 Mar 1939), 25.

79. ERVINE, ST. JOHN: "Mr. Yeats," *Obs,* 5 Feb 1939, 13.

80. ESSON, LOUIS: "Irish Memories and Australian Hopes," *Union Recorder,* 24 Nov 1938, 281-82.

81. ———: "Portrait of W. B. Yeats: Poet and Mystic. The Man I Knew," *Sydney Morning Herald,* 4 Feb 1939, 21.

Recalls two meetings ca. 1904 and 1918. See also BB179.

82. EVERETT, KATHERINE: *Bricks and Flowers: Memoirs.* London: Constable, 1949. x, 252 pp.

Yeats talking about the moon sometime around 1917, pp. 142-43.

83. FAY, GERARD: *Passenger to London.* NY: Macmillan, 1961. 222 pp.

"Dublin of the Books," 92-97, contains some Yeats memories.

84. FINCH, EDITH: *Carey Thomas of Bryn Mawr.* NY: Harper, 1947. ix, 341 pp.

Yeats's visit to Bryn Mawr in Dec 1903 is noted on pp. 234-35.

85. FITZGIBBON, MAJORIE: Sculpture of Yeats (photograph), *ILS,* 6:1 (Spring 1987), 14.

86. FLANAGAN, GERALD: "Yeats' Sussex Haven," *IrP,* 13 Nov 1965, 10.

Edith Shackleton Heald's Chantry House in Steyning. Illustrated.

87. FREEMAN, JOHN: *Literature and Locality: The Literary Topography of Britain and Ireland.* London: Cassell, 1963. xiii, 402 pp.

On some of the places associated with Yeats's life, pp. 44, 313-14, 323-25.

88. FREMANTLE, ANNE: *Three-Cornered Heart.* NY: Viking Press, 1971. xi, 316 pp.

See index for some Yeats reminiscences.

89. GARNETT, DAVID: "W. B. Yeats," *NSt,* 4 Feb 1939, 174.

Letter by Sean O'Faolain, 11 Feb 1939, 209, corroborating Garnett's statement that Yeats had a powerful political influence on his generation.

90. GIBBON, MONK: "The Advice of an Old Man," *IrT,* 24 June 1950, 6.
Recalls a meeting with Yeats, who expressed his cautious opinion of Gurdjieff's school at Fontainebleau.

91. GIBBS, PHILIP: *The Pageant of the Years: An Autobiography.* London: Heinemann, 1946. viii, 530 pp.
"Victorian Flirtation," 15-16; a short Yeats reminiscence.

92. GIBRAN, KAHLIL: *The Letters of Kahlil Gibran and Mary Haskell: Visions of Life as Expressed by the Author of "The Prophet."* Edited by Annie Salem Otto. Houston, Texas: No publisher given, 1970. xxv, 677 pp.
Gibran hears a Yeats address in Boston on 28 Sept 1911 and comments on his work, pp. 84-85. See also AC12.

93. GILLET, LOUIS: "W. B. Yeats (1865-1939)," *Revue des deux mondes,* 8th period / year 109 / 50:1 (1 Mar 1939), 219-23.

94. GLENDINNING, ALEX: "Commentary," *Nineteenth Century,* 125:745 (Mar 1939), 352-55.

95. GLENDINNING, VICTORIA: *Vita: The Life of V. Sackville-West.* London: Weidenfeld & Nicolson, 1983. xviii, 430 pp.
See pp. 80, 220, 278-79, 299 for a few Yeats reminiscences.

96. GRANT, JOY: *Harold Monro and the Poetry Bookshop.* Berkeley: U of California Press, 1967. x, 286 pp.
Yeats reading at the Poetry Bookshop, pp. 77-78, and passim (see index).

97. GRAY, HUGH: "The Spoken Word: W. B. Yeats," *List,* 23 Feb 1939, 439.
How the B.B.C. failed to present an adequate appreciation of Yeats's life and work when he died.

98. GREEVES, THOMAS AFFLECK: *Bedford Park: The First Garden Suburb. A Pictorial Survey.* London: Bingley, 1975. [63 pp.]
Illustration 73 shows No. 3 Blenheim Road, home of John Butler Yeats and his family.

99. GREGORY, HORACE: *The House on Jefferson Street: A Cycle of Memories.* NY: Holt, Rinehart & Winston, 1971. xi, 276 pp.
For Yeats reminiscences see pp. 252-54 and index.

100. GRIFFIN, WILLIAM: *Clive Staples Lewis: A Dramatic Life.* San Francisco: Harper & Row, 1986. xxv, 507 pp.
See pp. 24-25 for a short Yeats reminiscence.

101. GRUBB, H. T. HUNT: "A Poet Passes," *Poetry R,* 30:2 (Mar-Apr 1939), 149-51.

102. HAINING, PETER (ed): *The Hashish Club: An Anthology of Drug Literature.* London: Owen, 1975. 2 vols.
Vol. 1 contains a note on Yeats (pp. 189-90) and a reprint of "The Adoration of the Magi." Haining claims that Havelock Ellis made an experiment with Yeats by giving him mescaline and

quotes a report attributed to Yeats. In fact, the report was written by Ellis, not by Yeats, and published as "Mescal: A New Artificial Paradise," *ContempR,* 73:385 (Jan 1898), 130-41. See Warwick Gould: "Short-Cuts to Xanadu," *TLS,* 13 Feb 1976, 170.

103. HARVEY, ARNOLD: "Memories of Coole," *IrT,* 23 Nov 1959, 5; 24 Nov 1959, 7.

104. HAWARD, LAWRENCE: "W. B. Yeats: A Visit to Manchester Recalled," *MGuard,* 31 Jan 1939, 5.

105. HEADLAM, MAURICE: *Irish Reminiscences.* London: Hale, 1947. 244 pp.
See pp. 36-37, 48, 223-24.

106. H[ENDERSON], A[LICE] C[ORBIN]: "Too Far from Paris," *Poetry,* 4:3 (June 1914), 105-11.
Contains a note on the poetry reading by Yeats and Vachel Lindsay in Chicago.

107. HENN, T. R.: "The Return to the Valley," *Irish Library Bulletin,* 9:[10] (Oct 1948), 163-65.

108. HINE, REGINALD LESLIE: *Confessions of an Uncommon Attorney.* London: Dent, 1946 [1945]. xix, 268 pp.
Visited Yeats in 1908, pp. 151-53.

109. HOPE, ARTHUR JOSEPH: *Notre Dame: One Hundred Years.* Revised edition; introduction by Thomas J. Schlereth. South Bend, Ind.: Icarus Press, 1978. xxxii, 500 pp.
See pp. 274 and 419 for notes on Yeats's visits, the second of which (1933) did not produce a "hearty welcome . . . for he spoke mostly of an Ireland that was un-Catholic."

110. HORGAN, JOHN JOSEPH: *Parnell to Pearse: Some Recollections and Reflections.* Dublin: Browne & Nolan, 1948. viii, 359 pp.
Reminiscences of Yeats, pp. 82, 117-18; on *Cathleen ni Houlihan,* pp. 93-94 ("This powerful allegory . . . did more than hundreds of political speeches to influence the rising generation").

110a. HUNEKER, JAMES GIBBONS: *Steeplejack.* NY: Scribner's, 1925 [1920]. 2 vols.
Quotes from a letter which Yeats sent to him in 1903 (2:242-43). Huneker met Yeats "at the home of John Quinn" in May (i.e., March) 1914 (2:203; see also *Letters of James Gibbons Huneker.* Collected and edited by Josephine Huneker. NY: Scribner's, 1922, pp. 167, 241).

111. HUNTER, WILLIAM R.: "A Trio of Ireland's Literary Greats," *Stamps,* 186:2427 (17 Mar 1979), 702-4.
On the Yeats stamps issued in Ireland. See also Liam Miller: *The Dolmen Book of Irish Stamps.* Preface by Feargal Quinn. Mountrath: Dolmen Press, 1986. 61 pp. (p. 52).

112. IRELAND OF THE WELCOMES: "W. B. Yeats Special Issue," *Ireland of the Welcomes,* 28:3 (May-June 1979).
Contains only one article on Yeats, Liam Miller's "Yeats's West," 17-32; an illustrated survey of Yeats's West of Ireland.

113. JOHN, AUGUSTUS: *Chiaroscuro: Fragments of an Autobiography.*

First series. London: Cape, 1952. 285 pp.
See pp. 100-101.

114. JOHNSON, WILLIAM SAVAGE: *An Account of a Summer's Pilgrimage: Being the Journal of William Savage Johnson on a Trip to England, Wales and Ireland in 1925.* Meriden, Ct.: Bayberry Hill Press, 1972. iv, 59 pp.
See pp. 53-54.

115. JONES, E. AYKROYD: "The Sincerity of Yeats," *Focus,* 3 [i.e., 8]:6 (June 1965), 127-28.

116. JOYCE, STANISLAUS: *The Complete Dublin Diary.* Edited by George H. Healey. Ithaca: Cornell UP, 1971. xv, 189 pp.
See pp. 25, 26, 63.

117. KASSNER, RUDOLF: *Umgang der Jahre: Gleichnis--Gespräch--Essay --Erinnerung.* Erlenbach-Zürich: Rentsch, 1949, 398 pp.
See pp. 324-25.

117a. KAVANAGH, MATT: "Yeats Country," *IrT,* 2 Aug 1988, 13.
A portfolio of photographs.

118. KELLEHER, DANIEL LAWRENCE: *The Glamour of Dublin.* Dublin: Talbot Press, 1928 [1918]. 108 pp.
The first edition was published under the pseudonym D. L. Kay. "The Abbey Theatre," 17; "The High School: W. B. Yeats," 64.

119. KEYSERLING, HERMANN, COUNT: "W. B. Yeats: Recollections," *New English Weekly and New Age,* 31 Aug 1939, 256.

120. ————: *Reise durch die Zeit. II: Abenteuer der Seele.* Darmstadt: Holle, 1958. 428 pp. (Gesammelte Werke. 2.)
See p. 182 for a Yeats reminiscence (ca. 1903/4).

121. KILDARE, PETER: "The Day I Met W. B. Yeats," *Sunday Press,* 13 June 1965, 17.

122. KING, JAMES: *Interior Landscapes: A Life of Paul Nash.* London: Weidenfeld & Nicolson, 1987. xiv, 258 pp.
See pp. 60-61 for a short Yeats reminiscence. See also BG152.

123. VIK [i.e., KOVAČIĆ, IVAN GORAN]: "Smrt irskog pjesnika W. B. Yeatsa" [Death of Irish poet WBY], *Hrvatski dnevnik,* 4:1010 (1939), 6.

124. LAWRENCE, SIR ALEXANDER: "W. B. Yeats," *Times,* 3 Feb 1939, 14.
An anecdote on Yeats's belief in fairies.

125. LEACOCK, STEPHEN: *Too Much College or Education Eating Up Life: With Kindred Essays in Education and Humour.* NY: Dodd, Mead, 1940 [1939]. xi, 255 pp.
"Thinking of Tomorrow," 200. A supper party for Yeats when he lectured in Montreal. Yeats, thinking of the next day, wondered "if there is breakfast on the Boston train."

126. LEEMING, A. EMID: "Yeats and the Fairies," *IrT,* 22 Mar 1965, 8.
Recollections of a Yeats lecture.

127. LEGGE, M. DOMINICA: "Yeats and J. G. Legge," *TLS*, 6 Jan 1956, 7.
Identifies the J. G. Legge referred to in letters to Katharine Tynan.

128. Vig. [i.e., LENDIĆ, IVO]: "William Butler Yeats: Veliki irski pjesnik i dramatičar" [WBY: A great Irish poet and dramatist], *Hrvatska straža*, 11:29 (1939), 4.

129. LESLIE, SEYMOUR: *The Jerome Connexion*. London: Murray, 1964. x, 220 pp.
Yeats and the ghost at Gogarty's house, pp. 142-44.

130. LESLIE, SHANE: "How William Butler Yeats Became a Poet and Made Poets," *Ireland-American R*, [1]:4 [1940?], 86-90.
Discusses neither the first nor the second question but gives a sketchy biography with emphasis on Irish scenes.

131. LETTS, WINIFRED: "The Fays at the Abbey Theatre," *FortnR*, os 169 / ns 163:978 (June 1948), 420-23.
Includes reminiscences of Yeats.

132. L[INATI], C[ARLO]: Reminiscences of Yeats in 1902, *Convegno*, 4:4-5-6 (Apr-May-June 1923), 269-70.

133. LINDSAY, JACK: *Fanfrolico and After*. London: Bodley Head, 1962. 287 pp.
Chapter 11, "The London Aphrodite," 117-27, contains some remarks on Yeats, including reminiscences of a meeting. See also Lindsay's "The Modern Consciousness," *London Aphrodite*, 1 (Aug 1928), 3-24, where he refers to *A Vision* as "the only truly profound contribution to thought since Nietzsche" (p. 23).

134. LO DUCA, [GIUSEPPE]: "Yeats," *Larousse mensuel illustré*, 11:389 (July 1939), 460.

135. LYNCH, ARTHUR: *My Life Story*. London: Long, 1924. 319 pp.
Reminiscences of Yeats, whom he did not like, pp. 101-2.

136. LYND, ROBERT: "The Greatest Poet Is Dead," *News Chronicle*, 30 Jan 1939, 6.

137. MACCARTHY, DESMOND: "W. B. Yeats," *SunT*, 5 Feb 1939, 6.
Reprinted in CA50, pp. 428-33.

138. MCGILLION, JOSEPH: *Irish Lives*. Dublin: Folens, 1973. 96 pp.
"William Butler Yeats (1865-1939)," 54-56.

139. MCGRATH, JOANNE: "A Fitting Abode for a Towering Poet," *NYT*, 9 Mar 1975, section X, 11.
On Thoor Ballylee.

140. *The McGraw-Hill Encyclopedia of World Biography*. NY: McGraw-Hill, 1973. 12 vols.
Kathleen McGrory: "Yeats," 11:480-83.

141. MACKENNA, STEPHEN: "Notes on the Celtic Renaissance: The Personality of W. B. Yeats," *Gael*, 18:5 (Aug 1899), 132-34.
Gossip.

142. MACKENZIE, COMPTON: *My Life and Times*. London: Chatto & Windus, 1963-71. 10 vols.
Yeats talking on astrology in 1921, 5:207-8. See also 6:41.

143. MACLYSAGHT, EDWARD: *Changing Times: Ireland since 1898 as Seen by Edward MacLysaght*. Gerrards Cross: Smythe, 1978. 248 pp.
See p. 139.

144. MACMANUS, L. [i.e., CHARLOTTE ELIZABETH]: *White Light and Flame: Memories of the Irish Literary Revival and the Anglo-Irish War*. Dublin: Talbot Press, 1929. viii, 228 pp.
"Memories of the Irish Literary Revival," 1-73; reminiscences of Yeats, pp. 15-16; notes on *Diarmuid and Grania*, pp. 46-48.

145. MACMANUS, MICHAEL JOSEPH: *Adventures of an Irish Bookman: A Selection from the Writings*. Edited by Francis MacManus. Dublin: Talbot Press, 1952. xvi, 192 pp.
"How the Irish Literary Revival Began," 117-21. It began with *Poems and Ballads of Young Ireland* (1888).
"The Big House at Coole," 127-31; slight piece about Yeats and Lady Gregory at Coole.

146. MACNEICE, LOUIS: *The Strings Are False: An Unfinished Autobiography*. London: Faber & Faber, 1965. 288 pp.
Saw Yeats in 1935 ("his manner was hierophantic"), pp. 147-48.

147. MAGUIRE, WILLIAM JOSEPH: *Irish Literary Figures: Biographies in Miniature*. Dublin: Metropolitan Publishing Co., 1945. 221 pp.
"William Butler Yeats (1865-1939)," 195-98.

148. MANNING, MARY: "I Remember It Well: Some Bits of Autobiography," *JIL*, 15:3 (Sept 1986), 17-41.
Contains a short Yeats reminiscence, pp. 32-33.

149. MARTIN, SEAMUS: "The Swans Are Gone But Much Still Remains," *IrT*, 25 July 1984, 11.
On Coole Park and Thoor Ballylee.

150. MORLEY, FRANK: *Literary Britain: A Reader's Guide to Writers and Landmarks*. London: Hutchinson, 1980. 510 pp.
Several references to Yeats (see index).

151. MULCAHY, Mrs. J. B.: "A Pen Picture of W. B. Yeats," *Gael*, 22:12 (Dec 1903), 425.
Yeats on his first American lecture tour; with two rather unusual photographs.

152. NASH, PAUL: *Outline: An Autobiography and Other Writings*. London: Faber & Faber, 1949. 271 pp.
Visited Yeats ca. 1913 because he wanted to illustrate a book of his poems, but was glad that he did not get the job (p. 88).
See also BG122 and CD869.

153. *The New International Year Book: A Compendium of the World's Progress for the Year 1939*. NY: Funk & Wagnalls, 1940. xv, 822 pp.
See pp. 813-14 for an obituary notice.

154. NICHOLS, BEVERLEY: *25: Being a Young Man's Candid Recollections of His Elders and Betters*. London: Cape, 1926. 256 pp.
Reminiscences of Yeats in Oxford, pp. 42-44; reprinted in BA13,

1:135-36.

155. ———: *The Unforgiving Minute: Some Confessions from Childhood to the Outbreak of the Second World War.* London: Allen, 1978. vii, 311 pp.
See pp. 105-6.

156. NICOLSON, HAROLD: *Diaries and Letters, 1930-1939.* Edited by Nigel Nicolson. London: Collins, 1966. 448 pp.
A letter from Victoria Sackville-West to Nicolson, dated 9 Nov 1934, contains the following paragraph: "Then I went to luncheon with Virginia [Woolf], who gave me an imitation of Yeats telling her why he was occult. He has been confirmed in this theory because he saw a coat-hanger emerge from his cupboard and travel across the foot of his bed; next night, it emerged again, clothed in one of his jackets; the third night, a hand emerged from one of his cuffs; the fourth night--'Ah! Mrs Woolf, that would be a long story; enough to say, I finally recovered my potency'" (p. 188). See Yeats's poem "The Apparitions."

157. NOYES, HENRY: "William Butler Yeats," *Canadian Poetry Magazine,* 3:4 (Apr 1939), 5-10.

158. O'BRIEN, KATE: "Yeats Comes Home," *Spect,* 22 Sept 1948, 394.
Correspondence by St. John Ervine: "Yeats and Others," 1 Oct 1948, 432, questioning Yeats's "greatness."

159. O'BRIEN, SEUMAS: "Leaves from a Notebook," *Blarney Magazine,* 10 (Summer 1956), 26-32.
Includes reminiscences of Yeats, who came to see him in his sculptor's studio sometime before 1912.

160. [O'CONNOR, T. P. (?)]: "A Poet at Home. W. B. Yeats's Eyrie. Tea under Difficulties. A Pen Portrait of Mr. Yeats," *M.A.P.,* 20 Oct 1900, 369.
See the ironical note by "Seang Siúir": "Mr. Yeats's Jug," *Leader,* 3 Nov 1900, 155; and Yeats's letter, 10 Nov 1900, 173 (reprinted in *Uncollected Prose,* 2:243-44), denying that the meeting took place.

161. O'FAOLÁIN, SEÁN: "William Butler Yeats," *Spect,* 3 Feb 1939, 183.

162. O'NEILL, DERMOT: "William Butler Yeats," *New Northman,* 7:1 (Spring 1939), 3-4.

163. O'NEILL, SEAMUS: "W. B. Yeats," *Leader,* 25 Feb 1939, 639.

164. O'SULLIVAN, DONAL: *The Spice of Life and Other Essays.* Dublin: Browne & Nolan, 1948. ix, 126 pp.
See pp. 3-5.

165. OXBURY, HAROLD: *Great Britons: Twentieth-Century Lives.* Oxford: Oxford UP, 1985. x, 371 pp.
See pp. 362-63.

166. P., M.: "The Yeats[es]--Father and Son," *Theatre,* 19:158 (Apr 1914), 176, 211.

167. PFISTER, KURT: "William Yeats †," *Fränkischer Kurier,* 6 Feb 1939, 11.

168. POUND, EZRA: "Death of Yeats End of Irish Literary Revival, Says Pound, Noh Enthusiast," *Japan Times & Mail*, 5 June 1939, 3.
Yeats is only of marginal importance in this rambling piece (not listed in the 1983 edition of Donald C. Gallup's Pound bibliography). Reprinted on pp. 152-54 of Sanehide Kodama: *Ezra Pound & Japan: Letters & Essays*. Redding Ridge, Ct.: Black Swan Books, 1987. xvi, 256 pp., which also contains a few other Yeats references (no index).

169. PRATI, RAFFAELLO: "William Butler Yeats," *Circoli*, year 8 / series 4 / 2 (Feb 1939), 207-8.

170. PRIESTLEY, JOHN BOYNTON: *Margin Released: A Writer's Reminiscences and Reflections*. London: Heinemann, 1962. viii, 236 pp.
See p. 158.

171. PUDNEY, JOHN: "A Poet Comes Home," *Illustrated*, 9 Oct 1948, 16-18.

172. REID, FORREST: *Private Road*. London: Faber & Faber, 1940. 243 pp.
See pp. 76-77.

173. REYNOLDS, REGINALD: *My Life and Crimes*. London: Jarrolds, 1956. 260 pp.
Ethel Mannin's husband's reminiscences of Yeats, pp. 159-61. See also BB149-150.

174. RITTENHOUSE, JESSIE BELLE: *My House of Life: An Autobiography*. Boston: Houghton Mifflin, 1934. ix, 335 pp.
Recalls two meetings with Yeats, pp. 230-33.

175. ROBERTS, CECIL: *The Bright Twenties: Being the Third Book of an Autobiography, 1920-1929*. London: Hodder & Stoughton, 1970. 424 pp.
See pp. 33-36 for reminiscences of Yeats, including the coat-hanger story (see BG156).

176. ROBERTS, GEORGE: "Memoirs of George Roberts," *IrT*, 13 July 1955, 5.
Continued in issues of 14 July 1955, 5; 19 July 1955, 5; 1 Aug 1955, 5; 2 Aug 1955, 5. Reminiscences of Yeats, passim.

177. ROBERTSON, JILLIAN: "Yeats Mystery Unearthed," *Times*, 19 Aug 1986, 8.
The question of whether the wrong body was disinterred in Roquebrune and interred in Drumcliffe.

178. ROBERTSON, OLIVIA: *Dublin Phoenix*. London: Cape, 1957. 224 pp.
Memories of Yeats, pp. 27-29; note on *The Dreaming of the Bones*, pp. 189-90.

179. ROBINSON, LENNOX: "Journey's End," *Irish Library Bulletin*, 9:[10] (Oct 1948), 166.

180. RODGERS, W. R.: "Speak and Span," *List*, 23 May 1957, 829-30.

181. ROGERS, WILLIAM GARLAND: *Ladies Bountiful*. London: Gollancz, 1968. xiv, 236 pp.

Note on Yeats and Miss Horniman, pp. 10-12.

182. ROSS, MARGERY (ed): *Robert Ross, Friend of Friends: Letters to Robert Ross, Art Critic and Writer, Together with Extracts from His Published Articles*. London: Cape, 1952. 367 pp.
See pp. 278-79.

183. ROSSI, MARIO MANLIO: *Viaggio in Irlanda*. Milano: Doxa Editrice, 1932. 189 pp.
On Yeats, passim, especially pp. 140-44. An abridged version appeared as *Pilgrimage in the West*. Translated by J. M. Hone. Dublin: Cuala Press, 1933. viii, 53 pp.

184. RUGGLES, ELEANOR: *The West-Going Heart: A Life of Vachel Lindsay*. NY: Norton, 1959. 448 pp.
Lindsay meets Yeats in Chicago, 1 Mar 1914, pp. 216-18.

185. RYAN, DESMOND: *Remembering Sion: A Chronicle of Storm and Quiet*. London: Barker, 1934. 308 pp.
Reminiscences of the Abbey Theatre and of Yeats at the Thomas Davis Centenary, pp. 86-87, 164-65.

186. S., E.: "Der Dichter der irischen Wiedergeburt: Zum Tode von William Butler Yeats," *Berliner Börsenzeitung*, 2 Feb 1939, Beilage Volk und Kultur, 1.

187. S., M.: "Smrt pesnika Vilijama Batlera Jejtsa" [Death of poet WBY] *XX vek* [Dvadesiti vek], 2:2 (Feb 1939), 311-12.

188. SANDERS, DORA: "Man of Ireland," *Saturday Night*, 19 Nov 1932, 5.
Visited Yeats in Dublin.

189. SASSOON, SIEGFRIED: *Siegfried's Journey 1916-1920*. London: Faber & Faber, 1982 [1945]. 224 pp.
Short reminiscence of Yeats in 1920, pp. 176-78.

190. ———: *Diaries 1920-1922*. Edited and introduced by Rupert Hart-Davis. London: Faber & Faber, 1981. 304 pp.
See pp. 113-14.

191. SCHWARTZMAN, MYRON: "'Quinnigan's Quake!': John Quinn's Letters to James Joyce, 1921-1924," *BRH*, 83:1 (Spring 1980), 27-66.
Quinn's comments on Yeats's American interviews, pp. 45-46.

191a. SHANAHAN, ELLA: "Claim That Yeats Was Buried in Pauper's Grave," *IrT*, 6 Sept 1988, 1.
A claim made by Diana Souhami in a forthcoming book on the painter and photographer Hannah Gluckstein. See John Armstrong: "New Claim on Yeats Reburial," 12 Sept 1988, 7; correspondence by Eleanor French, 13 Sept 1988, 13; Anne and Michael Yeats, 6 Oct 1988, 11 (who refute the claim).

192. SINHA, SHRI MURARI: *Nobel Laureates of Literature 1901-1973. (With a Note on the Laureates of 1974)*. New Delhi: Chand, 1975. xlviii, 397 pp.
"William Butler Yeats (1865-1939)," 97-102. Inane.

193. SKELTON, ROBIN: "Thoor Ballylee," *Ireland of the Welcomes*, 15:1 (May-June 1966), 29-31.

194. SOUFFRIN-LE BRETON, EILEEN: "W. B. Yeats to Mallarmé," *TLS,* 26 Nov 1954, 759.
Yeats was to be introduced to Mallarmé by Verlaine and Henley, but the meeting did not take place.

195. SPEIRS, RUSSELL: "An Expert Use of Tact," *CSM,* 21 Oct 1974, 15.
Reminiscence of a Yeats lecture.

196. S[TAMM], R[UDOLF]: "William Butler Yeats," *National-Zeitung,* 1 Feb 1939, 2.

197. STARKIE, WALTER: *Scholars and Gipsies: An Autobiography.* London: Murray, 1963. xi, 324 pp.
Reminiscences of Yeats, passim (see index).

198. STEWART, DOUGLAS: *The Flesh and the Spirit: An Outlook on Literature.* Sydney: Angus & Robertson, 1948. viii, 281 pp.
"The Heroic Dream," 10-16; on Yeats and Maud Gonne as described by Hone.

199. STITT, PETER: "Stephen Spender," *Paris R,* 22:77 (Winter-Spring 1980), 119-54.
Interview, including a short Yeats reminiscence, pp. 121-22. See also CD1106.

200. STRINGER, ALFRED: "W. B. Yeats," *Saturday Night,* 9 Aug 1941, 25, 32.
Part of a series "Wild Poets I Have Known"; recalls a Yeats lecture.

201. STUART, FRANCIS: "Rencontre," in Genet: *William Butler Yeats* (1981, CA32), 441.
A short reminiscence.

202. SUTHERLAND, JAMES (ed): *The Oxford Book of Literary Anecdotes.* London: Oxford UP, 1975. ix, 382 pp.
See index for several anecdotes by and about Yeats.

203. SWIFT, GEORGE: "In Memoriam: William Butler Yeats," *America,* 25 Feb 1939, 498-99.
Lame attempt at a satirical evaluation.

204. TAGORE, RABINDRANATH: "Rabindranath's Message on the Passing Away of Yeats," *VQ,* 17:1 (May-July 1951), 28.
Reprinted as the frontispiece of *VQ,* 30:3 (1964-65).

205. TÉRY, SIMONE: "Visite à W.-B. Yeats, lauréat du Prix Nobel," *Nouvelles littéraires,* 24 Nov 1923, 6.

206. THOMAS, JOHN ORMOND: "W. B. Yeats Comes Home to Sligo," *Picture Post,* 9 Oct 1948, 10-13.

207. TIETJENS, EUNICE: *The World at My Shoulder.* NY: Macmillan, 1938. xiii, 341 pp.
Meetings with Yeats, pp. 59-61.

208. UNDERWOOD, VERNON PHILIP: *Verlaine et l'Angleterre.* Paris: Nizet, 1956. 511 pp.
A note on Yeats's visit, pp. 463-64.

209. VÉGH, GYÖRGY: "William Butler Jeats [sic]," *Vigilia,* 5:3 (Mar 1939), 184-86.

210. VIDAKOVIĆ, A.: "Vilijam Batler Jejts (1865-1939)," *Politika,* 25 Feb 1939, 10.

211. WAGNER, LUDWIG: "Ein grosser Dichter ist gestorben: Zum Tode von W. B. Yeats," *Münchener Neueste Nachrichten,* 6 Feb 1939, 4.
Reprinted with slight revisions in *Blätter der Städtischen Bühnen Frankfurt am Main,* 6:19 (1939), 219-21, 224.

212. WAITE, ARTHUR EDWARD: *Shadows of Life and Thought: A Retrospective Review in the Form of Memoirs.* London: Selwyn & Blount, 1938. 288 pp.
See p. 119.

213. WALLACE, MARTIN: *100 Irish Lives.* Newton Abbot: David & Charles / Totowa, N.J.: Barnes & Noble, 1983. 184 pp.
"W. B. Yeats 1865-1939: Towering Poet," 139-40.

213a. °WASSON, TYLER (ed): *Nobel Prize Winners: An H. W. Wilson Biographical Dictionary.* NY: Wilson, 1987. xxxiv, 1165 pp.
See pp. 1152-55.

214. WHITE, TERENCE DE VERE: "Yeats's Tower at Thoor Ballylee," *IrT,* 7 Dec 1963, 12.
A visit to the tower.

215. WILLIAMS, GEORGE G.: *Guide to Literary London.* London: Batsford, 1973. vii, 406 pp.
See index for several references to places associated with Yeats.

216. WILLIAMS, WILLIAM CARLOS: *The Autobiography.* NY: New Directions, 1967 [1951]. xii, 402 pp.
See pp. 114-15.

217. WINTLE, JUSTIN, and RICHARD KENIN (eds): *The Dictionary of Biographical Quotation of British and American Subjects.* London: Routledge & Kegan Paul, 1978. xviii, 860 pp.
See pp. 823-25.

218. WOOLF, LEONARD: *Beginning Again: An Autobiography of the Years 1911-1918.* London: Hogarth Press, 1964. 260 pp.
Yeats trying a psychic experiment and failing, pp. 142-43. A photograph of Yeats and Lytton Strachey, p. 145.

219. YEATS, W. B.: "Letter to M. Clifford Harrison." Edited by George Mills Harper, *YeSt,* 1 (Bealtaine 1971), 209-10.
A letter to a U of Virginia graduate student (1 Apr 1914).

220. YOUNG, EDITH: *Inside Out.* London: Routledge & Kegan Paul, 1971. vii, 167 pp.
Yeats as remembered by D. N. Dunlop, Mrs. Young's father, pp. 6-9.

221. ZWEIG, STEFAN: *Die Welt von Gestern: Erinnerungen eines Europäers.* Frankfurt: Suhrkamp, 1949 [1944]. 485 pp.
A recollection of Yeats reading his own poetry, pp. 181-82.

C THE WORKS (GENERAL SECTION)

CA Books, Pamphlets, and Selected Special Issues of Periodicals Exclusively on Yeats

1. AGENDA: Yeats issue, *Agenda,* 9:4--10:1 (Autumn/Winter 1971/72). For the individual contributions see CD1271, DB85, DC80, 170, DD471, 603.

2. ALLEN, JAMES LOVIC: *Yeats's Epitaph: A Key to Symbolic Unity in His Life and Work.* Washington, D.C.: UP of America, 1982. xi, 270 pp.

Incorporates "'Imitate Him If You Dare': Relationships between the Epitaphs of Swift and Yeats," *Studies,* 70:228/229 [i.e., 70: 278/279] (Summer/Autumn 1981), 177-86.

Contains chapters on the relationship of the epitaph in "Under Ben Bulben" to Yeats's reading of an essay on Rilke and to Swift's epitaph, on the image of the horseman and the horse in the epitaph and in Yeats's other works, on the relevance of Yeats's burial in Drumcliff Churchyard, and on the "two eternities."

Reviews:
- Alison Armstrong: "Casting a Cold Eye--Yeats's Epitaph," *ILS,* 2:1 (Spring 1983), 22.
- Steve Connelly, *Eire,* 18:3 (Fall 1983), 143-47.
- Karen Dorn, *YeA,* 3 (1985), 255-57.
- Jacqueline Genet, *EI,* 8 (Dec 1983), 394-95.
- Declan Kiberd, *IUR,* 14:2 (Autumn 1984), 301-3.
- Andrew Parkin, *YER,* 8:1&2 (1986), 137-39.
- Donald T. Torchiana, *Yeats,* 2 (1984), 265-68.

3. ——— (ed): *Yeats Four Decades After: Some Scholarly and Critical Perspectives.* Butler, Pa.: Kopper, 1979. iii, 84 pp. (Modern British Literature Monograph Series. 1.)

This is identical with the Yeats issue of *MBL,* 4:1 (Spring 1979). Contains: "Editor's Introduction: Yeats and Intentional Commission of the Intentional Fallacy," 1-4, and the following items: CD1008, DA6 in part, DC23, 89, 189, 365.

4. ARCHIBALD, DOUGLAS N.: *Yeats.* Syracuse: Syracuse UP, 1983. xv, 280 pp. (Irish Studies.)

Incorporates "Father and Son: John Butler and William Butler Yeats," *MR,* 15:3 (Summer 1974), 481-501.

Studies the process of Yeats's thought toward the achievement of an "ideal expression." Contains chapters on the appropriation of Coleridge, the relationship between Yeats and his father, his friendships with Mabel Beardsley, Maud Gonne, and Lady Gregory, his "engagements with and programs for Anglo-Ireland and Celtic Ireland," various political and public poems of 1913-39 (particularly "The Tower"), the occult and *A Vision,* antinomies in some poems, and the *Last Poems.* Analyzed in sections DD, EE, and FC.

Reviews:
- Elizabeth Bartlett, *National Forum,* 65:1 (Winter 1985), 45-46.
- Denis Donoghue: "A 'Southern Californian' Anglo-Irishman," *NYTBR,* 5 June 1983, 7, 28-29.
- Edward Engelberg: "A Recent Bio-Critical Study of Yeats," *ELT,* 27:2 (1984), 176-77.
- Eamon Grennan: "Beyond the Breakfast Table," *IrT,* 23 July

1983, 12.
- Wayne E. Hall, *VS,* 28:1 (Autumn 1984), 191-92.
- [Robert Hogan], *JIL,* 13:1&2 (Jan-May 1984), 143-44.
- L. M., *West Coast R of Books,* 9:6 (Nov/Dec 1983), 41.
- Roy McFadden: "He Never Got Hurt," *IrP,* 27 Aug 1983, 9.
- Janet Madden-Simpson: "Blurred Orb," *BooksI,* 77 (Oct 1983), 183-84.
- Leslie B. Mittleman, *Magill's Literary Annual,* 1984, 988-91.
- William H. O'Donnell, *Yeats,* 2 (1984), 268-72.
- Sidney Poger, *Eire,* 19:2 (Summer 1984), 152-54.
- Richard Taylor, *YeA,* 3 (1985), 282-84.
- Wolfgang Wicht, *ZAA,* 33:3 (1985), 277-78.

5. ARIEL: "A Yeats Number," *Ariel,* 3:3 (July 1972).
A. N. J[effares]: "Editorial," 3-4. For the individual contributions see CD350, 375, 470, DC121, DD119, 121, EE103, and FA72 in part.

6. ARROW: "W. B. Yeats Commemoration Number," *Arrow,* Summer 1939.
Contents: L[ennox] R[obinson]: "Foreword," 5.
John Masefield: "William Butler Yeats," 5-6; reprinted from *Author, Playwright, and Composer,* 49:3 (Spring 1939), 86-87.
F. R. Higgins: "As Irish Poet," 6-8.
Austin Clarke: "Poet and Artist," 8-9; reprinted from *Obs,* 5 Feb 1939, 8.
Richard Hayes: "His Nationalism," 10-11.
Gordon Bottomley: "His Legacy to the Theatre," 11-14; reprinted in CD291.
Edmund Dulac: "Without the Twilight," 14-16.
William Rothenstein, W. J. Turner, and Oliver St. John Gogarty: "Three Impressions," 16-20; reprinted in BA13, 2:248-56.
Lennox Robinson: "As Man of the Theatre," 20-21; reprinted in BA13, 2:256-59.
Portraits by John B. Yeats, Charles Shannon, Sean O'Sullivan; caricatures by Sir Max Beerbohm and Edmund Dulac.
Reviews:
- Anon.: "A Tribute to Yeats," *TAM,* 23:11 (Nov 1939), 837.
- Stephen Spender: "Honey-Bubblings of the Boilers," *NSt,* 11 Nov 1939, 686-87.

7. BERRYMAN, CHARLES BEECHER: *W. B. Yeats: Design of Opposites. A Critical Study*. NY: Exposition Press, 1967. 149 pp.
Based on "W. B. Yeats: Design of Opposites," °Ph.D. thesis, Yale U, 1965. 261 pp. (*DAI,* 26:8 [Feb 1966], 4624)
A rather narrow and rigid study, beset with frequent misunderstandings. Discusses *A Vision, The Island of Statues, The Player Queen, The Resurrection, John Sherman* and other prose fiction, "The Song of the Happy Shepherd," "The Sad Shepherd," "The Wanderings of Oisin," and "Under Ben Bulben."
Reviews:
- [Denis Donoghue]: "Lore of Opposites," *TLS,* 28 Sept 1967, 890.
- Paul H. Stacy: "Yeats's Dualities: Two Restatements," *HSL,* 2:1 (1970), 68-69.

8. BERTHOUD, JACQUES, and ALBERT JAMES SMITH: *Yeats: The Natural and the Supernatural / Yeats: Time and Death*. London: Audio Learning, 1979. Tape, length ca. 56 mins. (Audio Learning: English Literature Series. 59.)
A five-page accompanying booklet contains a summary, notes, and a bibliography.

9. BITHELL, JETHRO: *W. B. Yeats*. Translated [into French] by Franz Hellens. Bruxelles: Lamertin / Paris: Librairie Générale des Sciences, Arts et Lettres, [1913]. 49 pp.

Reprinted from *Masque*, series 2 / 1 (1912), 2-16; 2 (1912), 69-77. An essay on Yeats's life and work, including French translations of some of his poems. Anonymous review in *Academy*, 14 Sept 1912, 340.

10. BJERSBY, BIRGIT: *The Interpretation of the Cuchulain Legend in the Works of W. B. Yeats*. Upsala: Lundequist, 1950. 189 pp. (Upsala Irish Studies. 1.)

Reprinted: Philadelphia: West, 1978. On "The Death of Cuchulain" (later "Cuchulain's Fight with the Sea"), the Cuchulain plays, and "Cuchulain Comforted." "In this study we have tried to show how the Cuchulain writings present W. B. Yeats in three aspects, as Poet, as Man and as Interpreter of life. We have tried to prove that the Cuchulain works occupy a central place in Yeats' writings, that they mirror important events in his own life and that they are also closely associated with the problems of his outlook upon life [i.e., with *A Vision*]" (p. 164).

Reviews:
- Peter Allt, *ES*, 35:1 (Feb 1954), 31-33.
- William Becker, *DM*, 27:1 (Jan-Mar 1952), 46-48.
- ———: "On the Margin of Yeats," *Poetry*, 81:5 (Feb 1953), 331-34.
- Friedrich Biens, *SN*, 24:1&2 (1952), 155-57.
- Austin Clarke: "Footlights for Poetry," *IrT*, 7 Apr 1951, 6.
- [———]: "Aspects of Yeats's Poetry," *TLS*, 1 June 1951, 339.
- A. Norman Jeffares, *RES*, 4:13 (Jan 1953), 86-88.
- A. Koszul, *EA*, 5:3 (Aug 1952), 263-64.
- Roger McHugh: "Yeats, Synge, and the Abbey Theatre," *Studies*, 41:163-64 (Sept-Dec 1952), 333-40.
- Horace Reynolds: "'To Follow Yeats Down All the Diverse Paths,'" *CSM*, 12 June 1952, 13.
- W. H. Stenfert Kroese: "Yeats, gedetailleerd," *Litterair paspoort*, 7:53 (Jan 1952), 11.

11. BLÄTTER DER STÄDTISCHEN BÜHNEN FRANKFURT AM MAIN: "Gedenkheft zum Tode von William Butler Yeats," *Blätter der Städtischen Bühnen Frankfurt am Main*, 6:19 (1939).

For individual contributions see BG211 and EE117.

12. BLOOM, HAROLD: *Yeats*. NY: Oxford UP, 1970. xii, 500 pp.

A study based on two convictions: (1) Yeats was a romantic and the last representative, but also the betrayer of a tradition that began with Blake and Shelley; his achievement has to be judged against theirs; (2) Yeats's achievement has been overrated. On these tenets, Bloom attempts a revaluation of the entire work, which succeeds on its own terms but hardly on any others. He also discusses the influence of Wordsworth, Browning, and Pater, and invokes the parallel case of Wallace Stevens. Analyzed in sections DD, EE, FC, and FE. See also CD283.

Reviews:
- James L. Allen: "Recent Yeatsiana: The Failed Quest for Unity of Being," *JML*, 2:1 (Sept 1971), 148-54.
- Eavan Boland, *Critic*, 29:3 (Jan 1971), 80-82.
- James D. Boulger, *Thought*, 45:179 (Winter 1970), 620-23.
- W. Bronzwaer, *DQR*, 1:1 (1971), 42-43.
- Gerald L. Bruns, *Spirit*, 38:4 (Winter 1972), 41-45.
- Kenneth Connelly: "Yeats," *YR*, 60:3 (Mar 1971), 394-403.

- [G. S. Fraser]: "Saving Yeats from the Critics," *TLS*, 12 Mar 1971, 292.
- René Fréchet, *EA*, 28:1 (Jan-Mar 1975), 105-6.
- Allen Grossman: "Harold Bloom's Yeats," *VQR*, 46:3 (Summer 1970), 520-25.
- George Mills Harper, *Masterplots*, 1971, 349-51.
- John Hollander: "Let a Thousand Blooms. . . ," *Poetry*, 117:1 (Oct 1970), 43-45.
- A. Norman Jeffares, *RES*, 22:88 (Nov 1971), 514-17.
- Will C. Jumper, *Poet and Critic*, 6:1 (Fall 1970), 47-48.
- Augustine Martin, *Studies*, 60:237 (Spring 1971), 98-102.
- George P. Mayhew, *BA*, 45:2 (Spring 1971), 321-22.
- John Montague: "The Young and the Old Campaigner," *Guardian*, 3 Sept 1970, 7.
- Harry T. Moore, *SatR*, 20 June 1970, 37-39.
- J. R. Mulryne, *MLR*, 69:3 (July 1974), 629-30.
- Thomas Parkinson, *ELN*, 9:3 (Mar 1972), 234-35.
- Marjorie Perloff: "Yeats as Gnostic," *ConL*, 12:4 (Autumn 1971), 554-61.
- John Pick, *America*, 30 May 1970, 597-98.
- William H. Pritchard: "Mr. Bloom in Yeatsville," *PR*, 38:1 (Spring 1971), 107-12.
- John Raymond: "In Yeats' Shadow," *SunT*, 23 Aug 1970, 26.
- Howard Sergeant, *English*, 20:106 (Spring 1971), 26-27.
- Sandra Siegel: "Prolegomena to Bloom: The Opposing Virtue," *Diacritics*, 1:2 (Winter 1971), 35-38.
- Donald T. Torchiana, *MP*, 70:2 (Nov 1972), 168-74 (a particularly scathing review).
- ———: "Some Recent Books on W. B. Yeats," *JIL*, 5:2 (May 1976), 60-81.
- Helen Vendler, *JEGP*, 70:4 (Oct 1971), 691-96.
- Ann Wordsworth: "Wrestling with the Dead," *Spect*, 25 July 1970, 74.

13. ——— (ed): *William Butler Yeats*. Edited with an introduction by Harold Bloom. NY: Chelsea House, 1986. viii, 232 pp.

Contains 11 previously published pieces without their footnotes (unconvincingly judged as "the most useful criticism yet published" on Yeats's writings [p. vii]; not analyzed in this bibliography); an "Introduction" (pp. 1-22, a reprint of "Yeats, Gnosticism, and the Sacred Void" from CC29); a short chronology; and an altogether insufficient bibliography.

Reviewed by Richard J. Finneran: "Two on Yeats," *ELT*, 31:3 (1988), 320-24.

14. BRADFORD, CURTIS BAKER: *Yeats at Work*. Carbondale: Southern Illinois UP, 1965. xix, 407 pp.

Abridged edition: NY: Ecco Press, 1978. xv, 169 pp. Prints, and comments upon, the early drafts of the following poems, plays, and prose pieces: "The Hosting of the Sidhe," "The Host of the Air," "The Lover Asks Forgiveness," "Words," "The Wild Swans at Coole," "Nineteen Hundred and Nineteen," "The Tower" (section 3), "Lullaby," "The Mother of God," "Vacillation" (section 8), "Ribh Considers Christian Love Insufficient," "The Gyres," "The Circus Animals' Desertion," *At the Hawk's Well*, *The Words upon the Window-Pane*, *The Resurrection*, *A Full Moon in March*, *Purgatory*, "The Religion of a Sailor" from *The Celtic Twilight*, "The Rose of Shadow" and other material from *The Secret Rose*, sections from *Discoveries*, sections from *Autobiographies*, and extracts from *On the Boiler*.

Reviews:
- Rivers Carew, *DM,* 6:2 (Summer 1967), 92-94.
- Brian John: "Hurt into Poetry: Some Recent Yeats Studies," *JGE,* 18:4 (Jan 1967), 299-306.
- Walther Martin, *ZAA,* 14:3 (1966), 308-12.
- Giorgio Melchiori, *N&Q,* os 211 / ns 13:11 (Nov 1966), 430-31.
- J. R. Mulryne, *MLR,* 63:3 (July 1968), 692-93.
- Thomas Parkinson, *ELN,* 4:2 (Dec 1966), 154-56.
- George Brandon Saul, *Eire,* 4:3 (Autumn 1969), 127-29.
- Robert E. Scholes, *JEGP,* 66:2 (Apr 1967), 280-82.
- Priscilla W. Shaw: "The Yeats Centenary: Part of the Harvest," *VQR,* 42:1 (Winter 1966), 173-76.
- Jon Stallworthy, *RES,* 18:70 (May 1967), 225-27.
- August W. Staub: "Yeats: The Hundredth Year," *QJS,* 52:1 (Feb 1966), 81-85.
- Donald T. Torchiana: "Three Books on Yeats," *PQ,* 46:4 (Oct 1967), 536-56.
- Peter Ure, *ES,* 48:3 (June 1967), 264-68.
- Gertrude M. White, *Criticism,* 9:4 (Fall 1967), 392-93.

15. COLBY LIBRARY QUARTERLY: Yeats issue, *CLQ,* 15:2 (June 1979).
Contains: Douglas N. Archibald: "Announcements and Comments," 66-67; CC25, 212, CD355, DD720, and EE534.

16. COLLEGE LITERATURE: "Yeats Issue," *CollL,* 13:1 (Winter 1986).
See CC78, 343, CD257, 871, 1253, DC39, 176, DD32, 205, 444, 636, 662.

17. COLWELL, FREDERIC STEWART: "W. B. Yeats: The Dimensions of Poetic Vision," Ph.D. thesis, Michigan State U, 1966. v, 220 pp. (*DAI,* 27:4 [Oct 1966], 1053A)

Discusses dualism in *The Shadowy Waters;* Heraclitus and Plato as sources; Yeats's departure from the Platonic tradition in the figure of the Daimon; Unity of Being; primary and antithetical experience in the hero, the artist, the saint, and the fool; and "the lineaments of the Yeatsian myth as it unfolds from an operative dualism to paradoxical resolution" (p. 8) in *A Vision.*

18. *The Cornell Yeats.* Ithaca: Cornell UP, 1982--. In progress.
Unnumbered series. Published so far: *The Death of Cuchulain* (1982, see EE171), *Purgatory* (1986, see EE475), *The Early Poetry* (1987, EE390). The variorum edition of *The Secret Rose* (1981, FA74), although published by the same publisher, is not part of the series.

19. COWELL, RAYMOND (ed): *Critics on Yeats: Readings in Literary Criticism.* London: Allen & Unwin, 1971. ix, 114 pp. (Readings in Literary Criticism. 10.)

Contains "Introduction," vi-vii, and 33 snippets from previously published criticism (not analyzed in this bibliography). The selection is one-sided; almost all the material is on the poetry.

Reviews:
- Peter Faulkner, *DUJ,* os 64 / ns 33:2 (Mar 1972), 171-72.
- Phillip L. Marcus: "Approaching W. B.," *IrP,* 25 Sept 1971, 12.

20. *The Dolmen Press Yeats Centenary Papers MCMLXV.* Edited by Liam Miller with a preface by Jon Stallworthy. Dublin: Dolmen Press, 1965-68. xvi, 523 pp. in 12 parts.

Contents: Jon Stallworthy: "Preface," ix-xi; on the Cuala Press as a predecessor of the Dolmen Press; Liam Miller: "Introduction," xiii-xvi; and the following parts: CC129, CD7, 209, 253, 763, DC334, 383, DD285, 330, ED17, FD51, and FF12.

Reviews:

- Rivers Carew, *DM,* 6:2 (Summer 1967), 92-94.
- Austin Clarke: "Yeats Late and Early," *IrT,* 14 Sept 1968, 8.
- [Denis Donoghue]: "No Plays Like Noh Plays," *TLS,* 30 Mar 1967, 263; correspondence by G. S. Fraser, 6 Apr 1967, 296.
- [———]: "Lore of Opposites," *TLS,* 28 Sept 1967, 890.
- T. P. Dunning: "Innisfree Onwards," *IrI,* 23 Aug 1969, 6.
- William Empson: "A Time of Troubles," *NSt,* 23 July 1965, 123-24 (reprinted in CB149a).
- [G. S. Fraser]: "Surveying Yeats from China to Peru," *TLS,* 10 Feb 1966, 99.
- R. Fréchet, *EA,* 24:2 (Apr-June 1971), 211-12.
- T. R. Henn, *RES,* 20:79 (Aug 1969), 373-75.
- Gerhard Hoffmann, *Anglia,* 90:1/2 (1972), 266-70.
- Christine Longford: "Bold Fenian Men," *IrT,* 2 Sept 1967, 10.
- Augustine Martin, *Studies,* 57:225 (Spring 1968), 108-10.
- Austin Martin: "Yeats the 'Fenian in Practice,'" *IrP,* 3 June 1967.
- George P. Mayhew, *BA,* 43:3 (Summer 1969), 420-21.

21. DONOGHUE, DENIS (ed): *The Integrity of Yeats.* Cork: Mercier Press, 1964. 70 pp. (Thomas Davis Lectures.)

Reprinted °Philadelphia: West, 1976; °Norwood, Pa.: Norwood Editions, 1976. Contents: Denis Donoghue: "Yeats and the Modern Tradition: An Introduction," 9-20; and the following items: CA49 in part, DB56, DC165, and FG34.

22. ———, and JAMES RONALD MULRYNE (eds): *An Honoured Guest: New Essays on W. B. Yeats.* London: Arnold, 1965. viii, 196 pp.

Contents: Charles Tomlinson: "Yeats and the Practising Poet," 1-7. "Yeats gives us the sense of liberating scale, scale generated by--what remains for the practitioner the central and necessary miracle--the ability to remake himself and his verse."

Northrop Frye: "The Rising of the Moon: A Study of *A Vision,*" 8-33; reprinted in FC120.

T. R. Henn: "*The Green Helmet* and *Responsibilities,*" 34-53; the background and sources of the poems in these volumes.

Graham Martin: "*The Wild Swans at Coole,*" 54-72; on the inner coherence of the two volumes published under this title.

Donald Davie: "*Michael Robartes and the Dancer,*" 73-87; also concerned with the inner structure of the volume. Discusses its prominent theme, "the matter of woman's role in society," and syntactical aspects.

John Holloway: "Style and World in *The Tower,*" 88-105. Yeats's "common idiom" is by no means "colloquial" but rather a private language, through which he creates his own world. This is an interesting article, marred by obscure writing and garbled quotations.

Denis Donoghue: "On *The Winding Stair,*" 106-23; reprinted in CB131. "The question which storms and cries through the entire book: in a world of mutability, what remains, what is possible, where does Value reside? The answer, but not the whole story, is: in the imagination of Man."

J. R. Mulryne: "The *Last Poems,*" 124-42.

Peter Ure: "The Plays," 143-64.

Ian Fletcher: "Rhythm and Pattern in *Autobiographies,*" 165-89. Reprinted in CB160.

Reviews:

- Anon., *NYTBR,* 10 July 1966, 49.
- A. Norman Jeffares, *RES,* 18:69 (Feb 1967), 93-94.
- L. F. McNamara, *MQR,* 7:1 (Jan 1968), 68-69.
- John Montague, *CritQ,* 8:4 (Winter 1966), 381-83.
- Hermann Peschmann, *English,* 16:92 (Summer 1966), 67-69.
- Christopher Ricks: "Yeats & Facts," *Encounter,* 27:1 (July 1966), 50-54.
- V. K. Titlestad, *ESA,* 9:2 (Sept 1966), 215-17.

23. DONOGHUE, DENIS: *Yeats.* London: Fontana/Collins, 1971. 140 pp. (Fontana Modern Masters.)

An exposé of "Yeats's sensibility," developed through a consideration of key concepts. Yeats is a poet who judges imagination superior to experience, a man who wants to exert power through his work, whose most important article of faith is a "sense of consciousness as conflict," hence as drama.

Reviews:
- Anon., *Times,* 13 May 1971, 9.
- Gulliver Boyle: "Beautiful Women v. the Furies," *Teacher,* 6 Aug 1971, 7.
- Anthony Cronin: "Yeats Seminar," *IrP,* 26 June 1971, 12.
- Jacques Darras: "Mesures de Yeats," *Critique,* 31:338 (July 1975), 696-706.
- [G. S. Fraser]: "Yeats as a Modern Master," *TLS,* 17 Mar 1972, 311.
- Roy Fuller: "Trumpets?" *List,* 23 Sept 1971, 416-17.
- Claire Hahn, *Commonweal,* 28 Apr 1972, 196-97.
- Rolf Hermann Lass, *J of European Studies,* 1:4 (Dec 1971), 379.
- Christopher Lehmann-Haupt: "Sigmund Freud and W. B. Yeats," *NYT,* 18 Nov 1971, 45.
- Laurence Lerner: "The Circus Animals," *Spect,* 8 Jan 1972, 45-46.
- John P. White: "Conceptions of the Self," *Tablet,* 29 May 1971, 527.
- Terence de Vere White: "In the Bee-Loud Glade," *IrT,* 17 July 1971, 10; correspondence by Jeananne Crowley, 22 July 1971, 11.
- H. Williams, *New Edinburgh R,* 17 (1972), 25.

24. DUBLIN MAGAZINE: "W. B. Yeats Centenary Edition," *DM,* 4:2 (Summer 1965).

See CB59, CD832, FD37, and HD22.

25. EIGO SEINEN / THE RISING GENERATION: Yeats number, *Eigo Seinen,* 111:11 (1 Nov 1965).

18 essays on Yeats, two of which are in English (see CC329 and CD788). The Japanese items are not listed in this bibliography.

26. ELLMANN, RICHARD: *The Identity of Yeats.* NY: Oxford UP, 1964 [1954]. xxv, 342 pp. (Galaxy Books. GB126.)

Incorporates "The Art of Yeats: Affirmative Capability," *KR,* 15:3 (Summer 1953), 357-85; "Yeats without Analogue," *KR,* 26:1 (Winter 1964), 30-47 (appears as preface to the 1964 edition only and is reprinted in CB148a).

One of the basic Yeats studies; a description of the development of Yeats's work, particularly of the poetry. Analyzed in sections DD and EE.

Reviews:
- Hazard Adams: "Yeats the Stylist and Yeats the Irishman," *Accent,* 5:3 (Summer 1955), 234-37.

- Anon., *Adelphi,* 31:1 (1954), 93-94.
- Anon., *USQBR,* 10:4 (Dec 1954), 499-500.
- Sally Appleton, *Thought,* 30:117 (Summer 1955), 319-20.
- Reuben A. Brower: "The Incarnation of Yeats," *YR,* 44:2 (Dec 1954), 290-92.
- Rivers Carew, *DM,* 4:3/4 (Autumn-Winter 1965), 106-7.
- Austin Clarke: "Second Thoughts," *IrT,* 4 Sept 1954, 8.
- C. Day Lewis, *LMag,* 1:10 (Nov 1954), 85-88.
- Denis Donoghue, *Studies,* 43:[ ] (Winter 1954), 482-84.
- J. A. Dowling, *DM,* 30 [i.e., 29]:4 (Oct-Dec 1954), 56-58.
- Johannes Edfelt: *Utblick.* Stockholm: Bonnier, 1958, 218 pp. ("Nytt ljus över Yeats," 93-100).
- H. I'A. F[ausset]: "Yeats," *MGuard,* 24 Aug 1954, 4.
- [G. S. Fraser]: "Yeats Set in Place," *TLS,* 3 Sept 1954, 554; correspondence by J. M. Hone, 10 Sept 1954, 573, confirming that Yeats read Leibniz.
- Iain Hamilton: "All Metaphor," *Spect,* 6 Aug 1954, 176-77.
- T. R. Henn: "When That Story's Finished, What's the News?" *NSt,* 9 Oct 1954, 447-48.
- Hugh Kenner: "Unpurged Images," *HudR,* 8:4 (Winter 1956), 609-17.
- Chris McCully: "The Wild Old Wicked Man," *PNR,* 38 (10:6) (1984), 63-64.
- Vivian Mercier: "W. B. Yeats," *Commonweal,* 21 Jan 1955, 435-36.
- Raymond Mortimer: "The Progress of a Poet," *SunT,* 15 Aug 1954, 3.
- Herbert Read: "W. B. Yeats," *List,* 7 Oct 1954, 582, 585.
- T[erence] S[mith], *IrW,* 28 (Sept 1954), 67-68.
- G. T.: "A Study of Yeats," *IrI,* 20 Nov 1954, 6.
- George Whalley, *QQ,* 62:4 (Winter 1956), 617-21.

27. ENGELBERG, EDWARD: *The Vast Design: Patterns in W. B. Yeats's Aesthetic.* Toronto: U of Toronto Press, 1965 [1964]. xxxi, 224 pp. Second edition, expanded: Washington, D.C.: Catholic U of America Press, 1988. xxxv, 284 pp. Based on "The Herald of Art: A Study of W. B. Yeats' Criticism and Aesthetic," °Ph.D. thesis, U of Wisconsin, 1958. 528 pp. (*DAI,* 18:6 [June 1958], 2140); incorporates "Picture and Gesture in the Yeatsian Aesthetic," *Criticism,* 3:2 (Spring 1961), 101-20, and "Passionate Reverie: W. B. Yeats's Tragic Correlative," *UTQ,* 31:2 (Jan 1962), 201-22. Analyzed in section DD.

Reviews:

- Hazard Adams, *JEGP,* 64:3 (July 1965), 596-98.
- James L. Allen, *MP,* 62:4 (May 1965), 369-70.
- Harold Bloom: "Myth, Vision, Allegory," *YR,* 54:1 (Oct 1964), 143-49.
- Frederic S. Colwell, *QQ,* 71:3 (Autumn 1964), 446-47.
- David Fitzgerald, *Dubliner,* 3:3 (Autumn 1964), 56-57.
- [G. S. Fraser]: "From Sligo to Byzantium," *TLS,* 24 June 1965, 529-30.
- Paul J. Hurley, *CE,* 26:2 (Nov 1964), 170-71.
- Thomas Parkinson, *MQR,* 4:2 (Spring 1965), 146-47.
- Robert L. Peters, *Criticism,* 6:4 (Fall 1964), 386-87.
- B. Rajan: "Conflict, More Conflict!" *UTQ,* 35:3 (Apr 1966), 315-20.
- A. G. Stock, *BJA,* 4:4 (Oct 1964), 373-75.
- Peter Ure, *ES,* 47:2 (Apr 1966), 154-57.
- George T. Wright, *JAAC,* 23:3 (Spring 1965), 392-93.
- Dudley Young, *CambR,* 88:2113 (15 Jan 1966), 185-86.

28. ENGLISH: "W. B. Yeats: 1865-1939," *English,* 15:89 (Summer 1965).
Includes CA49, 124, CD968, DD469, DE2, HD169, and a review of CA48.

28a. FAGERBERG, SVEN: *Friheten att älska: Essäer* [The freedom to love: Essays]. Stockholm: Alba, 1986. 211 pp.
Much of the book is devoted to meditations on Yeats, especially on *At the Hawk's Well* and *The Only Jealousy of Emer;* they are written in the form of essays or dialogs with Fand, the author's adopted daughter.

29. FINNERAN, RICHARD J. (ed): *Critical Essays on W. B. Yeats.* Boston: Hall, 1986. viii, 258 pp.
The selection of the essays was made by the critics themselves; they were asked "to choose their own most appropriate essays for inclusion in this volume" (p. v). Contains "Introduction," 1-8 (a short survey of Yeats criticism) and 14 previously printed pieces (not analyzed in this bibliography).

30. FRASER, GEORGE SUTHERLAND: *W. B. Yeats.* London: Longmans, Green, for British Council and the National Book League, 1968 [1954]. 44 pp. (Writers and Their Work. 50.)
Mostly on the poetry, of which the later work is preferred to the earlier; underrates the plays and the prose. Reviewed by Kathleen Raine: "Master of Ideas," *NSt,* 12 June 1954, 764-65.
Reprinted in CB167 and DB90. For a revised version see *British Writers.* Edited under the auspices of the British Council. General editor Ian Scott-Kilvert. Volume VI: Thomas Hardy to Wilfred Owen. NY: Scribner's, 1983. xxxv, 460 pp. (pp. 207-24).

31. GENET, JACQUELINE: *William Butler Yeats: Les fondements et l'évolution de la création poétique. Essai de psychologie littéraire.* Villeneuve d'Ascq: Publications de l'Université de Lille III, 1976. 768 pp. (Etudes irlandaises. 3.)
Based on a °Doctorat d'Etat thesis, Université de Paris III, 1973. Discusses Yeats's biography; his poetry in chronological order; the mythological, religious, occult, philosophical, and literary sources; the poetic theory; and, as a summarizing conclusion, the concept of Unity of Being.
Reviews:
- Terence Brown, *IUR,* 6:2 (Autumn 1976), 256-59.
- Hubert Juin: "La formation d'une mythologie," *Monde,* 29 Oct 1976, 22.
- Johannes Kleinstück, *Erasmus,* 30:9 (10 May 1978), 278-79.
- Andrew Parkin, *CJIS,* 5:1 (June 1979), 112-14.
- Marilyn Gaddis Rose, *ACIS Newsletter,* 9:2 (Apr 1979), 2-3.
- Raymond Tschumi, *ES,* 58:4 (Aug 1977), 366-67.

32. ——— (ed): *William Butler Yeats.* Paris: Editions de l'Herne, 1981. 451 pp. (Cahiers de l'Herne. 40.)
For individual items see BG201, CA90, CB194, CD45, 112, 349, 658, 786, 1316, DB188, DD272, 448, 716, EE4, 46, 334, FA27, 45, FD32, FE62, 68, and G322. Includes J. Genet: "Bibliographie française," 442-51 (incomplete); a preface by Michael Yeats; translations of poems, plays and prose pieces; and several illustrations.
Reviews:
- Nicholas Grene, *EA,* 38:2 (Apr-June 1985), 240-41.
- Michel Le Bris: "L'Irlande à la vie à la mort," *Nouvel observateur,* 31 July 1982, 44-46.

- Eric Neuhoff: "Yeats: L'élégant irlandais," *Quotidien de Paris*, 25 Aug 1981, 28.

33. GILBERT, SANDRA: *The Poetry of William Butler Yeats*. NY: Monarch Press, 1965. 133 pp. (Monarch Notes and Study Guides. 00738.)

Introduction to the poetry and plays on the undergraduate level.

34. GREEN, HENRY MACKENZIE: *The Poetry of W. B. Yeats*. An address delivered before the Australian English Association, Sydney, on November 19, 1931. Sydney: Australasian Medical Publishing Co., 1931. 61 pp. (Australian English Association. Leaflet Dec 1931. No. 13.)

A sensible, though not very deep, introduction to Yeats's life and work; discusses his biography, his place in the history of English poetry (comparing him with Blake, Shelley, Keats, Milton, and others), the four phases of his poetical development, his verse structures, and the question of whether he is a poet of escape. Does not pretend to understand the later poetry.

35. GWYNN, STEPHEN (ed): *William Butler Yeats: Essays in Tribute*. Port Washington, N.Y.: Kennikat Press, 1965 [1940]. viii, 229 pp.

The first edition was entitled *Scattering Branches: Tributes to the Memory of W. B. Yeats*. Contents: S. Gwynn: "Scattering Branches," 1-14; i.e., paying homage.

Maud Gonne: "Yeats and Ireland," 15-33; reminiscences and MG's personal view of what WBY did and did not do for Ireland.

Sir William Rothenstein: "Yeats as a Painter Saw Him," 35-54; reminiscences with notes on Yeats's relationship with Tagore and Dorothy Wellesley.

Lennox Robinson: "The Man and the Dramatist," 55-114. See also BB207.

W. G. Fay: "The Poet and the Actor," 115-34.

Edmund Dulac: "Without the Twilight," 135-44.

F. R. Higgins: "Yeats as Irish Poet," 145-55.

C. Day Lewis: "A Note on W. B. Yeats and the Aristocratic Tradition," 157-82.

L. A. G. Strong: "William Butler Yeats," 183-229.

Reviews:

- Anon.: "To the Memory of W. B. Yeats: 'The Greatest Poet of His Time,'" *IrT*, 10 Aug 1940, 5.
- Anon.: "A Garland of Tributes to Yeats," *NYTBR*, 18 May 1941, 2.
- G. M. Brady, *DM*, 16:3 (July-Sept 1941), 64-65.
- James Burnham: "Yeats," *Commonweal*, 16 May 1941, 88-89.
- [Austin Clarke]: "Tributes to Yeats: Poetry and the Theatre," *TLS*, 3 Aug 1940, 376.
- Thomas Quinn Curtiss: "Yeats and the Irish Drama," *Decision*, 1:6 (June 1941), 78-80.
- Babette Deutsch: "Living Memories of W. B. Yeats," *NYHTB*, 11 May 1941, 2.
- J. J. H[ogan], *Studies*, 29:116 (Dec 1940), 650-53.
- Winfield Townley Scott: "The Foolish, Passionate Man," *Accent*, 1:4 (Summer 1941), 247-50.
- Stephen Spender: "Wise Man and Fool," *NSt*, 31 Aug 1940, 214-15.
- James Stephens: "Homage to W. B. Yeats," *Spect*, 12 July 1940, 40. Reprinted in CD1245.

36. HALL, JAMES, and MARTIN STEINMANN (eds): *The Permanence of Yeats*. NY: Collier Books, 1961 [1950]. ix, 371 pp. (Collier Books. BS11.)

Perhaps the best collection of previously published criticism, although it neglects the early work and is somewhat out of date now. For individual contributions see BA8 (review by Zabel), CB68, 106, 118, 422, 426, 484, 527, CC321, 338, DB10, 20, 52, 72, 124, 140, 162, 198, 228, DC59, 178, DD540, EB10, and G384.

Also contained: [The editors]: "The Seven Sacred Trances," 1-8; discusses the problem of belief in Yeats's poetry and concludes that "Yeats habitually translates from his private system to public symbols."

"A Select Bibliography of Articles and Books, in Whole or in Part, on Yeats," 349-71; about 460 pre-1950 items.

Reviews:

- M. C. Bradbrook, *MLR,* 46:3-4 (July-Sept 1951), 498-99.
- Malcolm Brown, *MLQ,* 13:4 (Dec 1952), 413-15.
- [Austin Clarke]: "Yeats and His Critics," *TLS,* 25 Aug 1950, 525-26.
- Babette Deutsch: "'High-Powered Exegesis' of William Butler Yeats, His Plays and Poems: A Critical Symposium Finds Authorities Disagreeing on Almost Every Aspect of Him Except His Greatness," *NYHTB,* 5 Feb 1950, 3.
- Richard Ellmann: "Philandering with the Sixth Sense," *SatR,* 15 Apr 1950, 49.
- Dudley Fitts: "Yeats Meets the Critics," *NYTBR,* 5 Feb 1950, 5.
- John M. Flynn: "Yeats Weathers the Test of Literary Permanence," *Chicago Sunday Tribune,* 5 Mar 1950, part 4, 10.
- James Gallagher: "W. B. Yeats's Permanence," *Spirit,* 17:2 (May 1950), 51-55.
- Isabel Gamble, *Poetry,* 76:4 (July 1950), 227-29.
- A. M. Klein: "The Masked Yeats," *Northern R,* 3:5 (June-July 1950), 43-45. Reprinted on pp. 282-84 of Klein's *Literary Essays and Reviews.* Edited by Usher Caplan and M. W. Steinberg. Toronto: U of Toronto Press, 1987. xxix, 424 pp.
- Robin Mayhead: "American Criticism," *Scrutiny,* 19:1 (Oct 1952), 65-75 (see 69-71).
- Vivian Mercier, *Commonweal,* 2 June 1950, 204-5.
- Thomas Riggs, *MLN,* 66:4 (Apr 1951), 280-81.
- G. S., *SF Chronicle,* 23 Apr 1950, This World section, 27.
- Donald A. Stauffer: "Measure of a Poet," *NewRep,* 20 Mar 1950, 20-21.
- W. D. T[empleman], *Personalist,* 32:2 (Apr 1951), 214.

37. HENN, THOMAS RICE: *The Lonely Tower: Studies in the Poetry of W. B. Yeats.* Revised edition. London: Methuen, 1965 [1950]. xxiv, 375 pp. (University Paperbacks. UP 126.)

On the Irish background, the theory of the mask and of self and anti-self, women in the poetry, the love poetry, Yeats and Synge, the Byzantium motif, the influence of painting, the poetry of the plays, and other subjects. The first edition includes a note on Yeats's collection of lantern slides intended for use on the American lecture tours.

Reviews:

- Anon., *Adelphi,* 27:2 (1951), 184, 187.
- Anon., *List,* 25 Jan 1951, 152-53.
- A. C. Boyd: "Commentary on Yeats," *Britain To-day,* 180 (Apr 1951), 46.
- M. C. Bradbrook: "The Country of Yeats and the Countries of His Mind," *CambR,* 72:1761 (21 Apr 1951), 428, 430.
- M.-L. Cazamian: "L'évolution de W. B. Yeats après ses dernières oeuvres," *EA,* 5:1 (Feb 1952), 50-54.
- Austin Clarke: "The Mind's Eye," *IrT,* 27 Jan 1951, 6.

- ———: "Yeats: A Centenary Tribute," *IrP,* 12 June 1965, 12.
- Mary Colum: "This Poet Was Quite Often 'Fighting Mad': A New Study of the Many Influences That Shaped the Ideas of W. B. Yeats," *NYTBR,* 10 Feb 1952, 1. See letter by Harry Goldgar: "Yeats and Mallarmé," 2 Mar 1952, 30; and reply by Mary M. Colum, 16 Mar 1952, 26.
- Babette Deutsch: "Some Backgrounds of the Art of Yeats: A New Study Centers on the Inter-relation of His Work and His Life," *NYHTB,* 10 Feb 1952, 4.
- Ronald Dunlop: "W. B. Yeats, 1865-1939," *PoetryA,* 6 (Oct 1965), 36-39.
- Richard Eberhart: "New Looks at Yeats," *VQR,* 28:4 (Autumn 1952), 618-21.
- Richard Ellmann: "Three Ways of Looking at a Triton," *SR,* 61:1 (Jan-Mar 1953), 149-56.
- Gareth Lloyd Evans: "Yeats: Mirror of His Age," *Birmingham Post,* 5 June 1965, II.
- K. F., *Irish Book Lover,* 31:6 (Nov 1951), 143.
- Kimon Friar: "Contrapuntal Serpent," *NewRep,* 28 Apr 1952, 17-18.
- Charles Graves: "Consistency in Yeats," *Scotsman,* 12 June 1965, Weekend Magazine, 2.
- P[atrick] K[avanagh], *Bell,* 16:5 (Feb 1951), 69-70, 72.
- Roy McFadden, *IrW,* 14 (Mar 1951), 63-65.
- Francis MacManus: "Yeats: The Tree Still Flourishes," *Sunday Press,* 13 June 1965, 21.
- Giorgio Melchiori, *N&Q,* os 211 / ns 13:3 (Mar 1966), 114-17.
- Edwin Muir: "Yeats and His Mask," *Obs,* 10 Dec 1950, 7.
- Richard Murphy: "Footnotes to Yeats," *Spect,* 23 Mar 1951, 390, 392.
- John Frederick Nims: "On the Trifles of W. B. Yeats' Perfection," *Chicago Sunday Tribune,* 17 Feb 1952, part 4, 8.
- Horace Reynolds: "'To Follow Yeats Down All the Diverse Paths,'" *CSM,* 12 June 1952, 13.
- Lennox Robinson, *Irish Library Bulletin,* 12:[2-3] (Feb-Mar 1951), 22.
- W. R. Rodgers: "The Poetry of Contraries," *NSt,* 6 Jan 1951, 18.
- Grover Smith, *New Mexico Q,* 23:3 (Autumn 1953), 325-26.
- K. R. Srinivasa Iyengar, *Aryan Path,* 22:5 (May 1951), 219-20.
- W. D. T[empleman], *Personalist,* 34:2 (Spring 1953), 205-6.
- [P. Tomlinson]: "Studies in the Poetry of Yeats," *TLS,* 16 Feb 1951, 104.
- Peter Ure, *Cambridge J,* 4:12 (Sept 1951), 762-66.

38. ———: *Last Essays.* Gerrards Cross: Smythe, 1976. 253 pp.
All essays are at least in part on Yeats. Contains: "'The Place of Shells,'" 13-25; on Sligo in Yeats's works, including notes on Yeats's prosody and on the International Yeats Summer School. Also in CA51.

"The Weasel's Tooth," 26-50; on Anglo-Irish attitudes and political violence.

"Choice and Chance," 51-64; in Yeats's life and works.

"The Centenary Yeats," 65-80: "My task . . . is to attempt the impossible . . . to set the poetry of Yeats, first, against his background, and to some extent my own: and then against our own climate of opinion forty years after he wrote his greatest poetry."

"Yeats and the Poetry of War," 81-97; revised from *PBA,* 51 (1965), 301-19. Discusses Yeats's treatment of the Easter Rising and the Irish civil war.

"The Rhetoric of Yeats," 98-118. Revised from CA48.

"The Lighter Side of the Irish Literary Revival," 119-36. The parodies and pastiches of Susan L. Mitchell and George Moore.

"The Sainthood of A. E.," 137-56.

"Yeats and the Picture Galleries," 157-72; reprinted from *SoR*, 1:1 (Jan 1965), 57-75; discusses the important and controversial motif of painters and paintings in Yeats's poetry and plays.

"George Moore," 173-90.

"J. M. Synge: A Reconsideration," 191-206.

"The Big House," 207-20.

"'The Property of the Dead,'" 221-39; the theme of death in Yeats's works.

"Towards the Values," 240-53; reprinted from *SoR*, 5:3 (July 1969), 833-49. Those who criticize Yeats for his style, occultism, politics, and other characteristics usually overlook the many real values that his work contains.

Reviews:

- Denis Donoghue: "The Last of Anglo-Ireland?" *Spect*, 21 Aug 1976, 21.
- J. R. Mulryne, *MLR*, 74:3 (July 1979), 686-87.

39. HERMATHENA: "Yeats Number," *Hermathena*, 101 (Autumn 1965).
See CB142, DD186, EC47, and review of DB144.

40. HIRST, DESIRÉE, and GEOFFREY MATHEWS: *W. B. Yeats: Poet of Love, Politics and the Other World. / W. B. Yeats: Yeats' Interest in Politics, the Paranormal and Old Age*. London: Audio Learning, 1983. Cassette, ca. 37 mins.

Includes "Supplementary Notes" (seven mimeographed pages).

41. HONE, JOSEPH MAUNSELL: *William Butler Yeats: The Poet in Contemporary Ireland*. Dublin: Maunsel, [1916]. vii, 134 pp. (Irishmen of To-day.)

Reprinted: °Folcroft, Pa.: Folcroft Library Editions, 1973; °Norwood, Pa.: Norwood Editions, 1976.

A study in three parts: early life and work; Irish and other influences; theater and later work. No index. In some ways this book is more satisfactory than Hone's later biography (BA8).

Reviews:

- [T. W. H. Crosland?]: "Irishmen of To-day," *Academy*, 12 May 1916, 10-11. "Yeats, as we all know, is a lesser poet than AE might have been."
- [Ellen M. Duncan]: "The Irish Renaissance," *Athenaeum*, 4601 (Jan 1916), 24-25.
- [Darrell Figgis]: "W. B. Yeats," *TLS*, 13 Jan 1916, 17. Attacks the alleged superficiality of Yeats's public rhetoric.
- [Charles Larcom Graves]: "Two Irishmen," *Spect*, 25 Dec 1915, 921-22.
- Crawford Neil: "W. B. Yeats," *New Ireland*, 18 Dec 1915, 98-100.
- R. Ellis Roberts: "W. B. Yeats," *BmL*, 50:299 (Aug 1916), 139-40.

42. IRISH BOOK: "Special Yeats Issue," *IrB*, 2:3/4 (Autumn 1963).
See AA5, 15, AE77, CD253, CE394, CF17, DD726, and FE31.

43. IRISH TIMES: *William Butler Yeats Aetat. 70*. [Dublin: Irish Times, 1935]. 16 pp.

Reprinted from *IrT*, 13 June 1935, 6-8. Contents: Anon.: "Ad

Multos Annos," 3-4.

Francis Hackett: "Place in World Letters: 'A Crucible of an Art,'" 5-6.

Sean O Faolain: "Philosophy of W. B. Yeats: Two Elements at War," 7-8. Mystery and intellect, self and anti-self.

F. R. Higgins: "The Poet of a Dream: Where 'Beauty Is Taut, Passion Precise,'" 8-9.

Denis Johnston: "Yeats as Dramatist: Tenacity of Purpose through Thirty Years," 10-11.

Aodh de Blacam: "Yeats and the Nation: A Surrender to Subjectivity. Why the Abbey Ideal Failed," 11-14. The Abbey failed because its dramatists came from the Ascendancy and were out of touch with the Irish people.

Andrew E. Malone: "Yeats and the Abbey: School of Dramatists and School of Acting," 15-16.

See also correspondence by Florence Lynch, 14 June 1935, 4; and Anon.: "World-Wide Greetings: Mr. Yeats's Birthday Mail. Plans for the Future," 15 June 1935, 6.

44. ———: *W. B. Yeats, 1865-1965: A Centenary Tribute*. [Dublin: Irish Times, 1965]. viii pp.

A supplement to the *Irish Times,* 10 June 1965, photographs by Jack MacManus and drawings by Ruth Brandt. Individual contributions listed under BB26, 40, 119, 146, CB55, CC166, CD7, 13, 48, 501, 701, 929, DB113, EC15, EF61, FD59, 79, and HD50.

45. IRISH WRITING: "W. B. Yeats: A Special Number," *IrW,* 31 (Summer 1955).

See CA124, CD208, DB132, DC10, EB76, FA79, and G1033.

Reviews:

- Denis Donoghue: "Mummy Truths to Tell," *IrT,* 24 Sept 1955, 6.
- Anthony Hartley, *Spect,* 2 Dec 1955, 778.
- John Jordan: "Yeats and Irish Writing," *IrP,* 17 Sept 1955, 4.

46. JAMES JOYCE QUARTERLY: "Yeats Issue," *JJQ,* 3:2 (Winter 1966).

See CE352, CH14, DA30, DC294, and EA41.

47. JEFFARES, ALEXANDER NORMAN: *W. B. Yeats: Man and Poet*. NY: Barnes & Noble, 1966 [1949]. ix, 365 pp. (Barnes & Noble Paperback. 421.)

Based on °"The Sources & Symbolism of the Later Poems of William Butler Yeats," Ph.D. thesis, Trinity College, Dublin, 1945; and on °"W. B. Yeats: Man and Poet," D.Phil. thesis, Oxford U, 1947. ix, 204, 243 pp.

As the title indicates, a biography-cum-criticism type of study. Valuable for background and firsthand information about the Yeats family and friends; the interpretations, however, do not go very deep. Contains numerous small inaccuracies.

Reviews:

- Anon., *DM,* 25:5 [i.e., 25:1] (Jan-Mar 1950), 54-56.
- A. W. J. Becker: "In Search of Yeats," *Isis,* 19 May 1949, 16.
- Thomas Bodkin: "W. B. Yeats," *Birmingham Post,* 17 May 1949, 2.
- Austin Clarke: "A Poet's Progress," *IrT,* 14 May 1949, 6.
- [———]: "An Interpreter of Yeats," *TLS,* 3 June 1949, 363.
- ———: "The Rending of the Veil," *Enquiry,* 2:1 (July 1949), 70-72.
- Mary Colum: "To a Yeatsian Urn," *SatR,* 28 Jan 1950, 14-16.
- Bruce Cutler: "Introductions and Conclusions," *Poetry,* 112:1 (Apr 1968), 52-56.

- Richard Ellmann, *MLN,* 66:5 (May 1951), 335-36.
- Isabel Gamble: "Two Views of Yeats," *Hopkins R,* 3:2 (Winter 1950), 52-54.
- Robert Greacen: "Masks and the Man," *Poetry Q,* 11:2 (Summer 1949), 115-17.
- Horace Gregory: "Yeats: A Self-Made Poet," *NYTBR,* 25 Dec 1949, 4, 14.
- H. W. Häusermann, *ES,* 30:5 (Oct 1949), 278-79.
- Lawrence Haward: "W. B. Yeats," *MGuard,* 3 June 1949, 4.
- F. W. van Heerikhuizen: "Gedreven door angst," *Litterair paspoort,* 7:53 (Jan 1952), 10-11.
- B. P. Howell, *Aryan Path,* 20:10 (Oct 1949), 462-63.
- John o' London: "More about W. B. Yeats," *John o' London's Weekly,* 24 June 1949, 375.
- Patrick Kavanagh: "A Running Commentary on Yeats," *Spect,* 13 May 1949, 650.
- John Lehmann: "W. B. Yeats," *Time and Tide,* 2 July 1949, 679-80.
- J. B. Leishman, *RES,* 1:4 (Oct 1950), 375-77.
- R[oger] McH[ugh], *Studies,* 39:155 (Sept 1950), 345-46.
- M. J. MacM[anus]: "Yeats: A New Study," *IrP,* 7 July 1949, 6.
- Vivian Mercier, *Commonweal,* 21 Oct 1949, 48-49.
- J. B. Morton: "William Butler Yeats," *Tablet,* 11 June 1949, 384-85.
- Hermann Peschmann: "Portrait in a Mirror," *Student,* 18 Jan 1951, 241-43.
- R. G. G. Price, *New English R,* 3:2 (Aug 1949), 142-43.
- Horace Reynolds: "Poet of Our Time," *CSM,* 29 Dec 1949, 11.
- A. Rivoallan, *EA,* 5:1 (Feb 1952), 80-81.
- Mario M. Rossi: "Yeats nella sua torre incantata," *Nazione,* 18 Mar 1950, 3.
- Cecil ffrench Salkeld: "The Growth of Genius," *IrW,* 9 (Oct 1949), 68-69.
- George Brandon Saul: "Jeffares on Yeats," *MLN,* 66:4 (Apr 1951), 246-49. Corrects numerous inaccuracies. See Jeffares's reply: "Saul on Jeffares," *MLN,* 67:7 (Nov 1952), 501-2.
- Elizabeth Schneider: "Two Studies of Yeats," *Nation,* 29 July 1950, 112-13.
- Edith Shackleton: "New Books," *Lady,* 19 May 1949, 454.
- George N. Shuster: "A Dutch Monument to a Great Irish Poet," *NYHTB,* 4 Dec 1949, 36.
- Rex Warner: "Man and Poet," *Books of the Month,* Aug 1949, 17.
- Neil Weiss: "The Material of Yeats' Poetry," *New Leader,* 5 Nov 1949, 9.
- H. O. W[hite], *Hermathena,* 74 (Nov 1949), 76-77.

48. ———, and KENNETH GUSTAV WALTER CROSS (eds): *In Excited Reverie: A Centenary Tribute to William Butler Yeats, 1865-1939*. London: Macmillan, 1965. viii, 354 pp.

Contains AD6, BB208, 209, CA38, 49, CC73, 92, CD22, 1241, DD45, EA41, FB1, FD59, FE93, HD75, 86, 107, and 171. Many of the following reviews are concerned with O'Brien's article on Yeats's politics (FD59).

Reviews:

- Anon.: "Poet's Centenary," *Economist,* 5 June 1965, 1179.
- Anon., *Quarterly R,* 303:646 (Oct 1965), 464-65.
- Rivers Carew: "Bread That Tastes Sour," *DM,* 4:3/4 (Autumn-Winter 1965), 91-93.
- Austin Clarke: "Yeats: A Centenary Tribute," *IrP,* 12 June 1965, 12.

- Cyril Connolly: "Notes Towards an Understanding of Yeats," *SunT,* 13 June 1965, 43. Reprinted in *The Evening Colonnade.* London: Bruce & Watson, 1973. 519 pp. (pp. 244-49).
- Patrick Cosgrave: "Yeats, Fascism and Conor O'Brien," *LMag,* 7:4 (July 1967), 22-41. Accuses O'Brien of garbling the facts and of lack of evidence.
- Donald Davie: "Bardolators and Blasphemers," *Guardian,* 12 June 1965, 7.
- Denis Donoghue: "Bend Sinister," *IrT,* 5 June 1965, 8. Correspondence by Anthony Cronin, 10 June 1965, 9; Grattan Freyer and Arland Ussher, 16 June 1965, 7; Dermot MacManus, 17 June 1965, 9; and others.
- William Empson: "A Time of Troubles," *NSt,* 23 July 1965, 123-24. Correspondence by Conor Cruise O'Brien: "Yeats's Politics," 27 Aug 1965, 284-85; Empson, 10 Sept 1965, 354. Empson's review and reply are reprinted in CB149a.
- Gareth Lloyd Evans: "Yeats: Mirror of His Age," *Birmingham Post,* 5 June 1965, II.
- [G. S. Fraser]: "From Sligo to Byzantium," *TLS,* 24 June 1965, 529-30. Correspondence by Owen Sheehy-Skeffington re Hanna Sheehy Skeffington and what she thought about Yeats and his "fascism," and the reviewer's answer, 8 July 1965, 579; by Anthony Comerford on Yeats and fascism, 15 July 1965, 597.
- Michael P. Gallagher, *Studies,* 54:214-15 (Summer-Autumn 1965), 284-88.
- Charles Graves: "Consistency in Yeats," *Scotsman,* 12 June 1965, Weekend Magazine, 2.
- Hilton Kramer: "The Politics of Yeats," *New Leader,* 22 Nov 1965, 22-23. Particularly on O'Brien's essay, which he endorses wholeheartedly.
- Francis MacManus: "Yeats: The Tree Still Flourishes," *Sunday Press,* 13 June 1965, 21.
- Giorgio Manganelli: "Un simposio per Yeats: Il mago astuto," *Mondo,* 17 Aug 1965, 9. Reprinted on pp. 72-75 in *La letteratura come menzogna.* Milano: Feltrinelli, 1967. 180 pp. (Materiali. 11.)
- John Montague, *CritQ,* 8:4 (Winter 1966), 381-83.
- Harry T. Moore: "Time Pardons Him for Writing Well," *SatR,* 11 Dec 1965, 39, 81.
- Frank O'Connor: "Yeats," *Sunday Independent,* 13 June 1965, 10.
- Sir Charles Petrie: "Recalling a Great Irish Poet," *ILN,* 12 June 1965, 24.
- W. R. Rodgers, *List,* 25 Nov 1965, 867-68.
- Martin Seymour-Smith: "The Honoured Guest," *Spect,* 11 June 1965, 760.
- Priscilla W. Shaw: "The Yeats Centenary: Part of the Harvest," *VQR,* 42:1 (Winter 1966), 173-76.
- John Unterecker, *CE,* 27:7 (Apr 1966), 580-81.
- Peter Ure, *RES,* 17:66 (May 1966), 224-27.
- Donald Weeks, *JAAC,* 25:4 (Summer 1967), 471-72.
- M[argaret] W[illy], *English,* 15:89 (Summer 1965), 185-86.

49. JEFFARES, ALEXANDER NORMAN: *The Circus Animals: Essays on W. B. Yeats.* London: Macmillan, 1970. x, 183 pp.

Reprinted and revised essays (first publications in parentheses): "Yeats's Mask," 3-14 (*ES,* 30:6 [Dec 1949], 289-98). The theory of the mask and the mask symbol in Yeats's works.

"Yeats, Public Man, 15-28 ("Yeats as Public Man," *Poetry,* 98:4 [July 1961], 253-63; "Yeats the Public Man," in Donoghue:

The Integrity of Yeats [1964, CA21], 21-32). Originally a review of *Senate Speeches* (W211R/S); comments on politics in Yeats's poetry.

"Poet's Tower," 29-46 ("Thoor, Ballylee," *ES,* 28:6 [Dec 1947], 161-68; "Poet's Tower," *Envoy,* 5:20 [July 1951], 45-55). The tower symbol in Yeats's poetry and the influence of Milton and Shelley.

"Yeats, Critic," 47-77 ("Yeats as Critic," *English,* 15:89 [Summer 1965], 173-76; "The Criticism of Yeats," *Phoenix,* 10 [Summer 1965], 27-45).

"Women in Yeats's Poetry," 78-102 (CA109, q.v.).

"Gyres in Yeats's Poetry," 103-14 ("'Gyres' in the Poetry of W. B. Yeats," *ES,* 27:3 [June 1946], 65-74). Includes comments on *A Vision.*

"John Butler Yeats, Anglo-Irishman," 117-46 ("John Butler Yeats," in CA48, 24-47; *DM,* 4:2 [Summer 1965], 30-37). Comments on the JBY-WBY relationship.

"Oliver St. John Gogarty, Irishman," 147-74 (*PBA,* 46 [1960], 73-98). Includes remarks on the Yeats-Gogarty relationship.

Reviews:
- Terence Brown: "Life as Art," *IrT,* 3 Oct 1970, 8.
- [G. S. Fraser]: "Saving Yeats from the Critics," *TLS,* 12 Mar 1971, 292.
- Robert Greacen: "Aspects of Yeats," *Tribune,* 27 Nov 1970, 10.
- John S. Kelly: "Pathways," *IrP,* 21 Nov 1970, 12.
- Brendan Kennelly: "Yeats, Ltd.," *Hibernia,* 9 Oct 1970, 13.
- Frank Lentricchia: "Yeats and Stevens," *ConL,* 14:2 (Spring 1973), 247-52.
- Norman H. MacKenzie: "The Yeats Canon and Recent Scholarship," *QQ,* 78:3 (Autumn 1971), 462-64.
- Laurence Perrine: "Latest from a One-Man Yeats-Factory," *SWR,* 56:2 (Spring 1971), 211-12.
- Hilary Pyle, *RES,* 23:89 (Feb 1972), 101-3.
- T. J. Verster, *UES,* 9:2 (June 1971), 36-38.

50. ——— (ed): *W. B. Yeats: The Critical Heritage.* London: Routledge & Kegan Paul, 1977. xvi, 483 pp.

"Introduction," 1-58; a review of Yeats criticism, contemporary and posthumous, which contains some inaccuracies. The body of the book contains 115 items of previously published criticism and biographical material, 1884-1939, again with several inaccuracies in the annotations. Reference is made to most of the items from individual entries in this bibliography.

Reviews:
- Terry Eagleton, *Books and Bookmen,* 23:5 (Feb 1978), 64.
- Richard J. Finneran: "W. B. Yeats: Some Recent Bibliographical and Editorial Work," *Review,* 1 (1979), 233-48.
- John Jordan: "Heady Brew," *Hibernia,* 13 Jan 1978, 23.
- John Kelly, *N&Q,* os 225 / ns 27:6 (Dec 1980), 564-65.
- Norman H. MacKenzie, *CJIS,* 4:2 (Dec 1978), 64-68.
- Christopher Murray, *IUR,* 8:1 (Spring 1978), 122-26.
- Hermann Peschmann: "Terrible Beauty," *TES,* 27 Jan 1978, 28.
- Patrick Rafroidi, *EI,* 3 (Dec 1978), 114-17.
- Lynn Thiesmeyer: "The Greening of the Yeats Industry," *EIC,* 30:3 (July 1980), 256-64.
- Weldon Thornton, *MLR,* 75:4 (Oct 1980), 867-68.

51. ——— (ed): *Yeats, Sligo and Ireland: Essays to Mark the 21st Yeats International Summer School.* Gerrards Cross: Smythe, 1980. x, 267 pp. (Irish Literary Studies. 6.)

Includes an introduction by the editor, a poem by Brendan Kennelly (not on Yeats, as far as I can see), and material from the following items: BB130, BD16, CA38, CB131, CC200, CD748, 1455, DC75, 155, 244, 308, DD214, 257, DE57, and EE368.
Reviews:
- Richard Burnham, *JIL,* 10:3 (Sept 1981), 112-13.
- Jacqueline Genet: "Yeatsiana," *EI,* 6 (Dec 1981), 246-48.
- George Mills Harper, *YeA,* 1 (1982), 235-36.
- J. R. Mulryne: "The Summer School in the Place of Shells," *THES,* 31 Oct 1980, 16.
- Daniel T. O'Hara, *VS,* 26:1 (Autumn 1982), 99-101.
- Charles F. Totten, *Eire,* 19:1 (Spring 1984), 153-56.
- Robert Welch, *IUR,* 11:2 (Autumn 1981), 236-37.

52. JOURNAL OF MODERN LITERATURE: "Special Yeats Number," *JML,* 4:3 (Feb 1975).
See CD40, 1061, 1237, DC327, EC31, FB30, FC2, 143, and FE14.

53. KEANE, PATRICK J. (ed): *William Butler Yeats: A Collection of Criticism.* NY: McGraw-Hill, 1973. v, 151 pp.
An eccentric collection. Contains 10 extracts from previously published criticism, mostly concerned with the later poetry (not analyzed in this bibliography), plus an introduction and a previously unpublished essay by the editor: "Embodied Song," which is concerned with antinomies in Yeats's poetry, but overwritten and really a pastiche of quotations. Includes a selected bibliography and a poem by M. L. Rosenthal: "Visiting Yeats's Tower" (reprinted from *The View from the Peacock's Tail: Poems.* NY: Oxford UP, 1972. viii, 52 pp. [pp. 48-49]), answered by the editor's poem "Reconciliation."

53a. KEANE, PATRICK J.: *Yeats's Interactions with Tradition.* Columbia: U of Missouri Press, 1987. xx, 332 pp.
Includes "Revolutions French and Russian: Burke, Wordsworth, and the Genesis of Yeats's 'The Second Coming,'" *BRH,* 82:1 (Spring 1979), 18-52; "Yeats's Counter-Enlightenment," *Salmagundi,* 68-69 (Autumn 1985), 125-45 (but not the drawing of Yeats by Lowell Boyers); "Faithful in His Fashion: Yeats and the Eros Chorus from Sophocles' *Antigone* ," *YER,* 8:1&2 (1986), 3-21. See also CD876.

An investigation into "Yeats's allusive interactions with the various traditions--literary, philosophic, occult--in which he was rooted and in the context of which he intended his work to be read" (p. 7). Discusses Yeatsian opposites and antinomies, his views of the Enlightenment and the French and Russian Revolutions, Neoplatonism, occultism, and the influence of or relationship with Blake, Burke, Dryden, Lady Gregory, Robert Gregory, Hardy, Homer, Kant, Locke, Milton, Newton, Nietzsche, Palmer, Plato, Plotinus, Pope, Porphyry, Shakespeare, Shelley, Sophocles, Tennyson, Virgil, Wordsworth, and others. Analyzed in sections DD, EE, FC.

Reviewed by Terence Diggory: "Yeats and Tradition," *ELT,* 31:4 (1988), 510-12.

54. KEEP, WILLIAM CORBIN: "Yeats and the Public," Ph.D. thesis, U of Washington, 1965. vi, 212 pp. (*DAI,* 27:1 [July 1966], 209A)
Discusses the influence of John Butler Yeats, Morris, O'Leary, Mitchel, the Rhymers, and Arnold.

55. KENNER, HUGH: *A Colder Eye: The Modern Irish Writers.* NY:

Knopf, 1983. xiv, 304 pp.

A relentlessly funny book whose first sentence does and does not describe the contents: "This book tries, within reasonable limits of space, to tell a coherent story, which could be subtitled *Yeats and His Shadow*." Yeats is discussed extensively, mostly under Irish aspects (language, literature, history, politics). He is also referred to in chapters on other writers (Synge, Joyce, Kavanagh, Clarke, etc.).

Reviews:

- Robert M. Adams: "Mulligan Stew," *NYRB,* 12 May 1983, 40, 42.
- Bruce Allen: "A Fresh Look at Ireland's Gift to 20th-Century Literature," *CSM,* 18 Oct 1983, 25.
- Stephen Brook: "Higher Chat," *NSt,* 5 Aug 1983, 26.
- Anthony Burgess: "The Realm of Irish Facts," *Obs,* 24 July 1983, 25. Reprinted on pp. 445-47 of *Homage to Qwert Yuiop: Essays*. London: Hutchinson, 1986. xiv, 589 pp. (American edition: *But Do Blondes Prefer Gentlemen? Homage to Qwert Yuiop, and Other Writings*. NY: McGraw-Hill, 1986.)
- Ronald Bush, *Criticism,* 26:3 (Summer 1984), 288-90.
- Denis Donoghue: "Ireland at Swim," *LRB,* 21 Apr--4 May 1983, 3-4.
- Doris L. Eder: "Yeats & Company," *VQR,* 60:4 (Autumn 1984), 729-33.
- Thomas Flanagan: "Ireland and the Modern Movement," *WashP,* 8 May 1983, Book World section, 1, 22.
- Gary Gach, *San Francisco R of Books,* 8:2 (July-Aug 1983), 11-12, 15.
- Michael Paul Gallagher: "One Kind of Book and not Another," *Month,* 246:1402 (July/Aug 1984), 279.
- Harry Goldgar: "An Eye on Irish Writers," *Times-Picayune,* 19 June 1983, section 3, 4.
- George Mills Harper, *Yeats,* 2 (1984), 286-89.
- Desirée Hirst: "Eyes on Ireland," *Tablet,* 29 Oct 1983, 1057-59.
- Rüdiger Imhof, *LWU,* 18:4 (1985), 361-63.
- Karl Keller, *LA Times,* 1 May 1983, Book Review section, 1.
- Herbert Kenny: "The Shanachie," *National R,* 22 July 1983, 881.
- Frank Kersnowski, *SSF,* 21:2 (Spring 1984), 169-70.
- David Krause: "Hugh Kenner Casts a Cocked Eye," *ILS,* 2:2 (Oct 1983), 21.
- Roger Lewis, *American Spectator,* 16:10 (Oct 1983), 34-36.
- Janet Madden-Simpson: "Blurred Orb," *BooksI,* 77 (Oct 1983), 183-84.
- K. Marre, *MFS,* 31:2 (Summer 1985), 377-80.
- Julian Moynahan: "Synge to Joyce," *NYTBR,* 31 July 1983, 10-11, 15.
- Timothy O'Keeffe: "The Irish Fact," *TES,* 26 Aug 1983, 16.
- Tom Paulin: "Do Letters Kill?" *New Criterion,* 2:3 (Nov 1983), 82-85.
- Stanley Reynolds: "Fool's Erin," *Punch,* 24 Aug 1983, 48-49.
- Gregory A. Schirmer: "Modernism and Ireland," *SR,* 92:3 (Summer 1984), lviii, lx, lxii.
- Clement Semmler: "The Ireland of W. B. Yeats," *Courier Mail,* 7 July 1984, 30.
- Daniel Taylor, *Magill's Literary Annual,* 1984, 173-77.

56. KLEINSTÜCK, JOHANNES: *W. B. Yeats oder: Der Dichter in der modernen Welt*. Hamburg: Leibnitz, 1963. 288 pp.

An uneven book, not much concerned with the problem announced in the subtitle (the poet in the modern world); mainly interested in Yeats's symbols, which are not linked to the "system." Analyzed in sections DD and FA.

Reviews:

- J. Blondel, *EA*, 18:3 (July-Sept 1965), 320-21.
- Ronald Dunlop: "W. B. Yeats, 1865-1939," *PoetryA*, 6 (Oct 1965), 36-39.
- Karl August Horst: "Ein vorbildlicher Interpret," *FAZ*, 17 Aug 1963, Bilder und Zeiten, [7].
- K. P. S. Jochum, *NS*, 14:3 (Mar 1965), 147-48.
- Christoph Kuhn: "Zu William Butler Yeats," *Du*, 23:7 (July 1963), 53.
- Walther Martin, *ZAA*, 14:1 (1966), 87-91.

57. KRAJEWSKA, WANDA: *William Butler Yeats*. Warszawa: Wiedza Powszechna, 1976. 395 pp.

In Polish. Contains chapters on the poetry, the plays, and the poetic and dramatic theories, also a note on the Yeats reception in Poland and a near-complete list of Polish Yeats translations.

Reviews:

- Barbara Cendrowska, *Pamiętnik teatralny*, 26:2 (1977), 245-47.
- Roża Jabłkowska, *KN*, 24:4 (1977), 546-50. (In English)
- Zbigniew Lewicki: "Yeats nareszcie przypomniany" [Yeats finally remembered], *Nowe książki*, 31 July 1977, 43-45.

58. KRANS, HORATIO SHEAFE: *William Butler Yeats and the Irish Literary Revival*. NY: Haskell House, 1966 [1904]. xi, 196 pp.

Incorporates "Mr. Yeats and the Irish Literary Revival," *Outlook*, 2 Jan 1904, 57-61. As the first monograph on Yeats, the book contains numerous small inaccuracies and hagiographical enthusiasms. Krans discusses the Irish literary revival, Yeats's poems based upon Irish myth, legend, and romance, as well as the entire output to date. Considering the little information available to Krans, his interpretations are fairly sound. Although he emphasizes Yeats's supposed mysticism and otherworldliness, he recognizes his ability as a leader of a literary and theatrical movement. Mainly of historical value.

Reviews:

- Anon., *BmL*, 28:164 (May 1905), 70.
- Anon.: "The Modern Irish Literary Revival and Its Leader," *Dial*, 37:439 (1 Oct 1904), 213.
- Anon.: "The 'Celtic Renascence,'" *Outlook* [London], 22 July 1905, 97-98.
- H. W. Boynton: "Books New and Old," *Atlantic Monthly*, 94:562 (Aug 1904), 269-76 (see pp. 270-71).
- C. [Percival Chubb?], *Ethical Record*, 5:5 (July 1904), 200-1.
- Treadwell Cleveland, *NYTBR*, 21 May 1904, 346. A letter referring to a review that I have not been able to locate.
- R. W. L[ynd]: "The Book World," *Black and White*, 22 Apr 1905, 563.
- Seathan MacDhonain, *Celtic R*, 2:1 (15 July 1905), 87-88.
- [Wilmer Cave France Wright], *Nation*, 5 May 1904, 351.

59. LE BROCQUY, LOUIS: *A la recherche de W. B. Yeats: Cent portraits imaginaires*. Paris: Musée d'art moderne de la Ville de Paris, 1976. [38 pp.]

Catalog of an exhibition, 15 Oct--28 Nov 1976. Contains a "Préface" by Jacques Lassaigne, "Les visages de Yeats" by John Montague, an introduction by Le Brocquy, a list of exhibited pieces and black-and-white reproductions of 26 portraits.

English edition: *Studies towards an Image of W. B. Yeats: The 1977 Edinburgh International Festival Exhibition*. Edinburgh:

Richard Demarco Gallery, 1977. [32 pp.]. Montague's "Faces of Yeats," is on pp. [7-8]; there is also a note by Le Brocquy: "Studies towards an Image of W. B. Yeats," [9]. Montague's note was reprinted in *EI,* 2 (Dec 1977), 41-43.

One of the portraits was published in Le Brocquy's *Images de W. B. Yeats, James Joyce, Samuel Beckett, Federico Garcia Lorca, Auguste Strindberg, Francis Bacon.* Paris: Galerie Jeanne Bucher, 1979. [60 pp.]

See also Le Brocquy's "Painting and Awareness," *EI,* 4 (Dec 1979), 149-62; Michael Peppiatt: "Interview with Louis Le Brocquy," *Art International,* 23:7 (Oct 1979), 60-66; and CD743.

The catalog was reviewed by Bryan Guinness, *Apollo,* 116:247 (Sept 1982), 201.

Another exhibition took place in Sligo, 12-30 Aug 1980; see *Images of Yeats.* Sligo: Sligo Art Gallery, 1980. [4 pp.].

Some of the Yeats heads and Le Brocquy's comments were published on pp. 28-32, 49, 57-58 of *Louis Le Brocquy and the Celtic Head Image.* An exhibition: September 26 through November 21, 1981. Introduction by Kevin M. Cahill. Essays by Proinsias MacCana and Anne Crookshank. Albany, N.Y.: New York State Museum, 1981. 64 pp.

60. LEVINE, HERBERT J.: *Yeats's Daimonic Renewal.* Ann Arbor: UMI Research Press, 1983. ix, 169 pp. (Studies in Modern Literature. 16.)

Based on "'Meditations upon a Mask': *Per Amica Silentia Lunae* and the Middle Poems and Plays of William Butler Yeats," Ph.D. thesis, Princeton U, 1977. v, 478 pp. (*DAI,* 38:7 [Jan 1978], 4158A-59A)

Incorporates: "Yeats at the Crossroads: The Debate of Self and Anti-Self in 'Ego Dominus Tuus,'" *MLQ,* 39:2 (June 1978), 132-53.

"The Inner Drama of Yeats's *Four Plays for Dancers* ," *CLQ,* 16:1 (Mar 1980), 5-18.

"'But Now I Add Another Thought': Yeats's Daimonic Tradition," *SLitI,* 14:1 (Spring 1981), 77-84.

"'Freeing the Swans': Yeats's Exorcism of Maud Gonne," *ELH,* 48:2 (Summer 1981), 411-26.

Argues that *Per Amica* and not *A Vision* occupies a central place in Yeats's poetic career, because it defines the concepts of self and antiself. Discusses the love poetry of the middle period; analyzed in sections DD and EE.

Reviews:

- Edward Engelberg, *Yeats,* 2 (1984), 298-300.
- Thomas Parkinson: "Yeats and Women," *ELT,* 27:2 (1984), 171-73.

61. LOIZEAUX, ELIZABETH BERGMANN: *Yeats and the Visual Arts.* New Brunswick: Rutgers UP, 1986. xix, 238 pp. (Illustrated)

Based on Elizabeth Wagner Bergmann: "Yeats's Poetry and the Pre-Raphaelite Tradition: From Painting to Sculpture," Ph.D. thesis, U of Michigan, 1980. vii, 244 pp. (*DAI,* 41:9 [Mar 1981], 4029A; reprinted *YeA,* 2 [1983], 100-101)

Incorporates "'Separating Strangeness': From Painting to Sculpture in Yeats's Theatre," *Yeats,* 1 (1983), 68-91; "Yeats's Early Landscapes," *Yeats,* 2 (1984), 144-64.

Contains chapters on Yeats and the Pre-Raphaelites, "Poems and Pictures: Yeats's Early Poetic Theory," the early poems, the plays, *A Vision* and the visual arts, and the visual arts in the later poetry. Discusses Yeats's views of painters and artists such as Blake, Burne-Jones, Calvert, Claude Lorrain, E. G.

Craig, Dulac, Horton, Michelangelo, William Morris, Nettleship, Palmer, Phidias, Poussin, Rossetti, and John Butler Yeats; also on the influence of the Nō. The illustrations include WBY's pastel of Coole Library, his sketch for a production of *The Countess Cathleen,* his *Head of a Young Man,* and an undated drawing by JBY of his son. Partly analyzed in sections DD and EE.

Reviews:
- Terence Diggory, *Yeats,* 5 (1987), 246-52.
- David Faldet, *Rocky Mountain R of Language and Literature,* 42:1-2 (1988), 88-89.
- Ian Fletcher: "Yeats: Letters and the Visual Arts," *ELT,* 30:4 (1987), 475-81.
- Bruce Gardiner, *VS,* 31:4 (Summer 1988), 612-14.
- Claude Rawson: "A Question of Potency," *TLS,* 24 July 1987, 783-85.

62. LONDON MERCURY: Yeats issue, *LMerc,* 39:233 (Mar 1939).
See BB165, CB428, and FD40.

63. LYNCH, DAVID: *Yeats: The Poetics of the Self.* Chicago: U of Chicago Press, 1979. ix, 240 pp.

Based on "Yeats's Final Questions: A Psychological Study," Ph. D. thesis, Brandeis U, 1973. v, 188 pp. (*DAI,* 34:7 [Jan 1974], 4270A). A psychoanalytical study of the life, some poems, and the Cuchulain plays. Yeats's particular problem is seen to be narcissistic rather than oedipal. Analyzed in sections DD, EE, and FA.

Reviews:
- Francis Baudry, *Psychoanalytic Q,* 50:1 (Jan 1981), 132-33.
- Gary T. Davenport: "The Narcissistic Yeats," *SR,* 88:1 (Winter 1980), xx-xxii.
- John P. Frayne, *JEGP,* 82:3 (July 1983), 457-59.
- George M. Harper: "Looking at Yeats through 'Selfish' Glasses," *SoR,* 16:2 (Spring 1980), 492-98.
- Herbert J. Levine, *YER,* 7:1&2 (June 1982), 138-39.
- Daniel O'Hara, *JML,* 8:3/4 (1980/81), 647.
- Marjorie Perloff, *MLQ,* 41:4 (Dec 1980), 389-95.
- William Pratt, *WLT,* 54:4 (Autumn 1980), 637.
- Hilary Pyle, *RES,* 32:127 (Aug 1981), 356-58.

64. MACLEISH, ARCHIBALD: *Yeats and the Belief in Life.* An address at the University of New Hampshire, January 17, 1957. [Durham]: U of New Hampshire, 1958. 20 pp.

Reprinted in *A Continuing Journey.* Boston: Houghton Mifflin, 1967. x, 374 pp. (pp. 12-25). The modern mind wishes "to know" and believes that knowledge is possible. This applies particularly to Yeats's life and work.

65. MACNEICE, LOUIS: *The Poetry of W. B. Yeats.* With a foreword by Richard Ellmann. NY: Oxford UP, 1969 [1941]. 207 pp. (Galaxy Book. GB269.)

This is still one of the sanest books written about Yeats. MacNeice discusses, among other things, the nineties and Irish background, the early poems, the style in the prose and in the plays, the later ballad technique and Yeats's politics. He defines Yeats's place in the poetry and thought of the 20th century, frequently invoking comparisons with Housman, D. H. Lawrence, Rilke, Eliot, and Auden.

Reviews:
- Anon., *List,* 11 Sept 1941, 383.

- Anon., *N&Q,* 180:9 (1 Mar 1941), 161-62.
- Cleanth Brooks, *MLN,* 58:4 (Apr 1943), 319-20.
- James Burnham: "Yeats," *Commonweal,* 16 May 1941, 88-89.
- S. C. C[hew]: "Yeats as Seen by Mr. MacNeice," *CSM,* 3 May 1941, Weekly Magazine section, 10.
- [Harold Child]: "The Mystery of Yeats: Stages in a Poet's Search for Himself," *TLS,* 29 Mar 1941, 150. Reprinted in *Essays and Reflections.* Edited with a memoir by S. C. Roberts. Cambridge: UP, 1948, xii, 185 pp. (pp. 12-19).
- Austin Clarke: "Poetry of W. B. Yeats: 'An Extremely Irascible Guide,'" *IrT,* 15 Mar 1941, 5.
- A[ustin] C[larke], *DM,* 16:2 (Apr-June 1941), 75-77.
- Maurice James Craig, *LLT,* 29:[1] (Apr 1941), 83-86.
- Babette Deutsch: "His Poetry Unique in Our Time," *NYHTB,* 1 June 1941, 10.
- E[lizabeth] D[rew], *Atlantic Monthly,* 167:5 (May 1941), Atlantic Bookshelf section, unpaged.
- Dudley Fitts: "MacNeice on Yeats," *SatR,* 3 May 1941, 6.
- F. W. van Heerikhuizen: "Een interessant boek over Yeats," *Litterair paspoort,* 2:12 (Nov 1947), 14-15.
- A. Norman Jeffares, *ES,* 27:1 (Feb 1946), 29-31.
- Samuel J. Looker: "Bar Gold and Paper Money," *Poetry Q,* 3:2 (Summer 1941), 51-53.
- W. H. M[ellers]: "A Book on Yeats," *Scrutiny,* 9:4 (Mar 1941), 381-83.
- E. H. W. Meyerstein: "Yeats, the Old and the New," *English,* 3:17 (Summer 1941), 223-25.
- Edwin Muir: "Yeats," *NSt,* 26 Apr 1941, 440.
- Roibeárd O Faracháin, *Bell,* 2:2 (May 1941), 93-95.
- F. T. Prince, *Dublin R,* 209:418 (July 1941), 101-3.
- Kathleen J. Raine, *Horizon,* 4:19 (July 1941), 66-71.
- Michael Roberts: "Mr. MacNeice on Yeats," *Spect,* 28 Feb 1941, 234.
- Winfield Townley Scott: "The Foolish, Passionate Man," *Accent,* 1:4 (Summer 1941), 247-50.
- William Soutar: "William Butler Yeats," *Adelphi,* 17:12 (Sept 1941), 425-27.
- George Woodcock, *Now,* 4 (Easter 1941), 28-30.

66. MALINS, EDWARD: *A Preface to Yeats.* London: Longman, 1974. xii, 212 pp.

A somewhat eccentric but useful book. It contains (1) a discussion of the historical and literary background, including sections on some of Yeats's sources (occultism, Neoplatonism, Vico, Berkeley, Burke, Blake, Nietzsche) and a discussion of *A Vision.* (2) Short interpretations of ten poems (analyzed in section DD). (3) A reference section with annotated lists of important persons in Yeats's life, a gazetteer of important places, an idiosyncratic list of "Yeats's symbols," etc.

Reviews:

- Denis Donoghue: "Aura, Atmosphere, and Spirit," *THES,* 1 Aug 1975, 17.
- Geoffrey Durrant, *CJIS,* 2:1 (May 1976), 58-59.
- George Mills Harper: "Always . . . Verify Your References, Sir!" *CEA,* 38:3 (Mar 1976), 34-37.
- A. Norman Jeffares: "Coughing in Ink," *SR,* 84:1 (Jan-Mar 1976), 157-67.
- Charles Mann, *ARBA,* 7 (1976), 623.

67. *Manuscripts of W. B. Yeats.* General editor: David R. Clark.

Various publishers, 1971--.
Published so far: *Druid Craft: The Writing of "The Shadowy Waters"* (1971, EE505); *The Writing of "The Player Queen"* (1977, EE429). A volume on *Sophocles' King Oedipus,* edited by David R. Clark and James B. McGuire, is promised for 1989.

68. MANVELL, ROGER: "W. B. Yeats: A Study of W. B. Yeats's Poetic Career with Special Reference to His Lyrical Poems," Ph.D. thesis, U of London, 1939. x, 323 pp.

69. MARCUS, PHILLIP LEDUC: *Yeats and the Beginning of the Irish Renaissance.* Ithaca: Cornell UP, 1970. xvii, 299 pp.
Based on "The Beginnings of the 'Irish Literary Renaissance,' 1885-1899," Ph.D. thesis, Harvard U, 1967, xiv, 315 pp. Incorporates "Old Irish Myth and Modern Irish Literature," *IUR,* 1:1 (Autumn 1970), 67-85.
Describes Yeats's activities between 1885 and 1899. Discusses the literary theories as related to Irish literature, the prose fiction (particularly *John Sherman*), some poems (most extensively "The Wanderings of Oisin"), and the controversies with Duffy, Dowden, and Eglinton. Also on Yeats's relationship to Katharine Tynan, Nora Hopper, Todhunter, Rolleston, Savage-Armstrong, Lionel Johnson, AE, Hyde, O'Grady, and Larminie, and on the beginnings of the Irish dramatic revival.
Second edition with a long new preface (pp. xi-xxxvi): Syracuse: Syracuse UP, 1987. xliii, 298 pp.
Reviews:
- Daniel J. Casey, *EngR,* 23:1 (Fall 1972), 73-74.
- [Austin Clarke]: "Young Irishman," *TLS,* 16 July 1971, 836.
- Anthony Cronin: "Poet above All," *IrP,* 6 Mar 1971, 12.
- Richard J. Finneran, *JML,* 3:3 (Fall 1974), 835-37.
- J. P. Frayne, *JEGP,* 71:2 (Apr 1972), 280-82.
- James MacKillop: "Yeats and the Gaelic Muse," *AntigR,* 11 (Autumn 1972), 97-109.
- George P. Mayhew, *BA,* 45:4 (Autumn 1971), 699-700.
- Michael O hAodha: "Poems and Ballads of Young Ireland," *Hibernia,* 6 Aug 1971, 16.
- Donald T. Torchiana: "Some Recent Books on Yeats," *JIL,* 5:2 (May 1976), 60-81.

70. [MASEFIELD, JOHN]: *Words Spoken at the Music Room, Boar's Hill, in the Afternoon of November 5th, 1930 at a Festival Designed in the Honour of William Butler Yeats, Poet.* [Oxford, 1931. 10 pp.]
Reprinted °San Francisco: David Magee & Albert Speresen, 1970; also in Masefield's *Recent Prose.* NY: Macmillan, 1933. ix, 294 pp. (pp. 193-97). "I suppose that any simpler age would have canonized him; of course, after first burning him at the stake."

71. MAXWELL, DESMOND ERNEST STEWART, and SUHEIL BADI BUSHRUI (eds): *W. B. Yeats, 1865-1965: Centenary Essays on the Art of W. B. Yeats.* Ibadan: Ibadan UP, 1965. xvi, 252 pp. (Illustrated)
Contains: A. Norman Jeffares: "Foreword," ix-x; "A Select Bibliography," 227-41 (about 350 items); and CB160, CC215, CD272, 1175, 1307, DB73, DC105, 111, DD514, EB107, EE129, 287, EG61, FA22, FD45, HD96, 137, and 162.
Reviews:
- Timothy Brownlow, *DM,* 5:1 (Spring 1966), 90-93.
- [G. S. Fraser]: "Surveying Yeats from China to Peru," *TLS,* 10 Feb 1966, 99.
- Sean Lucy: "Yeatsiana," *IrI,* 26 Feb 1966, 10.

- Christopher Ricks: "Yeats & Facts," *Encounter,* 21:1 (July 1966), 50-54.
- William Kean Seymour: "Reflections and Recollections," *ContempR,* 208:1202 (Mar 1966), 165-66.

72. [MAYHEW, JOYCE]: *Ad Multos Annos: William Butler Yeats in His Seventieth Year.* [Oakland: Mills College, Eucalyptus Press], 1935. [4 pp.]

73. MELCHIORI, GIORGIO: *The Whole Mystery of Art: Pattern into Poetry in the Work of W. B. Yeats.* London: Routledge & Kegan Paul, 1960. xiv, 306 pp.

Incorporates: "Yeats, simbolismo e magia," *Spettatore italiano,* 8:11 (Nov 1955), 453-65; "Leda and the Swan: The Genesis of Yeats's Poem," *EM,* 7 (1956), 147-239; "Yeats' Beast and the Unicorn," *DUJ,* os 51 / ns 20:1 (Dec 1958), 10-23; "La cupola di Bisanzio," *Paragone,* 11:128 (Aug 1960), 41-70.

Investigates the sources and shaping of Yeats's symbolism, more precisely the transformation of visual into poetic patterns. Discusses the unicorn symbolism in some plays; the imagery of swan, Helen of Troy, and tower; *A Vision;* the Byzantium poems; and other Yeats symbols. Analyzed in sections DD, EE, and FA.

Reviews:

- Robert Armstrong: "Threads of Tapestry," *Poetry R,* 52:1 (Apr-June 1961), 99-100.
- Thomas Bodkin: "Yeats Re-examined," *Birmingham Post,* 3 Jan 1961, 3. "He [Melchiori] does not seem to suspect that Yeats, though indisputably a great poet at his best, was at his worst an ill-educated and pretentious man."
- Austin Clarke: "Swan-Songs," *IrT,* 24 Dec 1960, 6.
- Donald Davie: "The Poet as Orator," *Guardian,* 17 Feb 1961, 6.
- T. R. Henn: "The Unity of Yeats," *NSt,* 13 Jan 1961, 60.
- [Rayner Heppenstall]: "Tame Swan at Coole," *TLS,* 17 Feb 1961, 97-98.
- A. Norman Jeffares, *RES,* 12:48 (Nov 1961), 437-39.
- Frank Kermode: "The Spider and the Bee," *Spect,* 31 Mar 1961, 448-49.
- J. B. Morton: "Yeats under the Microscope," *Tablet,* 8 Apr 1961, 330-31.
- R. F. Rattray, *Hibbert J,* 59:235 (July 1961), 373-74.
- W. D. T[empleman], *Personalist,* 44:1 (Winter 1963), 123-24.

74. MENON, VATAKKE KURUPATH NARAYANA: *The Development of William Butler Yeats.* With a preface by Sir Herbert J. C. Grierson. Edinburgh: Oliver & Boyd, 1960 [1942]. xiv, 92 pp.

Based on °"The Development of the Poetry of William Butler Yeats," Ph.D. thesis, U of Edinburgh, 1940. Grierson's preface recalls some meetings with Yeats. Menon gives a fairly straightforward account of Yeats's development, which neglects the more complex features of his life and work. He criticizes the earlier work and prefers the later. A short conclusion raises the question of Yeats's political and social prejudice but does not go very deep.

Reviews:

- Mulk Raj Anand, *LLT,* 36:[2] (Feb 1943), 130, 132.
- T[homas] B[odkin]: "A Study of W. B. Yeats," *Birmingham Post,* 15 Dec 1942, 2.
- A. M. C., *U of Edinburgh J,* 12:2 (Summer 1943), 124-25.
- M. D., *DM,* 18:4 (Oct-Dec 1943), 59-60.
- [Hugh I'Anson Fausset]: "Yeats Early and Late," *TLS,* 2 Jan

1943, 9.
- E. M. Forster: "An Indian on W. B. Yeats," *List,* 24 Dec 1942, 824.
- René Fréchet: "L'étude de Yeats: Textes, jugements et éclairissements," *EA,* 14:1 (Jan-Mar 1961), 36-47.
- P. J. Gannon, *Studies,* 32:125 (Mar 1943), 127-29.
- [Graham Hough]: "The Man and the Mask," *TLS,* 19 Aug 1960, 530.
- R. G. Lienhardt: "Hopkins and Yeats," *Scrutiny,* 11:3 (Spring 1943), 220-24.
- E. H. W. Meyerstein: "The Music of Death and Change," *English,* 4:23 (Summer 1943), 161-63.
- George Orwell: "W. B. Yeats," *Horizon,* 7:37 (Jan 1943), 67-71; reprinted in *The Collected Essays, Journalism and Letters.* Edited by Sonia Orwell and Ian Angus. London: Secker & Warburg, 1968. 4 vols. (2:271-76). Orwell concerns himself mostly with Yeats's politics and fascist leanings. See also Menander [i.e., Charles Morgan]: "Poetry and Prejudice," *TLS,* 20 Feb 1943, 87; correspondence by Orwell and Menander, 6 Mar 1943, 115. See also CD962.
- ———: "The Way of a Poet," *Time and Tide,* 17 Apr 1943, 325-26. A different review.
- F. T. Prince: "Yeats," *Poetry London,* 2:10 (Dec 1944), 238-39.

75. MISRA, BALA PRASAD: *William Butler Yeats.* Allahabad: Kitab Mahal, 1962. viii, 130 pp. (Masters of English Literature. 3.)
Reprinted: °Norwood, Pa.: Norwood Editions, 1977. Deals with the poetry and the plays only.

76. MODERN DRAMA: Yeats issue, *MD,* 7:3 (Dec 1964).
Contains BB74, 210, CA124, CD516, EA26, EB165, EC111, EE236, 415, 465, 505, and a review of EA8.

77. MOKASHI-PUNEKAR, SHANKAR: *The Later Phase in the Development of W. B. Yeats. (A Study in the Stream of Yeats's Later Thought and Creativity).* Dharwar: Karnatak U, 1966. xv, 285 pp. (Karnatak U Research Studies. 8. [i.e., 9.])
Discusses *A Vision* as the crowning achievement of Yeats's quest for Unity of Being. Deals with the love poetry; the motif of hatred and the ancestry motif in the poetry; Yeats's aristocratic politics; "Supernatural Songs"; and the influence of Shri Purohit Swami.
Reviewed by Prema Nandakumar: "The Aesthesis and Metaphysics of W. B. Yeats," *Aryan Path,* 39:10 (Oct 1968), 449-50.

78. MURPHY, D. J.: *William Butler Yeats: A Student's Guide to His Work.* Cork: Mercier Educational, 1974. 47 pp.
An introduction on the undergraduate level with sections on "Yeats's Critical Prose," his major symbols, language and style, the poems of the middle and late periods, and a chronology.

79. *New Yeats Papers.* Dublin: Dolmen Press, 1971-82. 20 vols.
For the individual volumes see BA7, BD8, 14, 23, CA90 (3), CC239, 247, CD1245, CF20, DA6, DD339, EA25, FA5, 8, FB24, FD27, 85, and FG28.

80. O'DONNELL, FRANK HUGH: *The Stage Irishman of the Pseudo-Celtic Drama.* London: Long, 1904. 47 pp.
Invective against Yeats from an extreme nationalist and Catholic point of view. See also EE120.

81. O'DRISCOLL, ROBERT, and LORNA REYNOLDS (eds): *Yeats and the Theatre*. Niagara Falls, N.Y.: Maclean-Hunter Press / Toronto: Macmillan of Canada, 1975. xiv, 288 pp. (Yeats Studies Series.)

Despite the title this is a somewhat heterogeneous collection. For the individual contributions see AE66, BF86, 87, CD775, EA10, EE18, 313, 370, 548, FD28, FG25. Includes "Suggested Guidelines for Catalogue of Yeats Manuscripts," 278-81.

Reviews:
- Diane Bessai, *NCTR,* 5:1 (Spring 1977), 64-66.
- Terence Brown, *IUR,* 6:1 (Spring 1976), 118-19.
- Lovat Dickson: "Know Yeats, Know Our Age in Courage, and Sensuality," *Globe and Mail,* 8 Mar 1975, 3.
- Denis Donoghue: "Yeatsiana," *Spect,* 19 July 1975, 84-85.
- Edward Engelberg: "Yeats on Stage," *SR,* 84:1 (Jan-Mar 1976), 167-74.
- Barton R. Friedman, *JML,* 5:4 (1976), 852-54.
- John Kelly, *Anglo-Irish Studies,* 3 (1977), 110-12.
- Milton Levin, *Eire,* 10:4 (Winter 1975), 148.
- F. S. L. Lyons: "Keeping Up with Yeats Studies," *IrT,* 19 Aug 1975, 8.
- ———: "Plays for Aristocrats," *TLS,* 10 Oct 1975, 1187.
- Sean McMahon: "The Painted Stage," *Hibernia,* 3 Oct 1975, 14.
- Giorgio Melchiori, *YES,* 9 (1979), 341.
- John Rees Moore, *ACIS Newsletter,* 7:1 (Feb 1977), 3-4.
- Andrew Parkin, *MD,* 19:1 (Mar 1976), 109-10.
- Ian Shaw, *Humanities Association R,* 28:2 (Spring 1977), 209-12.
- Reg Skene, *CTR,* 7 (Summer 1975), 151-52.
- Timothy Webb, *RES,* 28:112 (Nov 1977), 499-503.
- R. G. Yeed: "Yeats Studies Series," *JIL,* 5:2 (May 1976), 86-90.
- Lorna Young: "A Scholarly Look at Poet-Dramatist," *Citizen,* 28 Feb 1976, 74.

82. OREL, HAROLD: *The Development of William Butler Yeats: 1885-1900*. Lawrence: U of Kansas Publications, 1968. vii, 104 pp. (Humanistic Studies. 39.)

Includes "Dramatic Values, Yeats, and *The Countess Cathleen*," *MD,* 2:1 (May 1959), 8-16. A plea for a new assessment of the early Yeats, surveying his various activities of this period.

Reviews:
- Joe Lee Davis, *MQR,* 9:4 (Fall 1970), 280-81.
- Edward Engelberg, *VP,* 8:4 (Winter 1970), 354-56.
- Norman H. MacKenzie: "The Yeats Canon and Recent Scholarship," *QQ,* 78:3 (Autumn 1971), 462-64.
- George Brandon Saul, *Eire,* 4:1 (Spring 1969), 152-53.

83. °PACK, ROBERT: *On William Butler Yeats*. NY: McGraw-Hill, 1962. Tape recording, 60 mins.

84. *PdR Press Publications on William Butler Yeats*. Lisse (Holland): Peter de Ridder Press, 1981--?.

To the best of my knowledge, only one volume was published in this series; see DD626.

85. PETERSON, RICHARD F.: *William Butler Yeats*. Boston: Twayne, 1982. 228 pp. (Twayne's English Authors Series. 328.)

Written along the usual lines of the series: chronology, short biography, and chronological assessment of the major works. Includes a chapter on Yeats's "modernity." One of the better of the introductory studies.

Reviews:

- Michael André Bernstein, *Yeats*, 1 (1983), 216-18.
- James J. Blake: "Yeats Meets the Twayne," *ILS*, 2:1 (Spring 1983), 23.
- Richard Bonaccorso, *Eire*, 19:2 (Summer 1984), 159-60.
- Declan Kiberd, *IUR*, 14:2 (Autumn 1984), 301-3.
- Karina Williamson, *N&Q*, os 229 / ns 31:2 (June 1984), 275-77.

86. PHOENIX: Yeats centenary number, *Phoenix*, 10 (1965).
See CA49, CB487, DC202, 203, 422, DD83, FC29. Review: [G. S. Fraser]: "Surveying Yeats from China to Peru," *TLS*, 10 Feb 1966, 99.

87. POLLOCK, JOHN HACKETT: *William Butler Yeats*. London: Duckworth / Dublin: Talbot Press, 1935. 112 pp.
Reprinted: Folcroft, Pa.: Folcroft Editions, 1975. A personal but largely unprejudiced attempt to come to terms with Yeats's works and their development (especially their stylistic development). Remarkable for its sympathy with the earlier as well as the later work. Pollock is, however, not attracted by Yeats's "metaphysical speculations," which he explains as a serious lack of humor, and is silent when faced with more complex questions. In the end, he finds Yeats "lacking in depth of human experience" and a "poet of frustration and isolation."
Reviews:
- Anon.: "The Poetic Pilgrimage of W. B. Yeats," *IrT*, 27 Apr 1935, 7.
- Karl Arns, *Englische Studien*, 71:2 (Dec 1936), 276-77.
- [Austin Clarke], *TLS*, 23 May 1935, 332.
- G. Evans, *English Literary and Educational R*, 6:4 (Winter 1935-1936), 133-37.
- Desmond MacCarthy: "W. B. Yeats: His Seventieth Birthday," *SunT*, 30 June 1935, 8.
- P. S. O'H[egarty], *DM*, 10:3 (July-Sept 1935), 82-83.
- F[rancis] S[haw], *Studies*, 24:95 (Sept 1935), 492-93.

88. PRASAD, BAIDYA NATH: *W. B. Yeats as a Literary Critic and Other Essays*. Ranchi: Vishwamoham, 1971. xii, 134 pp.
Contains chapters on Yeats and Mohini Chatterjee and on Yeats and Sanskrit drama, on the parallels between Yeats and Hindi dramatist Jai Shankar Prasad, "Yeats as a Literary Critic," "Yeats's Early Dramatic Criticism," "Characterisation in Tragedy: Yeats's Views," "Yeats's Concept of Tragic Drama," and "In Scorn of the Counting-House" (his hatred of the bourgeoisie).
Reviews:
- Anon.: "Yeats and His Dialectics," *LHY*, 14:2 (July 1973), 163-65.
- R. Bangaruswami, *Aryan Path*, 43:4 (Apr 1972), 179.

89. PRITCHARD, WILLIAM H. (ed): *W. B. Yeats: A Critical Anthology*. Harmondsworth: Penguin, 1972. 390 pp.
Includes material from DB34. Contains 53 extracts from previously published criticism (not analyzed in this bibliography); some snippets from Yeats's own prose; two reviews of Yeats criticism by the editor (early criticism to 1940, pp. 17-28; later criticism after 1939, pp. 147-53); and a previously unpublished essay by Helen Vendler on the poetry: "Sacred and Profane Perfection in Yeats," 338-49, reprinted in *SoR*, 9:1 (Jan 1973), 105-17.
Reviews:
- John Bryson: "Unexpurgated Yeats," *Books and Bookmen*, 18:210 (Mar 1973), 52-53.

- Ian Fletcher: "The Traffic in Yeats," *TLS,* 2 May 1975, 490.
- Robert Nye: "Yeats as Bardic Poet," *Times,* 11 Jan 1973, 10.
- Kathleen Raine: "Man behind the Magic," *Sunday Telegraph,* 14 Jan 1973, 12.

90. RAINE, KATHLEEN: *Yeats the Initiate: Essays on Certain Themes in the Work of W. B. Yeats.* Mountrath: Dolmen Press / London: Allen & Unwin, 1986. xxiv, 449 pp. (Illustrated)

Most of the essays in this book are rewritten and republished pieces and are concerned with Neoplatonic themes and influences and with the Perennial Philosophy. Contents:

"Hades Wrapped in Cloud," 1-31; from Harper: *Yeats and the Occult* (1976, FC40), 80-107. A French version was published as "Hadès enveloppé de nuages," in CA32, 240-61. Mainly, as far as I can make it out, on the influence of Swedenborg.

"Fairy and Folk Tales of Ireland," 33-43; introduction to Yeats's collection, published in 1973 (see FA54).

"Ben Bulben Sets the Scene," 45-64; French version: "Ben Bulben fixe le décor," in CA32, 44-57; mostly on *The Celtic Twilight.*

"AE," 65-81; contains some references to Yeats.

"Yeats's Debt to Blake," 82-105; see CD264.

"From Blake to *A Vision*," 106-76; originally published as a pamphlet, Dublin: Dolmen Press, 1979. 64 pp. (New Yeats Papers. 17.) Incorporates "Mental Worlds of Blake and Yeats: Two Diagrams," *Eranos Jahrbuch,* 44 (1975), 133-65. Argues that the groundwork for the structure of *A Vision* is laid in Yeats's Blake and Swedenborg studies; discusses the charts and diagrams used by Blake and Yeats. Reviewed by Hazard Adams, *Blake,* 15:4 (Spring 1982), 187-88.

"Yeats, the Tarot and the Golden Dawn," 177-246; originally published as a pamphlet, Dublin: Dolmen Press, 1972. 60 pp. plus 42 illustrations (New Yeats Papers. 2.). Second edition, revised, Dolmen Press, 1976. vii, 78 pp. Incorporates "Yeats, the Tarot and the Golden Dawn," *SR,* 77:1 (Jan-Mar 1969), 112-48. On the relationship between Tarot symbols, Golden Dawn practices, and the Platonic myth in Yeats's philosophy and poetry.

Reviews of this pamphlet:

- Mowbray Allan, *BA,* 48:1 (Winter 1974), 154.
- [Austin Clarke]: "Power Pack," *TLS,* 1 June 1973, 620.
- William Empson: "Yeats and the Spirits," *NYRB,* 13 Dec 1973, 43-45; reprinted in CB149a.
- Mary Lappin: "Ritual and Magic," *Hibernia,* 22 Sept 1972, 10.
- Peter Sheal, *Four Decades,* 1:4 (July 1977), 307-10.

"Death-in-Life and Life-in-Death," 247-94; originally published as "Life in Death and Death in Life: Yeats's 'Cuchulain Comforted' and 'News for the Delphic Oracle,'" *SoR,* 9:3 (July 1973), 550-78. Revised and published as *Death-in-Life and Life-in-Death: "Cuchulain Comforted" and "News for the Delphic Oracle."* Dublin: Dolmen Press, 1974. 63 pp. (New Yeats Papers. 8.). Includes a note on *The Death of Cuchulain* and discusses the influence of Plotinus, Swedenborg, and Blake.

Reviews of this pamphlet:

- John Holloway: "Golden Dawn, Angry Light," *THES,* 17 Jan 1975, III.
- Graham Hough: "Yeats and the Magic of Power," *TLS,* 14 Feb 1975, 160.
- Edward Malins, *CJIS,* 1:1 (June 1975), 60-61.

- Elizabeth Young-Bruehl: "New Dolmen Yeats Papers," *JIL*, 5:2 (May 1976), 81-83.

"Blake, Yeats and Pythagoras," 295-330; first published in *Homage to Pythagoras: Papers from the 1981 Lindisfarne Corresponding Members Conference, Crestone, Colorado*. West Stockbridge, Mass.: Lindisfarne Association, 1982. 144 pp. (Lindisfarne Letter. 14.) (pp. 111-34).

"Yeats and Kabir," 331-58; first published in *Temenos*, 5 (1984), 7-28; on Yeats's interest in India and on echoes of Kabir in his poetry, especially in "Among School Children."

"Purgatory," 359-78; the introduction to a projected French version of the play by Pierre Leyris.

"Yeats and the Creed of St. Patrick," 379-407; on Yeats's attitude towards Christianity.

"Giraldus," 408-30; on the probable identity or model of Yeats's fictitious character.

"Yeats's Singing School: A Personal Acknowledgment," 431-49; discusses her own interest in Yeats and his influence on her.

Reviews of the entire collection:
- John Allitt, *Celtic Dawn*, 1 (Spring 1988), 20-26.
- John Hanratty: "Countries of the Mind," *BooksI*, 108 (Nov 1986), 228.
- Brian Keeble: "Yeats's Predestined Part," *Temenos*, 8 (1987), 246-51.
- Claude Rawson: "A Question of Potency," *TLS*, 24 July 1987, 783-85.

91. RAJAN, BALACHANDRA: *W. B. Yeats: A Critical Introduction*. London: Hutchinson, 1965. 207 pp.

Includes: "The Reality Within," *IJES*, 6 (1965), 44-55; "Yeats's 'Byzantium,'" *OJES*, 5:1 (1965), 57-61. Perhaps the best short introduction to Yeats; analyzed in sections DD and EE.

Reviews:
- Ronald Dunlop: "W. B. Yeats, 1865-1939," *PoetryA*, 6 (Oct 1965), 36-39.
- [G. S. Fraser]: "A New Eye on Yeats," *TLS*, 16 Sept 1965, 802.
- Charles Graves: "Consistency in Yeats," *Scotsman*, 12 June 1965, Weekend Magazine, 2.
- Giorgio Melchiori, *N&Q*, os 211 / ns 13:3 (Mar 1966), 114-17.
- Harry T. Moore: "Time Pardons Him for Writing Well," *SatR*, 11 Dec 1965, 39, 81.
- Hermann Peschmann, *English*, 16:92 (Summer 1966), 67-69.
- A. Ranganathan, *BA*, 41:1 (Winter 1967), 110.
- Jon Stallworthy, *RES*, 17:67 (Aug 1966), 342-44.
- August W. Staub: "Yeats: The Hundredth Year," *QJS*, 52:1 (Feb 1966), 81-85.
- J. Trautmann, *UES*, 8:2 (June 1970), 61.

92. REID, BENJAMIN LAWRENCE: *William Butler Yeats: The Lyric of Tragedy*. Norman: U of Oklahoma Press, 1961. xiii, 282 pp.

Reprinted: Westport, Ct.: Greenwood Press, 1977. Based on "W. B. Yeats and Generic Tragedy," °Ph.D. thesis, U of Virginia, 1957. 376 pp. (*DAI*, 17:11 [Nov 1957], 2615). Incorporates "Yeats and Tragedy," *HudR*, 11:3 (Autumn 1958), 391-410.

Discusses Yeats's theory of tragedy and tragic themes in his poetry, excludes the plays. Analyzed in sections DD and FC.

Reviews:
- Austin Clarke: "The Irish Liberal," *IrT*, 16 Dec 1961, 10.
- Patrick Cruttwell: "From Donne to Yeats," *HudR*, 15:3 (Autumn 1962), 451-54.

- H. R. MacCallum: "W. B. Yeats: The Shape Changer and His Critics," *UTQ,* 32:3 (Apr 1963), 307-13.
- Francis Murphy, *BA,* 36:3 (Summer 1962), 319-20.
- Thomas Whitaker: "Spiritual Arrogance and Impassioned Humility," *MR,* 3:4 (Summer 1962), 805-9.

93. REID, FORREST: *W. B. Yeats: A Critical Study.* London: Secker, 1915. 258 pp.

Reprinted: Folcroft, Pa.: Folcroft Press, 1969, and NY: Haskell House, 1972; incorporates "The Early Work of Mr. W. B. Yeats," *Irish R,* 1:11 (Jan 1912), 529-36. Contains the following chapters: Early Poems; Poems, 1890-1899; The Lyrical Dramas; Prose Tales and Sketches; Plays for an Irish Theatre; Collaboration [with Lady Gregory]; Philosophy; The Later Lyrics; Conclusion. Valuable as a document of the early Yeats reception, but somewhat dated. See also CD993 and 995.

Reviews:
- Anon., *Irish Book Lover,* 7:6 (Jan 1916), 113-14.
- Anon.: "Mr. Yeats's Poetry," *Nation* [London], 23 Oct 1915, 154, 156.
- Anon.: "Living Authors as Seen by the Critic," *NYTBR,* 28 Nov 1915, 478-79.
- [Harold Child]: "Mr. Yeats's Poetry," *TLS,* 30 Sept 1915, 331.
- [Basil de Sélincourt], *Athenaeum,* 16 Oct 1915, 259-60.
- Lawrence Gilman: "The Last of the Poets," *NAR,* 202:719 (Oct 1915), 592-97.
- [Charles Larcom Graves]: "A Study of Mr. Yeats's Poetry," *Spect,* 16 Oct 1915, 510-11.
- P[hilip] L[ittell]: "Books and Things," *NewRep,* 18 Dec 1915, 176.
- Crawford Neil: "W. B. Yeats," *New Ireland,* 18 Dec 1915, 98-100.

94. REVIEW OF ENGLISH LITERATURE: "W. B. Yeats Issue," *REL,* 4:3 (July 1963).

See A. N. J[effares]: "Editorial," 7-8, and CD523, DA45, EE333, FD74, HD168. Review by Roger McHugh: "Yeats: A Phoenix among Hawks, Rooks, and Sparrows," *Sunday Press,* 17 Nov 1963, 26.

95. RI͡APOLOVA, VERA ALEKSANDROVNA: *U. B. Ĭeĭts i irlandskai͡a khudozhestvennai͡a kul'tura: 1890*-e--*1930*-e *gody.* Moskva: "Nauka," 1985. 272 pp.

"WBY and Irish artistic culture from the 1890s to the 1930s." The first Russian monograph on Yeats, mainly concerned with the plays and the theatrical activities. Surprisingly enough, the author does not mention recent Russian Yeats criticism.

Reviews:
- V. Khorol'skiĭ: "Dramaturgii͡a V. B. Ĭeĭtsa," *Voprosy literatury,* 11 (Nov 1986), 268-74.
- M. Koreneva: "Magii͡a poeticheskogo teatra Ĭeĭtsa," *Teatr,* 4 (Apr 1987), 98-100.

96. SALVADORI, CORINNA: *Yeats and Castiglione: Poet and Courtier. A Study of Some Fundamental Concepts of the Philosophy and Poetic Creed of W. B. Yeats in the Light of Castiglione's "Il Libro del Cortegiano."* Dublin: Figgis, 1965. x, 109 pp.

Based on an °M.A. thesis, University College, Dublin, 1961. Includes a discussion of the Yeats-Lady Gregory relationship.

Reviews:
- Curtis Bradford: "A Yeats Gathering," *MLQ,* 28:1 (Mar 1967),

96-101.
- Timothy Brownlow, *DM*, 5:1 (Spring 1966), 90-93.
- Michael P. Gallagher, *Studies*, 54:214-215 (Summer-Autumn 1965), 284-88.
- Harry T. Moore: "Time Pardons Him for Writing Well," *SatR*, 11 Dec 1965, 39, 81.

97. SCHAUP, SUSANNE MARGARETE: "William Butler Yeats in deutscher Sicht," Dr.phil. thesis, U of Salzburg, [1968]. viii, 228 pp.

On the reception of Yeats in Germany, Switzerland, and Austria, the productions of his plays in these countries, and the German translations of his works. Includes a near-complete bibliography of German translations and criticism. See also "W. B. Yeats: Image of a Poet in Germany," *SHR*, 2:3 (Summer 1968), 313-23; on the sad case of an almost nonexistent Yeats reception in Germany (at least until recently) and some of the reasons for it.

98. SCHMALENBECK, HILDEGARD: "The Early Career of W. B. Yeats," Ph.D. thesis, U of Texas, 1957. ix, 414 pp. (*DAI*, 18:2 [Feb 1958], 593)

99. SCHRICKER, GALE C.: *A New Species of Man: The Poetic Persona of W. B. Yeats*. Lewisburg, Pa.: Bucknell UP, 1982. 214 pp.

Persona is defined as the synthesis of character and personality, which Yeats sought to establish in his prose and poetry. Mainly on *Autobiographies, A Vision,* and other prose works collected in *Mythologies,* less comprehensively on the poetry.

Reviews:
- Steve Connelly, *Eire*, 18:4 (Winter 1983), 152-58.
- Terence Diggory: "Casting a Cold 'I,'" *ILS*, 2:2 (Oct 1983), 19. See also Schricker: "An Incomplete Review Protested" and Diggory's reply, 3:1 (Spring 1984), 4.
- Richard Fallis, *Yeats*, 2 (1984), 314-18.
- Declan Kiberd, *IUR*, 14:2 (Autumn 1984), 301-3.
- Elizabeth Mackenzie, *N&Q*, os 231 / ns 33:4 (Dec 1986), 565-66.
- George O'Brien, *MLR*, 83:2 (Apr 1988), 430-32.
- Samuel Rees, *YER*, 8:1&2 (1986), 133-34.
- Jo Russell, *YeA*, 4 (1986), 261-62.

100. SEIDEN, MORTON IRVING: *William Butler Yeats: The Poet as Mythmaker, 1865-1939*. [East Lansing]: Michigan State UP, 1962. xiv, 397 pp.

Reprinted: °NY: Cooper Square, 1975. Based on "William Butler Yeats: His Poetry and Vision, 1914-1939," °Ph.D. thesis, Columbia U, 1952. 425 pp. (*DAI*, 12:4 [1952], 429). Incorporates "Patterns of Belief: Myth in the Poetry of William Butler Yeats," *AI*, 5:4 (Dec 1948), 258-300; "W. B. Yeats as a Playwright," *WHR*, 13:1 (Winter 1959), 83-98.

Sees *A Vision* as the center of Yeats's work and discusses the influences and preliminary prose works leading up to it, the work itself in its two versions and Yeats's own evaluation of it, and its influence on the poetry and plays. Analyzed in sections DD and FC.

Reviews:
- Daniel Albright, *WHR*, 31:3 (Summer 1977), 283-85.
- Austin Clarke: "An Irish Chronicle," *Poetry*, 103:3 (Dec 1963), 185-87.
- René Fréchet, *EA*, 31:1 (Jan-Mar 1978), 102-3.
- [A. Norman Jeffares]: "Thinking on Paper," *TLS*, 29 Mar 1963, 218.

- ———: "The Yeats Country," *MLQ*, 25:2 (June 1964), 218-22.
- Brendan Kennelly, *RES*, 28:110 (May 1977), 240-41.
- John Unterecker: "Yeats: Seer and Dramatist," *YR*, 52:4 (June 1963), 585-88.
- John B. Vickery, *WHR*, 18:2 (Spring 1964), 182-83.

101. SHENANDOAH: "Yeats and Ireland," *Shenandoah*, 16:4 (Summer 1965).

See BB39, 250, CD120, DC306, and HD73.

102. SKELTON, ROBIN, and ANN SADDLEMYER (eds): *The World of W. B. Yeats*. Revised edition. Seattle: U of Washington Press, 1967. x, 231 pp. (Washington Paperbacks. WP-23.)

The first edition was entitled *The World of W. B. Yeats: Essays in Perspective*. A symposium and catalogue on the occasion of the W. B. Yeats Centenary Festival held at the University of Victoria, February 14 to March 16, 1965. Dublin: Dolmen Press, 1965. 278 pp. The revised edition does not contain the catalogue. Its documentation is rather scrappy (unidentified quotations abound).

Contains: Ann Saddlemyer: "The Cult of the Celt: Pan-Celticism in the Nineties," pp. 3-5, and BD20, CC65, 66, CD47, 518, 819, 842, 1162, 1336, CF18, EB143, EE102, EF89, FC15, 25, FD69.

Reviews:
- Curtis Bradford: "A Yeats Gathering," *MLQ*, 28:1 (Mar 1967), 96-101.
- Ian Fletcher, *MLR*, 63:1 (Jan 1968), 228-29.
- Hermann Peschmann, *English*, 16:92 (Summer 1966), 67-69.
- Wulstan Phillipson, *Month*, os 221 / ns 35:1181 (Jan 1966), 60-61.
- Hilary Pyle, *DM*, 5:2 (Summer 1966), 94-95.
- B. Rajan: "Conflict, More Conflict!" *UTQ*, 35:3 (Apr 1966), 315-20.
- August W. Staub: "Yeats: The Hundredth Year," *QJS*, 52:1 (Feb 1966), 81-85.
- M. W. Steinberg: "Aspects of Yeats," *CanL*, 27 (Winter 1966), 67-69.
- John Unterecker, *CE*, 27:7 (Apr 1966), 580-81.
- Peter Ure, *ES*, 48:3 (June 1967), 264-68.

103. SNUKAL, ROBERT MARTIN: *High Talk: The Philosophical Poetry of W. B. Yeats*. Cambridge: UP, 1973. viii, 270 pp.

Based on °"Kantian and Neo-Kantian Elements in the Poetry of Yeats: A Study of the Controlling Metaphors of the Later Poetry," M.A. thesis, U of Manitoba, 1968. Discusses Yeats's indebtedness to Kant, Hegel, Coleridge, Wordsworth, and Whitehead; his symbolism, romanticism, philosophy, and concept of history; and related poems. Analyzed in section DD.

Reviews:
- Carlos Baker, *JML*, 4:5 (1975), 1148-49.
- William C. Barnwell, *Eire*, 12:4 (Winter 1977), 148-51.
- Lorraine Hall Burghardt, *MP*, 73:1 (Aug 1975), 97-100.
- [Denis Donoghue]: "Kant's Cousin Yeats," *TLS*, 31 Aug 1973, 996.
- Anthony Farrow, *Cithara*, 14:1 (Dec 1974), 126-30.
- A. Norman Jeffares: "The Great Purple Butterfly," *SR*, 82:1 (Winter 1974), 108-18.
- Brian John, *QQ*, 82:1 (Spring 1975), 133-34.
- Brendan Kennelly, *RES*, 26:101 (Feb 1975), 99-100.
- J. R. Mulryne, *MLR*, 70:1 (Jan 1975), 167-69.
- Hermann Peschmann, *English*, 23:116 (Summer 1974), 78-79.

- Z. J. Qureshi, *N&Q*, os 220 / ns 22:5 (May 1975), 228-30.
- Geoffrey Thurley: "Yeats Today," *SoRA*, 8:1 (Mar 1975), 74-85.
- T. J. Verster, *UES*, 12:3 (Sept 1974), 78-81.
- Thomas R. Whitaker, *ELN*, 12:3 (Mar 1975), 225-28.
- Georges-Denis Zimmermann, *ES*, 56:4 (Aug 1975), 368-70.

104. SOUTHERN REVIEW: "Special Yeats Issue," *SoR*, 7:3 (Winter 1941/42).

See CB118, 223, 301, 426, CC175, 321, 338, DB21, 72, 162, 199, DC59, 143, DD497, and FB48. See also CB222.

Reviews:
- Anon., *CE*, 3:3 (Mar 1942), 601-2.
- M. D., *DM*, 17:3 (July-Sept 1942), 54-55.

105. ———: "W. B. Yeats: Critical Perspectives," *SoR*, 5:3 (July 1969).

Contains a prefatory note by Donald E. Stanford, pp. 831-32; for individual items see CA38, 109, CB359, CD175, DC120, and FD82.

106. °SPENDER, STEPHEN: *W. B. Yeats*. NY: MacGraw-Hill, 1953. Tape recording, 49 minutes.

"The center of Yeats' vision is the inner life experience purged of the dross of actual living and transformed into a symbol which possesses a life outside the poet's subjectivity" (publisher's prospectus).

107. SPIVAK, GAYATRI CHAKRAVORTY: *Myself Must I Remake: The Life and Poetry of W. B. Yeats*. NY: Crowell, 1974. ix, 204 pp.

A modest and unsophisticated introduction for the general reader rather than the incipient scholar.

108. SRIVASTAVA, KAMTA C., and UJJAL DUTTA (eds): *Unaging Intellect: Essays on W. B. Yeats*. Delhi: Doaba House, 1983. viii, 208 pp.

See CB274, CD39, 146, 392, 988, 1174, DB68, 135, 171, DD557, EC14, EE233, 500, and FE84.

N.B.: "Unaging" appears to be a possible spelling; Yeats, however, wrote "Unageing," at least in the final version of "Sailing to Byzantium."

109. STARKIE, WALTER, and ALEXANDER NORMAN JEFFARES: *Homage to Yeats*. Papers read at a Clark Library Seminar, October 16, 1965. With an introduction by Majl Ewing. Los Angeles: William Andrews Clark Memorial Library, 1966. vi, 78 pp.

W. Starkie: "Yeats and the Abbey Theatre," 1-39; reprinted with slight revisions in *SoR*, 5:3 (July 1969), 886-921. Discusses the development of Yeats's writing for, and interest in, the theater, including some personal reminiscences.

A. N. Jeffares: "Women in Yeats's Poetry," 41-74; reprinted in CA49. On Maud Gonne, "Diana Vernon" (i.e., Olivia Shakespear), Lady Gregory, Iseult Gonne, and Mrs. Yeats.

110. STAUFFER, DONALD ALFRED: *The Golden Nightingale: Essays on Some Principles of Poetry in the Lyrics of William Butler Yeats*. NY: Hafner, 1971 [1949]. vii, 165 pp.

Incorporates "Yeats and the Medium of Poetry," *ELH*, 15:3 (Sept 1948), 227-46; "The Reading of a Lyric Poem," *KR*, 11:3 (Summer 1949), 426-40 ("The Wild Swans at Coole"). Discusses *A Vision*, Yeats's theory of the symbol, symbols in his poetry, the image of the swan, and the development of the poetry.

Reviews:

- Ray C. B. Brown: "The Song among the Reeds," *Voices*, 139 (Autumn 1949), 35-39.
- Austin Clarke: "Oedipus and Philomel," *IrT*, 10 Dec 1949, 6.
- Mary Colum: "To a Yeatsian Urn," *SatR*, 28 Jan 1950, 14-16.
- Richard Ellmann, *MLN*, 66:5 (May 1951), 335-36.
- John Farrelly, *NewRep*, 8 Aug 1949, 20.
- Isabel Gamble: "Two Views of Yeats," *Hopkins R*, 3:2 (Winter 1950), 52-54.
- Robert Hillyer: "Explaining Yeats," *NYTBR*, 26 June 1949, 7, 16.
- A. Norman Jeffares, *RES*, 2:7 (July 1951), 291-93.
- Leo Kennedy: "Lyrical Approach to Yeats," *Chicago Sun-Times*, 15 Aug 1949, 39.
- A. M. Klein: "The Masked Yeats," *Northern R*, 3:5 (June-July 1950), 43-45. Reprinted on pp. 282-84 of Klein's *Literary Essays and Reviews*. Edited by Usher Caplan and M. W. Steinberg. Toronto: U of Toronto Press, 1987. xxix, 424 pp.
- R[oger] McH[ugh], *Studies*, 39:155 (Sept 1950), 345-46.
- W. M. Parrish, *QJS*, 36:2 (Apr 1950), 263-64.
- Henry W. Wells: "Intellectual Godfathers," *CE*, 11:5 (Feb 1950), 294-96.
- George Whalley: "Yeats's Mind," *YR*, 39:1 (Sept 1949), 165-67.
- George F. Whicher: "The Lyricism of Yeats," *NYHTB*, 26 June 1949, 4.

111. STOCK, AMY GERALDINE: *W. B. Yeats: His Poetry and Thought*. Cambridge: UP, 1964 [1961]. xii, 255 pp.

Incorporates: "W. B. Yeats: The Poet of Loneliness," *Modern R*, 86:515 (Nov 1949), 405-7; "Art, Aristocracy and the Poetry of Yeats," *LCrit*, 3:2 (Summer 1957), 131-40. Mostly on Yeats's poetry and "ideas," with chapters on the Irish background, *The Countess Cathleen*, *The Land of Heart's Desire*, and *A Vision*.

Reviews:

- Hazard Adams, *JEGP*, 61:2 (Apr 1962), 439-40.
- H. H. Anniah Gowda, *LHY*, 3:2 (July 1962), 80-82.
- Anon.: "Poet as Thinker," *Economist*, 8 July 1961, 146.
- A[erol] A[rnold], *Personalist*, 43:2 (Spring 1962), 278-79.
- Amalendu Bose, *IJES*, 3 (1962), 158-67.
- V. L. O. Chittick, *MLQ*, 23:3 (Sept 1962), 272-73.
- Austin Clarke: "Poet of Loneliness," *IrT*, 1 July 1961, 8.
- Gustav Cross, *AUMLA*, 17 (May 1962), 112-14.
- David Daiches: "The Practical Visionary," *Encounter*, 19:3 (Sept 1962), 71-74.
- [G. S. Fraser]: "A Dragonish Cloud," *TLS*, 4 Aug 1961, 480.
- John Fraser, *DR*, 42:1 (Spring 1962), 99-100.
- René Fréchet, *EA*, 18:3 (July-Sept 1965), 321-22.
- Brian Inglis: "'I, the Poet. . . ,'" *Spect*, 30 June 1961, 956.
- A. Norman Jeffares, *MLR*, 57:2 (Apr 1962), 255-56.
- H. R. MacCallum: "W. B. Yeats: The Shape Changer and His Critics," *UTQ*, 32:3 (Apr 1963), 307-13.
- George Brandon Saul, *ArQ*, 18:1 (Spring 1962), 95-96.
- Irène Simon, *RLV*, 31:4 (1965), 406-13.
- Jon Stallworthy, *RES*, 13:52 (Nov 1962), 425-27.
- Derek Stanford, *English*, 13:78 (Autumn 1961), 237-38.
- John Unterecker, *CE*, 23:7 (Apr 1962), 605.
- Peter Ure, *DUJ*, os 55 / ns 24:3 (Jun 1963), 155-56.

112. SUGIYAMA, SUMIKO: *Yeats: Fatherland and Song*. Kyoto: Yamaguchi Shoten, 1985. x, 406 pp.

The treatment of the reality of Ireland in Yeats's works, i.e., its history and poetic tradition. Discusses the early poetry, the theatrical activities until 1909, *Poems Written in Discouragement*, "Coole and the Gregorys," the impact of the Easter 1916 rising, the Anglo-Irish tradition in the poetry of the thirties, and the later and last poems. Analyzed in section DD.

113. SZENTMIHÁLYI SZABÓ, PÉTER: *W. B. Yeats világa*. Budapest: Európa könyvkiado, 1978. 268 pp.
"WBY's world"; a chronological study of life, works, and background, intended as an introduction to Hungarian readers.

114. *Terres celtiques: Ecole d'été de Dublin*. 12e voyage d'études (1965/66). Lyon: Audin, [1966]. 83 pp.
Most of this issue is devoted to Yeats; it contains: Claude Jandard: "Les voyages d'Oisin et la quête d'un poète," 39-43; Michel Christolhomme: "Enfance et jeunesse de Yeats," 44-46; Henri Carette: "Yeats poète irlandais," 47-51; Dominique Cesseux: "L'influence de Sligo, son pays natal, sur le poète William Butler Yeats," 52-53; Henri Carette: "La religion de Yeats," 54-59; Madeleine Revelin: "Magie et poésie populaire," 60-61; Renée Hougouvieux: "William Butler Yeats poète national," 62-64; René Fréchet: "Quelques étapes de l'oeuvre de Yeats," 65-74; Noel Pichon: "Yeats et les contes de fées," 75-78.

115. ———. 13e voyage d'études (1966/67). Lyon: Ecole d'été de Dublin, [1967]. 121 pp.
Most of this issue is devoted to Yeats; it contains translations of previously published material, which is more easily available elsewhere and not listed separately in this bibliography.

116. TEXAS QUARTERLY: Yeats issue, *Texas Q*, 8:4 (Winter 1965).
Contains a facsimile of Yeats's handprints, pp. 150-51, and BB180, CD1007, DD301, and HD10.

117. THRESHOLD: "The Theatre of W. B. Yeats: Centenary 1965," *Threshold*, 19 (Autumn 1965). (Illustrated)
See CD139, 187, EB26, 94, 121, EC45, 116, and EF104.

118. TORCHIANA, DONALD THORNHILL: *W. B. Yeats & Georgian Ireland*. Evanston: Northwestern UP, 1966. xvi, 378 pp.
Based on "W. B. Yeats's Literary Use of Certain Anglo-Irish Augustans," °Ph.D. thesis, State U of Iowa, 1953. 289 pp. (*DAI*, 13:5 [1953], 815-16). Incorporates: "Senator Yeats, Burke, and Able Men," *Newberry Library Bulletin*, 5:8 (July 1961), 267-80; "W. B. Yeats, Jonathan Swift, and Liberty," *MP*, 61:1 (Aug 1963), 26-39.

A study of the complex relationship between Yeats and Protestant Ireland, especially of the 18th century, based on a great amount of widely scattered material (including unpublished writings, published interviews with Yeats, and reports of speeches and lectures). Discusses the influence on, and importance for, Yeats of Trinity College Dublin, Lady Gregory, Robert Gregory, Sir Hugh Lane, John Shawe-Taylor, Swift (particularly on *The Words upon the Window-Pane*), Burke, Berkeley, and Goldsmith. The last two chapters are concerned with Yeats's treatment of the Georgian heritage in his poems, in *On the Boiler*, and in *Purgatory*. Analyzed in sections DD and EE.

Reviews:
- Anon.: "The Anglo-Irish Tradition," *Economist*, 31 Dec 1966, 1398.
- Denis Donoghue: "The Politics of Poetry," *NYRB*, 6 Apr 1967,

22-25. David Levine's caricature of Yeats is not one of his best.
- David H. Greene, *MD,* 11:3 (Dec 1968), 336-38.
- Frank L. Kersnowski, *Eire,* 1:4 (Winter 1966), 94-95.
- Richard J. Loftus, *JEGP,* 66:4 (Oct 1967), 613-14.
- Hugh B. Staples, *JJQ,* 3:4 (Summer 1966), 299-302.
- R. S. Thomas, *CritQ,* 9:4 (Winter 1967), 380-83.
- Peter Ure, *N&Q,* os 213 / ns 15:2 (Feb 1968), 68-71.

119. TRI-QUARTERLY: "W. B. Yeats Centenary," *TriQ,* 4 [Fall 1965]. (Illustrated)

The lectures and discussions at the Yeats Festival of Northwestern University, Evanston, Ill., in April 1965. Contains Colton Johnson: "Editor's Foreword," 66-67; Donald T. Torchiana: "Some Dublin Afterthoughts," 138-43; and BB44, CB454, CC164, CD7, 48, CE171, DC310, FA44, FD59, and FG50.

120. UNIVERSITY REVIEW: "Special Yeats Edition," *UR,* 3:8 [1966?].

See BB145, 177, CB129, CD319, CE282, DD696, HD26, 102, and 154.

121. UNTERECKER, JOHN (ed): *Yeats: A Collection of Critical Essays.* Englewood Cliffs: Prentice-Hall, 1963. ix, 180 pp. (Twentieth Century Views. S-TC-23.)

Unterecker's introduction on Yeats as his own best interpreter (pp. 1-6) is a revision of "The Putting Together of W. B. Yeats," *Columbia U Forum,* 6:1 (Winter 1963), 41-44. The book contains 14 extracts from previously published criticism (not analyzed in this bibliography).

Reviews:
- Raymond Nelson: "Comments on Yeats," *Discourse,* 7:2 (Spring 1964), 203-7.
- George Brandon Saul, *ArQ,* 20:4 (Winter 1964), 363-64.

122. URE, PETER: *Towards a Mythology: Studies in the Poetry of W. B. Yeats.* NY: Russell & Russell, 1967 [1946]. 123 pp.

Reprinted: °Westport, Ct.: Greenwood Press, 1986. Defines myth as "a story, a framework of action and event, at once sufficiently firm to support passion and conflict, and sufficiently plastic for its meaning to be adapted to suit the personal poetic end" (p. 11). The poetic purpose is to translate the poet's inner landscape into poetry by means of the framework. Yeats's "stories" are those of Cuchulain, of his ancestors and friends, of *A Vision,* and of his fools, including Crazy Jane. Concludes that Yeats's framework was "a raft whose accommodation was severely limited to one" (p. 119). His poetry had little effect on his contemporaries. Analyzed in sections DD and EE.

Reviews:
- [Austin Clarke]: "Yeats's Hero and Fool," *TLS,* 11 Jan 1947, 24.
- Una Ellis-Fermor, *MLR,* 43:2 (Apr 1948), 267-69.
- A. Norman Jeffares, *ES,* 30:1 (Feb 1949), 23-25.
- J. B. Leishman, *RES,* 23:92 (Oct 1947), 372-74.

123. ———: *Yeats.* Edinburgh: Oliver & Boyd, 1963. viii, 129 pp. (Writers and Critics. 031.)

Good introduction to the poetry and the plays, including a short survey of Yeats research (pp. 119-26). Analyzed in sections DD and EE.

Reviews:
- Harry T. Moore: "Time Pardons Him for Writing Well," *SatR,* 11

Dec 1965, 39, 81.
- V. de S. Pinto, *CritQ,* 6:2 (Summer 1964), 186-87.

124. ———: *Yeats and Anglo-Irish Literature: Critical Essays*. Edited by C. J. Rawson with a memoir by Frank Kermode. Liverpool: Liverpool UP, 1974. xvi, 292 pp. (Liverpool English Texts and Studies. 12.)

Partial contents: "W. B. Yeats and the Growth of a Poet's Mind," 43-60. Written in 1947, previously unpublished.

"W. B. Yeats and the Irish Theme," 61-82. Written in 1947, previously unpublished.

"'The Statues': A Note on the Meaning of the Poem," 83-87; reprinted from *RES,* 25:99 (July 1949), 254-57.

"The Integrity of Yeats," 88-103; reprinted from *Cambridge J,* 3:2 (Nov 1949), 80-93. Defends Yeats against the charge that the later work is different from the early and that it lacks an awareness of ethical problems.

"Yeats's 'Demon and Beast,'" 104-13; reprinted from *IrW,* 31 (Summer 1955), 42-50.

"Yeats's Supernatural Songs," 114-29; reprinted from *RES,* 7:25 (Jan 1956), 38-51.

"A Source of 'Parnell's Funeral,'" 130-32; reprinted from *ES,* 39:6 (Dec 1958), 257-58. In Sordello di Goito via Ezra Pound.

"W. B. Yeats and the Musical Instruments," 133-50; written in 1968, previously unpublished. On music and musical instruments in Yeats's poetry and their function as keys to his art.

"Yeats and the Two Harmonies," 153-73; reprinted from *MD,* 7:3 (Dec 1964), 237-55. On prose and verse in the plays.

"The Hero on the World Tree: Yeats's Plays," 174-79; reprinted from *English,* 15:89 (Summer 1965), 169-72. Discusses the reputation and reception of the plays.

"The Plays," 180-203; reprinted from CA22.

"W. B. Yeats and the Shakespearian Moment," 204-24; reprint of *W. B. Yeats and the Shakespearian Moment: On W. B. Yeats's Attitude towards Shakespeare as Revealed in His Criticism and His Work for the Theatre*. A lecture delivered at Queen's University Belfast on 27 April 1966. Belfast: Institute of Irish Studies, 1969. 25 pp. On the concept of reverie as Yeats saw it in Shakespeare and as it appears in his own plays; also on "Unity of Being." Reviewed by Augustine Martin, *Studies,* 60:237 (Spring 1971), 98-102.

Reviews:
- Mowbray Allan, *BA,* 50:1 (Winter 1976), 176.
- Anthony Bradley, *Eire,* 11:2 (Summer 1976), 153-55.
- David Daiches: "A Dedicated Scholar-Critic," *THES,* 14 Feb 1975, 21.
- Denis Donoghue: "The Self and Its Roles," *TLS,* 17 Jan 1975, 51.
- René Fréchet, *EA,* 29:4 (Oct-Dec 1976), 624-25.
- David Grene, *MP,* 76:3 (Feb 1979), 319-23.
- Maurice Harmon, *IUR,* 5:1 (Spring 1975), 189-91.
- Elizabeth Mackenzie, *N&Q,* os 221 / ns 23:1 (Jan 1976), 34-36.
- J. R. Mulryne, *MLR,* 71:3 (July 1976), 646-48.
- David C. Nimmo, *Four Decades,* Special Review Supplement (Jan 1979), 16-18.
- F. G. F. Schulte, *DQR,* 7:1 (1977), 58-60.
- Georges-Denis Zimmermann, *ES,* 57:5 (Oct 1976), 464-68.

125. VENDLER, HELEN HENNESSY: *Yeats's "Vision" and the Later Plays.* Cambridge, Mass.: Harvard UP, 1963. xiii, 286 pp.

Based on "A Study of W. B. Yeats's *Vision* and the Plays Related to It," Ph.D. thesis, Radcliffe College, 1960. ii, 340 pp. A patient analysis of *A Vision* and a prejudiced and unbalanced criticism of the following plays: *At the Hawk's Well, Calvary, The Death of Cuchulain, The Dreaming of the Bones, A Full Moon in March, The Herne's Egg, The King of the Great Clock Tower, The Only Jealousy of Emer, The Player Queen, Purgatory,* and *The Resurrection*. Includes discussions of "Byzantium," "Cuchulain Comforted," "Leda and the Swan" (pp. 105-8, not listed in the index), and "The Second Coming."

Reviews:
- James L. Allen, *WHR*, 19:1 (Winter 1965), 90-92.
- [Austin Clarke]: "Closed-Circuit," *TLS*, 21 Nov 1963, 945. Correspondence by Peter Ure, 5 Dec 1963, 1020.
- ————: "An Irish Chronicle," *Poetry*, 103:3 (Dec 1963), 185-87.
- Padraic Fallon: "Documenting the Poet," *IrT*, 24 Aug 1963, 8.
- David Fitzgerald, *Dubliner*, 3:1 (Spring 1964), 68-70.
- Bernard Heringman, *MD*, 6:4 (Feb 1964), 464-65.
- A. Norman Jeffares: "The Yeats Country," *MLQ*, 25:2 (June 1964), 218-22.
- Rolf Lass, *Kilkenny Magazine*, 10 (Autumn-Winter 1963), 103-6.
- E. L. Mayo: "Place of a Hot Potato," *SatR*, 15 June 1963, 43.
- Richard M. Ohmann, *Wisconsin Studies in Contemporary Literature*, 5:3 (Autumn 1964), 276-78.
- V. de S. Pinto, *CritQ*, 16:2 (Summer 1964), 186-87.
- James Reaney: "How Not to Read Yeats," *Canadian Forum*, 43:513 (Oct 1963), 162-63.
- Howard Sergeant, *English*, 14:84 (Autumn 1963), 243-44.
- John Unterecker: "Yeats: Seer and Dramatist," *YR*, 52:4 (June 1963), 585-88.
- Peter Ure, *RES*, 15:60 (Nov 1964), 444-47.
- Sarah Youngblood, *Drama Survey*, 3:2 (Oct 1963), 319-20.

126. WEBSTER, BRENDA ANN SCHWABACHER: *Yeats: A Psychoanalytical Study*. Stanford: Stanford UP, 1973. ix, 246 pp.

Based on "Dream and the Dreamer in the Work of W. B. Yeats," Ph.D. thesis, U of California (Berkeley), 1967. iii, 374 pp. (*DAI*, 28:10 [Apr 1968], 4192A). Incorporates "Yeats' *The Shadowy Waters:* Oral Motifs and Identity in the Drafts," *AI*, 28:1 (Spring 1971), 3-16.

A somewhat unsatisfactory study of the relationship between Yeats's traumatic childhood experiences and the later work, particularly of his sexual fears, the nonexistent relationship with his mother, Lady Gregory as mother figure, the island and escape motifs, the father-son theme, the relationship with Maud Gonne and Olivia Shakespear, and the concept of the mask. Discusses some poems related to *A Vision*. Analyzed in sections DD, EE, and FA.

Reviews:
- Mowbray Allan, *BA*, 48:4 (Autumn 1974), 784.
- Anon.: "Freudian Grid," *Economist*, 13 Apr 1974, 74.
- Anon., *YR*, 64:1 (Oct 1974), viii, x.
- Brigid Brophy: "Dagda's Daughter," *NSt*, 3 May 1974, 627-28.
- Dwight Eddins: "An Image of Yeats," *PrS*, 48:3 (Fall 1974), 263-64.
- Monk Gibbon: "Castration on the Brain," *Hibernia*, 24 Mar 1974, 21.
- Claire Hahn: "Yeats Studies and the Parameters of Psychoanalytic Criticism," *L&P*, 24:4 (1974), 171-76.
- Carolyn G. Heilbrun, *Far-Western Forum*, 1:2 (May 1974), 282-84.

- Graham Hough: "Yeats and the Magic of Power," *TLS*, 14 Feb 1975, 160.
- A. Norman Jeffares: "The Great Purple Butterfly," *SR*, 82:1 (Winter 1974), 108-18.
- Patrick Keane: "Luminous Glimpse," *NewRep*, 19 Jan 1974, 24-26.
- Louis K. MacKendrick, *SHR*, 11:3 (Summer 1977), 315.
- J. R. Mulryne, *MLR*, 72:2 (Apr 1977), 420-21.
- Richard W. Noland: "Psychoanalysis and Yeats," *HSL*, 7:1 (1975), 33-47.
- John C. Sherwood, *WCR*, 10:3 (Feb 1976), 46-48.
- Richard P. Wheeler: "Yeats," *AI*, 32:3 (Fall 1975), 309-14.
- David P. Willbern, *Psychoanalytic Q*, 44:3 (July 1975), 488-90.
- Georges-Denis Zimmermann, *ES*, 56:5 (Oct 1975), 463-65.

127. °WEISS, THEODORE: *On William Butler Yeats*. NY: McGraw-Hill, 1966. Tape recording, 60 minutes.

Reissued: °NY: Norton, [1974?].

128. WHITAKER, THOMAS RUSSELL: *Swan and Shadow: Yeats's Dialogue with History*. Chapel Hill: U of North Carolina Press, 1964. xi, 340 pp.

Based on "W. B. Yeats and His Concept of History," Ph.D. thesis, Yale U, 1953. i, 377 pp. Incorporates: "W. B. Yeats: History and the Shaping Joy," *EIE*, 1959, 80-105; "The Dialectic of Yeats's Vision of History," *MP*, 57:2 (Nov 1959), 100-12; "The Early Yeats and the Pattern of History," *PMLA*, 75:2 (June 1960), 320-28; "Yeats's Alembic," *SR*, 68:4 (Oct-Dec 1960), 576-94; and "Yeats's 'Dove or Swan,'" *PMLA*, 76:1 (Mar 1961), 121-32.

This is less a study of how history is treated in Yeats's work than a discussion of his view of history. As such, history appears in two principal perspectives: as creative vision ("history is the landscape upon which the soul projects its image," p. 8), and as dramatic experience "of existential immersion in history, where the antiself may be . . . more disturbingly and dangerously confronted" (p. 9). Mainly on Yeats's poetry and related prose, especially *A Vision*. Chapters 7 and 9 discuss the Anglo-Irish background. Analyzed in sections DD, EE, and FA.

Reviews:

- Hayden Carruth: "On Yeats and Others," *Poetry*, 107:3 (Dec 1965), 192-94.
- D. J. Gordon, *MLR*, 63:3 (July 1968), 693-94.
- Geoffrey Hartman: "Insiders and Outsiders," *YR*, 54:2 (Dec 1964), 270-73.
- John Montague, *CritQ*, 8:4 (Winter 1966), 381-83.
- Timothy Rogers, *English*, 16:94 (Spring 1967), 152-54.
- Robert Scholes: "Yeats upon the Rood of Time," *ASch*, 34:1 (Winter 1964/65), 137-40.
- Helen Hennessy Vendler: "Assimilating Yeats," *MR*, 7:3 (Summer 1966), 590-97.
- P[eter] W[olfe], *PrS*, 39:1 (Spring 1965), 87-88.

129. WILSON, FRANCIS ALEXANDER CHARLES: *W. B. Yeats and Tradition*. London: Gollancz, 1958. 286 pp.

Incorporates "Patterns in Yeats's Imagery: *The Herne's Egg*," *MP*, 55:1 (Aug 1957), 46-52. Part of the book was revised and submitted as a thesis: "W. B. Yeats: The Last Plays. A Commentary on Yeats's Sources for the Narrative, Symbolism and Philosophy of His Plays *The King of the Great Clock Tower*, *A Full Moon in March*, *The Herne's Egg*, *Purgatory*, and *The Death of*

Cuchulain," Ph.D. thesis, Cambridge U, 1959. ii, 282 pp.

A controversial book. Besides the plays listed above, Wilson discusses *The Player Queen*, "Shepherd and Goatherd," "Chosen," "The Delphic Oracle upon Plotinus," "News for the Delphic Oracle," "The Black Tower," "Byzantium" (but see Empson, DD82), and "Cuchulain Comforted," by tracing their Neo-Platonic and Irish sources. He includes a defense of *A Vision*. Wilson's readers were irritated by his claim that this "ulterior body of knowledge" is indispensable for a full understanding of the texts and by his failure to explain the texts as plays or poems. The American edition, °NY: Macmillan, 1958, has a note on p. 12 in which Wilson responds to some criticism of the English edition. See also the next item and CD1085.

Reviews:
- Hazard Adams, *SAQ*, 58:3 (Summer 1959), 479-80.
- Anon., *List*, 13 Feb 1958, 287.
- Anon.: "Plato in Sligo," *Times*, 16 Jan 1958, 13.
- Aerol Arnold, *Personalist*, 41:1 (Winter 1960), 115-16.
- R. P. Blackmur: "Obscuris vera involvens," *KR*, 20:1 (Winter 1958), 160, 162-64, 166-68.
- Christine Brooke-Rose, *LMag*, 5:7 (July 1958), 77, 79, 81, 83.
- Christopher Busby: "Yeats and His Beliefs," *Dublin R*, 232:476 (Summer 1958), 178-81.
- Austin Clarke: "On the Track of W. B.," *IrT*, 25 Jan 1958, 6.
- Cyril Connolly: "Yeats's Use of Symbols," *SunT*, 12 Jan 1958, 8.
- Babette Deutsch: "The Poet and His Symbols," *NYHTB*, 17 May 1959, 5.
- Padraic Fallon: "Verse Chronicle," *DM*, 33:2 (Apr-June 1958), 39-45 (pp. 39-41).
- Hugh Fausset: "A Source-Book for Yeats," *MGuard*, 18 Feb 1958, 6.
- Helen Gardner: "Symbolic Equations," *NSt*, 1 Feb 1958, 141-42. Correspondence by Kathleen Raine: "A Little Song about a Rose," 8 Feb 1958, 170; H. Gardner, 15 Feb 1958, 202; F. A. C. Wilson, 1 Mar 1958, 273; H. Gardner, 8 Mar 1958, 305.
- John Edward Hardy: "After the New Criticism," *YR*, 48:3 (Mar 1959), 410-13.
- Thomas Hogan: "Old Man's Anger," *Spect*, 17 Jan 1958, 78.
- [Graham Hough]: "Yeats's Use of Symbolism," *TLS*, 24 Jan 1958, 43.
- G. F. Hudson, *Twentieth Century*, 163:975 (May 1958), 482-83.
- A. Norman Jeffares, *MLR*, 54:2 (Apr 1959), 271-73.
- Frank Kermode: "The Persecution of the Abstract," *Encounter*, 10:3 (Mar 1958), 77-78. See correspondence by T. R. Henn: "Studying Yeats," and answer by Kermode :5 (May 1958), 69-71; by F. A. C. Wilson, 11:1 (July 1958), 76.
- Thomas P. McDonnell, *CathW*, 188:1128 (Mar 1959), 520-22.
- John Rees Moore: "William Butler Yeats: A New View," *Evening Sun* [Baltimore], 28 Jan 1959, 30.
- Edwin Muir: "Ruthless Interpreter," *Obs*, 12 Jan 1958, 15.
- Harold Orel: "Views of a Vision," *PrS*, 33:3 (Fall 1959), 283-84.
- Thomas Parkinson: "Two Books on Yeats," *SR*, 66:4 (Oct-Dec 1958), 678-87.
- R. F. Rattray, *Hibbert J*, 56:222 (Apr 1958), 311-12.
- George Brandon Saul, *ArQ*, 15:2 (Summer 1959), 177-78.
- Eleanor M. Sickels, *Expl*, 18:1 (Oct 1959), R1.
- John Unterecker, *History of Ideas Newsletter*, 5:4 (Jan 1960), 80-82.

130. ———: *Yeats's Iconography*. London: Gollancz, 1960. 349 pp.

Written along the lines of the previous book (on which the author comments on pp. 304-6). Discusses *At the Hawk's Well, The Only Jealousy of Emer, The Cat and the Moon, Calvary, The Dreaming of the Bones,* "The Two Trees," "He Thinks of His Past Greatness When a Part of the Constellations of Heaven," "The Collar-Bone of a Hare," "The Wheel," "The Hour before Dawn," "Demon and Beast," "Solomon and the Witch," "At Algeciras," "Mohini Chatterjee," "The Statues," *A Vision,* and the unpublished play *The Bridegroom.*

Reviews:
- A[erol] A[rnold], *Personalist,* 43:2 (Spring 1962), 278-79.
- Birgit Bramsbäck, *SN,* 34:1 (1962), 168-70.
- Austin Clarke: "Hither and Thither," *IrT,* 23 July 1960, 6.
- David Daiches, *List,* 18 Aug 1960, 269-70.
- G. S. Fraser: "Hard Symbolic Bones," *NSt,* 27 Aug 1960, 280.
- W. R. Grey, *Focus,* 4:12 (Dec 1961), 289.
- [Graham Hough]: "The Man and the Mask," *TLS,* 19 Aug 1960, 530. Correspondence by Rupert and Helen Gleadow, 16 Sept 1960, 593.
- Frank Kermode: "A Bundle of Ideas," *Spect,* 5 Aug 1960, 220.
- R. F. Rattray, *Hibbert J,* 59:232 (Oct 1960), 101-3.

131. WRENN, CHARLES LESLIE: *W. B. Yeats: A Literary Study.* London: Murby, 1920. 16 pp.

Reprinted from *DUJ,* 22:3 (July 1919), 82-88; :4 (Nov 1919), 118-25. Reprinted: °Folcroft, Pa.: Folcroft Library Editions, 1973.

A somewhat labored essay by a conservative scholar who is out of sympathy with Yeats's later development. Wrenn was, however, one of the first critics to point to Neo-Platonic influences, but he did not pursue the topic.

132. *Yeats: An Annual of Critical and Textual Studies.* Volume 1. Edited by Richard J. Finneran. Ithaca: Cornell UP, 1983. 231 pp.

Contains AB9, BB192, CA61, CC242, CD708, 1206, FA74, FC124, G1563; reviews of CA85, CD872, DB116, EB122, EF97, FC80, FD19, 30, FE56; Carolyn Holdsworth (comp): "Dissertation Abstracts, 1982," 174-87; Mary FitzGerald: "Passim: Brief Notices," 227-31.

Reviews:
- Eric Domville, *CJIS,* 13:1 (June 1987), 180-81.
- Richard Kain: "No Time for Uncritical Appreciation," *ILS,* 3:1 (Spring 1984), 51.

133. ———. Volume 2. Edited by Richard J. Finneran. Ithaca: Cornell UP, 1984. 328 pp.

Contains AB10, CA61, CB242, CD1238, DB85, EC67, EE314, FB28, FF17; reviews of CA2, 4, 55, 60, 99, CC174, CD18, DA6, DB70, 210, FA25, FB24; Deborah Martin (comp): "Dissertation Abstracts, 1983," 258-64; Mary FitzGerald: "Passim: Brief Notices," 319-25; "Vale: F. S. L. Lyons," 327-28.

Reviews:
- Eric Domville, *CJIS,* 13:1 (June 1987), 180-81.
- Daniel T. O'Hara: "The Specialty of Self-Victimization in Recent Yeats Studies," *ConL,* 27:2 (Summer 1986), 285-89.
- Sidney Poger, *Eire,* 21:1 (Spring 1986), 151-52.

134. ———. Volume 3: A Special Issue on Yeats and Modern Poetry. Edited by George Bornstein and Richard J. Finneran. Ithaca: Cornell UP, 1985. 274 pp.

Contains AB11, CB360, CC48, 265, CD155, 218, 849, DD274, 463, EE31, G1581, and reviews of BA11, BC10, CC333, CD90, 975, DA25,

46, EA10, FC101, FE80; Deborah Martin Gonzales (comp): "Dissertation Abstracts, 1984," 206-16; Mary FitzGerald: "Passim: Brief Notices," 267-74.

135. ———. Volume IV, 1986. Edited by Richard J. Finneran. Ann Arbor: UMI Research Press, 1986. xvi, 231 pp. (Studies in Modern Literature. 61.)
Contains AB12, BB109, CD1099, 1279, DB3, DD51, 396, 648, FC133; reviews of AE78, CB332, CD31, DB123, EB101, EC12, EE6, FC47, FE17, 48; Deborah Martin Gonzales (comp): "Dissertation Abstracts, 1985," 177-86; Mary FitzGerald: "Passim: Brief Notices," 223-31. Reviewed by Robert C. Petersen: "Yeats Annual IV," *ELT*, 31:3 (1988), 336-39.

136. ———. Volume V, 1987. Edited by Richard J. Finneran. Ann Arbor: UMI Research Press, 1987. xvi, 270 pp. (Studies in Modern Literature. 76.)
Contains AB13, CC250, CD723, 1280, DB133, DD527, 767, EE513, G1634; reviews of CA61, CB274, CC132, 260, CD511, 1154, 1456, DA4, DB233, DC3; Gwenn De Mauriac (comp): "Dissertation Abstracts, 1986," 199-208; Mary FitzGerald: "Passim: Brief Notices," 265-70. Reviewed by Sheila Deane: "Yeats Annual V," *ELT*, 31:4 (1988), 507-10. (N.B.: Beginning with vol. VI, the annual will be published by the U of Michigan Press.)

137. *Yeats Annual* No. 1. Edited by Richard J. Finneran. London: Macmillan, 1982. xiii, 259 pp.
Contains CB160, CC213, CD1378, DB74, DD237, FC94, 138; reviews of CA51, CC345, 352, CD492, EA4, 32, EF20, FC64; Carolyn Holdsworth (comp): "Dissertation Abstracts, 1980," 207-20.
Reviews:
- Craig Wallace Barrow, *Eire*, 20:2 (Summer 1985), 147-49; reprinted in *Eire*, 21:3 (Fall 1986), 157-60.
- Sean Breslin: "U.S.W.B.," *IrP*, 2 Sept 1982, 6.
- Richard M. Kain: "The Yeats Annual," *ILS*, 2:1 (Spring 1983), 21.
- Elizabeth Mackenzie, *N&Q*, os 229 / ns 31:4 (Dec 1984), 542-44.

138. ——— No. 2. Edited by Richard J. Finneran. London: Macmillan, 1983. xi, 158 pp.
Contains CD340, 1141, 1394, DB281, DD644, FF16, G1550; reviews of BB136, CB185, CC324, CD576, 603, DA6, FA2, FB26, 31, FD22, 46, FE45, 84; Carolyn Holdsworth (comp): "Dissertation Abstracts, 1981," 96-106.
Reviews:
- Richard Kain: "No Time for Uncritical Appreciation," *ILS*, 3:1 (Spring 1984), 51.
- Janet Madden-Simpson: "Sailing from Byzantium," *BooksI*, 75 (July-Aug 1983), 129-30.

139. ——— No. 3. Edited by Warwick Gould. London: Macmillan, 1985. xix, 323 pp.
See AB3, AE58, 87, 106, BB123, CC67, 238, CD177, 258, 1148, 1168, DC348, DD259, 454, 615, EE130, 293, FA21, 74, FC47, 103, G1564, 1596, HD12; reviews of CA2, 4, CD18, DA6, 15, 25, EF97, FD19; "Editorial Miscellany," 285-94 (survey of recent publications).
Reviewed by Charles O'Neill: "Macmillan's Yeats Annuals," *ILS*, 5:2 (Fall 1986), 23.

140. ——— No. 4. Edited by Warwick Gould. London: Macmillan,

1986. xxi, 335 pp.

See AB4, AE9, 79, 107, CC252, CD333, 351, 549, 563, 1025, 1048, 1103, 1172, 1395, DB164, DD397, 427, EE31, 279, FC134; reviews of BC10, CA99, CC45, 174, CD975, EA10, 22, 36, EC12, FC47; also "Editorial Miscellany," 269-76 (short reviews of recent publications); "Recent Postgraduate Research," compiled by K. P. S. Jochum, Olympia Sitwell, and Warwick Gould, including "Dissertation Abstracts, 1982-1983," 297-322.

Reviews:
- Edward Engelberg: "Yeats Annual," *ELT,* 30:2 (1987), 249-51.
- Alison Armstrong Jensen: "Macmillan's Yeats Annuals," *ILS,* 5:2 (Fall 1986), 23.
- Alan Robinson, *RES,* 38:151 (Aug 1987), 405-6.
- Stephen Watt, *VS,* 31:1 (Autumn 1987), 115-18.

141. ——— No. 5. Edited by Warwick Gould. London: Macmillan, 1987. xxi, 341 pp.

See AB5, AE108, BB13, 120, 122, 222, 223, BC7, BF126, CD1225, 1454, DC356, DD143, 336, 724, EE7, 185, 295, 318, 490, FA39, FC34; reviews of CC201, CD511, DC3, FE48; Genevieve Brennan: "A Biographical Miscellany," 280-86.

142. *Yeats Association Bulletin.* Dublin: Dolmen Press, 1967-70. 3 issues (no more published).

No. 1 (Easter 1967): Contains news and notes and the constitution of the Association.
No. 2 (Spring 1968): See FG45; also news and notes.
No. 3 (Spring 1970): Contains news and a note on the Yeats memorial at Sandymount Green with a photograph.

143. *Yeats Club Review,* 1:1 (Summer 1987).

This is published in Oxford (PO Box 271, Oxford OX2 6DU). The first issue (16 unnumbered pages, including covers) contains notes on the club's activities, brief essays on "Yeats and Tagore" by Chris Morgan and "A Turn of the Century" by Dwina Murphy-Gibb, as well as other matter not concerned with Yeats. The club also publishes an annual, *Celtic Dawn* (see next item), and conducts poetry competitions.

143a. ———, 2 (Spring 1988).

Incorporated in *Celtic Dawn,* 1 (Spring 1988); contains EC3a, reviews of CA90 and HC42.

144. *Yeats Eliot Review.* Edited by Shyamal Bagchee. Edmonton: Department of English, U of Alberta, 1978-86. Edited by Russell E. Murphy. Little Rock: Department of English, U of Arkansas, 1987--.

A continuation of the *T. S. Eliot Review.* Several issues include a short "Bibliographical Update." Published so far:
5:1 (1978). See BD1, CB343, DA22, DD223, and review of CC182.
5:2 (1978). See CD599, 986, DD173, 585, and review of EC31.
6:1 (1979). See DD118, 147, 582, FA56.
6:2 (1979). See CC64, DD9, EB124, and review of EA29.
7:1&2 (June 1982). See CD531, DC206, DD37, 148, 164, 219, 589, and review of CA63.
8:1&2 (1986). See CA53a, CC138, DC319, DD106, 668, FC137, G1571, and reviews of CA2, 99, CB185, CD18, 576, EF20, FB24, 26.
9:1 (Fall 1987). Contains "An Editorial Introduction" by the new editor and DD506.
9:2 (Winter 1988). See CD175a and review of DC3.
9:3 (Spring 1988). See DC101a.

145. YEATS SOCIETY OF JAPAN: *Annual Report*. Tokyo: Yeats Society of Japan, 1966-1976. 9 issues, no more published.

1 (1966): News and notes; synopses of speeches made at the inauguration ceremony of the society; a congratulatory address by E. W. F. Tomlin; Frank Tuohy: "Yeats and Irish History," 6-9 (reprinted in CA25, CC329); synopses of the following papers: Iwas Mizuta: "W. B. Yeats and Zen Buddhism"; Yukio Oura: "On the Wisdom of W. B. Yeats"; William Johnston: "On *Cathleen ni Houlihan*," 9-11.

146. ———. 2 (1967).

News and notes; "Yeats and His Circle: A Series of Photographs for the Yeats Centenary," 5-8 (catalog of 48 items); "W. B. Yeats: Bibliography in Japan, 1966," 9; E. W. F. Tomlin: "The Continuity of Yeats," 10-15 (also in CA86 and CB487, q.v.); Shuji Yamamoto: "Yeats and Synge," 16-20 (the influence of Synge's poetry on Yeats).

147. ———. 3 (1968-69).

News and notes; Junzaburo Nishiwaki: "Yeats and Symbolism," 3-4 (synopsis); Hisashi Furukuwa: "Yeats and Noh," 5-6 (synopsis); Okifumi Komesu: "Brahman or Daimon: Yeats's Schooling in Eastern Thought," 7-18 (part 1, continued in next item; discusses the monistic-experiential aspect of the saint and the dualistic cognitive aspect of the artist and their Eastern sources); Hiromi Itoh: "Yeats: Archetypal Religious Perception," 18-19; Shotaro Oshima: "Address Given . . . before the Sligo Yeats Society and the Japan-Ireland Friendship Society (August 1968)," 21-24.

148. ———. 4 (1970).

News and notes; James Kirkup: "The Stones of Yeats," 5-19 (the stone imagery in the poems, includes a poem of his own, "The Sacrifice at the Grave of Yeats"); Okifumi Komesu: "Brahman or Daimon," 20-26 (part 2, see preceding entry); Shotaro Oshima: "A Message to the People of Ireland," 27-28.

149. ———. 5 (1970), combined with the society's *Bulletin* No. 5 (CA158).

"Tributes in Prose and Verse to Shotaro Oshima on the occasion of His Seventieth Birthday, Sept. 29, 1969," 1-26 (also published separately, see DA48); James Kirkup: "The Stones of Yeats," 27-41 (reprinted from CA148); Hiroshi Suzuki: "Shelley's Influence on 'The Second Coming,'" 42-46 ("Ozymandias" as a source); Ken'ichi Matsumara: "Fire and Bird," 47-51 (fire and bird imagery in the poems); Shotaro Oshima: "Irish Notes," 52-57 (on Michael Yeats, Mrs. Yeats, and the Yeats International Summer School). All the preceding items are on the left-to-right pages.

The following articles are in Japanese, printed on the right-to-left pages: Iwao Mizuta: "W. B. Yeats and Egan O'Rahilly," 1-9; Sachio Oura: "The Theme of *At the Hawk's Well*," 10-15; Yushiro Takahashi: "Allegory and Symbolism," 16-21; also some articles not on Yeats and synopses.

150. ———. 6 (1971).

News and notes; Roger McHugh: "Ah, Sweet Dancer--W. B. Yeats: Some Newly Discovered Letters and a New Poem," 4-14 (Margot Ruddock in "Sweet Dancer," "A Crazed Girl," "Beautiful Lofty Things," "The Man and the Echo," and "Margot"); Shotaro Oshima: "Yeats and Michio Ito," 15-20 (the importance of Ito's dance artistry for Yeats's plays); Ken'ichi Matsumara: "A Tree Image of W. B. Yeats," 21-25 (tree imagery in the poetry, especially "The Two Trees").

151. ———. 7 (1972).
News and notes; Frank Tuohy: "Yeats and Politics," 4-8 (negligible); Shotaro Oshima: "Yeats and the Noh," 9-18 (psychic phenomena in the Nō and in related plays by Yeats); Ken'ichi Matsumara: "'Sailing to Byzantium': A Note," 19-32 (the importance of "moment" and "memory"); material on the visit of Michael and Grainne Yeats.

152. ———. 8 (1973).
News and notes; Michael Yeats: "Words and Music," 7-18 (on his father's interest in Irish folk music and ballads). Reviewed by Elizabeth Mackenzie, *N&Q*, os 221 / ns 23:1 (Jan 1976), 34-36.

153. ———. 9 (1976).
News and notes; Michael Butler Yeats: "My Father and Ireland Today," 3-15 (less than half of the article is concerned with WBY, there is more on the present political situation in Ireland); Kazumi Yano: "Miscellaneous Notes on W. B. Yeats," 16-21 (mainly concerned with mistakes in Hone's biography BA8); Shotaro Oshima: "A Personal Reminiscence of Douglas Hyde (1860-1949)," 22-30 (includes Hyde's reminiscences of Yeats).

154. YEATS SOCIETY OF JAPAN: *Bulletin*. Tokyo: Yeats Society of Japan, 1966--. 16 issues published so far.
1 (Apr 1966): Tetsuro Sano: "The Meaning of Yeats's 'Memory,'" 1-12; Mariko Kai: "On Irish 'Mob Censorship,'" 13-19. Both articles are in Japanese, right-to-left paging. News and notes and a list of the society's members, pp. 32-19, partly in English, to be read left-to-right but paged in reverse.

155. ———. 2 (June 1967).
E. W. F. Tomlin: "The Continuity of Yeats," 1-6, also in CA146. The following items are in Japanese and printed and paged right-to-left: Shuji Yamamoto: "Yeats and Synge," 1-6; Taketoshi Furomoto: "On the Repetition in Yeats's Poetry," 7-20; Yushiro Takahashi: "Yeats and Mallarmé," 21-32; Saburo Onuki: "W. B. Yeats and the Chicago Critic," 33-37 (the Cleanth Brooks--Elder Olson approach); news and notes.

156. ———. 3 (Dec 1968).
All items are in Japanese, right-to-left: Junzaburo Nishiwaki: "Yeats and Symbolism," 1-2; Hisashi Furukawa: "Yeats and the Noh," 3-4; Joji Mori: "'The Black Tower': On the Study of Literature," 5-15; Masao Igarashi: "Yeats: His Poetry and Drama," 16-20; Tsunehiki Hoshino: "From *At the Hawk's Well* to *Takahime*," 21-28; synopses, news, and notes.

157. ———. 4 (Dec 1969).
All items are in Japanese, right-to-left: Takamichi Ninomiya: "Modernity of Modern Poetry," 1-5; Giichi Ouchi: "Songs about the Leprechaun," 7-11; Shiro Naito: "Influence of Zen upon 'The Statues,'" 12-20; Yasunari Shimizu: "W. B. Yeats's Anti-Democracy Reconsidered," 21-28 (obviously concerned with Harrison, CB190); Tonaji Hoashi: "In the Year 1891," 29-36; Shotaro Oshima: "Dublin Notes: Mr. Michael Yeats and the Late Mrs. W. B. Yeats," 37-39; synopses, news, and notes.

158. ———. 5 (1970).
See CA149.

159. ———. 6 (Oct 1971).
All items are in Japanese, right-to-left: Sadao Sasakura: "The Disintegration of Images in Yeats's Poetry," 1-6; Tatsuo Yamamoto: "Bernard Shaw and Ireland," 7-13; Minoru Hirooka: "Yeats and Roethke," 14-17; synopses, news, and notes.

160. ———. 7 (Dec 1972).
All items are in Japanese, right-to-left: Giichi Ouchi: "On Carolan," 1-4; Akiko Suzue: "*The Shadowy Waters:* Dream, Love, Reality," 5-10; Yoshiaki Inomata: "Yeats and Shakespeare," 11-17; Toshiichiro Okazaki: "Poetic Imagination," 18-23; synopses, news, and notes.

161. ———. 8 (Dec 1973).
All items are in Japanese, right-to-left: Ken Mori: "W. B. Yeats and French Symbolism (I)," 1-7 (there seem to be no further parts); Shiro Naito: "From Cubism to Zen--Yeats on the Eve of Fascism," 8-12; Hiroyuki Yamazaki: "Refrain in Yeats's Poetry--On 'Poetry of Insight and Knowledge,'" 13-18; Akio Matsuyama: "Yeats and Noh--On His *The Dreaming of the Bones*," 19-22; news and notes.

162. ———. 9 (July 1976).
All items are in Japanese, right-to-left: Taketoshi Furomoto: "Vernon Watkins's Three Poems on Yeats," 1-10; synopses of lectures.

163. ———. 10 (Nov 1979).
All items are in Japanese, right-to-left: Manji Kobayashi: "Another Reading of Yeats's Poetry," 1-11; Ikuyo Miura: "'Island' and 'Water,'" 12-18; reports, synopses, bibliography (not analyzed).

164. ———. 11 (Nov 1980): In Memory of Dr. Shotaro Oshima.
All items are in Japanese, right-to-left: "Tributes to the Memory of Dr. Shotaro Oshima," 1-16; Fumihiko Kato: "Reading 'The Dolls,'" 17-25; Sachiyo Kitadai: "Yeats's View of Apocalypse," 26-37; Ryuji Kobori: "On 'This or That' in Yeats," 38-48; Akio Matsuyama: "Yeats and Kyogen," 49-58; Yoko Yasuda: "Yeats's 'Old Man's Frenzy': His Last Struggle to Justify Himself," 59-65; reports, synopses, bibliography (not analyzed), 66-76.

165. ———. 12 (Oct 1981).
All items are in Japanese, right-to-left: Hiroyuki Yamasaki: "Yeats and Owen: Reconsiderations of Yeats's Exclusion of Owen's War Poems," 1-8 (from the *Oxford Book of Modern Verse*); Eiko Araki: "Yeatsian Geometry," 9-19; Mitsuko Ohno: "From *The King of the Great Clock Tower* to *A Full Moon in March:* Dramatic Unity and Noh," 20-30; Chie Oda: "A Study of the Swan Symbol in the Poetry of W. B. Yeats," 39-50; Toshimitsu Hasegawa: "Yeats in Irish Theatres," 51-62; reports, synopses, bibliography (not analyzed).

166. ———. 13 (Oct 1982).
Peter Milward: "Yeats, Eliot and Christian Tradition," 71-58 (in English, paged in reverse but to be read left-to-right). In Japanese (right-to-left): Toshitake Kunoki: "Arnold Bax and Yeats,"

1-10; Fuyuji Tanigawa: "Life for a Living Man: A Note on 'A Dialogue of Self and Soul,'" 11-20; Yoko Nakano: "Yeats and the Rose," 21-31; reports, synopses, reviews, bibliography (not analyzed).

167. ———. 14 (Oct 1983).
All items are in Japanese, right-to-left: Yoko Sato: "The Structure of *The Player Queen* ," 1-11; Saburo Moriguchi: "The Image of Cuchulain in the Works of W. B. Yeats," 12-21; Sumiko Sugiyama: "On 'The Black Tower,'" 22-41; Toshiichiro Okazaki: "On Yeats Studies in Japan," 42-49; Shoichiro Yasuda, Shozo Tsuji, Ryuji Kobori, and Hiromu Miyauchi: Symposium on "Byzantium," 50-82; reports, synopses, reviews, bibliography (not analyzed).

168. ———. 15 (Oct 1984).
Augustine Martin: "Kinesis[,] Stasis, Revolution in Yeatsean Drama," 90-80 (in English, paged in reverse but to be read left-to-right; also in EE69). In Japanese (right-to-left): Eiko Araki: "Yeats and the Fool," 1-14; Masanori Funakura: "Yeats and Rossetti," 15-23; Hiroshi Izubuchi: "Yeats's Misreading of Blake," 24-35; Manji Kobayashi, Kenichi Haya, Shiro Naito, and Hisayoshi Watanabe: Symposium on "Lapis Lazuli," 36-59; reports, synopses, reviews, bibliography (not analyzed).

169. ———. 16 (Oct 1985).
Ann Saddlemyer: "Yeats's Voices in the Theatre: *The Words upon the Window-Pane*," 125-110 (in English, paged in reverse but to be read left-to-right). In Japanese (right-to-left, some with English summary): Mitsuko Ohno: "The Woman in the Mirror: Yeats's Idea of Woman," 1-10, 108; Masami Nakao: "The People, the Land, and the Art: On 'In Memory of Major Robert Gregory,'" 11-20, 104-103; Iwao Mizuta, Ken'ichi Matsumara, Mark S. Suzuki, and Hiroshi Shimizu: Symposium on "The Man and the Echo," 21-47, 107-104; "Commemoration Essays," 48-76; reports, reviews, bibliography (not analyzed), 77-102.

170. ———. 17 (Oct 1986).
Yoko Nakano: "A Study of *Beyond the Grave: Letters on Poetry to W. B. Yeats from Dorothy Wellesley* [BC16]," 86-74; Augustine Martin: "Time and Place in *The Wild Swans at Coole* ," 93-87.

In Japanese, some with English summaries: Yoko Sato: "The Function of the Musicians in *At the Hawk's Well*," 1-14, 73-72. Shiro Naito: "Yeats and Pastoral," 15-25, 72-71. Seishi Matsuda: "A Paradoxical Vision of Life and Death in *Purgatory* ," 26-33, 71-70. Tadaaki Miyake: "*Purgatory* Another Cuchulain Play of W. B. Yeats," 34-41, 70-69. Akiko Suzue: "*Purgatory*--A Mother's Dream," 42-50, 69. An article on Yeats's "Suggestions and Corrections" (see CD1025) with extensive quotations from a Yeats letter, 68-62. Reviews and checklists (not analyzed in this bibliography).

171. *Yeats Studies: An International Journal.* Number 1: "Yeats and the 1890s." Editors: Robert O'Driscoll, Lorna Reynolds. Shannon: Irish UP, 1971. viii, 211 pp.
Introduction by the editors. For individual contributions see BD13, BG219, CB160, CD811, 1095, FA85, 88, FC36, 37.
Reviews:
- John Bryson: "Yeatsiana," *Books and Bookmen,* 17:199 (Apr 1972), 24.
- Norman H. MacKenzie, *QQ,* 78:4 (Winter 1971), 630-31.

- Phillip L. Marcus: "Approaching W. B.," *IrP*, 25 Sept 1971, 12.
- Augustine Martin, *Studies*, 61:241 (Spring 1972), 107-10.

172. ———. Number 2. "Theatre and the Visual Arts: A Centenary Celebration of Jack Yeats and John Synge." Editors: Robert O'Driscoll, Lorna Reynolds. Shannon: Irish UP, 1972. vi, 138 pp.

For relevant items see BB218 and EE189. N.B.: No other volume of *Yeats Studies* was published. According to a subscription note contained in no. 1, *Yeats and the Theatre* and *Yeats and the Occult* were to be nos. 3 and 5, respectively (see next item). No. 4 was to deal with John Butler Yeats, but hasn't materialized so far.

173. YEATS STUDIES SERIES. Various publishers, 1975-76.

Originally, five volumes were planned. Of these the following have been published so far: Robert O'Driscoll and Lorna Reynolds: *Yeats and the Theatre* (1975, CA81); George Mills Harper: *Yeats and the Occult* (1975, FC40); W. B. Yeats: *The Speckled Bird* (1976, FA82). The other two volumes are John Butler Yeats's unpublished memoir and a collection on Yeats and the Irish tradition; there seem to be no plans for publication.

174. YOUNGBLOOD, SARAH HELEN: "William Butler Yeats: The Mature Style," Ph.D. thesis, U of Oklahoma, 1958. vi, 252 pp. (*DAI*, 19:7 [Jan 1959], 1764)

175. ZWERDLING, ALEX: *Yeats and the Heroic Ideal*. NY: New York UP, 1965. ix, 196 pp.

Based on a °Ph.D. thesis, Princeton U, 1960. 249 pp. (*DAI*, 21:8 [Feb 1961], 2301). Incorporates "W. B. Yeats: Variations on the Visionary Quest," *UTQ*, 30:1 (Oct 1960), 72-85.

A discussion of the Irish hero, the aristocrat, the public hero, and the visionary in Yeats's work, unfortunately not by way of extended interpretations but rather in an assembly of snippets from various pieces and periods.

Reviews:
- Curtis Bradford: "A Yeats Gathering," *MLQ*, 28:1 (Mar 1967), 96-101.
- Brian John: "Hurt into Poetry: Some Recent Yeats Studies," *JGE*, 18:4 (Jan 1967), 299-306.
- Harry T. Moore: "Time Pardons Him for Writing Well," *SatR*, 11 Dec 1965, 39, 81.
- B. Rajan: "Conflict, More Conflict!" *UTQ*, 35:3 (Apr 1966), 315-20.
- Priscilla W. Shaw: "The Yeats Centenary: Part of the Harvest," *VQR*, 42:1 (Winter 1966), 173-76.
- Raney Stanford, *ELN*, 5:1 (Sept 1976), 67-68.
- Donald T. Torchiana: "Three Books on Yeats," *PQ*, 46:4 (Oct 1967), 536-56.
- Peter Ure, *ES*, 48:3 (June 1967), 264-68.

See also AE37, BA3.

CB Substantial Articles and Parts of Books

1. ACEVEDO, LUCIANO DE: "El poeta W. B. Yeats," *Cuba contemporánea*, year 12 / 34:136 (Apr 1924), 357-63.

2. ADKINSON, R. V.: "Criticizing Yeats," *RLV*, 33:5 (1967), 423-30.
Too many source studies and a "self-perpetuating process of re-interpretation" have obscured the essential question of why Yeats is worth reading and the position he occupies in his time.

3. *Aleksandr Solzhenitsyn, Rabindranath Tagore, Sigrid Undset, William Butler Yeats*. NY: Gregory, 1971. vi, 360 pp. (Nobel Prize Library.)
Per Hallström: "Presentation Address," 257-61 (reprint of CB187). Frank Kermode: "The Life and Works of William Butler Yeats," 349-58. Gunnar Ahlström: "The 1923 Prize," 359-60 (the reasons for choosing Yeats and not Hardy). See also CB536-537.

4. ALLEN, JAMES LOVIC: "The Road to Byzantium: Archetypal Criticism and Yeats," *JAAC*, 32:1 (Fall 1973), 53-64.
Archetypal criticism based on Jung and Frye fails to explain Yeats adequately; his own mythological views are much more akin to those of Philip Wheelwright.

5. ———: "From Puzzle to Paradox: New Light on Yeats's Late Career," *SR*, 82:1 (Winter 1974), 81-92.
The paradox that Yeats accepted both the physical and the spiritual world after about 1926 can be explained by reference to his belief in the tenets of *A Vision* and his conviction that he must live according to his phase. Contains a note on the epitaph in "Under Ben Bulben."

6. AMIRTHANAYAGAM, GUY (ed): *Writers in East-West Encounter: New Cultural Bearings*. London: Macmillan, 1982. xii, 218 pp.
G. Amirthanayagam: "Pontifex and Scapegoat: The Poet in Twentieth-Century Western Culture," 150-201; on Yeats, pp. 181-90 and passim.
Also published as °*Only Connect: Literary Perspectives East and West*. Adelaide: Centre for Research in the New Literatures in English / Honolulu: East-West Center, 1981. xiii, 335 pp.

7. AMORUSO, VITO, and FRANCESCO BINNI (eds): *I contemporanei: Letteratura inglese*. Roma: Lucarini, 1977. 2 vols.
Toni Cerutti: "William Butler Yeats," 1:209-37.

8. ANČEVSKI, ZORAN: "Vo nečistata prodavnica za otpad na srceto: Kon poezijata na V(ilijam) B(atler)--Jejts," *Stremež*, 24:1 (Jan 1980), 71-79.
"In the foul rag-and-bone shop of the heart"; an introduction to Yeats followed by translations, pp. 80-91.

9. ANON.: "Some Younger Reputations: Mr. W. B. Yeats," *Academy*, 4 Dec 1897, 488-89.
"To Mr. Yeats we look for a masterpiece, since his imagination is of the highest quality, and his execution not far beneath it."

10. ANON.: Editorials, *Catholic Bulletin*, 13:12 (Dec 1923), 817-19; 14:1 (Jan 1924), 5-7; :9 (Sept 1924), 745-50; :11 (Nov 1924), 929-38; 15:4 (Apr 1925), 291-94, 316-17; :7 (July 1925), 641-45; :9 (Sept 1925), 854-57; 16:1 (Jan 1926), 4-10; :3 (Mar 1926), 242-52; :5 (May

1926), 456-57; :6 (June 1926), 572-74; 18:7 (July 1928), 676-77; :10 (Oct 1928), 988-92; "The Soothsayers: To Captain Stephen Quinn," 21:7 (July 1931), 684-99.

Hysterical anti-Yeats diatribes, also in other issues of this period; in one of them (15:1 [Jan 1925], 1), the Ascendancy writers and politicians are called "The Cloacal Combine."

11. ANON.: "Centenary of the Birth of W. B. Yeats," *Eire-Ireland: Weekly Bulletin of the Department of External Affairs,* 706 (15 June 1965), 1-16.

12. ANON.: "An Irish National Theatre," *Irish Daily Independent and Daily Nation,* 8 Oct 1903, 4.

Criticizes Yeats's "eccentricities," his "unwholesome products," and his advocacy of artistic freedom. See the report of a Yeats speech in which he replies to this article, "Mr. Yeats and Ourselves," 9 Oct 1903, 6.

13. ANON.: "These Characters Remain," *IrT,* 27 Aug 1968, 11.

Editorial on the death of Mrs. Yeats. See also R. M. Fox: "Mrs. George Yeats: An Appreciation," 9 Sept 1968, 11; and CB16.

14. ANON.: "Mr. Yeats's Nobel Prize," *MGuard,* 16 Nov 1923, 8.

15. ANON.: "Mr. Yeats at Seventy," *NYT,* 30 June 1935, section IV, 8.

16. ANON.: "Georgina Yeats, Widow of Irish Poet, Dead at 75," *NYT,* 26 Aug 1968, 39.

See also CB13.

17. ANON.: "A Fine Poet: Mr. W. B. Yeats Visits Sheffield," *Sheffield Daily Telegraph,* 23 Nov 1922, 8.

Reprinted in BB177.

18. ANON.: "Yeats as Nobel Prize Winner," *Sun and the Globe,* 15 Nov 1923, 26.

19. ANON.: "William Butler Yeats årets Nobelpristagare," *Svenska dagbladet,* 15 Nov 1923, 11.

20. ANON.: "Personalities and Powers: William Butler Yeats," *Time and Tide,* 8 Aug 1924, 762-64.

21. ANON.: "Mr. W. B. Yeats: Award of Nobel Prize," *Times,* 15 Nov 1923, 12.

22. ANON.: "Mr. W. B. Yeats: An Appreciation," *Times,* 31 Jan 1939, 17.

Correspondence by D[orothy] W[ellesley], 9 Feb 1939, 19.

23. ANON.: "The Last Romantic," *Times,* 12 June 1965, 11.

24. ANON.: "Vacant Trinity Professorships," *TES,* 6 May 1913, 74.

Discusses the prospects of Yeats's appointment as Professor of English Literature: "He has not of late given the world much verse; the delicate and sensitive quality of his poetic gift was hardly of a nature to last into middle life. But he is and will remain an excellent interpreter of poetry. He has not, indeed, published much regular criticism, but the occasional brief essays which have accompanied the play-bills of the Abbey Theatre show that he can write of the literary art with the tact and penetration of one who is familiar with its secrets. On the other hand, it is impossible to imagine Mr. Yeats facing the routine duties of a university professor; it would be, to say the least, incongruous to ask this poet of fairyland to set examination papers and add up columns of marks."

See also "Mr. Yeats and the Chair," *Sinn Féin*, 3 May 1913, 5; and CB142, 144, and CF35.

25. ANON.: "The Week's Work," *United Ireland*, 9 Mar 1895, 4.
Editorial on Yeats's list of the thirty best Irish books, published in the *Dublin Daily Express*, 27 Feb 1895. Correspondence by D. F. Hannigan and Yeats, 16 Mar 1895, 3. See also Yeats's four letters in the *Daily Express* between 26 Jan and 8 Mar 1895 (all of them, including the list of books, in *Collected Letters*, 1:430-50). There is more correspondence in the *Daily Express* by other writers, including Edward Dowden's letter in the issue of 9 Mar 1895. For more information see the annotations in *Collected Letters*.

26. ANON.: "Mr. Yeats on Irish Literature," *United Ireland*, 17 Aug 1895, 1.
Criticizes Yeats's articles on "Irish National Literature" in *BmL*, July and Aug 1895, reprinted in *Uncollected Prose*, 1:359-73.

27. ANON.: "The Literary Movement in Ireland," *United Irishman*, 6 Jan 1900, 2.
On Yeats's article "The Literary Movement in Ireland," in *NAR*, Dec 1899, reprinted in *Uncollected Prose*, 2:184-96.

28. ANON.: "Yeats and the Nobel Prize," *World*, 16 Nov 1923, 10.

29. ARCHER, WILLIAM: *Poets of the Younger Generation*. London: Lane, 1902. vii, 565 pp.
"William Butler Yeats," 531-57. On the early poems and plays. Regards Yeats as "the quintessential spirit of Keltic eld," compares *The Countess Cathleen* with Maeterlinck's plays, and remarks with reference to the notes to *The Wind among the Reeds* that Yeats "is becoming more and more addicted to a petrified, fossilised symbolism, a system of hieroglyphs which may have had some inherent significance for their inventors, but which have now become matters of research, of speculation, of convention." Extract reprinted in CA50, pp. 123-29.

30. ARMSTRONG, ROBERT: *The Poetic Vision: Signposts and Landmarks in Poetry. Essays and Lectures*. London: Mitre Press, 1973. 133 pp.
"W. B. Yeats: The Man and His Poetry," 79-85.

31. ARNS, KARL: "Der Träger des Nobel-Preises," *Literatur*, 26:5 (Feb 1924), 261-65.

32. ———: "William Butler Yeats," *Schöne Literatur*, 30:6 (June 1929), 248-56.

33. ———: "W. B. Yeats: Zum 70. Geburtstag am 13. Juni," *Hamburger Fremdenblatt*, 12 June 1935, 2.

34. ATKINSON, F. M.: "A Literary Causerie," *Dana*, 10 (Feb 1905), 314-17.
Criticizes Yeats's "synthetic Celticism" and the "twilight" limi-

tations: "Where vigorous deedful life is required he can give nothing."

35. AUDEN, W. H.: "The Private Life of a Public Man," *Mid-Century*, 4 (Oct 1959), 8-15.
A misnomer. Although intended to be a review of *Mythologies* (W211P/Q), this is Auden's assessment of a poet whom he admires in some respects (his workmanship, his adaptability) and confesses not to understand in others. Auden is especially critical of Yeats's "system," of his early work, and of his ninetyish background.

36. A[YNARD], J[OSEPH]: "Le prix Nobel de littérature: W. B. Yeats," *Journal des débats politiques et littéraires*, 17 Nov 1923, 1.

37. ———: "W. B. Yeats: Lauréat du Prix Nobel," *Revue de Paris*, 31:1 (1 Jan 1924), 176-89.

38. BACKER, FRANZ DE: "William Butler Yeats," *DWB*, 39:4 (Apr 1939), 249-68.

39. BAGSHAW, WILLIAM: "W. B. Yeats," *Manchester Q*, 41:164 (Oct 1922), 227-48.

40. BALL, PATRICIA M.: *The Central Self: A Study in Romantic and Victorian Imagination*. London: Athlone Press, 1968. x, 236 pp.
Contains a note on Yeats, pp. 226-28, whose work constitutes "the apotheosis of the ego."

41. BARNWELL, W. C.: "James Dickey on Yeats: An Interview," *SoR*, 13:2 (Apr 1977), 311-16.
Mainly on three questions: "The importance of the Yeatsian system and the way we might best approach the verse by way of it; . . . the significance of Yeats's attitudes toward sexuality, experience, and closed forms in writing; the place of Yeats in our time."

41a. BARTLETT, THOMAS, a.o. (eds): *Irish Studies: A General Introduction*. Dublin: Gill & Macmillan, 1988. xiii, 241 pp.
Gerald Dawe, D. E. S. Maxwell, and Riana O'Dwyer: "Twentieth-Century Irish Literature," 173-91, and passim (see index).

42. BARTOŠ, JOSEF: "William Butler Yeats," *Lumír*, 34:7 (17 May 1906), 327-31; :8 (16 June 1906), 372-75; :9 (17 July 1906), 423-26.

43. BÁTI, LÁSZLÓ, and ISTVÁN KRISTÓ-NAGY (eds): *Az angol irodalom a huszadik században*. Budapest: Gondolat, 1970. 2 vols.
Ágnes Gergely: "William Butler Yeats," 1:103-21; 2:314-15.

44. BAUGH, ALBERT CROLL (ed): *A Literary History of England*. Second edition. London: Routledge & Kegan Paul, 1967 [1948]. xv, 1796, lxxx pp.
Samuel C. Chew and Richard D. Altick: "The Nineteenth Century and After (1789-1939)" contains a section on Yeats (pp. 1508-12, 1777-79).

45. BAX, CLIFFORD: *Some I Knew Well*. London: Phoenix House, 1951. 192 pp.
"W. B. Yeats: Chameleon of Genius," 97-103; and passim (see index).

46. BAYLEY, JOHN: *The Romantic Survival: A Study in Poetic Evolution*. London: Constable, 1957. vii, 231 pp.

"W. B. Yeats," 77-126. Yeats, Auden, and Dylan Thomas "found romanticism at low ebb, and its legacy rather a liability than an asset, but . . . were able to rediscover its original scope and richness" (p. 78). Comments on mask, conversation, and symbol in Yeats's poetry and includes a short comparison with Wilfred Owen.

Reviews:

- [G. S. Fraser]: "What is Romantic Poetry?" *TLS*, 5 Apr 1957, 208.
- Graham Hough: "Shrinking Poetry," *Spect*, 12 Apr 1957, 490.
- Peter Ure: "From Wordsworth to Yeats," *List*, 25 July 1957, 133-35.

47. BELL, MICHAEL (ed): *The Context of English Literature: 1900-1930*. London: Methuen, 1980. vii, 248 pp. (University Paperback. 696.)

M. Bell: "Introduction: Modern Movements in Literature," 1-93; on Yeats's "mythopoeic elusiveness," pp. 28-36, and passim (see index).

48. BERGONZI, BERNARD: *The Turn of a Century: Essays on Victorian and Modern English Literature*. London: Macmillan, 1973. x, 222 pp.

"Fin de Siècle," 17-39; reprint of "Aspects of the *fin de siècle*," in Arthur Pollard (ed): *The Victorians*. London: Barrie & Jenkins, 1970. 436 pp. (History of Literature in the English Language. 6.) (pp. 364-85). Comments passim on Yeats's attitude toward the nineties.

"Modern Reactionaries," 177-82; a review of CB190.

49. BERTI, LUIGI: *Boccaporto*. Firenze: Parenti, 1940. 293 pp. (Collezione di Letteratura. Saggi e memorie. 35.)

"Memoria per Yeats," 87-95. Incorporates: "Epigrafe per Yeats," *Nazione*, 11 Apr 1939, 5; "Memoria per Yeats," *Letteratura*, 3:12 (Oct 1939), 142-48.

50. BILLESKOV JANSEN, FREDERIK JULIUS, HAKON STANGERUP, and P. H. TRAUSTEDT (eds): *Verdens litteratur historie. Vol. 10: Århundredskifte 1890-1920*. København: Politikens Forlag, 1973. 637 pp.

Gunilla Bergsten and Staffan Bergsten: "Yeats--Irland, Maud og mystikken," 199-209.

51. BITHELL, JETHRO: "La littérature irlandaise contemporaine," *Signaux de France et de Belgique*, 1:8 (1 Dec 1921), 384-91.

Continued as "W. B. Yeats et les symbolistes irlandais," 1:10 (1 Feb 1922), 521-27. Reprinted in *Disque vert*, 1 (1970), 384-91, 521-27.

52. BLOOM, HAROLD: *The Ringers in the Tower: Studies in Romantic Tradition*. Chicago: U of Chicago Press, 1971. xii, 352 pp.

Numerous notes on Yeats, passim (see index).

53. BOGAN, LOUISE: *Selected Criticism: Prose, Poetry*. NY: Noonday Press, 1955. x, 404 pp.

"The Oxford Book of Modern Verse," 52-54.

"William Butler Yeats," 86-104; reprinted from *Atlantic Monthly*, 161:5 (May 1938), 637-44.

"On the Death of William Butler Yeats," 133-37; reprint of "The Cutting of an Agate," *Nation*, 25 Feb 1939, 234-35.

"The Later Poetry of William Butler Yeats," 202-6; combines "Verse," *New Yorker,* 1 June 1940, 73-75 (a review of *Last Poems and Plays* [W203/204]), and "Poet and Mage," *NewRep,* 17 Sept 1951, 19-20 (a review of *Collected Poems* [W211/211A]).

The entire Yeats material is reprinted in *A Poet's Alphabet: Reflections on the Literary Art and Vocation.* Edited by Robert Phelps and Ruth Limmer. NY: McGraw-Hill, 1970. xvii, 474 pp. (pp. 446-68).

54. ———: *Selected Letters of Louise Bogan, 1920-1970.* Edited and with an introduction by Ruth Limmer. NY: Harcourt Brace Jovanovich, 1973. xiv, 401 pp.

Numerous references to Yeats, passim (see index). Contains a parody of Yeats's poetic style, p. 152.

55. BOLAND, EAVAN: "A Young Writer's Reaction," *IrT,* 10 June 1965, iv.

Love and gratitude, especially for Yeats the master craftsman.

56. ———: "From Athens to Dublin," *Tablet,* 16 Mar 1968, 254.

Yeats gave Ireland "an image of herself."

57. BOSE, AMALENDU: "William Butler Yeats: A Study in Appreciation," *Dacca U Studies,* 4:1 (July 1939), [part 2], 45-65.

58. BOYD, ERNEST: *Ireland's Literary Renaissance.* Dublin: Figgis, 1968 [1916]. 456 pp.

Reprint of the revised edition (1922). Contains three chapters on Yeats (poems, plays, prose) that are still interesting (pp. 122-87). Grants that Yeats's poems are symbolical, but not mystical and not intellectual, and thereby underrates Yeats's wide, if eclectic reading. Deplores Yeats's experiments with the Nō. The prose impresses by its beauty, not by intellectual power.

Reviews:

- Anon.: "The Ango-Irishman," *Nation* [London], 9 Dec 1916, 362, 364.
- Anon.: "The Irish Renaissance," *NSt,* 11 Aug 1923, 528-29.
- Anon., *NAR,* 217:806 (Jan 1923), 138-40.
- [Harold Child]: "The New Irish Literature," *TLS,* 18 Jan 1917, 31.
- J. W. Cunliffe: "Recent Irish Literature," *Literary R,* 10 Feb 1923, 451.
- John Eglinton: "Anglo-Irish Literature," *Dial,* 74:4 (Apr 1923), 395-98.
- St. John Ervine: "Ireland's Literary Renaissance," *Obs,* 7 Jan 1917, 4.
- Sean Lucy: "Yeats' Poems in the Making," *IrI,* 26 Apr 1969, 6.
- D. L. M.: "Literary Men of Ireland," *BET,* 24 Jan 1917, section 2, 8.
- Augustine Martin: "Classic Survey," *Hibernia,* 14-27 Mar 1969, 20.
- Susan L. Mitchell: "Ireland's Literary Renaissance," *New Ireland,* 3:6 (16 Dec 1916), 92-93.
- R. H. C. [i.e., Alfred Richard Orage]: "Readers and Writers," *New Age,* 4 Jan 1917, 229-30; 11 Jan 1917, 254; 18 Jan 1917, 278. Correspondence by E. A. Boyd, 25 Jan 1917, 309-10; answer by R. H. C., 1 Feb 1917, 326-27. The three reviews, minus the correspondence, were reprinted in Orage's *Selected Essays and Critical Writings.* Edited by Herbert Read and Denis Saurat. London: Nott, 1935, v, 216 pp. (pp. 54-65).

- John C. Reville: "The Irish Revival," *America*, 18 Nov 1916, 137-38.
- W. P. Ryan, *BmL*, 51:306 (Mar 1917), 187-88.
- Solomon Eagle [i.e., J. C. Squire]: "Books in General," *NSt*, 6 Dec 1916, 257.
- Philip Tillinghast, *Publisher's Weekly*, 16 Sept 1916, 848-49.
- Katharine Tynan, *Studies*, 6:21 (Mar 1917), 164-65.

59. BRADBROOK, MURIEL CLARA: *Aspects of Dramatic Form in the English and the Irish Renaissance*. Brighton: Harvester / Totowa, N.J.: Barnes & Noble, 1983. xvi, 187 pp. (The Collected Papers of Muriel Bradbrook. 3.)

"Yeats and the Elizabethans," 131-45; reprint of "Yeats and Elizabethan Love Poetry," *DM*, 4:2 (Summer 1965), 40-55. Mainly on the influence of Spenser and Shakespeare on Yeats's love poetry.

"Yeats and the Legend of Ireland," 146-59; reprint of "A Dream within a Dream--Yeats and the Legend of Ireland," *Mosaic*, 10:2 (Winter 1977), 85-96.

"Yeats and the Noh Drama of Japan," 160-72.

60. BRADFORD, CURTIS B.: "Journeys to Byzantium," *VQR*, 25:2 (Spring 1949), 205-25.

"While Yeats saw the modern world as an ironic tragic spectacle and made sense of it, Eliot views it as a Christian mystic and makes less sense but still sense of it."

60a. BRAMSBÄCK, BIRGIT: "William Butler Yeats and the 'Bounty of Sweden,'" *MSpr*, 82:2 (1988), 97-106.

The award of the Nobel Prize and Yeats's reaction to it.

61. BRASH, W. BARDSLEY: "W. B. Yeats, 1865-1939," *London Q and Holborn R*, 164 (ser 6 / 8):3 (July 1939), 320-33.

Discusses the early works only.

62. BRATT, EYVIND: "En vittrad marmortriton" [A weathered marble triton], *Sydsvenska dagbladet snällposten*, 27 Sept 1969, 4.

63. ———: *Ön bortom ö-landet*. Göteborg: Zindermans, 1977. 147 pp.

"Ett artikulerat folk," 105-20; on the Irish literary renaissance (on Yeats, pp. 108-14).

64. BRÉGY, KATHERINE: "Yeats Revisited," *CathW*, 151:906 (Sept 1940), 677-86.

Written from a conservative Catholic point of view. Prefers the early work because the later is sexually too explicit.

65. BRENNAN, CHRISTOPHER: *The Prose*. Edited by A. R. Chisholm and J. J. Quinn. Sydney: Angus & Robertson, 1962. ix, 461 pp.

"Vision, Imagination and Reality," 19-39; reprinted from °*Australian Field*, 8 Mar 1902, 22 Mar 1902, 5 Apr 1902. Yeats is one of the few poets "who had not merely the capacity of visionary perception, but further the capacity to examine and test their perceptions, and who had given proof of the latter capacity concurrently with the exercise of the former."

"Blake after Many Years," 248-52; reprinted from °*Bulletin*, 5 Feb 1925. Partly on Blake's influence on Yeats.

66. BRION-GUERRY, LILIANE (ed): *L'année 1913: Les formes esthétiques de l'oeuvre d'art à la veille de la première guerre mondiale*.

Paris: Klincksieck, 1971. 1291 pp. in 2 vols. (Collection d'esthétique. 9.)

John Kelly: "*The Irish Review*," 2:1023-31 (written in French), discusses Yeats's involvement in this periodical (published 1911-14). Yeats is also referred to in other contributions (see index).

67. BRONOWSKI, J.: "W. B. Yeats," *CambR*, 54:1338 (8 June 1933), 475-76.

Yeats's poetry had sequence but no consequence. Yeats filled this gap between cause and effect by turning to mysticism.

68. BROOKS, CLEANTH: *Modern Poetry and the Tradition*. NY: Oxford UP, 1965 [1939]. xxxiv, 253 pp. (Galaxy Book. GB150.)

"Yeats: The Poet as Myth-Maker," 173-202; first published as "The Vision of William Butler Yeats," *SoR*, 4:1 (Summer 1938), 116-42; reprinted in CA36. Discusses *A Vision* and the poems related to it (see also FC136). Other references to Yeats, passim, especially pp. 60-64, revised from "Three Revolutions in Poetry: III. Metaphysical Poetry and the Ivory Tower," *SoR*, 1:3 (Winter 1935/36), 568-83; on "On a Picture of a Black Centaur" and "Byzantium."

69. ———: "W. B. Yeats: An Introduction," *Yale Literary Magazine*, 123:6 (May 1955), 18.

70. ———: *A Shaping Joy: Studies in the Writer's Craft*. London: Methuen, 1971. xix, 393 pp.

"The Modern Writer and His Community," 17-36; incorporates *The Writer and His Community*. Glasgow: Jackson, 1968. 31 pp. (W. P. Ker Memorial Lectures. 21.) Discusses Yeats's concept of unity of culture and unity of being in the context of 20th-century literature.

"Poetry and Poeticality," 87-101. The choice of evil as a subject for poetry and Yeats's opinion on this matter.

"W. B. Yeats as a Literary Critic," 102-25; reprinted from Peter Demetz, Thomas Greene, and Lowry Nelson (eds): *The Disciplines of Criticism: Essays on Literary Theory, Interpretation, and History* [Wellek Festschrift]. New Haven: Yale UP, 1968. x, 616 pp. (pp. 17-41). Discusses Yeats's views of poetry, the poet, and the cultural situation; specifically his views of Shelley, Shaw, Wilde, and Shakespeare. Frequent reference to "Ego Dominus Tuus."

"The American 'Innocence' in James, Fitzgerald, and Faulkner," 181-97; contains a note on "A Prayer for My Daughter," 195-97.

"The Unity of Marlowe's *Doctor Faustus*," 367-80; contains a note on *The Countess Cathleen*, 374-77.

71. BRUGSMA, REBECCA PAULINE CHRISTINE: *The Beginnings of the Irish Revival*. Part 1. Groningen: Noordhoff, [1933]. vii, 108 pp. (Doctor's thesis, U of Amsterdam, 1933.)

Discusses the following aspects: "The Origin of the Irish Revival," "W. B. Yeats and the Irish Revival," and "W. B. Yeats and the Irish Dramatic Movement." No more published.

72. BRYFONSKI, DEDRIA, and PHYLLIS CARMEL MENDELSON (eds): *Twentieth-Century Literary Criticism: Excerpts from Criticism of the Novelists, Poets, Playwrights, Short Story Writers, and Other Creative Writers, 1900-1960. Volume 1*. Detroit: Gale, 1978. x, 604 pp.

"William Butler Yeats 1865-1939," 552-84; a brief introduction

and about 30 extracts from previously published criticism.
Further selections appear in vol. 11, edited by Dennis Poupard (1983. 590 pp., pp. 504-42); in vol. 18, also edited by Poupard and James E. Person (1985. 591 pp., pp. 439-64).

73. BURGESS, ANTHONY: *Urgent Copy: Literary Studies*. London: Cape, 1968. 272 pp.
"Cast a Cold Eye: The Yeats Centenary," 62-67; reprinted from *Spect*, 15 Jan 1965, 73. Appreciates Yeats's poetry and plays, but considers his prose "dangerous."

74. CAMBON, GLAUCO: *La lotta con Proteo*. Milano: Bompiani, 1963. 318 pp. (Portico Critica e Saggi. 40.)
"Yeats e la lotta con Proteo" [Yeats and the fight with Proteus], 69-111; reprinted from *Aut aut*, 7:37 (Jan 1957), 1-34.

75. CAMERON, SUSAN ELIZABETH: "William Butler Yeats," *McGill U Magazine*, 4:1 (Jan 1905), 94-105.

76. Cattani [i.e., CATTAUI], GEORGES: "William Butler Yeats," *Journal des poètes*, 2:3 (29 Nov 1931), [3-4].

77. ———: *Trois poètes: Hopkins, Yeats, Eliot*. Paris: Egloff, 1947. 171 pp.
"William Butler Yeats et le réveil celtique," 45-63. A rambling essay on Yeats as symbolist, Celtic dreamer, and adept of mysticism. Includes "Rencontres avec Yeats: Un grand poète celtique vient de mourir à Menton," *Nouvelles littéraires*, 4 Feb 1939, 1, 9; "Rencontres avec W.-B. Yeats," *Lettres*, 4:3 (1946), 48-57. Reprinted with a few changes as "W. B. Yeats: 'La mémoire de la nature elle-même,'" *Journal de Genève*, 12-13 June 1965, I.

78. CAZAMIAN, MADELEINE L.: "Un poète irlandais: W. B. Yeats," *Revue germanique*, 7:2 (Mar-Apr 1911), 129-54.

79. ———: "Le poète de l'Irlande: W. B. Yeats," *Vie des peuples*, 12:45 (Jan 1924), 102-32.
On the early works only.

80. ———: *Le roman et les idées en Angleterre*. Paris: Belles Lettres, 1935-55. 3 vols. (Publications de la Faculté des Lettres de l'Université de Strasbourg. 15. 73. 125.)
"Esthétisme et renaissance celtique," 2:326-68; contains the following subsections: "W. B. Yeats: Formation esthétique et mystique," 327-32; "W. B. Yeats, théoricien," 333-35; "W. B. Yeats: Le culte de la Rose," 335-45. See also index to vols. 2-3.

81. CHAPPLE, J. A. V.: *Documentary and Imaginative Literature, 1880-1920*. London: Blandford Press, 1970. 395 pp.
On Yeats, pp. 238-61 and passim (see index).

82. CHATTERJEE, MANOJ KUMAR: "The Significance of the Later Works of Yeats," *VQ*, 17:1 (May-July 1951), 19-28.
The significance lies in the "continual intellectual adventure."

83. CHESTERTON, GILBERT KEITH: "Mr. Yeats and the Cosmic Moth," *America*, 22 July 1916, 357-58.
Yeats should be saved from his idolators and be subjected to genuine criticism to bring out his considerable qualities. Discusses *The Shadowy Waters*.

84. ———: *Irish Impressions*. NY: Lane, 1920 [1919]. 222 pp.
See especially pp. 78 ("Mr. W. B. Yeats, in the very wildest vision of a loneliness remote and irresponsible, is careful to make it clear that he knows how many bean-rows make nine"), 139-40, 182-83.

85. ———: *The Autobiography*. NY: Sheed & Ward, 1936. vii, 360 pp.
Incorporates "Some Literary Celebrities," *SatR*, 12 Sept 1936, 3-4, 13. Chesterton's estimate of Yeats appears on pp. 139-42, 146-50, 293-94.

86. CLARK, JAMES M.: "The Irish Literary Movement," *Englische Studien*, 49:1 (July 1915), 50-98.
On Yeats, passim.

87. [CLARKE, AUSTIN]: "Yeats's Inner Drama: A Poet of Two Reputations. Appeal of the Later Works," *TLS*, 4 Feb 1939, 72, 74.
See also [Austin Clarke]: "The Success of Yeats," on p. 73 of the same issue.

88. ———: "W. B. Yeats," *DM*, 14:2 (Apr-June 1939), 6-10.

89. ———: *The Celtic Twilight and the Nineties*. With an introduction by Roger McHugh. Dublin: Dolmen Press, 1969. 104 pp. (Tower Series of Anglo-Irish Studies. 1.)
On Yeats's Celtic Twilight period, pp. 31-49; "Yeats's Early Plays," 74-91; "Yeats's Later Plays," 92-104. Rambling and gossipy, but nevertheless valuable for some first-hand information, e.g., concerning the productions of Yeats's plays.
Reviews:
- Patrick Murray: "Yeats on Stage," *IrP*, 30 Aug 1969, 10.
- Eilean Ni Chuilleanain: "Twilight," *IrT*, 13 Sept 1969, 8.

90. CLARKE, EGERTON: "William Butler Yeats," *Dublin R*, 204:409 (Apr-May-June 1939), 305-21.
Includes an untitled poem written in memory of Yeats.

91. COLLINS, ARTHUR SIMONS: *English Literature of the Twentieth Century*. 4th edition. London: University Tutorial Press, 1965 [1951]. vii, 410 pp.
"Yeats," 14-21, and passim (see index).

92. COLLS, ROBERT, and PHILIP DODD (eds): *Englishness: Politics and Culture 1880-1920*. London: Croom Helm, 1986. vi, 378 pp.
Peter Brooker and Peter Widdowson: "A Literature for England," 116-63, contains some notes on Yeats.

93. COLUM, MARY M.: "The Later Yeats," *Poetry*, 7:5 (Feb 1916), 258-60.
The later Yeats is better than the earlier. Praises *The Green Helmet* as "his greatest dramatic work."

94. ———: "Yeats and the Mysteries," *NYHTB*, 13 July 1930, 1, 6.

95. COLUM, PADRAIC: "The Irish Literary Movement," *Forum*, 53:1 (Jan 1915), 133-48.

96. ———: "Youngest Ireland," *Seven Arts*, 2:11 (Sept 1917), 608-23.

97. ———: "The Promise of Irish Letters," *Nation*, 10 Oct 1923, 396-97.

98. ———: *The Road round Ireland*. NY: Macmillan, 1926. xvii, 492 pp.

"Dublin through the Abbey Theatre," 260-338; a series of sketches of Dublin literary life in the early years of the 20th century.

99. ———: "On the Centenary of William Butler Yeats." Introduced by Allan Nevins, *Proceedings of the American Academy of Arts and Letters*, series 2 / 16 (1966), 61-69.

Includes a poem "In Memory of William Butler Yeats," a reprint of "William Butler Yeats: The Arch Poet," *Programme for the Formal Opening of Thoor Ballylee on 20 June 1965*. [Dublin: Dolmen Press, 1965]. 4 pp. The poem is also included in BB44.

100. CONNOLLY, PETER (ed): *Literature and the Changing Ireland*. Gerrards Cross: Smythe / Totowa, N.J.: Barnes & Noble, 1982. ix, 230 pp. (Irish Literary Studies. 9.)

With one exception (Kiberd), these are the papers delivered at the IASAIL conference in Maynooth, July 1979. On Yeats: Declan Kiberd: "The Perils of Nostalgia: A Critique of the Revival," 1-24.

Vivian Mercier: "Victorian Evangelicalism and the Anglo-Irish Literary Revival," 59-101.

Suheil B. Bushrui: "Images of a Changing Ireland in the Works of W. B. Yeats," 103-32; on the manifestations of Yeats's "ideal nationalism" throughout his poetic career.

Stan Smith: "Historians and Magicians: Ireland between Fantasy and History," 133-56.

D. E. S. Maxwell: "Semantic Scruples: A Rhetoric for Politics in the North," 157-74; includes a section on Yeats's political poetry.

101. CONRAD, H. R.: "Englische Dichter der Neuzeit. I.: W. B. Yeats," *Neue Schweizer Rundschau*, ns 14:6 (Oct 1946), 360-68.

Sees Yeats's work, especially his poetry, in the context of his time.

102. CONRAD, PETER: *The Everyman History of English Literature*. London: Dent, 1985. xi, 740 pp.

"The Last Romantic?" 546-59, and passim (see index).

103. COUSINS, JAMES H.: "Yeats: The Occult Poet," *Herald of the Star*, 4:10 (11 Oct 1915), 443-45.

By turning to theosophy and occultism Yeats transcended his Irish preoccupations.

104. ———: "Yeats," *Madras Mail*, 16 Nov 1923, 6.

105. COWLEY, MALCOLM: *Think Back on Us. . . : A Contemporary Chronicle of the 1930's*. Edited with an introduction by Henry Dan Piper. Carbondale: Southern Illinois UP, 1967. xv, 400 pp.

"Yeats as Anthologist," 307-10; reprint of "A Poet's Anthology," *NewRep*, 16 Dec 1936, 221-22; a review of W250/251.

"Yeats and the Baptism of the Gutter," 324-28; reprint of "Poet in Politics," *NewRep*, 21 Sept 1938, 191-92; a review of W198. Correspondence (not reprinted) by Delmore Schwartz and Malcolm Cowley, 12 Oct 1938, 272-73; James P. O'Donnell, 7 Dec

1938, 133-34.
"Socialists and Symbolists," 328-32; reprinted from *NewRep*, 28 Sept 1938, 218-19; Yeats's example proves that a symbolic and not a realistic treatment of social problems produces better poetry.
"Yeats and O'Faolain," 336-42; reprinted from *NewRep*, 15 Feb 1939, 49-50; see CD1160.

106. CRAIG, HARDIN (ed): *A History of English Literature*. NY: Oxford UP, 1950. xiii, 697 pp.
Joseph Warren Beach: "The Literature of the Nineteenth and the Early Twentieth Century, 1798 to the First World War," 463-618; includes "William Butler Yeats: The Celtic Mythos," 592-95 (also in CA36); "The Drama in Ireland," 599-601.

106a. °*Critical Essays: A Presentation Volume for Professor V. S. Seturaman*. Madras: Macmillan India, 1987.
A. Norman Jeffares: "Anglo-Irish Literature: Some Critical Perspectives," 87-104; contains some notes on Yeats.

107. CRONIN, ANTHONY: "A Question of Modernity," *X: A Quarterly Review*, 1:4 (Oct 1960), 283-92.

108. ———: *Heritage Now: Irish Literature in the English Language*. Dingle, Co. Kerry: Brandon, 1982. 215 pp.
"William Butler Yeats: Containing Contradictions," 87-93.

109. ———: *An Irish Eye*. Dingle, Co. Kerry: Brandon, 1985. 141 pp.
"Farewell Kiltartan," 32-36. Yeats's hatred of the middle class will not do these days.

110. CROSS, GUSTAV: "'Unless Soul Clap Its Hands. . . ,'" *Sydney Morning Herald*, 12 June 1965, 14.

111. Quiller, A., Jr. [i.e., CROWLEY, ALEISTER]: "The Shadowy Dill-Waters or Mr. Smudge the Medium," *Equinox*, 1:3 (Mar 1910), 327-31.
Crowley ridicules Yeats, whom he calls "Weary Willie," "Attis with a barren fig-leaf," and "Peer Gynt without his courage and lightheartedness, O onion with many a stinking sheath, and a worm at the heart."

112. CUNLIFFE, JOHN WILLIAM, and ASHLEY HORACE THORNDIKE (eds): *The World's Best Literature*. NY: Warner Library, 1917. 30 vols.
James Cobourg Hodgins: "William Butler Yeats," 26:16260a-h. Also contained in °John William Cunliffe and others (eds): *Columbia University Course in Literature Based on the World's Best Literature*. NY: Columbia UP, 1928-29 (vol. 8).

113. DAICHES, DAVID: *The Present Age after 1920*. London: Cresset Press, 1962 [1958]. x, 376 pp. (Introductions to English Literature. 5.)
The American edition was published as *The Present Age in British Literature*. Bloomington: Indiana UP, 1962. x, 376 pp. Yeats, pp. 30-39 and passim (see index). For an earlier version of the book see DB168.

114. ———, and ANTHONY THORLBY (eds): *Literature and Western Civilization. The Modern World III: Reactions*. London: Aldus Books, 1976. 621 pp.
On Yeats passim (see index); his right-wing attitudes are dis-

cussed by Daiches in "Anti-Romanticism and Reaction," 459-82.

115. DAICHES, DAVID, and JOHN FLOWER: *Literary Landscapes of the British Isles: A Narrative Atlas*. London: Paddington Press, 1979. 287 pp.
"The Dublin of Yeats and Joyce: After Parnell," 214-34.

116. DARRAS, JACQUES: "Comme je la vois," *Critique*, 38:421-422 (June-July 1982), 603-11.
The author's view of Irish literature, including Yeats.

117. DATTA, SUDHINDRANATH: *The World of Twilight: Essays and Poems*. Bombay: Oxford UP, 1970. xxiv, 292 pp.
"W. B. Yeats and Art for Art's Sake," 185-203 (written in 1936).

118. DAVIDSON, DONALD: *Still Rebels, Still Yankees and Other Essays*. [Baton Rouge]: Louisiana State UP, 1957. x, 284 pp.
"Yeats and the Centaur," 23-30; reprinted from *SoR*, 7:3 (Winter 1941/42), 510-16; and from CA36. In his early work, especially his poetry, Yeats drew heavily on popular Irish lore; it was only one of many themes in the later work, which had no visible impact on the popular imagination.

119. DAVRAY, HENRY D.: "William Butler Yeats," *Ermitage*, 7:8 (Aug 1896), 88-96.

120. DAY, MARTIN STEELE: *History of English Literature: 1837 to the Present. A College Course Guide*. Garden City: Doubleday, 1964. xii, 442 pp. (Doubleday College Course Guides. U15.)
Yeats, pp. 239-49.

121. DAY LEWIS, C.: "W. B. Yeats," *New Masses*, 30:11 (7 Mar 1939), 22-23.

122. DEANE, SEAMUS: *Celtic Revivals: Essays in Modern Irish Literature 1880-1980*. London: Faber & Faber, 1985. 199 pp.
On Yeats passim (see index), especially in "The Literary Myths of the Revival," 28-37 (reprinted from CB403; on Yeats's myth of the ascendancy).
"Yeats and the Idea of Revolution," 38-50; revised from "Yeats, Ireland and Revolution," *Crane Bag*, 1:2 (1977), 56-64; also in CB194.
"O'Casey and Yeats: Exemplary Dramatists," 108-22; revised from *Threshold*, 30 (Spring 1979), 21-28; incorporates "Irish Politics and O'Casey's Theatre," *Threshold*, 24 (Spring 1973), 5-16.
Reviews:
- Denis Donoghue: "A Myth and Its Unmasking," *TLS*, 1 Nov 1985, 1239-40.
- Nicholas Murray: "To Sing the Burden of History," *NSt*, 6 Sept 1985, 26.
- Peter Sirr: "The Burden of History," *IrT*, 28 Sept 1985, 13.

123. ———: *A Short History of Irish Literature*. London: Hutchinson, 1986. 282 pp.
See "Irish Modernism: Poetry and Drama," 141-67, and the index for numerous other references.

124. DE BLACAM, AODH: "Yeats as I Knew Him," *IrM*, 67:789 (Mar 1939), 204-12.

A misnomer. Not a biographical article but a condemnation of much of the later work and a half-hearted appraisal of the earlier.

125. ———: "Yeats Reconsidered," *IrM,* 71:839 (May 1943), 209-17.
"How richly the highest part of his genius would have been at home if he had been reared in the Catholic culture!"

126. DE BREFFNY, BRIAN (ed): *The Irish World: The History and Cultural Achievements of the Irish People*. London: Thames & Hudson, 1977. 296 pp.
Phillip L. Marcus: "Literature and the Theatre," 213-26, and passim (see index).

127. *Decadence and the 1890s*. Associate editor Ian Fletcher. London: Arnold, 1979. 216 pp. (Stratford-upon-Avon Studies. 17.)
Yeats is referred to passim, especially in the following: Jan B. Gordon: "'Decadent Spaces': Notes for a Phenomenology of the *Fin de Siècle*," 30-58; John Lucas: "From Naturalism to Symbolism," 130-48 (see also FE58).

128. DICKINSON, ASA DON: *The Best Books of Our Time, 1901-1925*. Another clue to the literary labyrinth consisting of a list of one thousand best books published in the first quarter of the twentieth century selected by the best authorities accompanied by critical descriptions. NY: Wilson, 1931 [1928]. xiv, 405 pp.
This is an interesting compilation. Yeats received 18 endorsements (pp. 335-37), mainly for *Cathleen ni Houlihan, Reveries over Childhood and Youth,* and *The Land of Heart's Desire* in *Selected Poems* (1921). Yeats possesses, however, only a fraction of Galsworthy's "quality" (197 endorsements, the winner of the contest); he is also preceded by Wells (172), Bennett (137), Shaw (123), Synge (53), Moore (45), Maeterlinck (33), James Stephens (24), and Lord Dunsany (20). Less successful celebrities are Proust (7), Thomas Mann (6), Pirandello (6), Emily Dickinson (4), Hugo von Hofmannsthal (4), and Pound (4). Another list, *The Best Books of the Decade 1926-1935,* was published in 1937. Yeats has 116 endorsements for his *Collected Poems*. The winner is James Truslow Adams (733); Eliot gets 179 for his drama and criticism; Pound has disappeared. Among 13 books of poetry, Yeats has only tenth place, trailing Stephen Vincent Benét, Edna St. Vincent Millay, Frost, Robinson, MacLeish, Sandburg, and Elinor Wylie; but he is "better" than Sara Teasdale. In the 1936-45 list (published 1948), Yeats collects 215 votes for his prose and poetry (but does not appear in the list of 16 best books of poetry). Eliot gets 298 for his poetry and plays; the winner is Van Wyck Brooks (1,711).

129. DONOGHUE, DENIS: *The Ordinary Universe: Soundings in Modern Literature*. London: Faber & Faber, 1968. 320 pp.
"The Human Image in Yeats," 108-24; first published in *LMag,* 1:9 (Dec 1961), 51-65, and in *UR,* 3:8 [1966?], 56-70. In most of Yeats's volumes of poetry, the human image is curiously defective; it is either body or soul, rarely both, so that unity of being is never fully realized. The one exception, and hence his most splendid achievement, are the poems in *The Wild Swans at Coole*.

"Yeats and the Living Voice," 125-45; first published in *Studies,* 55:218 (Summer 1966), 147-65. Yeats was committed to an "oral culture." Unlike the symbolists and Eliot, he wrote poems as a means of communication. This also explains "why Yeats resorted to the drama."

130. ———: "The Hard Case of Yeats," *NYRB*, 26 May 1977, 3-4, 6, 8.
A review article in which Donoghue discusses Yeats's "status in modern literature." Correspondence by Robert Lowell: "Yeats's Vision," 14 July 1977, 41; and reply by Donoghue, ibid.

131. ———: *We Irish: Essays on Irish Literature and Society*. NY: Knopf, 1986. ix, 276 pp.
On Yeats see especially: "We Irish," 3-18.
"Romantic Ireland," 21-33; from Jeffares: *Yeats, Sligo, and Ireland* (1980, CA51), 17-30. Yeats's concept of Romantic Ireland is, in Schiller's terms, that of a sentimental poet unsuccessfully trying to recapture a naive relation to nature.
"Yeats: The Question of Symbolism," 34-51; from CB403.
"Yeats, Ancestral Houses, and Anglo-Ireland," 52-66. Also published in Desmond Guinness and Denis Donoghue: *Ascendancy Ireland*. Papers read at a Clark Library Seminar, 28 Sept 1985. Los Angeles: William Andrews Clark Memorial Library, U of California, 1986. ix, 54 pp. (pp. 31-52).
"On *The Winding Stair*," 67-88; from Donoghue and Mulryne: *An Honoured Guest* (1965, CA22), 106-23.
"Maud Gonne," 218-25.
Reviews:
- Thomas Flanagan: "The Quaking Bog," *NYRB*, 31 Mar 1988, 46-48.
- John Wilson Foster: "Letters from Denis: Donoghue's Irish Criticism," *Irish R*, 2 (1987), 107-12.
- Patrick Keane: "A Balanced Stance," *Salmagundi*, 73 (Winter 1987), 177-86.
- David Krause: "On Irish Poetics and Politics," *ILS*, 6:1 (Spring 1987), 5-6.
- Edna Longley: "Hauteur, Hauteur," *TLS*, 5 June 1987, 612.
- Julian Moynahan: "Thinking Otherwise," *NewRep*, 5 & 12 Jan 1987, 38-41.
- Margaret O'Brien: "Irishry," *EIC*, 38:1 (Jan 1988), 84-93.

132. DOORN, WILLEM VAN: "William Butler Yeats: A Lopsided Study," *ES*, 2:9 (June 1920), 65-77.
Also as a booklet, °Amsterdam: Swets & Zeitlinger, 1920. 16 pp.

133. DOTTIN, PAUL: "W. B. Yeats, poète national de l'Irlande," *Revue de France*, year 3 / 6:3 (1 Dec 1923), 665-72.

134. DOWLING, LINDA C.: *Language and Decadence in the Victorian Fin de Siècle*. Princeton: Princeton UP, 1986. xvi, 295 pp.
"Yeats and the Book of the People," 244-83, and passim (see index). Discusses the influence of Pater and Yeats's changing attitude and unending adherence to "Victorian literary Decadence," particularly in the stories of *The Secret Rose*.

135. DRĂGHICI, SIMONA: "Actualitatea lui William Butler Yeats" [The actuality of Yeats], *Secolul 20*, 5:12 (1965), 40-47.
General introduction to Yeats's life and work for Rumanian readers. Claims that Yeats's philosophy implies the possibility of perceiving an absolute truth, whereas his poetry does not. Yeats, not Auden and others, wrote the best political poetry of his time, although he did not propose any solutions to political problems.

Discusses "Lapis Lazuli" as very close to Yeats's idea of the ideal poem.

136. D[UNCAN], E[LLEN] M.: "The Writings of Mr. W. B. Yeats," *FortnR*, os 91 / ns 85:506 (Feb 1909), 253-70.
A chronological survey. The author has sometimes been wrongly identified as Edward Dowden, e.g., in CA50, where an extract is reprinted on pp. 169-72.

137. DYBOSKI, ROMAN: *Sto lat literatury angielskiej*. Warszawa: Pax, 1957. xx, 927 pp.
"Wkład Irlandii" [The contribution of Ireland], 803-50 ("William Butler Yeats . . . i George William Russell," 812-24).

138. EARNSHAW, HERBERT GEOFFREY: *Modern Writers: A Guide to Twentieth-Century Literature in the English Language*. Edinburgh: Chambers, 1968. vi, 266 pp.
"W. B. Yeats," 112-21.

139. EDGAR, PELHAM: "William Butler Yeats and the Irish Movement," *Globe*, 17 Dec 1904, Magazine section, 7.

140. ———: *Across My Path*. Edited by Northrop Frye. Toronto: Ryerson Press, 1952. xiv, 167 pp.
"The Enigma of Yeats," 145-53; reprinted from *QQ*, 46:4 (Winter 1939), 411-22.

141. EDWARDS, OLIVER: "W. B. Yeats and Ulster; and a Thought on the Future of the Anglo-Irish Tradition," *Northman*, 13:2 (Winter 1945), 16-21.
Discusses the reasons for Yeats's dislike of Ulster and says that true Anglo-Irish literature has a future only in Ulster, now that the Republic has a stifling censorship act.

142. EDWARDS, PHILIP: "Yeats and the Trinity Chair," *Hermathena*, 101 (Autumn 1965), 5-12.
The professorship of English literature. See also CB24, 144, and CF35.

143. EGLINTON, JOHN: "National Ideals," *United Irishman*, 16 Nov 1901, 3.
Answers Yeats's "John Eglinton" in the preceding number (see *Uncollected Prose*, 2:255-62).

144. ———: "Life and Letters," *IrSt*, 21 Feb 1920, 181.
On Yeats's nonappointment to the Trinity Chair of English Literature. See also CB24, 142, and CF35.

145. ———: *Irish Literary Portraits*. Freeport, N.Y.: Books for Libraries Press, 1967 [1935]. v, 158 pp.
Contents: "Introductory," 3-14. Some general remarks on the Irish literary revival, pointing out that Yeats was its greatest poet but failed as its spiritual leader. Yeats's and the revival's enemy was Trinity College, not the Irish people.

"Yeats and His Story," 17-35; reprinted from *Dial*, 80:5 (May 1926), 357-66. On Yeats's life and work, especially in their relation to Ireland, including some reminiscences.

Reviews:
- Anon.: "John Eglinton Returns," *IrT*, 6 July 1935, 7.
- Karl Arns, *Englische Studien*, 71:2 (Dec 1936), 294-96.

- [Alan Clutton Brock]: "Literary Portraits," *TLS*, 25 July 1935, 474.
- Heinz Höpf'l, *Neuphilologische Monatsschrift*, 7:6 (June 1936), 252-55.
- D. M.: "The Tragedy of Irish Literature," *IrP*, 19 June 1937, 7.
- A. L. Morton: "The Ireland of W. B. Yeats," *New English Weekly*, 5 Sept 1935, 330.
- T. C. M[urray]: "After a Long Silence," *IrI*, 25 June 1935, 4.
- Horace Reynolds: "James Joyce and Other Irish Writers," *NYTBR*, 8 Sept 1935, 3, 13.

146. ———: *Confidential, or Take It or Leave It*. London: Fortune Press, 1951. 54 pp.
"Apologia," 5-10. On Yeats and AE as leaders of the Irish literary revival.

147. ELIOT, THOMAS STEARNS: *After Strange Gods: A Primer of Modern Heresy*. The Page-Barbour Lectures at the University of Virginia, 1933. NY: Harcourt, Brace, 1934. 72 pp.
Reprinted [Folcroft, Pa.]: Folcroft Press, 1970. On Yeats, pp. 47-51. The supernatural world of the early Yeats was the wrong supernatural world: "It was not a world of spiritual significance, not a world of real Good and Evil, of holiness or sin, but a highly sophisticated lower mythology summoned, like a physician, to supply the fading pulse of poetry with some transient stimulant so that the dying patient may utter his last words."

148. E[LIOT], T. S.: "A Commentary," *Criterion*, 14:57 (July 1935), 610-13.
A surprisingly generous tribute to Yeats on the occasion of his 70th birthday: With his literary Irish nationalism, Yeats "performed a great service to the English language" and to English poetry.

148a. ELLMANN, RICHARD: *a long the riverrun: Selected Essays*. London: Hamilton, 1988. viii, 277 pp.
"The Uses of Decadence: Wilde, Yeats, Joyce," 3-17; see CC71a.
"Yeats without Analogue," 18-32; reprinted from the second edition of CA26.
"Ez and Old Billyum," 46-66, and "Gazebos and Gashouses," 78-97; reprinted from CD7.
"At the Yeatses'," 239-55; reprinted from the 1979 edition of BA3.

149. ELTON, OLIVER: *Modern Studies*. London: Arnold, 1907. viii, 342 pp.
"Living Irish Literature," 285-320. On Yeats, pp. 299-307; particularly on *Deirdre*.

149a. EMPSON, WILLIAM: *Argufying: Essays on Literature and Culture*. Edited with an introduction by John Haffenden. London: Chatto & Windus, 1987. ix, 657 pp.
"Yeats and the Spirits," 350-55; reprinted from *NYRB*, 13 Dec 1973, 43-45; a review of *Memoirs* (1972).
"A Time of Troubles," 343-49; a review of CA20, CA48 (including the reply to Conor Cruise O'Brien), and DA35 (qq.v.).
"Literary Criticism and the Christian Revival," 632-37; reprinted from *Rationalist Annual*, 83 (1966), 25-30; also in Karl Miller (ed): *Writing in England Today: The Last Fifteen Years*. Harmondsworth: Penguin, 1968. 362 pp. (pp. 168-74). Argues that

the "neo-Christian method of literary criticism leads frequently to . . . unpleasant misinterpretations" and discusses "Byzantium" as a relevant example.
Further references to Yeats passim (see index).

150. ENEHJELM, HELEN AF: "En stor irländsk diktare" [A great Irish poet], *Hufvudstadsbladet,* 12 June 1965, 7.

151. ESPMARK, KJELL: *Det litterära Nobelpriset: Principer och värderingar bakom besluten.* Stockholm: Norstedts, 1986. 202 pp.
On Yeats, pp. 60-64 and passim (see index).

152. EVANS, BENJAMIN IFOR: *English Literature between the Wars.* London: Methuen, 1948. ix, 133 pp.
"W. B. Yeats," 83-90. Yeats looked for "some formula through which the fragmentation of modern experience can be expressed."

152a. EYLER, AUDREY S., and ROBERT F. GARRATT (eds): *The Uses of the Past: Essays on Irish Culture.* Newark: U of Delaware Press, 1988. 195 pp.
Declan Kiberd: "The War against the Past," 24-54; includes a discussion of *Deirdre.*
Bonnie Kime Scott: "Feminist Theory and Women in Irish Writing," 55-63; responds in part to a paper by Conrad Balliet, "W. B. Yeats: Chauvinist/Feminist" (not included in this volume).
Hazard Adams: "Yeats, Joyce, and Criticism Today," 64-78. Sees *A Vision* as a critical model with which to arrive at an understanding of *Finnegans Wake.*
Robert Tracy: "Ghosts in the Churchyard: Ó Cadhain and Patterns," 79-97. Compares the treatment of the "persistently active dead" by Yeats and Máirtín Ó Cadhain in *Cré na Cille.*
Philip O'Leary: "Uneasy Alliance: The Gaelic League Looks at the 'Irish' Renaissance," 144-60; including Pearse's view of Yeats.

153. FALLIS, RICHARD: *The Irish Renaissance.* Syracuse: Syracuse UP, 1977. xvi, 320 pp.
A competent survey of Anglo-Irish literature from the 1880's onwards with careful attention given to its historical, political, and social contexts. Yeats figures prominently (see index).
Reviews:
- R. W. Desai: "Ireland Reborn," *Humanities R,* 1:2 (Oct-Dec 1979), 43-46.
- Denis Donoghue: "Ghostly Paradigms," *NSt,* 22 Sept 1978, 366, 368.
- Mary Joan Egan and Joseph J. Egan, *MFS,* 24:4 (Winter 1978-79), 596-97.
- Warren Leamon: "The Stage Irishman as Academic," *GaR,* 32:4 (Winter 1978), 910-15.
- Lorna Reynolds: "A Thorny Way," *Hibernia,* 7 Sept 1978, 12.

154. FARMER, ALBERT JOHN: *Le mouvement esthétique et "décadent" en Angleterre (1873-1900).* Paris: Champion, 1931. xvii, 413 pp. (Bibliothèque de la Revue de littérature comparée. 75.)
Several references to Yeats (see index), especially to his connection with the Rhymers' Club (pp. 261-75).

155. FERRANDO, GUIDO: "Il Premio Nobel ad un poeta irlandese," *Marzocco,* 2 Dec 1923, 1-2.

156. FIELD DAY THEATRE COMPANY: *Ireland's Field Day*. London: Hutchinson, 1985. viii, 120 pp.

The first three items are reprints of Field Day Pamphlets 4, 5, and 6, Derry: Field Day Theatre Company, 1984.

Seamus Deane: "Heroic Styles: The Tradition of an Idea," 43-58.

Richard Kearney: "Myth and Motherland," 59-80; discusses Yeats's "myth of Mother Ireland as spiritual or symbolic compensation for the colonial calamities of historical reality."

Declan Kiberd: "Anglo-Irish Attitudes," 81-105; contains some notes on Yeats's place in the Anglo-Irish tradition.

Denis Donoghue: "Afterword," 107-20; comments on the Yeats interpretations offered in the above contributions.

American edition: °Notre Dame, Ind.: U of Notre Dame Press, 1986. viii, 116 pp.; with an afterword by Thomas Flanagan.

157. FLEISHER, FREDERIC: "William Butler Yeats," *Hufvudstadsbladet*, 28 Jan 1964, 7-8.

158. FLEMING, LIONEL: *Head or Harp*. London: Barrie and Rockliff, 1965. 187 pp.

"The Synthesis," 149-56. Almost alone among the better-known 20th-century Irishmen, Yeats achieved a synthesis of heroic past and nationalistic present. Fleming, while on the staff of the *Irish Times*, met Yeats several times. On one occasion Yeats remarked: "It might surprise you to know what I am reading. It is Kipling. I dislike his works so much that I feel sure it must have something to teach me."

159. FLETCHER, IAN: "The 1890's: A Lost Decade," *VS*, 4:4 (June 1961), 345-54.

160. ———: *W. B. Yeats and His Contemporaries*. Brighton: Harvester Press, 1987. x, 350 pp.

Revised and expanded versions of previous publications. See especially: "Bedford Park: Aesthete's Elysium?" 43-82; first published in Fletcher (ed): *Romantic Mythologies*. London: Routledge & Kegan Paul, 1967. xiii, 297 pp. (pp. 169-207).

"Rhythm and Pattern in Yeats's *Autobiographies*," 127-52; reprinted from CA22.

"Yeats's Quest for Self-Transparency," 153-65; first published in *TLS*, 19 Jan 1973, 53-55. A review of *Memoirs*, discussing Yeats's autobiography in general and the relationship between draft and finished product in particular. See also correspondence by Denis Donoghue, *TLS*, 2 Feb 1973, 125.

"Poet and Designer: W. B. Yeats and Althea Gyles," 166-96; reprinted from *YeSt*, 1 (Bealtaine 1971), 42-79. The biographical connections set against a discussion of Yeats's theories of art.

"Yeats and Lissadell," 197-219; reprinted from Maxwell and Bushrui: *W. B. Yeats 1865-1965* (1965, CA71), 62-78. On the historical background of "In Memory of Eva Gore-Booth and Con Markiewicz."

"Yeats's 'Leda and the Swan' as Iconic Poem," 220-51; reprinted from *YeA*, 1 (1982), 82-113.

"Symons, Yeats and the Demonic Dance," 252-66; reprinted from *LMag*, 7:6 (June 1960), 46-60. The dance symbol in the poetry of Yeats and Symons.

Reviewed by Robert Hogan: "Yeats and Some Contemporaries," *ELT*, 31:2 (1988), 218-20.

161. F-t, T. [FOGELQVIST, TORSTEN]: "Nobelpriset i litteratur utdelat i går: Av Svenska akademin tilldelat irländaren William Butler Yeats," *Dagens nyheter,* 15 Nov 1923, 1, 7.

162. FORD, BORIS (ed): *The Modern Age.* Harmondsworth: Penguin Books, 1961. 560 pp. (Pelican Guide to English Literature. 7.)

See especially John Holloway: "The Literary Scene," 51-100; Graham Martin: "The Later Poetry of W. B. Yeats," 170-95; Grattan Freyer: "The Irish Contribution," 196-208.

163. ———: *The New Pelican Guide to English Literature.* Harmondsworth: Penguin Books, 1982-84. 9 vols.

Based on the preceding. See vol. 6: *From Dickens to Hardy.* 1982. 526 pp. (scattered remarks on Yeats).

Vol. 7: *From James to Eliot.* 1983. 592 pp. (John Holloway: "The Literary Scene," 61-112; Graham Martin: "The Later Poetry of W. B. Yeats," 230-54; Grattan Freyer: "The Irish Literary Scene," 255-74; and passim).

164. FORD, JULIA ELLSWORTH, and KATE V. THOMPSON: "The Neo-Celtic Poet--William Butler Yeats," *Poet Lore,* 15:4 (Winter 1904), 83-89.

165. FRANULIC, LENKA: *Cien autores contemporaneos.* 3rd edition. Santiago de Chile: Ercilla, 1952. 997 pp.

"William Butler Yeats," 975-83.

166. FRASER, GEORGE SUTHERLAND: *The Modern Writer and His World.* London: Deutsch, 1964 [1953]. 427 pp.

First published in Japan in °1950. Yeats, passim (see index).

167. ———: *Vision and Rhetoric: Studies in Modern Poetry.* London: Faber & Faber, 1959. 285 pp.

"The Romantic Tradition and Modern Poetry," 15-38; contains some remarks on Yeats's poetry.

"W. B. Yeats," 39-64; a reprint of CA30, q.v.

"Yeats and 'The New Criticism,'" 65-83; reprinted from *Colonnade,* 1:1 (Spring 1952), 6-12; :2 (Winter 1952), 14-21. Criticizes recent interpretations of "I Am of Ireland" by Walter E. Houghton (DC178) and of "Among School Children" by Delmore Schwartz (CB426).

168. FRENCH, R. D. B.: "Yeats as Poet and Politician," *Glasgow Herald,* 12 June 1965, 10.

169. FRENZ, HORST (ed): *Nobel Lectures Including Presentation Speeches and Laureates' Biographies: Literature, 1901-1967.* Amsterdam: Elsevier, 1969. xxi, 630 pp.

"William Butler Yeats," 193-212, includes "Presentation" by Per Hallström (see also CB187), Yeats's acceptance speech (apparently not published elsewhere), Yeats's lecture "The Irish Dramatic Movement" (see Wade 144), and a short biography.

170. FROTHINGHAM, EUGENIA BROOKS: "An Irish Poet and His Work," *Critic,* 44:1 (Jan 1904), 26-31.

171. GARBATY, THOMAS JAY: "*The Savoy* 1896: A Re-Edition of Representative Prose and Verse, with a Critical Introduction, and Biographical and Critical Notes," Ph.D. thesis, U of Pennsylvania, 1957. xxv, 719 pp. (*DAI,* 17:12 [Dec 1957], 3014-15)

See especially pp. 81-92, 94-98, 713-19, and index.

172. GENRE: "The Genres of the Irish Literary Revival," edited by Ronald Schleifer, *Genre,* 12:4 (Winter 1979).
Contains the editor's introduction, "Reviving Genres," 415-22, and CD97, 718, 843, 1335, FA17, and FG36.
Also issued as a book with the same title, Norman, Oklahoma: Pilgrim Books / Dublin: Wolfhound Press, 1980. v, 193 pp. Reviewed by Robert Boyle, *JJQ,* 18:2 (Winter 1981), 209-15.

173. GILLIE, CHRISTOPHER: *Movements in English Literature 1900-1940.* Cambridge: Cambridge UP, 1975. vii, 207 pp.
See pp. 74-80, 150-56, 170-73, and passim.

174. GLICKSBERG, CHARLES I.: "William Butler Yeats and the Role of the Poet," *ArQ,* 9:4 (Winter 1953), 293-307.
Yeats put the role of the poet above everything else and believed in it unswervingly.

175. [GOGARTY, OLIVER ST. JOHN]: "Literature and Civilization," *IrSt,* 24 Nov 1923, 325-26.
Praises Yeats for having won the Nobel Prize.

176. GREEN, MARTIN: *Yeats's Blessings on von Hügel: Essays on Literature and Religion.* London: Longmans, 1967. viii, 256 pp.
Yeats, pp. 1-5, 24-29, 59-61, 121-26, and passim (see index). Unlike von Hügel, Yeats was not a liberal humanist. The relevant passage in "Vacillation" proves that he did not understand von Hügel. I cannot help feeling, however, that Green mistakes Yeats for Richard Ellmann (consistently misspelled), who is another target of Green's attacks.

177. GREGORY, HORACE: "W. B. Yeats: An Irish Traveler to Byzantium," *Griffin,* 8:8 (Sept 1959), 2-14.

178. Entry canceled.

179. GRUBB, H. T. HUNT: "William Butler Yeats: His Plays, Poems and Sources of Inspiration," *Poetry R,* 26:5 (Sept/Oct 1935), 351-66; :6 (Nov/Dec 1935), 455-65.

180. GRZYBOWSKI, STANISŁAW: *Historia Irlandii.* Wrocław: Zakład Narodowy imienia Ossolińskich Wydawnictwo, 1977. 392 pp.
"Celtyckie odrodzenie 1864-1914" [The Celtic revival], 308-20.

181. GWYNN, STEPHEN: *Irish Books and Irish People.* Dublin: Talbot Press / London: Unwin, [1920]. vii, 120 pp.
"Introduction," 1-6: "Yeats and Synge have showed how completely it is possible to be Irish while using the English language."

182. ———: "Ebb and Flow," *FortnR,* os 144 / ns 138:824 (Aug 1935), 229-38.
Contains sections on "Yeats's Poetry and Work" and "The Irish Theatre."

183. ———: *Irish Literature and Drama in the English Language: A Short History.* London: Nelson, 1936. ix, 240 pp.
Numerous references to Yeats, especially to his plays; includes an "Appendix" on the Irish Academy of Letters (pp. 232-36).
Reviews:
- Anon.: "The Irish Revival," *Outlook* [Glasgow], 1:4 (July 1936), 84-86.

- Padraic Fallon, *DM*, 11:3 (July-Sept 1936), 66-68.
- H. T. Hunt Grubb: "A Poet's Friends," *Poetry R*, 27:4 (July-Aug 1936), 317-22.
- Francis MacManus: "Ireland with the English Mouth," *IrM*, 64:761 (Nov 1936), 744-50.
- Sean Moran: "A Survey of the Sham Irish: Mr. Stephen Gwynn's Review of Some English Writers," *Catholic Bulletin*, 26:8 (Aug 1936), 657-61.

184. HAERDTER, MICHAEL: "Den Deutschen unbekannt: 100. Geburtstag von William Butler Yeats," *FAZ*, 11 June 1965, 32.

185. HALL, WAYNE EDWARD: *Shadowy Heroes: Irish Literature of the 1890s*. Syracuse: Syracuse UP, 1980. xvii, 241 pp.
Based on "Irish Writers of the 1890's: The Literary Hero and the Landed Gentry," Ph.D. thesis, Indiana U, 1978. iv, 287 pp. (*DAI*, 39:2 [Aug 1978], 896A). The early writers as seen in, or rather alienated from, the contemporary Irish social, political, and religious context. See "W. B. Yeats: Prose Works and *The Countess Cathleen*," 155-75; "W. B. Yeats: *The Rose* and *The Wind among the Reeds*," 176-98; and passim.
Reviews:
- Phillip L. Marcus, *YeA*, 2 (1983), 129-35.
- Daniel T. O'Hara, *VS*, 26:1 (Autumn 1982), 99-101.
- Joseph Ronsley, *YER*, 8:1&2 (1986), 127-28.
- Robert Welch, *IUR*, 11:2 (Autumn 1981), 236-37.

186. HALLSTRÖM, PER: "William Butler Yeats," *Edda*, 5:1 (1916), 22-39.

187. ———: "The Nobel Prize in Literature for 1923," *Prix Nobel*, 1923, 61-65.
Reprinted in CB3; see also CB169, 536, 537.

188. °HARMON, MAURICE: *Modern Irish Literature*. NY: McGraw-Hill, 1968. Tape recording, 25 minutes.
"Covers the growth of Irish writing from 1800 to the present. Discusses and illustrates the main periods and the principal writers, including the leading figures of the Irish Literary Revival" (publisher's prospectus).

189. HARRISON, GEORGE BAGSHAWE (ed): *Major British Writers*. Enlarged edition. NY: Harcourt, Brace & World, 1959 [1954]. 2 vols.
Reuben A. Brower: "William Butler Yeats, 1865-1939," 2:779-818. Annotations to some poems and a general introduction.

190. HARRISON, JOHN R.: *The Reactionaries: Yeats, Lewis, Pound, Eliot, Lawrence. A Study of the Anti-Democratic Intelligentsia*. Introduction by William Empson. NY: Schocken Books, 1967 [1966]. 224 pp. (Schocken Paperback. SB205.)
Based on °"The Social and Political Ideas of W. B. Yeats, Wyndham Lewis, Ezra Pound, T. S. Eliot, and D. H. Lawrence," M.A. thesis, U of Sheffield, 1962.
"W. B. Yeats," 39-73; and passim. Yeats's view of democratic government, as expressed in poetry, prose, and letters, was one of "the election of those least able to govern by those least able to judge." His aristocratic view of political and sociological matters is clearly related to his literary style. Harrison admits, however, that Yeats "is probably the last poet who could legitimately reject our modern civilisation without being guilty of in-

tellectual and moral evasion." Generally, "Yeats, Lewis, Pound, and Eliot were really interested in society only in so far as it would allow the arts to flourish." The book has been criticized for its lack of substance and for its simplifications. See also CA157 and FD72.

Reviews:

- Bernard Bergonzi, *LMag*, 6:8 (Nov 1966), 88-91, 93-94; reprinted as "Modern Reactionaries" in CB48, pp. 177-82.
- Cyril Connolly: "Five Writers Accused," *SunT*, 21 Aug 1966, 21.
- Nigel Dennis: "Haters of the Herd," *Sunday Telegraph*, 21 Aug 1966, 15.
- D. J. Enright: "No Cheer for Democracy," *NSt*, 23 Sept 1966, 443-44; reprinted in *Man Is an Onion: Reviews and Essays*. London: Chatto & Windus, 1972. 222 pp. (pp. 163-69).
- Irving Howe: "Beliefs of the Masters," *NewRep*, 16 Sept 1967, 19-20, 22-23, 26.
- Graham Martin: "The Romantic Defence," *List*, 29 Sept 1966, 471-72.
- Philip Rahv, "An Open Secret," *NYRB*, 1 June 1967, 20-23; reprinted in *Literature and the Sixth Sense*. London: Faber & Faber, 1970. xv, 445 pp. (pp. 437-45).
- David H. Stewart, *CE*, 31:3 (Dec 1969), 330-34.
- Philip Toynbee: "Poetry and Fascism," *Obs*, 28 Aug 1966, 16.
- Geoffrey Wolff: "Writers and Politics," *ASch*, 37:2 (Spring 1968), 356-62.

191. HARTMAN, GEOFFREY H.: *Criticism in the Wilderness: The Study of Literature Today*. New Haven: Yale UP, 1980. xi, 323 pp.

Passim (see index), especially on "Leda and the Swan." See also DD367.

192. HARTNETT, MICHAEL: "W. B. Yeats: Evolution of a Style," *IrT*, 23 Feb 1971, 10.

"He was a professional English poet but an amateur Irish one." "There was no Irish Literary Renaissance: there *was* a school of 'Anglo-Irish' writers: they no longer exist."

On the same page there is a photograph of a bust of the young Yeats by Irene Broe.

193. HEATH-STUBBS, JOHN: *The Darkling Plain: A Study of the Later Fortunes of Romanticism in English Poetry from George Darley to W. B. Yeats*. London: Eyre & Spottiswoode, 1950. 221 pp.

Reprinted Philadelphia: West, 1977. See pp. 203-11. Although Yeats's flirtation with fascism and his occult interests should not be overlooked, it can be argued that "no poetry which satisfies our intellect and our senses together will, on ultimate examination, prove false."

194. HEDERMAN, MARK PATRICK, and RICHARD KEARNEY (eds): *The Crane Bag Book of Irish Studies (1977-1981)*. Dublin: Blackwater Press, 1982. 937 pp.

A reprint of vols. 1-5 of *The Crane Bag*. Major references to Yeats are to be found in the following contributions:

M. P. Hederman: "The Playboy versus the Western World (Synge's Political Role as Artist)," 59-65 (from 1:1, 1977).

Seamus Deane: "Unhappy and at Home: Interview with Seamus Heaney by Seamus Deane," 66-72 (from 1:1, 1977). Includes comments on Yeats's importance for modern Irish poetry.

John Hill: "An Archetype of the Irish Soul," 136-38 (from 1:2, 1977). Jungian archetypal imagery in *Cathleen ni Houlihan*.

Seamus Deane: "Yeats, Ireland, and Revolution," 139-47 (from 1:2, 1977; also in CB122). On Yeats's romantic politics, as seen in some poems and in *A Full Moon in March*.

R. Kearney: "Myth and Terror," 273-87 (from 2:1&2, 1978). Comments on "Easter 1916" and other poems with Irish nationalistic themes.

Augustine Martin: "What Stalked through the Post-Office?" 312-25 (from 2:1&2, 1978). A reply to Deane, above.

Declan Kiberd: "Writers in Quarantine? The Case for Irish Studies," 341-53 (from 3:1, 1979).

W. J. McCormack: "Yeats and a New Tradition," 362-72 (from 3:1, 1979). The Anglo-Irish tradition from the 18th century onwards. Incorporated in CB274.

Aidan Mathews: "Modern Irish Poetry: A Question of Covenants," 380-89 (from 3:1, 1979).

M. P. Hederman: "A Hidden Tradition," 403-7 (from 3:1, 1979).

W. J. McCormack: "Yeats' *Purgatory:* A Play and a Tradition," 453-64 (from 3:2, 1979). Incorporated in CB274.

R. Kearney: "Those Masterful Images," 491-501 (from 3:2, 1979). Discusses Yeats's concept of the imagination. French version: "Ces images magistrales," in CA32, 174-88.

Timothy Kearney: "Beyond the Planter and the Gael: Interview with John Hewitt and John Montague on Northern Poetry and The Troubles," 722-29 (from 4:2, 1980). Includes comments on Yeats as a political poet.

Peter Kuch: "Mananaan Mac Lir as Monoglot--George Russell and the Irish Language," 880-89 (from 5:2, 1981).

195. HEISELER, BERNT VON: "Erzählungen und Lyrik," *Deutsche Zeitschrift,* 47:9 (June 1934), 579-80.

196. ———: *Gesammelte Essays zur alten und neuen Literatur.* Stuttgart: Steinkopf, 1966-67. 2 vols.

"William B. Yeats," 1:264-75; reprinted from *Neue Rundschau,* year 50 / 2:8 (Aug 1939), 142-49; and *Sammlung,* 4 (1949), 257-63. Rhapsodic praise, particularly of the early plays.

197. HEŁSZTYNSKI, STANISŁAW: *Od Chaucera do Ezry Pounda.* Warszawa: Państwowy Instytut Wydawniczy, 1976. 188 pp.

"William Butler Yeats: Cztery fazy twórczości (1865-1939)," 87-97 ("Four phases of the literary work").

198. HEMINGWAY, ERNEST: *Dateline: Toronto. The Complete "Toronto Star" Dispatches, 1920-1924.* Edited by William White. NY: Scribner's, 1985. xxxi, 478 pp.

"'Nobelman' Yeats," 384-86; reprint of "Learns to Commune with the Fairies, Now Wins the $40,000 Nobel Prize: Yeats Also Elected Senator in the Irish Free State--Hair Hangs Down in a Lank Sweep on One Side of His Celtic Face," *Toronto Star Weekly,* 24 Nov 1923, 35.

"W. B. Yeats a Nighthawk," 427-28; reprint of "W. B. Yeats a Night Hawk Kept Toronto Host Up: Also Forgot His Hair Brush and Pyjamas--Room Looked like Premier Nitti's Wrecked House," 22 Dec 1923, 35.

Both articles were published anonymously.

199. HENN, THOMAS RICE: *Five Arches: A Sketch for an Autobiography. And "Philoctetes and Other Poems."* Gerrards Cross: Smythe, 1980. 326 pp.

Yeats is referred to passim (see index). Includes Henn's poem

"The Tower Revisited" (reprinted from *Acorn*, 3 [Autumn 1962], 15), p. 262 (see also note, p. 306).

200. HENNECKE, HANS: *Englische Gedichte von Shakespeare bis W. B. Yeats: Einführungen, Urtexte und Übertragungen*. Berlin: Kiepenheuer, 1938. 160 pp.
"William Butler Yeats," 153-55. Also contained in *Gedichte von Shakespeare bis Ezra Pound: Einführungen, Urtexte und Übertragungen*. Wiesbaden: Limes, 1955. 352 pp. (pp. 163-65). Factually inaccurate.

201. ———: *Dichtung und Dasein: Gesammelte Essays*. Berlin: Henssel, 1950. 274 p.
"William Butler Yeats und der europäische Symbolismus," 153-60 (reprinted from *Europäische Revue*, 15:3 [Mar 1939], 280-84), and passim (see index).

202. ———: *Kritik: Gesammelte Essays zur modernen Literatur*. Gütersloh: Bertelsmann, 1958. 301 pp.
"Dichtung--Philosophie--Gedicht: Zur Poetik von William Butler Yeats," 115-23; reprinted from *Jahresring*, [3] ([19]56/57), 52-55.

203. ———: "Späte Wege zu William Butler Yeats," *Neue deutsche Hefte*, 18:4 (1971), 25-52.
A general assessment of Yeats's modernity and his reception in Germany by way of a review of *Werke*, vols. 1-2 (CB540).

204. HIGHET, GILBERT: *The Powers of Poetry*. NY: Oxford UP, 1960. xv, 356 pp.
"The Old Wizard," 122-28; reprinted from *A Clerk of Oxenford: Essays on Literature and Life*. NY: Oxford UP, 1954. xii, 272 pp. (pp. 165-72).

205. HOFFMAN, CHRISTINE B.: "William Butler Yeats and the Nobel Prize," *Personalist*, 49:1 (Winter 1968), 103-15.
Nobel's stipulation that the prize for literature should go to somebody whose work shows "an idealistic tendency" was inspired by his reading of Shelley. Yeats's idealism can be traced to the same source.

206. HOGAN, J. J.: "W. B. Yeats," *Studies*, 28:109 (Mar 1939), 35-48.

207. HOGAN, ROBERT (ed): *The Macmillan Dictionary of Irish Literature*. London: Macmillan, 1980. xviii, 3-816 pp.
Yeats figures prominently (see index); the article devoted to him (pp. 701-26) is by Richard M. Kain.

208. HOLROYD, STUART: *Emergence from Chaos*. London: Gollancz, 1957. 222 pp.
"W. B. Yeats: The Divided Man," 113-37.

209. HORTMANN, WILHELM: *Englische Literatur im 20. Jahrhundert*. Bern: Francke, 1965. 204 pp. (Dalp-Taschenbücher. 379G.)
"William Butler Yeats und die irische Renaissance," 27-35; "W. B. Yeats," 71-74.

210. HOUGH, GRAHAM: *Image and Experience: Studies in a Literary Revolution*. London: Duckworth, 1960. ix, 228 pp.
The American edition was published as °*Reflections on a Literary*

Revolution. Washington, D.C.: Catholic U of America Press, 1960. 127 pp. Yeats, passim (see index).

211. ———: *Selected Essays*. Cambridge: Cambridge UP, 1978. viii, 247 pp.
"W. B. Yeats: A Study in Poetic Integration," 144-72; reprinted from *Eranos*, 40 (1971), 51-84. Yeats's personal and poetic development shows parallels to Jungian concepts, but also radical differences.

212. HOWARTH, HERBERT: "The Week of the Banquet," *LMag*, 5:1 (Apr 1965), 36-45.
What Yeats did and probably thought in the week after his 70th birthday. Includes an imagined conversation between Yeats, Gogarty, and Julian Bell.

213. ———: "Yeats: The Variety of Greatness," *WHR*, 19:4 (Autumn 1965), 335-43.

214. HUGO, L. H.: "'The Last Romantic': The Poetry and Thought of W. B. Yeats," *Lantern*, 15:2 (Dec 1965), 24-37.

215. HUMAYUN KABIR: *Poetry, Monads and Society*. Calcutta: U of Calcutta, 1941. xi, 203 pp. (Sir George Stanley Lectures 1941.)
"William Butler Yeats," 169-93. Yeats's work represents a synthesis of emotion and intellect and cannot be divided into different phases. A highly abstract essay almost devoid of illustrative quotations.

216. HUNEKER, JAMES: "Mystic, Poet and Dramatist: Career of William Butler Yeats, Irish Lyricist," *Sun* [NY], 27 Dec 1903, 3.
See also Huneker's "The Week's Output of Plays," ibid., 22 Nov 1903, section 3, 4; a preview of Yeats's American lecture tour.

217. IMAAL: "A Rather Complex Personality," *Leader*, 26 Sept 1903, 71-72.
Mocks Yeats's "symbolical" inclinations. Correspondence by Stephen Gwynn, 10 Oct 1903, 100; and Imaal, 17 Oct 1903, 122.

218. JACKSON, HOLBROOK: *The Eighteen Nineties: A Review of Art and Ideas at the Close of the Nineteenth Century*. New illustrated edition with an introduction by Christopher Campos. Hassocks: Harvester Press, 1976 [1913]. 304 pp.
On Yeats, pp. 150-56, and passim (see index).

219. ———: "Makers of Movements: No. XIII--William Butler Yeats and the Irish Literary Movement," *Bystander*, 25 Mar 1914, 622-24.
Includes the Alvin Langdon Coburn photograph (see BG60).

220. [———]: "Men of To-day and To-morrow III: Mr. William Butler Yeats," *To-day*, 1:3 (May 1917), 93-97.
Yeats withdraws more and more from the Irish literary movement that he helped to found.

221. JACKSON, SCHUYLER: "William Butler Yeats," *LMerc*, 11:64 (Feb 1925), 396-410.
Yeats is the only poet of his time who has been consistent in following his imagination, but now he seems to betray a certain fragmentation in his poetry and thought.

222. JANSSENS, GERARDUS ANTONIUS MARIA: *The American Literary Review: A Critical History, 1920-1950*. The Hague: Mouton, 1968. 341 pp. (Studies in American Literature. 26.)
Notes on the Yeats reception in American literary reviews, passim; see especially pp. 239-42 on the *Southern Review* Yeats issue (CA104).

223. JARRELL, RANDALL: *Kipling, Auden & Co.: Essays and Reviews 1935-1964*. NY: Farrar, Straus, and Giroux, 1980. xii, 381 pp.
"The Development of Yeats's Sense of Reality," 88-100; reprinted from *SoR*, 7:3 (Winter 1941/42), 653-66. The development of Yeats's thought and poetry falls into three phases: (1) neglect of reality (stereotyped poetry), (2) acknowledgment of reality (good poetry), (3) victory over reality (superb poetry). Yeats was driven to an acceptance of reality by his failure to create a unity of Irish culture in the early years of the century.

224. JEFFARES, ALEXANDER NORMAN: "W. B. Yeats: The Gift of Greatness," *Daily Telegraph*, 12 June 1965, 8.

225. ———: *Anglo-Irish Literature*. London: Macmillan, 1982. x, 349 pp. (Macmillan History of Literature.)
"William Butler Yeats," 148-60, and passim (see index).

226. ———: *Parameters of Irish Literature in English*. A lecture given at the Princess Grace Irish Library on Friday 25 April 1986 at 8.00 p.m. Gerrards Cross: Smythe, 1986. 44 pp.
Several references to Yeats.

227. JOHNSEN, WILLIAM ARNOLD: "Toward a Redefinition of the Modern," Ph.D. thesis, U of Illinois at Urbana-Champaign, 1970. iii, 210 pp. (*DAI*, 31:12 [June 1971], 6613A)
"W. B. Yeats," 87-102.

228. JOHNSON, PAUL: *Ireland: A History from the Twelfth Century to the Present Day*. London: Granada, 1981. 272 pp.
First published as °*Ireland: Land of Troubles*. London: Eyre Methuen, 1980. On Yeats, pp. 124-26, 157-59, 180-81.

229. JOURNET, DEBRA: "Yeats's Quarrel with Modernism," *SoR*, 20:1 (Winter 1984), 41-53.
"Unlike the Modernist who strives for formal autonomy, Yeats strives for conceptual intelligibility."

230. JURČINOVÁ, EVA: *Poutníci věčných cest: Essaye* [Pilgrims on eternal paths]. Turnov (Czechoslovakia): Müller, 1929. 117 pp. (Edice sever a ýýchod. 28.)
"Před prahem stoleti a na jeho prahu" [Before the threshold of the century and on the threshold], 9-24; contains a note on Yeats, 22-24. "Hlasy z irska" [The voices from Ireland], 25-52; on the early works.

231. KAHN, DEREK: "The Morality of W. B. Yeats," *Left R*, 2:6 (Mar 1936), 252-58.
A misnomer. Criticizes Yeats's "anti-democratic and anti-rational bias" and detects weak spots in his humanism. Concludes that Yeats "has written fine poetry, though he has not always taught good lessons."

232. KAIN, RICHARD MORGAN: *Dublin in the Age of William Butler*

Yeats and James Joyce. Norman: U of Oklahoma Press, 1962. xi, 216 pp. (Centers of Civilization Series. 7.)

Reprinted °Newton Abbott: David & Charles, 1972. The intelligent reader's Baedeker to Irish literature and literary Dublin; informative but not particularly deep. Yeats figures prominently. Documentation practically nil.

233. KARL, FREDERICK ROBERT: *Modern and Modernism: The Sovereignty of the Artist 1885-1925*. NY: Atheneum, 1985. xviii, 459 pp.

On Yeats, pp. 220-31; mainly on his occult interests, his early plays, particularly *Deirdre*, and "The Indian to His Love."

234. KAVANAGH, PATRICK: "Diary: Being Some Reflections on the 50th Anniversary of Irish Literature," *Envoy*, 1:1 (Dec 1949), 86-90.

Continued in subsequent issues; Yeats is mentioned passim. In one installment (3:10 [Sept 1950], 84-85), Kavanagh includes a parody of "Under Ben Bulben."

235. ———: *November Haggard: Uncollected Prose and Verse*. Selected, arranged and edited by Peter Kavanagh. NY: Peter Kavanagh Hand Press, 1971. vii, 229 pp.

"On a Liberal Education," 79-87; reprinted from *X: A Quarterly Review*, 2:2 (Aug 1961), 112-19. Kavanagh's quarrel with Yeats and the Irish literary revival (it "was responsible for many lies").

"Yeats," 229; reprinted from *Holy Door*, 3 (Spring 1966), 1. A poem, perhaps Kavanagh's best diatribe against Yeats.

236. ———: *Collected Pruse*. London: McGibbon & Kee, 1967. 288 pp.

"William Butler Yeats," 254-56; reprinted from *Kilkenny Magazine*, 6 (Spring 1962), 25-28. "Yeats, you have much to answer for."

See also "Auden and the Creative Mind," 247-53, for a few notes on Yeats.

237. ———: *Lapped Furrows: Correspondence 1933-1967 between Patrick and Peter Kavanagh with Other Documents*. Edited by Peter Kavanagh. NY: Peter Kavanagh Hand Press, 1969. vii, 307 pp.

Yeats, passim (see index).

238. Entry canceled.

239. KEARNEY, RICHARD (ed): *The Irish Mind: Exploring Intellectual Traditions*. Dublin: Wolfhound Press, 1985. 365 pp.

R. Kearney: "An Irish Intellectual Tradition? Philosophical and Cultural Contexts," 7-38, 311-18.

John Jordan: "Shaw, Wilde, Synge and Yeats: Ideas, Epigrams, Blackberries, and Chassis," 209-25, 340-42. Despite the title, very little is said about Yeats.

Elizabeth Cullingford: "The Unknown Thought of W. B. Yeats," 226-43, 343-45. A survey of Yeats's "beliefs."

240. KELLNER, LEON: *Die englische Literatur im Zeitalter der Königin Viktoria*. Leipzig: Tauchnitz, 1909. xxx, 703 pp.

"William Butler Yeats," 629-39. Insists on Yeats's otherworldliness, his lack of political interest, and his Celticism. The second edition of the book, *Die englische Literatur der neuesten Zeit von Dickens bis Shaw*. Leipzig: Tauchnitz, 1921. 402 pp., although announced as radically revised, prints virtually the same material on Yeats (pp. 368-76).

241. KELLY, JOHN STEPHEN: "The Political, Intellectual, and Social Background to the Irish Literary Revival to 1901," Ph.D. thesis, Cambridge U, 1971. vi, 392, vii, xv pp.
Contains individual chapters on O'Grady, Hyde, Yeats and the Irish National Theatre, including an account of the *Countess Cathleen* row. Lacks a table of contents.

242. ———: "Aesthete among the Athletes: Yeats's Contributions to *The Gael* ," *Yeats,* 2 (1984), 75-143.
A reconstruction of Yeats's contributions to this elusive weekly (1887-88); cites all surviving parts of the Finn Mac Cumhaill essay, the review of Katharine Tynan's *Shamrocks* (including John O'Leary's comments on Yeats's review), and his poem "The Protestants' Leap."

243. KENNEDY, JOHN MURRAY: *English Literature, 1880-1905*. London: Swift, 1912. vi, 340 pp.
On Yeats, pp. 280-89; he is described as "a compound of Gaelic bard and William Blake," i.e., as one whose adoption of Irish subject matter is tempered by a thorough knowledge of English poetry.

244. KENNY, HERBERT A.: *Literary Dublin: A History*. With illustrations by Charles Carroll. NY: Taplinger / Dublin: Gill & Macmillan, 1974. 336 pp.
See index for references to Yeats, particularly in "The Celtic Renaissance," 161-240, and "Modern Times," 241-318 (post-1916).

245. "Pat" [i.e., KENNY, PATRICK D.]: "Patriana. . . : Lady Gregory, Mr. Yeats, and Irish Realities," *Irish Peasant,* 3 Mar 1906, [4-5].
"Would it be too much to ask Mr. Yeats to come down to the ground, for just a little while, and to try something more directly and more obviously in touch with actual, human sympathies and imp[u]lses? I know my suggestion may appear a little vulgar, but Mr. Yeats is generous to critics, and after all, the theatre must have some more direct relation to national life."

246. K[EOHLER], T. G.: "Mr. Yeats," *Sinn Féin,* 6 July 1907, 3.
"Yeats could never have done the work which he has done but for the efforts of his predecessors--Moore, Mangan, and Ferguson."

247. KIBERD, DECLAN: "Inventing Irelands," *Crane Bag,* 8:1 (1984), 11-23.
Yeats's kind of the Irish Revival was not the only one; his pastoral Ireland "has now become a downright oppression."

248. KIDD, WALTER E. (ed): *British Winners of the Nobel Literary Prize*. Norman: U of Oklahoma Press, 1973. vii, 280 pp.
James V. Baker: "William Butler Yeats," 44-82.

249. KIDDER, RUSHWORTH M.: "Exploring an Inner Landscape: William Butler Yeats," *CSM,* 23 Aug 1982, 20-21.

250. KING, BRUCE (ed): *Literatures of the World in English*. London: Routledge & Kegan Paul, 1974. xi, 225 pp.
A. Norman Jeffares: "Ireland," 98-115. A survey of Anglo-Irish writers with frequent references to Yeats. See also the editor's introduction, pp. 16-19.

251. KITCHIN, LAURENCE: "The Ditch and the Tower," *List,* 14 Oct 1965, 575-77.
Yeats's authority and modernity.

252. KLEIN, LEONARD S. (ed): *Encyclopedia of World Literature in the 20th Century*. Revised edition. NY: Ungar, 1981-84. 4 vols.
David Castronovo: "Irish Literature," 2:458-63; Edward Hirsch: "Yeats, William Butler," 4:673-79.
Based on Wolfgang Bernard Fleischmann (ed): *Encyclopedia of World Literature in the 20th Century in Three Volumes*. An enlarged and updated edition of the Herder *Lexikon der Weltliteratur im 20. Jahrhundert*. NY: Ungar, 1967-71. 3 vols. (Melvin J. Friedman: "Irish Literature," 2:146-50; Richard Ellmann: "Yeats," 3:553-56).
Both articles are also in the German edition: *Lexikon der Weltliteratur im 20. Jahrhundert*. Freiburg: Herder, 1960-61. 2 vols. (Friedman: "Irische Literatur," 1:979-85; Ellmann: "Yeats," 2:1291-99).

253. KLEINSTÜCK, JOHANNES: "Im Kampf um Irlands Seele: Am 13. Juni vor hundert Jahren wurde W. B. Yeats geboren," *Welt,* 11 June 1965, 7.

254. KNOWER, E. T.: "A Modern Minstrel," *American R,* 3:4 (July-Aug 1925), 400-405.

255. KOEBNER, THOMAS (ed): *Zwischen den Weltkriegen*. Wiesbaden: Akademische Verlagsgesellschaft Athenaion, 1983. vii, 620 pp. (Neues Handbuch der Literaturwissenschaft. 20.)
Yeats is discussed by Franz Norbert Mennemeier: "Das neue Drama," 79-110; and by Heinz Kosok: "Die britische und anglo-irische Literatur," 417-54.

256. KOOMEN, MARTIN: *Het literaire Dublin: Opkomst en ondergang van de Ierse literaire beweging*. Amsterdam: Tabula, 1984. 141 pp.
"Literary Dublin: The rise and fall of the Irish literary movement"; Yeats figures prominently (see index).

257. KOROTICH, VITALIĬ: "Slova Uïl'i͡ama Ïtsa" [The word of William Yeats], *Vsesvit,* 11 (Nov 1973), 127-30.

258. KOSOK, HEINZ (ed): *Studies in Anglo-Irish Literature*. Bonn: Bouvier, 1982. viii, 496 pp. (Wuppertaler Schriftenreihe Literatur. 19.)
The papers written for the Wuppertal Symposium on Anglo-Irish Literature in July 1981. The following are on Yeats:
Hans Walter Gabler: "James Joyce and Ireland," 65-73.
John Wilson Foster: "The Revival of Saga and Historical Romance during the Irish Renaissance: The Ideology of Cultural Nationalism," 126-36.
Mary FitzGerald: "Some Problems of Nationality in the Early Irish Theatre," 148-54 (on Yeats and Lady Gregory).
Paul F. Botheroyd: "The Years of the Travellers: Tinkers, Tramps, and Travellers in Early Twentieth-Century Irish Drama and Society," 167-75.
S. N. R. Kazmi: "Poetry and Politics: A Case Study of W. B. Yeats," 198-204.
Fahmy F. Farag: "The Ireland That Sings: Yeats and the Heresy of Universal Education," 205-13.
Conrad A. Balliet: "Yeats and His Bloody Repetition," 214-26

(blood imagery in the poetry, especially in "Blood and the Moon").

Robert Welch: "Yeats's Crazy Jane Poems and Gaelic Love Song," 227-35.

Joseph T. Swann: "'Where All the Ladders Start': Language and Experience in Yeats's Later Poetry," 236-45.

Ronald Marken: "'The Strange Heart Beating': Prosodic Considerations of Yeats's Poetry," 246-53.

Andrew Parkin: "Yeats's Stage Diction," 254-61.

Christina Hunt Mahony: "The Influence of John Todhunter on the Plays of W. B. Yeats," 262-68.

Siga Asanga: "The Playwright in the Theatre: Dramatic Theory and Practice since W. B. Yeats," 455-65 (mainly on Nigerian playwrights John Pepper Clark and Wole Soyinka).

Robert Mahony: "Some Problems in Editing Anglo-Irish Dramatic Texts," 490-96.

259. KRISTENSEN, SVEN MØLLER (ed): *Fremmede digtere i det 20. århundrede*. København: Gad, 1967-68. 3 vols.

Peter P. Rohde: "William Butler Yeats," 1:69-85.

260. LANGBAUM, ROBERT: *The Modern Spirit: Essays on the Continuity of Nineteenth- and Twentieth-Century Literature*. NY: Oxford UP, 1970. xiii, 221 pp. (Galaxy Books. GB320.)

Yeats, passim (see index), especially in "The Mysteries of Identity: A Theme in Modern Literature," 164-84; reprinted from *ASch*, 34:4 (Autumn 1965), 569-86 (myth, mask, and character in Yeats's poetry).

261. LENNARTZ, FRANZ: *Ausländische Dichter und Schriftsteller unserer Zeit: Einzeldarstellungen zur schönen Literatur in fremden Sprachen*. 2nd edition. Stuttgart: Kröner, 1957 [1955]. vii, 749 pp. (Kröners Taschenausgabe. 217.)

Yeats, pp. 737-45.

262. LESTER, JOHN A.: *Journey through Despair, 1880-1914: Transformations in British Literary Culture*. Princeton: Princeton UP, 1968. xxiii, 211 pp.

On Yeats, passim (see index), especially on the concept of the mask.

263. LEWIS, WYNDHAM: "W. B. Yeats," *New Verse*, ns 1:2 (May 1939), 45-46.

264. ———: *Rude Assignment: A Narrative of My Career Up-to-Date*. London: Hutchinson, [1950]. 231 pp.

Some notes on Yeats, passim (see index). A new edition was published as *Rude Assignment: An Intellectual Autobiography*. Illustrated by the author, edited by Toby Foshay. Santa Barbara: Black Sparrow Press, 1984. 315 pp.

265. LICHNEROWICZ, JEANNE: "Le dernier Prix Nobel de littérature: W.-B. Yeats," *Revue bleue*, 61:23 (1 Dec 1923), 793-94.

An English summary was published as "The Latest Nobel Prize for Literature: William Butler Yeats," *American R of Reviews*, 69:2 (Feb 1924), 205-6.

266. ———: "William Butler Yeats," *Europe*, 5:18 (15 June 1924), 162-74.

267. LONGAKER, MARK, and EDWIN COURTLANDT BOLLES: *Contemporary English Literature*. NY: Appleton, 1953. xvii, 526 pp.
"The Celtic Renaissance," 34-66; on Yeats, pp. 35-43.

268. LYND, ROBERT: *Home Life in Ireland*. London: Mills & Boon, 1910 [1909]. xvi, 317 pp.
"Literature and Music," 305-17; on Yeats, pp. 305-9.

269. ———: *Old and New Masters*. NY: Scribner's, [1919]. 249 pp.
"W. B. Yeats," 156-70; reprinted in *Essays on Life and Literature*. London: Dent, 1951. xiv, 274 pp. (Everyman's Library. 990.), pp. 160-72. An essay in two parts: "His Own Account of Himself" and "His Poetry."

270. ———: *Ireland a Nation*. NY: Dodd, Mead, 1920. ix, 299 pp.
"The Witness of the Poets," 176-88. "A Note on Irish Literature," 187-217, includes an interview with Yeats "on the prospects and functions of an Irish theatre," 211-17; reprinted from *Daily News*, 6 June 1910, 4; reprinted in BA13, 1:64-68.

271. ———: "Letters to Living Authors.--IV.: Mr. W. B. Yeats," *John o' London's Weekly*, 10 Aug 1929, 608.
"I doubt whether the reading public . . . realizes yet what a good poet you are."

272. ———: *Books and Writers*. With a foreword by Richard Church. London: Dent, 1952. xv, 331 pp.
"William Butler Yeats," 76-84; includes "William Butler Yeats: A Great Poet Who Was a Missionary of Art," *John o' London's Weekly*, 10 Feb 1939, 735-36.

273. MCALINDON, T.: "Divine Unrest: The Development of William Butler Yeats," *IrM*, 83 [i.e., 82]:968 (Apr 1954), 152-59.

274. MCCORMACK, WILLIAM JOHN: *Ascendancy and Tradition in Anglo-Irish Literary History from 1789 to 1939*. Oxford: Clarendon Press, 1985. xi, 432 pp.
The Yeats chapters are revised versions of previously published articles: "Yeats and a New Tradition," *Crane Bag*, 3:1 (1979), 30-40; also in CB194.

"Yeats' *Purgatory:* A Play and a Tradition," *Crane Bag*, 3:2 (1979), 33-44; also in CB194.

"Sons and Fathers: W. B. Yeats and a Problem of Modernism," in CA108, 14-29.

On Yeats's place in the Anglo-Irish tradition, the historical approach to "Nineteen Hundred and Nineteen," the father-son conflict in *On Baile's Strand*, and *Purgatory* see pp. 293-367 and passim. See also CD132.

Reviews:

- Terence Brown, *Hermathena*, 140 (Summer 1986), 111-14.
- Denis Donoghue: "A Myth and Its Unmasking," *TLS*, 1 Nov 1985, 1239-40.
- Richard Fallis, *Clio*, 15:3 (Spring 1986), 321-23.
- William H. O'Donnell, *Yeats*, 5 (1987), 253-55.
- Mary Helen Thuente: "Two Books on Irish Literature," *ELT*, 30:1 (1987), 104-9.
- Robert Tracy, *VS*, 29:4 (Summer 1986), 619-20.

275. ———: *The Battle of the Books: Two Decades of Irish Cultural Debate*. Gigginstown, Mullingar: Lilliput Press, 1986. 94 pp.

Numerous references to Yeats (see index).

276. MACDONAGH, OLIVER, W. F. MANDLE, and PAURIC TRAVERS (eds): *Irish Culture and Nationalism, 1750-1950*. London: Macmillan, in association with Humanities Research Centre, Australian National University, Canberra, 1983. xi, 289 pp.

On Yeats see particularly Patrick Rafroidi: "Imagination and Revolution: The Cuchulain Myth," 137-48.

A. R. G. Griffiths: "Finland, Norway and the Easter Rising," 149-60 (on Yeats's view of Ibsen).

F. S. L. Lyons: "Yeats and the Anglo-Irish Twilight," 212-38.

Vincent Buckley: "Poetry and the Avoidance of Nationalism," 258-79; reprinted from *Threshold*, 32 (Winter 1982), 8-34.

277. MACGLOIN, T. P.: "Yeats's Faltering World," *SR*, 95:3 (Summer 1987), 470-84.

The faltering world is that of the Anglo-Irish, "devastated, doomed, and unredeemable."

278. MCGOWAN, JOHN P.: *Representation and Revelation: Victorian Realism from Carlyle to Yeats*. Columbia: U of Missouri Press, 1986. vii, 206 pp.

"Yeats: Poverty and the Tragic Vision," 175-202.

279. [MCGRATH, JOHN]: Answer to Yeats's letter on American and Irish literature, signed "A Student of Irish Literature," *United Ireland*, 24 Nov 1894, 1.

See Yeats's reply, 1 Dec 1894, 1. Yeats's letters are reprinted in *Collected Letters*, 1:408-9, 416-17.

280. MCGRORY, KATHLEEN, and JOHN UNTERECKER (eds): *Yeats, Joyce, and Beckett: New Light on Three Modern Irish Writers*. Lewisburg, Pa.: Bucknell UP, 1976. 184 pp.

J. Unterecker: "The Yeats Landscape," 23-34. Photographs.

Adrienne Gardner: "*Deirdre:* Yeats's Other Greek Tragedy," 35-38. The play's structural and thematic indebtedness to Greek tragedy.

J. Unterecker: "Interview with Anne Yeats," 39-45. Her reminiscences of her father, including notes on her stage set for *Purgatory*.

Austin Clarke: "Glimpses of W. B. Yeats," 46-51. Reprinted from BB39.

K. McGrory: "Scholarship Frowned into Littleness?" 52-70. A review of research, mainly of the period 1965-73.

Reviews:
- Craig Wallace Barrow, *Eire*, 12:3 (Fall 1977), 137-39.
- Enoch Brater, *JBeckS*, 6 (Autumn 1980), 142-43.
- Barbara Brothers, *JJQ*, 14:2 (Winter 1977), 225-27.

281. MCHUGH, ROGER: "Yeats: The Era of the Celtic Twilight," *IrI*, 12 June 1965, 8.

282. ———, and MAURICE HARMON: *Short History of Anglo-Irish Literature: From Its Origins to the Present Day*. Dublin: Wolfhound Press, 1982. 377 pp.

See especially the chapters "The Irish Literary Revival" and "After the Revival," pp. 125-325.

283. O'L., A. [i.e., MACKENNA, STEPHEN]: "Mr. W. B. Yeats: An Argument and an Appreciation (By an Admirer)," *FrJ*, 2 Jan 1909, 5.

284. MACLEOD, FIONA: "A Group of Celtic Writers," *FortnR,* os 71 / ns 65:385 (1 Jan 1899), 34-53.
Mainly on Yeats. Extract reprinted in CA50, pp. 100-103.

285. ———: *The Winged Destiny: Studies in the Spiritual History of the Gael.* London: Heinemann, 1925 [1904]. xiv, 393 pp. (The Collected Works. 5.)
"The Shadowy Waters," 320-45; reprint of "The Later Work of Mr. W. B. Yeats," *NAR,* 175:551 (Oct 1902), 473-85. See also [Francis Thompson]: "Fiona Macleod on Mr. W. B. Yeats," *Academy,* 25 Oct 1902, 444-45; reprinted in G144.

286. MACLIAMMÓIR, MICHEÁL: "W. B. Yeats: Poet and Patriot," *Ireland of the Welcomes,* 14:1 (May-June 1965), 14-20.

287. MACM[ANUS], M. J.: "Yeats, Shaw and the New Ireland," *IrP,* 10 Aug 1939, 8.
Yeats and Shaw are Irish, not English, writers.

288. MACNEICE, LOUIS: *Selected Literary Criticism of Louis MacNeice.* Edited by Alan Heuser. Oxford: Clarendon Press, 1987. xxiii, 279 pp.
"The Newest Yeats: *A Full Moon in March*," reprinted from *New Verse,* 19 (Feb-Mar 1936), 16; a review of W182.
"Yeats's Epitaph," 116-19; reprinted from *NewRep,* 24 June 1940, 862-63; a review of W203/204.
"Great Riches," 171-73; reprinted from *Obs,* 27 Aug 1950, 7; a review of W211/A.
"Yeats's Plays," 180-82; reprinted from *Obs,* 2 Nov 1952, 8; a review of W211D/E.
"Endless Old Things," 190-94; reprinted from *NSt,* 2 Oct 1954, 398; a review of W211J/K.
"The Variorum Edition of the Poems of W. B. Yeats," 216-20; reprinted from *LMag,* 5:12 (Dec 1958), 69, 71, 73, 75; a review of W211N.
"Yeats at Work," 239-41; reprinted from *List,* 21 Mar 1963, 521; a review of DA44.

289. MAGILL, FRANK N. (ed): *Cyclopedia of World Authors.* NY: Harper & Row, 1958. xiii, 1200 pp.
"William Butler Yeats," 1186-90.

290. ——— (ed): *Critical Survey of Poetry: English Language Series.* Englewood Cliffs: Salem Press, 1982. 8 vols.
James Lovic Allen: "William Butler Yeats," 7:3181-3209; a survey of life and works, including analyses of "Leda and the Swan," "The Second Coming," "Among School Children," and "Sailing to Byzantium."

291. MAHON, A.: "The Man Who Was Yeats," *IrI,* 10 June 1965, 14, 17.

292. MALONE, G. P.: "William Butler Yeats: A Centenary Tribute," *ContempR,* 207:1195 (Aug 1965), 96-99.

293. MALVIL, ANDRÉ: "William Butler Yeats: Suivi de traductions inédites," *Monde nouveau,* 10:8 (15 Oct 1928), 548-57.
For the translations (pp. 553-57) see Wade, p. 439.

294. MALYE, JEAN: *La littérature irlandaise contemporaine.* Paris: Sansot, 1913, 70 pp.
Based on a series of articles entitled "La renaissance celtique

en Irlande," *Entretiens idéalistes,* year 5 / 8:51 (25 Dec 1910), 281-91; 6 / 9:54 (25 Mar 1911), 113-26; :55 (25 Apr 1911), 198-209; °:56 (25 May 1911). On Yeats, pp. 53-70.

295. MAN, PAUL DE: *Blindness & Insight: Essays in the Rhetoric of Contemporary Criticism.* NY: Oxford UP, 1971. xiii, 189 pp.
On the concept of modernity in Yeats's introduction to the *Oxford Book of Modern Verse* and on his idea of the soul, pp. 170-72.

296. MARBLE, ANNIE RUSSELL: *The Nobel Prize Winners in Literature.* NY: Appleton, 1925. xiii, 312 pp.
"W. B. Yeats and His Part in the Celtic Revival," 253-63.

297. MARTINS, SOARES: "Introdução a W. B. Yeats," *Tempo presente,* 7 (Nov 1959), 31-36.

298. MASON, EUGENE: *A Book of Preferences in Literature.* London: Wilson, 1915. 213 pp.
"The Poet as Mystic: William Butler Yeats," 89-113.

299. MASTERMAN, CHARLES FREDERICK GURNEY: *In Peril of Change: Essays Written in Time of Tranquillity.* NY: Huebsch, [1905]. xvi, 332 pp.
"After the Reaction," 1-36; reprinted from *ContempR,* 86:468 (Dec 1904), 815-34, and *Living Age,* 244:3160 (28 Jan 1905), 193-208. After the imperialist reaction of late Victorianism, Yeats is one of the most promising representatives of a future literature of the golden age.

300. MATTHEWMAN, S[YDNEY]: "The Paradox of W. B. Yeats," *Decachord,* 4:17 (Nov-Dec 1928), 150-55.
"Here, then, is the paradox: in one person a man of abundant and vivid personality, working for others; for a whole people indeed; and a poet aloof, obscure and self-absorbed, working out his own problems for his own satisfaction and inviting only those of like mind to share in the result."

301. MATTHIESSEN, FRANCIS OTTO: *The Responsibilities of the Critic: Essays and Reviews.* Selected by John Rackliffe. NY: Oxford UP, 1952. xvi, 282 pp.
"Yeats: The Crooked Road," 25-40; reprinted from *SoR,* 7:3 (Winter 1941/42), 455-70.

302. MAXWELL, D. E. S.: "Views of Yeats," *Mosaic,* 12:3 (Spring 1979), 115-28.
How Yeats's contemporaries saw him and how he viewed the world. Compares his poetry with that of Edward Thomas and Thomas Hardy.

303. [MAY, DERWENT]: "Under Ben Bulben," *TLS,* 21 Jan 1965, 47.
Correspondence by Robert O'Driscoll, 18 Feb 1965, 132.

304. MAYNARD, THEODORE: *Our Best Poets English and American.* NY: Holt, 1922. xxi, 233 pp.
"W. B. Yeats: Fairies and Fog," 67-83. The later work is not as good as the earlier, because Yeats "has lost his sympathy for Ireland." But even the earlier verse "has not worn well."

305. MENON, NARAYANA: "W. B. Yeats and the Irish Literary Revival," *IndL,* 8:2 (1965), 12-22.

306. MERCIER, VIVIAN: *The Irish Comic Tradition*. Oxford: Clarendon Press, 1962. xx, 258 pp.
Notes on Yeats, passim (see index).

307. METSCHER, THOMAS: "Bürgerliche und sozialistische Literatur in Irland, von Swift bis O'Casey: Eine literarhistorische Skizze," *Gulliver*, 7 (1980), 7-35.
A Marxist-oriented survey sees Yeats as the main representative of Irish bourgeois literature.

308. MILLER, JOSEPH HILLIS: *Poets of Reality: Six Twentieth-Century Writers*. Cambridge, Mass.: Belknap Press of Harvard UP, 1965. xiii, 369 pp.
"W. B. Yeats," 68-130; and passim. The book sketches a development from Romanticism through Nihilism to a New Realism, i.e., the rediscovery of God. The new realists are, in different ways, Conrad, Yeats, Eliot, Dylan Thomas, Stevens, and William Carlos Williams. Miller concludes that Yeats's "affirmation of the infinite richness of the finite moment" (p. 11) defines his kind of reality. See also the review by William H. Pritchard: "The Circus Animals' Desertion," *MR*, 7:2 (Spring 1966), 387-94.

309. MIROIU, MIHAI: "William Butler Yeats, bardul irlandei moderne" [Poet of modern Ireland], *Studi de literatură universală*, 7 (1965), 195-215.
Includes a summary in English.

310. MIX, KATHERINE LYON: *A Study in Yellow: The "Yellow Book" and Its Contributors*. Lawrence: U of Kansas Press, 1960. ix, 325 pp.
Yeats, passim (see index).

311. *Moderne encyclopedie der wereldliteratuur*. Hilversum: Brand & de Boer, 1963-77. 9 vols.
W. Schrickx: Yeats, 9:424-28.

312. MOKASHI-PUNEKAR, SHANKAR: *The Indo-Anglian Creed and Allied Essays*. Calcutta: Writers Workshop, 1972. 72 pp.
"Adam's Curse and Cussedness: Yeats's Approach of English and Its Lesson to India," 19-27; first published in *Triveni*, 33:3 (Oct 1964), 35-41, with the subtitle "W. B. Yeats's Rebellion against British English and Its Lesson to India."

313. MOLUA: "Purging the Pride of Pollexfen," *Catholic Bulletin*, 16:9 (Sept 1926), 937-43.
Vitriolic.

314. ———: "Pollexfen Pride and the People: An Anthology (1912-1925) with a Practical Result (1925-1927)," *Catholic Bulletin*, 17:8 (Aug 1927), 821-25.
Yeats's contempt of Paudeen turned on him with a vengeance.

315. MONAHAN, MICHAEL: *Nova Hibernia: Irish Poets and Dramatists of Today and Yesterday*. Freeport, N.Y.: Books for Libraries Press, 1967 [1914]. vii, 274 pp.
"Yeats and Synge," 13-37; reprinted from *Papyrus*, series 3 / year 9 / 3:2 (Dec 1911), 1-8.

316. MONTGOMERY, K[ATHLEEN and] L[ETITIA]: "Some Writers of the Celtic Renaissance," *FortnR*, os 96 / ns 90:537 (Sept 1911), 545-61.
Mainly on Yeats.

317. MOORE, T. STURGE: "Yeats," *English,* 2:11 (Summer 1939), 273-78.

318. MORAN, D. P.: "A Hundred Years of Irish Humbug," *Claidheamh Soluis,* 19 May 1900, 149-51.
Attacks the Irish literary revival, particularly Rolleston and Yeats: "I never knew a man who can, with such impunity, cast insults at his race and nation as Mr. W. B. Yeats." Correspondence by T. W. Rolleston, 2 June 1900, 189.

319. [——— (?)]: "At the Abbey Theatre," *Leader,* 7 Jan 1905, 330-31.
"Mr. Yeats does not interest us" and neither does the Abbey.

320. MORAWSKI, STEFAN: "Kipling--Yeats--Auden," *Twórczość,* 5:6 (1949), 84-99.
A Marxist approach.

321. MORE, PAUL ELMER: *Shelburne Essays.* First series. NY: Putnam's, 1904. v, 253 pp.
"Two Poets of the Irish Movement," 177-92; reprinted from *Evening Post,* 12 Dec 1903, Book section, 1; extract reprinted in CA50, pp. 151-56. Compares Yeats and Lionel Johnson to the latter's advantage. Yeats's poetry is one of "defeat"; compared to the healthy robustness of the Irish sagas, Yeats's works are feeble and decadent products.

322. MORGAN, CHARLES: *The House of Macmillan (1843-1943).* London: Macmillan, 1943. xii, 248 pp.
See pp. 220-24 for the relationship between Yeats and his publisher, particularly for two negative reader's reports by Mowbray Morris and John Morley. See also CB326.

323. MORRALL, JOHN: "Personal Themes in the Public and Private Writings of W. B. Yeats," *UR,* 1:9 (Summer 1956), 28-36.
Yeats as he appears from his letters and other writings.

324. MOSES, MONTROSE J.: "W. B. Yeats and the Irish Players," *Metropolitan Magazine,* 35:3 (Jan 1912), 23-25, 61-62.
After praising Yeats and the Abbey Players profusely, Moses offers some criticism: "There is perhaps one unfortunate factor in the movement: both dramatist and actor are self-conscious of their nationality. They never once allow you to forget that they are Irish and that they represent the Irish drama."

325. MURPHY, SHEILA ANN: "William Butler Yeats: Enemy of the Irish People," *Literature & Ideology,* 8 (1971), 15-30.
The periodical is published by the Necessity for Change Institute of Ideological Studies, Dublin and Montreal, which favors the Maoist approach. The article "expose[s] the fascist and anti-people character of imperialist cultural propaganda in Ireland represented by writers like Yeats, Lady Gregory, and many others." The Irish people "refute and repudiate [Yeats] as part of their struggle against U.S. and British imperialism."

326. MURRAY, T. C.: "The Casting Out of Shaw and Yeats," *Bell,* 12:4 (July 1946), 310-17.
Essentially a review of the Shaw and Yeats sections in CB322.

327. NELSON, JAMES G.: *The Early Nineties: A View from the Bodley Head.* Cambridge, Mass.: Harvard UP, 1971. xv, 387 pp.

Yeats, passim (see index), especially in connection with the Rhymers' Club.

328. NEVILLE, TONY: *The Challenge of Modern Thought.* London: U Tutorial Press, 1977. 158 pp.
"Yeats: The Divided Self," 105-8.

329. *The New Encyclopaedia Britannica in 30 Volumes.* 15th edition. Chicago: Encyclopaedia Britannica. 1974. 30 vols.
Macropaedia, vols. 1-19; Micropaedia, vols. 1-11. See D[enis] Do[noghue]: "Yeats, William Butler," Macropaedia, 19:1075-78; and the index to further Yeats references in Micropaedia, 10: 809. For a revised version of Donoghue's article see the 32-volume edition of 1986 (12:829-31).

See also T. R. Henn's article on Yeats in *Encyclopaedia Britannica.* Chicago: Encyclopaedia Britannica, 1968. 24 vols. (23: 880-82); that by Lennox Robinson in the 1947 edition (23:882-83); and the unsigned article on Yeats in the 11th edition of 1910-11 (28:909-10).

330. NIEMOJOWSKA, MARIA: "Iryjski głos" [The Irish voice], *Poezja,* 3:3 (Mar 1967), 69-77.

331. NIST, JOHN: "In Defense of Yeats," *ArQ,* 18:1 (Spring 1962), 58-65.
Against Yvor Winters (DA50).

332. NORTH, MICHAEL: *The Final Sculpture: Public Monuments and Modern Poets.* Ithaca: Cornell UP, 1985. 263 pp.
Incorporates "The Paradox of the Mausoleum: Public Monuments and the Early Aesthetics of W. B. Yeats," *CentR,* 26:3 (Summer 1982), 221-38; "The Ambiguity of Repose: Sculpture and the Public Art of W. B. Yeats," *ELH,* 50:2 (Summer 1983), 379-400.

The treatment of public monuments in modern poetry reveals one of its major concerns, "the contradiction between hermeticism and public ambition." Yeats is one of the "preeminent modern examples of the kind of imaginative writer who hopes to build a culture to receive his own work partly by calling attention to other works of art" (p. 9). See "W. B. Yeats," 41-99, on statues in the poetry and particularly in "The Statues."
Reviews:
- Terence Diggory, *Yeats,* 4 (1986), 213-18.
- Sister Bernetta Quinn: "Modern Poets," *ConL,* 28:1 (Spring 1987), 133-41.
- Andrew Swarbrick: "Modern Perplexity," *CritQ,* 28:3 (Autumn 1986), 109-14.

333. NUTT, ALFRED: "Irish Writers and English Readers," *New Ireland,* 10 Oct 1903, 7.
Irish readers have come to appreciate Yeats because English readers have preceded them in this.

334. OATES, JOYCE CAROL: "Speaking of Books: The Formidable W. B. Yeats," *NYTBR,* 7 Sept 1969, 2.
Correspondence by Dennis E. Smith, Fireman, Engine Co. 82, New York Fire Dept., 5 Oct 1969, 25.

335. O'BRIEN, GEORGE: "In Search of an Audience: Notes on the Progress of Irish Literature, 1891-1941," *YES,* 11 (1981), 117-26.
Mainly on Yeats, Joyce, and O'Faolain.

336. O'BRIEN, JAMES H.: "Yeats's Search for Unity of Being," *Personalist*, 48:3 (Summer 1967), 361-71.
Yeats's relevance to his age "lies in his continued pursuit of unity of being" and in his preservation of the self.

337. O'CASEY, SEAN: *Blasts and Benedictions: Articles and Stories*. Selected and introduced by Ronald Ayling. London: Macmillan, 1967. xx, 314 pp.
Yeats is mentioned passim (see index), especially in the following items:
"O'Casey on O'Casey: A Word before Curtain-Rise (1954)," 85-87; reprint of the foreword to °*Selected Plays*. NY: Braziller, 1954.
"W. B. Yeats and *The Silver Tassie*," 99-102; reprinted from CD929, q.v.
"Literature in Ireland," 170-81; reprinted from *International Literature*, 11 (Nov 1939), 104-8 (not Dec 1939, as stated by Ayling).
"Ireland's Silvery Shadow (1946)," 182-87; reprinted from *Tribune*, 27 Sept 1946, 14-15.
"John Millington Synge," 35-41; first published in Russian in °*Britanskiĭ soi͡uznik*, June 1946.
"On the Banks of the Ban (1963)," 146-49; reprinted from °*NYT*, 5 Jan 1964. On the Abbey Theatre.
"A Protestant Bridget (1946)," 205-12; reprinted from *Bell*, 13:5 (Feb 1947), 64-72. A review of Lady Gregory's *Journals* (BB98).
"A Sprig of Rosemary among the Laurel (1962)," 213-15; reprinted from the foreword to Lady Gregory's *Selected Plays* (London: Putnam, 1962), pp. 7-9.

338. O'CONNOR, FRANK: "The Plays and Poetry of W. B. Yeats: An Appreciation," *List*, 8 May 1941, 675-76.

339. ———: *The Backward Look: A Survey of Irish Literature*. London: Macmillan, 1967. viii, 264 pp.
The American edition was published as °*A Short History of Irish Literature: A Backward Look*. NY: Putnam, 1967. Incorporates: "Willie Is So Silly," *Vogue*, 1 Mar 1965, 122, 189-91, 193-95; "All the Olympians," *SatR*, 10 Dec 1966, 30-32, 99; "W. B. Yeats," *Critic*, 25:3 (Dec 1966--Jan 1967), 50-59; "Bring In the Whiskey Now, Mary," *New Yorker*, 12 Aug 1967, 36-40, 42, 45, 48, 50, 55-56, 58, 60, 63-64, 66, 68, 70-71.
Based on lectures, rambling rather than scholarly; includes reminiscences of Yeats. See especially pp. 163-82 and passim.

340. ———: "Yeats," *JIL*, 4:1 (Jan 1975), 173-78.
Speech delivered at Drumcliffe, 13 June 1965.

341. O'CONNOR, ULICK: *Celtic Dawn: A Portrait of the Irish Literary Renaissance*. London: Hamilton, 1984. xii, 292 pp.
An American edition was published as °*All the Olympians: A Biographical Portrait of the Irish Literary Renaissance*. NY: Atheneum, 1984. Yeats figures prominently in this popular rather than scholarly account (see index).

342. O'CONOR, NORREYS JEPHSON: *Changing Ireland: Literary Backgrounds of the Irish Free State, 1889-1922*. Cambridge, Mass.: Harvard UP, 1924. xii, 259 pp.
A somewhat sketchy book. The parallel between literature and

politics, suggested by the title, is not pursued very far. See especially "Yeats and His Vision," 72-82 (the dream of restoring Ireland's "ancient spiritual dignity"); and "Lady Gregory: Folklorist," 192-96, reprint of "Visions of the Celtic World as Seen by Lady Gregory in the West of Ireland," *BET,* 16 June 1920, section 2, 6 (a review of W312).

343. O'DRISCOLL, ROBERT, and LORNA REYNOLDS: "The Untilled Field of W. B. Yeats," *YER,* 5:1 (1978), 28-31.
The opportunities for further research, particularly the study of unpublished manuscripts.

344. O'DRISCOLL, ROBERT (ed): *The Celtic Consciousness.* Mountrath, Portlaoise: Dolmen Press / Edinburgh: Cannongate Publishing, 1982. xxxi, 642 pp.
First published °Toronto: McClelland & Stewart, 1981. Yeats is referred to passim, especially in the following:
Lorna Reynolds: "The Irish Literary Revival: Preparation and Personalities," 383-99.
R. O'Driscoll: "The Aesthetic and Intellectual Foundations of the Celtic Literary Revival in Ireland," 401-25.
"Epilogue: The Celtic Hero," 610-19 (on the production of *The Celtic Hero,* a conflation of Yeats's Cuchulain plays, with photographs).

345. O'DUFFY, EIMAR: "William Butler Yeats," *Flambeau,* 6:12 (31 Dec 1923), 549-52.

346. O'FAOLAIN, SEAN: "W. B. Yeats," *English R,* 60:6 (June 1935), 680-88.
Yeats between romanticism and realism.

347. [————]: "Fifty Years of Irish Literature," *Bell,* 3:5 (Feb 1942), 327-34.
An introduction to a collection of Yeats clippings ("The Wisdom of W. B. Yeats," 335-39), demonstrating how right Yeats was about certain Irish literary phenomena.

348. The Editor [i.e., O'FAOLAIN, SEAN]: "Romance and Realism," *Bell,* 10:5 (Aug 1945), 373-82.
Yeats was a romantic, not a realist.

349. O'FAOLAIN, SEAN: "W. B. Yeats Comes Back to Erin," *SunT,* 12 Sept 1948, 2.

350. ————: *The Irish: A Character Study.* NY: Devin-Adair, 1949. x, 180 pp.
"The Writers," 156-80.

351. ————: "Ireland after Yeats," *BA,* 26:4 (Autumn 1952), 325-33.
Reprinted in *Bell,* 18:11 (Summer 1953), 37-48.

352. ————: "Fifty Years of Irish Writing," *Studies,* 51:201 (Spring 1962), 93-105.

353. ————: *Vive Moi! An Autobiography.* London: Hart-Davis, 1965. 288 pp.
O'Faolain's opinion of Yeats and some anecdotes, pp. 272-83.

354. O'LEARY, JOHN: "The National Publishing Company," *FrJ,* 8 Sept

1892, 5.
The Yeats--Sir Charles Gavan Duffy quarrel. For further letters and leaders by O'Leary, John F. Taylor, Yeats, and others, see preceding and subsequent issues and *Collected Letters,* 1:310-14.

355. OLIVERO, FEDERICO: *Correnti mistiche nella letteratura inglese moderna*. Torino: Bocca, 1932. 373 pp.
See especially chapter 6, "Il 'Celtic Twilight,'" and passim.

356. O LOCHLAINN, COLM: "William Butler Yeats," *British Annual of Literature,* 2 (1939), 24-30.

357. OREL, HAROLD (ed): *Irish History and Culture: Aspects of a People's Heritage*. Lawrence: UP of Kansas, 1976. ix, 387 pp.
See particularly H. Orel: "A Drama for the Nation," 251-69; and "The Irishry of William Butler Yeats," 291-307.
Marilyn Stokstad and Mary Jean Nelson: "The Arts in Twentieth-Century Ireland," 271-89 (mainly on Jack B. Yeats).

358. ORTENSI, ULISSE: "Letterati contemporanei: William Butler Yeats," *Emporium,* 21:124 (Apr 1905), 265-73.
With two unknown photographs.

359. PARKINSON, THOMAS: "The Modernity of Yeats," *SoR,* 5:3 (July 1969), 922-34.
"We should be grateful that Yeats was not trained in the designs of modern thought. . . . Yeats had another . . . important role in modern consciousness, to keep us aware of the obligations of the artist, to remind us of the kind of lonely courage that the poet has, perhaps above all men; and to hold before us a traditional ideal of artistic responsibility."

360. ———: *Poets, Poems, Movements*. Ann Arbor: UMI Research Press, 1986. ix, 330 pp. (Studies in Modern Literature. 64.)
"Yeats and Pound: The Illusion of Influence," 21-30; reprinted from *CL,* 6:3 (Summer 1954), 256-64. Pound's influence on Yeats was "minor and adventitious."
"Yeats' 'Nineteen Hundred and Nineteen,'" 117-28; reprinted from Benjamin Harrison Lehman and others: *The Image of the Work: Essays in Criticism*. Berkeley: U of California Press, 1955. ix, 265 pp. (U of California Publications. English Studies. 11.) (pp. 209-27, 264).
"W. B. Yeats," 131-52; reprinted from Bernard Bergonzi (ed): *The Twentieth Century*. London: Barrie & Jenkins, 1970. 415 pp. (History of Literature in the English Language. 7.): "W. B. Yeats," 49-74; Yeats was perhaps not the greatest modern poet but a great poet writing in the modern period. (There are further references to Yeats in the book; see index).
"Yeats and the Limits of Modernity," 203-12; reprinted from *Yeats,* 3 (1985), 60-71. "Yeats was a modern poet but not a modernist."
See index for further references.

361. PAUL-DUBOIS, LOUIS: "M. Yeats et le mouvement poétique en Irlande," *Revue des deux mondes,* year 99 / period 7 / 53:3 (1 Oct 1929), 558-83; :4 (15 Oct 1929), 824-46.

362. PAYNE, BASIL: "Debunking Yeats," *IrT,* 31 Mar 1962, 9.
Yvor Winters is right: Yeats was not a great Irish poet. Correspondence by James Liddy, 4 Apr 1962, 7; Basil Payne and

"Kathleen ni Houlihan," 7 Apr 1962, 7, 12.

363. PEARCE, DONALD: "Shadows Deep: Change and Continuity in Yeats," *CLQ,* 22:4 (Dec 1986), 198-204.
Includes comments on "When You Are Old" and "The Lake Isle of Innisfree."

363a. [PEARSE, P. H.]: "Mr. Yeats on His Failure," *Claidheamh Soluis,* 5 Mar 1904, 5.
The failure of Irish poetry written in English which does not reach the heart of the people.

364. PESCHMANN, HERMANN: "Craftsmanship, Integrity and Passion," *Poetry Q,* 12:3 (Autumn 1950), 175-80.

365. PETILLON, PIERRE-YVES: "En étrange pays, fragment d'une île (1891-1916)," *Critique,* 38:421-422 (June-July 1982), 537-60.

366. PHELAN, FRANCIS J.: "Aspects of a National Literature in the *United Irishman* and Other Periodicals of the Anglo-Irish Literary Revival, 1899-1906," Ph.D. thesis, University College, Dublin, 1966. ii, 312 pp.
"W. B. Yeats Contributes," 57-89, and passim.

367. PHELPS, ARTHUR L.: "William Butler Yeats," *Acta Victoriana,* 39:3 (Dec 1914), 153-54, 156-58, 160-62.

368. PINTO, VIVIAN DE SOLA: *Crisis in English Poetry, 1880-1940.* NY: Harper & Row, 1966 [1951]. 228 pp. (Harper Torchbooks. TB1260.)
Yeats, passim (see index), especially "Yeats and Synge," 85-111 (a general account of Yeats's life and work; almost nothing on Synge).

369. PLUNKETT, JAMES: *The Gems She Wore: A Book of Irish Places.* London: Hutchinson, 1972. 208 pp.
On Yeats, pp. 162-76 and passim (see index).

370. POGGIOLI, RENATO: "Qualis Artifex Pereo! or Barbarism and Decadence," *Harvard Library Bulletin,* 13:1 (Winter 1959), 135-59.
Yeats was "able to see that the nemesis of decadence might turn into a catharsis transcending decadence itself." Includes a discussion of the two Byzantium poems.

371. PORTER, RAYMOND J., and JAMES D. BROPHY (eds): *Modern Irish Literature: Essays in Honor of William York Tindall.* [New Rochelle, N.Y.]: Iona College Press / NY: Twayne, 1972. ix, 357 pp. (Library of Irish Studies. 1.)
Partial contents: Samuel Hynes: "Yeats and the Poets of the Thirties," 1-22; on Yeats's political poetry, particularly "The Second Coming," "Easter 1916," and "Lapis Lazuli," and his influence on Auden, MacNeice, Day Lewis, and Spender.
John Unterecker: "Interview with Liam Miller," 23-41; on the Dolmen Press and what it did for Irish literature; also on the Cuala Press.
Daniel J. Murphy: "Lady Gregory, Co-Author and Sometimes Author of the Plays of W. B. Yeats," 43-52. Lady Gregory was the co-author of almost every early Yeats play; *Cathleen ni Houlihan* seems to be entirely hers.
James F. Carens: "Gogarty and Yeats," 67-93.
Lester Conner: "The Importance of Douglas Hyde to the Irish

Literary Renaissance," 95-114; on Hyde and Yeats, passim.

Grover Smith: "Yeats, Gogarty, and the Leap Castle Ghost," 129-41. The ghost occurs in *A Vision* (1937), Book 3, Section 5; it is indebted to Gogarty and others.

E[dmund] L. Epstein: "Yeats' Experiments with Syntax in the Treatment of Time," 171-84. Static syntax and kinetic content in Yeats's poetry, especially in "Leda and the Swan."

Raymond J. Porter: "Language and Literature in Revival Ireland: The Views of P. H. Pearse," 195-214. Includes a discussion of what Pearse thought of Yeats and the dramatic revival.

David H. Greene: "Yeats's Prose Style: Some Observations," 301-14.

Thomas S. W. Lewis: "Some New Letters of John Butler Yeats," 335-54. Five letters (1920) to his cousin Frank Yeats, mostly concerned with the Yeats family.

372. POTEZ, HENRI: "W. B. Yeats et la renaissance poétique en Irlande," *Revue de Paris,* year 11 / 4:3 (1 Aug 1904), 597-618; :4 (15 Aug 1904), 848-66.

373. POURRAT, HENRI: "W. B. Yeats," *Nouvelle revue française,* ns year 11 / 22:124 (1 Jan 1924), 124-28.

374. PRAZ, MARIO: *Cronache letterarie anglosassoni.* Roma: Edizione di Storia e Letteratura, 1950-66. 4 vols. (Letture di pensiero e d'arte. 16. 17. 41. 42.)

"Rivalutazione dei romantici," 1:123-28, reprinted from °*Tempo,* 31 Oct 1950; contains a note on Yeats.

"Due antologie di versi," 2:23-31, reprinted from °*Stampa,* 8 Dec 1936; reviews *The Oxford Book of Modern Verse* (W250/251).

"Poeti maghi," 3:328-33, reprinted from °*Tempo,* 16 Apr 1965; on Blake and Yeats.

"L'usignolo d'oro," 4:70-76; on *A Vision.*

375. PREMINGER, ALEX, FRANK J. WARNKE, and O. B. HARDISON (eds): *Encyclopedia of Poetry and Poetics.* Princeton: Princeton UP, 1965. xxiv, 906 pp.

Not indexed. The following contributions contain major references to Yeats: R[ichard] H[arter] F[ogle]: "English Poetry," 236-37. J[ames] B[aird]: "Exoticism," 265. G[eorge] B[randon] S[aul]: "Irish Literary Renaissance," 403-4. P[adraic] C[olum] and G. B. S[aul]: "Irish Poetry," 404-6. E[arl] M[iner]: "Nō," 571. N[orman] F[riedman]: "Symbol," 833-36.

A revised and enlarged edition was published as *Princeton Encyclopedia of Poetry and Poetics.* Princeton: Princeton UP, 1974. xxiv, 992 pp.

376. PRESS, JOHN: *The Chequer'd Shade: Reflections on Obscurity in Poetry.* London: Oxford UP, 1958. vii, 229 pp.

References to Yeats, passim (see index).

377. ————: *A Map of Modern English Verse.* London: Oxford UP, 1969. xii, 282 pp.

"The Later Poetry of W. B. Yeats," 7-29, consists of an introduction (Yeats was neither a mystic nor a fanatic right-wing politician but a rather complex personality) and some samples from the poetry and criticism of Yeats and from Yeats criticism.

378. PROTOPOPESCU, DRAGOȘ: *Pagini englez.* București: Cultura națională, 1925. ii, 287 pp.

"William Butler Yeats," 98-105.

379. PUHALO, DUSAN: *Engleska književnost XIX-XX veka (1832-1950): Istorijsko-kritički pregled.* Beograd: Naučna knjiga, 1983. 324 pp.
"Vilijem B. Jejts (William Butler Yeats), 1865-1939," 247-64.

380. QVAMME, BØRRE: "William Butler Yeats 1865-1939," *Edda,* year 30 / 43:2 (1943), 99-107.

381. RAFROIDI, PATRICK: "W. B. Yeats: Sligo ou Byzance?" *LanM,* 60:1 (Jan-Feb 1966), 45-54.
Not Sligo *or* Byzantium, but Sligo *and* Byzantium.

382. ———: *L'Irlande: 2. Littérature.* Paris: Colin 1970. 239 pp. (Collection U2. 124.)
See especially "Un phénix renaissant," 37-58; "Aspects du théâtre irlandais-anglais," 59-107 (on Yeats, pp. 80-84).

383. RAINE, KATHLEEN, and MAX-POL FOUCHET (eds): *Aspects de la littérature anglaise (1918-1945).* Paris: Fontaine, [1947]. 479 pp.
Stephen Spender: "Quelques observations sur la poésie anglaise entre les deux guerres," 19-29; on Yeats, 25-26.
Edwin Muir: "W. B. Yeats," 94-104; reprinted from *Fontaine,* 7:37-40 (Dec 1944), 105-14; translated by Austin and Madeleine Gill.

384. RAINE, KATHLEEN: *The Inner Journey of the Poet and Other Papers.* Edited by Brian Keeble. London: Allen & Unwin, 1982. xi, 208 pp.
"The Inner Journey of the Poet," 25-39; reprint of a pamphlet with the same title, Ipswich: Golgonooza Press, 1976. 24 pp. Contains a note on "Sailing to Byzantium."
"Poetic Symbols as a Vehicle of Tradition," 40-79; reprinted from *Eranos-Jahrbuch,* 37 (1968), 356-409.
"Waste Land, Holy Land," 80-98; reprinted from *PBA,* 62 (1976), 379-97; also in FC67.

385. RAJAN, BALACHANDRA: "Now Days Are Dragon-Ridden," *ASch,* 32:3 (Summer 1963), 407-14.
"Reading Yeats in a time of crisis is a radical if not a liberal education. . . ."

386. RANDALL, JAMES: "An Interview with Seamus Heaney," *Ploughshares,* 5:3 (1979), 7-22.
Includes comments on Yeats.

387. RAY, GORDON NORTON (ed): *Masters of British Literature.* 2nd edition. Boston: Houghton Mifflin, 1962 [1958]. 2 vols.
Richard Ellmann: Yeats, 2:823-31.

388. READ, HERBERT: *Annals of Innocence and Experience.* London: Faber & Faber, 1946 [1940]. 236 pp.
Distrusts Yeats's Celtic Twilight phase (pp. 95-96) and comments on the exclusion of the war poets from the *Oxford Book of Modern Verse* (pp. 100-101).

389. READE, ARTHUR ROBERT: *Main Currents in Modern Literature.* London: Nicholson & Watson, 1935. 223 pp.
"The Anglo-Irish and W. B. Yeats," 41-56. Discusses Yeats as a symbolist rather than as an Irish writer.

390. REES, DAVID: "Another Troy," *Spect,* 16 Dec 1966, 789-90.
Yeats was "the great poet of our time."

391. REEVES, JAMES: *Commitment to Poetry.* NY: Barnes & Noble, 1969. vii, 295 pp.
Reeves does not like Yeats and his poetry and says so: "This perverse, despotic old man flogging his will to make himself a kind of pastiche of a great bardic figure" (pp. 6-7).

392. ——— (ed): *The Poets and Their Critics: Arnold to Auden.* London: Hutchinson, 1969. 279 pp. (Poets and Their Critics. 3.)
"William Butler Yeats," 108-36; a short introduction and reprints of several snippets from various critics.

393. REVOL, ENRIQUE LUIS: "La vida o la obra," *Revista de Occidente,* 2nd epoch, 4th year, 40 (July 1966), 109-13.
Yeats between "perfection of the life, or of the work."

394. ———: *Literatura inglesa del siglo XX.* Buenos Aires: Editorial Columbia, 1973. 455 pp. (Coleccion Nuevos Esquemas. 29.)
"Renacimiento irlandés: W. B. Yeats y J. M. Synge," 203-29.

395. REYNOLDS, HORACE: *A Providence Episode in the Irish Literary Renaissance.* Providence: Study Hill Club, 1929. 41 pp. (Study Hill Club Publication. 1.)
The contributions of some writers of the revival (among them Yeats) to the *Providence Sunday Journal.*

396. RIVOALLAN, A.: "William Butler Yeats, 1865-1939," *LanM,* 37:2 (Mar 1939), 188-93.

397. ROBINSON, NORMAN L.: "Poems of W. B. Yeats," *Central Literary Magazine,* 28:5 (Jan 1928), 185-94.

398. ROBSON, WILLIAM WALLACE: *Modern English Literature.* London: Oxford UP, 1970. xv, 172 pp.
Yeats, pp. 50-59 and passim (see index).

399. ———: *A Prologue to English Literature.* London: Batsford, 1986. 254 pp.
On Yeats, pp. 203-6 and passim (see index).

400. ROHDE, PETER PREISLER: *Engelsk litteratur, 1900-1947.* København: Athenaeum, 1948. 351 pp.
Yeats, pp. 26-40, 35-38, 167-70, and passim (see index).

401. ROLLINS, RONALD G.: "Portraits of Four Irishmen as Artists: Verisimilitude and Vision," *IUR,* 1:2 (Spring 1971), 189-97.
Verisimilitude and vision in the works of Synge, O'Casey, Yeats, and Joyce.

402. ROLT, LIONEL THOMAS CASWELL: *High Horse Riderless.* London: Allen & Unwin, 1947. 172 pp.
An attack against "modernism," quoting with approval Yeats as a poet and thinker who "remained faithful to traditional form" and who "possessed a most profound perception of our social maladies" (pp. 101-4).

403. RONSLEY, JOSEPH (ed): *Myth and Reality in Irish Literature.* Waterloo, Ont.: Wilfred Laurier UP, 1977. xiv, 329 pp.

On Yeats see particularly: David Greene, Thomas Kinsella, Jay Macpherson, Kevin Nowlan, Ann Saddlemyer: "Ancient Myth and Poetry: A Panel Discussion," 1-16.

Ann Saddlemyer: "Augusta Gregory, Irish Nationalist: 'After All, What Is Wanted but a Hag and a Voice?'" 29-40.

Henry Summerfield: "AE as a Literary Critic," 41-61.

Norman H. MacKenzie: "Hopkins, Yeats, and Dublin in the Eighties," 77-97; a "biocritical" article.

Denis Donoghue: "Yeats: The Question of Symbolism," 99-115; on the influence of Mallarmé; reprinted in CB131. See also CC19.

Balachandra Rajan: "The Poetry of Confrontation: Yeats and the Dialogue Poem," 117-28; especially on "Ego Dominus Tuus" and "A Dialogue of Self and Soul."

J. Ronsley: "Yeats as an Autobiographical Poet," 129-48.

David R. Clark: "After 'Silence,' the 'Supreme Theme': Eight Lines of Yeats," 149-73; reprinted in DA6.

Shotaro Oshima: "Between Shapes and Shadows," 175-81; on Yeats and the Nō.

Thomas Kilroy: "Two Playwrights: Yeats and Beckett," 183-95; particularly on *The Herne's Egg*.

J. C. C. Mays: "Mythologized Presences: *Murphy* in Its Time," 197-218; contains a note on Yeats and Beckett, pp. 202-4.

Andrew Parkin: "Imagination's Abode: The Symbolism of House Settings in Modern Irish Stage Plays," 255-63.

Seamus Deane: "The Literary Myths of the Revival: A Case for Their Abandonment," 317-29; reprinted in CB122.

404. ROONEY, PHILIP: "The Sligo of William Butler Yeats: Legendary Men Who Were Ancestors of the Poet," *IrP*, 10 Aug 1961, 9.

Continued as "Poet's Experiments in Telepathy," 11 Aug 1961, 8-9; "A Tinkle of Water in Fleet Street--'Innisfree,'" 12 Aug 1961, 9. Includes reminiscences.

405. ROSENFELD, PAUL L.: "William Butler Yeats," *Yale Literary Magazine*, 74:658 (Jan 1909), 146-53.

406. ROSENTHAL, M. L.: "On Yeats and the Cultural Symbolism of Modern Poetry," *YR*, 49:4 (June 1960), 573-83.

On the symbolic fusion of "man's day-to-day predicament" with "envisioned transformation" in Yeats's work.

407. ROSSITER, FRANK: "Yeats--'Great Minor Poet,'" *IrP*, 25 Aug 1967, 9.

A depreciation. Correspondence by "Iconoclast": "Philosophy of Yeats," 28 Aug 1967, 9; by "Celtic Codology": "Assessments of Yeats," 28 Oct 1967, 10; and by Hugh Murphy, 22 Nov 1967, 12.

408. ROYAL HIBERNIAN ACADEMY AND METROPOLITAN SCHOOL OF ART, DUBLIN: *Report by Committee of Inquiry into the Work Carried On by the Royal Hibernian Academy and the Metropolitan School of Art*. Dublin: HMSO, 1906. xxv, 98 pp.

Yeats's evidence, given on 13 Oct 1905, appears on pp. 60-61. See passim for reactions to this evidence.

409. [RUSSELL, GEORGE WILLIAM]: "Literature and Civilisation," *IrSt*, 24 Nov 1923, 325-26.

Yeats's share in "creating" an Irish civilization.

410. A. E. [i.e., RUSSELL, GEORGE WILLIAM]: *The Living Torch*. Edited by Monk Gibbon with an introductory essay. London: Macmil-

lan, 1937. xii, 382 pp.
A selection from AE's writings, including numerous paragraphs on Yeats (not analyzed in this bibliography).

411. RUTHVEN, KENNETH KNOWLES: *Critical Assumptions*. Cambridge: Cambridge UP, 1979. x, 263 pp.
See index for numerous short references to Yeats.

412. RYAN, WILLIAM PATRICK: *The Irish Literary Revival: Its History, Pioneers and Possibilities*. London: The Author, 1894, vii, 184 pp.
On Yeats, passim, especially pp. 29-30, 36, 50-51, 53-60, 66-68, 70, 75, 125-29, 132-36. He receives high praise as the most imaginative of the Irish writers.

413. ———: *Literary London: Its Lights & Comedies*. London: Smithers, 1898. 167 pp.
"The Passing of the Poets," 109-28, contains notes on Yeats: "If Mr. Yeats could go into Parliament, or edit *The Daily Chronicle*, or launch a newspaper syndicate, he would be a much larger figure to his age. But happily that is impossible."

414. ———: "Celts in the Workshop," *BmL*, 15:89 (Feb 1899), 136-37.
Yeats's treatment of legendary material is "arbitrary and obscure." "A good deal of his late work . . . seems merely trite English."

415. ———: *The Pope's Green Island*. London: Nisbet, 1912. vi, 325 pp.
"Materialism and Mysticism," 193-203: Yeats's "mysticism" is not accepted in Ireland.
"Ireland at the Play," 299-307; on the Irish dramatic movement. Contends that the Abbey is much more enjoyable without Yeats's theories about it.

416. S., B.: "William Butler Yeats," *Native Companion*, 1:6 (29 June 1907), 4-11.

417. SAMPLEY, ARTHUR M.: "Quiet Voices, Unquiet Times," *MQ*, 4:3 (Apr 1963), 247-56.
Yeats is one of the 20th-century poets who have "developed a reasoned and thoughtful solution for the spiritual problem of modern man."

418. SANDERS, ALAIN: "W. B. Yeats: Le miroir de son rêve," *Artus*, 15 (Winter 1983-84), 23-25.

419. SANDERS, SCOTT: "The Left-Handedness of Modern Literature," *TCL*, 23:4 (Dec 1977), 417-36.
Yeats belongs to those writers who believe in the holistic, synchronic, acausal, receptive, and intuitive functions of the mind.

420. SARKAR, SUBHAS: *Eliot and Yeats: A Study*. Calcutta: Minerva Associates, 1978. ix, 156 pp.
Not a comparison of the two poets but 18 separate essays of which four are on Yeats: "The Irish Heritage and W. B. Yeats," 128-33. "The Tragic Romance of W. B. Yeats," 134-41 (Maud Gonne). "W. B. Yeats' Contribution to Modern Poetry and Tradition," 142-45. "W. B. Yeats and the Indian Monk," 146-51; reprinted from *BDE*, ns 11:1 (1975-76), 21-24 (Shri Purohit Swami).

421. SARUKHANI͡AN, ALLA PAVLOVNA: *Sovremennai͡a irlandskai͡a literatura* [Contemporary Irish literature]. Moskva: Izdatel'stvo Nauka, 1973. 319 pp.

Contains chapters on the Easter Rising and its literature, the turning point in the Irish literary revival (i.e., after 1916), the development of realism in the twenties and thirties, Irish literature during World War II and in the first decade after the war, and the literature of discussion and protest in the sixties. On Yeats see pp. 28-30, 52-66, 84-86, 90-119, and passim.

Reviewed by Larisa Litvinova: "A Book on Present-Day Irish Literature," *Soviet Literature*, 3 (1976), 158-59.

422. SAVAGE, DEREK STANLEY: *The Personal Principle: Studies in Modern Poetry*. Port Washington: Kennikat Press, 1969 [1944]. viii, 196 pp.

"The Aestheticism of W. B. Yeats," 67-90; reprinted and revised from *KR*, 7:1 (Winter 1945), 118-34; also in CA36. See commentary by John Crowe Ransom: "The Severity of Mr. Savage," *KR*, 7:1 (Winter 1945), 114-17.

Savage claims that Yeats was an "aesthete," i.e., a watered-down symbolist. Yeats lacked "inner dynamism, the religious impulse to grasp hold of life and make it surrender its meaning," and there is something "inhuman, or soulless," in his poetry.

423. SCHIRMER, WALTER FRANZ: "William Butler Yeats 70 Jahre," *Berliner Tageblatt*, 14 June 1935, Beiblatt 1, unpaged.

424. ———: *Geschichte der englischen und amerikanischen Literatur von den Anfängen bis zur Gegenwart*. 6th edition, edited by Arno Esch. Tübingen: Niemeyer, 1983 [1937]. 2 vols.

Arno Esch: "W. B. Yeats und die keltische Renaissance," 2:855-59; "Das irische Drama," 2:907-14.

425. ———: "William Butler Yeats," *Tribüne*, 25:9 (1955/56), 77-80.

426. SCHWARTZ, DELMORE: *Selected Essays*. Edited by Donald A. Dike and David H. Zucker. Chicago: U of Chicago Press, 1970. xxiv, 500 pp.

"The Poet as Poet," 72-80; reprinted from *PR*, 6:3 (Spring 1939), 52-59.

"An Unwritten Book," 81-101; reprinted from *SoR*, 7:3 (Winter 1941/42), 471-91; and from CA36. Outline for a book that someone should write in the near future in order to show the real Yeats. The book should discuss the following topics: Yeats in Europe, Yeats in Ireland, Yeats in himself, and Yeats's lyric poems. See also AD7 and CB167.

427. SCOTT-JAMES, ROLFE ARNOLD: *Modernism and Romance*. London: Lane, 1908. xvi, 284 pp.

"The Self-Conscious Poet," 189-213; on Yeats, 192-97: His criticism and plays have stifled the lyrical impulse of his poetry.

428. ———: *The Day before Yesterday*. London: Muller, 1947. viii, 166 pp.

"June 1935," 35-38; reprinted from *LMerc*, 32:188 (June 1935), 105. On Yeats's 70th birthday.

"March 1939: The Farewell to Yeats," 160-65; reprinted from *LMerc*, 39:233 (Mar 1939), 477-80. Includes some reminiscences.

429. [———]: "The Defence of Culture," *Britain To-day*, 84 (Apr

1943), 1-4.
Is Yeats an Irish or an English poet?

430. SEKINE, MASARU (ed): *Irish Writers and Society at Large*. Gerrards Cross: Smythe / Totowa, N.J.: Barnes & Noble, 1985. x, 251 pp. (Irish Literary Studies. 22. / IASAIL--Japan Series. 1.)
Joan Coldwell: "The Bodkin and the Rocky Voice: Images of Weaving and Stone in the Poetry of W. B. Yeats," 16-30.
Maurice Harmon: "The Era of Inhibitions: Irish Literature 1920-60," 31-41.
A. Norman Jeffares: "Anglo-Irish Literature: Treatment for Radio," 42-95; four lectures prepared for the Australian Broadcasting Commission (see especially pp. 78-85).
Augustine Martin: "Prose Fiction in the Irish Literary Renaissance," 139-62 (includes a discussion of Yeats's fiction).
Robert Welch: "Some Thoughts on Writing a Companion to Irish Literature," 225-36 (includes notes on Yeats's "Irishness").

431. SERGEANT, HOWARD: *Tradition in the Making of Modern Poetry*. Volume 1. London: Britannicus Liber, 1951. v, 122 pp.
No other volume published. On Yeats's pre-1899 works, pp. 18-22, and passim (see index).

432. SEYMOUR-SMITH, MARTIN: *Guide to Modern World Literature*. London: Wolfe, 1973. xxi, 1206 pp.
On Yeats, pp. 228-32, 262; mainly on the poetry.

433. ———: *Who's Who in Twentieth Century Literature*. London: Weidenfeld & Nicolson, 1976. 414 pp.
See pp. 406-8.

434. ———: *Macmillan Guide to Modern World Literature*. London: Macmillan, 1985. xxviii, 1396 pp.
See pp. 240-43 for a short critical assessment of Yeats, who is said to lack intellect and sophistication.

435. SHAPIRO, KARL: "Modern Poetry as Religion," *ASch*, 28:3 (Summer 1959), 297-305.
Contains some notes on Yeats.

436. ———: *In Defense of Ignorance*. NY: Random House, 1960. xi, 339 pp.
"W. B. Yeats: Trial by Culture," 87-113; also included in *The Poetry Wreck: Selected Essays 1950-1970*. NY: Random House, 1975. xvii, 366 pp. (pp. 55-82). Yeats's idea of civilization was quite narrow.

437. ———: *To Abolish Children and Other Essays*. Chicago: Quadrangle Books, 1968. 288 pp.
"A *Malebolge* of Fourteen Hundred Books," 169-288: "Y/Yeats," 264-68; reprinted from *Carleton Miscellany*, 5:3 (Summer 1964), 110-14. "Yeats (unfortunately, from my philosophy) probably gave European poetry another millenium [sic] of life. In Yeats is summed up all the phoniness of the art of poetry and its practitioners and its adherents, its power and its meaninglessness."

438. SHEEHY, JEANNE: *The Rediscovery of Ireland's Past: The Celtic Revival 1830-1930*. London: Thames & Hudson, 1980. 208 pp.
The revival of Irish arts and crafts. On Yeats see particularly

"The Celtic Revival," 95-105; "Hugh Lane and the Gallery of Modern Art," 107-19; "The Arts and Crafts Movement," 147-75; and pp. 139-41 (on his tower).

439. SIEGMUND-SCHULTZE, DOROTHEA (ed): *Irland: Gesellschaft und Kultur*. Halle/Saale: Martin-Luther-Universität Halle-Wittenberg, 1976. 183 pp. (Wissenschaftliche Beiträge. 1976/28.)

Thomas Metscher: "Zur Entwicklung der bürgerlichen und sozialistischen Nationalliteratur in Irland," 96-147. There is a bourgeois and a socialist national literature in Ireland; Yeats belongs to the former. Discusses some of his poems with Irish nationalist themes, especially "September 1913" and "Easter 1916."

440. ———: *Irland: Gesellschaft und Kultur III*. Halle/Saale: Martin-Luther-Universität Halle-Wittenberg, 1982. 327 pp. (Wissenschaftliche Beiträge. 1982/8 [F35].)

D. Siegmund-Schultze: "St. Patrick of Ireland--An Inquiry into a National Symbol," 19-31, contains a brief note on "The Wanderings of Oisin."

Alla Saruchanian [Sarukhanîan]: "The Irish Literary Revival: Some Aspects," 115-24.

Maurice Goldring: "Intellectual Response to the Dublin Lockout and Strike, 1913-1914," 164-78.

Wolfgang Wicht: "Yeats and Joyce: Some General Remarks," 204-12.

440a. ———: *Irland: Gesellschaft und Kultur V*. Halle/Saale: Martin-Luther-Universität Halle-Wittenberg, 1987. 255 pp. (Wissenschaftliche Beiträge. 1987/40 [F71].)

David Pierce: "The Ireland of Yeats and Joyce," 175-82; discusses Yeats's view of Irish history.

Thomas Metscher: "On the Poetry of W. B. Yeats," 183-201; an analysis of "Among School Children" in terms of "materialist hermeneutics."

Rüdiger Hillgärtner: "The Difficulties of Self-Redemption: Contradictions in William Butler Yeats' Autobiographical Writings," 202-14: "The price Yeats has to pay for his retrospective proof that an inherent order has evolved from the contradictions and fragments of his life is high: he has to exorcise life from the mask."

441. [SINGER, BURNS]: "England Is Abroad," *TLS*, 18 Apr 1958, 201-2. The development of Yeats attests "the diminished importance of England's contribution to English literature." Correspondence by Vivian Mercier: "Yeats and 'The Fisherman,'" 6 June 1958, 313.

442. SKARTVEIT, ANDREAS (ed): *Fra skald til modernist: Dikterens rolle gjennom tidene*. Oslo: Dreyer, 1967. 116 pp. (Perspektivbøkene. 26.)

Kristian Smidt: "Dikterens jeg eller verket for seg? Noen engelske modernister i speilet" [The poet's I or the work as such? Some English modernists in the mirror], 97-110; on Yeats, passim. Reprinted in Smidt: *Konstfuglen og nattergalen: Essays om diktning og kritikk*. Oslo: Gyldendal, 1972. 206 pp. (pp. 75-85).

443. SKELTON, ROBIN, and DAVID RIDGLEY CLARK (eds): *Irish Renaissance: A Gathering of Essays, Memoirs, and Letters from "The Massachusetts Review."* Dublin: Dolmen Press, 1965. 167 pp.

The following items are on Yeats (first publications in parentheses):

W. B. Yeats: "Modern Ireland: An Address to American Audiences, 1932-1933," 13-25 (5:2 [Winter 1964], 256-68). Transcribed from the MS., and edited by Curtis Bradford.

David R. Clark: "W. B. Yeats: *The Shadowy Waters* (MS. Version): Half the Characters Had Eagles' Faces," 26-55 (6:1 [Autumn-Winter 1964], 151-80; now in EE505).

John Butler Yeats: "John Butler Yeats to Lady Gregory: New Letters," 56-64 (5:2, 269-77). Eight letters written between 18 June 1898 and 23 Sept 1907, edited by Glenn O'Malley and Donald T. Torchiana.

J. M. Synge: "Synge to MacKenna: The Mature Years," 65-79 (5:2, 279-95). Edited by Ann Saddlemyer. The letters contain some critical remarks on the Abbey and on Yeats's plays, especially *The Shadowy Waters.*

W. B. Yeats: "Discoveries: Second Series," 80-89 (5:2, 297-306). Transcribed from the MS. and edited by Curtis Bradford.

Austin Clarke: "A Centenary Celebration," 90-93 (5:2, 315-22). An account of the meeting held at the Thomas Davis Centenary in the Antient Concert Rooms on 20 Nov 1914. Yeats made a speech on this occasion; see also BF127.

W. B. Yeats: "A Fair Chance of a Disturbed Ireland: W. B. Yeats to Mrs. J. Duncan," 98-105 (5:2, 315-22). Edited by John Unterecker. Eleven letters written in 1918. Mrs. James Duncan seems to be the same as Ellen M. Duncan who wrote occasionally on Yeats (see index of names).

David Krause: "Sean O'Casey: 1880-1964," 139-57 (6:2 [Winter-Spring 1965], 233-51). Quotes some of O'Casey's remarks on Yeats.

Robin Skelton: "Twentieth-Century Irish Literature and the Private Press Tradition: Dun Emer, Cuala, & Dolmen Presses, 1902-1963," 158-67 (5:2, 368-77).

Reviews:

- [Austin Clarke]: "Mad Ireland," *TLS,* 22 Dec 1966, 1190.
- Harold Orel, *MD,* 9:4 (Feb 1967), 466.

444. SMITH, A. J. M.: "A Poet Young and Old--W. B. Yeats," *UTQ,* 8:3 (Apr 1939), 255-63.

445. SMITH, EDWIN: *Ireland.* Introduction by Micheál MacLiammoir. London: Thames & Hudson, 1966. 55 pp. plus 123 plates.

In his introduction, MacLiammoir refers repeatedly to Yeats (see especially pp. 44-53).

446. SMITH, JOHN: *The Arts Betrayed.* London: Herbert Press, 1978. 256 pp.

"Yeats Bartók," 59-87, 246-47. Yeats's organical growth into modernism, especially in his poetry, parallels Bartók's development.

447. SOMERVILLE, EDITH OENONE, and MARTIN ROSS: *Wheeltracks.* London: Longmans, 1923. x, 284 pp.

For Martin Ross's estimate of Yeats see the letters on pp. 229-34 (Mr. X being Mr. Y). Includes comments on *Diarmuid and Grania* and *The King's Threshold.*

448. SPALDING, PHILIP ANTHONY: *In the Margin: Being Extracts from a Bookman's Notebook.* [London: Adam Books, 1959]. 84 pp.

Reprinted from *Adam,* 25:262 (1957), 7-84. Yeats, passim (see index), especially pp. 39-42 (epigrams in praise of Yeats).

449. SPEAIGHT, ROBERT: "Salute to Yeats," *Colosseum*, 5:21 (Apr-June 1939), 131-38.
An appreciation of Yeats's aristocratic mind.

450. SPEARS, MONROE K.: *Dionysus and the City: Modernism in Twentieth-Century Poetry*. NY: Oxford UP, 1970. x, 278 pp.
Yeats, passim (see index); partly on his poetry as an instance of modernism, more on his modern critics.

451. SPENDER, STEPHEN: "The 'Egotistical Sublime' in W. B. Yeats," *List*, 16 Feb 1939, 377-78.

452. ———: "Movements and Influences in English Literature, 1927-1953," *BA*, 27:1 (Winter 1953), 5-32.
Yeats, passim; Spender regards him as E. M. Forster's opposite in his preference for "things" and his contempt for "people."

453. ———: *The Creative Element: A Study of Vision, Despair, and Orthodoxy among Some Modern Writers*. London: Hamilton, 1953. 199 pp.
Compares Arnold's "Dover Beach" and "The Second Coming," 33-34; discusses Yeats's and Rimbaud's use of "magic," 49-55; and deals with Yeats in "Hammered Gold and Gold Enamelling of Humanity," 108-24: "Where Yeats does convince us . . . is in his acceptance of the necessity of sacrifice in order that man may create the monuments of his own greatness." His insistent belief in the supernatural is less convincing. Compares Yeats and D. H. Lawrence.

454. ———, W. D. SNODGRASS, THOMAS KINSELLA, and PATRICK KAVANAGH: "Poetry since Yeats: An Exchange of Views," *TriQ*, 4 [Fall 1965], 100-106, 108-11.
After the academic efforts of the first three speakers, Kavanagh wrecked the discussion with some delightfully irreverent and irrelevant outbursts. The battle seems to have ended in chaos.

455. SPENDER, STEPHEN: "Form and Pressure in Poetry," *TLS*, 23 Oct 1970, 1226-28.
The effect of the "pressure of the modern time" on poetic form in Pound, Yeats, and others. Yeats is a poet of the "continuous tradition" who revised his subject matter almost organically like a plant, "gradually adapting to meet new conditions," but who retained the formal standards of his early romanticism.

456. ———: *Journals 1939-1983*. Edited by John Goldsmith. London: Faber & Faber, 1985. 510 pp.
Contains a few short notes on Yeats (see index) and a reminiscence of Mrs. Yeats (pp. 104-5).

457. SPINNER, KASPAR: "William Butler Yeats: Zum hundertsten Geburtstag (13. Juni)," *NZZ*, 12 June 1965, 20r-v.

458. SPIVEY, TED RAY: *The Coming of the New Man: A Study of Literature, Myth, and Vision since 1750*. NY: Vantage Press, 1970. 212 pp.
See pp. 53-56, 182-83.

459. SQUIRE, J. C.: "The Nobel Prize Winner: Mr. W. B. Yeats," *Obs*, 18 Nov 1923, 4.

460. STANFORD, DEREK (ed): *Poets of the 'Nineties: A Biographical Anthology*. London: Baker, 1965. 225 pp.

The introduction (pp. 17-45) quotes from Yeats passim; "W. B. Yeats, 1865-1939," 168-76, comments on Yeats's early poetry, neglecting almost entirely its "Irish" elements.

The introduction is reproduced in photocopy, without acknowledgment and revision, on pp. 5-33 of Stanford's *Introduction to the 'Nineties*. Salzburg: Institut für Anglistik und Amerikanistik, Universität Salzburg, 1987. 124 pp. (Salzburg Studies in English Literature. Poetic Drama & Poetic Theory. 78:1.)

461. STANFORD, DONALD E. (ed): *British Poets, 1880-1914*. Detroit: Gale, 1983. xi, 486 pp. (Dictionary of Literary Biography. 19.)

B. L. Reid: "William Butler Yeats," 399-452.

462. STARKIE, WALTER: "William Butler Yeats: Premio Nobel 1924 [sic]," *Nuova antologia*, series 6 / year 59 / 312:1249 (1 Apr 1924), 238-45.

463. STEAD, CHRISTIAN KARLSON: *The New Poetic: Yeats to Eliot*. Harmondsworth: Penguin Books, 1967 [1964]. 201 pp. (Pelican Book. A902.)

"W. B. Yeats, 1865-1916," 17-45, and passim (see index). Investigates the triangle between the poet, the audience, and "that area of experience which we call variously 'Reality,' 'Truth,' or 'Nature'" (p. 11). Too much distance from the audience results in aestheticism, too little in rhetoric. The perfect poem is one that exists "in an equilateral triangle, each point pulling equally in a moment of perfect tension" (p. 12). Discusses "The Fisherman" and "Easter 1916" as examples from Yeats's poetry.

There is a "revised edition" (Philadelphia: U of Pennsylvania Press, 1987), but a short new preface seems to be all there is by way of "revision." See also DB233.

464. STEPHENS, JAMES: *James, Seumas & Jacques: Unpublished Writings*. Chosen and edited with an introduction by Lloyd Frankenberg. London: Macmillan, 1964. xxxii, 288 pp.

Mostly B.B.C. broadcasts. See particularly: "Some Irish Books I Like," 61-66 (16 June 1937), with notes on Yeats's poetry.

"W. B. Yeats," 67-72 (5 Jan 1942); excerpt in "Yeats and the Telephone," *List*, 22 Jan 1942, 106. Reminiscences.

"Yeats as Dramatist," 73-76 (9 May 1943); reprint of "He Died Younger Than He Was Born," *List*, 17 June 1943, 728.

"'Byzantium,'" 77-86 (28 Dec 1944: "The Making of a Poem").

"Yeats and Music," 87-88 (3 Oct 1947, excerpt).

"Around and About Yeats," 89-95 (2 Jan 1948).

"Yeats the Poet," 96-100 (9 Jan 1948). See Vernon Watkins, "The Poetry of W. B. Yeats," *List*, 22 Jan 1948, 143.

"A. E.," 110-22 (27 Mar 1942 and 13 Jan 1948); reprinted from *List*, 9 Apr 1942, 467-68, and 22 Jan 1948, 144-45. Includes reminiscences of Yeats.

"Poets on Poetry," 168-75 (18 June 1946).

465. ———: *Uncollected Prose of James Stephens*. Edited by Patricia A. McFate. London: Macmillan, 1983. 2 vols.

"W. B. Yeats: A Tribute," 2:248-50; reprinted from *Obs*, 19 Sept 1948, 4 (also in CD1245). A few other references to Yeats in both volumes (see indexes).

466. STEWART, JOHN INNES MACKINTOSH: *Eight Modern Writers*. Oxford: Clarendon Press, 1963. ix, 704 pp. (Oxford History of English Literature. 12.)

"VII. Yeats," 294-421, 671-79. See the review by John Simon: "Unlucky J. I. M.," *PR*, 31:4 (Fall 1964), 632-37, 639 (quarrels with Stewart's Yeats interpretations).

467. STRELKA, JOSEPH PETER (ed): *Literary Theory and Criticism: Festschrift Presented to René Wellek in Honor of His Eightieth Birthday*. Bern: Lang, 1984. 2 vols.
Cleanth Brooks: "The American South and Yeats's Ireland," 2: 729-41 (the campaign for cultural autonomy).

467a. STRÖMBERG, KJELL R. G.: "Årets Nobelpris i litteratur till irländaren Yeats," *Stockholms-tidningen*, 15 Nov 1923, 1, 11.

468. STRONG, LEONARD ALFRED GEORGE: *Personal Remarks*. London: Nevill, 1953. 264 pp.
"William Butler Yeats," 13-33; revised from "W. B. Yeats: An Appreciation," *Cornhill Magazine*, 156:931 (July 1937), 14-29.

469. ———: "W. B. Yeats," *Spect*, 18 Nov 1938, 856-57.
Reprinted as "W. B. Yeats--Ireland's Grand Old Man," *Living Age*, 355:4468 (Jan 1939), 438-40; and in CA50, pp. 420-24.

470. STUART, T. P.: "Mr. Yeats and the Irish Heart," *Leader*, 26 Jan 1901, 352.
See the comments by the editor [D. P. Moran], ibid.; Stuart's rejoinder, 9 Feb 1901, 387-88, and editor's comments, ibid. A discussion about whether Yeats is or is not an Irish poet.

471. STURGEON, MARY C.: *Studies of Contemporary Poets*. Revised and enlarged. London: Harrap, 1920 [1916]. 440 pp.
"William Butler Yeats," 419-32.

472. SÜHNEL, RUDOLF, and DIETER RIESNER (eds): *Englische Dichter der Moderne: Ihr Leben und Werk*. Berlin: Schmidt, 1971. viii, 598 pp.
Johannes Kleinstück: "William Butler Yeats," 193-204.

473. SULLIVAN, DANIEL J.: "The Literary Periodical and the Anglo-Irish Revival, 1894-1914," Ph.D. thesis, University College Dublin, 1969. vi, 376 pp.
Frequent references to Yeats.

474. SYMONS, ARTHUR: *Studies in Prose and Verse*. London: Dent, 1922 [1904]. ix, 292 pp.
"Mr. W. B. Yeats," 230-41; a general discussion of the poetry and plays. Incorporates "Mr. Yeats as a Lyric Poet," *SatRL*, 6 May 1899, 553-54 (a review of W17 and W27, reprinted in CA50, pp. 109-13); "Mr. Yeats' New Play," *SatRL*, 29 Dec 1900, 824-25 (an anonymous review of W30/31); and an unidentified review of W56.

475. [TAGORE, RABINDRANATH]: "A Hindu on the Celtic Spirit," *American R of Reviews*, 49:1 (Jan 1914), 101-2.
Translated excerpts from an article published in °*Prabashi*.

476. ———: *Rabindra-racanābalī* [Rabindranath's works]. Calcutta: Visva-Bharati, 1939-65. 27 vols.
"Kabi Ietsh" [Poet Yeats], 26:521-28 (in Bengali). See CD1357.

477. TALLQVIST, C. E.: "William Butler Yeats: En studie," *Finsk* *tidskrift*, 102:2 (1927), 119-41; :4 (1927), 281-307.

478. TAYLOR, JOSEPH R.: "William Butler Yeats and the Revival of Gaelic Literature," *Methodist R*, 87:2 (Mar-Apr 1905), 189-202.
Yeats is quite outside the current revival of Gaelic language and literature. Although he is a good poet, he becomes increasingly obscure and thus less typically Irish.

479. TÉRY, SIMONE: *L'île des bardes: Notes sur la littérature irlandaise contemporaine*. Paris: Flammarion, 1925. 249 pp.
"W. B. Yeats," 57-98; based on "W. B. Yeats, poète irlandais: Lauréat du Prix Nobel," *Grande revue*, year 27 / 113:12 (Dec 1923), 259-72. Includes some personal reminiscences.
Reviews:
- C. P. Curran: "French Critics and Irish Literature," *IrSt*, 15 Aug 1925, 723-24.
- André Maurois: "La littérature irlandaise contemporaine," *Candide*, 13 Aug 1925, 3.

480. THAKUR, DAMODAR: *The Constant Pursuit: Studies in the Use of Myth and Language in Literature*. Patna: Novelty, 1964. ix, 206 pp.
"The Personality of W. B. Yeats: Heritage and Achievement," 193-201. In Yeats, "the separation between the man who suffers and the mind that creates seems not to have occurred." A rather sketchy essay.

481. THOMAS, EDWARD: *Letters from Edward Thomas to Gordon Bottomley*. Edited and introduced by R. George Thomas. London: Oxford UP, 1968. vi, 302 pp.
Yeats is mentioned passim (see index).

482. ———: *A Language Not to Be Betrayed: Selected Prose of Edward Thomas*. Selected and with an introduction by Edna Longley. Manchester: Carcanet Press, 1981. viii, xxii, 290 pp.
"W. B. Yeats," 79-87; extracts from G186, 234, 251, 275, 291, and 291a.

483. THORNTON, ROBERT KELSEY ROUGHT: "The Poets of the Rhymers' Club," M.A. thesis, Manchester U, 1961. iii, 269 pp.
"William Butler Yeats," 230-57.

484. TINDALL, WILLIAM YORK: *Forces in Modern British Literature, 1885-1956*. NY: Vintage Books, 1956 [1947]. xi, 316, xxi pp. (Vintage Books. V35.)
Includes "The Symbolism of W. B. Yeats," *Accent*, 5:4 (Summer 1945), 203-12; also in CA36. On the Irish literary revival, pp. 63-82; on Yeats's symbolism, 265-74; and passim (see index).

485. TOLIVER, HAROLD E.: *The Past That Poets Make*. Cambridge, Mass.: Harvard UP, 1981. vii, 256 pp.
"Yeats, Eliot, Hemingway: Hosting Other Phantoms," 85-100, and passim (see index).

486. TOMASI DI PALMA, GIUSEPPE [i.e., Giuseppe Tomasi di Lampedusa]: "W. B. Yeats e il risorgimento irlandese," *Opere e i giorni*, 5:11 (1 Nov 1926), 36-46.
Argues that the influence of the symbolists is merely technical and that the spirit of Yeats's work is characterized by his rootedness in his native country Ireland.

487. TOMLIN, ERIC WALTER FREDERICK: *Tokyo Essays*. Tokyo: Hokusaido Press, 1967. xi, 365 pp.
"The Continuity of Yeats," 142-48; reprinted from *Phoenix*, 10 (Summer 1965), 60-65; also in CA146. Argues that the difference between the early and the later Yeats is not as great as is usually thought.
"W. B. Yeats: Speech on the Occasion of the Centenary Celebrations, Waseda University 13 June, 1965," 149-51.

488. TYE, JAMES REGINALD: "Literary Periodicals of the Eighteen-Nineties: A Survey of the Monthly and Quarterly Magazines and Reviews," D.Phil. thesis, Oxford U, 1970. viii, 370 pp.
Contains some references to Yeats but unfortunately no index.

489. T[YNAN], K[ATHARINE]: "William Butler Yeats," *Magazine of Poetry*, 1:4 (Oct 1889), 454.

490. TYNAN, KATHARINE: "W. B. Yeats," *BmL*, 5:25 (Oct 1893), 13-14.
Summarized in *BmNY*, 2:4 (Dec 1895), 258-60. "He is full of literary activity and plans, many of which are sure to be fulfilled, for with all his dreamy temperament he has a gift of energy and perseverance. There is not one of the younger men to whose career one looks with keener hope and faith."

491. ———: "Neglect of Irish Writers," *CathW*, 87:517 (Apr 1908), 83-92.
The Irish neglect their best writers, Yeats included.

492. ——— (ed): *The Wild Harp: A Selection from Irish Poetry*. London: Sidgwick & Jackson, 1913. xxvi, 160 pp.
"Introductory," ix-xv, praises Yeats for his immeasurable service to Irish literature, but criticizes him for having given up poetry in favor of drama.

493. UNGVÁRI, TAMÁS: *Az eltűnt személyiseg nyomában: Tanulmányok* [On the search for the lost personality: Essay]. Budapest: Szépirodalmi Könyvkiadó, 1966. 450 pp.
"William Butler Yeats: Az ezoterikus forradalmár" [The esoteric revolutionary], 340-66.

494. UNTERECKER, JOHN: "W. B. Yeats: On His Centennial," *NYTBR*, 13 June 1965, 7, 34-36.

495. UNTERMEYER, LOUIS: *Makers of the Modern World: The Lives of Ninety-two Writers, Artists, Scientists, Statesmen, Inventors, Philosophers, Composers, and Other Creators Who Formed the Pattern of Our Century*. NY: Simon & Schuster, 1955. xx, 809 pp.
"William Butler Yeats," 336-44.

496. ———: *Lives of the Poets: The Story of One Thousand Years of English and American Poetry*. NY: Simon & Schuster, 1959. x, 758 pp.
"William Butler Yeats," 615-22; a somewhat simplistic account of Yeats's development.

497. ———: *The Paths of Poetry: Twenty-five Poets and Their Poems*. NY: Delacorte Press, 1966. 251 pp.
"Land of Heart's Desire," 218-22. For juvenile readers.

498. USSHER, ARLAND: *Three Great Irishmen: Shaw, Yeats, Joyce*. London: Gollancz, 1952. 160 pp.

Incorporates "The Magi," *DM*, 20:2 (Apr-June 1945), 18-21. See "W. B. Yeats: Man into Bird," 63-113, and passim. Discusses Yeats as a thinker, his occult interests, his isolation, and his antidemocratic bias.

Reviews:

- Anon.: "Four Provocative Irishmen," *Times*, 6 Aug 1952, 6.
- Thomas Bodkin: "Magi from the West," *Birmingham Post*, 12 Aug 1952, 3. This review contains what is perhaps the most malignant statement ever made about Yeats: "Yeats almost deserved the dishonouring tribute of condolence which Hitler's foreign office offered his family on his death."
- [Austin Clarke]: "Natives of Ireland," *TLS*, 29 Aug 1952, 560.
- Padraic Colum: "A Gaelic Trill," *SatR*, 5 Sept 1953, 11-12, 29.
- Gerard Fay: "Three Irishmen," *MGuard*, 26 Aug 1952, 4. "Done in the manner of the Synge Street shopkeeper."
- John Gassner, *TAM*, 38:8 (Aug 1954), 12.
- Alfred Kazin: "The Talker," *New Yorker*, 6 Feb 1954, 102, 105-106, 108.
- Walter Kerr: "The Giants of the Irish Revival," *Commonweal*, 7 Aug 1953, 446-47.
- A. J. L[eventhal], *DM*, 28:1 (Jan-Mar 1953), 72.
- H. Marshall McLuhan: "Through Emerald Eyes," *Renascence*, 6:2 (Spring 1954), 157-58.
- Raymond Mortimer: "Three Islanders," *SunT*, 10 Aug 1952, 3.
- Horace Reynolds: "A Triad of Literary Greatness," *NYTBR*, 26 July 1953, 3.
- W. R. Rodgers: "The Flesh behind the Skeleton," *NSt*, 27 Sept 1952, 353.
- Philip Toynbee: "An Irish Critic," *Obs*, 3 Aug 1952, 7.

499. VEGT, JAN VAN DER: *Naar Ierland varen*. 's Gravenhage: Nijgh & Van Ditmar, 1976. 215 pp. (Nieuwe Nijgh boeken. 76.)
"Dichters langs de wegen" [Poets by the way], 98-117. "Het land van Yeats" [Yeats country], 186-200; reprinted from *Kentering*, 14:6 (June 1975), 52-61 (Ireland, especially Sligo, in the poetry).

500. VITOR, E. D'ALMEIDA: "Vale a pena reler W. B. Yeats," *Minais Gerais: Suplemento literário*, 25 Aug 1979, 5.
"It pays to reread Yeats."

501. WADE, ALLAN: *Memories of the London Theatre 1900-1914*. Edited by Alan Andrews. London: Society for Theatre Research, 1983. ix, 54 pp.
Numerous references to Yeats (see index).

502. WAIN, JOHN: "The Meaning of Yeats," *Obs*, 13 June 1965, 26.
He spoke for his age and the age spoke through him.

503. WAKEFIELD, DAN: "Sailing to Byzantium: Yeats and the Young Mind," *Nation*, 23 June 1956, 531-32.
"That cold, metallic world of abstraction described . . . [in] 'Byzantium' and 'Sailing to Byzantium' seems to hold the climate most desired by the recently-graduated English majors."

504. W[ALSH], E[RNEST]: "Senator William Butler Yeats and Miss Harriet Monroe," *This Quarter*, 1:2 [Autumn-Winter 1926], 335-42.
A formidable and somewhat silly attack on Yeats and Miss Monroe. Has this to say about "No Second Troy," a poem that he dislikes particularly: "lines of baldness . . . that no hair tonic on earth or in Mr. Yeats' heavens could grow even a

charge of dandruff to dust over the smooth perfectly polished nothing of the crown."

505. WALSH, WILLIAM: *A Human Idiom: Literature and Humanity*. London: Chatto & Windus, 1964. 212 pp.
"Conclusion: To the Desert or the Cloister," 195-207. Yeats solved the problem of the relationship between the writer and his time by opting for the cloister.

506. WARNER, ALAN: *A Guide to Anglo-Irish Literature*. Dublin: Gill & Macmillan / NY: St. Martin's Press, 1981. viii, 295 pp.
"William Butler Yeats," 169-81.

507. WATTS, HAROLD H.: "W. B. Yeats: Poetry and 'Solutions,'" *Poetry New York,* 1 (1949), 15-21.
As a poet, Yeats had the right answers to his problems; as a public man, however, he was a failure because he had no solutions for the political and social problems of his time. But the lack of solutions is a source of strength in his poetry.

508. WEBB, W. L.: "Ireland's Tongue," *Guardian,* 12 June 1965, 7.

509. WEBER, RICHARD: "About Him . . . and About. . . ," *DM,* 10:1 (Winter/Spring 1973), 21-28.
Obiter dicta. Weber's attitude is best summed up in his poem "Envoy," published in the same issue (p. 69):
Despite the Nineties, the art of art,
The arrogance, the magic and the looking back,
The Moon, the Saint, the Fool and Hunchback;
Despite the lot, how he hits the heart!

510. WELLEK, RENÉ: "William Butler Yeats," *Literární noviny,* 19 July 1935, 5.

511. ———, and AUSTIN WARREN: *Theory of Literature*. NY: Harcourt, Brace, [1959] [1949]. xii, 368 pp. (Harvest Book. HB22.)
Yeats, passim (see index).

512. WELLS, WARRE BRADLEY: *Irish Indiscretions*. London: Allen & Unwin, [1923]. 230 pp.
See pp. 188-222; includes a comparison between AE and WBY and notes on the genesis of *If I Were Four-and-Twenty,* of which Wells was a witness, as well as on Yeats's dissatisfaction with the peasant plays performed at the Abbey.

513. WEST, PAUL: *The Wine of Absurdity: Essays on Literature and Consolation*. University Park: Pennsylvania State UP, 1966. xiv, 249 pp.
"W. B. Yeats," 5-18 [i.e., 3-18]. On the shaping of Yeats's thoughts in the nineties under the influence of Pater.

514. WEST, REBECCA: *The Strange Necessity: Essays and Reviews*. London: Cape, 1928. 344 pp.
See pp. 152-71 for a discussion of Anglo-Irish writers, of whom Yeats is taken to be a nonrevolutionary. Is dismayed by Yeats's "magical view of the universe" and his use of Irish folklore, which merely serves to fill the gaps in his "system." Contains factual inaccuracies of a rather crude sort; e.g., Synge left Ireland to write his plays and promptly came under the influence of Villiers de l'Isle Adam (p. 153).

515. WEYGANDT, CORNELIUS: "The Irish Literary Revival," *SR*, 12:4 (Oct 1904), 420-31.
On Yeats passim.

516. ———: "Literary Workers in Ireland To-day: The Irish Renaissance and What It Has Accomplished," *Book News Monthly*, 25:9 (May 1907), 575-89.

517. ———: *The Time of Yeats: English Poetry of To-day against an American Background*. NY: Russell & Russell, 1969 [1937]. xiii, 460 pp.
"William Butler Yeats and the Irish Literary Renaissance," 167-251. Is mostly out of sympathy with Yeats's later work and regards his "spiritistic" leanings as pernicious to his poetry. The book's title is misleading; there are only sporadic attempts to link the English or Irish poets to the "American background."

518. WHITE, TERENCE DE VERE: *The Anglo-Irish*. London: Gollancz, 1972. 293 pp.
"Yeats as an Anglo-Irishman," 39-51, and passim (see index). An informal sketch rather than a scholarly investigation; contains numerous small inaccuracies.

519. WHITRIDGE, ARNOLD: "William Butler Yeats, 1865-1939," *DR*, 19:1 (Apr 1939), 1-8.

520. WHITTEMORE, REED: *From Zero to the Absolute*. NY: Crown, 1967. xii, 210 pp.
See pp. 91-96: Yeats was "one of the great manipulators."

521. WILEY, PAUL L., and HAROLD OREL (eds): *British Poetry, 1880-1920: Edwardian Voices*. NY: Appleton-Century-Crofts, 1969. xliii, 681 pp.
"William Butler Yeats," 273-77; on the early works.

522. WILHELM, GERTRAUDE (ed): *Die Literatur-Nobelpreisträger: Ein Panorama der Weltliteratur im 20. Jahrhundert*. Düsseldorf: Econ, 1983. 384 pp. (Hermes Handlexikon.)
Christiane Klemm: Yeats, 370-75.

523. WILLIAMS, HAROLD: *Modern English Writers: Being a Study of Imaginative Literature, 1890-1914*. London: Sidgwick & Jackson, 1925. xii, 532 pp.
"Irish Poets and Playwrights," 173-240; on Yeats, pp. 183-93 and passim. First published as *Outlines of Modern English Literature*. London: Sidgwick & Jackson, 1920. 268 pp. (on Yeats, pp. 151-57, 172-74).

524. WILPERT, GERO VON (ed): *Lexikon der Weltliteratur*. Stuttgart: Kröner, 1975-80 [1963-68]. 2 vols.
Yeats, biographical entry, 1:1768-69; summaries and evaluations of some of his works by Johannes Kleinstück, 2:passim (see index).

525. WILSON, COLIN: *The Strength to Dream: Literature and the Imagination*. London: Gollancz, 1962. 224 pp.
"W. B. Yeats," 29-35, and passim (see index). Yeats sees the world and art "in terms of a self-destructive pessimism." Like H. P. Lovecraft, Wilde, and Strindberg, he wages an escapist "assault on rationality."

526. WILSON, EDMUND: "W. B. Yeats," *NewRep*, 15 Apr 1925, Spring Book Section, 8-10.

527. ———: *Axel's Castle: A Study in the Imaginative Literature of 1870-1930*. NY: Scribner's, 1963 [1931]. ix, 319 pp.
"W. B. Yeats," 26-64; based on "William Butler Yeats," *NewRep*, 25 Sept 1929, 141-48, and on "Yeats's Guide to the Soul," *NewRep*, 16 Jan 1929, 249-51 (a review of *A Vision*, W149). Reprinted in CA36. The classical text for the discussion of Yeats as a symbolist; besides, one of the first intelligent attempts to come to terms with Yeats's unorthodoxies.

528. WINTERS, ARTHUR YVOR: "A Study of the Post-Romantic Reaction in Lyrical Verse and Incidentally in Certain Other Forms," Ph.D. thesis, Stanford U, 1933. vii, 401 pp.
Yeats, passim (see index). Winters's dislike of Yeats was very pronounced even at this early stage. He accuses him of confusion, quoting as an example the last lines of "The Gift of Harun Al-Rashid." He has some praise for *The Only Jealousy of Emer*, but is unwilling to specify the quality of the play. Since these are the only Yeats texts discussed at any length, the basis for the judgment that T. Sturge Moore is a far greater poet than Yeats is ridiculously small.

529. WITTIG, KURT: "Die Nationalliteratur Irlands in englischer Sprache von 1889 bis 1939: Motive--Probleme--Charaktere," Habilitationsschrift, U of Halle, [1945]. i, 340 pp.
On Yeats, pp. 12-25 and passim.

530. WOODWARD, A. G.: "The Artist and the Modern World," *ESA*, 16:1 (Mar 1973), 9-14.
Yeats combined aestheticism and immediate experience.

531. YEATS, W. B.: "A Postscript to a Forthcoming Book of Essays by Various Writers," *All Ireland R*, 1 Dec 1900, 6.
Yeats's "Postscript" is followed by the comments of the editor (Standish O'Grady), who criticizes Yeats for having written his book for a London rather than a Dublin audience. Correspondence by Lady Gregory, 15 Dec 1900, 5. The "Postscript" was written for *Ideals in Ireland* (EE214) and is reprinted in *Uncollected Prose*, 2:244-46.

532. ———: "The Irish National Theatre and Three Sorts of Ignorance," *United Irishman*, 24 Oct 1903, 2.
Yeats's article (reprinted in *Uncollected Prose*, 2:306-8) is followed by the comments of the editor (Arthur Griffith?).

533. ———: Letter to the editor about the sources of Synge's *In the Shadow of the Glen*, *United Irishman*, 4 Feb 1905, 1.
Followed by a deprecatory reply of the editor (Arthur Griffith?). Correspondence by Yeats, Synge, and editor's comments, 11 Feb 1905, 1. See also Yeats's letter, 28 Jan 1905, 1. Yeats's letters and the editor's replies are reprinted in *Uncollected Prose*, 2:331-38.

534. ———: *Tragedie irlandesi*. Versione, proemio e note di Carlo Linati. Milano: Studio Editoriale Lombardo, 1914. xlviii, 139 pp.
"William Butler Yeats: Sua lirica, suoi drammi e la rinascenza celtico-irlandese," ix-xxxix.

535. ———: *Erzählungen und Essays.* Übertragen und eingeleitet von Friedrich Eckstein. Leipzig: Insel, 1916. 182 pp.

"Einleitung des Übersetzers," 5-27, discusses Yeats as the exemplary "Celtic" poet and the protagonist of the Irish literary revival. For reviews see G1352-1354.

536. ———: *Théâtre.* Translated by Madeleine Gibert, illustrated by Keogh. Paris: Rombaldi, 1962. 277 pp.

Gunnar Ahlström: "La 'petite histoire' de l'attribution du Prix Nobel à William Butler Yeats," 7-14; translated by Malou Höjer.

Per Hallström: "Discours de réception prononcé lors de la remise du Prix Nobel de littérature à William Butler Yeats le 10 décembre 1923," 15-22. See also CB3 and 187.

Franck [sic] Kermode: "La vie et l'oeuvre de William Butler Yeats," 23-56.

Pierre Barkan: "Bibliographie," 263-74.

537. ———: *William Butler Yeats: Premio Nobel per la litteratura 1923.* Milano: Fabbri, 1966. iii, 508 pp. (Collana Premi Nobel di Letteratura. 24.)

Contains the essays by Ahlström and Hallström (see preceding item) in Italian translation, pp. 5-23; also Roberto Sanesi: "La vita e l'opera di William Butler Yeats," 25-65; "Bibliografia," 491-508.

538. ———: *Le opere: Poesia, teatro, prosa.* Edited by Salvatore Rosati. Torino: UTET, 1969. xxviii, 690 pp. (Scrittori del mondo: I Nobel. [22].)

Salvatore Rosati: "William Butler Yeats," ix-xxviii.

539. ———: *Shi'un min Yaits: Shi'r, nathir, masrah* [Poetry, prose, drama]. Beirut: Matabi' Dar al-Nadwa, 1969. xix, 242 pp.

S. B. Bushrui: Introductions, pp. 1-36, 85-96, 143-77.

540. ———: *Werke.* Edited by Werner Vordtriede. Neuwied: Luchterhand, 1970-73. 6 vols.

W. Vordtriede: "William Butler Yeats--Urbild und Gegenwart," 1:7-29; reprinted from *Neue Deutsche Hefte,* 16:4 (1969), 61-82. The first volume contains notes to the poems and a chronology.

Susanne Schaup: Notes to the plays, 3:230-41; 4:202-16; introduction and notes to the autobiography, 6:7-8, 508-17.

For reviews see G1449-1463.

541. ———: *Antología.* Translated by Jaime Ferrán. Esplugas de Llobregat (Barcelona): Plaza & Janes, 1973. 127 pp.

"Viaje a W. B. Yeats," 7-14.

542. ———: *Ich hatte die Weisheit, die Liebe uns gibt.* Herausgegeben, mit einem Nachwort und Anmerkungen versehen von Karl Heinz Berger. Berlin: Volk und Welt, 1981. 231 pp.

"Nachwort," 207-19 (generally on Yeats's thought and development); "Anmerkungen," 220-22. For a review see G1548.

543. ———: *Izbrano delo* [Selected works]. Translated by Veno Taufer. Ljubljana: Cankarjeva založba v Ljubljani, 1983. 224 pp. (Nobelova nagrada za literatura 1923: Nobelovci. 76.)

"Opombe," 193-98 (explanatory notes); "Spremna beseda o avtorju" [Introductory lecture on the author], 199-218; "Yeats pris nas," 219 (short bibliography of translations and critical studies by Jože Munda).

544. Z., O.: "From a Modern Irish Portrait Gallery: V.--W. B. Yeats," *New Ireland R,* 2:10 (Dec 1894), 647-59.

I suspect that the author, who seems to have inside knowledge, is W. P. Ryan. Comments on the Yeats--Charles Gavan Duffy quarrel. The answer to this was "Kleinbier, the Poet" (HF70).

545. Z[ABEL], M. D.: "Yeats at Thirty and Seventy," *Poetry,* 47:5 (Feb 1936), 268-77.

546. ZACH, WOLFGANG, and HEINZ KOSOK (eds): *Literary Interrelations: Ireland, England and the World.* Tübingen: Narr, 1987. 3 vols. (SECL: Studies in English and Comparative Literature. 1-3.)

On Yeats see especially: Birgit Bramsbäck: "William Butler Yeats and Sweden," 1:51-60; translated and revised version of "William Butler Yeats och Sverige," *Tvärsnitt,* 8:1 (1986), 4-13. Yeats's visit to Sweden, his reception, and the Nobel Prize award.

Ivanka Koviloska-Poposka: "The Reception of Yeats in Macedonian," 1:61-67.

Theo D'haen: "Translation, Adaptation, Inspiration: The Creative Reception of Anglo-Irish Works in Dutch Literature," 1:81-89; refers to A. Roland Holst's interest in Yeats.

Mirko Jurak: "Irish Playwrights in the Slovene Theatre," 1:159-67; contains a note on the performance of *The Countess Cathleen* in the Slovene National Theatre, Ljubljana, in Feb 1933. See also EE138.

Richard Ellmann: "The Uses of Decadence: Wilde, Yeats, and Joyce," 2:27-39: "They are not decadents but counter decadents [who] went through decadence to come out on the other side." See also CC71a.

Johannes Kleinstück: "Yeats and Ibsen," 2:65-74.

Mária Kurdi: "Parallels between the Poetry of W. B. Yeats and Endre Ady," 2:75-83.

Csilla Bertha: "An Irish and a Hungarian Model of Mythical Drama: W. B. Yeats and Áron Tamási," 2:85-93.

Jacqueline Genet: "W. B. Yeats and W. H. Auden," 2:95-110.

Patrick O'Neill: "Ossian's Return: The German Factor in the Irish Literary Revival," 2:207-20; contains notes on Yeats's views of Goethe, Nietzsche, and Spengler.

Suheil Badi Bushrui: "Yeats, India, Arabia, and Japan: The Search for a Spiritual Philosophy," 2:221-34.

B. N. Prasad: "The Impact of W. B. Yeats on Modern Indian Poetry," 2:235-44.

Donald T. Torchiana: "W. B. Yeats and Italian Idealism," 2:245-54; Yeats's reading of Vico, Croce, and Gentile.

Margaret E. Fogarty: "The Fiction of Iris Murdoch: Amalgam of Yeatsian and Joycean Motifs," 2:323-34.

See also AE28, BB21, 32, 98, 126, BE106, CD1344.

CC Themes and Types

The arrangement in this section is alphabetical by author, not by subject (as in the first edition). Readers looking for specific topics are advised to consult the subject index.

1. ALDERSON SMITH, PETER: *W. B. Yeats and the Tribes of Danu: Three Views of Ireland's Fairies.* Gerrards Cross: Smythe, / Totowa, N.J.: Barnes & Noble, 1987. 350 pp. (Irish Literary Studies. 27.)

Includes "'Grown to Heaven like a Tree': The Scenery of *The*

Countess Cathleen," *Eire*, 4:3 (Fall 1979), 65-82; and "*The Countess Cathleen* and the Otherworld," *Eire*, 17:2 (Summer 1982), 141-46.

Discusses the early mythological cycles, the collections of Irish fairy tales and folklore, and fairy lore in Yeats's early works. Analyzed in sections DD, EE, and FA.

Reviews:

- James E. Doan: "Irish Myth and Yeats," *ILS*, 7:1 (Spring 1988), 13.
- John Hanratty: "Singing-Masters of the Soul," *BooksI*, 118 (Nov 1987), 218-19.
- Micheál O hAodha: "The Plumed and Skinny Shee," *IrT*, 21 Nov 1987, Weekend, 9. Correspondence by Alderson Smith, *IrT*, 22 Dec 1987, 9.

2. ———: "Who Was Red Hanrahan?" *Eire*, 22:3 (Fall 1987), 144-50.

Yeats's use of his sources in the creation of this character.

3. ALEXANDER, JEAN: "Yeats and the Rhetoric of Defilement," *REL*, 6:3 (July 1965), 44-57.

Images of defilement and corruption in Yeats's works.

4. ALLEN, JAMES LOVIC: "Bird Symbolism in the Work of William Butler Yeats," Ph.D. thesis, U of Florida, 1959. iii, 413 pp. (*DAI*, 20:8 [Feb 1960], 3288)

Includes a long chapter on Yeats and Frazer (pp. 308-53) and an essay on the tower motif (pp. 363-90).

5. ———: "William Butler Yeats's One Myth," *Personalist*, 45:4 (Autumn 1964), 524-32.

The one myth is a Platonic dualism; its central motif is the union of man and god. Discusses the poetry and *A Vision*.

6. ———: "Miraculous Birds, Another and the Same: Yeats's Golden Image and the Phoenix," *ES*, 48:3 (June 1967), 215-26.

Discusses the phoenix imagery.

7. ———: "Unity of Archetype, Myth, and Religious Imagery in the Work of Yeats," *TCL*, 20:2 (Apr 1974), 91-95.

The "union of man and God, the human and the divine, the natural and the supernatural" is Yeats's "dominant image-idea."

8. ———: "Yeats and Modernism," *MBL*, 2:1 (Spring 1977), 5-16.

9. ALLT, GEORGE DANIEL PETER: "W. B. Yeats," *Theology*, 42:248 (Feb 1941), 81-91.

Yeats was not a religious poet; in fact, some of his thoughts are dangerous doctrines. Christians should read him because he was above all an honest poet.

10. ———: "Yeats, Religion, and History," *SR*, 60:4 (Oct-Dec 1952), 624-58.

Discusses among other texts *Cathleen ni Houlihan*, *Calvary*, and *The Resurrection*.

11. ———: "The Anglo-Irish Literary Movement in Relation to Its Antecedents," Ph.D. thesis, Cambridge U, 1953. iv, 207 pp.; bibliographical references on opposite blank pages.

Deals with the life and works of Molyneux, Swift, Grattan, the Edgeworths, Thomas Moore, Mangan, Mitchel, Yeats, and Joyce.

See particularly "Yeats, Religion, Ireland, and History," 132-73; written along the same lines as the two preceding items.

12. ANGHINETTI, PAUL WILLIAM: "Alienation, Rebellion, and Myth: A Study of the Works of Nietzsche, Jung, Yeats, Camus, and Joyce," Ph.D. thesis, Florida State U, 1969. iii, 464 pp. (*DAI*, 30:5 [Nov 1969], 1974A-75A)

"Yeats: Transcendental Myth and the Conflict of Time and Eternity," 162-247.

13. ĀRĀR: *Cimpalisam*. Tirupputtur: Arivarankam, 1982. 232 pp.

In Tamil. On p. 2 the book's title is given as *Symbolism: An Introduction to the Critical Idiom. With a Comparative Study of Symbolism in Yeats and Bharati.*

14. ARGOFF, NORMA JEANNE FORDHAM: "The Hearth and the Road: The Countryman in the Works of W. B. Yeats," Ph.D. thesis, University College Dublin, 1980. v, 489 pp.

14a. ARMSTRONG, TIMOTHY DAVID: "The Poetry of Winter: The Idea and Nature of the Late Career in the Works of Hardy, Yeats and Stevens," Ph.D. thesis, U of London, 1986. 417 pp.

Abstract in *Index to Theses*, 37:1 (1988), 22. "W. B. Yeats," 179-268; discusses *A Vision*, the poetry of old age, *The King of the Great Clock Tower*, *A Full Moon in March*, *The Death of Cuchulain*, and *Purgatory*.

15. ARMYTAGE, WALTER HARRY GREEN: *Yesterday's Tomorrows: A Historical Survey of Future Societies*. London: Routledge & Kegan Paul, 1968. xi, 288 pp.

"Yeats and the Dissociation of Myth and Fact," 109-11; reprint of "The Yeatsian Dialectic," *Riverside Q*, 3:1 (Aug 1967), 48-51.

16. ASSOCIATION INTERNATIONALE DE LITTÉRATURE COMPARÉE / INTERNATIONAL COMPARATIVE LITERATURE ASSOCIATION: *Actes du VIe congrès / Proceedings of the 6th Congress*. Stuttgart: Bieber, 1975. iv, 816 pp.

Haskell M. Block: "Conceptions of the Literary Elite at the End of the Nineteenth Century," 391-95; contains a note on Yeats's elitism.

17. AYER, JAMES RODERICK: "End as Beginning: The Evolution of Apocalyptic Thought in the Work of W. B. Yeats," Ph.D. thesis, U of Massachusetts, 1977. xiii, 158 pp. (*DAI*, 38:1 [July 1977], 272A)

On *A Vision*, related poems, *Stories of Michael Robartes and His Friends*, and *The Herne's Egg*.

18. B.-d. V., A.: "Moderne engelsche mystiek: William Butler Yeats," *Gulden winckel*, 11:12 (15 Dec 1912), 177-80.

Explains the "mystical element" in Yeats as his desire to "bring mankind one step nearer to the earthly paradise." Thinks that he is a Catholic.

19. BALAKIAN, ANNA (ed): *The Symbolist Movement in the Literature of European Languages*. Budapest: Akadémiai Kiadó, 1982. 732 pp. (Comparative History of Literatures in European Languages. 2.)

Denis Donoghue: "Yeats: The Question of Symbolism," 279-93; on the influence of Mallarmé and Arthur Symons (see also CB131 and 403). Yeats is also referred to in some other contributions (see index), especially in the editor's "Conclusion," 681-98.

20. BARNWELL, WILLIAM CURTIS: "W. B. Yeats: The Scheme of Perfection," Ph.D. thesis, U of Florida, 1972. v, 123 pp. (*DAI*, 34:1 [July 1973], 303A-4A)

Discusses the influence of Shelley and Blake on Yeats's perfectionist thinking, of Castiglione on the aristocratic concept, and the concept of Unity of Being.

21. ———: "Utopia and the 'New Ill Breeding': Yeats and the Politics of Perfection," *Eire*, 10:1 (Spring 1975), 54-68.

Notes the failure of all that Yeats "had worked for and valued in public matters--the aristocratic perfection of social, political and cultural affairs."

22. BECKETT, J. C.: *The Anglo-Irish Tradition*. London: Faber & Faber, 1976. 159 pp.

On Yeats passim (see index).

23. ———: "The Irish Writer and His Public in the Nineteenth Century," *YES*, 11 (1981), 102-16.

Contains several references to Yeats.

24. BENCE-JONES, MARK: *Twilight of the Ascendancy*. London: Constable, 1987. xvii, 327 pp.

See index for some notes on Yeats as an Ascendancy figure.

25. BERGMANN, ELIZABETH W.: "Yeats's Gallery," *CLQ*, 15:2 (June 1979), 127-36.

Analyzes Yeats's reasons for selecting the portraits of himself as illustrations of his books and his discussions of portraits in *Autobiographies* and some poems. Notes the influence of John Butler Yeats.

26. BESSAI, DIANE ELIZABETH: "Sovereignty of Erin: A Study of Mythological Motif in the Irish Literary Revival," Ph.D. thesis, U of London, 1971. 531 pp.

Nationalism and the national literary heritage, particularly in Yeats.

27. BHALLA, M. M.: "A Ritual of a Lost Faith," *JJCL*, 7 (1967), 102-22.

Reprinted in *Thought* [Delhi], 24 May 1969, 14-16; 31 May 1969, 14-16. A discussion of ritualism and symbolism in Yeats's poetry and prose.

28. BLOCK, EDWIN FRANK: "The Transition to Modernism: The Reader's Role in Selected Works of Walter Pater, Arthur Symons, W. B. Yeats, and Hugo von Hofmannsthal," Ph.D. thesis, Stanford U, 1975. xii, 524 pp. (*DAI*, 36:1 [July 1975], 300A)

"William Butler Yeats and the Symbolist Essay," 213-65; "Readings of Symons' 'Extracts from the Journal of Henry Luxulyan' and Yeats' 'Rosa Alchemica,'" 266-367; "Some Lyrics of Yeats," 417-72 (on the early poetry).

29. BLOOM, HAROLD: *Poetry and Repression: Revisionism from Blake to Stevens*. New Haven: Yale UP, 1976. x, 293 pp.

"Yeats, Gnosticism, and the Sacred Void," 205-34; on anthithetical thinking in *A Vision*, "The Second Coming," "Byzantium," and "Cuchulain Comforted," reprinted in CA13. See also CD283.

30. BÖHM, RUDOLF: *Das Motto in der englischen Literatur des 19.*

Jahrhunderts. München: Fink, 1975. 281 pp.
Contains a few notes on mottos in Yeats's books.

31. BORNSTEIN, GEORGE: *Transformations of Romanticism in Yeats, Eliot, and Stevens*. Chicago: U of Chicago Press, 1976. xiii, 265 pp.
"The Last Romanticism of W. B. Yeats," 27-93. "The first part of this chapter argues that Yeats' concept of romanticism, his construal of romantic heroes as incarnations of passionate mood or as principles of mind, and his interpretation of specific romantics display psychological doctrines and mental actions making the poet's quest for images the paradigmatic imaginative act. The second part applies those conclusions to a reading of the mature poetry, particularly to the surprising number of Greater Romantic Lyrics" (p. 27). Analyzed in section DD.

For a shorter version see "Yeats and the Greater Romantic Lyric" on pp. 91-110 of G. Bornstein (ed): *Romantic and Modern: Revaluations of Literary Tradition*. Pittsburgh: U of Pittsburgh Press, 1977. xiii, 248 pp. Also in CD1a.

Reviews:
- Robert Buttel, *JML*, 7:4 (1979), 603-5.
- Michael G. Cooke, *SIR*, 18:2 (Summer 1979), 323-30.
- George Mills Harper: "Riders for the High Horse," *MQR*, 17:3 (Summer 1978), 414-23.
- Kerry McSweeney: "Romantic Continuities and Mutations: Browning to Stevens," *Humanities Association R*, 28:3 (Summer 1977), 257-67.
- John D. Margolis, *ELN*, 15:2 (Dec 1977), 148-53.
- Marjorie Perloff, *WSJour*, 1:2 (Summer 1977), 75-78.
- David Wagenknecht, *CL*, 31:2 (Spring 1979), 190-92.

32. BOSE, ABINASH CHANDRA: "Yeat[s]'s View of Life as Conflict," *Shakti*, 3:8 (Aug 1966), 30-31.

33. BOSE, AMALENDU: "The Decade of Yeats's *In the Seven Woods*," *JJCL*, 8 (1968), 96-109.

34. BOULGER, JAMES D.: "Personality and Existence in Yeats," *Thought*, 39:155 (Winter 1964), 591-612.
Mythological, historical (especially Berkeley), and contemporary figures (especially Yeats himself) in the poetry and prose.

35. ———: "Yeats and Irish Identity," *Thought*, 42:165 (Summer 1967), 185-213.
Yeats's increasing awareness of his Irish identity is shown in "Easter 1916." His later works (e.g., the Crazy Jane poems) demonstrate "his spiritual identification with the racial majority." Compares Yeats, Joyce, and Eugene O'Neill.

36. BOYCE, DAVID GEORGE: *Nationalism in Ireland*. London: Croom Helm / Dublin: Gill & Macmillan, 1982. 441 pp.
Several remarks on Yeats (see index).

37. BRADBURY, MALCOLM, and JAMES MCFARLANE (eds): *Modernism 1890-1930*. Harmondsworth: Penguin, 1976. 684 pp.
Yeats is discussed in several contributions (see index), especially in the editors' introduction: "The Name and Nature of Modernism," 19-55; M. Bradbury: "London 1890-1920," 172-90; Graham Hough: "The Modernist Lyric," 312-22; Richard Sheppard: "The Crisis of Language," 323-36; J. McFarlane: "Neo-modernist Drama: Yeats and Pirandello," 561-70.

37a. BRADY, CAROLEE: "'May These Characters Remain': Yeats's Masks of Old Age," °Ph.D. thesis, George Washington U, 1987. 255 pp. (*DAI*, 48:11 [May 1988], 2877A)
The masks of Crazy Jane, Oedipus, and Cuchulain.

38. BRIGGS, JULIA: *Night Visitors: The Rise and Fall of the English Ghost Story*. London: Faber & Faber, 1977. 238 pp.
On ghosts in Yeats's works, especially *The Words upon the Window-Pane, The Dreaming of the Bones, Purgatory,* and *A Vision,* pp. 200-4 and passim (see index).

39. BRODER, PEGGY FISHER: "Positive Folly: The Role of the Fool in the Works of W. B. Yeats," °Ph.D. thesis, Case Western Reserve U, 1969. 244 pp. (*DAI,* 30:9 [Mar 1970], 3902A)

40. BRONSON, EDWARD FULTON: "The Dance of Apocalypse: Yeats and Michael Robartes," °Ph.D. thesis, U of Maryland, 1982. 241 pp. (*DAI,* 43:5 [Nov 1982], 1550A-51A; reprinted *Yeats,* 1 [1983], 185-86; *YeA,* 4 [1986], 303-4)
"This dissertation . . . is an appreciation of the role of the fictive character Michael Robartes in Yeats's pursuit of unity" (abstract).

41. BROOKS, CLEANTH: *The Hidden God: Studies in Hemingway, Faulkner, Yeats, Eliot, and Warren*. New Haven: Yale UP, 1963. xi, 136 pp.
"W. B. Yeats: Search for a New Myth," 44-67. Religion is important to Yeats. Although he may explore it in strange contexts, he gives back to it a much-needed sense of urgency and a feeling of awe. Yeats's own beliefs are, however, difficult to determine.

42. BROWN, R. M. C. S.: "Yeats's Early Approach to Nationalism," M.Litt. thesis, Trinity College Dublin, 1970. xvi, 317 pp.

43. BROWN, TERENCE: *Ireland: A Social and Cultural History 1922-1979*. London: Fontana, 1981. 364 pp.
On Yeats and the Anglo-Irish tradition, pp. 129-34 and passim (see index). A new edition was published as *Ireland: A Social and Cultural History, 1922 to the Present*. Ithaca: Cornell UP, 1985. 303 pp.

44. BRÜGGEMANN, THEODOR: "Das christliche Element in W. B. Yeats' dichterischer Symbolik," Dr.phil. thesis, U of Münster, 1954. 205 pp.
Yeats's use of Christian symbolism is essentially that of someone outside Christianity, who is equally distanced from and attracted by it. Christian symbolism provides points of orientation in Yeats's poetry and assists him in his search for truth. Discusses "Vacillation," "Leda and the Swan," "The Mother of God," *Calvary, The Resurrection,* and other works.

45. BUCHTA, NORBERT K.: *Rezeption und ästhetische Verarbeitung romantischer Poetologie im lyrischen Werk William Butler Yeats'*. Königstein: Forum Academicum, 1982. v, 276 pp. (Hochschulschriften Literaturwissenschaft. 52.)
"The reception and aesthetic use of romantic poetology in WBY's poetry." Originally a Dr.phil. thesis, U of Frankfurt, 1978. Buchta argues, not always convincingly, that Yeats's reaction to romantic poetics shows that he believed in concepts that were essentially outmoded. This accounts for unrelieved tensions in his later works. See review by K. P. S. Jochum, *YeA,* 4 (1986), 249-51.

46. BURTON, RICHARD EDMUND: "The Spiring Treadmill and the Preposterous Pig: The Accommodation of Science in the Political, Occult, and Poetic Development of W. B. Yeats, 1885-1905," Ph.D. thesis, U of London, 1985. 294 pp. (Abstract in *Index to Theses*, 35:3 [1987], 1086-87)

The chapter on politics is mainly concerned with Yeats's protofascist leanings, that on occultism with the importance of theosophy. Discusses *Mosada, The Seeker, Time and the Witch Vivien, Where There Is Nothing,* and "The Two Trees." Science is represented among others by Darwin, Haeckel, Huxley, and Tyndall.

47. BUSH, DOUGLAS: *Mythology and the Romantic Tradition in English Poetry*. NY: Pageant Book Company, 1957 [1937]. xvi, 647 pp.

See index for scattered notes on Yeats.

48. BUSH, RONALD: "Yeats, Spooks, Nursery Rhymes, and the Vicissitudes of Later Modernism," *Yeats,* 3 (1985), 17-33.

Reincarnation in Yeats's works and thought.

49. BYARS, JOHN ARTHUR: "The Heroic Type in the Irish Legendary Dramas of W. B. Yeats, Lady Gregory, and J. M. Synge: 1903-1910," Ph.D. thesis, U of North Carolina, 1963. ii, 262 pp. (*DAI,* 24:8 [Feb 1964], 3333)

Discusses heroic types in Yeats's pre-1899 plays, poems, and prose, as well as in *On Baile's Strand, The King's Threshold, Where There Is Nothing, Deirdre,* and *The Green Helmet.*

50. CAHILL, SUSAN and THOMAS CAHILL: *A Literary Guide to Ireland.* NY: Scribner's, 1973. xvii, 333 pp.

On Yeats and the places associated with him (Coole Park, Sligo, Thoor Ballylee), passim, especially pp. 101-15, 167-86.

51. CALLAN, EDWARD: "W. B. Yeats on the Coming of Age: From 'Homo Sapiens' to 'L'homme clairvoyant,'" *DM,* 9:3 (Summer 1972), 34-46.

The concept of Anima Mundi, particularly in "Under Ben Bulben."

52. CARPENTER, ANDREW (ed): *Place, Personality, and the Irish Writer.* Gerrards Cross: Smythe, 1977. 199 pp. (Irish Literary Studies. 1.)

A. Norman Jeffares: "Place, Space, and Personality and the Irish Writer," 11-40; on the young Yeats's view of Western Ireland.

Robert O'Driscoll: "Return to the Hearthstone: Ideals of the Celtic Literary Revival," 41-68; on Yeats's view of the Celtic heritage in Irish culture.

F. S. L. Lyons: "The Parnell Theme in Literature," 69-95.

Short references to Yeats in some of the other contributions.

53. CASEY, DANIEL J., and ROBERT E. RHODES (eds): *Views of the Irish Peasantry 1800-1916*. Hamden, Ct.: Archon Books, 1977. 225 pp.

Alf MacLochlainn: "Gael and Peasant--A Case of Mistaken Identity?" 17-36.

James MacKillop: "Finn Mac Cool: The Hero and Anti-Hero in Irish Folk Tradition," 86-106; see also EE219.

Maurice Harmon: "Cobwebs before the Wind: Aspects of the Peasantry in Irish Literature from 1800-1916," 129-59.

John Unterecker: "Countryman, Peasant, and Servant in the Poetry of W. B. Yeats," 178-91; on "The Fisherman" and "The Tower."

54. CASSIDY, ROBERT LAWRENCE: "W. B. Yeats' Early Poetry and Prose: The Landscape of Art," Ph.D. thesis, U of Western Ontario,

1971. vi, 303 pp. (*DAI,* 33:2 [Aug 1972], 748A)
Discusses the work of the 1880s and 1890s, particularly "The Wanderings of Oisin." Also on the importance of Edward Dowden for Yeats's development.

55. CAZAMIAN, LOUIS: *Symbolisme et poésie: L'exemple anglais.* Paris: Presse française et étrangère, 1947. 254 pp.
See pp. 217-20 and 224-27 for a discussion of Yeats's symbolism in theory and practice ("The Wanderings of Oisin").

56. CENDROWSKA, GRAŻYNA: "Irlandzkie spory wokół literatury narodowej," *Acta Philologica,* 9 (1977), 21-41.
"The Irish national literature controversy"; Yeats is referred to passim.

57. CENTRE D'ETUDE DU THEATRE ANGLO-SAXON. GROUPE D'ETUDE THEORIQUE DU ROMAN DE LANGUE ANGLAISE: *De William Shakespeare à William Golding: Mélanges dédiés à la mémoire de Jean-Pierre Vernier.* Préface de Sylvère Monod. Rouen: Université de Rouen, 1984. 157 pp. (Publications de l'Université de Rouen. 84.)
Jacqueline Genet: "W. B. Yeats: La poétique du visible et de l'invisible," 11-25; on the manifestations of the supernatural in Yeats's works.

58. CHEADLE, B. D.: "Yeats and Symbolism," *ESA,* 12:2 (Sept 1969), 132-50.
Symbolist tendencies in Yeats's poetry and thought, symbolism being understood in both a historical and a general sense. Points out that even the early Yeats at his most symbolic is tempered by matter-of-factness. Discusses "Sailing to Byzantium."

59. CHESTERTON, GILBERT KEITH: *All Things Considered.* Henley-on-Thames: Darwen Finlayson, 1969 [1908]. 190 pp.
"Fairy Tales," 164-67. Yeats's ideas of the fairies are wrong. See also Chesterton's "Our Note Book," *ILN,* 15 Feb 1908, 224: "I doubt whether Mr. Yeats really knows his way about fairyland. He is not simple enough; he is not stupid enough."

60. CLARK, JAMES MIDGLEY: *The Vocabulary of Anglo-Irish.* St. Gallen: Zollikofer, 1917. iii, 48 pp. (Städtische Handelshochschule St. Gallen. Jahresbericht 17-18 [1915/16-1916/17]. Wissenschaftliche Beilage.)
Yeats, passim.

61. CLARK, ROSALIND ELIZABETH: "Goddess, Fairy Mistress, and Sovereignty: Women of the Irish Supernatural," Ph.D. thesis, U of Massachusetts, 1985. xiii, 558 pp. (*DAI,* 46:3 [Sept 1985], 704A)
Yeats's use of Irish mythological material in *The Death of Cuchulain, The Only Jealousy of Emer, Cathleen ni Houlihan,* and "The Wanderings of Oisin" is discussed passim, especially on pp. 218-33, 296-310, 320-28, 364-73, and 394-420.

62. CLINTON-BADDELEY, VICTOR CLINTON: *Words for Music.* Cambridge: UP, 1941. xi, 168 pp.
"W. B. Yeats & the Art of Song," 149-64, and passim (see index). "Music for him was an aid to the performance of poetry and nothing more" (p. 151). "He was not so much interested in the art of song as in the art of the public presentation of poetry" (p. 155).

63. COHEN, PAUL NATHAN: "'Words Alone Are Certain Good': Yeats and the Unity of the Arts," Ph.D. thesis, Rutgers U, 1977. vi, 214 pp. (*DAI*, 38:5 [Nov 1977], 2801A-2A)
Discusses Yeats's involvement in the arts, especially painting and music, and the theme of art in his works, also his collaboration with various artists.

64. ———: "Blindness in Yeats," *YER*, 6:2 (1979), 49-55.
Yeats's deficient eyesight explains his insistence on the importance of the imagination.

65. COLDWELL, JOAN: "'The Art of Happy Desire': Yeats and the Little Magazine," in Skelton and Saddlemyer: *The World of W. B. Yeats* (1967, CA102), 24-37.
Yeats occupies only a marginal place in this somewhat superficial chronicle.

66. ———: "'Images That Yet Fresh Images Beget': A Note on Book Covers," in Skelton and Saddlemyer: *The World of W. B. Yeats* (1967, CA102), 134-39.
The designs made for Yeats's books by Althea Gyles, Sturge Moore, and Charles Ricketts.

67. COLEMAN, ANTONY: "The Big House, Yeats, and the Irish Context," *YeA*, 3 (1985), 33-52.
Yeats's treatment of the big houses reveals that he wasn't rooted in Irish soil. He used his access to the Irish tradition for his own purposes.

68. COMANZO, CHRISTIAN: "L'élément féerique dans la littérature et l'art victoriens," thesis, Université de Lyon II, 1979. Lille: Atelier national de reproduction des thèses, Université de Lille III, 1983. ii, 1032 pp. in 2 vols.
See index for numerous references to Yeats.

69. CORNWELL, ETHEL FRAZIER: *The "Still Point": Theme and Variations in the Writings of T. S. Eliot, Coleridge, Yeats, Henry James, Virginia Woolf, and D. H. Lawrence*. New Brunswick: Rutgers UP, 1962. ix, 261 pp.
"Yeats and His System," 89-125, and passim. "His use of myth and his later development of a system was . . . Yeats's personal protest against the growing chaos of his world, and his personal solution to the problems of unity and coherence that so plague the modern artist" (p. 90).

70. CORSA, HELEN STORM: "Psychoanalytic Concepts of Creativity and Aging: The Fate of Creativity in Mid-Years and Old Age," *J of Geriatric Psychiatry*, 6:2 (1973), 169-83.
Yeats is an important example of creativity in old age and of a poet grappling with the question of old age.

71. COSTELLO, PETER: *The Heart Grown Brutal: The Irish Revolution in Literature from Parnell to the Death of Yeats, 1891-1939*. Dublin: Gill & Macmillan, 1977. xiii, 330 pp.
Yeats figures prominently, especially in the introduction and in chapters 2, 6, 8, and 16.
Reviews:
- Mary Joan Egan and Joseph J. Egan, *MFS*, 24:4 (Winter 1978/79), 597-98.
- R. F. Foster, *L&H*, 6:1 (Spring 1980), 131-32.

- Roger McHugh, *IUR*, 8:1 (Spring 1978), 126-28.
- Rosita Sweetman: "The Revolution That Failed," *BooksI*, 20 (Feb 1978), 14.

71a. CROSSLEY, CERI, and IAN SMALL (eds): *Studies in Anglo-French Cultural Relations: Imagining France*. London: Macmillan, 1988. ix, 247 pp.

Richard Ellmann: "The Uses of Decadence: Wilde, Yeats, Joyce," 17-33. Reprint of *The Uses of Decadence: Wilde, Yeats, Joyce*. Originally delivered at Bennington College as Lecture Six in the Ben Belitt Lectureship Series, September 28, 1983. Bennington, Vt.: Bennington College, 1983. iv, 26 pp. (Bennington Chapbooks in Literature.). See also CB148a and 546.

"Decadence . . . had its uses for Wilde, Yeats and Joyce, as a pivot around which they could organise their work. All in their different ways summon up an opposite to decadence, the promise of an 'unfashionable' age for which as artists they constitute themselves heralds. They are not decadents but counterdecadents."

72. DAICHES, DAVID: *Literary Essays*. Edinburgh: Oliver & Boyd, 1956. vii, 225 pp.

"Religion, Poetry and the 'Dilemma' of the Modern Writer," 206-25. See also "Theodicy, Poetry, and Tradition," in Stanley Romaine Hopper (ed): *Spiritual Problems in Contemporary Literature*. NY: Harper, 1957 [1952]. xvii, 298 pp. (Harper Torchbooks. TB21.), pp. 73-93.

Yeats "needed a religious tradition to work with, but he could not accept any tradition specifically denominated as religious" (p. 218).

73. ———: *More Literary Essays*. Chicago: U of Chicago Press, 1968. vii, 274 pp.

"Myth, Metaphor, and Poetry," 1-18; reprinted from *EDH*, 33 (1965), 39-55. "The search for archetypal images, for the contents of Yeats's Great Memory. . . , is not always the surest way of accounting for the suggestion of myth. . . . One could use all the symbols in the book and still achieve no adequate poetic expression."

"Yeats's Earlier Poems: Some Themes and Patterns," 133-49; reprinted from CA48.

74. DANAHER, KEVIN: "Folk Tradition and Literature," *JIL*, 1:2 (May 1972), 63-76.

Includes notes on Yeats, who is said to have never understood the Irish folk tradition.

75. DAVIE, DONALD: *Articulate Energy: An Inquiry into the Syntax of English Poetry*. London: Routledge & Kegan Paul, 1976 [1955]. xv, 173 pp.

Yeats's syntax, pp. 123-25, and passim (see index).

76. DAWE, GERALD, and EDNA LONGLEY (eds): *Across a Roaring Hill: The Protestant Imagination in Modern Ireland. Essays in Honour of John Hewitt*. Belfast: Blackstaff Press, 1985. xix, 242 pp.

See especially John Kelly: "Choosing and Inventing: Yeats and Ireland," 1-24.

W. J. McCormack: "'The Protestant Strain': Or, A Short History of Anglo-Irish Literature from S. T. Coleridge to Thomas Mann," 48-78.

Edna Longley: "Louis MacNeice: 'The Walls Are Flowing,'"

99-123 (contains notes on MacNeice's view of Yeats).
Short references to Yeats in some of the other contributions and in the editors' introduction.

77. DÉDÉYAN, CHARLES: *Le nouveau mal du siècle de Baudelaire à nos jours*. Paris: Société d'Édition d'Enseignement Supérieur, 1968-72. 2 vols.
On Yeats, 2:267-78 as part of the chapter "Rêve et tristesse des post-décadents."

78. DETTMAR, KEVIN J. H.: "'Evil Gathers Head': Yeats' Poetics of Evil," *CollL*, 13:1 (Winter 1986), 71-87.

79. DOMVILLE, ERIC W. (ed): *Editing British and American Literature, 1880-1920*. Papers given at the tenth annual Conference on Editorial Problems, University of Toronto, November 1974. NY: Garland, 1976. viii, 98 pp.
Michael Sidnell: "Yeats in the Light of Day: The Text and Some Editions," 49-63; on the problems facing the editor of the unpublished and published works.

80. DONOGHUE, DENIS: "Tradition, Poetry, and W. B. Yeats," *SR*, 69:3 (Summer 1961), 476-84.
Yeats's idea of tradition, including a note on "Byzantium."

81. DORSON, RICHARD MERCER: *The British Folklorists: A History*. London: Routledge & Kegan Paul, 1968. x, 518 pp.
"Ireland," 431-39; contains some notes on Yeats.

82. DUFFY, MAUREEN: *The Erotic World of Faery*. London: Hodder & Stoughton, 1972. 352 pp.
Note on Yeats and the faeries, pp. 301-5.

83. DUFOUR, MICHEL: "Le symbole de la rose dans l'oeuvre de W. B. Yeats," thesis, Doctorat de 3e cycle, Université de Caen, 1980. 326 pp.

84. DUNNE, TOM (ed): *The Writer as Witness: Literature as Historical Evidence*. Cork: Cork UP, 1987. xi, 244 pp. (Historical Studies. 16.)
Seamus Deane: "Irish National Character 1790-1900," 90-113, contains a note on Yeats's "pseudo-scientific" and esoteric approach to the Irish national character.

84a. DYSERINCK, HUGO, and KARL ULRICH SYNDRAM (eds): *Europa und das nationale Selbstverständnis: Imagologische Probleme in Literatur, Kunst und Kultur des 19. und 20. Jahrhunderts*. Bonn: Bouvier, 1988. 435 pp. (Aachener Beiträge zur Komparatistik. 8.)
J. Th. Leerssen: "'The Cracked Lookingglass of a Servant': Cultural Decolonization and National Consciousness in Ireland and Africa," 103-18; contains notes on Yeats's cultural nationalism.

85. EAGLETON, TERRY: *Criticism and Ideology: A Study in Marxist Literary Theory*. London: NLB, 1976. 191 pp.
"W. B. Yeats," 151-54, and passim (see index). On Yeats's cultural nationalism, derived from an aristocratic romantic idealism and in conflict with the realities of nationalist politics.

86. ———: "Politics and Sexuality in W. B. Yeats," *Crane Bag*, 9:2 (1985), 138-42.

87. EDDY, MICHAEL MAX: "The Grotesque in the Art of William Butler Yeats," Ph.D. thesis, Purdue U, 1984. vi, 169 pp. (*DAI*, 45:7 [Jan 1985], 2109A-10A; reprinted *Yeats*, 4 [1986], 178-79)

88. EDEL, LEON: *Stuff of Sleep and Dreams: Experiments in Literary Psychology*. London: Chatto & Windus, 1982. xiii, 353 pp.

"Portrait of the Artist as an Old Man," 138-63; revised from an article in *ASch*, 47:1 (Winter 1977/78), 52-68; also in David Dirck VanTassel (ed): *Aging, Death, and the Completion of Being*. Philadelphia: U of Pennsylvania Press, 1979. xix, 293 pp. (pp. 193-214). On Tolstoy, Henry James and Yeats.

89. EDWARDS, MICHAEL: "Yeats and the Moon," *Adam*, 34:334-336 (1969), 27-29.

90. EGERER, SISTER MARY ANNE MONICA: "The Rogueries of William Butler Yeats," Ph.D. thesis, Radcliffe College, 1962. iii, 609 pp.

Yeats's reading of and writing on Irish subjects, 1885-1900.

91. ELLMANN, RICHARD: *Wilde, Yeats, Joyce, and Beckett: Four Dubliners*. London: Hamilton, 1987. xii, 106 pp.

"W. B. Yeats's Second Puberty," 27-51. Reprint of a lecture with the same title, delivered at the Library of Congress on 2 Apr 1984, and published as a pamphlet Washington, D.C.: Library of Congress, 1985. 29 pp. Also published, without the photographs, in *NYRB*, 9 May 1985, 10, 12, 14-16, 18. Discusses the importance of the Steinach operation for Yeats's later work, especially for its treatment of sex; also on the revisions of *A Vision*.

"Samuel Beckett: Nayman of Noland," 79-104. Reprint of a lecture with the same title, delivered at the Library of Congress on 16 Apr 1985, and published as a pamphlet Washington, D.C.: Library of Congress, 1986. 31 pp. First published in *NYRB*, 24 Apr 1986, 27-28, 34-37. Includes notes on Yeats.

Reviews:
- Francis Doherty: "Dubliners All," *PNR*, 58 (14:2) (1987), 75-76.
- Roy Fuller, *LMag*, 27:4 (July 1987), 113-14.
- Declan Kiberd: "Ellmann and the Big Four," *IrT*, 13 June 1987, Weekend, 5
- Riana O'Dwyer: "Writers round Dublin," *ILS*, 7:1 (Spring 1988), 17.
- William H. Pritchard: "The Critic as Storyteller," *New Criterion*, 6:3 (Nov 1987), 67-70.
- Claude Rawson: "A Question of Potency," *TLS*, 24 July 1987, 783-85.
- Merle Rubin: "Quartet of Essays Traces the 'Doubleness' of Four Literary Dubliners," *CSM*, 24 Sept 1987, 20.
- Thomas C. Ware, *Eire*, 22:4 (Winter 1987), 153-55.

92. ENGELBERG, EDWARD: "'He Too Was in Arcadia': Yeats and the Paradox of the Fortunate Fall," in Jeffares and Cross: *In Excited Reverie* (1965, CA48), 69-92.

Yeats's Arcadia as fallen Eden in *The Island of Statues* and some poems; also on the influence of Pater.

93. ESTOK, MICHAEL JOHN: "Elements of Pastoral and Satiric Tradition in W. B. Yeats," °Ph.D. thesis, U of Toronto, 1971. 472 pp. (*DAI*, 33:9 [Mar 1973], 5120A)

94. EVANS, SIR BENJAMIN IFOR: *Literature and Science*. London: Allen & Unwin, 1954. 114 pp.

On Yeats, pp. 109-11.

95. EVERY, GEORGE: "Life. Life. Eternal Life," *Student World,* 31:2 (1938), 136-45.
On Yeats, religion, and "The Second Coming," pp. 139-42.

96. FARAG, FAHMY FAWZY: "W. B. Yeats's Antithetical Mask," *Annals of the Faculty of Arts,* 7 (1962), 21-28.

96a. ———: "Yeats and the Irish Dialectic," *ESC,* 7:4 (Dec 1981), 402-13.

97. FARRELLY, JAMES PATRICK: "Yeats and Ireland: The Interaction of Genius and *Genius Loci*," Ph.D. thesis, Boston U Graduate School, 1975. xi, 260 pp. (*DAI,* 35:12 [June 1975], 7902A-3A)

98. FAULKNER, PETER: *Modernism.* London: Methuen, 1977. x, 86 pp. (Critical Idiom. 35.)
See index for some notes on Yeats.

99. FEDER, LILLIAN: *Ancient Myth in Modern Poetry.* Princeton: Princeton UP, 1971. xiv, 432 pp.
"W. B. Yeats: Myth as Psychic Structure," 61-90. "W. B. Yeats: Prophecy and Control," 185-200 (part of a section entitled "Myth and Ritual"). "W. B. Yeats: History as Symbol," 277-93. Also passim, involving comparisons with Eliot, Pound, and Auden. Largely a psychoanalytical approach. Analyzed in sections DD and FC.

100. FINKELSTEIN, NORMAN MARK: "The Utopian Invariant: Interiority and Exteriority in Twentieth-Century Poetic Consciousness," °Ph.D. thesis, Emory U, 1980. 333 pp. (*DAI,* 41:7 [Jan 1981], 3104A-5A; reprinted *YeA,* 4 [1986], 306-7)
Yeats is given a place at the beginning of "poetic Modernism"; his early poetry is set against that of his Romantic precursors, his later poetry is compared with that of Ezra Pound.

101. FINNEGAN, T. A.: *Sligo: Sinbad's Yellow Shore.* Sligo: Keohane / Dublin: Dolmen Press, 1977. 91 pp.
Frequent references to Yeats.

102. FITCH, PATRICK ROLAND: "The Dialectical Function of the Imagination in the Poetry of Wordsworth, Keats, and Yeats," Ph.D. thesis, U of Tulsa, 1976. ix, 132 pp. (*DAI,* 37:3 [Sept 1976], 1561A-62A)
Chapter 4 ("The Double Vision of W. B. Yeats," 80-132) "is concerned primarily with Yeats's major symbols. Virtually all of these symbols are variations of the circle, which is, of course, the archetypal symbol of unity" (abstract).

103. FLANAGAN, THOMAS: "Yeats, Joyce, and the Matter of Ireland," *CritI,* 2:1 (Autumn 1975), 43-67.
Discusses "the very different manner in which each man [Yeats and Joyce] came to accept his identity as an Irish writer."

104. FLANNERY, MARY CATHERINE: *Yeats and Magic: The Earlier Works.* Gerrards Cross: Smythe, 1977, iv, 165 pp. (Irish Literary Studies. 2.)
Based on a °Ph.D. thesis with the same title, Indiana U, 1973. 290 pp. (*DAI,* 34:9 [Mar 1974], 5908A). Discusses Yeats's cabalistic and theosophical interests, the influence of Indian thought

and of Blake, the interest in Irish folklore and politics, the prose fiction, the autobiography, and "Ego Dominus Tuus."

Reviews:

- Brian Arkins, *Studies*, 41:283 (Autumn 1982), 322.
- Richard Allen Cave, *RES*, 30:117 (Feb 1979), 106-7.
- Leo Daly: "From Earth to Heaven," *BooksI*, 22 (Apr 1978), 56-57.
- Monk Gibbon: "Words, Words, Words!" *Hibernia*, 20 Apr 1978, 22.
- Desirée Hirst: "Along the Occult Path," *TLS*, 18 Aug 1978, 935.
- A. Norman Jeffares: "Irish Order of Mysteries," *THES*, 3 Mar 1978, 16.
- G. Lernout, *RBPH*, 63:3 (1985), 629-33.
- Phillip L. Marcus, *YES*, 11 (1981), 344-45.
- Lowry Nelson: "Now That It's Past Let's Call It Modernism," *YR*, 68:2 (Dec 1978), 266-70.
- Patrick Rafroidi, *EI*, 3 (Dec 1978), 114-17.
- Hilary Robinson, *IUR*, 8:2 (Autumn 1978), 272-73.

105. FLEMING, DEBORAH DIANE: "The Irish Peasant in the Work of W. B. Yeats and J. M. Synge," Ph.D. thesis, Ohio State U, 1985. vi, 233 pp. (*DAI*, 46:12 [June 1986], 3724A-25A; reprinted *Yeats*, 5 [1987], 202-3)

Concentrates on the poetry and prose and neglects the plays.

106. °FOX, F. S.: "Nationalism in the Lives and Works of W. B. Yeats and Alexander Blok: A Comparative Study," Ph.D. thesis, U of Manchester, 1982. (Abstract in *Index to Theses*, 35:1 [1986], 41)

107. FOX, STEVEN JAMES: "Art and Personality: Browning, Rossetti, Pater, Wilde, and Yeats," Ph.D. thesis, Yale U, 1972. iii, 310 pp. (*DAI*, 33:2 [Aug 1972], 751A)

"W. B. Yeats: The Struggle for Personality," 230-307; mainly on *Per Amica Silentia Lunae*, *A Vision*, and *The Autobiography*.

108. *France--Ireland: Literary Relations*. Lille: Université de Lille III / Paris: Editions universitaires, 1974. 269 pp. (Cahiers irlandais. 2./3.)

Margaret Stanley: "Yeats and French Painting," 167-81; on "certain analogies" and "accidental correspondences."

109. FRIEDMAN, BARTON R.: "Yeats, Johnson, and Ireland's Heroic Dead: Toward a Poetry of Politics," *Eire*, 7:4 (Winter 1972), 32-47.

Yeats's view of O'Leary, Parnell, and others, particularly in his poetry, compared with Lionel Johnson's.

110. FRYE, NORTHROP: *Fables of Identity: Studies in Poetic Mythology*. NY: Harcourt, Brace & World, 1963. vi, 265 pp.

"Yeats and the Language of Symbolism," 218-37; reprinted from *UTQ*, 17:1 (Oct 1947), 1-17.

111. ———: *The Secular Scripture: A Study of the Structure of Romance*. Cambridge, Mass.: Harvard UP, 1976. ix, 199 pp.

See index for some notes on history and myth in Yeats's works.

112. GARVER, JOSEPH C.: "Die Macht der Phantasie: Die 'heredity of influence' als literarisches Thema," *Saeculum*, 33:3-4 (1982), 287-311.

Contains some notes on heredity of influence (or telegony) in Yeats's works, particularly in *Purgatory*, where it appears as racial guilt.

113. GENET, JACQUELINE: "Du mythe agraire de J. G. Frazer à la poésie de W. B. Yeats ou la recréation des mythes de Dionysos et d'Attis," *CVE*, 9/10 (Oct 1979), 219-39.

114. GILL, RICHARD: *Happy Rural Seat: The English Country House and the Literary Imagination*. New Haven: Yale UP, 1972. xix, 305 pp.

The "big house" in Yeats's works, pp. 168-75 and passim (see index).

115. GLASSIE, HENRY: *All Silver and No Brass: An Irish Christmas Mumming*. Bloomington: Indiana UP, 1975. xx, 192 pp.

Notes on Yeats and Irish folklore, pp. 53-56 and passim (see index).

116. GLICKSBERG, CHARLES I.: "William Butler Yeats and the Hatred of Science," *PrS*, 27:1 (Spring 1953), 29-36.

Yeats was opposed to science, education, democracy, and reason, and addicted to dreams, visions, ghosts, fairies, and the imagination.

117. GMUCA, JACQUELINE LAURA: "A Preference for the Acorn, Not the Oak: A Study of Yeats's Romanticism through the Use of Imagery," Ph.D. thesis, Kent State U, 1980. iv, 229 pp. (*DAI*, 41:9 [Mar 1981], 4040A; reprinted *YeA*, 2 [1983], 99-100)

Discusses the imagery of birds, water, and Jesus Christ, and the influence of Keats, Shelley, and Blake.

118. GOLDEN, SEAN V.: "Traditional Irish Music in Contemporary Irish Literature," *Mosaic*, 12:3 (Spring 1979), 1-23.

Frequent references to Yeats.

119. GOLDRING, MAURICE: "Le mythe d'une civilisation rurale dans la Renaissance littéraire irlandaise," *Pensée*, 177 (Oct 1974), 117-26.

120. ———: *Faith of Our Fathers: The Formation of Irish Nationalist Ideology 1890-1920*. Translated by Frances de Burgh-Whyte. Dublin: Repsol, 1982. 112 pp.

Originally published as *Irlande: Idéologie d'une révolution nationale*. Paris: Editions sociales, 1975. 128 pp. See "Cultural Models," 41-73.

121. GOSE, ELLIOTT B.: *The World of the Irish Wonder Tale: An Introduction to the Study of Fairy Tales*. Dingle, Co. Kerry: Brandon, 1985. xxiv, 228 pp.

Short note on Yeats, pp. xvii-xviii.

122. GOSHI, KEIGO: [In Japanese] "W. B. Yeats and Aristocracy," *Humanities*, 14 (Dec 1967), 62-82.

With a summary in English.

123. GREGORY, LADY ISABELLA AUGUSTA: *Visions and Beliefs in the West of Ireland*. Collected and arranged by Lady Gregory with two essays and notes by W. B. Yeats. Gerrards Cross: Smythe. 1970 [1920]. 365 pp. (Coole Edition of the Works of Lady Gregory. 1.)

References to Yeats's interest in Irish folklore in the foreword by Elizabeth Coxhead, pp. 5-8, and in Lady Gregory's headnotes to the various sections of the compilation. For reviews of the first publication (Wade 312) see G1282-1289.

124. GRIERSON, H[ERBERT]: "Fairies--From Shakespeare to Mr. Yeats," *Dublin R,* 148:297 (Apr 1911), 271-84.

Reprinted in *Living Age,* 10 June 1911, 651-58. Yeats's fairies no longer have the innocence that Shakespeare gave them; they know sorrow and age.

124a. GRIEVE-CARLSON, GARY ROBERT: "The Cracked Tune That Chronos Sings: W. B. Yeats, Charles Olson, and the Idea of History," °Ph.D. thesis, Boston U, 1988. 378 pp. (*DAI,* 48:8 [Feb 1988], 2059A-60A)

125. GROBMAN, NEIL R.: "In Search of a Mythology: William Butler Yeats and Folklore," *NYFQ,* 30:2 (June 1974), 117-36.

Not very much on Yeats's use of folklore; most of the article is a rather general treatment of his use of myth.

126. GWYNN, STEPHEN: "Ireland Week by Week: The Honour to Mr. Yeats," *Obs,* 18 Nov 1923, 9.

Yeats and Irish nationality.

127. HAAS, RUDOLF, HEINZ-JOACHIM MÜLLENBROCK, and CLAUS UHLIG (eds): *Literatur als Kritik des Lebens: Festschrift zum 65. Geburtstag von Ludwig Borinski.* Heidelberg: Quelle & Meyer, 1975. 298 pp.

Johannes Kleinstück: "W. B. Yeats als Kritiker seines Landes und seiner Zeit," 237-46 ("Yeats as a critic of his country and of his time").

Volker Bischoff: "Der Dichter in der Gesellschaft: Audens 'In Memory of W. B. Yeats' und seine Yeats-Aufsätze," 264-78 ("The poet in society"; on Auden's poem [HD5] and essays on Yeats).

128. HANREZ, MARC (ed): *Espagne / écrivains: Guerre civile.* Paris: Pantheon Press France, 1975. 320 pp.

William Tinney: "Les écrivains irlandais," 55-64; contains a note on Yeats and the Spanish Civil War.

129. HARPER, GEORGE MILLS: *Yeats's Quest for Eden.* No. 9 of *DPYCP* (1966, CA20), 289-331.

The development of the pastoral Eden--Golden Age symbolism with particular reference to the influence of Blake.

130. HARRIS, DANIEL ARTHUR: *Yeats: Coole Park and Ballylee.* Baltimore: Johns Hopkins UP, 1974. x, 262 pp.

Based on "The Spreading Laurel Tree: Yeats and the Aristocratic Tradition," °Ph.D. thesis, Yale U, 1968. 421 pp. (*DAI,* 30:5 [Nov 1969], 1982A). Essentially on the poetry that Yeats wrote about Lady Gregory's estate and his own tower. Discusses the indebtedness to Irish tradition and the influence of Castiglione and Ben Jonson. Analyzed in section DD.

Reviews:

- Hazard Adams, *JML,* 4:5 (1975), 1144-46.
- J. C. Beckett, *MLR,* 72:1 (Jan 1977), 163-66.
- Eavan Boland: "Crossing the Bridge," *Hibernia,* 21 Mar 1975, 19.
- Anthony Bradley, *Eire,* 11:2 (Summer 1976), 151-52.
- Virginia Cooke, *QQ,* 84:2 (Summer 1977), 329-30.
- F. Farag, *Four Decades,* 2:2 (July 1978), 110-11.
- Richard J. Finneran: "W. B. Yeats," *ConL,* 17:1 (Winter 1976), 142-47.
- John P. Frayne, *JEGP,* 77:2 (Apr 1978), 290-92.
- David Grene, *MP,* 76:3 (Feb 1979), 319-23.
- A. Norman Jeffares: "Coughing in Ink," *SR,* 84:1 (Jan-Mar

1976), 157-67.
- F. S. L. Lyons: "Strange Enchantments," *TLS*, 7 May 1976, 547.
- Jeannette Clare McDonnell, *CollL*, 2:2 (Spring 1975), 149.
- Robert D. Spector, *BA*, 49:3 (Summer 1975), 554.
- Donald T. Torchiana: "Some Recent Books on W. B. Yeats," *JIL*, 5:2 (May 1976), 60-81. (Very negative)
- ———, *PQ*, 55:1 (Winter 1976), 145-48.
- John Unterecker, *MLQ*, 37:4 (Dec 1976), 395-98.
- Georges-Denis Zimmermann, *ES*, 57:5 (Oct 1976), 464-68.

131. HARRIS, JAY, and JEAN HARRIS: *The Roots of Artifice: On the Origin and Development of Literary Creativity*. NY: Human Sciences Press, 1981. 320 pp.

A "neuropsychological" study. Contains "Yeats: A Poet Looking to Old Age," 264-73; "'The Tower' by William Butler Yeats," 273-84. See also pp. 163-64 for a note on "Leda and the Swan."

132. HASSETT, JOSEPH M.: *Yeats and the Poetics of Hate*. Dublin: Gill & Macmillan / NY: St. Martin's Press, 1986. ix, 189 pp.

On hate in Yeats's thinking and poetry, particularly the Crazy Jane and Ribh poems. Discusses the relationship to Blake, T. H. Huxley, Locke, Swift, and John Butler Yeats; includes a chapter on *Per Amica Silentia Luna*e. Analyzed in section DD.

Reviews:
- Michael H. Begnal, *Eire*, 23:1 (Spring 1988), 147-48.
- Tom Clyde: "Bananas and the Oozalum Bird," *BooksI*, 106 (Sept 1986), 167-68.
- Sean Dunne: "A Healthy Hate," *ILS*, 5:2 (Fall 1986), 24-25.
- Edward Engelberg, *Yeats*, 5 (1987), 226-30.
- Declan Kiberd: "Taking Stock of Yeats," *TLS*, 13 Feb 1987, 166.
- Thomas Parkinson: "Yeats and Hate," *ELT*, 30:4 (1987), 473-75.
- Peter Sirr: "Yeatsian Love and Hate," *IrT*, 30 Aug 1986, 14.

133. HAYDN, HIRAM: "The Last of the Romantics: An Introduction to the Symbolism of W. B. Yeats," *SR*, 55:2 (Apr-June 1947), 297-323.

134. HEALY, J. V.: "Yeats and His Imagination," *SR*, 54:4 (Autumn 1946), 650-59.

On Yeats's religion and beliefs. Actually, less than half of the article is concerned with Yeats.

135. HENN, T. R.: "W. B. Yeats and the Irish Background," *YR*, 42:3 (Mar 1953), 351-64.

136. HESSE, EVA, MICHAEL KNIGHT, and MANFRED PFISTER: *Der Aufstand der Musen: Die "Neue Frau" in der englischen Moderne*. Passau: Haller, 1984. 153 pp.

"The revolt of the muses: The 'new woman' in modern English literature"; contains many references to Yeats's alleged anti-emancipatory view of women. See pp. 18-19, 56-57 (on Florence Farr), 64-74 (on Maud Gonne), 83-96 (on Lady Gregory).

137. HILL, DOUGLAS: "Yeats and the Invisible People of Ireland," *Brigham Young U Studies*, 7:1 (Autumn 1965), 61-67.

Yeats's belief in the fairies was genuine and part of his peculiarly Irish outlook.

138. HIRSCH, EDWARD: "Wisdom and Power: Yeats and the Commonwealth of Faery," Ph.D. thesis, U of Pennsylvania, 1979. iv, 659 pp. (*DAI*, 40:7 [Jan 1980], 4168A; reprinted *YeA*, 1 [1982], 208-9)

See also an article with the same title, *YER*, 8:1&2 (1986), 22-40.

139. HOBSBAUM, PHILIP: "The Romantic Dichotomy," *BJA*, 16:1 (Winter 1976), 32-45.
Contains a note on Yeats's kind of romanticism.

140. HÖNNIGHAUSEN, LOTHAR: *Präraphaeliten und Fin de Siècle: Symbolistische Tendenzen in der englischen Spätromantik*. München: Fink, 1971. 492 pp. plus 46 illustrations.
Yeats, passim (see index).

141. HOFFMAN, DANIEL: *Barbarous Knowledge: Myth in the Poetry of Yeats, Graves and Muir*. NY: Oxford UP, 1967. xvi, 266 pp.
Irish myths in Yeats's works, particularly in the ballads, in "The Tower," and in the Cuchulain plays (discussed as "Yeats's most successful version of the epic theme," p. 87). Analyzed in sections DD, EE, and FA.
Reviews:
- James D. Boulger, *Thought*, 43:168 (Spring 1968), 128-30.
- Patrick Cosgrave: "Barbarous Scholarship," *LMag*, 7:5 (Aug 1967), 83-86. Correspondence by Hoffman and Cosgrave's reply, :10 (Jan 1968), 109-12.
- Bruce Cutler: "Introductions and Conclusions," *Poetry*, 112:1 (Apr 1968), 52-56.
- Denis Donoghue, *MLQ*, 29:1 (Mar 1968), 120-21.
- Robert S. Kinsman, *Western Folklore*, 28:1 (Jan 1969), 63-64.
- A. D. Nuttal, *RES*, 19:75 (Aug 1968), 349.
- William Sylvester, *CE*, 29:1 (Oct 1967), 62-65.
- R. S. Thomas, *CritQ*, 9:4 (Winter 1967), 380-83.
- Peter Ure, *MLR*, 65:1 (Jan 1970), 161-62.

142. HOFFMAN, FREDRICK JOHN: *The Imagination's New Beginning: Theology and Modern Literature*. Notre Dame: U of Notre Dame Press, 1967. xiv, 105 pp. (University of Notre Dame Ward-Phillips Lectures in English Language and Literature. 1.)
On Yeats, pp. 10-15. "Despite his practice of shying away from Christianity, Yeats was fascinated by the metaphysical suggestiveness of Christ. The Incarnation remained a central attraction for him, though he preferred his own definition of it."

143. HOLLIS, JAMES RUSSELL: "Patterns of Opposition and Reconciliation in the Life and Work of W. B. Yeats," Ph.D. thesis, Drew U, 1967. iii, 453 pp. (*DAI*, 28:5 [Nov 1967], 1819A)

144. HONE, J. M.: "The Later Writings of Mr. Yeats," *NSt*, 24 Apr 1915, 62-64.
Irish themes in the writings after the collected edition of 1908, with special reference to the influence of Synge.

145. ———: "A Letter from Ireland," *LMerc*, 2:9 (July 1920), 341-43.
Criticizes Yeats's views on religion.

146. HOUGH, GRAHAM: *The Last Romantics*. London: Duckworth, 1961 [1949]. xix, 284 pp.
Reprinted NY: AMS Press, 1978. "Yeats," 216-62; reprinted from *Cambridge J*, 2:5 (Feb 1949), 259-78; :6 (Mar 1949), 323-42. Subtitles: The Rejection of Rhetoric, The Search for a Mythology, The Mask and the Great Wheel (including a discussion of *Per Amica Silentia Lunae* and *A Vision*), His Beliefs.

"Conversation in Limbo," 263-74; between Yeats and H. G. Wells.

See also the review by Austin Clarke: "The Last Ditch," *IrT*, 12 Nov 1949, 6.

147. HOWARD, M. F.: "A Poet of Dreamland: W. B. Yeats," *Quest* [London], 4:3 (Apr 1913), 484-93.

The importance of dreams, originating in the great memory, particularly in *The Shadowy Waters*.

148. HOWARTH, HERBERT: *The Irish Writers, 1880-1940: Literature under Parnell's Star*. London: Rockliff, 1958. x, 318 pp.

The Yeats chapter (pp. 110-64) discusses Irish themes and allegiances.

Reviews:

- [Austin Clarke]: "Dubliners," *TLS*, 6 Feb 1959, 72.
- René Fréchet: "Les écrivains irlandais et la réalité: Note brève," *EA*, 12:4 (Oct-Dec 1959), 338-44.
- Monk Gibbon, *LMag*, 6:8 (Aug 1959), 73, 75-77.
- John Hewitt, *MLR*, 54:4 (Oct 1959), 631.
- J. Mitchell Morse, *CL*, 12:4 (Fall 1960), 374-76.

149. HUTCHINSON, JOHN: *The Dynamics of Cultural Nationalism: The Gaelic Revival and the Creation of the Irish Nation State*. London: Allen & Unwin, 1987. viii, 343 pp.

"The Gaelic Revival (c. 1890-1921): Its Secular Propounders and Religious Roots," 114-50, discusses Yeats's cultural nationalism.

150. JASPER, DAVID (ed): *Images of Belief in Literature*. London: Macmillan, 1984. ix, 195 pp.

John Coulson: "Religion and Imagination (Relating Religion and Literature)--A Syllabus," 7-23; contains frequent references to Yeats.

151. JEFFARES, A. NORMAN: "The Anglo-Irish Temper," *EDH*, 36 (1970), 84-112.

A survey of Anglo-Irish literature from the end of the 17th century to the present day. Three elements combine to produce the Anglo-Irish temper: the classical and English literary convention, the native Irish tradition and oral literature, and the urge to write for a national audience. On Yeats, passim.

152. JOANNON, PIERRE: "Sources anglo-irlandaises de l'idéologie nationaliste irlandaise," *EI*, 6 (Dec 1981), 137-56.

Contains references to Yeats.

153. JOHN, BRIAN: "'To Hunger Fiercely after Truth': Daimonic Man and Yeats's Insatiable Appetite," *Eire*, 9:1 (Spring 1974), 90-103.

The imagery of hunger and appetite in Yeats's works and its sources in Dante and Carlyle.

154. JOHNSON, MARY LYNN, and SERAPHIA DEVILLE LEYDA (eds): *Reconciliations: Studies in Honor of Richard Harter Fogle*. Salzburg: Institut für Anglistik und Amerikanistik, Universität Salzburg, 1983. ix, 261 pp. (Salzburg Studies in English Literature: Romantic Reassessment. 96.)

James Lovic Allen: "Yeats's Romanticized Reconciliation with the Church of Ireland," 219-34. Yeats's final reconciliation with the Church of Ireland is connected with his interest in the early Irish church and its Druidic rituals, in St. Columba, and in early Christian monasticism. His use of Ribh points into the same direction.

155. JOHNSON, WENDELL STACY: *Sons and Fathers: The Generation Link in Literature 1780-1980*. NY: Lang, 1985. vii, 237 pp. (Studies in Romantic and Modern Literature. 1.)

"Sons and Fathers: Yeats, Joyce, and Faulkner," 153-202; discusses the Cuchulain plays, "Sailing to Byzantium," "A Prayer for My Daughter," and "A Prayer for My Son."

155a. JORDAN, CARMEL PATRICIA: *A Terrible Beauty: The Easter Rebellion and Yeats's "Great Tapestry."* Lewisburg, Pa.: Bucknell UP, 1987. 132 pp.

Based on "A Terrible Beauty: The Mask of Cuchulain in 'Easter 1916,'" Ph.D. thesis, Fordham U, 1984. iii, 198 pp. (*DAI*, 46:4 [Oct 1985], 989A). Discusses the Gaelic-Irish tradition behind Yeats's concept of the mask and his view of the Easter 1916 uprising, also the Cuchulain plays and their connections with "Easter 1916."

156. JORDAN, JOHN: "Yeats and the Irish Language," *Hibernia*, 4 Jan 1974, 34.

157. JOURNET, DEBRA SOMBERG: "W. B. Yeats, D. H. Lawrence and Modernism," °Ph.D. thesis, McGill U, 1980. (*DAI*, 41:3 [Sept 1980], 1064A; reprinted *YeA*, 1 [1982], 215-16)

Yeats and Lawrence "deliberately place themselves outside a Modernist tradition" (abstract).

158. KAIN, RICHARD M.: "*Genius Loci:* The Spirit of Place in Irish Literature," *DM*, 10:2 (Summer 1973), 33-41.

159. KANTAK, V. Y.: "Yeats's Meditation on 'the Bestial Floor,'" *JJCL*, 7 (1967), 64-84.

The sexual theme and its indebtedness to Indian sources.

160. KEANE, PATRICK J.: "The Human Entrails and the Starry Heavens: Some Instances of Visual Art as Patterns for Yeats's Mingling of Heaven and Earth," *BRH*, 84:3 (Autumn 1981), 366-91. (Illustrated)

The "role played by visual art in Yeats's attempts to make intelligible his own central theme: the interpenetration of the human and the spiritual." Discusses the influence of Blake.

160a. KEARNEY, RICHARD: *Transitions: Narratives in Modern Irish Culture*. Dublin: Wolfhound Press, 1988. 318 pp.

Includes previously published material, heavily revised and therefore not listed separately. See especially "Yeats and the Conflict of Imaginations," 19-30; on Yeats's "vacillation between the rival claims of 'vision' and 'desire'" or tradition and modernism, and on the fallacies inherent in his concept of Unity of Culture, including a note on "The Byzantine Imagination."

"Yeats and the Symbolism of Sacrifice," 216-18; mainly on "Easter 1916."

161. KEE, ROBERT: *The Green Flag: A History of Irish Nationalism*. London: Weidenfeld & Nicolson, 1972. xvi, 877 pp.

"Growth of National Consciousness," 426-37; on Yeats and the early days of the Irish literary revival.

162. KEEBLE, BRIAN: "'Myself Must I Remake': W. B. Yeats and Unity of Being," *Studies in Mystical Literature,* 1:2 (Winter 1980), 154-85.

163. KEHOE, CONSTANCE DE MUZIO: "The Tradition of the Irish Poet in the Work of William Butler Yeats," Ph.D. thesis, Trinity College Dublin, 1966. vi, 255 pp.

164. KELLEHER, JOHN V.: "Yeats's Use of Irish Materials," *TriQ,* 4 [Fall 1965], 115-25.
The phrases "lebeen-lone" in "The Three Beggars" and "Clooth-na-Bare" in "The Hosting of the Sidhe" and "Red Hanrahan's Song about Ireland," as well as the use of the Cuchulain myth.

165. KELLY, JOHN S.: "The Fall of Parnell and the Rise of Irish Literature: An Investigation," *Anglo-Irish Studies,* 2 (1976), 1-23.
Investigates Yeats's claim that the Irish literary revival began with the fall and death of Parnell in 1891.

166. KENNELLY, BRENDAN: "The Gaelic Epic," *IrT,* 10 June 1965, vi-vii.
Yeats's Cuchulain.

167. ———: "Modern Irish Poets and the Irish Epic," Ph.D. thesis, Trinity College Dublin, 1967. vi, 459 pp.
Discusses "The Wanderings of Oisin," *At the Hawk's Well, The Green Helmet, On Baile's Strand, The Only Jealousy of Emer,* and *Deirdre,* pp. 220-63.

168. KERMODE, FRANK: *Romantic Image.* NY: Vintage Books, 1964 [1957]. xi, 173 pp. (Vintage Book. V260.)
An essay on the troublesome relation between the artist and society. "Artists and contemplatives" have two chances of escape from the world of action, "the making of Images and death" (p. 30). The reconciliation of action and contemplation in a poetic symbol is "the flowering of . . . the Romantic Image" (p. 43). Yeats is the prime example. Kermode concentrates on "In Memory of Major Robert Gregory" and the view of Gregory as the artist isolated from society, the image of the dancer and of Salome in Yeats's poetry, prose, and plays, and the use of tree imagery that Yeats learned from Blake. Discusses the connections with Pater, Wilde, Symons, Hulme's imagism, and Eliot's concept of the dissociation of sensibility.
Reviews:
- Hazard Adams, *JAAC,* 17:4 (June 1959), 529-30.
- A. Alvarez, *Universities Q,* 12:2 (Feb 1958), 206, 208, 210, 212, 214, 216.
- John Bayley: "Image and Intent," *Spect,* 21 June 1957, 817.
- [G. S. Fraser]: "The Dancer and the Tree," *TLS,* 17 May 1957, 304.
- H. Marshall McLuhan: "Romanticism Reviewed," *Renascence,* 12:4 (Summer 1960), 207-9.
- Thomas Parkinson: "Two Books on Yeats," *SR,* 66:4 (Oct-Dec 1958), 678-85.
- Robert L. Peters: "By Way of Definition," *VN,* 14 (Fall 1958), 18-19.
- Peter Ure: "From Wordsworth to Yeats," *List,* 25 July 1957, 133-35. Correspondence by Janice Bull, 1 Aug 1957, 174, and by Ure, 8 Aug 1957, 209.

169. KHOROL'SKIĬ, V. V.: "Simbolizm U. B. Ĭetsa (Evoli͡ut͡sii͡a tvor-

cheskogo metoda)," *Problemy metoda i zhanra v zarubezhnoĭ literature*, 6 (1981), 146-59.
"The symbolism of WBY (The evolution of the creative method)."

170. KIBERD, DECLAN: *Men and Feminism in Modern Literature*. London: Macmillan, 1985. xii, 250 pp.
"W. B. Yeats: Robartes' Quarrel with the Dancer," 103-35, and passim (see index). On Yeats's view of woman in his life and poetry, particularly the New Woman, the dancer and the *anima* figure.

171. KIESSLING, NICOLAS: *The Incubus in English Literature: Provenance and Progeny*. Pullman: Washington State UP, 1977. vii, 104 pp.
See pp. 82-86.

171a. KINAHAN, FRANK: *Yeats, Folklore, and Occultism: Contexts of the Early Work and Thought*. Boston: Unwin Hyman, 1988. xxiii, 255 pp.
Based on "The Moon upon the Tide: A Study in the Early Poetry of William Butler Yeats," Ph.D. thesis, Harvard U, 1973. iii, 260 pp.
Discusses Yeats's poetry and prose up to the mid-1890s as dominated by the influences of Irish folklore and occultism (the connection with the Golden Dawn); contains chapters on "The Wanderings of Oisin" and the rose symbol (especially in "The Rose of Battle," "The Rose of the World," and "The Rose upon the Rood of Time").

172. KIRBY, SHEELAH: *The Yeats Country: A Guide to the Sligo District and Other Places in the West of Ireland Associated with the Life and Writings of W. B. Yeats*. With drawings by Ruth Brandt and an appreciation by Kathleen Raine. Revised edition. Dublin: Dolmen Press, 1977 [1962]. 93 pp.
Reprinted in 1985. A collection of notes on Yeats's allusions to West of Ireland places (Sligo and surroundings, Thoor Ballylee, Coole Park and surroundings).
Reviews:
- [Austin Clarke]: "Poetic Haunts," *TLS*, 25 Jan 1963, 62.
- J[ames] D[elehanty], *Kilkenny Magazine*, 8 (Autumn-Winter 1962), 56-58.
- Denis Donoghue: "Countries of the Mind," *Guardian*, 11 Jan 1963, 5.
- T. R. Henn, *MLR*, 58:4 (Oct 1963), 627.
- A. Norman Jeffares: "The Yeats Country," *MLQ*, 25:2 (June 1964), 218-22.

173. KLIMEK, THEODOR: *Symbol und Wirklichkeit bei W. B. Yeats*. Bonn: Bouvier, 1967. viii, 223 pp. (Abhandlungen zur Kunst-, Musik- und Literaturwissenschaft. 45.)
Originally a Dr.phil. thesis, U of Hamburg, 1966. Discusses Yeats's concept of the symbol in his poetry and prose, also his use of the terms image, allegory, metaphor, emblem, and the relation between symbol and reality. Unfortunately the book does not contain an index.

174. KLINE, GLORIA CORNELIA: *The Last Courtly Lover: Yeats and the Idea of Woman*. Ann Arbor: UMI Research Press, 1983. xiii, 199 pp. (Studies in Modern Literature. 6.)
Based on "'That Fierce Virgin': Mythopoesis of Courtly Love in the Works of W. B. Yeats," Ph.D. thesis, Florida State U, 1976.

v, 272 pp. (*DAI*, 37:7 [Jan 1977], 4368A)

"In all instances--artistic, personal, cultural--the woman at the center provides the image around which the unities that Yeats thought the greatest good could be achieved--Unity of Being and Unity of Culture." Discusses Maud Gonne, Mrs. Yeats, Lady Gregory, Margot Ruddock, and Dorothy Wellesley, and "those poems and plays which present the woman as an elevated figure who has a spiritual influence on man, can provide him a unifying image, and for that reason is reverently, sometimes fearfully, pursued or 'courted' by him" (pp. 2-4).

Reviews:

- David R. Clark, *Yeats,* 2 (1984), 289-97.
- Karen Dorn, *YeA,* 4 (1986), 258-60.
- Peter van de Kamp, *IUR,* 15:1 (Spring 1985), 108-11.
- Lucy McDiarmid: "Yeats and Women," *ILS,* 3:2 (Fall 1984), 29.
- George O'Brien, *MLR,* 83:2 (Apr 1988), 430-32.
- Thomas Parkinson: "Yeats and Women," *ELT,* 27:2 (1984), 171-73.

175. KNIGHTS, LIONEL CHARLES: *Explorations: Essays in Criticism Mainly on the Literature of the Seventeenth Century.* London: Chatto & Windus, 1951 [1946]. xii, 199 pp.

"Poetry and Social Criticism: The Work of W. B. Yeats," 170-85; first published as "W. B. Yeats: The Assertion of Values," *SoR,* 7:3 (Winter 1941/42), 426-41. On the aristocratic concept and the idea of life in Yeats's poetry and thought.

176. KOLJEVIĆ, NIKOLA: "O Eliotu, o Jejtsu, o tradiciji," *Izraz,* year 20 / 40:11 (Nov 1976), 385-417.

"On Eliot, on Yeats, on tradition."

177. KRANS, HORATIO S.: "Ethical Aspects of Wm. B. Yeats's Work," *Ethical Record,* 5:5 (July 1904), 170-74.

178. KREMEN, KATHRYN REBECCA: *The Imagination of the Resurrection: The Poetic Continuity of a Religious Motif in Donne, Blake, and Yeats.* Lewisburg, Pa.: Bucknell UP, 1972. 344 pp.

Based on a °Ph.D. thesis, Brandeis U, 1970. 444 pp. (*DAI,* 31:10 [Apr 1971], 5366A). On Yeats, passim (especially pp. 260-307); analyzed in section DD. See review by John B. Vickery, *JML,* 3:3 (Feb 1974), 400-2.

179. KRIVINA, T. M.: "O nekotorykh osobennostia͡kh vzglia͡da V. B. Ĭeĭtsa na irlandskiĭ fol'klor na rannem ėtape tvorchestva," *Gert͡senovskie chteniia͡,* 27 (1975), Literaturovedenie: Nauchnye doklady, 160-65.

"On some peculiarities of Yeats's views of Irish folklore in the early phase of his work."

180. LAITY, CASSANDRA: "From Fatal Woman to New Woman: Yeats' Changing Image of Woman in His Art and Aesthetic," Ph.D. thesis, U of Michigan, 1984. iii, 209 pp. (*DAI,* 45:12 [June 1985], 3646A; reprinted *Yeats,* 4 [1986], 181)

Discusses relevant poems and plays, particularly *The Shadowy Waters, Deirdre,* and *The Player Queen.* See also CD435.

181. ————: "Yeats's Changing Image of Maud Gonne," *Eire,* 22:2 (Summer 1987), 56-69.

The image of Maud Gonne in the plays, poems, and *A Vision.*

182. LANGBAUM, ROBERT: *The Mysteries of Identity: A Theme in Modern Literature*. NY: Oxford UP, 1977. xi, 383 pp.

Incorporates "The Exteriority of Self in Yeats's Poetry and Thought," *NLH,* 7:3 (Spring 1976), 579-97.

See particularly "Reconstitution of Self--Yeats: The Religion of Art," 145-247; with the following subsections: "Exteriority of Self," "The Self as a Work of Art," and "The Self as God." Includes extended analyses of *The Player Queen,* stories from *The Secret Rose, Per Amica Silentia Lunae,* and *A Vision*. Analyzed in sections DD, EE, and FA.

Reviews:

- Christopher Butler: "The Self in Dissolution," *TLS,* 18 Aug 1978, 927.
- Ian Fletcher, *VP,* 17:3 (Autumn 1979), 278-81.
- A. D. Nuttall: "A Quickening Book," *YER,* 5:1 (1978), 58-60.
- Thomas Parkinson, *MP,* 78:1 (Aug 1980), 108-11.

183. LASS, ROLF HERMANN: "The Irish Ireland Myth: A Study of the Irish Idea of Nationality, Its Native and European Roots, and Its Bearing on the Work of W. B. Yeats," Ph.D. thesis, U of Cambridge, 1970. iii, 312 pp.

Discusses Yeats's early prose, some poems (particularly "The Old Age of Queen Maeve," "The Two Kings," "The Grey Rock," "The Hour Before Dawn," and "Under the Round Tower"), as well as *The Player Queen, The King of the Great Clock Tower, A Full Moon in March,* and *The Herne's Egg*.

184. LECHNER, EMIL THEODORE: "Experience of the Numinous in Yeats, Jung, and Bonhoeffer," Ph.D. thesis, Rice U, 1974. ix, 230 pp. (*DAI,* 35:5 [Oct 1974], 2280A-81A)

See particularly "The Yeatsian Symbol," 38-79. "The approach of Yeats to Jung and Jung to Yeats may be treated through their common adherence to a sense of divinity within, that is, to the felt outward movement, rather than simple presence, of a numinous power arising from self, rather than descending from above" (p. iii).

184a. LEITH, JAMES A. (ed): *Symbols in Life and Art: The Royal Society of Canada Symposium in Memory of George Whalley / Les symboles dans la vie et dans l'art: La Société royale du Canada colloque à la mémoire de George Whalley*. Kingston, Ont.: McGill-Queen's UP, 1987. xi, 151 pp.

Norman H. MacKenzie: "Reflections," 133-51; includes notes on Yeats's use of symbols.

185. LENOSKI, DANIEL S.: "The Artist as a Force for Change in W. B. Yeats," *Albion,* 10:1 (Spring 1978), 76-90.

Yeats's views on the relationship between artist and society, as expressed in his prose, poetry, and plays.

186. ———: "W. B. Yeats and Celtic Spiritual Power," *CJIS,* 5:1 (June 1979), 26-51.

187. ———: "Yeats, Eglinton, and Aestheticism," *Eire,* 14:4 (Winter 1979), 91-108.

Discusses and rejects Eglinton's charge that Yeats was guilty of "some of the worst abuses of aestheticism."

188. ———: "W. B. Yeats: God and Imagination," *ESC,* 6:1 (Spring 1980), 84-93.

The function of the imagination in shaping Yeats's view of God.

189. ———: "The Symbolism of the Early Yeats: Occult and Religious Backgrounds," *SLitI,* 14:1 (Spring 1981), 85-100.

190. LENSE, EDWARD LOUIS: "W. B. Yeats in Paradise," Ph.D. thesis, Ohio State U, 1975. iv, 281 pp. (*DAI,* 36:3 [Sept 1975], 1528A-29A)
Images of paradise and related concepts such as Tir na nOg, the golden bird, and Byzantium in the poetry, prose, and plays. Includes a chapter on *A Vision.*

191. LEWALD, H. ERNEST (ed): *The Cry of Home: Cultural Nationalism and the Modern Writer.* Knoxville: U of Tennessee Press, 1972. xii, 400 pp.
Robert Tracy: "Ireland: The Patriot Game," 39-57; comments on Yeats and the political implications of the Irish literary revival.

192. LIEBERSON, GODDARD (producer): *The Irish Uprising 1916-22.* With a foreword by Eamon de Valera. NY: Macmillan, 1966. xvi, 164 pp. (CBS Legacy Collection Book.)
Thomas P. O'Neill: "The Springs of 1916," 1, 4, 6, 8, 12, 18, 24; one of them the Irish literary revival which, Yeats notwithstanding, was political in nature.
Benedict Kiely: "A Terrible Beauty," 117, 121, 129, 132, 138, 144, 147, 158, 160; on the literary aspects of the rising.

193. LINDER, ANN PLANUTIS: "The Devil in the Garden: The Vision of Paradise in European Romantic Literature," °Ph.D. thesis, Rutgers U, 1975. 242 pp. (*DAI,* 36:10 [Apr 1976], 6674A)
Includes a discussion of Yeats's "attempt to create a paradise of art that is also artificial" (abstract).

194. LINEHAN, MARY CLARE: "Mysticism and Some Irish Writers: An Examination of the Work of G. W. Russell (A. E.), William Butler Yeats, and John Eglinton," Ph.D. thesis, Pennsylvania State U, 1928. ii, 151 pp.
"William Butler Yeats," 69-125. Yeats's "sense of artistry is best served by the use of sensuous pictures dictated by a highly developed emotional imagination pursued through the labyrinth of the occult and the magical. But scarcely is he a mystic" (p. 125).

195. LIPSKI, W. DE: "Note sur le symbolisme de W. B. Yeats," *EA,* 4:1 (Jan-Mar 1940), 31-42.
Yeats's concept of symbolism as related to the subconscious.

196. LUCAS, JAMES LAVARD: *The Religious Dimensions of Twentieth-Century British and American Literature: A Textbook in the Analysis of Types.* Washington, D.C.: UP of America, 1982. x, 295 pp.
"William Butler Yeats: The Heterodox Platonist," 65-82. Christianity in some poems and in *Calvary* and *The Resurrection.*

197. LUCY, SEÁN: "The Irishness of Yeats," *CJIS,* 3:2 (Nov 1977), 6-17.
Defends the position that Yeats was an Irish poet.

198. LYONS, FRANCIS STEWART LELAND: "W. B. Yeats and the Public Life of Ireland," *New Divinity,* 7:1 (Summer 1976), 6-25.

199. ———: *Culture and Anarchy in Ireland 1890-1939.* The Ford

Lectures delivered in the University of Oxford in the Hilary Term of 1978. Oxford: Clarendon Press, 1979. vii, 184 pp.

Numerous and extended passages on Yeats's place in the Irish cultural politics of his time (see index).

200. ———: "Yeats and Victorian Ireland," in Jeffares: *Yeats, Sligo and Ireland* (1980, CA51), 115-38.

On Yeats's various cultural activities and quarrels at the end of the 19th century, particularly his controversy with Edward Dowden.

201. MCDIARMID, LUCY: *Saving Civilization: Yeats, Eliot, and Auden between the Wars*. Cambridge: Cambridge UP, 1984. xxi, 144 pp.

Incorporates "Poetry's Landscape in Auden's Elegy for Yeats," *MLQ,* 38:2 (June 1977), 167-77; and "The Living Voice in the Thirties: Yeats, Eliot, Auden," *YES,* 11 (1981), 161-77. A discussion of the social and political views of the three poets. For Auden's elegy see HD5.

Reviews:

- Bernard Bergonzi, *YES,* 18 (1988), 353-54.
- David Bradshaw: "L'entre deux guerres," *EIC,* 36:4 (Oct 1986), 352-55.
- Denis Donoghue: "Poets in Their Places," *NewRep,* 17 Dec 1984, 38-40.
- F. Farag, *CJIS,* 11:2 (Dec 1985), 87-88.
- Vincent Fitzpatrick: "Art and Politics in Yeats, Auden, and Eliot," *VQR,* 62:2 (Spring 1986), 360-65.
- Andrew Gibson, *YeA,* 5 (1987), 272-76.
- Nicholas Grene, *N&Q,* os 231 / ns 33:3 (Sept 1986), 423-24.
- Steven Helmling, *Kritikon Litterarum,* 13:1-4 (1984), 108-10.
- Maureen Murphy: "Saving 'Civilization' with Yeats," *ILS,* 3:2 (Fall 1984), 28.
- Sidney Poger, *Eire,* 20:2 (Fall 1985), 150-52.
- Sister Bernetta Quinn: "Modern Poets," *ConL,* 28:1 (Spring 1987), 133-41.

202. MCGARRY, JAMES P.: *Place Names in the Writings of W. B. Yeats*. Edited and with additional material by Edward Malins and a preface by Kathleen Raine. Gerrards Cross: Smythe, 1976. 99 pp.

More precisely, places in Ireland. Includes a list of corrections to the two *Prolegomena* by G. B. Saul (AA10-11), some photographs, and two maps as end papers.

203. MCGOVERN, KEVIN JOSEPH: "The Influence of Irish Fairy Lore in the Thought of W. B. Yeats," Ph.D. thesis, U of North Carolina at Chapel Hill, 1978. iv, 331 pp. (*DAI,* 40:1 [July 1979], 272A-73A)

Contains chapters on "The Written Tradition," "Occult Studies," "The Oral Tradition," and "Spiritualism and Fairy."

204. MACGREEVY, THOMAS: "The Gaelic and the Anglo-Irish Culture," *IrSt,* 7 Mar 1925, 816-17.

A defense of Yeats as an Irish writer.

205. MACHAC, LEOPOLD: "William Butler Yeats als Mystiker und Symbolist," Dr.phil. thesis, U of Wien, 1954. ix, 281 pp.

Of little value.

206. MACKILLOP, JAMES: "'Beurla on It': Yeats, Joyce, and the Irish Language," *Eire,* 15:1 (Spring 1980), 138-48.

A comparison of both writers' knowledge and use of Irish.

207. MADDEN, WILLIAM A.: "The Victorian Sensibility," *VS*, 7:1 (Sept 1963), 67-97.
Notes Yeats's "modern" (rather than "romantic") sensibility.

208. MAHON, CECIL MICHAEL: "The Fascination of What's Difficult: W. B. Yeats; the Mask as Esthetic and Discipline," Ph.D. thesis, U of California (Santa Barbara), 1966. viii, 226 pp. (*DAI*, 28:7 [Jan 1968], 2689A)

209. MALINS, EDWARD, and PATRICK BOWE: *Irish Gardens and Demesnes from 1830*. London: Barrie & Jenkins, 1980. 190 pp.
"'Gardens Where a Soul's at Ease,'" 137-49; the gardens and houses associated with Yeats's life and work (Lissadell, Coole, Thoor Ballylee, etc.).

210. MALMQVIST, GÖRAN (ed): *Modern Chinese Literature and Its Social Context*. Stockholm: Nobel Foundation, [1977]. ii, 217 pp. (Nobel Symposium. 32.)
Irene Eber: "Chinese Views of Anglo-Irish Writers and Their Works in the 1920's," 46-75. Chinese writers viewed Anglo-Irish literature as an example of the literature of small, oppressed and weak peoples, comparable to Polish and Yiddish literature. Discusses the reception of Yeats, Lady Gregory, and Synge; mentions several translations of Yeats into Chinese and about 20 Chinese articles on Yeats (both of which I have not attempted to trace and to incorporate into this bibliography).

211. MARCUS, PHILLIP L.: "Yeats and the Image of the Singing Head," *Eire*, 9:4 (Winter 1974), 86-93.
The source in Irish mythology and its treatment in "The Binding of the Hair," "A Very Pretty Little Story," *The King of the Great Clock Tower*, and *A Full Moon in March*.

212. ———: "Artificers of the Great Moment: An Essay on Yeats and National Literature," *CLQ*, 15:2 (June 1979), 71-92.
Yeats's views on what an Irish national literature should be like; refers to his defense of Synge and the Lane Gallery, also to "The Grey Rock."

213. ———: "Incarnation in 'Middle Yeats,'" *YeA*, 1 (1982), 68-81.
"Middle Yeats" is defined as the period 1900-1917.

214. MATHIEU-CASTELLANI, GISÈLE (ed): *La métamorphose dans la poésie baroque française et anglaise: Variations et résurgences*. Actes du Colloque international de Valenciennes, 1979. Tübingen: Narr / Paris: Place, 1980. iv, 250 pp. (Études littéraires françaises. 7.)
Jacqueline Genet: "Les métamorphoses chez W. B. Yeats," 219-35.

215. MAXWELL, D. E. S.: "Swift's Dark Grove: Yeats and the Anglo-Irish Tradition," in Maxwell and Bushrui: *W. B. Yeats, 1865-1965* (1965, CA71), 18-32.
Discusses Yeats's efforts to grasp the Anglo-Irish 18th century from the insecure standpoint of the 20th, his view of Swift, and Swift's influence on his verse.

216. ———: "Yeats and the Irishry," *CJIS*, 1:1 (June 1975), 27-38.
Reprinted in *Threshold*, 29 (Autumn 1978), 3-14. On Ireland and the Irish as imagined by Yeats, "who was never much inhibited by facts"; also on his views on the peasant plays submitted to the Abbey.

217. MELNICK, DANIEL: "Yeats's Image of Culture," *SLitI*, 14:1 (Spring 1981), 111-21.

218. MILLER, KARL: *Doubles: Studies in Literary History*. Oxford: Oxford UP, 1985. xiii, 468 pp.
See index for several notes on Yeats.

219. MILLER, SUSAN FISHER: "'Rooting Mythology in the Earth': W. B. Yeats at Ballylee," Ph.D. thesis, Northwestern U, 1986. viii, 293 pp. (*DAI*, 47:8 [Feb 1987], 3033A)
Discusses the importance of Thoor Ballylee for Yeats's poetry, the influence of Milton, Morris, Martyn and the importance of architect William Scott, Yeats's unpublished correspondence with the Irish Congested Districts Board, and provides a biographical context. One chapter was published as "Hopes and Fears for the Tower: William Morris's Spirit at Yeats's Ballylee," *Eire*, 21:2 (Summer 1986), 43-56.

220. MIYOSHI, MASAO: *The Divided Self: A Perspective on the Literature of the Victorians*. NY: New York UP, 1969. xix, 348 pp.
See index for notes on the motif of the divided self in Yeats's early works, especially in *John Sherman*.

221. MOKASHI[-PUNEKAR], S. R.: "W. B. Yeats and Anglo-Phobia: A Lesson to India," *Triveni*, 30:2 (Oct 1960), 46-52.

222. MOORE, MARIANNE: *The Complete Prose of Marianne Moore*. Edited and with an introduction by Patricia C. Willis. NY: Viking, 1986. xi, 724 pp.
"Wild Swans," 39-41; reprinted from *Poetry*, 13:1 (Oct 1918), 42-44; a review of W118. Reprinted in CA50, pp. 211-12.
"Words for Music Perhaps," 294-96; reprinted from *Poetry*, 42:1 (Apr 1933), 40-44; a review of W164 and W168.
"The Hawk and the Butterfly," 312-16; reprinted from *Westminster Magazine*, 23:1 (Spring 1934), 63-66. On the antinomies in Yeats's "system."

223. MORISON, JOHN L.: "Modern Irish Literature: A Study in Nationalism," *QQ*, 30:1 (July-Aug-Sept 1922), 66-90.
"Irish folk-beliefs have found in Mr. Yeats their poet-laureate. For the rest, it is dangerous to take from so highly individualized a genius notable qualities and claim them as peculiarly Irish" (p. 83).

224. MURPHY, MAUREEN: "'What Stood in the Post Office / With Pearse and Connolly?': The Case for Robert Emmet," *Eire*, 14:3 (Fall 1975), 141-43.
The importance of Cuchulain to Yeats and Pearse (who abandoned him in favor of Emmet).

225. MYLES, PERCY: Review of Lady Wilde's *Ancient Cures, Charms, and Usages of Ireland*, *Academy*, 27 Sept 1890, 266-67.
Criticizes the unnamed editor of *Irish Fairy and Folk Tales* (Yeats, of course), who "goes out of his way to gibe at the honest folklorist who tells what he has actually heard, not what he thinks he might have heard, or what he thinks his audience would like to hear." Reply by Yeats: "Poetry and Science in Folk-Lore," 11 Oct 1890, 320 (reprinted in *Uncollected Prose*, 1:173-74); letter by Alfred Nutt, 18 Oct 1890, 344.

226. NAITO, SHIRO: *Yeats and Zen: A Study of the Transformation of His Mask.* Kyoto: Yamaguchi, 1984. ix, 182 pp.
Incorporates, presumably, "Yeats and Zen Buddhism," *Eastern Buddhist,* 5:2 (Oct 1972), 171-78. Comments on the relationship between Yeats and Yone Noguchi and Daisetz Suzuki, and discusses "Among School Children," "Byzantium," "A Dialogue of Self and Soul," "The Gyres," "Lapis Lazuli," "The Man and the Echo," "The Black Tower," "Cuchulain Comforted," "Long-legged Fly," "The Statues," and "A Bronze Head." Includes a chapter on "The Masks in Yeats's Ballad Poetry"; also reproductions of Yeats letters to Suzuki (22 May 1928) and to Kazumi Yano (18 Nov 1927).

227. NALBANTIAN, SUZANNE: *The Symbol of the Soul from Hölderlin to Yeats: A Study in Metonymy.* London: Macmillan, 1977. vii, 151 pp.
See index for some notes on Yeats's concept of the soul.

228. NAPIER, WILLIAM MICHAEL: "Critical Method in the Early Reviewers of W. B. Yeats: A Bibliographical and Critical Study," Ph.D. thesis, U of Leeds, 1973. ix, 384 pp.
The critical study covers pp. 1-255; the bibliography pp. 256-370. "The commentary is not intended primarily as a contribution to Yeats studies. . . . Its main concern is with the nature and value of the criticism, the theories and preconceptions on which it is based, and the justice and justifications of its judgements" (p. iii). Valuable.

229. NIEMOJOWSKA, MARIA: *Zapisy zmierzchu: Symboliści angielscy i ich romantyczny rodowód.* Warszawa: Czytelnik, 1976. 492 pp.
See index for notes on Yeats's activities in the 1890's.

230. NOON, WILLIAM T.: "Yeats and the Human Body," *Thought,* 30: 117 (Summer 1955), 188-98.
The dichotomy of body and soul in Yeats's thought and poetry with references to *A Vision.*

231. ———: "The Lion and the Honeycomb: What Has Scripture Said. An Incarnational Perspective on Joyce and Yeats," *Newsletter of the Conference on Christianity and Literature,* 19:3 (Spring 1970), 18-24.
Refers to "Vacillation" and von Hügel.

232. O'BRIEN, CONOR CRUISE (ed): *The Shaping of Modern Ireland.* London: Routledge & Kegan Paul, 1960. vi, 201 pp.
Donald Davie: "The Young Yeats," 140-51. Discusses Yeats's views on the relationship between art and politics, the Young Irelanders, O'Leary, Parnell, the *Playboy* controversy, and the Lane pictures.

233. O'BRIEN, CONOR CRUISE: "An Unhealthy Intersection," *New R,* 2:16 (July 1975), 3-8.
Reprinted in *IrT,* 21 Aug 1975, 10; 22 Aug 1975, 10. The intersection of poetry and politics, with Yeats as an example.

234. O'BRIEN, FRANCIS WILLIAM, and others: *Divided Ireland: The Roots of the Conflict. A Study into the Causes of Disorders in North Ireland.* Rockford, Ill.: Rockford College Press, 1971. 77 pp.
Arra M. Garab: "Yeats and Irish Nationalism," 17-25.

235. °O'BRIEN, MICHAEL GERARD: "Dreams and Ancient Things: History and the Imagination in the Work of W. B. Yeats," Ph.D. thesis,

McMaster U, 1978.

236. Ó BROIN, LEÓN: *Protestant Nationalists in Revolutionary Ireland: The Stopford Connection*. Dublin: Gill & Macmillan / Totowa, N.J.: Barnes & Noble, 1985. vi, 234 pp.
Several references to Yeats (see index).

237. O'CONNOR, WILLIAM VAN: "The Poet as Esthetician," *QR of Literature*, 4:3 (1948), 311-18.

238. O'DONNELL, WILLIAM H.: "Portraits of W. B. Yeats: This Picture in the Mind's Eye," *YeA*, 3 (1985), 81-103.
Yeats's opinions of portraits and studio photographs, especially of himself. Includes a "Preliminary Checklist of Portraits of W. B. Yeats."

239. O'DRISCOLL, ROBERT: *Symbolism and Some Implications of the Symbolic Approach: W. B. Yeats during the Eighteen-Nineties*. Dublin: Dolmen Press, 1975. 84 pp. (New Yeats Papers. 9.)
On Yeats's concept of symbolism, his commentary on Blake, the early narrative prose, the poems in *The Wind among the Reeds*, *Where There Is Nothing*, and *The Unicorn from the Stars*.
Reviews:
- Warwick Gould: "Symbols and Systems," *TLS*, 25 Feb 1977, 218.
- Daniel S. Lenoski, *CJIS*, 2:2 (Dec 1976), 86-88.
- F. S. L. Lyons: "Keeping Up with Yeats Studies," *IrT*, 19 Aug 1975, 8.
- St. John Sweeney, *JIL*, 5:2 (May 1976), 84.
- Timothy Webb, *RES*, 28:112 (Nov 1977), 499-503.

240. Ó GLAISNE, RISTEÁRD: "Yeats agus an Ghaeilge" [Yeats and the Irish language], *Ultach*, 42:7 (July 1965), 3-5.

241. O'HEGARTY, P. S.: "W. B. Yeats and Revolutionary Ireland of His Time," *DM*, 14:3 (July-Sept 1939), 22-24.
Nationalism in the early works.

242. O HEHIR, BRENDAN: "Kickshaws and Wheelchairs: Yeats and the Irish Language," *Yeats*, 1 (1983), 92-103.

243. Ó HÓGAIN, DÁITHÍ: *The Hero in Irish Folk History*. Dublin: Gill & Macmillan, 1985. x, 354 pp.
See pp. 314-21 for notes on Yeats's indebtedness to Irish folklore.

244. OLNEY, JAMES: *Metaphors of Self: The Meaning of Autobiography*. Princeton: Princeton UP, 1972. xv, 342 pp.
On autobiographical themes in Yeats's work, passim (see index).

245. ———: "Sex and the Dead: *Daimones* of Yeats and Jung," *SLitI*, 14:1 (Spring 1981), 43-60.
The origin of the concept of the daimon in classical antiquity and its appropriation by Yeats and Jung.

246. Ó MUIRITHE, DIARMAID (ed): *The English Language in Ireland*. Cork: Mercier Press, 1977. 149 pp.
John Garvin: "The Anglo-Irish Idiom in the Works of Major Irish Writers," 100-14; includes some notes on Yeats.

246a. O'NEIL, DANIEL J.: "Enclave Nation-Building: The Irish Expe-

rience," *J of Ethnic Studies*, 15:3 (1987), 1-25.
Contains some critical notes on Yeats's nationalism.

247. O'SHEA, EDWARD JOSEPH: *Yeats as Editor*. Dublin: Dolmen Press, 1975. 80 pp. (New Yeats Papers. 12.)
Includes "Yeats's Revisions in *Fairy and Folk Tales*," *SFQ*, 38:1 (Sept 1974), 223-32. Discusses the editorial work in *Fairy and Folk Tales of the Irish Peasantry*, *Stories from Carleton*, *Representative Irish Tales*, *A Book of Irish Verse*, the Blake and Spenser editions, *Beltaine*, *Samhain*, *The Arrow*, and *The Oxford Book of Modern Verse*, also the involvement in the Dun Emer and Cuala Press publications.

For a more detailed study see O'Shea's unpublished Ph.D. thesis with the same title, Northwestern U, 1976. ix, 303 pp. (*DAI*, 37:7 [Jan 1977], 4373A-74A).

Reviews:
- Warwick Gould: "Symbols and Systems," *TLS*, 25 Feb 1977, 218.
- F. S. L. Lyons: "Keeping Up with Yeats Studies," *IrT*, 19 Aug 1975, 8.
- Timothy Webb, *RES*, 28:112 (Nov 1977), 499-503.

248. O'SULLIVAN, SEAN (ed): *Folktales of Ireland*. Foreword by Richard M. Dorson. London: Routledge & Kegan Paul, 1969 [1966]. xliii, 321 pp.
The foreword discusses the contributions of some writers of the Irish literary revival (including Yeats) to the exploration of Irish folklore.

249. O'TOOLE, FINTAN: "Going West: The Country versus the City in Irish Writing," *Crane Bag*, 9:2 (1985), 111-16.
Contains some notes on Yeats's view of the Irish peasant.

250. PATRIDES, C. A.: "Gaiety Transfiguring All That Dread: The Case of Yeats," *Yeats*, 5 (1987), 117-32.
The context of Yeats's concept of tragic joy, discussed with reference to "Lapis Lazuli," his literary criticism, the Oedipus plays, the figure of the fool in *On Baile's Strand*, *The Hour-Glass*, and *The Herne's Egg*, the influence of Shakespeare, and Crazy Jane.

251. PEARCE, DONALD ROSS: "The Significance of Ireland in the Work of W. B. Yeats," Ph.D. thesis, U of Michigan, 1948. iv, 373 pp. (*Microfilm Abstracts*, 9:1 [1949], 133-34)

252. ———: "The Systematic Rose," *YeA*, 4 (1986), 195-200.
The "alchemical rose of the Nineties . . . was reborn first as the visionary moon of the middle years, then as the privileged 'antithetical' phases of the System."

253. PFISTER, MANFRED, and BERND SCHULTE-MIDDELICH (eds): *Die 'Nineties: Das englische Fin de siècle zwischen Dekadenz und Sozialkritik*. München: Francke, 1983. 422 pp. (UTB. 123.)
Richard Taylor: "Die mystisch-okkulte Renaissance: Rituelle Magie und symbolistische Dichtung," 100-14, and passim (see index).

254. PITNER, MARIA GRAY: "The Aristocratic Mask of William Butler Yeats," Ph.D. thesis, Florida State U, 1979. iii, 172 pp. (*DAI*, 40:7 [Jan 1980], 4059A; reprinted *YeA*, 1 [1982], 207-8)

255. PITTWOOD, ERNEST H.: "The Celtic Spirit in Literature," *Holborn R*, os 71 / ns 20:[4] (Oct 1929), 461-69.
The Celtic spirit of "wonder, reverence, faith," as found in Yeats's works.

256. POPOT, RAYMONDE: "Mythes et nationalisme: L'exemple irlandais," *Gaéliana,* [1] (1979), 39-61.
Discusses Yeats's use of Irish mythology, particularly his treatment of the Cuchulain and Deirdre myths.

257. PORTER, RAYMOND J.: "The Irish Messianic Tradition," *Emory UQ,* 22:1 (Spring 1966), 29-35.
Yeats's treatment of the theme of the deliverer.

258. PRUITT, VIRGINIA DIANE: "Yeats, Old Age, and Death: The Dynamic of the Mask," Ph.D. thesis, U of Virginia, 1974. xvii, 188 pp. (*DAI,* 35:8 [Feb 1975], 5422A)

259. ———: "Yeats, the Mask, and the Poetry of Old Age," *J of Geriatric Psychiatry,* 15:1 (1982), 99-112.
Discusses the concept of the mask, a "psychodynamic," as a key to Yeats's life and poetry. "If in . . . a physical sense . . . Yeats spent his youth being old, in . . . an emotional sense . . . he did not come into possession of his youth until he was middle-aged."

260. PUTZEL, STEVEN DANIEL: *Reconstructing Yeats: "The Secret Rose" and "The Wind among the Reeds."* Dublin: Gill & Macmillan / Totowa, N.J.: Barnes & Noble, 1986. xi, 242 pp.
Based on "Yeats's Use of Irish Folklore and Mythology in the 1890's," Ph.D. thesis, U of Toronto, 1980. v, 375 pp. (*DAI,* 41:6 [Dec 1980], 2601A; reprinted *YeA,* 1 [1982], 218-19). Discusses the construction of a symbolic system in the two early collections. Analyzed in sections DD and FA.
Reviews:
- Terence Brown: "A Book Hard to Warm To," *ILS,* 5:2 (Fall 1986), 23.
- Carolyn Holdsworth, *Yeats,* 5 (1987), 255-63.
- Declan Kiberd: "Taking Stock of Yeats," *TLS,* 13 Feb 1987, 166.
- Stephen Watt, *VS,* 31:1 (Autumn 1987), 115-18.

261. ———: "The Black Pig: Yeats's Early Apocalyptic Beast," *Eire,* 17:3 (Fall 1982), 86-102.
The sources of the image in Irish folklore and mythology.

262. QUIN, C. C. W.: "W. B. Yeats and Irish Tradition," *Hermathena,* 97 (1963), 3-19.
Yeats was an "ignorant plunderer and raider in the field of Gaelic literature . . . but he shows his scholarship and artistry and his taste in the use he makes of [it]."

263. QUINN, SISTER M. BERNETTA: *The Metamorphic Tradition in Modern Poetry: Essays on the Work of Ezra Pound, Wallace Stevens, William Carlos Williams, T. S. Eliot, Hart Crane, Randall Jarrell, and W. B. Yeats.* New Brunswick: Rutgers UP, 1955. xi, 263 pp.
"William Butler Yeats: The Road to Tír-na-n-Og," 207-36; on the metamorphosis motif in Yeats's works. See review by A. Norman Jeffares, *MLR,* 52:1 (Jan 1957), 108-10.

264. RAINE, KATHLEEN: "A Traditional Language of Symbols," *List,* 9 Oct 1958, 559-60.
Platonic symbolism in Blake and Yeats.

265. RAJAN, BALACHANDRA: "Its Own Executioner: Yeats and the Fragment," *Yeats,* 3 (1985), 72-87.
Unlike Pound and Eliot, "who seek the whole in parts," Yeats holds that completeness is a "delusion."

266. RANCY, CATHERINE: *Fantastique et décadence en Angleterre 1890-1914.* Paris: CNRS, 1982. ix, 224 pp.
See index for some notes on Yeats.

267. RAWSON, CLAUDE J., and MARJORIE PERLOFF: *Yeats and the Romantic Tradition. Yeats: Imagination and Symbolism.* London: Audio Learning, 1976. 1 cassette.
The talks are summarized by John Sutherland and Keith Walker in a supplementary booklet (6 pp.).

268. REID, BENJAMIN LAURENCE: *Tragic Occasions: Essays on Several Forms.* Port Washington, N.Y.: Kennikat Press, 1971. ix, 188 pp.
"The House of Yeats," 163-88; reprinted from *HudR,* 18:3 (Autumn 1965), 331-50. On "the meaning of nobility in the life and work of Yeats."

269. REID, MARGARET J. C.: *The Arthurian Legend: Comparison of Treatment in Modern and Mediaeval Literature. A Study in the Literary Value of Myth and Legend.* London: Methuen, 1970 [1938]. viii, 277 pp.
Note on Irish mythology in Yeats's works, pp. 257-60.

270. REIMAN, DONALD H.: "Wordsworth, Shelley, and the Romantic Inheritance," *RP&P,* 5:2 (1981), 1-22.

270a. RENEHAN, R[OBERT]: "The *Heldentod* in Homer: One Heroic Ideal," *Classical Philology,* 82:2 (Apr 1987), 99-116.
Contains notes on Yeats's use of Cuchulain.

271. RESCH, ANDREAS (ed): *Fortleben nach dem Tode.* Innsbruck: Resch, 1980. 787 pp. (Imago Mundi. 7.)
Wilhelm Gauger: "Postmortale Welt und Poesie," 179-220; contains a section on Yeats's treatment of the motif of life-after-death, especially in "Shepherd and Goatherd."

272. REYNOLDS, HORACE: "Yeats on Irish Wonders," *Tuftonian,* 2:2 (Jan 1942), 87-88.
Introduction to Yeats's essay, "Irish Wonders." See *Uncollected Prose,* 1:138-41.

273. RHEE, YOUNG SUCK: "The Poetics of Etherealization: Female Imagery in the Work of W. B. Yeats," Ph.D. thesis, U of Nebraska, 1985. viii, 260 pp. (*DAI,* 46:10 [Apr 1986], 3043A; reprinted *Yeats,* 5 [1987], 201-2)

274. RICHARDS, DAVID: "Literature and Anthropology: The Relationship of Literature to Anthropological Data and Theory, with Special Reference to the Works of Sir Walter Scott, W. B. Yeats, and Wole Soyinka," Ph.D. thesis, Cambridge U, 1982. iii, 223 pp.
Abstract printed in *YeA,* 4 (1986), 300. Discusses Yeats's "disillusionment with 'scientific' analytical methods and the streng-

thening of a metaphysical and speculative approach" as well as its effects on "Yeats's perception of poetic symbols and national politics" (abstract). See especially "Yeats and Anthropology," 59-105, with particular emphasis on "Meditations in Time of Civil War" and *The Death of Cuchulain*.

275. RIGHTER, WILLIAM: *Myth and Literature*. London: Routledge & Kegan Paul, 1975. viii, 132 pp.
See pp. 29-37 for notes on Yeats's mythmaking.

276. RIVOALLAN, ANATOLE: *Présence de Celtes*. Paris: Nouvelle Librairie Celtique, [1957]. iii, 444 pp.
"Le romantisme de W. B. Yeats," 200-203 (part of the section "Celtisme et romantisme"). "Les Celtes et le théâtre," 292-97 (the Abbey Theatre). Also passim (see index).

277. ROBINSON, ALAN DAVID: *Poetry, Painting and Ideas, 1885-1914*. London: Macmillan, 1985. xv, 280 pp.
American edition published as °*Symbol to Vortex: Poetry, Painting and Ideas, 1885-1914*. NY: St. Martin's Press, 1985. Numerous remarks on Yeats (see index), especially on his indebtedness to Symbolism and on his relationships with F. S. Flint, T. E. Hulme, and Ezra Pound.

278. ROGERS, DAVID: "Yeats and Eliot on 'Traditional Culture': A Few Long Thoughts," *Spirit*, 45:1 (Spring/Summer 1977), 1-12.

279. ROSE, ALAN: "The Impersonal Premise in Wordsworth, Keats, Yeats, and Eliot," Ph.D. thesis, Brandeis U, 1969. ix, 220 pp. (*DAI*, 30:6 [Dec 1969], 2548A)
"The Modern Poet: Yeats and Eliot," 152-97.

280. ROSE, JONATHAN: *The Edwardian Temperament 1895-1919*. Athens: Ohio UP, 1986. xiv, 275 pp.
See index for some notes on Yeats's interest in theosophy and the doctrine of the mask.

281. ROSSI, MARIO M.: "Yeats--and Philosophy," *Cronos*, 1:3 (Fall 1947), 19-24.
The philosophy in the poetry and plays, not in the "philosophical" works.

282. RUNNELS, JAMES ALAN: "Mother, Wife, and Lover: Symbolic Women in the Work of W. B. Yeats," °Ph.D. thesis, Rutgers U, 1973. 277 pp. (*DAI*, 34:1 [July 1973], 336A)

283. RUPRECHT, HANS-GEORGE: "Mémoire (r) poésie: Mythe et 'pratique discursive,'" *CRCL*, 2:2 (Spring 1975), 97-110.
A rather impenetrable structuralist essay; contains a note on Yeats's "Great Memory." N.B.: "(r)" means "relation."

284. A. E. [i.e., RUSSELL, GEORGE WILLIAM]: *Song and Its Fountain*. London: Macmillan, 1932. vii, 133 pp.
AE's opinion of Yeats's theory of self and anti-self and of *The Shadowy Waters*, pp. 9-12.

285. R[YAN, W. P.]: "The Best Irish Books," *New Ireland R*, 3:2 (Apr 1895), 122-32.
Discusses Yeats's list of the best thirty Irish books (see *Uncollected Prose*, 1:355-56, and *Collected Letters*, 1:440-45, 452-53).

286. SAHA, PROSANTA KUMAR: "The Dialectics of the Cuchulain Theme in Yeats' Works," *Thought* [Delhi], 8 June 1963, 12-14; 15 June 1963, 12-14.

287. ———: "Yeats's Cuchulain Works: Computer-Aided Analysis of Theme, Style, and Concordances," Ph.D. thesis, Western Reserve U, 1966. ix, 917 pp. (*DAI*, 28:2 [Aug 1967], 693A-94A)

287a. SAINERO [SÁNCHEZ], RAMÓN: *Leyendas celtas en la literatura irlandesa*. Madrid: Akal, 1985. 215 pp. (Akal bolsillo. 149.)
Contains paraphrases of several of Yeats's works indebted to Irish legends and myths, passim, and a general discussion of the poetry and plays, pp. 184-97.

288. SALVESEN, CHRISTOPHER: "Ireland and Its Dead Yeats," *New Society*, 10 June 1965, 26-28.
Yeats's Irish nationalism and Ireland's reaction to him.

289. SAROT, ELLIN: "Snared in an Evil Time: Responses to War in the Work of W. B. Yeats, Wilfred Owen, and Sylvia Plath," Ph.D. thesis, Columbia U, 1979. vii, 221 pp. (*DAI*, 40:5 [Nov 1979], 2686A)
See especially "Heroic Reverie," 22-53.

290. SARWAR, SELIM: "Apocalyptic Imagery in Four Twentieth-Century Poets: W. B. Yeats, T. S. Eliot, Robert Lowell, and Allen Ginsberg," Ph.D. thesis, McGill U, 1983. viii, 329 pp. (*DAI*, 44:5 [Nov 1983], 1452A; reprinted *Yeats*, 2 [1984], 263-64, and *YeA*, 4 [1986], 318)
"W. B. Yeats: Beyond the Romantic Apocalypse," 86-146; mainly on *The Countess Cathleen, Where There Is Nothing, The Unicorn from the Stars, The Player Queen,* the poems in *The Wind among the Reeds* and *Responsibilities,* and *A Vision*.

291. SCHNEIDER, ULRICH: "Yeats' Byzanz-Bild im Kontext seiner Zeit," *Anglia*, 95:3-4 (1977), 426-49.
Discusses the historical and political context of the poems and Yeats's admiration for Byzantine art, not so much the poems themselves.

292. SCHRICKER, GALE C.: "Old Nurse: W. B. Yeats and the Modern Fairy Tale," *Eire*, 19:2 (Summer 1984), 38-54.

293. SCOTT, NATHAN ALEXANDER (ed): *The Climate of Faith in Modern Literature*. NY: Seabury Press, 1964. xvi, 239 pp.
E. Martin Browne: "The Christian Presence in the Contemporary Theater," 128-41; contains a note on *The Resurrection*.
Ralph J. Mills: "The Voice of the Poet in the Modern City," 142-76; comments on Yeats as an anti-Christian poet, pp. 164-67.

294. SELDEN, RAMAN: *Criticism and Objectivity*. London: Allen & Unwin, 1984. vi, 170 pp.
"Eliot, Yeats and Pound," 131-37; on the concept of the mask.

295. SEPEDA, TONI: "Yeats and Women: The Nineteenth Century," Ph.D. thesis, U of Reading, 1980 [i.e., 1981]. iv, 423 pp.
The influence of Yeats's female acquaintances on his work.

296. SEWARD, BARBARA: *The Symbolic Rose*. NY: Columbia UP, 1960. xi, 233 pp.
"Yeats and Transition," 88-117; on the sources and function of the rose symbol in Yeats's works.

297. SHARMA, P. P.: "The Double Vision of W. B. Yeats," *IJES*, 16 (1975-76), 119-25.
The dialectical mode of apprehending opposites and antinomies.

298. SHAW, FRANCIS: "The Celtic Twilight," *Studies*, 23:89 (Mar 1934), 25-41.
A severe criticism of the term, of which "Twilight" may be correct but "Celtic" certainly isn't. As conceived by Yeats, "Celtic" does not describe Irish literature and culture. See next item.

299. ———: "The Celtic Twilight. Part II.--The Celtic Element in the Poetry of W. B. Yeats," *Studies*, 23:90 (June 1934), 260-78.
The so-called Celtic works are neither Celtic nor Irish. They are simply romantic, whereas genuine Celtic tradition is realistic. Yeats's critics, however, were more instrumental in creating the cliché than Yeats himself.

300. SHEVARDNADZE, PAATA EDUARDOVICH: *Problema "impersonal'nosti" v tvorchestve U. B. Ĭitsa*. Avtoreferat dissertatsii kandidata filologicheskikh nauk. Tbilisi: Tbilisskiĭ ordena trudovogo krasnogo znameni gosudarstvennyĭ universitet, 1984. 16 pp.
A dissertation abstract. "The problem of 'impersonality' in the work of WBY"; see also DC201.

301. SINISTRARI, LUDOVICO MARIA: *Demoniality*. Translated into English from the Latin (with introduction and notes) by Montague Summers. London: Fortune Press, [1927]. xliii, 127 pp.
Summers notes that Yeats's Irish fairies are "none other than the incubi of whom Sinistrari speaks" (pp. xxix-xxxii).

302. SMITH, EVANS LANSING: "The Descent to the Underworld: Towards an Archetypal Poetics of Modernism," Ph.D. thesis, Claremont Graduate School, 1986. vii, 265 pp. (*DAI*, 47:5 [Nov 1986], 1736A)
"Yeats and Conrad: Daimon and Demon," 26-46, sees Yeats's underworld as a "granary . . . the repository of the fundamental forms of the poetic imagination" (p. 34). The relationship with Conrad remains largely unexplored.

303. SMYTH, DONNA ELLEN: "The Figure of the Fool in the Works of W. B. Yeats, Samuel Beckett, and Patrick White," Ph.D. thesis, U of London, 1972. 465 pp.
"W. B. Yeats," 22-111.

304. SOCIÉTÉ DES ANGLICISTES DE L'ENSEIGNEMENT SUPÉRIEUR: *Rhétorique et communication*. Actes du Congrès de Rouen (1976). Paris: Didier, 1979. 473 pp. (Études anglaises. 75.)
Jacqueline Genet: "La spirale yeatsienne," 383-95.

305. SOCIÉTÉ FRANÇAISE D'ÉTUDES IRLANDAISES: *Actes du Colloque Littérature et arts visuels en Irlande: 22 octobre 1982, Grand Palais, Paris*. Rennes: Société française d'études irlandaises, [1983]. 72 pp.
Jacqueline Genet: "W. B. Yeats et les arts visuels," 27-40; Dorothy Walker: "Literature and Contemporary Irish Art," 41-48 (refers to the Yeats portraits of Patrick Collins and Louis le Brocquy).

306. SPANOS, WILLIAM V.: "Heidegger, Kierkegaard, and the Hermeneutic Circle: Towards a Postmodern Theory of Interpretation of Dis-Closure," *Boundary 2*, 4:2 (Winter 1976), 455-88.
Contains a short note on Yeats's concept of Unity of Being in

his cyclical concept of time.

307. SPIEGEL, ALAN: "From Divided to Shared Love in the Art of Yeats," *Renascence*, 26:2 (Winter 1974), 59-71.
The antinomial treatment of the love theme in Yeats's works.

308. SRIGLEY, M. B.: "The Mathematical Muse," *DM*, 31:3 (July-Sept 1956), 13-21.
The importance of mathematics for Yeats's poetry and thought, especially in *A Vision*.

309. STACE, W. T.: "The Faery Poetry of Mr. W. B. Yeats," *British R*, 1:1 (Jan 1913), 117-30.
Reprinted in *Living Age*, 22 Feb 1913, 483-90. Concentrates on "The Wanderings of Oisin" and *The Land of Heart's Desire*.

310. STAMM, RUDOLF: "Kunst und Gesellschaft im Werk von George Bernard Shaw und William Butler Yeats," *NZZ*, 24 June 1973, 49-50.
"Art and society in the works of GBS and WBY."

311. STAUFFER, DONALD A.: "The Modern Myth of the Modern Myth," *EIE*, 1947, 23-49.
On Yeats, pp. 36-49; particularly on *A Vision*.

312. STEIN, ARNOLD: "Yeats: A Study in Recklessness," *SR*, 57:4 (Oct-Dec 1949), 603-26.
"Sprezzatura" in Yeats's works and their indebtedness to Castiglione. Discusses "The Magi," "Leda and the Swan," "Nineteen Hundred and Nineteen," and "Easter 1916."

313. STEWART, ROBERT CALDWELL: "Those Masterful Images: A Study of Yeats's Symbols of Unity and Joy as Aspects of Romanticism," Ph.D. thesis, Yale U, 1969. v, 197 pp. (*DAI*, 29:11 [May 1969], 4021A-22A)

314. STRELKA, JOSEPH P. (ed): *Anagogic Qualities of Literature*. University Park: Pennsylvania State UP, 1971. vii, 335 pp. (Yearbook of Comparative Criticism. 4.)
Désirée Hirst: "Symbolism and the Changing Climate in Thought: A Problem in Literary Criticism," 132-48; comments on Yeats's neoplatonic symbolism.

315. SULLIVAN, ALVIN (ed): *British Literary Magazines: The Victorian and Edwardian Age, 1837-1913*. Westport, Ct.: Greenwood Press, 1984. xxvi, 561 pp.
Includes discussions of Yeats's association with *Green Sheaf*, *Dome*, *Samhain*, *Savoy*, *Scots Observer*, and *Arrow* (see index).

316. ——— (ed): *British Literary Magazines: The Modern Age, 1914-1984*. Westport, Ct.: Greenwood Press, 1986. xxxi, 629 pp.
See index for some references to Yeats.

317. SZABO, ANDREW: "The Poet and Society: Problems of Communication with Special Reference to the Work of W. B. Yeats," M.A. thesis, U of Bristol, 1963. 377 pp.

318. TAKADA, ERIKO: "The Quest of William Butler Yeats for Human Integrity," *Bulletin of Seisen College*, 25 (1977), 19-39.
On Cuchulain as Yeats's Celtic embodiment of Christ, especially in *On Baile's Strand*.

319. TAKAYANAGI, SHUN'ICHI: "Yeats and T. S. Eliot: Aging and Apocalypse," *English Literature and Language*, 13 (1976), 19-34.

320. TANIGUCHI, JIRO: *A Grammatical Analysis of Artistic Representation of Irish English with a Brief Discussion of Sounds and Spelling*. Revised and enlarged edition. Tokyo: Shinozaki Shorin, 1972 [1955]. xxx, 419 pp.
Uses material from Yeats's plays and prose passim.

321. TATE, ALLEN: *Essays of Four Decades*. Chicago: Swallow Press, [1968]. xi, 640 pp.
"Yeats's Romanticism: Notes and Suggestions," 299-309. Reprinted from *SoR*, 7:3 (Winter 1941/42), 591-600, and various collections of Tate's essays; also in CA36.

321a. THOMAS, CALVIN: "Knowledge and Embodiment in Yeats," *South Central R*, 4:4 (Winter 1987), 53-60.
Yeats's antinomies have to be understood as interpenetrating and interdependent, not as conflicting, structures.

322. THOMPSON, WILLIAM IRWIN: *The Imagination of an Insurrection: Dublin, Easter 1916. A Study of an Ideological Movement*. NY: Oxford UP, 1967. xiii, 262 pp.
Reprinted with a new two-page preface, West Stockbridge, Mass.: Lindisfarne Press, 1982. Discusses the historical and literary conditions that led to the Easter Rising and the aftermath in the works of Yeats (particularly in "Easter 1916)") and others.
See also Conor Cruise O'Brien: "Two-faced Cathleen," *NYRB*, 29 June 1967, 19-21; John Wilson Foster: "Apocalypse Then and Now," *CJIS*, 9:2 (Dec 1983), 87-91.

323. THORNTON, ROBERT KELSEY ROUGHT: *The Decadent Dilemma*. London: Arnold, 1982. viii, 215 pp.
See pp. 75-86 (Yeats and the Dowson legend) and 165-71.

324. THUENTE, MARY HELEN: *W. B. Yeats and Irish Folklore*. Dublin: Gill & Macmillan, 1980. x, 286 pp.
Based on "W. B. Yeats and Nineteenth-Century Irish Literary Tradition," Ph.D. thesis, U of Kansas, 1973. ii, 242 pp. (*DAI*, 34:6 [Dec 1973], 3360A-61A).
Incorporates "W. B. Yeats and Celtic Ireland, 1885-1900," *Anglo-Irish Studies*, 4 (1979), 91-104; "W. B. Yeats and Nineteenth-Century Folklore," *JIL*, 6:3 (Sept 1977), 64-79; material from the next item and from FE113.
Argues that in the 1880s and 1890s Yeats was more "involved with Irish folklore than with Irish mythology" (p. 3) and discusses his anthologies *Fairy and Folk Tales of the Irish Peasantry*, *Irish Fairy Tales*, and *Representative Irish Tales*, as well as *The Celtic Twilight*, the abortive *Irish Adventurers* series, the collection *The Secret Rose*, and *Stories from Carleton*.
Reviews:
- Hazard Adams: "Yeats and Folklore," *ILS*, 2:1 (Spring 1983), 21.
- Sean Breslin: "Yeats Folk," *IrP*, 19 Feb 1981, 10.
- Gary Davenport: "Yeats and Belief," *SR*, 89:3 (Summer 1981), 469-73.
- Ben Forkner, *Clio*, 12:2 (Winter 1983), 202-4.
- Miriam Fuchs, *Eire*, 16:4 (Winter 1981), 141-43.
- Benedict Kiely: "Mr. Yeats and the Pooka," *IrT*, 4 July 1981, Weekend section, 4.

- F. S. L. Lyons: "Freedom from Fact," *TLS*, 13 Mar 1981, 280.
- Janet Madden-Simpson: "Source and Symbol," *BooksI*, 52 (Apr 1981), 61-62.
- Phillip L. Marcus, *YeA*, 2 (1983), 129-35.
- James H. O'Brien, *CJIS*, 9:2 (Dec 1983), 100-102.
- Daniel T. O'Hara, *VS*, 26:1 (Autumn 1982), 99-101.
- Dáithi Ó hÓgain, *IUR*, 11:2 (Autumn 1981), 247-50.
- Frank Stack: "Folklore," *THES*, 13 Mar 1981, 12.
- Brian Tippett, *L&H*, 8:2 (Autumn 1982), 265-66.

325. ———: "'Traditional Innovations': Yeats and Joyce and Irish Oral Tradition," *Mosaic*, 12:3 (Spring 1979), 91-104.
Yeats's works and *Finnegans Wake* "demonstrate that the Literary Renaissance indeed marked the rebirth or renewal of the forms and techniques of Irish oral narrative traditions in written literature."

326. TILLYARD, EUSTACE MANDEVILLE WETENHALL: *Poetry Direct and Oblique*. London: Chatto & Windus, 1945 [1934]. 116 pp.
Note on Yeats's symbolism, pp. 62-68.

327. TINDALL, WILLIAM YORK: *The Literary Symbol*. Bloomington: Indiana UP, 1962 [1955]. ix, 278 pp.
On Yeats's symbolism, passim (see index); on "Sailing to Byzantium," pp. 247-53.

328. TREVOR, WILLIAM: *A Writer's Ireland: Landscape in Literature*. London: Thames & Hudson, 1984. 192 pp.
On Yeats, passim (see index).

329. TUOHY, FRANK: "Yeats and Irish History," *Eigo Seinen*, 111:11 (1 Nov 1965), 734-36.
Reprinted from CA145.

330. UNTERECKER, JOHN EUGENE: "A Study of the Function of Bird and Tree Imagery in the Works of W. B. Yeats," Ph.D. thesis, Columbia U, 1956, x, 281 pp. (*DAI*, 17:3 [1957], 637-38)

331. VEGT, JAN VAN DER: "Het maanlicht in de ogen: Iets over elfen en hun verwanten," *Bzzlletin*, 10:92 (Jan 1982), 61-64.
"The moonlight in the eyes; some remarks on fairies and their relatives"; on Yeats and the fairies.

332. VICKERS, CLINTON JOHN: "Image into Symbol: The Evolution of the Dance in the Poetry and Drama of W. B. Yeats," °Ph.D. thesis, U of Massachusetts, 1974. 205 pp. (*DAI*, 35:1 [July 1974], 484A)
Includes a chapter on the rituals of the Golden Dawn.

333. VLASOPOLOS, ANCA: *The Symbolic Method of Coleridge, Baudelaire, and Yeats*. Detroit: Wayne State UP, 1983. 219 pp.
Based on "Reintegration of the Mind: Symbolization in Coleridge, Baudelaire, and Yeats," °Ph.D. thesis, U of Michigan, 1977. 282 pp. (*DAI*, 38:11 [May 1978], 6704A). See the chapter "Yeats: The Quest for Unity of Being," 135-91; especially in the poetry.
Reviews:
- Hazard Adams, *MLS*, 16:4 (Autumn 1986), 93-94.
- Michael André Bernstein, *Yeats*, 3 (1985), 257-60.
- R. Bienvenu, *RLC*, 59:4 (Oct-Dec 1985), 472-73.
- Lore Metzger, *Wordsworth Circle*, 15:3 (Summer 1984), 127-29.
- Suzanne Nalbantian, *YCGL*, 34 (1985), 142-43.

334. *Voprosy istorii i teorii literaturnoĭ kritiki.* Tîumen': Tîumenskiĭ gosudarstvennyĭ universitet, 1976. 109 pp. (Nauchnye trudy. 29.)
V. V. Khorol'skiĭ: "Ĭets i irlandskiĭ fol'klor," 49-65.

335. WALKER, SANDRA ELIZABETH COWAN: "'All That Most Ancient Race': A Study of Ultonian Legend in Anglo-Irish Literature," Ph.D. thesis, U of Toronto, 1976. xiv, 366 pp. (*DAI*, 39:3 [Sept 1978], 1527A)

336. WARD, MARGARET: *Unmanageable Revolutionaries: Women and Irish Nationalism.* Dingle, Co. Kerry: Brandon / London: Pluto Press, 1983. ix, 296 pp.
"Inghinidhe na hEireann and the Birth of the Irish Theatre," 55-57, and passim (see index).

337. WARNER, ALAN: "How Irish Are the Irish Writers?" *Theoria*, 42 (June 1974), 1-17.
Some notes on Yeats's attempts to "combine literature and nationality."

338. WARREN, AUSTIN: *Rage for Order: Essays in Criticism.* Ann Arbor: U of Michigan Press, 1959 [1948]. vii, 165 pp. (Ann Arbor Paperbacks. AA33.)
"William Butler Yeats: The Religion of a Poet," 66-83; reprint of "Religio Poetae," *SoR*, 7:3 (Winter 1941/42), 624-38; also in CA36. Discusses Yeats's religious and quasi-religious convictions and their sources.

339. WATANABE, JUNKO: "The Symbolism of W. B. Yeats: His Doctrine of 'the Mask,'" *Kyoritsu Women's Junior College: Collected Essays by Members of the Faculty*, 11 (1968), 50-67.

340. WATSON, GEORGE: *Politics and Literature in Modern Britain.* London: Macmillan, 1977. 190 pp.
See index for some notes on Yeats.

341. WATSON, GEORGE JOSEPH: *Irish Identity and the Literary Revival: Synge, Yeats, Joyce, and O'Casey.* London: Croom Helm, 1979. 326 pp.
Includes "Yeats's View of History: 'The Contemplation of Ruin,'" *Maynooth R*, 2:2 (Nov 1976), 27-46. See "W. B. Yeats: From 'Unity of Culture' to 'Anglo-Irish Solitude,'" 87-150, and passim.
The book's "unifying theme is each writer's attempt to grapple with, or define, the nature or meaning of Irish identity, and the resultant effect on the content and form of his art" (p. 13). "However painful the question of identity may be for the Irish in real life, it has functioned . . . as a superb catalyst to the production of some of the great art of the century" (p. 34). Analyzed in sections DD and EE.
Reviews:
- Brian Cosgrove, *Studies*, 69:273 (Spring 1980), 104-5.
- Cairns Craig, *Aberdeen UR*, 48:3 (Spring 1980), 333-36.
- Patricia Craig: "Sorrowful and Senile," *NSt*, 23 Nov 1979, 813-14.
- Patrick Diskin, *N&Q*, os 227 / ns 29:4 (Aug 1982), 373-75.
- Peter Faulkner, *DUJ*, 74:2 (June 1982), 316-17.
- Christopher Fitz-Simon, *Drama*, 134 (Autumn 1979), 87, 89.
- Nicholas Grene, *Hermathena*, 130 & 131 (1981), 140-42.
- Declan Kiberd, *RES*, 32:125 (Feb 1981), 97-99.
- Joseph Leondar Schneider, *MFS*, 26:2 (Summer 1980), 318-19.

- Stan Smith: "Anglo-Irish Solitudes," *Literary R,* 4 (16-29 Nov 1979), 20.

342. WATTS, HAROLD HOLLIDAY: *Hound and Quarry*. London: Routledge & Kegan Paul, 1953. viii, 304 pp.

"W. B. Yeats and Lapsed Mythology," 174-87; revised from *Renascence,* 3:2 (Spring 1951), 107-12. Yeats used myth, particularly Celtic myth, in order to erect a barrier between himself and the society in which he lived. The original users of the myth would not have understood him at all.

"W. B. Yeats: Theology Bitter and Gay," 188-208; revised from *SAQ,* 49:3 (July 1950), 359-77. Yeats's religious thinking was solipsistic.

343. WEATHERLY, JOAN: "Yeats, the Tarot, and the Fool," *CollL,* 13:1 (Winter 1986), 112-21.

344. WEISNER, CLAUS JÜRGEN: "Dialektische Ästhetik und antithetische Struktur in W. B. Yeats' theoretischen Schriften und lyrischem Werk," Dr.phil. thesis, U of Freiburg, 1970. iii, 417 pp.

Includes an English summary, pp. 412-15; reprinted in *EASG,* 1970, 43. An ill-organized and cluttered attempt to discuss antithetical structures in Yeats's thought and poetry, particularly in the early work.

345. WELCH, ROBERT: *Irish Poetry from Moore to Yeats*. Gerrards Cross: Smythe, 1980. 248 pp. (Irish Literary Studies. 5.)

"Yeats and Oisin," 205-27; on Irish themes in the early works, especially in "The Wanderings of Oisin." The essays on Thomas Moore, J. J. Callanan, Mangan, Ferguson, de Vere, and Allingham include references to Yeats.

Reviews:

- James F. Kilroy, *YeA,* 1 (1982), 252-54.
- David Lloyd, *IUR,* 11:2 (Autumn 1981), 244-46.
- John Montague: "Breaking the Silence," *IrT,* 23 Aug 1980, 11.

346. ———: "Yeats, Myth and History," *Gaéliana,* 8 (1986), 91-101.

347. WIENER, PHILIP P. (ed): *Dictionary of the History of Ideas: Studies of Selected Pivotal Ideas*. NY: Scribner, 1973-74. 5 vols.

See René Wellek: "Symbol and Symbolism in Literature," 4:337-45.

348. WILLIAMS, CAROL ELIZABETH: "Gyres in a Sphere: Yeats and History," Ph.D. thesis, Syracuse U, 1980. xxiv, 228 pp. (*DAI,* 41:8 [Feb 1981], 3598A; reprinted *YeA,* 2 [1983], 98-99)

Discusses Yeats's writings on Blake and Shelley, *A Vision,* and relevant poems.

349. WILLIAMS, MELVIN G.: "Yeats and Christ: A Study in Symbolism," *Renascence,* 20:4 (Summer 1968), 174-78, 222.

The Christ figure in the poetry and plays.

350. WILSON, BRUCE MATTHEW: "The Artifice of Eternity: Yeats and the Purgatorial Vision," Ph.D. thesis, U of Virginia, 1977. xii, 172 pp. (*DAI,* 38:9 [Mar 1978], 5470A)

Discusses the influence of the Nō, *The Dreaming of the Bones, Purgatory,* the romantic inheritance, and Yeats's and D. H. Lawrence's cyclical views of self and history.

351. WYATT, DAVID: *Prodigal Sons: A Study of Authorship and Au-*

thority. Baltimore: Johns Hopkins UP, 1980. xxi, 174 pp.
"Yeats and Synge: The Cuchulain Complex," 26-51, 158-60. For "Cuchulain" read "Oedipus." Discusses *On Baile's Strand*, other plays, several poems, and the Yeats-Synge relationship. See review by James Olney, *YeA*, 1 (1982), 255-59.

352. YAMADA, MASAAKI: [In Japanese] "Sing the Peasantry: Yeats's Irish Background," *SELit*, 57:2 (Dec 1980), 157-73.
English synopsis in English Number (1981), 130-31.

353. YAMASAKI, HIROYUKI: [In Japanese] "Yeats and Allegory," *HSELL*, 29:Special Number (1984), 51-62; English summary, 70-71.

354. YEATS, W. B.: *The Celtic Twilight and a Selection of Early Poems*. Introduction by Walter Starkie. NY: New American Library, 1962. 222 pp. (Signet Classic. CP120.)
"Introduction," ix-xxv [i.e., 9-25]; on the early biography and works.

355. ———, and THOMAS KINSELLA: *Davis, Mangan, Ferguson? Tradition and the Irish Writer*. Dublin: Dolmen Press, 1970. 72 pp. (Tower Series of Anglo-Irish Studies. 2.)
Roger McHugh: "Foreword," 7-11; discusses the influence of Davis, Mangan, and Ferguson on Yeats.
Thomas Kinsella: "The Irish Writer," 55-70; includes "The Irish Writer," *Eire*, 2:2 (Summer 1967), 8-15, and "Irish Literature--Continuity of the Tradition," *Poetry Ireland*, 7&8 (Spring 1968), 109-16. Yeats's relationship with the past is essentially that of a broken tradition. He is an isolated figure in 20th-century Irish literature.
For reviews see G1405-1411.

356. ——— (ed): *Fairy and Folk Tales of Ireland*. Edited by W. B. Yeats, with a foreword by Benedict Kiely. NY: Macmillan, 1983. xx, 387 pp.
"Foreword," ix-xx.

357. YOSHINO, MASAAKI: [In Japanese] "Yeats's Dance Image," *Studies in English Language and Literature*, 28 (1978), 21-35.
English summary on pp. 163-64.

358. ZANGER, JULES: "Living on the Edge: Indian Captivity Narrative and Fairy Tale," *Clio*, 13:2 (Winter 1984), 123-32.
Contains notes on Yeats's views of the fairies.

CD Influences, Parallels, and Contrast Studies, Including Biographical Relations with Other Persons

This section is subdivided into three parts. The first part includes general studies of influence; the second part lists national literatures in alphabetical arrangement. The relative shortness of the Japanese section is due to the fact that the considerable amount of material on the influence of the Nō has been relegated to a separate section (ED). The third part comprises relationships with individual authors and persons, in alphabetical order of their names. Many of these persons (Eliot, MacNeice, Pound and others) have published *on* Yeats; with a few exceptions these items are not found here. Readers are therefore advised to check the index of names for relevant items. Index IA should also be consulted for names of authors and persons not represented by separate entries (e.g., Hans Christian Andersen, William Archer). A few important authors such as Coleridge are, however, included by way of references.

The possibility that some material is missing from this section is greater than elsewhere in the bibliography; there is a certain difficulty in guessing which author or poet might serve as an occasion or excuse for comparison with Yeats.

Part 1: General Studies

1. BACHCHAN, HARBANS RAI: *W. B. Yeats and Occultism: A Study of His Works in Relation to Indian Lore, the Cabbala, Swedenborg, Boehme and Theosophy*. Foreword by T. R. Henn. Delhi: Motilal Banarsidass, 1965. xxii, 296 pp.

Based on a Ph.D. thesis, Cambridge U, 1954. xvi, 395 pp. Indian lore is represented by Mohini Chatterjee, Tagore, Purohit Swami, and the *Upanishads*, theosophy by Madame Blavatsky. Contains a chapter on *The Herne's Egg* (pp. 185-206), as well as notes on the influence of Blake and MacGregor Mathers. Unfortunately, no Yeats criticism published after 1954 has been taken into account.

1a. BORNSTEIN, GEORGE: *Poetic Remaking: The Art of Browning, Yeats, and Pound*. University Park: Pennsylvania State UP, 1988. xi, 164 pp.

A study of poetic influence that assembles, with one exception, reprinted and revised essays. For these see CC31, CD33, 355, 1238, 1378.

2. BOYD, STEPHEN KENT: "On the Way to the Rag-and-Bone Shop: A Developmental Study of W. B. Yeats's Use of Eastern Iconologies," Ph.D. thesis, U of Nebraska--Lincoln, 1983. v, 191 pp. (*DAI*, 44:8 [Feb 1984], 2476A-77A; reprinted *Yeats*, 3 [1985], 206-7, and *YeA*, 4 [1986], 302-3)

Contains short chapters on Indian themes in the early poetry, *The Speckled Bird, Per Amica Silentia Lunae, A Vision,* the relationship with Tagore and J. H. Cousins, "Supernatural Songs," and *Last Poems*.

3. CARPENTER, WILLIAM MORTON: "W. B. Yeats's Literary Use of the Renaissance," Ph.D. thesis, U of Minnesota, 1967. i, 253 pp. (*DAI*, 28:12 [June 1968], 5010A-11A)

Discusses Yeats's poetry and prose, especially *A Vision*.

4. CHRISTY, ARTHUR EDWARD (ed): *The Asian Legacy and American Life*. NY: Day, 1945. xi, 276 pp.

William York Tindall: "Transcendentalism in Contemporary Literature," 175-92; discusses Eastern influences on Yeats and his indebtedness to Madame Blavatsky.

5. CRONIN, ANTHONY: "Some Aspects of Yeats and His Influence," *Bell,* 16:5 (Feb 1951), 52-58.

Yeats was an important poet but exerted no influence on his generation and was essentially not a "contemporary figure."

6. DUME, THOMAS LESLIE: "William Butler Yeats: A Survey of His Reading," Ph.D. thesis, Temple U, [1950]. iv, 378 pp.

Does not trace influences but wants to establish precisely which books Yeats read; arranges his material as follows: works relating to Ireland and other Celtic material; magic, alchemy, mysticism, witchcraft; the East: theosophy, India, China, Japan, Arabia; psychical research; ancient Greece, Rome, Egypt, and Byzantium; science, history, philosophy; English and American literature. Valuable; an updated study would be very welcome.

7. ELLMANN, RICHARD: *Eminent Domain: Yeats among Wilde, Joyce, Pound, Eliot, and Auden*. NY: Oxford UP, 1967. vii, 159 pp.

Incorporates: "Gazebos and Gashouses: Yeats and Auden," *IrT*, 10 June 1965, iii; "Yeats & Eliot," *Encounter*, 25:1 (July 1965), 53-55, also as "Eliot's Conversion," *TriQ*, 4 [Fall 1965], 77-78, 80; "Ez and Old Billyum," from CD1040; *Yeats and Joyce*. No. 11 of *DPYCP* (1967, CA20), 445-79. The Auden and the Pound essays are also in CB148a.

Discusses the "poetic commerce" (mutual appropriations) between Yeats and the five poets, more precisely the biographical connections, and the aesthetic, critical, poetic, and dramatic similarities. Valuable study, but not exhaustive.

Reviews:

- Bernard Benstock, *JJQ*, 5:3 (Spring 1968), 267-69.
- Thomas W. Bergmann: "Getting Down to Cases," *NAR*, os 253 / ns 5:4 (July-Aug 1968), 39-40.
- Bernard Bergonzi, *RES*, 20:78 (May 1969), 251.
- Curtis Bradford: "Yeats and His Contemporaries," *Chicago Sun-Times Book Week*, 22 Oct 1967, 6-7.
- Cyril Connolly: "A Choice of Critics," *SunT*, 3 Mar 1968, 28.
- Patrick Cruttwell: "How Many Ways of Looking at a Poem?" *HudR*, 21:1 (Spring 1968), 197-207 (pp. 199-201).
- Denis Donoghue: "Clashing Symbols," *NYTBR*, 10 Dec 1967, 12, 14, 16.
- Edward Engelberg, *VS*, 12:3 (Mar 1969), 387-89.
- [G. S. Fraser]: "Yeats as Pickpocket," *TLS*, 25 July 1968, 787.
- George Mills Harper, *SAQ*, 67:3 (Summer 1968), 564.
- Daniel Hoffman: "Old Ez and Uncle William," *Reporter*, 37:7 (2 Nov 1967), 59-62.
- K. P. S. Jochum, *Anglia*, 88:3 (1970), 418-19.
- Robert Langbaum: "Literary Relations," *VQR*, 44:2 (Spring 1968), 333-37.
- W. K. Rose, *AL*, 40:3 (Nov 1968), 415-16.
- Kevin Sullivan: "Yeats and All That Crowd," *Nation*, 13 Nov 1967, 501-2.
- John Unterecker: "The Yeats Circle," *ConL*, 10:1 (Winter 1969), 150-52.
- Peter Ure, *ES*, 52:1 (Feb 1971), 84-85. Note by Kristian Smidt: "Eliot and Yeats," :4 (Aug 1971), 399.
- H. L. Weatherby: "Knowledge and Forgiveness," *SR*, 77:1 (Jan-Mar 1969), 171-76.

8. FARAG, FAHMY FAWZY: "Oriental Mysticism in W. B. Yeats," Ph.D. thesis, U of Edinburgh, 1959. ii, 261 pp.

Discusses *A Vision* and the poems and plays related to it.

9. GREGG, FREDERICK JAMES: "W. B. Yeats and Those He Has Influenced," *Vanity Fair* [NY], 5:2 (Oct 1915), 71.

Slight.

10. HANNA, NASHED GIRGIS: "Oriental Influence on the Poetry of W. B. Yeats," Ph.D. thesis, University College Galway, 1975. ix, 358 pp.

The orient is defined as Egypt, Byzantium, Arabia, India, and Japan; there is a chapter on each of these five areas.

11. ITO, H.: [In Japanese] "W. B. Yeats and the Buddhistic Philosophy," *J of Indian and Buddhist Studies,* 13:1 (1965), 180-82; 14:2 (1966), 770-75.

12. JAMESON, GRACE EMILY: "Mysticism in AE and Yeats in Relation to Oriental and American Thought," Ph.D. thesis, Ohio State U, 1932. iii, 185 pp.

Contains chapters on Yeats and Ireland, the East, Plato, and Blake.

13. JEFFARES, NORMAN: "The Literary Influence," *IrT,* 10 June 1965, vi.

14. SANBORN, CLIFFORD EARLE: "W. B. Yeats and the Winds of Doctrine: The Literary Environments of His Early Life and Their Contribution to His Theory of Poetry," Ph.D. thesis, U of Toronto, 1959. ii, 306 pp.

Contains chapters on "Yeats and Young Ireland"; "The Celtic Twilight as a Moulder of Poetic Theory"; "Yeats, Symons, and the French Symbolists"; "Yeats and the Aesthetic Movement" (mainly on the Rhymers' Club); "Yeats and Shelley"; and "The Occult and Poetic Theory in Yeats."

15. SMITH, ELLEN ROSSER: "Yeats's Cultural Touchstone: The Period from Dante to Shakespeare," Ph.D. thesis, U of Michigan, 1968. vii, 209 pp. (*DAI,* 29:3 [Sept 1968], 914A)

Yeats's knowledge of the art and literature of the 13th through the 16th centuries and their influence on his work.

16. WILSON, BRUCE M.: "'From Mirror after Mirror': Yeats and Eastern Thought," *CL,* 34:1 (Winter 1982), 28-46.

See also CA31, CC295, DA5, 37, EC77.

Part 2
African Literatures

See CC274, CD141-44, 324-25, 957, CE238.

American Literature and Culture

17. BISCHOFF, VOLKER: *Amerikanische Lyrik zwischen 1912 und 1922: Untersuchungen zur Theorie, Praxis und Wirkungsgeschichte der "New Poetry."* Heidelberg: Winter, 1983. 399 pp. (Britannica et Americana. 3. Folge. 2.)

On Yeats's importance for 20th-century American poetry, passim.

18. DIGGORY, TERENCE E.: *Yeats & American Poetry: The Tradition of the Self.* Princeton: Princeton UP, 1983. xix, 263 pp.

Based on °"The Presence of W. B. Yeats in American Poetry," Ph.D. thesis, Oxford U, 1976. On Yeats's view of 19th-century American poetry (particularly Whitman), the Yeats-Pound relationship, and Yeats's influence on Lindsay, Frost, Williams, Stevens, Eliot, Jeffers, Tate, Ransom, Robert Penn Warren, Horace Gregory, MacLeish, Roethke, Berryman, and Lowell.

Reviews:
- Robert Belflower, *RES,* 37:145 (Feb 1986), 133-34.
- George Bornstein, *Yeats,* 2 (1984), 275-78.

- Denis Donoghue: "A 'Southern Californian' Anglo-Irishman," *NYTBR*, 5 June 1983, 7, 28-29.
- Herbert J. Levine: "The Importance of Being Yeats," *VQR*, 60:1 (Winter 1984), 174-76.
- Peter Makin, *YES*, 17 (1987), 338-39.
- Vivian Mercier: "Putting Himself in His Place," *TLS*, 25 Jan 1985, 80.
- Thomas F. Merrill, *JIL*, 12:3 (Sept 1983), 86-89.
- James Olney: "Modernism, Yeats, and Eliot," *SR*, 92:3 (Summer 1984), 451-66.
- Michael O'Neill, *DUJ*, os 77 / ns 46:1 (Dec 1984), 129-30.
- Marjorie Perloff, *YeA*, 3 (1985), 271-75.
- Julia M. Reibetanz, *YER*, 8:1&2 (1986), 136-37.
- Joseph Ronsley, *QQ*, 92:1 (Spring 1985), 173-75.
- Willard Spiegelman: "Of Influence, No End," *Salmagundi*, 65 (Autumn 1984), 146-52.
- Leonora Woodman, *AL*, 56:2 (May 1984), 295-96.

19. GALLAGHER, BRIAN: "About Us, For Us, Near Us: The Irish and Harlem Renaissances," *Eire*, 16:4 (Winter 1981), 14-26.
Detects numerous parallels; Yeats's work is a good example.

20. SHIPLEY, WILLIAM MAURICE: "The Rhetoric of Black and Irish Revolutionary Poetry," Ph.D. thesis, U of Illinois at Urbana-Champaign, 1975. ix, 206 pp. (*DAI*, 37:3 [Sept 1976], 1523A)
"The goals and aspirations of Irish poetry during the Cultural Renaissance (1890-1900) and the 'revolutionary' periods, respectively, are quite similar to the Harlem Renaissance (1920-1930) and the 'revolutionary' period in America between 1960 and 1970" (p. v). Includes a discussion of Yeats's poetry.

21. TAPSCOTT, STEPHEN: "The Poem of Trauma," *APR*, 13:6 (Nov/Dec 1984), 38-47.
Discusses Yeats's influence on American poetry, particularly Roethke and Berryman, and has some notes on "Easter 1916."

See also AE98, BF160, CB467, 485, CC69, 124a, 290, CD6, 203-204, 212-18 and note, 221-22 and note, 283 and note, 288-90, 296-98, 309, 369, 385, 439-40 and note, 455-56, 459-60 and note, 540-43, 590-91 and note, 617, 716, 749, 759 and note, 812-15, 816, 820 and note, 849, 945, 959 and note, 1000, 1005-6 and note, 1015, 1017-74 and note, 1081-82 and note, 1085, 1093, 1118-27 and note, 1165, 1169, 1242, 1249a-51 and note, 1376 and note, 1384-88 and note, 1416, 1429-32, 1434-36 and note, 1438, 1447, 1448-49 and note, 1450-51, DB17, DC30, 229, 247, 397, DD269, 738, FB8, 38, 39.

Arabic Literature

22. BUSHRUI, S. B.: "Yeats's Arabic Interests," in Jeffares and Cross: *In Excited Reverie*, (1965, CA48), 280-314.
Particularly on *A Vision*, and "The Gift of Harun Al-Rashid."

23. GHAMRAWI, AHMED ABDEL-WAHAB EL-: *W. B. Yeats and the Culture of the Middle East*. Cairo: Anglo-Egyptian Bookshop, 1979. 136 pp.
Based on "Some Eastern and Esoteric Aspects in the Work of W. B. Yeats," Ph.D. thesis, U of Exeter, 1977. vi, 372 pp. Discusses Yeats's interest in Arabic literature and the *Arabian Nights* and "The Gift of Harun Al-Rashid." The Ph.D. thesis contains chapters on the association with Madame Blavatsky, the Theoso-

phists, the Golden Dawn, and on the Leo Africanus manuscript.

See also AC1, 12, CB546, CD6, 10, FC112a.

Australian Literature

See CD292, 563-64.

Belgian Literature

See CD781-83 and note.

Canadian Literature

See CD342, 561, 773, 823, 1227-28, DC229.

Chinese Literature

24. EBER, IRENE: *Voices from Afar: Modern Chinese Writers on Oppressed Peoples and Their Literature*. Ann Arbor: Center for Chinese Studies, U of Michigan, 1980. xxiv, 162 pp. (Michigan Papers in Chinese Studies. 38.)

See index for notes on the reception of Yeats by Chinese writers; includes bibliographical citations which I have not followed up.

See also CC210, CD6, 1390 and note.

Classical Literature

25. DAVIS, DOROTHY ROSALIA: "Parallelism between Classical Tragedy and the Tragedy of William Butler Yeats," Ph.D. thesis, Boston U, 1937. x, 138 pp.

Discusses parallels in subject and plot, the use of chorus and masks, and the devices of foreshadowing, irony, and peripety. Includes a chapter on the Aristotelian quality of Yeats's plays.

26. DOWGUN, RICHARD: "Responses to Tragedy: Hazlitt to T. S. Eliot," °Ph.D. thesis, U of Pennsylvania, 1982. 267 pp. (*DAI*, 43:3 [Sept 1982], 807-8A)

"This dissertation examines the responses to Greek and Shakespearean tragedy of Hazlitt, Coleridge, Arnold, Pater, Yeats, Eliot, and several lesser-known nineteenth-century critics" (abstract).

27. INGALLS, JEREMY: "The Classics and New Poetry," *CJ*, 40:2 (Nov 1944), 77-91.

Notes some classical sources of Yeats's poetry, pp. 79-81.

28. STANFORD, WILLIAM BEDELL: *Ireland and the Classical Tradition*. Dublin: Figgis, 1976. x, 261 pp.

"Anglo-Irish Literature," 90-112; on Yeats's knowledge of Classical literature and his use of Classical themes. See also pp. 125-27 on the Irish coinage, and passim.

29. THOMSON, JAMES ALEXANDER KERR: *The Classical Background of*

English Literature. London: Allen & Unwin, 1962 [1948]. 272 pp.
See pp. 259-60: "Yeats had a somewhat false picture in his mind of classical antiquity, seeing it as it were through a veil of romantic mysticism."

See also CA17, CD6.

Danish Literature

See DD506, 543, 554, 752.

Dutch Literature

See CD1128-36 and note.

Egyptian Literature

See CD6, 10.

English (British) Literature, Art, and Culture

30. *Approaches to the Study of Twentieth-Century Literature: Proceedings of the Conference in the Study of Twentieth-Century Literature*. Second session, May 3-5, 1962. East Lansing: Michigan State U, [1963?]. vi, 131 pp.
David H. Greene: "Recent English and Irish Drama," 31-39, plus discussion about Yeats's influence on contemporary drama, 54-56. Greene maintains that Yeats exerted no influence.
John J. Espey on Pound and Yeats, 126-28.

31. BAKER, CARLOS: *The Echoing Green: Romanticism, Modernism, and the Phenomena of Transference in Poetry*. Princeton: Princeton UP, 1984. xiii, 378 pp.
"Living It All Again: W. B. Yeats and English Romanticism," 149-85, and passim (see index). On the influence of Keats, Shelley, and Blake. See review by Hugh Witemeyer, *Yeats,* 4 (1986), 187-89.

32. BEDIENT, CALVIN: "The Thick and the Thin of It: Contemporary British and Irish Poetry," *KR,* ns 3:3 (Summer 1981), 32-48.
Yeats is referred to passim.

33. BORNSTEIN, GEORGE: "Victorians and Volumes, Foreigners and First Drafts: Four Gaps in Postromantic Influence Study," *RP&P,* 6:2 (1982), 1-9.
Incorporated in CD1a; contains some notes on Yeats.

34. COLBERT, JUDITH ANNE: "The Passionate Artifice: Yeats and the Later Renaissance," °Ph.D. thesis, U of Western Ontario, 1978. (*DAI,* 39:9 [Mar 1979], 5501A)
The influence of Jonson, Donne, and Milton.

35. COUGHLAN, SISTER JEREMY: "The Pre-Raphaelite Aesthetic and the Poetry of Christina Rossetti, William Morris, and William Butler Yeats," Ph.D. thesis, U of Minnesota, 1967. ii, 206 pp. (*DAI,* 28:2 [Aug 1967], 622A-23A)

"Pre-Raphaelitism in the Poetry of William Butler Yeats," 163-98.

35a. CRAWFORD, FRED D.: *British Poets of the Great War.* Selinsgrove: Susquehanna UP, 1988. 269 pp.
Contains some notes on Yeats's view of the poets of World War I and on his own war poetry.

36. DOWLING, LINDA C.: "The Aesthetes and the Eighteenth Century," *VS,* 20:4 (Summer 1977), 357-77.
Contains some notes on Yeats.

37. FALLIS, RICHARD: "Yeats and the Reinterpretation of Victorian Poetry," *VP,* 14:2 (Summer 1976), 89-100.
Yeats's views of Tennyson, Arnold, Browning, Hardy, Hopkins, and Morris.

37a. GASSENMEIER, MICHAEL, and NORBERT H. PLATZ (eds): *Beyond the Suburbs of the Mind: Exploring English Romanticism. Papers Delivered at the Mannheim Symposium in Honour of Hermann Fischer.* Essen: Verlag Die blaue Eule, 1987. 242 pp. (Studien zur englischen Romantik. 2.)
Werner Huber: "Irish Writers and the English Romantics," 79-94; contains notes on Yeats's indebtedness to the Romantic poets.

37b. GENIUZHENE, IZOL'DA-GABRIELE: "U. B. Ĭets i poety XX veka," *Literatūra,* 29:3 (1987), 42-48.
"WBY and 20th-century poetry," with a summary in English.

38. HUNT, JOHN DIXON: *The Pre-Raphaelite Imagination, 1848-1900.* Lincoln: U of Nebraska Press, 1968. xv, 262 pp.
Passim (see index).

38a. JORDAN, FRANK (ed): *The English Romantic Poets: A Review of Research and Criticism.* Fourth edition. NY: Modern Language Association, 1985. xiii, 765 pp.
Numerous references to Yeats (see index), especially in the Blake chapter.

39. MCALINDON, T.: "Yeats and the English Renaissance," *PMLA,* 82:2 (May 1967), 157-69.
Revised in Srivastava and Dutta: *Unaging Intellect* (1983, CA108), 30-43. On the relationship between Yeats and Morris, Nietzsche, Shakespeare, Spenser, and Ben Jonson.

40. MAXWELL, D. E. S.: "Time's Strange Excuse: W. B. Yeats and the Poets of the Thirties," *JML,* 4:3 (Feb 1975), 717-34.
Especially MacNeice and Auden; includes a note on Yeats's political convictions.

41. MORRISON, BLAKE: *The Movement: English Poetry and Fiction of the 1950s.* Oxford: Oxford UP, 1980. x, 326 pp.
Some remarks on Yeats's influence (see index).

42. OHMANN, RICHARD M.: *Shaw: The Style and the Man.* Middletown: Wesleyan UP, 1962. xv, 200 pp.
"Appendix I," 169-85, offers a statistical comparison of the stylistic peculiarities in the prose of the following writers: Shaw, Yeats (*Per Amica Silentia Lunae*), Bertrand Russell, Sidney and Beatrice Webb, Chesterton, and Wilde.

43. PETERS, ROBERT LOUIS: "The Poetry of the 1890's: Its Relation to the Several Arts," Ph.D. thesis, U of Wisconsin, 1952. ix, 516 pp.
Pre-Raphaelite elements in Yeats's poetry, pp. 56-62; the influence of Blake's and Horton's drawings on Yeats's poetry, pp. 115-31; on "The Man Who Dreamed of Faeryland," pp. 155-58.

44. PRESS, JOHN: *Rule and Energy: Trends in British Poetry since the Second World War*. London: Oxford UP, 1963. xi, 245 pp.
Notes on Yeats's influence on the poetry after 1945, passim (see index).

45. RAFROIDI, PATRICK: "La tradition poétique," in Genet: *William Butler Yeats*, (1981, CA32), 60-73.
The English poetic tradition as a shaping influence.

46. SHIRES, LINDA M.: *British Poetry of the Second World War*. London: Macmillan, 1985. xv, 174 pp.
See index for some notes on Yeats's influence.

47. SKELTON, ROBIN: "A Literary Theatre: A Note on English Poetic Drama in the Time of Yeats," in Skelton and Saddlemyer: *The World of W. B. Yeats* (1967, CA102), 103-10.
John Davidson, Charles Doughty, Stephen Phillips, John Masefield, W. W. Gibson, Lascelles Abercrombie, T. Sturge Moore, and Gordon Bottomley.

48. SPENDER, STEPHEN: "The Influence of Yeats on Later English Poets," *TriQ*, 4 [Fall 1965], 82-89.
Revised as "The Poet and the Legend: An Evaluation," *IrT*, 10 June 1965, i-ii. Yeats's volume *The Tower* had the greatest influence on the poets of Spender's generation, especially Auden. Yeats was admired for the "threefold responsibility" shown in his life and work: responsibility toward belief, toward political action, and toward art. Invokes frequent comparisons with Eliot.

49. TOLLEY, A. TREVOR: *The Poetry of the Thirties*. London: Gollancz, 1975. 445 pp.
See index for scattered notes on Yeats's influence on the poets of the thirties.

50. ———: *The Poetry of the Forties*. Manchester: Manchester UP, 1985. xi, 394 pp.
Several short references to Yeats (see index).

51. WALTON, GEOFFREY: "The Age of Yeats or the Age of Eliot? Notes on Recent Verse," *Scrutiny*, 12:4 (Autumn 1944), 310-21.

52. WEATHERHEAD, ANDREW KINGSLEY: *Stephen Spender and the Thirties*. Lewisburg: Bucknell UP, 1975. 241 pp.
Scattered notes on Yeats's influence on the poets of the thirties.

53. WELLS, HENRY WILLIS: *New Poets from Old: A Study in Literary Genetics*. NY: Columbia UP, 1940. xi, 356 pp.
See pp. 252-59 for a discussion of various influences on Yeats's poetry, notably the influence of Donne.

54. WILDI, MAX: "The Influence and Poetic Development of W. B. Yeats," *ES*, 36:5 (Oct 1955), 246-53.
The mutual influence of Yeats--Symons, Yeats--T. Sturge Moore, Yeats--Pound, and others.

See also AE21, 24, BA22, BB109, 240, BC1, BE67, BF129, 160, CA4, 53a, 60, 66, 90, 103, 118, 209, CB70, 134, 158, 302, 320, 371, CC45, 46, 69, 100, 132, 146, 168, 247, 277, 333, CD6, 82, 150-72 and note, 176-77, 179-201 and notes, 205-11, 224-77 and note, 284-85 and note, 291 and note, 293-95 and note, 299-303, 306-8 and note, 311, 313, 318 and note, 318a, 320, 322-23 and notes, 341, 344-50 and note, 352 and note, 360-62, 364-67 and notes, 370-74 and note, 379-84 and notes, 394-427 and note, 429, 433-38 and note, 454, 454a and note, 458 and note, 475 and note, 486-96 and notes, 526, 527 and note, 529-38 and notes, 551-54 and note, 559-60 and note, 565-78 and notes, 605-10 and notes, 618-20 and note, 705-12 and note, 721-23 and note, 725-40 and notes, 745, 750, 751-57 and notes, 760, 762, 764 and note, 772, 776-79 and note, 802-11 and notes, 817 and note, 851-70 and notes, 879, 887, 962, 965-72 and note, 977-93 and note, 1009, 1016 and note, 1082a-83, 1086-87, 1102-6 and notes, 1138-41 and notes, 1166-67 and note, 1171-86 and notes, 1210-24 and note, 1226-26a, 1229-32, 1238-41 and note, 1243 and note, 1261-89 and notes, 1377-83 and notes, 1391, 1418-28 and notes, 1438a-46 and note, 1452-58 and notes, CE204, DA6, 24, DB10, 146, DC84, 191, 231, 299, 336, 348, DD44, 93, 94, 200, 235, 252, 380, 387, 393, 463, 475, 477, 506, 516, 544, 599, 715, 724, EA40, EE33, 39, EF90, FA24, FB15, 32, FC39, 54, 63, 122, 140, FE26, 82, FF17, G682.

French Art and Literature

55. BALAKIAN, ANNA: *The Symbolist Movement: A Critical Appraisal.* NY: New York UP, 1977 [1967]. xv, 220 pp.
On *Deirdre* and *The Shadowy Waters* as examples of Yeats's "symbolist theater," pp. 148-55; on "Leda and the Swan," the "symbolist masterpiece constructed in the very spirit of Mallarmé's understanding of symbolist technique," pp. 171-73. See index for further references.

56. BATE, A. J.: "Yeats and the Symbolist Aesthetic," *MLN,* 98:5 (Dec 1983), 1214-33.
The influence of French symbolism.

57. BOWRA, CECIL MAURICE: *The Heritage of Symbolism.* London: Macmillan, 1951 [1943]. vii, 232 pp.
"William Butler Yeats 1865-1939," 180-218. Symbolism in Yeats's theory and practice and its indebtedness to French sources, particularly Mallarmé.
Reviews:
- Anon.: "W. B. Yeats and Symbolism," *Poetry R,* 34:2 (Mar-Apr 1943), 126-28.
- Lawrence Leighton: "Criticism from Oxford," *KR,* 6:1 (Winter 1944), 146-50. Thinks that the Yeats chapter is the weakest in the book.

58. GRILL, RICHARD: "Der junge Yeats und der französische Symbolismus," Dr.phil. thesis, U of Freiburg, 1952. vii, 179 pp.
The influence of Mallarmé, Verlaine, and Villiers de l'Isle Adam on Yeats's early critical, dramatical, and poetical work.

59. HASSAN, IHAB H.: "French Symbolism and Modern British Poetry: With Yeats, Eliot, and Edith Sitwell as Indices," Ph.D. thesis, U of Pennsylvania, 1953. vi, 533 pp. (*DAI,* 13:2 [1953], 232-33)
"William Butler Yeats," 326-96, and passim.

60. KILLEN, A. M.: "Some French Influences in the Works of W. B. Yeats at the End of the Nineteenth Century," *Comparative Literature Studies*, 2:8 (1942), 1-8.
The influence of Sâr Péladan, Villiers de l'Isle Adam, and Mallarmé.

61. PAULY, MARIE-HÉLÈNE: "W. B. Yeats et les symbolistes français," *RLC*, 20:1 (Jan-Mar 1940), 13-33.

62. SABIN, MARGERY: *English Romanticism and the French Tradition*. Cambridge, Mass.: Harvard UP, 1976. xv, 294 pp.
See index for some notes on Yeats.

63. STANLEY, MARGARET: "W. B. Yeats et la France," thesis, Doctorat du 3e cycle, Université de Lille III, 1977. iii, 390 pp.
In three parts: "Les contacts: Londres, l'influence paternelle, Bedford Park, Yeats en France, Maud Gonne." "La France dans l'oeuvre de Yeats." "La fortune de Yeats en France."

64. STARKIE, ENID: *From Gautier to Eliot: The Influence of France on English Literature, 1851-1939*. London: Hutchinson, 1960. 236 pp.
See pp. 115-28 and passim.

65. TEMPLE, RUTH ZABRISKIE: *The Critic's Alchemy: A Study of the Introduction of French Symbolism into England*. New Haven: College and University Press, [1962] [1953]. 345 pp.
Scattered notes, passim (see index).

See also BG194, 208, CA61, 161, CB453, CC12, 71a, 108, CD14, 173-75a and note, 178, 304, 334, 452-53, 457, 462, 604, 786-92 and note, 1164, 1404 and note, 1408-14 and note, 1415, 1464, DA11, DB116, 203, DC26, 71, 112, 194, 201, 226, DD174, 240, 731-35, EA12, 39, EC4, FA38, FB8, FE20.

German Literature and Culture and Other Literatures in German

66. HUMBLE, MALCOLM EDWARD: "German Contacts and Influences in the Lives and Works of W. B. Yeats and D. H. Lawrence, with Special Reference to Friedrich Nietzsche," Ph.D. thesis, U of Cambridge, 1969. xvii, 488 pp.
Discusses Yeats's acquaintance with Germans and German literature in general and with Goethe, Wagner, Boehme, Kant, Hegel, Spengler, and Nietzsche in particular.

67. O'NEILL, PATRICK: *Ireland and Germany: A Study in Literary Relations*. NY: Lang, 1985. 358 pp. (Canadian Studies in German Language and Literature. 33.)
See index for several inadequate notes on the Yeats reception in Germany and his relationship to German literature.

68. RENZ, JOAN KELLOGG: "Yeats and the Germans: A Dramatic Kinship Once Removed," Ph.D. thesis, U of Connecticut, 1979. ix, 245 pp. (*DAI*, 40:10 [Apr 1980], 5433A-34A; reprinted *YeA*, [1982], 211-12)
Part I discusses the German influence on Yeats (Boehme, Goethe, Nietzsche, Rilke); part II the German response to Yeats (criticism and performances of his plays); part III Yeats's influence on Henry von Heiseler, Werner Egk, and Hugo von Hofmannsthal.

69. SMITH, ROBERT JEROME: "Thou Shalt Be Irish: A Study of the Influence of German Romantic Folk-Ideology on the Irish Literary Revival," *KanQ,* 13:2 (Spring 1981), 103-13.

See also CA53a, 103, CB176, CC231, CD286 and note, 287, 359, 461 and note, 464-66 and note, 476, 550 and note, 555, 562 and note, 696-99 and note, 746-47, 795 and note, 871-86 and note, 1107-10 and note, 1168, 1237 and note, 1253, 1417 and note, 1433, DD192, EC17, 46, 107, EE417, FC126.

Greek Literature, Art, and Philosophy (ancient)

70. GRAB, FREDERIC DANIEL: "William Butler Yeats and Greek Literature," Ph.D. thesis, U of California (Berkeley), 1965. ii, 327 pp. (*DAI,* 26:2 [Aug 1965], 1040-41)

See also CA53a, 61, 90, CB280, CD6, 149, 428, 876, 1007-13 and notes, 1236, DC356, DD40, 124, 170, 547, EC43, EE187, 190, 398.

Greek Literature (modern)

See CD1170.

Hungarian Literature

See CB546, CD1375, 1375a and note.

Indian Literature and Culture

71. ARONSON, ALEX: "Yeats on India," *Aryan Path,* 16:4 (Apr 1945), 131-33.

"And more than once he found in India what was so sadly lacking in the West: an intuitive approach to life, a religion born of an inner need, a challenge to materialism."

72. BARUA, D. K.: "Yeats, India, and Indian Criticism," *BDE,* 7:2 (1971-72), 90-99.

The reception of Yeats by Indian critics.

73. CHABRIA, R. G.: "Yeats and India," *Aryan Path,* 42:10 (Dec 1971), 436-40.

74. GORDON, WILLIAM A.: "Eastern Religion and the Later Yeats," *DR,* 55:4 (Winter 1975/76), 720-37.

Eastern religion is to be understood as Hinduism.

75. GRÜNWALD, CONSTANZE: "Yeats und die Versuchung des Ostens: Die Rolle der indischen transzendentalen Philosophie in Yeats' Dichtung seit seiner Begegnung mit Shri Purohit Swami, 1931," Dr.phil. thesis, U of München, 1979. iv, 260 pp. (*DAI,* 46:1 [Mar 1985], p. 33, item 10/209 C; reprinted *Yeats,* 4 [1986], 180)

76. GUHA, NARESH: "W. B. Yeats and India: The Story of a Relationship till the Advent of Tagore in the West," *JJCL,* 3 (1963), 41-79.

The influence of Mohini Chatterjee and the influence through AE and Madame Blavatsky.

77. ———: "The Upanisads, Patañjali, Apparitions, and W. B. Yeats (A New Approach to *A Vision*)," *JJCL*, 4 (1964), 104-24.

78. ———: *W. B. Yeats: An Indian Approach*. Preface by Richard Ellmann. Calcutta: Jadavpur U, 1968. 170 pp.

Based on a Ph.D. thesis, Northwestern U, 1962. iii, 164 pp. (*DAI*, 23:12 [June 1963], 4684). Discusses Yeats's relations with Mohini Chatterjee, Madame Blavatsky, Tagore (with reference to the concept of Unity of Being), and Purohit Swami; his interest in theosophy, Hinduism, Patañjali, and the Upanishads; Indian themes in the poetry; *The Shadowy Waters, The Herne's Egg*, and *A Vision*.

Reviews:
- P. C. Chatterji: "A Poet's Captivations," *Thought* [Delhi], 20 Dec 1969, 17-18.
- C. N. Srinath, *LCrit*, 8:4 (Summer 1969), 81-84.
- A. G. Stock, *YCGL*, 22 (1973), 98-99.

79. JADAVPUR UNIVERSITY: DEPARTMENT OF COMPARATIVE LITERATURE: *W. B. Yeats and India: Centenary 1865-1965*. A seminar and festival at Jadavpur University, 25 to 27 December 1965. Calcutta: Department of Comparative Literature, Jadavpur U, 1965. 9 pp.

A program with a note on the "Purpose and Scope of This Seminar on Yeats and India," apparently written by Naresh Guha.

80. JAIN, SUSHIL KUMAR: "Indian Elements in the Poetry of Yeats: On Chatterji and Tagore," *CLS*, 7:1 (Mar 1970), 82-96.

81. KANTAK, V. Y.: "Yeats's Indian Experience," *IJES*, 6 (1965), 80-101.

Although some of Yeats's Indian sources were not reputable, his affinity with, and understanding of, Indian thought was closer than in most of his Western contemporaries.

82. KHAN, S. M.: "Indian Elements in the Works of W. B. Yeats, T. S. Eliot and Aldous Huxley," Ph.D. thesis, U of Nottingham, 1956. iv, 321 pp.

On Yeats, pp. 21-35, 65-131, and passim.

83. KUEHN, NANDINI PILLAI: "The Influence of Indian Thought on the Poetry of W. B. Yeats," Ph.D. thesis, U of Michigan, 1973. vii, 142 pp. (*DAI*, 35:1 [July 1974], 459A-460A)

84. LYNCH, JOHN JOSEPH: "William Butler Yeats and India," °Ph.D. thesis, New York U, 1977. 280 pp. (*DAI*, 38:4 [Oct 1977], 2112A-13A)

85. PRASAD, BAIDYANATH: "Yeats and India," *Quest*, 75 (Mar-Apr 1972), 65-67.

86. RAJAN, B.: "Yeats and Indian Philosophy," *List*, 4 Sept 1947, 392-93.

87. RAMAMRUTHAM, J. V.: "Indian Themes in the Poetry of W. B. Yeats," *LHY*, 1:2 (July 1960), 43-48.

88. RAO, K. BHASKARA: "The Impact of Theosophy on the Poetry of W. B. Yeats," *Aryan Path*, 26:12 (Dec 1955), 545-52.

Particularly through Indian authors. Stresses the idea of incarnation as central to Yeats's "theosophical" poetry.

89. RAVINDRAN, SANKARAN: "William Butler Yeats and India: Indian Ideas of Art, Religion, and Philosophy in Yeats' Works, 1885-1939," Ph.D. thesis, U of Kansas, 1986. vii, 210 pp. (*DAI*, 47:6 [Dec 1986], 2171A; reprinted *Yeats*, 5 [1987], 207-8)

Includes discussions of the early "Indian" poems, the relationship with Tagore and Shri Purohit Swami (based on an examination of nearly 115 unpublished letters), the Upanishadic concept of self, *The Herne's Egg*, and impersonality in poetry. There is also "A Descriptive and Critical Study of Secondary Material on Yeats's Relationship to India," 194-210 (far from exhaustive).

90. SHAH, RAMESH CHANDRA: *Yeats and Eliot: Perspectives on India*. Atlantic Highlands: Humanities Press, 1983. xi, 174 pp.

Compares the impact of Indian culture and literature on Yeats and Eliot. Discusses the influence of Mohini Chatterjee, Tagore, and Purohit Swami and the concept of Unity of Being.

Reviews:

- Shyamal Bagchee, *CRCL*, 13:4 (Dec 1986), 689-92.
- E. P. Bollier, *Yeats*, 3 (1985), 249-52.
- Sisirkumar Ghosh, *LCrit*, 20:4 (1985), 118-21.

91. VISWANATHAN, S.: "Yeats and the Swan: The Poet's Use of an Indian Tradition," *Aryan Path*, 39:8 (Aug 1968), 340-45.

See also CA88, 90, CB546, CC13, 104, 159, CD1, 2, 6, 10, 630, 1077-79 and note, 1353-74 and note, 1400-3, DB172, DC111, 147a, 185, 210, 262, 276, DD233, 275, 725, EE277-79, FC142, FE29, 48, 84, G1243-52.

Irish Literature (written in English and in Irish) and Irish Culture

92. ALMQVIST, BO, BREANDÁN MAC AODHA, and GEARÓID MAC EOIN (eds): *Hereditas: Essays and Studies Presented to Professor Séamus Ó Duilearga*. Dublin: Folklore of Ireland Society, 1975. xxiii, 431 pp.

This is identical with *Béaloideas*, 39-41 (1971-73).

Birgit Bramsbäck: "William Butler Yeats and Folklore Material," 56-68; reprinted in EC12. On the importance of Irish folklore for Yeats's works, quoting a long list of possible sources.

Sheila O'Sullivan: "W. B. Yeats's Use of Irish Oral and Literary Tradition," 266-79. The sources of "Under the Moon," "The Song of Wandering Aengus," "The Hosting of the Sidhe," *Cathleen ni Houlihan*, "A Love Song," "The Happy Townland," "Running to Paradise," "Under Ben Bulben," and others.

93. BARRY, SEBASTIAN (ed): *The Inherited Boundaries: Younger Poets of the Republic of Ireland*. Edited with an introduction by Sebastian Barry. Mountrath, Portlaoise: Dolmen Press, 1986. 192 pp.

"Introduction," 13-29; contains some references to Yeats.

94. BOLAND, EAVAN, LIAM MILLER, SEAMUS HEANEY, and MICHAEL HARTNETT: "The Future of Irish Poetry: A Discussion," *IrT*, 5 Feb 1970, 14.

Yeats is mentioned passim.

94a. BOYD, TIMOTHY WAYNE: "Assuming a Feathered Mantle: Forms of Poetic Succession in Ireland from Myth to the Early Yeats," °Ph.D. thesis, Princeton U, 1987. 248 pp. (*DAI*, 48:9 [Mar 1988], 2330A)

Contains a chapter on the indebtedness of the early Yeats to the Anglo-Irish tradition and to Ferguson (abstract).

95. BRADLEY, ANTHONY (ed): *Contemporary Irish Poetry: An Anthology*. Berkeley: U of California Press, 1980. xvii, 430 pp.
The "Introduction," 1-26, contains a few references to Yeats; there are no Yeats texts in the anthology.

96. BRADLEY, WILLIAM: "The Poetry of *The Nation*, 1842-1848: A Descriptive and Critical Study with Some Reference to the Influence on the Poetic Development of W. B. Yeats," Ph.D. thesis, U of London, 1977. 380 pp.
See pp. 288-348 for Yeats's criticism of "Young Ireland" poetry and for his quarrel with Sir Charles Gavan Duffy over the New Irish Library.

97. BROWN, TERENCE: "After the Revival: The Problem of Adequacy and Genre," *Genre*, 12:4 (Winter 1979), 565-89.
Contains references to Yeats. See also CB172.

98. ———: *Northern Voices: Poets from Ulster*. Dublin: Gill & Macmillan, 1975. viii, 248 pp.
Some remarks on Yeats (see index).

99. CADENHEAD, I. E. (ed): *Literature and History*. Tulsa: U of Tulsa, 1970. vii, 102 pp. (U of Tulsa [Department of English] Monograph Series. 9.)
James H. Matthews: "History to Literature: Alternatives to History in Modern Irish Literature," 73-87. Mainly on Irish poetry after 1940 (Clarke and Kavanagh), including notes on Yeats.

100. CAHALAN, JAMES M.: *Great Hatred, Little Room: The Irish Historical Novel*. Syracuse: Syracuse UP, 1983. xv, 240 pp.
Several references to Yeats (see index).

101. CONCERNING POETRY: "Concerning Irish Poetry Since Yeats," *CP*, 14:2 (Fall 1981).
For extended references to Yeats in this special issue see Robert F. Garratt: "Introduction," 1-3; Terence Brown: "An Ulster Renaissance: Poets from the North of Ireland, 1965-1980," 5-23; Dillon Johnston: "Devlin's Poetry: Love in Abeyance," 27-43; James Liddy: "'Pity and Love Are beyond Our Buoys': The 'Simple Tale' of Austin Clarke's Politics," 47-57; and particularly Anthony G. Bradley: "Pastoral in Modern Irish Poetry," 79-96.

102. DENMAN, PETER: "Man into Myth: The Figure of Yeats in the Poetry of His Successors," *Gaéliana*, 2 (1980), 11-22.

103. DONALDSON, ALLAN ROGERS: "The Influence of Irish Nationalism upon the Early Development of W. B. Yeats," M.A. thesis, U of London, 1953 [i.e., 1954]. iii, 290 pp.
Discusses Yeats's work to 1914; contains chapters on "Irish Nationalism and Irish Nationalist Literature," "The Irish Literary Movement and the Decadents," and "The Irish Theatre Movement."

104. DONOGHUE, DENIS: "Irische Literatur nach Yeats und Joyce", *Dokumente*, 14:3 (June 1958), 233-35.
The Irish writers of today have not really assimilated the literary work of Joyce and Yeats.

105. DUNN, DOUGLAS (ed): *Two Decades of Irish Writing: A Critical Survey*. Cheadle: Carcanet Press, 1975. v, 260 pp.
Yeats's pervading influence on Irish literature is discussed pas-

sim (see index); particularly by Seamus Deane: "Irish Poetry and Irish Nationalism," 4-22; Michael Allen: "Provincialism and Recent Irish Poetry: The Importance of Patrick Kavanagh," 23-36; Donald Davie: "Austin Clarke and Padraic Fallon," 37-58 (also in *Poetry Nation,* 3 [1974], 80-101); and Edna Longley: "Searching the Darkness: Richard Murphy, Thomas Kinsella, John Montague, and James Simmons," 118-53.

106. EDWARDS, OWEN DUDLEY (ed): *Conor Cruise O'Brien Introduces Ireland.* London: Deutsch, 1969. 240 pp.

Kevin Sullivan: "Literature in Modern Ireland," 135-47: Between the extremes of Yeats and Joyce lies the whole body of modern Irish literature.

James Plunkett: "Dublin Streets: Broad and Narrow," 189-94; contains some reminiscences of Yeats (p. 193).

107. FAUCHEREAU, SERGE: "Introduction," "Quelques aînés," "La génération d'après-guerre," *Lettres nouvelles,* 1 (Mar 1973), 6-12, 19-28, 97-104.

Introductions to a special number, "Écrivains irlandais d'aujourd'hui." Yeats is mentioned passim.

108. FREYER, GRATTAN (ed): *A Prose and Verse Anthology of Modern Irish Writing.* With a preface by Conor Cruise O'Brien. Dublin: Irish Humanities Centre, 1978. xvi, 309 pp.

"Preface," x-xvi, includes notes on Yeats; see also Freyer's headnotes to the individual writers.

108a. FRIBERG, HEDDA: "Irish Writing in the Late 20th Century: A Report of a Conversation with Two Irish Critics," *MSpr,* 80:3 (1986), 210-20.

The critics are Declan Kiberd and Fintan O'Toole; several references to Yeats.

108b. GOODBY, J.: "Inner Emigres: A Study of Seven Irish Poets (1955-85)," °Ph.D. thesis, U of Leeds, 1986.

Abstract in *Index to Theses,* 36:4 (1988), 1395-96. On Kinsella, Montague, Heaney, Hartnett, Mahon, Paulin, Muldoon, and their indebtedness to their forerunners, including Yeats.

109. GRANT, DAMIAN: "Body Poetic: The Function of a Metaphor in Three Irish Poets," *Poetry Nation,* 1 (1973), 112-25.

Personifications of Ireland in John Montague, Seamus Heaney, and Paul Muldoon, with some references to Yeats's influence.

110. GRENNAN, ÉAMON: "Careless Father: Yeats and His Juniors," *Eire,* 14:3 (Fall 1979), 96-111.

What Yeats said about his younger contemporaries in "Under Ben Bulben" and in the introduction to the *Oxford Book of Modern Verse.*

111. HARMON, MAURICE (ed): *Irish Poetry after Yeats. Seven Poets: Austin Clarke, Richard Murphy, Patrick Kavanagh, Thomas Kinsella, Denis Devlin, John Montague, Seamus Heaney.* Portmarnock: Wolfhound Press, 1979. 231 pp.

"Introduction," 9-30; passim on Yeats. A different version was published as "Irish Poetry after Yeats," *EI,* 2 (Dec 1977), 45-62.

112. HARMON, MAURICE: "Yeats et la jeune poésie irlandaise," in Genet: *William Butler Yeats,* (1981, CA32), 425-40.

Yeats's influence on Austin Clarke, Patrick Kavanagh, Thomas Kinsella, John Montague, Seamus Heaney, and others.

112a. HENDERSON, LYNDA: "Yeats and the Development of Theatre Languages in Ireland," *Gaêliana*, 8 (1986), 117-31.
The re-emergence of Yeatsian ideas on the theater in some Irish plays of the 1980s.

113. HOLLOWAY, JOHN: "Yeats and the Penal Age," *CritQ*, 8:1 (Spring 1966), 58-66.
The influence of the Gaelic poetry of the 18th century on Yeats's poetry and on *Cathleen ni Houlihan*.

114. *Iz sovremennoĭ irlandskoĭ poezii: Ostin Klark, Tomas Kinsella, Dzhon Montegîu, Sheĭmas Khini, Sheĭmas Din*. Perevod s angliĭskogo. Moskva: "Raduga," 1983. 216 pp.
A. Sarukhanîan: "Golosa irlandii" [Ireland's voices], 5-18; contains several references to Yeats.

115. JOHNSTON, DILLON: *Irish Poetry after Joyce*. Notre Dame: U of Notre Dame Press / Mountrath: Dolmen Press, 1985. xv, 336 pp.
"Yeats's Legacy: An Antithetical Art," 13-28, and passim on Yeats's "troubling presence" in Irish poetry after 1941.

116. KENNELLY, BRENDAN: "Contemporary Irish Poetry," *Tablet*, 15 Mar 1969, 264-66.
Contains some notes on Yeats.

117. ——— (ed): *The Penguin Book of Irish Verse*. Harmondsworth: Penguin Books, 1970. 428 pp.
"Introduction," 29-42; stresses Yeats's role as a unifying force and powerful influence.

118. KERSNOWSKI, FRANK: *The Outsiders: Poets of Contemporary Ireland*. Fort Worth: Texas Christian UP, 1975. viii, 201 pp. (Texas Christian University Monographs in History and Culture. 12.)
See index for references to Yeats.

119. LITERARY REVIEW: "Irish Poetry after Yeats," *LitR*, 22:2 (Winter 1979).
See particularly Adrian Frazier: "Irish Poetry after Yeats," 133-44; "On Language and Invention," 197-204, an interview with Brendan Kennelly. Reviewed by Kevin P. Reilly: "Re-membering [. . .]," *Eire*, 15:3 (Fall 1980), 120-26.

120. MONTAGUE, JOHN: "Under Ben Bulben," *Shenandoah*, 16:4 (Summer 1965), 21-24.
Also published as "Living under Ben Bulben," *Kilkenny Magazine*, 14 (Spring-Summer 1966), 44-47. Maintains that Yeats's "direct influence on Irish poetry has been disastrous."

121. ——— (ed): *The Faber Book of Irish Verse*. London: Faber & Faber, 1974. 400 pp.
"In the Irish Grain," 21-39; several references to Yeats.

122. MURPHY, DANIEL: *Imagination & Religion in Anglo-Irish Literature 1930-1980*. Blackrock, Co. Dublin: Irish Academic Press, 1987. 228 pp.
Contains some remarks on Yeats, especially in the chapters on Kavanagh, O'Faolain, and Clarke.

123. MURPHY, MAUREEN O'ROURKE, and JAMES MACKILLOP (eds): *Irish Literature: A Reader*. Syracuse: Syracuse UP, 1987. xxiii, 454 pp.
Several references to Yeats (see index); does not contain any Yeats texts.

124. O'BRIEN, FRANK: *Filíocht ghaeilge na linne seo: Staidéar critiúil*. Baile Átha Cliath: An Clóchomhar Tta, 1968. xi, 347 pp.
"Contemporary Gaelic poetry: A critical study." Yeats is mentioned passim (see index).

125. O'FAOLAIN, SEAN: "Ireland's Literature Now Yeats Is 70: Sean O'Faolain Evaluates the Poet's Debt to Ireland and Her Debt to Him," *NYTBR*, 16 June 1935, 2, 14.

126. Ó HAILÍN, TOMAS: "Yeats agus filíocht na Gaeilge," *Comhar*, 7:12 (Dec 1948), 10-11.
"Yeats and Irish poetry."

127. O'LOUGHLIN, MICHAEL: *After Kavanagh: Patrick Kavanagh and the Discourse of Contemporary Irish Poetry*. Dublin: Raven Arts Press, 1985. 38 pp.
Contains some references to Yeats.

128. O'SULLIVAN, DONAL (ed): *Songs of the Irish: An Anthology of Irish Folk Music and Poetry with English Verse Translations*. Dublin: Browne & Nolan, 1960. xi, 199 pp.
"Introduction," 1-12; notes the influence of Irish folksong on Yeats.

129. POWER, PATRICK E. C.: *The Story of Anglo-Irish Poetry (1800-1922)*. Cork: Mercier Press, 1967. 187 pp.
"This . . . study . . . is an attempt to discover just how far the principal poets of the time were influenced by Gaelic literature and folklore" (p. 7). See particularly "Style--Poets of the Revival," 152-71; on Yeats, passim (see index).

130. *Problemy realizma v zarubezhnoĭ literature XIX-XX vekov: Mezhvuzovskiĭ sbornik nauchnykh trudov*. Moskva: Moskovskiĭ ordena trudovogo krasnogo znameni oblastnoĭ pedagogicheskiĭ institut imeni N. K. Krupskoĭ, 1983. 136 pp.
I. K. Eremina: "Irlandskie poety-uchastniki vosstanii͡a 1916 g. v Dubline i U. B. Ĭits," 128-34. "Irish poets as participants of the 1916 rising in Dublin and WBY."

131. RAFROIDI, PATRICK: *L'Irlande et le romantisme: La littérature irlandaise-anglaise de 1789 à 1850 et sa place dans le mouvement occidental*. Paris: Éditions universitaires, 1972. x, 787 pp. (Études irlandaises. 1.)
Notes on Yeats and the Irish romantics, passim (see index). A translation was published as *Irish Literature in English: The Romantic Period (1789-1850)*. Gerrards Cross: Smythe, 1980. 2 vols. For Yeats references see index in vol. 1.

132. SCHIRMER, GREGORY A.: "Yeats's Ghost and Irish Poetry Today," *SR*, 95:3 (Summer 1987), 485-90.
Includes a review of CB274.

133. SMITH, MICHAEL: "Irish Poetry since Yeats: Notes towards a Corrected History," *DQ*, 5:4 (Winter 1971), 1-26.

134. Eagle, Solomon [i.e., SQUIRE, J. C.]: "The Critic at Large: Irish Literature To-Day," *Outlook* [London], 16 July 1921, 53.
On the minor poets and their indebtedness to Yeats.

135. TORCHIANA, DONALD T.: "Contemporary Irish Poetry," *ChiR*, 17: 2-3 (1964), 152-68.
"Contemporary Irish poetry written in English can show nothing comparable to the poetry of Yeats."

See also AD8, 9, AE37, 96, CA41, 54, 55, 69, 109, 118, 129, 130, CB152a, 194, 241, 247, 258, 351, CC1, 2, 26, 130, 148, 155a, 345, 355, CD6, 12, 14, 32, 145-47 and note, 189, 191-92, 202 and note, 209-10 and note, 310, 312 and note, 314-17 and note, 326-32 and note, 333, 335-40 and notes, 343, 363 and note, 368, 375-78 and note, 386-87 and note, 390-93 and note, 430-32 and note, 441-51 and note, 463, 467-74 and notes, 477-85 and note, 497-525 and notes, 544-48 and note, 549, 556-58 and note, 579-85 and note, 611-16 and note, 621-95 and note, 700-4 and note, 713-15, 717-19 and note, 724 and note, 741-44 and note, 748, 761, 763 and note, 765-71 and note, 774-75, 780, 784, 793-94 and note, 796-801 and notes, 818-19 and note, 821-22 and note, 824-48 and note, 850 and note, 888-944 and note, 946-56 and notes, 958 and note, 960-61, 963-64 and note, 973-76 and note, 994-99 and note, 1004, 1010, 1014, 1080, 1088-92, 1094-1101, 1111-17 and note, 1137 and note, 1142-63 and note, 1187-1208 and note, 1209, 1225, 1233-35, 1244-49 and note, 1254-56 and note, 1290-1352 and note, 1389 and note, 1393-99 and note, 1460-68 and notes, DA18, 40, DB92, 95, 146, DC71, 248, 250, 383, DD182, 183, 185, 189, 265 and note, 427, 454, 486-88 and note, 521, 611, 710, 711, 714, 722, EA12, 25, EB156, EC28, ED10, EE54, 75, 196, 292, EF32, 54, 55, FA35, 39, 49, 52, 53, 55, 57, FB22, 23, 33, FC54, FD46, 57, 73, 77, FE26, 29, 97.

Italian Literature and Culture

136. WILSON, ROGER SHADE: "W. B. Yeats's Myth of the Italian Renaissance," Ph.D. thesis, U of Colorado, 1971. vi, 213 pp. (*DAI*, 32: 12 [June 1972], 7015A-16A)
Contains a chapter on the treatment of the Italian Renaissance in *A Vision* and an appendix listing references to it in Yeats's poems, prose, and letters.

See also CA96, CB546, CC20, 37, 130, 312, CD305, 351, 353-58 and note, 1407 and note, DA6, DD45, 232, 400, 404, 441, 459, 533, EC107, FC127.

Japanese Literature and Culture

137. MCDONALD, KEIKO IWAI: "In Search of the Orient: W. B. Yeats and Japanese Tradition," Ph.D. thesis, U of Oregon, 1974. v, 170 pp. (*DAI*, 35:6 [Dec 1974], 3753A)
Contains chapters on *At the Hawk's Well* and the Nō, *The Dreaming of the Bones* and *Nishikigi*, and the influence of Zen on the imagery of Yeats's poems.

138. MINER, EARL: *The Japanese Tradition in English and American Literature*. Princeton: Princeton UP, 1958. xxi, 312 pp.
"'An Aristocratic Form': Japan in the Thought and Writing of William Butler Yeats," 232-65; with subsections on Yeats's criti-

cism, poetry, and plays.

139. OSHIMA, SHOTARO: *W. B. Yeats and Japan*. Tokyo: Hokuseido Press, 1965. xiv, 198 pp.

Includes: "A Recent Letter of Mr. W. B. Yeats and a New Version of the 'Youth and Age' etc.," *SELit*, 9:3 (July 1929), 463-66; "W. B. Yeats and Japan in His Relation with the Zen Philosophy and the 'Noh,'" *Bulletin of the Graduate Division of Literature of Waseda U*, 9 (1963), 1-25; "The Poetry of Symbolic Tradition in the East and the West," ibid., 10 (1964), 1-29; "Yeats and the Japanese Theatre," *Threshold*, 19 (Autumn 1965), 89-102.

Contains letters from Yeats to Oshima, Hyde, Frederick Langbridge, Makoto Sangu, Yone Noguchi, Kazumi Yano; from Mrs. Yeats, Jack B. Yeats, and Hyde to Oshima.

Four autograph poems sent to Oshima by Yeats; interviews with Yeats, Jack B. Yeats, Elizabeth C. Yeats, and Junzo Sato; and 43 photographs.

"Yeats and the 'Noh' Plays" (the influence on Yeats's dramatic theory and practice); "Yeats and the Zen Philosophy" (in the poetry); "'Meru'" (the Taoist influence); "The Elements" (stone and water imagery in the poetry); "'Buddha's Emptiness'" (Buddhistic influence, particularly in "The Statues").

Junzo Sato: "A Sketch of My Life."

"Books and Periodicals on Yeats in Japan" (a review of research); "Bibliography of Yeats in Japan" (translations and criticism. As explained in the introduction to this bibliography, I have excluded most of the items listed by Oshima with the exception of those written in English).

Reviews:
- Rachel Burrows: "Yeats's Debt to Japan," *IrT*, 17 Dec 1965, 9.
- Rivers Carew, *DM*, 5:1 (Spring 1966), 81.
- James Kirkup, *JapQ*, 12:4 (Oct-Dec 1965), 540-42.
- Giorgio Melchiori, *N&Q*, os 211 / ns 13:3 (Mar 1966), 114-17.
- William E. Naff, *CL*, 19:1 (Winter 1967), 80-83.
- Patrick O'Flanagan, *MN*, 21:3-4 (1966), 420-21.
- Frank Tuohy, *SELit*, 43:2 (Mar 1967), 284-86.
- F. A. C. Wilson, *MLR*, 63:2 (Apr 1968), 469-70.

See also AB6, CB546, CC226, CD6, 10, 528, 588-89 and note, 720, 1257 and note, DD176, ED1-35 and note, EE18, 46, FE101.

Latin Literature

See CA53a, CD6, 319, 384, 1075, DD46.

Norwegian Literature

See CD586-87 and note.

Oriental (and Eastern) Literature

See CA147, CD2, 4, 6, 10, 12, 16, 23, DC111, 113a.

Polish Literature

See CD1437, EC58.

Portuguese Literature

See CD1001-3.

Romanian Literature

140. ALBU, RODICA: "W. B. Yeats and Romanian Poetry: Suggestions for a Tentative Comparative Approach," *ASUI,* 27 (1981), 95-106.
Compares Yeats's poetry with that of Mihail Eminescu and Lucian Blaga.

See also CD140, 223 and note.

Russian Literature

See CD281-82 and note, 785.

Spanish Literature and Literature in the Spanish Language

See CD321, 592-603 and note, 758 and note, 1405, DC247.

Swedish Literature

See CD1252 and note, 1258-60 and note.

Part 3
Chinua Achebe

141. BROWN, LLOYD W.: "Cultural Norms and Modes of Perception in Achebe's Fiction," *Research in African Literatures,* 3:1 (Spring 1972), 21-35.
Includes a note on Achebe's debt to Yeats.

142. GUHA, NARESH: "The Design of a Novel from Africa," *JJCL,* 16/17 (1978/79), 26-37.
Yeats's influence on Achebe's *Things Fall Apart.*

143. INNES, CATHERINE LYNETTE, and BERNTH LINDFORS (eds): *Critical Perspectives on Chinua Achebe.* London: Heinemann, 1979. iv, 316 pp.
A. G. Stock: "Yeats and Achebe," 86-91; reprinted from *J of Commonwealth Literature,* 5 (1968), 105-11. Relates Achebe's *Things Fall Apart* to *A Vision.*

144. MELONE, THOMAS: "Architecture du monde: Chinua Achebe et W. B. Yeats," *Conch,* 2:1 (Mar 1970), 44-52.
Unity of Being in Yeats and Unity of Humanity in Achebe.

William Allingham

145. BROWN, MALCOLM: "Allingham's Ireland," *IUR,* 13:1 (Spring 1983), 7-13.

146. JEFFARES, A. NORMAN: "Yeats, Allingham, and the Western Fic-

tion," *CJIS,* 6:2 (Dec 1980), 2-17.
Reprinted in Srivastava and Dutta: *Unaging Intellect* (CA108, 89-106). Discusses Allingham's influence on *John Sherman* and *The Speckled Bird.*

147. JORDAN, JOHN: "Adieu to Belashanny," *Hibernia,* 12 Apr 1974, 13.

See also CC345, DA11, FE69.

George Antheil

148. WHITESITT, LINDA: *The Life and Music of George Antheil 1900-1959.* Ann Arbor: UMI Research Press, 1983. xxi, 351 pp. (Studies in Musicology. 70.)
See index for notes on Yeats and Antheil, particularly on the music for *Fighting the Waves* (HC337).

See also BB7.

Aristotle

149. MCMAHAN, NOREEN DEE: "Tragedy or Eternal Return: Yeats's and Nietzsche's Reversal of Aristotle," Ph.D. thesis, U of Texas at Austin, 1984. x, 328 pp. (*DAI,* 46:4 [Oct 1985], 990A; reprinted *Yeats,* 4 [1986], 182-83)
Includes a chapter on *Where There Is Nothing* and *Purgatory.*

See also CD25.

Matthew Arnold

150. FAVERTY, FREDERIC E.: *Matthew Arnold the Ethnologist.* NY: AMS Press, 1968 [1951]. vii, 241 pp. (Humanities Series. 27.)
"The Celt," 111-61; contains some remarks on Yeats.

151. GOLDBERG, M. K.: "Arnold and Yeats--A Note," *CJIS,* 3:2 (Nov 1977), 41-43.
"Both Arnold and Yeats felt the typically Victorian need to work their way out of romanticism's disenchanted web."

152. LEVIN, HARRY (ed): *Perspectives of Criticism.* Cambridge, Mass.: Harvard UP, 1950. xvii, 248 pp. (Harvard Studies in Comparative Literature. 20.)
John V. Kelleher: "Matthew Arnold and the Celtic Revival," 197-221. Includes a few notes on Yeats.

153. MCNALLY, JAMES: "Cast a Cold Eye on Yeats on Arnold," *VP,* 25:2 (Summer 1987), 173-80.
Arnold's influence on Yeats's poetry.

154. MUSGROVE, S[IDNEY]: "Yeats and Arnold: A Common Rhythm," *Southerly,* 3:3 (Dec 1942), 25-26.
Yeats's irregular meters were anticipated in Arnold's "Haworth Churchyard." See A. W. V.: "Voice and Verse," *N&Q,* 185:1 (3 July 1943), 20-21, who asks indignantly: "What sort of an ear can this Australian have?"

155. SCHUCHARD, RONALD: "Yeats, Arnold, and the Morbidity of Modernism," *Yeats,* 3 (1985), 88-106.

See also CA54, CB453, CD37, DA11, DC192, 374, DD44, 212, FE18, 84, FF16.

W. H. Auden

156. BLAIR, JOHN G.: *The Poetic Art of W. H. Auden*. Princeton: Princeton UP, 1965. ix, 210 pp.
See pp. 91-95: Auden was influenced by Yeats's use of the occasional poem; in turn, Auden's prime achievement in this genre is his elegy on Yeats.

157. CALLAN, EDWARD T.: *Auden: A Carnival of Intellect*. NY: Oxford UP, 1983. xiii, 299 pp.
"Disenchantment with Yeats: From Singing-Master to Ogre," 143-62; first published in *Commonweal,* 13 May 1977, 298-303. Mainly on Auden's Yeats elegy and the opera *Elegy for Young Lovers* in which several characters are modelled on Yeats and his circle.

158. CARPENTER, HUMPHREY: *W. H. Auden: A Biography*. London: Allen & Unwin, 1981. xvi, 495 pp.
On Auden's Yeats poem, pp. 255-57; also scattered notes on the Auden-Yeats relationship (see index).

159. CROSSMAN, RICHARD: "Remembering and Forgetting: W. H. Auden Talks to Richard Crossman about Poetry," *List,* 22 Feb 1973, 238-40.
Auden comments on Yeats.

160. DAALDER, JOOST: "Yeats and Auden: Some Verbal Parallels," *N&Q,* os 218 / ns 20:9 (Sept 1973), 334-36.
In the poetry.

161. FINLAY, CAROLYN ROBERTS: "The Miner of Falun as Operatic Motif," *Mosaic,* 15:2 (June 1982), 47-56.
Note on Yeats as a possible source for Auden and Kallman's *Elegy for Young Lovers*.

162. GENET, JACQUELINE: "W.-B. Yeats et W.-H. Auden," *Trames,* 2 (Apr 1979), 57-78.

163. °GLOVERSMITH, FRANK: *Marxism and Literature*. Brighton: U of Sussex, 1975.
Four tape recordings in the U of Sussex Library; no. 4 is on Auden and Yeats.

164. GLOVERSMITH, FRANK (ed): *Class, Culture and Social Change: A New View of the 1930s*. Brighton: Harvester / Atlantic Highlands, N.J.: Humanities Press, 1980. 285 pp.
F. Gloversmith: "Changing Things: Orwell and Auden," 101-41; contains a note on Yeats and Auden, pp. 134-37.

165. HYNES, SAMUEL: *The Auden Generation: Literature and Politics in England in the 1930s*. London: Bodley Head, 1976. 428 pp.
See pp. 349-53.

166. MENDELSON, EDWARD: *Early Auden*. London: Faber & Faber, 1981. xxiii, 407 pp.

Several references to Yeats (see index).

167. PLIMPTON, GEORGE (ed): *Writers at Work: The "Paris Review" Interviews*. Fourth Series. London: Secker & Warburg, 1977. xvii, 459 pp.

Michael Newman: "W. H. Auden," 243-69; reprinted from *Paris R*, 14:57 (Spring 1974), 32-69. Contains brief comments on Yeats, especially on p. 265 where Auden says that Yeats had a bad influence on him.

168. RAICHURA, SURESH, and AMRITJIT SINGH: "A Conversation with W. H. Auden," *SWR*, 60:1 (Winter 1975), 27-36.

Includes a few comments on Yeats.

169. SPEARS, MONROE K.: *The Poetry of W. H. Auden: The Disenchanted Island*. NY: Oxford UP, 1963. x, 394 pp.

See index for several short references to Yeats, pointing out parallels and influences.

170. WILLIAMS, EDITH WHITEHURST: "Auden, Yeats, and the Word 'Silly': A Study in Semantic Change," *SoAR*, 46:4 (Nov 1981), 17-33.

Auden's use of the word "silly" in his elegy suggests the old meanings of "blessed" and "innocent" and helps to define his complex relationship to Yeats.

See also CA65, CB46, 236, 320, 371, 546, CC99, 127, 201, CD7, 40, 48, DC151, 162, 295, DD455, FE56. Auden's Yeats elegy is listed under HD5, the *Elegy for Young Lovers* under HE1.

Francis Bacon (born 1909)

171. BOXER, DAVID WAYNE: "The Early Works of Francis Bacon," °Ph.D. thesis, Johns Hopkins U, 1975. 385 pp. (*DAI*, 36:12 [June 1976], 7697A)

Includes a discussion of the literary sources of Bacon's paintings, among them the poems of Yeats.

172. SYLVESTER, DAVID: *Interviews with Francis Bacon 1962-1979*. New and enlarged edition. London: Thames & Hudson, 1980. 176 pp.

Bacon notes the influence of Yeats's poetry on his work, p. 152.

Honoré de Balzac

173. ARONSON, ALEX: "Yeats and Balzac," *VQ*, 47:1&2 (May-Oct 1981), 107-23.

174. BENSON, CARL: "Yeats and Balzac's *Louis Lambert*," *MP*, 49:4 (May 1952), 242-47.

On Yeats's essay "Louis Lambert" (1934) and Balzac's influence on *A Vision*.

175. FULLWOOD, DAPHNE: "Balzac and Yeats," *SoR*, 5:3 (July 1969), 935-49.

175a. WONHAM, HENRY B.: "'Nature and Supernatural with the Selfsame Ring Are Wed': Yeats, Balzac, and the Advantages of Monism," *YER*, 9:2 (Winter 1988), 39-53.

Balzac and Yeats "belong to a single occult tradition," both are influenced by Swedenborg.

See also EE490, FD73.

George Barker

176. FODASKI, MARTHA: *George Barker*. NY: Twayne, 1969. 190 pp. (Twayne's English Authors Series. 90.)
Compares the poetry of Yeats and Barker, pp. 138-43 and passim.

177. FRASER, ROBERT HUGH: "George Barker and the English Poets: 'The Minor Bird on the Bough,'" Ph.D. thesis, U of London, 1984. 526 pp.
"'The Pilgrimage along the Drogheda Road': George Barker, W. B. Yeats and the Idea of Ireland," 282-309. See also Fraser's article with the same title in *YeA*, 3 (1985), 133-47.

Charles Baudelaire

178. DAVIS, EDWARD: *Yeats's Early Contacts with French Poetry*. Pretoria: U of South Africa, 1961. 63 pp. (Communications of the University of South Africa. C29.)
Reprinted °Folcroft: Folcroft Library Editions, 1974; °Norwood, Pa.: Norwood Editions, 1976.
Neither "Irishness" nor the "mumbo-jumbo of the occultists" (p. 3) contributed significantly to Yeats's poetic development. He was profoundly influenced by Baudelaire, nevertheless highly original. Reviewed by Peter Ure, *N&Q*, os 208 / ns 10:10 (Oct 1963), 400.

See also CC333, DB203.

Sir Arnold Bax

179. BAX, SIR ARNOLD: *Farewell, My Youth*. London: Longmans, Green, 1943. 112 pp.
"Celtic," 41-48. Says that Yeats influenced his stories, poems, and plays, written under the pseudonym Dermot O'Byrne.

180. FOREMAN, LEWIS: *Bax: A Composer and His Times*. London: Scolar Press, 1983. xx, 491 pp.
Contains notes on Bax and Yeats (see index). See also HC17-18.

See also CA166, HC18.

Aubrey Beardsley

181. WEINTRAUB, STANLEY: *Beardsley: A Biography*. NY: Braziller, 1967. xvii, 285 pp.
A revised edition was published as *Beardsley*. Harmondsworth: Penguin, 1972. 287 pp. See index for notes on Yeats and Beardsley.

182. ———: *Aubrey Beardsley: Imp of the Perverse*. University Park: Pennsylvania State UP, 1976. xiv, 292 pp.

See index for some notes on Yeats.

See also BB14, DD250, EE505, FB2.

Mabel Beardsley

183. EASTON, MALCOLM: *Aubrey and the Dying Lady: A Beardsley Riddle*. London: Secker & Warburg, 1972. xxxii, 272 pp.
On Yeats and Mabel Beardsley, pp. 232-39, and passim (see index).

See also CA4, FB2.

Samuel Beckett

184. ARMSTRONG, GORDON: "Symbols, Signs, and Language: The Brothers Yeats and Samuel Beckett's Art of the Theater," *CompD,* 20:1 (Spring 1986), 38-53.
Jack Yeats, not WBY, had the greater influence on Beckett's theater practice.

185. BAIR, DEIRDRE: *Samuel Beckett: A Biography*. NY: Harcourt, Brace, Jovanovich, 1978. xiv, 736 pp.
See index for a few notes on the Yeats-Beckett relationship.

186. BRATER, ENOCH (ed): *Beckett at 80 / Beckett in Context*. NY: Oxford UP, 1986. x, 238 pp.
Katharine Worth: "Beckett's Auditors: *Not I* to *Ohio Impromptu*," 168-92; contains some notes on Yeats's influence.

187. COHN, RUBY: "The Plays of Yeats through Beckett Coloured-Glasses," *Threshold,* 19 (Autumn 1965), 41-47.
Apart from a few echoes in Beckett's plays, both writers share a principal attitude, "a purgatorial view of earthly life."

188. GADDIS, MARILYN: "The Purgatory Metaphor of Yeats and Beckett," *LMag,* 7:5 (Aug 1967), 33-46.
Parallels, parodies, and continuations of Yeatsian themes, types, and structures in *Waiting for Godot* and *Endgame*.

189. HARRINGTON, JOHN PATRICK: "The Irish Beckett: A Study of the Irish Contexts of His Work through the Second World War and the Development of His Prose Style," Ph.D. thesis, Rutgers U (New Brunswick), 1980. xiii, 278 pp. (*DAI,* 40:12 [June 1980], 6290A)
Comments on Yeats's "presence" in *Murphy* (pp. 143-58) and in *Watt* (pp. 184-87). See also by the same author: "'That Red Branch Bum Was the Camel's Back': Beckett's Use of Yeats in *Murphy*," *Eire,* 15:3 (Fall 1980), 86-96.

190. JEFFARES, A. NORMAN: "Foreword," *Hermathena,* 141 (Winter 1986), 7-9.
To a special Beckett edition, comments on Yeats's influence.

191. LONG, CAROL SUE: "Samuel Beckett, Irishman," Ph.D. thesis, Northwestern U, 1972. xiii, 209 pp. (*DAI,* 33:6 [Dec 1972], 2939A)
See especially pp. 183-99; includes a discussion of the character of the fool in Yeats and Beckett.

192. MAYS, J. C. C.: "Young Beckett's Irish Roots," *IUR*, 14:1 (Spring 1984), 18-33.
One of the roots being Yeats's work.

193. MERCIER, VIVIAN: *Beckett/Beckett*. NY: Oxford UP, 1977. xvii, 254 pp.
See index.

194. PARKIN, ANDREW: "Similarities in the Plays of Yeats and Beckett," *Ariel*, 1:3 (July 1970), 49-58.

195. PILLING, JOHN: *Samuel Beckett*. London: Routledge & Kegan Paul, 1976. x, 244 pp.
See index.

196. ROLLINS, RONALD GENE: "Old Men and Memories: Yeats and Beckett," *Eire*, 13:3 (Fall 1978), 106-19.
Compares *Purgatory* and *Krapp's Last Tape*.

197. ———: *Divided Ireland: Bifocal Vision in Modern Irish Drama*. Lanham, Md.: UP of America, 1985. xi, 104 pp.
See pp. 25-34 on Yeats and Beckett and on *Purgatory*.

198. WORTH, KATHARINE: "Yeats and Beckett," *Gaéliana*, 6 (1984), 203-13.
On Yeats echoes in Beckett's television play . . . *but the clouds*. . . (BBC 2, 1977; the title comes from "The Tower").

See also CB403, CC91, 303, EA38, 40, EB123, 147, 158a, 175, EE481.

Sir Max Beerbohm

199. FELSTINER, JOHN: *The Lies of Art: Max Beerbohm's Parody and Caricature*. London: Gollancz, 1973. xx, 283, xi pp.
See index for some notes on Beerbohm's view of Yeats.

200. GRUSHOW, IRA: "The Chastened Dandy: Beerbohm's 'Hilary Maltby and Stephen Braxton,'" *PLL*, 8:Supplement (Fall 1972), 149-64.
The character of Braxton in this story is modeled on Yeats.

201. ———: *The Imaginary Reminiscenes of Sir Max Beerbohm*. Athens: U of Ohio Press, 1984. xvii, 287 pp.
See pp. 78-79 and passim.

See also BB17, CE52.

Brendan Behan

202. O'CONNOR, ULICK: *Brendan Behan*. London: Coronet Books, 1972 [1970]. 328 pp.
Yeats is mentioned passim (see index).

See also DD213.

Saul Bellow

203. GORDON, ANDREW: "Shakespeare's *The Tempest* and Yeats's 'Sailing to Bysantium' [sic] in *Seize the Day*," *Saul Bellow J*, 4:1 (Fall-Winter 1985), 45-51.

204. MALONEY, STEPHEN R.: "Half-way to Byzantium: *Mr. Sammler's Planet* and the Modern Tradition," *SCR*, 6:1 (Nov 1973), 31-40.
Notes the indebtedness of the novel to "Sailing to Byzantium."

Arnold Bennett

205. MUNRO, JOHN M.: "'Byzantium' or the Imperial Palace? Ultimate Vision or Variable Compromise?" *Venture*, 5:2 (Apr 1969), 93-105.
The imperial palace is to Bennett what Byzantium is to Yeats.

F. R. Benson

206. TREWIN, JOHN COURTENAY: *Benson and the Bensonians*. London: Barrie & Rockliff, 1960. xv, 302 pp.
See pp. 126-31 on the production of *Diarmuid and Grania*.

George Berkeley

207. BERMAN, DAVID (ed): *George Berkeley: Essays and Replies*. Blackrock, Co. Dublin: Irish Academic Press, 1986. i, 171 pp.
D. Berman: "George Berkeley: Pictures by Goldsmith, Yeats and Luce," 9-23, reprinted from *Hermathena*, 139 (Winter 1985), 9-23. Yeats's view of Berkeley was indebted to Goldsmith's (although he did not know it) and was rightly criticized by A. A. Luce (CD211).

208. DAVIE, DONALD: "Yeats, Berkeley, and Romanticism," *IrW*, 31 (Summer 1955), 36-41.
Reprinted in S. P. Rosenbaum (ed): *English Literature and British Philosophy: A Collection of Essays*. Chicago: U of Chicago Press, 1971. vii, 365 pp. (pp. 278-84). Yeats based his rejection of romanticism in "Among School Children" on his reading of Berkeley.

209. FAULKNER, PETER: *Yeats & the Irish Eighteenth Century*. No. 5 of *DPYCP* (1965, CA20), 109-24.
Discusses the importance of Berkeley, Burke, and Swift.

210. KEARNEY, RICHARD: "Berkeley and the Irish Mind," *EI*, 11 (1986), supplement "Berkeley et l'Irlande," 27-43.
Contains notes on Yeats's view of Berkeley.

211. LUCE, ARTHUR ASTON: *Berkeley's Immaterialism: A Commentary on His "A Treatise Concerning the Principles of Human Knowledge."* London: Nelson, 1950 [1945]. xii, 163 pp.
Reprinted °NY: Russell & Russell, 1968. In the preface (pp. vii-ix), Luce refers to the Yeats-Berkeley relationship. See CD207.

See also BA14, BB211, CA66, 118, CC34, CD1261-62, DD61, FC140.

John Berryman

212. BAWER, BRUCE: *The Middle Generation: The Lives and Poetry of*

Delmore Schwartz, Randall Jarrell, John Berryman, and Robert Lowell. Hamden, Ct.: Archon Books, 1986. ix, 216 pp.

"Berryman and the Influence of Yeats," 90-103; see also passim.

212a. BERRYMAN, JOHN: *We Dream of Honour: John Berryman's Letters to His Mother.* Edited by Richard J. Kelly. NY: Norton, 1988. xxiii, 405 pp.

Many references to Yeats, including a letter from him and an account of Berryman's meeting with him (see index).

213. CONARROE, JOEL: *John Berryman: An Introduction to the Poetry.* NY: Columbia UP, 1977. xxiii, 215 pp.

Notes Yeats's influence on Berryman (see index).

214. HAFFENDEN, JOHN: *The Life of John Berryman.* Boston: Routledge & Kegan Paul, 1982. xiii, 451 pp.

Several notes on Yeats and Berryman (see index), including the account of a meeting in 1937.

215. LINEBARGER, J. M.: *John Berryman.* Boston: Twayne, 1974. 176 pp. (Twayne's United States Authors Series. 244.)

See index.

216. MAZZARO, JEROME: *Postmodern American Poetry.* Urbana: U of Illinois Press, 1980. xi, 203 pp.

"The Yeatsian Mask: John Berryman," 112-38; revised from "John Berryman and the Yeatsian Mask," *R of Existential Psychology and Psychiatry,* 12:2 (1973), 141-62. Yeats is also referred to in the chapters on Theodore Roethke and Sylvia Plath (see index).

217. SIMPSON, EILEEN: *Poets in Their Youth: A Memoir.* London: Faber & Faber, 1982. ix, 272 pp.

John Berryman reminisces about Yeats, pp. 128-30, and passim (see index).

218. THORNBURY, CHARLES: "John Berryman and the 'Majestic Shade' of Yeats," *Yeats,* 3 (1985), 121-72.

With numerous quotations from unpublished Berryman papers and poems on Yeats. For the published poems see HD14.

See also CD18, 21.

R. I. Best

219. WHITE, TERENCE DE VERE: "Richard Irvine Best and His Irish Literary Contemporaries," *IUR,* 7:2 (Autumn 1977), 168-83.

Augustine Birrell

220. Ó BROIN, LEON: *The Chief Secretary: Augustine Birrell in Ireland.* London: Chatto & Windus, 1969. viii, 232 pp.

Quotations from the Birrell-Yeats correspondence, pp. 159-60.

R. P. Blackmur

221. FRASER, RUSSELL: *A Mingled Yarn: The Life of R. P. Blackmur.* NY: Harcourt Brace Jovanovich, 1981. xxv, 357 pp.

See index for notes on Blackmur and Yeats, especially on pp. 106-7.

222. JONES, JAMES T.: *Wayward Skeptic: The Theories of R. P. Blackmur*. Urbana: U of Illinois Press, 1986. ix, 217 pp.
"The Outsider at the Heart of Things: Blackmur on Stevens, Eliot, and Yeats," 139-47.

See also DB21, DC229, DD496.

Lucian Blaga

223. ALBU, RODICA: "The Poetry of Yeats and Blaga: Suggestions for a Comparative Analysis," *Synthesis*, 12 (1985), 15-22.

See also CD140.

William Blake

224. ADAMS, HAZARD: *Blake and Yeats: The Contrary Vision*. NY: Russell & Russell, 1968 [1955]. xxii, 328 pp. (Cornell Studies in English. 40.)
Based on "Structure of Myth in the Poetry of William Blake and W. B. Yeats," °Ph.D. thesis, U of Washington, 1953. 558 pp. (*DAI*, 14:1 [1954], 105-6). Discusses "the question of influence . . . , Blake's aesthetic theory and . . . Yeats's interpretation of that theory. . . , the pattern of Blake's symbolism, with special emphasis upon those symbols Yeats later made his own . . . , [and] Yeats's system" (pp. xiii-xiv). Analyzed in sections DD, FA, and FE.
Reviews:
- Anon., *USQBR*, 12:2 (June 1956), 170-71.
- Anon., *YR*, 45:4 (June 1956), vi, viii.
- Sven Armens: "Suprarational Sources for Poetry," *Western R*, 21:1 (Autumn 1956), 69-76.
- Austin Clarke: "Blake and Yeats," *IrT*, 14 Jan 1956, 6.
- Peter F. Fisher, *QQ*, 64:1 (Spring 1957), 155-57.
- L. H., *DM*, 31:3 (July-Sept 1956), 52-53.
- T. R. Henn, *MLR*, 52:2 (Apr 1957), 263-65.
- Nicholas Joost, *Renascence*, 9:3 (Spring 1957), 147-49.
- V. G. Kiernan, *Science and Society*, 21:2 (Spring 1957), 185-87.
- Calvin D. Linton, *ASch*, 25:3 (Summer 1956), 378.
- William Van O'Connor, *CE*, 18:2 (Nov 1956), 127.
- Thomas Parkinson, *MP*, 54:4 (May 1957), 281-84.
- William D. Templeman, *Personalist*, 40:1 (Winter 1959), 86-87.

225. BENTLEY, GERALD EADES, and MARTIN K. NURMI: *A Blake Bibliography: Annotated Lists of Works, Studies, and Blakeana*. Minneapolis: U of Minnesota Press, 1964. xix, 393 pp.
On the Ellis-Yeats edition, passim, especially pp. 19-20; it is described as remarkable and original, but very inaccurate and more characteristic of its compilers than of Blake.

226. BENTLEY, GERALD EADES: *Blake Books*. Annotated catalogues of William Blake's writings in illuminated printing, in conventional typography and in manuscript and reprints thereof. Reproductions of his designs, books with his engravings, catalogues, books he owned,

and scholarly and critical works about him. Oxford: Clarendon Press, 1977. xii, 1079 pp.
Passim (see index).

227. BERTHOLF, ROBERT J., and ANNETTE S. LEVITT (eds): *William Blake and the Moderns*. Albany, N.Y.: State U of New York Press, 1982. xv, 294 pp.
See Hazard Adams: "The Seven Eyes of Yeats," 3-14; Robert F. Gleckner: "Joyce's Blake: Paths of Influence," 135-63 (Yeats is referred to passim).

228. BILLIGHEIMER, RACHEL VICTORIA: "Wheels of Eternity: Circle Symbolism in the Works of W. B. Yeats and W. Blake," °Ph.D. thesis, York U (Downsview, Ont.), 1980. (*DAI*, 42:7 [Jan 1982], 3143A; reprinted *Yeats*, 1 [1983], 177-78)

229. ———: "The Eighth Eye: Prophetic Vision in Blake's Poetry and Design," *CLQ*, 22:2 (June 1986), 93-110.
Includes some notes on Yeats.

230. ———: "The Dance as Vision in Blake and Yeats," *UES*, 24:2 (Sept 1986), 11-16.

231. ———: "The Female in Blake and Yeats," *CEA*, 48:4/49:1 (Summer-Fall 1986), 137-44.
Mainly on *The King of the Great Clock Tower* and *A Full Moon in March*.

232. BLAKE, WILLIAM: *The Poetic Books of William Blake*. Collected, and their myth and meaning explained by Edwin John Ellis and William Butler Yeats. London: Quaritch, 1891. [4 pp.]
A folded sheet, marked "In Preparation," including a facsimile of the title page (later modified) and an anonymous description of the projected edition. There is a copy in the National Library of Ireland.

233. ———: *The Poetical Works of William Blake*. Edited by John Sampson. Oxford: Clarendon Press, 1905. xxxvi, 384 pp.
Frequent references to the Ellis-Yeats edition.

234. ———: *Vala or The Four Zoas*. A facsimile of the manuscript, a transcript of the poems, and a study of its growth and significance by G. E. Bentley. Oxford: Clarendon Press, 1963. xviii, 220 pp. and illustrations.
Some notes on the Ellis-Yeats edition, passim (see index).

235. ———: *The Works of William Blake: Poetic, Symbolic and Critical*. Edited with lithographs of the illustrated "Prophetic Books," and a memoir and interpretation by Edwin John Ellis and William Butler Yeats. London 1893. NY: AMS Press, 1979. 3 vols.
This reprint contains an introduction by G. F. [i.e., G. E.] Bentley: "The Works of William Blake (Introduction to the AMS Edition)," 1-16 preceding p. v in vol. 1 (not in the 1973 AMS reprint). Bentley comments on the making, the scope, and the reliability of the Ellis-Yeats edition. For reviews of the 1893 edition see G1164-1170.

236. BÖKER, UWE: "Die Anfänge der europäischen Blake-Rezeption," *Arcadia*, 16:3 (1981), 266-83.
"The beginnings of Blake's European reputation."

237. BOGOEVA, LJILJANA: "U traganju za identitetom: Primer Vilijama Blejka i Vilijama Batlera Jejtsa," *Gradina,* 15:9 (Sept 1980), 44-53.
"On the search for identity: The example of WB and WBY."

238. BOLDEREFF, FRANCES MOTZ: *A Blakean Translation of Joyce's "Circe."* Woodward, Pa.: Classic Non-Fiction Library, 1965. xii, 178 pp.
Based on the Ellis-Yeats edition.

239. CARLSON, CRAIG BURNHAM: "The Shock of New Material: The Development of W. B. Yeats's Literary Use of William Blake," Ph.D. thesis, U of Exeter, 1972. xxviii, 377 pp.

240. CHISLETT, WILLIAM: *The Classical Influence in English Literature in the Nineteenth Century and Other Essays and Notes.* Boston: Stratford Company, 1918. xvii, 150 pp.
"The Influence of William Blake on William Butler Yeats," 88-95. Blake influenced Yeats's critical theories, not so much his poetry and plays.

241. CROMPTON, LOUIS WILLIAM: "Blake's Nineteenth-Century Critics," Ph.D. thesis, U of Chicago, 1954. iv, 289 pp.
"Blake and Symbolism: William Butler Yeats," 235-78.

242. DE SELINCOURT, BASIL: *William Blake.* Port Washington, N.Y.: Kennikat Press, 1972 [1909]. xi, 298 pp.
Contains a few notes on the Ellis-Yeats edition (see index).

243. DORFMAN, DEBORAH: *Blake in the Nineteenth Century: His Reputation from Gilchrist to Yeats.* New Haven: Yale UP, 1969. xv, 314 pp. (Yale Studies in English. 170.)
"The Ellis-Yeats Edition," 190-226, and passim (see index). The edition, "albeit brilliant and revolutionary, must be one of the most idiosyncratic and poorly put-together among literary critiques. It does, however, still illuminate Blake despite dense, obscure, and dubious mystical doctrine" (p. 192).

244. FITE, MONTE D.: "Yeats as an Editor of Blake: Interpretation and Emendation in *The Works of William Blake, Poetic, Symbolic, and Critical*," Ph.D. thesis, U of North Carolina at Chapel Hill, 1968. vii, 468 pp. (*DAI*, 31:1 [July 1970], 355A)

245. FLETCHER, IAN: "The Ellis-Yeats-Blake Manuscript Cluster," *BC,* 21:1 (Spring 1972), 72-94.
Description of the MSS. acquired by the University of Reading concerning the Ellis-Yeats edition, with quotations from unpublished Yeats material. A note indicates that the whole material is currently being edited for publication by Fletcher and Robert O'Driscoll. No such edition seems to have materialized so far.

246. GARDNER, CHARLES: *Vision & Vesture: A Study of William Blake in Modern Thought.* Port Washington: Kennikat Press, 1966 [1916]. xi, 226 pp.
"W. B. Yeats," 156-65, and passim (see index).

247. GENET, JACQUELINE: "Blake et Yeats: Deux modes d'approche d'une même tradition," *EI,* 8 (Dec 1983), 21-39.
Neoplatonism in Blake's "The Mental Traveller" and in Yeats's "Shepherd and Goatherd," *The Resurrection,* and *A Full Moon in March.*

248. GUTHRIE, WILLIAM NORMAN: *The Vital Study of Literature and Other Essays*. Chicago: Sergel, 1912. 380 pp.
"William Blake--Poet and Artist," 268-321; reprinted from *SR*, 5:3 (July 1897), 328-48; :4 (Oct 1897), 438-56. Comments on the Ellis-Yeats edition.

249. HÖNNIGHAUSEN, LOTHAR: "Aspekte des Blake-Verständnisses in der Ästhetik des neunzehnten Jahrhunderts," *Zeitschrift für Kunstgeschichte*, 33:1 (1970), 41-53.
"Aspects of the Blake reception in the aesthetics of the 19th century."

250. HOLMBERG, CAROL E.: "A Study of William Blake's Fourfold Perceptive Process as Interpreted by William Butler Yeats," °Ph.D. thesis, U of Minnesota, 1971. 271 pp. (*DAI*, 32:5 [Nov 1971], 2666A)

251. JAMESON, GRACE: "Irish Poets of To-day and Blake," *PMLA*, 53:2 (June 1938), 575-92.

252. KEYNES, GEOFFREY: *A Bibliography of William Blake*. NY: Grolier Club, 1921. xvi, 516 pp.
Notes on Yeats's Blake editions, pp. 275-76.

253. LISTER, RAYMOND: *Beulah to Byzantium: A Study of Parallels in the Works of W. B. Yeats, William Blake, Samuel Palmer & Edward Calvert*. No. 2 of *DPYCP*, (1965, CA20), 29-68. (Illustrated)
An expanded version of "Yeats and Edward Calvert," *IrB*, 2:3/4 (Autumn 1963), 72-80.

254. ———: "W. B. Yeats as an Editor of William Blake," *Blake Studies*, 1:2 (Spring 1969), 123-38.
As an editor, Yeats was a failure. His comments on Blake's symbolism have some value, as has his and Ellis's insistence on Blake's sanity. The real value of the edition lies in what it meant to his poetry.

255. MCCORD, JAMES: "John Butler Yeats, 'The Brotherhood,' and William Blake," *BRH*, 86:1 (Spring 1983), 10-32.
Frequent references to WBY and his Blake studies. The Brotherhood included J. T. Nettleship and Edwin J. Ellis.

256. MARGOLIOUTH, H. M.: "William Blake's Family," *N&Q*, 193:14 (10 July 1948), 296-98.
Demolishes the Ellis-Yeats theory that Blake was of Irish extraction.

257. MARVEL, LAURA: "Blake and Yeats: Visions of Apocalypse," *CollL*, 13:1 (Winter 1986), 95-105.

258. MASTERSON, DONALD, and EDWARD O'SHEA: "Code Breaking and Myth Making: The Ellis-Yeats Edition of Blake's *Works* ," *YeA*, 3 (1985), 53-80.
Discussion of the preparation undertaken by the editors, their work on Swedenborg and Boehme, and "The Two Trees" as a related poem.

259. NOYES, ALFRED: "William Blake," *BmL*, 30:180 (Sept 1906), 201-8.
Comments adversely on Yeats's use of Blake.

260. PEATTIE, R. W.: "William Michael Rossetti's Aldine Edition of

Blake," *Blake,* 12:1 (Summer 1978), 4-9.
Contains previously unpublished notes by Rossetti on Yeats's Blake projects.

261. *Perekhodnye esteticheskie i͡avlenii͡a v literaturnom prot͡sesse XVIII-XX vekov: Sbornik nauchnykh trudov.* Moskva: Moskovskiĭ ordena Lenina i ordena trudovogo krasnogo znameni gosudarstvennyĭ pedagogicheskiĭ institut imeni V. I. Lenina, 1981. 168 pp.
V. Khorol'skiĭ: "Tradit͡sii angliiskogo romantizma v mirovozzrenii i tvorcheskom metode U. B. Ĭetsa," 125-40. "Traditions of English romanticism in the world views and the creative method of WBY"; mainly on the influence of Blake and Shelley.

262. PIRKHOFER, A[NTON] M.: "Zur Bildersprache von Blake und Yeats," *Anglia,* 75:2 (1957), 224-33.
Blake's influence on the imagery of Yeats's poetry and plays.

263. QUINN, KERKER: "Blake and the New Age," *VQR,* 13:2 (Spring 1937), 271-85.

264. RAINE, KATHLEEN: *Defending Ancient Springs.* London: Oxford UP, 1967. vi, 198 pp.
Reprinted Ipswich: Golgonooza Press, 1985. "Yeats's Debt to William Blake," 66-87; reprinted from *Texas Q,* 8:4 (Winter 1965), 165-81; also in *DM,* 5:2 (Summer 1966), 27-47; reprinted in CA90. Places Yeats, Blake, and others in the tradition of the Perennial Philosophy, i.e., the Platonic and Neo-Platonic tradition of the myth and the beautiful. See index for further notes.
Reviews:
- [Peter Green]: "Unreasonable Gods," *TLS,* 11 July 1968, 717-19.
- K. P. S. Jochum, *Anglia,* 89:1 (1971), 143-45.
- Ants Oras: "Kathleen Raine: The Ancient Springs and Blake," *SR,* 80:1 (Jan-Mar 1972), 200-211.

265. ———: *Blake and Tradition.* London: Routledge & Kegan Paul, 1969. 2 vols. (A. W. Mellon Lectures in the Fine Arts. 11 [1962]. Bollingen Series. 35.)
On Yeats, 1:306-25 and passim (see index).

266. RAY, WILLIAM ERNEST: "William Blake and the Critical Development of William Butler Yeats," °Ph.D. thesis, U of North Carolina at Chapel Hill, 1971. 290 pp. (*DAI,* 32:5 [Nov 1971], 2652A)

267. ROSENFELD, ALVIN H. (ed): *William Blake: Essays for S. Foster Damon.* Providence: Brown UP, 1969. xlvi, 498 pp.
Hazard Adams: "Blake and the Postmodern," 3-17.

268. RUDD, MARGARET ELIZABETH: *Divided Image: A Study of William Blake and W. B. Yeats.* London: Routledge & Kegan Paul, 1953. xv, 239 pp.
Reprinted NY: Haskell House, 1970. Based on "William Blake and W. B. Yeats: A Study of Poetry and Mystical Vision," Ph.D. thesis, U of Reading, 1951. x, 340 pp.
Blake and Yeats are both "concerned with the drama of inner life" (p. 189). But where Blake identifies poetry with prophecy, Yeats equates it with magic. For Blake's belief Yeats substitutes vacillation. Comments on Yeats's "system" and on his poetry.
Reviews:
- Anon., *Month,* 11:2 (Feb 1954), 126-27.
- Anon., *NSt,* 4 Apr 1953, 407.

- Austin Clarke: "The Pierian Spring," *IrT*, 11 Apr 1953, 6.
- T. R. Henn, *CambR*, 74:1816 (6 June 1953), 579-80.
- Edwin Muir: "Magician or Poet," *Obs*, 22 Feb 1953, 9.
- [Arland Ussher]: "Mysticism and Magic," *TLS*, 27 Feb 1953, 138.
- Rex Warner: "Blake and Yeats," *Spect*, 3 Apr 1953, 423.

269. SCHORER, MARK: "Magic as an Instrumental Value: Blake and Yeats," *Hemispheres*, 2:5 (Spring 1945), 49-54.
The relations of both poets to the metaphysical were magical, not mystical. Neither was a visionary.

270. ———: *William Blake: The Politics of Vision*. NY: Vintage Books, 1959 [1946]. xiv, 450, xxviii pp.
Passim (see index).

271. STARLING, ROY: "The Ellis and Yeats Edition of William Blake's *Vala:* Text and Commentary," °Ph.D. thesis, Florida State U, 1981. 461 pp. (*DAI*, 42:6 [Dec 1981], 2691A; reprinted *YeA*, 2 [1983], 106)

272. STEVENSON, W. H.: "Yeats and Blake: The Use of Symbols," in Maxwell and Bushrui: *W. B. Yeats, 1865-1965* (1965, CA71), 219-25.
Both poets differ significantly in their symbolism and imagery.

273. STRELKA, JOSEPH P. (ed): *Literary Criticism and Myth*. University Park: Pennsylvania State UP, 1980. xiii, 285 pp. (Yearbook of Comparative Criticism. 9.)
Haskell M. Block: "The Myth of the Artist," 3-24; on Blake and Yeats as myth-making artists.

274. SUTTON, DOROTHY MOSELEY: "Soul Clap Its Hands and Sing: Yeats's Debt to Blake," °Ph.D. thesis, U of Kentucky, 1981. 214 pp. (*DAI*, 42:7 [Jan 1982], 3157A; reprinted *Yeats*, 1 [1983], 174-75, and *YeA*, 4 [1986], 320-21)

275. TWITCHELL, JAMES B.: "'The Mental Traveller,' Infinity, and the 'Arlington Court Picture,'" *Criticism*, 17:1 (Winter 1975), 1-14.
Contains a note on Yeats's view of Blake's poem.

276. WALTER, JAKOB: *William Blakes Nachleben in der englischen Literatur des neunzehnten und zwanzigsten Jahrhunderts*. Schaffhausen: Bachmann, 1927. ix, 100 pp. (Dr.phil. thesis, U of Zürich)
"Blake's reputation in the English literature of the 19th and 20th centuries"; on Blake and Yeats see pp. 59-95.

277. WITTREICH, JOSEPH ANTHONY (ed): *Nineteenth-Century Accounts of William Blake*. Gainesville, Fla.: Scholars' Facsimiles & Reprints, 1970. ix, 289 pp.
See pp. viii, 247-49.

See also BA14, BB155, BE108, BF129, CA12, 34, 53a, 61, 66, 90, 168, CB65, 374, CC20, 104, 117, 129, 132, 160, 168, 178, 239, 247, 264, 348, CD1, 12, 31, 38a, 43, 355, 604, 644-46, 663, DA6, DB127, DC245, 411, DD2, 128, 411, 547, 588, EC17, EE106, 290, 538, FC45a, 76, 101, FE18, 20, 26, 29, 45, 60, 109, G1164-75.

H. P. Blavatsky

278. BARRATT, GRAHAME W.: "W. B. Yeats: Defender of H. P. Blavatsky," *Prediction*, 31:8 (Aug 1965), 12-13.

279. GOLDFARB, RUSSELL M.: "Madame Blavatsky," *J of Popular Culture*, 5:3 (Winter 1971), 660-72.
Contains some references to Yeats. This is part of an "In-Depth" supplement to the journal, also published separately as: °Galbreath, Robert (ed): *The Occult: Studies and Evaluations*. Bowling Green, Ohio: Bowling Green Popular Press, 1972. 126 pp.

279a. LINVILLE, WILLIAM RAYMOND: "Helena Petrovna Blavatsky, Theosophy, and American Thought," °Ph.D. thesis, U of Hawaii, 1983. (*DAI*, 45:2 [Aug 1984], 561A)
Includes a discussion of the Yeats-Blavatsky relationship.

280. MEADE, MARION: *Madame Blavatsky: The Woman behind the Myth*. NY: Putnam, 1980. 528 pp.
See pp. 392, 400-405, 410, 421, 439.

See also BB201, 203, 224, CD1, 4, 23, 76, 78, DD123, 507, FC47, 63.

Aleksandr Blok

281. KHOROL'SKIĬ, V. V.: "Simbolizm A. Bloka i U. B. Ĭitsa (Nekotorye problemy tipologii evropeĭskogo simbolizma)," *Voprosy russkoi literatury*, 45 (1985), 90-96.
"The symbolism of Blok and WBY: Some problems of the typology of European symbolism."

282. *Poeziia A. Bloka i fol'klorno-literaturnye traditsii: Mezhvuzovskiĭ sbornik nauchnykh trudov*. Omsk: Omskiĭ gosudarstvennyĭ ordena "Znak Pocheta" Pedagogicheskiĭ Institut imeni A. M. Gor'kogo, 1984. 140 pp.
V. V. Khorol'skiĭ: "A. Blok i U. B. Ĭets: Puti simbolizma [Developments of symbolism]," 118-25; contains only a few notes on the rose symbol in Yeats's poetry.

See also CC106, DC132, EC4.

Harold Bloom

283. FITE, DAVID: *Harold Bloom: The Rhetoric of Romantic Vision*. Amherst: U of Massachusetts Press, 1985. xiv, 230 pp.
Bloom's treatment of Yeats (especially in CA12 and CC29) is discussed at length in "Yeats and the Spectre of Modernism," 35-54, and "Vision's Revision: The Anxiety of Influence," 55-90.

See also DC229.

Wilfrid Scawen Blunt

284. FINNERAN, RICHARD J.: "W. B. Yeats and Wilfrid Scawen Blunt: A Misattribution," *IUR*, 8:2 (Autumn 1978), 203-7.
The anonymous report of a visit of several poets with Blunt in *The Times* of 20 Jan 1914 was not written by Yeats but by Richard Aldington. Quotes the Yeats text in BF110.

285. LONGFORD, ELIZABETH [PAKENHAM, COUNTESS OF]: *A Pilgrimage* *of Passion: The Life of Wilfrid Scawen Blunt*. London: Weidenfeld & Nicholson, 1979. xii, 467 pp.

Several references to Yeats (see index).

See also BB76, 89, BF110, CD519.

Jacob Boehme

286. °KNEAVEL, ANN: "Affinities between William Butler Yeats and Jacob Boehme," Ph.D. thesis, U of Ottawa, 1980.

See also CD1, 66, 68, 258, EC17.

Heinrich Böll

287. MCGOWAN, MORAY: "Pale Mother, Pale Daughter? Some Reflections on Böll's Leni Gruyten and Katharina Blum," *GL&L*, 37:3 (Apr 1984), 218-28.

Comments on Böll's use of Yeats in his *Gruppenbild mit Dame* and *Die verlorene Ehre der Katharina Blum*.

Louise Bogan

288. FRANK, ELIZABETH: *Louise Bogan: A Portrait*. NY: Columbia UP, 1986. xvi, 462 pp.

Notes on Yeats's influence on Louise Bogan's poetry (see index).

289. MIDDLEBROOK, DIANE WOOD: *Worlds into Words: Understanding Modern Poems*. NY: Norton, 1980 [1978]. xvi, 139 pp.

"Liberation: Poetry of William Butler Yeats and Louise Bogan," 47-63; compares "Sailing to Byzantium" and "The Alchemist."

290. RIDGEWAY, JAQUELINE: *Louise Bogan*. Boston: Twayne, 1984. xii, 146 pp. (Twayne's United States Authors Series. 461.)

See index for a few notes on Yeats's influence.

Gordon Bottomley

291. BOTTOMLEY, GORDON: *A Stage for Poetry: My Purposes with My Plays*. Kendal: Wilson, 1948. xvi, 78 pp.

Bottomley acknowledges his indebtedness to Yeats's Nō experiments, pp. 9, 13, 20-21, 26. See also CA6.

See also ED7.

Bertolt Brecht

See DD192, EC46, 107.

C. J. Brennan

292. MEREWETHER, MARY A.: "Brennan and Yeats: An Historical Survey," *Southerly*, 37:4 (1977), 389-406.

Robert Bridges

293. BRIDGES, ROBERT, and W. B. YEATS: *The Correspondence of Robert Bridges and W. B. Yeats*. Edited by Richard J. Finneran. London: Macmillan, 1977. xviii, 68 pp.

The editor comments on the Yeats-Bridges relationship (pp. xi-xviii). The edition contains 27 letters from Bridges to Yeats (8 of them in BC1); 15 letters from Yeats to Bridges (14 of them in *Letters*, W211J/K); one letter from Yeats to Mrs. Bridges; Yeats's "Mr. Robert Bridges" (1897); a list of Yeats books in Bridges's library; and a list of Bridges books in Yeats's library.

Reviews:
- Jane Brown, *Eire*, 14:4 (Winter 1979), 153.
- Richard Ellmann: "The Centre Holds," *NSt*, 13 Jan 1978, 53-54.
- Roy Fuller: "Between Poets," *TLS*, 3 Feb 1978, 114.
- Warwick Gould: "The Poet at the Breakfast Table," *English*, 27:128-129 (Summer-Autumn 1978), 222-39.
- Iain Hamilton: "Letters between Two Poets," *Country Life*, 19 Jan 1978, 163.
- William G. Holzberger: "Remembering the Bard of Boar's Hill," *MQR*, 19:1 (Winter 1980), 117-27.
- Lynn Thiesmeyer: "The Greening of the Yeats Industry," *EIC*, 30:3 (July 1980), 256-64.

294. BRIDGES, ROBERT: *The Selected Letters of Robert Bridges with the Correspondence of Robert Bridges and Lionel Muirhead*. Edited by Donald E. Stanford. Newark: U of Delaware Press / London: Associated University Presses, 1983-84. 2 vols.

See index in vol. 2 for references and letters to Yeats. These letters are also in CD293.

295. FINNERAN, RICHARD J.: "Yeats and Bridges," *TLS*, 10 Mar 1978, 284.

Correspondence by A. A. Daryush, 14 Apr 1978, 417, on the absence of poems by Elizabeth Daryush (Bridges's daughter) from the *Oxford Book of Modern Verse*.

See also BB166, CD565.

Cleanth Brooks

296. BOVÉ, PAUL A.: "Cleanth Brooks and Modern Irony: A Kierkegaardian Critique," *Boundary 2*, 4:3 (Spring 1976), 727-59.

Discusses Brooks's treatment of Yeats.

297. SIMPSON, LEWIS P. (ed): *The Possibilities of Order: Cleanth Brooks and His Work*. Baton Rouge: Louisiana State UP, 1976. xx, 254 pp.

Robert Penn Warren: "A Conversation with Cleanth Brooks," 1-124, contains numerous references to Yeats.

298. WELLEK, RENÉ: "Cleanth Brooks: Critic of Critics," *SoR*, 10:1 (Jan 1974), 125-52.

See pp. 147-49.

Robert Browning

299. BOGERT, JUDITH B. W.: "Robert Browning's Influence upon the

Aesthetes and Decadents of the 1890's in England," Ph.D. thesis, Pennsylvania State U, 1975. iii, 221 pp. (*DAI*, 36:11 [May 1976], 7430A-31A)

"Yeats: A Dangerous Influence," 104-35.

300. FLOWERS, BETTY S.: *Browning and the Modern Tradition*. London: Macmillan, 1976. viii, 208 pp.

See index for a few notes.

301. GARRATT, ROBERT F.: "Browning's Dramatic Monologue: The Strategy of the Double Mask," *VP*, 11:2 (Summer 1973), 115-25.

Notes the parallels to Yeats's theory of the mask in *A Vision*.

302. SHMIEFSKY, MARVEL: "Yeats and Browning: The Shock of Recognition," *SEL*, 10:4 (Autumn 1970), 701-21.

Emphasizes the concept of Unity of Being.

303. WOODARD, CHARLES R.: "Browning and Three Modern Poets: Pound, Yeats, and Eliot," Ph.D. thesis, U of Tennessee, 1953. iv, 288 pp.

"Browning and William Butler Yeats," 165-217. Both poets share "prose precision," the use of colloquialisms in poetic language, the concern with syntax, and "the preoccupation with the mask."

See also CA12, CC107, CD1a, 37, 1378, DD94, 237, 572, 764, FE84.

Ferdinand Brunetière

304. BARNET, SYLVAN: "W. B. Yeats and Brunetière on Drama," *N&Q*, os 214 / ns 16:7 (July 1969), 255-56.

Some of Yeats's ideas on farce and tragedy can also be found in Brunetière.

Giordano Bruno

305. SCHRICKX, W.: "On Giordano Bruno, Wilde, and Yeats," *ES*, 45: Supplement presented to R. W. Zandvoort on the occasion of his 70th birthday (1964), 257-64.

The concept of Anima Mundi traced from Bruno to Yeats via Pater, Wilde, and Frederick York Powell.

A. H. Bullen

306. SIDGWICK, FRANK: *Frank Sidgwick's Diary and Other Material Relating to A. H. Bullen, & The Shakespeare Head Press at Stratford-upon-Avon*. Oxford: Blackwell for Shakespeare Head Press, 1975. xii, 13-90 pp.

Yeats is mentioned passim, especially in Paul Morgan: "Arthur Henry Bullen (1857-1920) and the Shakespeare Head Press," 69-85.

See also AE72.

Basil Bunting

307. TERRELL, CARROLL F. (ed): *Basil Bunting Man and Poet*. Orono, Maine: National Poetry Foundation, 1981. 442 pp.

See index for a few short notes on Yeats and Bunting.

308. WILLIAMS, JONATHAN, and TOM MEYER: "A Conversation with Basil Bunting," *St. Andrews R*, 4:2 (Spring and Summer 1977), 21-32.
Includes a few comments on Yeats.

Edmund Burke

See CA53a, 66, 118, 209, CD879, 1261-62.

Witter Bynner

309. BYNNER, WITTER: *The Works of Witter Bynner: Selected Letters.* Edited and with an introduction by James Kraft. NY: Farrar, Straus, Giroux, 1981. xxv, 275 pp.
Some references to Yeats (see index). Apparently Yeats and Bynner knew each other and exchanged letters, none of them included in this selection.

William Byrne

310. SWORDS, L. F. K.: "How to Read the Poems of William Byrne: W. B. Yeats and William Byrne," *Vexilla Regis*, 5 (1956), 104-10.
Yeats is a good poet, but so is William Byrne. (I dissent; the two examples from Byrne are not very inspiring.)

Lord Byron

311. ADAMS, HAZARD: "Byron, Yeats, and Joyce: Heroism and Technic," *SIR*, 24:3 (Autumn 1985), 399-412.

Joseph Campbell

312. CAMPBELL, JOSEPH: "Northern Autobiography," *JIL*, 8:3 (Sept 1979), 60-96.
Contains some remarks on Yeats.

See also DA22, DC71, DD544.

Stella Patrick Campbell

313. PETERS, MARGOT: *Mrs. Pat: The Life of Mrs. Patrick Campbell.* London: Bodley Head, 1984. ix, 533 pp.
The index is incomplete and omits the Yeats references. Yeats figures in chapter 26 ("1908-1909"), pp. 281-84, 497 (Mrs. Campbell as Deirdre) and pp. 292-93, 498 (on *The Player Queen*).

William Carleton

314. BOUÉ, ANDRÉ: *William Carleton, 1794-1869: Romancier irlandais.* Lille: Service de reproduction des thèses, 1973. viii, 579 pp.
Contains some notes on Carleton and Yeats (see index).

315. MONTEIRO, GEORGE: "An Unrecorded Review by Yeats," *N&Q*, os 219 / ns 21:1 (Jan 1974), 28.

A review of Carleton's *The Traits and Stories of the Irish Peasantry* in *BmNY*, 3:6 (Aug 1896), 549-50; not reprinted in *Uncollected Prose*.

316. SULLIVAN, EILEEN: "Yeats and Carleton," *Carleton Newsletter*, 5:2 (Apr 1975), 12-14.

Annotated excerpts from Yeats's letters dealing with Carleton.

317. WOLFF, ROBERT LEE: *William Carleton: Irish Peasant Novelist. A Preface to His Fiction*. NY: Garland, 1980. vii, 156 pp.

See index.

See also CC247, FB23, G1155.

Thomas Carlyle

318. JOHN, BRIAN: "Yeats and Carlyle," *N&Q*, os 215 / ns 17:12 (Dec 1970), 455.

The description of Keats in "Ego Dominus Tuus" resembles Carlyle's objections to Keats.

See also CC153, DB127, DD219, FB32, FC122.

Joyce Cary

318a. FISHER, BARBARA: *The House as a Symbol: Joyce Cary and "The Turkish House."* Amsterdam: Rodopi, 1986. vii, 241 pp. (Costerus. ns 55.)

Notes parallels between Cary and Yeats, pp. 43-45 and passim.

Sir Roger Casement

See CD763, 975, DA18, DD486-88 and note.

Baldassare Castiglione

See CA96, CC20, 130, 312, DD232, 533.

Catullus

319. O'MEARA, JOHN J.: "Yeats, Catullus, and 'The Lake Isle of Innisfree,'" *UR*, 3:8 [1966?], 15-24.

Similarities in the poetry of Catullus and Yeats.

George Chapman

320. BRADFORD, CURTIS: "W. B. Yeats: A Quotation," *N&Q*, os 201 / ns 3:10 (Oct 1956), 455.

Asks for identification of two lines of poetry in "A General Introduction for My Work." See answer by Anthony W. Shipps, os 211 / ns 13:8 (Aug 1966), 306: the source is Chapman's *The Shadow of Night*.

Alfonso Chase

321. KALINA DE PISZK, ROSA: "La paradoja como elemento unificador en *El tigre luminoso* de Alfonso Chase," *Káñina,* 7:2 (July-Dec 1983), 39-42.
Notes the influence of Yeats.

Mohini Chatterjee (or Chatterji)

See CA88, CD1, 76, 78, 80, 90, DC111, FE84.

Geoffrey Chaucer

322. BLENNER-HASSETT, ROLAND: "Yeats' Use of Chaucer," *Anglia,* 72:4 (1955), 455-62.
The concept of "Annus Mundus" or "Annus Magnus" in *A Vision* derives from Chaucer, not from Milton.

See also DB50, DD46, 460, FF16.

G. K. Chesterton

323. DERUS, DAVID L.: "Chesterton and W. B. Yeats: Vision, System and Rhetoric," *Chesterton R,* 2:2 (Spring-Summer 1976), 197-214.
The influence of Yeats's views on religion and of his system on Chesterton.

See also CD42.

John Pepper Clark

324. °ASANGA, SIGA: "Theory and Practice in the Plays of John Pepper Clark and Wole Soyinka, as Related to the Irish Dramatic Movement, 1899-1939," Ph.D. thesis, U of Ottawa, 1978.

325. MADUAKOR, OBI: "On the Poetry of War: Yeats and J. P. Clark," *African Literature Today,* 14 (1984), 68-76.
A comparison.

See also CD957.

Austin Clarke

326. [DEANE, SEAMUS]: "The Irelands of Austin Clarke," *TLS,* 1 Dec 1972, 1459-60.
Compares Yeats and Clarke.

327. HALPERN, SUSAN EVE HIRSHFELD: *Austin Clarke, His Life and Works.* Dublin: Dolmen Press, 1974. 219 pp.
See index for remarks on Yeats and Clarke.

328. IRISH UNIVERSITY REVIEW: "Austin Clarke Special Issue," *IUR,* 4:1 (Spring 1974).
Several articles with frequent references to Yeats.

329. JORDAN, JOHN: "Austin Clarke, Theodore de Banville, and Yeats," *Poetry Ireland*, 16 (Mar 1980), [3-6].
Clarke's version of Banville's *Le Baiser* (1887), called *The Kiss* (1942), reveals his attitude towards Yeats.

330. O'NEILL, CHARLES LEE: "Circumventing Yeats: Austin Clarke, Thomas Kinsella, Seamus Heaney," °Ph.D. thesis, New York U, 1987. 386 pp. (*DAI*, 48:3 [Sept 1987], 655A-56A)

331. SCHIRMER, GREGORY ALAN: *The Poetry of Austin Clarke*. Notre Dame: U of Notre Dame Press / Mountrath, Portlaoise: Dolmen Press, 1983. viii, 167 pp.
Several references to Yeats (see index).

332. TAPPING, G. CRAIG: *Austin Clarke: A Study of His Writings*. Dublin: Academy Press, 1981. 362 pp.
Frequent references to Yeats (not indexed).

See also BA10, BC1, CA55, CD105, 112, 122, 449, DB92, 95, 212, DC249, FB23.

Paul Claudel

See CD787, EA39, EC4.

Edward Clodd

333. BRENNAN, GENEVIEVE: "Yeats, Clodd, *Scatological Rites* and the Clonmel Witch Burning," *YeA*, 4 (1986), 207-15.
Yeats's reaction to one of the least palatable instances of Irish folk superstition and his contacts with the folklorist Edward Clodd.

Jean Cocteau

334. ISKANDAR, FAYEZ: "Yeats and Cocteau: Two Anti-Romanticists," *Cairo Studies in English*, 1963/66, 119-35.
Yeats's solution of the problem of modern verse drama was "aesthetic perfection," whereas Cocteau presented "a 'coarsened' version of poetry where prosaicisms contribute as much to dramatic effect as poeticisms."

S. T. Coleridge

See CA4, 103, CC69, 333, CD1009, CE204, DD44, 93, 200, 387, 393, 463, 475, 477, FC140.

Mary M. Colum

335. RIMO, PATRICIA ANN: "Mary Colum: Woman of Letters," Ph.D. thesis, U of Delaware, 1982. iv, 232 pp. (*DAI*, 43:7 [Jan 1983], 2345A-46A)
For Mary Colum's view of Yeats see chapter IV, "Creative Autobiography," 129-83.

Padraic Colum

336. BOLAND, EAVAN: "The Unknown Dimension of Padraic Colum," *IrT,* 16 Sept 1981, 12.

Colum on Yeats: "Yeats hurt me . . . he expected too much of me."

337. IRISH TIMES: "Padraic Colum 1881-1981: A Tribute to the Centenary of His Birth," *IrT,* 8 Dec 1981, 8.

Yeats is referred to passim.

338. MURPHY, ANN ADELAIDE: "Padraic Colum: A Critical Study of the Plays and Poems," Ph.D. thesis, New York U, 1980. viii, 309 pp. (*DAI,* 41:6 [Dec 1980], 2600A)

See especially "W. B. Yeats, Douglas Hyde, AE: Beginnings of the Irish Renaissance," 48-71.

See also AE15, BA10, BC1.

Norreys Connell
(i.e., Conal O'Riordan)

339. JOURNAL OF IRISH LITERATURE: "A Conal O'Riordan Number," *JIL,* 14:3 (Sept 1985).

References to Yeats in Judith O'Riordan's introduction, including a reprint of Yeats's speech preceding the performance of *The Piper* (see BF72), pp. 3-9, and in the chronology, pp. 107-13.

340. PETERSON, RICHARD F., and GARY PHILLIPS: "W. B. Yeats and Norreys Connell," *YeA,* 2 (1983), 46-58.

Yeats's involvement in the performance of Connell's *The Piper* (1907) and Connell's short tenure as managing director of the Abbey (1909).

See also BF73.

A. E. Coppard

341. SAUL, GEORGE BRANDON: "Literary Parallels: Yeats and Coppard," *N&Q,* 168:18 (4 May 1935), 314.

Two Coppard quotations originate from a phrase in *Reveries over Childhood and Youth.*

John Coulter

342. ANTHONY, GERALDINE: *John Coulter.* Boston: Twayne, 1976. 176 pp. (Twayne's World Author's Series. 400.)

See pp. 21, 23-24, 35, 38, 113, 139-40, 147.

See also BB45-46.

James H. Cousins

343. DUMBLETON, WILLIAM A.: *James Cousins.* Boston: Twayne, 1980. 145 pp. (Twayne's English Authors Series. 280.)

See index for references to Yeats.

Abraham Cowley

344. COHANE, J. J.: "Cowley and Yeats," *TLS*, 10 May 1957, 289.
A stanzaic form used by Cowley reappears in some Yeats poems.

Edward Gordon Craig

345. BABLET, DENIS: *Edward Gordon Craig*. Translated by Daphne Woodward. NY: Theatre Arts Books, 1966. ix, 207 pp.
Translation of °*Edward Gordon Craig*. Paris: L'Arche, 1962. On Craig, Yeats, and the Abbey Theatre, pp. 128-30; other references to Yeats, passim (see index).

346. CRAIG, EDWARD GORDON: *Index to the Story of My Days: Some Memoirs 1872-1907*. London: Hulton Press, 1957. vii, 308 pp.
Contains two letters from Yeats to Craig, 1901-2 (pp. 239, 242).

347. INNES, CHRISTOPHER: *Edward Gordon Craig*. Cambridge: Cambridge UP, 1983. xiv, 240 pp.
Contains a few notes on Craig and Yeats (see index).

348. THILLIEZ, CHRISTIANE: "W. B. Yeats--E. G. Craig: Autour d'une correspondance inédite," thesis, Doctorat de 3e cycle, Université de Lille III, 1977. vii, 556 pp.
Contains chapters on the life and work of Craig, Yeats's early plays (until 1901), the Craig-Yeats collaboration and Yeats's plays, 1902-1909; also an edition of Craig's letters to Yeats and vice versa, together with French translations. Illustrated.

349. ———: "L'apprentissage du théâtre," in Genet: *William Butler Yeats* (1981, CA32), 74-92.
Craig's influence on Yeats's dramatic theory and practice.

350. TOMLINSON, ALAN: "W. B. Yeats and Gordon Craig," *Ariel*, 3:3 (July 1972), 48-57.
Craig's influence on Yeats's dramatic theory and his plays.

See also AE12, BC1, BE63, 64, BF92, CA61, CD1103, EA10, 12, 25, 40, EB135, 143, 155, ED18, EE288, 291, EF90, FG3, 25, 52.

Benedetto Croce

351. TORCHIANA, DONALD T.: "Yeats and Croce," *YeA*, 4 (1986), 3-11.

See also CB546.

Aleister Crowley

352. HEIM, WILLIAM JAMES: "Aleister Crowley and W. B. Yeats: A Study in Magic and Art," Ph.D. thesis, Indiana U, 1974. iii, 145 pp. (*DAI*, 35:10 [Apr 1975], 6667A-68A)
Largely on magic and occultism, not very much on Yeats or on his relationship with Crowley.

See also BA14, BB49, 70, FC82.

Dante Alighieri

353. ELLIS, STEVE [i.e., Ellis, Stephen Paul]: *Dante and English Poetry: Shelley to T. S. Eliot.* Cambridge: Cambridge UP, 1983. viii, 280 pp.

Based on "The Poets' Dante from Shelley to T. S. Eliot," Ph.D. thesis, London U, 1981. 303 pp. Incorporates "Yeats and Dante," *CL,* 33:1 (Winter 1981), 1-17.

See "W. B. Yeats and Dante's Mask," 140-70, and passim (see index). Discusses "Ego Dominus Tuus," *Per Amica Silentia Lunae* and *A Vision* (1925). Review by John Bayley: "Power Systems," *LRB,* 15 Mar--4 Apr 1984, 10-11.

354. JOHN, ALAN ARTHUR: "Yeats and Dante," Ph.D. thesis, U of Chicago, 1981. ii, 198 pp.

355. MCDOUGAL, STUART Y. (ed): *Dante among the Moderns.* Chapel Hill: U of North Carolina Press, 1985. xiii, 175 pp.

George Bornstein: "Yeats's Romantic Dante," 11-38; reprinted from *CLQ,* 15:2 (June 1979), 93-113; incorporated in CD1a. Sees Yeats's "fascination with Dante" as part of his preoccupation with the Romantics, particularly Blake, Keats, and Shelley.

356. MELCHIORI, GIORGIO: "Yeats and Dante," *EM,* 19 (1968), 153-79.

357. SPURR, DAVID: "A Celtic *Commedia:* Dante in Yeats' Poetry," *Rackham Literary Studies,* 8 (Spring 1977), 99-116.

358. VANCE, THOMAS: "Dante, Yeats, and Unity of Being," *Shenandoah,* 17:2 (Winter 1966), 73-85.

Yeats's affinity of mind with Dante was greater than that of Eliot, Pound, or Joyce. It rests on a common "visionary structure" that Yeats called Unity of Being. Comments on "Ego Dominus Tuus," "Cuchulain Comforted," and *A Vision.*

See also CC153, CD15, 604, DD96, 218-20.

Max Dauthendey

359. LANGE, VICTOR, and HANS-GERT ROLOFF (eds): *Dichtung, Sprache, Gesellschaft.* Akten des IV. internationalen Germanisten-Kongresses 1970 in Princeton. Frankfurt/Main: Athenäum, 1971. x, 635 pp. (Beihefte zum Jahrbuch für internationale Germanistik. 1.)

O[liver] H. Edwards: "Dauthendey und Yeats: Ihre Begegnungen in den neunziger Jahren," 289-90. Summary of a lecture. See also BB52.

John Davidson

360. MCLEOD, ROBERT DUNCAN: *John Davidson: A Study in Personality.* Glasgow: Holmes, 1957. 35 pp.

See pp. 14-16.

361. TOWNSEND, JAMES BENJAMIN: *John Davidson: Poet of Armageddon.* New Haven: Yale UP, 1961. xvii, 555 pp. (Yale Studies in English. 148.)

See pp. 141-50 and passim for a comparison of Davidson's and Yeats's characters and works.

Donald Davie

362. DEKKER, GEORGE (ed): *Donald Davie and the Responsibilities of Literature*. Manchester: Carcanet Press in association with The National Poetry Foundation, Orono, Maine, 1983. vi, 153 pp.
Several references to Yeats, particularly in Bernard Bergonzi: "Davie and Pound," 31-48; Augustine Martin: "Donald Davie and Ireland," 49-63.

Thomas Osborne Davis

363. SCHILLER, JOHANNES: *Thomas Osborne Davis: Ein irischer Freiheitssänger*. Wien: Braumüller, 1915. xiv, 237 pp. (Wiener Beiträge zur englischen Philologie. 46.)
"Das Fortwirken der jungirischen (Davis'schen) Dichtung bis auf die heutige Zeit," 198-203; a short discussion of Davis's impact on later Irish poetry, contains some notes on Yeats.

See also CC355, DA11, DC71, FA35, FD41.

C. Day Lewis

364. TENNYSON, HALLAM: "Shortly before His Death C. Day Lewis Talked to Hallam Tennyson," *List*, 27 July 1972, 108-10.
Day Lewis comments on Yeats's influence on his poetry.

See also CB371, CD887.

Walter de la Mare

365. CLARKE, W. T.: "The Soul's Quest for Ideal Beauty in W. B. Yeats, Walter de la Mare, and John Masefield," *London QR*, 147 (series 5 / 33):294 (Apr 1927), 165-73.
"W. B. Yeats voices the soul's dissatisfaction with present good and present beauty, while Walter de la Mare and John Masefield treat respectively of what may be distinguished as the poetic, and the more distinctively spiritual, realizations of the quest."

366. LOGES, MARY KAISER: "The Poetry of Walter de la Mare: A Re-Evaluation," Ph.D. thesis, U of Denver, 1985. iii, 276 pp. (*DAI*, 46:11 [May 1986], 3349A)
"De la Mare and W. B. Yeats: The Symbolist Mode," 50-58, and passim.

See also DB36.

Thomas De Quincey

367. PETERFREUND, STUART: "'The Second Coming' and *Suspiria de Profundis:* Some Affinities," *AN&Q*, 15:3 (Nov 1976), 40-43.
Verbal and doctrinal parallels between De Quincey's essay and Yeats's poem.

See also DD373.

John Devoy

368. DEVOY, JOHN: *Devoy's Post Bag, 1871-1928.* Edited by William O'Brien and Desmond Ryan. Introduction by P. S. O'Hegarty. Dublin: Fallon, 1948-53. 2 vols.
Contains a short letter from Yeats to Devoy, 13 Nov 1903, 2:350-51; Yeats is also mentioned in a letter by Patrick McCartan, 2:392.

Joan Didion

369. STRANDBERG, VICTOR: "Passion and Delusion in *A Book of Common Prayer* ," *MFS,* 27:2 (Summer 1981), 225-42.
Notes Yeats's influence on Joan Didion.

John Donne

370. DUNCAN, JOSEPH ELLIS: *The Revival of Metaphysical Poetry: The History of a Style, 1800 to the Present.* Minneapolis: U of Minnesota Press, 1959. ix, 227 pp.
"Yeats, Donne and the Metaphysicals," 130-42. The affinities between Yeats's thought and the Metaphysicals, and the influence of Donne and Herbert on Yeats's poetry.

371. KUITI, CHITTARANJAN: "Beaconlight to the Modern Poet," *J of the Department of English, U of Calcutta,* 16:2 (1980-81), 20-34.
Donne's influence on Yeats's poetry.

372. MARTZ, LOUIS L.: "Donne and the Meditative Tradition," *Thought,* 34:133 (Summer 1959), 269-78.
Notes some Donne-Yeats parallels.

373. STEIN, ARNOLD: *John Donne's Lyrics: The Eloquence of Action.* Minneapolis: U of Minnesota Press, 1962. ix, 244 pp.
Some scattered notes (see index).

374. WILLY, MARGARET: "The Poetry of Donne: Its Interest and Influence Today," *E&S,* 7 (1954), 78-104.

See also CC178, CD34, 53, DC7, 345.

Edward Dowden

375. ELLIOTT, MAURICE: "Yeats and the Professors," *Ariel,* 3:3 (July 1972), 5-30.
The influence of, and relationship with, Dowden and Frederick York Powell.

376. LUDWIGSON, KATHRYN MILLER: "Transcendentalism in Edward Dowden," Ph.D. thesis, Northwestern U, 1963. 234 pp. (*DAI,* 25:1 [July 1964], 479-80)
On the Yeats-Dowden relationship and Dowden's rejection of the Irish literary revival, pp. 4-18, 174-218.

377. ———: *Edward Dowden.* NY: Twayne, 1973. 170 pp. (Twayne's English Authors Series. 148.)
"Relation to the Yeatses and Irish Literature," 43-47, "His Aloof-

ness from the Irish Literary Renaissance," 127-52, and passim.

378. MULRYNE, RONNIE: "Yeats and Edward Dowden: Critical Clinamen," *Gaéliana,* 5 (1984), 137-53.

See also CA69, CC54, 200, FE7.

Ernest Dowson

379. GAWSWORTH, JOHN: "The Dowson Legend," *EDH,* 17 (1938), 93-123.
Yeats's portrait of Dowson in *Autobiographies* is incorrect and based on rumor (pp. 101-2).

380. GOLDFARB, RUSSELL M.: "The Dowson Legend Today," *SEL,* 4:4 (Autumn 1964), 653-62.
Yeats is one of those guilty of having invented and perpetuated falsehoods about Dowson.

381. LONGAKER, MARK: *Ernest Dowson.* Philadelphia: U of Pennsylvania Press, 1967 [1945]. xv, 308 pp.
See "The Rhymers' Club," 80-110, and passim.

See also CC323, DA11.

John Dryden

382. BARNARD, JOHN: "Dryden: History and 'The Mighty Government of the Nine,'" *English,* 32:143 (Summer 1983), 129-53.
First published in *U of Leeds R,* 24 (1981), 13-42. Contains a short comparison between Dryden's "Absalom and Achitophel" and "Easter 1916."

383. SPENCER, THEODORE: *Selected Essays.* Edited by Alan C. Purves. New Brunswick: Rutgers UP, 1966. xii, 368 pp.
"Antaeus, or Poetic Language and the Actual World," 10-27; reprinted from *ELH,* 10:3 (Sept 1943), 173-92. Compares Dryden's and Yeats's use of language.
"William Butler Yeats," 308-20; reprinted from *Hound & Horn,* 7:1 (Oct-Dec 1933), 164-74. Originally a review of *Words for Music Perhaps* (W168), actually a defense of Yeats's poetry against the charges made by Yvor Winters (see CD854).

384. SWAMINATHAN, S. R.: "Virgil, Dryden, and Yeats," *N&Q,* os 217 / ns 19:9 (Sept 1972), 328-30.
Mainly on Virgil/Dryden echoes in "Two Songs from a Play."

See also CA53a.

W. E. B. Du Bois

385. SHIPLEY, W. MAURICE: "Reaching Base to Geary: Comparative Studies in the 'Dreams' of W. B. Yeats and W. E. B. Du Bois," *Crisis,* 83:733 (June-July 1976), 195-98, 200-1.
Discusses Yeats's and Du Bois's attempts "to channel the creative arts of the Irish and black people, respectively, into a more meaningful, substantially fulfilling art; an art that took its original impulse from history, legend, and myth."

Sir Charles Gavan Duffy

386. HEANEY, SEAMUS: "A Tale of Two Islands: Reflections on the Irish Literary Revival," *Irish Studies,* 1 (1980), 1-20.
Compares Yeats's "notions of an Ireland renewed through the influence of books" with those of Sir Charles Gavan Duffy and comments more generally on his role in Anglo-Irish literature.

387. PEARL, CYRIL: *The Three Lives of Gavan Duffy*. Kensington, Australia: New South Wales UP, 1979. vii, 237 pp.
See pp. 225-28.

See also CA69, CB354, 544, CD96, FD16.

Edmund Dulac

388. HOBBY, DIANA POTEAT: "William Butler Yeats and Edmund Dulac, a Correspondence: 1916-1938," Ph.D. thesis, Rice U, 1981. v, 286 pp. (*DAI,* 42:3 [Sept 1981], 1160A; reprinted *YeA,* 2 [1983], 103-4)
Prints the correspondence and other unpublished material by Yeats, Dulac, Cecil Salkeld, and others.

389. WHITE, COLIN: *Edmund Dulac*. London: Studio Vista, 1976. 208 pp.
Yeats is mentioned passim (see index), especially on pp. 81-86 (on the first performance of *At the Hawk's Well*).

See also BC1, CA61, EA25.

Lord Dunsany

390. AMORY, MARK: *Biography of Lord Dunsany*. London: Collins, 1972. 288 pp.
On the uneasy Yeats-Dunsany relationship, pp. 61-78 and passim (see index).

John Eglinton

391. BRYSON, MARY E.: "'Our One Philosophical Critic': John Eglinton," *Eire,* 10:2 (Summer 1975), 81-88.
Includes references to Yeats.

392. MCHUGH, ROGER: "Yeats and 'Our One Irish Critic,'" in Srivastava and Dutta: *Unaging Intellect* (1983, CA108), 85-88.

393. SCOTT, BONNIE K.: "John Eglinton: A Model for Joyce's Individualism," *JJQ,* 12:4 (Summer 1975), 347-57.
Includes notes on Yeats.

See also CA69, CC187, 194.

Sir Edward Elgar

394. YOUNG, PERCY MARSHALL: *Elgar O. M.: A Study of a Musician*. Revised edition. London: White Lion, 1973 [1955]. 447 pp.
On Elgar and Yeats and the music for *Diarmuid and Grania,* pp.

96-97 (for the score see HC110). Quotes a Yeats letter dated 23 March [1903].

T. S. Eliot

395. ALVAREZ, ALFRED: *The Shaping Spirit: Studies in Modern English and American Poets*. London: Chatto & Windus, 1958. 191 pp.
The American edition was published as *Stewards of Excellence: Studies in Modern English and American Poets*. NY: Scribner's, 1958.
"Eliot and Yeats: Orthodoxy and Tradition," 11-47; reprinted from *Twentieth Century*, 162:966 (Aug 1957), 149-63; :967 (Sept 1957), 224-34. "Eliot uses tradition, Yeats is in it." Eliot's poetry is intelligent, Yeats's emotional. Yeats's poetry is good despite its mythological trappings and despite *A Vision*, the early poetry is negligible, and the prose of *Autobiographies* belongs to the 19th century, whereas the poetry written at the same time belongs to the 20th. Discusses "Sailing to Byzantium."

396. BRAYBROOKE, NEVILLE (ed): *T. S. Eliot: A Symposium for His Seventieth Birthday*. London: Hart-Davis, 1958. 221 pp.
G. S. Fraser: "W. B. Yeats and T. S. Eliot," 196-216.

396a. BROOKS, HAROLD FLETCHER: *T. S. Eliot as Literary Critic*. London: Woolf, 1987. 160 pp.
Contains some notes on Yeats and Eliot (see index).

397. BROWN, CHRISTOPHER: "Eliot on Yeats: 'East Coker, II,'" *T. S. Eliot R*, 3:1&2 (1976), 22-24.

398. BUSH, RONALD: *T. S. Eliot: A Study in Character and Style*. NY: Oxford UP 1983. xvi, 287 pp.
On Yeats and Eliot, pp. 231-36 and passim.

399. CANARY, ROBERT H.: *T. S. Eliot: The Poet and His Critics*. Chicago: American Library Association, 1982. xiii, 392 pp.
Scattered remarks on what the critics said about the Yeats-Eliot relationship (see index).

400. DONOGHUE, DENIS: *A Foreign Mind: Yeats and Eliot*. Milton Keynes: Open U, 1976. Cassette and booklet. (Open University Audio Tapes. A 306. 07/08.)
"Professor Donoghue examines some of the evidence on which we might construct a view of what Eliot thought of Yeats, and Yeats of Eliot" (booklet). The cassette also includes a recording of *Purgatory*, produced by Nuala O'Faolain, spoken by Cyril Cusack and Jim Norton, introduced by Arnold Kettle (see DA17).

401. ———: "On 'Gerontion,'" *SoR*, 21:4 (Oct 1985), 934-46.
Comments on the Eliot-Yeats relationship.

402. EAGLETON, TERRY: *Exiles and Emigrés: Studies in Modern Literature*. London: Chatto & Windus, 1970. 227 pp.
Contrasts the use of myth in the poetry of Yeats and Eliot, pp. 174-77.

403. ELIOT, T. S.: "Tradition and the Practise of Poetry." Introduction and afterword by A. Walton Litz, *SoR*, 21:4 (Oct 1985), 873-88.
A lecture delivered at University College Dublin on 24 Jan 1936.

The introduction and the afterword discuss the Eliot-Yeats relationship.

403a. ———: *The Letters of T. S. Eliot*. Edited by Valerie Eliot. Volume 1: 1898-1922. London: Faber & Faber, 1988. xxxi, 639 pp.
Contains several notes on Yeats (see index), but no letters to him.

404. GARDNER, HELEN: *The Composition of "Four Quartets."* London: Faber & Faber, 1978. xiii, 239 pp.
On Eliot's use of Yeats in "Little Gidding," pp. 64-69, 186-89.

405. HOWARTH, HERBERT: *Notes on Some Figures behind T. S. Eliot*. Boston: Houghton Mifflin, 1964. xv, 396 pp.
Some notes on Yeats and Eliot, passim (see index).

406. JAY, GREGORY S.: *T. S. Eliot and the Poetics of Literary History*. Baton Rouge: Louisiana State UP, 1983. xiii, 256 pp.
Eliot's treatment of Yeats in "Little Gidding," pp. 235-41.

407. JOHNSON, MAURICE: "The Ghost of Swift in *Four Quartets*," *MLN*, 64:4 (Apr 1949), 273.
A hidden allusion to Yeats and Swift in "Little Gidding," confirmed by Eliot in a private letter.

408. KENNER, HUGH: "A Thousand Lost Golf Balls," *Notre Dame English J*, 14:3 (Summer 1982), 169-76.
Compares Yeats's and Eliot's use of myth; refers to "No Second Troy."

409. KERMODE, FRANK: "Eliot's Dream," *NSt*, 19 Feb 1965, 280-81.
Compares the later poetry of Yeats and Eliot.

410. ———: *Continuities*. London: Routledge & Kegan Paul, 1968. viii, 238 pp.
"A Babylonish Dialect," 67-77; reprinted from *SR*, 74:1 (Winter 1966), 225-37.

411. KOHLI, DEVINDRA: "Yeats and Eliot: The Magnitude of Contrast?" *Quest*, 58 (Monsoon 1968), 42-46.
The differences between the poets are great, yet they have one thing in common: their insistence on the individual's responsibility to remake his soul.

412. KOLJEVIĆ, NIKOLA: "Jejts prema Eliotu: Delimično upoređenje," *Letopis matice srpske*, year 141 / 396:1 (July 1965), 59-78.
"Y and E, a partial comparison"; compares the poetry.

413. LEAVIS, FRANK RAYMOND: *English Literature in Our Time & the University: The Clark Lectures, 1967*. London: Chatto & Windus, 1969. vii, 200 pp.
Compares Yeats and Eliot on pp. 136-37, 148; thinks that Eliot is the greater poet and deplores the fact that the academic attention has gone to Yeats. On the basis of my own experience with Yeats and Eliot bibliographies, I would submit that the last statement is statistically wrong.

414. LUCY, SEÁN: *T. S. Eliot and the Idea of Tradition*. London: Cohen & West, 1960. xiii, 222 pp.
Passim (see index).

415. MCCUTCHION, DAVID: "Yeats, Eliot and Personality," *Quest,* 50 (Monsoon 1966), 13-24.
Yeats's and Eliot's personalities and their ideas of personality compared.

416. Ó MUIRÍ, PÁDRAIG S.: "Filíocht agus reiligiún. Yeats agus Eliot: Comparáid" [Poetry and religion. . .], *Feasta,* 18:4 (July 1965), 7-9.

417. RAJAN, BALACHANDRA: *The Overwhelming Question: A Study of the Poetry of T. S. Eliot.* Toronto: U of Toronto Press, 1976. viii, 153 pp.
Numerous remarks on Yeats and Eliot (see index).

418. SCHNEIDER, ELISABETH: *T. S. Eliot: The Pattern in the Carpet.* Berkeley: U of California Press, 1975. x, 226 pp.
See index for comparisons between Yeats's and Eliot's poetry; special attention is given to "The Second Coming."

419. SELTZER, JOANNE: "The Kings of the Cats," *PRR,* 1:1 (Nov 1977), 34-38.
Discusses Eliot's Yeats lecture of 1940 (DB72).

420. SMIDT, KRISTIAN: *The Importance of Recognition: Six Chapters on T. S. Eliot.* Tromsø: Norbye, 1973. 95 pp.
"T. S. Eliot and W. B. Yeats," 81-95; revised from *RLV,* 31:6 (1965), 555-67. Both poets criticized each other; each objected to the other's style and philosophy. Discusses Yeats's influence on Eliot's poetry, plays, and criticism.

421. °SMITH, CAROL H.: *Women in Yeats and Eliot.* De Land, Fla.: Everett/Edwards, 1976. 1 cassette.

422. SMITH, GROVER: *T. S. Eliot's Poetry and Plays: A Study in Sources and Meaning.* Chicago: U of Chicago Press, 1965 [1956]. xii, 342 pp. (Phoenix Books. P54.)
Detects several Yeats echoes in Eliot's poetry (see index).

422a. TAMPLIN, RONALD: *A Preface to T. S. Eliot.* London: Longman, 1988. xii, 195 pp.
"W. B. Yeats," 87-89, and passim (see index).

423. UNGER, LEONARD: *T. S. Eliot: Moments and Patterns.* Minneapolis: U of Minnesota Press, 1966. vii, 196 pp. (Minnesota Paperbacks. MP3.)
Some notes concerning Yeats's and Eliot's poetry, passim (see index).

424. ———: *Eliot's Compound Ghost: Influence and Confluence.* University Park: Pennsylvania State UP, 1981. vii, 131 pp.
Yeats echoes in "Little Gidding," pp. 112-13.

425. VERMA, RAJENDRA: *Time and Poetry in Eliot's "Four Quartets."* Atlantic Highlands, N.J.: Humanities Press, 1979. xi, 201 pp.
Numerous references to Yeats (see index).

426. WATTS, HAROLD H.: "The Tragic Hero in Eliot and Yeats," *CentR,* 13:1 (Winter 1969), 84-100.
Discusses the "anti-anti-heroes" in Eliot's and Yeats's plays, who share an important quality: "They repudiate the world and its autocratic control over modern persons."

427. WHITE, GINA: "Modes of Being in Yeats and Eliot," *Modern Occasions,* 1:2 (Winter 1971), 227-37.
Sexuality and the self in the poetry of Yeats and Eliot.

See also AE23, CA65, 166, CB60, 190, 485, CC31, 69, 99, 168, 176, 201, 265, 278, 279, 290, 294, 319, CD7, 18, 48, 51, 59, 82, 90, 1048, DA21, DB14, 24, 172, 209, 233, 242, DC19, 20, 35, 68, 101a, 106, 118, 123, 132, 134, 192, 264, 295, 364, 417, DD113, 193, 239, 320, 371, 399, 402, 577, 601, 663, EB123, 124, 158a, EC33, EE3, 33, 361, 465, FC31a, FD19, 33, FE17, 36, 88, FG6, 9.

Euripides

428. MERRITT, ROBERT GRAY: "Euripides and Yeats: The Parallel Progression of Their Plays," Ph.D. thesis, Tulane U, 1963. ii, 181 pp. (*DAI,* 24:8 [Feb 1964], 3463)
Discusses *On Baile's Strand, The Shadowy Waters, At the Hawk's Well, Calvary, Purgatory,* and *The Resurrection.*

W. Y. Evans-Wentz

429. EVANS-WENTZ, WALTER YEELING: *The Fairy-Faith in Celtic Countries.* With a foreword by Kathleen Raine. Gerrards Cross: Smythe, 1977. xxxviii, 524 pp.
The book was originally published in 1911 and dedicated to AE and Yeats. In the foreword to the reprint (pp. xi-xx) reference is made to Yeats's influence on Evans-Wentz.

Padraic Fallon

430. HARMON, MAURICE: "The Poetry of Padraic Fallon," *Studies,* 64: 255 (Autumn 1975), 269-81.
Comments on Fallon's Yeats poems (see HD50).

431. HOWE, PARKMAN: "The Head Still Singing: The Poetry of Padraic Fallon," *Lines R,* 52/53 (May 1975), 8-21.
Discusses Yeats's influence on Fallon.

432. SIRR, PETER: "Some Distinction: Padraic Fallon's *Athenry,*" *Eire,* 20:3 (Fall 1985), 93-108.
Discusses Fallon's view of Yeats.

See also CD105, DB95.

Florence Farr

433. D'ARCH SMITH, TIMOTHY: *The Book of the Beast.* [Wellingborough?]: Crucible, 1987. 128 pp.
"Pregnant with Mandrakes: Florence Farr," 98-103; originally published as introduction to a reprint of her *Egyptian Magic.* Wellingborough: Aquarian Press, 1982. xvii, 85 pp. (pp. ix-xv).

434. JOHNSON, JOSEPHINE: *Florence Farr: Bernard Shaw's "New Woman."* Gerrards Cross: Smythe, 1975. xiv, 222 pp.
On Yeats, passim (the index is unreliable), especially on Golden Dawn involvements and "Speaking to the Psaltery" performances.

435. LAITY, CASSANDRA: "W. B. Yeats and Florence Farr: The Influence of the 'New Woman' Actress on Yeats's Changing Images of Women," *MD,* 28:4 (Dec 1985), 620-37.
See also CC180.

436. PETERS, MARGOT: *Bernard Shaw and the Actresses.* Garden City: Doubleday, 1980. xv, 461 pp.
Notes on Yeats passim, especially in connection with Florence Farr.

437. SHAW, GEORGE BERNARD, and W. B. YEATS: *Florence Farr, Bernard Shaw, W. B. Yeats: Letters.* Edited by Clifford Bax. London: Home & Van Thal, 1946 [1942]. x, 67 pp.
Reprinted °Shannon: Irish UP, 1971. xvi, 96 pp. See C. Bax: "Prefatory Note," v-vii; GBS: "An Explanatory Word from Mr. Shaw," viii-x; George Yeats: "A Foreword to the Letters of W. B. Yeats," 33-35. For reviews see G1320-1332.

438. WALL, VINCENT: *Bernard Shaw: Pygmalion to Many Players.* Ann Arbor: U of Michigan Press, 1973. xii, 171 pp.
On Florence Farr, Shaw and Yeats, pp. 52-54.

See also AE104a, BB61, BC1, CC136, CD1198a, EF90, FC17, 37, 39, 54, FE109, FF1-18 and note, G1320-32.

William Faulkner

439. BROOKS, CLEANTH: *William Faulkner: Toward Yoknapatawpha and Beyond.* New Haven: Yale UP, 1978. xviii, 445 pp.
"Faulkner and W. B. Yeats," 329-44, revised version of "William Faulkner and William Butler Yeats: Parallels and Affinities," on pp. 139-58 of George Herbert Wolfe (ed) *Faulkner: Fifty Years after "The Marble Faun."* University: U of Alabama Press, 1976. iv, 188 pp.; discusses parallels in cultural background and thematic material. See index for further references to Yeats.

440. IZUBUCHI, HIROSHI: [In Japanese] "Faulkner and Yeats--An Essay," *William Faulkner,* 4:1 (Dec 1981), 1-14; English summary, 15-16.
Points out the similarities in both writers' views of history.

See also CC155, DD113.

Frank and William Fay

See EA12, 25, EB156, EF32, 54, 55.

Sir Samuel Ferguson

441. BROWN, MALCOLM: *Sir Samuel Ferguson.* Lewisburg, Pa.: Bucknell UP, 1973. 101 pp.
Contains a few notes on Ferguson's influence on Yeats, passim.

442. CLARK, DAVID R.: "Yeats's Fishermen and Samuel Fergusons's 'Willy Gilliland,'" *Irish Studies,* 1 (1980), 73-83.
Ferguson's ballad "Willy Gilliland" influenced "The Fisherman" and "The Tower."

442a. MARTIN, AUGUSTINE: "Apocalypse Then: Pastorini, Ferguson, Mangan, Yeats," *Gaéliana*, 8 (1986), 55-62.
Contains a short note on the indebtedness of Yeats's apocalyptic imagery to Ferguson and Mangan.

443. ROCHE DOLAN, MARY: "La influencia de Sir Samuel Ferguson sobre el joven Yeats," *Miscelania,* 3 (Mar 1984), 65-76.

See also CC345, 355, CD94a, DA11, DC71, 248, DD293, 710, FA35, FE69.

George Fitzmaurice

444. CLARKE, AUSTIN: "A Spark of Genius . . . Smothered by Yeats and Lady Gregory," *IrP,* 22 May 1963, 8.
Fitzmaurice told Clarke that his play *The Linnaun Shee* (i.e., "The Fairy Lover") was a satire on Yeats. If this is the case, the satire is weak; the play seems to allude to both *The Land of Heart's Desire* and *Cathleen ni Houlihan*. It is available in vol. 1 of Fitzmaurice's *The Plays*. Dublin: Dolmen Press, 1967 (pp. 39-55).

445. CONBERE, JOHN P.: "The Obscurity of George Fitzmaurice," *Eire,* 6:1 (Spring 1971), 17-26.
Yeats rejected Fitzmaurice's play *The Dandy Dolls* either because it did not fit in his own concept of what Irish drama should be or because he felt that Fitzmaurice satirized his heroic mode.

446. COOKE, JOHN: "'Tis Mysterious Surely and Fantastic Strange: Art and Artists in Three Plays of George Fitzmaurice," *IRA,* 1 (1980), 32-55.
Includes a comparison with *The King's Threshold.*

447. COUGHLIN, MATTHEW NICHOLAS: "Birth Astride a Grave: Theme and Structure in George Fitzmaurice's Dark Comedies," Ph.D. thesis, U of Iowa, 1975. xii, 231 pp. (*DAI,* 36:8 [Feb 1976], 4859A-60A)
Compares *The Dandy Dolls* with *The Countess Cathleen,* pp. 111-14.

448. GELDERMAN, CAROL WETTLAUFER: "In Defense of George Fitzmaurice," Ph.D. thesis, Northwestern U, 1972. ii, 232 pp. (*DAI,* 33:10 [Apr 1973], 5722A)
Contains an appendix "William Butler Yeats and George Fitzmaurice," 210-23.

449. ———: *George Fitzmaurice*. Boston: Hall/Twayne, 1979. 163 pp. (Twayne's English Authors Series. 252.)
Incorporates "Austin Clarke and Yeats's Alleged Jealousy of George Fitzmaurice," *Eire,* 8:2 (Summer 1973), 62-70. See "William Butler Yeats and the Obscurity of George Fitzmaurice," 131-39, and passim. Maintains that Clarke's allegation that Yeats was jealous of Fitzmaurice's achievement is without foundation.

450. SLAUGHTER, HOWARD KEY: "Fitzmaurice and the Abbey," *ETJ,* 22:2 (May 1970), 146-54.
Comments on Yeats's unjustly low opinion of Fitzmaurice's work.

451. ———: *George Fitzmaurice and His Enchanted Land.* Dublin: Dolmen Press, 1972. 62 pp. (Irish Theatre Series. 2.)
Comments on the Yeats-Fitzmaurice relationship.

Gustave Flaubert

452. BLOCK, HASKELL M.: "Flaubert, Yeats, and the National Library," *MLN,* 67:1 (Jan 1952), 55-56.
Discusses Yeats's letter to the *Irish Times,* 8 Oct 1903 (reprinted in *Uncollected Prose,* 2:305).

453. O'CONNOR, JOHN R.: "Flaubert: *Trois Contes* and the Figure of the Double Cone," *PMLA,* 95:5 (Oct 1980), 812-26.
Notes the possible influence on Yeats's concept of interpenetrating gyres. See Richard J. Finneran: "Yeats's Sources," *PMLA,* 96:3 (May 1981), 420.

Ford Madox Ford

454. Hueffer, Ford Madox [later FORD, FORD MADOX]: *Collected Poems.* London: Goschen, 1914. 227 pp.
In the preface, Ford notes his indebtedness to Yeats and apologizes for having once thought that Yeats was merely a "literary" poet (pp. 25-27).

E. M. Forster

454a. FORSTER, EDWARD MORGAN: *Commonplace Book.* Edited by Philip Gardner. Stanford: Stanford UP, 1985. xxv, 372 pp.
Several references to Yeats (see index), especially to "The Magi" (pp. 208-9).

See also CB452.

Jeanne Robert Foster

455. Londreville [i.e., LONDRAVILLE], RICHARD: "Jeanne Robert Foster," *Eire,* 5:1 (Spring 1970), 38-44.
Preview of an edition of her papers that will include several unpublished Yeats items. The edition hasn't materialized so far.

456. MCDOWELL, EDWIN: "A New Yorker's Link with Literary Figures," *NYT,* 3 Sept 1984, 12.
Jeanne Robert Foster, John Quinn's friend, whose collection of letters, diaries, and manuscripts is now in the Rare Books and Manuscripts Division of the New York Public Library. The collection includes correspondence with Yeats.

Anatole France

457. MCNALLY, JAMES: "A Brief Confluence: Yeats and Anatole France," *Humanities in the South,* 54 (Fall 1981), 6-7.
Some images in "Sailing to Byzantium" seem to be indebted to chapter X of Anatole France's novel *Penguin Island.*

Sir James George Frazer

458. VICKERY, JOHN B.: *The Literary Impact of "The Golden Bough."* Princeton: Princeton UP, 1973. ix, 435 pp.

Incorporates "*The Golden Bough* and Modern Poetry," *JAAC*, 15:3 (Mar 1957), 271-88. "William Butler Yeats: The Tragic Hero as Dying God," 179-232, and passim (see index); particularly on the poetry. Analyzed in section DD.

See also CC4, 113, DC8.

Robert Frost

459. NITCHIE, GEORGE W.: *Human Values in the Poetry of Robert Frost: A Study of a Poet's Convictions*. Durham, N.C.: Duke UP, 1960. xiii, 242 pp.

Discusses Yeats's influence on Frost, pp. 203-13 and passim (see index).

460. PRITCHARD, WILLIAM H.: *Frost: A Literary Life Reconsidered*. NY: Oxford UP, 1984. xix, 286 pp.

See index for some notes on Yeats and Frost.

See also BB241, CD18, DC112, DD175.

Stefan George

461. VIERECK, PETER: "Context for George's 'Gleaning' and Yeats Parallels," *LitR*, 26:1 (Autumn 1982), 95-99.

Stefan George's poem "Nach der Lese" ("After the gleaning") is the German equivalent of "The Lake Isle of Innisfree."

See also DA38, FE13.

Gérard de Nerval

462. HUBERT, CLAIRE MARCOM: "The Still Point and the Turning World: A Comparison of the Myths of Gérard de Nerval and William Butler Yeats," Ph.D. thesis, Emory U, 1965. xxi, 337 pp. (*DAI*, 26:2 [Aug 1965], 1042-43)

Monk Gibbon

463. MACKENZIE, NORMAN: "The Monk Gibbon Papers," *CJIS*, 9:2 (Dec 1983), 5-24.

Comments on the Yeats-Gibbon relationship. See also BA4.

J. W. von Goethe

464. EDWARDS, OLIVER: "Aspects of Goethe's Poetry," *RLV*, 15:4 (Aug 1949), 210-21.

Contains a section "Yeats and Goethe," 219-21.

465. PERLOFF, MARJORIE: "Yeats and Goethe," *CL*, 23:2 (Spring 1971), 125-40.

466. WOOTTON, CAROL [i.e., Wootton, Alice Carolyn May]: *Selective Affinities: Comparative Essays from Goethe to Arden*. NY: Lang, 1983. 183 pp. (American University Studies. Series 3: Comparative Literature. 3.)

Based on "Goethe and Yeats: A Parallel Development towards the Whole Man," °Ph.D. thesis, U of Oregon, 1974. 120 pp. (*DAI*, 35:2 [Aug 1974], 1130A).

See "Goethe and Yeats within the Context of European Romanticism," 11-32; "The Courtly Tradition: An Aspect of the Life and Works of Goethe and W. B. Yeats," 33-59; "Goethe, Yeats and the Problem of Old Age: The Final Phase," 153-68.

See also CB546, CD66, 68, DC226, DD34.

Oliver St. John Gogarty

467. CARENS, JAMES FRANCIS: *Surpassing Wit: Oliver St. John Gogarty, His Poetry and His Prose*. NY: Columbia UP, 1979. ix, 266 pp.

Passim (see index).

468. EDWARDS, OWEN DUDLEY: "Gogarty: The Man behind the Folklore Figure," *IrT*, 20 May 1978, 9.

469. HUXLEY, DAVID JOSEPH: "A Study of the Works of Oliver St. John Gogarty," M.A. thesis, U of Sheffield, 1969. xii, 290 pp.

Contains a discussion of Yeats's estimate of Gogarty's work, and a chapter on "The Yeats Connexion."

470. ———: "Yeats and Dr. Gogarty," *Ariel*, 3:3 (July 1972), 31-47.

The influence of Gogarty's poetry on Yeats's.

471. LYONS, JOHN BENIGNUS: *Oliver St. John Gogarty*. Lewisburg, Pa.: Bucknell UP, 1976. 89 pp.

Some references to Yeats; contains Gogarty's bawdy parody of "The Pity of Love," p. 18.

472. ———: *Oliver St. John Gogarty: The Man of Many Talents. A Biography*. Dublin: Blackwater Press, 1980. 348 pp.

See index.

472a. ———: "Oliver St. John Gogarty," *Dublin Historical Record*, 38:1 (Dec 1984), 2-13.

Comments on the Yeats-Gogarty relationship.

473. O'CONNOR, ULICK: *The Times I've Seen: Oliver St. John Gogarty. A Biography*. NY: Obolensky, 1963. xiii, 365 pp.

English edition: *Oliver St. John Gogarty: A Poet and His Times*. London: Cape, 1964. 316 pp. Yeats is mentioned passim.

474. REGAN, MARY J.: "The Poetry of Oliver St. John Gogarty: A Study of the Irish and Classical Elements," °Ph.D. thesis, New York U, 1974. 288 pp. (*DAI*, 35:7 [Jan 1975], 4548A-49A)

Discusses Gogarty's affinities with and indebtedness to Yeats, according to abstract.

See also BB79-88, 120, 209, BC1, CA49, CB371, CD763, DC71, FB23, HA2.

Oliver Goldsmith

475. SWARBRICK, ANDREW (ed): *The Art of Oliver Goldsmith*. London: Vision Press / Totowa, N.J.: Barnes & Noble, 1984. 200 pp.

W. J. McCormack: "Goldsmith, Biography and the Phenomenology of Anglo-Irish Literature," 168-94; includes a discussion of Yeats's placing of Goldsmith in the Anglo-Irish tradition.

See also CA118, CD207.

Yvan Goll

476. PERKINS, VIVIEN: *Yvan Goll: An Iconographical Study of His Poetry*. Bonn: Bouvier, 1970. vi, 198 pp. (Studien zur Germanistik, Anglistik und Komparatistik. 5.)
"Esotericism in Poetry: Goll and Yeats," 163-66; a comparison.

Iseult Gonne

See AE96, CA109, DA40, DC207, DD427, 454.

Maud Gonne

477. BRADFORD, CURTIS: "Yeats and Maud Gonne," *TSLL*, 3:4 (Winter 1962), 452-74.
Maud Gonne in Yeats's life and poetry.

478. CARDOZO, NANCY: *Maud Gonne: Lucky Eyes and a High Heart*. London: Gollancz, 1979. xi, 468 pp.
American edition: °*Lucky Eyes and a High Heart: The Life of Maud Gonne*. Indianapolis: Bobbs-Merrill, 1978. Contains numerous references to Yeats (see index).
Reviews:
- Kay Boyle, *NewRep*, 28 Oct 1978, 36-38.
- Geoffrey Grigson: "The Irish Joan of Arc," *Country Life*, 22 Mar 1979, 867.
- Willis E. McNelly, *Magill's Literary Annual*, 1979, 409-13.
- Dorothy Parker: "A Terrible Beauty Is Born: Maud Gonne," *CSM*, 8 Jan 1979, B1, B7.
- William H. Pritchard: "La Belle Dame Sans Merci," *NYTBR*, 3 Dec 1978, 7, 108-9.
- Ellen Torgerson: "Yeats, Gonne: Telling the Lovers from the Love," *LA Times*, 3 Dec 1978, Book Review, 18.
- Susan Wood: "Yeats's Muse and Ireland's Mistress," *WashP*, 12 Nov 1978, Book World, E10.

479. COXHEAD, ELIZABETH: *Daughters of Erin: Five Women of the Irish Renascence*. London: Secker & Warburg, 1965. 236 pp.
Short biographies of Maud Gonne, Constance Markievicz, Sarah Purser, Sara Allgood, and Maire O'Neill. Numerous references to Yeats, passim.

480. FAGERBERG, SVEN: *Maud Gonne och myterna om kvinnan*. Linköping: Lindberg, 1978. 212 pp.
"MG and the myth of woman." Yeats figures prominently in this rather scantily documented biography.

481. JOCHUM, K. P. S.: "Maud Gonne on Synge," *Eire*, 6:4 (Winter 1971), 65-70.
Includes comments on Yeats.

482. LEVENSON, SAMUEL: *Maud Gonne*. NY: Reader's Digest Press / Crowell, 1976. xi, 436 pp.

A popular rather than a scholarly biography with few quotations identified. Frequent references to Yeats.

Reviews:
- Denis Donoghue: "The Hard Case of Yeats," *NYRB*, 26 May 1977, 3-4, 6, 8.
- Mary Ellmann: "Queen Cathleen," *New R*, 4:44 (Nov 1977), 51-52.
- Edward Engelberg: "Perspectives on Yeats," *New Boston R*, 3:2 (Fall 1977), 14-15.
- Roy Foster: "A New Woman among the Nationalists," *TLS*, 30 Sept 1977, 1112.
- Julian Moynahan: "The Poet, His Love, and His Plays," *NYTBR*, 27 Feb 1977, 8, 10.
- David C. Nimmo, *Four Decades*, Special Review Supplement (Jan 1979), 16-18.
- Conor Cruise O'Brien: "Incendiary Passions," *Obs*, 28 Aug 1977, 24.
- Frank Tuohy: "Officer Class," *NSt*, 16 Sept 1977, 374-75.
- Terence Winch: "The 'Irish Joan of Arc' and William Butler (Willie) Yeats," *WashP*, 24 Feb 1977, D5.

483. MACLIAMMÓIR, MICHÉAL: "Michéal MacLiammóir Recalls Maud Gonne MacBride," *JIL*, 6:2 (May 1977), 45-61.

Interview conducted by Conrad A. Balliet with frequent references to Yeats.

484. PRATT, LINDA RAY: "Maud Gonne: 'Strange Harmonies amid Discord,'" *Biography*, 6:3 (Summer 1983), 189-208.

Yeats's view of Maud Gonne and hers of him.

See also AE37, 104, BA3, 14, BB9, 10, 93, 142, 203, BC1, BG198, CA4, 35, 60, 109, 126, CB131, 420, CC136, 174, 181, CD63, DA3, 40, 48, DC23, 207, 227, 228, 305a, 370, 391, 403, 413, DD45, 66, 427, 454, 479, 643, 768, EA12, FB23, FC54, FD57, FE109.

Eva Gore-Booth

485. YEATS, W. B.: Letter to Eva Gore-Booth, edited with a note by Ian Fletcher, *REL*, 4:3 (July 1963), between pp. 24-25.

See also AE37, DD265a, 266 and note.

Edmund Gosse

486. THWAITE, ANN: *Edmund Gosse: A Literary Landscape 1849-1928*. London: Secker & Warburg, 1984. viii, 567 pp.

Several references to Yeats (see index).

See also AE26, FB32.

R. B. Cunninghame Graham

487. WATTS, C. T.: "A Letter from W. B. Yeats to R. B. Cunninghame Graham," *RES*, 18:71 (Aug 1967), 292-93.

Harley Granville-Barker

488. KENNEDY, DENNIS: *Granville Barker and the Dream of Theatre.* Cambridge: Cambridge UP, 1985. xiv, 231 pp.
See index for a few notes on Yeats.

See also AE100, FG3.

Robert Graves

489. [FRASER, G. S.]: "Graves, 1965," *TLS,* 7 Oct 1965, 898.
Includes a Yeats-Graves comparison.

490. GRAVES, ROBERT: *In Broken Images: Selected Letters of Robert Graves 1914-1946.* Edited, with commentary, by Paul O'Prey. London: Hutchinson, 1982. 372 pp.
Deprecatory notes on pp. 171, 262, 305-6. See also Graves's letter, "Robert Graves's Poems," *Daily Mail,* 8 Feb 1939, 10, containing the following sneer: "As for the late W. B. Yeats, . . . his father told our father some 40 years ago: 'Willie has discovered a very profitable by-path in poetry.' This remains a just criticism."

491. ———: *Between Moon and Moon: Selected Letters of Robert Graves 1946-1972.* Edited, with a commentary and notes, by Paul O'Prey. London: Hutchinson, 1984. 323 pp.
See pp. 24, 180, 193-95.

492. KEANE, PATRICK J.: *A Wild Civility: Interactions in the Poetry and Thought of Robert Graves.* Columbia: U of Missouri Press, 1980. v, 110 pp.
On Graves's views of Yeats, pp. 34-50 and passim. See review by Donald E. Stanford, *YeA,* 1 (1982), 237-43.

493. *On Poets & Poetry: Second Series.* Salzburg: Institut für Anglistik und Amerikanistik, Universität Salzburg, 1980. i, 101 pp. (Salzburg Studies in English Literature: Poetic Drama & Poetic Theory. 27.)
Anita Weinzinger: "Graves's Criticism of Contemporary Poets," 49-101; contains a discussion of Graves's views of Yeats, pp. 67-73.

494. SEYMOUR-SMITH, MARTIN: *Robert Graves: His Life and Work.* London: Hutchinson, 1982. xiv, 608 pp.
Discusses Graves's aversion to Yeats on pp. 250-52, 324-25 and passim (see index).

495. WILSON, COLIN: "Some Notes on Graves's Prose," *Shenandoah,* 13:2 (Winter 1962), 55-62.
Largely on the question of why Graves doesn't like Yeats.

See also CD563, DB103, DC264, DD380.

John Gray

496. MCCORMACK, M. JERUSHA: "The Person in Question: John Gray. A Critical and Biographical Study," Ph.D. thesis, Brandeis U, 1973. vi, 276 pp. (*DAI,* 34:7 [Jan 1974], 4211A-12A)
Contains a few references to Yeats.

Lady Gregory

497. ADAMS, HAZARD: *Lady Gregory*. Lewisburg: Bucknell UP, 1973. 106 pp.
On Yeats, passim.

498. CHISLETT, WILLIAM: *Moderns and Near-Moderns: Essays on Henry James, Stockton, Shaw, and Others*. NY: Grafton Press, 1928. 226 pp.
"On the Influence of Lady Gregory on William Butler Yeats," 165-67.

499. [CLARKE, AUSTIN]: "Lady Gregory, the Abbey, Yeats, Moore, Synge," *TLS*, 16 July 1970, 761-62.

500. COXHEAD, ELIZABETH: *Lady Gregory: A Literary Portrait*. 2nd edition, revised and enlarged. London: Secker & Warburg, 1966 [1961]. xii, 227 pp.
Chapter 7, "Collaboration--Yeats," 98-107, attempts to disprove two attacks on Lady Gregory's reputation: "that she interfered with and spoilt Yeats's plays, and that he really wrote the best of hers." The one play that was certainly written by both, *The Unicorn from the Stars*, has its best parts in what must be credited to her. Criticizes Yeats for not doing Lady Gregory justice in his *Dramatis Personae*.

501. ———: "The Lifelong Friendship: Yeats and Lady Gregory," *IrT*, 10 June 1965, vi.

502. DALMASSO, MICHÈLE: *Lady Gregory et la renaissance irlandaise*. Aix-en-Provence: Université de Provence, 1982. iv, 691 pp.
Numerous references to Yeats (see index).

503. DEDIO, ANNE: *Das dramatische Werk von Lady Gregory*. Bern: Francke, 1967. 135 pp. (Cooper Monographs. 13.)
Contains some material on Yeats's theatrical activities, and a note on parallels between Lady Gregory's and Yeats's plays.

504. FITZGERALD, MARY MARGARET. "The Dominant Partnership: W. B. Yeats and Lady Gregory in the Early Irish Theatre," Ph.D. thesis, Princeton U, 1973. xiii, 259 pp. (*DAI*, 34:4 [Oct 1973], 2066A)
Based on the unpublished Lady Gregory papers in the Berg Collection; discusses the efforts of Yeats and Lady Gregory to found and maintain a theater in Dublin and their collaboration in play writing.

505. GREGORY, LADY ISABELLA AUGUSTA: "The Letters of Lady Gregory to John Quinn." Edited by Daniel Joseph Murphy. Editor's Ph.D. thesis, Columbia U, 1961. vii, 237 pp. (*DAI*, 22:9 [Mar 1962], 3204)
Letters written between 1906 and 1924, several of them dealing with Yeats.

506. ———: "Letters from Lady Gregory: A Record of Her Friendship with T. J. Kiernan." Edited by Daniel J. Murphy, *BNYPL*, 71:10 (Dec 1967), 621-61; 72:1 (Jan 1968), 19-63; :2 (Feb 1968), 123-31.
Letters written between 1924 and 1932, some of them concerning Yeats and Abbey affairs.

507. ———: *Cuchulain of Muirthemne: The Story of the Men of the Red Branch of Ulster Arranged and Put into English*. With a preface by W. B. Yeats and a foreword by Daniel Murphy. Gerrards Cross:

Smythe, 1970. 272 pp. (Coole Edition of the Works of Lady Gregory. 2.)

The "Foreword," 7-10, contains references to Yeats.

508. ———: *The Translations and Adaptations and Her Collaborations with Douglas Hyde and W. B. Yeats: Being the Fourth Volume of the Collected Plays*. Edited and with a foreword by Ann Saddlemyer. Gerrards Cross: Smythe, 1971. xix, 376 pp. (Coole Edition of the Works of Lady Gregory. 8.)

"Foreword," vii-xii, contains notes on the collaboration with Yeats in *The Unicorn from the Stars* and *Heads or Harps*.

509. ———: *Poets and Dreamers*. Studies and translations from the Irish by Lady Gregory including nine plays by Douglas Hyde. With a foreword by T. R. Henn. Gerrards Cross: Smythe, 1974. 287 pp. (Coole Edition of the Works of Lady Gregory. 11.)

Henn's "Foreword," 5-10, refers to Yeats passim. See also "A Red-Letter Day in Killeenan," 248-50; reprinted from the *Tuam News*, 31 Aug 1900 (a description of a "concourse" in honor of Raftery, which included a speech by Yeats).

510. ———: *Selected Plays of Lady Gregory*. Chosen and with an introduction by Mary FitzGerald. Gerrards Cross: Smythe / Washington, D.C.: Catholic U of America Press, 1983. 377 pp. (Irish Drama Selections. 3.)

"Introduction," 11-19, on the Yeats--Lady Gregory collaboration.

511. KOHFELDT, MARY LOU: *Lady Gregory: The Woman behind the Irish Renaissance*. London: Deutsch, 1985. xiii, 367 pp.

Based on Mary Lou Kohfeldt Stevenson: "Lady Gregory: A Character Study," Ph.D. thesis, U of North Carolina at Chapel Hill, 1977. xiv, 295 pp. (*DAI*, 38:6 [Dec 1977], 3490A-91A); incorporates Mary Lou Stevenson: "Lady Gregory and Yeats: Symbiotic Creativity," *JRUL*, 40:2 (Dec 1978), 63-77. Yeats figures prominently in a book remarkable for its rather gushy style.

Reviews:

- James F. Carens, *Yeats*, 5 (1987), 235-43.
- Roy Foster: "Sacrifice and Inspiration," *TLS*, 12 July 1985, 778.
- David Krause: "No Justice to Lady Gregory," *ILS*, 4:2 (Fall 1985), 28-29.
- James Pethica, *YeA*, 5 (1987), 257-60.

512. KOPPER, EDWARD A.: *Lady Isabella Persse Gregory*. Boston: Twayne, 1976. 160 pp. (Twayne's English Authors Series. 194.)

Frequent references to Yeats.

513. MIKHAIL, EDWARD HALIM (ed): *Lady Gregory: Interviews and Recollections*. London: Macmillan, 1977. xii, 113 pp.

Reprinted pieces; Yeats is referred to passim.

514. MIZEJEWSKI, LINDA: "Patriarchy and the Female in Lady Gregory's *Grania*," *Eire*, 22:1 (Spring 1987), 122-38.

Frequent references to Yeats.

515. MONTGOMERY, BENILDE: "The Presence of Parnell in Three Plays by Lady Gregory," *IRA*, 3 (1982), 106-23.

Includes some notes on Yeats.

516. MURPHY, DANIEL J.: "Yeats and Lady Gregory: A Unique Dramatic Collaboration," *MD*, 7:3 (Dec 1964), 322-28.

517. SADDLEMYER, ANN: *In Defence of Lady Gregory, Playwright.* Dublin: Dolmen Press, 1966. 131 pp.
Includes notes on the Yeats-Lady Gregory relationship.

518. ———: "Image-Maker for Ireland: Augusta, Lady Gregory," in Skelton and Saddlemyer: *The World of W. B. Yeats* (1967, CA102), 161-68.

519. ———, and COLIN SMYTHE (eds): *Lady Gregory Fifty Years After.* Gerrards Cross: Smythe / Totowa, N.J.: Barnes & Noble, 1987. xiv, 464 pp. (Irish Literary Studies. 13.)
Numerous references to Yeats, especially in the following: Colin Smythe: "Chronology," 1-12.
Gabriel Fallon: Extracts from an unpublished history of the Abbey Theatre, 30-34.
Elizabeth Longford: "Lady Gregory and Wilfrid Scawen Blunt," 85-97; also on the Blunt-Yeats relationship.
Gareth W. Dunleavy: "The Pattern of Three Threads: The Hyde-Gregory Friendship," 131-42.
Maureen Murphy: "Lady Gregory and the Gaelic League," 143-62.
John Kelly: "'Friendship Is the Only House I Have': Lady Gregory and W. B. Yeats," 179-257; also on the Yeats-Robert Gregory relationship, and the Gregory and Coole Park poems.
Robert Welch: "A Language for Healing," 258-73 (the Irish language).
Colin Smythe: "Lady Gregory's Contributions to Periodicals: A Checklist," 322-45; includes the collaborations with Yeats.
Richard Allen Cave: "Robert Gregory: Artist and Stage Designer," 347-400; includes comments on Gregory's designs for Yeats's plays, i.e., *On Baile's Strand, Deirdre,* and *The Hour-Glass.*

520. SMYTHE, COLIN: *A Guide to Coole Park, Co. Galway, Home of Lady Gregory.* With a foreword by Anne Gregory. Revised edition. Gerrards Cross: Smythe, 1983 [1973]. 72 pp.
Numerous references to Yeats, including photographs and a reproduction of his pastel of Lady Gregory's house.

521. SZEKERESSNÉ FLACHNER, MARGIT MÁRIA: *Lady Augusta Gregory az ir nemzeti szinpad megalapítása.* Doktori értekezés. Budapest: Országos központi községi nyomda r.-t., 1931. 64 pp. (A Kir. Magyar pázmány Péter Tudományegyetem. Angol philologiai intézetének kiadványai. 7.)
"Lady Gregory and the foundation of the Irish national theater"; Yeats is referred to passim.

522. THUENTE, MARY HELEN: "Lady Gregory and 'The Book of the People,'" *Eire,* 15:1 (Spring 1980), 86-99.
Lady Gregory as folklorist, includes some remarks on Yeats.

523. YEATS, W. B.: "Some New Letters from W. B. Yeats to Lady Gregory." Edited by Donald T. Torchiana and Glenn O'Malley, *REL,* 4:3 (July 1963), 9-47.

See also AC64, AE24, 37, 73, 92-94, 100, BB97, 98, 100, 155, 170, BF162, CA4, 53a, 93, 96, 109, 112, 118, 126, CB258, 337, 371, 403, CC49, 130, 136, 174, CD584, 724, 1082, 1280, DC10, 207, 391, 413, DD437, EA12, 25, EE74, 161, 196, 538, EF32, 39, 97, FA11, 25, 85, 86, FE29, FG51.

Robert Gregory

524. SMYTHE, COLIN (ed): *Robert Gregory 1881-1918: A Centenary Tribute with a Foreword by His Children*. Gerrards Cross: Smythe, 1981. 40 pp.

See also AE37, CA53a, 112, 118, CC168, CD519, DC135, 261, 386, DD267-70 and note, 276-83 and note, 483-84 and note.

Arthur Griffith

525. Ó LÚING, SEÁN: *Art Ó Gríofa*. Dublin: Sáirséal agus Dill, 1953. 430 pp.

"Art Ó Gríofa, J. M. Synge agus W. B. Yeats," 144-50, and passim on Griffith and Yeats (see index).

See also BB43, EE55, FD24.

Ivor Gurney

526. GURNEY, IVOR: *War Letters*. A selection edited by R. K. R. Thornton. Manchester: Mid Northumberland Arts Group / Carcanet New Press, 1983. 271 pp.

Several references to Yeats (see index). See also HC136.

Althea Gyles

527. HOLAHAN, MARY F.: "Althea Gyles: Visions of the Celtic Twilight," Ph.D. thesis, U of Delaware, 1978. x, 169 pp. and illustrations on pp. 170-211. (*DAI*, 36:4 [Oct 1978], 1892A)

"William Butler Yeats: Mysticism, Symbolism, and the Occult" and "Gyles' Designs for William Butler Yeats and Oscar Wilde," 75-102, and passim.

See also BB70, CB160, CC66.

Hagiwara

528. TSUKIMURA, REIKO: "The Language of Symbolism in Yeats and Hagiwara," Ph.D. thesis, Indiana U, 1967. vii, 207 pp. (*DAI*, 28:9 [Mar 1968], 3689A)

A. H. Hallam

529. FRIEDMAN, NORMAN: "Hallam on Tennyson: An Early Aesthetic Doctrine and Modernism," *SLitI*, 8:2 (Fall 1975), 37-62.

Hallam's ideas on the uniqueness of poetry as an art were recognized and taken up by Yeats in his criticism and poetry.

See also FE17, 29, 84.

Thomas Hardy

530. ALEXANDER, EDWARD: "*Fin de Siècle, Fin du Globe:* Yeats and

Hardy in the Nineties," *BuR*, 23:2 (Fall 1977), 142-63.
As poets "in transition from Victorianism to modernism" Hardy and Yeats reacted differently to 19th-century ideas.

531. BAWER, BRUCE: "Two on a Tower: Hardy and Yeats," *YER*, 7:1&2 (June 1982), 91-108.
On the similarities rather than differences between both poets.

532. BROOKS, JEAN R.: *Thomas Hardy: The Poetic Structure*. London: Elek, 1971. 336 pp.
Includes a short comparison between Yeats and Hardy as poets writing about old age, pp. 77-79.

533. DAVIE, DONALD: *Thomas Hardy and British Poetry*. London: Routledge & Kegan Paul, 1973. viii, 192 pp.
Several notes comparing Hardy and Yeats, passim (see index). See also the anonymous review, "The Choice of Yeats or Hardy," *TLS*, 13 July 1973, 793-94, which refers to the influence of Yeats on Philip Larkin. The review was written by Clive James and is reprinted in his *At the Pillars of Hercules*. London: Faber & Faber, 1979. 224 pp. ("Yeats *v*. Hardy in Davie's Larkin," 64-70).

534. Hueffer, Ford Madox [later FORD, FORD MADOX]: "The Poet's Eye. III," *New Freewoman*, 1:7 (15 Sept 1913), 126-27.
Compares the poetry of Yeats and Hardy.

535. HARDY, THOMAS: *The Collected Letters of Thomas Hardy*. Edited by Richard Little Purdy and Michael Millgate. Oxford: Clarendon Press, 1978-88. 7 vols.
See vol. 4, 1909-1913 (1984) for references to Yeats in letters to Lady Gregory; one about the fairy poetry (p. 37), and one in connection with the Civil List pension (p. 113); on Yeats's visit to present Hardy with a medal (pp. 216-18).
Vol. 5, 1914-1919 (1985), contains a reference to "The Lake Isle of Innisfree," p. 151.
For further notes on Yeats see index in vol. 7.

536. HEPBURN, JAMES: *Critic into Anti-Critic*. Columbia, S.C.: Camden House, 1984. xi, 238 pp. (Studies in English and American Literature, Linguistics, and Culture. 3.)
"Leda and the Dumbledore," 115-24; reprinted from *SR*, 88:1 (Winter 1980), 52-66; compares Yeats and Hardy, particularly "Leda and the Swan" and "An August Midnight."

537. HOFFPAUIR, RICHARD: "Yeats or Hardy?" *SoR*, 19:3 (Summer 1983), 519-47.
"Too many poets have taken their cue from W. B. Yeats and too few from Thomas Hardy."

538. SHANKS, EDWARD: "The Nobel Prize: Mr. Yeats's Award and the Case of Mr. Thomas Hardy," *Evening Standard*, 20 Nov 1923, 7.
Hardy should have received the prize to satisfy British hopes.

See also BB167, CA53a, CB3, 302, CC14a, CD37, CE99, DB233, DC192, 394.

Wilson Harris

539. WALSH, WILLIAM (ed): *Readings in Commonwealth Literature*.

Oxford: Clarendon Press, 1973. xxi, 448 pp.
W. J. Howard: "Wilson Harris's *Guiana Quartet:* From Personal Myth to National Identity," 314-28; notes the influence of Yeats.

Robert Hayden

540. BLOUNT, MARCELLUS: "A Dialogue of Poets: The Syndesis of W. B. Yeats and Robert Hayden," *Obsidian,* 8:1 (Spring 1981 [i.e., 1982]), 27-41.

541. HATCHER, JOHN: *From the Auroral Darkness: The Life and Poetry of Robert Hayden.* Oxford: Ronald, 1984. xii, 342 pp.
See index for some references to Yeats's influence.

542. O'SULLIVAN, MAURICE J.: "The Mask of Allusion in Robert Hayden's 'The Diver,'" *CLAJ,* 17:1 (Sept 1973), 85-92.
Discusses the Yeats allusions.

543. WILLIAMS, PONTHEOLLA TAYLOR: *Robert Hayden: A Critical Analysis of His Poetry.* Urbana: U of Illinois Press, 1987. xviii, 243 pp.
See index for notes on Yeats's influence.

Seamus Heaney

544. COBB, ANN VALENTINE: "Seamus Heaney: Poet in a Destitute Time," °Ph.D. thesis, Tufts U, 1986. 107 pp. (*DAI,* 47:10 [Apr 1987], 3761A)
Discusses the influence of Yeats, according to abstract.

545. CORCORAN, NEIL: *Seamus Heaney.* London: Faber & Faber, 1986. 192 pp.
See index for several references to Yeats.

546. HEANEY, SEAMUS: "A Raindrop on a Thorn: An Interview with Seamus Heaney," *DQR,* 9:1 (1979), 24-37.
Interview conducted by Robert Druce, with comments on Yeats.

547. OPPEL, HORST: *Die Suche nach Irlands Vergangenheit und einer anglo-irischen Dichtersprache in Seamus Heaneys "North."* Wiesbaden: Steiner, 1979. 37 pp. (Akademie der Wissenschaften und der Literatur Mainz: Abhandlungen der geistes- und sozialwissenschaftlichen Klasse. Jahrgang 1979, Nr. 1.)
"The search for Ireland's past and for an Anglo-Irish poetic language. . . ," includes frequent comparisons with Yeats.

548. STALLWORTHY, JON: "The Poet as Archaeologist: W. B. Yeats and Seamus Heaney," *RES,* 33:130 (May 1982), 158-74.

548a. TAPSCOTT, STEPHEN: "Poetry and Trouble: Seamus Heaney's Irish Purgatorio," *SWR,* 71:4 (Autumn 1986), 519-35.
Discusses Yeats's influence.

See also CB194, CD112, 330, 1455, DB92, 95, DC14a, 195.

William Heffernan

549. NASH, NANCY RUTKOWSKI: "Yeats and Heffernan the Blind," *YeA,* 4 (1986), 201-6.

Henry von Heiseler

550. GRONICKA, ANDRÉ VON: *Henry von Heiseler: A Russo-German Writer*. NY: King's Crown Press, 1944. ix, 224 pp. (Columbia University Germanic Studies. ns 16.)

See index for notes on Heiseler's indebtedness to Yeats and his translations of Yeats's plays. See also EG28 and 72.

See also CD68, EE124.

W. E. Henley

551. ALEXANDER, JULIA ANN: "William Ernest Henley, Editor: *The National Observer*, the *Magazine of Art*, and the *New Review*," Ph.D. thesis, U of Texas at Austin, 1974. ix, 320 pp. (*DAI*, 35:8 [Feb 1975], 5334A)

"The Case against Henley (Yeats, Shaw, Meynell)," 234-58, discusses Henley's revisions or non-revisions of Yeats's contributions to these reviews.

552. FLORA, JOSEPH M.: *William Ernest Henley*. NY: Twayne, 1970. 171 pp. (Twayne's English Authors Series. 107.)

Scattered notes on Yeats and Henley, passim (see index).

553. GUILLAUME, ANDRÉ: *William Ernest Henley et son groupe: Néo-romantisme et impérialisme à la fin du XIXe siècle*. Paris: Klincksieck, 1973. 467 pp.

On Henley and Yeats passim (see index).

See also BG194.

George Herbert

554. MCFARLAND, RONALD E.: "George Herbert and Yeats's 'Sailing to Byzantium,'" *Four Decades*, 1:1 (Jan 1976), 51-53.

Stanza III of Yeats's poem is indebted to Herbert's sonnet "Love (II)."

See also CD370.

Hermann Hesse

555. COLLINS, ROBERT A., and HOWARD D. PEARCE (eds): *The Scope of the Fantastic: Culture, Biography, Themes, Children's Literature. Selected Essays from the First International Conference on the Fantastic in Literature and Film*. Westport, Ct.: Greenwood Press, 1985. xii, 284 pp. (Contributions to the Study of Science Fiction and Fantasy. 11.)

Bradford Crain: "Masks, Mirrors, and Magic: Fantasy as Autobiography in the Works of Hesse and Yeats," 91-97.

F. R. Higgins

556. BYRNE, J. PATRICK: "Manager of the Abbey: The Late F. R. Higgins," *Accent*, 2:2 (Winter 1942), 92-94.

Suggests that Yeats's later ballads were influenced by Higgins.

557. CLARKE, R. DARDIS: "In Quest of an Abbey Managing Director," *IrT,* 12 Jan 1982, 8.

558. [O'FAOLAIN, SEAN]: "Frederick Robert Higgins (1897-1941)," *Bell,* 1:5 (Feb 1941), 53-55.
Higgins's poetry compared with Yeats's.

See also BB209, DB95.

Geoffrey Hill

559. HART, HENRY: *The Poetry of Geoffrey Hill.* Carbondale: Southern Illinois UP, 1986. xiv, 306 pp.
Numerous remarks on Hill and Yeats (see index).

560. SHERRY, VINCENT: *The Uncommon Tongue: The Poetry and Criticism of Geoffrey Hill.* Ann Arbor: U of Michigan Press, 1987. xi, 274 pp.
See index for some notes on Hill and Yeats.

See also DC14a.

Jack Hodgins

561. HORNER, JAN C.: "Irish & Biblical Myth in Jack Hodgins' *The Invention of the World*," *CanL,* 99 (Winter 1983), 6-18.
Notes the allusions to "Under Ben Bulben."

Hugo von Hofmannsthal

562. HAMBURGER, MICHAEL: *Hugo von Hofmannsthal: Zwei Studien.* Göttingen: Sachse & Pohl, 1964. 134 pp. (Schriften zur Literatur. 6.)
See "Gedichte und kleine Dramen," 11-62, for some comparisons of Yeats's and Hofmannsthal's plays. First published on pp. xiii-lxiii of Hofmannsthal's *Poems and Verse Plays.* Edited and introduced by Michael Hamburger. With a preface by T. S. Eliot. NY: Pantheon Books, 1961. lxiii, 562 pp. (Bollingen Series. 33:2.). Eliot's "Preface" (pp. xi-xii) also refers to Yeats's verse plays.

See also CC28, CD68, DC167, 270a, EC4.

Homer

See CA53a, CD876, DD447.

A. D. Hope

563. HOPE, A. D.: "Coming to Grips with Proteus," *YeA,* 4 (1986), 161-71.
Hope on his relationship to Yeats and on his Yeats poems (here reprinted). One of them, "The Spectre of W. B. Yeats to Robert Graves," is on Graves's mistreatment of Yeats. See also HD75-77.

564. ———: "Daytime Thoughts about the Night Shift: Alec Hope Talks to Peter Kuch and Paul Kavanagh," *Southerly,* 46:2 (1986), 221-31.
Hope comments on Yeats's influence.

Gerard Manley Hopkins

565. ABAD GARCÍA, MARIA PILAR: "G. M. Hopkins y W. B. Yeats escriben a Robert Bridges," *ES* [Valladolid], 13 (Sept 1983), 133-84.
Discusses the Yeats-Bridges and Yeats-Hopkins relationships.

566. EMMONS, JEANNE CARTER: "Hopkins and Yeats: Pre-Raphaelite Influence and Poetic Experience," *Hopkins Q,* 8:2 (Summer 1981), 75-83.

567. GILES, RICHARD F. (ed): *Hopkins among the Poets: Studies in Modern Responses to Gerard Manley Hopkins.* Hamilton, Ont.: International Hopkins Association, 1985. viii, 128 pp. (International Hopkins Association Monograph Series. 3.)
Norman H. MacKenzie: "Yeats and Hopkins," 7-11.

568. HOWARTH, R. G.: "Yeats and Hopkins," *N&Q,* 188:10 (19 May 1945), 202-4.
Yeats's indebtedness to Hopkins's "sprung rhythm."

569. WASWO, RICHARD (ed): *On Poetry and Poetics.* Tübingen: Narr, 1985. 212 pp. (SPELL: Swiss Papers in English Language and Literature. 2.)
Gregory T. Polletta: "Hopkins and Modern Poetics," 63-91; includes some notes comparing the poetry of Hopkins and Yeats.

See also BA4, CB403, CD37, 710, DB115, 165, DC21, 68, 88, EE389.

Herbert Horne

570. KERMODE, FRANK: *Forms of Attention.* Chicago: U of Chicago Press, 1985. xv, 93 pp.
"Botticelli Recovered," 2-31, contains some remarks on Herbert Horne and Yeats.

See also CD811.

A. E. F. Horniman

571. FLANNERY, JAMES W.: *Miss Annie F. Horniman and the Abbey Theatre.* Dublin: Dolmen Press, 1970. 40 pp. (Irish Theatre Series. 3.)
Miss Horniman's interest in the Abbey was doubly motivated; by her emotional attachment to Yeats and by her desire to have "an instrument for the expression of her personal artistic ambitions" (p. 14).

572. GREENWICH THEATRE, LONDON: *A Festival for Miss Horniman: April-July 1978.* [London: Greenwich Theatre, 1978. 20 pp.]
Leaflet describing the program, including frequent references to Yeats. Part of the program was *The Golden Cradle*, an evening with plays by Synge, Lady Gregory, as well as Yeats's *The Cat and the Moon, Purgatory,* and *The Pot of Broth;* see *Cue*, 53 (June 1978).

573. MALINS, EDWARD: "Annie Horniman, Practical Idealist," *CJIS,* 3:2 (Nov 1977), 18-26.
Contains some notes on Yeats.

See also BC1, BG181, EA12, 25, EF32, FC39, 54.

W. T. Horton

574. FINNERAN, RICHARD J., and GEORGE MILLS HARPER: "'He Loved Strange Thought': W. B. Yeats and William Thomas Horton," in Harper: *Yeats and the Occult* (1975, FC40), 190-223.

575. GRABSKA, ELŻBIETA (ed): *Moderniści o sztuce: Wybrała, opracowała i wstępem opatrzyla E. G.* Warszawa: Państwowe Wydawnictwo Naukowe, 1971. 556 pp.

"Wstęp do *Księgi obrazów* W. T. Hortona [1898]," 300-9; a translation by Róża Jabłkowska of Yeats's introduction to Horton's *A Book of Images* (Wade 255), together with notes (see index).

576. HARPER, GEORGE MILLS: *W. B. Yeats and W. T. Horton: The Record of an Occult Friendship*. London: Macmillan, 1980. x, 160 pp.

Traces the biographical connections and occult interests of Yeats and Horton, prints all of Horton's 33 surviving letters to Yeats, and summarizes or prints 86 Yeats letters to Horton.

Reviews:

- Jacqueline Genet: "Yeatsiana," *EI*, 6 (Dec 1981), 246-48.
- F. S. L. Lyons: "Beware the Dark Horse," *TLS*, 13 Feb 1981, 160.
- Elizabeth Mackenzie, *N&Q*, os 228 / ns 30:1 (Feb 1983), 90-92.
- Andrew Parkin, *CJIS*, 10:1 (June 1984), 147-51.
- Rory Ryan, *UES*, 19:2 (Sept 1981), 47-48.
- Ann Saddlemyer, *YeA*, 2 (1983), 138-40.
- Michael Sidnell, *DR*, 61:4 (Winter 1981/82), 752-54.
- Henry Summerfield, *YER*, 8:1&2 (1986), 139-40.

See also BC1, CA61, CD43, 635.

Ted Hughes

577. FAAS, EKBERT: *Ted Hughes: The Unaccommodated Universe*. With selected writings by Ted Hughes & two interviews. Santa Barbara: Black Sparrow Press, 1980. 229 pp.

In the interviews Hughes refers repeatedly to Yeats.

578. HIRSCHBERG, STUART: *Myth in the Poetry of Ted Hughes: A Guide to the Poems*. Dublin: Wolfhound Press, 1981. 239 pp.

On Yeats echoes in Hughes's poetry, pp. 140-41.

T. E. Hulme

See CC168, 277, DC299, FF17.

Douglas Hyde

579. DALY, DOMINIC: *The Young Douglas Hyde: The Dawn of the Irish Revolution and Renaissance, 1874-1893*. Foreword by Erskine Childers. Dublin: Irish UP, 1974. xix, 232 pp.

Quotes extensively from Hyde's unpublished journals, which contain frequent references to Yeats.

580. DUNLEAVY, GARETH W.: *Douglas Hyde*. Lewisburg, Pa.: Bucknell UP, 1974. 92 pp.

Yeats is referred to passim.

581. HYDE, DOUGLAS: *Abhráin Grádh Chúige Connacht. Love Songs of Connacht.* Being the fourth chapter of *The Songs of Connacht.* Introduction by Micheál Ó hAodha. Shannon: Irish UP, 1969. x, viii, 158 pp.

Reprint of the 1893 edition with a short new introduction in which Ó hAodha establishes the connections with Yeats (pp. v-x).

582. MCMAHON, SEÁN: "*Casadh an tSugáin:* The First Irish Play," *Eire,* 12:4 (Winter 1977), 73-85.

583. ———: "Art and Life Blended: Douglas Hyde and the Literary Revival," *Eire,* 14:3 (Fall 1979), 112-25.

584. THOMAS, W. C. ELVET: *Balchder Erin.* Abertawe [Swansea]: Davies, 1978. 155 pp.

Contains chapters (in Welsh) on Hyde, Lady Gregory, and Synge (pp. 66-94), with frequent references to Yeats.

585. WELCH, ROBERT: *A History of Verse Translation from the Irish 1789-1897.* Gerrards Cross: Smythe / Totowa, N.J.: Barnes & Noble, 1988. xi, 200 pp. (Irish Literary Studies. 24.)

Some references to Yeats, especially in the chapter on Hyde, which was first published as "Douglas Hyde and His Translations of Gaelic Verse," *Studies,* 64:255 (Autumn 1975), 243-57.

See also AE23, BA22, BC1, BF16, CA69, 153, CB241, 371, CD519, DC248, EE518, FA57, FD16, FE109.

Henrik Ibsen

586. ASOCIACIÓN ESPAÑOLA DE ESTUDIOS ANGLO-NORTEAMERICANOS: *Homenaje a Esteban Pujals Fontrodona.* Oviedo: Servicio de Publicaciones, Universidad de Oviedo, 1981. Unpaged.

Ramón Sainero Sánchez: "Ibsen y el movimiento literario irlandés," no. 20; contains some notes on Yeats.

587. FOX, R. M.: "Ibsen and Yeats: Pioneers of National Drama," *Aryan Path,* 26:4 (Apr 1955), 154-58.

Biographical parallels rather than influences.

See also CB276, 546, EA12, EB140, EE538, FG2, 7.

Michio Ito

588. CALDWELL, HELEN: *Michio Ito: The Dancer and His Dances.* Berkeley: U of California Press, 1977. xi, 184 pp. (Illustrated)

On Yeats and Ito passim (see index); on *At the Hawk's Well,* pp. 37-54.

589. CARRUTHERS, IAN: "A Translation of Fifteen Pages of Ito Michio's Autobiography *Utsukushiku naru Kyoshitsu* ," *CJIS,* 2:1 (May 1976), 32-43.

On Pound, Yeats, and the performance of *At the Hawk's Well.*

See also CA150.

Randall Jarrell

590. JARRELL, RANDALL: *Randall Jarrell's Letters: An Autobiographical and Literary Selection.* Edited by Mary Jarrell. Boston: Houghton Mifflin, 1985. xix, 540 pp.
Several references to Yeats (see index).

Robinson Jeffers

591. BENNETT, MELBA BERRY: *The Stone Mason of Tor House: The Life and Work of Robinson Jeffers.* Los Angeles: Ward Ritchie Press, 1966. xvi, 264 pp.
Several notes on Jeffers and Yeats (see index).

See also CD18, DB14.

Juan Ramón Jiménez

592. CARILLA, EMILIO: "Juan Ramón Jiménez y William Butler Yeats," *A la luz,* 12-13 (1980-81), 18-24.
Compares "A Coat" with "Vino, primero, pura."

593. COKE-ENGUIDANOS, MERVYN: "Juan Ramón en su contexto esteticista, romántico y modernista," *Cuadernos hispanoamericanos,* 376-378 (Oct-Dec 1981), 532-46.
The influence of Yeats on Juan Ramón Jiménez.

594. GICOVATE, BERNARDO: *La poesía de Juan Ramón Jiménez: Obra en marcha.* Esplugues de Llobregat: Ariel, 1973. 241 pp.
Some notes on Yeats and Jiménez, pp. 134-42, and passim.

595. JOHNSON, R[OBERT]: "Juan Ramón Jiménez, Rabindranath Tagore, and 'La poesía desnuda,'" *MLR,* 60:4 (Oct 1965), 534-46.
Notes Yeats's influence on Jiménez.

596. PATTON, KATHRYN HART: "The Evolution of the Rose: From Form to Flame," *U of Mississippi Studies in English,* 12 (1971), 65-78.
The rose symbol in the poetry of Yeats and Jiménez.

597. PEREZ ROMERO, CARMEN: *Juan Ramón Jiménez y la poesía anglosajona.* Cáceres: Universidad de Extremadura, Seminario da Critica Literaria, 1981. 176 pp. (Colección El Criticón. 1.)
"El simbolismo de W. B. Yeats y su incidencia en la poesía juanramoniana," 119-22; "Cotejo de 'A Coat' y 'Vino, primero, pura,'" 123-39; "'La Rosa' en W. B. Yeats y en Juan Ramón Jiménez," 141-63 (the rose image); "Traducciones de Yeats," 165-70.

598. WILCOX, JOHN CHAPMAN: "W. B. Yeats and Juan Ramón Jiménez: A Study of Influence and Similarities and a Comparison of the Themes of Death, Love, Poetics, and the Quest for Fulfilment in Time," Ph.D. thesis, U of Texas at Austin, 1976. xiv, 476 pp. (*DAI,* 37:8 [Feb 1977], 5114A)

599. ———: "Enticing Yeats to Spain: Zenobia and Juan Ramón Jiménez," *YER,* 5:2 (1978), 5-13.

600. ———: "William Butler Yeats: Un 'lírico del Norte' en la poesía de Juan Ramón Jiménez," *Insula,* 36:416-417 (July-Aug 1981), 8.

601. ———: "'Naked' versus 'Pure' Poetry in Juan Ramón Jiménez, with Remarks on the Impact of W. B. Yeats," *Hispania*, 66:4 (Dec 1983), 511-21.

Comments on "A Coat" and "Crazy Jane Talks with the Bishop."

602. ———: *Self and Image in Juan Ramón Jiménez: Modern and Post-Modern Readings*. Urbana: U of Illinois Press, 1987. xvii, 207 pp.

See index for a few notes on Yeats.

603. YOUNG, HOWARD T.: *The Line in the Margin: Juan Ramón Jiménez and His Readings in Blake, Shelley, and Yeats*. Madison: U of Wisconsin Press, 1980. xxiii, 295 pp.

"Yeats," 109-61, and passim. "It is clear that during one of the most active and fruitful intervals of Juan Ramón's life Yeats was the English-language poet uppermost in his mind" (p. 118).

Reviews:

- Michael André Bernstein, *YeA*, 2 (1983), 136-37.
- Richard A. Cardwell, *Hispanic R*, 51:1 (Winter 1983), 115-17.
- Carl W. Cobb, *Anales de la literatura española contemporánea*, 6 (1981), 354-56.
- John P. Devlin, *Bulletin of Hispanic Studies*, 60:1 (Jan 1983), 77-78.
- Dario Fernández-Morera, *CRCL*, 11:2 (June 1984), 317-19.
- Armando Miguelez, *Revista de estudios hispánicos*, 17:2 (May 1983), 304-6.
- Paul R. Olson, *CL*, 37:4 (Autumn 1985), 378-79.
- John C. Wilcox, *MLN*, 96:2 (Mar 1981), 457-59.
- ———, *Blake*, 16:4 (Spring 1983), 235-39.

See also DC262, DD75.

Joachim of Fiore

604. REEVES, MARJORIE, and WARWICK GOULD: *Joachim of Fiore and the Myth of the Eternal Evangel in the Nineteenth Century*. Oxford: Clarendon Press, 1987. x, 365 pp.

"W. B. Yeats: A Noble Antinomianism," 202-71; especially on "The Tables of the Law," *Where There Is Nothing, The Unicorn from the Stars,* and *A Vision,* also on Yeats's indebtedness to Blake, Dante, Lionel Johnson, Nietzsche, and Ernest Renan.

"A Note on James Joyce and Joachim," 271-78; on Joyce's indebtedness to "The Tables of the Law."

Reviewed by George M. Harper, *SoAR*, 52:4 (Nov 1987), 131-35.

See also EE490.

Augustus John

605. HOLROYD, MICHAEL: *Augustus John: A Biography*. London: Heinemann, 1974-75. 2 vols.

"Images of Yeats," 1:259-63; see also indexes in both volumes.

See also BB87, BG113.

Lionel Johnson

606. CLIFTON, GERALD KENT: "'Lost in Light': A Study of Lionel Johnson's Poetry," Ph.D. thesis, U of California, Irvine, 1978. ix, 269 pp. (*DAI*, 39:4 [Oct 1978], 2252A-53A)
See particularly pp. 5-20.

607. °LHENRY-EVANS, ODETTE: "Lionel Johnson 1867-1902: Étude biographique et critique," thesis, Doctorat de l'Université, U of Lille, 1964. 315 pp.

608. MILLAR, DAVID HASWELL: "Lionel Johnson, 1867-1902: A Biographical and Critical Study," M.A. thesis, Queen's U, Belfast, 1947. iv, 228 pp.
See pp. 47-82 and passim for a discussion of literary and biographical relations between Johnson and Yeats (via the Rhymers' Club and the Irish literary revival).

609. PATRICK, ARTHUR W.: *Lionel Johnson (1867-1902), poète et critique*. Paris: Rodstein, 1939. 254 pp.
"La renaissance littéraire irlandaise," 53-64; notes Yeats's influence on Johnson.

610. ROGERS, JOHN ELTON: "Lionel Johnson: A Reassessment of His Work," M.A. thesis, U of Manchester, 1967. ii, 281 pp.
Contains a chapter on "Johnson, the Celt," 228-68, and numerous references to Yeats.

See also AE24, 37, BC3, CA69, CB321, CC109, CD604, 983, 1440, DA11, FA13, 24, 91, HD83.

Denis Johnston

611. DODD, PHILIP (ed): *Modern Selves: Essays on Modern British and American Autobiography*. London: Cass, 1986. vii, 192 pp.
Shirley Neuman: "Autobiography, Epistemology and the Irish Tradition: The Example of Denis Johnston," 118-38; contains some references to Yeats.

612. FERRAR, HAROLD: *Denis Johnston's Irish Theatre*. Dublin: Dolmen Press, 1973. 144 pp. (Irish Theatre Series. 5.)
See especially "Introduction," 7-18.

613. HENDERSON, GORDON: "An Interview with Denis Johnston," *JIL*, 2:2&3 (May-Sept 1973), 31-44.
Includes comments on Yeats.

614. RONSLEY, JOSEPH (ed): *Denis Johnston: A Retrospective*. Gerrards Cross: Smythe, 1981. xii, 276 pp. (Irish Literary Studies. 8.)
See especially Christine St. Peter: "*The Old Lady:* In Principio," 10-23; D. E. S. Maxwell: "Waiting for Emmet," 24-37.

615. ST. PETER, MARY CHRISTINE: "Denis Johnston's *The Old Lady Says "No!"*: The Gloriable Nationvoice," Ph.D. thesis, U of Toronto, 1979. vii, 302 pp. (*DAI*, 40:12 [June 1980], 6295A)
Contains some references to Yeats.

616. ———: "Denis Johnston, the Abbey and the Spirit of the Age," *IUR*, 17:2 (Autumn 1987), 187-206.

Discusses the troubled Yeats-Johnston relationship.

See also CD1115.

LeRoi Jones (Imamu Amiri Baraka)

617. BENSTON, KIMBERLY W.: *Baraka: The Renegade and the Mask.* New Haven: Yale UP, 1976. xxi, 290 pp.
Compares Yeats's Crazy Jane poems with LeRoi Jones's Crow Jane poems, pp. 116-19.

Ben Jonson

618. COLBERT, JUDITH A.: "Masks of Ben Jonson in W. B. Yeats's *The Green Helmet* and *Responsibilities*," *CJIS*, 7:1 (June 1981), 32-48.
"Jonson's importance for Yeats [was] . . . that he offered masks for the poet as craftsman and as social satirist and idealist, . . . allowing him to make his earliest and most radical escape from the mannerisms of the nineties."

619. DONALDSON, IAN: "Volpone," *EIC*, 22:2 (Apr 1972), 216-18.
On Yeats and Jonson.

620. NICHOLS, JOHN GORDON: *The Poetry of Ben Jonson.* London: Routledge & Kegan Paul, 1969. x, 177 pp.
"Jonson and Yeats," 161-62.

See also CC130, CD34, 39, DB133a.

James Joyce

621. ATHERTON, JAMES S.: *The Books at the Wake: A Study of Literary Allusions in James Joyce's "Finnegans Wake."* London: Faber & Faber, 1959. 308 pp.
Note on Yeats allusions, p. 290, and passim (see index).

622. BATES, RONALD, and HARRY J. POLLOCK (eds): *Litters from Aloft.* Papers delivered at the second Canadian James Joyce Seminar, McMaster University. Tulsa: U of Tulsa, 1971. ix, 111 pp. (U of Tulsa Department of English Monograph Series. 13.)
M. J. Sidnell: "A Daintical Pair of Accomplasses: Joyce and Yeats," 50-73. Mainly on parallel motives in "The Wanderings of Oisin" and *Finnegans Wake*.

623. BEJA, MORRIS, PHILLIP HERRING, MAURICE HARMON, and DAVID NORRIS (eds): *James Joyce: The Centennial Symposium.* Urbana: U of Illinois Press, 1986. xvii, 234 pp.
Ellen Carol Jones (ed): "Yeats and Joyce," 21-30. Transcription of a panel discussion between A. Walton Litz, Giorgio Melchiori (who comments on the tower image of both writers), and Richard Ellmann.

624. BOLDEREFF, FRANCES MOTZ: *Reading Finnegans Wake.* Woodward, Pa.: Classic Nonfiction Library, 1959. xxii, 210; x, 285 pp.
On Yeats's influence, especially that of *A Vision:* 1:59-60, 63-66, 69, 74-80, 82-83, 101-3, 108, 122, 126, 128, 130, 132-33, 135, 139, 141-47, 153, 162; 2:54, 74, 82, 247, 280. Rather eccentric.

625. ———: *Hermes to His Son Thoth: Being Joyce's Use of Giordano Bruno in Finnegans Wake.* Woodward, Pa.: Classic Nonfiction Library, 1968. 289 pp.
Claims that Yeats preceded Joyce insofar as his "living delicate response to the times [he] lived in characterizes the genuinely creative spirit." Quotes in support Yeats's "The Adoration of the Magi" (pp. 232, 244-50).

626. BOWEN, ZACK, and JAMES F. CARENS (eds): *A Companion to Joyce Studies.* Westport, Ct.: Greenwood Press, 1984. xiv, 818 pp.
On the Joyce-Yeats relationship, pp. 54-57, and passim (see index).

627. BRAY, PAUL LYONS: "The Influence of Theories of History on the Style of James Joyce's *Finnegans Wake*," °Ph.D. thesis, City U of New York, 1986. 321 pp. (*DAI*, 47:3 [Sept 1986], 907A)
Includes a discussion of Yeats's theory of history.

628. BRIVIC, SHELDON: "The Mind Factory: Kabbalah in *Finnegans Wake*," *JJQ*, 21:1 (Fall 1983), 7-30.
Notes correspondences with Phase 22 of *A Vision*.

629. BUSHRUI, SUHEIL BADI, and BERNARD BENSTOCK (eds): *James Joyce: An International Perspective.* Gerrards Cross: Smythe / Totowa, N.J.: Barnes & Noble, 1982. xiii, 301 pp. (Irish Literary Studies. 10.)
Vivian Mercier: "John Eglinton as Socrates: A Study of 'Scylla and Charybdis,'" 65-81; and Ann Saddlemyer: "James Joyce and the Irish Dramatic Movement," 190-212, contain some notes on Yeats. See also the index for further Yeats references.

630. CAHILL, KEVIN M. (ed): *The American Irish Revival: A Decade of "The Recorder"--1974-1983.* Port Washington, N.Y.: Associated Faculty Press, 1984. xxiii, 807 pp.
Pieces reprinted from *The Recorder* (published by the American Irish Historical Society, NY).
Contains: Kevin Sullivan: "James Joyce and Anglo-Ireland," 81-91, reprinted from 43 (1982), 24-34; Narayan Hegde: "Yeats, India and Long Island," 145-52, reprinted from 41 (1980), 86-93 (on Yeats's interest in India and on the Yeats archives at SUNY, Stonybrook).

631. CARVER, CRAIG MURRAY: "The Esoteric Joyce," Ph.D. thesis, U of Wisconsin, Madison, 1978. vii, 307 pp. (*DAI*, 39:9 [Mar 1979], 5500A)
Contains a chapter on the influence of *A Vision;* Yeats is also mentioned passim. See the same author's "James Joyce and the Theory of Magic," *JJQ*, 15:3 (Spring 1978), 201-14.

632. COLLINS, BEN L.: "Joyce's Use of Yeats and of Irish History: A Reading of 'A Mother,'" *Eire*, 5:1 (Spring 1970), 45-66.
Joyce uses *Cathleen ni Houlihan* satirically.

633. CURRAN, CONSTANTINE PETER: *James Joyce Remembered.* [Foreword by Padraic Colum]. NY: Oxford UP, 1968. x, 129 pp.
On Joyce and Yeats, passim.

634. DAVIES, STAN GÉBLER: *James Joyce: A Portrait of the Artist.* London: Davis-Poynter, 1975. 328 pp.
Some notes on Yeats and Joyce (see index).

635. DAY, ROBERT ADAMS: "How Stephen Wrote His Vampire Poem," *JJQ*, 17:2 (Winter 1980), 183-97.
Contains remarks on Joyce's use of Yeats. Correspondence by Richard J. Finneran, *JJQ*, 18:2 (Winter 1981), 221 (Yeats and W. T. Horton).

636. DEMING, ROBERT H. (ed): *James Joyce: The Critical Heritage*. London: Routledge & Kegan Paul, 1970. 2 vols.
Reprinted items; Yeats is referred to passim (see index).

637. DUNCAN, EDWARD: "James Joyce & the Primitive Celtic Church," *Alphabet*, 7 (Dec 1963), 17-38.
On *The Tables of the Law* and *Stephen Hero*, pp. 21-25.

638. ELLMANN, RICHARD: "Joyce and Yeats," *KR*, 12:4 (Autumn 1950), 618-38.

639. ———: *James Joyce*. New and revised edition. NY: Oxford UP, 1982 [1959]. xviii, 887 pp.
On Joyce and Yeats passim (see index).

640. ———: *Ulysses on the Liffey*. London: Faber & Faber, 1972. xviii, 208 pp.
Yeats is mentioned passim (see index).

641. ———: *The Consciousness of Joyce*. London: Faber & Faber, 1977. ix, 150 pp.
See index for notes on Joyce and Yeats.

642. FACKLER, HERBERT V.: "Stephen Dedalus Rejects Forgotten Beauty: A Yeats Allusion in *A Portrait of the Artist as a Young Man*," *CLAJ*, 12:2 (Dec 1968), 164-67.
An allusion to "He Remembers Forgotten Beauty," which reveals the difference between Joyce/Stephen and Yeats/Robartes in artistic and Irish matters.

643. FUEGER, WILHELM: "Forerunners," *WN*, 12:1 (Feb 1975), 16.
A Vision, Nietzsche, and *Finnegans Wake*.

644. GANDOLFO, ANITA MARIE: "Every Man's Wisdom: Literary Affiliation among Blake, Yeats, and Joyce," Ph.D. thesis, City U of New York, 1977. iv, 328 pp. (*DAI*, 38:3 [Sept 1977], 1408A)
A study "of the transmission of ideas" from Blake to Yeats and Joyce.

645. ———: "This Is Doubbllinnbbayyates: A Further Blake-Joyce Note," *WN*, 14:5 (Oct 1977), 77-79.

646. ———: "Whose Blake Did Joyce Know and What Difference Does It Make?" *JJQ*, 15:3 (Spring 1978), 215-21.
"Yeats is the only *single* source for all of Joyce's allusions to Blake."

647. GECKLE, GEORGE L.: "Stephen Dedalus and W. B. Yeats: The Making of the Villanelle," *MFS*, 15:1 (Spring 1969), 87-96.
The villanelle is indebted to "He Remembers Forgotten Beauty," the aesthetic theory to Yeats's essay "The Symbolism of Poetry."

648. GIFFORD, DON: *Joyce Annotated: Notes for "Dubliners" and "A Portrait of the Artist as a Young Man."* Second edition, revised and

enlarged. Berkeley: U of California Press, 1982. ix, 308 pp.
Numerous references to Yeats (see index). The first edition was published as °*Notes for Joyce: "Dubliners" and "A Portrait of the Artist as a Young Man."* NY: Dutton, 1967.

649. ———, and ROBERT J. SEIDMAN: *Notes for Joyce: An Annotation of James Joyce's "Ulysses."* NY: Dutton, 1974. xiv, 554 pp.
See index for allusions to Yeats.

650. GLASHEEN, ADALINE: *Third Census of Finnegans Wake: An Index of the Characters and Their Roles.* Revised and expanded from the *Second Census* [1963]. Berkeley: U of California Press, 1977. lxxxiv, 314 pp.
Index of Yeats in *Finnegans Wake,* p. 313. "His use in FW is vast and needs study."

651. ———: "Joyce and Yeats," *WN,* ns 4:1 (Feb 1967), 30.
Explains six Yeats allusions in *Finnegans Wake.*

652. ———: "The Yeats Letters and *FW*," *WN,* ns 10:5 (Oct 1973), 76.
Verbal parallels (some of them tenuous) between some Yeats letters and *Finnegans Wake.*

653. GOZZI, FRANCESCO: *La poesia di James Joyce.* Bari: Adriatica Editrice, 1974. 225 pp. (Biblioteca di studi inglesi. 28.)
Contains notes on the influence of Yeats's poetry on Joyce's.

653a. HARKNESS, MARGUERITE: *The Aesthetics of Dedalus and Bloom.* Lewisburg: Bucknell UP, 1984. 212 pp.
See index for numerous references to Yeats, especially to his aestheticism and to "The Symbolism of Poetry."

654. HART, CLIVE: *Structure and Motif in "Finnegans Wake."* London: Faber & Faber, 1962. 271 pp.
Notes on Yeats's influence, particularly that of *A Vision,* passim (see index).

655. HODGART, MATTHEW: *James Joyce: A Student's Guide.* London: Routledge & Kegan Paul, 1978. viii, 196 pp.
See index for references to Yeats.

656. HUDDLESTON, SISLEY: *Bohemian Literary and Social Life in Paris: Salons, Cafés, Studios.* London: Harrap, 1928. 451 pp.
The anecdote of Joyce saying to Yeats: "You are too old to be influenced by me," pp. 263-64. See also CD671.

657. IRISH TIMES: "James Joyce: A Special Supplement of the *Irish Times,*" *IrT,* 2 Feb 1982. 8 pp.
See particularly Micheál Ó hAodha: "The Would-Be Playwright," 8.

658. JACQUET, CLAUDE: "Joyce," in Genet: *William Butler Yeats* (1981, CA32), 412-24.
Joyce's use of *A Vision* in *Finnegans Wake.*

659. JOYCE, JAMES: *Chamber Music.* Edited with an introduction and notes by William York Tindall. NY: Columbia UP, 1954. vii, 236 pp.
Passim (see index).

660. ———: *The Critical Writings*. Edited by Ellsworth Mason and Richard Ellmann. NY: Viking Press, 1964 [1959]. 288 pp. (Viking Compass Book. C145.)

Passim (see index), especially in the following pieces: "The Day of the Rabblement," 68-72; first published in F. J. C. Skeffington and James A. Joyce: *Two Essays*. Dublin: Gerrard, [1901]. 8 pp. (pp. 7-8), an onslaught on the Irish Literary Theatre for surrendering to the "popular will."

"The Holy Office," 149-52; reprinted from a °broadside published 1904/5 (?). Contains a parody of "To Ireland in the Coming Times."

661. ———: *A Portrait of the Artist as a Young Man*. Text, criticism, and notes edited by Chester G. Anderson. NY: Viking Press, 1968. vi, 570 pp.

See p. 541 for an index of the references to *The Countess Cathleen* and p. 549 for those to Michael Robartes.

662. JOYCE, STANISLAUS: *My Brother's Keeper*. Edited with an introduction by Richard Ellmann, with a preface by T. S. Eliot. London: Faber & Faber, 1958. 258 pp.

On Yeats and Joyce, pp. 182-85, 206-7, and passim (see index). Extract reprinted in BA13, 1:24-27.

663. KEANE, PATRICK J.: "Time's Ruins and the Mansions of Eternity or, Golgonooza and Jerusalem, Yes; Bloomusalem and Beulah, No; Ithaca, Yes and No: Another Joyce-Blake Parallel at the End of Bloomsday," *BRH*, 86:1 (Spring 1983), 33-66.

Notes that Joyce's knowledge of Blake was based on the Ellis-Yeats edition.

664. KENNER, HUGH: *Dublin's Joyce*. London: Chatto & Windus, 1955. xii, 372 pp.

See especially "Yeats and *Chamber Music*," 39-41 (a comparison of Yeats's and Joyce's poetry); "Yeats as Tragic Hero," 45-46; "Yeats, Dedalus, and Mr. Duffy," 46-48 (Mr. Duffy of "A Painful Case"); pp. 158-61 on the influence of *The Tables of the Law* and *The Adoration of the Magi*.

665. KENNY, THOMAS JOSEPH: "His Plagiarist Pen: James Joyce's Marginal Markings in the Books of His Personal Library," Ph.D. thesis, New York U, 1975. v, 386 pp. (*DAI*, 36:6 [Dec 1975], 3690A-91A)

References to books by Yeats on pp. 59-64 and 173-75.

666. KLEINSTÜCK, JOHANNES: *Die Erfindung der Realität: Studien zur Geschichte und Kritik des Realismus*. Stuttgart: Klett-Cotta, 1980. 160 pp.

"Joyce and Yeats," 113-33; on the differences between Joyce's and Yeats's kind of realism.

667. LYONS, F. S. L.: "James Joyce's Dublin," *Twentieth-Century Studies*, 4 (Nov 1970), 6-25.

The literary, social, and political Irish background of Joyce's early career. Yeats is mentioned passim.

668. MACCABE, COLIN (ed): *James Joyce: New Perspectives*. Brighton: Harvester Press, 1982. xiv, 198 pp.

Seamus Deane: "Joyce and Nationalism," 168-83; compares Yeats's and Joyce's views on nationalism.

669. MCCARTHY, PATRICK A.: "Joyce's *Finnegans Wake,* 3.18-21," *Expl,* 43:3 (Spring 1985), 26-28.
Yeats's advice to Synge to visit the Aran Islands.

670. MCCORMACK, WILLIAM J., and ALISTAIR STEAD (eds): *James Joyce and Modern Literature.* London: Routledge & Kegan Paul, 1982. xiii, 222 pp.
W. J. McCormack: "Nightmares of History: James Joyce and the Phenomenon of Anglo-Irish Literature," 77-107.

671. MCGREEVY, THOMAS: "James Joyce," *TLS,* 25 Jan 1941, 43-44.
Denies, on the authority of both Yeats and Joyce, that Joyce said, "You are too old to be influenced by me." See also CD656.

672. MAGALANER, MARVIN, and RICHARD MORGAN KAIN: *Joyce: The Man, the Work, the Reputation.* NY: New York UP, 1956. xiv, 377 pp.
On Yeats and Joyce, pp. 68-70 and passim (see index).

673. MOORE, JOHN REES: "Artifices for Eternity: Joyce and Yeats," *Eire,* 3:4 (Winter 1968), 66-73.

674. *Nordic Rejoycings 1982--In Commemoration of the Centenary of the Birth of James Joyce.* S.l.: James Joyce Society of Sweden and Finland, [1982]. 148 pp.
Apparently edited by Johannes Hedberg. See Birgit Bramsbäck: "Allusions to Yeats in *Stephen Hero* and *A Portrait of the Artist as a Young Man*," 9-25.

675. O'HANLON, JOHN, and DANIS ROSE: "Specific Use of Yeats's *A Vision* in *Finnegans Wake* ," *WN,* 16:3 (June 1979), 35-44.

676. OWENS, COILIN DON: "*Dubliners* and the Irish Tradition," Ph.D. thesis, Kent State U, 1975. iv, 320 pp. (*DAI,* 36:6 [Dec 1975], 3698A-99A)
Notes the allusions to Yeats.

677. PARRINDER, PATRICK: "Joyce-sur-mer," *CVE,* 23 (Apr 1986), 87-97.
Notes that Joyce "found precedents for some of his sea-imagery" in poems by Yeats.

678. POWER, ARTHUR: *Conversations with James Joyce.* Edited by Clive Hart. London: Millington, 1974. 111 pp.
See p. 93.

679. SCHENONI, LUIGI: "Some Comments upon Joyce's Meeting with Yeats," *WN,* 14:2 (Apr 1977), 31-32.

680. SCHOLES, ROBERT: "James Joyce, Irish Poet," *JJQ,* 2:4 (Summer 1965), 255-70.
Compares Joyce's poems "Tilly" and "Ecce Puer" with Yeats's "The Dedication to a Book of Stories Selected from the Irish Novelists" and "A Cradle Song," respectively.

681. ———, and RICHARD M. KAIN (eds): *The Workshop of Daedalus: James Joyce and the Raw Materials for "A Portrait of the Artist as a Young Man."* Evanston: Northwestern UP, 1965. xiv, 287 pp.
See index for notes on Yeats.

682. SCOTT, BONNIE KIME: "James Joyce in His Irish Milieu," Ph.D. thesis, U of North Carolina at Chapel Hill, 1973. vii, 416 pp. (*DAI,*

34:9 [Mar 1974], 5993A)
See especially pp. 234-73.

683. ———: "Joyce and the Dublin Theosophists: 'Vegetable Verse' and Story," *Eire,* 13:2 (Summer 1978), 54-70.
The form of mysticism practiced by the Dublin theosophists (including Yeats) is reflected in Joyce's work.

684. ———: "The Woman in the Straw Hat: A Transitional Priestess in *Stephen Hero,*" *JJQ,* 16:4 (Summer 1979), 407-16.
Notes the use of "The Adoration of the Magi" in Joyce's novel.

685. SULTAN, STANLEY: *The Argument of Ulysses.* Columbus: Ohio State UP, 1964. xv, 485 pp.
Notes on Yeats in *Ulysses,* passim (see index).

686. THORNTON, WELDON: *Allusions in Ulysses: An Annotated List.* Chapel Hill: U of North Carolina Press, 1968. ix, 554 pp.
Index to Yeats allusions in *Ulysses,* p. 554.

687. TINDALL, WILLIAM YORK: *James Joyce: His Way of Interpreting the Modern World.* NY: Scribner's, 1950. ix, 134 pp.
See index for scattered notes on Yeats and Joyce.

688. ———: "James Joyce and the Hermetic Tradition," *JHI,* 15:1 (Jan 1954), 23-39.
Yeats's occult interests and their influence on Joyce.

689. ———: *A Reader's Guide to James Joyce.* NY: Noonday Press, 1959. xi, 304 pp.
On Yeats in Joyce's work (mostly interpreted as a father image), passim (see index).

690. TORCHIANA, DONALD T.: *Backgrounds for Joyce's Dubliners.* Boston: Allen & Unwin, 1986. xiv, 283 pp.
See index for numerous references to Yeats.

691. TRENCH, W. F.: "Dr. Yeats and Mr. Joyce," *IrSt,* 30 Aug 1924, 790.
Horrified complaint that the poet of the beautiful sees in "foul-minded" Joyce a genius.

692. VALMARANA, PAOLO: "Joyce e Yeats: Due volti dell'Irlanda," *Popolo,* 11 Oct 1964, 5.
"J and Y: Two faces of Ireland."

693. VOELKER, JOSEPH C.: "'He Lumped the Emancipates Together': More Analogues for Joyce's Mr. Duffy," *JJQ,* 18:1 (Fall 1980), 23-34.
The influence of *The Tables of the Law.*

694. WITT, MARION: "A Note on Joyce and Yeats," *MLN,* 63:8 (Dec 1948), 552-53.
A Yeats allusion in *Ulysses.*

695. WOLFF-WINDEGG, PHILIPP: "Auf der Suche nach dem Symbol--J. Joyce und W. B. Yeats," *Symbolon,* 5 (1966), 39-52.
As Yeats's work matured, his symbolism became colder and less obtrusive. Joyce is diametrically opposed; the symbolism of *Finnegans Wake* is enormously inflated, obscure, and finally a victim of the built-in mechanism. Discusses *Purgatory.*

See also AE24, 86, BB209, 219, BC4, BF160, CA55, CB152a, 258, 440, 440a, 546, CC12, 35, 71a, 103, 155, 206, 325, 341, CD7, 227, 238, 311, 604, 828, 1189, DC64, FA7, 23, 31, FB41, 42, FC16, 31a.

C. G. Jung

696. HOLLIS, JAMES R.: "Convergent Patterns in Yeats and Jung," *Psychological Perspectives,* 4:1 (Spring 1973), 60-68.

697. OLNEY, JAMES: "'A Powerful Emblem': The Towers of Yeats and Jung," *SAQ,* 72:4 (Autumn 1973), 494-515.
The actual towers and their symbolical implications.

698. ———: "The Esoteric Flower: Yeats and Jung," in Harper: *Yeats and the Occult* (1975, FC40), 27-54.
The common root of Yeats's philosophy and Jung's psychology in Platonism.

699. WALL, RICHARD J., and ROGER FITZGERALD: "Yeats and Jung: An Ideological Comparison," *L&P,* 13:2 (Spring 1963), 44-52.
Spiritus mundi, the mask, and opposites and antinomies and the Jungian counterparts.

See also CB194, 211, CC12, 184, 245, DA3, DC372, EE6, FC64, 109, 126.

Immanuel Kant

See CA53a, 103, CD66.

Patrick Kavanagh

700. GARRATT, ROBERT F.: "Patrick Kavanagh and the Killing of the Irish Revival," *CLQ,* 17:3 (Sept 1981), 170-83.

701. KAVANAGH, PATRICK: "George Moore's Yeats," *IrT,* 10 June 1965, ii.
Rather Kavanagh's Yeats, and what a curious character that is.

702. KAVANAGH, PETER (ed): *Patrick Kavanagh: Man and Poet.* Orono, Maine: National Poetry Foundation, 1986. 499 pp.
Numerous references to Yeats in texts by and about Kavanagh (see index).

703. LIDDY, JAMES: "Open Letter to the Young about Patrick Kavanagh," *Lace Curtain,* 1 [1970?], 55-57.
Why Kavanagh is a better poet and model than Yeats.

704. WARNER, ALAN: *Clay Is the Word: Patrick Kavanagh, 1904-1967.* Dublin: Dolmen Press, 1973. 144 pp.
Passim (see index).

See also CA55, CD105, 112, 122, DB92, 95, 212, DC195, 249.

John Keats

705. BAKER, CARLOS: "The Poet as Janus: Originality and Imitation in Modern Poetry," *Proceedings of the American Philosophical Society,* 128:2 (June 1984), 167-72.

Compares "Sailing to Byzantium" and "The Fascination of What's Difficult" with passages in Keats's poetry.

706. DARUWALA, MANECK HOMI: "The Myth of the Poet: Studies in Keats, Wilde, and Yeats," Ph.D. thesis, U of Rochester, 1981. xi, 454 pp. (*DAI,* 42:5 [Nov 1981], 2138A; reprinted *YeA,* 2 [1983], 104-5)

On Yeats, pp. 187-376, and passim.

707. ENDE, STUART A.: *Keats and the Sublime.* New Haven: Yale UP, 1976. xviii, 201 pp.

"Coda: Yeats's Dialogues with the Voice of Enchantment," 160-84 (Yeats's poetics compared with Keats's).

708. HARPER, GEORGE MILLS: "'Out of a Medium's Mouth': Yeats's Theory of 'Transference' and Keats's 'Ode to a Nightingale,'" *Yeats,* 1 (1983), 17-33.

Yeats's use of Keats's ode in his development of a theory of transference, as illustrated in the records of his and Mrs. Yeats's experiments in automatic writing.

709. JONES, JAMES LAND: "Keats and Yeats: 'Artificers of the Great Moment,'" *XUS,* 4:2 (May 1965), 125-50.

The early Yeats (before 1916) was closer to Shelley, the later closer to Keats.

710. ———: "Keats and the Last Romantics: Hopkins and Yeats," °Ph.D. thesis, Tulane U, 1969. 301 pp. (*DAI,* 30:6 [Dec 1969], 2530A)

711. ———: *Adam's Dream: Mythic Consciousness in Keats and Yeats.* Athens: U of Georgia Press, 1975. xiv, 226 pp.

"My central purpose is to show that the poetry of Keats and Yeats is informed by a set of assumptions, a mode of apprehension, which marks it as a certain kind of poetry: Romantic poetry. . . , characterized in particular by the elements of mythic thinking" (p. 11). The most detailed discussion is that of "Vacillation" (pp. 128-33).

Reviews:

- Richard Bonaccorso, *Eire,* 16:1 (Spring 1981), 152-53.
- George Bornstein, *Keats-Shelley J,* 26 (1977), 139-42.
- Michael Goldberg, *CJIS,* 3:2 (Nov 1977), 50-52.
- M[ichael] Goldberg, *Humanities Association R,* 28:1 (Winter 1977), 112-14.
- Barry Gradman, *Wordsworth Circle,* 7:3 (Summer 1976), 257-63.
- George Mills Harper, *SAB,* 42:2 (May 1977), 102-4.
- A. Norman Jeffares: "Coughing in Ink," *SR,* 84:1 (Jan-Mar 1976), 157-67.
- Priscilla Johnston, *JML,* 5:4 (1976), 849-51.

712. MAGAW, MALCOLM: "Yeats and Keats: The Poetics of Romanticism," *BuR,* 13:3 (Dec 1965), 87-96.

See also CA34, CC102, 117, 279, CD31, 318, 355, 1224, 1457, DA11, DB196, DC303, DD93, 503, 506, 510, 514, 532, 554, 715.

Patrick Kennedy

713. ALSPACH, RUSSELL K.: "The Use by Yeats and Other Irish Writers of the Folklore of Patrick Kennedy," *JAF,* 59:234 (Oct-Dec 1946), 404-12.

Yeats used Kennedy in "The Priest and the Fairy," "Baile and Ailinn," "The Wanderings of Oisin," and *The King's Threshold.*

Brendan Kennelly

714. OTTO, ERWIN: *Das lyrische Werk Brendan Kennellys: Eine Beschreibung der Gedichte auf dem Hintergrund des Dichtungsverständnisses und der spezifisch irischen Erfahrungen des Autors sowie der Tradition irisch-englischer Dichtung.* Frankfurt: Lang, 1977. iv, 352 pp. (Europäische Hochschulschriften. Reihe XIV: Angelsächsische Sprache und Literatur. 39.)

Contains a chapter on Kennelly's place in Anglo-Irish literature with frequent references to Yeats, pp. 211-80.

Tom Kettle

715. LYONS, JOHN BENIGNUS: *The Enigma of Tom Kettle: Irish Patriot, Essayist, Poet, British Soldier 1880-1916.* Dublin: Glendale Press, 1983. 351 pp.

See index for some notes on Yeats and Kettle.

Galway Kinnell

716. KINNELL, GALWAY: *Walking Down the Stairs: Selections from Interviews.* Ann Arbor: U of Michigan Press, 1978. xv, 112 pp.

Short note on Yeats's influence on Kinnell, pp. 42-43, 49.

Thomas Kinsella

717. DUNN, JAMES HENRY: "Thomas Kinsella and the Matter of Ireland: From Fairybog to Finistère," Ph.D. thesis, U of Massachusetts, 1984. vii, 240 pp. (*DAI,* 45:1 [July 1984], 179A-80A)

Compares Kinsella's "Death of a Queen" with Yeats's *Deirdre,* pp. 33-38; discusses Kinsella's views on Yeats's place in the Irish tradition, pp. 61-71, 215-22.

718. KENNER, HUGH: "Thomas Kinsella: An Anecdote and Some Reflections," *Genre,* 12:4 (Winter 1979), 591-99.

Considers the influence of Yeats. See also CB172.

719. MCGUINNESS, ARTHUR E.: "'Bright Quincunx Newly Risen': Thomas Kinsella's Inward 'I,'" *Eire,* 15:4 (Winter 1980), 106-25.

Contains a few notes on the influence of Yeats.

See also CD105, 112, 330, DB92, 95, DC71.

Komparu Zenchiku

720. KIM, MYUNG WHAN: "Zenchiku's Philosophy of Wheels and the Yeatsian Parallel," *Literature East & West,* 15:4--16:1-2 (Dec 1971, Mar 1972, June 1972), 647-61.

Zenchiku's wheels and Yeats's gyres in *A Vision.*

W. S. Landor

721. DAVIE, DONALD: "Attending to Landor," *Ironwood,* 12:2 (Fall 1984), 103-11.
Comments on "Men Improve with the Years" and "Easter 1916."

722. LOGAN, JAMES V., JOHN E. JORDAN, and NORTHROP FRYE (eds): *Some British Romantics: A Collection of Essays.* Columbus: Ohio State UP, 1966. vii, 343 pp.
Vivian Mercier: "The Future of Landor Criticism," 41-85; on Yeats and Landor, pp. 45-47.

723. SUPER, R. H.: "Dining with Landor," *Yeats,* 5 (1987), 143-49.
Landor's influence on Yeats's poetry.

See also DD655.

Sir Hugh Lane

724. GREGORY, LADY ISABELLA AUGUSTA: *Sir Hugh Lane: His Life and Legacy.* With a foreword by James White. Gerrards Cross: Smythe, 1973. 324 pp. (Coole Edition of the Works of Lady Gregory. 10.)
"Hugh Lane's Life and Achievement, with Some Account of the Dublin Galleries," 21-187; first published separately, London: Murray, 1921. xv, 290 pp. Contains numerous references to Yeats, quotations from conversations with him and from his letters as well as from Lady Gregory's letters to him (see index).
"Letters to the Press Etc. from Lady Gregory and W. B. Yeats," 216-47, contains the interview in BE84 (but not the reply).

See also BB98, CA118, CB438, CC232, DC366, FD13 and index IE s.v. Lane pictures.

Philip Larkin

725. LARKIN, PHILIP: *The North Ship.* London: Faber & Faber, 1966 [1945]. 48 pp.
In the introduction, pp. 7-10 (not in the first edition), Larkin notes his indebtedness to Yeats.

726. MOTION, ANDREW: *Philip Larkin.* London: Methuen, 1982. 92 pp.
On Yeats and Larkin, pp. 12-17, 33-38.

727. PRESS, JOHN: "W. B. Yeats, Thomas Hardy, and Philip Larkin," *AJES,* 3:2 (1978), 153-65.
How and why Larkin turned from Yeats's influence to that of Hardy.

728. RÜCKERT, INGRID: *The Touch of Sympathy: Philip Larkin und Thom Gunn. Zwei Beiträge zur englischen Gegenwartsdichtung.* Heidelberg: Winter, 1982. 342 pp. (Anglistische Forschungen. 162.)
Discusses the influence of Yeats on Larkin and Gunn on pp. 33-61, 65-71, and passim (see index).

728a. TIERCE, MICHAEL THOMAS: "Eggs, Small Beer, and Hardy: The Poetry and Prose of Philip Larkin," °Ph.D. thesis, U of Tennessee, 1985. 245 pp. (*DAI,* 46:3 [Sept 1985], 700A)

Refers to Larkin's rejection of Yeats in favor of Hardy, according to abstract.

729. TIMMS, DAVID: *Philip Larkin*. Edinburgh: Oliver & Boyd, 1973. vi, 138 pp.
Discusses the influence of Yeats, especially in chapters 2 and 3, pp. 22-91.

730. TOLLEY, A. T.: "Philip Larkin's Unpublished Book *In the Grip of Light*," *Agenda*, 22:2 (Summer 1984), 76-86.
Notes the influence of Yeats.

731. WEATHERHEAD, A. KINGSLEY: "Philip Larkin of England," *ELH*, 38:4 (Dec 1971), 616-30.
Contains notes on Yeats's influence on Larkin.

See also CD533, DB146, FE10.

D. H. Lawrence

732. BALBERT, PETER, and PHILLIP L. MARCUS (eds): *D. H. Lawrence: A Centenary Consideration*. Ithaca: Cornell UP, 1985. 263 pp.
P. L. Marcus: "Lawrence, Yeats, and 'the Resurrection of the Body,'" 210-36. Yeats is also referred to in Sandra M. Gilbert: "Potent Griselda: 'The Ladybird' and the Great Mother," 130-61.

733. BRUNNER, KARL, HERBERT KOZIOL, and SIEGFRIED KORNINGER (eds): *Anglistische Studien: Festschrift zum 70. Geburtstag von Professor Friedrich Wild*. Wien: Braumüller, 1958. x, 249 pp. (Wiener Beiträge zur englischen Philologie. 66.)
Franz Stanzel: "G. M. Hopkins, W. B. Yeats, D. H. Lawrence und die Spontaneität der Dichtung," 179-93. Mythology and the theory of self and anti-self helped Yeats to establish a distance between reality and poetry. In this he differs from Lawrence's "expressionism." Stanzel does not discuss the Yeats-Hopkins relationship.

734. GILBERT, SANDRA M.: *Acts of Attention: The Poems of D. H. Lawrence*. Ithaca: Cornell UP, 1972. xv, 329 pp.
Yeats is mentioned passim (see index).

735. GORDON, DAVID J.: *D. H. Lawrence as a Literary Critic*. New Haven: Yale UP, 1966. ix, 172 pp. (Yale Studies in English. 162.)
See pp. 94-101, 108-10.

736. NEWMAN, PAUL B.: "The Natural Aristocrat in Letters," *UKCR*, 31:1 (Oct 1964), 23-31.
On Lawrence's *Women in Love*, frequently invoking Yeats in support of the argument.

737. SMAILES, T. A.: "D. H. Lawrence, Poet," *Standpunte*, 23:85 (Aug 1969), 24-36.
Includes a comparison with Yeats.

738. THOMPSON, LESLIE M.: "The Christ Who Didn't Die: Analogues to D. H. Lawrence's *The Man Who Died* ," *D. H. Lawrence R*, 8:1 (Spring 1975), 19-30.
Notes that Yeats's view of Christianity anticipates Lawrence's view.

See also CA65, CB190, 453, CC69, 157, 350, CD66, 878a, DB127, 204, DD544, 601, EE38.

T. E. Lawrence

739. HYDE, HARFORD MONTGOMERY: *Solitary in the Ranks: Lawrence of Arabia as Airman and Private Soldier*. London: Constable, 1977. 288 pp.

See pp. 215-16.

740. LAWRENCE, ARNOLD WALTER (ed): *Letters to T. E. Lawrence*. Second impression. London: Cape, 1964. 216 pp.

Contains one letter by Yeats to T. E. Lawrence and one to Mrs. G. B. Shaw, pp. 213-14.

See also BC5.

W. J. Lawrence

741. DREWNIANY, PETER JOHN: "The Collected Theater Criticism of W. J. Lawrence in *The Stage*," Ph.D. thesis, U of Delaware, 1981. iv, 547 pp. (*DAI*, 42:11 [May 1982], 4831A)

Refers repeatedly to Lawrence's hostility to Yeats's plays. His only review of a Yeats play in *The Stage*, of *The Hour-Glass*, was published in the issue of 28 Nov 1912 and is here reprinted on pp. 151-54.

See also Drewniany's: "W. J. Lawrence's Irish Theater Criticism in *The Stage* ," *IRA*, 4 (1983), 42-56.

742. HOGAN, ROBERT: *"Since O'Casey" and Other Essays on Irish Drama*. Gerrards Cross: Smythe / Totowa, N.J.: Barnes & Noble, 1983. 176 pp. (Irish Literary Studies. 15.)

"Yeats Creates a Critic," 11-24 (W. J. Lawrence), and passim.

Louis le Brocquy

743. WALKER, DOROTHY: *Louis le Brocquy*. With an introduction by John Russell. Dublin: Ward River Press, 1981. 167 pp.

See pp. 56-58 and 146-50 for notes on le Brocquy's Yeats images (listed under CA59), including his own comments.

J. S. Le Fanu

744. MCCORMACK, WILLIAM J.: *Sheridan Le Fanu and Victorian Ireland*. Oxford: Clarendon Press, 1980. xii, 310 pp.

Contains a few notes on Yeats (see index).

See also DD207.

Richard Le Gallienne

745. DOWLING, LINDA C.: "'Rose Accurst': Yeats and Le Gallienne," *VP*, 16:3 (Autumn 1978), 280-84.

The indebtedness of Le Gallienne's poem "Beauty Accurst" to Yeats's "The Rose of the World."

Wilhelm Lehmann

746. BÖHM, RUDOLF, and HENNING WODE (eds): *Anglistentag 1986 Kiel: Vorträge*. Giessen: Hoffmann, 1987. 535 pp. (Tagungsberichte des Anglistentags Verbands deutscher Anglisten. 8.)
Axel Goodbody: "Wilhelm Lehmann and English Literature," 63-86; on Lehmann's preoccupation with Yeats.

747. SCRASE, DAVID: *Wilhelm Lehmann: A Critical Biography. Volume I: The Years of Trial (1880-1918)*. Columbia, S.C.: Camden House, 1984. xiii, 191 pp. (Studies in German Literature, Linguistics and Culture. 13:1.)
See index for several references to Lehmann's interest in Yeats.

C. J. Lever

748. JEFFARES, A. NORMAN: "Yeats and the Wrong Lever," in Jeffares: *Yeats, Sligo and Ireland* (1980, CA51), 98-111.
Yeats seems not to have known Lever's best works.

Ira Levin

749. MCMANIS, JO AGNEW: "*Rosemary's Baby:* A Unique Combination of Faust, Leda, and the Second Coming," *McNR,* 20 (1971-72), 33-36.

Alun Lewis

750. DEVINE, KATHLEEN: "Alun Lewis's 'A Fragment,'" *Poetry Wales,* 19:1 (1983), 37-43.
Discovers echoes of Yeats's poetry.

C. S. Lewis

751. CHRISTOPHER, JOE R.: "'From the Master's Lips': W. B. Yeats as C. S. Lewis Saw Him," *Bulletin of the New York C. S. Lewis Society,* 6:1 (1974), 14-19.
The biographical connections and Lewis's satirizing of Yeats in *Dymer* (see next item).

752. LEWIS, CLIVE STAPLES: *Narrative Poems*. Edited by Walter Hooper. London: Bles, 1969. xiv, 178 pp.
"Dymer," first published in 1926 under the pseudonym Clive Hamilton, contains a "Preface by the Author to the 1950 Edition," pp. 3-6, in which Lewis admits his debts to Yeats and explains that the Magician in Canto VI owes something to Yeats's "physical appearance."

753. ———: *They Stand Together: The Letters of C. S. Lewis to Arthur Greeves (1914-1963)*. Edited by Walter Hooper. London: Collins, 1979. 592 pp.
See index for references to Yeats, including reminiscenes.

See also BB137.

Wyndham Lewis

754. ANON.: "Miss Sitwell, Mr. Yeats, and Mr. Wyndham Lewis," *Yorkshire Post*, 30 Oct 1930, 6.
About Yeats's letter to Wyndham Lewis, printed in the latter's *Satire and Fiction* (1930, reprinted in *Letters*, p. 776). Correspondence by Wyndham Lewis, 6 Nov 1930, 6.

755. MEYERS, JEFFREY: *The Enemy: A Biography of Wyndham Lewis*. London: Routledge & Kegan Paul, 1980. xv, 391 pp.
See especially pp. 156-57.

756. ——— (ed): *Wyndham Lewis: A Revaluation. New Essays*. London: Athlone Press, 1980. viii, 276 pp.
Timothy Materer: "Lewis and the Patriarchs: Augustus John, W. B. Yeats, T. Sturge Moore," 47-63.

757. WAGNER, GEOFFREY: *Wyndham Lewis: A Portrait of the Artist as the Enemy*. Westport, Ct.: Greenwood Press, 1973 [1957]. xvi, 363 pp.
Some notes on Yeats (see index).

See also BB139, 229, BC1, CB190, CD1026, DD637, FB38, FE29.

John Locke

See CA53a, CC132, DD235.

Federico García Lorca

758. BAUMGARTEN, MURRAY: "Lyric as Performance: Lorca and Yeats," *CL*, 27:4 (Fall 1977), 328-50.
Parallels between Lorca's and Yeats's aesthetic theories, poetic practice, and concepts of poetry as an "act of performance."

See also EB32, EC71.

Robert Lowell

759. COSGRAVE, PATRICK: *The Public Poetry of Robert Lowell*. London: Gollancz, 1970. 222 pp.
Compares Yeats and Lowell passim (see index).

See also CC290, CD18, DB50, DC19, 20.

Malcolm Lowry

760. SLATER, ARDIS M.: "A Vision of the Valley: Mesoamerican and Yeatsian Planes of Malcolm Lowry's *Under the Volcano*," °Ph.D. thesis, Kent State U, 1986. 309 pp. (*DAI*, 47:9 [Mar 1987], 3437A)
Discusses the influence of *A Vision* and "The Second Coming" on Lowry's novel.

T. W. Lyster

761. MACLOCHLAINN, ALF: "An Unrecorded Yeats Item," *IrB*, 1:3

(1960/61), 61-65.

Prints and comments upon Yeats's speech given at the ceremony of the unveiling of the memorial to T. W. Lyster. See *Uncollected Prose,* 2:470-72.

George MacBeth

762. MACBETH, GEORGE: "Ancestors and Allegiances," *LMag,* 6:11 (Nov 1959), 21-27.

Names Yeats as one of his literary ancestors.

Patrick McCartan

763. YEATS, W. B.: *Yeats and Patrick McCartan: A Fenian Friendship.* Letters with a commentary by John Unterecker & an address on Yeats the Fenian by Patrick McCartan. No. 10 of *DPYCP* (1967, CA20), 333-443.

The commentary chronicles Yeats's friendship with McCartan and provides material on some of the matters that interested Yeats during this period, e.g., the Irish Academy of Letters, the Casement affair, and the fund set up for him by an American committee (including the role played by Gogarty). Reprints, with slight omissions and changes, McCartan's address (FD49) and includes an appendix on the principal activities of the Academy until Spring 1965.

See also AE24, BB84.

Hugh MacDiarmid

764. MACDIARMID, HUGH: *The Letters of Hugh MacDiarmid.* Edited with an introduction by Alan Bold. London: Hamilton, 1984. xxxv, 910 pp.

Several references to Yeats (see index).

See also BB141, G1132.

Thomas MacDonagh

765. JORDAN, JOHN: "MacDonagh and Yeats," *Hibernia,* 25 May 1973, 22.

See also Jordan's "*The Irish Review,*" 8 June 1973, 12.

766. MACDONAGH, THOMAS: *When the Dawn Is Come: A Tragedy in Three Acts.* Introduction by Chester Garrison, textual commentary by Johann Norstedt. Chicago: De Paul U, 1973. i, 52 pp. (Irish Drama Series. 9.)

"Introduction ," 1-13; "Textual Commentary," 44-51. On Yeats and MacDonagh, passim.

767. NORSTEDT, JOHANN A.: *Thomas MacDonagh: A Critical Biography.* Charlottesville: UP of Virginia, 1980. xi, 175 pp.

"Yeats, Synge, and the Abbey Theatre, 1907-8," 52-61, and passim (see index).

768. ———: "The Gift of Reputation: Yeats and MacDonagh," *Eire,* 19:3 (Fall 1984), 135-42.

769. PARKS, EDD WINFIELD, and AILEEN WELLS PARKS: *Thomas MacDonagh: The Man, the Patriot, the Writer*. Athens: U of Georgia Press, 1967. xiv, 151 pp.
On Yeats and MacDonagh, passim.

770. RYAN, STEPHEN P.: "W. B. Yeats and Thomas MacDonagh," *MLN*, 76:8 (Dec 1961), 715-19.
The biographical connections.

See also G351.

Patrick MacDonogh

771. MACDONOGH, CAROLINE: "Notes on MacDonogh and Yeats," *Gaéliana*, 4 (1982), 205-15.
Yeats echoes in MacDonogh's poetry.

Arthur Machen

772. PETERSEN, KARL MARIUS: "Arthur Machen and the Celtic Renaissance in Wales," Ph.D. thesis, Lousiana State U, 1973. vi, 215 pp. (*DAI*, 34:6 [Dec 1973], 3426A-27A)
On Yeats's "The Celtic Element in Literature," 41-50. Yeats is also mentioned passim.

Hugh MacLennan

773. BARTLETT, DONALD R.: "MacLennan and Yeats," *CanL*, 89 (Summer 1981), 74-84.
MacLennan's nationalism and his views of culture, education, politics, and cyclical history in *Return of the Sphinx* are similar to Yeats's thoughts.

Micheál MacLiammóir

774. MACLIAMMÓIR, MICHEÁL: *An Oscar of No Importance: Being an Account of the Author's Adventures with His One-Man Show about Oscar Wilde, "The Importance of Being Oscar."* London: Heinemann, 1968. vi, 234 pp.
Wilde fascinated, Yeats influenced MacLiammóir (p. 222). Several other references to Yeats, passim (see index).
For MacLiammóir's one-man show "Talking about Yeats" see HE22.

775. ———: "How Yeats Influenced My Life in the Theatre," in O'Driscoll and Reynolds: *Yeats and the Theatre* (1975, CA81), 1-3.

Louis MacNeice

776. BROWN, TERENCE: *Louis MacNeice: Sceptical Vision*. Dublin: Gill & Macmillan / NY: Barnes & Noble, 1975. vi, 215 pp.
Contains a few notes on Yeats and MacNeice (see index).

777. HABERER, ADOLPHE: *Louis MacNeice 1907-1963: L'homme et la poésie*. Lille: Atelier national de reproduction des thèses, 1986. ix,

1000 pp. in 2 vols.
Numerous references to Yeats (see index).

778. MAXWELL, DESMOND E. S.: "Louis MacNeice and the 'Low Dishonest Decade,'" *Modernist Studies,* 1:1 (1974), 55-69.
Discusses Yeats's role as a model for MacNeice.

779. SMITH, ELTON EDWARD: *Louis MacNeice.* NY: Twayne, 1970. 232 pp. (Twayne's English Authors Series. 99.)
See pp. 97-104 and index.

See also CB371, CC76, CD40, DB146.

Eoin MacNeill

780. TIERNEY, MICHAEL: *Eoin MacNeill: Scholar and Man of Action 1867-1945.* Edited by F. X. Martin. Oxford: Clarendon Press, 1980. xxii, 409 pp.
See pp. 66-69.

Maurice Maeterlinck

781. °CNUDDE-KNOWLAND, A.: "Maurice Maeterlinck and English and Anglo-Irish Literature: A Study of Parallels and Influences," D.Phil. thesis, Oxford U, 1984.

782. DRAPER, JOHN W.: "Yeats and Maeterlinck: A Literary Parallel," *Colonnade,* 7:7 (Apr 1914), 240-45.
A comparison of their plays.

783. HUYGELEN, PAUL: "Maeterlinck and England," Ph.D. thesis, U of London, [1954]. xiii, 498 pp.
"W. B. Yeats," 383-87. "The extent of Maeterlinck's impact . . . remains . . . a matter of literary controversy."

See also CB29, DC167, EA12, 28, 40, EB123, 155, EE503, G266.

J. P. Mahaffy

784. STANFORD, WILLIAM BEDELL, and ROBERT BRENDAN MCDOWELL: *Mahaffy: A Biography of an Anglo-Irishman.* London: Routledge & Kegan Paul, 1971. xiv, 281 pp.
See pp. 113-15.

V. V. Maîakovskiĭ

785. ASSOCIATION INTERNATIONALE DE LITTÉRATURE COMPARÉE / INTERNATIONAL COMPARATIVE LITERATURE ASSOCIATION: *Trois grandes mutations littéraires: Renaissance--Lumières--Début du vingtième siècle / Three Epoch-Making Literary Changes: Renaissance--Enlightenment--Early Twentieth Century.* Edited by Béla Köpeczi and György M. Vajda. Stuttgart: Bieber, 1980. 931 pp. (Actes du VIIIe Congrès / Proceedings of the 8th Congress. Vol. 1.)
George Gibian: "The Historical View and the Inward Look: Revolution and Love in Mayakovsky and Yeats," 819-31; compares several poems on the subjects of history and love.

Stéphane Mallarmé

786. BACKÈS, JEAN-LOUIS: "Mallarmé," in Genet: *William Butler Yeats* (1981, CA32), 397-407.
His influence on Yeats.

787. FULLWOOD, DAPHNE: "The Influence on W. B. Yeats of Some French Poets (Mallarmé, Verlaine, Claudel)," *SoR*, 6:2 (Apr 1970), 356-79.

788. GARDINER, KENNETH: "Thoughts on Yeats and Mallarmé," *Eigo Seinen*, 111:11 (1 Nov 1965), 736-39.

789. MALLARMÉ, STÉPHANE: *Correspondance*. Edited by Henri Mondor and Lloyd James Austin. Paris: Gallimard, 1959-85. 11 vols.
See vol. 6 (1981), pp. 223, 225, 230, 237, 238, for Yeats's letter to Mallarmé and some notes.

790. MAN, PAUL MICHAEL DE: "Mallarmé, Yeats, and the Post-Romantic Predicament," Ph.D. thesis, Harvard U, 1960. viii, 125, i, 191 pp.
An extract from this appears in CD1456.

791. REVARD, STELLA: "Yeats, Mallarmé, and the Archetypal Feminine," *PLL*, 8:Supplement (Fall 1972), 112-27.
The influence of *Hérodiade* on several poems, on *The Shadowy Waters, The King of the Great Clock Tower,* and *A Full Moon in March.*

792. SPIVAK, GAYATRI CHAKRAVORTY: "A Stylistic Contrast between Yeats and Mallarmé," *Lang&S*, 5:2 (Spring 1972), 100-107.
Yeats and Mallarmé had a common theme but a different "stylistic tendency."

See also BG194, CA37 (review Colum), 155, CB403, CC19, CD55, 57, 58, 60, 1279, DD39, EC17, FE13, G112.

James Clarence Mangan

793. DONAGHY, HENRY J.: *James Clarence Mangan*. NY: Twayne, 1974. 141 pp. (Twayne's English Authors Series. 171.)
See pp. 122-26.

794. FREITAG, HANS-HEINRICH, and PETER HÜHN (eds): *Literarische Ansichten der Wirklichkeit: Studien zur Wirklichkeitskonstitution in der englischsprachigen Literatur. To Honour Johannes Kleinstück.* Frankfurt/M: Lang, 1980. viii, 450 pp. (Anglo-American Forum. 12.)
H.-H. Freitag: "Die Vision als Form der Wirklichkeitserfahrung bei Mangan und Yeats," 173-90. Mangan inspired Yeats's visionary/realistic poetry; compares Mangan's "A Vision of Connaught in the Thirteenth Century" with "Meditations in Time of Civil War."

See also CC345, 355, CD442a, DC71, 248, DD158, FA35, FE18.

Thomas Mann

795. CONVERSI, LEONARD: "Mann, Yeats and the Truth of Art," *YR*, 56:4 (June 1967), 506-23.

Opposites and antinomies in Mann and Yeats.

See also CD878a.

Constance Markievicz (or Markiewicz)

796. MARRECO, ANNE: *The Rebel Countess: The Life and Times of Constance Markievicz*. Philadelphia: Chilton Books, 1967. xiii, 330 pp.
On Yeats, passim (see index).

797. NORMAN, DIANA: *Terrible Beauty: A Life of Constance Markievicz 1886-1927*. London: Hodder & Stoughton, 1987. 320 pp.
See index for some notes on Yeats.

798. SMITH, D. J.: "The Countess and the Poets: Constance Gore-Booth Markievicz in the Work of the Irish Writers," *JIL,* 12:1 (Jan 1983), 3-63.

799. VAN VORIS, JACQUELINE: *Constance de Markievicz in the Cause of Ireland*. Amherst: U of Massachusetts Press, 1967. 384 pp.
Yeats's connections with the countess and the Gore-Booth family are referred to passim (see index).

See also AE37, CD479, DC99, DD265a, 266 and note, 427.

Edward Martyn

800. COURTNEY, SISTER MARIE-THÉRÈSE: *Edward Martyn and the Irish Theatre*. NY: Vantage Press, 1956. 188 pp.
Chapter 3, "Theatre," 65-148, refers to the Yeats-Martyn relationship.

801. GWYNN, DENIS: *Edward Martyn and the Irish Revival*. London: Cape, 1930. 349 pp.
"The Irish Literary Theatre," 113-70; corrects some statements that Yeats made about Martyn.

See also BB155, BC1, CC219, CD842, EA12, 25, EF27.

Andrew Marvell

See DA24, DC231, DD506, 599.

John Masefield

802. DREW, FRASER: "The Irish Allegiances of an English Laureate: John Masefield and Ireland," *Eire,* 3:4 (Winter 1968), 24-34.

802a. DWYER, JUNE: *John Masefield*. NY: Ungar, 1987. xii, 120 pp.
Notes Yeats's influence on Masefield (see index).

803. MASEFIELD, JOHN: *So Long to Learn*. NY: Macmillan, 1952. iv, 181 pp.
Yeats's influence on Masefield and reminiscenes, pp. 93-110.

804. ———: *Letters to Reyna*. Edited by William Buchan. London:

Buchan & Enright, 1983. 509 pp.
Letters written 1952-1967 to "Reyna" (Audrey Napier-Smith); several references to Yeats (see index).

805. SMITH, CONSTANCE BABINGTON: *John Masefield: A Life*. Oxford: Oxford UP, 1978. xvi, 261 pp.
See index. An extract was published as "Bank Clerk and Poet. Constance Babington Smith on how the young John Masefield, born one hundred years ago this week, fell under the spell of W. B. Yeats," *Times*, 3 June 1978, 7.

806. YEATS, W. B.: "W. B. Yeats to John Masefield: Two Letters." Edited by Paul Delany, *MR*, 11:1 (Winter 1970), 159-62.

See also BA12, BC1, CD365, DA22.

S. L. MacGregor Mathers

807. COLQUHOUN, ITHELL: "Two Pupils and a Master," *Prediction*, 37:10 (Oct 1971), 12-14.
MacGregor Mathers, the master, and Yeats and Aleister Crowley, the pupils.

808. ———: *Sword of Wisdom: MacGregor Mathers and "The Golden Dawn."* London: Spearman, 1975. 307 pp.
On Yeats passim (see index).

809. FENNELLY, LAURENCE WILLIAM: "S. L. Macgregor Mathers and the Fiction of W. B. Yeats," °Ph.D. thesis, Florida State U, 1973. 130 pp. (*DAI*, 34:6 [Dec 1973], 3389A)
Discusses Yeats's occult interests, his involvement in the Golden Dawn, and "Rosa Alchemica," *The Speckled Bird*, and *A Vision*.

810. ———: "W. B. Yeats and S. L. MacGregor Mathers," in Harper: *Yeats and the Occult* (1975, FC40), 285-306.
The biographical connections and the Golden Dawn involvement.

See also BA14, CD1, FC17, 37, 39, 54.

Moina Mathers

See BC1, FC39, 54.

Elkin Mathews

810a. NELSON, JAMES G.: "Elkin Mathews, W. B. Yeats, and the Celtic Movement in Literature," *JML*, 14:1 (Summer 1987), 17-33.
Mainly about the publication of *The Wind among the Reeds* (Wade 27), including numerous quotations from unpublished letters.

811. YEATS, W. B.: "Letters to Herbert Horne, Ernest Radford, and Elkin Mathews." Edited by Ian Fletcher, *YeSt*, 1 (Bealtaine 1971), 203-8.
Prints and annotates four letters to Mathews, one to Horne, and one to Radford.

William Meredith

812. FITZ GERALD, GREGORY, and PAUL FERGUSON: "The Frost Tradition: A Conversation with William Meredith," *SWR*, 57:2 (Spring 1972), 108-17.

Meredith comments on Yeats's influence on him.

James Merrill

813. BLOOM, HAROLD (ed): *James Merrill*. NY: Chelsea House, 1985. viii, 214 pp.

Leslie Brisman: "Merrill's Yeats," 189-98; on allusions to Yeats (particularly to "Lapis Lazuli") in Merrill's poetry. Further references to Yeats in some of the other contributions (see index).

814. YENSER, STEPHEN: *The Consuming Myth: The Work of James Merrill*. Cambridge, Mass.: Harvard UP, 1987. xiii, 367 pp.

See index for some references to Yeats.

Stuart Merrill

815. HENRY, MARJORIE LOUISE: *La contribution d'un américain au symbolisme français: Stuart Merrill*. Paris: Champion, 1927. x, 291 pp. (Bibliothèque de la Revue de littérature comparée. 34.)

See pp. 109, 264.

Josephine Miles

816. HAMMOND, KARLA M.: "An Interview with Josephine Miles," *SoR*, 19:3 (Summer 1983), 606-31.

Yeats was the most enduring influence on Josephine Miles.

John Milton

817. UNGER, LEONARD: "Yeats and Milton," *SAQ*, 61:2 (Spring 1962), 197-212.

The influence of *Areopagitica* on Yeats's prose style and poetic theories; Miltonic imagery in Yeats's poetry, particularly in "The Second Coming."

See also CA34, 49, 53a, CC219, CD34, EE165.

Susan L. Mitchell

818. KAIN, RICHARD MORGAN: *Susan L. Mitchell*. Lewisburg: Bucknell UP, 1972. 103 pp.

Numerous remarks on Yeats; includes an unpublished parody of "The Lake Isle of Innisfree" (p. 49).

819. SKELTON, ROBIN: "Aide to Immortality: The Satirical Writings of Susan L. Mitchell," in Skelton and Saddlemyer: *The World of W. B. Yeats* (1967, CA102), 199-206.

See also CA38.

Harriet Monroe

820. WILLIAMS, ELLEN: *Harriet Monroe and the Poetry Renaissance: The First Ten Years of "Poetry" 1912-22*. Urbana: U of Illinois Press, 1977. xiv, 312 pp.
See index for references to Yeats.

See also BC1.

John Montague

821. FRAZIER, ADRIAN: "John Montague's Language of the Tribe," *CJIS*, 9:2 (Dec 1983), 57-75.
Comments on Yeats's influence on Montague and on "Blood and the Moon."

822. INGERSOLL, EARL, and BEN HOWARD: "'Elegiac Cheer': A Conversation with John Montague," *LitR*, 31:1 (Fall 1987), 23-31.
Includes comments on Yeats.

See also CD105, 112, DB92, 95.

Brian Moore

823. GREEN, ROBERT: "The Function of Poetry in Brian Moore's *The Emperor of Ice Cream* ," *CanL*, 93 (Summer 1982), 164-72.
"Easter 1916" is one of the poems central to this novel.

George Moore

824. BROWN, MALCOLM: *George Moore: A Reconsideration*. Seattle: U of Washington Press, 1955. xix, 235 pp.
On Yeats and Moore, passim (see index)

825. BRUNIUS, AUGUST: *Engelska kåserier*. Stockholm: Bonniers, 1927. 227 pp.
"Yeats och Moore: Två typer ur 'den irländska renässansen," 91-126; reprinted from *Vår tid*, 8 (1923), 75-95.

826. CAVE, RICHARD ALLEN: *A Study of the Novels of George Moore*. Gerrards Cross: Smythe, 1978. 271 pp. (Irish Literary Studies. 3.)
See index for a few notes on Yeats.

827. DONOVAN, BRIAN GREENWOOD: "George Moore's Fictive Autobiography," Ph.D. thesis, U of Minnesota, 1974. xvii, 235 pp. (*DAI*, 35:8 [Feb 1975], 5396A-97A)
Discusses Moore's treatment of Yeats, pp. 146-231 and passim.

828. FARROW, ANTHONY: "Currents in the Irish Novel: George Moore, James Joyce, Samuel Beckett," Ph.D. thesis, Cornell U, 1972. vi, 264 pp. (*DAI*, 33:10 [Apr 1973], 5719A-20A)
On Yeats's "presence" in the works of Moore and Joyce see especially pp. 41-106, 151-53.

829. ———: *George Moore*. Boston: Twayne, 1978. 169 pp. (Twayne's English Authors Series. 244.)
See index for references to Yeats.

830. GILOMEN, WALTHER: "George Moore and His Friendship with W. B. Yeats," *ES,* 19:3 (June 1937), 116-20.
On the mutual treatment in the respective autobiographies.

831. HARRIS, ELIZABETH HALL: "The Irish George Moore: A Biographical and Critical Interpretation," Ph.D. thesis, Stanford U, 1976. iii, 432 pp. (*DAI,* 37:10 [Apr 1977], 6498A)
Yeats is mentioned passim.

832. HENN, T. R.: "Moore and Yeats," *DM,* 4:2 (Summer 1965), 63-77.

833. HONE, JOSEPH: *The Life of George Moore.* NY: Macmillan, 1936. 515 pp.
Yeats is mentioned passim (see index).

834. HUGHES, DOUGLAS A. (ed): *The Man of Wax: Critical Essays on George Moore.* NY: New York UP, 1971. xxvi, 364 pp.
Reprinted essays; references to Yeats passim (see index).

835. HUNEKER, JAMES: "The Seven Arts," *Puck,* 25 Apr 1914, 9, 17.
What Moore did to Yeats in his autobiography.

835a. LANGENFELD, ROBERT: "Grand Themes in the Satiric Characterizations of George Moore's *Hail and Farewell,*" *EI,* 13:1 (June 1988), 63-79.
On Moore's satiric portrait of Yeats "in a Juvenalian manner."

836. MCFATE, PATRICIA: "*The Bending of the Bough* and *The Heather Field:* Two Portraits of the Artists," *Eire,* 8:1 (Spring 1973), 52-61.
Includes comments on the Yeats-Moore relationship.

837. MACY, JOHN: *The Critical Game.* NY: Boni & Liveright, 1922. 335 pp.
"George Moore and Other Irish Writers," 305-14.

838. MICHIE, DONALD M.: "A Man of Genius and a Man of Talent," *TSLL,* 6:2 (Summer 1964), 148-54.
The Yeats-Moore collaboration in *Diarmuid and Grania* and its effect on some other Yeats works.

839. MOORE, GEORGE: *The Untilled Field.* With a foreword by T. R. Henn. Gerrards Cross: Smythe, 1976 [1903]. xxv, 348 pp.
Moore's preface, pp. xvii-xxii, first included in the revised edition of 1914, mentions Yeats passim.

840. OWENS, GRAHAM (ed): *George Moore's Mind and Art: Essays.* Edinburgh: Oliver & Boyd, 1968. xi, 182 pp. (Essays Old and New. 2.)
See especially William F. Blissett: "George Moore and Literary Wagnerism," 53-76; and Herbert Howarth: "Dublin, 1899-1911: The Enthusiasms of a Prodigal," 77-98.

841. RUTTLEDGE, PAUL: "Stage Management in the Irish National Theatre," *Dana,* 5 (Sept 1904), 150-52.
See also the correction in a note by the editor [John Eglinton], 8 (Dec 1904), 256. Mainly on W. G. Fay. "Paul Ruttledge" has been identified as George Moore; see Jack Wayne Weaver: "'Stage Management in the Irish National Theatre': An Unknown Article by George Moore," *ELT,* 9:1 (1966), 12-17. Weaver argues that Moore disguised his identity by adopting as a pseudonym the

name of the hero in *Where There Is Nothing*, a bone of contention between himself and Yeats.

842. SADDLEMYER, ANN: "'All Art Is Collaboration'? George Moore and Edward Martyn," in Skelton and Saddlemyer: *The World of W. B. Yeats* (1967, CA102), 169-88.

843. SCHLEIFER, RONALD: "George Moore's Turning Mind: Digression and Autobiographical Art in *Hail and Farewell*," *Genre*, 12:4 (Winter 1979), 473-503.

Contains references to Yeats. See also CB172.

844. SHERMAN, STUART PRATT: *On Contemporary Literature*. NY: Holt, 1917. vii, 312 pp.

On Yeats see "The Aesthetic Naturalism of George Moore," 120-68; "The Exoticism of John Synge," 190-210.

845. WEAVER, JACK WAYNE: "A Story-Teller's Holiday: George Moore's Irish Renaissance, 1897 to 1911," Ph.D. thesis, U of North Carolina at Chapel Hill, 1966. xiv, 214 pp. (*DAI*, 27:9 [Mar 1967], 3067A-68A)

846. ———: "An Exile Returned: Moore and Yeats in Ireland," *Eire*, 3:1 (Spring 1968), 40-47.

Moore's collaboration and quarrel with Yeats. Comments on *Diarmuid and Grania* and *Where There Is Nothing*.

847. WELCH, ROBERT (ed): *The Way Back: George Moore's "The Untilled Field" & "The Lake."* Dublin: Wolfhound Press, 1982. 140 pp.

Yeats is referred to passim (see index), especially in Declan Kiberd: "George Moore's Gaelic Lawn Party," 13-27, 127-28.

848. WHITE, CLYDE PATRICK: "George Moore: From Naturalism to Pure Art," °Ph.D. thesis, U of Virginia, 1970. 258 pp. (*DAI*, 31:9 [Mar 1971], 4800A)

Discusses the Yeats-Moore relationship.

See also AC54a, BA4, BB84, 86, 155, 209, BC1, 6, BE112a, 135, CA38, EA12, 25, EE95, 212-32 and note, 537, FA7, FB5, 6, 23, 25, G758, 770, HA2.

Marianne Moore

849. DIGGORY, TERENCE: "American Responses to Yeats's Prose: Marianne Moore and Allen Ginsberg," *Yeats*, 3 (1985), 34-59.

Thomas Moore

850. BURGESS, ANTHONY: "The Milesian Firbolg," *TLS*, 29 July 1977, 909-10.

A review of Terence de Vere White's *Tom Moore* (1977), includes some remarks on Yeats.

See also CC345, DD253.

T. Sturge Moore

851. EASTON, MALCOLM: "T. Sturge Moore and W. B. Yeats," *Apollo*,

92 (Oct 1970), 298-300.
Sturge Moore's covers for Yeats's books and Yeats's estimate of them.

852. ——— (ed): *T. Sturge Moore (1870-1944): Contributions to the Art of the Book & Collaboration with Yeats.* Catalogue of an exhibition compiled and edited together with an introduction by Malcolm Easton. Hull: U of Hull, 1970. 55 pp.
"Introduction: The Yeats Covers in Their Context," 7-13; discusses the Moore-Yeats relationship and Moore's book covers.

853. EASTON, MALCOLM: "Thomas Sturge Moore: Wood-Engraver," *PrL,* 4:1 (Spring 1971), 24-37.

854. WINTERS, YVOR: *Uncollected Essays and Reviews.* Edited and introduced by Francis Murphy. London: Lane, 1974. xxi, 320 pp.
"T. Sturge Moore," 139-52; reprinted from *Hound & Horn,* 6:3 (Apr-June 1933), 534-45. Includes frequent comparisons with Yeats ("Mr. Moore is a greater poet than Mr. Yeats"). See answer by Theodor Spencer, CD383.
Winters refers to the quarrel in his *In Defense of Reason.* Denver: Swallow, 1947. vii, 611 pp. (pp. 490-92).
Other notes on Yeats passim (see index).

855. YEATS, W. B., and THOMAS STURGE MOORE: *W. B. Yeats and T. Sturge Moore: Their Correspondence, 1901-1937.* Edited by Ursula Bridge. London: Routledge & Kegan Paul, 1953. xix, 214 pp.
Reprinted °Westport, Ct.: Greenwood Press, 1978. "Introduction," ix-xix; "Notes," 186-202. For reviews see G1333-1347 and note.

See also AE9, BA14, BB103, 136, CB528, CC66, CD54, DB164, EA25, EF90, FC20, 29, 140, FE46.

William Morris

856. FAULKNER, PETER: *William Morris and W. B. Yeats.* Dublin: Dolmen Press, 1962. 31 pp.
See also Faulkner's "W. B. Yeats and William Morris," *Threshold,* 4:1 (Spring-Summer 1960), 18-27; "Morris and Yeats," *J of the William Morris Society,* 1:3 (Summer 1963), 19-23. Discusses the biographical connections; Morris's influence on Yeats as a poet, "generous personality," and social critic; and Yeats's assessment of Morris's work.
Reviews:
- Bruce Arnold, *Dubliner,* 5 (Sept-Oct 1962), 61-62.
- Denis Donoghue: "Countries of the Mind," *Guardian,* 11 Jan 1963, 5.
- Ian Fletcher, *MLR,* 58:4 (Oct 1963), 626.

857. GRENNAN, MARGARET R.: *William Morris: Medievalist and Revolutionary.* NY: Russell & Russell, 1970 [1945]. xi, 173 pp.
See pp. 108-9, 118, 129, 151-52.

858. GRIGSON, GEOFFREY: *The Contrary View: Glimpses of Fudge and Gold.* London: Macmillan, 1974. xi, 243 pp.
"The Happiness of His Poems," 80-90; contains some remarks on Morris and Yeats.

859. HOARE, DOROTHY MACKENZIE: *The Works of Morris and of Yeats* *in Relation to Early Saga Literature*. NY: Russell & Russell, 1971 [1937]. x, 179 pp.

Based on a Ph.D. thesis, Cambridge U, 1930. v, 180, cxvii pp. Reprinted °Norwood, Pa.: Norwood Editions, 1975; °Philadelphia: West, 1977.

Contains chapters on "The Irish Movement" (pp. 77-110, with a section on "The Poetry of Yeats") and on "The Dreamer in Contact with Irish Saga" (pp. 111-39, with sections on Yeats and his *Deirdre* version). Concludes that for Morris and for the early Yeats the "sagas offered both liberation and escape." The escape was twofold: "First, from life to the sagas; and secondly, from the actuality which the sagas reveal to the dreaming and stilled refuge, with all harshness eliminated, which they made of them" (p. 143).

Reviews:
- Anon., *N&Q*, 173:4 (24 July 1937), 72.
- Edith C. Batho, *MLR*, 33:2 (Apr 1938), 289-90.
- M. L. Cazamian, *EA*, 2:1 (Jan-Mar 1938), 58.
- A[ustin] C[larke], *DM*, 12:4 (Oct-Dec 1937), 64-65.
- A[odh] DeB[lacam]: "Yeats a 'Minor Poet'?" *IrP*, 8 June 1937, 7. Correspondence by Sean O Faolain, 9 June 1937, 8.
- I. K.: "Morris and Yeats and Early Saga Literature," *ContempR*, 152:862 (Oct 1937), 508-9.
- [C. S. Lewis]: "The Sagas and Modern Life: Morris, Mr. Yeats, and the Originals," *TLS*, 29 May 1937, 409.
- J. M. N.: "Sagas and the Poets," *Time and Tide*, 25 Sept 1937, 1271.
- Margaret Schlauch, *MP*, 35:4 (May 1938), 469-70.
- J. A. Smith, *Medium Aevum*, 8:3 (Oct 1939), 240-41.

860. LOURIE, MARGARET A.: "The Embodiment of Dreams: William Morris' 'Blue Closet' Group," *VP*, 15:3 (Autumn 1977), 193-206.
Yeats's "inwardness" is partly due to the influence of Morris.

861. MCALINDON, T.: "The Idea of Byzantium in William Morris and W. B. Yeats," *MP*, 64:4 (May 1967), 307-19.
Morris was one of the influences on Yeats's idea of Byzantium. Discusses Yeats's cultural theories and *A Vision*, not so much the Byzantium poems.

862. TALBOT, NORMAN: "Women and Goddesses in the Romances of William Morris," *SoRA*, 3:4 (1969), 339-57.

863. THOMPSON, EDWARD PALMER: *William Morris: Romantic to Revolutionary*. London: Lawrence & Wishart, 1955. 908 pp.
See pp. 643-44 and index.

See also CA54, 61, CC219, CD35, 37, 39, 1138, DA6, 10, 11, FD22, 57.

Edwin Muir

864. CLARKE, AUSTIN: "The Yeats Tradition," *IrT*, 27 Mar 1943, 2.
Yeats's influence on poets Edwin Muir and Sean Jennett.

865. MACINTYRE, LORN M.: "The Poetry of Edwin Muir," *Akros*, 13:78 (Aug 1978), 8-17.
Notes the influence of Yeats.

Iris Murdoch

866. GERSTENBERGER, DONNA: *Iris Murdoch*. Lewisburg, Pa.: Bucknell UP, 1975. 85 pp.
Chapter 2, pp. 51-69, includes a comparison between the novel *The Red and the Green* and Yeats's "Easter 1916."

867. SCANLAN, MARGARET: "Fiction and the Fictions of History in Iris Murdoch's *The Red and the Green*," *Clio*, 9:3 (Spring 1980), 365-78.
Comments on the Yeats allusions in the novel.

See also CB546.

Gilbert Murray

868. ARCHER, CHARLES: *William Archer: Life, Work, and Friendships*. London: Allen & Unwin, 1931. 451 pp.
Contains a letter from Gilbert Murray to Archer, 10 Jan 1903, written "in a state of enthusiasm over Yeats," p. 271.

868a. WILSON, SIR DUNCAN: *Gilbert Murray O M: 1866-1957*. Oxford: Clarendon Press, 1987. xiv, 474 pp.
See index for some references to Yeats; apparently he and Murray corresponded with each other.

See also BC1, DA18, EF90.

Paul Nash

869. CAUSEY, ANDREW: *Paul Nash*. Oxford: Clarendon Press, 1980. xix, 511 pp.
Some references to Yeats. See also BG122 and 152.

J. T. Nettleship

870. PALEY, MORTON D.: "John Trivett Nettleship and the 'Blake Drawings,'" *Blake*, 14:4 (Spring 1981), 185-94.

See also CA61.

Friedrich Nietzsche

871. BATTAGLIA, ROSEMARIE: "Yeats, Nietzsche, and the Aristocratic Ideal," *CollL*, 13:1 (Winter 1986), 88-94.

872. BOHLMANN, OTTO: *Yeats and Nietzsche: An Exploration of Major Nietzschean Echoes in the Writings of William Butler Yeats*. London: Macmillan, 1982. xviii, 222 pp.
An investigation arranged under such topics as "Conflict, Will, Power," "The Tragic Disposition," "Realism, Aesthetics, Art," "The Hero," and "Cyclical History." I think, however, that Bohlmann sees too many Nietzschean echoes and does not evaluate their importance in comparison to other "influences."
Reviews:
- G. K. Blank, *CLS*, 22:4 (Winter 1985), 549-51.
- John Burt Foster, *SAB*, 48:3 (Sept 1983), 90-92.

- F. S. L. Lyons: "Strong Enchantment," *TLS*, 31 Dec 1982, 1438.
- William J. Maroldo: "Echoes of Nietzsche in Yeats," *ILS*, 2:1 (Spring 1983), 22.
- James Olney: "Modernism, Yeats, and Eliot," *SR*, 92:3 (Summer 1984), 451-66.
- David S. Thatcher, *Yeats*, 1 (1983), 188-91.

873. BRIDGWATER, PATRICK: *Nietzsche in Anglosaxony: A Study of Nietzsche's Impact on English and American Literature*. Leicester: Leicester UP, 1972. 236 pp.

"'That Strong Enchanter' (W. B. Yeats)," 67-90; reprinted from R. W. Last (ed): *Affinities: Essays in German and English Literature Dedicated to the Memory of Oswald Wolff (1897-1968)*. London: Wolff, 1971. x, 353 pp. (pp. 68-87). Also passim (see index).

874. FOSTER, JOHN BURT: *Heirs to Dionysus: A Nietzschean Current in Literary Modernism*. Princeton: Princeton UP, 1981. xiv, 475 pp.

Several references to Yeats and Nietzsche (see index).

875. HELLER, ERICH: *Die Wiederkehr der Unschuld und andere Essays*. Frankfurt/M: Suhrkamp, 1977. 270 pp. (Suhrkamp Taschenbuch. 396.)

"Als der Dichter Yeats zum ersten Mal Nietzsche las" [When the poet Yeats read Nietzsche for the first time], 29-48; reprinted from Carl-Joachim Friedrich and Benno Reifenberg (eds): *Sprache und Politik: Festgabe für Dolf Sternberger zum sechzigsten Geburtstag*. Heidelberg: Schneider, 1968. 545 pp. (pp. 116-31).

See also Heller's "Yeats and Nietzsche: Reflections on a Poet's Marginal Notes," *Encounter*, 33:6 (Dec 1969), 64-72; reprinted in *The Disinherited Mind: Essays in Modern German Literature and Thought*. Fourth edition. London: Bowes & Bowes, 1975. xvii, 358 pp. (pp. 327-47).

876. KEANE, PATRICK J.: "Yeats and Nietzsche: The 'Antithetical' Vision," Ph.D. thesis, New York U, 1971. xxxvi, 402 pp. (*DAI*, 33:9 [Mar 1973], 5182A)

Discusses the concepts of heroic mask and tragic joy, Yeats's alleged fascism, his views of Plato and Homer, and the poems "A Dialogue of Self and Soul" and "What Then?" See also CA53a.

877. KNIGHT, GEORGE WILSON: *Christ and Nietzsche: An Essay in Poetic Wisdom*. London: Staples Press, 1948. 244 pp.

Scattered notes, passim (see index).

878. MARTIN, STODDARD: *Art, Messianism and Crime: A Study of Antinomianism in Modern Literature and Lives*. London: Macmillan, 1986. vi, 218 pp.

Discusses Nietzsche's influence on Yeats, pp. 65-72. See index for further references.

878a. MAY, KEITH M.: *Nietzsche and Modern Literature: Themes in Yeats, Rilke, Mann and Lawrence*. London: Macmillan, 1988. ix, 175 pp.

"Yeats and Aristocracy," 16-44, and passim. Does not consider texts or criticism in German.

879. O'BRIEN, CONOR CRUISE: *The Suspecting Glance*. London: Faber & Faber, 1972. 91 pp.

"Burke, Nietzsche, and Yeats," 67-91. The influence of Nietzsche prompted Yeats's withdrawal from popular Irish nationalism and his abandonment of a generally liberal attitude. Burke was important for a reconciliation of Yeats's liberal and fascist tendencies. Comments briefly on several relevant poems.

880. OPPEL, FRANCES NESBITT: *Mask and Tragedy: Yeats and Nietzsche, 1902-10*. Charlottesville: UP of Virginia, 1987. xi, 255 pp.
Based on "Yeats and Nietzsche: Mask and Tragedy, 1902-1910," °Ph.D. thesis, Rutgers U, 1983. 367 pp. (*DAI*, 44:12 [June 1984], 3697A; reprinted *Yeats*, 3 [1985], 211-12, and *YeA*, 4 [1986], 316-17).
Discusses *Deirdre, The King's Threshold, On Baile's Strand, The Player Queen, The Shadowy Waters, Where There Is Nothing, A Vision,* and some poems, especially "Adam's Curse" and "Never Give All the Heart." Unfortunately, the author does not consider any German-language material and is thus unaware of Timm's *William Butler Yeats und Friedrich Nietzsche* (CD885).

881. PASLEY, MALCOLM (ed): *Nietzsche: Imagery and Thought. A Collection of Essays*. London: Methuen, 1978. x, 262 pp.
Patrick Bridgwater: "English Writers and Nietzsche," 220-58; on Yeats, pp. 248-52.

882. REYNOLDS, LORNA: "Collective Intellect: Yeats, Synge and Nietzsche," *E&S*, 26 (1973), 83-98.
Poetry and philosophy as manifestations of unity of being in Yeats, Synge, and Nietzsche, and the influence of Nietzsche and Synge on Yeats in his efforts to formulate a "new syntax."

883. THATCHER, DAVID S.: "A Misdated Yeats Letter on Nietzsche," *N&Q*, os 213 / ns 15:8 (Aug 1968), 286-87.
The letter to John Quinn, dated 26 Sept 1902 in *Letters* (p. 380), was presumably written between 27 Dec 1902 and 3 Jan 1903.

884. ———: *Nietzsche in England, 1890-1914: The Growth of a Reputation*. Toronto: U of Toronto Press, 1970. xi, 331 pp.
"William Butler Yeats," 139-73 and passim (see index).

885. TIMM, EITEL FRIEDRICH: *William Butler Yeats und Friedrich Nietzsche*. Würzburg: Königshausen & Neumann, 1980. ix, 331 pp. (Epistemata: Reihe Literaturwissenschaft. 2.)
Originally a Dr.phil. thesis, U of Kiel; English summary in *EASG*, 1980, 89-90.
The most thorough investigation of this topic. Discusses the influence of Nietzsche on Yeats's ideas and on his poetics of mask and symbol, also on the images of the sea, the dance, the tree of life, and the circle (or gyre).
Reviewed by Wolfgang Wicht, *ZAA*, 33:3 (1985), 278-79.

886. WESTERBECK, COLIN LESLIE: "The Dancer and the Statue: A Reading of the Poetry of Shelley, Keats, and Yeats in Terms of Friedrich Nietzsche's *The Birth of Tragedy* ," °Ph.D. thesis, Columbia U, 1973. 261 pp. (*DAI*, 34:5 [Nov 1973], 2664A)
Discusses "The Song of the Happy Shepherd," "An Irish Airman Foresees His Death," "The Fisherman," "Among School Children," "Lapis Lazuli," "The Circus Animals' Desertion," and "Under Ben Bulben."

See also BB128, CA53a, 66, CB546, CC12, CD39, 66, 68, 149, 604, 643, DB175, 196, DC42, EC17, EE491, 534, 536, 538, FC127, FE29, 78, FG23, 26.

Alfred Noyes

887. SAUL, GEORGE BRANDON: "Yeats, Noyes, and Day Lewis," *N&Q*, 195:12 (10 June 1950), 258.
A Yeats echo in a Noyes poem and a Day Lewis echo in "Vacillation." See correction by Alfred Noyes, :15 (22 July 1950), 309.

Flann O'Brien (i.e., Brian O'Nolan)

888. POWER, P. C.: "Climbing the Mountain," *DM*, 9:1 (Autumn 1971), 68-73.
The indebtedness of *An Beal Bocht* to "The Hour before Dawn."

George O'Brien

889. MEENAN, JAMES: *George O'Brien: A Biographical Memoir*. Dublin: Gill & Macmillan, 1980. xi, 218 pp.
See especially pp. 112-22; quotes passages from O'Brien's unpublished recollections.

Sean O'Casey

890. ACHILLES, JOCHEN: *Drama als Form: Der Wandel zu nichtrealistischer Gestaltungsweise im Werk Sean O'Caseys*. Frankfurt/M: Lang, 1979. x, 373 pp. (Regensburger Arbeiten zur Anglistik und Amerikanistik. 16.)
On Yeats's view of *The Silver Tassie*, pp. 321-31.

891. ANON.: "Mr. O'Casey's New Play: Why It Was Rejected. Mr. Yeats on the Dramatist's Job. The War and the Stage," *Obs*, 3 June 1928, 19.
The letters concerning the *Silver Tassie* affair; see CD929.

892. ANON.: "Cleanse the Theatre," *Standard* [Dublin], 30 Aug 1935, 8.
On the *Silver Tassie* affair: "Mr. W. B. Yeats is no literary leader for a catholic country."

893. AYLING, RONALD (ed): *Sean O'Casey: Modern Judgments*. London: Macmillan, 1969. 274 pp.
On Yeats see especially William A. Armstrong: "Sean O'Casey, W. B. Yeats and the Dance of Life," 131-42. On O'Casey's use and implied criticism of Yeats in his description of Mild Millie in *Drums under the Window* and *Red Roses for Me*. O'Casey did not approve of Yeats's romantic conception of Cathleen ni Houlihan and of his later pessimistic view of Irish society.
David Krause: "A Self Portrait of the Artist as a Man," 235-51. Abridged version of *A Self-Portrait of the Artist as a Man: Sean O'Casey's Letters*. Dublin: Dolmen Press, 1968. 39 pp. (Dolmen Chapbook. 6.)

894. ——— (ed): *O'Casey: The Dublin Trilogy. "The Shadow of a Gunman," "Juno and the Paycock," "The Plough and the Stars." A Casebook*. London: Macmillan, 1985. 207 pp.
Numerous references to Yeats in Ayling's introduction and in the reprinted pieces (see index).

895. BENSTOCK, BERNARD: *Sean O'Casey*. Lewisburg: Bucknell UP, 1970. 123 pp.
Yeats is mentioned passim.

896. ———: *Paycocks and Others: Sean O'Casey's World*. Dublin: Gill & Macmillan / NY: Barnes & Noble, 1976. x, 318 pp.
On Yeats and O'Casey, passim (see index).

897. BESIER, WERNER: *Der junge O'Casey: Eine Studie zum Verhältnis von Kunst und Gesellschaft*. Bern: Lang, 1974. iv, 431 pp. (Europäische Hochschulschriften: Reihe XIV--Angelsächsische Sprache und Literatur. 22.)
Passim (see index).

898. BROMAGE, MARY C.: "The Yeats-O'Casey Quarrel," *Michigan Alumnus QR*, 64:14 (1 Mar 1958), 135-44.
About *The Silver Tassie*.

899. COWASJEE, SAROS: *Sean O'Casey: The Man behind the Plays*. Edinburgh: Oliver & Boyd, 1963. xv, 265 pp. (Biography and Criticism. 2.)
Yeats is mentioned passim. Contains a long chapter on the *Silver Tassie* row.

900. ———: "O'Casey Seen through Holloway's Diary," *REL*, 6:3 (July 1965), 58-69.
Contains some notes on the Yeats-O'Casey relationship.

901. FALLON, GABRIEL: "Sean O'Casey and W. B. Yeats vs. Canons of Dramatic Art," *Leader*, 27 Aug 1938, 586-87.
Yeats criticized *The Silver Tassie* because it betrays the author's "opinions," but his own *Purgatory* is no better.

902. ———: *Sean O'Casey: The Man I Knew*. London: Routledge & Kegan Paul, 1965. x, 213 pp.
Reminiscences of Yeats defending *The Plough and the Stars*, pp. 91-93; on the *Silver Tassie* row, pp. 108-16.

903. ———: "The First Production of *The Plough and the Stars*," *SOCR*, 2:2 (Spring 1976), 167-75.
Includes notes on Yeats. N.B.: The whole issue commemorates the first production of O'Casey's play and contains numerous references to Yeats.

904. FITZGERALD, MARY: "How the Abbey Said No: Readers' Reports and the Rejection of *The Silver Tassie* ," *OCA*, 1 (1982), 73-87.
Discusses the involvement of Yeats and Lady Gregory; quotes from unpublished material.

905. GENESON, PAUL: "The Yeats-O'Casey Relationship: A Study in Loyal Opposition," *SOCR*, 2:1 (Fall 1975), 52-57.

906. HOGAN, ROBERT: *The Experiments of Sean O'Casey*. NY: St. Martin's Press, 1960. viii, 215 pp.
See appendix on the *Silver Tassie* controversy, pp. 184-206.

907. HUNT, HUGH: *Séan O'Casey*. Dublin: Gill & Macmillan, 1980. v, 153 pp. (Gill's Irish Lives.)
See index for references to Yeats.

908. IRISH TIMES: "Sean O'Casey: A Centenary Tribute," *IrT,* 1 Apr 1980, 8-9.
Several articles with frequent references to Yeats.

909. JACQUOT, JEAN (ed): *Le théâtre moderne: Hommes et tendances.* Paris: Editions du Centre national de la recherche scientifique, 1958. 372 pp.
René Fréchet: "Sean O'Casey: Un épisode de la vie du théâtre anglais," 321-36. Includes notes on Yeats's plays.

910. JOHNSTON, DENIS: "Joxer in Totnes: A Study in Sean O'Casey," *IrW,* 13 (Dec 1950), 50-53.
O'Casey & Johnston vs. Ireland & Yeats.

911. JORDAN, JOHN: "The Passionate Autodidact: The Importance of *Litera Scripta* for O'Casey," *IUR,* 10:1 (Spring 1980), 59-76.
Comments on O'Casey's quotations from Yeats.

911a. KENNEALLY, MICHAEL: *Portraying the Self: Sean O'Casey & the Art of Autobiography.* Gerrards Cross: Smythe / Totowa, N.J.: Barnes & Noble, 1988. xv, 268 pp. (Irish Literary Studies. 26.)
Several references to Yeats, but unfortunately no index.

912. KILROY, THOMAS (ed): *Sean O'Casey: A Collection of Critical Essays.* Englewood Cliffs: Prentice-Hall, 1975. ix, 174 pp. (Twentieth Century Views. 121.)
Mostly reprinted pieces with frequent references to Yeats.

913. KLEIMAN, CAROL: *Sean O'Casey's Bridge of Vision: Four Essays on Structure and Perspective.* Toronto: U of Toronto Press, 1982. xiv, 148 pp.
Several references to Yeats and *The Silver Tassie* (see index).

914. KOPELEV, LEV ZALMANOVICH (ed): *Sovremennai͡a zarubezhnai͡a drama.* Moskva: Akademii͡a Nauk SSSR, 1962. 383 pp.
E. Kornilova: "Dramaturgii͡a Shona O'Keĭsi," 63-131. Contains some references to Yeats.

915. KOSOK, HEINZ: *Sean O'Casey: Das dramatische Werk.* Berlin: Schmidt, 1972. 419 pp.
On Yeats and O'Casey, passim, especially pp. 372-75. English edition, revised and updated: *Sean O'Casey the Dramatist.* Translated by the author and Joseph T. Swann. Gerrards Cross: Smythe / Totowa, N.J.: Barnes & Noble, 1985. xiv, 409 pp. (Irish Literary Studies. 19.)

916. KRAUSE, DAVID: *Sean O'Casey: The Man and His Work.* An enlarged edition. NY: Macmillan, 1975 [1960]. xiii, 390 pp.
Includes "The Playwright's Not for Burning," *VQR,* 34:1 (Winter 1958), 60-76 (on the *Silver Tassie* row). Discusses the Yeats-O'Casey relationship, including a comparison of their dramatic theories, passim (see index).

917. ———: "O'Casey and Yeats and the Druid. (Some Reflections Provoked by the Recent Publication of O'Casey's *Blasts and Benedictions*)," *MD,* 11:3 (Dec 1968), 252-62.
The *Silver Tassie* quarrel and how and why O'Casey became reconciled with Yeats.

918. ———: *Sean O'Casey and His World.* London: Thames & Hudson,

1976. 128 pp.
See index.

919. ——— and ROBERT G. LOWERY (eds): *Sean O'Casey: Centenary Essays*. Gerrards Cross: Smythe, 1980. ix, 257 pp. (Irish Literary Studies. 7.)
On Yeats see particularly: Ronald Ayling: "Sean O'Casey and the Abbey Theatre, Dublin," 13-40.
Mary FitzGerald: "Sean O'Casey and Lady Gregory: The Record of a Friendship," 67-99.
David Krause: "The Druidic Affinities of O'Casey and Yeats," 100-20; affinities in the treatment of Irish politics in the poetic and dramatic works, the dramatic experiments, and the battles with an incomprehending Irish public.

920. LOWERY, ROBERT G. (ed): *Essays on Sean O'Casey's Autobiographies*. London: Macmillan, 1981. xviii, 249 pp.
Numerous references to Yeats (see index).

921. ———: "The Autobiographies: An Historical Approach," *OCA*, 1 (1982), 97-140.
On references to and quotations from Yeats in O'Casey's autobiography.

922. ———: *Sean O'Casey's Autobiographies: An Annotated Index*. Westport, Ct.: Greenwood Press, 1983. xxxiii, 489 pp.
See pp. 367-69, 419, 455.

923. ——— (ed): *A Whirlwind in Dublin: "The Plough and the Stars" Riots*. Westport, Ct.: Greenwood Press, 1984. xiii, 122 pp. (Contributions in Drama and Theatre Studies. 11.)
An annotated anthology of contemporary reactions to the first performance in 1926; see index for references to Yeats.

924. MCCANN, SEAN (ed): *The World of Sean O'Casey*. London: New English Library, 1966. 252 pp. (Four Square Books. 1610.)
On O'Casey and Yeats, passim, especially in Donal Dorcey: "The Great Occasions," 50-72; on the reception of *The Plough and the Stars*.
Anthony Butler: "The Abbey Daze," 92-105. On the *Silver Tassie* affair. Speculates about the reasons for Yeats's behavior and concludes that he was jealous.

925. MIKHAIL, EDWARD HALIM, and JOHN O'RIORDAN (eds): *The Sting and the Twinkle: Conversations with Sean O'Casey*. London: Macmillan, 1974. xii, 184 pp.
Interviews and conversations, mostly reprinted from newspapers. See index for references to Yeats.

926. MOYA, CARMELA: "L'univers de Sean O'Casey d'après les autobiographies," thesis, Doctorat de 3e cycle, Université de Paris (Sorbonne), 1970. xii, 296 pp.
See index for some remarks on Yeats.

927. MURRAY, CHRISTOPHER: "Tomas MacAnna in Interview about the Later O'Casey Plays at the Abbey Theatre," *IUR*, 10:1 (Spring 1980), 130-45.
MacAnna contends that when Yeats rejected *The Silver Tassie* he also rejected "Total Theatre."

928. O'CASEY, EILEEN: *Sean*. Edited with an introduction by J. C. Trewin. London: Macmillan, 1971. 318 pp.
On the *Silver Tassie* row, pp. 83-103.

929. [O'CASEY, SEAN]: "The Abbey Directors and Mr. O'Casey," *IrSt*, 9 June 1928, 268-72.
Letters about *The Silver Tassie* to and from O'Casey, Lennox Robinson, Yeats, Lady Gregory, and Walter Starkie; reprinted in *IrT*, 10 June 1965, vii-viii, CB337, and in various publications about O'Casey (see index IE s.v. Silver Tassie affair).
For contemporary reactions see the following items: Anon.: "A Dublin Tempest," *Literary Digest*, 4 Aug 1928, 24-25.
Anon.: "Ploughing the Star," *MGuard*, 4 June 1928, 8 (correspondence by O'Casey, 12 June 1928, 22).
Harry Bergholz: "Sean O'Casey," *Englische Studien*, 65:1 (1930), 49-67.
A. Brulé: "Sean O'Casey et le théâtre moderne," *Revue anglo-américaine*, 6:1 (Oct 1928), 53-57.
Sean O'Faolain: "The Case of Sean O'Casey," *Commonweal*, 11 Oct 1935, 577-78.
Walter Starkie: "The Plays of Sean O'Casey," *Nineteenth Century and After*, 104:618 (Aug 1928), 225-36 (correspondence by O'Casey, :619 [Sept 1928], 399-402).

930. O'CASEY, SEAN: *The Letters of Sean O'Casey*. Edited by David Krause. London: Cassell, 1975--. 3 vols.
Volume 1: 1910-41. 1975. xxx, 972 pp. Contains letters from Yeats to O'Casey; material on the *Silver Tassie* affair (pp. 225-326); Yeats's report on O'Casey's *The Crimson in the Tricolour* (pp. 102-3); a letter by George O'Brien to Yeats about *The Plough and the Stars* and Yeats's reply (pp. 144-47); and letters from O'Casey to Yeats. See also index for further references to Yeats.
Volume 2: 1942-54. 1980. xxix, 1200 pp. See index for references to Yeats.
Volume 3: Not yet published (December 1988).

930a. O'CONNOR, GARRY: *Sean O'Casey: A Life*. London: Hodder & Stoughton, 1988. x, 448 pp.
Numerous references to Yeats (see index). Prints two Yeats caricatures by O'Casey, pp. 253-54.

931. O'FLAHERTY, LIAM: "The Plough and the Stars," *IrSt*, 20 Feb 1926, 739-40.
Criticizes Yeats for defending O'Casey's play.

932. Ó HAODHA, MICHEÁL (ed): *The O'Casey Enigma*. Dublin: Mercier Press, 1980. 126 pp.
Some references to Yeats.

933. O'RIORDAN, JOHN: *A Guide to O'Casey's Plays: From the Plough to the Stars*. London: Macmillan, 1984. xi, 419 pp.
See index for references to Yeats.

934. PASACHOFF, NAOMI S.: "Unity of Theme, Image, and Diction in *The Silver Tassie*," *MD*, 23:1 (Mar 1980), 58-64.
Refutes Yeats's criticism that the play lacks unity and contains irrelevancies.

935. PETERSON, RICHARD F.: "Polishing Up the *Silver Tassie* Contro-

versy: Some Lady Gregory and W. B. Yeats Letters to Lennox Robinson," *SOCR,* 4:2 (Spring 1978), 121-29.
Unpublished letters to Robinson show Yeats's arrogance in dealing with O'Casey.

936. REYNOLDS, HORACE: "Riot in the Abbey," *American Spectator,* 3:26 (Dec 1934), 14-15.
The controversial production of *The Plough and the Stars* and Yeats's speech of defense.

937. SCRIMGEOUR, JAMES R.: *Sean O'Casey.* Boston: Hall, 1978. 186 pp. (Twayne's English Authors Series. 245.)
"Yeats vs. O'Casey," 126-28.

938. °*Sean O'Casey.* [London]: National Broadcasting Co., released by Encyclopaedia Britannica Films, 1958. Black-and-white film, 28 minutes.
"Dramatist Sean O'Casey visits with a young American friend at his home on the Devon coast in England, surrounded by his family and his books. He tells of the poverty of his youth, discusses great playwrights whom he has known and admired--including Shaw, Yeats, and Lady Gregory, and speaks of the great hope he has for the world" (from the description in the National Union Catalog).

939. SIMMONS, JAMES: *Sean O'Casey.* London: Macmillan, 1983. ix, 187 pp.
"*The Silver Tassie* Rejected," 92-115, and passim (see index).

940. SMITH, GUS: "Clash with Yeats," *Sunday Independent,* 30 Mar 1980, 11.
O'Casey's clash with Yeats; negligible.

941. SMITH, HUGH: "And Back Home," *NYT,* 14 July 1935, section IX, 1.
About the *Silver Tassie* affair. Correspondence by O'Casey: "Mr. O'Casey Dissents," 11 Aug 1935, IX, 1, defending Yeats as a great man and poet.

942. TABORSKI, BOLESŁAW: *Nowy teatr elżbietański.* Kraków: Wydawnictwo literackie, 1967. 520 pp.
". . . A dla mnie bukiet czerwonych róż: O dramaturgii Seana O'Caseya" [Red roses for me: On Sean O'Casey's dramatic art], 55-98. Contains notes on Yeats.

943. WORTH, KATHARINE: "O'Casey, Synge and Yeats," *IUR,* 10:1 (Spring 1980), 103-17.
The influence of Yeats's plays on O'Casey's.

944. YEATS, W. B.: "Sean O'Casey's Story," *Time and Tide,* 27 May 1933, 640.
Letter to the editor protesting the suppression of O'Caseys "I Wanna Woman" (reprinted in EF104 and 105). See the silly answers by John Gibbons and William Thomson, 3 June 1933, 670, criticizing Yeats's position.

See also AC7, 65, AE94, 98, 100, BB170, BF170, CB122, 337, 443, CC341, CD969, 1115, 1201, CG13, DD213, EA40, EE63, FB12, 23, FD73, HB12.

Flannery O'Connor

945. BYARS, JOHN A.: "W. B. Yeats and *Wise Blood*," *Flannery O'Connor Bulletin*, 14 (1985), 88-93.
Two episodes in Flannery O'Connor's novel seem to be indebted to "The Last Gleeman" in *The Celtic Twilight*.

Frank O'Connor

946. HELWIG, WERNER: "Letzter Besuch bei Frank O'Connor," *Neue Rundschau*, 82:1 (1971), 192, 194-96.
O'Connor talks about Yeats.

947. MATTHEWS, JAMES H.: *Voices: A Life of Frank O'Connor*. NY: Atheneum, 1983. xi, 453 pp.
Numerous references to Yeats, especially in chapter 10: "The Abbey: A Fantasy in Five Acts," 124-48.

948. REID, B. L.: "The Teller's Own Tale: The Memoirs of Frank O'Connor," *SR*, 84:1 (Jan-Mar 1976), 76-97.

949. TOMORY, WILLIAM M.: *Frank O'Connor*. Boston: Twayne, 1980. 198 pp. (Twayne's English Authors Series. 297.)

950. WOHLGELERNTER, MAURICE: *Frank O'Connor: An Introduction*. NY: Columbia UP, 1977. xxiv, 222 pp.
See index.

See also BB176, FB23.

Sean O'Faolain

950a. BONACCORSO, RICHARD: *Sean O'Faolain's Irish Vision*. Albany: State U of New York Press, 1987. viii, 167 pp.
On O'Faolain's indebtedness to Yeats see pp. 40-44, 102-7, and passim.

951. HARMON, MAURICE: *Sean O'Faolain: A Critical Introduction*. Dublin: Wolfhound Press, 1984 [1966]. xix, 236 pp.
See index for notes on O'Faolain's indebtedness to Yeats, especially regarding the concept of unity of being and the romantic-heroic tradition.

952. SAMPSON, DENIS: "'Admiring the Scenery': Sean O'Faolain's Fable of the Artist," *CJIS*, 3:2 [i.e., 3:1] (June 1977), 72-79.
Notes O'Faolain's indebtedness to Yeats.

See also CB105, CD122, FB23.

Liam O'Flaherty

953. SHEERAN, PATRICK F.: *The Novels of Liam O'Flaherty: A Study in Romantic Realism. Part I: Background & Profile. Part II: Analysis*. Dublin: Wolfhound Press, 1976. 319 pp.
Numerous references to O'Flaherty's battle with the Irish literary revival and with Yeats (see index).

954. ZNEIMER, JOHN: *The Literary Vision of Liam O'Flaherty*. Syracuse: Syracuse UP, 1971. xiii, 207 pp.
Contains some comments on the Yeats-O'Flaherty relationship, pp. 10-13, 15-20.

Standish James O'Grady

955. HAGAN, EDWARD ALPHONSUS: *"High Nonsensical Words": A Study of the Works of Standish James O'Grady*. Troy, N.Y.: Whitston, 1986. viii, 229 pp.
See index for references to Yeats.

956. MARCUS, PHILLIP LEDUC: *Standish O'Grady*. Lewisburg: Bucknell UP, 1970. 92 pp.
Refers repeatedly to O'Grady's influence on Yeats.

See also BC1, CA69, CB241, DD57, FE32.

Christopher Okigbo

957. °MADUAKOR, HEZZY OBIAJURU: "Landscape as Symbol in the Poetry of Christopher Okigbo, John Pepper Clark, Wole Soyinka, and Lenrie Peters: As Related to the Poetry of W. B. Yeats," Ph.D. thesis, U of Ottawa, 1977. xix, 339 pp.

John O'Leary

958. BOURKE, MARCUS: *John O'Leary: A Study in Irish Separatism*. Athens: U of Georgia Press, 1967. xi, 251 pp.
Refers to O'Leary's influence on Yeats, passim (see index).

See also AE24, 37, BA21, 22, 147, CA54, CB242, CC109, 232, DC385, EA12, FA51, FD16, 22, 49, 57, FE78, 109.

Eugene O'Neill

959. KRAJEWSKA, WANDA: "Irlandskość Eugene'a O'Neill," *Przegląd humanistyczny*, 10:4 (1966), 51-66.
Discusses the influence of Yeats.

See also CC35, EE416.

Joseph O'Neill

960. LYNCH, M. KELLY: "The Smiling Public Man: Joseph O'Neill and His Works," *JIL*, 12:2 (May 1983), 3-72.
On Yeats and O'Neill, pp. 10-12.

William Orpen

961. ARNOLD, BRUCE: *Orpen: Mirror to an Age*. London: Cape, 1981. 448 pp.
Yeats is referred to passim (see index), especially in "The Irish Cultural Renaissance," 123-86.

George Orwell

962. FLEMING, DEBORAH: "George Orwell's Essay on W. B. Yeats," *Eire*, 19:4 (Winter 1984), 141-47.
Orwell's review of Menon (CA74).

Seumas O'Sullivan (James Starkey)

963. BURNHAM, RICHARD: "The Development of Seumas O'Sullivan and *The Dublin Magazine*," Ph.D. thesis, University College Dublin, 1977. iv, 356 pp.
"W. B. Yeats," 237-53; comments on *Diarmuid and Grania, The Words upon the Window-Pane*, and *Fighting the Waves*.

964. RUSSELL, JANE: *James Starkey / Seumas O'Sullivan: A Critical Biography*. Rutherford, N.J.: Fairleigh Dickinson UP, 1987. 148 pp.
"A. E., Yeats, and the 'School' of Thought," 79-87; "Seumas O'Sullivan and Drama," 97-104, and passim on the strained Yeats-O'Sullivan relationship.

See also BB85, DC71.

Wilfred Owen

965. COHEN, JOSEPH: "In Memory of W. B. Yeats--and Wilfred Owen," *JEGP*, 58:4 (Oct 1959), 637-49.
Author's correction, 59:1 (Jan 1960), 171. Yeats excluded Owen from the *Oxford Book of Modern Verse* because his work did not reflect "the joy of battle."

966. DAS, SASI BHUSAN: *Aspects of Wilfred Owen's Poetry*. Calcutta: Roy & Roy, 1979. ix, 477 pp.
See "W. B. Yeats's Charges against Wilfred Owen," 380-437 (reprinted from *Modern R*, 139:2, 3, 4, 5 [Feb, Mar, Apr, May 1976], 114-25, 195-207, 274-82, 297-304) and passim.

967. JOHNSTON, JOHN HUBERT: *English Poetry of the First World War: A Study in the Evolution of Lyric and Narrative Form*. Princeton: Princeton UP, 1964. xvi, 354 pp.
Some notes on Yeats and Owen, passim (see index).

968. PESCHMANN, HERMANN: "Yeats and the Poetry of War," *English*, 15:89 (Summer 1965), 181-84.
Yeats's exclusion of Owen from the *Oxford Book of Modern Verse* betrays a lack of insight into the "*raison d'être* of the new verse."

969. SEXTON, MÁIRE: "W. B. Yeats, Wilfred Owen, and Sean O'Casey," *Studies*, 70:227 [i.e., 277] (Spring 1981), 88-95.
Yeats's aversion to Owen's poetry, dating perhaps from 1919, helps to explain his unjustified rejection of *The Silver Tassie*. Yeats felt O'Casey's play to be influenced by Owen.

970. STALLWORTHY, JON: "W. B. Yeats and Wilfred Owen," *CritQ*, 11:3 (Autumn 1969), 199-214.
On Yeats echoes in Owen's poetry and Yeats's failure to appreciate Owen's work. Maintains that Owen's work conforms in several important respects to Yeats's idea of poetry and implies

that Yeats forsook his own convictions when he rejected it.

971. ———: *Wilfred Owen*. London: Oxford UP / Chatto & Windus, 1974. xiv, 333 pp.
See pp. 213-14, 244-45, 265n.

972. WHITE, GERTRUDE M.: *Wilfred Owen*. NY: Twayne, 1969. 156 pp. (Twayne's English Authors Series. 86.)
"Yeats and *The Oxford Book of Modern Verse*," 116-21, and passim.

See also CA165, CB46, CC289, DD600.

Charles Stewart Parnell

973. O'GRADY, THOMAS BRENDAN: "'A Certain Fascination': Parnell in the Irish Literary Imagination," Ph.D. thesis, U of Notre Dame, 1985. v, 239 pp. (*DAI*, 45:12 [June 1985], 3647A)
Frequent references to Yeats's view of Parnell, especially on pp. 157-75.

974. O'KEEFE, TIMOTHY J.: "The Art and Politics of the Parnell Monument," *Eire*, 19:1 (Spring 1984), 6-25.
Includes a note on Yeats's views.

975. STEINMAN, MICHAEL ARTHUR: *Yeats's Heroic Figures: Wilde, Parnell, Swift, Casement*. London: Macmillan, 1983. ix, 197 pp.
Based on "Great Men in Their Pride: Studies in Yeats's Heroic Figures. Wilde, Parnell, Swift, Casement," °Ph.D. thesis, State U of New York at Stony Brook, 1981. 536 pp. (*DAI*, 42:3 [Sept 1981], 1165A; reprinted *YeA*, 2 [1983], 102-3).
Contains two chapters each on Wilde and Swift, one on Parnell, and a note on Casement. Discusses Yeats's involvement with these "heroes" and, rather briefly, those of his works dealing with them.
Reviews:
- Anon., *Scriblerian and the Kit-Cats*, 20:1 (Autumn 1987), 94-95.
- Douglas Archibald, *Yeats*, 3 (1985), 252-54.
- Richard Burton, *YeA*, 4 (1986), 263-64.
- Jacqueline Genet, *EI*, 9 (Dec 1984), 343-44.
- Phillip L. Marcus, *ILS*, 3:2 (Fall 1984), 29.
- Daniel T. O'Hara: "The Specialty of Self-Victimization in Recent Yeats Studies," *ConL*, 27:2 (Summer 1986), 285-89.
- Rory Ryan, *UES*, 22:2 (Sept 1984), 51-52.
- George J. Watson: "Heroic Examples," *THES*, 24 Feb 1984, 18.
- Terence de Vere White: "The Heroic Cult," *IrT*, 18 Feb 1984, 12.

976. ———: "Yeats's Parnell: Sources of His Myth," *Eire*, 18:1 (Spring 1983), 46-60.
Partly identical with the Parnell chapter in the preceding item.

See also CC52, 109, 148, 165, 232, FD16, 57.

Walter Pater

977. BAGCHI, JASODHARA: "Yeats and Pater," *Essays and Studies* [Department of English, Jadavpur U], 1 (1968), 61-72.

978. BAROLSKY, PAUL: *Walter Pater's Renaissance*. University Park: Pennsylvania State UP, 1987. xiv, 214 pp.
See index for a few notes on Yeats and Pater.

979. BIZOT, RICHARD: "Pater and Yeats," *ELH*, 43:3 (Fall 1976), 389-412.

980. BLOCK, ED: "Walter Pater, Arthur Symons, W. B. Yeats, and the Fortunes of the Literary Portrait," *SEL*, 26:4 (Autumn 1986), 759-76.
Pater's portrait essays provided structural models for both Symons and Yeats. Discusses "The Happiest of the Poets" and "Discoveries" as indebted to Pater's deductive principle.

981. ENGLER, BALZ: *Reading and Listening: The Modes of Communicating Poetry and Their Influence on the Texts*. Bern: Francke, 1982. 144 pp. (Cooper Monographs. 30.)
Note on Yeats's arrangement of Pater's Mona Lisa section in the *Oxford Book of Modern Verse*, pp. 29-31.

982. FLETCHER, IAIN: "Leda and St. Anne," *List*, 21 Feb 1957, 305-7.
Pater's influence on Yeats and Yeats's interpretation of Pater in the *Oxford Book of Modern Verse*.

983. L'HOMME, CHARLES EDMUND: "The Influence of Walter Pater: A Study in the Making of the Modern Literary Mind," Ph.D. thesis, Columbia U, 1965. xiii, 405 pp. (*DAI*, 29:8 [Feb 1969], 2715A)
"W. B. Yeats and the Rhymers' Club," 190-326. Yeats was influenced by Pater via Lionel Johnson and Arthur Symons.

984. MCGRATH, FRANCIS CHARLES: "Heroic Aestheticism: W. B. Yeats and the Heritage of Walter Pater. The Role of Paterian Aesthetics in Yeats's Drama," Ph.D. thesis, U of Texas at Austin, 1973. xii, 298 pp. (*DAI*, 34:9 [Mar 1974], 5981A-82A)
Particularly on *On Baile's Strand, At the Hawk's Well, Purgatory, A Vision,* and "Rosa Alchemica"; also on Shakespeare's influence. See the following items.

985. ———: "Heroic Aestheticism: Yeats, Pater, and the Marriage of Ireland and England," *IUR*, 8:2 (Autumn 1978), 183-90.

986. ———: "'Rose [sic] Alchemica': Pater Scrutinized and Alchemized," *YER*, 5:2 (1978), 13-20.

987. ———: "Paterian Aesthetics in Yeats' Drama," *CompD*, 13:1 (Spring 1979), 33-48.
Pater's influence on Yeats's dramatic theories and his view of Shakespeare; on *The Shadowy Waters* and *On Baile's Strand*.

988. ———: "W. B. Yeats's Double Vision of Walter Pater," in Srivastava and Dutta: *Unaging Intellect* (1983, CA108), 72-84.

989. ———: *The Sensible Spirit: Walter Pater and the Modernist Paradigm*. Tampa: U of South Florida Press, 1986. xi, 299 pp.
Numerous references to Yeats (see index).

990. MONSMAN, GERALD: "Pater and His Younger Contemporaries," *VN*, 48 (Fall 1975), 1-9.
Pater's influence on Yeats and others.

991. ———: *Walter Pater*. London: Prior / Boston: Twayne, 1977. 213 pp. (Twayne's English Authors Series. 207.)
See pp. 161-64 and passim.

992. NATHAN, LEONARD P. [LEONARD E.?]: "W. B. Yeats's Experiments with an Influence," *VS*, 6:1 (Sept 1962), 66-74.
Pater's influence on Yeats's view of literature.

993. SUDRANN, JEAN: "Victorian Compromise and Modern Revolution," *ELH*, 26:3 (Sept 1959), 425-44.
On Pater, with a few notes on Yeats.

See also CA12, CB134, 513, CC28, 92, 107, 168, CD305, EA28, EB32, FE20, 27, 60, 78, 82.

Patrick (Padraic) Pearse

994. CLAUSEN, CHRISTOPHER: *The Moral Imagination: Essays on Literature and Ethics*. Iowa City: U of Iowa Press, 1986. xii, 195 pp.
"Padraic Pearse: The Revolutionary as Artist," 125-38; reprinted from *ShawR*, 19:2 (May 1976), 83-92; contains notes on Yeats.

995. EDWARDS, RUTH DUDLEY: *Patrick Pearse: The Triumph of Failure*. London: Gollancz, 1977. xvii, 384 pp.
See index for some remarks on Yeats and Pearse.

996. JORDAN, JOHN: "Pearse and Yeats," *Hibernia*, 27 Apr 1973, 12.

997. LE ROUX, LOUIS N.: *Patrick H. Pearse*. Adapted from the French and revised by the author; translated into English by Desmond Ryan. Dublin: Talbot Press, 1932. xiii, 440 pp.
French edition: *°L'Irlande militante: La vie de Patrice Pearse*. Rennes: Imprimerie commerciale de Bretagne, 1932. 336 pp. See pp. 47, 133-34, 152, 155, 224.

998. MITCHELL, JOAN TOWEY: "Yeats, Pearse, and Cuchulain," *Eire*, 11:4 (Winter 1976), 51-65.
Similarities and differences between Pearse and Yeats, especially in their treatment of the Cuchulain myth.

999. PORTER, RAYMOND J.: *P. H. Pearse*. NY: Twayne, 1973, 168 pp. (Twayne's English Authors Series. 154.)
See index for references to Yeats.

See also CB152a, 371, CC224, DC115.

Walker Percy

1000. OAKES, RANDY W.: "W. B. Yeats and Walker Percy's *The Second Coming*," *NConL*, 14:1 (Jan 1984), 9-10.
Percy's use, in his novels, of Yeats's poem.

Fernando Pessoa

1001. *Actas do II Congresso internacional de estudos Pessoanos (Nashville, 31 de Março / 2 de Abril, 1983)*. Oporto: Centro de Estudos Pessoanos, 1985. 687 pp.

Sol Biderman: "Arcane Imagery in Yeats and Fernando Pessoa," 79-90; discusses Rosicrucianism and the image of Mount Abiegnos. See also next item.

1002. BIDERMAN, SOL: "Mount Abiegnos and the Masks: Occult Imagery in Yeats and Pessoa," *Luso-Brazilian R,* 5:1 (June 1968), 59-74.
Mount Abiegnos, the rose, Rosicrucianism, initiation, and mask in the poetry of Yeats and Pessoa. The link seems to have been Annie Besant, who was read by both.

1003. GARCÍA, RUBEN: "The Unexpected Affinities: W. B. Yeats and Fernando Pessoa," *J of the American Portuguese Society,* 10:1 (Spring 1976), 29-37.

George Petrie

1004. BOYNE, PATRICIA: "Scholarly Seedtime of the Irish Literary Revival: A Study of the Lives and Work of George Petrie, Eoin O'Curry, and John O'Donovan Related to the Development of Irish Literature in English," Ph.D. thesis, University College Dublin, 1977. vi, 200 pp.
Contains notes on the influence of these writers on Yeats.

Luigi Pirandello

See CC37, EC107, FC127.

Sylvia Plath

1005. LANE, GARY (ed): *Sylvia Plath: New Views on the Poetry.* Baltimore: Johns Hopkins UP, 1979. xiv, 266 pp.
Barnett Guttenberg: "Plath's Cosmology and the House of Yeats," 138-52. See index for further Yeats references.

1006. WAGNER, LINDA WELSHIMER (ed): *Critical Essays on Sylvia Plath.* Boston: Hall, 1984. viii, 231 pp.
Sandra M. Gilbert: "In Yeats' House: The Death and Resurrection of Sylvia Plath," 204-22.

See also CC289, CD216, DC20.

Plato

1007. RAINE, KATHLEEN: "Yeats and Platonism," *Texas Q,* 10:4 (Winter 1967), 161-81.
Reprinted in *DM,* 7:1 (Spring 1968), 38-63.

1008. TORCHIANA, DONALD T.: "Yeats and Plato," *MBL,* 4:1 (Spring 1979), 5-16.

See also CA17, 53a, 90, CD12, 264, 876, DD50, 539.

Plotinus

1009. ESTERLY, JAMES DAVID: "Yeats, Plotinus, and Symbolic Perception," Ph.D. thesis, U of Cambridge, 1972. v, 281 pp., with interleaved footnotes.

Also on the influence of Coleridge; concentrates on Yeats's poetry with particular reference to "Sailing to Byzantium."

1010. MOTES, MARTIN RICHARD: "'Plotinus for a Friend': MacKenna's Translation of Plotinus and W. B. Yeats's *A Vision* and Later Poetry," Ph.D. thesis, Miami U [Oxford, Ohio], 1973. iv, 159 pp. (*DAI*, 34:8 [Feb 1974], 5195A)

On *Words for Music Perhaps*, "A Woman Young and Old," "Supernatural Songs," "A Dialogue of Self and Soul," and "Vacillation."

1011. RITVO, ROSEMARY PUGLIA: "Plotinistic Elements in Yeats's Prose Works," °Ph.D. thesis, Fordham U, 1973. 214 pp. (*DAI*, 34:1 [July 1973], 334A)

In *A Vision* and *Per Amica Silentia Lunae*.

1012. ———: "*A Vision* B: The Plotinian Metaphysical Basis," *RES*, 26:101 (Feb 1975), 34-46.

1013. ———: "Plotinus's Third *Ennead* and Yeats's *A Vision* (1925)," *N&Q*, os 221 / ns 23:1 (Jan 1976), 19-21.

See also BA14, CA53a, 90.

Horace Plunkett

1014. WEST, TREVOR: *Horace Plunkett: Co-operation and Politics. An Irish Biography*. Gerrards Cross: Smythe / Washington, D.C.: Catholic U of America Press, 1986. xviii, 288 pp.

On Yeats, pp. 87-93, and passim (see index).

E. A. Poe

1015. KÜHNELT, HARRO HEINZ: *Die Bedeutung von Edgar Allan Poe für die englische Literatur: Eine Studie anlässlich des 100. Todestages des Dichters*. Innsbruck: Wagner, 1949. 320 pp.

"William Butler Yeats," 301-3. Yeats's concept of poetry, his preoccupation with dreams and mysticism, and his distrust of the moral element in poetry have close parallels in Poe.

Alexander Pope

1016. RAWSON, CLAUDE: "The Proper Study of Pope," *TLS*, 14 Mar 1975, 275.

See also CA53a.

Porphyry

See CA53a, DC356, DD40, 170.

Ezra Pound

1017. ACKROYD, PETER: *Ezra Pound and His World*. With 111 illustra-

tions. London: Thames & Hudson, 1980. 127 pp.
Yeats is mentioned passim (see index).

1018. AGOSTINO, NEMI D': "La fin de siècle inglese e il giovane Ezra Pound," *EM*, 6 (1955), 135-62.
Contains some notes on the WBY/EP relationship.

1019. BACIGALUPO, MASSIMO: "Linea ligure angloamericana: Pound, Yeats," *Studi di filologia e letteratura* (Università degli studi di Genova), 5 (1980), 477-533.
Pound and Yeats in Rapallo; includes discussions of *A Vision*, the poems in *The Winding Stair*, and "Byzantium."

1020. BAUMANN, WALTER: *The Rose in the Steel Dust: An Examination of the Cantos of Ezra Pound*. Bern: Francke, 1967. 211 pp. (Schweizer anglistische Arbeiten / Swiss Studies in English. 58.)
"Yeats and Conversation," 127-30, and passim (see index).

1021. BORNSTEIN, GEORGE: *The Postromantic Consciousness of Ezra Pound*. Victoria, B.C.: U of Victoria, 1977. 84 pp. (ELS Monograph Series. 8.)
Yeats is mentioned passim.

1022. ——— (ed): *Ezra Pound among the Poets*. Chicago: U of Chicago Press, 1985. xii, 238 pp.
A. Walton Litz: "Pound and Yeats: The Road to Stone Cottage," 128-48.

1023. BROOKE-ROSE, CHRISTINE: *A ZBC of Ezra Pound*. London: Faber & Faber, 1971. x, 297 pp.
On Yeats and Pound, passim (see index); especially on allusions to Yeats in the *Cantos*.

1024. BUSH, RONALD: *The Genesis of Ezra Pound's Cantos*. Princeton: Princeton UP, 1976. xv, 327 pp.
"Yeats and the Noh," 102-11, and passim (see index).

1024a. CARPENTER, HUMPHREY: *A Serious Character: The Life of Ezra Pound*. London: Faber & Faber, 1988. xiii, 1005 pp.
Many references to Yeats, including quotations from unpublished letters (see index).

1025. CHIBA, YOKO: "Ezra Pound's Versions of Fenollosa's Noh Manuscripts and Yeats's Unpublished 'Suggestions & Corrections,'" *YeA*, 4 (1986), 121-44.

1026. DASENBROCK, REED WAY: *The Literary Vorticism of Ezra Pound & Wyndham Lewis: Towards the Condition of Painting*. Baltimore: Johns Hopkins UP, 1985. xii, 271 pp.
See index for some notes on Yeats.

1027. DAVIE, DONALD: "Yeats and Pound," *DM*, 30:4 (Oct-Dec 1955), 17-21.
Although both are prime examples of the "poet as sage," they are very different in other aspects. Yeats would have placed Pound in the subjective phase, opposite his own.

1028. ———: *Ezra Pound: Poet as Sculptor*. London: Routledge & Kegan Paul, 1965. viii, 261 pp.
Passim (see index).

1029. ———: *Trying to Explain*. Ann Arbor: U of Michigan Press, 1979. viii, 213 pp.

"Ezra Pound and the English," 150-64, reprinted from *Paideuma*, 7:1&2 (Spring & Fall 1978), 297-307 (includes notes on the Yeats-Pound relationship); "A Fascist Poem: Yeats's 'Blood and the Moon,'" 165-73.

1030. DAVIS, KAY: *Fugue and Fresco: Structures in Pound's "Cantos."* Orono, Maine: National Poetry Foundation, 1984. 125 pp.

Discusses Yeats's view of Pound in *A Packet for Ezra Pound* in connection with the fugue structure of the *Cantos* (pp. 76-81) and the frescoes in the Schifanoia Palace, Ferrara (pp. 94-97).

1031. EDWARDS, JOHN HAMILTON: "A Critical Biography of Ezra Pound: 1885-1922," Ph.D. thesis, U of California (Berkeley), 1952. vi, 319 pp.

Passim, especially pp. 97-102, 132-36.

1032. "Ezra Pound: A Commemorative Symposium," *Paideuma*, 3:2 (Fall 1974), 151-68.

Oliver Edwards on the friendship of Yeats and Pound, pp. 166-68.

1033. FRASER, GEORGE SUTHERLAND: *Ezra Pound*. Edinburgh: Oliver & Boyd, 1962 [1960]. vi, 118 pp. (Writers and Critics. 001.)

See pp. 93-97.

1034. GOODWIN, KENNETH L.: *The Influence of Ezra Pound*. London: Oxford UP, 1966. xvi, 230 pp.

"Pound and Yeats," 75-105. Pound's influence on Yeats's poetry and plays was not as pervasive as is usually believed.

1035. GORDON, ROBERT: "'Old Yeats,' Young Willie, and 'This Queer Creature Ezra Pound,'" *Montclair J of Social and Behavioral Sciences*, 2:1 (Summer 1973), 68-73.

"Old Yeats . . . had only a small part at best to play in the relationship of his son and . . . Ezra Pound. But JBY's and Pound's own association, entirely separate of Willie's and Ezra's, is a tiny, curious sidelight in the literary history of the time."

1036. GROVER, PHILIP (ed): *Ezra Pound: The London Years, 1908-1920*. NY: AMS Press, 1978. xvi, 166, [26] pp.

William Pratt: "Ezra Pound and the Image," 15-30, mentions Yeats passim.

1037. HÄUSERMANN, H. W.: "W. B. Yeats's Criticism of Ezra Pound," *ES*, 29:4 (Aug 1948), 97-109.

Also in *SR*, 57:3 (July-Sept 1949), 437-55. Especially on Yeats's treatment of Pound in *A Vision*.

1038. HAGEMANN, E. R.: "Incoming Correspondence to Dorothy and Ezra Pound at the Lilly Library," *Paideuma*, 12:1 (Spring 1983), 131-56.

The Lilly Library at Indiana U, Bloomington. The collection includes Yeats material.

1039. HALL, DONALD: "Ezra Pound: An Interview," *Paris R*, 7:28 (Summer-Fall 1962), 22-51.

Pound on Yeats, pp. 29-30, 36.

1040. HESSE, EVA (ed): *New Approaches to Ezra Pound: A Co-ordinated Investigation of Pound's Poetry and Ideas*. London: Faber & Faber, 1969. 406 pp.

Richard Ellmann: "Ez and Old Billyum," 55-85; reprinted from *KR*, 28:4 (Sept 1966), 470-95. Reprinted in CD7.

Other articles in the book comment on the Yeats-Pound relationship, passim (see index).

The book is not identical with the following compilation by the same editor: *Ezra Pound: 22 Versuche über einen Dichter*. Frankfurt/Main: Athenäum, 1967. 456 pp., which contains a German translation of Ellmann's article (pp. 17-44) and other material on the Yeats-Pound relationship, passim (see index).

1041. HEYMANN, CLEMENS DAVID: *Ezra Pound: The Last Rower. A Political Profile*. NY: Viking Press, 1976. xii, 372 pp.

See index for some notes on WBY and EP.

1042. HUTCHINS, PATRICIA: "Yeats and Pound in England," *Texas Q*, 4:3 (Autumn 1961), 203-16.

Biographical connections.

1043. ———: *Ezra Pound's Kensington: An Exploration, 1885-1913*. London: Faber & Faber, 1965. 180 pp.

Passim (see index).

1044. JACKSON, THOMAS H.: *The Early Poetry of Ezra Pound*. Cambridge, Mass.: Harvard UP, 1968. xvi, 261 pp.

Compares the early poetry of Pound and Yeats, passim (see index), especially pp. 47-60, 129-40, 152-53, and 191-94.

1045. ———: "The Poetic Politics of Ezra Pound," *JML*, 3:4 (Apr 1974), 987-1011.

Compares the political attitudes of Yeats and Pound, pp. 996-97.

1046. KENNER, HUGH: *The Poetry of Ezra Pound*. Norfolk, Ct.: New Directions, [1951]. 342 pp.

Scattered notes on the WBY/EP relationship, passim (see index).

1047. ———: *The Pound Era*. London: Faber & Faber, 1972. xiv, 606 pp.

Passim (see index).

1048. LONGENBACH, JAMES BURTON: *Modernist Poetics of History: Pound, Eliot, and the Sense of the Past*. Princeton: Princeton UP, 1987. xviii, 280 pp.

Based on "A Sense of the Past: Pound, Eliot, and Modernist Poetics of History," Ph.D. thesis, Princeton U, 1985. xi, 325 pp. (*DAI*, 46:5 [Nov 1985], 1277A-78A). See "Pater and Yeats: The Dicta of the Great Critics," 29-44, and passim (see index). Discusses Yeats's influence on Pound and Eliot.

The following two items have been extracted from the thesis: "The Order of the Brothers Minor: Pound and Yeats at Stone Cottage 1913-1916," *Paideuma*, 14:2-3 (Fall-Winter 1985), 395-403.

"The Secret Society of Modernism: Pound, Yeats, Olivia Shakespear, and the Abbé de Montfaucon de Villars," *YeA*, 4 (1986), 103-20. Mainly on Pound's interest in *Le Comte de Gabalis* by Montfaucon de Villars, which was translated by Olivia Shakespear. Yeats seems to have played a minor role in this matter by rekindling Pound's interest in occult literature.

1048a. ———: "The Odd Couple: Pound and Yeats Together," *NYTBR*, 10 Jan 1988, 1, 26-28.
In Stone Cottage, 1913-16.

1048b. ———: *Stone Cottage: Pound, Yeats, and Modernism*. NY: Oxford UP, 1988. xviii, 329 pp.
Incorporates "The Secret Society . . ." from CD1048. A description of the collaboration of both poets during the winters 1913-16, which centers more on Pound than on Yeats. Discusses *At the Hawk's Well, Per Amica Silentia Lunae*, and other works, also the influence of the Nō.
Reviews:
- Denis Donoghue: "Pound's Book of Beasts," *NYRB*, 2 June 1988, 14-16.
- Steven Helmling: "Masking the Needs of Art," *KR*, 10:4 (Fall 1988), 124-29.
- David Wyatt: "Cottagemates," *VQR*, 64:4 (Autumn 1988), 739-43.

1049. MCDOWELL, COLIN, and TIMOTHY MATERER: "Gyre and Vortex: W. B. Yeats and Ezra Pound," *TCL*, 31:4 (Winter 1985), 343-67.
"Pound worked in the same esoteric tradition that Yeats developed."

1049a. MAKIN, PETER: *Pound's Cantos*. London: Allen & Unwin, 1985. xviii, 331 pp.
Several notes on Yeats's influence on Pound (see index).

1050. MULLINS, EUSTACE: *This Difficult Individual, Ezra Pound*. NY: Fleet Publishing Corporation, 1961. 388 pp.
See pp. 56-69 and passim for biographical connections.

1051. NAGY, NICOLAS CHRISTOPH DE: *The Poetry of Ezra Pound: The Pre-Imagist Stage*. Bern: Francke, 1960. 184 pp. (Cooper Monographs. 4.)
See chapters 3, 4C, and 5, passim.

1052. NORMAN, CHARLES: *Ezra Pound*. Revised edition. London: Macdonald, 1969 [1960]. xvii, 493 pp.
See especially "Pound and Yeats," 128-45, and "Pound and Yeats in Rapallo," 296-304. Discusses biographical connections.

1053. OLSON, CHARLES: *Charles Olson & Ezra Pound: An Encounter at St. Elizabeths*. Edited by Catherine Seelye. NY: Grossman, 1975. xxvi, 147 pp.
On Yeats passim; see especially "Thoughts on Yeats. Ideas on Ezra Pound," 23-24.
"This Is Yeats Speaking," 25-31; reprinted from *PR*, 13:1 (Winter 1946), 139-42. Also in Olson's *Human Universe and Other Essays*. Edited by Donald Allen. NY: Grove Press, 1967. v, 160 pp. (pp. 99-102). Olson defends Pound by speaking through an imagined Yeats.

1054. PERLOFF, MARJORIE: *The Dance of the Intellect: Studies in the Poetry of the Pound Tradition*. Cambridge: Cambridge UP, 1985. xii, 243 pp.
Passim (see index).

1055. POUND, EZRA: "On Criticism in General," *Criterion*, 1:2 (Jan 1923), 143-56.
Pound records his debt to Yeats in six lines (p. 144).

1056. ———: *Pound/Joyce: The Letters of Ezra Pound to James Joyce, with Pound's Essays on Joyce*. Edited and with commentary by Forrest Read. NY: New Directions, [1967]. vi, 314 pp.

Numerous references to Yeats, passim. Reprints Pound's "Le Prix Nobel," *Querschnitt,* 4:1 (Spring 1924), 41-44, which is actually not so much on Yeats as on British literary politics.

1057. ———, and FORD MADOX FORD: *Pound/Ford: The Story of a Literary Friendship. The Correspondence between Ezra Pound and Ford Madox Ford and Their Writings about Each Other*. Edited with an introduction and narrative commentary and notes by Brita Lindberg-Seyersted. London: Faber & Faber, 1982. xxiv, 222 pp.

Several short references to Yeats (see index).

1058. POUND, EZRA: *Ezra Pound and Dorothy Shakespear: Their Letters 1909-1914*. Edited by Omar Pound and A. Walton Litz. NY: New Directions, 1984. xv, 399 pp.

Many references to Yeats, Georgie Hyde-Lees (Mrs. W. B. Yeats), and Olivia Shakespear (see index).

1059. READ, HERBERT: *The True Voice of Feeling: Studies in English Romantic Poetry*. London: Faber & Faber, 1953. 382 pp.

"Ideas into Action: Ezra Pound," 116-38; notes Pound's influence on Yeats.

1060. RECK, MICHAEL: *Ezra Pound: A Close-Up*. NY: McGraw-Hill, 1967. xiii, 205 pp.

Passim (see index).

1061. REES, THOMAS: "Ezra Pound and the Modernization of W. B. Yeats," *JML,* 4:3 (Feb 1975), 574-92.

1062. REISING, RUSSELL J.: "Yeats, the Rhymers' Club, and Pound's Hugh Selwyn Mauberly," *JML,* 12:1 (Mar 1985), 179-82.

Pound's treatment of the members of the Rhymers' Club reflects his reaction to two Yeats lectures.

1063. RUTHVEN, K. K.: "Propertius, Wordsworth, Yeats, Pound and Hale," *N&Q,* os 213 / ns 15:2 (Feb 1968), 47-48.

On a supposed Yeats parody in Pound's "Homage to Sextus Propertius." Actually, I think that Pound does not parody, but only refers obliquely to, Yeats's "The Withering of the Boughs."

1064. SCHNEIDAU, HERBERT N.: "Pound and Yeats: The Question of Symbolism," *ELH,* 32:2 (June 1965), 220-37.

Yeats's influence on Pound.

1065. ———: *Ezra Pound: The Image and the Real*. Baton Rouge: Louisiana State UP, 1969. ix, 210 pp.

Passim (see index).

1066. SCHULTZ, ROBERT: "A Detailed Chronology of Ezra Pound's London Years, 1908-1920," *Paideuma,* 11:3 (Winter 1982), 456-72; 12:2-3 (Fall-Winter 1983), 357-73.

1067. SITWELL, EDITH: "Yeats e la soluzione di Pound," *Fiera letteraria,* 5:46 (16 Nov 1950), 3.

1068. STOCK, NOEL: *The Life of Ezra Pound*. An expanded edition. San Francisco: North Point Press, 1982 [1970]. xxi, 478 pp.

Scattered notes (see index).

1069. TERRELL, CARROLL F.: *A Companion to the Cantos of Ezra Pound*. Berkeley: U of California Press, 1980-84. 2 vols.
For an index to Yeats references see 2:785.

1070. TORREY, EDWIN FULLER: *The Roots of Treason: Ezra Pound and the Secrets of St. Elizabeths*. NY: McGraw-Hill, 1984. xx, 339 pp.
See index for some remarks on Yeats, especially with reference to his occult interests which Pound is said to have shared.

1071. TYTELL, JOHN: *Ezra Pound: The Solitary Volcano*. NY: Doubleday, 1987. xv, 368 pp.
See index for notes on the Yeats-Pound relationship.

1072. WALLACE, EMILY MITCHELL: "Some Friends of Ezra Pound: A Photographic Essay," *YR*, 75:3 (June 1986), 331-56.

1073. WILLIAMS, WILLIAM CARLOS: *The Selected Letters*. Edited with an introduction by John C. Thirlwall. NY: McDowell, Obolensky, 1957. xix, 348 pp.
Some notes on the Yeats-Pound relationship, passim (see index).

1074. WITEMEYER, HUGH: *The Poetry of Ezra Pound: Forms and Renewal, 1908-1920*. Berkeley: U of California Press, 1969. xiv, 220 pp.
Discusses Yeats's influence on Pound, Yeats allusions in Pound's poetry, and Yeats's concept of the mask in relation to Pound's personae, passim (see index).

See also AE33, BA14, BB37, 94, 185, BC8-9, CA124, CB190, 360, CC99, 100, 265, 277, 294, CD1a, 7, 18, 30, 54, 303, 589, 1302, 1415, DA6, DB24, 209, 233, 242, DC233, 397, 417, DD447, 461, 644, 646, EA25, EB54, ED1, 16, 31, FD19, FE17, 29, 36, 43, 101, FF17, G571, 586.

Propertius

1075. ARKINS, BRIAN: "Yeats and Propertius," *Liverpool Classical Monthly*, 10:5 (May 1985), 72-73.
Part of a projected study of Greek and Roman themes in Yeats's works; discusses "A Thought from Propertius."

Marcel Proust

1076. WILSON, EDMUND: "Proust and Yeats," *NewRep*, 5 Oct 1927, 176-77, 177a.
Proust and Yeats as symbolists.

Shri Purohit Swami

1077. HEGDE, NARAYAN: "W. B. Yeats and Shri Purohit Swami: A Study of Yeats's Last Indian Phase," Ph.D. thesis, State U of New York at Stony Brook, 1980. vi, 199 pp. (*DAI*, 41:4 [Oct 1980], 1580; reprinted *YeA*, 1 [1982], 216-17)
Contains chapters on "The Five Indian Essays," *A Vision*, "Supernatural Songs," and *The Herne's Egg*.

1078. MOKASHI PUNEKAR, [SHANKAR]: "An Introduction to Shri Purohit

Swami and the Anadhoota Geeta," *LCrit*, 11:3 (Winter 1974), 95-97.

1079. NAIK, M. K., S. K. DESAI, and S. T. KALLAPUR (eds): *The Image of India in Western Creative Writing*. Dharwar: Karnatak U / Madras: Macmillan, 1971. viii, 404 pp.
Shankar Mokashi-Punekar: "Sri Purohit Swami and W. B. Yeats," 127-48.

See also BC1, CA77, CB420, CD1, 75, 78, 89, 90, 1401, 1402, EE277.

Sarah Purser

1080. O'GRADY, JOHN NOEL: "Sarah Henrietta Purser: Her Life and Her Work," Ph.D. thesis, University College Dublin, 1974. 2 vols.
Some references to Yeats in vol. 1 (see index); note on the pastel of Yeats in vol. 2, item 285.

See also CD479.

Thomas Pynchon

1081. LENSE, EDWARD: "Pynchon's *V*," *Expl*, 43:1 (Fall 1984), 60-61.
An allusion to the Golden Bird in "Sailing to Byzantium."

1081a. MCCARRON, WILLIAM E.: "Pynchon and Yeats," *NConL*, 18:3 (May 1988), 6-7.
A reference to "Sailing to Byzantium" in *Gravity's Rainbow*.

John Quinn

1082. KAVANAGH, PETER: *The John Quinn Letters: A Pandect*. NY: Peter Kavanagh Hand Press, 1960. iii, 52 pp.
Extracts from letters from Yeats to Quinn, and Quinn to Yeats, pp. 21-25. Further references to Yeats, some of them not very flattering, in letters from AE, Lady Gregory, Arthur Symons, and Lily Yeats. The originals are in the New York Public Library where, according to Kavanagh, they can be read but must not copied or quoted. Kavanagh made his selections from memory; they "are not verbatim irrespective of the style used." The book had to be withdrawn because of legal action.

See also AE68, 83, 88, BB84, 199, BC1, 10, BG191.

Kathleen Raine

1082a. HUK, ROMANA CHRISTINA: "Tradition, Synthesis, Vision, and Voice: Kathleen Raine's Poetry in Perspective," °Ph.D. thesis, U of Notre Dame, 1987. 404 pp. (*DAI*, 48:7 [Jan 1988], 1775A)
Discusses the influence of Yeats.

1083. ROSEMERGY, JANET MARY CRAMER: "Kathleen Raine, Poet of Eden: Her Poetry and Criticism," °Ph.D. thesis, U of Michigan, 1981. 305 pp. (*DAI*, 42:9 [Mar 1982], 3995A)
Includes a comparison with Yeats.

See also CA90.

Balachandra Rajan

1084. WOODCOCK, GEORGE: "Balachandra Rajan: The Critic as Novelist," *World Literature Written in English,* 23:2 (1984), 442-51.
Notes Yeats's influence on Rajan's novels.

John Crowe Ransom

1085. RANSOM, JOHN CROWE: *Selected Letters.* Edited by Thomas Daniel Young and George Core. Baton Rouge: Louisiana State UP, 1984. xv, 430 pp.
Contains a few notes on Yeats (see index), particularly with reference to Wilson's *W. B. Yeats and Tradition* (CA129).

See also CD18.

James Reeves

1086. REEVES, JAMES: "Yeats and the Muses," *Time and Tide,* 17 May 1958, 613.
Quotes from two letters written to Reeves, in which Yeats refuses the inclusion of his poems in the *Oxford Book of Modern Verse.*

1087. ———: "Yeats & Reeves," *NSt,* 30 Oct 1964, 651.
Comments on the exclusion of Laura Riding and himself from the *Oxford Book of Modern Verse.*

Forrest Reid

1088. BRYAN, MARY: *Forrest Reid.* Boston: Twayne, 1976. 173 pp. (Twayne's English Authors Series. 199.)
On Reid and Yeats, pp. 46-50.

1089. BURLINGHAM, RUSSELL: *Forrest Reid: A Portrait and a Study.* With an introduction by Walter de la Mare. London: Faber & Faber, 1953. 259 pp.
See pp. 196-202 and passim for Reid's book on Yeats (CA93).

1090. MCIVOR, PETER: "Forrest Reid, *Uladh,* and the Ulster Literary Theatre," *Eire,* 17:2 (Summer 1982), 134-41.

1091. SIMMONS, JAMES: "Forrest Reid on Yeats," *Threshold,* 28 (Spring 1977), 60-67.
An assessment of Reid's Yeats book (CA93).

1092. TAYLOR, BRIAN: *The Green Avenue: The Life and Writings of Forrest Reid, 1875-1947.* Cambridge: Cambridge UP, 1980. xiv, 218 pp.
See index.

Kenneth Rexroth

1093. GARDNER, GEOFFREY (ed): *For Rexroth.* NY: Ark, 1980. xvii, 415 pp. (Ark. 14.)
Emiko Sakurai: "The Noh Plays of Kenneth Rexroth: A Study of the Fusion of the Classical Greek and Japanese Traditions," 63-80; comments on Yeats's influence.

The Rhymers' Club

1094. ALFORD, NORMAN: *The Rhymers' Club*. [Victoria, B.C.]: Cormorant Press, 1980. x, 165 pp.
"William Butler Yeats: 1890-1896," 45-65, and passim.
Reviews:
- Karl Beckson: "The Legends of the Rhymers' Club: A Review Article," *VP*, 19:4 (Winter 1981), 397-406.
- Ian Fletcher: "The Wavering Kind," *TLS*, 14 Aug 1981, 939.

1095. BECKSON, KARL: "Yeats and the Rhymers' Club," *YeSt*, 1 (Bealtaine 1971), 20-41.
What the Rhymers' Club meant to Yeats and vice versa.

1096. GANNON, PATRICIO (ed): *Poets of the Rhymers' Club*. With a preface. Buenos Aires: Colombo, 1953. 75 pp.
"Preface," 11-21.

1097. GARDINER, BRUCE: "The Rhymers' Club: A Social and Intellectual History," Ph.D. thesis, Princeton U, 1983. iv, 252 pp. (*DAI*, 43:12 [June 1983], 3919A; reprinted *YeA*, 4 [1986], 308-9)
Frequent references to Yeats. See particularly "An Irish Answer," 143-73; "The Irish Literary Society and the New Irish Library," 190-200.

1098. GARDNER, JOANN LYNN: "Myth and Poetic Survival: A Study of W. B. Yeats and the Rhymers' Club of the 1890's," °Ph.D. thesis, Johns Hopkins U, 1984. 326 pp. (*DAI*, 44:11 [May 1984], 3388A; reprinted *Yeats*, 3 [1985], 208-9, and *YeA*, 4 [1986], 309)

1099. ———: "The Rhymers' Club Reviews and Yeats's Myth of Failure," *Yeats*, 4 (1986), 33-54.
The influence of the reviews of the first *Book of the Rhymers' Club* on Yeats's views of the Rhymers. Includes a complete list of the reviews.

1100. KING, PETER: "W. B. Yeats: The Rhymers and Reality," *1837-1901*, 2 (Oct 1977), 37-48.

1101. RUTENBERG, DANIEL: "A Study of Rhymers' Club Poetry," Ph.D. thesis, U of Florida, 1967. iii, 192 pp. (*DAI*, 31:1 [July 1970], 402A)

For further references to the Rhymers' Club see Index IB.

Dorothy M. Richardson

1102. ROSE, SHIRLEY: "Dorothy Richardson Recalls Yeats," *Eire*, 7:1 (Spring 1972), 96-102.
Discusses the material listed in BB204.

Charles Ricketts

1103. BINNIE, ERIC: *The Theatrical Designs of Charles Ricketts*. Ann Arbor: UMI Research Press, 1985. xiii, 185 pp. (Theater and Dramatic Studies. 23.)
See especially "The Irish Plays," 59-86; on the designs made by Ricketts for *On Baile's Strand* and *The King's Threshold* (illustrated), also on the screens made by Edward Gordon Craig.

1104. DELANEY, J. G. P.: "'Heirs of the Great Generation': Yeats's Friendship with Charles Ricketts and Charles Shannon," *YeA*, 4 (1986), 53-73.

1105. FLETCHER, IFAN KYRLE: "Charles Ricketts and the Theatre," *TN*, 22:1 (Autumn 1967), 6-23.
Yeats was indirectly responsible for Ricketts's career as a stage designer. Ricketts designed three plays for him: *Deirdre, The King's Threshold,* and *On Baile's Strand.*

See also BB205, BC1, CC66, EB143, EF90.

Laura Riding

1106. JACKSON, LAURA (RIDING): "Literary Mentioning," *Paris R*, 23: 79 (Spring 1981), 301-4.
Refutes a Yeats story about herself as related by Stephen Spender in 22:77 (Winter-Spring 1980), 121-22. See BG199.

See also CD1087.

Rainer Maria Rilke

1107. CLARKE, AUSTIN: "The Commerce of Poetry," *IrT*, 23 Feb 1946, 4.
Compares Yeats and Rilke.

1108. MASON, EUDO COLECESTRA: *Rilke, Europe, and the English-Speaking World*. Cambridge: UP, 1961. xvi, 257 pp.
See pp. 111-13.

1109. MERIVALE, PATRICIA: "'Ultima Thule': Ghosts and Borderlines in Yeats and Rilke," *CL*, 30:3 (Summer 1978), 249-67.

1110. ROSE, WILLIAM: "A Letter from W. B. Yeats on Rilke," *GL&L*, 15:1 (Oct 1961), 68-70.

See also CA2, 65, CD68, 878a, DC215, 402, DD363, 370, G828.

Lennox Robinson

1111. O'NEILL, MICHAEL JOSEPH: *Lennox Robinson*. NY: Twayne, 1964. 192 pp. (Twayne's English Authors Series. 9.)
Yeats is mentioned passim.

1112. PEAKE, DONALD JAMES: "Selected Plays of Lennox Robinson: A Mirror of the Anglo-Irish Ascendancy," Ph.D. thesis, Southern Illinois U, 1972. v, 236 pp. (*DAI*, 33:9 [Mar 1973], 5340A)
Contains references to Yeats.

1113. PETERSON, RICHARD F.: "The Crane and the Swan: Lennox Robinson and W. B. Yeats," *JIL*, 9:1 (Jan 1980), 69-76.

1114. PHILLIPS, GARY: "Lennox Robinson on the Dublin Drama League: A Letter to Gabriel Fallon," *ICarbS*, 4:2 (Spring-Summer 1981), 75-82.
Contains a few references to Yeats.

1115. SPINNER, KASPAR: *Die alte Dame sagt: Nein! Drei irische Dra-*

matiker: Lennox Robinson, Sean O'Casey, Denis Johnston. Bern: Francke, 1961. vi, 210 pp. (Schweizer anglistische Arbeiten. 52.)
Some remarks on Yeats passim (no index).

1116. WORLEY, LLOYD DOUGLAS: "Four Lost Comedies by Lennox Robinson," Ph.D. thesis, Southern Illinois U at Carbondale, 1979. viii, 788 pp. (*DAI*, 40:4 [Oct 1979], 2081A)
Frequent references to Yeats.

1117. WORTH, KATHARINE: "A Place in the Country," *TLS*, 2 Sept 1983, 929.
A review of Robinson's *Selected Plays* (1983); comments on the Yeats-Robinson relationship.

See also AE97, BC1, EB147.

Theodore Roethke

1118. BOWERS, NEAL: *Theodore Roethke: The Journey from I to Otherwise*. Columbia: U of Missouri Press, 1982. xi, 228 pp.
On Yeats's influence passim (see index).

1119. HEYEN, WILLIAM HELMUTH: "Essays on the Later Poetry of Theodore Roethke," Ph.D. thesis, Ohio U, 1967. iv, 132 pp. (*DAI*, 28:8 [Feb 1968], 3185A)
"The Yeats Influence: Roethke's Formal Lyrics of the 1950's," 44-92; a revised version of this chapter was published in *John Berryman Studies*, 3:4 (Fall 1977), 17-63.

1120. LA BELLE, JENIJOY: *The Echoing Wood of Theodore Roethke*. Princeton: Princeton UP, 1976. x, 174 pp.
On Yeats's influence on Roethke, pp. 109-17, and passim (see index). Incorporates "Theodore Roethke's Dancing Masters in 'Four for Sir John Davies,'" *CP*, 8:2 (Fall 1975), 29-35 (one of them is Yeats).

1121. MAKI, JACQUELINE R.: "The Dance: Roethke's Legacy from Yeats," *Kentucky Philological Association Bulletin*, 8:1 (1981), 9-23.
Yeats's influence on Roethke's dance symbolism.

1122. MALKOFF, KARL: *Theodore Roethke: An Introduction to the Poetry*. NY: Columbia UP, 1966. x, 246 pp.
Passim (see index).

1123. MARTZ, LOUIS LOHR: *The Poem of the Mind: Essays on Poetry English and American*. NY: Oxford UP, 1966. xiii, 231 pp.
Notes the influence of Yeats's "The Magi" on Roethke's "Frau Bauman, Frau Schmidt, and Frau Schwartze," pp. 175-76.

1124. PARINI, JAY: *Theodore Roethke: An American Romantic*. Amherst: U of Massachusetts Press, 1979. xi, 204 pp.

1125. STIFFLER, RANDALL: *Theodore Roethke: The Poet and His Critics*. Chicago: American Library Association, 1986. xviii, 211 pp.
"The Influence of W. B. Yeats," 139-56; a review of what the critics said about the Roethke-Yeats relationship.

1126. SULLIVAN, ROSEMARY: *Theodore Roethke: The Garden Master*. Seattle: U of Washington Press, 1975. xv, 220 pp.

1127. VANDERWERKEN, DAVID L.: "Roethke's 'Four for Sir John Davies' and 'The Dying Man,'" *RS*, 41:2 (June 1973), 125-35.

See also CA159, CD18, 21, 216, DC112, DD239.

Adriaan Roland Holst

1128. BOSSAERT, HENRI: "De keltische en mythologische facetten in het werk van A. Roland Holst," *Vlaamse gids*, 56:6 (June 1972), 7-12.
Includes notes on Yeats's influence.

1129. ———: "A. Roland Holst, W. B. Yeats en de kunstidealen van het franse symbolisme," *Nieuw vlaams tijdschrift*, 26:2 (Feb 1973), 155-76.

1130. DRAAK, MAARTJE: "De gecompliceerde bronnen van Holst's Ierse prozaverhalen," *Nieuwe taalgids*, 68:1 (1975), 31-45.
Discusses Yeats's influence on Roland Holst's prose works.

1131. SÖRENSEN, FREDDY: "Een vergelijking: Adiraan [sic] Roland Holst en William Butler Yeats," *Ruimten*, 3:12 (1964), 22-38.
A detailed comparison of the poetry of both poets.

1132. STENFERT KROESE, WILLEM HERMAN: *De mythe van A. Roland Holst*. Amsterdam: De Bezige Bij, 1951. iii, 110 pp.
On the influence of Yeats on Roland Holst, pp. 6-33.

1133. VEGT, JAN VAN DER: "A. Roland Holst en William Butler Yeats," *Syllabus*, Oct 1966, 3-5.

1134. ———: *De brekende spiegel: Ontwikkeling, samenhang, achtergronden bij A. Roland Holst*. 's Gravenhage: Nijgh & Van Ditmar, 1974. 362 pp. (Nieuwe Nijgh boeken. 61.)
Numerous remarks on the influence of Yeats (see index).

1135. VESTDIJK, SIMON: *Voor en na de explosie: Opstellen over poezie*. Den Haag: Bert Balcker / Daamen, 1960. 208 pp.
"Nestoriaanse overpeinzingen: A. Roland Holst," 9-17; reprinted from *Gids*, 119:3 (Mar 1956), 203-9. Compares the poetry of Yeats and Roland Holst and discusses Roland Holst's Yeats translations.

1136. WIJNGAARDS, N.: "*The Shadowy Waters* van W. B. Yeats en A. Roland Holst," *Spiegel der letteren*, 6:3 (1963), 197-209.

See also CB546.

T. W. Rolleston

1137. ROLLESTON, CHARLES HENRY: *Portrait of an Irishman: A Biographical Sketch of T. W. Rolleston*. London: Methuen, 1939. xv, 189 pp.
See index for references to Yeats. Reprints an article from an unidentified issue of *Irish Weekly Independent*, 1896, in which Rolleston comments on Yeats's poetry (pp. 20-21). This may have been "Irish Literary Revival: An Interesting Lecture by Mr. T. W. Rolleston," *Irish Weekly Independent*, 1 Feb 1896, 12-13.

See also CA69.

Dante Gabriel Rossetti

1138. FALDET, DAVID STEVEN: "Visual Art and the Poetics of Rossetti, Morris, and Yeats," °Ph.D. thesis, U of Iowa, 1986. 327 pp. (*DAI*, 47:9 [Mar 1987], 3433A)

1139. PISTORIUS, ALAN PHIL: "D. G. Rossetti and Early Yeats," Ph.D. thesis, U of California (Berkeley), 1973. ii, 310 pp. (*DAI*, 34:10 [Apr 1974], 6654A)

See also CA61, 168, CC107, DA11.

Margot Ruddock

1140. YEATS, W. B., and MARGOT RUDDOCK: *Ah, Sweet Dancer: A Correspondence*. Edited by Roger McHugh. London: Macmillan, 1970. 142 pp.

Contains 35 letters from Margot Ruddock to Yeats and her essay "Almost I Tasted Ecstasy" (reprinted from BB213); also notes and editorial introduction. For reviews see G1390-1402 and note.

See also BB109, 229, CA150, CC174.

John Ruskin

1141. LEVINE, HERBERT J.: "Yeats's Ruskinian Byzantium," *YeA*, 2 (1983), 25-34.

"Yeats's habit of evaluating an historic civilization through its art stems from his early and lifelong acquaintance with the work of John Ruskin," especially from Ruskin's treatment of Venice.

See also DB165.

G. W. Russell (AE)

1142. AUROBINDO, SRI [i.e., Aurobindo Ghose]: *Letters of Sri Aurobindo (On Poetry and Literature)*. Third series. Bombay: Sri Aurobindo Circle, 1949. xvi, 350 pp.

"Yeats and AE," 308-10 (written Aug 1934); "Yeats and the Occult," 310-13 (on occult themes in the poetry).

1142a. BURLEIGH, MARIAN: "George Russell (AE)--The Painter of the Irish Renaissance," Ph.D. thesis, New York U, 1978. x, 362 pp. (*DAI*, 39:4 [Oct 1978], 1889A)

Yeats is mentioned passim.

1143. DANIELS, WILLIAM LAWS: "AE: 1867-1967," *UR*, 4:2 (Summer 1967), 107-20.

Contains numerous references to Yeats.

1144. ———: "The Early AE: Prose, Poetry, Life, 1867-1905," Ph.D. thesis, Harvard U, 1968. 3 vols.

On Yeats, passim. Quotes copiously from MS. sources.

1145. DAVIS, ROBERT BERNARD: *George William Russell ("AE")*. Boston: Twayne, 1977. 163 pp. (Twayne's English Authors Series. 208.)

See index for some notes on the Yeats-AE relationship.

1146. EGLINTON, JOHN: *A Memoir of AE: George William Russell.* London: Macmillan, 1937, vii, 291 pp.
On Yeats and AE, passim.

1147. FIGGIS, DARRELL: *AE (George W. Russell): A Study of a Man and a Nation.* Dublin: Maunsel, 1916. vii, 159 pp.
On Yeats, pp. 26-29, 133-38.

1148. FOSTER, JOHN WILSON: "*The Interpreters:* A Handbook to AE and the Irish Revival," *Ariel,* 11:3 (July 1980), 69-82.

1149. GIBBON, MONK: "The Early Years of George Russell (AE) and His Connection with the Theosophical Movement," Ph.D. thesis, Trinity College, Dublin, 1947/48. iv, 399 pp.
"Correspondence with Yeats," 301-13.

1150. ———: "AE: The Years of Mystery," *DM,* 31:1 (Jan-Mar 1956), 8-21.
Includes some references to Yeats.

1151. ———: "AE and the Early Days of Theosophy in Dublin," *DM,* 32:3 (July-Sept 1957), 25-37.
Some references to Yeats's theosophical interests.

1152. KAIN, RICHARD M., and JAMES H. O'BRIEN: *George Russell (A. E.).* Lewisburg, Pa.: Bucknell UP, 1976. 93 pp.

1153. KINDILIEN, CARLIN T.: "The George Russell Collection at Colby College: A Check List," *CLQ,* 4:2 (May 1955), 31-55.
Colby College possesses several (unpublished?) letters dealing with Yeats.

1154. KUCH, PETER: *Yeats and A. E.: "The Antagonism That Unites Dear Friends."* Gerrards Cross: Smythe / Totowa, N.J.: Barnes & Noble, 1986. xiii, 291 pp.
Based on "W. B. Yeats and George Russell: An Enquiry into Their Literary Associations," M.Litt. thesis, Oxford U, 1978. ix, 349 pp.

Discusses the period 1884-1907, with particular reference to both poets' interest in theosophy and spiritism, Irish literature and tradition, and the revival of the theater. Numerous quotations from AE's unpublished letters to Yeats and from some unpublished Yeats letters.

Analyzes the following works: "The Rose of the World," *Deirdre, Diarmuid and Grania, The Hour-Glass, The Shadowy Waters, Where There Is Nothing,* "An Irish Visionary," "Rosa Alchemica," and "Three Irish Poets."

Reviews:
- James F. Carens, *Yeats,* 5 (1987), 243-46.
- Eileen Douglas, *Studies,* 36:301 (Spring 1987), 121.
- Jacqueline Genet: "Frères ennemis," *EI,* 13:1 (June 1988), 234-37.
- Robert Greacen: "Poet and Puritan," *BooksI,* 115 (July/Aug 1987), 135-36.
- John Hanratty: "Literature," *Linen Hall R,* 3:4 (Winter 1986), 31.
- Declan Kiberd: "Taking Stock of Yeats," *TLS,* 13 Feb 1987, 166.
- Derek Mahon: "The Hare and the Tortoise," *IrT,* 26 July 1986, 11.
- Maureen Murphy, *ILS,* 6:1 (Spring 1987), 25-26.

1155. MCFATE, PATRICIA ANN: "AE's Portraits of the Artists: A Study of *The Avatars*," *Eire*, 6:4 (Winter 1971), 38-48.
Finds Yeats to be one of the characters in this novel.

1156. ———: "*The Interpreters:* AE's Symposium and *Roman à Clef*," *Eire*, 11:3 (Autumn 1976), 82-92.
Yeats and others as they appear in the novel under pseudonyms.

1157. MÖR, IAN: "W. B. Yeats and A. E. (George Russell)," *Theosophical R*, 37:218 (Oct 1905), 105-17.
Yeats's mysticism is magical: he wants an Ireland of artists. AE's mysticism is visionary: he wants an Ireland of saints.

1158. O'BRIEN, JAMES H.: "A. E. and the Self," *ArQ*, 22:3 (Autumn 1966), 258-68.
Includes frequent comparisons with Yeats.

1159. O'CONNOR, FRANK: "Two Friends: Yeats and A. E.," *YR*, 29:1 (Sept 1939), 60-88.
Reprinted, *YR*, 75:1 (Autumn 1985), 40-62.

1160. O'FAOLAIN, SEAN: "AE and W. B.," *VQR*, 15:1 (Winter 1939), 41-57.
A shorter version was published as "Yeats and the Younger Generation," *Horizon*, 5:25 (Jan 1942), 43-54. Discusses Yeats's and AE's occult interests; John Butler Yeats's influence on his son; WBY's gregariousness, which proves his affinity with the 18th century rather than with the romantics (although he writes like a hermit); and the development of his poetry. See also CB105.

1161. RICHARDSON, MALCOLM: "AE's *Deirdre* and Yeats's Dramatic Development," *Eire*, 20:4 (Winter 1985), 89-105.
AE's play showed Yeats "that a heroic, familiar, Irish theme could be presented in a way both non-naturalistic and stylized without sacrificing the heroic energy to which he sought to make the audience respond."

1162. SKELTON, ROBIN: "Division and Unity: AE and W. B. Yeats," in Skelton and Saddlemyer: *The World of W. B. Yeats* (1967, CA102), 189-98.

1163. SUMMERFIELD, HENRY: *That Myriad-Minded Man: A Biography of George William Russell "A. E." 1867-1935*. Gerrards Cross: Smythe, 1975. xiii, 354 pp.
Numerous references to Yeats. See also the review by Denis Donoghue: "The Master Mystic," *TLS*, 26 Mar 1976, 334.

See also BA4, BB170, 209, 214, BC1, 11, CA38, 69, 90, CB194, 403, 464, 512, CC194, CD12, 76, 964, 1082, CE47, DC284, DD313, EE174, 189, 199, FC54, 76.

George Sand

1164. THOMSON, PATRICIA: *George Sand and the Victorians: Her Influence and Reputation in Nineteenth Century England*. London: Macmillan, 1977. ix, 283 pp.
See pp. 208-10 for a note on Yeats's interest in George Sand, which may be responsible for his reference to Jacques de Molay in "Meditations in Time of Civil War."

George Santayana

1165. HUGHSON, LOIS: *Thresholds of Reality: George Santayana and Modernist Poetics*. Port Washington, N.Y.: Kennikat Press, 1977. xii, 180 pp.

"Yeats and His Enchanted Stone," 116-38. In the poetic development of Yeats and Santayana "we see the same drive to articulate the worlds of experience and imagination."

Siegfried Sassoon

1166. STEWART, JAMES FLOYD: "A Descriptive Account of Unpublished Letters of Siegfried Sassoon in the University of Texas Collection," Ph.D. thesis, U of Texas at Austin, 1972. xx, 422 pp. (*DAI*, 33:9 [Mar 1973], 5202A)

Yeats is referred to on pp. 16, 29, 38, 194, 211-13, 228, 236, 237, 250-51, 306, 315, 334, 349. It appears that Sassoon did not like his work.

1167. WELLAND, DENNIS: "Sassoon on Owen," *TLS*, 31 May 1974, 589-90.

Quotes some disparaging remarks made by Sassoon on Yeats.

See also BG189, 190, DC237.

Arthur Schopenhauer

1168. NEVO, RUTH: "Yeats and Schopenhauer," *YeA*, 3 (1985), 15-32.

The influence on "Meru" and other poems and on *A Vision*.

Delmore Schwartz

1169. SCHWARTZ, DELMORE: *Portrait of Delmore: Journals and Notes of Delmore Schwartz 1939-1959*. Edited and introduced by Elizabeth Pollet. NY: Farrar, Straus, Giroux, 1986. xix, 663 pp.

See index for some notes on Yeats.

George Seferis

1170. PADEL, RUTH: "Homer's Reader: A Reading of George Seferis," *Proceedings of the Cambridge Philological Society*, os 211 / ns 31 (1985), 74-132.

Notes on Seferis's knowledge and use of Yeats, pp. 79, 123, 126.

Olivia Shakespear

1171. FRENCH, WILLIAM: "For 'Gentle Graceful Dorothy,' a Tardy Obit," *Paideuma*, 12:1 (Spring 1983), 89-112.

1172. HARWOOD, JOHN: "Olivia Shakespear and W. B. Yeats," *YeA*, 4 (1986), 75-98.

See also Deirdre Toomey: "An Afterword on *Rupert Armstrong*," 99-102.

See also BC1, CA109, 126, CD1058, DC207, FA24.

William Shakespeare

1173. DESAI, RUPIN WALTER: *Yeats's Shakespeare*. Evanston: Northwestern UP, 1971. xxiv, 280 pp.
Based on "Yeats and Shakespeare," Ph.D. thesis, Northwestern U, 1968. iv, 420 pp. (*DAI*, 29:7 [Jan 1969], 2255A-56A).
Surveys Shakespeare productions that Yeats saw or may have seen and his Shakespeare criticism; discusses Shakespeare's place in *A Vision* and Shakespeare echoes in the plays and in "The Statues." Analyzed in section EE. Valuable.
Reviews:
- John P. Cunningham, *LCrit*, 10:3 (Winter 1972), 74-78.
- Donald T. Torchiana: "Some Recent Books on Yeats," *JIL*, 5:2 (May 1976), 60-81.

1174. ———: "'There Struts Hamlet': Yeats and the Hamlet Mask," *Hamlet Studies*, 1:1 (Apr 1979), 45-50.
Reprinted in Srivastava and Dutta: *Unaging Intellect* (1983, CA108), 44-51.

1175. KLEINSTÜCK, JOHANNES: "Yeats and Shakespeare," in Maxwell and Bushrui: *W. B. Yeats, 1865-1965* (1965, CA71), 1-17.
Links Yeats's uneasy and complex attitude toward Ireland and things Irish to his equally ambiguous use of Shakespeare. Comments on "Lapis Lazuli."

1176. MELCHIORI, GIORGIO: *Shakespeare's Dramatic Meditations: An Experiment in Criticism*. Oxford: Clarendon Press, 1976. xi, 206 pp.
Note on Shakespeare and Yeats's gyre symbolism, pp. 185-87.

1177. RAM, ALUR JANKI: "Yeats on Shakespeare," *Phoenix*, 11 (1967), 53-71.
Incorporates "Yeats and Shakespeare's Tragic Vision," *English Miscellany* [Dehli], 3 (1965), 103-18, where the author's name is spelled Alur Janaki Ram. On Shakespeare in Yeats's theory of tragedy and Shakespearean echoes in Yeats's poetry.

1178. SCOFIELD, MARTIN: *The Ghosts of Hamlet: The Play and Modern Writers*. Cambridge: Cambridge UP, 1980. xi, 202 pp.
Note on Yeats's view of Hamlet, pp. 8-9.

1179. SEN, TARAKNATH (ed): *Shakespeare Commemoration Volume*. Calcutta: Presidency College, Department of English, 1966. xii, 382 pp.
Gayatri Chakravorty [Spivak]: "Shakespeare in Yeats's *Last Poems* ," 243-84. Particularly on Yeats's use of Timon and Hamlet and on "An Acre of Grass," "Lapis Lazuli," and "A Bronze Head."

1180. SHAKESPEARE, WILLIAM: *Henry V*. Edited by Gary Taylor. Oxford: Clarendon Press, 1982. ix, 330 pp.
Criticizes Yeats's view of Henry, pp. 73-74.

1181. UNGER, LEONARD: "Yeats and *Hamlet*," *SoR*, 6:3 (Summer 1970), 698-709.
Hamlet as a source for "That the Night Come."

1182. WEISS, THEODORE: *The Breath of Clowns and Kings: Shakespeare's Early Comedies and Histories*. London: Chatto & Windus, 1971. vii, 339 pp.
See pp. 205-8 and passim (see index).

See also BF155, CA53a, 124, 160, CB59, 70, CC124, 250, CD15, 26, 39, 984, 987, DD240, 320, 453, 516, 590, 704, 705, EA28, EB32, EF20, 73, FG41

William Sharp / Fiona Macleod

1183. ALAYA, FLAVIA: *William Sharp--"Fiona Macleod": 1855-1905*. Cambridge, Mass.: Harvard UP, 1970. xiv, 261 pp.
Passim (see index).

1184. HALLORAN, WILLIAM FRANK: "William Sharp and Fiona Macleod: The Development of a Literary Personality, 1890-1900," Ph.D. thesis, Duke U, 1965. x, 356 pp. (*DAI*, 26:2 [Aug 1965], 1041)
Contains some references to Yeats, including quotations from letters written to him.

1185. ———: "W. B. Yeats and William Sharp: The Archer Vision," *ELN*, 6:4 (June 1969), 273-80.
Yeats's belief in psychic phenomena was undermined by a hoax perpetrated by Sharp.

1186. LAHEY-DOLEGA, CHRISTINE: "Brief Observations on the Life and Work of William Sharp (Fiona Macleod)," *BSUF*, 21:4 (1980), 18-26.

See also BB221, BC1, DC336, FA24, FC54, G144.

G. B. Shaw

1187. ADAMS, ELSIE BONITA: *Bernard Shaw and the Aesthetes*. Columbus: Ohio State UP, 1972. xxv, 193 pp.
Notes on Yeats, passim, especially pp. 144-46 (a comparison of Shaw's *As Far as Thoughts Can Reach* with "Sailing to Byzantium").

1188. ANON.: "*Blanco Posnet* in Dublin: Textual Alterations. Lord Aberdeen's Explanation," *Morning Post*, 24 Aug 1909, 6.
Quotes a letter from Shaw to Yeats as well as a letter by Lord Aberdeen to Lady Gregory and her reply.

1189. BARR, ALAN PHILIP: *Victorian Stage Pulpiteer: Bernard Shaw's Crusade*. Athens: U of Georgia Press, 1973. xiv, 188 pp.
"Shaw's Irish Contemporaries," 41-54, compares the views on religion held by Shaw, Yeats, and Joyce.

1190. BEARD, WILLIAM RUSSELL: "Shaw's *John Bull's Other Island:* A Critical, Historical and Theatrical Study," Ph.D. thesis, U of London, 1974. 383 pp.
See pp. 142-52.

1191. BROWN, IVOR: *Shaw in His Time*. London: Nelson, 1965. ix, 212 pp.
"Shaw's Ireland," 1-20, refers to the Irish literary scene at the turn of the century and to Yeats.

1192. CARY, ELIZABETH LUTHER: "Apostles of the New Drama," *Lamp*, 27:6 (Jan 1904), 593-98.
Yeats and Shaw compared.

1193. CROMPTON, LOUIS: *Shaw the Dramatist*. Lincoln: U of Nebraska Press, 1969. xi, 261 pp.
See pp. 29-44 for Shaw's reaction to Yeats and his use of *The Land of Heart's Desire* in *Candida*.

1194. FERRAR, HAROLD: "The Caterpillar and the Gracehoper: Bernard Shaw's *John Bull's Other Island*," *Eire*, 15:1 (Spring 1980), 25-45.

1195. GIBBS, A. M.: "Yeats, Shaw, and Unity of Culture," *SoRA*, 6:3 (1973), 189-203.

1196. GRENE, NICHOLAS: *Bernard Shaw: A Critical View*. London: Macmillan, 1984. xi, 173 pp.
Chapter 5, "A Geographical Conscience," contains notes on Yeats's reaction to *John Bull's Other Island*.

1197. ———: "Shaw in Ireland: Visitor or Returning Exile?" *Shaw*, 5 (1985), 45-62.

1198. HOLROYD, MICHAEL (ed): *The Genius of Shaw: A Symposium*. London: Hodder & Stoughton, 1979. 238 pp.
Terence de Vere White: "An Irishman Abroad," 31-41.

1198a. ———: *Bernard Shaw. Volume I: The Search for Love 1856-1898*. London: Chatto & Windus, 1988. viii, 486 pp.
The standard biography; two more volumes are projected. Contains some notes on Yeats, especially on the Florence Farr, Shaw, and Yeats triangle (see index).

1199. JENCKES, NORMA MARGARET: "*John Bull's Other Island:* A Critical Study of Shaw's Irish Play and Its Theatrical and Socio-Political Context," Ph.D. thesis, U of Illinois at Urbana-Champaign, 1974. iv, 186 pp. (*DAI*, 35:7 [Jan 1975], 4526A)
Frequent references to Yeats. See also the same author's "The Rejection of Shaw's Irish Play: *John Bull's Other Island*," *Eire*, 10:1 (Spring 1975), 38-53.

1200. NETHERCOT, ARTHUR H.: "Who *Was* Eugene Marchbanks?" *ShawR*, 15:1 (Jan 1972), 2-20.
Yeats was certainly not one of the models.

1201. PARKER, R. B.: "Bernard Shaw and Sean O'Casey," *QQ*, 73:1 (Spring 1966), 13-34.
Several references to Yeats.

1202. °SETHNA, K. D.: "Shaw and Yeats," *Mother India*, 2:11 (Nov 1950), 6-7.

1203. SHAW, GEORGE BERNARD: *The Diaries 1885-1897: With Early Autobiographical Notebooks and Diaries, and an Abortive 1917 Diary*. Edited and annotated by Stanley Weintraub. University Park: Pennsylvania State UP, 1986. 2 vols.
See index for references to Yeats in 1888 and 1892-95.

1204. SIDNELL, MICHAEL J.: "John Bull's Other Island: Yeats and Shaw," *MD*, 11:3 (Dec 1968), 245-51.

1205. SILVER, ARNOLD: *Bernard Shaw: The Darker Side*. Stanford: Stanford UP, 1982. xiii, 353 pp.
On Shaw's reaction to *The Land of Heart's Desire* and on *Can-*

dida as a parody of Yeats's play, pp. 88-96.

1206. WEINTRAUB, STANLEY: "Uneasy Friendship: Shaw and Yeats," *Yeats*, 1 (1983), 125-53.
An earlier and shorter version appeared as °"Shaw and His Fellow Townsmen Yeats and Joyce," *GBS: Newsletter of the Bernard Shaw Society of Japan*, 10 (Dec 1982).

1207. WILSON, COLIN: *Bernard Shaw: A Reassessment*. London: Hutchinson, 1969. xiv, 306 pp.
On Shaw and Yeats, pp. 136-39, and passim (see index). Thinks that Marchbanks in *Candida* is modeled on Yeats.

1208. WINSTEN, STEPHEN: *Shaw's Corner*. London: Hutchinson, 1952. 238 pp.
Shaw on Yeats, pp. 167-68.

See also AE81, BA8 (review Hackett), BB73, 209, BC1, 12-13a, BE33, 61, 134, BF104, CB70, 287, CC310, CD42, 436-38, EB84, 115, 123, 140, EE491, EF39, 46, 95, FG3, 44, G1320-32.

Francis Sheehy-Skeffington

1209. LEVENSON, LEAH: *With Wooden Sword: A Portrait of Francis Sheehy-Skeffington, Militant Pacifist*. Boston: Northeastern UP / Dublin: Gill & Macmillan, 1983. xii, 270 pp.
Some notes on Yeats and Sheehy-Skeffington (see index).

P. B. Shelley

1210. ALLOTT, MIRIAM (ed): *Essays on Shelley*. Liverpool: Liverpool UP, 1982. xviii, 286 pp. (Liverpool English Texts and Studies. 19.)
M. Allott: "Attitudes to Shelley: The Vagaries of a Critical Reputation," 1-38, contains some references to Yeats.

1211. BERNSTEIN, HELMUT: "Shelleys Dichtung im Lichte der Kritik nachviktorianischer Dichter," Dr.phil. thesis, U of Frankfurt, 1954. iii, 130 pp.
"Symbolsistische [sic] Kritik: W. B. Yeats," 43-61. Negligible.

1212. BLOOM, HAROLD: *Shelley's Mythmaking*. New Haven: Yale UP, 1959. viii, 279 pp. (Yale Studies in English. 141.)
Passim (see index).

1213. ———: *The Visionary Company: A Reading of English Romantic Poetry*. Garden City: Doubleday, 1961. xvii, 460 pp.
See pp. 229-30, 322-26, and passim.

1214. BORNSTEIN, GEORGE JAY: *Yeats and Shelley*. Chicago: U of Chicago Press, 1970. xv, 239 pp.
Based on "The Surfeited Alastor: William Butler Yeats's Changing Relation to Percy Bysshe Shelley," Ph.D. thesis, Princeton U, 1966. viii, 321 pp. (*DAI*, 27:11 [May 1967], 3832A-33A).
A more balanced assessment than most of Yeats-Shelley studies listed here. Includes a discussion of the rose symbol; analyzed in sections DD and EE.
Reviews:
- Terence Brown, *IUR*, 1:2 (Spring 1971), 276-78.

- Gerald L. Bruns, *Spirit*, 38:4 (Winter 1972), 41-45.
- Richard J. Finneran: "Progress Report on the Yeats Industry," *JML*, 3:1 (Feb 1973), 129-33.
- John S. Kelly: "Pathways," *IrP*, 21 Nov 1970, 12.
- Timothy Webb, *RES*, 22:87 (Aug 1971), 376-78.

1215. ———: "Yeats's Copy of Shelley at the Pforzheimer Library," *BRH*, 82:1 (Spring 1979), 53-62.
The importance of *The Selected Works of Percy B. Shelley* (1866) for Yeats's views of Shelley. Quotes Yeats's annotations.

1216. BUTTER, PETER H.: *Shelley's Idols of the Cave*. Edinburgh: Edinburgh UP, 1954. vii, 228 pp. (Edinburgh U Publications. Language & Literature. 7.)
Scattered notes, passim (see index).

1217. DALSIMER, ADELE MINTZ: "The Unappeasable Shadow: Shelley's Influence on Yeats," °Ph.D. thesis, Yale U, 1971. 270 pp. (*DAI*, 32:12 [June 1972], 6969A-70A)

1218. ———: "My Chief of Men: Yeats's Juvenilia and Shelley's *Alastor*," *Eire*, 8:2 (Summer 1973), 71-90.
On *The Island of Statues, The Seeker, Mosada,* and "The Two Titans."

1219. DUERKSEN, ROLAND A.: *Shelleyan Ideas in Victorian Literature*. The Hague: Mouton, 1966. 208 pp. (Studies in English Literature. 12.)
See pp. 153-60, 200-201.

1220. GRIGSON, GEOFFREY (ed): *The Mint: A Miscellany of Literature, Art, and Criticism*. London: Routledge, 1946. xii, 220 pp.
H. W. Häusermann: "W. B. Yeats's Idea of Shelley," 179-94.

1221. HOLLANDER, JOHN (ed): *Modern Poetry: Essays in Criticism*. London: Oxford UP, 1968. ix, 520 pp.
Harold Bloom: "Yeats and the Romantics," 501-20.

1222. MERRITT, H. C.: "Shelley's Influence on Yeats," *YES*, 1 (1971), 175-84.
The development of Yeats's estimate of Shelley and the influence of Shelley's symbols on Yeats's poetry.

1223. NORMAN, SYLVA: "Twentieth-Century Theories of Shelley," *TSLL*, 9:2 (Summer 1967), 223-37.

1224. PEARCE, DONALD: "Yeats and the Romantics," *Shenandoah*, 8:2 (Spring 1957), 40-57.
Shelley's skylark, Keats's nightingale, and Yeats's golden bird. Comments on both Byzantium poems and on "Coole Park 1929."

See also CA12, 34, 49, 53a, 149, CB70, 205, CC20, 117, 270, 348, CD14, 31, 261, 355, 709, 1239, 1457, DA11, DB17, DD33, 44, 93, 96, 244, 534a, 547, 608, 617, 777, FE26.

George Sigerson

1225. TOOMEY, DEIRDRE: "Bards of the Gael and Gall: An Uncollected Review by Yeats in *The Illustrated London News*," *YeA*, 5 (1987), 203-11.

Review of a book by Sigerson, published 14 Aug 1897, here reprinted. The introduction comments on the Sigerson-Yeats relationship.

Edith Sitwell

1226. GLENDINNING, VICTORIA: *Edith Sitwell: A Unicorn among Lions.* London: Weidenfeld & Nicolson, 1981. xiv, 395 pp.
See index for a few notes on Yeats and Edith Sitwell.

1226a. RAND, THOMAS WAYNE: "The Letters of Edith Sitwell to Siegfried Sassoon," °Ph.D. thesis, Washington State U, 1986. 278 pp. (*DAI*, 47:10 [Apr 1987], 3764A)
Previously unpublished letters containing references to Yeats, according to abstract.

See also CD59.

A. J. M. Smith

1227. FERNS, JOHN: *A. J. M. Smith.* Boston: Twayne, 1979. 148 pp. (Twayne's World Authors Series. 535.)
See index for some notes on Smith's interest in Yeats.

1228. MACLAREN, I. S.: "The Yeatsian Presence in A. J. M. Smith's 'Like an Old, Proud King in a Parable,'" *Canadian Poetry,* 4 (Spring/Summer 1979), 59-64.

Pamela Colman Smith

1229. CALDWELL, MARTHA B.: "Pamela Colman Smith: A Search," *Southeastern College Art Conference R,* 7:2 (Fall 1974), 33-38.
Contains a few references to Yeats.

1230. COLDWELL, JOAN, and ANN SADDLEMYER: *Pamela Colman Smith: An Exhibition of Her Work.* McMaster University Art Gallery 15-24 February 1977. [Hamilton, Ont., 1977. 12 pp.]
Yeats is referred to passim.

1231. COLDWELL, JOAN: "Pamela Colman Smith and the Yeats Family," *CJIS,* 3:2 (Nov 1977), 27-34.

1232. PARSONS, MELINDA BOYD: *To All Believers--The Art of Pamela Colman Smith.* Wilmington, Del.: Delaware Art Museum, 1975. [28 pp.]
Catalog of an exhibition; several references to Yeats.

See also EF90.

Somerville and Ross
(E. OE. Somerville and Martin Ross)

1233. COLLIS, MAURICE: *Somerville and Ross: A Biography.* London: Faber & Faber, 1968. 286 pp.
Martin Ross's unflattering impressions of Yeats, pp. 128-31.

1234. CUMMINS, GERALDINE: *Dr. E. OE. Somerville: A Biography.* Being the first biography of the leading member of the famous literary partnership of E. OE. Somerville and Martin Ross, with a new bibliography of first editions compiled by Robert Vaughan and a preface by Lennox Robinson, Litt.D. London: Dakers, 1952. xv, 271 pp.

"Some Literary Celebrities (AE., Yeats, G. B. S., The Founding ot the Irish Academy of Letters)," 70-82. Negligible.

1235. POWELL, VIOLET: *The Irish Cousins: The Books and Background of Somerville and Ross*. London: Heinemann, 1970. x, 214 pp.

Yeats is mentioned passim (see index).

Sophocles

1236. SOPHOCLES: *King Oedipus in the Translation by W. B. Yeats*. With selections from the *Poetics* of Aristotle, translated by G. M. A. Grube. Edited and with an introduction and notes by Balachandra Rajan. Toronto: Macmillan of Canada, 1969. vii, 99 pp.

See the introduction, pp. 1-12, for comments on Yeats's interest in Sophocles.

See also CA53a, DA6, DD134, EA10, ED16, EE312-27 and note, 391-92 and note, 398, G547-49.

Wole Soyinka

See CC274, CD324, 957.

Stephen Spender

See CB371, CD52, EE33, 39, FB15.

Oswald Spengler

1237. CALLAN, EDWARD: "W. B. Yeats's Learned Theban: Oswald Spengler," *JML*, 4:3 (Feb 1975), 593-609.

Discusses Spengler's influence on Yeats's poetry.

See also CB546, CD66, DD637.

Edmund Spenser

1238. BORNSTEIN, GEORGE: "The Making of Yeats's Spenser," *Yeats*, 2 (1984), 21-29.

Now incorporated in CD1a. Discusses the marginalia that Yeats wrote into the Spenser edition on which he built his own selection, and generally Yeats's interest in Spenser.

1239. DAVIDSON, RICHARD BARTLETT: "Yeats's Images of Spenser: A Question of Literary Influence," Ph.D. thesis, U of Colorado, 1973. x, 180 pp. (*DAI*, 34:12 [June 1974], 7700A-1A)

Includes discussions of the influence of Shelley, of *A Vision*, and of "Shepherd and Goatherd" and "In Memory of Major Robert Gregory."

1240. REANEY, JAMES: "The Influence of Spenser on Yeats," Ph.D.

thesis, U of Toronto, 1958. Abstract (6 pp.) plus iii, 281 pp.
"The early influence of Spenser is . . . seen to be related to Yeats' failure to understand Spenser. As Yeats developed, certain things he says about Spenser after 1906 imply that he no longer regards the Elizabethan poet as having an imperfect, divided genius, but as a poet who successfully fused . . . aesthetics and morality into an imaginative synthesis. This thesis explores both these early and late attitudes to Spenser as well as the area between them" (abstract).

1241. STOCK, A. G.: "Yeats on Spenser," in Jeffares and Cross: *In Excited Reverie* (1965, CA48), 93-101.
Includes comments on *The Island of Statues*.

See also CB59, CC247, CD39, EE538, G1194.

Jack Spicer

1242. FINKELSTEIN, NORMAN M.: "Jack Spicer's Ghosts and the Gnosis of History," *Boundary 2*, 9:2 (Winter 1981), 81-100.
Notes the influence of Yeats's theory of the daimon on Spicer's work.

W. F. Stead

1243. HARPER, GEORGE MILLS: "William Force Stead's Friendship with Yeats and Eliot," *MR*, 21:1 (Spring 1980), 9-38.

See also BC1.

James Stephens

1244. BRAMSBÄCK, BIRGIT: *James Stephens: A Literary and Bibliographical Study*. Upsala: Lundequist, 1959. 209 pp. (Upsala Irish Studies. 4.)
"Introductory Chapter on James Stephens: A Literary Study," 13-54; mentions Yeats passim (see index).

1245. FINNERAN, RICHARD J.: *The Olympian and the Leprechaun: W. B. Yeats and James Stephens*. Dublin: Dolmen Press, 1978. 36 pp. (New Yeats Papers. 16.)
Traces the biographical connections; includes Yeats's Polignac Prize speech (Wade 308; see also BF108), two uncollected writings by Stephens on Yeats (review of CA35, CB465), and a list of books by Stephens in Yeats's library and vice versa.
Reviews:
- Audrey S. Eyler, *ACIS Newsletter*, 11:3 (Oct 1981), 5.
- Brian John, *CJIS*, 5:1 (June 1979), 130-33.
- Robert Welch, *IUR*, 11:2 (Autumn 1981), 236-37.

1246. MCFATE, PATRICIA: *The Writings of James Stephens: Variations on a Theme of Love*. London: Macmillan, 1979. xiv, 183 pp.
See index.

1247. MARTIN, AUGUSTINE: *James Stephens: A Critical Study*. Dublin: Gill & Macmillan, 1977. xii, 177 pp.
Numerous references to Yeats (see index).

1248. PYLE, HILARY: *James Stephens: His Work and an Account of His Life*. London: Routledge & Kegan Paul, 1965. xi, 196 pp.
On Yeats and Stephens, passim (see index), especially pp. 56-57 and 80-83 (their methods of reciting verse).

1249. STEPHENS, JAMES: "Three Unpublished Letters from James Stephens." Edited by Richard J. Finneran, *PLL*, 6:1 (Winter 1970), 77-88.

See also BC14, BF108, DC284, FA11, FB23.

Wallace Stevens

1249a. BERGER, CHARLES: *Forms of Farewell: The Late Poetry of Wallace Stevens*. Madison: U of Wisconsin Press, 1985. xviii, 198 pp.
Frequent comparisons between the poetry of Stevens and Yeats (see index).

1250. BLESSINGTON, FRANCIS G., and GUY ROTELLA (eds): *The Motive for Metaphor: Essays on Modern Poetry in Honor of Samuel French Morse*. Boston: Northeastern UP, 1983. xv, 175 pp.
Robert Buttel: "The Incandescence of Old Age: Stevens and Yeats in Their Late Poems," 48-59; reprinted from *APR*, 12:1 (Jan-Feb 1983), 42-44.

1251. SHOENBERG, E. I.: "Wallace Stevens's 'Page from a Tale': An Exploration of the Poem and Its Sources," *WSJour*, 6:1-2 (Spring 1982), 39-45.
One of the sources is "The Lake Isle of Innisfree."

See also CA12, CC14a, 31, CD18, DB14, 203, DC35, DD108, 162, 517, FE55.

August Strindberg

1252. LAPISARDI, FREDERICK S.: "The Same Enemies: Notes on Certain Similarities between Yeats and Strindberg," *MD*, 12:2 (Sept 1969), 146-54.
In dramatic theory and practice.

See also EC10, FG7.

Josef Strzygowski

1253. MURPHY, RUSSELL: "Josef Strzygowski and Yeats' 'A Starlit or a Moonlit Dome,'" *CollL*, 13:1 (Winter 1986), 106-11.
Strzygowski's influence on *A Vision* and "Byzantium."

Francis Stuart

1254. BARNWELL, WILLIAM C.: "Looking to the Future: The Universality of Francis Stuart," *Eire*, 12:2 (Summer 1977), 113-25.
Contains a short Yeats-Stuart comparison.

1255. NATTERSTAD, JERRY H.: "Francis Stuart: A Critical Biography," Ph.D. thesis, Southern Illinois U, 1972. iv, 117 pp.
Contains some references to Yeats.

1256. ———: "An Interview," *JIL,* 5:1 (Jan 1976), 16-31.
With Francis Stuart who comments on Yeats (see pp. 22-23).

See also BA10, BB59a.

Daisetz Suzuki

1257. DOHERTY, GERALD: "The World That Shines and Sounds: W. B. Yeats and Daisetz Suzuki," *IRA,* 4 (1983), 57-75.
Suzuki's influence on Yeats, especially on the poetry.

See also CC226.

Emanuel Swedenborg

1258. ISLAM, SYED MANZOORUL: "Gyres and Spirits: An Exploration of Some Parallels between W. B. Yeats and Emanuel Swedenborg," °Ph.D. thesis, Queen's U (Kingston, Ont.), 1981. (*DAI,* 42:8 [Feb 1982], 3610A; reprinted *Yeats,* 1 [1983], 179-80, and *YeA,* 4 [1986], 313-14)

1259. L[INDH], F. G.: "Nobelpristagaren Mr. W. B. Yeats," *Nya Kyrkans Tidning,* 48:12 (Dec 1923), 151-52.
Yeats, entertained by Mrs. O. W. Nordenskiöld while in Stockholm, notes his "high estimation of Swedenborg."

1260. ODHNER, SIGRID CYRIEL: "Gleanings from Swedish Periodicals," *New Church Life,* 44:4 (Apr 1924), 235-36.
Quotations from preceding item and from BE108.

See also BE108, CA90, CD1, 175a, 258.

Jonathan Swift

1261. ARCHIBALD, DOUGLAS NELSON: "W. B. Yeats's Encounters with Swift, Berkeley, and Burke," Ph.D. thesis, U of Michigan, 1966. xvii, 300 pp. (*DAI,* 28:1 [July 1967], 220A-21A)
Includes an interpretation of "Lapis Lazuli," pp. 278-94.

1262. ———: "Yeats's Encounters: Observations on Literary Influence and Literary History," *NLH,* 1:3 (Spring 1970), 439-70.
Yeats's "encounters with Swift, Berkeley, and Burke" as a basis for a general discussion of the problem of literary influence.

1263. DALSIMER, ADELE M.: "Yeats's Unchanging Swift," *Eire,* 9:2 (Summer 1974), 65-89.

1264. DONOGHUE, DENIS: *Jonathan Swift: A Critical Introduction.* Cambridge: UP, 1969. viii, 235 pp.
Swift and Yeats, passim (see index). Discusses parallels rather than influences.

1265. HONE, JOSEPH M.: "A Letter from Ireland," *Poetry,* 44:4 (July 1934), 215-20.

1266. JOHNSON, MAURICE: *The Sin of Wit: Jonathan Swift as a Poet.* Syracuse: Syracuse UP, 1950. xvii, 145 pp.
"Eliot, Hardy, Joyce, Yeats, and the Ghost of Swift," 130-35.

1267. MCHUGH, ROGER, and PHILIP EDWARDS (eds): *Jonathan Swift, 1667-1967: A Dublin Tercentenary Tribute*. Dublin: Dolmen Press, 1967. xix, 231 pp.

Louis A. Landa: "Jonathan Swift: 'Not the Greatest of Divines,'" 38-60, rejects Yeats's image of Swift as fierce and brooding ("Blood and the Moon"); so does Austin Clarke: "The Poetry of Swift," 94-115, quoting *The Words upon the Window-Pane*.

1268. RAWSON, CLAUDE JULIEN (ed): *Focus: Swift*. London: Sphere, 1971. 270 pp.

John Traugott: "Swift, Our Contemporary," 239-64; revised from *UR*, 4:1 (Spring 1967), 11-34.

1269. RAWSON, CLAUDE JULIEN: *Gulliver and the Gentle Reader: Studies in Swift and Our Time*. London: Routledge & Kegan Paul, 1973. x, 190 pp.

"'Tis Only Infinite Below: Swift, with Reflections on Yeats, Wallace Stevens and R. D. Laing," 60-83; reprinted from *EIC*, 22:2 (Apr 1972), 161-81.

1270. ROLLINS, RONALD G.: "Enigmatic Ghosts of Swift in Yeats and Johnston," *Eire*, 18:2 (Summer 1983), 103-15.

Mainly on *The Words upon the Window-Pane*.

1271. SISSON, C. H.: "Yeats and Swift," *Agenda*, 9:4--10:1 (Autumn-Winter 1971/72), 34-38.

Yeats's understanding of Swift was very limited.

1272. VOIGT, MILTON: *Swift and the Twentieth Century*. Detroit: Wayne State UP, 1964. vii, 205 pp.

See pp. 131-33.

1273. VOZAR, LEA BERTANI: "Yeats, Swift, Irish Patriotism, and 'Rationalistic Anti-Intellectualism,'" *MSE*, 3:4 (Fall 1972), 108-16.

See also AE98, BB211, CA2, 118, CC132, 215, CD209, 975, DC143, DD62, EB147, EE548-64.

Arthur Symons

1274. BECKSON, KARL: *Arthur Symons: A Life*. Oxford: Clarendon Press, 1987. xi, 402 pp.

Many references to Yeats, including quotations from letters to and from Yeats.

1275. ELLMANN, RICHARD: *Golden Codgers: Biographical Speculations*. London: Oxford UP, 1973. xi, 193 pp.

"Discovering Symbolism," 101-12; on Yeats and Symons. See also CD1287.

1276. LHOMBREAUD, ROGER: *Arthur Symons: A Critical Biography*. London: Unicorn Press, 1963. xii, 333 pp.

Passim (see index).

1277. MORRIS, BRUCE D.: "Arthur Symons and W. B. Yeats: A Biographical and Critical Study," Ph.D. thesis, U of Denver, 1977. xvii, 237 pp. (*DAI*, 38:2 [Aug 1977], 809A-10A)

1278. ———: "Symons, Yeats, and the *Knave of Hearts*," *N&Q*, os

229 / ns 31:4 (Dec 1984), 509-11.
Yeats's corrections and comments in the MS. version and Symons's response.

1279. ———: "Elaborate Forms: Symons, Yeats, and Mallarmé," *Yeats*, 4 (1986), 99-119.
Yeats's reaction to Symons's Mallarmé translations.

1280. ———: "Reassessing Arthur Symons's Relationship with Lady Gregory," *Yeats*, 5 (1987), 107-15.
The relationship as it influenced both writers' attitude towards Yeats.

1281. MUNRO, JOHN M.: "Arthur Symons, 'The Symphony of Snakes,' and the Development of the Romantic Image," *ELT*, 7:3 (1964), 143-45.
Notes Yeats's influence on Symons. Commentary by Edward Baugh and Munro, :4 (1964), 228-30.

1282. ———: "Arthur Symons and W. B. Yeats: The Quest for Compromise," *DR*, 45:2 (Summer 1965), 137-52.

1283. ———: *Arthur Symons*. NY: Twayne, 1969. 174 pp. (Twayne's English Author's Series. 76.)
See pp. 56-81 and passim on the Yeats-Symons relationship. Concludes that Symons owes more to Yeats than vice versa. Prints a letter from Mrs. Rhoda Symons to Yeats, pp. 153-54.

1284. SARGEANT-QUITTANSON, RÉGINE: "Arthur Symons et les mouvements décadents des années 1890," thesis, Doctorat de 3e cycle, U of Reims, 1981. xv, 345, 248 pp.
On Yeats and Symons, 1:105-11, and passim (see index).

1285. STANFORD, DEREK: "Arthur Symons as a Literary Critic (1865-1945): A Centenary Assessment," *QQ*, 72:3 (Autumn 1965), 533-41.
Reprinted in *ContempR*, 207:1197 (Oct 1965), 210-16; :1198 (Nov 1965), 265-68; and as "Arthur Symons and Modern Poetics," *SoR*, 2:2 (Spring 1966), 347-53 (surely a waste of space). "It sometimes appears as if they [Yeats and Symons] were co-authors of each other's books [of criticism]."

1286. STERN, CAROL SIMPSON: "Arthur Symons's Literary Relationships, 1882-1900: Some Origins of the Symbolist Movement," Ph.D. thesis, Northwestern U, 1968. iv, 266 pp. (*DAI*, 29:7 [Jan 1969], 2282A-83A)
See especially pp. 104-16, 151-62, 207-11.

1287. SYMONS, ARTHUR: *The Symbolist Movement in Literature*. With an introduction by Richard Ellmann. NY: Dutton, 1958 [1899]. xxi, 164 pp. (Dutton Paperback. D21.)
Ellmann's introduction (pp. vii-xvi) mentions Yeats passim. Symons dedicated the book to Yeats in a two-page appreciation.

1287a. ———: *An Anonymous Review of W. B. Yeats's "Ideas of Good and Evil" in the 27 June 1903 "Athenaeum."* Edited, with Notes and an Introduction by Bruce Morris. Edinburgh: Tragara Press, 1988. 20 pp.
Reprinted from *Athenaeum*, 27 June 1903, 807-8; an extract is reprinted in CA50, pp. 135-38, where the author is not identified. In the introduction Morris discusses the mutual Symons-Yeats influence (pp. 3-7).

1288. WILDI, MAX: *Arthur Symons als Kritiker der Literatur*. Heidelberg: Winter, 1929. 145 pp. (Anglistische Forschungen. 67.)
Passim, especially pp. 51-60.

1289. WITT, MARION: "A Note on Yeats and Symons," *N&Q*, os 205 / ns 7:12 (Dec 1960), 467-69.
Symons echoes in several Yeats poems.

See also AE24, BC7, CB160, CC19, 28, 168, CD14, 54, 983, 1082, 1440, DC281a, EA12, 40, EF90, FA24, FE29, 89.

J. M. Synge

1290. ANDERSON, PATRICK: "Down among the Nuts," *Spect*, 9 Aug 1968, 196-97.
Includes some remarks on the mutual Yeats-Synge influence.

1291. ANON.: "Yeats Meets His Critics: Throws Open the Abbey Theatre for a Free Discussion of *The Playboy of the Western World*. Talk Is Plain on Both Sides," *Gaelic American*, 2 Mar 1907, 2.

1292. ANON.: "Paints the *Playboy* in Glowing Colors," *Gaelic American*, 21 Oct 1911, 1, 10.
The subtitles are revealing: "William Butler Yeats makes ineffectual attempt to defend the monstrosity as a work of 'art,' but still insists it is true to life and a picture of 'The Mind of Ireland.' His plea completely refuted by the gross brutality of the text. All who know Ireland pronounce it insulting and debasing. Loyalists and Castle hacks give it 'The Seal of Ireland's Approval.'"
See similar onslaughts in preceding and following issues until about March 1912 ("Yeats doesn't chaw sawdust any more. The dog returns to his vomit. Yeats slanders American Irish.").

1293. ANON.: "Mr. Yeats and Some Others," *Weekly Sun*, 15 June 1907, 3.
Yeats was right to call the police because *The Playboy*, although a "ridiculous play," deserves to be seen in its entirety.

1294. BAŁUTOWA, BRONISŁAWA: "Wpływ kultury ludowej na odrodzenie irlandzkiego. (John Millington Synge)" [The influence of folk culture on the renaissance of the Irish theater], *Prace polonistyczne*, 9 (1951), 281-305.
Yeats is mentioned passim.

1295. BENSON, EUGENE: *J. M. Synge*. London: Macmillan, 1982. xii, 167 pp.
Numerous references to Yeats (see index), especially in the chapter "Synge and the Theatre," 34-50.

1296. BICKLEY, FRANCIS: *J. M. Synge and the Irish Dramatic Movement*. London: Constable / Boston: Houghton Mifflin, 1912. 97 pp.
Reprinted °NY: Russell & Russell, 1968. See "Yeats and the Movement," 49-66 (on the early work); "The Irish Theatre," 67-85 (on Yeats's plays); and passim.

1297. BOURGEOIS, MAURICE: *John Millington Synge and the Irish Theatre*. London: Constable, 1913. xvi, 338 pp.
Reprinted °NY: Blom, 1965. Numerous references to Yeats, especi-

ally to *Deirdre* (see index).

1298. BROOKS, SYDNEY: "The Irish Peasant as a Dramatic Issue," *Harper's Weekly*, 9 May 1907, 344.
Comments on the *Playboy* row and Yeats's involvement in it.

1299. BUSHRUI, SUHEIL BADI (ed): *Sunshine and the Moon's Delight: A Centenary Tribute to John Millington Synge, 1871-1909*. With a foreword by A. Norman Jeffares. Gerrards Cross: Smythe / Beirut: American U of Beirut, 1972. 356 pp.
See especially A. Norman Jeffares: "Foreword," 9-15; Robert O'Driscoll: "Yeats's Conception of Synge," 159-71; Richard M. Kain: "The *Playboy* Riots," 173-88; S. B. Bushrui: "Synge and Yeats," 189-203.

1300. COLUM, PADRAIC: "Letter from Mr. Padraic Colum, Author of *The Land*," *Evening Telegraph*, 31 Jan 1907, 2.
About *The Playboy*. The same page carries a report of the disturbances and two letters commenting on Yeats's views.

1301. FAULK, C. S.: "John Millington Synge and the Rebirth of Comedy," *SHR*, 8:4 (Fall 1974), 431-48.

1302. FAULKNER, PETER: "Yeats, Ireland, and Ezra Pound," *Threshold*, 18 [1963?], 58-68.
When Yeats met Pound for the first time, he was past the Symbolist stage in his aesthetics. This was largely due to Synge's influence, which is therefore much more important than Pound's.

1303. FOSTER, JOHN WILSON: "*The Aran Islands* Revisited," *UTQ*, 51:3 (Spring 1982), 248-63.

1304. GARTON, JANET (ed): *Facets of European Modernism: Essays in Honour of James McFarlane Presented to Him on His 65th Birthday, 12 December 1985*. Norwich: U of East Anglia, 1985. 372 pp.
Simon Williams: "John Millington Synge: Transforming Myths of Ireland," 79-98; includes comments on Yeats.

1305. GASSNER, JOHN: *Masters of the Drama*. NY: Random House, 1940. xvii, 804 pp.
"John Millington Synge and the Irish Muse," 524-74; includes notes on Yeats.

1306. GERSTENBERGER, DONNA: *John Millington Synge*. NY: Twayne, 1964. 157 pp. (Twayne's English Authors Series. 12.)
On Yeats and Synge, passim (see index).

1307. ———: "Yeats and Synge: 'A Young Man's Ghost,'" in Maxwell and Bushrui: *W. B. Yeats, 1865-1939* (1965, CA71), 79-87.

1308. GREENE, DAVID HERBERT: "Synge's Unfinished *Deirdre*," *PMLA*, 63:4 (Dec 1948), 1314-21.
Yeats is mentioned passim.

1309. ———, and EDWARD MILLINGTON STEPHENS: *J. M. Synge, 1871-1909*. NY: Macmillan, 1959. xiii, 321 pp.
The standard biography; Yeats and the Abbey Theatre are referred to passim (see index). Contains quotations from unpublished Yeats letters to Lady Gregory.

1310. GRENE, NICHOLAS, and ANN SADDLEMYER: "Stephen MacKenna on Synge: A Lost Memoir," *IUR*, 12:2 (Autumn 1982), 141-51.
Contains some references to Yeats.

1311. HARMON, MAURICE (ed): *J. M. Synge: Centenary Papers, 1971*. Dublin: Dolmen Press, 1972. xv, 202 pp.
Jon Stallworthy: "The Poetry of Synge and Yeats," 145-66 and passim.

1312. HART, WILLIAM E.: "The Dramatic Art of J. M. Synge: Critic and Creator," Ph.D. thesis, University College Dublin, 1968. vii, 289 pp.
"Yeats--The Dramatic Movement--Synge," 237-56, and passim.

1313. HIRSCH, EDWARD: "The Gallous Story and the Dirty Deed: The Two *Playboys*," *MD*, 26:1 (Mar 1983), 85-102.
The Yeatsian reading of the play versus the response of the original audience.

1314. HONE, J. M.: "A Memory of *The Playboy*," *SatRL*, 22 June 1912, 776-77.
Reprinted in *Irish Book Lover*, 4:1 (Aug 1912), 7-8. How Yeats defended the play.

1315. IRISH TIMES: "John Millington Synge Born 16th April 1871," *IrT*, 16 Apr 1971, 8.
Several articles with frequent references to Yeats.

1316. JEFFARES, A. NORMAN: "Jeunesse à Dublin," in Genet: *William Butler Yeats*, (1981, CA32), 23-36.

1317. JOHNSON, TONI O'BRIEN: *Synge: The Medieval and the Grotesque*. Gerrards Cross: Smythe / Totowa, N.J.: Barnes & Noble, 1982. viii, 209 pp. (Irish Literary Studies. 11.)
Several references to Yeats (see index).

1318. JOHNSTON, DENIS: *John Millington Synge*. NY: Columbia UP, 1965. 48 pp. (Columbia Essays on Modern Writers. 12.)
Compares Yeats and Synge briefly, especially *The Land of Heart's Desire* and *In the Shadow of the Glen*, p. 14.

1319. KAIN, RICHARD M.: "A Scrapbook of the '*Playboy* Riots,'" *Emory UQ*, 22:1 (Spring 1966), 5-17.
Includes notes on Yeats's involvement.

1320. KIBERD, DECLAN: *Synge and the Irish Language*. London: Macmillan, 1979. xi, 294 pp.
Discusses the relationship between Yeats and Synge and Yeats and the Irish language.

1321. KILROY, JAMES (ed): *The "Playboy" Riots*. Dublin: Dolmen Press, 1971. 101 pp. (Irish Theatre Series. 4.)
Reprints numerous contemporary reviews and articles from newspapers and periodicals (some of them also contained in BB177). The following items show Yeats's involvement: "Abbey Theatre Scenes: Mr. Yeats's Appeal for a Fair Hearing," 25-31; from *FrJ*, 30 Jan 1907, 7 (see also BE31).
"Interviews with Mr. W. B. Yeats," 31-34; from the same issue.
"Police Prosecution [. . .]: Mr. W. B. Yeats Examined," 47-

51; from *FrJ*, 31 Jan 1907, 8 (the Piaras Beaslai case).

"The Poet Is Pleased: Interview with Mr. Yeats," 64-65; from *IrI*, 1 Feb 1907, 5.

Part of an interview with Yeats about William Boyle's defection from the Abbey, pp. 80-81; from *FrJ*, 4 Feb 1907, 4 (see also BE31).

"Parricide and Public: Discussion at the Abbey Theatre," 81-88; from *FrJ*, 5 Feb 1907, 6-7. Includes Yeats's contributions.

Criticism of Yeats's defense of the play, pp. 89-91; partial reprint of "The Playboy of the West: The Freedom of the Theatre," *Sinn Féin*, 9 Feb 1907, 2.

"Brittania Rule-the-Wave: A Comedy (In One Act and in Prose)," 91-94; reprinted from *Sinn Féin*, 9 Feb 1907, 3. A parody of *Cathleen ni Houlihan*, attributed to AE; also in *Nationality*, 29 Jan 1916, 5-6.

1322. KILROY, THOMAS: "Synge the Dramatist," *Mosaic*, 5:1 (Fall 1971), 9-16.
Includes a note on the Yeats-Synge relationship.

1323. KING, MARY C.: *The Drama of J. M. Synge*. London: Fourth Estate, 1985. ix, 229 pp.
Some remarks on Yeats (see index).

1324. KUYPER, SJOERD: "In het voetspoor van John M. Synge: Naar de Aran eilanden," *Bzzlletin*, 8:76 (May 1980), 68-87.
Contains a few notes on Yeats.

1325. LEAMON, WARREN: "Yeats, Synge, Realism and 'The Tragic Theatre,'" *SoR*, 11:1 (Jan 1975), 129-38.
Yeats's view of Synge, explained on the basis of an analysis of Yeats's essay "The Tragic Theatre."

1326. LEECH, CLIFFORD: "John Synge and the Drama of His Time," *MD*, 16:3/4 (Dec 1973), 223-37.

1327. MIKHAIL, EDWARD HALIM (ed): *J. M. Synge: Interviews and Recollections*. Foreword by Robin Skelton. London: Macmillan, 1977. xiv, 138 pp.
Reprinted pieces; frequent references to Yeats.

1328. MISRA, K. S.: *The Plays of J. M. Synge: A Critical Study*. New Delhi: Caxton Press, 1977. vii, 193 pp.
See the introduction, pp. 1-30.

1329. MORTIMER, MARK: "Yeats and Synge: An Inappropriate Myth," *Studies*, 66:264 (Winter 1977), 292-98.
Yeats was only partly responsible for Synge's decision to go to the Aran Islands.

1330. O'CONNOR, FRANK: "A Classic One-Act Play," *Radio Times*, 3 Jan 1947, 4.
Riders to the Sea. Compares Yeats and Synge.

1331. O'DONOGHUE, D. J.: "The Synge Boom: Foreign Influences," *IrI*, 21 Aug 1911, 4.
Comments on Yeats's ideas about Synge. Further correspondence in subsequent issues.

1332. O'MANGAIN, H. C.: "The National Drama," *Evening Telegraph*, 4

Feb 1907, 4.
Subheading: "Mr. Henry Mangan discusses Mr. Yeats, Mr. Synge, Mr. Boyle, and Lady Gregory." The same page carries letters by Boyle, Alice Milligan, D. J. O'Donoghue, and W. O'Leary Curtis, commenting on Yeats's position in the *Playboy* affair.

1333. PRICE, ALAN: *Synge and Anglo-Irish Drama*. London: Methuen, 1961. xi, 236 pp.
Includes a chapter on "Yeats and Synge," 51-68.

1334. R.: "Synge a Yeats" [Synge and Yeats], *Jeviště*, 2:43 (27 Oct 1921), 638-40.
More on Synge than on Yeats.

1335. ROCHE, ANTHONY: "The Two Worlds of Synge's *The Well of the Saints* ," *Genre*, 12:4 (Winter 1979), 439-50.
Frequent references to Yeats.

1336. SADDLEMYER, ANN: "'A Share in the Dignity of the World': J. M. Synge's Aesthetic Theory," in Skelton and Saddlemyer: *The World of W. B. Yeats* (1967, CA102), 207-19.

1337. ———: *J. M. Synge and Modern Comedy*. Dublin: Dolmen Press, 1968. 32 pp.
Comments on Yeats's inadequate understanding of Synge: "In seeing Synge only through Yeats's glass darkly, not only the man but to an important extent the plays--and certainly the audience's reaction to them--remain incomplete."

1338. ———: "J. M. Synge on the Irish Dramatic Movement: An Unpublished Article," *MD*, 24:3 (Sept 1981), 276-81.
"The Dramatic Movement in Ireland," written in 1906, reprinted here, a short sketch of the development from 1899 to 1906.

1339. SIDNELL, MICHAEL J.: "Synge's Playboy and the Champion of Ulster," *DR*, 45:1 (Spring 1965), 51-59.
The sources of the play in the Cuchulain saga and some comparisons with Yeats.

1340. SKELTON, ROBIN: *J. M. Synge and His World*. London: Thames & Hudson, 1971. 144 pp.
Numerous references to Yeats (see index).

1341. ———: *The Writings of J. M. Synge*. London: Thames & Hudson, 1971. 190 pp.
Yeats is mentioned passim (see index).

1342. ———: "The Politics of J. M. Synge," *MR*, 18:1 (Spring 1977), 7-22.

1343. STEPHENS, EDWARD MILLINGTON: *My Uncle John: Edward Stephens's Life of J. M. Synge*. Edited by Andrew Carpenter. London: Oxford UP, 1974. xviii, 222 pp.
See index.

1344. SYNGE, JOHN MILLINGTON: *Collected Works*. London: Oxford UP, 1962-68. 4 vols. to date.
1. *Poems*. Edited by Robin Skelton (1962). Contains an introduction by Skelton, pp. xi-xxix, with some references to Yeats.
2. *Prose*. Edited by Alan Price (1966). Contains an introduction

by Price, pp. x-xvi, with some references to Yeats, and among others the following items:

a. "An Epic of Ulster," 367-70; reprinted from *Speaker*, 7 June 1902, 284-85; a review of Wade 256.

b. "Le mouvement intellectuel irlandais," 378-82; reprinted from °*Européen*, 31 May 1902, 12-13.

c. "The Old and New in Ireland," 383-86; reprinted with the addition of a discarded passage from *Academy*, 6 Sept 1902, 238-39, where it was published anonymously. On Yeats, passim.

3. *Plays: Book I*. Edited by Ann Saddlemyer (1968). The editor's introduction, pp. xi-xxxi, contains references to Yeats.
4. *Plays: Book II*. Edited by Ann Saddlemyer (1968). The editor's introduction, pp. xi-xxxiii contains references to Yeats.
5. Was to contain a bibliography; it is, however, unlikely to be published.

1345. ———: *The Plays and Poems*. Edited with an introduction and notes by T. R. Henn. London: Methuen, 1963. xi, 363 pp.

"Synge and Yeats," 308-11.

1346. ———: *Letters to Molly: John Millington Synge to Maire O'Neill, 1906-1909*. Edited by Ann Saddlemyer. Cambridge, Mass.: Belknap Press of Harvard UP, 1971. xxxiv, 330 pp.

Numerous references to Yeats (see index), some of them not very flattering (see, e.g., pp. 113-14 for Synge's unmitigated jealousy). See also CD1349.

1347. ———: *The Playboy of the Western World*. Edited by Malcolm Kelsall. London: Benn, 1975. xxxv, 87 pp.

See the "Introduction," ix-xxxiii.

1348. ———: *The Well of the Saints*. Edited with an introduction and notes by Nicholas Grene. Washington, D.C.: Catholic U of America Press / Gerrards Cross: Smythe, 1982. ix, 80 pp.

Notes on Yeats in the "Introduction," especially pp. 1-5.

1349. ———: *The Collected Letters of John Millington Synge*. Edited by Ann Saddlemyer. Oxford: Clarendon Press, 1983-84. 2 vols.

Volume 1: 1871-1907. xxx, 385 pp. Includes material from CD1346. Contains 16 letters to Yeats, previously published in EF97. See also the index for other references to Yeats.

Volume 2: 1907-1909. 1984. xvii, 270 pp. Contains several letters to Yeats, previously published in EF97. Yeats is also frequently referred to in other letters (see index).

1350. *The Synge Manuscripts in the Library of Trinity College, Dublin*. A catalogue prepared on the occasion of the Synge centenary exhibition, 1971. Dublin: Dolmen Press, 1971. 55 pp.

The following items are of interest: An article, "The Dramatic Movement in Ireland" (MS. 4347); a collection of documents relating to theater business including press opinions of Abbey plays (MS. 4355); notes on Yeats's Blake edition (MS. 4378); two diaries recording meetings with Yeats (MSS. 4417-18); and some letters from Yeats (MSS. 4424-29).

Announced for publication on microfilm: °*The J. M. Synge Manuscripts from the Library of Trinity College, Dublin*. Brighton: Harvester Press Microform Publications, 1988 [?]. (Manuscripts of the Irish Literary Renaissance. Series 3.)

1351. THORNTON, WELDON: *J. M. Synge and the Western Mind.* Gerrards Cross: Smythe, 1979. 169 pp. (Irish Literary Studies. 4.)
See index.

1352. YEATS, W. B.: "Memorandum Prepared for the Synge Estate by W. B. Yeats," *Long Room,* 24-25 (Spring-Autumn 1982), 39-40.
A memorandum prepared after Synge's death, reprinted from item 4364 of the Synge collection in Trinity College Library, Dublin. See note by Mary C. King on p. 9.

See also AC51, 55, 60, AE37, BB50, 155, 170, 177, 209, BC2, BE30-32, 52, 53, 55, 57, 58, 61, 106, BF59, 70, 83, 114, 117, 119, 120, 122, 125, CA37, 38, 55, 146, 155, CB194, 337, 443, 533, CC49, 105, 144, 212, 232, 341, 351, CD584, 844, 882, DB258, DC348, 386, DD267, EA12, 40, EB90, 147, EE174, 180, 186, 189, 199, 519, EF32, 39, 46, 97, 101, FB14, FE20, 29, FG7, 51, G298-301, 536, 550.

Rabindranath Tagore

1353. ANNIAH GOWDA, H. H.: "Ideas into Drama: Yeats and Tagore as Playwrights," *LHY,* 2:1 (Jan 1961), 63-76.
"Yeats and Tagore express beautiful ideas, but their medium may be described as archaic and undramatic. They try to come to grips with the actualities of life but do not reduce the distance between the stage and the audience."

1354. CHAKRAVORTY, BYOMKESH CHANDRA: *Rabindranath Tagore: His Mind and Art. Tagore's Contribution to English Literature.* New Delhi: Young India Publications, 1971. 304 pp.
See pp. 273-78.

1355. CHAUDHERY, SUMITA MITRA: "William Butler Yeats and Rabindranath Tagore: A Comparative Study," Ph.D. thesis, U of Michigan, 1973. vi, 220 pp. (*DAI,* 34:4 [Oct 1973], 1898A-99A)

1356. DASGUPTA, PRANABENDU: "One or Two Aspects of the 'Subjective Tradition' in the Plays of W. B. Yeats and Rabindranath Tagore," *JJCL,* 4 (1964), 46-67.
The aspects are character and symbol.

1357. DASGUPTA, R. K. (ed): *Rabindranath Tagore and William Butler Yeats: The Story of a Literary Friendship.* A souvenir of the 100th anniversary of the birth of Yeats observed at the 104th anniversary of the birth of Tagore. Delhi: Department of Modern Indian Languages, U of Delhi, 1965. iv, 36 pp.
Contents: Tagore: "W. B. Yeats," 1-7; a translation of an essay originally published in Bengali in 1912 (see CB476). Tagore explains Yeats's achievement in modern English poetry as the "individual expression of his soul."

Yeats: Several pieces on Tagore, among others the introduction to Wade 263, the preface to Wade 267, and the letter from Wade 318.

"W. B. Yeats on Tagore (Speech at a Reception to Tagore at the Trocadero Restaurant, London, 10 July 1912)," 13 (source not given, apparently not published elsewhere; but see BF99) and "Tagore's Reply," 13-14.

"Sri Aurobindo on W. B. Yeats," 15-17; four snippets from letters and various publications (1917-49).

Abinash Chandra Bose: "My Interview with W. B. Yeats," 18-

24, on 1 June 1937; for a fuller account see BB20.
R. K. DasGupta: "Rabindranath Tagore and W. B. Yeats," 25-34.
"Rabindranath's Message on the Passing Away of Yeats," MS. facsimile opposite p. 34 (see also BG204).
"Chronology of Rabindranath's Association with W. B. Yeats," 35-36. Rather sketchy.

1358. DATTA, HIRENDRANATH: "Tagore and Yeats," *VQ,* 17:1 (May-July 1951), 29-34.

1359. FALLON, PADRAIC: "Poetic Labourers: Yeats and Tagore," *IrT,* 30 June 1962, 9.

1360. GUHA, NARESH: "Yeats and Rabindranath: A Study in Tradition and Modern Poetry," *Quest,* 36 (Winter 1962-63), 9-19.
Revised as "Discovery of a Modern Poet," *Mahfil,* 3:1 (1966), 58-73. Reprinted in Aby Sayeed Ayyub and Amlan Datta (eds): *Ten Years of "Quest."* Bombay: Manaktalas, 1966. xi, 407 pp. (pp. 135-53).

1361. HURWITZ, HAROLD MARVIN: "Rabindranath Tagore and England," Ph.D. thesis, U of Illinois, 1959. iv, 223 pp. (*DAI,* 20:8 [Feb 1960], 3294-95)
See pp. 76-88.

1362. ———: "Tagore's English Reputation," *WHR,* 16:1 (Winter 1962), 77-83.

1363. ———: "Yeats and Tagore," *CL,* 16:1 (Winter 1964), 55-64.
Biographical connections and mutual interests.

1364. KRIPALANI, KRISHNA: *Rabindranath Tagore: A Biography.* London: Oxford UP, 1962. ix, 417 pp.
Scattered references, passim (see index).

1365. LAGO, MARY M.: "The Parting of the Ways: A Comparative Study of Yeats and Tagore," *IndL,* 6:2 (1963), 1-34.
Reprinted in *Mahfil,* 3:1 (1966), 32-57. "The similarities were in reality superficial . . . by the age of seventy, Yeats and Tagore had moved steadily away from each other in opposite directions, Yeats going away from reality to a private world of myth, and Tagore coming closer to the world of men."

1366. ———: *Rabindranath Tagore.* Boston: Twayne, 1976. 176 pp. (Twayne's World Authors Series. 402.)

1367. MITRA, SAURĪNDRA: *Khyāti akhyātira nepathye.* Kalikātā [Calcutta]: Ānanda Pābaliśārsa, 1977. 618 pp.
In Bengali. On Tagore's relations with Western writers such as Yeats and Romain Rolland (British Library catalog).

1368. NARASIMHAIAH, C. D.: "The Reputation of English *Gitanjali:* Tagore and His Critics," *LCrit,* 9:4 (Summer 1971), 1-22.
Yeats's introduction to *Gitanjali* "is in the nature of a literary scandal of the first magnitude and does little credit to Yeats's poetic, much less to his critical faculty."

1369. PONNUSWAMY, KRISHNA: "Yeats and Tagore: A Comparative Study of Their Plays," °Ph.D. thesis, Madurai Kamaraj U (India), 1984.

437 pp. (*DAI*, 46:7 [Jan 1986], 1933A-34A; reprinted *Yeats*, 5 [1987], 200)

1370. RANGANATHAN, SUDHA: "Rabindranath Tagore's *Malini* and W. B. Yeats's *The Countess Cathleen:* A Study in 'Hominisation,'" *OJES*, 9:1 (1972), 51-54.

1371. SEN, NABANEETA DEV: "The Reception of Rabindranath Tagore in England, France, Germany, and the United States," Ph.D. thesis, Indiana U, 1964. vi, 167 pp. (*DAI*, 26:4 [Oct 1965], 2192-93)

Yeats is mentioned passim. Negligible.

1372. SINGH, B. M.: "Yeats and *Gitanjali*," *RUSEng*, 9 (1976), 41-46.

1373. THOMPSON, EDWARD JOHN: "Memories of Tagore: E. P. Thompson Introduces His Father E. J. Thompson's Account of a Stay with the Bengali Poet," *LRB*, 22 May 1986, 18-19.

Thompson and Tagore comment adversely on Yeats's introduction to *Gitanjali*.

1374. UDDIN, QAZI NASIR: "Horizon of Expectations: The Reception of Rabindranath Tagore in the United States and Britain (1913-41)," Ph.D. thesis, State U of New York at Binghamton, 1985. viii, 237 pp. (*DAI*, 46:5 [Nov 1985], 1272A-73A)

See especially chapter 3, "Tagore and Britain," 57-95, for a discussion of the Yeats-Tagore relationship.

See also BB211, BC1, BF99, 102, CA35, 143, CD1, 2, 78, 80, 89, 90, CE317, DC147a, 262, DD727, EB31, EE277.

Áron Tamási

1375. BERTHA, CSILLA: "A mitikus-költői dráma két változata: W. B. Yeats és Tamási Aron játékai," *Egri Ho Si Minh Tanárkepző Főiskola tudományos közleményei*, 17 (1984), 391-403.

Includes a summary in English entitled "An Irish and a Hungarian Model of Mythic Drama: W. B. Yeats and Áron Tamási."

1375a. ———: "Mythical Vision: Parallels between the Drama of W. B. Yeats and Áron Tamási," *Acta Litteraria Academiae Scientiarum Hungaricae*, 29:1-2 (1987), 113-38.

The parallels are explained by the use of myth and ritual.

See also CB546.

Allen Tate

1376. SCHÖPP, JOSEPH C.: *Allen Tate: Tradition als Bauprinzip dualistischen Dichtens*. Bonn: Bouvier, 1975. vi, 265 pp. (Abhandlungen zur Kunst-, Musik- und Literaturwissenschaft. 168.)

Several notes on Tate's reception of Yeats (see index).

See also CD18.

Thomas Taylor

1377. TAYLOR, THOMAS: *Thomas Taylor the Platonist: Selected Writ-*

ings. Edited with introductions by Kathleen Raine and George Mills Harper. Princeton: Princeton UP, 1969. xiii, 544 pp. (Bollingen Series. 88.)

Passim (see index).

See also DD143.

Alfred Lord Tennyson

1378. BORNSTEIN, GEORGE: "Last Romantic or Last Victorian: Yeats, Tennyson, and Browning," *YeA*, 1 (1982), 114-32.

Now incorporated in CD1a.

1379. GLASSER, MARVIN: "The Early Poetry of Tennyson and Yeats: A Comparative Study," Ph.D. thesis, New York U, 1962. v, 227 pp. (*DAI*, 24:10 [Apr 1964], 4174)

See also CA53a, CD37, DA11, 24, DB165, DC303, DD94, 121, 307, 580.

Dylan Thomas

1380. ASTLEY, RUSSELL: "Stations of the Breath: End Rhyme in the Verse of Dylan Thomas," *PMLA*, 84:6 (Oct 1969), 1595-605.

Involves frequent comparisons with Yeats.

1381. KERSHNER, R. B.: *Dylan Thomas: The Poet and His Critics*. Chicago: American Library Association, 1976. xiii, 280 pp.

See index for notes on the Yeats-Thomas relationship.

See also CB46, CD1425, DC88, DD28, FG23.

Edward Thomas

See CB302, DB146, DC191.

Francis Thompson

1382. DANCHIN, PIERRE: *Francis Thompson: La vie et l'oeuvre d'un poète*. Paris: Nizet, 1959. 554 pp.

See pp. 433-34 and passim (see index).

1383. ———: "A propos de l'acceuil de W. B. Yeats par la critique anglaise," *EA*, 30:3 (July-Sept 1977), 346-49.

Discusses Thompson's views of Yeats and lists his published Yeats criticism. Correspondence by F. M. G. Atkinson and Danchin, ibid., 350.

Henry David Thoreau

1384. DUNCAN, MARGARET S.: "New England Dawn and Keltic Twilight (Notes on the Theosophy of Henry Thoreau and the Poems of W. B. Yeats)," *Theosophical R*, 27:157 (15 Sept 1900), 63-72.

1385. GLICK, WENDELL: "Yeats's Early Reading of *Walden*," *Boston Public Library Q*, 5:3 (July 1953), 164-66.

Comments on the composition of "The Lake Isle of Innisfree."

1386. POGER, SIDNEY: "Yeats as Azad: A Possible Source in Thoreau," *Thoreau JQ,* 5:3 (1973), 13-15.
Comments on *Purgatory.*

1387. RYAN, GEORGE E.: "Shanties and Shiftlessness: The Immigrant Irish of Henry Thoreau," *Eire,* 13:3 (Fall 1978), 54-78.
Note on Yeats and Thoreau, pp. 75-76.

1388. SCHWARTZMAN, JACK: "Yes, Ladies, There Is an Innisfree! (Thoreau's Influence on Yeats)," *Nassau R,* 1:4 (Spring 1968), 14-25.

See also DD290, 758.

John Todhunter

1389. MORIARTY, DAVID JAMES: "John Todhunter: Child of the Coming Century," Ph.D. thesis, U of Wisconsin--Madison, 1979. xvii, 950 pp. (*DAI,* 40:6 [Dec 1979], 3320A-21A)
On Yeats, passim.

See also CA69, CB258, FE109.

Tu Fu

1390. WANG, AN-YAN TANG: "Subjectivity and Objectivity in the Poetic Mind: A Comparative Study of the Poetry of William Butler Yeats and Tu Fu," °Ph.D. thesis, Indiana U, 1981. 63 pp. (*DAI,* 42:7 [Jan 1982], 3152A; reprinted *Yeats,* 1 [1983], 175-77, and *YeA,* 4 [1986], 321-22)
Tu Fu lived from 712 to 770.

See also FE92.

W. J. Turner

1391. HÄUSERMANN, H. W.: "W. B. Yeats and W. J. Turner, 1935-1937 (With Unpublished Letters)," *ES,* 40:4 (Aug 1959), 233-41; 41:4 (Aug 1960), 241-53.
Discusses the collaboration on the *Oxford Book of Modern Verse, The Ten Principal Upanishads,* the broadsides, and the poetry broadcasts.

1392. NIMMO, DAVID C.: "W. B. Yeats and W. J. Turner," *ES,* 56:1 (Feb 1975), 32-33.
For inclusion in the *Oxford Book of Modern Verse* Yeats changed a Turner poem to make it agree with his own doctrines.

Katharine Tynan

1393. FALLON, ANN CONNERTON: *Katharine Tynan.* Boston: Twayne, 1979. 191 pp. (Twayne's English Author's Series. 272.)
"Tynan, Yeats, and the Irish Literary Revival," 49-74, and passim.

1394. HOLDSWORTH, CAROLYN: "'Shelley Plain': Yeats and Katharine Tynan," *YeA*, 2 (1983), 59-92.

1395. KAMP, PETER G. W. VAN DE: "Some Notes on the Literary Estate of Pamela Hinkson," *YeA*, 4 (1986), 181-86.

Discusses the relationship between Yeats and Katharine Tynan (Pamela Hinkson's mother) on the basis of unpublished material.

1396. MOLONEY, SISTER FRANCIS INÉS: "Katharine Tynan Hinkson: A Study of Her Poetry," Ph.D. thesis, U of Pennsylvania, 1952. iii, 158 pp. (*DAI*, 14:10 [1954], 1726-27)

On Yeats and Katharine Tynan, passim, especially pp. 48-58. Claims on the authority of letters written by KT's nephew that KT and WBY contemplated marriage at one time.

1397. ROSE, MARILYN GADDIS: *Katharine Tynan*. Lewisburg: Bucknell UP, 1974. 97 pp.

1398. WALSH, CAROLINE: "In Search of Katharine Tynan," *IrT*, 28 Aug 1981, 8.

1399. YEATS, W. B.: *Letters to Katharine Tynan*. Edited by Roger McHugh. Dublin: Clonmore & Reynolds / London: Burns, Oates & Washburn, 1953. 190 pp.

"Introduction," 11-22; on Yeats's early life and works and his relationship with KT; also headnotes to the individual sections and notes on pp. 152-84. For reviews see G946-966.

See also BA22, BB113, 114, 245-249, BC1, CA69, CB242, CE195, FE69, 77.

Upanishads

1400. DAVENPORT, A.: "Yeats and the Upanishads," *RES*, 3:9 (Jan 1952), 55-62.

1401. LAL, P. (trans): *The Īśā Upaniṣad: With an Essay on "The Difficulties of Translation" (Based on a Study of the Yeats-Purohit Version of the Īśā-Upaniṣad)*. Calcutta: Writer's Workshop, 1968. 16 pp.

Compares the Yeats-Purohit versions with a literal translation and concludes that the former is a mixture of successes and failures.

1402. MASSON, J.: "Yeats's *The Ten Principal Upanishads*," *JJCL*, 9 [1971?], 24-31.

"Nearly every passage is inaccurate, and what is more important, the inaccuracies are never on the side of poetry." Moreover, many of the most splendid passages are missing in the translations. The inference is that Purohit Swami misinformed Yeats seriously.

1403. TIEN, RENÉ: "La pensée indienne selon Yeats," *Gaéliana*, 7 (1985), 45-55.

See also G1243-1252 and index IE s.v. Upanishads.

Paul Valéry

1404. ALEXANDER, IAN W.: "Valéry and Yeats: The Rehabilitation of Time," *Scottish Periodical,* 1:1 (Summer 1947), 77-106.

"Yeats's whole development may be described as the progressive discovery of concrete experience, and it is in this that he may best be brought into parallel with Valéry." This development ends "in a rehabilitation of Time and Being." Valéry, unlike Yeats, however, is no idealist.

See also DC215.

Ramón María del Valle-Inclán

1405. LYON, JOHN: *The Theatre of Valle-Inclán.* Cambridge: Cambridge UP, 1983. viii, 229 pp.

Compares Yeats's and Valle-Inclán's symbolist aesthetics and dramatic theories, pp. 10-24.

Bram van Velde

1406. BONNEFOY, YVES: "A propos de Yeats et de Bram van Velde," *Solaire,* 18-19 (Autumn 1977), [26-30].

Reprinted in Bonnefoy's °*Trois remarques sur la couleur.* Losne: Bouchard, 1978, 43 pp. A comparison between Yeats's *The Resurrection* and the lithographs of Bram van Velde.

Paul Verlaine

See BG194, 208, CD58, 787, DD174.

Giovanni Battista Vico

1407. ELLMANN, RICHARD: "Yeats and Vico," *ILS,* 2:2 (Oct 1983), 1, 19.

See also CA66, CB546.

Villiers de l'Isle Adam

1408. ANZALONE, JOHN B.: "The First English Translation of *Axël*," *Bulletin du Bibliophile,* 2 (1980), 149-60.

1409. FRIEDMAN, MELVIN J.: "A Revaluation of *Axël*," *MD,* 1:4 (Feb 1959), 236-43.

1410. GOLDGAR, HARRY: "Deux dramaturges symbolistes: Villiers de l'Isle Adam et William Butler Yeats," thesis, Doctorat d'Université (Lettres), U of Paris, 1948. vii, 410 pp.

Contains chapters on Yeats in Paris, the French influence on Yeats in general and of Villiers de l'Isle Adam in particular, "romantisme," religion, mysticism, mythology, and symbolism in both poets, especially in their plays.

1411. °HAMILTON, MARY GERTRUDE: "Villiers de l'Isle Adam and W.

B. Yeats: The Alchemical Model and the Phantasmagoric Imagination," Ph.D. thesis, U of Alberta, 1980. xii, 595 pp.

1412. PARKS, LLOYD CLIFFORD: "The Influence of Villiers de l'Isle Adam on W. B. Yeats," Ph.D. thesis, U of Washington, 1959. v, 215 pp. (*DAI*, 20:7 [Jan 1960], 2784-85)

1413. ———: "The Influence of Villiers de l'Isle Adam on W. B. Yeats," *Nineteenth-Century French Studies*, 6:3&4 (Spring-Summer 1978), 258-76.

1414. ROSE, MARILYN GADDIS: "Yeats's Use of *Axël*," *CompD*, 4:4 (Winter 1970/71), 253-64.

Particularly in *The Countess Cathleen*.

See also CD58, 60, EA12, 28, EC10, 17, EE498, FE29.

François Villon

1415. BORNSTEIN, GEORGE J., and HUGH H. WITEMEYER: "From *Villain* to Visionary: Pound and Yeats on Villon," *CL*, 19:4 (Fall 1967), 308-20.

Yeats's view of Villon was originally indebted to Pound, but changed later as his literary theory developed.

Kurt Vonnegut

1416. NELSON, JON ERIC: "Yeats and Vonnegut: The Artist as Myth-maker," *Lutheran Q*, 25:2 (May 1973), 124-35.

Richard Wagner

1417. MARTIN, STODDARD: *Wagner to "The Waste Land": A Study of the Relationship of Wagner to English Literature*. London: Macmillan, 1982. xi, 277 pp.

"Yeats," 121-34, and passim (see index).

See also CD66, 840, EA12, EC17, FG26.

A. E. Waite

1418. GILBERT, R. A.: "'The One Deep Student': Yeats and A. E. Waite," *YeA*, 3 (1985), 3-13.

"Utterly opposed to each other as they were in all things occult, each man evidently respected the other." Quotes from Waite's unpublished diaries.

Peter Warlock

1419. COPLEY, IAN ALFRED: *The Music of Peter Warlock: A Critical Survey*. London: Dobson, 1979. xvii, 334 pp.

Numerous references to Yeats and to Warlock's settings of his poems.

1420. GRAY, CECIL: *Peter Warlock: A Memoir of Philip Heseltine*.

London: Cape, 1934. 319 pp.
Several references to Yeats and to Warlock's settings of his poems, especially on pp. 182, 186, 248-50.

For Warlock's settings see HC304-307.

Vernon Watkins

1421. HIRST, DESIRÉE: "Vernon Watkins and the Influence of W. B. Yeats," *Poetry Wales,* 12:4 (Spring 1977), 84-100.

1422. LA BELLE, JENIJOY: "Vernon Watkins: Some Observations on Poetry," *AWR,* 65 (1979), 100-6.
Lecture notes, taken down verbatim and later corrected by Watkins. Several notes are concerned with Yeats.

1423. MCCASLIN, SUSAN ELIZABETH: "Vernon Watkins, Metaphysical Poet," °Ph.D. thesis, U of British Columbia, 1984. (*DAI,* 45:12 [June 1985], 3635A)
Discusses the influence of Yeats.

1424. WATKINS, GWEN: "Vernon Watkins & W. B. Yeats," *Poetry Wales,* 12:4 (Spring 1977), 64-65.
Letter from Gwen Watkins to J. P. Ward and an extract from a lecture by Watkins on modern poetry (1966).

1425. ————: *Portrait of a Friend.* Llandysul: Gomer Press, 1983. xv, 226 pp.
On the Vernon Watkins--Dylan Thomas relationship with several references to Yeats (see index).

For Watkins's poems on Yeats see HD187-190. See also BB62, CA162.

Dorothy Wellesley

1426. HASSETT, JOSEPH M.: "Slouching towards Intimacy," *Harvard Magazine,* 84:4 (Mar-Apr 1982), 7-8.
An essay on "the lumbering pace at which W. B. Yeats and Lady Dorothy Wellesley achieved intimacy of address in their correspondence."

1427. O'SHEA, EDWARD: "Yeats as Editor: Dorothy Wellesley's *Selections,*" *ELN,* 11:2 (Dec 1973), 112-18.
Yeats's MS. annotations to, and changes in, DW's *Poems of Ten Years.*

1428. YEATS, W. B.: *Letters on Poetry from W. B. Yeats to Dorothy Wellesley.* With an introduction by Kathleen Raine. London: Oxford UP, 1964 [1940]. xiii, 202 pp. (Oxford Paperback. 82.)
Includes letters from DW to WBY, two sections of comments and recorded conversations, and an account of Yeats's last days. Kathleen Raine's introduction (pp. ix-xiii, not in the 1940 edition) defends Yeats's more unpopular views about poetry and politics. For reviews see G1290-1319 and note.

See also AE23, BB109, 229, 256, BC16, CA35, 170, 174, DC207, DD66.

Eudora Welty

1429. CARSON, FRANKLIN D.: "'The Song of Wandering Aengus': Allusions in Eudora Welty's *The Golden Apples*," *NMW*, 6:1 (Spring 1973), 14-18.

1430. COTHRAN, DIANNE ALLBRITTON: "Myth and Eudora Welty's Mississippi: An Analysis of *The Golden Apples*," °Ph.D. thesis, Florida State U, 1982. 134 pp. (*DAI*, 46:1 [July 1985], 151A)
Discusses the influence of Yeats.

1431. PRENSHAW, PEGGY WHITMAN (ed): *Eudora Welty: Critical Essays*. Jackson: UP of Mississippi, 1979. xviii, 446 pp.
Danièle Pitavy-Souques: "Technique as Myth: The Structure of *The Golden Apples*," 258-68 (the use of "The Song of Wandering Aengus").

1432. YAEGER, PATRICIA S.: "'Because a Fire Was in My Head': Eudora Welty and the Dialogic Imagination," *PMLA*, 99:5 (Oct 1984), 955-73.
Eudora Welty's use of "The Song of Wandering Aengus" and "Leda and the Swan" in *The Golden Apples*.
A revised version of this article was published under the same title in *Mississippi Q*, 39:4 (Fall 1986), 561-86, and reprinted in Albert J. Devlin (ed): *Welty: A Life in Literature*. Jackson: UP of Mississippi, 1987. xi, 3-310 pp. (pp. 139-67).

Zacharias Werner

1433. DISKIN, PATRICK: "Yeats's *Purgatory* and Werner's *Der vierundzwanzigste Februar*," *N&Q*, os 224 / ns 26:4 (Aug 1979), 340-42.
Zacharias Werner's romantic drama (1809/15) may have been a source of Yeats's play.

Walt Whitman

1434. ASSOCIATION INTERNATIONALE DE LITTÉRATURE COMPARÉE / INTERNATIONAL COMPARATIVE LITERATURE ASSOCIATION: *Comparative Literature*. Edited by Werner P. Friederich. Chapel Hill: U of North Carolina Press, 1959. 2 vols. (Actes du 2e congrès / Proceedings of the 2nd Congress. U of North Carolina Studies in Comparative Literature. 23. 24.)
Herbert Howarth: "Whitman and the Irish Writers," 2:479-88; reprinted as "Whitman among the Irish," *LMag*, 7:1 (Jan 1960), 48-55.

1435. QUINN, JAMES E.: "Yeats and Whitman, 1887-1925," *Walt Whitman R*, 20:3 (Sept 1974), 106-9.
Mostly quotations; slight.

1436. TRAUBEL, HORACE: *With Walt Whitman in Camden January 21 to April 7, 1889*. Edited by Sculley Bradley. Philadelphia: U of Pennsylvania Press, 1953. xviii, 528 pp.
Whitman reads and marks Yeats's essay on Ferguson (1886, *Uncollected Prose*, 1:87-104), pp. 347-50.

See also CD18.

Kazimierz Wierzyński

1437. DUDEK, JOLANTA: "The Poetics of W. B. Yeats and K. Wierzyński: A Parallel," D.Phil. thesis, Oxford U, 1979. xii, 240 pp.
Compares "The Tower" with Wierzyński's poem "Piąta pora roku" by analyzing the poems in the context of each poet's works and of the national and European literary traditions.

Richard Wilbur

1438. HERZMAN, RONALD B.: "A Yeatsian Parallel from Richard Wilbur's 'Merlin Enthralled,'" *NConL*, 2:5 (Nov 1972), 10-11.
A parallel from "Leda and the Swan."

Oscar Wilde

1438a. ACKROYD, PETER: *The Last Testament of Oscar Wilde*. London: Hamilton, 1983. v, 185 pp.
A novel in form of a diary with some references to Yeats (e.g., pp. 7, 82-83, 99).

1439. CHAMBERLIN, J. E.: *Ripe Was the Drowsy Hour: The Age of Oscar Wilde*. NY: Seabury Press, 1977. xv, 222 pp.
Some notes on Yeats and Wilde.

1440. CHARLESWORTH, BARBARA: *Dark Passages: The Decadent Consciousness in Victorian Literature*. Madison: U of Wisconsin Press, 1965. xvi, 155 pp.
On Yeats and Wilde, Lionel Johnson, and Symons, passim (see index).

1441. DARUWALA, MANECK HOMI: "Good Intentions: The Romantic Aesthetics of Oscar Wilde's Criticism," *VIJ*, 12 (1984), 105-32.
Discusses Wilde's influence on Yeats's poetry and criticism.

1442. ELLMANN, RICHARD: *Oscar Wilde*. London: Hamilton, 1987. xiv, 632 pp.
Numerous references to Yeats (see index).

1443. HYDE, HARFORD MONTGOMERY: *Oscar Wilde: A Biography*. London: Eyre Methuen, 1976. xiii, 410 pp.
See index for a few notes on Wilde and Yeats.

1444. KOHL, NORBERT: *Oscar Wilde: Das literarische Werk zwischen Provokation und Anpassung*. Heidelberg: Winter, 1980. 703 pp. (Anglistische Forschungen. 143.)
Note on Yeats's "edition" of the "Ballad of Reading Gaol" in the *Oxford Book of Modern Verse*, pp. 472-74.

1445. KORNINGER, SIEGFRIED (ed): *Studies in English Language and Literature Presented to Professor Dr. Karl Brunner on the Occasion of His Seventieth Birthday*. Wien: Braumüller, 1957. x, 290 pp. (Wiener Beiträge zur englischen Philologie. 65.)
Rudolf Stamm: "W. B. Yeats und Oscar Wildes 'Ballad of Reading Goal,'" 210-19. An English version of this article appears in DD630. Yeats's cuts in Wilde's poem, as printed in the *Oxford Book of Modern Verse*, improve it considerably, but then it is no longer a poem by Wilde.

1446. RHYNEHART, J. G.: "Wilde's Comments on Early Works of W. B. Yeats," *IrB*, 1:4 (Spring 1962), 102-4.

See also BC17, CB70, 546, CC71a, 107, 168, CD7, 42, 305, 706, 975, DC71, DD630, EA12, 40, EE260, 261, 332, 503, FE78, 82, G417.

Tennessee Williams

1447. PRESLEY, DELMA E., and HARI SINGH: "Epigraphs to the Plays of Tennessee Williams," *NMW*, 3:1 (Spring 1970), 2-12.
On a quotation from "Sailing to Byzantium" in *The Milk Train Doesn't Stop Here Any More*, pp. 9-11.

William Carlos Williams

1448. JACKSON, THOMAS H.: "Positivism and Modern Poetics: Yeats, Mallarmé, and William Carlos Williams," *ELH*, 46:3 (Fall 1979), 509-40.
Williams's modernism and critique of positivism was partly anticipated by Yeats and Mallarmé.

1449. KENNER, HUGH: "The Minims of Language," *TLS*, 27 Apr 1984, 451-52.
Compares Williams and Yeats.

See also BG216, CD18.

Yvor Winters

1450. FRASER, SHIRLEY STERNBERG: "Yvor Winters: The Critic as Moralist," Ph.D. thesis, Louisiana State U, 1972. viii, 226 pp. (*DAI*, 33:5 [Nov 1972], 2370A)
"William Butler Yeats," 132-39; on Winters's Yeats essay (DA50).

1451. SEXTON, RICHARD J.: *The Complex of Yvor Winters' Criticism*. The Hague: Mouton, 1973. ix, 412 pp. (De Proprietatibus Litterarum. Series maior. 6.)
"The Poetry of W. B. Yeats," 276-82; a rather uncritical summary of Winters's essay (DA50).

Virginia Woolf

1452. WOOLF, VIRGINIA: *The Letters*. Edited by Nigel Nicolson and Joanne Trautmann. London: Hogarth Press, 1975-80. 6 vols.
See indexes to vols. 2-6.

1453. ———: *The Diary of Virginia Woolf*. Introduction by Quentin Bell, edited by Anne O. Bell. London: Hogarth Press, 1977-84. 5 vols.
There are references to Yeats in vols. 3-5 (see indexes).

See also CC69, DD113.

William Wordsworth

1454. BARON, MICHAEL: "Yeats, Wordsworth and the Communal Sense:

The Case of 'If I Were Four-and-Twenty,'" *YeA*, 5 (1987), 62-82.
The relevance of the Wordsworth references to Yeats's writings.

1455. HEANEY, SEAMUS: *Preoccupations: Selected Prose 1968-1978*. NY: Farrar, Straus, Giroux, 1980. 226 pp.
"The Makings of a Music: Reflections on Wordsworth and Yeats," 61-78; reprint of a pamphlet with the same title, Liverpool: Liverpool UP, 1978. iii, 18 pp. (Kenneth Allott Lectures. 1.) Wordsworth viewed "the poetic act as essentially an act of complaisance with natural impulses and tendencies. It is otherwise with Yeats. With him the act is not one of complaisance but of control."
"Yeats as an Example?" 98-114; also in Jeffares: *Yeats, Sligo and Ireland* (1980, CA51), 56-72.
Review by John Bayley: "Seamus Heaney's Prose," *List*, 20 Nov 1980, 691-92, which includes a Yeats-Heaney comparison.

1456. MAN, PAUL DE: *The Rhetoric of Romanticism*. NY: Columbia UP, 1984. xi, 327 pp.
"Symbolic Landscape in Wordsworth and Yeats," 125-43; first published on pp. 22-37 of Reuben Arthur Brower and Richard Poirier (eds): *In Defense of Reading: A Reader's Approach to Literary Criticism*. NY: Dutton, 1963 [1962]. x, 3-311 pp. (Dutton Paperback. D113.). Compares Wordsworth's "Composed by the Side of Grasmere Lake" with "Coole Park and Ballylee, 1931."
"Image and Emblem in Yeats," 145-238, 301-13, 315-19; an excerpt from CD790.
Reviews:
- George Bornstein, *Yeats*, 5 (1987), 222-26.
- Northrop Frye: "In the Earth, or in the Air?" *TLS*, 17 Jan 1986, 51-52.
- Daniel T. O'Hara: "The Specialty of Self-Victimization in Recent Yeats Studies," *ConL*, 27:2 (Summer 1986), 285-89.

1457. PERKINS, DAVID: *The Quest for Permanence: The Symbolism of Wordsworth, Shelley, and Keats*. Cambridge, Mass.: Harvard UP, 1959. xi, 305 pp.
Scattered notes, passim (see index).

1458. ———: *Wordsworth and the Poetry of Sincerity*. Cambridge, Mass.: Harvard UP, 1964. xi, 285 pp.
Scattered notes, passim (see index).

See also CA12, 53a, 103, CC102, 270, 279, DB203, DC192, 218, 301, 374, DD44, 93, 113, 223, 534a, 582, FB32.

Mrs. Georgie Yeats (Georgie Hyde-Lees)

1459. DAILEY, SUSAN RAMSAY: "'My Delight and Comfort': The Influence of Georgie Hyde-Lees on the Life of W. B. Yeats and the Aesthetic Development of His Work," °Ph.D. thesis, Catholic U of America, 1987. 203 pp. (*DAI*, 48:5 [Nov 1987], 1209A)

See also BA3, BB23, CA109, CC174, CD1058, DC391, DD427.

Jack Butler Yeats

1460. MCGUINNESS, NORA MAHONEY: "The Creative Universe of Jack B.

Yeats," Ph.D. thesis, U of California, Davis, 1984. viii, 435 pp. (*DAI,* 46:2 [Aug 1985], 421A)

On "the familial events which contributed to making him [Jack Yeats] the distanced outsider," including WBY's contribution.

1461. PYLE, HILARY: "'Men of Destiny': Jack B. and W. B. Yeats. The Background and the Symbols," *Studies,* 66:262-263 (Summer-Autumn 1977), 188-213.

1462. ROSE, MARILYN GADDIS: "The Kindred Vistas of W. B. and Jack B. Yeats," *Eire,* 5:1 (Spring 1970), 67-79.

Spatial relations in WBY's poems and JBY's paintings.

1463. ———: *Jack B. Yeats: Painter and Poet.* Bern: Lang, 1972. 51 pp. (European University Papers. Series 18, vol. 3.)

"Complementary Views: W. B. Yeats, Synge, Joyce, Beckett," 37-47.

1464. ———: "The Helens of Gustave Moreau and Jack B. Yeats: Influence or Parallel?" *Eire,* 15:3 (Fall 1980), 65-74.

Jack Yeats's knowledge of Moreau is due to WBY's mediation.

See also BB193, BD1, 12, EE293, 340.

John Butler Yeats

1465. BENNETT, DIANE CHRISTINA: "My Father's Studio: John Butler Yeats and William Butler Yeats," Ph.D. thesis, U of California, Irvine, 1976. xiv, 330 pp. (*DAI,* 38:9 [Mar 1978], 5490A-91A)

1465a. CULLEN, FINTAN: *The Drawings of John Butler Yeats (1839-1922): Essay and Catalogue.* With a brief biography by William M. Murphy; foreword by Daniel Robbins. Albany, N.Y.: Albany Institute of History & Art and the Department of the Arts and the Department of English of Union College, 1987. 115 pp.

On WBY see the contributions by Murphy and Cullen; reproductions of drawings of WBY and notes, pp. 44-45, 58-59, 66-67.

1466. MURPHY, WILLIAM M.: "Father and Son: The Early Education of W. B. Yeats," *REL,* 8:4 (Oct 1967), 75-96.

Biographical connections and JBY's influence on WBY.

1467. OLNEY, JAMES: "Father and Son: J. B. Yeats and W. B. Yeats," *SAQ,* 79:3 (Summer 1980), 321-28.

See also AE37, BA3, 15, BB260, BC1, 18-20, BD3, 18, 24, CA4, 49, 54, 61, 126, CC25, 132, CD63, 1035, 1160, FA77, FD57, FE27, 29, 78.

Zozimus (Michael Moran)

1468. GULIELMUS DUBLINIENSIS HUMORIENSIS [i.e., Joseph Tully?]: *Memoir of the Great Original Zozimus (Michael Moran), the Celebrated Dublin Street Rhymer and Reciter: With His Songs, Sayings and Recitations.* A facsimile edition with an introduction by Thomas Wall. Blackrock, Co. Dublin: Carraig Books, 1976. iv, 34 pp. (Carraig Chapbooks. 6.)

Wall's introduction (pp. iii-iv) refers to Yeats's interest in Zozimus.

CE Less Substantial Material

1. *Academic American Encyclopedia*. Princeton, N.J.: Aretê Publishing Company, 1980. 21 vols.
Eamon Grennan: "Yeats, William Butler," 20:321.

2. ADLARD, JOHN: "An Unnoticed Yeats Item," *N&Q*, os 214 / ns 16:7 (July 1969), 255.
Annotations to an article by Bryan J. Jones: "Traditions and Superstitions Collected at Kilcurry, County Louth, Ireland," *Folk-lore*, 10:1 (Mar 1899), 122-23. Yeats's notes are reprinted in *Uncollected Prose*, 2:145-47.

3. ALBERT, EDWARD: *A History of English Literature*. 3rd edition revised by J. A. Stone. London: Harrap, 1960 [1923]. 624 pp.
"William Butler Yeats," 482-86.

4. ALEXANDER, H.: "Några irländska författere" [Some Irish writers], *Dagens tidning*, 5 Jan 1920, page number not available.

5. ANDERSON, GEORGE K., and EDA LOU WALTON (eds): *This Generation*. Revised edition. Chicago: Scott, Foresman, 1949 [1939]. xvi, 1065 pp.
"William Butler Yeats," 91-93.

6. ANON.: "The Moderns: VII. William Butler Yeats," *America*, 1 Dec 1923, 166.
"Of some of his work, there can be no word spoken in dispraise; but in regard to other writings [i.e., those offensive to Catholics], silence is charity."

7. ANON.: Note on recent sales of the first edition of *Mosada*, *BC*, 12:4 (Winter 1963), 437-38.
The highest price paid was $3,750.

8. ANON.: "Ireland and the Theatre," *Claidheamh Soluis*, 19 Mar 1910, 7.
Yeats and the Gaelic League.

9. ANON.: "The Visit of William Butler Yeats: Mr. Yeats Maintains That Propaganda Cannot Take the Place of Art. Mr. Yeats's Activities through George Moore's Eyes," *Current Opinion*, 56:4 (Apr 1914), 294-95.

10. ANON.: "Setna rocznica urodzin Yeatsa" [Centenary of Y's birth], *Dialog*, 10:8 (Aug 1965), 135-37.

11. ANON.: "Yeats: Sunday Next Will Be the Centenary of the Poet's Birth," *Evening Herald*, 11 June 1965, 6.

12. ANON.: "A Dublin Literary Coterie Sketched by a Non-Pretentious Observer," *Evening Telegraph*, 14 Jan 1888, [2].
According to Monk Gibbon (BA4, p. 58), Sappho is Katharine Tynan, O'Reilly is AE, and Augustus Fitzgibbon is Yeats.

13. ANON.: "William Butler Yeats: The Life and Labours of a Young Celtic Poet," *Irish Emerald*, 23 Jan 1897, 56.

14. ANON.: "An Alchemist's Forge--Where Yeats Drew Out Crumbs of Gold," *IrI*, 22 Nov 1963, 14.

Report of John Masefield's speech at the opening of the Yeats Room in the New Ambassador's Hotel, Woburn Place, London.

15. ANON.: "Poet's Tower to Be Restored: Plan for W. B. Yeats's Castle," *IrT,* 25 Oct 1963, 11.
See also the editorial on p. 9.

16. ANON.: "Det keltiske element in literaturen," *Kringsjaa,* 12:1 (15 July 1898), 69-74.
Summary of "The Celtic Element in Literature" (Wade, p. 355).

17. ANON.: "Irske hekse-doktere," *Kringsjaa,* 16:7 (15 Oct 1900), 489-93.
Summary of "Irish Witch Doctors" (Wade, p. 359).

18. ANON.: [The Showing Up of Pensioner Yeats], *Leader,* 25 Nov 1911, 348-49.
Sneers; see also preceding and subsequent issues.

19. ANON.: "Why Yeats Is a Nobel Prize Man," *Literary Digest,* 8 Dec 1923, 26-27.
Extracts from press notices.

20. ANON.: "Mr. W. B. Yeats," *Literary Year-Book,* 1897, 174-75.
A survey of his publications to date.

21. ANON.: "Seeker for Truth," *MD: Medical Newsmagazine,* 9:8 (Aug 1965), 180-87.

22. ANON.: "A Lille: Un hommage à Yeats," *Monde,* 6 Apr 1965, 12.
The Yeats festival and exhibition, organized by the 5th Congrès de la Société des anglicistes de l'enseignement supérieur.

23. ANON.: [Note on Yeats as a possible future Poet Laureate], *NSt,* 26 Apr 1930, 71.
See also "The Next Poet Laureate--Some Pleas for Possible Candidates," *Public Opinion,* 2 May 1930, 413; "Dr. Bridges and His Successor," *Week-end R,* 26 Apr 1930, 220-21; Charles Powell: "The Laureateship: Dr. Bridge[s]'s Successor. A Review of the Claims: Kipling, Watson, Masefield, Yeats," *Obs,* 27 Apr 1930, 19 (Yeats's "claim, stripped of all circumstance, is surely unchallengeable").

24. ANON.: "An Irish Poet Crowned," *NY Evening Post,* 16 Nov 1923, 8.
With the Nobel Prize.

25. ANON.: "Do We Deserve This Compliment?" *NYT,* 25 Sept 1924, 22.
Yeats's favorable opinion of the Pennsylvania Railroad Station in New York.

25a. ANON.: "Changes in Oratory," *NYT,* 25 Aug 1925, 16.
On Yeats's statement that "the day of oratory is past."

26. ANON.: "William Butler Yeats--Poezja i polityka," *Odgłosy,* 4 July 1965, 9.

27. ANON.: "Literary Gossip," *Outlook* [London], 16 Apr 1898, 344-46.
Criticizes "The Broken Gates of Death" for lack of factual accuracy. See Yeats's reply (reprinted in *Letters,* pp. 297-98) and the answer by the "friendly paragraphist," 23 Apr 1898, 377.

28. ANON.: "The Man and the Myth: William Butler Yeats 1865-1965," *Queen*, 2 June 1965, 70-77.
One page of text and 12 photographs by John Hedgecoe with captions from Yeats's works.

29. ANON.: Note on Yeats in Croatian, *Radio Zagreb*, 8:1 (1952), 8.

30. ANON.: "The World in One Small Room. . . : William Butler Yeats," *Senior Scholastic*, 47:5 (15 Oct 1945), 20.

31. ANON.: "An Important Centenary," *Shavian*, 3:3 (Winter 1965), 34-35.

32. ANON.: Note on Yeats as the "most able exponent of the Celtic movement," *Sketch*, 26 Jan 1898, 12.
Includes a caricature by W. T. Horton. Reprinted in *BmNY*, 7:1 (Mar 1898), 5-6.

33. ANON.: "A New Literary Impulse," *Speaker*, 11 Mar 1893, 276-77.
On the founding of the Irish Literary Society, London: "From Mr. Yeats, with his exquisite feeling for form, much is to be expected in the future, especially if he can emancipate himself from the little 'sheeogue' and 'luricaun' way of looking at everything." Correspondence by T. W. Rolleston, 18 Mar 1893, 312.

34. ANON.: Warning to Yeats not to "pose" on his American lecture tour, *Theatre*, 3:30 (Aug 1903), 186.

35. ANON.: "Cast a Cold Eye," *Time*, 6 Oct 1952, 41.
On the difficulties of erecting a Yeats memorial in Ireland.

36. ANON.: "D. Litt. for Mr. W. B. Yeats," *Times*, 27 May 1931, 14.
The Oxford degree. See also CE371.

37. ANON.: "A Tribute to W. B. Yeats," *Times*, 29 June 1939, 12.
Preview of a program at the Ellen Terry Barn Theatre with a note on *Purgatory*.

38. ANON.: "T. P.'s Portrait Gallery--VI.," *T. P.'s Weekly*, 26 Nov 1909, 703.
"He takes all beauty for his province, and lives in the Euston Road."

39. ANON.: "İngiliz ozanı William Butler Yeats" [The English poet WBY], *Yeni insan*, 5:2 (Feb 1967), 10-11.

40. ARMSTRONG, ALISON: "Like a Long-Legged Fly. . . ," *ILS*, 2:1 (Spring 1983), 19-20.
Introduction to "A Yeats Broadside," which will be an occasional feature of the *ILS*.

41. ARNS, KARL: *Grundriss der Geschichte der englischen Literatur von 1832 bis zur Gegenwart*. Paderborn: Schöningh, 1941. 235 pp.
"Die keltische Renaissance und die neuen Anglo-Iren," 205-24; on Yeats, pp. 207-11.

42. ARRIETA, RAFAEL ALBERTO: "Un soneto di William Butler Yeats," *Prensa*, 13 June 1965, Secciones illustrades, no. 1, p. 2.
An introductory note and a translation of "Leda and the Swan."

43. ASTALDI, MARIA LUISA: *Il poeta e la regina e altre letture inglesi*. Firenze: Sansoni, 1963. 284 pp.
"Un grande poeta del novecento: W. B. Yeats," 107-10.

44. ATKINS, JOHN: "Soul against the Intellect. W. B. Yeats: The Point of Balance," *Books and Bookmen,* 2:12 (Sept 1957), 11.

45. ATKINSON, BROOKS: "Critic at Large: The Yeats Brothers Remain a Dominant Force in Ireland's Cultural Life," *NYT,* 14 Dec 1962, 5.

46. ———: *Brief Chronicles*. NY: Coward-McCann, 1966. 255 pp.
"The Yeats Boys," 44-46; presumably identical with the preceding.

47. ATKINSON, F. G.: "'Mighty Beautiful Stuff': Two New A. E. Letters and Some Footnotes to the Irish Renaissance," *EA,* 29:1 (Jan-Mar 1976), 64-71.
The letters were written to Sir Arthur Quiller-Couch and contain some references to Yeats.

48. BARKER, VERNON DUCKWORTH: "Regionális irodalmi kísérlet nagybritanniában," *Erdélyi Helikon,* 3:9 (Nov 1930), 785-89.
A survey of 20th-century Irish literature in English, with notes on Yeats. Continued as "Ír drámaírók," 4:1 (Jan 1931), 76-79.

49. BARZUN, JACQUES: *Race: A Study in Superstition*. Revised, with a new preface. NY: Harper & Row, 1965. xxiv, 263 pp.
Note on whether Yeats was typically Irish, pp. 213-14.

50. BATES, KATHARINE LEE: "William Butler Yeats: The Irish Poet Who Is Now Visiting America," *BET,* 11 Nov 1903, 16.
Subheadings: "A sketch of his career and work and an estimate of their value--His great labors for the Celtic Revival--His ascetic devotion to his art--An important figure in literature." An extract was published as "The 'Standard-Bearer' of the Celtic Revival," *Literary Digest,* 28 Nov 1903, 737-38.

51. BAYLEY, JOHN: "W. B. Yeats," *Cahiers du Centre de Recherches sur les Pays du Nord et du Nord-Ouest,* 1 (1978), 53-57.

52. BEERBOHM, MAX: *Beerbohm's Literary Caricatures: From Homer to Huxley*. Selected, introduced, and annotated by J. G. Riewald. London: Lane, 1977. 295 pp.
See pp. 98-101, 152-53, 186-87 for Yeats caricatures and notes.

53. BEGLEY, MONIE: *Rambles in Ireland and: A County-by-County Guide for Discriminating Travellers*. Old Greenwich, Ct.: Devin-Adair, 1977. x, 374 pp.
See index for some notes on Yeats.

54. BENCE-JONES, MARK: *The Remarkable Irish: Chronicle of a Land, a Culture, a Mystique*. NY: McKay, 1966. xi, 243 pp.
Yeats, passim (see index).

55. ———: "A Yeats Pilgrim in Sligo," *Country Life,* 27 May 1971, 1284-86.

56. BICKLEY, FRANCIS: "The Development of William Butler Yeats," *Thrush,* 1:2 (Jan 1910), 147-51.
Reprinted in *Living Age,* 26 Mar 1910, 802-5.

57. BING, JUST: *Verdens-litteraturhistorie: Grunnlinjer og hovedverker*. Oslo: Aschehoug, 1928-34. 3 vols.
Yeats, 3:496-98.

58. BIRMINGHAM, GEORGE A.: "The Literary Movement in Ireland," *FortnR*, os 88 / ns 82:492 (Dec 1907), 947-57.
Reprinted in *Living Age*, 25 Jan 1908, 235-43. On Yeats, passim.

59. ———: *An Irishman Looks at His World*. London: Hodder & Stoughton, 1919. 307 pp.
"--And Scholars--Ireland's Culture," 102-22. "Ireland, in spite of its springtime of promise, has failed to create a national kind of literature because Ireland does not want literature of any kind, national or other." Yeats is one of the unwanted.

60. BLACK, E. L. (ed): *Nine Modern Poets: An Anthology*. London: Macmillan, 1968 [1966]. x, 230 pp.
"W. B. Yeats," 1-5.

61. BLAMIRES, HARRY: *A Short History of English Literature*. London: Methuen, 1974. viii, 536 pp.
See pp. 397-98, 410-14.

62. ———: *Twentieth-Century English Literature*. London: Macmillan, 1982. xii, 304 pp. (Macmillan History of Literature.)
"The Irish Movement," 32-36; "W. B. Yeats," 90-93; and passim (see index).

63. ———: (ed): *A Guide to Twentieth Century Literature in English*. London: Methuen, 1983. xiv, 312 pp.
H. Blamires: Yeats, 309-11.

64. BLEI, FRANZ: *Zeitgenössische Bildnisse*. Amsterdam: De Lange, 1940. 345 pp.
"William Butler Yeats," 162-63.

65. BLOEM, J. C.: "William Butler Yeats," *Nieuwe Rotterdamsche Courant*, 17 Nov 1923, Lett. Bijbl., 1.

66. BLOOM, HAROLD (ed): *Twentieth-Century British Literature*. NY: Chelsea House, 1985-87. 5 vols.
"W. B. Yeats," 5:3153-3212; a short introduction and 12 extracts from previously published criticism (not analyzed in this bibliography).

67. BOEHRINGER, ERICH, and WILHELM HOFFMANN (eds): *Robert Boehringer: Eine Freundesgabe*. Tübingen: Mohr, 1957. viii, 772 pp.
W. M. Jablonski: "Bemerkenswertes aus dem Leben und der Gedankenwelt des irischen Dichters William Butler Yeats" [Memorabilia from the life and thought of the Irish poet WBY], 325-29.

68. BÖKER, UWE, HORST BREUER, and ROLF BREUER: *Die Klassiker der englischen Literatur: Von Geoffrey Chaucer bis Samuel Beckett*. Düsseldorf: Econ Taschenbuch Verlag, 1985. 256 pp. (Hermes Handlexikon.)
U. Böker: "William Butler Yeats," 237-42.

69. *Bol'shaia͡ sovetskaia͡ ėnt͡siklopediia͡*. Moskva: Gos. Nauchno isd-vo "Bol'shaia͡ sovetskaia͡ ėnt͡siklopediia͡," 1948-58. 51 vols.
Ĭits, 19:185.

70. BORUM, POUL: *Poetisk modernisme: En kritisk introduktion.* København: Vendelkaers, 1966. 279 pp.
Yeats, pp. 60-62 and passim (see index).

71. BOTHEROYD, SYLVIA, and PAUL F. BOTHEROYD: *Irland: Kunst- und Reiseführer mit Landeskunde.* Stuttgart: Kohlhammer, 1985. 408 pp.
A Baedeker with some references to Yeats (see index).

72. BOURGEOIS, MAURICE: "William Butler Yeats," *Comoedia,* 1 Jan 1924, 4.

72a. BRACK, O. M. (ed): *Twilight of Dawn: Studies in English Literature in Transition.* Tucson: U of Arizona Press, 1987. xiv, 245 pp.
Some references to Yeats, particularly in Wendell Harris: "Richard Le Gallienne and the Romanticism of the 1890's," 168-79.

73. BRADY, CHARLES A.: "Ireland and the Two Eternities," *America,* 22 Mar 1941, 663-64.
"The three wraths of Ireland: the anger of St. Patrick; the rage of Swift; the defiance of Yeats."

74. BRADY, GERARD K.: "Yeats's Tower," *IrT,* 16 Sept 1960, 7.
The history of Thoor Ballylee before Yeats bought it. Correspondence by Gabriel Fallon, 17 Sept 1960, 7, 9.

75. BRANCATI, VIVALDA: "William Butler Yeats, dal sogno alla realtà: Dopo aver guardato al mondo fittizio delle leggende e tradizioni irlandesi divenne il cantore della disillusione," *Persona,* 8:3 (1967), 12.
"WBY from dream to reality: After having seen the fictitious world of Irish legends and traditions, he becomes the singer of disillusion."

76. BREÁDÚN, DEAGLÁN DE: "Yeats Letters Collected," *IrT,* 15 Aug 1984, 8.
Announcement that the first of at least 12 volumes of Yeats letters will be published early in 1985. See BA22.

77. BROCKHAUS: *Der Grosse Brockhaus.* 16th edition. Wiesbaden: Brockhaus, 1952-58. 13 vols.
"Yeats," 12:625.

78. BROPHY, LIAM: "W. B. Yeats: That Hazy Mixed-up Kid," *Friar,* 23:4 (Apr 1965), 13-19.

79. BRUNIUS, AUGUST: *Modern engelsk litteratur.* Stockholm: Natur och Kultur, 1923. 142 pp. (Natur och Kultur. 17.)
Yeats, passim (see index).

80. BUCHANAN, GEORGE: "Pages from a Journal," *Rann,* 15 (Spring 1952), 11-13.
Includes some notes on Yeats.

81. BULLOCK, ALAN, and OLIVER STALLYBRASS (eds): *The Harper Dictionary of Modern Thought.* NY: Harper & Row, 1977. xix, 684 pp.
Also published as *The Fontana Dictionary of Modern Thought.* London: Fontana, 1977. See p. 680 for an index to several short references to Yeats.

82. BULLOCK, ALAN, and R. B. WOODINGS (eds): *The Fontana Bio-*

graphical Companion to Modern Thought. London: Collins, 1983. xxv, 867 pp.

E[ric] H[omberger]: Yeats, 839-40.

83. CAHILL, PAUL [pseudonym]: "Cast a Cold Eye on Yeats," *Word*, June 1965, [7-10].

84. CARTIANU, ANA, and IOAN AUREL PREDA (eds): *Dicționar al literaturii engleze*. București: Editora Științifică, 1970. 440 pp.

L[iliana] P[opovici-Teodoreanu]: Yeats, 381-83.

85. ČERMÁK, FRANTIŠEK: "Baladický básník svobody" [Ballad poet of liberty], *Rude pravo*, 13 June 1965, [6].

86. CHAMBERLIN, J. E.: "From High Decadence to High Modernism," *QQ*, 87:4 (Winter 1980), 591-610.

Contains a few notes on Yeats.

87. *Chambers's Cyclopaedia of English Literature*. Edited by David Patrick, revised and expanded by J. Liddell Geddie and J. C. Smith. London: Chambers, 1938. 3 vols.

Yeats, 3:709. There is a different article in an earlier edition, Philadelphia: Lippincott, 1902-4. 3 vols. (3:711: Yeats is a good poet, but not an Irish poet.)

88. *Chambers's Encyclopaedia*. New revised edition. London: International Learning System, 1968. 15 vols.

M[ichael] R[oberts]: Yeats, 14:764. Also in 1964 edition.

89. CHASSÉ, CHARLES: "Le lauréat du Prix Nobel: W. B. Yeats, poète irlandais," *Figaro: Supplément littéraire*, 24 Nov 1923, 1-2.

90. CHIAMPI, RUBENS: "Yeats's View of Women," *ITA-Humanidades*, 7 (1971), 137-45.

Negligible.

91. CHIARI, JOSEPH: *The Aesthetics of Modernism*. London: Vision Press, 1970. 224 pp.

See index for some rather general remarks on Yeats.

92. CHURCH, RICHARD: *British Authors: A Twentieth-Century Gallery with 53 Portraits*. London: Longmans, Green, 1948 [1943]. 145 pp.

"W. B. Yeats, 1865-1939," 40-42.

93. CLARK, DAVID: "Yeats on Hatred," *Pax*, 12:3 (Christmas 1957), 20-22.

Yeats was no pacifist, but his hatred was nonviolent.

94. CLEARY, JAMES MANSFIELD (ed): *Proud Are We Irish: Irish Culture and History as Dramatized in Verse and Song*. Chicago: Quadrangle Books, 1966. xvi, 239 pp.

Reprints some Yeats items and adds short comments.

95. CLEEVE, BRIAN: *Dictionary of Irish Writers*. Cork: Mercier Press, 1967-71. 3 vols.

See 1:142-43. Reissued as Anne M. Brady and Brian Cleeve: *A Biographical Dictionary of Irish Writers*. Mullingar: Lilliput Press, 1985. xii, 388 pp. (See pp. 251-53.)

96. CLEMENS, KATHARINE: "Some Reflections on William Butler Yeats,"

Mark Twain Q, 6:1 (Summer-Fall 1943), 17-18.
"Yeats's mental life had been mostly confusion."

97. COLBY, ELBRIDGE: "Irish Literary Patriotism," *CathW,* 99:591 (June 1914), 361-66.
The works of Seumas MacManus are more representative of the Irish people than are those of Yeats.

98. *Collier's Encyclopedia.* With bibliography and index. NY: Crowell-Collier, 1969. 24 vols.
Russell K. Alspach: Yeats, 23:687-89. Also in 1963 edition.

99. COLLINS, VERE H.: *Talks with Thomas Hardy at Max Gate 1920-1922.* London: Duckworth, 1978 [1928]. xvi, 85 pp.
Hardy makes short comments on Yeats: "Yeats is not a Sinn Feiner." "I don't suppose he believes in Sinn Fein. I don't suppose he knows what he believes" (p. 19).

100. COLUM, MARY MAGUIRE: *From These Roots: The Ideas That Have Made Modern Literature.* Port Washington, N.Y.: Kennikat Press, 1967 [1937]. xiii, 386 pp.
"The Outside Literatures in English: The Irish and the American," 260-311; on Irish literature, pp. 260-69, with some remarks on Yeats.

101. COLUM, PADRAIC: "Irish Poetry," *BmNY,* 54:2 (Oct 1921), 109-15.
Yeats's contribution to the revival was the idea "of a culture that would be personal and aristocratic."

102. ———: "A Dublin Letter," *SatR,* 15 Feb 1936, 24.
Thoughts on Yeats's 70th birthday and a note on *The King of the Great Clock Tower.*

103. COMBS, GEORGE HAMILTON: *These Amazing Moderns.* St. Louis: Bethany Press, 1933. 270 pp.
"Moore, Synge, and Yeats--An Irish Stew," 220-47. Lectures of the minister of Country Club Christian Church, Kansas City, Mo., sponsored by the young married people's class. Typical quotation: "His poems are delicately beautiful but not seldom lacking sufficient starch of an idea to stand up to. . . . While he seems to have been a pretty poor Christian he was a real patriot."

104. CONNOLLY, CYRIL: *The Modern Movement: One Hundred Key Books from England, France and America, 1880-1950.* NY: Atheneum, 1966. ix, 149 pp.
Yeats is represented by *Responsibilities, Later Poems* (1922), *The Tower,* and *The Winding Stair.*

105. CONNOLLY, JOSEPH: *Collecting Modern First Editions.* London: Studio Vista, 1977. xvi, 175 pp.
A note on scarce Yeats editions, pp. 174-75.

106. COOKE, JOHN DANIEL, and LIONEL STEVENSON: *English Literature of the Victorian Period.* NY: Appleton-Century-Crofts, 1949. xiii, 438 pp.
Yeats, pp. 124-25, 132, 211-14.

107. COOLE, T.: "The Poet--Clues to His Identity," *Claidheamh Soluis,* 12 Mar 1910, 8-9.
A reflection on the question "Can Mr. Yeats, as an Irishman,

have the sincerity so necessary for the great poet?"

108. COOMBES, HARRY: "Yeats and Synge, Sligo and the H-Block," *Haltwhistle Q,* 10 (Spring 1983), 7-16.
Rambling.

109. COURTNEY, NEIL: "Triumphant Life of W. B. Yeats," *Age,* 12 June 1965, 21.

110. COURTNEY, WINIFRED F. (ed): *The Reader's Adviser: A Guide to the Best in Literature.* 11th edition, revised and enlarged. NY: Bowker, 1968. 2 vols.
Yeats, 1:153-54, 935-36, 1024-25.

111. COUSINS, JAMES HENRY: *Modern English Poetry: Its Characteristics and Tendencies.* Madras: Ganesh, [1921]. xiii, 214, ii pp. (Keiogijuku U, Tokyo, Public Lectures in Literature, Autumn 1919.)
"Poets of the Irish Literary Revival," 85-116; on Yeats, passim.

112. ———: "Culture and National Renaissance: The Irish Example," *VQ,* 17:3 (Nov 1951--Jan 1952), 179-90.

113. COUSTER, P. J.: "Un poète irlandais--W. B. Yeats," *Echanges et recherches,* 2:5 (Mar 1939), 296-99.

114. COX, AEDAN: "A Weaver of Symbols," *Hermes,* [1:1] (Feb 1907), 7-11.

115. C[RAIG], M[AURICE] J[AMES]: "W. B. Y.," *Thoth,* 1 (27 Jan 1939), [4].
"Yeats is probably the last man of letters whom people will have the leisure to make into a legendary figure."

116. [CRONE, J. S.?]: "Mr. Yeats' Confessions," *Irish Book Lover,* 15:2 (Apr 1925), 19-21.

117. CRONIN, COLM: "A Visit to Thoor Ballylee," *IrP,* 4 Aug 1966, 9.

118. CROSLAND, THOMAS WILLIAM HODGSON: *The Wild Irishman.* London: Laurie, 1905. 183 pp.
"W. B. Yeats," 112-22. Silly.

119. CUMBERLAND, GERALD: *Set Down in Malice: A Book of Reminiscences.* NY: Brentano's, 1919. 286 pp.
"People I Would Like to Meet," 263-72; one of them Yeats, in order to find out why he is so self-deluded.

120. CUNLIFFE, JOHN WILLIAM: *English Literature during the Last Half Century.* NY: Macmillan, 1919. viii, 315 pp.
"The Irish Movement," 223-43; on Yeats, pp. 225-31.

121. ———: *English Literature in the Twentieth Century.* NY: Macmillan, 1933. vii, 341 pp.
"The Irish Renaissance," 100-124; with a section on Yeats, pp. 101-5.

122. ———: *Leaders of the Victorian Revolution.* NY: Appleton-Century-Crofts, 1934. viii, 343 pp.
"William Butler Yeats," 305-11.

123. CUNO, JOHN MARSHALL: "Irish TV Items," *CSM*, 10 Mar 1965, 4.
A review of a CBS program that featured a reading and discussion of Yeats's love poems and a commentary by David Greene.

124. CVEK, VOJTĚCH: "Buditel ostrova světců" [The reviver of the island of saints], *Katolické noviny*, 29 June 1975, 5.

125. CZERNIAWSKI, ADAM: Note on Yeats in Polish, accompanying a translation of "Easter 1916," *Kultura*, 10 (Oct 1965), 65.

126. DAICHES, DAVID (ed): *The Penguin Companion to Literature: Britain and the Commonwealth*. London: Lane / Penguin Press, 1971. 576 pp.
G. S. F[raser] and J[ohn] K[elly]: "Yeats," 568-69.

127. DALY, JAMES JEREMIAH: *A Cheerful Ascetic and Other Essays*. Freeport, N.Y.: Books for Libraries Press, 1968 [1931]. vii, 147 pp.
"The Paganism of Mr. Yeats," 87-102; reprinted from *CathW*, 115: 689 (Aug 1922), 595-605. Deplores Yeats's pagan ways, but is rather uninformed.

128. D'ANNA, EDUARDO: "W. B. Yeats," *Lagrimal trifurca*, 1 (Apr-June 1968), 23-24.
Short introductory note followed by translations of six poems.

129. DAVIS, ROBERT HOBART: *Man Makes His Own Mask: Text and Portraits*. Foreword by Benjamin de Casseres. NY: Huntington Press, 1932. viii, 239 pp.
Note on Yeats and his portrait photograph, pp. 234-35. Says that "W. B. Yeats and W. Bird, whose drawings appear at interval in *Punch*, are one and the same person," but this is not correct. W. Bird was a pseudonym of Jack B. Yeats.

130. DEAN-SMITH, MARGARET: "Celtic Twilight," *N&Q*, os 207 / ns 9:1 (Jan 1962), 30.
Attempts a lexical definition.

131. DEANE, SEAMUS: *Irish Writers 1886-1986*. Dublin: Eason, 1986. [24 pp.] (Irish Heritage Series. 57.)

132. DE BLACAM, AODH: *A First Book of Irish Literature: Hiberno-Latin, Gaelic, Anglo-Irish. From the Earliest Times to the Present Day*. Dublin: Talbot Press, [1934]. xii, 236 pp.
"Renascent Ireland," 211-28; a survey and short author sketches from a conservative, Catholic, and nationalistic point of view. See his opinion of Yeats: "His idiosyncratic temperament has withdrawn him from the great central themes on which high literature must rest."

133. DELANEY, MARY MURRAY: *Of Irish Ways*. Minneapolis: Dillon Press, 1973. xii, 356 pp.
"Language and Literature," 231-47.

134. DE MAURO, LISA: "The Rugged, Quicksilver Beauty of Yeats's Sligo," *NYT*, 4 Oct 1981, section 10, XX1, 15.

135. DE SANTANA, HUBERT: "Publishing Feat in Toronto Lures Yeats' Ghost Back," *Toronto Star*, 3 Jan 1976, H 5.
On the University of Toronto Yeats Studies series project (see CA172).

136. DESMOND, SHAW: "Dunsany, Yeats, and Shaw: Trinity of Magic," *BmNY,* 58:3 (Nov 1923), 260-66.

137. DEVANE, JAMES: "Is an Irish Culture Possible?" *Ireland To-day,* 1:5 (Oct 1936), 21-31.
Includes some notes on Yeats's place in Irish culture.

138. DICKINSON, PATRIC: *The Good Minute: An Autobiographical Study.* London: Gollancz, 1965. 239 pp.
Quotations from Yeats's poems, passim, serve as a kind of moral life support.

139. DÍEZ-CANEDO, ENRIQUE: *Conversaciones literarias. Segunda serie: 1920-1924.* México: Mortiz, 1964. 267 pp.
"Yeats, Premio Nobel," 222-24; reprinted from *España,* 8 Dec 1923, 4.

140. *Dizionario Motta della letteratura contemporanea.* Milano: Motta, 1982. 4 vols.
L. A.: "Yeats," 4:1814-15; a summary of Eliot's article (DB72).

141. *Dizionario universale della letteratura contemporanea.* Milano: Mondadori, 1959-63. 5 vols.
"Celtic Revival," 1:750-51; Yeats, 4:1205-9.

142. DODD, LORING HOLMES: *Celebrities at Our Hearthside.* Boston: Dresser, Chapman & Grimes, 1959. ix, 402 pp.
"An Irish Laureate: William Butler Yeats," 368-72.

143. DOUGLAS, ALFRED, LORD: Text of the telegram sent to Yeats on the publication of the *Oxford Book of Modern Verse, Daily Express,* 30 Nov 1936, 6.
"Your omission of my work from the absurdly-named Oxford Book of Modern Verse is exactly typical of the attitude of the minor to the major poet. For example Thomas Moore, the Yeats of the 19th century, would undoubtedly have excluded Keats and Shelley from any anthology he had compiled. And why drag in Oxford? Would not shoneen Irish be a more correct description?"
See note by William Hickey, 2 Dec 1936, 6, quoting Sir Arthur Quiller-Couch in support of Douglas.

144. ———: *Without Apology.* London: Secker, 1938. 316 pp.
For Lord Alfred's Yeats complex see pp. 21-24 ("a minor Irish poet"), 46 (a "very minor poet"), 117, and 136.

145. DOWDEN, EDWARD: *Letters of Edward Dowden and His Correspondents.* London: Dent / NY: Dutton, 1914. xvi, 415 pp.
Some references to Yeats (see index), especially pp. 350-51 in a letter written in 1907, in which Dowden indicates that it would be better for Yeats to stay out of the movement.

146. [DOWNES, ROBERT PERCEVAL]: "Mr. W. B. Yeats," *Great Thoughts,* series 4 / vol. 36 / part 5 (Mar 1902), 356-58.
To Yeats, "romance is reality." Fortunately he does not belong to that large part of the human world that is ruled by the "almighty dollar."

147. DOWNES, ROBERT P.: "William Butler Yeats," *Great Thoughts,* series 7 / 8:1140 (30 Jan 1915), 214-16. (With an unknown photograph)

148. DUNCAN, RONALD: "Yeats," *Townsman,* 2:7 (Aug 1939), 19-21.

149. DUNN, JOSEPH, and PATRICK JOSEPH LENNOX (eds): *The Glories of Ireland.* Washington, D.C.: Phoenix, 1914. ix, 357 pp.
Joseph Holloway: "The Irish Theatre," 304-9; Horatio S. Krans: "The Irish Literary Revival," 317-25.

150. DUNSANY, LORD [EDWARD JOHN MORETON DRAX PLUNKETT]: "Four Poets: AE, Kipling, Yeats, Stephens," *Atlantic Monthly,* 201:4 (Apr 1958), 77-78, 80.

151. ECKHOFF, LORENTZ: *The Aesthetic Movement in English Literature.* Oslo: University Press, 1959. 34 pp.
Based on "Den estetiske bevegelse," *Edda,* year 34 / 47:2 (1947), 81-97. Yeats, passim.

152. *Écrivains anglais et irlandais.* Recueil 1. Paris: Casterman, 1973. 264 pp. (Littérature de notre temps.)
Patrick Rafroidi: "William Butler Yeats," 241-43.

153. EKA: "Yeats magányos mühelye" [The lonely workshop of Yeats], *Másvilág: Bölcsészindex,* 1986, 55-57.
A short introduction to Yeats's work, following a Hungarian translation of *Purgatory.*

154. ELLMANN, RICHARD: "The Uses of Adversity," *American P.E.N.,* 4:1 (Winter 1972), 15-17.
Comparative affluence in later life may have influenced the quality of Yeats's works.

155. EMBLER, WELLER: "Rage against Iniquity," *Arts in Society,* 6:1 (Spring/Summer 1969), 80-93.
On the nineties, with some references to Yeats.

156. EMERSON, DOROTHY: "William Butler Yeats," *Scholastic,* 28:6 (7 Mar 1936), 12.

157. EMT.: "100-året for Yeats: Irland fejrer sin nationaldigter den 13. juni," *Jyllands posten,* 4 June 1965, 19.

158. *Enciclopedia cattolica.* Città del Vaticano: Enciclopedia cattolica, 1949-54. 12 vols.
Augusto Guidi: Yeats, 12:1732-33.

159. *Enciclopedia europea.* Milano: Garzanti, 1977-81. 12 vols.
Giovanni Giudici: Yeats, 11:1107-8.

160. *Enciclopedia filosofica.* 2nd edition. Firenze: Sansoni, 1967. 6 vols.
A[lbino] Babolin: Yeats, 6:1180-81.

161. *Enciclopedia italiana di scienze, lettere ed arti.* Roma: Istituto della Enciclopedia italiana (Treccani), 1929-39. 36 vols.
M[ario] P[raz]: "W. B. Yeats," 35:833.

162. *Encyclopaedia of Ireland.* Dublin: Figgis / NY: McGraw-Hill, 1968. 463 pp.
Eavan Boland: "The Literary Revival," 354-58; Brendan Kennelly: "Modern Writing," 358-61; Anon.: "Theatre," 372-79.

163. *Encyclopaedia universalis.* Paris: Encyclopaedia universalis France, 1968. 21 vols.
D. F[ernandez]: Yeats, 16:1021-23.

164. *Encyclopedia Americana.* International edition. NY: Americana Corporation, 1968. 30 vols.
Peter Kavanagh: Irish Literary Revival, 15:341-47; Richard Ellmann: Yeats, 29:659-60.

165. ENGLE, PAUL: "The Ireland of Yeats," *Saturday Evening Post,* 243:3 (Winter 1971), 91-93.
Saturday Eveningish.

166. ERVINE, ST. JOHN GREER: "The Loneliest Poet: W. B. Yeats," *John o' London's Weekly,* 5 July 1919, 375.

167. *Essays in Memory of Barrett Wendell by His Assistants.* Cambridge, Mass.: Harvard UP, 1926. ix, 320 pp.
Norreys Jephson O'Conor: "A Note on Yeats," 285-89. Yeats is a personal, not so much an Irish, poet.

168. EVANS, OLIVE: "Topics: Centennial of a Poet," *NYT,* 12 June 1965, 30.

169. FARRELL, JAMES THOMAS: *On Irish Themes.* Edited with an introduction by Dennis Flynn; foreword by William V. Shannon. Philadelphia: U of Pennsylvania Press, 1982. xiii, 201 pp.
"Observations on the First Period of the Irish Renaissance," 40-44; reprint of "The Irish Cultural Rennaissance [sic] in the Last Century," *IrW,* 25 (Dec 1953), 50-53. See index for other references to Yeats. The article is also contained in Farrell's *Literary Essays 1954-1974.* Collected and edited by Jack Alan Robbins. Port Washington, N.Y.: Kennikat Press, 1976. ix, 147 pp. (pp. 58-62, misdated).

170. FARREN, ROBERT: "Yeats: An Anniversary Tribute, 1941," *Irish Library Bulletin,* 9:[10] (Oct 1948), 161-63.

171. FAY, WILLIAM P.: "A Yeats Centenary," *TriQ,* 4 [Fall 1965], 68-70.
Yeats was "a great Irishman," says the Irish ambassador to the United States.

172. FEHR, BERNHARD: *Die englische Literatur des 19. und 20. Jahrhunderts: Mit einer Einführung in die englische Frühromantik.* Berlin-Neubabelsberg: Akademische Verlagsgesellschaft Athenaion, 1923. iv, 524 pp. (Handbuch der Literaturwissenschaft. [1].)
"Die keltische Renaissance," 452-61 (on Yeats, 454-57). "Das Drama der keltischen Renaissance," 497-506 (on Yeats, 500-503).

173. ———: "William Butler Yeats, der Träger des Nobelpreises," *NZZ,* 21 Nov 1923, 1-2.

174. FISHER, LOIS H.: *A Literary Gazetteer of England.* NY: McGraw-Hill, 1980. xi, 740 pp.
See index for references to Yeats.

175. FLANAGAN, THOMAS: *The Irish Novelists, 1800-1850.* NY: Columbia UP, 1959. xiii, 362 pp.
See index for some scattered references to Yeats.

176. FORD, MARY K.: "Is the Celtic Revival Really Irish?" *NAR*, 183: 601 (19 Oct 1906), 771-75.
No, it is not--at least not in the works of Yeats, which are altogether inferior to those of Ethna Carberry and Moira O'Neill.

177. FOWLER, ALASTAIR: *A History of English Literature: Forms and Kinds from the Middle Ages to the Present*. Oxford: Blackwell, 1987. x, 395 pp.
"Modernist Poetry and Drama," 343-62, contains notes on Yeats.

178. FOX, R. M.: "Yeats and His Circle," *Aryan Path*, 20:7 (July 1949), 306-9.

179. ———: "W. B. Yeats and the Abbey Theatre," *IrP*, 19 June 1965, 8.

180. FRÉCHET, RENÉ: "Le centenaire de Yeats," *EA*, 18:3 (July-Sept 1965), 225-27.

181. FREUDENTHAL, M[ARIE]: "Von irischer Art und Kunst," *Bühne und Welt*, year 11 / 21:6 (Dec 1908), 245-49.
On Yeats, pp. 245-47; includes two photographs of a performance of *The Hour-Glass*.

182. FRIEDRICH, W. G.: "The Popularity of Yeats," *Cresset*, 28:8 (June 1965), 14-15.
"The main reason for Yeats' popularity is no doubt the fact that many of his best poems deal, not with esoteric matters, but with such universal things as love, friendship, youth, old age, and death."

183. FRIIS-MØLLER, KAI (ed): *Irland*. København: Branner, 1918. vii, 183 pp.
K. Friis-Møller: "Irlands harpe," 161-73; contains some notes on Yeats.

184. FRYE, NORTHROP: *Anatomy of Criticism: Four Essays*. Princeton: Princeton UP, 1957. x, 383 pp.
Scattered notes on Yeats, passim (see index).

185. FULFORD, ROBERT: "The Scholar and Promoter of Celtic Culture in Canada," *Saturday Night*, 90:3557 (July/Aug 1975), 9.
What Robert O'Driscoll has done for Yeats studies.

186. FULLER, ROY: *Professors and Gods: Last Oxford Lectures on Poetry*. London: Deutsch, 1973. 176 pp.
A few remarks on Yeats.

187. FURUMOTO, TAKETOSH: "W. B. Yeats's Missing Review," *TLS*, 4 Jan 1974, 12.
The elusive periodical *The Gael* (Dublin, 1887-88), of which no copy is said to have survived. For a more complete account see CB242.

188. GANT, ROLAND: "Lights in the Darkness: No. 5: W. B. Yeats," *Opus*, 13 (New Year 1943), 25-28.

189. GARDINER, BRUCE: "Decadence: Its Construction and Contexts," *SoRA*, 18:1 (March 1985) 22-43.
Contains some notes on Yeats.

190. GARDNER, JOANN: "A Footnote on the *Weekly Review*," *ELT*, 26:3 (1983), 198-99.
Allan Wade's note on this periodical (in *Letters*, p. 159) is wrong; it was not a theosophical publication.

191. GARGÀRO, F.: "Da William Butler Yeats," *Rassegna italiana*, 176 (Jan 1933), 1-2.

192. GARNIER, CHARLES-MARIE: "W. B. Yeats: Fleurs de regrets et couronne de souvenirs," *Yggdrasill*, year 4 / 3:35 (25 Mar 1939), 190-91.

193. GHAURI, H. R.: "Yeats, Pound, Eliot, Joyce: Lawrence's Secret Sharers," *Ariel* [University of Sind], 7 (1981-82), 54-74.
There is very little on Yeats in this article, and his share in Lawrence's work (or vice versa) is not made clear.

194. GHOSE, SISIRKUMAR: *Modern and Otherwise*. Delhi: P.K., [1974]. x, 321 pp.
"Mainly a Matter of Masks," 83-99.

195. GIBBON, MONK: "Personality: Determined or Determinable?" *Hibernia*, 27 Apr 1973, 17.
Yeats's personality as seen through his correspondence with Katharine Tynan.

196. GIBBONS, TOM: *Rooms in the Darwin Hotel: Studies in English Literary Criticism and Ideas, 1880-1920*. Nedlands: U of Western Australia Press, 1973. xi, 164 pp.
Mainly on Havelock Ellis, Symons, and Orage; Yeats is mentioned passim (see index).

197. GILL, RICHARD: "Invitation to Garsington," *VQR*, 50:2 (Spring 1974), 198-214.
Lady Ottoline Morrell's residence; contains a few notes on Yeats.

198. [GOLDRING, DOUGLAS]: *Dublin: Explorations and Reflections by an Englishman*. Dublin: Maunsel, 1917. vii, 271 pp.
For a few remarks on Yeats see "The Intellectuals," 165-91, "Literature in Dublin," 192-239, and "The Theatre in Dublin," 240-57.

199. GORDON, DAVID: "The Twilight of the Celtic Twilight," *America*, 24 July 1937, 379-80.
Lest it be forgot: "The true Gael is and must be a Catholic Christian." Yeats, however, poor man, has "drunk deep at the poisonous wells of Madame Blavatsky." He "bastardized" the Gaelic language.

200. GRABOWSKI, ZBIGNIEW: "Życie umysłowe zagranicą: Ostatnie nagrody literackie," *Przeglad współczesny*, 3 (1924), 132-34.
"Cultural life abroad: Recent literary prizes."

201. GRAHAM, RIGBY: "Thoor Ballylee: The Castle Home of W. B. Yeats," *American Book Collector*, 21:4 (1971), 11-13.
See also "Letter from Dublin," *AN&Q*, 10:7 (Mar 1972), 107-8.

202. °GRAHAM, ROBIN: "How to Get a Rise Out of Yeats," *Opus* [U of Rhodesia, Salisbury], 2nd series, 1 (1977), 5-7.

203. *Grande dizionario enciclopedico Utet.* 3rd edition. Torino: Unione tipografico-editrice torinese, 1966-75. 20 vols.
V[ittoria] Rad[icati]: Yeats, 19:769-70.

204. GREENBERG, MARTIN: *The Hamlet Vocation of Coleridge and Wordsworth.* Iowa City: U of Iowa Press, 1986. xiv, 209 pp.
The Coleridge chapter contains a note on Yeats's "Hamletism," pp. 87-89.

205. GRIGSON, GEOFFREY, and CHARLES HARVARD GIBBS-SMITH (eds): *People: A Volume of the Good, Bad, Great & Eccentric Who Illustrate the Admirable Diversity of Man.* NY: Hawthorn, 1956. x, 470 pp.
"Custom and Ceremony," 466-67.

206. GRZEBIENIOWSKI, TADEUSZ: "Irlandja współczesna: Stan literatury" [Contemporary Ireland: The literary situation], *Droga,* 1935, 250-68.
On Yeats, passim.

207. HADEN-GUEST, ANTHONY: "Yeats Country," *Daily Telegraph,* 26 Feb 1965, Weekend Telegraph, 18-23. (Illustrated)

208. HALL, DONALD: *The Weather for Poetry: Essays, Reviews, and Notes on Poetry, 1977-81.* Ann Arbor: U of Michigan Press, 1982. xvi, 335 pp.
"To Imitate Yeats," 306-8; reprinted from *Kentucky R,* 1:1 (Autumn 1979), 61-62. Yeats is a "model for artistic morality."

209. HALLERT, BIRGITTA, STIG GUNNAR SKOOT, and GÖRAN STRÖM: *Nobelpriset i litteratur 1901-1982.* Stockholm: Marieberg, 1983. 350 pp.
See pp. 110-13.

210. HARLEY, E. S.: "A Note on a Yeats Quotation," *BDE,* 5:16&17 (1963), 1.
Attempts to track down the source of "Think like a wise man but express yourself like the common people," reputedly said by Yeats to Lady Gregory.

211. HARVEY, SIR PAUL: *The Oxford Companion to English Literature.* 4th edition revised by Dorothy Eagle. Oxford: Clarendon Press, 1967 [1932]. x, 961 pp.
Yeats, pp. 903-4. For a new edition see Margaret Drabble (ed): *The Oxford Companion to English Literature.* 5th edition. Oxford: Oxford UP, 1985. xii, 1155 pp. (pp. 1093-94.)

212. HASSALL, CHRISTOPHER: *Edward Marsh: Patron of the Arts. A Biography.* London: Longmans, 1959. xvi, 732 pp.
Scattered references to Yeats, passim (see index), particularly pp. 95-96 on the genesis of *The Shadowy Waters,* and 383-84 on the first performance of *At the Hawk's Well.*

213. HAWKINS, HUNT: "W. B. Yeats: A Profile," *Florida State U Bulletin: Research in Review,* 81:2 (Spring 1987), 16.

214. HEALY, THOMAS: "A. E. Talks of Irish Letters," *Commonweal,* 2 Nov 1927, 632-34.
Interview. Yeats, in AE's words, "belongs to what we call 'the literature of dream.'"

215. HEDLUND, TOM: "Var det bara 'dårskap'?" [Was this only folly?], *Svenska dagbladet,* 27 July 1976, 8.

216. HEINEY, DONALD W.: *Essentials of Contemporary Literature.* Great Neck, N.Y.: Barron's Educational Series, 1954. xviii, 555 pp.
See pp. 310-13.

217. ———, and LENTHIEL HOWELL DOWNS: *British.* Woodbury, N.Y.: Barron's Educational Series, 1974. x, 286 pp. (Essentials of Contemporary Literature of the Western World. 2.)
See pp. 124-29.

217a. HEINRICH-JOST, INGRID: "Liebessklave der Elfen," *FAZ,* 29 Apr 1988, Magazin, 66-72, 74-75.
"Love slave of the fairies"; subtitled "A poet enchants the world: WBY considered himself to be the true heir of the Irish magicians, as intimate with spirits as with his neighbors."

218. HEISELER, BERNT VON: "Erzählungen und Lyrik," *Deutsche Zeitschrift,* 47:9 (June 1934), 579-80.

219. HENDERSON, PHILIP: *Literature and a Changing Civilisation.* London: Lane, 1935. xi, 180 pp. (XXth Century Library. 15.)
Yeats, pp. 95-98.

220. HENN, T. R.: *Address on the Occasion of the Gift of Duras House, Kinvara, to An Óige, Irish Youth Hostel Association, to Be Dedicated to the Memory of W. B. Yeats, Lady Gregory, Edward Martyn, and Florimond, Count de Basterot.* Kinvara, 20 August 1961. Dublin: Irish Times, 1961. 4 pp.
See also Wulstan Phillipson: "An Irish Occasion," *Month,* 26:6 (Dec 1961), 356-62.

221. HERHOLTZ, FRITZ: "Die neuirische Literaturbewegung. (The Irish Literary Revival)," *Xenien,* 7:[7] (July 1914), 412-16.

222. HERLITSCHKA, HERBERT E.: Note on Yeats in German, *Merkur,* 9:12 (Dec 1955), 1134.

223. HERTS, BENJAMIN RUSSELL: *Depreciations.* NY: Boni, 1914. 171 pp.
"The Shadowy Mr. Yeats," 33-39; reprinted from *Forum,* 52:6 (Dec 1914), 911-14. His works are "comatose" and produce "yawns."

224. H[EWITT], J. H.: "William Butler Yeats, 1865-1939," *Belfast Municipal Museum and Art Gallery Quarterly Notes,* 60 (Mar 1939), 6-7.
On the H. M. Paget painting of April 1889.

225. HEY: "Slavný Irčan" [A famous Irishman], *Lidová demokracie,* 13 June 1975, 5.

226. HICKEY, D. J., and J. E. DOHERTY: *A Dictionary of Irish History since 1800.* Dublin: Gill & Macmillan, 1980. viii, 615 pp.
See pp. 612-14.

227. HICKS, GRANVILLE: *Figures of Transition: A Study of British Literature at the End of the Nineteenth Century.* NY: Macmillan, 1939. xvii, 326 pp.
Yeats, passim (see index).

228. HIGGINS, AIDAN: "The Heroe's Portion: Chaos or Anarchy in the

Cultic Twoilet," *R of Contemporary Fiction,* 3:1 (Spring 1983), 108-14.
Contains a few remarks on Yeats.

229. HISGEN, RUUD, and ADRIAAN VAN DER WEEL (eds): *Ierse stemmen: Bloemlezing van moderne schrijvers uit het West-Eiland.* 's Gravenhage: Nijgh & Van Ditmar, 1981. 208 pp. (Nijgh & Van Ditmar's paperbacks. 311.)
An anthology of modern Irish literature; contains a few references to, but no texts by, Yeats (see index).

230. HODGART, M. J. C.: "Misquotation as Re-Creation," *EIC,* 3:1 (Jan 1953), 28-38.
On Yeats's misquotation of Burns's "Open the Door to Me, O" in *Ideas of Good and Evil,* pp. 36-37.

231. HOLM, INGVAR: *Fran Baudelaire till första världskriget.* Stockholm: Bonnier, 1964. 267 pp. (Bonniers allmänna litteratur-historia. 6.)
"Irländskt," 126-36; on Yeats, pp. 131-36.

232. HONE, J. M.: "W. B. Yeats: A Character Sketch," *Everyman,* 27 June 1913, 328-29.

233. HUET, G. H. M. VAN: "Grootste moderne engels schrijvende dichter: William Butler Yeats," *Haagse post,* 9 June 1956, 16.
"Greatest modern poet of the English language."

234. HÜTTEMANN, HERTA [i.e., GERTA]: "William Butler Yeats," *Germania,* 1 June 1928, supplement "Das neue Ufer," 1-2.

235. HURLEY, MICHAEL (ed): *Irish Anglicanism, 1869-1969.* Essays on the role of Anglicanism in Irish life presented to the Church of Ireland on the occasion of the centenary of its disestablishment by a group of Methodist, Presbyterian, Quaker, and Roman Catholic scholars. Dublin: Figgis, 1970. xi, 236 pp.
Thomas P. O'Neill: "Political Life: 1870-1921," 101-9; contains a note on Yeats, pp. 107-8. Augustine Martin: "Anglo-Irish Literature," 120-32; on Yeats, passim.

236. HYMAN, STANLEY EDGAR: *The Armed Vision: A Study in the Methods of Modern Literary Criticism.* NY: Knopf, 1948. xv, 417, xxii pp.
Notes on what some of the modern critics thought of Yeats, passim (see index).

237. I.: "Mr. W. B. Yeats," *To-Day,* 27 Apr 1904, 366.
A sketch "from the life" by A. S. Forrest appears on p. 367.

238. INNES, C. L.: "Through the Looking Glass: African and Irish Nationalist Writing," *African Literature Today,* 9 (1978), 10-24.
Contains a few notes on Yeats.

239. *The Ireland of Today.* Reprinted with some additions from the London *Times.* Boston: Small, Maynard, 1915. xiii, 419 pp.
Based in part on the Irish number of the *Times,* 17 Mar 1915. See pp. 121-37, passim.

240. *Irlanda.* Con cartina geografica e molte illustrazioni in tavole fuori testo. Roma: Edizioni Roma, 1940. 160 pp.
Serafino Riva: "Profilo della letteratura irlandese," 33-53; Renato Simoni: "Carattere del teatro irlandese," 55-69.

241. *L'Irlande*. Paris: Larousse, 1981. 160 pp. (Mondes et voyages.)
Catherine Salles: "La littérature," 150-57.

242. *Irlandskie teatral'nye miniatîury*. Leningrad: Iskusstvo, 1961. 96 pp.
"Uil'îam Batler Eĭts," 5-10; translation of *The Pot of Broth* by N. Rakhmanova, 11-20.

243. IZZO, CARLO: *Storia della letteratura inglese*. Milano: Nuova Accademia, 1961-63. 2 vols.
Yeats, 2:658-62 and passim (see index).

244. JACKSON, ROBERT WYSE: *A Memorial Service Preached at Drumcliffe on the Occasion of the Centenary of the Birth of William Butler Yeats*. Dublin: Dolmen Press / Sligo: Keohane, [1965]. 4 pp.

245. JAECKLE, ERWIN: *Zirkelschlag der Lyrik*. Zürich: Fretz & Wasmuth, 1967. 302 pp.
"Flucht nach Byzanz: William Butler Yeats," 116-19. A one-sided sketch of Yeats's metaphysical leanings, written in a sometimes incomprehensible style.

246. JARNES, BENJAMIN (ed): *Enciclopedia de la literatura*. México: Editora central, [1946?]. 6 vols.
Yeats, 6:387-89.

247. JOHNSON, COLTON: "Some Unnoticed Contributions to Periodicals by W. B. Yeats," *N&Q*, os 217 / ns 19:2 (Feb 1972), 48-52.
These are now in *Uncollected Prose*, vol. 2.

248. JOHNSON, LOUIS: "Yeats Regained," *Numbers*, 1:4 (Oct 1955), 38-40.

249. JOHNSTON, CHARLES, and CARITA SPENCER: *Ireland's Story*. New edition with an additional chapter 1904-1922. Boston: Houghton Mifflin, 1923 [1905]. xv, 422 pp.
"The Irish Literary Revival," 370-79.

250. JONES, E. W.: Note on Yeats, *SR*, 34:4 (Oct-Dec 1926), 492-94.

251. [JORDAN, JOHN]: "Editorial," *Poetry Ireland R*, 8 [1983], 5-6.

252. KAIN, RICHARD M.: "The Yeats Centenary in Ireland," *JJQ*, 3:2 (Winter 1966), 130-38.

253. KARRER, WOLFGANG, and EBERHARD KREUTZER: *Daten der englischen und amerikanischen Literatur von 1890 bis zur Gegenwart*. Köln: Kiepenheuer & Witsch, 1973. 301 pp.
Yeats, passim (see index).

254. KATONA, ANNA: *A huszadik századi angol irodalom főirányai / Main Trends of Twentieth Century English Literature*. Budapest: Tankönyvkiadó, 1975. 84 pp.
"The Irish Renaissance," 25-31.

255. KEARNEY, TOM: "Yeats Country: Little Changes," *WashP*, 22 Aug 1971, K7.

256. KELLEHER, DANIEL LAWRENCE: *Ireland of the Welcomes*. 4th edition revised. Dublin: Irish Tourist Association, 1948. 119 pp.

"W. B. Yeats at Lough Gill," 104-5.

257. KELLY, BLANCHE MARY: *The Voice of the Irish*. NY: Sheed & Ward, 1952. xi, 340 pp.
A compact literary history of Ireland, written from a conservative Catholic point of view. On Yeats, passim (see index). Contains numerous factual errors and ill-advised judgments.

258. KEMP, PETER: "High and Low Talk," *TLS*, 1 July 1983, 699.
Review of a TV program, "Makers: Joyce, Yeats, and Wilde," B.B.C., Channel 4, with Richard Ellmann and Seamus Heaney.

259. KERMODE, FRANK: "A Memory for Poetry," *Daily Telegraph*, 26 Jan 1974, 9.
Kermode's reminiscences of his past preoccupation with Yeats.

260. KIELY, BENEDICT: *Modern Irish Fiction: A Critique*. Dublin: Golden Eagle Books, 1950. xv, 179 pp.
Contains some general remarks on Yeats (see index), but nothing on his prose fiction.

261. ——— (ed): *Dublin*. Oxford: Oxford UP, 1983. vii, 112 pp.
An anthology with several references to Yeats (see index).

262. KINSELLA, THOMAS: "A Yeats Festival on the Shores of Lake Michigan," *Hibernia*, 29:6 (June 1965), 9.
At Northwestern University; see also CA119.

263. ———: "W. B. Yeats: The Last Romantic," *Daily Egyptian*, 12 Feb 1966, 2.

264. KIRSCH, HANS-CHRISTIAN: *Einladung nach Irland*. München: Langen-Müller, 1971. 240 pp. (Einladung nach. . . . 13.)
Thoor Ballylee and Yeats country, Co. Sligo, pp. 100-102, 130-34.

265. K[OHL], N[IELS] V[ON]: "Irerens kaerlighed til det skjulte liv" [The Irishman's love of the hidden life], *Kristeligt dagblad*, 5 Aug 1965, 7.

266. KOSOK, HEINZ, and HORST PRIESSNITZ (eds): *Literaturen in englischer Sprache: Ein Überblick über englischsprachige Nationalliteraturen ausserhalb Englands*. Bonn: Bouvier, 1977. vi, 261 pp. (Gesamthochschule Wuppertal: Schriftenreihe Literaturwissenschaft. 5.)
H. Kosok: "Irische Literatur in englischer Sprache unter britischer Herrschaft," 5-20; contains a few notes on Yeats.

266a. KP: "Irský národní básník," *Lidová demokracie*, 13 June 1985, 5.
Note on the 120th anniversary of Yeats's death.

267. KREUZER, HELMUT (ed): *Jahrhundertende--Jahrhundertwende (I. Teil)*. Wiesbaden: Athenaion, 1976. viii, 475 pp. (Neues Handbuch der Literaturwissenschaft. 18.)
See index for some notes on Yeats.

268. KROJER, MAXIM: "Twintig jaar geleden overleed: William Butler Yeats," *Periscoop*, 9:4 (Feb 1959), 11.
"Died 20 years ago: WBY." A short assessment, mainly of the plays.

269. K[UBIAK], Z[YGMUNT]: Note on Yeats in Polish, *Tygodnik powszechny*, 22 May 1966, 4.

270. LAFFONT, [ROBERT], and [VALENTINO] BOMPIANI: *Dictionnaire des oeuvres de tous les temps et de tous les pays: Littérature, philosophie, musique, sciences*. Paris: S.E.D.E., 1968 [1953]. 5 vols.
Contains synopses of *Cathleen ni Houlihan* (1:337), *The Countess Cathleen* (1:488), *Deirdre* (1:627), *The Land of Heart's Desire* (3:698), *Poems*, 1895 (4:33), *The Tower* (4:579), and *The Wind among the Reeds* (4:667) as Yeats's most memorable works.

271. ——— (eds): *Dictionnaire biographique des auteurs*. Paris: S.E.D.E., 1964 [1957]. 2 vols.
Bernard Noël: "W. B. Yeats," 2:722-23.

272. LANDER, JEANNETTE: "Möglichkeiten und Unmöglichkeiten einer deutschen William Butler Yeats-Ausgabe," *Diagonale*, 2:5 (1967), 45-50.
"Possibilities and impossibilities of a German Yeats edition"; a short note on the problems of translating Yeats into German with three translations of "Sailing to Byzantium."

272a. LANE, DENIS, and CAROL MCCRORY LANE (eds): *Modern Irish Literature: A Library of Literary Criticism*. NY: Ungar, 1988. xv, 736 pp.
"Yeats, William Butler (1865-1939)," 665-84; 22 extracts from previously published criticism.

273. LAROUSSE: *Grand Larousse encyclopédique en dix volumes*. Paris: Larousse, 1960-64. 10 vols.
Yeats, 10:980.

274. LAUTERBACH, EDWARD S., and W. EUGENE DAVIS: *The Transitional Age in British Literature, 1880-1920*. Troy, N.Y.: Whitston, 1973. xiii, 323 pp.
A short survey of the period and selected checklists. On Yeats, passim (see index); checklist, pp. 307-11 (insufficient).

275. LAW, HUGH ALEXANDER: *Anglo-Irish Literature*. With a foreword by A. E. [i.e., George William Russell]. London: Longmans Green, 1926. xviii, 302 pp.
Reprinted Folcroft, Pa.: Folcroft Library Editions, 1974. A defense of Anglo-Irish literature as distinct from English and Irish literature; contains only a few references to Yeats.

275a. LEE, BRIAN: *Poetry and the System*. Retford: Brynmill Press, 1983. 39 pp.
Contains some notes on Yeats who insisted on "the wholeness of the language as a condition of fulness of life."

276. LEGOUIS, EMILE, LOUIS CAZAMIAN, and RAYMOND LAS VERGNAS: *A History of English Literature*. Revised edition. London: Dent, 1971 [1926]. xxiii, 1488 pp.
"The Celtic Revival," 1281-91; on Yeats, passim.

277. LEHMANN, WILHELM: "Im keltischen Zwielicht. Von William Butler Yeats," *Berliner Tageblatt*, 28 July 1913, supplement "Der Zeitgeist," [2].
A short introduction to a translation of extracts from *The Celtic Twilight*.

278. LETTS, WINIFRED M.: "W. B. Yeats in Sligo," *Great Thoughts*, series 11 / 8:2659 (Nov 1934), 75-76.

279. LEVENSON, MICHAEL H.: *A Genealogy of Modernism: A Study of English Literary Doctrine 1908-1922*. Cambridge: Cambridge UP, 1984. xiii, 250 pp.
See index for a few remarks on Yeats.

280. LEVIN, HARRY: *Contexts of Criticism*. Cambridge, Mass.: Harvard UP, 1957. xiii, 294 pp. (Harvard Studies in Comparative Literature. 22.)
Scattered notes on Yeats, passim (see index).

281. LIDDY, JAMES, and ANTHONY CRONIN: "Two Offerings for W. B. Yeats," *Arena*, 4 (Spring 1965), 42-43.
Reprinted in *This Was Arena*. Introduced by James Liddy. Naas, Co. Kildare: Malton Press, 1982. 115 pp. (pp. 112-13).

282. LIDDY, JAMES: "A Note on Yeats," *UR*, 3:8 [1966?], 71.
Yeats's hallmark is his "arrogant will to stay an individual."

283. hbl [i.e., LIISBERG, HENRIK BERING]: "W. B. Yeats," *Information*, 12 June 1965, 4.

284. L[ITTELL], P[HILIP]: "Books and Things," *NewRep*, 18 Feb 1920, 358.
Why one should like to meet Yeats in person.

285. LOWRY, HELEN BULLITT: "Another 'Contemptible Little Army': Minor Poets. Imaginative Account of What Happened When Yeats Told a Meeting of the Clan He Didn't Have Time to Read American Verse," *NYT*, 15 Feb 1920, IV, 7.

286. LUCEY, CHARLES: *Ireland and the Irish: Cathleen ni Houlihan Is Alive and Well*. Garden City: Doubleday, 1970. viii, 256 pp.
"Where Poets Walk Proudly," 123-40; on Yeats, passim.

287. LYNCH, ARTHUR: *Our Poets!* London: Remington, 1894. viii, 92 pp.
"Contemporary Irish Literature," 56-59; Yeats is considered promising but derivative.

288. LYSAGHT, PADDY: *An Irish Literary Quiz Book*. Dingle, Co. Kerry: Brandon, 1984. 91 pp.
The Yeats quiz is on pp. 9-10 (17 questions); he also figures in some other quizzes. Unfortunately, the book contains some terrible mistakes.

289. M., T.: "The Irish Literary Renascence," *Weekly Sun*, 16 Dec 1894, Literary Supplement, 14.
A new Irish literature is on its way with Yeats as one of its most notable figures, but his work "is richer in promise than in performance."

290. MAC AODHA, BREANDAN S.: "The Big House in Western Ireland: The Background to Yeats's Writing," *Gaéliana*, 6 (1984), 217-23.
A historical description of the great Irish estates, with only scant attention given to Yeats.

291. MCAULEY, JAMES: "A Moment's Memory to That Laurelled Head," *Australian*, 12 June 1965, 9.

292. ———: "Driving through Kiltartan to the Yeats Tower," *Hibernia*, 29:10 (Oct 1965), 17.

293. MCBRIEN, PETER: "Those Irish Pagans!" *Dublin R*, 177:355 (Oct-Nov-Dec 1925), 179-92.
Diatribe against Yeats as a member of the "Liffey School of English Literature [which] was born with chronic anaemia."

294. MACCALLUM, THOMAS WATSON, and STEPHEN TAYLOR (eds): *The Nobel Prize-Winners and the Nobel Foundation, 1901-1937*. With an introduction by Gilbert Murray. Zürich: Central European Times Publishing Co., 1938. xi, 599 pp.
"William Butler Yeats," 298-99.

295. MACCARTAN, HUGH A.: "Some National Poets," *Sinn Féin*, 26 Dec 1908, 3-4.
Yeats is not really one of them.

296. MCCUTCHION, DAVID: "Yeats Centenary Festival at Jadavpur," *JJCL*, 5 (1965), 117-21.

297. MACDONALD, QUENTIN: "William Butler Yeats and the 'Celtic Movement,'" *Book News Monthly*, 22:262 (June 1904), 1024-25.
Yeats belongs to the "Celtic Movement," not to the "Irish Literary Revival," but the difference is not explained.

298. MCGARRY, J. P.: "The Yeats Country," *Ireland of the Welcomes*, 6:2 (July-Aug 1957), 31-33.

299. MCGLYNN, EDNA M.: "The Megaliths of the Yeats Country," *Delta Kappa Gamma Bulletin*, 40:3 (Spring 1974), 21-31.

300. MCGURRIN, JAMES: *Bourke Cockran: A Free Lance in American Politics*. NY: Scribner's, 1948. xvii, 361 pp.
Cockran's support of Yeats is noted on pp. 230-32.

301. MCMAHON, SEAN (comp): *A Book of Irish Quotations*. Dublin: O'Brien Press, 1984. 222 pp.
Yeats, pp. 163-65 (25 quotations). See also the subject index, p. 221, for quotations referring to Yeats.

302. MCPARLAND, EDWARD: "Lissadell, Co. Sligo: The Property of the Gore-Booth Family," *Country Life*, 6 Oct 1977, 914-17. (Illustrated)

303. MCQUILLAN, OLIVER: "W. B. Yeats," *Young Citizen*, Oct 1967, 2.

304. MCQUILLAND, LOUIS J.: "W. B. Yeats, Poseur and Poet," *Vanity Fair*, 4 Sept 1907, 311-12.
"Mr. Yeats is as great a poet as he is a *poseur*, which is saying much." Nevertheless, "he does often transcend the limits of allowable poetic absurdity."

305. MAGILL, FRANK N. (ed): *English Literature: Romanticism to 1945*. Pasadena, Cal.: Salem Softbacks, 1981. xv, 836 pp.
Previously published as *Masterpieces of World Literature in Digest Form* (3rd series, 1960; 4th series, 1969). "William Butler Yeats," 818-32.

306. MAGUIRE, ALASTAIR: "Mr. W. B. Yeats, the True Interpreter of the Irish Mind," *National Student*, 1:5 (July 1911), 149-51.

307. MALORY, THOMAS, THOMAS SACKVILLE, and W. B. YEATS: *Testi*. Roma: De Santis, [1967]. 239 pp. (Università degli studi di Roma. Facoltà di magistero. Anno accademico 1966-67.)
See pp. 175-79 for a short general introduction to Yeats.

308. *Mały słownik pisarzy angielskich i amerykańskich*. Warszawa: Wiedza Powszechna, 1971. 548 pp.
K[rystyna] S[lamirowska]: Yeats, 541-42.

309. MANGANIELLO, DOMINIC: "The Artist as Magician: Yeats, Joyce, and Tolkien," *Mythlore*, 10:2 (Summer 1983), 13-15, 25.

310. MANLEY, SEON, and SUSAN BELCHER: *O, Those Extraordinary Women! Or the Joys of Literary Lib*. Philadelphia: Chilton Book Co., 1972. xii, 331 pp.
"The High Style of Cathleen ni Houlihan," 261-82; on Constance Markievicz, Maud Gonne, and Lady Gregory. Yeats is mentioned passim.

311. MANNING, OLIVIA: *The Dreaming Shore*. London: Evans, 1950. 202 pp.
"Yeats' Country," 149-63; a description of County Sligo.

312. MARSHALL, PERCY: *Masters of English Poetry*. London: Dobson, 1966. 242 pp.
"William Butler Yeats (1865-1939)," 198-213. Rather naive and weak on facts.

313. MARTIN, AUGUSTINE: *Anglo-Irish Literature*. Dublin: Department of Foreign Affairs, 1980. 71 pp. (Aspects of Ireland. 7.)
See pp. 32, 36-37, and passim.

314. MATTHEWS, HAROLD: "Yeats and the Irish Theatre," *Theatre World*, 61:485 (June 1965), 35-36.

315. MAUGHAM, WILLIAM SOMERSET: *W. Somerset Maugham's Introduction to Modern English and American Literature*. NY: New Home Library, 1943. xxi, 618 pp.
Note on Yeats, pp. 600-601; he is described as a pompous and vain but nevertheless great poet.

316. Brother Leo [MEEHAN, FRANCIS JOSEPH GALLAGHER]: *English Literature: A Survey and a Commentary*. Boston: Ginn, 1928. xiii, 738 pp.
"The Irish Literary Revival," 624-40.

317. MENEZES, ARMANDO: *Airy Nothings: Essays in Literary Criticism*. Dharwar: Karnatak U, 1977. x, 278 pp.
"William Butler Yeats (A 25th Death-Anniversary Tribute)," 59-64; "Yeats and Tagore," 137-40 (reprinted in *Goa Today*, 15:2 [Sept 1980], 16-17).

318. MITCHELL, KEITH: "So Hard and Late: W. B. Yeats, 1865-1939," *Tablet*, 12 June 1965, 657-58.
Yeats was a good poet with an unacceptable mysticism and unsympathetic political views.

319. MITGANG, HERBERT: "To Begin With," *NYTBR*, 4 Sept 1983, 23.
Yeats as a "champion modern supplier of epigraphs" for other writers' works.

320. MOLE, JOHN: "Poetry and Rhetoric," *TLS*, 3 Aug 1984, 869.
Letter to the editor, locating the source of the dictum "We make out of the quarrel with others, rhetoric, but of the quarrel with ourselves, poetry" in *Per Amica Silentia Lunae*.

321. MONOD, SYLVÈRE: *Histoire de la littérature anglaise: De Victoria à Elizabeth II*. Paris: Colin, 1970. 392 pp.
"W. B. Yeats," 198-202.

322. M[ONROE], H[ARRIET]: "Mr. Yeats and the Poetic Drama," *Poetry*, 16:1 (Apr 1920), 32-38.
Takes a Yeats address as a starting point for a general discussion of the poetic drama. Not really on Yeats.

323. MOORE, ISABEL: "William Butler Yeats," *BmNY*, 18:4 (Dec 1903), 360-63.

323a. MOORE, JOHN REES: "Irish Story," *SR*, 95:3 (Summer 1987), 494-505.
A review article with some notes on Yeats.

324. MORÁN, FRANCISCO JOSÉ, and MATÍAS DÍEZ ALONSO: *Historia de los Premios Nobel: Literatura*. Léon: Everest, 1971. 334 pp.
"William Butler Yeats," 117-21.

325. MORGAN, GERALD: "Cofio bardd: Canmlwyddiant geni W. B. Yeats" [Remembering the poet: The centenary of Yeats's birth], *Barn*, 33 (July 1965), 250-51.

326. MORISSET, HENRI: "William Butler Yeats," *Esprit*, 7:84 (1 Sept 1939), 776-80.

327. MORTON, J. B., and VIOLET CLIFTON: "William Butler Yeats: Two Appreciations," *Tablet*, 4 Feb 1939, 136-37.
Includes reminiscences.

328. MOULT, THOMAS: "The Bard of Houlihan," *Apple (of Beauty and Discord)*, 1:4 (1920), 220, 222, 224.

329. MROCZKOWSKI, PRZEMYSŁAW: *Historia literatury angielskiej: Zarys*. Wrocław: Zakład narodowy im. Ossolińskich, 1981. 627 pp.
See pp. 538-39, 553-55.

330. MUDDIMAN, BERNARD: *The Men of the Nineties*. London: Danielson, 1920. iv, 146 pp.
Yeats is mentioned passim (see index).

331. MULLIK, B. R.: *Yeats*. Delhi: Chand, 1961. iv, 61 pp. (Studies in Poets for M.A. and B.A. Students of English Literature in Indian Universities. 19.)
Practically worthless.

332. MURPHY, EDWARD FRANCIS (comp): *The Macmillan Treasury of Relevant Quotations*. London: Macmillan, 1979. viii, 658 pp.
Originally °*The Crown Treasury of Relevant Quotations*. NY: Crown, 1978. Contains numerous Yeats quotations (see p. 613).

333. *Die Musik in Geschichte und Gegenwart: Allgemeine Enzyklopädie der Musik*. Kassel: Bärenreiter, 1949-79. 16 vols.
Hans Ferdinand Redlich: Yeats, 14:932-33.

334. NELSON, WALTER W.: *Oscar Wilde in Sweden and Other Essays*. Dublin: Dublin UP, 1965. v, 84 pp.
"Anglo-Irish and Scandinavian Authors Rewarded with the Nobel Prize in Literature," 38-50; contains a few vague remarks on the Yeats reception in Sweden.

335. NEMEROV, HOWARD: *Reflexions on Poetry & Poetics*. New Brunswick: Rutgers UP, 1972. xii, 235 pp.
"William Butler Yeats," 52-55; reprinted from Louis Kronenberger (ed): *Brief Lives: A Biographical Guide to the Arts*. London: Lane / Penguin Press, 1972. xxii, 900 pp. (pp. 894-97).

336. *New Catholic Encyclopedia*. NY: McGraw-Hill, 1967. 15 vols.
Stephen P. Ryan and John Montague: "Irish Poetry," 7:654-57. Cleanth Brooks: "Yeats," 14:1067-68: "His poetry returns to Christianity the dimension of awe."

337. NICHOLSON, NORMAN: *Man & Literature*. London: SCM Press, 1944 [1943]. 218 pp.
"W. B. Yeats," 188-92. "It is a rather curiously Irish type of Natural Man that he presents to us."

338. *Nobel: The Man and His Prizes*. Edited by the Nobel Foundation. Norman: U of Oklahoma Press, 1951. 620 pp.
Note by Anders Österling on the reasons for giving Yeats and not Hardy the prize for literature, pp. 119-20.

339. *Nobel-díjas írók antológiája: Harmincnégy arcképpel* [Thirty-one portraits]. Budapest: Káldor kőnyvkiadóvállalat, 1935. xii, 583 pp.
Dezső Kosztolányi: "William Butler Yeats," 403-5; translations of seven poems, 407-10.

340. *Nobelprisen 50 år: Forskare, diktare, fredskämpar*. Stockholm: Sohlmans, 1950. 512 pp.
Anders Österling: Yeats, pp. 109-10.

341. NOWLAN, KEVIN B., and T. DESMOND WILLIAMS (eds): *Ireland in the War Years and After, 1939-51*. Dublin: Gill and Macmillan, 1969. ix, 216 pp.
Augustine Martin: "Literature and Society, 1938-51," 167-84; mentions Yeats passim.

342. O'BRIEN, FLANN [i.e., Brian O'Nolan]: *The Hair of the Dogma: A Further Selection from "Cruiskeen Lawn."* Edited and with a preface by Kevin O'Nolan. London: Hart-Davis, MacGibbon, 1977. vii, 183 pp.
"W. B. Loud Glade," 151-53. "Some of these fine days I hope to present here the definitive appraisal of Yeats, for, by dad, fact it is that all critical matter already in print concerning him is of quite exceptional obtuseness and scandalous presumption."

343. Ó CEARBHAILL, DIARMUID (ed): *Galway: Town and Gown 1484-1984*. Dublin: Gill & Macmillan, 1984. xxv, 310 pp.
Some references to Yeats in Patrick Diskin: "Galway's Literary Associations," 206-22; and Patrick F. Sheeran: "The Absence of Galway City from the Literature of the Revival," 223-44.

344. O'CONNELL, DANIEL: *The Opposition Critics: The Antisymbolist Reaction in the Modern Period*. The Hague: Mouton, 1974. xi, 172 pp. (De Proprietatibus Litterarum. Series Minor. 14.)
See index for a few notes on Yeats.

345. O'CONNOR, ULICK: "Let's Honour Yeats," *Sunday Independent,* 24 Aug 1958, 8.
"Yeats, who so personifies our people, should have a statue in the middle of Dublin." Correspondence by C. F. N., 31 Aug 1958, 11; by O'Connor: "Pearse Stood Up for Yeats," 21 Sept 1958, 11; by C. F. N., 28 Sept 1958, 15.

346. O'DONOVAN, J.: "The Celtic Revival of Today," *Irish Ecclesiastical Record,* series 4 / year 32 / 5:375 (Mar 1899), 238-56.
"What is it which is flooding so many masterminds, which is gradually seeking its way through the land in tiny rivulets, soon to join into a mighty river in which the men of Ireland are to bathe and arise with hearts and minds re-vivified? It is the revival of the Celt." One of these purifying streams is Yeats, who is pronounced thoroughly Celtic in spirit.

347. O'GLASAIN, PADRAIC: "Yeats: Symbolist or Mystic?" *Ave Maria,* ns 54:3 (19 July 1941), 71-74.
Since mystics can only be Catholic, Yeats was of necessity a symbolist.

348. OLLES, HELMUT (ed): *Literaturlexikon 20. Jahrhundert.* Reinbek bei Hamburg: Rowohlt, 1971. 850 pp.
J[ohannes] K[leinstück]: Yeats, pp. 840-42.

349. O'NEILL, GEORGE: "Some Aspects of Our Anglo-Irish Poets: The Irish Literary Theatre. Foreign Inspiration of Alleged Irish Plays," *Irish Catholic,* 23 Dec 1911, 5.
Attacks Yeats.

350. ORKNEY, MICHAEL: "William B. Yeats: A Character Sketch," *IrI,* 21 Mar 1908, 4.

351. O'RORKE, TERENCE: *The History of Sligo: Town and Country.* Dublin: Duffy, [1890]. 2 vols.
Note on Yeats whose Irish themes are said to be "racy of the soil," 2:534.

352. OSGOOD, CHARLES GROSVENOR: *The Voice of England: A History of English Literature.* 2nd edition with a chapter on English literature since 1910 by Thomas Riggs. NY: Harper, 1952 [1935]. xv, 671 pp.
Yeats, passim (see index).

353. OUSBY, IAN: *Blue Guide: Literary Britain and Ireland.* London: Black / NY: Norton, 1985. 424 pp. and maps.
"William Butler Yeats," 405-9.

354. OWENS, BEDA: "William Butler Yeats," *Eirigh,* 60:6 (June 1968), 30-32.

355. *The Oxford Dictionary of Quotations.* Third edition. Oxford: Oxford UP, 1979. xx, 907 pp.
See pp. 584-87.

356. PALMSTIERNA, ERIK: *Åtskilliga egenheter: Karaktärstudier och silhuettklipp.* Stockholm: Tidens Förlag, 1950. 326 pp.
"W. B. Yeats," 242-44. Reprint of "W. B. Yeats: Ett silhuettklipp," *Dagens nyheter,* 6 Feb 1939.

357. PANHUIJSEN, JOS[EPH]: "Herzien, herdenken: William Butler Yeats"

[To review, to commemorate: WBY], *Stem,* 19:3 (Mar 1939), 321-24.

358. PARROT, THOMAS MARC, and WILLARD THORP (eds): *Poetry of the Transition, 1850-1914.* NY: Oxford UP, 1932. xli, 622 pp.
"William Butler Yeats, 1865--," 290-93.

359. PAUL, W. J. (ed): *Modern Irish Poets.* Belfast: Belfast Steam-Printing Co., 1894-97. 2 vols.
"W. B. Yeats," 1:136-38.

360. PAUL-DUBOIS, LOUIS: "Le mystère d'une renaissance littéraire: La littérature irlandaise contemporaine," *Revue des deux mondes,* period 8 / year 107 / 41:1 (1 Sept 1937), 176-97.

361. [PEARSE, P. H.]: "Some Thoughts," *Claidheamh Soluis,* 10 Feb 1906, 7.
"Do Mr. Yeats and his fellows hold a place in the intellectual present of Ireland. . . ?" Answer: No.

362. PFISTER, KURT: "Der irische Dichter William Yeats," *Frankfurter Zeitung,* 14 Feb 1934, 1.

362a. PHILLIPS, LOUIS: "Yeats-Shelley Merger Stuns Wall Street," *NYT,* 15 Nov 1988, A31.
Since the Yeats Corporation has taken over, all of Shelley's works will be published under the name of Yeats. . . .

363. PLARR, VICTOR GUSTAVE: *Men and Women of the Time: A Dictionary of Contemporaries.* 14th edition. London: Routledge, 1895. ix, 984 pp.
See pp. 918-19.

364. PLIMPTON, GEORGE (ed): *Writers at Work: The "Paris Review" Interviews.* Fourth series. London: Secker & Warburg, 1977. xvii, 459 pp.
Edmund Keeley: "George Seferis," 147-78. Interviewed in Dec 1968, includes two short comments on Yeats, pp. 161, 172.

365. PŁOŃSKI, JERZY: "Z nad Tamizy" [From the Thames], *Życie,* 19 Feb 1898, 92-93.
A survey of Yeats's work to date.

366. POLLARD, ARTHUR (ed): *Webster's New World Companion to English and American Literature.* London: Compton Russell, 1973. xi, 850 pp.
M. S[haw]: Yeats, 752-54.

367. P[OORE], C[HARLES]: "Honors for Yeats, Now 70: 'The Re-Creator of Irish Literature' Will Revisit Dublin, the Scene Years Ago of His Picturesque Battles for a National Drama," *NYT,* 9 June 1935, VII, 14.

368. PORTER, KATHERINE ANNE: *The Collected Essays and Occasional Writings.* NY: Delacorte Press, 1970. xiii, 496 pp.
"From the Notebooks: Yeats, Joyce, Eliot, Pound," 298-300; reprinted from *SoR,* 1:3 (July 1965), 570-73.

369. POUND, EZRA: *ABC of Reading.* London: Faber & Faber, 1961. 206 pp.
Two Yeats anecdotes, pp. 44, 197-98.

370. POWELL, LAWRENCE CLARK: *Books in My Baggage: Adventures in Reading and Collecting*. Cleveland: World, 1960. 257 pp.
"Ripeness Is All," 56-60: "To collect Yeats is . . . a joy."

371. [POYNTON, ARTHUR BLACKBURNE]: Oration of the Public Orator in presenting the honorary degree of D. Litt. to W. B. Yeats on 26 May 1931, *Oxford U Gazette*, 3 June 1931, 628.
See also CE36.

372. PRAMPOLINI, GIACOMO: *Storia universale della letteratura*. Torino: Unione tipografico-editrice, 1959-61. 7 vols.
"La rinascita celtica," 6:743-55; on Yeats, pp. 743-46.

373. PRICE, NANCY: *Into an Hour-Glass*. London: Museum Press, 1953. 245 pp.
Praises Yeats as an inspiring man and poet, pp. 165-67.

374. PRITCHARD, WILLIAM HARRISON: *Seeing through Everything: English Writers 1918-1940*. London: Faber & Faber, 1977. 234 pp.
See index for scattered remarks on Yeats.

375. PURBECK, PETER: "Television: The Casual Discussion," *List*, 9 Mar 1939, 543.
Review of a B.B.C. program in which Gogarty and Clinton-Baddeley chatted about Yeats.

376. PYLES, THOMAS: *Selected Essays on English Usage*. Edited by John Algeo. Gainesville: University Presses of Florida, 1979. xiv, 223 pp.
"Bollicky Naked," 124; reprinted from *American Speech*, 24:4 (Dec 1949), 255. Explains this uninhibited phrase that appears in Yeats's letter to Olivia Shakespear of 26 Aug 1936 (printed in Hone's biography, p. 448 of the 1943 English edition, p. 480 of the 1943 American edition). In *Letters*, someone saw fit to alter the phrase to "she was without a stitch on her" (p. 861). "She" was Jean Forbes-Robertson.

377. QUILLER-COUCH, A. T.: "Sundry Poets--X.: Mr. Yeats," *Daily News*, 27 Apr 1903, 8; 11 May 1903, 8; 18 May 1903, 8.
This is really a bad joke. "Q" discusses Yeats only in the last paragraph of the last installment, where he labels Yeats's diction "foreign," i.e., not London English.

378. QUINN, STEPHEN: "The Position of W. B. Yeats," *Catholic Bulletin*, 29:3 (Mar 1939), 183-84.
See also Quinn's "Further Placings for W. B. Yeats," :4 (Apr 1939), 241-44. Yeats was an English writer because he was an intolerable embarrassment to Ireland.

378a. RAINES, HOWELL: "Ancient Places That Anchor Yeats's Poems: Rambles from Ben Bulben to Ballylee," *NYT*, 11 Oct 1987, section X, 15, 33.

379. RAIZISS, SONA: *The Metaphysical Passion: Seven Modern American Poets and Seventeenth-Century Tradition*. Philadelphia: U of Pennsylvania Press, 1952. xv, 327 pp.
Yeats is mentioned passim (see index).

380. RAUCH, KARL: "William Butler Yeats und die magische Dichtung," *Deutsche Rundschau*, 81:8 (Aug 1955), 837-40.
Visionary and magical elements in Yeats's works. Slight.

381. REBORA, PIERO: *La letteratura inglese del novecento*. Firenze: Edizione le lingue estere, 1950. 227 pp.
"La rinascita irlandese," 61-72; on Yeats, pp. 64-67.

382. REES, LESLIE: "W. B. Yeats," *Australian English Association Bulletin,* 1:10 (Apr 1939); contained in *Union Recorder,* 13 Apr 1939, 43.

383. RICHARDSON, KENNETH (ed): *Twentieth Century Writing: A Reader's Guide to Contemporary Literature*. London: Newnes, 1969. viii, 751 pp.
David L. Parkes: "Yeats," 668-70.

384. RIFLER, PERCY STENT: "Men of the Times: VII.--Mr. W. B. Yeats," *Irish Truth,* 14 Nov 1903, 3658.
A satirical sketch.

385. RIVA, SERAFINO: *La tradizione celtica* e *la moderna letteratura irlandese. I. John Millington Synge*. Roma: "Religio," 1937. v, 319 pp.
Contains "La triade crepuscolare: John M. Synge, W. B. Yeats, George W. Russell (AE)," 148-56; and "William Butler Yeats," 162-68. No more published.

386. RIVOALLAN, ANATOLE: *L'Irlande*. Paris: Colin, 1950 [1934]. iv, 220 pp. (Collection Armand Colin. 170.)
"La littérature irlandaise," 117-34; on Yeats, pp. 128-34.

387. [ROBINSON, LENNOX]: *Augustus John: Yeats*. Address to be made at a presentation on November 23rd, 1955. [Dublin, 1955. 4 pp.]
Mimeographed text about the presentation of a bust, copy in National Library of Ireland, P.2355.

388. ROGERS, PAT (ed): *The Oxford Illustrated History of English Literature*. Oxford: Oxford UP, 1987. xvi, 528 pp.
Bernard Bergonzi: "Late Victorian to Modernist, 1880-1930," 379-430; includes some passages on Yeats.

389. ROLAND HOLST, A.: "William Butler Yeats herdacht," *Verslagen en mededelingen van de Koninklijke Vlaamse Academie voor Taal en Letterkunde,* 1-2-3-4 (Jan-Feb-Mar-Apr 1964), 5-6.

390. ROONEY, PHILIP: "Landmarks in the Yeats Country," *Ireland of the Welcomes,* 1:2 (July-Aug 1952), 5-8.

391. ROSATI, SALVATORE: Note on Yeats in Italian, *Nuova antologia,* series 7 / year 69 / 295:1491 (1 May 1934), 142-45.

391a. ROTHENSTEIN, SIR WILLIAM: *Contemporaries: Portrait Drawings. With Appreciations by Various Hands*. London: Faber & Faber, 1937. 112 pp.
A portrait of Yeats, dated 1923, appears between pp. 109-11; appreciation by L. A. G. S[trong], pp. 111-12.

392. ROUTH, HAROLD VICTOR: *English Literature and Ideas in the Twentieth Century: An Inquiry into Present Difficulties and Future Prospects*. London: Methuen, 1950 [1946]. viii, 204 pp.
"William Butler Yeats," 63-68. Yeats "demonstrated that the most convincing and inexhaustible symbol is oneself." Weak on facts.

393. RUTHERFORD, MALCOLM: "Thoor Ballylee," *Spect,* 25 June 1965, 806.
The reopening ceremony.

394. SADDLEMYER, ANN: "On 'Paragraphs from Samhain' and Some Additional Yeats Letters," *IrB,* 2:3/4 (Autumn 1963), 127-28.
Bibliographical note on letters to Winifred Letts and erroneous descriptions of the following:
(a) *Paragraphs from the Forthcoming Number of "Samhain":* Not a description of Wade 244A but of Wade 244B.
(b) *Paragraphs from Samhain:* Actually *Paragraphs from Samhain 1909,* reprinted in EF39.

395. SAHER, P. J.: *Symbole: Die magische Geheimsprache der Poesie (Zur Psycho-Kybernetik der logischen Begriffsformen im östlichen Denken und in der abendländischen Romantik).* Ratingen: Henn, 1968. 328 pp.
Some worthless and inaccurate notes on Yeats, pp. 184-86, 259.

396. SALE, ROGER: *Modern Heroism: Essays on D. H. Lawrence, William Empson, & J. R. R. Tolkien.* Berkeley: U of California Press, 1973. xi, 261 pp.
Contains some notes on Yeats, especially pp. 243-44.

397. *Salmonsens Konversations Leksikon.* København: Schultz, 1915-30. 26 vols.
Yeats, 25:537.

398. SAMPSON, GEORGE: *The Concise History of English Literature.* 3rd edition. Cambridge: UP, 1970 [1941]. xiii, 976 pp.
"Anglo-Irish Literature and the Irish Literary Revival in the Age of Synge and Yeats," 716-33. On Yeats, pp. 723-25 and passim (see index).

399. SARRAZIN, GREGOR: "Keltische Renaissance in der neuesten englischen Literatur," *Internationale Monatsschrift für Wissenschaft, Kunst und Technik,* 7:8 (May 1913), 967-86.

400. SAUL, GEORGE BRANDON (ed): *Age of Yeats: Irish Literature.* NY: Dell, 1964. 382 pp. (Laurel Masterpieces of World Literature. Dell Books. 0049.)
"The Irish Renaisssance," 13-25; "Concise Notes on Authors Included," 363-82. On Yeats, pp. 378-81.

401. SCHMIELE, WALTER (ed): *Englische Geisteswelt von Bacon bis Eliot.* Darmstadt: Holle, 1953. 366 pp.
Note on Yeats, pp. 227-28.

402. SCHNEDITZ, WOLFGANG: "'. . . als ein Weg des Schicksals, als eine Stimme': Zum Werk des Iren W. B. Yeats und des Walisers Dylan Thomas" [As a course of fate, as a voice: On the work of the Irishman WBY and the Welshman DT], *Salzburger Nachrichten,* 4 Apr 1956, 3.

403. SCHUCHART, MAX: "Yeats in de Ierse legatie," *Vrij Nederland,* 1 Dec 1951, 6.
Report of a recital of Yeats's poetry, mostly by A. Roland Holst, in the Irish embassy at The Hague.

404. SCOTT-JAMES, ROLFE ARNOLD: *Fifty Years of English Literature,*

1900-1950. With a Postscript, 1950 to 1955. London: Longmans Green, 1956 [1950]. xi, 282 pp.
"The Irish Literary Movement," 89-98; on Yeats, pp. 94-98.

405. SEEHASE, GEORG (ed): *Englische Literatur im Überblick*. Leipzig: Reclam, 1986. 597 pp.
Wolfgang Wicht: "Ideologische und ästhetische Differenzierung der Literatur 1917-1939," 351-407, contains some remarks on Yeats (especially pp. 359-61, 367-70).

406. SELIGO, IRENE: "Ein Dichter des 20. Jahrhunderts: William Butler Yeats, gestorben 28. Januar 1939," *Frankfurter Zeitung*, 5 Feb 1939, 1-2.
Comments on *Cathleen ni Houlihan*.

407. SERRANO PONCELA, SEGUNDO: *La literatura occidental*. Caracas: Ediciones de la Biblioteca de la Universidad Central de Venezuela, 1971. vii, 720 pp. (Colección Arte y Literatura. 2.)
"William Butler Yeats, poeta irlandés," 632-35.

408. SHORTER, CLEMENT: Letter to the editor, *Daily News*, 4 May 1904, 4.
Criticizes Yeats for declaring Lady Gregory's *Cuchulain of Muirthemne* to be "the best book that has come out of Ireland in my time." See Yeats's reply, 11 May 1904, 4, claiming that *Gods and Fighting Men* is an even better book. Incidentally, this last letter contains a statement that Yeats was later to repudiate: "Swift, Burke, and Goldsmith . . . hardly seem to me to have come out of Ireland at all." Yeats's letter is reprinted in *Uncollected Prose*, 2:327-28.

409. SIDGWICK, F[RANK]: "William Butler Yeats," *English Illustrated Magazine*, 29:3 (June 1903), 286-88.
Reprinted in *Gael*, 22:8 (Aug 1903), 266-67.

410. SIDNELL, M. J.: "Unicorn Territory?" *Canadian Forum*, 45:531 (Apr 1965), 2-3.
The Yeats centenary celebrations at the U of Victoria.

411. SINGH, GHAN SHYAM: "Il centenario di W. B. Yeats: Il poeta contro il tempo," *Mondo*, 28 Dec 1965, 9.

412. SKOUMAL, ALOYS: "Wiliam [sic] Butler Yeats," *Kulturně politický kalendář*, 1965, 383.

413. SLEDGE, LINDA CHING: *Shivering Babe, Victorious Lord: The Nativity in Poetry and Art*. Grand Rapids: Eerdmans, 1981. x, 189 pp.
See pp. 154, 156-57.

414. SOMLYÓ, GYÖRGY: *Szélrózsa 2: Huszadik század*. Budapest: Magvető könyvkiadó, 1965. 588 pp.
Note on Yeats, p. 515; translations of six Yeats poems, pp. 51-54.

415. SPICER-SIMSON, THEODORE: *Men of Letters of the British Isles: Portrait Medallions from the Life*. With critical essays by Stuart P. Sherman and a preface by G. F. Hill. NY: Rudge, 1924. 134 pp.
"W. B. Yeats," 131-33; medallion facing p. 131.

416. SPIESS-FAURE, DOMINIQUE, and JACQUES PONTHOREAU: *Ecrivains*

britanniques: Les auteurs du XXe s. Paris: Librairie Larousse, 1979. 128 pp. (Encyclopoche Larousse. 52.)
"William Butler Yeats," 117-22.

417. STANDOP, EWALD, and EDGAR MERTNER: *Englische Literaturgeschichte*. 4th edition, revised and enlarged. Heidelberg: Quelle & Meyer, 1983 [1967]. 755 pp.
"Die irische Renaissance," 591-605.

418. STAPLETON, MICHAEL: *The Cambridge Guide to English Literature*. Cambridge: Cambridge UP, 1983. xiii, 993 pp.
See pp. 984-90.

419. STEIN, ERNST: "Kulissen liebte ich und Spielerscharen: Der Dichter William Butler Yeats, den Deutschland noch kaum zur Kenntnis genommen hat," *Zeit*, 22 Nov 1963, I.
"Players and painted stage took all my love: The poet WBY, almost unnoticed in Germany."

419a. STEWART, ANN: *National Gallery of Ireland: Fifty Irish Portraits*. Dublin: National Gallery of Ireland, 1984. vi, 54 pp.
Notes on Yeats and reproduction of Edmund Dulac's portrait, pp. 43-47.

420. °STOJANOVIĆ ZOROVAVELJ, VLADAN: "Tri barda," *Novosti*, 5 Dec 1923, 885.

421. STONYK, MARGARET: *Nineteenth-Century English Literature*. London: Macmillan, 1983. xiv, 307 pp. (Macmillan History of Literature.)
On Yeats, pp. 255-58 and passim (see index).

422. STURM, F. P.: "The Irish Literary Movement," *Aberdeen Free Press*, 9 June 1906, 5.
See also BB240.

423. SULLIVAN, BARRY: "Der Turm von Ballylee: Über den irischen Dichter W. B. Yeats," *Englische Rundschau*, 8:13 (20 June 1958), 200.
"The Tower of Ballylee: On the Irish poet WBY."

424. SURKOV, ALEKSEĬ ALEKSANDROVICH (ed): *Kratkai͡a literaturnai͡a ėnt͡siklopedii͡a*. Moskva: Sovetskai͡a ėnt͡siklopedii͡a, 1962-78. 9 vols.
E. I͡A. Dombrovskai͡a: "Ĭits, Ĭets, Eĭts," 3:266-68.

425. SUŠKO, MARIO: Note on Yeats, *Republika*, 22:5 (May 1966), 209.

426. *Svensk Uppslagbok*. Malmö: Norden, 1954-63. 32 vols.
[Harold] E[lovson]: "Yeats," 32:142-44.

427. SWINGLER, RANDALL: "The English Twilight," *Our Time*, 1:3 (May 1941), 5-9.

427a. SWINNERTON, FRANK: *The Georgian Scene: A Literary Panorama*. NY: Farrar & Rinehart, 1934. x, 522 pp.
"William Butler Yeats," 260-63. Also in *The Georgian Literary Scene: A Panorama*. London: Hutchinson, 1938 [1935]. xii, 532 pp. (pp. 271-73).

427b. SZENCZI, MIKLÓS, TIBOR SZOBOTKA, and ANNA KATONA: *Az angol irodalom története*. Budapest: Gondolat, 1972. 703 pp.
A. Katona: "Az ír reneszánsz," 564-75.

428. *Tagore's Friend (Irish Poet--William Butler Yeats)*. Lahore: Tagore Memorial Publications, [1942?]. 15 pp.
A short survey of Yeats's works; little on the Yeats-Tagore relationship. Reprinted in °Dewan Ram Parkash (ed): *Tagore Centenary Souvenir*. New Delhi: Tagore Memorial Publications, 1961. 403 pp. (pp. 138-44).

429. TATE, SIR ROBERT WILLIAM: *Orationes et epistolae dublinenses (1914-40)*. Dublin: Hodges, Figgis, 1941. xix, 205 pp.
"Comitia hiemalis, die vicesimo decembris, 1922, habita: Litt.D. Willelmus Butler Yeats," 51; the formal Latin oration at Trinity College, Dublin.

430. TEODORESCU, ANDA: "W. B. Yeats," *Contemporanul,* 3 Dec 1965, 2.

431. TEUBER, HANS: "Ein Stück Zeitgeschichte: Irische Literatur des 20. Jahrhunderts," *Parlament,* 24:2-3 (12 Jan 1974), 5.

432. THOMPSON, FRANCIS: *The Letters*. Edited by John Evangelist Walsh. NY: Hawthorn Books, 1969. 272 pp.
A few references to Yeats, passim (see index).

433. THORPE, JAMES: *Frontiersmen of the Spirit: Four Masters of Twentieth-Century Literature. William Butler Yeats, James Joyce, Wallace Stevens, Conrad Aiken*. San Marino: Huntington Library, 1980. 24 pp.
Contains a short sketch of Yeats's life and works as part of an opening address for an exhibition at the Huntington Library.

434. THURLEY, GEOFFREY: "A Footnote on Yeats," *Icarus,* 47 (Dec 1965), 20-23.
A somewhat confused essay on the question "What does Yeats get to know . . . about the world in general?"

435. THWAITE, ANTHONY: "W. B. Yeats," *TLS,* 7 Sept 1984, 995.
Corrects a misattribution (a phrase attributed to Yeats is actually by Meredith).

436. T[ITUS], E[DWARD] W.: "Criticism à l'irlandaise," *This Quarter,* 3:4 (Apr-May-June 1931), 570-84.
Contains some notes on Yeats, especially in the section "Patriotism and Inspiration," 571-72.

437. TUCKER, WILLIAM JOHN: "The Celt in Contemporary Literature," *CathW,* 146:876 (Mar 1938), 650-57.
On Yeats's early works (despite the title of the article), passim.

438. TURNER, W. J.: "Words and Tones," *NSt,* 22 July 1939, 141-42.
Review of a reading of Yeats's poetry at the Ellen Terry Barn Theatre, including some remarks on why Yeats loved folksongs.

439. *20th-Century Drama*. Introduction by Simon Trussler. London: Macmillan, 1983. vii, 316 pp. (Great Writers Student Library. 11.)
A. Norman Jeffares: Yeats, 304-10; a bibliography and a three-page essay; reprinted from James Vinson and D. L. Kirkpatrick (eds): *Great Writers of the English Language: Dramatists*. London: Macmillan, 1979. viii, 648 pp. (pp. 629-34). Also in Vinson and Kirkpatrick: *Great Writers of the English Language: Poets*. London: Macmillan, 1979. x, 1141 pp. (pp. 1104-9).

440. *20th-Century Poetry*. Introduction by Stan Smith. London: Macmillan, 1983. vii, 526 pp. (Great Writers Student Library. 9.)
Reprints the contribution by Jeffares from the preceding item. Yeats is also referred to in the introduction, pp. 1-28.

441. USSHER, ARLAND: "Literaturbrief aus Irland," *Neue deutsche Literatur,* 13:11 (Nov 1965), 151-65.
A short sketch of the revival; on Yeats, passim.

442. ———: "Irish Literature," *ZAA,* 14:1 (1966), 30-55.
Another brief survey of the history of Irish literature; on Yeats as a model escapist writer, pp. 48-52.

443. ———: *From a Dark Lantern: A Journal*. Edited and arranged by Roger Nyle Parisious. Dalkey: Cuala Press, 1978. iv, 79 pp.
Contains several obiter dicta on Yeats.

444. ———: *The Journal of Arland Ussher*. Edited by Adrian Kenny. Dublin: Raven Arts, 1980. 32 pp.
See pp. 18-19 and passim.

445. VALLARDI: *Grande enciclopedia Vallardi*. Milano: Vallardi, 1967-70. 16 vols.
Yeats, 15:955-56.

446. VAN DOREN, CARL, and MARK VAN DOREN: *American and British Literature since 1890*. NY: Century, 1925. xi, 350 pp.
"Irish Literature," 273-309; on Yeats, pp. 275-79, 288-91, 307-8, and passim (see index).

447. VENGEROVA, ZIN[AIDA ATHANAS'EVNA]: "Molodaia͡ Anglii͡a (Literaturnaia͡ khronika)" [Young England: A literary chronicle], *Cosmopolis,* 15 (Mar 1897), 186-203.
On "Vill'i͡am Jets," 198-200.

448. VIOLA, WILHELM: "Der Dichter des *Einhorns von den Sternen*," [The poet of *The Unicorn from the Stars*], *Tribüne,* 25:10 (1955/56), 98-99.

449. *W. B. Yeats 1865-1939: A Tribute in Bronze by Henry Moore Erected by Admirers of the Poet October 1967*. [Dublin, 1967. 4 pp.]
A pamphlet with a photograph of the sculpture, erected in St. Stephen's Green. There is a copy in the National Library of Ireland (IR.92.p.85).
See also Anon.: "Tone, Emmet, Yeats--Three Memorials in St. Stephen's Green," *Oibre,* 6 (Sept 1968), 6-9.
Anon.: "Moore Memorial to Yeats Unveiled: Juncture of Great Talents," *IrT,* 27 Oct 1967, 13. (Includes the text of the speech made by the Taoiseach, Jack Lynch; illustrated.)
Anon.: "Green Sculpture Honours Yeats," *IrT,* 1 Sept 1986, 6.
Bruce Arnold: "Moore's New Yeats Memorial Examined," *Sunday Independent,* 5 Nov 1967, 25.
Gabriel Fallon: "Dublin Letter," *America,* 12 Oct 1957, 46-47 (the proposal to erect the memorial). See also CE35.
For another photograph see *ILS,* 2:2 (Oct 1983), 17.

450. WADE, STEPHEN: "Anglo-Irish Literature," *English Today,* 8 (Oct-Dec 1986), 37-40.
Contains some notes on Yeats.

451. WAGNER, LUDWIG: "William Butler Yeats," *30. Januar* [Dreissigster Januar], 1:12 (Feb 1934), 91-93.

452. WAIN, JOHN: *Professing Poetry*. London: Macmillan, 1977. x, 396 pp.
Some notes on Yeats (see index).

453. WALL, MERVYN: "An Interview with Mervyn Wall. Conducted by Gordon Henderson," *JIL*, 11:1&2 (Jan-May 1982), 3-18.
Includes a few comments on Yeats.

454. WALSH, THOMAS: "The Collected Yeats," *Commonweal*, 19 Nov 1924, 39.
"We owe him many thanks, but little veneration."

455. WARD, ALFRED CHARLES: *English Literature: Chaucer to Bernard Shaw*. London: Longmans, Green, 1958 [1953]. xxi, 781 pp.
Yeats, pp. 725-28 and passim (see index).

456. ———: *Twentieth-Century Literature, 1901-1950*. London: Methuen, 1956. viii, 248 pp.
"The Irish Theatre," 110-18, contains some critical remarks on Yeats's early plays. On Yeats's early poetry, pp. 150-53. Virtually nothing on his later work.

457. WARNER, OLIVER: *English Literature: A Portrait Gallery*. London: Chatto & Windus, 1964. xvii, 205 pp.
Yeats, pp. 180-81, including the Howard Coster photograph.

458. WARNER, REX: "O poiētēs W. B. Yeats (1865-1939)," *Angloellēnikē epitheōrēsē*, vol. B (Apr 1946), 38-40.
Includes a translation of "The Second Coming" by George Seferis, entitled "E deutéra parousía."

459. WATERS, MAUREEN: *The Comic Irishman*. Albany: State U of New York Press, 1984. vii, 204 pp.
See index for some notes on Yeats.

460. WEBER, BROM (ed): *Sense and Sensibility in Twentieth-Century Writing: A Gathering in Memory of William Van O'Connor*. Carbondale: Southern Illinois UP, 1970. xvii, 174 pp.
Earl Miner: "The Double Truth in Modern Poetic Criticism," 16-25; mentions Yeats passim.

461. *Die Weltliteratur: Biographisches, literarhistorisches und bibliographisches Lexikon in Übersichten und Stichwörtern*. Wien: Hollinek, 1951-53. 3 vols.
"Anglo-irische Literatur," 1:58-59; "Irische Literatur," 2:812-16; "Yeats," 3:1948-49.

462. WELTMANN, LUTZ: "William Butler Yeats: Der mathematische Symbolist," *Europa*, 16:6 (June 1965), 62-63.

463. WHEELER, ETHEL: "The Fairyland of Heart's Desire," *Great Thoughts*, series 4 / 8:948 (Oct 1901), 375-76.

464. WILLIAMSON, CLAUDE CHARLES HORACE: *Writers of Three Centuries 1789-1914*. London: Richards, 1920. 515 pp.
"W. B. Yeats and the Irish School," 444-51.

465. WILSON, EDMUND: *Letters on Literature and Politics 1912-1972*. Edited by Elena Wilson, introduction by Daniel Aron, foreword by Leon Edel. NY: Farrar, Straus & Giroux, 1977. xxxvii, 768 pp.
See index for short notes on Yeats.

466. WIMSATT, WILLIAM KURTZ: *Hateful Contraries: Studies in Literature and Criticism*. Lexington: U of Kentucky Press, 1965. xix, 260 pp.
A few scattered notes on Yeats, passim (see index).

467. WINKLER PRINS: *Algemeene encyclopaedie*. 5th edition. Amsterdam: Elsevier, 1932-38. 16 vols.
Willem van Doorn: "Yeats," 16:568.

468. WINTLE, JUSTIN (ed): *Makers of Modern Culture*. London: Routledge & Kegan Paul, 1981. xviii, 605 pp.
Joseph Bain: Yeats, 582-84.

469. WOOD-MARTIN, WILLIAM GREGORY: *Traces of the Elder Faiths of Ireland: A Folklore Sketch. A Handbook of Irish Pre-Christian Traditions*. Port Washington, N.Y.: Kennikat Press, 1970 [1902]. 2 vols.
Notes on Yeats's view of the fairies, 1:254-55; see also 2:320 where "Mr. Yates" is described as being "more Irish than the Irish themselves."

470. WRATISLAW, THEODORE: *Three Nineties Studies: W. B. Yeats, John Gray, Aubrey Beardsley*. Edinburgh: Tragara Press, 1980. 22 pp.
"William Butler Yeats," 7-12; reprint of "La garde joyeuse: VII. William Butler Yeats," *Artist and J of Home Culture*, 14:167 (1 Oct 1893), 297-98, where it was published under the intials T. W. G. W.
For a commentary see "North and South," *United Ireland*, 11 Nov 1893, 1; a letter by the editor of *The Artist* and the editor's reply, *United Ireland*, 2 Dec 1893, 1.

471. YEATS, W. B.: *Blaesten mellem sivene: Digte og skuespil*. Paa dansk ved Valdemar Rørdam. København: Haase, 1924. xi, 226 pp.
"Forord," vii-xi; notes, 223-26.

472. ———: *Gedichte*. Auswahl, Übertragung und Nachwort von H. E. Herlitschka. Zürich: Arche, 1958. 84 pp. (Die kleinen Bücher der Arche. 222-223.)
"Nachwort," 71-84.

473. ———: *Racconti, liriche*. Edited, translated and introduced by Giuseppe Sardelli. Milano: Fabbri, 1969. 256 pp. (I grandi della letteratura. 61.)
Introduction, pp. 7-10.

474. YOUNG, VERNON: "The Music of What Happens," *Parnassus*, 11:2 (Fall/Winter 1983--Spring/Summer 1984), 323-35.
Contains notes on Yeats's part in the Irish literary revival.

475. ZADURA, BOHDAN: "W. B. Yeats: Dramat przezwyciężony" [The drama of overcoming], *Kultura*, 7:5 (2 Feb 1969), 3.

CF The Cuala Press

1. ANON.: "Cuala Industries," *Irish Life*, 23 Feb 1917, 259-61.

2. BASKIN, LISA UNGER: "A Gathering from the Dun Emer Press & the Cuala Press," *MR*, 28:3 (Autumn 1987), [525-49]. (Illustrated)

3. CAVE, RODERICK: *The Private Press*. Second edition, revised and enlarged. NY: Bowker, 1983 [1971]. xvi, 389 pp.
See pp. 183-84.

4. DURKAN, MICHAEL J.: "The Dun Emer and the Cuala Press," *Wesleyan Library Notes*, 4 (Spring 1970), 7-18.

5. FOX, R. M.: "She's Printer to the Poets," *British Printer*, [65:4] (Jan-Feb 1953), 33-35.
On Mrs. Yeats.

6. ———: "The Name on the Knocker Is Yeats," *Ireland of the Welcomes*, 14:1 (May-June 1965), 21-22.

7. GIBBON, MONK: "At the Cuala Press," *IrT*, 29 Sept 1969, 12.

8. °GOODWIN, AILEEN M.: *The Cuala Press in Ireland: A Woman's Contribution to Fine Printing*. [Dublin: Cuala Press, ca. 1925]. 8 pp.

9. HAAS, IRVIN: "Miss Elizabeth Yeats and the Cuala Press with a List of Books Printed at the Cuala Press," *American Book Collector*, 4:9/10 (Sept-Oct 1933), 133-38.

10. HORWILL, HERBERT W.: "Yeats as a Printer," *NYTBR*, 24 Oct 1926, 13.

11. KENNER, HUGH: "'The Most Beautiful Book,'" *ELH*, 48:3 (Fall 1981), 594-605.
Mainly about the hand-set Dijon edition of Joyce's *Ulysses*, prefaced by remarks about the Dun Emer Press and the Cuala Press.

12. KIERNAN, T. J.: "Fifty Years of the Cuala Press," *Biblionews*, 7:8 (July 1954), 27-29.

13. *°A List of Books Published by the Dun Emer Press and the Cuala Press Founded in Nineteen Hundred and Three by Elizabeth Corbet Yeats*. With a preface by Liam Miller. Dublin: Cuala Press, 1972. xvi pp.

14. MACGLYNN, LOCHLINN: "In the Golden Land of Yeats," *IrP*, 23 May 1946, 7.

15. MARRINER, ERNEST C.: "Fifty Years of the Cuala Press," *CLQ*, 3:11 (Aug 1953), 171-83.

16. [MAXWELL, WILLIAM]: *The Dun Emer Press, Churchtown, Dundrum, July 1903--September 1907. The Cuala Press, Churchtown, Dundrum, October 1908--July 1923; Merrion Square Dublin, October 1923--October 1924; Lower Baggot Street Dublin, from May 1925*. A complete list of the books, pamphlets, leaflets, and broadsides printed by Miss Yeats, with some notes by the compiler. [Edinburgh]: Privately printed, 1932. 67 pp.

17. MILLER, LIAM: "The Dun Emer Press," *IrB,* 2:2 (Spring 1963), 43-52; :3/4 (Autumn 1963), 81-90.

18. ———: "The Dun Emer and Cuala Press," in Skelton and Saddlemyer: *The World of W. B. Yeats* (1967, CA102), 111-14, 127-33.

19. [———]: *A Brief Account of the Cuala Press, Formerly the Dun Emer Press Founded by Elizabeth Corbet Yeats in MCMIII.* Dublin: Cuala Press, 1971. [8 pp.]

20. ———: *The Dun Emer Press, Later the Cuala Press.* With a preface by Michael B. Yeats. Dublin: Dolmen Press, 1973. 131 pp. (New Yeats Papers. 7.)

21. MURDOCH, RICHARD: "The Cuala Press, 1902-1984," *ILS,* 3:2 (Fall 1984), 30-31.

22. MURDOCH, W. G. BLAIKIE: "The Cuala Press and the Yeats Family," *Bruno's R of Two Worlds,* 4:1 (June 1922), 23-25.

This may be identical with "The Cuala Press," *Bookman's J and Print Collector,* 6:10 (July 1922), 107-11.

23. NATIONAL BOOK LEAGUE: *The Cuala Press 1903-1973.* An exhibition arranged by the National Book League to celebrate the seventieth anniversary of the Cuala Press, 11-30 June 1973. London: National Book League, 1973. 32 pp.

A catalog, compiled by Liam Miller, preface by Clifford Simmons, listing books, broadsides, and occasional publications by the Dun Emer Press and the Cuala Press until 1946 and after 1971. The same catalog was issued by the Dolmen Press when the exhibition was transferred to Trinity College Dublin (Oct 1973--Mar 1974).

24. O'SULLIVAN, PHILIP: "Hand-Printing Press Revived," *IrI,* 6 Oct 1969, 6.

25. PIONDAR, SEAN: "Her Fortune Is in Books," *Sunday Graphic and Sunday News,* 10 Jan 1937, 37.

Mainly on Elizabeth C. Yeats.

26. *Pressmarks and Devices Used at the Dun Emer Press and the Cuala Press.* Preface by the Liam Miller. Dalkey, Co. Dublin: Cuala Press, 1977. [35 pp.]

27. QUIDNUNC: "An Irishman's Diary," *IrT,* 14 Sept 1953, 5.

Correspondence by Katherine MacCormack, 16 Sept 1953, 5.

28. RANSOM, WILL: *Private Presses and Their Books.* NY: Bowker, 1929. 493 pp.

Contains some notes on the press and a checklist (see index).

29. SMYTHE, COLIN: "Rebirth of the Cuala Press: The Famous Little Publishing Enterprise So Closely Connected with the Yeats Family Has Recently Been Revived," *Ireland of the Welcomes,* 21:4 (Nov-Dec 1972), 31-35. (Illustrated)

A revised version was published as "The Cuala Press 1903-1973," *PrL,* series 2 / 6:3 (Autumn 1973), 107-13.

30. TICKELL, ADELINE HILL: "The Dun Emer Press," *Book-Lover's Magazine,* 8:1 (1908), 6-14.

31. TOMKINSON, GEOFFREY STEWART: *A Select Bibliography of the Principal Modern Presses Public and Private in Great Britain and Ireland.* With an introduction by B. H. Newdigate. London: First Edition Club, 1928. xxv, 238 pp.

"The Cuala Press," 32-38.

32. TURNER, G. W. "The Cuala Industries," *Lady's Pictorial,* 2 Sept 1916, 301-2.

33. YEATS, ANNE: "Talk Given by Miss Anne Yeats at the Opening of the Cuala Press Exhibition in the Long Room, Old Library, on 24 October 1973," *Long Room,* 9 (Spring-Summer 1974), 38-39.

At Trinity College Dublin.

34. YEATS, LILY [i.e., Yeats, Susan Mary]: *Elizabeth Corbet Yeats. Born March 11th. 1868. Died January 16th. 1940.* [Dublin: Cuala Press, 1940. 4 pp.]

35. YEATS, MICHAEL BUTLER: *"Something to Perfection Brought": The Cuala Press.* Published on the occasion of an exhibition of an Irish literature collection given to Stanford University by James A. Healey. Stanford: Associates of the Stanford University Libraries and the Department of Special Collection, 1976. [28 pp.]

Contains an introduction by Oswalda Deva, describing the collection; a four-page essay on the Cuala Press by Michael Yeats; several reproductions of inscriptions in Cuala Press books, six of them by WBY; and a reprint of an extract from a letter by John Butler Yeats on the Trinity Chair proposal (see CB24, 142, 144).

See also AA15, 19, 84, CA20, CB371, 443, CC247.

CG The Irish Academy of Letters

1. ANON.: "The Pollexfen Peacock Parade: Dismal Drip from Westmoreland Street," *Catholic Bulletin,* 22:10 (Oct 1932), 773-75.

See also "Shaw and Yeats and Their Tribe," 23:9 (Sept 1933), 693-96 (". . . parade of putridity. . . .").

2. ANON.: "Academy of Immorality [. . .]: A Real Insult to Ireland," *Catholic Mind,* 3:11 (Nov 1932), 247-48.

3. ANON.: "Irish Academy of Letters: Names of Those Selected. Mr. Yeats Expects Refusals. The Creation of Modern Ireland," *IrT,* 19 Sept 1932, 7.

See also the editorial on p. 6.

4. ANON.: "The New Irish Academy: Dublin Priest's Criticism. Lecture in the Theatre Royal," *IrT,* 14 Nov 1932, 7-8.

Long summary of a lecture by the Rev. P. J. Gannon, S.J., on "The Irish Academy of Letters--Unwelcomed and Unauthorised."

5. ANON.: "An Academy for Irish Letters," *Literary Digest,* 22 Oct 1932, 16.

6. ANON.: "An Academy of Absentees," *Tablet,* 24 Sept 1932, 394-95.

"An impudent usurpation. . . ."

7. ANON.: "An Irish Academy of Letters: Mr. W. B. Yeats's Proposal," *Times*, 4 Apr 1932, 9.

8. BODEN, R. ERIC: "Ireland's Academy of Letters," *NYTBR*, 29 Jan 1933, 6, 14.

9. BOYD, ERNEST: "An Unacademic Academy," *Nation*, 14 Dec 1932, 590.
Defends the project.

10. CLARKE, R. DARDIS: "Half a Century of the Irish Academy of Letters," *IrT*, 14 Sept 1982, 8.

11. GWYNN, STEPHEN: "The Irish Academy of Letters," *FortnR*, os 138 / ns 132:791 (Nov 1932), 653-54.

12. [MANNING, MARY ?]: "Processional," *Motley*, 1:5 (Oct 1932), 6-7.

13. O'CASEY, SEAN: "Laurel Leaves and Silver Trumpets," *American Spectator*, 1:2 (Dec 1932), 4.
O'Casey's unfavorable opinion of the academy and of Yeats's "Noh" plays. But he does not "hate" Yeats as has been frequently alleged: "I myself have gone about, arm in arm with him a thousand times, and sincerely hope to renew these delightful experiences. . . ."

14. O'HEGARTY, P. S.: "About the Academy of Letters," *Motley*, 2:2 (Feb 1933), 10-12.
Wants to see some members replaced because of lack of merit: Gogarty, Higgins, O'Faolain, O'Flaherty, and others. See also "More about the Academy," :3 (Mar 1933), 4-7.

15. T., O.: "The New Academy: To Throw Bad Eggs at Mrs. Grundy? Mr. Yeats' History," *United Irishman*, 24 Sept 1932, 5.

16. TALBOT, FRANCIS: "The Irish Academy of Literature," *America*, 10 Dec 1932, 240-41.
Vicious attack on Yeats' project and on his attempts to abolish censorship.

See also BC5, 13a, BE121, 122, 136, BF175, 185, CB183, CD763, 1234, FD46, G589.

CH The Yeats International Summer School

No completeness is attempted in this section. The activities of the Yeats International Summer School in Sligo (usually held in August of every year) are reported in the *Irish Times* and other Irish newspapers.

1. ALDERSON SMITH, PETER: "Majority: The International Yeats Summer School," *Eire*, 16:4 (Winter 1980), 129-34.

2. ALLEN, ROSEMARY: "21 Years of the Yeats School in Sligo," *IrT*, 22 Aug 1980, 8.

3. ANON.: "The Yeats Summer School," *ILS*, 5:1 (Spring 1986), 13.
Includes "A Student's View" by Gabriel Fitzmaurice.

4. ANON.: "Yeats's Work Takes on Added Grandeur for Students Visiting the Irish Poet's Sources of Inspiration," *NYT,* 29 Aug 1963, 31.

5. ANON.: "Interpreters of Yeats: Sligo Summer School," *TES,* 30 Aug 1963, 235.

6. ANON.: "Thoughts on Yeats: Ghosts and Computers," *TES,* 28 Aug 1964, 277.

6a. BORCHMEYER, DIETER, and TILL HEIMERAN (eds): *Weimar am Pazifik: Literarische Wege zwischen den Kontinenten. Festschrift für Werner Vordtriede zum 70. Geburtstag.* Tübingen: Niemeyer, 1985. xiv, 399 pp.

Susanne Schaup: "Unter dem Rücken Ben Bulbens" [Under Ben Bulben's back], 306-15; an impressionistic essay on the summer school and some of its participants.

7. BROWNLOW, TIMOTHY: "One Dear Perpetual Place," *DM,* 4:3/4 (Autumn-Winter 1965), 94-96.

8. CAREW, RIVERS: "Yeats: The Summer School in Sligo," *Hibernia,* 29:3 (Mar 1965), 26.

9. ———: "The Yeats Summer School in Sligo: Successful Cultural Venture," *Hibernia,* 31:8 (Aug 1967), 7.

10. COXHEAD, ELIZABETH: "The Dreaming of the Abbey," *Guardian,* 1 Aug 1961, 5.

Also on Duras House.

11. CURTAYNE, ALICE: "Ireland," *Critic,* 21:1 (Aug-Sept 1962), 48-50.

12. DURYEE, MARY BALLARD: "William Butler Yeats in Modern Ireland," *Recorder,* 28 (Dec 1965), 7-9.

13. EARLY, ELEANOR: "Ireland's Yeats Country," *NYT,* 10 July 1966, section X, 29.

14. FRIEND, ROBERT: "The Sixth Yeats International Summer School," *JJQ,* 3:2 (Winter 1966), 139-40.

15. GALLAGHER, MICHAEL PAUL: "Yeats, the Mountain and the Temple," *Month,* 244:1382 / ns 15:11 (Nov 1982), 388.

Evensong address at Drumcliffe Church on the opening of the School, Aug 1982.

16. GIBBON, MONK: "The Yeats Country," *Ireland of the Welcomes,* 9:2 (July-Aug 1960), 12-14.

17. GUILLOUX, FRANÇOIS: "Yeats International Summer School," *EI,* 2 (Dec 1977), 320-26.

18. HENN, T. R.: "Yeats Summer School," *TLS,* 25 Mar 1960, 193.

19. KELLY, JOHN: "The Evenin' Boozer to Sligo," *CambR,* 89A:2155 (28 Oct 1967), 55-57.

20. MATSON, LESLIE: "Conviviality and Challenge: Leslie Matson Recalls the Yeats International Summer School in Sligo," *BooksI,* 113 (May 1987), 87-88.

21. Gopaleen, Myles na [O'BRIEN, FLANN; i.e., Brian O'Nolan]: "Cruiskeen Lawn: Eng. Lit.," *IrT*, 15 Jan 1965, 8.

22. RAFROIDI, PATRICK: "The First Yeats International Summer School, Sligo, Eire (13-27 août 1960)," *EA*, 13:4 (Oct-Dec 1960), 502-3.

23. SPEAIGHT, ROBERT: "A Centenary in Sligo: The Yeats Summer School," *Tablet*, 28 Aug 1965, 952-53.

24. WARD, DAVID F.: "'Under Bare Ben Bulben's Head': The Yeats International Summer School," *JJQ*, 4:1 (Fall 1966), 46-49.

25. WARD, HERMAN M.: "Thanne Longen Folk to Goon on Pilgrimages," *EJ*, 51:4 (Apr 1962), 287-88.

See also CA38, 51, 149, HE4.

D THE POETRY

DA Books and Pamphlets Exclusively on Yeats

1. ALBRIGHT, DANIEL FRANK: *The Myth against Myth: A Study of Yeats's Imagination in Old Age*. London: Oxford UP, 1972. ix, 195 pp.

Based on a °Ph.D. thesis, Yale U, 1970. 264 pp. (*DAI*, 31:6 [Dec 1970], 2903A). "This book is a study of Yeats's image of the human mind, his painstaking construction of his own personality by means of poetry" (p. 1). Analyzes "The Circus Animals' Desertion," *The King of the Great Clock Tower*, "News for the Delphic Oracle," "The Tower," and "The Wanderings of Oisin."

Reviews:

- Michael H. Begnal, *Eire*, 8:3 (Autumn 1973), 114-15.
- John Boland: "Poet's Self-Portrait," *Hibernia*, 16 Feb 1973, 14.
- Frederic S. Colwell, *QQ*, 80:4 (Winter 1973), 645-46.
- Edward Engelberg, *Far-Western Forum*, 1:2 (May 1974), 285-86.
- Ian Fletcher: "The Traffic in Yeats," *TLS*, 2 May 1975, 490.
- Frank Kinahan, *MP*, 73:2 (Nov 1975), 210-14.
- Phillip L. Marcus: "Memoir and Myth," *IrP*, 20 Jan 1973, 10.
- J. M. Morrison, *BA*, 48:1 (Winter 1974), 151.
- J. R. Mulryne, *YES*, 5 (1975), 326-28.
- Harold Orel, *JEGP*, 72:4 (Oct 1973), 578-80.
- Roger N. Parisious, *DM*, 10:1 (Winter/Spring 1973), 125-30.
- Hermann Peschmann, *English*, 22:113 (Summer 1973), 83-84.
- Timothy Webb, *RES*, 25:98 (May 1974), 239-42.
- Georges-Denis Zimmermann, *ES*, 55:3 (June 1974), 297-98.

2. BEUM, ROBERT: *The Poetic Art of W. B. Yeats*. NY: Ungar, 1969. xvii, 161 pp.

Incorporates: "Yeats's Octaves," *TSLL*, 3:1 (Spring 1961), 89-96; "Yeats the Rhymer," *PLL*, 1:4 (Autumn 1965), 338-50; "Yeats's Idealized Speech," *MQR*, 4:4 (Fall 1965), 227-33.

A study of style, meter, and rhyme in the poems (particularly the later ones), including a short chapter on the drama.

Reviews:

- Terence Brown, *IUR*, 1:2 (Spring 1971), 276-78.
- Edward Engelberg, *ConL*, 11:2 (Spring 1970), 303-9.
- Arra M. Garab: "The Legacy of Yeats," *JML*, 1:1 (1970), 137-40.
- Richard M. Kain, *Eire*, 4:3 (Autumn 1969), 123-27.

3. BHARGAVA, ASHOK: *The Poetry of W. B. Yeats: Myth as Metaphor*. Atlantic Highlands, N.J.: Humanities Press / New Delhi: Arnold-Heinemann, 1980. 261 pp.

Based on °"Yeats's Idea of Myth, with Special Reference to His Poetry from 1919 to 1933," Ph.D. thesis, U of Manchester, 1976. On the role of myth in Yeats's thinking, in his poetry after 1919, and in *A Vision*. Includes discussions of Jungian parallels, the importance of Celtic mythology, and human embodiments of myth (particularly Maud Gonne).

4. CAVANAUGH, CATHERINE: *Love and Forgiveness in Yeats's Poetry*. Ann Arbor: UMI Research Press, 1986. xi, 174 pp. (Studies in Modern Literature. 57.)

Based on "Redemptive Tragedy: Love and Forgiveness in Yeats's Poetry," °Ph.D. thesis, State U of New York at Binghamton, 1984. 400 pp. (*DAI*, 45:4 [Oct 1984], 1120A; reprinted *Yeats*, 3 [1985], 215). Mainly on "The Three Bushes," "A Man Young and Old," "A

Woman Young and Old," the Crazy Jane poems, the Ribh poems in "Supernatural Songs," and "The Wild Old Wicked Man." Analyzed in section DD.
Reviews:
- Michael H. Begnal, *Eire,* 23:1 (Spring 1988), 147-48.
- Thomas Parkinson, *Yeats,* 5 (1987), 220-22.

5. CHATTERJEE, BHABATOSH: *The Poetry of W. B. Yeats.* Calcutta: Orient Longmans, 1962. xiii, 163 pp.
Reprinted Folcroft, Pa.: Folcroft Press 1970. "This book is a study in certain aspects of Yeats' non-dramatic verse, seen against the background of the poet's life and the political, philosophical and literary influences that worked on him. The two chief aims of the book are to show the development of Yeats's mind and craft, and to examine the richness and complexity of his symbolism" (p. ix).
Reviews:
- Amalendu Bose: "W. B. Yeats: His Poetry and Thought," *IJES,* 3 (1962), 158-67.
- A. Choudhuri, *VQ,* 27:3&4 (1961/62), 285-87.
- Frank Kermode, *RES,* 15:57 (Feb 1964), 119.
- Peter Ure, *N&Q,* os 208 / ns 10:10 (Oct 1963), 400.
- F. A. C. Wilson, *MLR,* 58:3 (July 1963), 468-69.

6. CLARK, DAVID RIDGLEY: *Yeats at Songs and Choruses.* Amherst: U of Massachusetts Press, 1983. xxiv, 283 pp. (Illustrated)
Incorporates: "The Manuscripts of W. B. Yeats' 'Crazy Jane on the Day of Judgment,'" *Malahat R,* 48 (Oct 1978), 32-76; subsequently revised and published as *That Black Day: The Manuscripts of "Crazy Jane on the Day of Judgment."* Mountrath, Portlaoise: Dolmen Press, 1980. 55 pp. (New Yeats Papers. 18.)
Reviews of the pamphlet:
- James Lovic Allen, *ACIS Newsletter,* 12:1 (Feb 1982), 6.
- Janet Madden-Simpson, *BooksI,* 52 (Apr 1981), 61-62.
- William H. O'Donnell, *YeA,* 2 (1983), 109-11.

°"W. B Yeats's 'Three Things' in the Light of the Manuscripts," *Soundings,* 14:1 (Spring 1977), 43-52; previously published as "Stretching and Yawning with Yeats and Pound," *Malahat R,* 29 (Jan 1974), 104-17.

"After 'Silence,' the 'Supreme Theme': Eight Lines of Yeats," reprinted from CB403.

"Yeats' Dragons: The Sources of 'Michael Robartes and the Dancer' and 'Her Triumph' as Shown in the Manuscripts," *Malahat R,* 57 (Jan 1981), 35-88.

"Yeats's 'From *Oedipus at Colonus*': Transcriptions of the Manuscripts, and Two Comments," *MBL,* 4:1 (Spring 1979), 63-82.

Prints MSS. versions of the poems mentioned and of "After Long Silence," "Colonus' Praise," and "From the *Antigone*" and traces their development to the first published versions in order to arrive at a better understanding of the meaning. Discusses literary and pictorial sources (Sophocles, Blake, Morris, Pound, Bordone, Bellini, Crivelli, Tintoretto, Burne-Jones, and others).
Reviews:
- Eavan Boland: "Critics and Readers," *IrT,* 30 July 1983, 12.
- George Bornstein: "Yeats's Texts and Contexts," *MLS,* 16:2 (Spring 1986), 82-87.
- Ian Fletcher, *YeA,* 3 (1985), 258-63.
- J. P. Frayne, *JEGP,* 84:2 (Apr 1985), 284-86.
- Jacqueline Genet, *EI,* 8 (Dec 1983), 395-96.
- George Mills Harper: "Remembering Greece," *ILS,* 2:2 (Oct

1983), 18.
- Janet Madden-Simpson: "A Case of Mental Vampirism," *BooksI,* 72 (Apr 1983), 62.
- Thomas Parkinson, *Yeats,* 2 (1984), 272-75.

7. COWELL, RAYMOND: *W. B. Yeats.* London: Evans, 1969. 160 pp. (Literature in Perspective.)

A study of "Yeats's life, poetry and thought" (p. 37), aimed at the "ordinary reader" and neglecting almost entirely the prose and the plays.

Reviews:
- Anon., *Teacher,* 14 Mar 1969, 17.
- Patrick Murray: "'W. B.' Plain," *IrP,* 15 Feb 1969, 10.
- J. Trautmann, *UES,* 8:2 (June 1970), 61.

8. CULLINGFORD, ELIZABETH (ed): *Yeats: Poems, 1919-1935. A Casebook.* London: Macmillan, 1984. 238 pp.

Editor's introduction, pp. 8-22, a survey of the more important criticism of Yeats's poetry. This is followed by reprinted pieces (not analyzed in this bibliography).

Reviews:
- Seamus Deane: "Yeats and the Occult," *LRB,* 18-31 Oct 1984, 27.
- Jacqueline Genet, *EA,* 39:2 (Apr-June 1986), 236-37.
- Peter van de Kamp, *IUR,* 15:1 (Spring 1985), 108-11.
- Declan Kiberd: "Taking Stock of Yeats," *TLS,* 13 Feb 1987, 166.
- James Simmons, *N&Q,* os 231 / ns 33:2 (June 1986), 267.

9. CURRIE, W. T., and GRAHAM HANDLEY: *Brodie's Notes on W. B. Yeats: Selected Poetry.* London: Pan Educational, 1978. 119 pp.

Contains a biographical introduction, "Guidelines to Topics in the Poetry of Yeats," and "Poem Summaries and Textual Notes" for 150 poems.

10. DENTON, MARILYN JEWELL: "The Form of Yeats' Lyric Poetry," Ph.D. thesis, U of Wisconsin, 1957. vii, 225 pp. (*DAI,* 17:12 [Dec 1957], 3012)

"This dissertation suggests that Yeats gave far more attention to poetic form than is generally recognized. The writer consulted Yeats's MS notebooks and 'found passages illustrating his method of composing poems'; with Mrs. Yeats's assistance, transcribed those which illustrated Yeats's concern with form. She discusses in detail his indebtedness to certain poets, including William Morris. She lists Yeats's poems according to their verse forms. She discusses his scattered writings about poetic form. A noteworthy study" (from the evaluation in AC79).

11. EDDINS, DWIGHT LYMAN: *Yeats: The Nineteenth Century Matrix.* University, Ala.: U of Alabama Press, 1971. x, 173 pp.

Based on a Ph.D. thesis, Vanderbilt U, 1967. vii, 178 pp. (*DAI,* 28:10 [Apr 1968], 4123A). Discusses the development of the early poetry from a pictorial to a dramatic mode, seen against the influence, and compared with the poetry, of Keats, Shelley, Thomas Davis, Allingham, Ferguson, Tennyson, Rossetti, Morris, Lionel Johnson, Dowson, Arnold, the Golden Dawn, and French symbolism. Analyzed in sections DD and EE.

Reviews:
- Richard J. Finneran, *JML,* 3:3 (Feb 1974), 835-37.
- [G. S. Fraser]: "Yeats as a Modern Master," *TLS,* 17 Mar 1972, 311.

- Donna Gerstenberger, *OhR,* 14 (Fall 1972), 106-8.
- T. R. Henn, *RES,* 23:90 (May 1972), 234-35.
- Richard M. Kain, *Eire,* 6:4 (Winter 1971), 134-36.
- Donald T. Torchiana: "Some Recent Books on W. B. Yeats," *JIL,* 5:2 (May 1976), 60-81.

12. °ELLMANN, RICHARD: *Yeats.* Wakefield: Sussex Tapes, 1971. (Sussex Tapes: Approach to Criticism Series. A 17.)

A tape recording, length ca. 60 mins.; contains two lectures and a booklet with summaries, bibliography, and notes (14 pp.). The first lecture is on "The Poetry of Yeats," the second on "Three Poems" ("The Lake Isle of Innisfree," "Sailing to Byzantium," and "Crazy Jane Talks with the Bishop").

13. FARRINGTON, BRIAN: *Malachi-Stilt-Jack: A Study of W. B. Yeats and His Work.* London: Connolly Publications, [1965?]. 12 pp.

A lecture read to the Connolly Association and Irish Self-Determination League, London, June 1965. Attempts to bring Yeats's "good" poetry and "bad" politics into line, but does not go very deep. Reviewed by Brendan Kennelly, *Hermathena,* 102 (Spring 1966), 96-97.

14. FAULKNER, PETER: *Yeats.* Milton Keynes: Open UP, 1987. viii, 104 pp. (Open Guides to Literature.)

Mainly concerned with the poems in *The Tower* and *The Winding Stair.* Analyzed in section DD.

15. FINNERAN, RICHARD J.: *Editing Yeats's Poems.* London: Macmillan, 1983. x, 144 pp.

A companion to the new edition of the poems (DA51). Its purpose is, "first, to outline the variety and complexity of the problems encountered in editing Yeats's poems; and, secondly, to explain and to defend the solutions adopted for the new text" (p. ix). See also DB86.

Reviews:

- Daniel Albright: "The Magician," *NYRB,* 31 Jan 1985, 29-32.
- John P. Frayne, *JEGP,* 86:1 (Jan 1987), 139-44.
- Jacqueline Genet, *EI,* 8 (Dec 1983), 396-97.
- Warwick Gould: "The Editor Takes Possession," *TLS,* 29 June 1984, 731-33.
- Seamus Heaney: "A New and Surprising Yeats," *NYTBR,* 18 Mar 1984, 1, 35-36; reprinted in *Yeats,* 3 (1985), 260-66.
- Elizabeth Jennings: "How Yeats's Work Unfolded," *Daily Telegraph,* 31 Aug 1984, 6.
- Elizabeth Mackenzie, *N&Q,* os 231 / ns 33:4 (Dec 1986), 565-66.
- Cóilin Owens: "The Poems of W. B. Yeats," *ILS,* 3:2 (Fall 1984), 28.
- Michael J. Sidnell: "Unacceptable Hypotheses: The New Edition of Yeats's Poems and Its Making," *YeA,* 3 (1985), 225-43.

16. FURBANK, PHILIP NICHOLAS: *W. B. Yeats.* Prepared by P. N. Furbank for the Course Team. Milton Keynes: Open UP, 1976. 61 pp. (The Open University. Arts: A Third Level Course. Twentieth Century Poetry: Units 14-17.)

An introduction to the poetry and to *A Vision* (which, according to Furbank, is illuminated by the poetry and not the other way round). Reviewed by David C. Nimmo, *Four Decades,* Special Review Supplement (Jan 1979), 16-18.

17. ———: *W. B. Yeats.* Milton Keynes: Open UP, 1983. vi, 104 pp.

plus 1 audio cassette and cassette notes (8 pp.)
Presumably a revised version of the preceding item; essentially a guide to the poetry with an appendix on *A Vision*. The cassette contains poems and songs read or sung by Yeats, Basil Bunting, and others; also *Purgatory*, spoken by Cyril Cusack and Jim Norton, produced by Nuala O'Faolain (see CD400).

18. GARAB, ARRA M.: *Beyond Byzantium: The Last Phase of Yeats's Career*. DeKalb: Northern Illinois UP, 1969. ix, 133 pp.
Based on the more adequately titled "Beyond Byzantium: Studies in the Later Poetry of William Butler Yeats," °Ph.D. thesis, Columbia U, 1962. 200 pp. (*DAI*, 26:3 [Sept 1965], 1645-46).
Incorporates: "Yeats's 'Dark betwixt the Polecat and the Owl,'" *ELN*, 2:3 (Mar 1965), 218-20; "Yeats and the Forged Casement Diaries," *ELN*, 2:4 (June 1965), 289-92; "Fabulous Artifice: Yeats's 'Three Bushes' Sequence," *Criticism*, 7:3 (Summer 1965), 235-49; "Times of Glory: Yeats's 'The Municipal Gallery Revisited,'" *ArQ*, 21:3 (Autumn 1965), 243-54.
Mainly concerned with the poems of the last decade, 1929-39. Discusses the time and escape theme, the Crazy Jane poems, the place of "The Gyres" in Yeats's poetry, "Lapis Lazuli," the Casement poems (identifying Gilbert Murray as one of Yeats's villains), "Three Songs to the One Burden," and other poems.
Reviews:
- James L. Allen: "Recent Yeatsiana: The Failed Quest for Unity of Being," *JML*, 2:1 (Sept 1971), 148-58.
- James Brazell, *Eire*, 10:1 (Spring 1975), 144-46.
- W. Bronzwaer, *DQR*, 1:1 (1971), 42-43.
- William M. Carpenter, *MP*, 68:4 (May 1971), 398-400.
- Edward Engelberg, *ConL*, 11:2 (Spring 1970), 303-9.
- René Fréchet, *EA*, 28:1 (Jan-Mar 1975), 106-7.
- George P. Mayhew, *BA*, 45:1 (Jan 1971), 129-30.
- Charles Molesworth: "He Kept a Sword Upstairs," *Nation*, 11 Jan 1971, 58, 60.
- Howard Sergeant, *English*, 20:106 (Spring 1971), 26-27.
- Paul H. Stacy: "Yeats's Dualities: Two Restatements," *HSL*, 2:1 (1970), 68-69.
- [F. A. C. Wilson], *WCR*, 5:3 (Jan 1971), 66.

19. GREEN, HOWARD LEWIS: "The Poetry of W. B. Yeats: A Critical Evaluation," Ph.D. thesis, Stanford U, 1952. v, 510 pp.
On Yeats's theories of poetry and his poems. A thesis supervised by Yvor Winters and written along the lines of his criticism, but less hostile to Yeats.

20. HACKETT, VIRGINIA M.: "The Poetic Sequences of William Butler Yeats," Ph.D. thesis, New York U, 1973. 470 pp. (*DAI*, 34:3 [Sept 1973], 1279A)
Discusses "Upon a Dying Lady," "Meditations in Time of Civil War," "A Man Young and Old," "Words for Music Perhaps," "A Woman Young and Old," "Supernatural Songs," "The Three Bushes," "Nineteen Hundred and Nineteen," and "Vacillation."

21. HESSENBERGER, ERNST: *Metapoesie und Metasprache in der Lyrik von W. B. Yeats und T. S. Eliot*. Passau: Haller, 1986. xiv, 395 pp.
Originally a Dr.phil. thesis, U of Passau, 1986. Discusses "poetic statements on poetry and linguistic reflexions on language" in the poems of both writers in order to connect them with their poetic theories. No index.

22. HIRSCHBERG, STUART: *At the Top of the Tower: Yeats's Poetry Explored through "A Vision."* Heidelberg: Winter, 1979. 145 pp. (Anglistische Forschungen. 135.)

Based on "*A Vision* and Yeats's Quest for a Unified Aesthetic Myth," Ph.D. thesis, New York U, 1972. ii, 337 pp. (*DAI*, 33:11 [May 1973], 6357A). Contains chapters on *A Vision* and *Per Amica Silentia Lunae* and incorporates the following:

"Yeats's 'On Woman,'" *CJIS*, 1:2 (Nov 1975), 34-35.

"The Shaping Role of *A Vision* in Yeats's 'Crazy Jane' Poems," *CJIS*, 4:1 (June 1978), 45-53.

"A Dialogue between Realism and Idealism in Yeats's 'Ego Dominus Tuus,'" *CLQ*, 11:2 (June 1975), 129-32.

"Yeats and the Meditative Poem," *Eire*, 9:4 (Winter 1974), 94-101 (on "Meditations in Time of Civil War").

"Why Yeats Saw Himself as a '*Daimonic* Man' of Phase 17: A Complementary View," *ELN*, 11:3 (Mar 1974), 202-5 (because of astronomical and astrological reasons).

"Yeats' 'The Phases of the Moon,' 118-23," *Expl*, 32:9 (May 1974), item 75.

"Yeats' 'Crazy Jane and Jack the Journeyman,'" *Expl*, 37:2 (Winter 1979), 21.

"Yeats' 'Crazy Jane Reproved,'" *Expl*, 37:2 (Winter 1979), 22.

"Yeats' 'A Dialogue of Self and Soul,'" *Expl*, 37:2 (Winter 1979), 23-24.

"Campbell's 'Monomyth' and the Exploration Pattern in Yeats's 'A Dialogue of Self and Soul,'" *Exploration*, 1 (1973), 47-52.

"The Visionary Landscape of Yeats's 'The Tower,'" *LWU*, 10:3 (1977), 194-201.

"Yeats's 'The Phases of the Moon': Towards a Lunar Myth," *Notre Dame English J*, 9:2 (Spring 1974), 73-76.

"Yeats's 'Vision of Evil' in 'Meditations in Time of Civil War,'" *NConL*, 4:3 (May 1974), 13-14.

"The Influence of the Japanese Noh Play, *Nishikigi*, on Yeats's 'Crazy Jane' Poems," *NConL*, 6:3 (May 1976), 2-3.

"Masefield's Influence in Yeats's 'Under Ben Bulben,'" *NConL*, 6:4 (Sept 1976), 8-12.

"Beyond Tragedy: Yeats's View of History in 'The Gyres,'" *RS*, 42:1 (Mar 1974), 50-55.

"The Shaping Role of *A Vision* on W. B. Yeats's 'The Double Vision of Michael Robartes,'" *Studies*, 68:269-270 (Spring/Summer 1979), 109-13.

"The 'Whirling Gyres' of History," *Studies*, 68:272 (Winter 1979), 305-14.

"'All Souls' Night': A Prototype for 'Byzantium,'" *YER*, 5:1 (1978), 44-50.

"An Encounter with the Supernatural in Yeats's 'The Spirit Medium,'" in Harper: *Yeats and the Occult* (1975, FC40), 311-16.

Reviews:
- Eitel F. Timm, *LWU*, 14:4 (Dec 1981), 240-41.
- Wolfgang Wicht, *ZAA*, 31:1 (1983), 72-73.

23. JEFFARES, ALEXANDER NORMAN: *The Poetry of W. B. Yeats*. Great Neck, N.Y.: Barron's Educational Series, 1961. 64 pp. (Studies in English Literature. 4.)

The English edition was published as °*W. B. Yeats: The Poems*. London: Arnold, 1961. The series attempts to give "close critical analyses and evaluations of individual works" and to present "studies of individual plays, novels and groups of poems and essays" (p. 5). In this sense, the booklet is a failure--the subject is much too large. On its own terms, however, it is a useful short introduction to Yeats's poetry.

Reviews:

- Birgit Bramsbäck, *SN,* 34:1 (1962), 171-72.
- R. P. Draper, *CritQ,* 3:3 (Autumn 1961), 274.

24. ———: *A Commentary on the Collected Poems of W. B. Yeats.* Stanford: Stanford UP, 1968. xxxiv, 563 pp.

Explains, poem by poem, allusions, references, and obscurities, but does not interpret. The value of the book is indisputable, but some criticism has to be made: (1) More interpretations should have been cited, not just those dealing with bibliographical and background material. (2) Sometimes Jeffares belabors the obvious or quotes too copiously from material that is easily accessible elsewhere. (3) There is, regrettably, no index of names. See also the following item.

Reviews:

- Anon.: "Coughing in Ink: The Scholiast upon Yeats," *Human World,* 4 (Aug 1971), 73-86. An extremely hostile review.
- Merlin Bowen, *MP,* 67:3 (Feb 1970), 294-95.
- Edward Engelberg, *VP,* 8:4 (Winter 1970), 354-56.
- [G. S. Fraser]: "Open Yeats," *TLS,* 2 Jan 1969, 7. Suggests that some lines in "Sailing to Byzantium" show similarities to Marvell's "The Garden." See correspondence by Francis Noel Lees, 23 Jan 1969, 69, where the disputed lines are traced back to Tennyson; by Fraser, ibid.; and by Morchard Bishop, 30 Jan 1969, 112.
- Arra M. Garab: "The Legacy of Yeats," *JML,* 1:1 (1970), 137-40.
- Geoffrey Grigson: "Use and Misuse of Folklore," *Country Life,* 2 Jan 1969, 43.
- George Mills Harper: "To Know All about Everything: Facts about Yeats," *CEA,* 32:7 (Apr 1970), 14.
- T. R. Henn, *CambR,* 90:2186 (31 Jan 1969), 240-41.
- Brendan Kennelly: "Yeats and Blake," *Hibernia,* 29 Nov--12 Dec 1968, 14.
- Heinz Kosok, *NS,* 20:3 (Mar 1971), 167-68.
- R. H. Lass, *Criticism,* 11:4 (Fall 1969), 391-93.
- John Rees Moore, *ACIS Newsletter,* Spring 1970, 13-15.
- John Mosier, *NOR,* 1:4 (Summer 1969), 387-88.
- Hermann Peschmann, *English,* 19:103 (Spring 1970), 28-29.
- Peter Ure: "About Yeats," *Guardian,* 20 Dec 1968, 7.
- Stanley Weintraub, *BA,* 43:2 (Spring 1969), 266.

25. ———: *A New Commentary on the Poems of W. B. Yeats.* London: Macmillan, 1984. xxxix, 543 pp.

New and revised edition of the previous item, still without an index and without more than cursory reference to previously published criticism and interpretation.

Reviews:

- Daniel Albright: "The Magician," *NYRB,* 31 Jan 1985, 29-32.
- Seamus Deane: "Yeats and the Occult," *LRB,* 18-31 Oct 1984, 27.
- Denis Donoghue: "Textual Choices," *THES,* 8 June 1984, 20.
- Richard J. Finneran: "W. B. Yeats: A Commentary on the New Commentary," *Review,* 7 (1985), 163-89. See also DB86.
- Warwick Gould: "The Editor Takes Possession," *TLS,* 29 June 1984, 731-33.
- Josephine Johnson, *LPer,* 6:2 (Apr 1986), 103-4.
- Augustine Martin: "Yeats: Vision and Revision," *IrT,* 16 June 1984, 12.
- John Montague: "What to Make of W. B. Yeats," *Guardian,* 14 June 1984, 21.

- James Olney, *Yeats*, 3 (1985), 229-38.
- Michael J. Sidnell: "Unacceptable Hypotheses: The New Edition of Yeats's Poems and Its Making," *YeA*, 3 (1985), 225-43.

26. ———: *W. B. Yeats*. London: Routledge & Kegan Paul, 1971. x, 118 pp. (Profiles in Literature Series.)

An introduction to Yeats's poetry under subject headings such as love poetry, poems related to *A Vision*, self, classicism, Ireland, friendship, heroic gesture. Analyzed in section DD.

Reviews:
- Anon.: "Coughing in Ink: The Scholiast upon Yeats," *Human World*, 4 (Aug 1971), 73-86.
- Gulliver Boyle: "Beautiful Women v. the Furies," *Teacher*, 6 Aug 1971), 7.
- Anthony Cronin: "Yeats Seminar," *IrP*, 26 June 1971, 12.
- Bryn Davies, *Wascana R*, 6:2 (1972), 75-78.
- Michael Hartnett: "Handbook on Yeat's [sic]," *IrT*, 22 May 1971, 10.
- John Jordan: "Introduction to Yeats' Poetry," *IrI*, 8 May 1971, 6.

27. ———: *W. B. Yeats: Selected Poems*. Notes by A. N. Jeffares. London: Longman / York Press, 1986. 112 pp. (York Notes.)

Notes on about 90 poems, commentary, hints for study, etc.

28. KOCH, VIVIENNE: *W. B. Yeats: The Tragic Phase. A Study of the Last Poems*. [Hamden, Ct.]: Archon Books, 1969 [1951]. 151 pp.

Interpretations, with strong emphasis on the sexual theme, of the following poems: "The Wild Old Wicked Man," "An Acre of Grass," "The Statues," "A Bronze Head," "The Gyres," "The Man and the Echo," "The Three Bushes," "The Lady's First (Second and Third) Song." See also DD333.

Reviews:
- Anon., *List*, 17 May 1951, 807.
- William Becker, *DM*, 27:1 (Jan-Mar 1952), 46-48.
- ———: "On the Margin of Yeats," *Poetry*, 81:5 (Feb 1953), 331-34.
- Helen Bevington, *SAQ*, 52:1 (Jan 1953), 157.
- M. C. Bradbrook: "La critique à la Robinson," *NSt*, 9 June 1951, 658-59.
- M.-L. Cazamian: "L'évolution de W. B. Yeats après ses dernières oeuvres," *EA*, 5:1 (Feb 1952), 50-54.
- Austin Clarke: "The Fire-born Moods," *IrT*, 12 May 1951, 6.
- [———]: "Aspects of Yeats's Poetry," *TLS*, 1 June 1951, 339.
- Stanley K. Coffman, *BA*, 27:3 (Summer 1953), 305.
- Babette Deutsch: "Yeats Study," *NYHTB*, 24 Aug 1952, 9.
- Richard Eberhart: "New Looks at Yeats," *VQR*, 28:4 (Autumn 1952), 618-21.
- Richard Ellmann: "Three Ways of Looking at a Triton," *SR*, 61:1 (Jan-Mar 1953), 149-56.
- Kimon Friar: "Contrapuntal Serpent," *NewRep*, 28 Apr 1952, 17-18.
- F. W. van Heerikhuizen: "Gedreven door angst," *Litterair paspoort*, 7:53 (Jan 1952), 10-11.
- Roger McHugh: "Yeats, Synge and the Abbey Theatre," *Studies*, 41:163-64 (Sept-Dec 1952), 333-40.
- Ewart Milne: "The Glittering Eye," *IrW*, 16 (Sept 1951), 54-58.
- W. W. Robson: "Yeats's Last Poems," *Dublin R*, 225:453 (Third Quarter 1951), 83-86.
- Grover Smith, *New Mexico Q*, 23:3 (Autumn 1953), 324-25.

- Peter Ure, *Cambridge J,* 5:9 (June 1952), 571-72.
- Earl R. Wasserman, *MLN,* 68:3 (Mar 1953), 185-90.

29. LAL, D. K.: *W. B. Yeats: Selected Poems (A Study of Yeats's Important Poems).* Bareilly: Prakash Book Depot, 1971. viii, 114 pp.
Contains a general introduction and notes on 33 poems. Full of mistakes and misprints; negligible.

30. LEVINE, BERNARD: *The Dissolving Image: The Spiritual-Esthetic Development of W. B. Yeats.* Detroit: Wayne State UP, 1970. 181 pp.
Based on "The Dissolving Image: A Concentrative Analysis of Yeats' Poetry," Ph.D. thesis, Brown U, 1965. vi, 376 pp. (*DAI,* 26:6 [Dec 1965], 3341-42). Includes: "Yeats' Aesthetics and His Concept of Self," *Universitas,* 4 (1966), 138-48; "'High Talk': A Concentrative Analysis of a Poem by Yeats," *JJQ,* 3:2 (Winter 1966), 124-29; "A Psychopoetic Analysis of Yeats's 'Leda and the Swan,'" *BuR,* 17:1 (Mar 1969), 85-111.
Views the poetry "as external form dissolving toward its invisible center, the spiritual demesne of the speaker's self-transforming awareness" (pp. 9-10). Analyzed in sections DD and EE.
Reviews:
- James L. Allen: "Recent Yeatsiana: The Failed Quest for Unity of Being," *JML,* 2:1 (Sept 1971), 148-54.
- Giles Gunn, *MP,* 69:1 (Aug 1971), 87-91.
- T. R. Henn, *RES,* 23:89 (Feb 1972), 100-101.
- Elizabeth Mackenzie, *N&Q,* os 218 / ns 20:9 (Sept 1973), 359-60.
- Norman H. MacKenzie: "The Yeats Canon and Recent Scholarship," *QQ,* 78:3 (Autumn 1971), 462-64.
- Howard Sergeant, *English,* 20:106 (Spring 1971), 26-27.

31. MORTON, RICHARD: *Notes on the Poetry of William Butler Yeats.* Toronto: Coles Publishing Co., 1971. iii, 80 pp. (Coles Notes. 1119.)
Also published as *An Outline of the Poetry of William Butler Yeats.* Toronto: Forum House, 1971. iii, 80 pp.

32. MUNDRA, S. C.: *W. B. Yeats and His Poetry (With Critical Introduction and Exhaustive Notes).* Bareilly: Prakash Book Depot, 1971. viii, 264 pp.
Contains a general introduction to Yeats life and work and notes on 25 poems. Somewhat elementary.

33. *Notes on W. B. Yeats's Poetry.* London: Methuen, 1980. v, 88 pp. (Methuen Notes: Study Aid Series.)
No author given; Cyril Kemp is listed as copyright holder. An introduction to the poetry on the undergraduate level, including short chapters on the Irish historical and political background and Yeats's spiritual and mystical interests.

34. O'DONNELL, WILLIAM H.: *The Poetry of William Butler Yeats: An Introduction.* NY: Ungar, 1986. xvi, 192 pp.
Contains a chronology, a short biography, chapters on "Backgrounds for Reading Yeats's Poems" and "Yeats and Modern Poetry," and short interpretations of some 35 poems. Analyzed in section DD.
Reviews:
- Richard J. Finneran: "Two on Yeats," *ELT,* 31:3 (1988), 320-24.
- Earl G. Ingersoll, *Eire,* 22:4 (Winter 1987), 158-59.

35. PARKINSON, THOMAS FRANCIS: *W. B. Yeats, Self-Critic: A Study of His Early Verse, and The Later Poetry.* Two vols. in one. Berkeley:

U of California Press, 1971. xv, 196; xi, 260 pp.

Part 1, first published in 1951, is based on °"Yeats as a Critic of His Early Verse," Ph.D. thesis, U of California (Berkeley), 1949. Incorporates "W. B. Yeats: A Poet's Stagecraft," *ELH*, 17:2 (June 1950), 136-61. Discusses the revisions of the early poems (1889-1901) up to 1933 and the interaction of dramatic and lyric writing during that period; also on *On Baile's Strand*, *The Shadowy Waters*, and Yeats's dramatic theories.

Part 2 was first published in 1964. Incorporates: "The Sun and the Moon in Yeats's Early Poetry," *MP*, 50:1 (Aug 1952), 50-58; "Intimate and Impersonal: An Aspect of Modern Poetics," *JAAC*, 16:3 (Mar 1958), 373-83; "Vestiges of Creation," *SR*, 69:1 (Winter 1961), 80-111. Discusses Yeats's iconography (swan, sun, and moon), prosody, and poetics as emerging from the poetry, as well as the revisions from MS. to printed version.

Both parts are analyzed in sections DD and EE.

Reviews of Part 1:
- Anon., *List*, 17 July 1952, 111, 113.
- Anon., *USQBR*, 8:1 (Mar 1952), 28-29.
- [Austin Clarke]: "A Poet's Revision," *TLS*, 5 Sept 1952, 582.
- Richard Eberhart: "New Looks at Yeats," *VQR*, 28:4 (Autumn 1952), 618-21.
- Richard Ellmann: "Three Ways of Looking at a Triton," *SR*, 61:1 (Jan-Mar 1953), 149-56.
- Martin Price: "Three Critiques of Modern Poetry," *YR*, 41:3 (Mar 1952), 458-61.
- Horace Reynolds: "'To Follow Yeats Down All the Diverse Paths,'" *CSM*, 12 June 1952, 13.

Reviews of Part 2:
- James L. Allen, *MP*, 62:4 (May 1965), 369-70.
- ———, *WHR*, 19:1 (Winter 1965), 90-92.
- Anon., *Quarterly R*, 303:643 (Jan 1965), 115-16.
- Harold Bloom: "Myth, Vision, Allegory," *YR*, 54:1 (Oct 1964), 143-49.
- Donald Davie: "Bardolators and Blasphemers," *Guardian*, 12 June 1965, 7.
- William Empson: "A Time of Troubles," *NSt*, 23 July 1965, 123-24; reprinted in CB149a.
- Edward Engelberg, *MQR*, 5:1 (Winter 1966), 65-66.
- Peter Faulkner, *DUJ*, os 57 / ns 26:3 (June 1965), 180-81.
- [G. S. Fraser]: "From Sligo to Byzantium," *TLS*, 24 June 1965, 529-30.
- T. R. Henn, *MLR*, 60:3 (July 1965), 440-41.
- John Montague, *CritQ*, 8:4 (Winter 1966), 381-83.
- W. R. Rodgers, *List*, 25 Nov 1965, 867-68.
- Peter Ure, *RES*, 16:63 (Aug 1965), 328-31.
- Thomas R. Whitaker, *ELN*, 2:2 (Dec 1964), 150-54.
- George T. Wright, *JAAC*, 23:3 (Spring 1965), 392-93.

Reviews of the Combined Edition:
- Gabriella Corradini Favati, *RLMC*, 27:2 (June 1974), 157-60.
- Donna Gerstenberger, *OhR*, 14:1 (Fall 1972), 106-8.
- Irene Haugh: "Yeats at Work," *IrT*, 12 Aug 1972, 10.

36. PERLOFF, MARJORIE GABRIELLE: *Rhyme and Meaning in the Poetry of Yeats*. The Hague: Mouton, 1970. 249 pp. (De Proprietatibus Litterarum. Series Practica. 5.)

Based on a Ph.D. thesis, Catholic U of America, 1965. vi, 232 pp. (*DAI*, 26:11 [May 1966], 6721-22). Includes about a hundred pages of statistical tables.

As indicated in the book's title, this is a study of the vari-

ous contributions made by rhyme in establishing the meaning of Yeats's poems. One chapter is devoted to the Byzantium poems; other substantial discussions are analyzed in section DD.
Reviews:
- [G. S. Fraser]: "Saving Yeats from the Critics," *TLS,* 12 Mar 1971, 292.
- Giles Gunn, *MP,* 69:1 (Aug 1971), 87-91.
- Stanley Poss, *JML,* 3:3 (Feb 1974), 839-41.

37. RAI, VIKRAMADITYA: *The Poetry of W. B. Yeats.* Delhi: Doaba House, 1971. viii, 261 pp.
Contains chapters on "The Making of the Poet" (nationalism, magic, various influences) and on "Yeats and the Romantic Tradition" (mask, symbolism, and "system"), followed by notes on some 80 poems and a chapter on the stylistic development.

38. SALINGER, HELLMUT: *William Butler Yeats: Seine Gedichte und Gedanken.* Bern: Francke, 1983. 183 pp.
A study of the development of the poetry, including a chapter on "occultism and philosophy," and an extended comparison with Stefan George. Analyzed in section DD.

39. SCHILLER, DANIEL HENRY: "W. B. Yeats: The Evolution of a Prosodic Style," Ph.D. thesis, Columbia U, 1977. vi, 309 pp. (*DAI,* 38:5 [Nov 1977], 2780A-81A)
A chronological survey of the poetry.

40. SEN, SRI CHANDRA: *Four Essays on the Poetry of Yeats.* Santiniketan: Visva-Bharati, 1968. v, 141 pp.
Contents: "The Irish Element in the Evolution of the Poetry of W. B. Yeats," 1-33; reprinted from *BDE,* 4:1&2 (1963), 13-25, :3&4 (1963), 1-13.
"The Love Lyrics of Yeats," 34-67; reprinted from *BDE,* 5:16&17 (1963), 13-38. Discusses the "island" theme, the "Maud Gonne Cycle," and the "Iseult [Gonne] Group of Poems."
"Time-Theme in the Poetry of Yeats," 68-108; reprinted from *BDE,* 5:18&19 (1964), 82-112.
"A Critical Study of Yeatsian Vocabulary," 109-41; reprinted from *VQ,* 31:2 (1965-66), 133-69.

41. °SENGUPTA, SUDHAYU KUMAR: "The Poetical Development of W. B. Yeats with a Study of Some Texts," Ph.D. thesis, U of Leeds, 1936. 2 vols.

42. SLAN, JONATHAN HART: "The Relationship of W. B. Yeats's Essays and *A Vision* to the Development of His Poetry," Ph.D. thesis, U of Toronto, 1974. viii, 274 pp. (*DAI,* 36:3 [Sept 1975], 1537A-38A)

43. SPIVAK, GAYATRI CHAKRAVORTY: "The Great Wheel: Stages in the Personality of Yeats's Lyric Speaker," Ph.D. thesis, Cornell U, 1967. ix, 296 pp. (*DAI,* 28:10 [Apr 1968], 4188A)
Investigates the relationship between the poetry and *A Vision* and claims that "the chronology of the Phases of the Moon is intimately linked to the successive periods of Yeats's poetry" (p. viii). Mainly on "The Wild Swans at Coole," "The Tower," "The Black Tower," and "Cuchulain Comforted."

44. STALLWORTHY, JON HOWIE: *Between the Lines: Yeats's Poetry in the Making.* Oxford: Clarendon Press, 1965 [1963]. xi, 262 pp.
Based on a B.Litt. thesis, Oxford U, 1960. iv, 312 pp. Discusses

Yeats's principles of revision in general and the following poems in particular: "The Second Coming" (but see DD603), "A Prayer for My Daughter," "The Sorrow of Love," "The Gift of Harun Al-Rashid," "Sailing to Byzantium," "Chosen," "Parting," "In Memory of Eva Gore-Booth and Con Markiewicz," "Coole Park, 1929," "Memory," "Consolation," "After Long Silence," "The Nineteenth Century and After," "The Results of Thought," "An Acre of Grass," "A Bronze Head," and "The Black Tower."

Reviews:

- Timothy Brownlow, *Dubliner,* 3:2 (Summer 1964), 71-73.
- Robert Conquest: "Celtic Highlight," *Spect,* 3 May 1963, 577-78; reprinted in *The Abomination of Moab.* London: Temple Smith, 1979. x, 277 pp. (pp. 16-18).
- Stephen Fanning, *Kilkenny Magazine,* 10 (Autumn-Winter 1963), 127, 129, 131.
- D. J. Gordon and Ian Fletcher: "Only a Magnifying Glass," *Review,* 9 (Oct 1963), 53-58. Criticizes the discussion of "In Memory of Eva Gore-Booth and Con Markiewicz" and "After Long Silence."
- [A. Norman Jeffares]: "Thinking on Paper," *TLS,* 29 Mar 1963, 218.
- ————: "The Yeats Country," *MLQ,* 25:2 (June 1964), 218-22.
- Louis MacNeice: "Yeats at Work," *List,* 21 Mar 1963, 521. Reprinted in CB288.
- Horace Reynolds: "'It Is Myself That I Remake,'" *CSM,* 26 Sept 1963, 13.
- Howard Sergeant, *English,* 14:83 (Summer 1963), 203-5.
- Peter Ure, *RES,* 15:60 (Nov 1964), 444-47.
- Helen Hennessy Vendler: "Assimilating Yeats," *MR,* 7:3 (Summer 1966), 590-97.

45. ————: *Vision and Revision in Yeats's "Last Poems."* Oxford: Clarendon Press, 1969. xi, 182 pp.

Incorporates: "Two of Yeats's Last Poems," *REL,* 4:3 (July 1963), 48-69.

"W. B. Yeats and the Dynastic Theme," *CritQ,* 7:3 (Autumn 1965), 247-65; on the "concern with the ties of blood" in Yeats's poetry and in other 20th-century poets, notably Robert Lowell, Anne Sexton, Philip Larkin, Anthony Thwaite, and Tony Connor (the paragraphs on Sexton, etc., are not reprinted in the book).

"W. B. Yeats's 'Under Ben Bulben,'" *RES,* 17:65 (Feb 1966), 30-53.

Discusses and prints the early drafts of "Lapis Lazuli," "The Man and the Echo," "The Three Bushes," "The Lady's First (Second and Third) Song," "The Lover's Song," "The Chambermaid's First (and Second) Song," "The Spur," "Long-legged Fly," "The Statues," and "Under Ben Bulben." The interpretations are prefaced by the shortened article from *CritQ* and an essay on "The Prophetic Voice," both of which have very little to do with the main argument.

Reviews:

- Curtis Bradford, *MLQ,* 31:1 (Mar 1970), 133-35.
- Patrick Diskin, *N&Q,* os 219 / ns 21:10 (Oct 1974), 388-89.
- Edward Engelberg, *ConL,* 11:2 (Spring 1970), 303-9.
- Roy Fuller: "Terrors of Fame," *List,* 13 Feb 1969, 212-13.
- Giles Gunn, *MP,* 69:1 (Aug 1971), 87-91.
- Edwin Honig: "On Knowing Yeats," *VQR,* 45:4 (Autumn 1969), 700-704.
- A. Norman Jeffares, *RES,* 21:84 (Nov 1970), 532.
- Thomas Kinsella: "Art and Labour," *IrP,* 29 Mar 1969, 12.

- Sean Lucy: "Yeats's Poems in the Making," *IrI,* 26 Apr 1969, 6.
- V. K. Moelwyn-Hughes, *UES,* 7:3 (Sept 1969), 117-18.
- J. R. Mulryne, *MLR,* 65:4 (Oct 1970), 893-94.
- Hermann Peschmann, *English,* 19:103 (Spring 1970), 28-29.
- R[obin] S[kelton], *Malahat R,* 11 (July 1969), 127-28.

46. THURLEY, GEOFFREY: *The Turbulent Dream: Passion and Politics in the Poetry of W. B. Yeats.* St. Lucia: U of Queensland Press, 1983. viii, 235 pp.

Discusses "root-words" in the poetry, especially "dream" and "disturb" and their equivalents and derivatives, also Yeats's "thought-processes" and his views on Irish history and politics.

Reviewed by K. P. S. Jochum, *Yeats,* 3 (1985), 254-57.

47. TINDALL, WILLIAM YORK: *W. B. Yeats.* NY: Columbia UP, 1966. 48 pp. (Columbia Essays on Modern Writers. 15.)

48. *Tributes in Prose and Verse to Shotaro Oshima, President of the Yeats Society of Japan, on the Occasion of His Seventieth Birthday, September 29th 1969.* Tokyo: Hokuseido Press, 1970. iii, 30 pp.

Also published in CA149. Partial contents:

A. Norman Jeffares: "Pallas Athene Gonne," 4-7; the sources for the mythologizing treatment of Maud Gonne in Yeats's poems.

Brendan Kennelly: "Yeats and Unity," 8-9.

Sheelah Kirby: "The Importance of Place and Place-Names in the Poetry of W. B. Yeats," 10-12.

James Kirkup: "W. B. Yeats and the Dolls," 13-21; the doll symbol in Yeats's poetry.

Roger McHugh: "A Note on Some Later Poems of W. B. Yeats," 22-23.

Kathleen Raine: "Written with Yeats's Pen: For Shotaro Oshima, Aetat 70," 24. Poem.

Frank Tuohy: "W. B. Yeats: Some Thoughts in 1970," 28-30.

49. UNTERECKER, JOHN: *A Reader's Guide to William Butler Yeats.* NY: Noonday Press, 1963 [1959]. x, 310 pp. (Noonday Paperback. 138.)

The book "is intended to supplement Yeats's *Collected Poems* by providing for the reader some of the basic information he will need in order to come to an intelligent evaluation of those poems" (p. vii). Substantial notes are analyzed in section DD.

Reviews:

- Austin Clarke: "A Scholar in Elfland," *IrT,* 31 Oct 1959, 6.
- René Fréchet: "L'étude de Yeats: Textes, jugements et éclairissements," *EA,* 14:1 (Jan-Mar 1961), 36-47.
- T. R. Henn, *List,* 5 Nov 1959, 788, 791.
- Thomas Hogan: "The Light Is Dark Enough," *Guardian,* 27 Nov 1959, 15.
- F. J. K.: "Guide to Yeats--Or Is It?" *IrI,* 19 Dec 1959, 8. It is not.
- Thomas Parkinson: "The Respect of Monuments," *SR,* 68:1 (Jan-Mar 1960), 143-49.
- Charles Poore: "Books of the Times," *NYT,* 8 Aug 1959, 15.
- Martin Steinmann, *CE,* 22:6 (Mar 1961), 443-44.

50. WINTERS, YVOR: *The Poetry of W. B. Yeats.* Denver: Swallow, 1960. 24 pp. (Swallow Pamphlets. 10.)

Reprinted in *TCL,* 6:1 (Apr 1960), 3-24; *Dubliner,* 2 (Mar 1962), 7-33; and with slight revisions in *Forms of Discovery: Critical and Historical Essays on the Forms of the Short Poem in Eng-*

lish. [Denver]: Swallow, 1967. xxii, 377 pp. (pp. 204-34).
Extracts Yeats's "beliefs" from his poetry and finds that he does not like them. Hence Yeats's poetry is not "great." Dislikes Yeats's dramatizations of other people and thinks that the respective poems are inflated. See CB331, 362, CD854, 1450-1451.
Reviews:
- [G. S. Fraser]: "Yeats in Winters's Grip," *TLS*, 18 Feb 1965, 126.
- John B. Gleason, *Ramparts*, 2:1 (May 1963), 94-96.
- John R. Moore: "Swan or Goose," *SR*, 71:1 (Jan-Mar 1963), 123-33.

51. YEATS, W. B.: *The Poems: A New Edition*. Edited by Richard J. Finneran. Dublin: Gill & Macmillan / London: Macmillan, 1984. xxv, 747 pp.
Reissued in 1984 with three major printing errors corrected and an errata slip included. The American edition (NY: Macmillan) was published late in 1983; second revised printing, 1984. See Richard Garnett: "Finneran's Yeats," *LRB*, 1-14 Nov 1984, 4.
Apart from the texts, the edition contains explanatory notes to Yeats's notes (pp. 600-8), the "Music from *New Poems*, 1938" (pp. 609-12), explanatory notes to the poems (pp. 613-708), and textual notes (pp. 709-17). Finneran's letter announcing this proposed edition was published in *TLS*, 10 Sept 1976, 1117. See also DA15 and DB86. For reviews see G1572-1597.

52. ———: *Poems of W. B. Yeats: A New Selection*. Selected, with an introduction and notes, by A. Norman Jeffares. London: Macmillan, 1984. xxi, 428 pp.
"Introduction," vii-xviii; "William Butler Yeats: Biographical Summary," 309-12; "Notes," 313-86; "Appendix I: Yeats's Technique as a Poet," 387-93; "Appendix II: Glossary of Irish People and Places in the Poems," 394-407; "Appendix III: Pronunciation of Irish Names," 408-13; "Appendix IV: Maps," 414-18; "Bibliography," 419-20. For reviews see G1600-1603.

53. YOUNG, DUDLEY: *Out of Ireland: A Reading of Yeats's Poetry*. Cheadle, Cheshire: Carcanet Press, 1975. 169 pp.
Reprinted Dingle, Co. Kerry: Brandon, 1982. Concentrates on "The Grey Rock," "Easter 1916," "In Memory of Major Robert Gregory," "Nineteen Hundred and Nineteen," "Lapis Lazuli," "Meditations in Time of Civil War," "Blood and the Moon," "The Tower," "Parnell's Funeral," "High Talk," "The Circus Animals' Desertion," "The Black Tower," and *Purgatory*.
Reviews:
- J. S. Atherton: "The Evidence of the Poem," *TLS*, 6 Feb 1976, 129.
- Ian Fletcher, *JBeckS*, 2 (Summer 1977), 105-7.
- René Fréchet, *EA*, 31:1 (Jan-Mar 1978), 103-4.
- Daniel A. Harris, *JML*, 5:4 (1976), 846-48.
- A. Norman Jeffares: "Coughing in Ink," *SR*, 84:1 (Jan-Mar 1976), 157-67.
- Grevel Lindop: "Poet in Outlandish Clothes," *PNR*, 7 (5:3) (1978), 17-19.
- Shirley Toulson: "Land of Great Hatred and Little Room," *TES*, 10 Sept 1976, 27.

See also AA10, AF1, 2, 4, CA22, 26, 27, 31, 33, 34, 36-38, 49, 57, 60, 61, 63, 65, 68, 73, 77, 92, 100, 103, 110-12, 122, 123, 128, CD10, 224, 711, 1009, 1379, EA3.

DB Substantial Articles and Parts of Books

1. AAS, L.: "William Butler Yeats og hans verker lyrik, prosadiktning og kritik," *Ord och bild,* 36:3 (Mar 1927), 145-52.
Mainly on the poetry, not much on the prose.

2. ADAMS, HAZARD: "The 'Book' of Yeats's Poems," *Cornell R,* 1 (Spring 1977), 119-28.
The *Collected Poems* and *A Vision* as coherent books.

3. ———: "Constituting Yeats's Poems as a Book," *Yeats,* 4 (1986), 1-16.

4. ALBRIGHT, DANIEL: *Lyricality in English Literature.* Lincoln: U of Nebraska Press, 1985. xi, 276 pp.
Frequent references to Yeats's poetry.

5. ALDINGTON, RICHARD: *A. E. Housman & W. B. Yeats: Two Lectures.* Hurst, Berks.: Peacocks Press, 1955. 36 pp.
"W. B. Yeats," 20-35; a rambling essay on Yeats's poetry together with some reminiscences.

6. ALLEN, DON CAMERON (ed): *The Moment of Poetry.* Baltimore: Johns Hopkins Press, 1962. vii, 135 pp. (Percy Graeme Turnbull Memorial Lectures on Poetry. 1961.)
Reprinted in Allen (ed): *A Celebration of Poets.* Baltimore: Johns Hopkins Press, 1967. xi, 241 pp. References to Yeats's poetry in the essays by John Holmes and May Sarton (see index); see also Richard Wilbur: "Round About a Poem of Housman's," 73-98, who criticizes "King and No King" for its obscurity (pp. 92-95).

7. ALSPACH, RUSSELL KING: "A Consideration of the Poets of the Literary Revival in Ireland, 1889-1929," Ph.D. thesis, U of Pennsylvania, 1942. iii, 122 pp.
"William Butler Yeats (1865-1939)," 50-74, presents an enthusiastic account of Yeats's development up to *The Tower.*

8. APPLEWHITE, JAMES: *Seas and Inland Journeys: Landscape and Consciousness from Wordsworth to Roethke.* Athens: U of Georgia Press, 1985. ix, 236 pp.
"Romantic Duality and Unity of Being," 162-95; on *Autobiographies* and some poems. Analyzed in section DD.

9. *Approaches to the Study of Twentieth-Century Literature: Proceedings of the Conference in the Study of Twentieth-Century Literature.* Third session, May 17-18, 1963. East Lansing: Michigan State U, [1964?]. vi, 186 pp.
M. L. Rosenthal: "Alienation of Sensibility and 'Modernity,'" 49-59; repeatedly on Yeats's poetry, especially "Her Anxiety."

10. AUDEN, W. H.: "Yeats as an Example," *KR,* 10:2 (Spring 1948), 187-95.
Reprinted in CA36. Yeats's influence on later poets has been great, but the "side summed up in the *Vision* . . . has left virtually no trace." Yeats's main legacies are the transformation of the occasional poem "into a serious reflective poem of at once personal and public interest" and the release of regular stanzaic poetry "from iambic monotony."

11. BABIĆ, MILICA: "Tragom Jejtsove pesničke reči," *Izraz,* year 23 /

46:9 (Sept 1979), 232-36.
"In search of Yeats's poetic language"; also in *Mostovi*, 10:2 (Apr-June 1979), 153-57.

12. BANERJEE, JAYGOPAL: "W. B. Yeats," *Calcutta R*, series 3 / 26:3 (Mar 1928), 277-91; 27:1 (Apr 1928), 81-101; :2 (May 1928), 141-67; :3 (June 1928), 361-73; 28:1 (July 1928), 109-25; :2 (Aug 1928), 221-39; :3 (Sept 1928), 421-32; 29:1 (Oct 1928), 93-122.
A study of the development of Yeats's poetry, of his symbolism, and of his mysticism. Originally a series of lectures, hence somewhat elementary.

13. BARNES, TERENCE ROBERT: *English Verse: Voice and Movement from Wyatt to Yeats*. Cambridge: UP, 1967. ix, 324 pp.
See pp. 298-320. Yeats was not an esoteric or obscure but a public poet. Comments on "Sailing to Byzantium," "Byzantium," "Among School Children," "Coole Park and Ballylee 1931," and "The Circus Animals' Desertion."

14. BECKER, EDWARD LINDLEY: "The Moment of Vision in W. B. Yeats, Wallace Stevens, T. S. Eliot, and Robinson Jeffers," Ph.D. thesis, U of California, Berkeley, 1980. iv, 323 pp. (*DAI*, 41:7 [Jan 1981], 3101A; reprinted *YeA*, 2 [1983], 97-98)
"The moment of vision is an instant of supreme awareness in which reality is perceived whole" (p. 1).

15. BENSKO, JOHN RICHARD: "Narrative in the Modern Short Poem," Ph.D. thesis, Florida State U, 1985. iv, 299 pp. (*DAI*, 46:8 [Feb 1986], 2297A)
See pp. 87-92.

16. BERRY, FRANCIS: *Poetry and the Physical Voice*. NY: Oxford UP, 1962. x, 205 pp.
On Yeats's method of recording his own poetry, pp. 180-82.

17. BERTHOFF, WARNER: *Literature and the Continuances of Virtue*. Princeton: Princeton UP, 1986. xi, 294 pp.
"The Analogies of Lyric: Shelley, Yeats, Frank O'Hara," 223-73.

18. BLACKBURN, JOHN (ed): *Hardy to Heaney: Twentieth Century Poets. Introductions and Explanations*. Edinburgh: Oliver & Boyd, 1986. 208 pp.
Victor Ashton: "W. B. Yeats," 18-31.

19. BLACKBURN, THOMAS: *The Price of an Eye*. London: Longmans, 1961. 170 pp.
"W. B. Yeats and the Contemporary Dream," 30-49; includes "The Contemporary Dream," *LMag*, 6:1 (Jan 1959), 39-44. Yeats's poetry endures because he was in touch with the deeper levels of the human being and of his age, which in turn speak through his poetry.

20. BLACKMUR, RICHARD PALMER: *The Expense of Greatness*. Gloucester, Mass.: Smith, 1958 [1940]. v, 305 pp.
"The Later Poetry of W. B. Yeats," 74-105; reprinted from *SoR*, 2:2 (Autumn 1936), 339-62; reprinted in CA36, DB21, and 22; also in *Selected Essays*. Edited and with an introduction by Denis Donoghue. NY: Ecco Press, 1986. v, 372 pp. (pp. 145-69). The locus classicus for the discussion of "magic" in Yeats's poetry.

21. ———: *Language as Gesture: Essays in Poetry*. London: Allen & Unwin, 1961 [1952]. vi, 440 pp.

"The Later Poetry of W. B. Yeats," 80-104; reprinted from DB20, q.v.

"W. B. Yeats: Between Myth and Philosophy," 105-23; reprint of "Between Myth and Philosophy: Fragments of W. B. Yeats," *SoR*, 7:3 (Winter 1941/42), 407-25; reprinted in DB22. "Yeats commonly hovered between myth and philosophy, except for transcending flashes, which is why he is not one of the greatest poets. . . . His curse was . . . that he could not create, except in fragments, the actuality of his age" (p. 122).

"Lord Tennyson's Scissors: 1912-1950," 422-40; reprinted from *KR*, 14:1 (Winter 1952), 1-20; reprinted in DB22. Yeats, Eliot, and Pound are the only 20th-century poets whose work will survive.

For a criticism of Blackmur's view of Yeats see John Wain: *Essays on Literature and Ideas*. London: Macmillan, 1964. xi, 270 pp. ("R. P. Blackmur," 145-55).

22. ———: *Form and Idea in Modern Poetry*. Garden City: Doubleday, 1957. vii, 388 pp. (Doubleday Anchor Books. A96.)

See DB20 and 21.

23. ———: "The Key and the Hook," *Bennington R*, 2:1 (Winter 1968), 3-10.

A plea for the poetry as poetry; comments on "A Deep-Sworn Vow," "Vacillation," "Chosen," and "Long-legged Fly."

24. BLOOMFIELD, MORTON WILFRED (ed): *Allegory, Myth, and Symbol*. Cambridge, Mass.: Harvard UP, 1981. x, 390 pp. (Harvard English Studies. 9.)

J. Hillis Miller: "The Two Allegories," 355-70; on Yeats's early poetry and on *Ideas of Good and Evil*.

Ronald Bush: "The 'Rhythm of Metaphor': Yeats, Pound, Eliot, and the Unity of Image in Postsymbolist Poetry," 371-88.

25. BOLT, SYDNEY (ed): *Poetry of the 1920s: An Anthology*. London: Longmans, 1967. x, 272 pp.

"W. B. Yeats (1865-1939)," 32-35. Particularly on "Among School Children." "It is . . . the function of style in the poetry of W. B. Yeats to prevent the reader from using his own judgment. The style takes him captive."

26. BRADBROOK, H. L.: "The Development of Yeats's Poetry," *Contemporaries*, 2:1 (Summer 1935), 201-6.

27. BRATT, EYVIND: "Dikt och tanke hos Yeats" [Poetry and thought in Y], *Svenska dagbladet*, 27 June 1969, 4.

28. BRAUN, JOHN THEODORE: *The Apostrophic Gesture*. The Hague: Mouton, 1971. 217 pp. (De Proprietatibus Litterarum. Series Maior. 17.)

Based on a Ph.D. thesis, U of Washington, 1967. vi, 338 pp. (*DAI*, 28:5 [Nov 1967], 1813A-14A).

"The Apostrophic Gesture in the Poetry of Yeats," 99-208. "Reading a poem, we participate in a threefold apostrophic gesture: turning aside, turning toward, returning" (p. 9). Discusses Yeats's poetic theory (especially his theory of the mask) and ten of his poems in the light of the apostrophic gesture. Analyzed in section DD.

29. BRENNER, RICA: *Poets of Our Time*. NY: Harcourt, Brace, 1941. xii, 411 pp.

"William Butler Yeats," 357-411.

30. BRKIĆ, SVETOZAR: *Svetla lovina*. Beograd: Nolit, 1972. 484 pp.

"V. B. Jejts i njegove razvojne faze" [WBY and his phase of development], 17-34; reprinted in next item.

"Bizantija kao pesnička inspiracija" [Byzantium as poetic inspiration], 137-48, reprinted from *Književnost*, year 24 / 49:9 (Sept 1969), 262-68.

31. ———, and MIODRAG PAVLOVIĆ (eds): *Antologija savremene engleske poezije*. Second edition, revised. Beograd: Nolit, 1975. 384 pp.

"V. B. Jejts i njegove razvojne faze," 14-25, reprinted from preceding item.

"Viljem Batler Jejts," 124-32; introduction to translations of 10 poems.

32. BRONOWSKI, JACOB: *The Poet's Defence: The Concept of Poetry from Sidney to Yeats*. Cleveland: World, 1966 [1939]. xii, 258 pp.

"William Butler Yeats," 229-52, and passim (see index). "Almost every poem he has written debates the same theme: the poet's place in the world. Far more pointedly than his criticism, Yeats's poems debate a theory of poetry."

33. BROOKE, STOPFORD AUGUSTUS, and THOMAS WILLIAM ROLLESTON (eds): *A Treasury of Irish Poetry in the English Tongue*. Revised and enlarged. NY: Macmillan, 1932 [1900]. xiv, 610 pp.

T. W. Rolleston: "W. B. Yeats," 492-98; written in 1899.

34. BROWER, REUBEN ARTHUR (ed): *Twentieth-Century Literature in Retrospect*. Cambridge, Mass.: Harvard UP, 1971. vii, 363 pp. (Harvard English Studies. 2.)

William H. Pritchard: "The Uses of Yeats's Poetry," 111-32; also in CA89.

35. BUCKLEY, VINCENT: *Poetry and the Sacred*. London: Chatto & Windus, 1968. viii, 244 pp.

"W. B. Yeats and the Sacred Company," 172-204; incorporates some material from "W. B. Yeats and the Dramatic Lyric," *Melbourne Critical R*, 2 (1959), 12-28.

"Yeats's concern with the past, racial or personal, gay or bitter, was at every stage religious in nature." This is especially true of the "dramatic" poems, those that celebrate Yeats's friends and, eventually, himself. Discusses "The Man and the Echo," "The Curse of Cromwell," "Easter 1916," "Sailing to Byzantium," and other poems.

36. BULLOUGH, GEOFFREY: *The Trend of Modern Poetry*. Edinburgh: Oliver & Boyd, 1941 [1934]. vii, 191 pp.

"W. B. Yeats and Walter de la Mare," 27-43. Both write "poetry of dream."

37. ———: *Mirror of Minds: Changing Psychological Beliefs in English Poetry*. London: Athlone Press, 1962. viii, 271 pp.

On Yeats as a representative of the "hermetic approach" in modern poetry, pp. 242-44.

38. BUSH, DOUGLAS: *English Poetry: The Main Currents from Chaucer to the Present*. NY: Oxford UP, 1963 [1952]. 222 pp. (Galaxy Book.

GB93.)

See pp. 199-202 and passim (see index).

39. BUSHRUI, SUHEIL BADI: "Shi'r Yaits" [Yeats's poetry], *Aswat,* 8 (1962), 6-27.

40. ————: "Yaits wa-Tajdid Islub al-Shi'r" [Yeats and modern poetic technique], *Shi'r,* 10:40 (Autumn 1968), 47-60.

41. CHURCH, RICHARD: *Eight for Immortality.* London: Dent, 1941. ix, 113 pp.

"The Later Yeats," 41-54; reprinted from *FortnR,* os 154 / ns 148:884 (Aug 1940), 193-99. The kind of article in which poets "sing."

42. CLARKE, AUSTIN: "Irish Poetry To-day," *DM,* 10:1 (Jan-Mar 1935), 26-32.

43. ————: "Poetry in Ireland To-day," *Bell,* 13:2 (Nov 1946), 155-61.

Contains some references to Yeats.

44. ————: *Poetry in Modern Ireland.* With illustrations by Louis Le Brocquy. Cork: Mercier Press for the Cultural Relations Committee of Ireland, [1961?] [1951]. 77 pp. (Irish Life and Culture. 2.)

See pp. 47-52.

45. CLAYES, STANLEY A., and JOHN GERRIETTS: *Ways to Poetry.* NY: Harcourt Brace Jovanovich, 1975. xxii, 378 pp.

"William Butler Yeats (1865-1939)," 196-213, and passim (see index); an anthology with notes and comments.

46. CLINTON-BADDELEY, V. C.: "Reading Poetry with W. B. Yeats," *LMag,* 4:12 (Dec 1957), 47-53.

How Yeats wanted poetry, especially his own poetry, to be read.

47. ————: "The Written and the Spoken Word," *E&S,* 18 (1965), 73-82.

Contains a note on the reciting and recording of Yeats's poems.

48. COHEN, JOHN MICHAEL: *Poetry of This Age, 1908-1965.* 2nd impression, revised. London: Hutchinson, 1966 [1960]. 256 pp.

On Yeats, pp. 69-79 and passim (see index).

49. COLUM, PADRAIC: "Yeats's Lyrical Poems," *IrW,* 2 (June 1947), 78-85.

50. COOPER, PHILIP: "Lyric Ambivalence: An Essay on the Poetry of William Butler Yeats and Robert Lowell," Ph.D. thesis, U of Rochester, 1967. viii, 313 pp. (*DAI,* 28:6 [Dec 1967], 2241A)

Discusses among other texts "The Two Trees," "Sailing to Byzantium," "Crazy Jane Talks with the Bishop," "Vacillation," *Purgatory* (linked to Chaucer's *Pardoner's Tale*), and *A Vision.*

51. COX, CHARLES BRIAN, and ANTHONY EDWARD DYSON (eds): *The Twentieth-Century Mind: History, Ideas, and Literature in Britain.* London: Oxford UP, 1972. 3 vols.

Volume 1: *1900-1918.* xiii, 526 pp. John Wain: "Poetry," 360-413 (passim on Yeats); D. J. Palmer: "Drama," 447-74 (on the Irish dramatic revival, 464-68); Graham Hough: "Criticism," 475-84 (see pp. 475-78).

Volume 2: *1918-1945*. xi, 514 pp. John Wain: "Poetry," 307-72 (see pp. 354-63).

52. DAICHES, DAVID: *Poetry and the Modern World: A Study of Poetry in England between 1900 and 1939*. Chicago: U of Chicago Press, 1940. x, 247 pp.

On Yeats, passim, especially pp. 128-89 (partly reprinted in CA36). Explains Yeats's poetic development as a search for a system that would enable the poet to symbolize experience completely. Eventually, in the last poems, the system conquered its creator.

53. ———, and WILLIAM CHARVAT (eds): *Poems in English, 1530-1940*. Edited with critical and historical notes and essays. NY: Ronald Press, 1950. xli, 763 pp.

Notes on Yeats's poems, pp. 731-36, especially on "To a Shade," "The Second Coming," "Byzantium," and "Long-legged Fly."

54. DAICHES, DAVID: *A Critical History of English Literature*. London: Secker & Warburg, 1963 [1960]. viii, 1169 pp. in 2 vols.

On Yeats's plays, pp. 1109-10; on his poetry, 1117-23.

55. DALE, PETER: "'Where All the Ladders Start. . . ,'" *Agenda*, 9:4--10:1 (Autumn-Winter 1971/72), 3-13.

Yeats's "ability to re-create a recognisable reality while endeavouring to see beyond it" is more important than "his do-it-yourself system."

56. DAVIE, DONALD: *The Poet in the Imaginary Museum: Essays of Two Decades*. Edited by Barry Alpert. Manchester: Carcanet, 1977. xxi, 322 pp.

"Yeats, the Master of a Trade," 125-32; reprinted from Donoghue: *The Integrity of Yeats* (1964, CA22), 59-70. Yeats as the master of the technical skills of writing poetry. Also passim (see index).

57. DAY LEWIS, CECIL: *Notable Images of Virtue: Emily Brontë, George Meredith, W. B. Yeats*. Toronto: Ryerson Press, 1954. xiii, 77 pp. (Chancellor Dunning Trust Lectures. 6.)

Reprinted Folcroft, Pa.: Folcroft Library Editions, 1974; Norwood, Pa.: Norwood Editions, 1976; Philadelphia: West, 1977.

"W. B. Yeats and Human Dignity," 53-77. Dignity, aristocracy, and the ceremony of innocence in Yeats's poetry.

58. ———: *The Lyric Impulse*. Cambridge, Mass.: Harvard UP, 1965. ix, 164 pp. (Charles Eliot Norton Lectures. 1964-65.)

Notes on Yeats's poetry, passim (see index), especially on "Politics," pp. 136-37.

59. DEL RE, GABRIELE: *L'età vittoriana e l'età contemporanea nella letteratura inglese*. Roma: Gremese, 1974. 179 pp. (Essenziale. 4.)

See pp. 109-20.

60. DEUTSCH, BABETTE: *Potable Gold: Some Notes on Poetry and This Age*. NY: Norton, 1929. viii, 96 pp.

See pp. 73-84.

61. ———: *This Modern Poetry*. NY: Norton, 1935. 284 pp.

Passim (see index).

62. ———: *Poetry in Our Time: A Critical Survey of Poetry in the English-Speaking World, 1900-1960*. 2nd edition, revised and enlarged. NY: Doubleday, 1963 [1952]. xix, 457 pp.
"A Vision of Reality," 287-320, and passim (see index).

63. DREW, ELIZABETH, and JOHN L. SWEENEY: *Directions in Modern Poetry*. NY: Norton, 1940. 296 pp.
"W. B. Yeats," 148-71, and passim (see index).

64. DREW, ELIZABETH: *Poetry: A Modern Guide to Its Understanding and Enjoyment*. NY: Norton, 1959. 288 pp.
Yeats, passim (see index), especially on "Sailing to Byzantium" and "Leda and the Swan."

65. ———, and GEORGE CONNOR: *Discovering Modern Poetry*. NY: Holt, Rinehart, & Winston, 1961. xix, 426 pp.
Comments on several Yeats poems, passim.

66. DUMBLETON, WILLIAM A.: *Ireland: Life and Land in Literature*. Albany: State U of New York Press, 1984. xii, 195 pp.
An introduction for the general reader, not a scholarly analysis. See especially "Dreams and Idylls: Yeats' Early Poetry," 87-97; "The Later Poems of Yeats," 127-45.

67. DUNLOP, R. T.: "Yeats," *Teaching of English*, 20 (June 1971), 38-43.
Lecture on the continuity of the subject matter in the poetry.

68. DUTTA, UJJAL: "Poetry and Its Cultural Determinants: The Case of W. B. Yeats," in Srivastava and Dutta: *Unaging Intellect* (1983, CA108), 194-208.
"Yeats did not create any great poetry of Irish history or of Irish life."

69. ĐUZEL, BOGOMIL: "Vilijam Batler Jejts--Poetot kako tvorec na mitovi" [Poet as creator of myth], *Razgledi*, series 3 / 4:8 (1962), 754-62.

70. DYSON, ANTHONY EDWARD: *Yeats, Eliot, and R. S. Thomas: Riding the Echo*. London: Macmillan, 1981. xx, 339 pp.
"Yeats's Poetry: The Major Phase, 1916-1939. No Enemy But Time," 1-184; a sequence of interpretations of some 40 poems, loosely connected by the intention to provide "practical criticism" and to read the poems as expressions of the poet's "striving towards meanings beyond any that syntax can contain" (p. xiii). Analyzed in section DD.
Reviews:
- Felicity Currie, *CritQ*, 24:3 (Autumn 1982), 65-71.
- Leon Hugo, *UES*, 21:2 (Sept 1983), 55-56.
- Denis Sampson: "An Old-Fashioned Book," *ILS*, 2:2 (Oct 1983), 18.
- Donald E. Stanford, *Yeats*, 2 (1984), 279-86.

71. ELIOT, THOMAS STEARNS: *The Use of Poetry and the Use of Criticism: Studies in the Relation of Criticism to Poetry in England*. London: Faber & Faber, 1964 [1933]. 156 pp.
Eliot disapproves of Yeats's "mysticism" and praises the later, saner poetry, p. 140.

72. ———: *On Poetry and Poets*. London: Faber & Faber, 1961

[1957]. 262 pp.

"The Music of Poetry," 26-38; reprint of a pamphlet of the same title, Glasgow: Jackson, 1942. 28 pp. (Glasgow University Publications. 57.) Contains a note on Yeats reading poetry aloud, pp. 31-32.

"Poetry and Drama," 72-88; reprint of a pamphlet of the same title, London: Faber & Faber, 1951. 35 pp. Contains a note on *Purgatory*, p. 78.

"Yeats," 252-62; reprint of "The Poetry of W. B. Yeats," *Purpose*, 12:3/4 (July-Dec 1940), 115-27; also in *SoR*, 7:3 (Winter 1941/42), 442-54, and in CA36. A slightly revised extract appeared as "William Butler Yeats: A Tribute," *Ireland-American R*, 5 [1941?], 183-84. A praise of the later poetry and plays. See also CD419.

73. ENGELBERG, EDWARD: "The New Generation and the Acceptance of Yeats," in Maxwell and Bushrui: *W. B. Yeats 1965-1965* (1965, CA71), 88-101.

Yeats is popular with the undergraduates, because his poetry lends itself to an extrinsic and political approach.

74. ———: "Absence and Presence in Yeats's Poetry," *YeA*, 1 (1982), 48-67.

75. *English Poetry*. London: Sussex Books, 1976. 239 pp.

Transcripts of recorded talks, edited by Alan Sinfield. See Laurence Lerner: "Reading Modern Poetry," 150-68 (on "Lapis Lazuli"), and Richard Ellmann and Peter Wilson: "W. B. Yeats" 170-85 (on "The Lake Isle of Innisfree," "Sailing to Byzantium," and "Crazy Jane Talks with the Bishop").

The so-called Sussex Tapes were published as follows: *Four Modern Poets: An Introduction to Criticism*. East Ardsley, Wakefield: Educational Productions, 1971. 1 cassette plus introductory booklet (17 pp.). Contains the material by Lerner.

W. B. Yeats. 1971. 1 cassette plus introductory booklet (13 pp.). Contains the material by Ellmann.

76. ENRIGHT, DENIS JOSEPH: *Literature for Man's Sake: Critical Essays*. Tokyo: Kenkyusha, 1955. v, 209 pp.

Reprinted [Norwood, Pa.]: Norwood Editions, 1976. "The Poetic Development of W. B. Yeats," 129-44. From deathwish and dream (early poetry) to reality, precision, and life (later poetry).

77. ERZGRÄBER, WILLI, and UTE KNOEDGEN (eds): *Moderne englische Lyrik: Englisch und Deutsch*. Zweite Auflage. Ausgewählt, kommentiert und herausgegeben von Willi Erzgräber und Ute Knoedgen. Mit einer Einleitung von Willi Erzgräber. Stuttgart: Reclam, 1984 [1976]. 623 pp.

See the introduction, pp. 23-27, and the notes, pp. 439-47. The translations appear on pp. 93-117.

78. EVANS, BENJAMIN IFOR: "The Poetry of W. B. Yeats," *FortnR*, os 151 / ns 145:867 (Mar 1939), 351-53.

79. ———: *Tradition and Romanticism: Studies in English Poetry from Chaucer to W. B. Yeats*. London: Methuen, 1940. ix, 213 pp.

"W. B. Yeats and the Continuance of Tradition," 201-8.

80. O Faracháin, Riobárd [FARREN, ROBERT]: "Elements for a Credo," *IrM*, 64:761 (Nov 1936), 751-55; :762 (Dec 1936), 828-35; 65:763 (Jan

1937), 39-45; :764 (Feb 1937), 106-10; :765 (Mar 1937), 197-202; :766 (Apr 1937), 258-63.

Subtitles: The Conceptual in the Poetry of Yeats, The Image in Yeats, Rhythm in Yeats; also a note on Yeats's poetic theory.

81. FARREN, ROBERT: *The Course of Irish Verse in English*. London: Sheed & Ward, 1948. xii, 171 pp.

See pp. 64-78.

82. O'F., R. [———]: "Yeats the Poet," *RTV Guide*, 11 June 1965, 6.

The same issue contains the program of the Yeats centenary productions, p. 6; Niall Sheridan: "Portrait of a Poet," 6; a note on *Deirdre* by Michael Garvey, p. 7; and Gabriel Fallon: "Yeats as a Dramatist," 7.

83. FAULKNER, PETER: "Yeats: Anti-Humanist?" *New Humanist*, 88:11 (Mar 1973), 455-56.

Yeats's poetry proves that he was, after all, a humanist.

84. FIGGIS, DARRELL: *Studies and Appreciations*. London: Dent, 1912. vii, 258 pp.

"Mr. W. B. Yeats' Poetry," 119-37; reprinted from *New Age*, 4 Aug 1910, 325-28.

85. FINNERAN, RICHARD J.: "A Note on the Scribner Archive at the Humanities Research Center," *Yeats*, 2 (1984), 227-32.

The relevance of the Scribner Archive at the HRC (U of Texas at Austin) to an edition of Yeats's poems.

86. ———: "The Order of Yeats's Poems," *IUR*, 14:2 (Autumn 1984), 165-76.

Re-examines the issues raised in DA15, 25, and some of the reviews of the new edition of the poems (DA51, G1572-1597).

87. FLETCHER, IAN: "The Vulnerable Yeats," *NSt*, 27 June 1969, 918.

88. Hueffer, Ford Madox [later FORD, FORD MADOX]: "Impressionism: Some Speculations," *Poetry*, 2:6 (Sept 1913), 215-25.

89. [———]: "Literary Portraits--XXXIX: Mr. W. B. Yeats and His New Poems," *Outlook* [London], 6 June 1914, 783-84.

With *Responsibilities* (W110, reviewed here), Yeats is no longer grotesque and irritating. Of the earlier poems, "The Lake Isle of Innisfree" is particularly bad; Ford improves it as follows:

> At Innesfree [sic] there is a public-house;
> They bord you well for ten and six a week.
> The mutton is not good, but you can eat
> Their honey. I am going there to take
> A week or so of holiday to-morrow.

90. FRASER, GEORGE SUTHERLAND: *Essays on Twentieth-Century Poets*. Leicester: Leicester UP, 1977. 255 pp.

"W. B. Yeats," 11-28; reprint of CA30, also in CB167.

"Seven Poems by Yeats," 29-44; reprinted from *Notes on Literature*, 10 (May 1962), 1-9; 63 (Oct 1966), 1-9. On "The Wild Swans at Coole," "Easter 1916," "Sailing to Byzantium," "In Memory of Major Robert Gregory," "The Municipal Gallery Revisited," "The Second Coming," and "Two Songs from a Play."

"Yeats and the Ballad Style," 45-60; reprinted from *Shenan-*

doah, 21:3 (Spring 1970), 177-94.
"Yeats: Two Dream Poems," 61-79; on "The Cap and Bells," "His Dream," and related poems.

91. ———: *A Short History of English Poetry*. Shepton Mallet: Open Books, 1981. x, 386 pp.
See pp. 286-90, 302-5, and passim.

92. FRAZIER, ADRIAN WOODS: "Under Ben Bulben: Irish Poetry after Yeats," Ph.D. thesis, Washington U, 1979. ii, 208 pp. (*DAI,* 40:2 [Aug 1979], 842A)
See "The Ascendancy Poetry of Yeats" (published separately in *SR,* 88:1 [Winter 1980], 67-85) and "Yeats among the Irish Poets: 1925-39" (Clarke, Kavanagh, Kinsella, Montague, Heaney).

93. FRÉCHET, RENÉ: "Un poète en quête de sa vérité: W. B. Yeats," *Foi. Education,* 31:56 (July-Aug 1961), 49-56.

94. GALLAGHER, MICHAEL P.: "Yeats, Syntax, and the Self," *ArQ,* 26:1 (Spring 1970), 5-16.
The three stages in Yeats's development as poet and critic are described as the dominance of words, the substitution of syntax for words, and the discovery of the "self" or unity of being. Discusses "Among School Children" and the influence of the *Upanishads.*

95. GARRATT, ROBERT F.: *Modern Irish Poetry: Tradition and Continuity from Yeats to Heaney*. Berkeley: U of California Press, 1986. xii, 322 pp.
"Tradition and Isolation: W. B. Yeats," 16-43, and passim (see index). On Yeats's place in Anglo-Irish poetry and his influence on other writers, particularly Clarke, Coffey, Fallon, Heaney, Higgins, Kavanagh, Kinsella, and Montague.
Reviews:
- Terence Brown, *IUR,* 17:2 (Autumn 1987), 317-20.
- Mary Helen Thuente: "Yeatsian Tradition," *ELT,* 31:2 (1988), 220-26.

96. GARRETT, JOHN: *British Poetry since the Sixteenth Century: A Students' Guide*. London: Macmillan, 1986. viii, 248 pp.
"The Last Romantic: W. B. Yeats," 200-12; particularly on "The Lake Isle of Innisfree" and "Sailing to Byzantium."

97. GERARD, MARTIN: "It Means What It Says," *X: A Quarterly Review,* 2:2 (Aug 1961), 100-107.
The problem of poetry and belief, with Yeats's poetry as object of demonstration.

98. GILBERT, KATHARINE: *Aesthetic Studies: Architecture & Poetry*. Durham, N.C.: Duke UP, 1952. vii, 145 pp.
Some notes on Yeats's poetry in the chapters "Recent Poets on Man and His Place," 51-81, and "A Spatial Configuration in Five Recent Poets," 85-97.

99. GILKES, MARTIN: *A Key to Modern English Poetry*. London: Blackie, 1937. vi, 178 pp.
"William Butler Yeats," 153-65.

100. GOLDGAR, HARRY: "Yeats and the Black Centaur in French," *Western R,* 15:2 (Winter 1951), 111-22.

On the difficulties of translating Yeats's poetry into French, with particular reference to "On a Picture of a Black Centaur by Edmund Dulac."

101. ———: "Note sur la poésie de William Butler Yeats," *Bayou,* 22 [i.e., 21]:72 (Winter 1958), 547-52.

102. GOMES, EUGENIO: *D. H. Lawrence e outros.* Pôrto Alegre: Edição da livraria do globo Barcellos, Bertaso, 1937. 329 pp.
"W. B. Yeats," 79-110; on the early poetry and plays.

103. GRAVES, ROBERT: *The Crowning Privilege: Collected Essays on Poetry.* Garden City: Doubleday, 1956. 311 pp.
"These Be Your Gods, O Israel!" 119-42; reprinted from *EIC,* 5:2 (Apr 1955), 129-50, and *NewRep,* 27 Feb 1956, 16-18; 5 Mar 1956, 17-18. Letters by Delmore Schwartz and W. M. Laetsch, 19 Mar 1956, 20-22; Karl Shapiro, 2 Apr 1956, 3, 23; and others.
A savage attack on Yeats's poetry; Graves accuses him of having nothing to say. See Peter Ure: "Yeats and Mr. Graves," *TLS,* 12 June 1959, 353.

104. GRENNAN, EAMON: "Leaving Cert Poetry: Yeats," *IrT,* 10 Dec 1983, 14.
The poems chosen for the Leaving Certificate are "No Second Troy," "September 1913," "The Fisherman," "Sailing to Byzantium," "Among School Children," and "The Circus Animals' Desertion."

105. GRIGSON, GEOFFREY (ed): *The Arts To-Day.* London: Lane / Bodley Head, 1935. xv, 301 pp.
Louis MacNeice: "Poetry To-Day," 25-67; Humphrey Jennings: "The Theatre To-Day," 189-216.

106. GROSS, HARVEY SEYMOUR: *Sound and Form in Modern Poetry: A Study of Prosody from Thomas Hardy to Robert Lowell.* Ann Arbor: U of Michigan Press, 1964. xii, 334 pp.
"William Butler Yeats," 48-55.

107. GRUBB, FREDERICK: *A Vision of Reality: A Study of Liberalism in Twentieth-Century Verse.* London: Chatto & Windus, 1965. 246 pp.
"Tragic Joy: W. B. Yeats," 25-45, and passim (see index). This is an essay on some themes in Yeats's poetry. What they have to do with liberalism is not explained.

108. HAMBURGER, MICHAEL: *The Truth of Poetry: Tensions in Modern Poetry from Baudelaire to the 1960s.* London: Weidenfeld & Nicolson, 1969. ix, 341 pp.
See pp. 72-80, 86-90, and passim (see index). Mainly concerned with the "modernity" and the "politics" of Yeats's poetry.

109. HANLEY, EVELYN ALICE: *Nature in Theme and Symbol: Wordsworth to Eliot.* NY: Heath Cote, 1972. 94 pp.
"William Butler Yeats (1865-1939): Celtic Analogist of the Tradition," 59-66. "In summation: Yeats's approach to nature is predicated on the mystic concept that man is incapable of a total comprehension of the forces that govern the universe."

110. HART, RICHARD HOOD: "The Lyric as Fictive Rhetoric: Skeptical Deconstructions of Poems in the Major British Tradition," °Ph.D. thesis, U of Texas at Austin, 1983. 250 pp. (*DAI,* 45:3 [Sept 1984],

849A)
Contains a chapter on Yeats's poetry, according to abstract.

111. HEANEY, SEAMUS: "John Bull's Other Island," *List,* 29 Sept 1977, 397, 399.

112. HENN, T. R. "The Wisdom of W. B. Yeats," *List,* 21 Dec 1950, 790-91, 793.
Yeats's "philosophy," as shown in his poetry.

113. ———: "The Poetry: A Stone with Many Facets," *IrT,* 10 June 1965, ii.

114. HEXTER, GEORGE J.: "The Philosophy of William Butler Yeats," *Texas R,* 1:3 (Jan 1916), 192-200.
As contained in the poetry.

115. HILL, ROBERT W.: "A Phenomenological Approach to Hopkins and Yeats," *Hopkins Q,* 5:2 (Summer 1978), 51-67.
Discusses the question whether Yeats's art and subject matter in his poetry is phenomenological and finds that "the only thing he seems to be phenomenologically sure about is language."

116. HOUSTON, JOHN PORTER: *French Symbolism and the Modernist Movement: A Study of Poetic Structures.* Baton Rouge: Louisiana State UP, 1980. xvii, 298 pp.
"Death, Renewal, and Redemption in Apollinaire, Montale, Lorca, Yeats, and Rilke," 227-68; see also pp. 27-30. Reviewed by Ian Fletcher, *Yeats,* 1 (1983), 198-202.

117. HUGHES, PAUL FENTON: *For the Birds: An Essay in Symbolism.* Richmond, Va.: Cavalier Press, 1969. xi, 40 pp.
"The Tradition of Yeats," 1-7; maintains that Yeats was a poet of the oral and not of the graphic tradition. "Fish as a Protean Symbol in the Poetry of W. B. Yeats," 9-14. "The Symbolic Stone in Yeats's Poems, 1921-1939," 17-22.

118. IONKIS, GRETA ĖVRIVIADOVNA: *Angliĭskai͡a poezii͡a XX veka: 1917-1945.* Moskva: Vysshai͡a shkola, 1980, 200 pp.
"Uil'i͡am Batler Ĭets," 126-47.

119. IREMONGER, VALENTIN: "The Byzantine Poems of Yeats," *Bell,* 19:10 (Nov 1954), 36-44.
The Byzantium poems point to a general problem in Yeats's poetry: "Yeats's mind veered between the symbol and the reality but, lacking sympathy with, or understanding of, ordinary life, failed to establish any connecting link between the two."

120. IRIBARREN BORGES, IGNACIO: *Una revolución literaria y sus autores: Yeats, Joyce, Pound, Eliot.* Caracas: Monte Avila, 1980. 139 pp.
"William B. Yeats (1865-1939)," 21-49; reprint of "El viejo bardo," *Revista nacional de cultura,* 36:225 (June-July 1976), 50-68.

121. ISON, R.: "More Thoughts on W. B. Yeats," *Teaching of English,* 20 (June 1971), 60-64.
Personal concerns in Yeats's poetry.

122. IZZO, CARLO (trans and ed): *Poesia inglese contemporanea da Thomas Hardy agli apocalittici.* Introduzione, versione e note di Carlo Izzo. Modena: Guanda, 1950. lxxxvii, 599 pp.

Passim (see index).

123. JACK, IAN: *The Poet and His Audience*. Cambridge: Cambridge UP, 1984. viii, 198 pp.

"Yeats: Always an Irish Writer," 144-68. The aim of the book is "to throw light on the careers of six major poets by considering how far the audiences for which they wrote seem to have influenced their poetry" (p. 3). The other poets are Dryden, Pope, Byron, Shelley, and Tennyson, who are not connected with Yeats. The main idea of the Yeats chapter is that he created "the taste by which his poetry is enjoyed" and that he "educated his audience."

Reviews:
- Andrew Carpenter, *Yeats*, 4 (1986), 202-4.
- Seamus Deane: "Yeats and the Occult," *LRB*, 18-31 Oct 1984, 27.

124. JEFFARES, A. NORMAN: "W. B. Yeats and His Methods of Writing Verse," *Nineteenth Century and After*, 139:829 (Mar 1946), 123-28.

Reprinted in CA36. The MSS. reveal that Yeats had two methods of writing verse, spontaneous composition that underwent few changes before it was published, and (more often) laborious writing and rewriting that he was careful to hide in the published version.

125. ———: "Yeats as Modern Poet," *Mosaic*, 2:4 (Summer 1969), 53-58.

Yeats's poetry is popular with the young, because his subjects appeal to them and because he cares for his audience.

126. JENNINGS, ELIZABETH: *Seven Men of Vision: An Appreciation*. London: Vision Press, 1976. 249 pp.

"W. B. Yeats: A Vision of Joy," 11-44.

127. JOHN, BRIAN: *Supreme Fictions: Studies in the Work of William Blake, Thomas Carlyle, W. B. Yeats, and D. H. Lawrence*. Montreal: McGill-Queen's UP, 1974. xiv, 318 pp.

"W. B. Yeats and the Wisdom of Daimonic Images," 149-229, and passim. Incorporates "Yeats's 'Crazy Jane Reproved,'" *Eire*, 4:4 (Winter 1969), 52-55. Discusses "Among School Children," "A Man Young and Old," "Meditations in Time of Civil War," "Nineteen Hundred and Nineteen," "Sailing to Byzantium," "The Tower," "Two Songs from a Play," and "A Woman Young and Old."

Reviews:
- John Paul Russo: "The Energy Question," *TLS*, 10 Oct 1975, 1186.
- Michael Steig, *ESC*, 2:1 (Spring 1976), 117-23.

128. JOHNSON, WALTER RALPH: *The Idea of Lyric: Lyric Modes in Ancient and Modern Poetry*. Berkeley: U of California Press, 1982. xi, 214 pp.

Note on Yeats as lyric performer before an imagined audience, pp. 15-17.

129. JONES, LLEWELLYN: *First Impressions: Essays on Poetry, Criticism, and Prosody*. NY: Knopf, 1925. 249 pp.

"The Later Poetry of W. B. Yeats," 137-48; reprinted from *NAR*, 219:821 (Apr 1924), 499-506. Defends Yeats against Middleton Murry's criticism (G384).

130. JURKIĆ-ŠUNJIĆ, MIRA: "Tragična ljepota u poeziji W. B. Yeatsa,"

Telegram, 15 Apr 1966, 12.
"Tragic beauty in the poetry of Yeats."

131. KAVANAGH, PATRICK: On Yeats's poems, *RTV Guide,* 22 Jan 1965, 23.

132. KENNER, HUGH: *Gnomon: Essays on Contemporary Literature.* NY: Obolensky, 1958. vii, 301 pp.
"The Sacred Book of the Arts," 9-29; reprinted from *IrW,* 31 (Summer 1955), 24-35, and *SR,* 64:4 (Oct-Dec 1956), 574-90. Yeats wrote and composed *books* of poetry, in which the arrangement of the poems is deliberate and meaningful.
"At the Hawk's Well," 198-214; a review of *Letters* (W211J/K).

133. ———: "The Three Deaths of Yeats," *Yeats,* 5 (1987), 87-94. Yeats's various poetical summings-up in the course of his development.

133a. ———: *A Sinking Island: The Modern English Writers.* NY: Knopf, 1988. xi, 292 pp.
"Yeats," 76-86, and passim (see index). Mainly on the changes in Yeats's poetic style due to the influence of Ben Jonson.

134. KERMODE, FRANK, and JOHN HOLLANDER (eds): *The Oxford Anthology of English Literature.* NY: Oxford UP, 1973. 2 vols.
Kermode and Hollander: "William Butler Yeats," 2:1679-1735; a selection from the poetry and the autobiography with introductory material (pp. 1679-83, 1721-23) and numerous notes.

135. KHANNA, KRISHNAKUMAR: "From Ideology to Art: Yeats's Poetry of Remembrance," in Srivastava and Dutta: *Unaging Intellect* (1983, CA108), 52-71.
A Marxist approach.

136. KING, ALEC: *The Unprosaic Imagination: Essays and Lectures on the Study of Literature.* Edited by Francis King. Nedlands: U of Western Australia Press, 1975. xv, 223 pp.
"Yeats: The Poet," 138-43; "An Early Poem of Yeats and the Plight of the Poet," 144-56 ("The Rose of Battle"); "Poetry and Philosophy: In Defence of Yeats's *A Vision,*" 157-68.

137. Forsman, Rafael [later KOSKIMIES, RAFAEL]: *Runoilijoita ja kiistamiehiä* [Poets and critics]. Porvoo: Söderström, 1926. 223 pp.
"Piirteitä W. B. Yeatsin runoudesta" [Extracts from Yeats's poetry], 155-70.

138. KUBAL, DAVID L.: "Our Last Literary Gentlemen: The Bourgeois Imagination," *BuR,* 22:2 (Fall 1976), 27-49.
Includes a discussion of Yeats's poetry which despite of a growing maturity remained dreamlike to the end.

139. KURATANI, NAOOMI: "Out of a Dead End--W. B. Yeats," *Mukogawa Women's U Bulletin,* 15 (1968), H99-117; 16 (1969), H127-42.

140. LEAVIS, FRANK RAYMOND: *New Bearings in English Poetry: A Study of the Contemporary Situation.* Ann Arbor: U of Michigan Press, 1960 [1932]. vii, 238 pp. (Ann Arbor Paperbacks. AA36.)
See pp. 27-50. Yeats's poetry has developed into "disillusion and waste" and is "little more than a marginal comment on the main activities of his life." Also in CA36.

141. ———, and QUEENIE DOROTHY LEAVIS: *Lectures in America*. London: Chatto & Windus, 1969. vii, 152 pp.

F. R. L.: "Yeats: The Problem and the Challenge," 59-81. Reprinted in F. R. Leavis: *Valuation in Criticism and Other Essays*. Collected and edited by G. Singh. Cambridge: Cambridge UP, 1986. vii, 305 pp. (pp. 88-92).

The problem is contained in the questions of what Yeats's achievement as a poet really was and how many of his poems are "great." The answers are (as far as I understand Leavis's somewhat redundant and idiosyncratic argument) that Yeats's work poses the continual question, "What *is* literary history?" and that he did not write many great poems. Discusses the two Byzantium poems and "Among School Children."

Reviews:

- [Clive James]: "Distillations from FRL and QDL," *TLS*, 20 Mar 1969, 297-98. The Yeats piece isn't up to the standard of the rest of the book. Reprinted as "F. R. Leavis in America" in Clive James: *The Metropolitan Critic*. London: Faber & Faber, 1974. 267 pp. (pp. 150-58).
- William H. Pritchard: "Discourses in America," *EIC*, 19:3 (July 1969), 336-47.

142. LEHMANN, JOHN: *The Open Night*. London: Longmans Green, 1952. ix, 128 pp.

"The Man Who Learnt to Walk Naked," 15-22; reprinted from John Lehmann (ed): *Orpheus: A Symposium of the Arts*. London: Lehmann, 1948-49. 2 vols. (1:96-102).

143. ——— (ed): *The Craft of Letters in England: A Symposium*. London: Cresset Press, 1956. vii, 248 pp.

Roy Fuller: "Poetry: Tradition and Belief," 74-97.

144. LERNER, LAURENCE: "W. B. Yeats: Poet and Crank," *PBA*, 49 (1963), 49-67.

Also issued separately as a pamphlet, °London: Oxford UP, 1964. Discusses "the relation between the value of a poem and the value of its subject matter," or more bluntly, "How is it that the greatest poet of the century, a poet of wisdom and understanding of the heart, a sage as well as a singer--how is it that he expounded in his poems such absurd, such eccentric, such utterly crackpot ideas?" Criticizes *A Vision*.

Reviewed by Brendan Kennelly, *Hermathena*, 101 (Autumn 1965), 60.

145. LOMBARDO, AGOSTINO: *La poesia inglese dall estetismo al simbolismo*. Roma: Edizione di Storia e letteratura, 1950. 303 pp. (Letture di pensiero e d'arte. 12.)

See pp. 67-68, 97-100, 249-88, and passim; particularly on the early poetry.

146. LONGLEY, EDNA: *Poetry in the Wars*. Newcastle: Bloodaxe, 1986. 264 pp.

Incorporates "Poetry and Politics in Northern Ireland," *Crane Bag*, 9:1 (1985), 26-40. Many references to Yeats (see index), particularly to "Nineteen Hundred and Nineteen" (pp. 14-21) and in discussions of Edward Thomas, Louis MacNeice, Philip Larkin, Derek Mahon, and poetry in Northern Ireland.

147. LUCAS, JOHN: *Modern English Poetry: From Hardy to Hughes. A Critical Survey*. London: Batsford, 1986. 218 pp.

"W. B. Yeats: The Responsibilities of the Poet," 103-29.

148. LUCY, SEÁN (ed): *Irish Poets in English: The Thomas Davis Lectures in Anglo-Irish Poetry*. Cork: Mercier Press, 1973. 238 pp.
A. Norman Jeffares: "Yeats," 105-17, and passim (see index).

149. MAC A'GHOBHAINN, IAIN: "Bardachd W. B. Yeats" [Yeats and the profession of the poet], *Gairm*, 64 (Autumn 1968), 363-69, 371-72.

150. MACCARTHY, DESMOND: *Criticism*. London: Putnam, 1932. xiii, 311 pp.
"Yeats," 81-88.

151. MACDONAGH, THOMAS: *Literature in Ireland: Studies Irish and Anglo-Irish*. Dublin: Talbot Press, 1916. xiii, 248 pp.
On Yeats's poetry, passim; particularly on his use of Gaelic names and on his prosody.

152. MACLEISH, ARCHIBALD: *A Time to Speak: The Selected Prose*. Boston: Houghton Mifflin, 1941. vii, 210 pp.
"Public Speech and Private Speech in Poetry," 59-69; revised from *YR*, 27:3 (Mar 1938), 536-47. There is no difference between Yeats the man and Yeats the poet. He *is* a poet. Yeats himself read this and approved of it (see *Letters*, p. 908).

153. ———: *Poetry and Experience*. Boston: Houghton Mifflin, 1961. ix, 204 pp.
"The Public World: Poems of W. B. Yeats," 115-47.

154. MACNEICE, LOUIS: "Subject in Modern Poetry," *E&S*, 22 (1937), 144-58.

155. ———: *Modern Poetry: A Personal Essay*. 2nd edition with an introduction by Walter Allen. Oxford: Clarendon Press, 1968 [1938]. xxiii, 205 pp.
Passim, especially pp. 23-25, 78, 80-83, 131, 143-44, 168-69, 194-95.

156. MAINUSCH, HERBERT, and DIETRICH ROLLE (eds): *Studien zur englischen Philologie: Edgar Mertner zum 70. Geburtstag*. Frankfurt/Main: Lang, 1979. 238 pp.
Willi Erzgräber: "W. B. Yeats als Lyriker," 167-88. The development of Yeats's poetry with particular reference to "The Man Who Dreamed of Faeryland," "Sailing to Byzantium," "A Dialogue of Self and Soul," "The Second Coming," and "Lapis Lazuli."

157. MANGANELLI, GIORGIO: "I simboli assediavano Yeats: La poesia di Yeats accompagna la lirica inglese da Swinburne ad Eliot," *Fiera letteraria*, 4:10 (6 Mar 1949), 3.

158. MARTIN, W. R.: "Yeats's 'Heaven Blazing into the Head,'" *ESA*, 15:2 (Sept 1972), 93-98.
Discusses the poems under the following aspect: "The persona begins in a certain drift of thought and feeling, then makes a discovery *in the course of the poem;* this brings an intense excitement and a deeper insight, and causes a different flow of thought and feeling, often a reversal of that of the beginning."

159. MARTZ, LOUIS LOHR: *The Poetry of Meditation: A Study in English Religious Literature of the Seventeenth Century*. New Haven: Yale

UP, 1955 [1954]. xv, 375 pp. (Yale Studies in English. 125.)
"'Unity of Being' and the Meditative Style," 321-30.

160. MAY, DERWENT: "Trzy wiersze W. B. Yeatsa--Przykład nowoczesnej krytyki angielskiej" [Three poems of WBY--An example of modern English criticism], *Zeszyty naukowe uniwersytetu Łodzkiego. Seria I: Nauki humanistyczno-społeczne,* 25 (1962), 173-82.
Contains interpretations of "Memory," "Crazy Jane on the Day of Judgment," and "Mad as the Mist and Snow."

161. MILLER, JOSEPH HILLIS: *The Linguistic Moment: From Wordsworth to Stevens*. Princeton: Princeton UP, 1985. xxi, 446 pp.
"Yeats," 316-48, and passim (see index). Mainly on "Nineteen Hundred and Nineteen."

162. MIZENER, ARTHUR: "The Romanticism of W. B. Yeats," *SoR,* 7:3 (Winter 1941/42), 601-23.
Reprinted in CA36. Yeats's later poetry differs from the earlier not in its themes but in their realization. The early poetry is committed to fancy, the later to fact.

163. MOORE, JOHN R.: "Yeats as a Last Romantic," *VQR,* 37:3 (Summer 1961), 432-49.
Misnomer; does not discuss Yeats's romanticism but rather the development of his thought as reflected in his poetry.

164. MOORE, THOMAS STURGE: "'Do We or Do We Not, Know It?': An Unpublished Essay on W. B. Yeats," *YeA,* 4 (1986), 145-56.
Followed by Warwick Gould: "Thomas Sturge Moore and W. B. Yeats--An Afterword," 157-60. Moore's essay was probably written in 1929 and discusses Yeats's poetry.

165. MORRIS, CHRISTOPHER D.: "World into Word: Tennyson, Ruskin, Hopkins, and the Nineteenth-Century Loss of Certainty," °Ph.D. thesis, State U of New York at Buffalo, 1972. 224 pp. (*DAI,* 33:8 [Feb 1973], 4427A)
Includes a discussion of Yeats's poetry.

166. MORRIS, LLOYD REGINALD: *The Celtic Dawn: A Survey of the Renascence in Ireland, 1889-1916*. NY: Cooper Square, 1970 [1917]. xix, 251 pp.
On Yeats's poetry and poetic theories, pp. 38-60; on his plays and dramatic theories, pp. 94-112; and passim.

167. MORTIMER, ANTHONY: *Modern English Poets: Seven Introductory Essays*. Toronto: Forum House, 1968. 159 pp.
"W. B. Yeats," 83-111.

168. MUIR, EDWIN: *The Present Age from 1914*. London: Cresset Press, 1939. 309 pp. (Introductions to English Literature. 5.)
For a second edition of the book see CB113. On Yeats, pp. 45-47, 52-61, and passim.

169. ———: *The Estate of Poetry*. Cambridge, Mass.: Harvard UP, 1962. xix, 118 pp. (Charles Eliot Norton Lectures. 1955-56.)
"W. B. Yeats," 42-60. Yeats was a poet with a definite Irish audience for his poems.

170. MULHOLLAND, ROSA: "Our Poets: No. 23--William B. Yeats," *IrM,* 17:193 (July 1889), 365-71.

Reprinted from °*Melbourne Advocate,* 9 Mar 1889. Ireland has earned the right to have a famous poet and Yeats is a likely candidate. Unfortunately his subject matter isn't all too Irish.

171. MULRYNE, R[ONALD]: "No Fabulous Symbol: Yeats and the Language of Poetry," *Gaéliana,* 5 (1983), 67-78.
Reprinted in Srivastava and Dutta: *Unaging Intellect* (1983, CA108), 1-13.

172. NAIK, M. K., and others (eds): *Indian Response to Poetry in English: A Collection of Critical Essays by Different Authors Presented to Dr. Vinayak Krishna Gokak on His Sixtieth Birthday.* Madras: Macmillan, 1970. ix, 285 pp.
Amalendu Bose: "Yeats from a Personal Angle," 142-49; reprinted from *BDE,* 5:1 (1969-70), 62-69; on Indian influences. Darshan Singh Maini: "Yeats: The Poet and the Pundit," 150-61. C. P. K. Tharagan: "Beyond the Veil: Some Vision Poems of Yeats and Eliot," 162-69; discusses poems indebted to *A Vision.*

173. NEMEROV, HOWARD: *Figures of Thought: Speculations on the Meaning of Poetry & Other Essays.* Boston: Godine, 1978. vii, 199 pp.
See pp. 15-17 (on "Lapis Lazuli") and 170-83, first published as "Poetry and History," *VQR,* 51:2 (Spring 1975), 309-28.

174. NOGUCHI, YONE: *Through the Torii.* London: Mathews, 1914. xi, 208 pp.
"A Japanese Note on W. B. Yeats," 110-17; reprinted from *Academy,* 6 Jan 1912, 22-23. The impression made by Yeats's poetry on an early Japanese visitor to England.

175. OATES, JOYCE CAROL: *The Edge of Impossibility: Tragic Forms in Literature.* NY: Vanguard Press, 1972. xi, 259 pp.
"Yeats: Violence, Tragedy, Mutability," 139-61; reprinted from *BuR,* 17:3 (Dec 1969), 1-17. In the poems and plays; comments on the influence of Nietzsche.
"Tragic Rites in Yeats's *A Full Moon in March,*" 163-87; reprinted from *AR,* 29:4 (Winter 1969/70), 547-60.

176. O'HARA, JAMES DONALD: *Poetry.* NY: Newsweek Books, 1977 [1976]. 192 pp.
See pp. 128-34.

177. OLIVERO, FEDERICO: *Studi sul romanticismo inglese.* Bari: Laterza, 1914. iii, 335 pp.
"William Butler Yeats," 105-69 ("Le liriche," 107-19; "I drammi," 120-69).

178. PACK, ROBERT: *Affirming Limits: Essays on Mortality, Choice, and Poetic Form.* Amherst: U of Massachusetts Press, 1985. viii, 264 pp.
"Lyric Narration: The Chameleon Poet," 23-40; reprinted from *HudR,* 37:1 (Spring 1984), 54-70. On the lyric poet "recreating himself as something other than what he is in fact," with several examples from Yeats's poetry.
"Yeats as Spectator to Death," 151-73; reprinted from *DQ,* 19:4 (Spring 1985), 93-110. On death in Yeats's poetry, especially in "A Dialogue of Self and Soul," "Lapis Lazuli," and "John Kinsella's Lament for Mrs. Mary Moore."
"The Tears of Art," 236-59; reprinted from *KR,* 7:1 (Winter 1985), 15-32; contains a note on "Coole Park, 1929."

179. PALIWAL, BRIJ BHUSHAN: *The Poetic Revolution of the Nineteen Twenties*. New Delhi: Chand, 1974. xv, 217 pp.
"W. B. Yeats," 100-19, and passim (see index). Discusses some poems written after 1920.

180. PARKINSON, THOMAS: "The Individuality of Yeats," *Pacific Spectator,* 6:4 (Autumn 1952), 488-99.

181. PARTRIDGE, ASTLEY COOPER: *Language and Society in Anglo-Irish Literature*. Dublin: Gill & Macmillan / Totowa, N.J.: Barnes & Noble, 1984. 380 pp.
"Nationalism and the Language of Poetry," 156-93 (on Yeats's poetry); "Dramatic Language in the Theatre," 194-235 (on the language of his plays); and passim (see index).

182. PAVLOVIC, MIODRAG: *Poetika modernog*. Beograd: "Vuk karadžić," 1981. 334 pp. (Izbrana dela Miodraga Pavlovića. 4.)
"O poeziji V. B. Jejtsa," reprinted from *Književnost,* 10:11 (Nov 1955), 363-76.

183. PEARCE, DONALD: "Flames Begotten of Flame," *SR,* 74:3 (July-Sept 1966), 649-68.
Traditional elements in Yeats's poetry, particularly in the two Byzantium poems.

184. PERKINS, DAVID: *A History of Modern Poetry: From the 1890s to the High Modernist Mode*. Cambridge, Mass.: Belknap Press of Harvard UP, 1976. xv, 623 pp.
See particularly "The Victorian Tradition and the Celtic Twilight," 15-29; "*Ars Victrix:* The London Avant-Garde," 30-59; "The Irish Scene," 252-66; "William Butler Yeats," 565-602.

185. ———: *A History of Modern Poetry: Modernism and After*. Cambridge, Mass.: Belknap Press of Harvard UP, 1987. xiii, 694 pp.
Numerous references to Yeats (see index).

186. PHELPS, WILLIAM LYON: *The Advance of English Poetry in the Twentieth Century*. NY: Dodd, Mead, 1933 [1918]. xv, 343 pp.
"The Irish Poets," 157-93; a revised version of "The Advance of English Poetry in the Twentieth Century, Part VI," *BmNY,* 47:1 (Mar 1918), 58-72. On Yeats, pp. 163-71.

187. PILLAT, ION: *Portrete lirice*. Edited by Virgil Nemoianu. București: Editura pentru literatură universală, 1969. xv, 405 pp.
"Sufletul irlandez in poesie: William Butler Yeats" [The Irish spirit in poetry], 310-28; written before 1936. Mainly on the early poetry.

187a. PLAKOTARE, ALEXANDRA: "E poieze tou W. B. Yeats (1865-1939)," *Epoches,* 32 (Dec 1965), 37-43.

188. POPOT, RAYMONDE: "Du refuge à l'envol," in Genet: *William Butler Yeats* (1981, CA32), 189-239.
Yeats's "espace poétique."

189. POUND, EZRA: "Status Rerum," *Poetry,* 1:4 (Jan 1913), 123-27.
At present, Yeats is "the only poet worthy of serious study."

190. POWER, PATRICK E. C.: "Irish Poets and the Countryside 1885-1947," Ph.D. thesis, University College Galway, [1968]. ix, 322 pp.

Discusses "nature" poetry, pastoral poetry, "peasant" poetry, and symbolist poetry written by various Irish poets, including Yeats (pp. 15-33, 84-99, 195-218, and passim).

191. PRESS, JOHN: *The Fire and the Fountain: An Essay on Poetry*. London: Methuen, 1966 [1955]. x, 256 pp. (University Paperbacks. 159.)

On Yeats, passim (see index).

192. PRIESTLEY, JOHN BOYNTON: *Literature and Western Man*. London: Heinemann, 1960. xiii, 512 pp.

On Yeats, pp. 398-404 and passim (see index).

193. PRITCHARD, WILLIAM H.: *Lives of the Modern Poets*. London: Faber & Faber, 1980. xii, 316 pp.

"W. B. Yeats: Theatrical Nobility," 49-82; more or less on the development of the poetry. See review by P. N. Furbank: "The Poet as Character," *TLS*, 26 Sept 1980, 1068.

194. *Problemy tvorcheskogo metoda (Mezhvuzovskiĭ sbornik)*. Ti͡umen': Ti͡umenskiĭ gosudarstvennyĭ universitet, 1979. 153 pp. (Nauchnye trudy: Sbornik. 67.)

V. V. Khorol'skiĭ: "Pozdni͡ai͡a lirika V. B. Ĭeĭtsa: Temy, konflikty, stil'" [The later lyrics of WBY: Subjects, conflicts, style], 110-19.

195. PUHALO, DUŠAN: "Poetske vrednosti jejtsove lirike" [The poetic values of Yeats's lyric work], *Letopis matice srpske*, year 135 / 384: 2-3 (Sept 1959), 144-58.

196. RAGUSSIS, MICHAEL: *The Subterfuge of Art: Language and the Romantic Tradition*. Baltimore: Johns Hopkins UP, 1978. xii, 244 pp.

"W. B. Yeats: The Vision of Evil and Poetic Objectivity in 'Nineteen Hundred and Nineteen,'" 85-108; also on "The Song of the Happy Shepherd," "The Sad Shepherd," and *A Vision*.

"W. B. Yeats: 'Her Vision in the Wood' as Tragic Art: A 'Hollow Image of Fulfilled Desire,'" 109-32; the treatment of the Venus-Adonis myth, includes comparisons with Keats and Nietzsche.

197. RAJAN, BALACHANDRA: *The Form of the Unfinished: English Poetics from Spenser to Pound*. Princeton: Princeton UP, 1985. viii, 319 pp.

See index for some notes on Yeats's poems.

198. RANSOM, JOHN CROWE: "Yeats and His Symbols," *KR*, 1:3 (Summer 1939), 309-22.

Reprinted in CA36. A defense of the later poetry at the expense of the earlier and a discussion of its symbols, which are taken to be not dependent on Yeats's esoteric speculations.

199. ———: "The Irish, the Gaelic, the Byzantine," *SoR*, 7:3 (Winter 1941/42), 517-46.

On the "naturalistic," "ontological," and "religionistic" aspects of Yeats's poetry. Discusses the Byzantium poems, "On a Picture of a Black Centaur," "Two Songs from a Play," "The Lake Isle of Innisfree," "After Long Silence," "Against Unworthy Praise," "Easter 1916," and "Among School Children."

200. RAY, NIRENDRA NATH: "The Poetry of W. B. Yeats (1865-1939)," *VQ*, 30:3 (1964-65), 177-96.

201. READ, HERBERT: "Révolte et réaction dans la poésie anglaise moderne," *Présence,* 5:1 (Apr 1946), 49-64.
A revised version was published as "Poetry in My Time," *Texas Q,* 1:1 (Feb 1958), 87-100.

202. ———: *The Tenth Muse: Essays in Criticism.* London: Routledge & Kegan Paul, 1957. xi, 331 pp.
"The Image in Modern Poetry," 117-38. "Sotto Voce: A Plea for Intimacy," 146-56; reprinted from *BBC Q,* 4:1 (Apr 1949), 1-6; discusses Yeats's dramatic theories and suggests that he might have been a successful writer of radio plays.

203. REGUEIRO, HELEN: *The Limits of Imagination: Wordsworth, Yeats, and Stevens.* Ithaca: Cornell UP, 1976. 224 pp.
Based on "Issue and Return: The Poetic Imagination in Wordsworth, Baudelaire, Yeats, Stevens, and Bonnefoy," °Ph.D. thesis, Brown U, 1970. 550 pp. (*DAI,* 40:10 [Apr 1980], 5433A; reprinted *YeA,* 1 [1982], 210-11). Yeats's poetry is discussed on pp. 95-145; analyzed in section DD.
Reviews:
- George Bornstein, *WSJour,* 2:1&2 (Spring 1978), 35-37.
- Robert Buttel, *JML,* 7:4 (1979), 603-5.
- Frances Ferguson, *GaR,* 31:2 (Summer 1977), 511-16.
- Kerry McSweeney: "Romantic Continuities and Mutations: Browning to Stevens," *Humanities Association R,* 28:3 (Summer 1977), 257-67.
- D. E. S. Maxwell, *Four Decades,* 1:4 (July 1977), 282-83.

204. RICHARDS, IVOR ARMSTRONG: *Poetries and Sciences.* A reissue of *Science and Poetry* (1926, 1935) with commentary. NY: Norton, 1970. 123 pp.
On Yeats's early poetry and D. H. Lawrence, pp. 70-75: Yeats and Lawrence "present two further ways of dodging those difficulties which come from being born into this generation rather than into some earlier age." The Yeats material is not included in the 1926 edition. It was first published as "A Background for Contemporary Poetry," *Criterion,* 3:12 (July 1925), 511-28.

205. ———: *Coleridge on Imagination.* Bloomington: Indiana UP, 1965 [1934]. xxv, 237 pp.
See pp. 207, 215, 217.

206. RIVOALLAN, ANATOLE: *Littérature irlandaise contemporaine.* Paris: Hachette, 1939. ix, 203 pp.
On Yeats's early plays, pp. 16-20; on the early poetry, pp. 45-55; on the later poetry, pp. 104-13; and passim (see index).
Reviews:
- Austin Clarke, *DM,* 15:2 (Apr-June 1940), 70-71.
- Ch.-M. Garnier, *LanM,* 38:1 (Jan-Mar 1940), 67-69.
- Armand Rébillon, *Annales de Bretagne,* 47 (1940), 267-70.

207. ROSENTHAL, MACHA LOUIS: *The Modern Poets: A Critical Introduction.* NY: Oxford UP, 1960. xii, 288 pp.
"Yeats and the Modern Mind," 28-48.

208. ———: *Poetry and the Common Life.* NY: Oxford UP, 1974. xi, 148 pp.
See pp. 25-37 ("Among School Children") and index.

209. ———: *Sailing into the Unknown: Yeats, Pound, and Eliot.* NY:

Oxford UP, 1978. xi, 224 pp.

"Structure and Process: Yeats's Civil War Sequences," 26-44 (on "Meditations in Time of Civil War" and "Nineteen Hundred and Nineteen"). "Yeats the Modern Lyric Poet: Around *The Tower*," 116-55. See index for further references.

Reviews:

- Harry Goldgar: "Yeats, Pound, Eliot Book Deals with the *Poetry*," *Times-Picayune*, 23 April 1978, section 3, 12.
- John Kelly: "Speak Easy," *New R*, 5:2 (Autumn 1978), 108-11.
- Robert Langbaum: "Lyrical Reading," *NYTBR*, 2 Apr 1978, 14, 36.
- Agnes McDonald, *Magill's Literary Annual*, 1979, 632-35.
- Charles Molesworth, *GaR*, 33:1 (Spring 1979), 230-33.
- Theodore Weiss: "The Many-Sidedness of Modernism," *TLS*, 1 Feb 1980, 124-25; reprinted in *The Man from Porlock: Engagements 1944-1981*. Princeton: Princeton UP, 1982. vii, 321 pp. (pp. 131-44).

210. ———, and SALLY M. GALL: *The Modern Poetic Sequence: The Genius of Modern Poetry*. NY: Oxford UP, 1983. xiv, 508 pp.

On Yeats's poetic sequences and on the order of *Last Poems*, pp. 96-145 and passim (see index). Analyzed in section DD. Reviewed by Raeburn Miller, *Yeats*, 2 (1984), 309-13.

210a. ROSENTHAL, MACHA LOUIS: *The Poet's Art*. NY: Norton, 1987. xvi, 160 pp.

A few notes on Yeats's poetry, especially on "The People" (see index).

211. A. E. [RUSSELL, GEORGE WILLIAM]: *Some Irish Essays*. Dublin: Maunsel, 1906. 39 pp. (Tower Press Booklets. 1.)

"Nationality and Cosmopolitanism in Art," 9-20; reprinted from FE23. "The Poet of Shadows," 35-39; reprinted from *Reader*, 2:3 (Aug 1903), 249-50; reprinted in G343. See also passim.

212. SCHMIDT, MICHAEL: *A Reader's Guide to Fifty Modern British Poets*. London: Heinemann, 1979. 432 pp.

Also issued as *An Introduction to Fifty Modern British Poets*. London: Pan Books, 1979. "W. B. Yeats (1865-1939)," 44-56; a biographical sketch and an account of the poetry. Yeats is also referred to in the chapters on Austin Clarke (pp. 173-80) and Patrick Kavanagh (pp. 207-12).

213. SCHRICKX, W.: "William Butler Yeats, symbolist en visionair dichter," *Vlaamse gids*, 49:6 (June 1965), 380-96.

214. SCHWARTZ, DELMORE: "Speaking of Books," *NYTBR*, 13 June 1954, 2.

Yeats's preoccupation with the theater helped him to improve his lyrical style. The later poetry is utterly unlike the earlier.

215. SERVOTTE, HERMAN: *Literatuur als levenskunst: Essays over hedendaagse engelse literatuur*. Antwerpen: Nederlandsche Boekhandel, 1966. 136 pp.

"Van Innisfree naar Byzantium: W. B. Yeats (1865-1939)," 97-113; reprinted from *DWB*, 110:1 (1965), 13-27. Sketches the development of Yeats's poetry.

216. ———: *English Literature: Poetry in the Twentieth Century. Lecture Notes*. Leuven: Acco, [1980]. ii, 144 pp.

"William Butler Yeats (1865-1939)," 19-40.

217. SETHNA, K. D.: "W. B. Yeats--Poet of Two Phases," *Mother India,* 1:10 (25 June 1949), 4-5, 8.
Reprinted in *Mother India,* 18:8 (July 1966), 17-27. The early poetry was "his richest from the viewpoint of poetry proper," whereas the later poetry, especially that written in a more realistic style, is often an aesthetic failure.

218. SHAW, PRISCILLA WASHBURN: *Rilke, Valéry and Yeats: The Domain of the Self.* New Brunswick: Rutgers UP, 1964. xiv, 278 pp.
Based on °"The Concept of Self in Rilke, Valéry and Yeats," Ph.D. thesis, Yale U, 1960. "William Butler Yeats: A Balance of Forces," 175-273; the balance of self and world in Yeats's poetry, particularly in "Leda and the Swan."
Reviews:
- Robert M. Adams: "Critical Cases," *NYRB,* 22 Oct 1964, 19-21.
- Geoffrey Hartman: "Insiders and Outsiders," *YR,* 54:2 (Dec 1964), 270-73.
- Joseph N. Riddel, *Modern Language J,* 49:3 (Mar 1965), 193-95.

219. SIEGMUND-SCHULTZE, DOROTHEA (ed): *Irland: Gesellschaft und Kultur IV.* Halle: Martin Luther Universität Halle-Wittenberg, 1985. viii, 231 pp. (Wissenschaftliche Beiträge. 1985/34 [F56].)
Thomas Metscher: "Reality and the Dream: On the Poetry of W. B. Yeats," 221-31; mainly on "The Fiddler of Dooney," "Among School Children," and "Easter 1916."

220. SISSON, CHARLES HUBERT: *The Avoidance of Literature: Collected Essays.* Edited by Michael Schmidt. Manchester: Carcanet Press, 1978. ix, 581 pp.
"W. B. Yeats," 255-74; slightly revised from *Ishmael,* 1:1 (Nov 1970), 38-59. Also in *English Poetry, 1900-1950: An Assessment.* London: Hart-Davis, 1971. 267 pp. (pp. 155-79).

221. SITWELL, EDITH: *Aspects of Modern Poetry.* London: Duckworth, 1934. 264 pp.
"William Butler Yeats," 73-89. Yeats's poetry is not an escape from life, it *is* life.

222. SITWELL, OSBERT, EDITH, and SACHEVERELL: *Trio: Dissertations on Some Aspects of National Genius.* Delivered as the Northcliffe Lectures at the University of London in 1937. London: Macmillan, 1938. viii, 248 pp.
Edith Sitwell: "Three Eras of Modern Poetry," 95-187; on Yeats, pp. 114-21.

223. SKELTON, ROBIN: "The Workshop of W. B. Yeats," *CP,* 1:2 (Fall 1968), 17-26.
The use of refrain in "The Apparitions," "Three Songs to the One Burden," and "What Then"; meter and sound in "The Municipal Gallery Revisited"; and some general remarks on Yeats's poetry.

224. SOUTHWORTH, JAMES GRANVILLE: *Sowing the Spring: Studies in British Poetry from Hopkins to MacNeice.* Oxford: Blackwell, 1940. viii, 178 pp.
"Age and William Butler Yeats," 33-45.

225. SPALDING, P. A.: "The Last of the Romantics: An Appreciation of W. B. Yeats," *Congregational Q,* 17:3 (July 1939), 332-45.

226. SPARROW, JOHN: *Sense and Poetry: Essays on the Place of Meaning in Contemporary Verse*. London: Constable, 1934. xxiv, 156 pp.
See pp. 13-14, 35-36, 77-80, 85-87, and passim.

227. ———: "Extracts from the Lecture on Tradition and Revolt in English Poetry," *British Institute of the U of Paris: The Bulletin,* 12 (Apr-May 1939), 15-23.

228. SPENDER, STEPHEN: *The Destructive Element: A Study of Modern Writers and Beliefs*. London: Cape, 1935. 284 pp.
Reprinted Folcroft, Pa.: Folcroft Library Editions, 1970. "Yeats as a Realist," 115-31; reprinted from *Criterion,* 14:54 (Oct 1934), 17-26; also in CA36. There is realism in Yeats's later poetry, but little awareness of contemporary issues (with the exception of "The Second Coming").

229. ———: "A Double Debt to Yeats," *List,* 4 Oct 1956, 513, 515.

230. ———: *The Struggle of the Modern*. London: Hamilton, 1963. xiii, 266 pp.
See pp. 29-30, 41-42, 44-45, 48, 50, 91, 113, 139, 162-64, 167, 215, 252-53, 259.

231. SPIVAK, GAYATRI CHAKRAVORTY: "'Principles of the Mind': Continuity in Yeats's Poetry," *MLN,* 83:6 (Dec 1968), 882-99.
The Wind among the Reeds is the first collection to exhibit one of Yeats's persistent preoccupations, the dramatization of the lyric self in the guise of Michael Robartes and other characters.

232. STAUFFER, DONALD ALFRED: *The Nature of Poetry*. NY: Norton, 1946. 291 pp.
On Yeats's symbolism, pp. 168-75; on "Sailing to Byzantium," pp. 243-46; and passim (see index).

233. STEAD, CHRISTIAN KARLSON: *Pound, Yeats, Eliot and the Modernist Movement*. London: Macmillan, 1986. vii, 393 pp.
A complementary book to Stead's *The New Poetic* (CB463). Yeats's poetry is discussed in "Part I: The Rise of Modernism," 9-83, and in "Some Reflections on the Poetry of Hardy and Yeats," 131-59. Analyzed in section DD. Reviewed by George Bornstein, *Yeats,* 5 (1987), 222-26.

234. SYMONS, ARTHUR: "Some Makers of Modern Verse," *Forum,* 66:6 (Dec 1921), 476-88.
Yeats "is never quite human--life being the last thing he has learnt."

235. TAMAMUSHI, KAZUKO: "Stillness and Dance--The Paradox of Art in W. B. Yeats," *Essays and Studies in British & American Literature,* 15:1 (Summer 1967), 65-89.

236. THOMAS, C. T., and others (eds): *Focus on Literature: Essays in Memory of C. A. Sheppard*. Madras: Macmillan India, 1982. xvi, 313 pp.
Nissim Ezekiel: "The Writing of Poetry," 135-42; comments on Yeats's laborious process of composition.

237. THWAITE, ANTHONY: *Essays on Contemporary English Poetry: Hopkins to the Present Day*. Tokyo: Kenkyusha, 1957. ix, 222 pp.
"W. B. Yeats," 30-47. Republished as *Contemporary English Poet-*

ry: An Introduction. London: Heinemann, 1959. viii, 168 pp. (pp. 28-41). Revised as *Twentieth-Century English Poetry: An Introduction.* London: Heinemann, 1978. x, 134 pp. (pp. 19-29).

238. TOWNSHEND, GEORGE: *The Genius of Ireland and Other Essays.* Dublin: Talbot Press, [1930]. 120 pp.
On the "idealistic" poetry of AE and Yeats, pp. 35-51.

239. TROTTER, DAVID: *The Making of the Reader: Language and Subjectivity in Modern American, English, and Irish Poetry.* London: Macmillan, 1984. viii, 272 pp.
On Yeats's poetry, pp. 58-67 and passim (see index).

240. TURNER, W. J.: "Music and Words," *NSt,* 24 July 1937, 146-47.
The relation between poetry and song, particularly in Yeats's poetry.

241. UYSAL, AHMET E.: "New Ideas and Trends in English Poetry during the First Quarter of the XXth Century," *Ankara Üniversitesi Dil ve Tarih-Coğrafya Fakültesi dergisi,* 22:3/4 (July-Dec 1964), 163-220.
On Yeats, pp. 167-74 and passim.

242. *A Vitalist Seminar: Studies in the Poetry of Peter Russell, Anthony L. Johnson and William Oxley.* Salzburg: Institut für Anglistik und Amerikanistik, Universität Salzburg, 1984. 313 pp. (Salzburg Studies in English Literature. Poetic Drama & Poetic Theory. 77.)
Anthony L. Johnson: "A Glance at Yeats, Eliot, Pound," 5-21. In his poetry, "Yeats was the only one of the three who was capable of displaying past, present and future as a single range of interconnected, interacting consciousness."
———: "Signifier and Signified in Verbal Art," 22-53; includes comments on the prosody of "The Wild Swans at Coole" and "After Long Silence."

243. WAGNER, ROBERT DEAN: "The Last Illusion: Examples of Spiritual Life in Modern Literature," Ph.D. thesis, Columbia U, 1952. iii, 260 pp. (*DAI,* 12:5 [1952], 624-25)
"Yeats and the Heresy of Paradox," 124-51.

244. WALSH, CHAD, and EVA T. WALSH: *Twice Ten: An Introduction to Poetry.* NY: Wiley, 1976. xxi, 435 pp.
"W. B. Yeats," 128-54; an introduction, reprints of several poems, and extended notes on the following: "The Stolen Child," "Adam's Curse," "The Dolls," "Crazy Jane Talks with the Bishop," and "Long-legged Fly."

245. WALSH, WILLIAM: *The Use of Imagination: Educational Thought and the Literary Mind.* London: Chatto & Windus, 1959. 252 pp.
"The Notion of Character in Education and Literature, and W. B. Yeats," 183-98; largely a reprint of "Columbia and Byzantium: The Notion of Character in Education and Literature," *Cambridge J,* 7:2 (Nov 1953), 101-13. Yeats's "universe of poetry" contains what pragmatical education lacks most: imagination.

246. WARD, DAVID: "Yeats's Conflicts with His Audience, 1897-1917," *ELH,* 49:1 (Spring 1982), 143-63.
Attempts to show "how Yeats's poems carry the stamp of historical forces in the sociological and psychological processes which he experienced as he produced them."

247. WARD, JOHN POWELL: *Poetry and the Sociological Idea*. Brighton: Harvester, 1981. xi, 242 pp. (Harvester Studies in Contemporary Literature and Culture. 6.)
"This book is not a sociology of poetry. Rather it implies that no such thing could usefully exist" (p. ix). See pp. 157-63.

248. Entry canceled.

249. WATKINS, VERNON: "New Year 1965," *List*, 7 Jan 1965, 22-23.

250. ———: *Yeats & Owen: Two Essays*. Frome: Hunting Raven Press, 1981. ii, 31 pp.
"The Poetry of W. B. Yeats," 1-18; sketches the poetic development. "War & Poetry: The Reactions of Owen & Yeats," 21-31; reprinted from *Labrys*, 1 (Feb 1978), [27-34]; mostly on Owen with a few notes on Yeats. Reviewed by Peter Phillips, *Poetry Wales*, 18:3 (1983), 56-57.

251. ———: "For Whom Does a Poet Write?" *Temenos*, 1 (1981), 93-96.
Previously unpublished lecture (1957), partly on Yeats, followed by texts of some poems which Watkins read on the occasion, including his own "A Photograph of Yeats," 99-100, apparently not in *Collected Poems* (HD190).

252. WELTE, WERNER (ed): *Sprachtheorie und angewandte Linguistik: Festschrift für Alfred Wollmann zum 60. Geburtstag*. Tübingen: Narr, 1982. xiii, 275 pp. (Tübinger Beiträge zur Linguistik. 195.)
Manfred Pfister: "Sailing to Innisfree: Stilwandel und ideologische Entwicklung in der Lyrik von W. B. Yeats" [Change of style and ideological development in the poetry of WBY], 113-30. Compares "The White Birds" and "Sailing to Byzantium" and finds that Yeats, early and late, exhibits "transcendental irrationality, an elitist hero cult, and dreams of authoritarian hierarchies," while rejecting critical observation and democratic pluralism.

253. WHALLEY, GEORGE: *Poetic Process*. London: Routledge & Kegan Paul, 1953. xxxix, 256 pp.
Notes on Yeats's poetry and criticism, passim (see index).

254. WHIGHAM, PETER: "Poetry in the First Half of the Twentieth Century II: Yeats, Pound, Eliot, and Auden," *European*, 69 (12:3) (Nov 1958), 168-73.

255. WICHT, WOLFGANG: "Die entromantisierte Metapher: Yeats' Umwertung einer Tradition," *ZAA*, 31:3 (1983), 211-27.
"The de-romanticized metaphor: Yeats's revaluation of a tradition." Discusses the relationship between nature and art and maintains that Yeats's devaluation of ideals results in human isolation but also in poetical productivity. Mainly on the two Byzantium poems.

256. WILLIAMS, CHARLES: *Poetry at Present*. Oxford: Clarendon Press, 1930. xii, 216 pp.
"William Butler Yeats," 56-69. Defends the later poetry, which he considers to be of Elizabethan magnitude. Includes "End Piece," a poem on Yeats.

257. WILLIAMS, JOHN: *Twentieth-Century British Poetry: A Critical Introduction*. London: Arnold, 1987. x, 117 pp.
On Yeats, passim (the index is unreliable).

258. WILLIAMS, JOHN ELLIS CAERWYN (ed): *Literature in Celtic Countries: Taliesin Congress Lectures*. Cardiff: U of Wales Press, 1971. 218 pp.

"Introduction," 5-19; contains some notes on Yeats and Synge. Austin Clarke: "Anglo-Irish Poetry," 153-74; on Yeats, passim.

259. WRIGHT, JAMES: "The Music of Poetry," *APR*, 15:2 (Mar-Apr 1986), 43-47.

Posthumously published version of a talk given in 1967; comments on Yeats's "traditional" poetry and on "Adam's Curse."

260. YEATS, W. B.: *Poèmes choisis*. Traduction, préface et notes par Madeleine L. Cazamian. Paris: Aubier, 1954. 383 pp.

The introduction (pp. 7-96) provides the biographical background and analyzes the poetry by grouping it according to themes. Notes on pp. 365-72. See G1371.

261. ———: *Poemas*. Selección, versión y prólogo de Jaime Ferran. Madrid: Rialp, 1957. 115 pp. (Adonais. 140.)

"Introducción a W. B. Yeats," 11-20.

262. ———: *The Variorum Edition of the Poems*. Edited by Peter Allt and Russell K. Alspach. NY: Macmillan, 1957. xxxv, 884 pp.

Reprinted as the °First Macmillan Hudson River Edition, NY: Macmillan, 1987.

T. R. Henn: "George Daniel Peter Allt," xi-xiv; an obituary with comments on Allt's Yeats studies.

"Introduction," xv-xvi; "Order and Placement of Poems," 858-63, the order and placement of poems in each of the individual volumes used for this edition. For reviews see G1039-1059.

263. ———: "A Critical Edition of Selected Lyrics of William Butler Yeats." Edited by Thomas Lee Watson, Editor's Ph.D. thesis, U of Texas, 1958. xii, 405 pp. (*DAI*, 19:5 [Nov 1958], 1080)

Contains a long introduction (pp. 1-90) in which the editor discusses the continuity of Yeats's poetic production, and an altogether unsatisfactory "edition" of about 120 poems. The editorial work consists mostly of printing one or perhaps two texts of a poem and appending a few biographical notes.

264. ———: *Versek*. Edited with introduction and notes by Tamás Ungvári. Budapest: Európa Könyvkiadó, 1960. 244 pp.

"William Butler Yeats," 5-29; "Jegyzetek," 229-37. See also G1377.

265. ———: *Poesie*. Traduzione, introduzione e note di Roberto Sanesi. Milano: Lerici, 1961. 513 pp. (Poeti europei. 8.)

"Introduzione," 7-80; "Biografia," 81-86; "Note ai testi," 441-78; "Bibliografia," 479-99. See also DB273 and G1378.

266. ———: *Selected Poems and Two Plays*. Edited and with an introduction by M. L. Rosenthal. NY: Macmillan, 1965 [1962]. xli, 236 pp. (Macmillan Paperbacks. 93.)

"The Poetry of Yeats," xv-xxxix; "Notes," 210-22; "Glossary of Names and Places," 223-30.

Reissued as *Selected Poems and Three Plays*. Third edition. Edited and with a new foreword and revised introduction and notes by M. L. Rosenthal. NY: Collier Books, 1986. xl, 248 pp. "Introduction: The Poetry of Yeats," xv-xl; "Notes," 219-34; "Glossary of Names and Places," 235-41; also a rather insufficient bibliography.

267. ———: *Selected Poetry*. Edited with an introduction and notes by A. Norman Jeffares. London: Macmillan, 1967 [1962]. xxi, 232 pp. (Papermac. P97.)
"Introduction," xiii-xxi; "Notes," 209-20. For reviews see G1133-1135.

268. ———, GEORGE BERNARD SHAW, and EUGENE O'NEILL: *Gedichten / Toneel*. Met inleidingen door W. H. Stenfert Kroese [etc.]. Haarlem: De Toorts, 1964. 419 pp.
W. H. Stenfert Kroese: "W. B. Yeats," 9-23.

269. YEATS, W. B.: *Quaranta poesie*. Prefazione e traduzione di Giorgio Melchiori. Torino: Einaudi, 1983 [1965]. xi, 163 pp. (Collezione di poesia. 15.)
"Prefazione," v-viii; "Nota bibliografica," ix-xi; "Note," 137-56. For reviews see G1381-1383.

270. ———: *Versuri*. Translated by Aurel Covaci. București: Editura pentru literatură universală, 1965. 288 pp.
Mihai Miroiu: "William Butler Yeats--Dialectica unei conștiințe poetice" [Dialectics of a poetic conscience], 5-28.

271. ———: *Runoja*. Translation, introduction and notes by Aale Tynni. Porvoo, Helsinki: Söderström, 1966. 212 pp.
"William Butler Yeats: Ihminen ja runoilija" [Man and poet], 11-29; "Selityksiä" [Explanations], 201-12. See also G1384.

272. ———: *The Poems*. Selected, edited and introduced by William York Tindall. Illustrated with drawings by Robin Jacques. NY: Printed at the Thistle Press for the Members of the Limited Editions Club, 1970. xviii, 135 pp.
"Introduction," v-xiii. See also G1413.

273. ———: *Poesie*. Traduzione, introduzione e note di Roberto Sanesi. Milano: Mondadori, 1974. 336 pp. (Gli Oscar. L145.)
"Introduzione," 11-63; written in 1960-61, probably identical with that used in DB265. "Biografia," 65-68. "Bibliografia," 69-82; contains virtually no items published after 1960. "Note ai testi," 309-35. See also G1517.

274. ———: *Choix de poèmes*. Introduction, choix, commentaires et traduction par René Fréchet. Paris: Aubier-Montaigne, 1975. 256 pp.
"Introduction," 11-70. For reviews see G1518-1520.

275. °———: *Selected Poems*. Selected by M. L. Rosenthal, illustrated by Liam Roberts. Franklin Center, Pa.: Franklin Library, 1979. 300 pp. (The 100 Greatest Books of All Time.)
Includes notes by the editor, 22 pp. inserted.

276. ———: *W. B. Yeats*. Edited with an introduction and notes by Tetsuro Sano. Kyoto: Yamaguchi Shoten, 1981. viii, 267 pp.
Introduction (in Japanese), pp. 3-31; poems, plays, and prose in English; reprint of Laurence Lerner's "W. B. Yeats: Poet and Crank" (DB144; why this of all Yeats criticism?), pp. 183-206; notes (in Japanese), pp. 209-42; bibliography, pp. 245-65.

277. ———: *Antología poética*. Introducción, selección, y traducción por E. Caracciolo Trejo. Madrid: Espasa-Calpe, 1984. 232 pp.
"Introducción," 11-26.

278. ———: [In Hebrew]: *Collected Poems*. Translated by Eliezra Eig-Zakov. S.l.: Cana Publishing House, 1985. 207 pp.
Contains an introduction, pp. 9-18.

279. YEH, MAX WEI: "Poetry, Art, and the Structure of Thought," °Ph.D. thesis, U of Iowa, 1971. 314 pp. (*DAI*, 32:3 [Sept 1971], 1489A-90A)
According to the abstract, on Yeats among others, particularly on "Among School Children."

280. YORK, R. A.: *The Poem as Utterance*. London: Methuen, 1986. viii, 214 pp.
"Yeats," 109-27; discusses the poetry as "imitated utterance," with particular reference to "Leda and the Swan."

281. ZIMMERMAN, LEE: "Singing amid Uncertainty: Yeats's Closing Questions," *YeA*, 2 (1983), 35-45.
The questions at the close of several poems.

See also AA7, AC3, 4, 17, 18, 29, 54, 76, 104, BA4, 10, BB15, 66, 77, 101, 109, 129, 165, BF136, 147, 156-58, 161, 163, 172, 177, 189, CA40, 53, 69, 89, 90, 93, 109, 124, 148-50, 155, 159, 161, 163, 165, CB46, 58, 68, 70, 100, 101, 129, 160, 162, 163, 167, 179, 189, 194, 223, 258, 260, 302, 308, 360, 371, 383, 384, 422, 426, 430, 446, 450, 463, 464, 540, 546, CC4-7, 14a, 17, 28, 35, 37, 49, 54, 92, 100, 105, 109, 117, 132, 168, 174, 180, 181, 190, 196, 215, 219, 299, 332, 333, 348, 351, CD2, 3, 7, 8, 20, 27, 31, 35, 43, 57, 58, 75, 78, 80, 83, 87-89, 113, 136, 137-39, 153, 223, 254, 262, 268, 319, 325, 344, 357, 370, 371, 395, 409, 412, 418, 427, 458, 470, 477, 519, 528, 529, 534, 558, 569, 596, 597, 598, 723, 785, 791, 794, 817, 859, 879, 885, 919, 957, 1002, 1044, 1101, 1131, 1135, 1137, 1142, 1160, 1165, 1168, 1177, 1222, 1237, 1249a, 1250, 1257, 1289, 1311, 1357, 1384, 1390, 1422, 1424, 1441, 1455, 1456, 1462, DD257, 505, EA29, EB86, FA67, FB30, 48, FC22, 29, 47, 53, 64, 76, 97, 101, 106, 108, 113, 117, 121, 142, FD18a, 29, 32, 51, 57, FE5, 16, 36, 48, 61, 68, 73, 106, FG23, 53, G2-30, 42-60, 85-129, 241-51 and note, 313-14, 391-94, 428-41 and note, 469-77, 511-13, 556-62, 605-32 and note, 696-724, 889-919 and note, 971, 1039-59 and note, 1130-35, 1266, 1369, 1371-72, 1376-78, 1381-85, 1413, 1460, 1517-20, 1548, 1572-97, 1600-3, HB10, 11.

DC Themes and Types

See headnote to section CC for an explanation of the structure of this section.

1. ADAMS, HAZARD: "Yeatsian Art and Mathematic Form," *CentR*, 4:1 (Winter 1960), 70-88.
Mathematics in the poetry (especially "The Statues") and in *A Vision*.

2. ———: *The Contexts of Poetry*. Boston: Little, Brown, 1963. xiii, 200 pp.
On Yeats, passim (see index), especially pp. 72-74 (the revisions of "Leda and the Swan"), 159-62 ("drama into character" in some poems), and 175-77 ("The Symbolism of Poetry").

3. ADAMS, [JOHN] JOSEPH: *Yeats and the Masks of Syntax*. NY: Columbia UP, 1984. viii, 111 pp.
Based on "A Syntactic Approach to Yeats," Ph.D. thesis, Colum-

bia U, 1975. vi, 219 pp. (*DAI*, 36:12 [June 1976], 8068A). Syntactical (not stylistic) analyses of the poetry, arranged according to linguistic criteria, not according to individual poems.
Reviews:
- Rosemary A. Battaglia, *YER*, 9:2 (Winter 1988), 66-68.
- Edmund L. Epstein, *Yeats*, 5 (1987), 209-20.
- Jacqueline Genet, *EI*, 10 (Dec 1985), 308-9.
- Kathleen Wales, *YeA*, 5 (1987), 260-66.

4. ADAMS, ROBERT MARTIN: "Now That My Ladder's Gone--Yeats without Myth," *Accent*, 13:3 (Summer 1953), 140-52.
Particularly on "Byzantium."

5. AGOSTINO, NEMI D': "La poesia di William Butler Yeats: Il 'periodo del sole' (1900-1919)," *EM*, 5 (1954), 149-202.

6. AITKEN, ADAM J., R. W. BAILEY, and N. HAMILTON-SMITH (eds): *The Computer and Literary Studies*. Edinburgh: UP, 1973, xi, 369 pp.
D. R. Tallentire: "Towards an Archive of Lexical Norms: A Proposal," 39-60. Discusses the shortcomings of the concordance of Yeats's poems (AF4) and lists the "word-frequency distribution" in this concordance.

6a. AL-ARISHI, ALI YAHYA, and WILLIAM L. TARVIN: "The Position of the Question in Yeats' Poetry," *JIL*, 17:1 (Jan 1988), 31-37.
The terminal questions, a unique phenomenon in English poetry.

7. ALLEN, JAMES L.: "Yeats's Use of the Serious Pun," *SoQ*, 1:2 (Jan 1963), 153-66.
Also on the influence of Donne.

8. ———: "The Golden Bird on *The Golden Bough:* An Archetypal Image in Yeats's Byzantium Poems," *DilR*, 11:2 (Apr 1963), 168-221.
Yeats's indebtedness to Frazer, specifically in his use of the archer-star and the golden bird and bough symbolism. Discusses "Parnell's Funeral" and the two Byzantium poems.

9. ALLT, G. D. P.: "Yeats and the Revision of His Early Verse," *Hermathena*, 64 (Nov 1944), 90-101; 65 (May 1945), 40-57.

10. ———: "Lady Gregory and Yeats's Cult of Aristocracy, *IrW*, 31 (Summer 1955), 19-23.
The aristocratic image of Lady Gregory in Yeats's poetry.

11. ALSPACH, RUSSELL KING: *Irish Poetry from the English Invasion to 1798*. 2nd edition revised. Philadelphia: U of Pennsylvania Press, 1964 [1943]. xi, 146 pp.
Some references, passim.

12. ———: "Some Textual Problems in Yeats," *SB*, 9 (1957), 51-67.

13. ALTIERI, CHARLES FRANCIS: "Yeats and the Tradition of the Literary Ballad," Ph.D. thesis, U of North Carolina at Chapel Hill, 1969. ii, 339 pp. (*DAI*, 31:1 [July 1970], 350A)
On Yeats's ballads and ballad theories.

14. ———: "From a Comic to a Tragic Sense of Language in Yeats's Mature Poetry," *MLQ*, 33:2 (June 1972), 156-71.
Particularly on "A Prayer for My Daughter" and "Coole Park and Ballylee, 1931."

14a. ANNWN, DAVID: *Inhabited Voices: Myth and History in the Poetry of Geoffrey Hill, Seamus Heaney and George Mackay Brown.* Frome, Somerset: Bran's Head Books, 1984. xv, 244 pp.

"W. B. Yeats," 16-26, and passim; on myth in Yeats's poetry.

15. ANTIPPAS, ANDY P.: "A Note on Yeats's 'Crazy Jane' Poems," *ES,* 49:6 (Dec 1968), 557-59.

The relationship with *A Vision.*

16. ARGOFF, N. JEANNE: "Yeats's Innovations in the Ballad Form," *CLQ,* 16:2 (June 1980), 106-17.

Yeats's ballads in theory and practice.

17. ARMSTRONG, ROBERTA R.: "Yeats as Nineteenth Century Poet," *VIJ,* 4 (July 1975), 45-58.

18. BABU, M. SATHYA: "Christian Themes and Symbols in the Later Poetry of W. B. Yeats," Ph.D. thesis, U of Wisconsin, 1968. vi, 259 pp. (*DAI,* 29:9 [Mar 1969], 3123A)

Includes chapters on "Statements on Religion in Yeats's Prose" and "Two Christian Plays," i.e., *Calvary* and *The Resurrection.*

19. BAGG, ROBERT ELY: "The Sword Upstairs: Essays on the Theory and Historical Development of Autobiographical Poetry," Ph.D. thesis, U of Connecticut, 1965. ix, 223 pp. (*DAI,* 26:9 [Mar 1966], 5408)

"The Self vs. Impersonality in Yeats, Eliot and Lowell," 186-217.

20. ———: "The Rise of Lady Lazarus," *Mosaic,* 2:4 (Summer 1969), 9-36.

Discusses "the context in which some exceptional modern poets discovered the self's various uses and its vulnerability." The poets are Yeats, Eliot, and Lowell, seen as predecessors of Sylvia Plath.

21. BAKER, WILLIAM EDWIN: *Syntax in English Poetry, 1870-1930.* Berkeley: U of California Press, 1967. xii, 197 pp. (Perspectives in Criticism. 18.)

Passim (see index), especially pp. 84-94, a comparison of Hopkins's and Yeats's syntactical peculiarities. It appears that Hopkins was far less orthodox than Yeats.

22. BALLIET, CONRAD A.: "The Adjective as Symbol," *Mosaic,* 12:3 (Spring 1979), 105-14.

Adjectives in Yeats's poetry.

23. ———: "W. B. Yeats: The Pun of a Gonne," *MBL,* 4:1 (Spring 1979), 44-50.

Gonne/gone puns in the poetry, indicating a preoccupation with Maud Gonne.

24. BANERJEE, AMITAVA: *Spirit above Wars: A Study of the English Poetry of the Two World Wars.* Madras: Macmillan, 1975. vii, 232 pp.

Contains some notes on Yeats.

25. BANFIELD, STEPHEN: *Sensibility and English Song: Critical Studies of the Early 20th Century.* Cambridge: Cambridge UP, 1985. 2 vols.

"The Celtic Twilight," 1:248-74, includes discussions of several musical settings of Yeats's poems. See also index, 2:619, for a select bibliography of these settings.

26. BARFOOT, C. C., F. H. BEUKEMA, and J. C. PERRYMAN (eds): *Time and Tide*. Writings offered to A. G. H. Bachrach by members of the Department of English on the occasion of his retirement from the Chair of English Literature in the University of Leiden. Leiden: Rijksuniversiteit, 1980. x, 313 pp.

Peter van de Kamp: "Some Notes on Yeats's Little and Intense Poems," 179-91. Stylistic analyses of some short poems and their indebtedness to French symbolism.

27. BARKER, VARA SUE TAMMINGA: "W. B. Yeats: Poetry as Meditation," °Ph.D. thesis, U of Texas at Austin, 1984. 318 pp. (*DAI*, 47:6 [Dec 1986], 2165A; reprinted *Yeats*, 5 [1987], 206-7)

28. BARTLETT, PHYLLIS: *Poems in Process*. NY: Oxford UP, 1951. ix, 267 pp.

On Yeats's methods of composition and revision, passim.

29. BARTON, RUTH PENDERGRASS: "'The Natural Words in the Natural Order': A Study of W. B. Yeats' Verse Syntax," Ph.D. thesis, U of Wisconsin, 1969. v, 298 pp. (*DAI*, 30:12 [June 1970], 5438A)

29a. BAUŽYTĖ, GALINA: "Būties vientisumo problema V. B. Jeitso poezijoje," *Literatūra*, 28:3 (1986), 57-66.

With a summary in English, entitled "Unity of Being in the Poetry of W. B. Yeats."

30. BEACH, JOSEPH WARREN: *Obsessive Images: Symbolism in the Poetry of the 1930's and 1940's*. Edited by William Van O'Connor. Minneapolis: U of Minnesota Press, 1960. xv, 396 pp.

On Yeats's use of the word "ceremony" and its reverberations in American poetry, pp. 3-12.

31. BEATTY, RICHMOND C.: "The Heritage of Symbolism in Modern Poetry," *YR*, 36:3 (Mar 1947), 467-77.

Note on Yeats, pp. 473-75.

32. BECKSON, KARL (ed): *Aesthetes and Decadents of the 1890's: An Anthology of British Poetry and Prose*. Edited with an introduction and notes by Karl Beckson. NY: Vintage Books, 1966. xli, 310 pp. (Vintage Book. V342.)

"Introduction," xvii-xl, passim on Yeats.

33. BEHAR, JACK: "Notes on Literature and Culture," *CentR*, 18:3 (Summer 1974), 197-220.

Contains a note on Yeats's poetry and history, pp. 207-8.

34. BELL, MICHAEL: "The Assimilation of Doubt in Yeats's Visionary Poems," *QQ*, 80:3 (Autumn 1973), 383-97.

Discusses "Lapis Lazuli," "The Second Coming," "The Gyres," and "Byzantium."

35. BENZIGER, JAMES: *Images of Eternity: Studies in the Poetry of Religious Vision from Wordsworth to T. S. Eliot*. Carbondale: Southern Illinois UP, 1962. ix, 324 pp.

"Modern Instances: Yeats / Stevens / Eliot," 226-49.

36. BERGER, HARRY: "Biography as Interpretation, Interpretation as Biography," *CE*, 28:2 (Nov 1966), 113-25.

The "fictional or dramatic image of career and self" in Yeats's poetry.

37. BESSAI, DIANE E.: "'Dark Rosaleen' as Image of Ireland," *Eire,* 10:4 (Winter 1975), 62-84.

38. BIANCHI, RUGGERO: *La poetica dell'imagismo.* Milano: Mursia, 1965. 243 pp. (Civiltà letteraria del novecento. Sezione inglese-americana. 1.)

Notes on Yeats and Imagism (see index), especially pp. 15-17.

39. BILLIGHEIMER, RACHEL V.: "'Passion and Conquest': Yeats' Swans," *CollL,* 13:1 (Winter 1986), 55-70.

The image of the swan in various poems.

40. ———: "Self and Soul in W. B. Yeats," *Eire,* 21:4 (Winter 1986), 52-65.

41. BLONDEL, JACQUES: *Imaginaire et croyance: Etudes de poésie anglaise.* Grenoble: Presses universitaires de Grenoble, 1976. ii, 195 pp. (Publications de la Faculté des Lettres de Clermont-Ferrand. 36.)

"L'expérience poétique de W. B. Yeats," 167-69; "Symbolisme et christianisme: De l'imagisme au symbolisme," 181-87.

42. BODKIN, MAUD: *Studies of Type-Images in Poetry, Religion, and Philosophy.* London: Oxford UP, 1951. xii, 184 pp.

Passim, especially on "The Second Coming" (with reference to Nietzsche), "A Prayer for My Son," and "Sailing to Byzantium."

43. BOKLUND, GUNNAR: "Time Must Have a Stop: Apocalyptic Thought and Expression in the Twentieth Century," *DQ,* 2:2 (Summer 1967), 69-98.

See pp. 94-96 ("As an apocalyptic writer James Thurber is much preferable to William Butler Yeats").

44. BOLAND, EAVAN: "Precepts of Art in Yeats's Poetry," *DM,* 4:1 (Spring 1965), 8-13.

Reflections on the poet's art in "Adam's Curse," "Sailing to Byzantium," and "The Circus Animals' Desertion."

45. BOSE, ABINASH CHANDRA: *Three Mystic Poets: A Study of W. B. Yeats, A. E. and Rabindranath Tagore.* With an introduction by J. H. Cousins. Kolhapur: School & College Bookstall, 1945. xx, 156 pp.

Based on "Mysticism in Poetry: With an Illustrative Study of A. E., W. B. Yeats, and Rabindranath Tagore," Ph.D. thesis, Trinity College, Dublin, 1937. x, 406 pp. Reprinted °Philadelphia: West, 1977.

"William Butler Yeats," 1-46. "Yeats belongs less to the class of mystics who also happen to be poets than to the class of poets who, owing to the special bent of their genius, come to be regarded as mystics. His mysticism is not . . . of the directly transcendental or religious type. . . . Yeats's poetic inspiration . . . is more purely aesthetic and humanistic" (p. 1).

46. BOWEN, JAMES K.: "Consummation, Completeness, and Crazy Jane: Totality through Union," *RS,* 39:2 (June 1971), 147-50.

47. BOWRA, CECIL MAURICE: *In General and Particular.* Cleveland: World, 1964. 248 pp.

"The Prophetic Element," 223-40; reprint of a pamphlet of the same title, London: Oxford UP, 1959. 19 pp. (English Association Presidential Address, 1959.) Contains some remarks on prophecies in Yeats's poetry.

48. ———: *Poetry & Politics, 1900-1960*. Cambridge: UP, 1966, viii, 157 pp.
See pp. 56-61, particularly on "The Black Tower."

49. BOZEK, PHILLIP EDWARD: "The Temporal Semantic of Poetic Texts: A Study of Selected Poems of W. B. Yeats," Ph.D. thesis, Southern Illinois U at Carbondale, 1979. x, 397 pp. (*DAI*, 40:6 [Dec 1979], 3310A)
The expression of time in "When You Are Old," "The Wild Swans at Coole," "The Lake Isle of Innisfree," "The Second Coming," "Sailing to Byzantium," and "Among School Children"; a study of semantics and style.

50. BRENKMAN, JOHN PRESTON: "Narcissus in the Text: Toward an Analysis of the Literary Subject in Ovid, Petrarch, and Yeats," Ph.D. thesis, U of Iowa, 1974. iii, 215 pp. (*DAI*, 35:12 [June 1975], 7861A-62A)
"I try to develop a procedure of reading literary texts that acknowledges their tendency to be stratified into a network of operations that are actively in contradiction with one another" (abstract). "Yeats: The Subject in Process," 118-85; discusses *A Vision* and some poems related to it.

51. BRIGGS, KATHARINE MARY: *The Fairies in Tradition and Literature*. London: Routledge & Kegan Paul, 1967. x, 261 pp.
See pp. 172-73: "With Yeats's poetry a different note came into our literature, for he believed in the fairies."

52. BROADBENT, JOHN BARCLAY: *Poetic Love*. London: Chatto & Windus, 1964. x, 310 pp.
Several notes on Yeats (see index), especially on "Among School Children" (pp. 4-7, 38).

53. BROOKE, NICHOLAS: "Crazy Jane and 'Byzantium,'" *E&S*, 27 (1974), 68-83.
The relationship between sensual and spiritual life in "Byzantium" and the Crazy Jane poems.

54. BROOKE-ROSE, CHRISTINE: *A Grammar of Metaphor*. London: Secker & Warburg, 1958. xi, 343 pp.
Passim on Yeats's metaphors.

55. BROWN, FORMAN G.: "Mr. Yeats and the Supernatural," *SR*, 33:3 (July 1925), 323-30.
In the poetry and the plays.

56. BROWN, TERENCE: "Dublin in Twentieth-Century Writing: Metaphor and Subject," *IUR*, 8:1 (Spring 1978), 7-21.
In Yeats's poetry and elsewhere.

57. BRUNNER, LARRY GEORGE: *Tragic Victory: The Doctrine of Subjective Salvation in the Poetry of W. B. Yeats*. Troy, N.Y.: Whitston, 1987. viii, 184 pp.
Based on "The Doctrine of Subjective Salvation in the Poetry of W. B. Yeats," Ph.D. thesis, Duke U, 1973. vii, 288 pp. (*DAI*, 34:11 [May 1974], 7222A).
"The aim of this study is to investigate the nature of the Yeatsian answer to tragic despair, to analyse its appearance in his poetry, to determine the reasons for its failure and consequent rejection by the poet, and to recognize possible alterna-

tives available to him after this rejection" (p. 3). Does not consider any Yeats criticism published after 1971.
Reviews:
- Arra M. Garab, *Christianity and Literature,* 37:3 (Spring 1988), 62-63.
- John Hanratty: "Singing-Masters of the Soul," *BooksI,* 118 (Nov 1987), 218-19.
- Mary Helen Thuente: "Yeatsian Tradition," *ELT,* 31:2 (1988), 220-26.

58. BUCKLEY, ERNEST BRUCE: "Mummy Truths: A Study of the Development of the Gyre Symbolism in the Poetry of W. B. Yeats," °Ph.D. thesis, U of Toronto, 1975. (*DAI,* 38:10 [Apr 1978], 6116A-17A)

59. BURKE, KENNETH: "On Motivation in Yeats," *SoR,* 7:3 (Winter 1941/42), 547-61.
A Vision and some related poems. Reprinted in CA36.

60. BURNSHAW, STANLEY: "Three Revolutions in Modern Poetry," *SR,* 70:3 (Summer 1962), 418-50.
Note on Yeats's symbols, pp. 443-44.

61. BUSH, DOUGLAS: *Pagan Myth and Christian Tradition in English Poetry.* Jayne Lectures for 1967. Philadelphia: American Philosophical Society, 1968. xvii, 112 pp. (Memoirs of the American Philosophical Society. 72.)
On Yeats, pp. 66-79 and passim (see index), especially on "Two Songs from a Play" and "Leda and the Swan."

62. BYRD, THOMAS L.: *The Early Poetry of W. B. Yeats: The Poetic Quest.* Port Washington, N.Y.: Kennikat Press, 1978. 151 pp.
Based on a Ph.D. thesis with the same title, U of Florida, 1968. iv, 174 pp. (*DAI,* 29:10 [Apr 1969], 3573A).
"This study will concentrate upon Yeats's very personal adaptation of the pastoral genre and an important theme or set of metaphors that not only is included in the pastoral but also serves to unify the early poetry: the figure of the poet-seeker and the poetic quest for truth" (p. 4). Analyzed in sections DD, EE, and FA.

63. ———, and CAROLYN GLENN KARHU: "The Stone as a Symbol in the Lyric Poetry of W. B. Yeats," *XUS,* 8:3 (Nov 1969), 28-35.

64. CANTOR, JAY: *The Space Between: Literature and Politics.* Baltimore: Johns Hopkins UP, 1981. xviii, 163 pp.
"History in the Revolutionary Moment," 17-57; on Yeats's poetry and the relationship with Joyce.

65. CARPENTER, LUCAS: "Yeats' Crazy Jane Poems," *CP,* 11:2 (Fall 1978), 55-65.

66. CASTEIN, HANNELORE: *Die anglo-irische Strassenballade.* München: Fink, 1971. 146 pp. (Motive. 3.)
English summary in *EASG,* 1971, 81. Discusses the influence of street ballads on Yeats's poetry, pp. 94-102.

67. CECI, LOUIS GABRIEL: "The Syntax of Vision: The Aesthetic Use of Grammatical Structures in the Visionary Poems of W. B. Yeats," Ph.D. thesis, Northwestern U, 1981. 401 pp. (*DAI,* 42:5 [Nov 1981], 2137A; reprinted *YeA,* 2 [1983], 105-6)

68. CERVO, NATHAN: "Hopkins, Yeats, Eliot: The Pre-Raphaelite Heritage," *PRR*, 2:1 (Nov 1978), 45-62.
Pre-Raphaelite echoes in Yeats's poetry and his views of Pre-Raphaelitism.

69. CHEADLE, B. D.: "A Perspective on Modernism in English Poetry," *ESA*, 19:2 (Sept 1976), 65-81.
Contains a few notes on Yeats's poetry.

70. CHITTICK, V. L. O.: "Yeats the Dancer," *DR*, 39:3 (Autumn 1959), 333-48.

71. CLARK, DAVID RIDGLEY: *Lyric Resonance: Glosses on Some Poems of Yeats, Frost, Crane, Cummings, & Others* [. . .]. Amherst: U of Massachusetts Press, 1972. ix, 274 pp.
Incorporates: "Poussin and Yeats's 'News for the Delphic Oracle,'" *Wascana R*, 2:1 (1967), 33-44; "Out of a People to a People," *Malahat R*, 22 (Apr 1972), 25-41.
"W. B. Yeats," 11-54, in three sections: "Out of a People to a People" (Yeats and the Anglo-Irish poetry of the 19th century, particularly Davis, Mangan, and Ferguson, and the reverberations in Yeats's own poetry); an interpretation of "He Bids His Beloved Be at Peace"; and an interpretation of "News for the Delphic Oracle" (commenting on the relationship between Yeats's poem and Poussin's painting "The Marriage of Peleus and Thetis," actually "Acis and Galatea").
"Some Irish Poems," 55-102; by Wilde, Gogarty, Seumas O'Sullivan, Joseph Campbell, and Thomas Kinsella, with references to Yeats.

72. CLEARFIELD, ANDREW MARK: *These Fragments I Have Shored: Collage and Montage in Early Modernist Poetry*. Ann Arbor: UMI Research Press, 1984. xii, 150 pp. (Studies in Modern Literature. 36.)
Note on the "modernism" of Yeats's poetry, pp. 47-50.

73. COHEN, PAUL: "Yeats as Portraitist," *CJIS*, 5:2 (Dec 1979), 31-37.
Portraits in Yeats's works, especially in his poetry.

74. ———: "Words for Music: Yeats's Late Songs," *CJIS*, 10:2 (Dec 1984), 15-26.
Yeats's "interest in the relationship between poetry and music."

75. CONNER, LESTER I.: "A Matter of Character: Red Hanrahan and Crazy Jane," in Jeffares: *Yeats, Sligo and Ireland* (1980, CA51), 1-16.
Discusses Yeats's method of inventing these two "mythological" characters.

76. CORRADINI FAVATI, GABRIELLA: *L'alchimia del sogno e della rosa: Studio sulla poesia del giovane Yeats*. Pisa: Pacini, 1977. 143 pp.
Contains chapters on "The Lake Isle of Innisfree"; Yeats's "celticismo"; his "faeryland"; the images of dream, life, and death; Christian and pagan motifs; and the symbol of the rose.

77. COSENTINO, GIACOMO: *Studies in Yeats's Later Poems*. Catania: Artigrafiche La Stampa, 1974. 70 pp.
Republished, slightly revised but without reference to previous publication as *The Search for Reality in Yeats's Later Poems*. Catania: C.U.E.C.M., 1986. 80 pp. On the fools and rogues in the later poetry and on "A Woman Young and Old," "Words for Music Perhaps," and "Supernatural Songs."

78. Entry canceled.

79. COUSINS, JAMES HENRY: *New Ways in English Literature*. Madras: Ganesh, 1919 [1917]. xv, 196 pp.
"William Butler Yeats, Poet and Occultist," 43-52; reprinted as "Yeats the Nobel Prizeman and His Poetry," *VQ*, 2:2 (July 1924), 156-61. His most important sources are theosophy and Neo-Platonism.

80. COX, KENNETH: "The Poetry of Yeats and Its Place or Places between Vision and Action," *Agenda*, 9:4--10:1 (Autumn-Winter 1971/72), 46-55.
On the vocabulary, syntax, and rhythm of Yeats's poetry.

81. CRONIN, ANTHONY: "Guns and Yeats," *NYT*, 24 Aug 1971, 37.
Yeats's poetry and the motif of political violence.

82. DAICHES, DAVID: "Jane Austen, Karl Marx, and the Aristocratic Dance," *ASch*, 17:3 (Summer 1948), 289-96.
The dance motif and the country house ideal in Jane Austen and in Yeats's poetry.

83. ———: *Time and the Poet*. Cardiff: U of Wales Press, 1965. 30 pp. (W. D. Thomas Memorial Lecture. 23 Feb 1965.)
Some notes on Yeats, pp. 28-30 and passim.

84. DAVENPORT, GUY: *Every Force Evolves a Form: Twenty Essays*. San Francisco: North Point Press, 1987. x, 173 pp.
"The Artist as Critic," 68-83; first published as part of "Claiming Kin: Artist, Critic and Scholar as Family," *Shenandoah*, 36:1 (1985-86), 35-86. Contains a note on the Crazy Jane poems and their indebtedness to Meredith's poem "Jump-to-Glory Jane."

85. DAVID, PAUL: "Structure in Some Modern Poets," *New English Weekly*, 26 July 1945, 131-32.
Yeats had difficulties in writing poems "with a beginning, a middle and an ending."

86. DAVIE, DONALD: *Purity of Diction in English Verse*. London: Routledge & Kegan Paul, 1969 [1952]. viii, 217 pp.
A few scattered notes on Yeats (see index).

87. ———: "Landscape as Poetic Focus," *SoR*, 4:3 (Summer 1968), 685-91.

88. DEANE, SHEILA MCCOLM: "The Bardic Style in the Poetry of Gerard Manley Hopkins, William Butler Yeats, and Dylan Thomas," °Ph.D. thesis, U of Western Ontario, 1987. (*DAI*, 48:6 [Dec 1987], 1458A)

89. DECKER, SHARON D.: "Love's Mansion: Sexuality in Yeats's Poetry," *MBL*, 4:1 (Spring 1979), 17-32.

90. DE LOGU, PIETRO: "L'Arcadia di W. B. Yeats," *Annali della Facoltà di lingue e letterature straniere di Ca' Foscari*, 16:2 (1977), 21-47.
On the early poetry and *The Island of Statues*.

91. DEL RE, GABRIELE: "Esoterismo e passione nella poesia di W. Butler Yeats," *Cristallo*, 16:1 (Apr 1974), 85-102.

92. DEMERS, PIERRE E.: "Yeats' Great Wheel and the Use of Christian Myths and Symbols in His Poems," *FJS*, 2 (1969), 33-51.

93. DEUTSCH, BABETTE: "Religious Elements in Poetry," *Menorah J*, 29:1 (Jan-Mar 1941), 21-48.
See pp. 24-30.

94. DIXON, CHRISTOPHER J.: *Fin de Siècle: Poetry of the Late Victorian Period 1860-1900*. London: Norton Bailey, 1968. viii, 165 pp.
"Introduction," 1-26.

95. DODSON, DIANE MARTHA: "A Theory of Tragedy," °Ph.D. thesis, North Texas State U, 1981. 155 pp. (*DAI*, 42:3 [Sept 1981], 1136A)
"In Chapter III the body of Yeats's lyric poetry is examined as an expression of the tragic vision" (abstract).

96. DOUGHERTY, ADELYN: *A Study of Rhythmic Structure in the Verse of William Butler Yeats*. The Hague: Mouton, 1973. 136 pp. (De Proprietatibus Litterarum. Series Practica. 38.)
Based on Adelyn O'Connell's Ph.D. thesis with the same title, Catholic U of America, 1966. v, 163 pp. (*DAI*, 27:9 [Mar 1967], 3057A). A heavily statistical study.

97. ———: "'Traditional Metres' and 'Passionate Syntax' in the Verse of William Butler Yeats," *Lang&S*, 14:3 (Summer 1981), 216-25.

98. DUCLOS, MICHÈLE: "L'Irlande dans la poésie de W. B. Yeats," *Annales du Groupe d'études et de recherches britanniques*, 1 (1976), 59-77.

99. DUGGAN, EILEEN: "Dedication, the Artist's Discipline," *America*, 10 June 1939, 210-11.
Constance Markievicz in Yeats's poetry.

100. DURRANT, GEOFFREY: "Cast a Cold Eye," *Acorn*, 4 (Spring 1963), 9-15.
Reprinted from °*Trek*, 1945. Yeats's later poetry is better than the earlier "damp" romanticism.

101. DURRELL, LAWRENCE: *A Key to Modern British Poetry*. Norman: U of Oklahoma Press, 1964 [1952]. xii, 209 pp.
On symbolism and theosophy in Yeats's early poetry, pp. 104-10.

101a. DUTTA-ROY, SONJOY: "The Rooted Bard and the Rootless Satirist: Tradition and Modernity in Yeats and Eliot," *YER*, 9:3 (Spring 1988), 119-23.
Yeats's view of his ancestors in his poetry, especially in "The Curse of Cromwell," compared to Eliot's.

102. EARLE, RALPH HARDING: "Yeats's Passionate Syntax," Ph.D. thesis, U of North Carolina at Chapel Hill, 1985. vi, 191 pp. (*DAI*, 47:2 [Aug 1986], 535A; reprinted *Yeats*, 5 [1987], 204-5)
The syntax of "Sailing to Byzantium," "Ancestral Houses," "A Prayer for My Daughter," "A Dialogue of Self and Soul," "Among School Children," "Leda and the Swan," and the sonnets.

103. EGLESON, JANET FRANK: "Christ and Cuchulain: Interrelated Archetypes of Divinity and Heroism in Yeats," *Eire*, 4:1 (Spring 1969), 76-85.
Discusses the pertinent poems and plays.

104. ELEANOR, MOTHER MARY: "The Debate of the Body and the Soul," *Renascence,* 12:4 (Summer 1960), 192-97.

105. EMSLIE, MACDONALD: "Gestures in Scorn of an Audience," in Maxwell and Bushrui: *W. B. Yeats 1865-1965* (1965, CA71), 102-26.
Arrogance in the poetry.

106. ENGELBERG, EDWARD: "Space, Time and History: Towards the Discrimination of Modernisms," *Modernist Studies,* 1:1 (1974), 7-27.
The view of history in the poetry of Yeats and Eliot.

107. ENGSBERG, RICHARD CARL: "Two by Two: Analogues of Form in Poetry and Music," Ph.D. thesis, New York U, 1968. xiii, 436 pp. (*DAI,* 30:1 [July 1969], 278A)
Includes discussions of Yeats's poetry.

108. ENSCOE, GERALD: *Eros and the Romantics: Sexual Love as Theme in Coleridge, Shelley and Keats.* The Hague: Mouton, 1967. 178 pp. (Studies in English Literature. 45.)
See pp. 170-71.

109. EPSTEIN, EDMUND L.: *Language and Style.* London: Methuen, 1978. xii, 92 pp.
Some notes on Yeats's poems, particularly on "An Irish Airman Foresees His Death," "Lapis Lazuli," "The Cold Heaven," and "Who Goes with Fergus?" (see index).

110. FAIRCHILD, HOXIE NEALE: *Religious Elements in English Poetry.* NY: Columbia UP, 1939-68. 6 vols.
On Yeats, 5:181-91, 539-50, and passim (see index); vol. 6, passim (see index).

111. FARAG, F. F.: "Oriental and Celtic Elements in the Poetry of W. B. Yeats," in Maxwell and Bushrui: *W. B. Yeats 1865-1965* (1965, CA71), 33-53.
Yeats adapted Celtic lore to suit traditions that he had come to know through the influence of Mohini Chatterjee.

112. FARRELL, LEIGH ANN DAWES: "The Archetypal Image: An Interpretation of the Poetry of Theodore Roethke, Arthur Rimbaud, W. B. Yeats, and Robert Frost," °Ph.D. thesis, U of Washington, 1983. 245 pp. (*DAI,* 44:11 [May 1984], 3377A; reprinted *Yeats,* 3 [1985], 209-10, and *YeA,* 4 [1986], 305-6)
Includes a "study of the persistent feminine figures in Yeats's poetry" (abstract).

113. FASS, BARBARA F.: "The Little Mermaid and the Artist's Quest for a Soul," *CLS,* 9:3 (Sept 1972), 291-302.
Contains a note on Yeats's poetry.

113a. FLANAGAN, KATHLEEN THERESA: "The Orient as Pretext for Aesthetic Revolution in Modern Poetry in English," °Ph.D. thesis, U of North Carolina at Chapel Hill, 1987. 220 pp. (*DAI,* 48:9 [Mar 1988], 2331A)
On oriental themes in Yeats's poetry, according to abstract.

114. FLEMING, DAVID: "A Vision of History: Yeats's Mystical Pattern and Historical References in the Later Lyrics," *Delta Epsilon Sigma Bulletin,* 9:1 (Mar 1964), 18-29.
The importance of *A Vision* for "Sailing to Byzantium," "Medita-

tions in Time of Civil War," "Two Songs from a Play," "Leda and the Swan," and "Under Ben Bulben."

115. FOSTER, JOHN WILSON: "Yeats and the Easter Rising," *CJIS*, 11:1 (June 1985), 21-34.
"Easter 1916" and related poems and the borrowings from Pearse.

116. FOSTER, THOMAS CARLETON: "What Will Suffice: Culture, History, and Form in Modern Literature," °Ph.D. thesis, Michigan State U, 1981. 208 pp. (*DAI*, 42:6 [Dec 1981], 2670A; reprinted *YeA*, 4 [1986], 307-8)
Contains a chapter attempting to connect "Yeats's political concerns with the development of his mythology" in the poetry (abstract).

117. FRANK, LUANNE (ed): *Literature and the Occult: Essays in Comparative Literature*. Arlington: U of Texas at Arlington, 1977. viii, 273 pp.
Wayne Shumaker: "The Uses of the Occult in Literature," 19-30, criticizes the "wrong sort of use" of the occult in Yeats's poetry.

118. FRANKLIN, LAURA MABEL: "The Development of Yeats's Poetic Diction," Ph.D. thesis, Northwestern U, 1956. vii, 212 pp. (*DAI*, 16:12 [1956], 2456-57)
Includes statistical tables and a comparison with Eliot's diction.

119. FRIEDMAN, ALBERT B.: *The Ballad Revival: Studies in the Influence of Popular on Sophisticated Poetry*. Chicago: U of Chicago Press, 1961. vii, 376 pp.
"Epilogue: The Ballad in Modern Verse," 327-56.

120. FRYE, NORTHROP: *The Stubborn Structure: Essays on Criticism and Society*. London: Methuen, 1970. xii, 316 pp.
"The Top of the Tower: A Study of the Imagery of Yeats," 257-77; reprinted from *SoR*, 5:3 (July 1969), 850-71.

121. FULLWOOD, DAPHNE: "The Early Poetry of W. B. Yeats," *Ariel*, 3:3 (July 1972), 80-90.

122. FUSSELL, PAUL: *Poetic Meter and Poetic Form*. NY: Random House, 1965. xiii, 208 pp. (Studies in Language and Literature. SLL3.)
Passim (see index).

123. GARDNER, HELEN: *Poems in the Making*. Southampton: U of Southampton, 1972. 29 pp. (Gwilym James Memorial Lecture at the University of Southampton. 1.)
Compares Yeats's and Eliot's methods of drafting and revising their poems.

124. GEAREN, ANN MARIE: "Helen, Crazy Jane, and the Dance Queens: The Developing Image of Woman in the Poetry and Plays of W. B. Yeats," Ph.D. thesis, U of Chicago, 1980. v, 218 pp.

125. GENET, JACQUELINE: "La symbolique de l'arbre dans la poésie de W. B. Yeats," *Travaux et mémoires*, [1] (Sept 1974), 15-36.

126. ———: "La conception de l'histoire dans la poésie de W. B. Yeats," *EI*, 1 (Dec 1976), 63-83.

127. ———: "W. B. Yeats et les problèmes politiques irlandais," *Cahiers du Centre de Recherches sur les Pays du Nord et du Nord-Ouest*, 1 (1978), 87-104.
Mainly as reflected in the poetry.

128. GENIUSHENE, IZOL'DA-GABRIELE LI͡AONO: "Some Traits of the Development of W. B. Yeats's Poetic Diction," *Tartu Riikliku Ülikooli Toimetised: Uchenye zapiski / Tartuskogo gosudarstvennogo unversiteta: Acta et commentationes Universitatis Tartuensis*, 426 (1977) / *Trudy po romano-germanskoĭ filologii*, 7 (1977), 14-31.
Mainly on the symbol of the rose. N.B.: Elsewhere, the author's name appears as Izolda-Gabrielė Geniušienė.

129. ———: "The Rose Symbol in the Early Poetry of W. B. Yeats," *Literatūra*, 19:3 (1977), 47-53.

130. ———: *Pozdni͡ai͡a poezii͡a U. B. Ieĭtsa: Problema metoda*. Avtoreferat disserta͡tsii . . . kandidata filologicheskikh nauk. Moskva: Moskovskiĭ. . . gosudarstvennyĭ universitet im. M. V. Lomonosova, 1984. 26 pp.
"Yeats's late poetry: The problem of method"; a dissertation abstract.

130a. ———: "Simbolicheskiĭ mifologizm v pozdneĭ poezii U. B. Ietsa," *Literatūra*, 28:3 (1986), 67-72.
With a summary in English, entitled "Symbolical Mythology in the Late Poetry of W. B. Yeats."

131. GERETY, JANE: "Poetry and Magic: A Study of Yeats's Poems of Meditation," °Ph.D. thesis, U of Michigan, 1982. 250 pp. (*DAI*, 43:10 [Apr 1983], 3324A; reprinted *Yeats*, 2 [1984], 259-60, and *YeA*, 4 [1986], 309-10)

132. GIFFORD, HENRY: *Poetry in a Divided World*. The Clark Lectures 1985. Cambridge: Cambridge UP, 1986, ix, 111 pp.
Discusses Yeats's "position in Irish life" as reflected in his poetry and the "affinities and opposition" between Yeats and Blok, pp. 38-44. See pp. 60-61 for a Yeats-Eliot comparison.

133. GOGGIN, EDWARD WILLIAM: "Blest: Cohesion and Ironic Deflation in Six Short Poem Sequences of W. B. Yeats," °Ph.D. thesis, Fordham U, 1985. 305 pp. (*DAI*, 47:3 [Sept 1986], 910A; reprinted *Yeats*, 5 [1987], 205-6)
Discusses "Upon a Dying Lady," "A Man Young and Old," "Meditations in Time of Civil War," "A Woman Young and Old," "Supernatural Songs," and "The Three Bushes."

134. GOLDEN, WILLIAM FRANCIS: "I. Jonson on Colonization. II. A Study of Transcendent Moments in the Poetry of Eliot and Yeats [. . .]," °Ph.D. thesis, Rutgers U, 1974. 109 pp. (*DAI*, 35:1 [July 1974], 402A)
On Yeats's search for myth.

135. GOLDSTEIN, LAURENCE: *The Flying Machine and Modern Literature*. London: Macmillan, 1986. xv, 253 pp.
On the Robert Gregory poems, 89-93.

136. GOMES, EUGENIO: *A neve e o girassol*. São Paulo: Conselho estadual de cultura: Comissão de literatura, 1967. 127 pp. (Coleção ensaio. 46.)

"Yeats e a velhice" [Yeats and old age], 89-92.

137. GOODMAN, ANN: "Phonological Aspects of Metaphor in Anglo-American Poetry," *Sigma,* 6 (1981), 109-21.
A section on "sound association in metaphor" contains examples taken from Yeats's poetry.

138. GOSHI, KEIGO: [In Japanese] "On W. B. Yeats's Historical Poems," *Humanities,* 6 (Sept 1957), 7-25.
With a summary in English.

139. GRAMM, CHRISTIE DIANE: "The Development of Prophecy in the Poetry of W. B. Yeats," °Ph.D. thesis, U of Oregon, 1985. 131 pp. (*DAI,* 46:7 [Jan 1986], 1948A; reprinted *Yeats,* 5 [1987], 199)

140. GREEN, J. T.: "Symbolism in Yeats's Poetry," *Fort Hare Papers,* 4:3 (June 1969), 13-23.
"Through symbolism he discovered a medium to create an extremely lively and concrete poetry about himself." Includes a discussion of Yeats's theory of symbolism.

141. GREENE, ROLAND ARTHUR: "Origins and Innovations of the Western Lyric Sequence," Ph.D. thesis, Princeton U, 1985. ix, 450 pp. (*DAI,* 45:12 [June 1985], 3631A; reprinted *Yeats,* 4 [1986], 180-81)
"The Modern Temper in the Lyric Sequence: Interval and Innovation in Two Sequences by Yeats," 214-94; on "A Man Young and Old" and "A Woman Young and Old."

142. GREER, SAMMYE CRAWFORD: "Yeats's Lyric Personae," Ph.D. thesis, U of Kentucky, 1970. iv, 251 pp. (*DAI,* 31:10 [Apr 1971], 5401A-2A)

143. GREGORY, HORACE: *The Shield of Achilles: Essays on Beliefs in Poetry.* NY: Harcourt, Brace, 1944. xii, 211 pp.
"On William Butler Yeats and the Mask of Jonathan Swift," 136-55; Swift in the poetry and in *The Words upon the Window-Pane.*
First published in *SoR,* 7:3 (Winter 1941/42), 492-509; reprinted in *Spirit of Time and Place: Collected Essays.* NY: Norton, 1973. xiii, 316 pp. (pp. 122-35), which also includes G1042.

144. GREGORY, VERE RICHARD TRENCH: *The House of Gregory.* Dublin: Browne & Nolan, 1943. xv, 210 pp.
Comments briefly on Yeats's "Gregory poems," pp. 136-41.

145. GRGAS, STIPE: "William Butler Yeats: Pjesnik i njegov sistem" [WBY: The poet and his system], *Radovi: Filozofski fakultet Zadar. Razdio filoloških znanosti,* 24 (1984/85), 223-30.
With a summary in English. Discusses the importance of *A Vision* to the later poetry.

146. GRIERSON, HERBERT JOHN CLIFFORD: *Lyrical Poetry from Blake to Hardy.* London: Hogarth Press, 1928. 159 pp. (Hogarth Lectures on Literature. 5.)
See pp. 148-52 on the early poetry.

147. GRIFFIN, JASPER: *The Mirror of Myth: Classical Themes & Variations.* London: Faber & Faber, 1986. 144 pp. (T. S. Eliot Memorial Lectures 1984.)
Chapter 1, "Myth and Paradigm," 9-42, contains some notes on the use of Classical myth in Yeats's poetry.

147a. GRIMES, LINDA SUE: "William Butler Yeats' Transformations of Eastern Religious Concepts," °Ph.D. thesis, Ball State U, 1987. 186 pp. (*DAI*, 48:11 [May 1988], 2866A-67A)
Yeats's "use of Upanishad philosophy in his poetry," including a comparison of the poetry of Yeats and Tagore.

148. GROSS, HARVEY SEYMOUR: *The Contrived Corridor: History and Fatality in Modern Literature*. Ann Arbor: U of Michigan Press, 1971. xiv, 202 pp.
Based on "The Contrived Corridor: A Study in Modern Poetry and the Meaning of History," Ph.D. thesis, U of Michigan, 1955. vii, 202 pp. (*DAI*, 15:4 [1955], 583). "W. B. Yeats," 74-99; on the poems related to *A Vision*.

149. GURD, PATTY: *The Early Poetry of William Butler Yeats*. Lancaster, Pa.: New Era Printing Company, 1916. iii, 101 pp.
A Dr.phil. thesis, U of Zürich, 1916. Reprinted °Folcroft, Pa.: Folcroft Press, 1978.

150. HAGENBÜCHLE, ROLAND, and JOSEPH T. SWANN (eds): *Poetic Knowledge: Circumference and Centre*. Papers from the Wuppertal Symposium 1978. Bonn: Bouvier, 1980. vi, 181 pp. (Gesamthochschule Wuppertal: Schriftenreihe Literaturwissenschaft. 18.)
J. Hillis Miller: "The Rewording Shell: Natural Image and Symbolic Emblem in Yeats's Early Poetry," 75-86; particularly in "The Sad Shepherd" and "The Song of the Happy Shepherd."

151. HAHN, HANS-JOACHIM: *Die Krisis des Lyrischen in den Gedichten von W. B. Yeats und W. H. Auden: Eine Untersuchung struktureller Wandlungen moderner Lyrik*. Göppingen: Kümmerle, 1971. xii, 245 pp. (Göppinger akademische Beiträge. 31.)
Originally a Dr.phil. thesis, U of Tübingen, 1971; English summary in *EASG*, 1971, 141-43. A largely unsuccessful attempt to explain the change in Yeats's poetic style in 1901-10.

152. HAHN, SISTER M. NORMA: "W. B. Yeats's Search for Reality: A Study of the Imagery of His Later Poetry," Ph.D. thesis, Fordham U, 1960. iii, 204, 14 pp.

153. HANEY-PERITZ, JANICE: "Refraining from the Romantic Image: Yeats and the Deformation of Metaphysical Aestheticism," *SIR*, 25:1 (Spring 1986), 3-37.
Discusses the Crazy Jane poems, "I Am of Ireland," "Long-legged Fly," "What Then," and other poems.

154. HARDY, BARBARA: *The Advantage of Lyric: Essays on Feeling in Poetry*. London: Athlone Press, 1977. ix, 142 pp.
"Passion and Contemplation in Yeats's Love Poetry," 67-83; reprinted from *Modernist Studies*, 1:2 (1974), 7-19.

155. ———: "The Wildness of Crazy Jane," in Jeffares: *Yeats, Sligo and Ireland* (1980, CA51), 31-55.

156. HARMON, MAURICE: "Literature and Nationalism in Ireland since 1922," *KN*, 25:4 (1978), 473-86.
Discusses Yeats's political poetry.

157. HARRIS, WENDELL: "Innocent Decadence: The Poetry of *The Savoy*," *PMLA*, 77:5 (Dec 1962), 629-36.
Contains some remarks on Yeats, pp. 630-31.

158. HARTMAN, GEOFFREY H.: *Beyond Formalism: Literary Essays, 1958-1970*. New Haven: Yale UP, 1970. xvi, 396 pp.
"The Poet's Politics," 247-57; and passim (see index).

159. HAYES, R.: "W. B. Yeats, a Catholic Poet?" *IrM,* 56:658 (Apr 1928), 179-86.

160. HAYLEY, BARBARA: "Artifex and Artifact: 'Ingenious Lovely Things' in the Poetry of W. B. Yeats," *Gaéliana,* 7 (1985), 35-43.

161. HEANEY, SEAMUS: "The Interesting Case of John Alphonsus Mulrennan," *Planet,* 41 (Jan 1978), 34-40.
Discusses the "Irish indigenous experience" in Yeats's poetry.

162. HEINZELMAN, KURT: *The Economics of the Imagination*. Amherst: U of Massachusetts Press, 1980. xiii, 330 pp.
"The Art of Labor," 137-65; on the relationship between art and labor in Yeats's poetry and in Auden's elegy (HD5), pp. 156-65.

163. HENDERSON, PHILIP: *The Poet and Society*. London: Secker & Warburg, 1939. vii, 248 pp.
"Politics and W. B. Yeats," 132-53.

164. HENN, T. R.: "A Note on Yeats," *CambR,* 60:1740 (10 Feb 1939), 225-27.
The outstanding quality of the later poetry (which is much better than the earlier) is "wisdom."

165. ———: "Yeats's Symbolism," in Donoghue: *The Integrity of Yeats* (1964, CA21), 33-46.
Particularly the tower and swan symbolism.

166. ———: "The Rhetoric of Yeats," in Jeffares and Cross: *In Excited Reverie* (1965, CA48), 102-22.

167. HERTZ, DAVID MICHAEL: "The Tuning of the Word: The Musico-Literary Poetics of Symbolism," Ph.D. thesis, New York U, 1983. iii, 406 pp. (*DAI,* 44:12 [June 1984], 3678A)
"The Tuned Word: Musico-Literary Ambiguity in Lyrics of Hofmannsthal, Yeats and Maeterlinck," 236-86; discusses some early poems, particularly "He Gives His Beloved Certain Rhymes," "He Bids His Beloved Be at Peace," and "The Travail of Passion."

168. HEWITT, JERENE: "The Epigram in English," Ph.D. thesis, U of California, Irvine, 1981. xv, 689 pp. (*DAI,* 42:11 [May 1982], 4819A)
On Yeats's epigrams, pp. 304-13.

169. *The Hidden Harmony: Essays in Honor of Philip Wheelwright*. NY: Odyssey Press, 1966. ix, 195 pp.
Sister M. Bernetta Quinn: "Symbolic Landscape in Yeats: County Galway," 145-71. See also DC306.

170. HILL, GEOFFREY: "'The Conscious Mind's Intelligible Structure': A Debate," *Agenda,* 9:4--10:1 (Autumn-Winter 1971/72), 14-23.
Yeats's politics and poetry do not correlate in a "grammar of assent." Discusses "Easter 1916" and "The Second Coming."

171. HIRSCH, EDWARD: "Yeats's Apocalyptic Horsemen," *IRA,* 3 (1982), 71-92.
The image of the Sidhe in the guise of Herodias's daughters.

172. HOFFMAN, BRYANT EDWARD: "This Sedentary Trade: Aesthetic Unity and the Poet-*Persona* in the Lyric Poetry of William Butler Yeats," Ph.D. thesis, Rutgers U, 1975. vi, 259 pp. (*DAI*, 36:2 [Aug 1975], 903A)

173. HOFSTADTER, ALBERT: *Agony and Epitaph: Man, His Art, and His Poetry*. NY: Braziller, 1970. xix, 268 pp.

"The Poem Is Not a Symbol," 129-48; reprinted from *Philosophy East and West*, 19:3 (July 1969), 221-33. On symbols in Yeats's poetry, particularly in the two Byzantium poems.

174. HOLTON, ROSEMARY THERESE: "A Study of Romanticism in the Lyric Poetry of William Butler Yeats," Ph.D. thesis, U of Ottawa, 1951. ix, 251 pp.

"Yeats was a Romantic in his poetry as in his life from first to last. The type of Romanticism changed from the languorous to the despairing to the passionate, but it was Romanticism throughout" (p. vi).

175. HONE, J. M.: "The Political Poems of Mr. Yeats," *Outlook* [London], 4 Feb 1922, 89-90.

176. HOPENWASSER, NANDA: "Crazy Jane: Writer of Her Own Justification," *CollL*, 13:1 (Winter 1986), 9-20.

177. HOSKINS, KATHARINE BAIL: *Today the Struggle: Literature and Politics in England during the Spanish Civil War*. Austin: U of Texas Press, 1969. xvii, 294 pp.

See pp. 28-31.

178. HOUGHTON, WALTER E.: "Yeats and Crazy Jane: The Hero in Old Age," *MP*, 40:4 (May 1943), 316-29.

The heroic theme in Yeats's poetry and its final crystallization in *Words of Music Perhaps*. Reprinted in CA36. See also CB167.

179. HUBANK, ROGER W. J.: "Unity of Being in the Poetry of W. B. Yeats," Ph.D. thesis, U of Nottingham, 1964. iii, 749, iv pp.

180. HÜHN, PETER: *Das Verhältnis von Mann und Frau im Werk von William Butler Yeats*. Bonn: Bouvier, 1971. vi, 243 pp. (Studien zur englischen Literatur. 5.)

Originally a Dr.phil. thesis, U of Hamburg; English summary in *EASG*, 1971, 136-38. Discusses the themes of love, time and eternity in the poetry and in *The Shadowy Waters, The Only Jealousy of Emer, The King of the Great Clock Tower,* and *A Full Moon in March*. A somewhat one-sided intrinsic study that sees the female characters as either *femmes fatales* or images of perfection.

181. HUGHES, PATRICK MICHAEL: "The Literature of National Identity: A Case Study of Revitalization in 19th Century Colonial Ireland," Ph.D. thesis, City U of New York, 1983. viii, 376 pp. (*DAI*, 44:10 [Apr 1984], 3177A)

"The Remembrance of Things Past: The Literature of National Identity in 19th Century Ireland," 265-346; comments on Yeats's political poetry.

182. HUME, MARTHA HASKINS: "Yeats: Aphorist and Epigrammatist. A Study of *The Collected Poems*," °Ph.D. thesis, U of Colorado, 1969. v, 114 pp. (*DAI*, 30:10 [Apr 1970], 4454A)

183. HYNES, SAMUEL: "All the Wild Witches: The Women in Yeats's Poems," *SR*, 85:4 (Fall 1977), 565-82.

184. IONKIS, GRETA ĖVRIVIADOVNA: *Ėsteticheskie iskanii͡a poetov anglii (1910-1930)*. Kishinev: "Shtiint͡sa," 1979. 140 pp.
"Simbolizm i 'mifologii͡a' V. B. Ĭetsa," 76-89, 128-31. (Aesthetic experiments of English poets; The symbolism and "mythology" of WBY).

185. ISLAM, SHAMSUL: "The Influence of Eastern Philosophy on Yeats's Later Poetry," *TCL*, 19:4 (Oct 1973), 283-90.
Especially in "Supernatural Songs."

186. JACOBS, EDWARD CRANEY: "Yeats and the Artistic Epiphany," *Discourse*, 12:3 (Summer 1969), 292-305.
The reconciliation of opposites in Yeats's poetry is achieved in an epiphany, which emphasizes unity and separateness at the same time. Discusses "The Phases of the Moon," "The Double Vision of Michael Robartes," and "Byzantium."

187. JAYNES, JOSEPH T.: "A Search for Trends in the Poetic Style of W. B. Yeats," *Association for Literary and Linguistic Computing Journal (ALLC Journal)*, 1:1 (Summer 1980), 11-18.
A computer-aided investigation into the syntax of Yeats's poetry.

188. JENSEN, EJNER: "The Antinomical Vision of W. B. Yeats," *XUS*, 3:3 (Dec 1964), 127-45.
The struggle of opposites in *A Vision*, "The Wanderings of Oisin," "Ego Dominus Tuus," "Byzantium," "A Dialogue of Self and Soul," "Lapis Lazuli," and other poems.

189. JOCHUM, K. P. S.: "Yeats's Sonnets," *MBL*, 4:1 (Spring 1979), 33-43.
Especially on "The Folly of Being Comforted," "At the Abbey Theatre," "Leda and the Swan," and "Meru."

190. JOHNSON, ANTHONY L.: "Actantial Modelling of the Love Relationship in W. B. Yeats: From 'He Wishes for the Cloths of Heaven' to 'Leda and the Swan,'" *Linguistica e letteratura*, 2:1 (1977), 155-79.

191. ———: "The Poetry of Suggestion: W. B. Yeats and Edward Thomas," *PoT*, 8:1 (1987), 85-104.
A linguistic approach to the use of signifiers in Yeats's poetry, compared to the use in Thomas's poetry. Also published on pp. 361-81 of °Franco Marucci and Adriano Bruttini (eds): *La performance del testo*. Siena: Ticci, 1986. xv, 437 pp.

192. JONES, GRANIA FRANCES: "Aspects of Time and Eternity with References to Some English Poetry from Wordsworth to Eliot," °Ph.D. thesis, U of Toronto, 1975. (*DAI*, 39:3 [Sept 1978], 1525A)
Time, history, memory, and eternity in the poetry of Yeats, Wordsworth, Arnold, Hardy, and Eliot.

193. JONES, LLEWELLYN: "Poetry and Devotion--V: William Butler Yeats," *Christian Register Unitarian*, 16 Feb 1939, 105-7.

194. JONG, MAX DE: "W. B. Yeats en Denis de Rougemont," *Criterium*, 9 (June 1946), 433-37.
Yeats's love poetry and its parallels in de Rougemont's *L'amour*

et l'occident.

195. KEANE, MICHAEL JAMES: "Private and Public Voices in Irish Poetry: W. B. Yeats, Patrick Kavanagh, and Seamus Heaney," Ph.D. thesis, U of Michigan, 1984. iii, 268 pp. (*DAI*, 45:7 [Jan 1985], 2097A-98A; reprinted *Yeats*, 4 [1986], 177-78)
Discusses Yeats's public and political poetry, his version of the Anglo-Irish tradition, and the theme of violence.

196. KELLY, ROBERT WILLIAM: "Time and the Personae in the Collected Poems of William Butler Yeats--A Dialectic of Time and Eternity," Ph.D. thesis, St. John's U, 1977. iii, 139 pp. (*DAI*, 38:1 [July 1977], 282A-83A)
"Escape" in the early poems, "confrontation" in the middle poems, "synthesis" in the later poems.

197. KHAMISANI, AMENA: "Themes and Symbolism in W. B. Yeats' Poetry," *Ariel* [U of Sind], 4:1 (1976-77), 7-27.

198. KHANNA, URMILLA: "The Tower Symbol in the Poetry of Yeats," *English Miscellany* [Delhi], 3 (1965), 9-18.

199. KHOROL'SKIĬ, VIKTOR VASIL'EVICH: *Poeziia U. B. Ĭetsa 1880-kh--1920-kh godov (Evoliutsiia obraznoĭ sistemy)*. Avtoreferat dissertatsii. Moskva: Moskovskiĭ ordena Lenina i ordena trudovogo krasnogo znameni gosudarstvennyĭ pedagogicheskiĭ institut imeni V. I. Lenina, 1978. 15 pp.
"The poetry of WBY from the 1880s to the 1920s: The evolution of the system of imagery."

200. ———: "Politicheskaia lirika U. B. Ĭetsa 1910-kh godov," *Problemy metoda i zhanra v zarubezhnoĭ literature: Sbornik trudov*, 2 (1978), 71-78.
"The political poetry of WBY in the 1910s."

201. KIASASHVILI, NICO (ed): [In Georgian] *Three Essays on John Donne, W. B. Yeats and T. S. Eliot*. Tbilisi: Tbilisi UP, 1984. v, 144 pp.
The Russian bibliographical description is as follows: KARUMIDZE, ZURAB LEVANOVICH, and others: *Dzhon Donn . . . Uil'iam Batler Ĭits . . . Tomas Sternz Eliot*. . . . Pod red. Niko Kiasashvili. Tbilisi: Izdatel'stvo Tbilisskogo universiteta, 1984.
Paata Eduardovich Shevardnadze: "W. B. Yeats: Impersonal Emotion," 62-96; in Georgian, with summaries in Russian and English. Relates the "impersonality" of Yeats's later poetry to the influence of Bergson's "élan vital." See also CC300.

202. KIM JONG GIL: "The Topography of Yeats's Poetry," *Phoenix*, 10 (Summer 1965), 84-95.
On the Irish landscapes described in some poems.

203. KIM U-CHANG: "The Embittered Sun: Reality in Yeats's Poetry," *Phoenix*, 10 (Summer 1965), 66-83.

204. Entry canceled.

205. KINGSLEY, LAWRENCE WILSON: "The Modern Elegy: The Epistemology of Loss," °Ph.D. thesis, U of Wisconsin (Madison), 1973. 425 pp. (*DAI*, 34:2 [Aug 1973], 779A-80A)

206. KISHEL, JOSEPH: "Yeats's Elegies," *YER*, 7:1&2 (June 1982), 78-90.

207. KOHLI, DEVINDRA: "Intelligence of Heart: Women in Yeats's Poetry," *IJES*, 8 (1967), 83-105.
Maud Gonne, Lady Gregory, Iseult Gonne, Olivia Shakespear, and Dorothy Wellesley.

208. KOLJEVIĆ, SVETOZAR: "Viljem Batler Jejts: Autobiografija kao poezija," *Izraz*, year 20 / 40:5 (May 1976), 769-79.
"WBY: Autobiography as poetry"; discusses autobiographical themes in the poetry.

209. KROGFUS, MILES EDWARD: "Knowledge and Sweeter Ignorance: The Strategies of Yeats's Poetic Structures," °Ph.D. thesis, U of Minnesota, 1982. 257 pp. (*DAI*, 43:11 [May 1983], 3604A; reprinted *Yeats*, 2 [1984], 260-61, and *YeA*, 4 [1986], 314-15)
On the use of sentence and line, refrain and repeated phrase, dialogue, and the metaphors of lightning and threshold.

210. KUEHN, NANDINI PILLAI: "The Influence of Indian Thought on the Poetry of W. B. Yeats," Ph.D. thesis, U of Michigan, 1973. vii, 142 pp. (*DAI*, 35:1 [July 1974], 459A-60A)

211. KUIĆ, RANKA: "Jeitsova lubavna lirika" [Yeats's love poetry], *Književne novine*, 21:355 (7 June 1969), 3, 12.
Reprinted in *Mostovi*, 1:1 (Jan-Mar 1970), 30-38.

212. KURDI, MÁRIA: "A kettősség élménye Yeats költészetében," *FK*, 26:2 (Apr-June 1980), 194-204.
"The experience of dualism in Y's poetry."

213. LAKIN, R. D.: "Unity and Strife in Yeats' Tower Symbol," *MQ*, 1:4 (July 1960), 321-32.
The symbol betrays dissonance, thus the poet's impotence, and points to the lack of final answers in Yeats's poetry.

214. LANDER, JEANNETTE [i.e., Seyppel, Jeannette]: *William Butler Yeats: Die Bildersprache seiner Lyrik*. Stuttgart: Kohlhammer, 1967. 168 pp. (Sprache und Literatur. 41.)
Based on the more adequately titled °"Wasserbilder in der Lyrik von W. B. Yeats," Dr.phil. thesis, Freie Universität Berlin, 1966. Discusses the imagery of water (and related images) in Yeats's poetry.
Reviews:
- Willi Erzgräber, *Neusprachliche Mitteilungen*, 22:1 (1969), 47-49.
- Rosemarie Gläser, *ZAA*, 19:2 (1971), 195-97.
- Egon Werlich, *Praxis des neusprachlichen Unterrichts*, 15:2 (1968), 196-97.

215. LATIMER, DAN RAYMOND: "Problems in the Symbol: A Theory and Application in the Poetry of Valéry, Rilke, and Yeats," Ph.D. thesis, U of Michigan, 1972. v, 610 pp. (*DAI*, 33:11 [May 1973], 6316A)
"Yeats," 422-586, and passim.

216. LEIGH, DAVID J.: "'The Whirl Becomes a Sphere': Concept and Symbol in Yeats' Poetry of Beatitude," *Christianity and Literature*, 26:2 (Winter 1977), 18-29.
"Transcendent union" in the poetry.

217. LEONARD, JENNIFER L.: "Wise and Crazy Jane," *Chrysalis,* 1:2 (Summer 1986), 131-35.

218. °LEPPARD, D. G.: "An Investigation into the Theory and Structure of Metaphor, with Special Reference to Wordsworth and Yeats," D.Phil. thesis, Oxford U, 1984.

219. LERNER, LAURENCE DAVID: *The Truest Poetry: An Essay on the Question What Is Literature*. London: Hamilton, 1960. xi, 221 pp.

Note on the opposition of life and abstraction in Yeats's poetry, pp. 118-20; note on "The Second Coming," pp. 134-35.

220. LINDENBERGER, HERBERT: *Historical Drama: The Relation of Literature and Reality*. Chicago: U of Chicago Press, 1975. xiv, 194 pp.

Notes on Yeats's "historical" poems, pp. 135, 139-41.

221. LOFTUS, RICHARD JOSEPH: "Yeats and the Easter Rising: A Study in Ritual," *ArQ,* 16:2 (Summer 1960), 168-77.

222. ———: *Nationalism in Modern Anglo-Irish Poetry*. Madison: U of Wisconsin Press, 1964. xi, 362 pp.

See pp. 38-46. Yeats was the only poet of truly nationalist stature, because he was able to withstand the pressures that the middle class brought to bear on the Irish writers.

223. MAC AODHA, BREANDAN S.: "Place Names in Yeats's Poetry and Plays," *Gaéliana,* 6 (1984), 225-31.

Yeats avoids Irish place names and those few that he does use "grate on both eye and ear."

224. MACCATHMHAOIL, SEOSAMH [i.e., Joseph Campbell]: "A Plea for the Patriotic Ballad," *Nationist,* 28 Sept 1905, 31-33.

Yeats is to blame (with his cry "Art for art's sake, not Ireland's") that here is no Irish patriotic poetry. Correspondence by Padraic Colum: "Nationality in Verse," 19 Oct 1905, 77-78.

225. MCCUTCHION, DAVID: "The Heroic Mind of W. B. Yeats," *VQ,* 27:1 (1961), 42-62.

226. ———: "Beast or Angel? Romantic Ambiguities in Goethe, Musset, Stendhal and Yeats," *JJCL,* 2 (1962), 31-67.

Antinomies in Yeats's poetry, pp. 55-67.

227. MCDONNELL, JANE RUTHERFORD TAYLOR: "'Dove or Swan': A Study of the Themes of Wisdom and Power in the Poetry and Plays of W. B. Yeats," Ph.D. thesis, Washington U, 1974, ii, 194 pp. (*DAI,* 35:9 [Mar 1975], 6148A-49A)

Contains chapters on "Women and the Issues of Power" (mainly on Maud Gonne), "The Artist and History," "Heroic Revery [sic]: Wisdom and Power in the Plays," and "Tragic Joy."

228. MACGREEVY, THOMAS: "Maud Gonne MacBride," *Father Mathew Record,* 46:6 (June 1953), 1-3.

Includes a note on Maud Gonne in Yeats's poetry.

229. MACHIN, RICHARD, and CHRISTOPHER NORRIS (eds): *Post-Structuralist Readings of English Poetry*. Cambridge: Cambridge UP, 1987. x, 406 pp.

Daniel O'Hara: "Yeats in Theory," 349-68. The reception of Yeats by various schools of literary criticism, notably by Blackmur,

Frye, Bloom, and de Man. Includes a short analysis of "Her Vision in the Wood."

230. MCHUGH, ROGER: "Yeats and Irish Politics," *UR*, 2:13 [1961?], 24-36.
Reprinted in *Texas Q*, 5:3 (Autumn 1962), 90-100.

231. MACINNES, MAIRI: "Marvell in Yorkshire, Yeats in Sligo," *PNR*, 28 [9:2] (1982), 29-33.
Reprinted in *Cumberland Poetry R*, 1:2 (Spring 1982), 76-89; discusses the garden metaphor in Marvell's and Yeats's poetry.

232. MACMANUS, FRANCIS (ed): *The Years of the Great Test*. Cork: Mercier Press, 1967. 183 pp.
Francis MacManus: "The Literature of the Period," 115-26. Anglo-Irish literature from 1925 to 1939; on Yeats, "this most political of genuine poets," pp. 123-26.

233. MACSWEEN, R. J.: "Yeats and His Language," *AntigR*, 14 (Summer 1973), 17-24.
The style of Yeats's poetry and Pound's influence on it.

234. MAGRINI, GIACOMO: "La bellezza e la pedagogia in Yeats," *Strumenti critici*, 45 (July 1981), 283-307.
In the poetry.

235. MALHOTRA, R. K.: "W. B. Yeats: Contrast as a Structural Device in His Poetry," *Panjab U Research Bulletin (Arts)*, 14:2 (Oct 1983), 157-65.

236. MALINS, EDWARD: "Coole Park," *Quarterly Bulletin of the Irish Georgian Society*, 13:1 (Jan-Mar 1970), 20-28.
Coole Park in Yeats's poetry.

237. MALLON, THOMAS: "All Soul's Nights: Yeats, Sassoon, and the Dead," *Irish Studies*, 1 (1980), 85-99.
In their poetry Yeats and Sassoon share a preoccupation with the influence of the dead upon the living.

238. MANDL, OTTO WILLIAM: "Rational Elements in the Poetry of William Butler Yeats," Dr.phil. thesis, U of Wien, 1954. ii, 149 pp.
Yeats's poetry is intellectual rather than emotional.

239. MANSERGH, NICHOLAS: *The Irish Question, 1840-1921: A Commentary on Anglo-Irish Relations and on Social and Political Forces in Ireland in the Age of Reform and Revolution*. Toronto: U of Toronto Press, 1965. 316 pp.
First published as °*Ireland in the Age of Reform and Revolution*. London: Allen & Unwin, 1940. 272 pp. Discusses Irish politics in Yeats's poetry and his political convictions, pp. 245-66.

240. MARSH, DERICK: "The Artist and the Tragic Vision: Themes in the Poetry of W. B. Yeats," *QQ*, 74:1 (Spring 1967), 104-18.
Particularly in "Long-legged Fly" and "Lapis Lazuli."

241. MARTIN, AUGUSTINE: "To Make a Right Rose Tree: Reflections on the Poetry of 1916," *Studies*, 55:217 (Spring 1966), 38-49.

242. MARTIN, GRAHAM: "Fine Manners, Liberal Speech: An Note on the Public Poetry of W. B. Yeats," *EIC*, 11:1 (Jan 1961), 40-59.

243. MAXWELL, D. E. S.: "Yeats and Modernism," *CJIS*, 3:2 [i.e., 3:1] (June 1977), 14-31.
Modernism in the poetry.

244. ———: "The Shape-Changers," in Jeffares: *Yeats, Sligo and Ireland* (1980, CA51), 153-69.
The metamorphosis of reality into art in the poetry.

245. °MAXWELL-MAHON, W. D.: "The Prophetic Mind: An Aspect of the Poetry of Blake and Yeats," *UES*, 2:1 (Mar 1964), 11-16.

246. MAYER, DAVID R.: "Flannery O'Connor and the Peacock," *Asian Folklore Studies*, 35:2 (1976), 1-16.
Includes a note on the peacock image in Yeats's poetry.

247. MEGGISON, LAUREN LOUISE: "Keepers of the Flame: Hermeticism in Yeats, H. D., and Borges," °Ph.D. thesis, U of California, Irvine, 1987. 281 pp. (*DAI*, 48:2 [Aug 1987], 386A)
Mainly on "The Two Trees" and the Crazy Jane poems, according to abstract.

247a. MEIHUIZEN, NICHOLAS: "Yeats and the Crazy Energy of Old Age," *UES*, 26:1 (Apr 1988), 22-25.
Particularly in "Those Dancing Days Are Gone," "A Prayer for Old Age," and "Ribh Considers Christian Love Insufficient."

248. MEIR, COLIN: *The Ballads and Songs of W. B. Yeats: The Anglo-Irish Heritage in Subject and Style*. London: Macmillan, 1974. viii, 141 pp.
Based on a °Ph.D. thesis, U of Essex, 1971/72. Contains chapters on "Popular Nationalism: 1885-1892," "Imaginative Nationalism," the influence of Gaelic material via Callanan, Ferguson, Walsh, Mangan, and Hyde, and the influence of the Anglo-Irish dialect. Discusses the various forms of Yeats's ballads, including the political ballads.
Reviews:
- J. C. Beckett, *MLR*, 71:1 (Jan 1976), 152-54.
- Terence Brown, *IUR*, 6:2 (Autumn 1976), 256-59.
- Denis Donoghue: "That Anglo-Irish Man," *THES*, 18 Apr 1975, 17.
- Serge Fauchereau: "Multiple Yeats," *Quinzaine littéraire*, 208 (16-30 Apr 1975), 13-14.
- Monk Gibbon: "Search for the Holy Grail," *Hibernia*, 24 Jan 1975, 18.
- Graham Hough: "Yeats and the Magic of Power," *TLS*, 14 Feb 1975, 160.
- Eileen Kennedy, *Eire*, 10:4 (Winter 1975), 146-48.
- Elizabeth Mackenzie, *N&Q*, os 221 / ns 23:1 (Jan 1976), 34-36.
- Vincent Mahon, *RES*, 27:107 (Aug 1976), 372-73.
- F. G. F. Schulte, *DQR*, 7:1 (1977), 58-60.
- Eugene Watters: "DEDI-cation," *IrP*, 28 Dec 1974, 8.
- Georges-Denis Zimmermann, *ES*, 57:5 (Oct 1976), 464-68.

249. ———: "Narrative Verse in Yeats, Clarke, and Kavanagh," *Gaéliana*, 4 (1982), 219-36.

250. ———: "Yeats's Minstrel Voice," *Gaéliana*, 5 (1983), 81-98.
Irish ballads as sources of Yeats's poetry.

251. ———: "Yeats's Search for a Natural Language," *Eire*, 19:3

(Fall 1984), 77-91.
In theory and poetic practice.

252. METZ, GERALD MARVIN: "The Timeless Moment in the Poetry of W. B. Yeats," Ph.D. thesis, U of Minnesota, 1972. 161 pp. (*DAI*, 33:10 [Apr 1973], 5736A)
Contains chapters on the early poetry and prose and on sex, art, history, and knowledge in the poetry.

253. MIGNOT, ALAIN: "Littérature de l'Insurrection de Paques 1916," thesis, Doctorat de 3e Cycle, Université de la Sorbonne Nouvelle, Paris III, [1975]. i, 345 pp.
"L'exaltation du mythe: W. B. Yeats," 13-72.

254. MILES, JOSEPHINE: *Major Adjectives in English Poetry from Wyatt to Auden*. Berkeley: U of California Press, 1946. v, pp. 305-426. (U of California Publications in English. 12:3.)
"Modern Quality," 389-407, contains a few notes on Yeats.

255. ———: *The Continuity of Poetic Language: Studies in English Poetry from the 1540's to the 1940's*. Berkeley: U of California Press, 1948-51. xiii, 542 pp. in 3 parts. (U of California Publications in English. 19.)
Statistical investigation of the vocabulary; on Yeats, part 3.

256. ———: *Eras & Modes in English Poetry*. Berkeley: U of California Press, 1957. xi, 233 pp.
"The Classical Mode of Yeats," 178-202; a study of Yeats's poetic vocabulary.

257. ———: *Poetry and Change: Donne, Milton, Wordsworth, and the Equilibrium of the Present*. Berkeley: U of California Press, 1974. v, 243 pp.
Some notes on Yeats's poetic diction, especially on pp. 148-49.

258. MILLS, JOHN GASCOIGNE: "On the Poetry and Politics of W. B. Yeats," *Ochanomizu Joshi Daigaku Jimbun Kagaku Kiyō*, 14 (1961), 1-6.

259. MILNER, IAN: "Yeats and the Poetry of Violence," *Acta Universitatis Carolinae, Philologica*, 3 / *Prague Studies in English*, 13 (1969), 97-107.
The poems of anarchy and violence ("The Second Coming," "Nineteen Hundred and Nineteen") are effective because they use the mask of traditional form. Formlessness would have made them unsuccessful.

260. MINAJAGI, S. B.: "W. B. Yeats's Poetic Ritual: 'Contraries' and Their Consummation," *LCrit*, 10:1 (Winter 1971), 50-61.

261. MINOCK, DANIEL WILLIAM: "Conceptions of Death in the Modern Elegy and Related Poems," Ph.D. thesis, Ohio State U, 1975. vi, 207 pp. (*DAI*, 36:3 [Sept 1975], 1496A-97A)
On the Robert Gregory poems, especially "In Memory of Major Robert Gregory," pp. 54-63.

262. MIRZA, GAIL ANNE B.: "The Hindu Concept of Pure Consciousness in the Poetry of Juan Ramón Jiménez, Rabindranath Tagore, and W. B. Yeats: A Comparative Study," °Ph.D. thesis, State U of New York at Binghamton, 1977. 351 pp. (*DAI*, 38:4 [Oct 1977], 2103A)

263. MISE, RAYMOND: "Yeats' Crazy Jane Poems," *Paunch*, 25 (Feb 1966), 18-30.

264. MISHRA, VIDYANATH: *Aspects of Myth in Modern Poetry (A Study of Yeats, Eliot and Graves)*. Patna: Anupam Publications, 1981. xi, 570 pp.

Arranged thematically with chapters on the imagery and symbolism of the four elements; organic vegetation and growth; the animal world; "birth, copulation, death"; cosmology; aesthetic creation; and "poetic myth."

265. MITCHELL, JOAN TOWEY: "Hero and Poet Reconciled," *English*, 23:115 (Spring 1974), 29-33.

In the poetry and plays, hero and poet "seem wholly antithetical beings"; in the later works, however, Yeats attempts a reconciliation. Mainly on "Cuchulain Comforted."

266. MOFFETT, CAROLYN: "Through the Looking Glass: An Analysis of the Mirror Imagery in the Poetry of William Butler Yeats," *McNR*, 27 (1980-81), 80-92.

267. MOKASHI-PUNEKAR, SHANKAR: *Interpretations of the Later Poems of W. B. Yeats*. Dharwar: Karnatak U, 1973. xxiv, 268 pp.

The poems beginning with *Responsibilities*. Analyzed in section DD. Reviewed by G. Srirama Murty, *Triveni*, 50:4 (Jan-Mar 1982), 87-88.

268. [MONAHAN, MICHAEL]: "A Poet of the Mystic," *Papyrus*, 1:6 (Dec 1903), 13.

269. MONIS, PATRICIO V.: "The Literary Symbol in Modern Literature," *Unitas*, 48:1 (Mar 1975), 7-190.

On Yeats's symbols, "The Second Coming," and "Leda and the Swan," pp. 98-111.

270. MONTGOMERY, LYNA LEE: "The Phoenix: Its Use as a Literary Device in English from the 17th Century to the 20th Century," *D. H. Lawrence R*, 5:3 (Fall 1972), 268-323.

On Yeats's use of the image, pp. 307-10.

270a. MORGAN, CAROL: "Stanza Structures in the Poetry of Hugo von Hofmannsthal and W. B. Yeats," Ph.D. thesis, University of East Anglia, 1984. iii, 284, 53, 39 pp.

Abstract in *Index to Theses*, 36:2 (1988), 468. See especially "Yeats and the Quatrain," 106-37; "Yeats and the Eight-Line Stanza," 138/39-93. Discusses "The Ballad of Moll Magee," "Down by the Salley Gardens," "The Cap and Bells," "A Coat," "The Coming of Wisdom with Time," "The Balloon of the Mind," "Gratitude to the Unknown Instructors," "The Song of Wandering Aengus," "In Memory of Major Robert Gregory," "Sailing to Byzantium," "A Dawn Song," and "Nineteen Hundred and Nineteen."

271. MORRIS, JOHN ANTHONY: *Writers and Politics in Modern Britain (1880-1950)*. London: Hodder & Stoughton, 1977. vii, 109 pp.

On Yeats's political poetry, pp. 12-17 and passim.

272. MUINZER, LOUIS A.: *Coole Park and Ballylee: Study Guide*. Belfast: Photographic Unit, Queen's U, 1976. 28 pp.

To the QUB documentary film *Coole Park and Ballylee*, a visual evocation of Yeats's poems concerned with these places.

273. MUNCH-PEDERSEN, OLE: "Crazy Jane: A Cycle of Popular Literature," *Eire*, 14:1 (Spring 1979), 56-73.
Crazy Jane's antecedents in 19th-century popular literature, beginning with a ballad by Matthew Gregory Lewis.

274. MURAWSKA, KATARZYNA: "An Image of Mysterious Wisdom Won by Toil: The Tower as Symbol of Thoughtful Isolation in English Art and Literature from Milton to Yeats," *Artibus et historiae*, 3:5 (1982), 141-62.
An extensively researched and illustrated article on the iconographical sources and predecessors of the tower image in Yeats's poetry.

275. MURPHY, FRANK HUGHES: *Yeats's Early Poetry: The Quest for Reconciliation*. Baton Rouge: Louisiana State UP, 1975. xi, 172 pp.
Based on "The Theme of Reconciliation in the Early Poetry of Yeats," °Ph.D. thesis, U of North Carolina, 1971. 200 pp. (*DAI*, 32:9 [Mar 1972], 5193A). Discusses the poetry up to the first edition of *A Vision* (1925). Analyzed in section DD.
Reviews:
- Richard J. Finneran: "W. B. Yeats," *ConL*, 17:1 (Winter 1976), 142-47.
- Warwick Gould: "Symbols and Systems," *TLS*, 25 Feb 1977, 218.
- George Mills Harper: "'Always . . . Verify Your References, Sir!'" *CEA*, 38:3 (Mar 1967), 34-37.
- A. Norman Jeffares: "Coughing in Ink," *SR*, 84:1 (Jan-Mar 1976), 157-67.
- Priscilla Johnston, *JML*, 5:4 (1976), 849-51.
- Eileen Kennedy, *Eire*, 12:3 (Fall 1977), 135-37.
- Phillip L. Marcus, *YES*, 8 (1978), 353-54.
- James E. Swinnen, *NOR*, 5:1 (1976), 88-89.
- Thomas L. Watson: "Yeats's Quest for Reconciliation," *SoR*, 13:3 (July 1977), 628-36.

276. MURSHID, K. S.: "Yeats and the Saint's Mask," *Dacca U Studies*, 10:1 (June 1961), 79-96.
Beggar, saint, and mask in Yeats's poetry, and the pertinent Indian influences.

277. NAPOLI, JOANNE LENORE: "The Meaning of the Dancer in the Poetry of William Butler Yeats," °Ph.D. thesis, U of Massachusetts, 1972. 153 pp. (*DAI*, 33:6 [Dec 1972], 2945A)
Discusses the occult sources and the concept of Unity of Being.

278. NARASIMHAIAH, C. D.: "W. B. Yeats: Poetry as an Act of Generosity," *JJCL*, 8 (1968), 1-20.
The theme of generosity in "poems dealing with love, national politics, theatre business, and old age."

279. NASH, J. P.: "Materialist Revolutionary Art and Metaphysical Reactionary Art: Eisenstein and Yeats, Eliot, Pound," Ph.D. thesis, Trinity College Dublin, 1977. v, 541 pp. (*DAI*, 38:4 [Summer 1978], 538, item 4646C)
Discusses the role of occultist metaphysics in some of Yeats's poems, particularly on pp. 117-383.

280. NASSAR, EUGENE PAUL: "Illusion as Value: An Essay on a Modern Poetic Idea," *Mosaic*, 7:4 (Summer 1974), 109-23.
Contains a note on Yeats's poetry.

281. NEWSON, RONALD: "W. B. Yeats and the Irish Movement," *VQ*, 1:4 (Feb 1936), 18-28.
Misnomer; slight article on Irish themes in Yeats's poetry.

281a. NICHOLS, ASHTON: *The Poetics of Epiphany: Nineteenth-Century Origins of the Modern Literary Moment*. Tuscaloosa: U of Alabama Press, 1987. xv, 256 pp.
"Yeats: The Artificer of the 'Great Moment,'" 181-90, and passim (see index). On epiphanies in the poetry, particularly "A Memory of Youth," also in *Per Amica Silentia Lunae*. Comments on the influence of Symons.

282. NIMS, JOHN FREDERICK: *A Local Habitation: Essays on Poetry*. Ann Arbor: U of Michigan Press, 1985. xi, 306 pp.
"Yeats and the Careless Muse," 145-69; reprinted from Robert Scholes (ed): *Learners and Discerners: A Newer Criticism. Discussions of Modern Literature*. Charlottesville: UP of Virginia, 1964. ix, 177 pp. (pp. 29-60). Discusses the motif of carelessness in Yeats's poetry.

283. NOON, WILLIAM THOMAS: *Poetry and Prayer*. New Brunswick: Rutgers UP, 1967. xiv, 354 pp.
"William Butler Yeats," 129-56, and passim (see index). Although Yeats separated poetry and religion sharply and opted for the former, he was always trying, unintentionally, to blur the distinction.

284. O'BRIEN, JAMES HOWARD: "Theosophy and the Poetry of George Russell (AE), William Butler Yeats, and James Stephens," Ph.D. thesis, U of Washington, 1956. v, 367 pp. (*DAI*, 16:11 [1956], 2167-68)
On Yeats see pp. 139-276 and passim.

285. O'DONNELL, JAMES PRESTON: *Sailing to Byzantium: A Study in the Development of the Later Style and Symbolism in the Poetry of William Butler Yeats*. Cambridge, Mass.: Harvard UP, 1939. 95 pp. (Harvard Honors Theses in English. 11.)
Reprinted °NY: Octagon Books, 1971. See also the anonymous review in *IrT*, 20 Apr 1940, 5.

286. OGBAA, KALU: "Yeats and the Irish Revolution," *Commonwealth Q*, 4:15 (Sept 1980), 1-12.
Yeats's nationalism in his poetry is both orthodox and romantic.

287. O'LOCHLAINN, COLM: *Anglo-Irish Song Writers since Moore*. Dublin: At the Sign of the Three Candles, [1950]. 23 pp. ([Bibliographical Society of Ireland Publications, 6:1.])
Yeats's only real song is "Down by the Salley Gardens," his other "songs" being "rather too delicate and precious ever to get into the pedlar's pack, or the balladmonger's sheaf."

288. OLSEN, LANCE: "The Ironic Dialectic in Yeats," *CLQ*, 19:4 (Dec 1983), 215-20.
Various types of ironic dialectic in the poetry.

289. O'NEILL, WILLIAM: "Yeats on Poetry and Politics," *MQ*, 25:1 (Autumn 1983), 64-73.
Mostly on politics in Yeats's poetry.

290. OPITZ, MICHAEL J.: "Poetry as Appropriate Epistemology: Gregory Bateson and W. B. Yeats," °Ph.D. thesis, U of Minnesota, 1985.

250 pp. (*DAI*, 46:10 [Apr 1986], 3042A; reprinted *Yeats*, 5 [1987], 201)

An approach to Yeats's poetry through the epistemological theories of scientist Gregory Bateson.

291. PACEY, DESMOND: "Children in the Poetry of Yeats," *DR*, 50:2 (Summer 1970), 233-48.

292. PALL, SANTOSH: "The Dancer in Yeats," *Studies*, 65:258 (Summer 1976), 113-27.

The dancer symbol in the poetry and plays.

293. PAREKH, PUSHPA NAIDU: "Response to Failure as Reflected in the Poetry of G. M. Hopkins, His Contemporaries (Francis Thompson and Lionel Johnson), and the Moderns," Ph.D. thesis, Louisiana State U, 1986. v, 245 pp. (*DAI*, 47:9 [Mar 1987], 3436A-37A)

Includes a short discussion of the "anti-heroic clown persona" (abstract) in Yeats's poetry (pp. 190-93).

293a. PARKIN, ANDREW T. L.: "Public and Private Voices in the Poetry of Yeats, Montague and Heaney," *AAA*, 13:1 (1988), 29-38.

Not a comparative study but separate treatments of Yeats on the one hand and the other two poets on the other.

294. PARKINSON, THOMAS: "Yeats and the Love Lyric," *JJQ*, 3:2 (Winter 1966), 109-23.

295. PARTRIDGE, ASTLEY COOPER: *The Language of Modern Poetry: Yeats, Eliot, Auden*. London: Deutsch, 1976. 351 pp.

"W. B. Yeats," 71-136, and passim (see index). Concentrates on prosody, language and style. Analyzed in section DD.

296. PAULIN, TOM: "The Politics of English Verse," *Poetry R*, 76:1-2 (June 1986), 34-38.

Discusses Yeats's political poetry.

297. PERLOFF, MARJORIE G.: "'Heart Mysteries': The Later Love Lyrics of W. B. Yeats," *ConL*, 10:2 (Spring 1969), 266-83.

Not all of the poems celebrate a sexual "mythology of earth." Discusses "Quarrel in Old Age," "The Results of Thought," and "A Bronze Head."

298. PERRINE, LAURENCE: "Yeats's Response to the Experience of Rejected Love," *MBL*, 2:1 (Spring 1977), 58-63.

In the poems the response is a paradigm of Yeats's attitude toward all of life.

299. PHARE, ELSIE ELIZABETH: "Extract from an Essay on the Devotional Poetry of T. S. Eliot," *Experiment*, 6 (Oct 1930), 27-32.

Misnomer; mostly concerned with Christianity and Byzantinism in some of Yeats's poems and the influence of T. E. Hulme.

300. PICCHI, FERNANDO: *Esoterismo e magia nelle poesie di W. B. Yeats*. Firenze: Nardini, 1977. 263 pp.

Contains chapters on the involvement in the Dublin Hermetic Society and the Golden Dawn, *A Vision*, and the relevant poetry.

301. POTTS, ABBIE FINDLAY: *The Elegiac Mode: Poetic Form in Wordsworth and Other Elegists*. Ithaca: Cornell UP, 1967. xii, 460 pp.

"Flute Song Yesterday: W. B. Yeats," 358-94, and passim (see index). On elegiac forms and themes in Yeats's poetry and plays and the classical and Wordsworthian influence behind them.

302. PRESLEY, JOHN W.: "Strategies for Detemporalizing Language in Modern Literature," *Lang&S*, 18:3 (Summer 1985), 293-301.
Comments on the stylistic means used by Yeats to express timelessness in his poetry.

303. PRINCE, JEFFREY ROBERT: "Havens of Intensity: Aestheticism in the Poetry of Keats, Tennyson, and Yeats," °Ph.D. thesis, U of Virginia, 1971. 350 pp. (*DAI*, 32:8 [Feb 1972], 4629A-30A)

304. PROSKY, MURRAY: "Landscapes in the Poetry of W. B. Yeats," Ph.D. thesis, U of Wisconsin, 1966. vi, 246 pp. (*DAI*, 28:2 [Aug 1967], 691A)

304a. PRUITT, RAYMOND D., and VIRGINIA D. PRUITT: "W. B. Yeats on Old Age, Death, and Immortality," *CLQ*, 24:1 (Mar 1988), 36-49.
Mainly in the poetry and "Under Ben Bulben."

305. PRUITT, VIRGINIA D.: "W. B. Yeats: Rage, Order, and the Mask," *Eire*, 21:2 (Summer 1986), 141-46.
The "psychodynamics of the mask" as related to "order-inducing rage" in some of Yeats's poems.

305a. °PYUN, SHI-JA: "The Image of Maud Gonne in Yeats's Poetry," *Phoenix* [Seoul], 12 (Spring 1968), 57-80.

306. QUINN, SISTER M. BERNETTA: "Symbolic Landscape in Yeats: County Sligo," *Shenandoah*, 16:4 (Summer 1965), 37-62.
See also DC169.

307. QUIVEY, JAMES R.: "Yeats and the Epigram: A Study of Technique in the Four-Line Poems," *Discourse*, 13:1 (Winter 1970), 58-72.

307a. RACE, WILLIAM H.: *Classical Genres and English Poetry*. London: Croom Helm, 1988. xix, 235 pp.
See index for references to Yeats's poetry, particularly to "A Coat," "An Irish Airman Foresees His Death," and "A Prayer for My Son."

308. RAFROIDI, PATRICK: "Yeats, Nature and the Self," in Jeffares: *Yeats, Sligo and Ireland* (1980, CA51), 189-96.
Sketchy note on the nature poetry and its relation to the poet's self.

309. RAINES, CHARLES A.: "Yeats' Metaphors of Permanence," *TCL*, 5:1 (Apr 1959), 12-20.

310. RAJAN, B.: "Yeats and the Absurd," *TriQ*, 4 [Fall 1965], 130-31, 133-37.
Discusses the absurd element in the poetry and the plays. Although Yeats had a sense of the absurd, he was no nihilist; the absurd was only one of many attitudes.

311. RAMRATNAM, MALATI: *W. B. Yeats and the Craft of Verse*. Lanham, Md.: UP of America, 1985. x, 135 pp.
Based on "Studies in the Craftsmanship of W. B. Yeats," Ph.D. thesis, Brandeis U, 1973. iv, 176 pp. (*DAI*, 34:7 [Jan 1974], 4281A). Contains chapters on "The Poet as Craftsman," "The Idea

of the Poetic Word," "Complex Words and Compound Epithets," "Verbal Allusiveness and Meaning," "The Making of the Stanza," and "The Art of the Dramatic Poem."

312. RATCLIFFE, DENIS: "The Nature of Being as a Preoccupation in Twentieth Century Poetry," Ph.D. thesis, U of Nottingham, 1977. ii, 457 pp.

"W. B. Yeats's Poetry," 63-112, 378-85; discusses the concept of self, particularly in "Ego Dominus Tuus," "The Second Coming," "Leda and the Swan," and the Byzantium poems.

313. RAVINDRAN, SANKARAN: "Mask, Divided Self, and Modernity in Yeats's Poetry," *J of Literature and Aesthetics*, 3:4 (Oct-Dec 1983), 16-23.

314. RAYAN, KRISHNA: "When the Green Echoes or Doesn't," *Malahat R*, 14 (Apr 1970), 30-38.

Image and discourse in poetry, including some notes on Yeats.

315. ———: *Text and Sub-Text: Suggestion in Literature*. London: Arnold, 1987. xi, 236 pp.

"Micro-suggestion in Yeats," 38-49; reprint of "Yeats and the 'Little and Intense' Poem," *EIC*, 25:4 (Oct 1975), 407-18. On Yeats's short poems.

316. R[IDING], L[AURA], R[OBERT] G[RAVES], and H[ARRY] K[EMP]: "Politics and Poetry," *Epilogue*, 3 (Spring 1937), 6-51.

Contains some critical asides on Yeats, "who believes in poems but not in poetry" (p. 46).

317. RIES, LAWRENCE R.: *Wolf Masks: Violence in Contemporary Poetry*. Port Washington, N.Y.: Kennikat Press, 1977. vi, 162 pp.

See index for notes on Yeats's poetry.

318. ROBBINS, MARY SUSANNAH: "Yeats: The Perspective of Style," °Ph.D. thesis, Boston College, 1973. 50 pp. (*DAI*, 34:10 [Apr 1974], 6655A)

319. ROBERTS, BARBARA: "Yeats's Rhetorical Imperative," *YER*, 8:1&2 (1986), 64-71.

On the use of imperatives in the poetry.

320. ROBINSON, LENNOX: "I Sometimes Think . . . How Few Are Our Ballads," *IrP*, 26 Mar 1955, 8.

On Yeats's ballads.

321. ———: "Yeats: The Early Poems," *REL*, 6:3 (July 1965), 22-33.

322. RODGERS, AUDREY T.: *The Universal Drum: Dance Imagery in the Poetry of Eliot, Crane, Roethke, and Williams*. University Park: Pennsylvania State UP, 1979. ix, 196 pp.

Frequent notes on dance and dancer in Yeats's poetry (see pp. 21-23 and index).

323. ROSE, PHYLLIS HOGE: "Yeats and the Dramatic Lyric," Ph.D. thesis, U of Wisconsin, 1958. v, 519 pp. (*DAI*, 18:6 [June 1958], 2130)

324. ROTHFUSS, HEINRICH: "Wandlungen in der späten Lyrik William Butler Yeats'," Dr.phil. thesis, U of Tübingen, 1966. xi, 299 pp.

A study of Yeats's "system" poems and of the revisions of the later poems in the light of his growing concern with philosophical "objectivity." Rothfuss fails to distinguish between different uses of the "system" and does not offer a convincing explanation of "objective." At times he becomes completely unintelligible. Numerous mistakes in both text and bibliography.

325. RUTLEDGE, ROBERT CLINTON: "The Development of the Poetry of William Butler Yeats as Reflected in His Metaphors," °Ph.D. thesis, George Washington U, 1966. 234 pp. (*DAI*, 27:6 [Dec 1967], 1836A)

326. RYBOWSKI, TADEUSZ: "Niektóre problemy przekładu poetyckiego: Uwagi warsztatowe na przszykładzie utworów Williama Butlera Yeatsa," *Acta Universitatis Wratislaviensis*, 905 / *Studia Linguistica*, 10 (1986), 41-51.

On the problem of translating Yeats's poems into Polish.

327. RYF, ROBERT S.: "Yeats's Major Metaphysical Poems," *JML*, 4:3 (Feb 1975), 610-24.

Antinomial poems; e.g., "Sailing to Byzantium," "The Tower," "Among School Children," and "Byzantium."

328. SAMSON, Mme. [ ]: "The Sacred in the Poetry of W. B. Yeats," *Confluents*, 2 (1975), 117-25.

329. SARAJAS, ANNAMARI: *Viimeiset romantikot: Kirjallisuuden aatteiden vaihtelua 1880-luvun jälkeen* [The last romantics: Thoughts on the literary revolution after 1880]. Porvoo-Helsinki: Söderström, 1962. 271 pp.

"Yeatsin runouden kansallinen romantiikka" [Yeats: Folk romanticism in his poetry], 38-67.

330. SÂRBU, RODICA: "W. B. Yeats: Avatarurile batrînului întelept," *ASUI*, 24 (1978), 121-24.

"WBY: The metamorphoses of the wise old man"; the theme of old age in Yeats's poetry.

331. Entry canceled.

332. SASAKURA, SADAO: "W. B. Yeats, an Eternal Wanderer," *Ibaraki Daigaku Kyōyōbu Kiyō. Bulletin / Bulletin: College of General Education, Ibaraki U, Mito, Japan*, 4 (1972), 109-34.

In Japanese; English synopsis on pp. 109-11. On self, anti-self, and Unity of Being in Yeats's poetry.

333. SAUL, GEORGE BRANDON: "Yeats and His Poems," *TLS*, 31 Mar 1950, 208.

The problem of dating Yeats's poems. Correspondence by Allan Wade, 7 Apr 1950, 215.

334. ———: *In . . . Luminous Wind*. No. 7 of *DPYCP* (1966, CA20), 197-256.

Contains the following essays: "The Short Stories of William Butler Yeats," 199-204; reprinted in FA28.

"Yeats's Verse before *Responsibilities*," 205-16; reprinted from *ArQ*, 16:2 (Summer 1960), 158-67.

"A Frenzy of Concentration: Yeats's Verse from *Responsibilities* to *The King of the Great Clock Tower*," 217-36; reprinted from *ArQ*, 20:2 (Summer 1964), 101-16.

"Coda: The Verse of Yeats's Last Five Years," 237-44; reprinted from *ArQ*, 17:1 (Spring 1961), 63-68.

"The Winged Image: A Note on Birds in Yeats's Poems," 245-56; reprinted from AC76.

334a. SAYLOR, CAROL CLOUGH: "That Other Heracles: Yeats's Counter Epic of Cuchulain," °Ph.D. thesis, U of Oklahoma, 1987. 204 pp. (*DAI*, 48:8 [Feb 1988], 2070A)

A "psychoanalytically oriented study" of the Cuchulain poems and plays.

335. SCHLEIFER, RONALD: "Forms of Intensity: A Study of Yeats's Middle Verse," Ph.D. thesis, Johns Hopkins U, 1974. v, 367 pp. (*DAI*, 35:12 [June 1975], 7923A)

Contains chapters on the early poetry, "Narrative in *In the Seven Woods*," "The Poetry of Masks in *The Green Helmet*," and "Tragedy and *Responsibilities*." See also DD273.

336. SCHOCH, OLGA: "Macpherson, Fiona Macleod, Yeats (Ein Stilvergleich)," [Dr.phil. thesis, U of Wien, 1931]. v, 153 pp.

A rather impressionistic study of "poetic style."

337. SCHRAMM, RICHARD: "The Line Unit: Studies in the Later Poetry of W. B. Yeats," *Ohio UR*, 3 (1961), 32-41.

On "A Deep Sworn Vow," "After Long Silence," and "The Mother of God."

338. SCHWEISGUT, ELSBETH: *Yeats' Feendichtung*. Darmstadt: Bender, 1927. 61 pp.

A Dr.phil. thesis, U of Giessen, 1927 [i.e., 1928]; on the fairy poetry.

339. SCOTT, NATHAN ALEXANDER: *The Broken Center: Studies in the Theological Horizon of Modern Literature*. New Haven: Yale UP, 1968 [1966]. xviii, 237 pp.

See pp. 41-42 for a note on the quest for eternity in Yeats's poetry.

340. SEEBER, HANS ULRICH: *Moderne Pastoraldichtung in England: Studien zur Theorie und Praxis der pastoralen Versdichtung in England nach 1800 mit besonderer Berücksichtigung von Edward Thomas (1878-1917)*. Frankfurt/Main: Lang, 1979. 398 pp. (Neue Studien zur Anglistik und Amerikanistik. 16.)

"Die produktive Aneignung der pastoralen Tradition um 1900 (Yeats, Davidson, Housman, Imagisten)" [The productive appropriation of the pastoral tradition around 1900], 143-60.

341. SEGREST, MABELLE MASSEY: "The Tree of Life in the Poetry of W. B. Yeats," °Ph.D. thesis, Duke U, 1979. 191 pp. (*DAI*, 40:10 [Apr 1980], 5440A-41A; reprinted *YeA*, 1 [1982], 212-13)

342. SEIDEN, MORTON IRVING: "A Psychoanalytic Essay on William Butler Yeats," *Accent*, 6:3 (Spring 1946), 178-90.

A one-sided piece of literary criticism. Interprets "The Wanderings of Oisin" and "The Cap and Bells" as illustrations of the Oedipus complex, "made manifest in the artist's sense of psychic impotence."

343. SHARMA, P. P.: "Yeats: Poet of Unified Sensibility," *VQ*, 40:2 (Aug-Oct 1974), 140-53.

Unity of Being in the poetry.

344. SHARROCK, ROGER: "Yeats and Death," *J of English Language and Literature,* 29:1 (Spring 1983), 189-208.
Yeats's view of death as expressed in some of his poems.

345. SHAWCROSS, JOHN T.: "A Consideration of Title-Names in the Poetry of Donne and Yeats," *Names,* 31:3 (Sept 1983), 159-66.
There are "made-up names for effect, actual names for certain connotations or meaning, and names that have little effect other than an anchoring in time" in the titles of Yeats's poems.

346. SHIH, HUNG-CHU: *William Butler Yeats's Prophetic Poetry.* T'aipei shih: Ching sheng wen wu kung ying kung ssu, min kuo 69 [1980]. iii, 62 pp.

347. SIDNELL, MICHAEL J.: "Mr. Yeats, Michael Robartes and Their Circle," in Harper: *Yeats and the Occult* (1975, FC40), 225-54.
Michael Robartes in the poetry and in *A Vision.*

348. ———: "Yeats, Synge and the Georgians," *YeA,* 3 (1985), 105-23.
Yeats's middle poetry as related to that of the Georgian poets (who were very much influenced by Synge).

349. SIMMONS, JAMES: "The Diction of Yeats," *Confrontation,* 6 (Spring 1973), 71-85.
In Yeats's poetry and political statements.

350. SINHA, V. N. : "The Theme of Escape in W. B. Yeats's Early Poetry," *J of the Department of English, Sana'a U,* 1 (June 1975), 51-66.

351. ———: "Yeats's 'Remarking [sic] of Himself' in Some Early Poems," *J of the Department of English, Sana'a U,* 5 (Sept 1978), 63-73.

352. SKELTON, ROBIN: *The Poet's Calling.* London: Heinemann / NY: Barnes & Noble, 1975. x, 214 pp.
"The Problem of Poetic Authority," 152-69; revised version of "W. B. Yeats: The Poet as Synopsis," *Mosaic,* 1:1 (Oct 1967), 7-21. On the unifying force of the figure of the Master-Poet Yeats in his poems; see also index for further references.

353. SLAVITT, DAVID: "The Significance of W. B. Yeats as a Modern Poet," *Yale Literary Magazine,* 123:6 (May 1955), 19-24.
On the Crazy Jane poems.

354. SMITH, BARBARA HERRNSTEIN: *Poetic Closure: A Study of How Poems End.* Chicago: U of Chicago Press, 1968. xvi, 289 pp.
Some notes on Yeats's poetry (see index).

355. SMITH, ERIC: *A Dictionary of Classical Reference in English Poetry.* Cambridge: Brewer / Totowa, N.J.: Barnes & Noble, 1984. xiii, 308 pp.
Index to classical references in Yeats's poetry, p. 307.

356. SMITH, STAN: "Porphyry's Cup: Yeats, Forgetfulness and the Narrative Order," *YeA,* 5 (1987), 15-45.
The motif of forgetfulness in the fictive stories contained in some of his poems and its source in Neoplatonism.

357. SOCIÉTÉ DES ANGLICISTES DE L'ENSEIGNEMENT SUPÉRIEUR: *Littérature--linguistique--civilisation--pédagogie*. Actes du Congrès de Grenoble (1973). Paris: Didier, 1976. 357 pp. (Études anglaises. 65.)
Jacqueline Genet: "La poétique de l'eau chez W. B. Yeats," 225-38; discusses water imagery in the poetry.

358. ———: *Autour de l'idée de nature: Histoire des idées et civilisation. Pédagogie et divers*. Actes du Congrès de Saint-Etienne (1975). Paris: Didier, 1977. 316 pp. (Études anglaises. 74.)
Jacqueline Genet: "La dialectique de la nature et de l'esprit dans la poésie de W. B. Yeats," 137-57.

359. ———: *Linguistique, civilisation, littérature*. Actes du Congrès de Tours (1977). Paris: Didier, 1980. 294 pp. (Études anglaises. 76.)
Christiane Joseph-Trividic: "De 'Ile' au 'Pêcheur': Le fonctionnement de l'image dans quelques poèmes de Yeats," 132-42. Discusses Unity of Being in several poems, particularly "The Lake Isle of Innisfree," "The Fisherman," "Easter 1916," and "On a Political Prisoner."

360. SOHNGEN, MARY, and ROBERT J. SMITH: "Images of Old Age in Poetry," *Gerontologist*, 18:2 (Apr 1978), 181-86.
"Study of the texts of 127 poems listed under 'old age' in *Granger's Index to Poetry*, indicates strongly negative attitudes about physical, emotional, social losses. The reading of poetry, a sensitizing experience, serves to reinforce negative stereotypes persistent in the media of mass culture." Yeats's poems of old age fit into this pattern.

361. SONOI, EISHU: "Yeats's Tree," *Studies in English Language and Literature*, 27 (1977), 109-13.
The tree image in the poetry.

362. SPANOS, WILLIAM V.: "Sacramental Imagery in the Middle and Late Poetry of W. B. Yeats," *TSLL*, 4:2 (Summer 1962), 214-27.

363. SPEAR, HILDA D.: *Remembering, We Forget: A Background Study to the Poetry of the First World War*. London: Davis-Poynter, 1979. 159 pp.
Note on why Yeats did not write war poetry, pp. 41-43.

364. SPIVEY, TED R.: "The Apocalyptic Symbolism of W. B. Yeats and T. S. Eliot," *Costerus*, 4 (1972), 193-214.

365. ———: "Yeats and Eliade: Shamanism and the Modern Poet," *MBL*, 4:1 (Spring 1979), 51-62.
In some of his poems Yeats assumes the role of the shaman as defined by Mircea Eliade; i. e., he attempts "to recover momentarily in a state of ecstasy a sense of the lost paradisial condition of man."

366. STANGE, G. ROBERT: "The Case of Hugh Lane's Paintings," *Texas Q*, 2:2 (Summer 1959), 180-87.
Hugh Lane in Yeats's poems.

367. STILZ, GERHARD: "Die Darstellung und Funktion des Tieres in der englischen Lyrik des 20. Jahrhunderts," Dr.phil. thesis, U of Tübingen, 1968. iv, 200 pp.
Notes on animals in Yeats's poetry, passim (see index).

368. STOCK, A. G.: "Symbolism and Belief in the Poetry of W. B. Yeats," *VQ,* 27:3-4 (1961-62), 181-96.

369. ———: "From the National to the Universal," *DM,* 4:3-4 (Autumn-Winter 1965), 28-35.
Concentrates on "To Ireland in the Coming Times" and "Nineteen Hundred and Nineteen."

370. ———: "The World of Maud Gonne," *IJES,* 6 (1965), 56-79.
Includes some comments on Yeats's attitude toward her and his treatment of her in his poetry.

371. ———: "W. B. Yeats and the Poetry of Violence," *JJCL,* 12 (1974), 74-85.

372. STROUD, JOANNE HERBERT: "Archetypal Symbols in the Poetry of W. B. Yeats," Ph.D. thesis, U of Dallas, 1975. vii, 211 pp. (*DAI,* 37:1 [July 1976], 302A)
A Jung-Yeats comparison.

373. STURTEVANT, DONALD F.: "The Public and Private Minds of W. B. Yeats," *Thoth,* 4:2 (Spring 1963), 74-82.
Largely concerned with the relationship between Yeats's system (particularly the concept of Anima Mundi) and his poetry.

374. SULERI, SARA: "Once Out of Nature: The Uses of System in Wordsworth, Arnold, Yeats," °Ph.D. thesis, Indiana U, 1983. 212 pp. (*DAI,* 44:12 [June 1984], 3699A; reprinted *Yeats,* 3 [1985], 212-13, and *YeA,* 4 [1986], 320)
Focuses "on the representation of systematic philosophy in the poetry of Wordsworth, Matthew Arnold, and Yeats" (abstract).

375. SULLIVAN, JOHN JOSEPH: "The Great Design: Yeats's Rearrangement of His Poems," Ph.D. thesis, U of Virginia, 1966. iv, 215 pp. (*DAI,* 27:12 [June 1967], 4266A-67A)

376. SUŠKO, MARIO: "Ptice B. Miljkovića i W. B. Yeatsa" [The birds of Miljković and Yeats], *Telegram,* 19 Nov 1965, 10.

377. ———: "O problemu romantičkog i simboličkog u poeziji W. B. Yeatsa," *Izraz,* year 10 / 20:8-9 (Aug-Sept 1966), 234-57.

378. ———: "V. B. Jejts: Poezija simbola," *Život,* 16:1-2 (Jan-Feb 1967), 43-52.

379. ———: *Duh i glina.* Sarajevo: Veselin Masleša, 1978. 284 pp.
"W. B. Yeats i ideja suprotnosti" [WBY and the idea of opposites], 69-119; reprinted from *Forum* [Zagreb], year 8 / 18:10 (Oct-Nov 1969), 745-80.

380. SUZUKI, FUMIE: "The Visionary Image of Love and Death in the Poems of W. B. Yeats," *Essays and Studies in British & American Literature,* 9:1 (Winter 1961), 39-72.

381. *Talks to Teachers of English.* Newcastle-upon-Tyne: Department of Education, Kings's College, 1959. 68 pp.
Peter Butter: "The Symbolist Movement in Poetry and Drama," 27-52; on symbolism in Yeats's poetry, particularly in "A Dialogue of Self and Soul," pp. 40-45.

382. TARVIN, WILLIAM LESTER: "Yeats's Rhetorical Art: Dimensions of Rhetoric in the Non-Dramatic Poetry of William Butler Yeats," Ph.D. thesis, U of Alabama, 1972. iii, 195 pp. (*DAI,* 33:10 [Apr 1973], 5752A)

383. TELFER, GILES W. L.: °"The Idea of the Gael in English Poetry, 1807-1914," D.Phil. thesis, Oxford U, 1967.

See also by the same author *Yeats's Idea of the Gael,* No. 4 of *DPYCP* (1965, CA20), 85-108. Yeats's idea of the Gael is peculiarly his own and very different from the originals. He comes closest to his Gaelic sources in "The Wanderings of Oisin."

384. THIESMEYER, LYNN JANET: "Figures of Style: Rhetoric, Poetics, and Syntax in Yeats's Poetry," Ph.D. thesis, Princeton U, 1980. x, 226 pp. (*DAI,* 41:7 [Jan 1981], 3122A; reprinted *YeA,* 2 [1983], 96-97)

"The purpose of this dissertation is to use traditional rhetoric and poetics in analyzing the stylistic devices of . . . Yeats's poetry" (abstract).

385. THOMPSON, FRANCIS J.: "Poetry and Politics: W. B. Yeats," *Hopkins R,* 3:1 (Fall 1949), 3-17.

Yeats did not stop being a political poet after he had outgrown his Celtic Twilight phase. Notes the influence of John O'Leary.

386. TRACY, ROBERT: "Energy, Ecstasy, Elegy: Yeats and the Death of Robert Gregory," *Eire,* 19:1 (Spring 1984), 26-47.

Compares the ways in which Yeats treats Cuchulain, Synge, Robert Gregory, and other heroes, and discusses "In Memory of Major Robert Gregory" and "An Irish Airman Foresees His Death."

387. TSCHUMI, RAYMOND: *Thought in Twentieth-Century English Poetry*. London: Routledge & Kegan Paul, 1950. 299 pp.

A Docteur ès lettres thesis, U of Genève, 1950. Reprinted °NY: Octagon Books, 1972; °Folcroft, Pa.: Folcroft Library Editions, 1972.

"Yeats's Philosophical Poetry," 129-73; discusses *A Vision* and the poems related to it, including a section on "Yeats's Historical Vision" and on the two Byzantium poems.

388. TUDOR, KATHLEEN RICHARDSON: "The Androgynous Mind in W. B. Yeats, D. H. Lawrence, Virginia Woolf, and Dorothy Richardson," Ph.D. thesis, U of Toronto, 1972. vi, 209 pp. (*DAI,* 35:2 [Aug 1974], 1126A-27A)

"Marriage of Opposites--W. B. Yeats," 16-54; masculine/feminine oppositions in *A Vision* and some later poems.

389. TURNER, W. J.: "Broadside Songs," *NSt,* 7 Dec 1935, 848-50.

Yeats's broadside songs have "the simplicity and directness of the old folk songs."

390. TUVE, ROSEMOND: *Elizabethan and Metaphysical Imagery: Renaissance Poetics and Twentieth-Century Critics*. Chicago: U of Chicago Press, 1947. xiv, 442 pp.

Notes on Yeats's imagery, passim (see index). See William Empson: "Donne and the Rhetorical Tradition," *KR,* 11:4 (Autumn 1949), 571-87; comments on the reading of "Byzantium," pp. 576-77.

391. VANDERHAAR, MARGARET MARY: "Yeats's Relationship with Women and Their Influence on His Poetry," Ph.D. thesis, Tulane U, 1966. ii,

154 pp. (*DAI,* 27:5 [Nov 1966], 1387A)
Mainly Maud Gonne, Lady Gregory, and Mrs. Yeats. The biographical parts are derived from the standard publications and do not constitute original research.

392. VEEDER, WILLIAM RICHARD: *W. B. Yeats: The Rhetoric of Repetition*. Berkeley: U of California Press, 1968. vii, 56 pp. (U of California Publications. English Studies. 34.)
A study of the various forms of verbal repetition in the poetry.

393. VENABLES, J. W.: "W. B. Yeats and His Poetry," *Holborn R,* os 62 / ns 11:4 (Oct 1920), 501-12.
Yeats as an Irish poet.

394. *Victorian Poetry*. London: Arnold, 1972. 304 pp. (Stratford-upon-Avon Studies. 15.)
Arnold Goldman: "The Oeuvre Takes Shape: Yeats's Early Poetry," 196-221. Lorna Sage: "Hardy, Yeats and Tradition," 254-75. Also passim (see index).

395. VORDTRIEDE, WERNER: *Novalis und die französischen Symbolisten: Zur Entstehungsgeschichte des dichterischen Symbols*. Stuttgart: Kohlhammer, 1963. 196 pp. (Sprache und Literatur. 8.)
See pp. 80-86 for a discussion of garden/paradise symbolism in Yeats's poetry.

396. *Vremen svi͡azui͡ushchai͡a nit'. (Problemy filosofii istorii v tvorchestve zarubezhnykh pisateleĭ XVII-XX vv.)*. Kishinev: Shtiint͡sa, 1981. 164 pp.
G. E. Ionkis: "Kont͡sept͡sii͡a istorii i ee voploshchenie v poezii U. B. Ĭetsa (10-30-e gg. XX v.)," 118-33. "The concept of history and its application in the poetry of WBY (from the 1910's to the 1930's)."

397. WALDMAN, ANNE, and MARILYN WEBB (eds): *Talking Poetics from Naropa Institute: Annals of the Jack Kerouac School of Disembodied Poetics*. Boulder: Shambala Publications, 1978-79. 2 vols.
Lewis MacAdams: "Poetry and Politics," 2:347-62; on Yeats, Pound, and Olson.

398. WARDLE, JUDITH FRANCES: "Myth and Image in Three Romantics: A Study of Blake, Shelley, and Yeats," Ph.D. thesis, Queen's U, Belfast, 1971. iv, 617 pp.
"William Butler Yeats," 395-590; mainly on the poetry and the theoretical writings.

399. WASSERMAN, ROSANNE: "Helen of Troy: Her Myth in Modern Poetry," °Ph.D. thesis, City U of New York, 1986. 451 pp. (*DAI,* 47:4 [Oct 1986], 1340A)
Contains a chapter on Yeats.

400. WATKINS, VERNON: "W. B. Yeats, poète religieux," *Critique,* 9:78 (Nov 1953), 913-30.
Also published as "W. B. Yeats--The Religious Poet," *TSLL,* 3:4 (Winter 1962), 473-88.

401. WATSON-WILLIAMS, HELEN: "All the Olympians: W. B. Yeats and His Friends," *English,* 14:83 (Summer 1963), 178-84.
Yeats's friends in his poetry.

402. WEBB, EUGENE: *The Dark Dove: The Sacred and Secular in Modern Literature*. Seattle: U of Washington Press, 1975. xi, 280 pp.
"The One and the Many: The Ambiguous Challenge of Being in the Poetry of Yeats and Rilke," 88-110.

403. WEINRAUB, RICHARD BRUCE: "Yeats and the Femme Fatale," °Ph.D. thesis, U of Oregon, 1983. 215 pp. (*DAI*, 45:1 [July 1984], 194A; reprinted *Yeats*, 3 [1985], 213-14)
Discusses, according to abstract, the femme fatale in the poetry, particularly Maud Gonne and Crazy Jane.

404. WEISSMAN, JUDITH: "'Somewhere in Ear-Shot': Yeats's Admonitory Gods," *Pequod*, 14 (1982), 16-31.
Yeats's truly visionary poetry can be found in his elegies.

405. WESTBROOK, EDWARD BRUCE: "The Tower Symbol in the Poetry of William Butler Yeats," °Ph.D. thesis, U of North Carolina at Chapel Hill, 1973. 184 pp. (*DAI*, 34:5 [Nov 1973], 2664A)

406. WHALLEY, GEORGE: "Yeats' Quarrel with Old Age," *QQ*, 58:4 (Winter 1951/52), 497-507.

406a. ———: "Literary Romanticism," *QQ*, 72:2 (Summer 1965), 232-52.
Contains notes on "Coole Park and Ballylee, 1931," "Lapis Lazuli," and "The Second Coming."

407. WILDER, AMOS NIVEN: *The Spiritual Aspects of the New Poetry*. NY: Harper, 1940. xxiv, 262 pp.
"W. B. Yeats and the Christian Option," 196-204, and passim (see index). Yeats's paganism and rejection of Christianity, as shown in his poetry, account for his "'numbness' to the intricacies of personal feeling."

408. ———: *Modern Poetry and the Christian Tradition: A Study in the Relation of Christianity to Culture*. NY: Scribner's, 1952. xix, 287 pp.
Passim (see index).

409. WILLIAMS, DESMOND (ed): *The Irish Struggle, 1916-1926*. London: Routledge & Kegan Paul, 1966. vii, 193 pp.
Francis MacManus: "Imaginative Literature and the Revolution," 19-30.

410. WILLIAMS, GWYN: "The Drowned Man in English Poetry," *Litera*, 8 (1965), 62-90.
Note on Yeats, pp. 81-82.

411. WILNER, ELEANOR RAND: *Gathering the Winds: Visionary Imagination and Radical Transformation of Self and Society*. Baltimore: Johns Hopkins UP, 1975. vii, 196 pp.
"The Uncommon Eye: Vision in the Poetry of Blake, Beddoes, and Yeats," 47-134; on Yeats, pp. 106-34. Discusses dualistic thinking and materialistic imagination in the poetry.

412. WILSON, COLIN: *Poetry & Mysticism*. London: Hutchinson, 1970. 227 pp.
"W. B. Yeats," 125-60, and passim. Reprinted °San Francisco: City Lights Books, 1986.

413. WITT, MARION: "William Butler Yeats," *EIE*, 1946, 74-101.

Yeats's biography in his poetry, notably his relationships with Maud Gonne and Lady Gregory and his "supernatural" preoccupations (particularly in "Ego Dominus Tuus").

414. ———: "A Competition for Eternity: Yeats's Revision of His Later Poems," *PMLA*, 64:1 (Mar 1949), 40-58.

415. WOLFE, STEPHEN: "The Half-Way House: Some Eastern Thoughts in Yeats' Poetry," *Doshisha Studies in English*, 23 (Dec 1979), 112-37.

Discusses the "noticeable effect" that Zen had on Yeats's poetry.

416. WOOD, ANDELYS: "Yeats and Measurement," *SoAR*, 50:4 (Nov 1985), 65-80.

The idea of measurement in the poetry, particularly in "Under Ben Bulben" and "The Statues."

417. WRIGHT, GEORGE THADDEUS: *The Poet in the Poem: The Personae of Eliot, Yeats, and Pound*. Berkeley: U of California Press, 1962 [1960]. xiv, 167 pp. (California Paperback. CAL71.)

Based on °"Modern Poetry and the *Persona:* The Device and Its Aesthetic Context, as Exhibited in the Work of Eliot, Yeats, and Pound," Ph.D. thesis, U of California (Berkeley), 1956/57. Reprinted °NY: Gordian Press, 1974. (Perspectives in Criticism. 4.)

The persona is the embodied representative of the poet in his work. With Eliot, Yeats, and Pound, "it is the poem, not the speaker, through which the poet speaks, and which therefore serves as his persona" (p. 59). "Yeats: The Tradition of Myself," pp. 88-123, discusses the mask and self in the poetry.

Reviews:

- Donna Gerstenberger, *WHR*, 15:3 (Summer 1961), 285-86.
- A. R. Jones, *MLR*, 56:4 (Oct 1961), 601-2.
- Peter Ure, *RES*, 13:50 (May 1962), 214-15.

418. YAMASAKI, HIROYUKI: "Yeats's Attitude toward 'Tragic Joy,' with Special Reference to Its Change," *HSELL*, 25:Special Number (1980), 91-102.

Discusses some relevant poems and essays.

419. YEATS, GRAINNE: "Some Unexpected Ballad Makers," *Ireland of the Welcomes*, 19:5 (Jan-Feb 1971), 11-14.

420. YEATS, MICHAEL: "W. B. Yeats and Irish Folk Song," *SFQ*, 31:2 [i.e., 30:2] (June 1966), 153-78.

Discusses the influence of Irish folksong (particularly Gaelic folksong) on Yeats's poetry, his ballad poetry and the reasons for its failure to become popular, and his ideas about music and singing.

421. YEATS, W. B.: *Liebesgedichte* [Love poems]. Herausgegeben und mit einem Nachwort versehen von Werner Vordtriede. Darmstadt: Luchterhand, 1979 [1976]. 113 pp. (Sammlung Luchterhand. 218.)

Notes to the poems, pp. 55-60; "Nachwort," pp. 100-11.

422. YI CH'ANG-PAE: [In Korean] "Yeats's Later Poetry," *Phoenix*, 10 (Summer 1965), 96-110.

423. YOSHINO, MASAAKI: [In Japanese] "On Yeats's Imagination: What the Ballylee Scene Means," *SELit*, 55:1 (Sept 1978), 61-73.

English summary in English Number (1979), 254-55. On the importance of Yeats's tower to his poetry.

424. YOUNGBLOOD, SARAH: "The Structure of Yeats's Long Poems," *Criticism,* 5:4 (Fall 1963), 323-35.
The long poems ("The Statues" and "Meditations in Time of Civil War") are fusions of the discursive and imagistic modes of poetry.

425. ZIMMERMANN, GEORGES-DENIS: "Irish Political Street Ballads and Rebel Songs, 1780-1900," Docteur ès lettres thesis, U of Genève, 1965. 342 pp. (Genève: La Sirène, 1966)
Also published as *°Songs of the Irish Rebellion: Political Street Ballads and Rebel Songs, 1780-1900.* Hatboro, Pa.: Folklore Associates, 1967. 342 pp. Scattered notes on Yeats, passim (see index).

426. ———: "Yeats, the Popular Ballad and the Ballad-Singers," *ES,* 50:2 (Apr 1969), 185-97.

DD Single Poems and Books of Poetry

This section lists discussions of single poems and of individual books of poetry, such as *Responsibilities.* It is arranged alphabetically by individual poems or books of poetry. Together with the cross references, it serves as a complete index to all the interpretations of poems listed in this bibliography. Cross references are made to analyzed books and articles. These items have been analyzed whenever they contain coherent interpretations of poems and, in the case of books, reliable indexes; they are marked accordingly. It should be noted that this section does not list all of Yeats poems. The titles of poems are those used in the *Variorum Edition* (Wade 211N). Yeats's early dramatic attempts *Mosada, The Island of Statues, Time and the Witch Vivien, The Seeker,* and *The Shadowy Waters,* are listed in section EE. No cross references have been made to musical renderings in section HC.

Some standard monographs on the poetry have not been analyzed because they are concerned with virtually the whole body of Yeats's poems and are essential reading for any research on this subject. For these books see CA22, 37, 65, 85, 110, 111, DA2, and 25.

"An Acre of Grass"

1. NELSON, T. G. A.: "Yeats' 'An Acre of Grass,'" *Expl,* 42:2 (Winter 1984), 14-16.

2. NIMMO, D. C.: "Yeats' 'An Acre of Grass,'" *Expl,* 29:6 (Feb 1971), no. 50.
Yeats's use of Blake.

3. PERRINE, LAURENCE: "Yeats' 'An Acre of Grass,'" *Expl,* 22:8 (Apr 1964), no. 64.

4. SPANOS, WILLIAM V.: "The Sexual Imagination in Yeats's Late Poetry: A Reading of 'An Acre of Grass,'" *CEA,* 32:1 (Oct 1969), 16-18.

5. TAUBE, MYRON: "Yeats' 'An Acre of Grass,' 10," *Expl,* 26:5 (Jan 1968), no. 40.
"The mill of the mind" refers to J. S. Mill.

See also CA53a, 91, CD1179, DA28, 34, 35(II), 44, DB70, DC295, DD294.

"Adam's Curse"

6. CIARDI, JOHN: *Dialogue with an Audience*. Philadelphia: Lippincott, 1963. 316 pp.

"The Morality of Poetry: Epilogue to an Avalanche," 105-15; reprinted from *SatR*, 30 Mar 1957, 11-14, 34. The poem is an example of the poet's contempt of "counterfeit sentimentality."

7. PESKIN, S. G.: "W. B. Yeats and 'Adam's Curse,'" *UES*, 19:1 (Apr 1981), 11-17.

The poem as an illustration of Yeats's attitude towards the modern world and Christian belief.

8. THEUMER, ERICH: "W. B. Yeats: 'Adam's Curse,'" *NS*, 16:7 (July 1967), 305-11.

9. WARD, DAVID: "'Adam's Curse' and the Value of Artistic Labour," *YER*, 6:2 (1979), 41-48.

See also BA3, CA4, 12, CD880, DA34, 35(I), 36, 49, DB28, 244, 259, DC44.

"After Long Silence"

10. DAVIS, WILLIAM V.: "'The Coming among Us of the Dead': Yeats's 'After Long Silence,'" *McNR*, 27 (1980-81), 45-49.

11. MILLETT, FRED BENJAMIN: *The Rebirth of Liberal Education*. NY: Harcourt, Brace, 1945. xi, 179 pp.

Quotes two interpretations "from students of very high academic standing," one "false" and one "true," pp. 166-68.

12. PARISH, JOHN E.: "The Tone of Yeats' 'After Long Silence,'" *WHR*, 16:4 (Summer 1962), 377-79.

Criticizes the Brooks-Warren interpretation (DD168).

13. PERRINE, LAURENCE: "Yeats's Supreme Theme," *CP*, 10:1 (Spring 1977), 13-15.

14. SUTHERLAND, RONALD: "Structural Linguistics and English Prosody," *CE*, 20:1 (Oct 1958), 12-17.

Prosodic interpretation of the poem.

See also CA26, 66, DA6, 26, 35(II), 36, 44, DB199, 242, DC337, DD168.

"Against Unworthy Praise"

See DB199.

"All Soul's Night"

15. MOORE, RICHARD: "The Balancer: Yeats and His Supernatural System," *YR*, 72:3 (Spring 1983), 385-98.

Mainly on this poem.

See also CA12, 26, CD224, DA14, 22, 49, DB70, DD680, FC49, 64.

"All Things Can Tempt Me"

See DA34, 36, DC275.

"Among School Children"

16. ANTUNES, FUTIN BUFFARA: "From Personal to Impersonal: A Textual Analysis of Yeats's 'Among School Children,'" *Estudos anglo-americanos,* 1 (1977), 25-37.

17. ARMSTRONG, ISOBEL: *Language as Living Form in Nineteenth-Century Poetry.* Brighton: Harvester / Totowa, N.J.: Barnes & Noble, 1982. xiv, 220 pp.
See pp. 210-18.

18. BODDEN, HORST, and HERBERT KAUSSEN: *Modellanalysen englischer Lyrik.* Stuttgart: Klett, 1974. 176 pp.
"William Butler Yeats: 'Among School Children,'" 135-51.

19. BROOKS, CLEANTH: *The Well Wrought Urn: Studies in the Structure of Poetry.* NY: Harcourt, Brace, 1959 [1947]. xiv, 300 pp. (Harvest Book. HB11.)
"Yeats's Great Rooted Blossomer," 178-91; also on "Sailing to Byzantium." See also DD30.

20. CHASE, RICHARD: "Myth as Literature," *EIE,* 1947, 3-22.
Note on this poem and on "Leda and the Swan," 18-20.

21. ———: *Quest for Myth.* Baton Rouge: Louisiana State UP, 1949. xi, 150 pp.
See pp. 120-21.

22. DAWSON, LEVEN MAGRUDER: "'Among School Children': 'Labour' and 'Play,'" *PQ,* 52:2 (Apr 1973), 286-95.
Relates the poem to 19th-century English socialism.

23. EIDE, ELLING O.: "Unai Otome as Helen of Troy," *MN,* 25:3-4 (1970), 455-58.
The influence of the Nō play *Motomezuka* in the translation of Marie Stopes on this poem.

24. EIJKELBOOM, J[AN]: "Notities bij 'Onder schoolkinderen,'" *Tweede ronde,* 3:1 (Spring 1982), 53-54.
"Notes on 'Among School Children.'"

25. FEINBERG, STEPHEN: "Yeats' 'Among School Children,'" *Expl,* 33:6 (Feb 1975), no. 45.

26. HANSON, CHRIS: "Yeats: 'Among School Children,'" *Critical Survey,* 6:1&2 (Summer 1973), 90-94.

27. HEANEY, SEAMUS: *Among School Children.* A lecture dedicated to the memory of John Malone. Belfast: John Malone Memorial Committee, [1985?]. 16 pp.
Contains notes on Yeats's poem.

28. HOLBROOK, DAVID: *Dylan Thomas: The Code of Night.* London: Athlone Press, 1972. viii, 271 pp.
See pp. 15-18.

29. ———: *Lost Bearings in English Poetry*. London: Vision Press, 1977. 255 pp.
"What Can Creativity Do? W. B. Yeats's 'Among School Children,'" 194-203. See also index for further references to Yeats's poetry.

30. HOŠEK, CHAVIVA, and PATRICIA PARKER (eds): *Lyric Poetry: Beyond New Criticism*. Ithaca: Cornell UP, 1985. 375 pp.
Jonathan Culler: "Changes in the Study of the Lyric," 38-54, discusses Cleanth Brooks's reading (DD19), pp. 44-46.

31. KAY, WALLACE G.: "'As Recollection or the Drug Decide': Images and Imaginings in 'Among School Children' and *Blowup*," *SoQ*, 12:3 (Apr 1974), 225-32.
Common to Yeats's poem, Antonioni's film and Cortazar's story (on which the film is based) is "the concern with the relationship between image, imagining, and perceived reality."

32. LENSING, GEORGE S.: "'Among School Children': Questions as Conclusions," *CollL*, 13:1 (Winter 1986), 1-8.

33. LINEBARGER, JAMES M.: "Yeats's 'Among School Children' and Shelley's 'Defence of Poetry,'" *N&Q*, os 208 / ns 10:10 (Oct 1963), 375-77.

34. LUCAS, JOHN: "Yeats and Goethe," *TLS*, 21 Nov 1968, 1321.
Connects the last four lines of the poem with Goethe's *Wilhelm Meister* and *Werther*.

35. MAN, PAUL DE: *Allegories of Reading: Figural Language in Rousseau, Nietzsche, Rilke, and Proust*. New Haven: Yale UP, 1979. xi, 305 pp.
"Semiology and Rhetoric," 3-19; contains a note on this poem. See also DD42a.

36. MIR, MAQSOOD HAMID: "The Phenomenological Response Theory: A Model for Synthesizing Reader Response and Literary Text in Teaching College English," °Ph.D. thesis, U of Louisville, 1983. 150 pp. (*DAI*, 44:11 [May 1984], 3390A-91A)
Includes a discussion of this poem.

37. PEARCE, DONALD: "Ghostly Paradigms of Things in 'Among School Children,'" *YER*, 7:1&2 (June 1982), 51-68.

38. RADCLIFFE, EVAN: "Yeats and the Quest for Unity: 'Among School Children' and Unity of Being," *CLQ*, 21:3 (Sept 1985), 109-21.

39. RAO, N. M.: "Yeats's 'Among School Children': Text and Context," *AJES*, 11:1 (1986), 98-108.
The context implies frequent references to Mallarmé.

40. ROSENBAUM, S. P.: "Yeats' 'Among School Children,' V," *Expl*, 23:2 (Oct 1964), no. 14.
The Porphyry reference. See also Charles C. Walcutt, 26:9 (May 1968), no. 72.

41. SCHIFFER, REINHOLD, and HERMANN J. WEIAND (eds): *Insight III: Analyses of English and American Poetry*. Frankfurt/Main: Hirschgraben, 1969. 366 pp.
R. Schiffer: "'Among School Children,'" 350-61; Peter H. Butter: "'The Wild Swans at Coole,'" 362-66.

42. SETURAMAN, V. S.: "Yeats and His Modern Critics," *Aryan Path,* 30:10 (Oct 1959), 457-61.
Mainly on what the critics did with this poem.

42a. SOKOLSKY, ANITA: "The Resistance to Sentimentality: Yeats, de Man, and the Aesthetic Education," *Yale J of Criticism,* 1:1 (Fall 1987), 67-86.
De Man (see DD35) and Schiller are the theoretical models for a reading of this poem as "a flamboyant conversion of an aesthetic into a sentimental education."

43. TERWILLIGER, PATRICIA J.: "A Re-Interpretation of Stanzas VII and VIII of W. B. Yeats's 'Among School Children,'" *Boston U Studies in English,* 5:1 (Spring 1961), 29-34.

44. THOMPSON, WILLIAM IRWIN: "Collapsed Universe and Structured Poem: An Essay in Whiteheadian Criticism," *CE,* 28:1 (Oct 1966), 25-39.
The five-part structure of location, implication, association, crisis, and resolution in Coleridge ("Dejection: An Ode"), Wordsworth ("Tintern Abbey"), Shelley ("Ode to the West Wind"), Arnold ("Dover Beach"), and Yeats's poem.

45. TORCHIANA, DONALD T.: "'Among School Children' and the Education of the Irish Spirit," in Jeffares and Cross: *In Excited Reverie* (1965, CA48), 123-50.
A reading of the poem against Yeats's ideas of education, as derived from Maria Montessori and Gentile. Includes a note on Maud Gonne.

46. UTLEY, FRANCIS LEE: "Stylistic Ambivalence in Chaucer, Yeats and Lucretius--The Cresting Wave and Its Undertow," *UKCR,* 37:3 (Mar 1971), 174-98.
On Yeats's poem, pp. 192-98.

47. VERHOEFF, ABRAHAM: *The Practice of Criticism: A Comparative Analysis of W. B. Yeats' "Among School Children."* Utrecht: Elinkwijk, [1966]. vii, 149 pp.
A Dr. in de letteren thesis, U of Utrecht, 1966. A comparison of previous interpretations of the poem, which concludes that no ultimately satisfactory results have been achieved so far. Verhoeff's own interpretation attempts to show that the poem is a typical Yeats poem and in effect not a very good one. Its reputation is largely based on its inferior half.
See review by Uta Janssens, *Neophilologus,* 52:3 (July 1968), 343-44.

48. WAIN, JOHN (ed): *Interpretations: Essays on Twelve English Poems.* London: Routledge & Kegan Paul, 1955. xv, 237 pp.
John Wain: "W. B. Yeats: 'Among School Children,'" 194-210.

49. WALCUTT, CHARLES C.: "Yeats' 'Among School Children' and 'Sailing to Byzantium,'" *Expl,* 8:6 (Apr 1950), no. 42.

50. WITT, ROBERT W.: "Yeats, Plato, and the Editors," *T. S. Eliot Newsletter,* 1:1 (Spring 1974), 4-5.
"Plato's parable" is not a Platonic concept of love but a satire on foolish theories.

See also BA3, 20, CA4, 12, 26, 27, 56, 63, 73, 90-92, 100, 103, 123,

CB167, 290, 440a, CC31, 178, 182, 226, CD208, 886, 1214, DA4, 14, 30, 34, 35(II), 36, 38, 49, DB13, 25, 70, 94, 104, 127, 141, 199, 208, 219, 279, DC49, 52, 102, 267, 327, DD168, 279, 359, 445, 537, 657, 680, FC64, FE80, HD53.

"Anashuya and Vijaya"

See DA11, DC62, 275.

"Ancestral Houses" (part 1 of "Meditations in Time of Civil War")

See DC102.

"Another Song of a Fool"

51. HARPER, GEORGE MILLS, and SANDRA L. SPRAYBERRY: "Complementary Creation: Notes on 'Another Song of a Fool' and 'Towards Break of Day,'" *Yeats,* 4 (1986), 69-85.

The role of Mrs. Yeats's automatic writing in the drafting of the two poems; reproduces the drafts of "Towards Break of Day."

"The Apparitions"

52. SKELTON, ROBIN: *Poetic Truth.* London: Heinemann, 1978. x, 131 pp.

See index for notes on this poem, "Sailing to Byzantium," and "The Second Coming."

See also BG156, 175, CA12, DB223, FC49, 56a.

"Are You Content?"

See DB70.

"At Algeciras--A Meditation upon Death"

See CA12, 103, 130, DA14, 36, 49.

"At Galway Races"

See DA30.

"At the Abbey Theatre"

See CA63, 128, DC189, DD240, HD82.

"Baile and Aillinn"

53. DUNSEATH, T. K.: "Yeats and the Genesis of Supernatural Song," *ELH,* 28:4 (Dec 1961), 399-416.

Also on "Ribh at the Tomb of Baile and Aillinn" and "Supernatural Songs."

See also CD713, HF24.

"The Ballad of Earl Paul"

54. H[AYES], R[ICHARD] [?]: "An Old Yeats Ballad," *DM,* 2:2 (Apr-June 1927), 59-61.

"The Ballad of Father Gilligan"

55. "A LOVER OF ORIGINALITY": "Father Gilligan," *Academy,* 12 Mar 1892, 255.

Points out that Yeats's poem plagiarizes a poem by one Tristram St. Martin. See Yeats's reply, 19 Mar 1892, 280 (reprinted in *Collected Letters,* 1:291-92), and letter by Tristram St. Martin, 26 Mar 1892, 303.

See also DA11, DC275, DD606.

"The Ballad of Father O'Hart"

See CC141.

"The Ballad of Moll Magee"

See DA11, DC270.

"The Ballad of the Foxhunter"

See DA35(I).

"The Balloon of the Mind"

See DC270a.

"Beautiful Lofty Things"

See CA150, DA26, 49, DD214, HD164.

"Before the World Was Made" (part 2 of "A Woman Young and Old")

56. DILTZ, BERT CASE: *Sense or Nonsense: Contemporary Education at the Crossroads*. Toronto: McClelland & Stewart, 1972. 190 pp.

See pp. 104-5.

See also DD417.

"Beggar to Beggar Cried"

See CC141.

"The Black Tower"

57. DISKIN, PATRICK: "A Source for Yeats's 'The Black Tower,'" *N&Q,* os 206 / ns 8:3 (Mar 1961), 107-8.
Standish O'Grady's *Finn and His Companions*. See additional note by Diskin, os 210 / ns 12:7 (July 1965), 278-79.

58. KEITH, W. J.: "Yeats's Arthurian Black Tower," *MLN,* 75:2 (Feb 1960), 119-23.

59. MATTHEWS, SUSAN: "Defiance and Defeat in W. B. Yeats' 'The Black Tower,'" *CP,* 5:2 (Fall 1972), 22-26.

60. SPIVAK, GAYATRI: "Allégorie et histoire de la poésie: Hypothèse de travail," *Poétique,* 2:8 (1971), 427-41.
Contains notes on the use of allegory in this poem.

See also CA4, 12, 112, 128, 129, 156, 167, CC130, 226, DA43, 44, 49, 53, DC48, 267, DD466.

"The Blessed"

See CC1, 260.

"Blood and the Moon"

61. FLEMING, NOEL: "Berkeley and Idealism," *Philosophy,* 60:233 (July 1985), 309-25.
Contains a note on this poem.

62. MEYERS, JEFFREY: "Yeats' 'Blood and the Moon,'" *Expl,* 30:6 (Feb 1972), no. 50.
The Swift allusions.

See also CA12, 91, 112, 118, 128, CB258, CC99, 130, 132, CD821, 1029, 1267, DA14, 35(II), 49, 53, DC267.

"Broken Dreams"

63. FRÉCHET, RENÉ: "Deux poèmes de W. B. Yeats," *CCEI,* 9 (1984), 7-13.
French translations of this poem and "The Statues" and notes.

See also DA35(I).

"A Bronze Head"

64. DENHAM, ROBERT D.: "Yeats' 'A Bronze Head,'" *Expl,* 29:2 (Oct 1970), no. 14.

65. SPIESS, REINHARD F.: "Observations Concerning Yeats's *Last Po-*

ems and Wittgenstein's *Tractatus Logico-Philosophicus*," *RLV*, 42:1 (1976), 82-86.

The philosophical implications of this poem (the reference to McTaggart) and, less importantly, of "The Circus Animals' Desertion" as related to Yeats's possible knowledge of Wittgenstein.

66. WILSON, F. A. C.: "Yeats's 'A Bronze Head': A Freudian Investigation," *L&P*, 22:1 (1972), 5-12.

Also generally on the type of the masculine woman in Yeats's poetry (Maud Gonne and Dorothy Wellesley).

See also CA12, 91, CC226, CD1179, DA28, 36, 44, 49, DC267, 297, DD337.

"Byzantium"

67. ALLEN, JAMES LOVIC: "Charts for the Voyage to Byzantium: An Annotated Bibliography of Scholarship and Criticism on Yeats's Byzantium Poems, 1935-1970," *BNYPL*, 77:1 (Autumn 1973), 28-50.

About 120 items.

68. ARKINS, BRIAN: "A New Source for Yeats' Poem 'Byzantium,'" *Byzantion*, 57:1 (1987), 172-73.

O. M. Dalton's *Byzantine Art and Archaeology* (1911).

69. AUTY, R. A.: "'Byzantium,'" *TLS*, 11 Aug 1950, 501.

Is it "A starlit or a moonlit dome disdains" or "distains"? See the letters by Gwendolen Murphy, 25 Aug 1950, 533 ("distains"); Richard Murphy, 1 Sept 1950, 549 ("disdains"); Maurice Craig, ibid. (points to difficulties in "The Municipal Gallery Revisited"); Peter Ure and Dennis Silk, 8 Sept 1950, 565 (on other textual difficulties); Gwendolen Murphy, 15 Sept 1950, 581 ("distains"); John Christopherson, ibid. ("disdains"); Vernon Watkins and Bonamy Dobrée, 22 Sept 1950, 597 ("disdains"); Gwendolen Murphy, 3 Nov 1950, 693 (remains unconvinced).

70. BEAUMONT, JOHN HOWLAND: "A Letter from Byzantium," *CSM*, 15 Aug 1979, 21.

A meditation on the Byzantium poems during a stay in the Kalahari desert.

71. BEN-MERRE, DIANA ARBIN: "The Poet Laureate and the Golden Bird: A Note on Yeats's Byzantium Poems," *CJIS*, 5:1 (June 1979), 100-103.

The importance of Yeats's "The Question of Laureateship" (*BmL*, Nov 1892, reprinted in *Collected Letters*, 1:324-26) for the interpretation of both Byzantium poems.

72. BEVINGTON, HELEN: *Beautiful Lofty People*. NY: Harcourt Brace Jovanovich, 1974. xi, 228 pp.

"Byzantium without Yeats," 111-17; on the real Byzantium which Yeats never saw and which is totally different from the one imagined in his poems. "A Tourist to Byzantium," 118; a poem.

73. BUNN, JAMES HARRY: "The Palace of Art: A Study of Form in Retrospective Poems about the Creative Process," °Ph.D. thesis, Emory U, 1969. 185 pp. (*DAI*, 30:10 [Apr 1970], 4400A)

Includes interpretations of the two Byzantium poems.

74. CECI, LOUIS G.: "The Case for Syntactic Imagery," *CE,* 45:5 (Sept 1983), 431-49.
Discusses the syntax of this poem and "Two Songs from a Play."

75. CERNUDA, LUIS: *Poesía y literatura.* Barcelona: Editorial Seix Barral, 1964. 2 vols. (Biblioteca breve. 150. 205.)
"W. B. Yeats: 'Bizancio,'" 1:112-15; reprinted from *México en la cultura,* 453 (24 Nov 1957), 3; a translation plus some notes (see also DD79).
"Yeats," 2:163-83; reprinted from *Cultura universitaria,* 72-73 (July-Sept 1960), 45-55. A review of *Letters* (W211J/K).
"Jiménez y Yeats," 2:249-56; reprinted from *Palabra y el hombre,* 7:28 (Oct-Dec 1963), 591-94.
The Yeats material is reprinted in Cernuda's *Prosa completa.* Barcelona: Barral, 1975. 1611 pp. (pp. 806-9, 1058-73, 1116-20).

76. CHATTERJEE, VISVANATH: *Aspects of Literature.* Calcutta: Progressive Publishers, 1978. xi, 189 pp.
"A Reading of Yeats's Byzantine Poems," 113-23; reprinted from *BDE,* ns 9:2 (1973-74), 14-22.

77. COPENHAVEN, CARLA: "Mastering the Images: Yeats's Byzantium Poems," *REAL,* 2 (1984), 319-53.

78. DAICHES, DAVID: *God and the Poets.* The Gifford Lectures, 1983. Oxford: Clarendon Press, 1984. ix, 227 pp.
See pp. 216-17.

79. DIETZ, BERND: "Luis Cernuda, traductor de poesía inglesa y alemana," *Cuadernos hispanoamericanos,* 350 (Aug 1979), 283-99.
Comments on Cernuda's translation of this poem (see DD75).

80. EIJKELBOOM, J[AN]: "Yeats en Byzantium," *Revisor,* 10:6 (Dec 1983), 71-73.
Short note on, and Dutch translations of, both Byzantium poems.

81. ELVIN, LIONEL: *Introduction to the Study of Literature.* Volume 1: Poetry. London: Sylvan Press, 1949. 224 pp.
See pp. 211-17.

82. EMPSON, WILLIAM: "Mr. Wilson on the Byzantium Poems," *REL,* 1:3 (July 1960), 51-56.
Criticizes F. A. C. Wilson's interpretations of both Byzantium poems (CA129).

83. ———: "The Variants for the Byzantium Poems," *Phoenix,* 10 (Summer 1965), 1-26.
Discusses the symbolism of the poems and its sources. Reprinted in Raj Kumar Kaul (ed): *Essays Presented to Amy G. Stock, Professor of English, Rajasthan University, 1961-65.* Jaipur: Rajasthan UP, 1965. viii, 195 pp. (pp. 111-36); and, slightly revised, as "Yeats and Byzantium," *Grand Street,* 1:4 (Summer 1982), 67-95.
Also contained in Empson's *Using Biography.* London: Chatto & Windus / Hogarth Press, 1984. viii, 259 pp. (pp. 163-86).

84. FRASER, G. S.: "Yeats's 'Byzantium,'" *CritQ,* 2:3 (Autumn 1960), 253-61.
Correspondence by John Wain, :4 (Winter 1960), 372-73; by Joan Grundy, 3:2 (Summer 1961), 168-69.

84a. FRIAR, KIMON: "*A Vision* and the Byzantium Poems," *Greek Heritage*, 1:3 (1964), 82-83, 85-89.

85. HAMARD, JEAN: "'Byzantium' de W. B. Yeats," *LanM*, 60:1 (Jan-Feb 1966), 54-63.

86. HUBERMAN, ELIZABETH: "To Byzantium Once More: A Study of the Structure of Yeats's 'Byzantium,'" *Essays in Literature*, 1:2 (Fall 1974), 193-205.

87. ISER, WOLFGANG: "Manieristische Metaphorik in der englischen Dichtung," *GRM*, os 41 / ns 10:3 (1960), 266-87.
See especially pp. 278-84.

88. JACKAMAN, ROB: "Byzantium Revisited: A Look at the Direction of Yeats's Philosophical Journey in the Poem 'Byzantium,'" *SoRA*, 8:3 (Nov 1975), 236-46.
"Byzantium" contains "a physical counterbalance to the spiritual experience conveyed in 'Sailing to Byzantium.'"

89. JEFFARES, A. NORMAN: "The Byzantine Poems of W. B. Yeats," *RES*, 22:85 (Jan 1946), 44-52.

90. ———: "Yeats's Byzantine Poems and the Critics," *ESA*, 5:1 (Mar 1962), 11-28.

91. ———: "Notes on Pattern in the Byzantine Poems of W. B. Yeats," *RLV*, 31:4 (1965), 353-59.
Syntactical and rhetorical patterns.

92. JERNIGAN, JAY: "The Phoenix as Thematic Symbol in Yeats's 'Byzantium,'" *Michigan Academician*, 1:3&4 (Spring 1969), 93-99.

93. KNIGHT, GEORGE WILSON: *The Starlit Dome: Studies in the Poetry of Vision*. With an introduction by W. F. Jackson Knight and an appendix on "Spiritualism and Poetry." London: Methuen, 1959 [1941]. xiv, 330 pp.
References to this poem on pp. 79, 93, 97, 175, 184, 202, 219, 225, 231, 233, 310-11; to "Sailing to Byzantium" on p. 310; in connection with a discussion of Wordsworth, Coleridge, Shelley, and Keats.

94. ———: *Neglected Powers: Essays on Nineteenth and Twentieth Century Literature*. London: Routledge & Kegan Paul, 1971. 515 pp.
"Poetry and the Arts: Tennyson, Browning, O'Shaughnessy, Yeats," 243-59; reprinted from *E&S*, 22 (1969), 88-104. See pp. 255-59 for a note on both Byzantium poems.

95. KOSTELANETZ, ANNE: "Irony in Yeat[s]'s Byzantium Poems," *Tennessee Studies in Literature*, 9 (1964), 129-42.

96. LEES, F. N.: "Yeats's 'Byzantium,' Dante, and Shelley," *N&Q*, os 202 / ns 4:7 (July 1957), 312-13.

97. MCDOWELL, FREDERICK P. W. (ed): *The Poet as Critic*. Evanston: Northwestern UP, 1967. xiii, 114 pp.
Murray Krieger: "*Ekphrasis* and the Still Movement of Poetry; or, *Laokoön* Revisited," 3-26; reprinted in Krieger: *The Play and Place of Criticism*. Baltimore: Johns Hopkins Press, 1967. xiv, 256 pp. (pp. 105-28). Notes on both Byzantium poems, passim.

98. MANDEL, SIEGFRIED: "The Nightingale in the Loom of Life," *Mosaic,* 9:3 (Spring 1976), 117-34.
Contains a note on the bird in the two Byzantium poems, a descendant of the "miraculous nightingale of myth and poetry."

99. MASSON, DAVID I.: "Word and Sound in Yeats' 'Byzantium,'" *ELH,* 20:2 (June 1953), 136-60.
See also Denis Davison, *Theoria,* 7 (1955), 111-14; correspondence by C. J. D. Harvey, 8 (1956), 66-67.

100. ———: "The 'Musical Form' of Yeats's 'Byzantium,'" *N&Q,* 198:9 (Sept 1953), 400-401.

101. ———: "Poetic Sound-Patterning Reconsidered," *Proceedings of the Leeds Philosophical and Literary Society,* 16:5 (May 1976), 61-124.
See pp. 112-15.

102. MATTHEWS, ROGER: "Byzantium: Approach or Arrival?" *Eigo Seinen,* 111:7 (July 1965), 440-42; :8 (Aug 1965), 514-17.
On both Byzantium poems.

103. MITCHELL, JOAN TOWEY: "'Byzantium': Vision as Drama," *CP,* 6:2 (Fall 1973), 66-71.

104. MIYAUCHI, HIROMU: "The Byzantium Poems: A Verbal Criticism," *SELit,* 53:English number (1977), 53-71.

105. NEVO, RUTH: "Again, Byzantium," *Lang&S,* 9:4 (Fall 1976), 247-59.
The poem is deliberately ambiguous and "enacts the creative process itself."

106. OLDFIELD, LAURIE: "Hades' Bobbin and the Mummy Cloth: Images of Poet and Language in Yeats's 'Byzantium,'" *YER,* 8:1&2 (1986), 72-75.

107. PALL, SANTOSH: "The Soul Must Dance: Yeats's 'Byzantium,'" *Temenos,* 2 (1982), 25-44.
Extract from a doctorate thesis, °"Yeats and the Sacred Dance" (U of Delhi); the author is herself a dancer of the Indian traditional dance.

108. PERLIS, ALAN D.: "Yeats' Byzantium and Stevens' Rome: A Comparison of Two Poems," *WSJour,* 2:1&2 (Spring 1978), 18-25.
This poem and "To an Old Philosopher in Rome."

109. PERLOFF, MARJORIE: "Symbolism / Anti-Symbolism," *Centrum,* 4:2 (Fall 1976), 69-103.
See pp. 72-73, 89.

110. ROPPEN, GEORG, and RICHARD SOMMER: *Strangers and Pilgrims: An Essay on the Metaphor of Journey.* Bergen: Norwegian Universities Press, 1964. 388 pp. (Norwegian Studies in English. 11.)
G. Roppen: "Yeats: To Byzantium," 337-52; an interpretation of both Byzantium poems.

111. SARANG, VILAS: "The Byzantium Poems: Yeats at the Limits of Symbolism," *CP,* 11:2 (Fall 1978), 49-54.
Discusses the symbols of the temporal and the timeless.

112. °SEN, S. C.: "'Byzantium,'" *BDE,* 1:3 (1960).

113. SENGELLI, NAZAN FERIDE: "Literary Continuity Traced through the Progression in the Use of Time in Wordsworth, Faulkner, Virginia Woolf, T. S. Eliot, and Yeats," °Ph.D. thesis, George Peabody College for Teachers, 1977. 156 pp. (*DAI,* 38:5 [Nov 1977], 2766A)
Discusses the Byzantium poems.

114. SRIVASTAVA, AVADESH K.: "Yeats's 'Byzantium,'" *OJES,* 15 (1979), 15-20.

115. WHITE, ALISON: "Yeats' 'Byzantium,' 20, and 'Sailing to Byzantium,' 30-32," *Expl,* 13:2 (Nov 1954), no. 8.
The bird symbolism.

116. YEATS, W. B.: *Byzantium.* Paintings by David Finn. Redding Ridge, Ct.: Black Swan Books, 1983. 96 pp.
Contains: "A Way of Experiencing Yeats's Byzantium," 6-11; the two Byzantium poems; 36 paintings which "represent a very intense effort . . . to work out a series of visual expressions of the profound and elusive ideas I became aware of through these poems"; and an afterword by John Walsh, pp. 92-93. See also G1571.

See also BA3, CA8, 12, 26, 27, 37, 56, 73, 91, 100, 103, 125, 126, 129, 167, CB68, 149a, 370, 464, 503, CC29, 31, 80, 99, 132, 178, 226, 291, CD224, 458, 861, 1019, 1224, 1253, DA11, 14, 22, 26, 30, 34, 35(II), 36, 49, DB8, 13, 28, 30, 53, 70, 119, 141, 183, 199, 203, 255, DC4, 8, 34, 53, 173, 186, 188, 267, 312, 327, 387, 390, DD308, 439, 494, 502, 503, 509, 512, 515, 536, 550, 561, 709, EC70, FC64, 137, FD19, FE55, 59, 80, G1571.

"The Cap and Bells"

117. BAILEY, JAMES: "Linguistic Givens and Their Metrical Realization in a Poem by Yeats," *Lang&S,* 8:1 (Winter 1975), 21-33.

118. COWART, DAVID: "Identity and Sexuality: Yeats's 'The Cap and Bells' and Its Contexts," *YER,* 6:1 (1979), 38-44.
The poem anticipates some of the ideas treated in *A Vision.*

119. LONDRAVILLE, RICHARD: "The Manuscript of 'The Queen and the Jester,'" *Ariel,* 3:3 (July 1972), 67-68 and plates I-IV.
An early version of the poem.

120. LOWDEN, SAMUEL MARION: *Understanding Great Poems.* Harrisburg: Handy Book Corporation, 1927. 340 pp.
"'The Cap and Bells' by William Butler Yeats," 217-28.

121. MILNE, FRED L.: "Yeats's 'The Cap and Bells': A Probable Indebtedness to Tennyson's 'Maud,'" *Ariel,* 3:3 (July 1972), 69-79.

122. NATTERSTAD, J. H.: "Yeats' 'The Cap and Bells,'" *Expl,* 25:9 (May 1967), no. 75.

See also CA12, 26, 126, CC260, DA30, DB90, DC270a, 342, DD770, HF4, 42.

"The Cat and the Moon"

123. BENSON, CARL: "Yeats's 'The Cat and the Moon,'" *MLN*, 68:4 (Apr 1953), 220-23.
A source in Madame Blavatsky.

124. SMITH, GROVER: "Yeats, Minnaloushe, and the Moon," *Western R*, 11:4 (Summer 1947), 241-44.
The relationship with *A Vision* and a source in Demetrius. See also Smith: "Yeats' 'The Cat and the Moon,'" *N&Q*, 195:2 (21 Jan 1950), 35, where the source is corrected to be Plutarch.

124a. VAX, LOUIS: *La poésie philosophique*. Paris: Presses universitaires françaises, 1985. 200 pp. (Littératures modernes. 38.)
Contains a note on this poem (pp. 79-82).

See also CD224, DB70, DC267, 275, DD606, EE46-51 and note.

"The Chambermaid's First (and Second) Song"

See DA45, 49, DB70.

"The Choice"

See DA34, 49, DB70.

"Chosen" (part 6 of "A Woman Young and Old")

See CA53a, 73, 129, DA44, DB23.

"The Circus Animals' Desertion"

125. LAIDLAW, J. C. (ed): *The Future of the Modern Humanities*. The papers delivered at the Jubilee Congress of the Modern Humanities Research Association. Cambridge: MHRA, 1969. ix, 137 pp. (Publications of the Modern Humanities Research Association. 1.)
Conor Cruise O'Brien: "Imagination and Politics," 73-85; draws a parallel between the "rag and bone shop" and the thought of Karl Marx, pp. 73-75.

126. SHAW, ROBERT B.: "Farewells to Poetry," *YR*, 70:2 (Jan 1981), 187-205.
Contains a note on this poem.

See also CA4, 12, 14, 53a, 91, 92, CC31, 99, CD886, DA1, 34, 35(II), 36, 49, 53, DB13, 28, 70, 104, DC44, 267, DD332, 337, 549, 657, FC64, HD164.

"The Cloak, the Boat, and the Shoes"

127. BLOCK, ED: "Lyric Voice and Reader Response: One View of the Transition to Modern Poetics," *TCL*, 24:2 (Summer 1978), 154-68.
Comments on this poem, "The Song of the Old Mother," and "The Fish."

"A Coat"

128. GLECKNER, ROBERT F.: "Blake and Yeats," *N&Q,* os 200 / ns 2:1 (Jan 1955), 38.
A Blake echo in the poem.

129. RADFORD, COLIN, and SALLY MINOGUE: *The Nature of Criticism.* Brighton: Harvester Press / Atlantic Highlands: Humanities Press, 1981. x, 180 pp.
See pp. 68-83.

See also CD592, 597, 601, DA49, DC270a, 307a, DD294.

"The Cold Heaven"

130. CECI, LOUIS G.: "Iconic Features in the Noun Phrases of Yeats's 'The Cold Heaven,'" *Lang&S,* 16:2 (Spring 1983), 138-50.

131. LUCY, SEÁN: "Metre and Movement in Anglo-Irish Verse," *IUR,* 8:2 (Autumn 1978), 151-77.
Contains a prosodic analysis of the poem.

See also CA12, 103, 123, CC1, 260, DA4, 49, DB233, DC109, 275, 295, DD384, FC49.

"The Collar-Bone of a Hare"

132. SAUL, GEORGE BRANDON: "Yeats's Hare," *TLS,* 11 Jan 1947, 23.
The date of this poem and of "Two Songs of a Fool." Correspondence by Marion Witt, 18 Oct 1947, 535.

133. WITT, MARION: "Yeats' 'The Collar-Bone of a Hare,'" *Expl,* 7:3 (Dec 1948), no. 21.

See also CA130, DC275.

"Colonel Martin"

See BF78.

"Colonus' Praise"

134. ARKINS, BRIAN: "Yeats's Version of Colonus' Praise," *Classical and Modern Literature,* 7:1 (Fall 1986), 39-42.
Yeats's poem radically alters the meaning of the original Sophoclean ode.

See also CA103, DA6, DD680.

"Come Gather round Me, Parnellites"

135. STERNFELD, FREDERICK W.: "Poetry and Music--Joyce's *Ulysses,*" *EIE,* 1956, 16-54.
Notes on the music of this poem and of "The Three Bushes," pp. 21-24, 28, 34.

"The Coming of Wisdom with Time"

136. BROWN, WENTWORTH K., and STERLING P. OLMSTEAD: *Language and Literature*. NY: Harcourt, Brace & World, 1962. ix, 371 pp.
Contains notes on this poem, pp. 63-64, and on "The Lamentation of the Old Pensioner," pp. 201-3.

See also DC270a.

"Conjunctions"

See DC267.

"Consolation"

See CA53a, DA44.

"Coole Park and Ballylee, 1931"

136a. BEDIENT, CALVIN: "Sensible Ecstasies," *Antaeus*, 59 (Autumn 1987), 185-99.

137. CARNE-ROSS, D. S.: "A Commentary on Yeats' 'Coole [Park] and Ballylee, 1931,'" *Nine*, 1:1 (Oct 1949), 21-24.
Comment by Ronald Bottrall, 2:1 (Jan 1950), 67.

138. CLUYSENAAR, ANNE: *Aspects of Literary Stylistics: A Discussion of Dominant Structures in Verse and Prose*. NY: St. Martin's Press, 1976. 160 pp.
The English edition was published as *Introduction to Literary Stylistics. . . .* London: Batsford, 1976. On this poem, pp. 82-84, 110; "The Song of Wandering Aengus," pp. 101-6.

139. PERLOFF, MARJORIE: "'*Another* Emblem There': Theme and Convention in Yeats's 'Coole Park and Ballylee, 1931,'" *JEGP*, 69:2 (Apr 1970), 223-40.

140. POLSKA AKADEMIA NAUK: INSTYTUT BADAŃ LITERACKICH: *Poetics. Poetyka. Poetika*. Warszawa: Państwowe wydawnictwo naukowe / 's Gravenhage: Mouton, 1961. xiii, 895 pp. (First International Conference of Work-in-Progress Devoted to Problems of Poetics, Warsaw, August 18-27, 1960.)
Donald Davie: "The Relation between Syntax and Music in Some Modern Poems in English," 203-14.

See also CA4, 12, 112, 118, 128, CC130, 141, CD1456, DA34, 35(II), 36, 49, DB13, 70, DC14, 406a, DD549, HA2, 3.

"Coole Park, 1929"

See CA4, 12, 112, 118, CC31, 130, CD1224, DA14, 26, 36, 44, 49, DB70, 178.

"A Cradle Song"

141. MCDOWELL, MARGARET B.: "Folk Lullabies: Songs of Anger, Love, and Fear," *Women's Studies,* 5:2 (1977), 205-18.

See also CD680.

"A Crazed Girl"

142. FREYER, GRATTAN: "W. B. Yeats," *TLS,* 20 Apr 1946, 187.
Misprints in this poem and in "Three Marching Songs."

See also CA150, DA49, DB203.

"The Crazed Moon"

143. HASSETT, JOSEPH M.: "'The Crazed Moon' and the Myth of Dionysus," *YeA,* 5 (1987), 232-37.
The myth in the Neoplatonic interpretation by Thomas Taylor.

See also CA128, CC31, CD224, DA49.

"Crazy Jane and Jack the Journeyman"

144. PERRINE, LAURENCE: "Yeats's 'Crazy Jane and Jack the Journeyman,'" *CEA,* 34:3 (Mar 1972), 22-23.

145. WALCUTT, CHARLES C.: "Yeats's 'Crazy Jane and Jack the Journeyman,'" *Expl,* 39:3 (Spring 1981), 40-41.

See also DA22, 35(II). N.B.: For this and other Crazy Jane poems see also index IE s.v. Crazy Jane.

"Crazy Jane and the Bishop"

146. HUTCHINGS, GEOFFREY: "Reading Poetry Aloud," *ESA,* 23:1 (1980), 31-39.
Includes notes on this poem and on "The Second Coming."

See also CA26, DA34.

"Crazy Jane Grown Old Looks at the Dancers"

147. LITTLE, MATTHEW: "'The Lion's Tooth' in Yeats's 'Crazy Jane Grown Old Looks at the Dancers,'" *YER,* 6:1 (1979), 51-53.
The reference is to the dandelion.

"Crazy Jane on God"

148. WRIGHT, GEORGE T.: "Yeats's Expressive Style," *YER,* 7:1&2 (June 1982), 109-16.

See also CA26.

"Crazy Jane on the Day of Judgment"

See DA6, DB160.

"Crazy Jane on the King"

149. FINNERAN, RICHARD J.: "The Composition and Final Text of W. B. Yeats's 'Crazy Jane on the King,'" *ICarbS*, 4:2 (Spring-Summer 1981), 67-74.
Reprints and discusses the various versions of the poem.

150. YEATS, W. B.: "Crazy Jane on the King," *Amherst Literary Magazine*, 10:2 (Summer 1964), 4-5.
With an introduction by Rolfe Humphries stating that he got the MS. of the poem in 1946. It was contained in the notebook of Oliver St. John Gogarty, who had set it down from memory. See also Archibald MacLeish: "Why Not?" ibid., 6-7.
This issue of the *Amherst Literary Magazine* "commemorates the fiftieth anniversary of William Butler Yeats' visit to Amherst College," but does not contain anything else on Yeats apart from the two items cited above. The visit took place in March 1914; see BF120.

"Crazy Jane on the Mountain"

See DD317.

"Crazy Jane Reproved"

151. THOMPSON, J. B.: "The Tables Turned: An Analysis of Yeats's 'Crazy Jane Reproved,'" *ESA*, 11:2 (Sept 1968), 173-83.

See also CA26, DA22, DB127.

"Crazy Jane Talks with the Bishop"

152. ATKINS, ANSELM: "The Vedantic Logic of Yeats' 'Crazy Jane,'" *Renascence*, 19:1 (Fall 1966), 37-40.
In this poem, Jane's paradox echoes the Vedantic "logic of mutual exclusion."

153. FINNEY, KATHE DAVIS: "Crazy Jane Talks with Jonathan Culler: Using Structuralism to Teach Lyric Poetry," *CEA*, 43:3 (Mar 1981), 29-36.
Mainly on this poem.

154. GALLAGHER, PHILIP: "Teaching and Publishing: The Yolk, the White, the One Shell," *MSE*, 9:2 (1983), 13-23.
On the "Johannine Christology" of the poem.

155. JOHNSON, W. R.: "Crazy Jane & Henry More," *Furioso*, 3:2 (Winter 1947), 50-53.
A PFLA article ("PVBLICATIONS-OF-THE-FVRIOSO-LANGVAGE-ASSOCIATION"), hence somewhat facetious.

156. KRELL, DAVID FARRELL: "Pitch: Genitality/Excrementality from

Hegel to Crazy Jane," *Boundary 2,* 12:2 (Winter 1984), 113-41.
The poem is taken as a peg to hang on "several complaints concerning Hegel's view of genitality/excrementality" and "a suspicion concerning the heavenly mansion of idealist philosophy as a whole."

157. LERNER, LAURENCE: *The Frontiers of Literature*. Oxford: Blackwell, 1988. ix, 291 pp.
See pp. 113-14 and 230-32 on this poem and on "Leda and the Swan." The latter is reprinted from Laurence Lerner (ed): *Reconstructing Literature*. Oxford: Blackwell, 1983. v, 218 pp. ("Titles and Timelessness," 179-204).

158. SUTTON, D. C.: "A Yeats Borrowing from Mangan," *N&Q,* os 219 / ns 21:10 (Oct 1974), 374.
A line from this poem is indebted to a poem by Mangan.

159. WATSON, THOMAS RAMEY: "Yeats's 'Crazy Jane Talks with the Bishop,'" *Expl,* 42:3 (Spring 1984), 35-36.
Crazy Jane defends sensuality by alluding to incarnational theology.

See also CA12, 26, CD601, DA12, 26, DB50, 75, 244, DD281.

Crossways

160. *On Poets & Poetry: Sixth Series. A Salzburg Miscellany: English and American Studies 1964-1984.* Salzburg: Institut für Anglistik und Amerikanistik, Universität Salzburg, 1984. 2 vols. (Salzburg Studies in English Literature: Poetic Drama & Poetic Theory. 27.)
Renate Thallinger: "William Butler Yeats[:] *Crossways* and *The Rose*,'" 1:188-227.

"Cuchulain Comforted"

161. BLACKFORD, RUSSELL: "Withheld Meaning in Yeats's 'Cuchulain Comforted,'" *AUMLA,* 57 (May 1982), 24-30.

162. BLOOM, HAROLD: *Figures of Capable Imagination*. NY: Seabury Press, 1976. xiii, 273 pp.
"Death and the Native Strain in American Poetry," 89-102; reprinted from *Social Research,* 39:3 (Autumn 1972), 449-62. Compares this poem with Stevens's "The Owl in the Sarcophagus."

See also CA10, 12, 53a, 90, 125, 129, CC29, 226, CD358, DA36, 38, 43, 49, DC265, 267, FE80.

"Cuchulain's Fight with the Sea"

163. OMIDSALAR, MAHMOUD: "W. B. Yeats' 'Cuchulainn's [sic] Fight with the Sea,'" *AI,* 42:3 (Autumn 1985), 315-34.
Notes the curious fact that in the revised version of the poem Cuchulain's son is also called Cuchulain, and develops this into a psychoanalytical interpretation of the oedipal motifs.

See also CA10, DA11.

"The Curse of Cromwell"

164. ALLEN, JAMES LOVIC: "House, Horse, and Hound: Emblems of Nobility in Yeats's 'The Curse of Cromwell,'" *YER,* 7:1&2 (June 1982), 69-77.

See also CA112, 118, 128, CC141, DB35, DC101a, FD46.

"The Dawn"

See DA30.

"A Dawn Song"

See DC270a.

"Death"

165. COOMBES, HENRY: *Literature and Criticism.* Baltimore: Penguin Books, 1966 [1953]. 160 pp.
See pp. 75-77.

166. MARKEN, RONALD: "Yeats's 'Death': A Reading," *IUR,* 10:2 (Autumn 1980), 244-50.

167. MÜLLER, WOLFGANG G.: *Das lyrische Ich: Erscheinungsformen gattungseigentümlicher Autor-Subjektivität in der englischen Lyrik.* Heidelberg: Winter, 1979. 246 pp. (Anglistische Forschungen. 142.)
"Yeats' 'Death' als Beispiel der Urteilslyrik," 225-27; the poem as an example of "poetry of statement."

See also DB70.

"The Dedication to a Book of Stories Selected from the Irish Novelists"

See CD680, DA30, 35(I).

"A Deep-Sworn Vow"

168. BROOKS, CLEANTH, and ROBERT PENN WARREN: *Understanding Poetry*. 3rd edition. NY: Holt, Rinehart & Winston, 1965 [1938], xxiv, 584 pp.
Comments on this poem, pp. 160-64; on "After Long Silence," 164-66 (see also DD12); on "Among School Children," 335-38; on "Two Songs from a Play," 403-9.
The 4th edition (1976) drops the interpretations of the last two poems. The other interpretations are somewhat shorter.

See also DA36, 38, DB23, DC337, HD54.

"The Delphic Oracle upon Plotinus"

169. BARNWELL, WILLIAM C.: "The Blandness of Yeats's Rhadaman-

thus," *ELN,* 14:3 (Mar 1977), 206-10.
The meaning of the word "bland" in the poem.

170. PEARCE, DONALD: "Yeats's 'The Delphic Oracle upon Plotinus,'" *N&Q,* os 199 / ns 1:4 (Apr 1954), 175-76.
A source in Porphyry. Note by Peter Ure, :8 (Aug 1954), 363.

See also CA26, 129.

"Demon and Beast"

See CA12, 124, 130, DA30, 36, DC275, DD316, 448.

"A Dialogue of Self and Soul"

171. CHUTO, JACQUES: "Yeats's 'A Dialogue of Self and Soul,'" *EI,* 3 (Nov 1974), 33-37. (In French)

172. FELDMAN, STEVE: "Four Short Prefaces to the 'Dialogue of Self and Soul' by W. B. Yeats," *Continental,* 4 (June 1949), 22-27.

173. FRIEDMAN, NORMAN: "Permanence and Change: What Happens in Yeats's 'Dialogue of Self and Soul'?" *YER,* 5:2 (1978), 21-30.

174. REVARD, STELLA: "Verlaine and Yeats's 'A Dialogue of Self and Soul,'" *PLL,* 7:3 (Summer 1971), 272-78.

175. SINGH, B. M.: "Look at the Sea," *RUSEng,* 10 (1977), 22-26.
Compares this poem with Frost's "Neither Out Far nor in Deep."

176. WITT, MARION: "Yeats' 'A Dialogue of Self and Soul,'" *Expl,* 5:7 (May 1957), no. 48.
Explains the Japanese background for the "emblems of the day."

See also BA3, CA4, 12, 53a, 63, 91, 92, 126, 166, CB403, CC130, 226, CD876, 1010, DA14, 22, 34, 36, 49, DB70, 156, 178, 203, DC102, 188, 295, 381, DD217, 371, 445, 569, FC64.

"The Dolls"

177. BALLIET, CONRAD A.: "'The Dolls' of Yeats and the Cradle of Christ," *RS,* 38:1 (Mar 1970), 54-57.
The poem describes the birth of Christ.

178. JOHNSON, RUSSELL I.: "The Vulgarity of His Death: Yeats and the Uncontrollable Mystery," *Spirit,* 38:1 (Spring 1971), 35-38.
Also on "The Magi."

179. PROFFITT, EDWARD: *Poetry: An Introduction & Anthology.* Boston: Houghton Mifflin, 1981. xv, 463 pp.
See pp. 74-75.

180. SCHOLES, ROBERT: *Elements of Poetry.* NY: Oxford UP, 1969. ix, 86 pp.
Note on the symbolism of the poem, pp. 43-45.

See also CA164, DA4, DB244.

"The Double Vision of Michael Robartes"

181. SHARMA, T. R. S.: "The Buddha as Symbol in W. B. Yeats: A Study of Two Poems," *LCrit,* 7:4 (Summer 1967), 32-41.
The other poem is "The Statues."

See also CA12, 26, 60, 100, 122, 126, 128, CC31, 99, CD224, DA22, 36, 49, DC186, 267.

"Down by the Salley Gardens"

182. DARLEY, ARTHUR, and P. J. MCCALL (eds): *Feis Ceoil Collection of Irish Airs Hitherto Unpublished. Volume 1.* Dublin: Feis Ceoil Association, 1914.
No. 33 is this poem (p. 14). The source note on p. 43 reads: "From MS. of Mr. James Cogley, Duffrey Hill, Enniscorthy. The song is well known in South Leinster. Mr. W. B. Yeats has re-written it. The old song began:--
Down by the sally gardens my own true love and I did meet,
She passed the sally gardens a-tripping with her snow-white feet,
She bid me take life easy, just as the leaves fall from each tree,
But I being young and foolish with my true love would not agree."

183. HENDERSON, WILLIAM (ed): *Victorian Street Ballads: A Selection of Popular Ballads Sold in the Street in the Nineteenth Century.* London: Country Life, 1937. 160 pp.
Yeats's source was "The Rambling Boys of Pleasure," pp. 16-17.

184. JANOUŠEK, MIROSLAV: "Na okraj literárních jubileí 1985. (Anglická e americká literatura)," *Cizí jazyky ve škole,* 28:5 (1984/85), 168-78.
Contains a phonological analysis of the poem.

185. MOONEY, CANICE: "Yeats and 'The Salley Gardens,'" *Irish Book Lover,* 31:4 (Apr 1950), 86-87.
The source of the poem is an 18th-century Irish MS. (Franciscan Library, Killiney, MS. A22). See notes by P. S. O'H[egarty], :5 (Feb 1951), 105; A[ustin] C[larke], :6 (Nov 1951), 133-34.

186. SHIELDS, H. E.: "Yeats and the 'Salley Gardens,'" *Hermathena,* 101 (Autumn 1965), 22-26.
The source of the poem and the music written for it.

187. TOPOROV, VLADIMIR N.: "William Butler Yeats: 'Down by the Salley Gardens.' An Analysis of the Structure of Repetition," *PTL,* 3:1 (Jan 1978), 95-115.
A linguistic analysis.

188. WALL, RICHARD: "Yeats and the Folk Tradition," *CJIS,* 11:2 (Dec 1985), 47-48.
The poem has moved "from the literary to the folk domain."

189. WILGUS, D. K.: "'Rose Connely': An Irish Ballad," *JAF,* 92:364 (Apr-June 1979), 172-95.

See also DC70a, 287, HF55, 67.

"A Dream of Death"

See DA36, 38.

"Easter 1916"

190. ALTHAMMER, CHARLOTTE, and ROLF BREUER (eds): *Anglo-Irish Literature: A Reader*. Frankfurt/Main: Hirschgraben, 1981. 2 vols.
An anthology designed for use in German high schools, contains *Cathleen ni Houlihan* and "Easter 1916" (vol. 1) as well as notes on how to prepare these texts for class (2:18-31, 39-41).

191. ATTRIDGE, DEREK: *The Rhythms of English Poetry*. London: Longman, 1982. xiv, 395 pp. (English Language Series. 14.)
See pp. 326-29.

192. BAXANDALL, LEE (ed): *Radical Perspectives in the Arts*. Harmondsworth: Penguin, 1972. 388 pp.
Meredith Tax: "Introductory: Culture Is Not Neutral, Whom Does It Serve?" 15-29, contains a note on revolutionary politics in this poem and Brecht's "An die Nachgeborenen," pp. 18-22.

193. BRASCH, CHARLES: *The Universal Dance: A Selection from the Critical Prose Writings of Charles Brasch*. Edited by J. L. Watson. Dunedin: U of Otago Press, 1981. 232 pp.
Several references to Yeats, especially in the chapters "Writer and Reader" (pp. 126-29: a comparison with Eliot) and "Poetry and Politics" (pp. 186-200: comments on "Easter 1916").

194. BRYSON, LYMAN, and others (eds): *Symbols and Values: An Initial Study*. NY: Cooper Square, 1964 [1954]. xviii, 827 pp. (Symposium of the Conference on Science, Philosophy, and Religion. 13.)
M. L. Rosenthal: "Cultural and Rhetorical Symbols in Contemporary American Poetry," 315-39; contains a note on this poem, pp. 315-18.

195. COLLINS, BEN L.: "A Note on the Historicity of Yeats's Stanzaic Pattern in 'Easter 1916,'" *Eire*, 3:1 (Spring 1968), 129.
Easter Monday, 24 Apr [19]16, reappears in the poem in two 24-line stanzas, 4 stanzas in all, and two 16-line stanzas.

196. COX, CHARLES BRIAN, and ANTHONY EDWARD DYSON: *Modern Poetry: Studies in Practical Criticism*. London: Arnold, 1963. 168 pp.
"'Easter 1916' by W. B. Yeats," 57-65; reprinted from *Critical Survey*, 1:1 (Autumn 1962), 28-32.

197. EAGLETON, TERRY: "History and Myth in Yeats's 'Easter 1916,'" *EIC*, 21:3 (July 1971), 248-60.

198. ———: *Against the Grain: Essays 1975-1985*. London: Verso, 1986. ix, 199 pp.
"Poetry, Pleasure and Politics," 173-80; reprinted from *Formations of Pleasure*. London: Routledge & Kegan Paul, 1983. vii, 172 pp. (pp. 58-65). Discusses the reasons for liking or not liking the line "A terrible beauty is born."

199. EDWARDS, THOMAS R.: *Imagination and Power: A Study of Poetry on Public Themes*. London: Chatto & Windus, 1971. ix, 232 pp.
Interpretation of the poem against a background of Yeats's po-

litical and aesthetic convictions, pp. 185-97, 200-12.

200. FOLEY, T. P.: "A Source for Yeats's 'Terrible Beauty,'" *N&Q,* os 229 / ns 31:4 (Dec 1984), 509.
A deleted variant in Coleridge's "The British Stripling's War-Song."

201. FRASER, G. S.: "A Yeats Borrowing," *TLS,* 25 Feb 1965, 156.
"All changed, changed utterly" may have come from a similar phrase in M. I. Ebbutt's *Hero-Myths* (EE107).

202. FUJIMOTO, REIJI: [In Japanese] "Easter Rising and Yeats's 'Easter 1916,'" *Studies in Language and Culture,* 4 (1978), 1-22.
English summary, pp. 23-24. Continued as "A Mythopoeic Process in Yeats's Poetry: Immortalization of the Easter Heroes," 5 (1979), 39-54; English summary, 55-56.

203. JACKAMAN, ROB: "Black and White: The Balanced View in Yeats's Poetry," *Ariel,* 9:4 (Oct 1978), 79-91.
Balanced opposites in this poem and in "Nineteen Hundred and Nineteen."

204. JONES, R. T.: *Studying Poetry: An Introduction.* London: Arnold, 1986. vi, 74 pp.
See pp. 16-21.

205. JORDAN, CARMEL: "The Stone Symbol in 'Easter 1916' and the Cuchulain Plays," *CollL,* 13:1 (Winter 1986), 36-43.

206. LE PAN, DOUGLAS: "Some Observations on Myth and Legend--Irish and Canadian," *Transactions of the Royal Society of Canada,* series 4 / 17 (1979), 85-97.
Includes a discussion of this poem.

207. MCMULLAN, D. H.: "Yeats and O. Henry," *TLS,* 28 Nov 1968, 1339.
Yeats may have taken the phrase "A terrible beauty is born" from a short story by O. Henry. See Austin Clarke: "Yeats and Le Fanu," 12 Dec 1968, 1409, where the line is traced to a poem by Le Fanu.

208. MALONEY, STEPHEN: "Yeats's Meaningful Words: The Role of 'Easter 1916' in His Poetic Development," *EngR,* 22:2 (Winter 1971), 11-18.

209. MAYHEW, GEORGE: "A Corrected Typescript of Yeats's 'Easter 1916,'" *HLQ,* 27:1 (Nov 1963), 53-71.

210. OLOFSSON, TOMMY: "Om W. B. Yeats' 'Easter 1916,'" *Studiekamraten,* 57:4/5 (1975), 75-77.
Mainly on the historical background.

210a. ———: "En fruktansvärd skönhet: Om Yeats och den irländska befrielsekampen," *Lyrikvannen,* 34:2-3 (1987), 108-20.
"A terrible beauty: On Yeats and the Irish struggle for freedom," an analysis of the poem and its political background. See corrections by Birgit Bramsbäck, 34:4 (1987), 229-30.

211. PATE, WILLARD (ed): "Interview with Richard Wilbur," *SCR,* 3:1 (Nov 1970), 5-23.
See pp. 8-9.

212. PERLOFF, MARJORIE: "Yeats and the Occasional Poem: 'Easter 1916,'" *PLL*, 4:3 (Summer 1968), 308-28.
Includes a comparison with Arnold's "Haworth Churchyard."

213. ROLLINS, RONALD G.: "O'Casey, Yeats and Behan: A Prismatic View of the 1916 Easter Week Rising," *SOCR*, 2:2 (Spring 1976), 196-207.

214. VENDLER, HELEN: "Four Elegies," in Jeffares: *Yeats, Sligo and Ireland* (1980, CA51), 216-31.
This poem, "In Memory of Eva Gore-Booth and Con Markiewicz," "Beautiful Lofty Things," and "The Municipal Gallery Revisited."

215. WATANABE, HISAYOSHI: [In Japanese] "An Inquiry into Yeats's 'Terrible Beauty,'" *SELit*, 58:2 (Dec 1981), 143-53.
English synopsis in English Number, 1982, pp. 150-151.

216. YOSHINO, MASAAKI: [In Japanese] "'Easter 1916': A Poet's Witness," *Studies in English Language and Literature*, 32 (Jan 1982), 13-26. (English summary, p. 98)

See also BA20, CA4, 91, 112, 122, CB194, 371, 439, 463, CC35, 155a, 160a, 312, 322, 341, CD21, 382, 721, 823, 866, CE125, DA26, 34, 49, 53, DB35, 70, 90, 219, DC115, 170, 359, DD427, 518, 549, EE12, FC64, FD19, 46, HD42.

"Ego Dominus Tuus"

217. CRONIN, ANTHONY: *A Question of Modernity*. London: Secker & Warburg, 1966. 130 pp.
Note on the relationship between Yeats's mystical thought, this poem, and "A Dialogue of Self and Soul," pp. 43-44, 47-48.

218. HAYWOOD, ERIC (ed): *Dante Readings*. Dublin: Irish Academic Press, 1987. 150 pp.
Seamus Heaney: "Envies and Identifications: Dante and the Modern Poet," 29-46; reprinted from *IUR*, 15:1 (Spring 1985), 5-19.

219. RAJAN, TILOTTAMA: "The Romantic Backgrounds of Yeats's Use of Dante in 'Ego Dominus Tuus,'" *YER*, 7:1&2 (June 1982), 120-22.
Carlyle as a link between Yeats and Dante.

220. SPIVAK, GAYATRI CHAKRAVORTY: *In Other Worlds: Essays in Cultural Politics*. NY: Methuen, 1987. xxi, 309 pp.
"Finding Feminist Readings: Dante--Yeats," 15-29, 270-74; reprinted from *Social Text*, 3 (Fall 1980), 73-87; also in Ira Konigsberg (ed): *American Criticism in the Poststructuralist Age*. Ann Arbor: U of Michigan, 1981. xxvii, 186 pp. (pp. 42-65). On this poem and *Per Amica Silentia Lunae* as "versions of the inbuilt exploitation of the figure of the woman in two autobiographical and self-deconstructive texts."

See also BA3, CA12, 60, 92, 126, CB70, 403, CC104, 130, 178, 182, CD318, 353, 358, DA22, 49, DB70, 203, DC189, 275, 312, 413, FC96.

"The Empty Cup" (part 5 of "A Man Young and Old")

See DD409.

"Ephemera"

See DA49, DC275, 295.

"The Everlasting Voices"

See CC260, DC62, DD770.

"A Faery Song"

See HA2.

"The Fairy Pedant"

See DC62.

"Fallen Majesty"

See DB233.

"The Fascination of What's Difficult"

See CA66, CD705, DA34, 46, 49.

"Father and Child" (part 1 of "A Woman Young and Old")

See CA53a, DD782.

"Fergus and the Druid"

See DA26, 34, 35(I), DC62, 275.

"The Fiddler of Dooney"

221. COMBECHER, HANS: *Deutung englischer Gedichte: Interpretationen zur Sammlung "The Word Sublime."* Frankfurt/Main: Diesterweg, 1965. 2 vols.

Notes on this poem and "The Lake Isle of Innisfree," 1:5-8.

See also CC260, DB219, HF11.

"The Fish"

222. MCFARLAND, RONALD E.: "'The Finny Prey': Some Observations on Fish in Poetry," *CentR,* 31:2 (Spring 1987), 167-82.

See pp. 173-75.

See also CC260, DA38, DD127, 770.

"The Fisherman"

223. BAGCHEE, SHYAMAL: "Anxiety of Influence: 'Resolution and Independence' and Yeats's 'The Fisherman,'" *YER*, 5:1 (1978), 51-57.
Yeats's reworking of Wordsworth's poem.

224. EDWARDS, OLIVER: "Yeats's 'The Fisherman,'" *Wales*, 7:25 (Spring 1947), 222-23.
On the misleading punctuation of the poem and how it affects its meaning.

225. LUCE, ARTHUR ASTON: *Fishing and Thinking*. London: Hodder & Stoughton, 1959. 191 pp.
See pp. 79-84.

226. MERCIER, VIVIAN: "Yeats and 'The Fisherman,'" *TLS*, 6 June 1958, 313.
On the punctuation of the poem.

See also CA63, 91, 92, 112, 118, CB441, 463, CC53, CD442, 886, DB104, DC359, DD294.

"The Folly of Being Comforted"

227. DREW, ELIZABETH: *Discovering Poetry*. NY: Norton, 1933. 224 pp.
See pp. 108-11.

228. MAIN, CHARLES FREDERICK, and PETER J. SENG (eds): *Poems: Wadsworth Handbook and Anthology*. San Francisco: Wadsworth, 1961. xxvii, 372 pp.
See pp. 264-66.

229. MAIXNER, PAUL R.: "Yeats' 'The Folly of Being Comforted,'" *Expl*, 13:1 (Oct 1954), no. 1.

230. PENDLETON, THOMAS A.: "'The Folly of Being Comforted': Three Versions and Three Voices," *Wascana R*, 15:1 (Spring 1980), 87-95.
The revisions result in a "basic incoherence."

231. SENG, PETER J.: "Yeats' 'The Folly of Being Comforted,'" *Expl*, 17:7 (Apr 1959), no. 48.

See also DA35(I), DC189, 295.

"For Anne Gregory"

232. ZLOGAR, RICHARD: "Yeats's 'For Anne Gregory,'" *Expl*, 35:2 (Winter 1976), 17.
The indebtedness to Castiglione's *The Courtier*.

See also CA103, DB70.

"The Four Ages of Man" (part 9 of "Supernatural Songs")

233. SARANG, VILAS: "W. B. Yeats: 'The Four Ages of Man,'" *N&Q*, os 223 / ns 25:4 (Aug 1978), 327.

A correspondence with traditional Hindu beliefs.

See also DA26, 49.

"Fragments"

234. BLY, ROBERT (ed): *News of the Universe: Poems of Twofold Consciousness*. Chosen and introduced by Robert Bly. San Francisco: Sierra Club Books, 1980. xiv, 305 pp.
"A Meditation on a Yeats Poem," 286-93.

235. JEFFARES, A. NORMAN: "Notes on Yeats's 'Fragments,'" *N&Q*, 194:13 (25 June 1949), 279-80.
Sources in John Locke and Arthur O'Shaughnessy.

See also CA26, 53a, 128, CD224, DC267, DD680.

"Friends"

See DA35(I), DB233.

"A Friend's Illness"

236. LEACH, ELSIE: "Yeats's 'A Friend's Illness' and Herbert's 'Vertue,'" *N&Q*, os 207 / ns 9:6 (June 1962), 215.

"From *Oedipus at Colonus*" (part 11 of "A Man Young and Old")

See DA6, 26.

"From the *Antigone*" (part 11 of "A Woman Young and Old")

See CA53a, DA6, DD781.

"The Gift of Harun Al-Rashid"

237. HARRIS, DANIEL A.: "'The Figured Page': Dramatic Epistle in Browning and Yeats," *YeA*, 1 (1982), 133-94.
Compares the poem with its source, Browning's "An Epistle Containing the Strange Medical Experience of Karshish, the Arab Physician."

See also CB528, CD22, 23, DA30, 44, DD680, FC64.

"The Glove and the Cloak"

238. WITT, MARION: "An Unknown Yeats Poem," *MLN*, 70:1 (Jan 1955), 26.
Bibliographical note.

"Gratitude to the Unknown Instructors"

See DC270a.

The Green Helmet and Other Poems

239. BOGEN, DONALD HOWARD: "Composition and the Self in Three Modern Poets: W. B. Yeats, T. S. Eliot, and Theodore Roethke," Ph.D. thesis, U of California, Berkeley, 1976. iii, 294 pp. (*DAI*, 37:9 [Mar 1977], 5813A-14A)
See "'Je me trouve': The Composition of *The Green Helmet and Other Poems*," 58-107.

240. CARPENTER, WILLIAM M.: "The *Green Helmet* Poems and Yeats's Myth of the Renaissance," *MP*, 67:1 (Aug 1969), 50-59.
Traces the ideological and stylistic influences of what Yeats considered to be the main characteristic traits of the Renaissance: unity of intellect and emotion. Discusses the allusions to Ronsard and Shakespeare in "At the Abbey Theatre" and "These Are the Clouds."

See also CA22, CD618, DC335, G292-97.

"The Grey Rock"

241. ALSPACH, RUSSELL K. "Yeats's 'The Grey Rock,'" *JAF*, 63:247 (Jan-Mar 1950), 57-71.
The bibliography and sources of the poem.

See also CA122, CC183, 212, DA49, 53, DC267, 275.

"The Gyres"

242. BALLIET, CONRAD A.: "Old Rocky Face in 'The Gyres' of W. B. Yeats," *N&Q*, os 215 / ns 17:12 (Dec 1970), 455-56.
The rocky face is Ben Bulben's.

243. BIERMAN, ROBERT: "Yeats' 'The Gyres,'" *Expl*, 19:7 (Apr 1961), no. 44.

244. JEFFARES, A. NORMAN: "Yeats's 'The Gyres': Sources and Symbolism," *HLQ*, 15:1 (Nov 1951), 87-97.
The sources can be found in Yeats's own writings and in Shelley's *Hellas*.

245. SICKELS, ELEANOR M.: "Yeats' 'The Gyres,' 6," *Expl*, 15:9 (June 1957), no. 60.
The function of Empedocles.

See also CA12, 14, 26, 92, CC99, 132, 229, CD224, DA22, 18, 28, 30, 35(II), 49, DB203, DC34, DD332, 337.

"The Happy Townland"

See CD92, DC275.

"The Hawk"

See DC267.

"He and She" (part 6 of "Supernatural Songs")

246. RUBENSTEIN, JEROME S.: "Three Misprints in Yeats's Collected Poems," *MLN,* 70:3 (Mar 1955), 184-87.

In this poem, "The Host of the Air," and "Whence Had They Come?"

See also DC267.

"He Bids His Beloved Be at Peace"

See BA3, DA30, CC1, 260, DC71, 167, 295.

"He Gives His Beloved Certain Rhymes"

See DC167.

"He Hears the Cry of the Sedge"

247. DOYLE, ESTHER M., and VIRGINIA HASTINGS FLOYD (eds): *Studies in Interpretation.* Amsterdam: Rodopi, 1972. x, 362 pp.

Chester C. Long: "The Poem's Text as a Technique of Performance in Public Group Readings of Poetry," 325-39.

See also CC1, CD1214, DA30.

"He Mourns for the Change That Has Come upon Him. . . ."

See CC1, 260, DD770.

"He Remembers Forgotten Beauty"

248. BRADY, FRANK, JOHN PALMER, and MARTIN PRICE (eds): *Literary Theory and Structure: Essays in Honor of William K. Wimsatt.* New Haven: Yale UP, 1973. viii, 429 pp.

Hugh Kenner: "Some Post-Symbolist Structures," 379-93.

See also CC1, 260, CD642, 647, DA30, DD770.

"He Reproves the Curlew"

See CC1, DD770.

"He Tells of the Perfect Beauty"

See DD498, 771.

"He Thinks of His Past Greatness. . . ."

See CA130, CC1, 260, DD770.

"He Wishes for the Cloths of Heaven"

249. RICKERT, EDITH: *New Methods for the Study of Literature*. Chicago: U of Chicago Press, 1927. xiii, 275 pp.
Establishes a tone pattern of the poem, pp. 226-27.

See also CC260, DA26, 34, DC190, 295.

"He Wishes His Beloved Were Dead"

See CC1, 260.

"The Heart of the Woman"

See CC260, DA30, 36, 38, DC275.

"Her Anxiety"

See DB9.

"Her Courtesy"
(part 1 of "Upon a Dying Lady")

250. PIWINSKI, DAVID J.: "Yeats's 'Her Courtesy,'" *Expl*, 42:1 (Fall 1983), 32-33.
Allusions to Aubrey Beardsley.

"Her Triumph" (part 4 of "A Woman Young and Old")

See DA6.

"Her Vision in the Wood"
(part 8 of "A Woman Young and Old")

See CA103, CC99, CD458, DA35(II), DB196, DC229, DD556, 778.

"The Hero, the Girl and the Fool"

251. SAHA, P. K.: "A Linguistic Approach to Style," *Style*, 2:1 (Winter 1968), 7-31.
See pp. 17-27.

See also DD680.

"High Talk"

252. DAVIE, DONALD: "Poets on Stilts: Yeats and Some Contemporaries," *PNR,* 30 (9:4) (1982), 14-17.
A discussion of this poem, leading to statements about Yeats's insecure place among the best poets of the century.

253. JOHN, BRIAN: "Yeats' 'High Talk,'" *Expl,* 29:3 (Nov 1970), no. 22.
A source in Thomas Moore.

254. REED, VICTOR: "Yeats' 'High Talk,' 9-11," *Expl,* 26:6 (Feb 1968), no. 52.

See also CA92, DA30, 49, 53.

"The Hills of Mourne"

See AE110.

"His Confidence"

255. BADER, ARNO LEHMAN (ed): *To the Young Writer.* Ann Arbor: U of Michigan Press, 1965. vii, 196 pp. (Hopwood Lectures. 2.)
Archibald MacLeish: "Why Can't They Say What They Mean?" 33-51; contains a note on the obscurity of this poem, pp. 35-38.

"His Dream"

See AE98, DB90.

"His Phoenix"

256. CHESTERTON, GILBERT KEITH: *Christendom in Dublin.* London: Sheed & Ward, 1932. 72 pp.
Note on the phoenix symbol, pp. 51-52.

See also CA73, DA49.

"The Host of the Air"

See CA14, CC141, 260, DD246.

"The Hosting of the Sidhe"

See CA14, CC164, 260, CD92, DA38, DC275, DD770.

"Hound Voice"

257. MARTIN, AUGUSTINE: "Hound Voices Were They All: An Experiment in Yeats Criticism," in Jeffares: *Yeats, Sligo and Ireland* (1980, CA51), 139-52.
The best commentary is found in Yeats's other poems.

See also DA49, DC267, FD73.

"The Hour before Dawn"

See CA130, CC1, 183, CD888, DA49, DC267.

"How Ferencz Renyi Kept Silent"

258. GÁL, ISTVÁN: "Yeats magyar balladája," *Nagyvilág,* 16:11 (Nov 1971), 1729-30.

259. GOULD, WARWICK: "How Ferencz Renyi Spoke Up, Part Two," *YeA,* 3 (1985), 199-205.
Variants in the later reprintings of the poem.

260. MOLNÁR, FERENC A.: "Egy magyar szabadsághős, Rényi Ferencz legendája az angol, finn, ír és a lengyel irodalomban," *FK,* 21:2 (Apr-June 1975), 198-214.
"The legend of a Hungarian hero of liberty, Ferencz Rényi, in English, Finnish, Irish, and Polish literature."

261. SZERB, ANTAL: "Yeats magyar tárgyú költeménye" [A Yeats poem on a Hungarian subject], *Debreceni szemle,* 4:5 (May 1930), 255-56.

See also DA11.

"I Am of Ireland"

262. GROSS, MARTHA: "Yeats' 'I Am of Ireland,'" *Expl,* 17:2 (Nov 1958), no. 15.

263. SICKELS, ELEANOR M.: "Yeats' 'I Am of Ireland,'" *Expl,* 15:2 (Nov 1956), no. 10.

See also CA26, 112, CB167, DC153.

"I Saw a Shepherd Youth. . . ."

See AA6.

"I Walked among the Seven Woods of Coole"

See CC130.

"An Image from a Past Life"

See CA26, 126, DA36, DC267, FC49.

"In Church"

264. DISHER, M. WILLSON: "A Yeats Poem?" *TLS,* 27 June 1942, 322.
Correspondence by Seumas O'Sullivan, 25 July 1942, 367.

"In Memory of Alfred Pollexfen"

265. MURPHY, WILLIAM M.: "'In Memory of Alfred Pollexfen': W. B. Yeats and the Theme of Family," *IUR*, 1:1 (Autumn 1970), 31-47.

"In Memory of Eva Gore-Booth and Con Markiewicz"

265a. BAYLEY, JOHN: *The Short Story: Henry James to Elizabeth Bowen*. Brighton: Harvester Press, 1988. viii, 197 pp.
Analyzes this poem because it tells us "a lot about the internal workings of the short story form" (pp. 23-26).

266. PERLOFF, MARJORIE: "Spatial Form in the Poetry of Yeats: The Two Lissadell Poems," *PMLA*, 82:5 (Oct 1967), 444-54.
The other poem is "On a Political Prisoner."

See also CA53a, 118, CB160, DA26, 35(II), 36, 44, 49, DB70, DD214.

"In Memory of Major Robert Gregory"

267. BAGG, ROBERT: "The Electromagnet and the Shred of Platinum," *Arion*, 8:3 (Autumn 1969), 407-29.
Comments on Yeats's use of "John Synge," pp. 412-14.

268. PERLOFF, MARJORIE: "The Consolation Theme in Yeats's 'In Memory of Major Robert Gregory,'" *MLQ*, 27:3 (Sept 1966), 306-22.

269. SACKS, PETER M.: *The English Elegy: Studies in the Genre from Spenser to Yeats*. Baltimore: Johns Hopkins UP, 1985. xv, 376 pp.
"Yeats: 'In Memory of Major Robert Gregory,'" 260-98; "Epilogue: The English Elegy after Yeats; a Note on the American Elegy," 299-328.

270. WITT, MARION: "The Making of an Elegy: Yeats's 'In Memory of Major Robert Gregory,'" *MP*, 48:2 (Nov 1950), 112-21.

See also CA4, 12, 53a, 60, 91, 92, 103, 112, 122, 169, CC31, 130, 168, CD1214, 1239, DA36, 38, 49, 53, DB70, 90, 233, DC261, 270a, 295, 386, DD613, FC49, FD19.

"In Tara's Halls"

See DC267.

"In the Seven Woods"

271. HOWARTH, HERBERT: "Yeats' 'In the Seven Woods,' 6," *Expl*, 17:2 (Nov 1958), no. 14.

See also CC130, DA35(I), DC275.

In the Seven Woods

271a. ADAMS, HAZARD: "The Early Poems of *In the Seven Woods*," *ADE Bulletin*, 87 (Fall 1987), 8-11.

The poems in this volume are related to each other in the sense that they form a *book* of poems.

272. LUCY, SEAN: "Vers la maturité," in Genet: *William Butler Yeats* (1981, CA32), 146-58.
Discusses the poems in this collection.

273. SCHLEIFER, RONALD: "Narrative in Yeats's *In the Seven Woods*," *JNT*, 6:3 (Fall 1976), 155-74.
Presumably an extract from DC335.

274. SIDNELL, MICHAEL J. "'Tara Uprooted': Yeats's *In the Seven Woods* in Relation to Modernism," *Yeats*, 3 (1985), 107-20.

See also CC33, DC335, G222-223.

"The Indian to His Love"

275. KUEHN, NANDINI PILLAI: "Yeats' 'The Indian to His Love,'" *Expl*, 33:3 (Nov 1974), no. 23.
On the "operation of Indian mythology in the poem."

See also CB233, CD1214, DA11, 35(I), 49, DC62, 275.

"Into the Twilight"

See CC1, 260, DA34, HF47.

"An Irish Airman Foresees His Death"

276. BEACHAM, WALTON: *The Meaning of Poetry: A Guide to Explication*. Boston: Allyn & Bacon, 1974. xii, 308 pp.
See pp. 248-53 for an interpretation by Beacham and George Newtown.

277. BRAMANN, JORN K.: *Wittgenstein's Tractatus and the Modern Arts*. Rochester, N.Y.: Adler, 1985. xv, 204 pp.
"Yeats: 'An Irish Airman Foresees His Death,'" 127-29. The connection between this poem and Wittgenstein's *Tractatus* is not explained.

278. DRAPER, R. P.: "Style and Matter," *RLV*, 27:1 (1961), 15-23.
Contains a rhetorical and stylistical analysis of the poem.

279. FOWLER, ROGER: *Linguistic Criticism*. Oxford: Oxford UP, 1986. vii, 190 pp.
Note on this poem and "Among School Children," pp. 90-93.

280. RODWAY, ALLAN: *The Craft of Criticism*. Cambridge: Cambridge UP, 1982. x, 192 pp.
"W. B. Yeats: 'An Irish Airman Foresees His Death,'" 134-37.

281. ROGERS, WILLIAM ELFORD: *The Three Genres and the Interpretation of Lyric*. Princeton: Princeton UP, 1983. ix, 278 pp.
On this poem and "Crazy Jane Talks with the Bishop," pp. 86-94; on "Leda and the Swan," pp. 107-9.

282. STOVEL, NORA FOSTER: "The Aerial View of Modern Britain: The Airplane as a Vehicle for Idealism and Satire," *Ariel,* 15:3 (July 1984), 17-32.
Contains a note on this poem.

283. VOGT, FRIEDRICH E.: "Übertragung eines fremdsprachigen Gedichts," *Deutschunterricht,* 2:3 (1950), 101-8.
How to translate the poem into German. The resulting "model version" is, to my mind, unsuccessful.

See also CA53a, 66, 118, CC130, CD109, 886, DA38, DB70, DC307a, 386, DD381, 708.

"John Kinsella's Lament for Mrs. Mary Moore"

See DA34, DB178.

"Kanva on Himself"

See DA35(I&II), DD429.

"King and No King"

See CA26, DB6.

"The Lady's First (Second and Third) Song"

See DA28, 45.

"The Lake Isle of Innisfree"

284. AHRENS, RÜDIGER: "Antithetische Literaturbetrachtung im Englischunterricht: Das Gedicht und seine Parodie, dargestellt an W. B. Yeats' 'The Lake Isle of Innisfree,'" *Neusprachliche Mitteilungen,* 27:1 (Feb 1974), 42-48.
Yeats's poem and the parody by G. F. Bradby (HF5).

285. ALSPACH, RUSSELL K.: *Yeats and Innisfree.* No. 3 of *DPYCP* (1965, CA20), 69-83.
On the genesis of the poem and the reverberations of its imagery and symbolism in the later work.

286. CLEYMAET, R.: "Yeats's 'Lake Isle of Innisfree,'" *RLV,* 9:5-6 (1943), 218-23.

287. COOPER, CHARLES WILLIAM, and JOHN HOLMES: *Preface to Poetry.* NY: Harcourt, Brace, 1946. xxiii, 737 pp.
On the rhythm and sound pattern of the poem, pp. 122-26.

288. D'AVANZO, MARIO L.: "Yeats' 'The Lake Isle of Innisfree' and the Song of Solomon," *McNR,* 20 (1971-72), 15-18.
The poem is indebted to the "Song of Solomon."

289. DEIGHTON, E. LONSDALE (comp): *The British Legion Album in Aid of Field-Marshall Earl Haig's Appeal for Ex-Service Men of All Ranks.*

London: Cassell, [1924]. Unpaged.
Contains the poem in Yeats's handwriting, dated 30 Nov 1922.

290. FRANCIS, ROBERT: "Of Walden and Innisfree," *CSM*, 6 Nov 1952, 12.
Why Thoreau left Walden and Yeats did not plant the nine bean rows.

291. GOULD, WARWICK: "Yeats as Aborigine," *Four Decades*, 2:2 (July 1978), 65-76, 126.
On the literary context of the poem.

292. GRAVES, ROBERT: *The Common Asphodel: Collected Essays on Poetry 1922-1949*. London: Hamilton, 1949. xi, 335 pp.
Contains a savage attack on the poem, pp. 186-88; revised from Laura Riding and Robert Graves: *A Pamphlet against Anthologies*. London: Cape, 1928. 192 pp. (pp. 95-102).

293. "GULLIVER": "The Open Window," *Bell*, 5:4 (Jan 1943), 324-25.
The influence of Sir Samuel Ferguson.

294. HEDBERG, JOHANNES (ed): *Poets of Our Time--English Poetry from Yeats to Sylvia Plath*. Stockholm: Almqvist & Wiksell, 1970. 179 pp.
"Yeats," 70-92, contains explanatory notes to this poem, "The Song of Wandering Aengus," "A Coat," "The Fisherman," "Sailing to Byzantium," and "An Acre of Grass."

295. HOWARTH, R. G.: "Yeats's 'My Own Music,'" *N&Q*, 189:8 (20 Oct 1945), 167-68.
The rhythm of the poem is not Yeats's "own music"; it is indebted to numerous predecessors. See additional note by Howarth, 190:8 (20 Apr 1946), 175.

296. HUNTER, C. STUART: "Return to *la bonne vaux:* The Symbolic Significance of Innisfree," *MLS*, 14:3 (Summer 1984), 70-81.
The poem as a description of a secluded numinous place.

297. *Interpretat͡siia khudozhestvennogo teksta v i͡azykovom vuze: Sbornik nauchnykh trudov*. Leningrad: Leningradskiĭ ordena trudovogo krasnogo znameni gosudarstvennyĭ pedagogicheskiĭ institut imeni A. I. Gert͡sena, 1981. 156 pp.
T. I. Sil'man: "Lingvisticheskai͡a interpretat͡sii͡a liriki poetov 'Irlandskogo Vozrozhdenii͡a,'" 82-95; a linguistic analysis.

298. KILGANNON, TADHG: *Sligo and Its Surroundings: A Descriptive and Pictorial Guide to the History, Scenery, Antiquities and Places of Interest in and around Sligo*. Sligo: Kilgannon, 1926. xxiv, 360 pp.
"Inishfree Island," 179-82.

299. KOCH, KENNETH: "Inspiration and Work: How Poetry Gets to Be Written," *CLS*, 17:2, Part II (June 1980), 206-19.
Note on this poem and "The Second Coming," pp. 214-15.

300. KREUZER, JAMES R.: *Elements of Poetry*. NY: Macmillan, 1962. xiii, 256 pp.
See pp. 117-19.

301. MULVANY, TOM: "The Genesis of a Lyric: Yeats's 'The Lake Isle of Innisfree,'" *Texas Q*, 8:4 (Winter 1965), 160-64.

302. O'GORDON, HANNAH JEAN: "As It Appears to Me," *EJ*, 33:3 (Mar 1944), 157-58.
The "vivisection" of a "friendly lyric."

303. PRITCHARD, FRANCIS HENRY: *Studies in Literature: An Aid to Literary Appreciation and Composition*. London: Harrap, 1919. 205 pp.
See pp. 27-30.

304. QUILLER-COUCH, SIR ARTHUR: *On the Art of Writing*. Cambridge: UP, 1936 [1916]. vii, 218 pp.
Short note on the "vowel-play" of this poem, pp. 124-25.

305. ROLA, DIONISIA: "On Yeats' 'The Lake Isle of Innisfree,'" *DilR*, 14:2 (Apr 1966), 133-34.

306. SEN, MIHIR KUMAR: *Fresh Grounds in English Literature*. New Delhi: Chand, 1974. ix, 174 pp.
"The 'Nine Bean-rows' in 'The Lake Isle of Innisfree': An Explication," 126-40.

307. SLOAN, GARY: "Yeats, Tennyson, and 'Innisfree,'" *VN*, 54 (Fall 1978), 29-31.
Notes Tennyson's "immense thematic and phraseological shadow over Yeats's first wellknown poem."

308. STEIN, AGNES: *The Uses of Poetry*. NY: Holt, Rinehart & Winston, 1975. xxxiii, 410 pp.
Note on this poem, pp. 262-64; on "Byzantium," 303-4.

309. STONOR, OLIVER: "Three Men of the West," *John o' London's Weekly*, 1 July 1933, 469, 472.
A visit to the place to find out why it inspired the poem.

310. THOMAS, GILBERT: *Builders and Makers: Occasional Studies*. London: Epworth Press, 1944. 219 pp.
"Poets on Holiday," 202-5. Yeats never built the cabin in the bee-loud glade because he was better off with his imagination.

311. TILLEKERATNE, NIHAL: "'The Lake Isle of Innisfree,'" *Community*, 3:1 (Apr 1959), 57-58.

312. YEATS, W. B.: *The Lake Isle of Innisfree*. With a facsimile of the poem in the poet's handwriting, also an appreciative note by George Sterling. Oakland: Mills College, Bender Collection, 1924. [8 pp.]
"A Note on 'The Lake Isle of Innisfree,'" [5-7].

See also BC15, CB363, 404, CD319, 461, 535, 818, 1251, 1385, 1388, DA12, 26, 30, 34, 35(II), 38, DB75, 89, 96, 199, DC49, 76, 359, DD221, 696, HA2, 3, HD49, HF2, 5, 6, 7, 17, 20, 28, 32, 38, 41, 42, 57, 58.

"The Lamentation of the Old Pensioner"

313. DANIELS, WILLIAM: "Yeats's 'Old Pensioner' and His 'Visionary': 1890-1925," *IUR*, 1:2 (Spring 1971), 178-88.
The revisions of this poem and of the related essay "An Irish Visionary." Comments on the influence of AE.

See also DA30, 35(I), 49, DD136.

"Lapis Lazuli"

314. BEATY, JEROME, and WILLIAM H. MATCHETT: *Poetry from Statement to Meaning.* NY: Oxford UP, 1965. xi, 353 pp.
See pp. 255-62; on "Sailing to Byzantium," pp. 245-46.

315. CALARCO, NATALE JOSEPH: *Tragic Being: Apollo and Dionysus in Western Drama.* Minneapolis: U of Minnesota Press, 1968. ix, 202 pp.
See pp. 3-4, 14, 108, 183.

316. DOHERTY, GERALD: "W. B. Yeats and Zen: A Reading of Two Poems," *Young East,* ns 5:2 (Spring 1979), 5-15.
This poem, "Demon and Beast," and the Lankavatara Sutra.

317. ESTRIN, BARBARA L.: "Alternating Personae in Yeats' 'Lapis Lazuli' and 'Crazy Jane on the Mountain,'" *Criticism,* 16:1 (Winter 1974), 13-22.

318. GALLATIN, MICHAEL: *Shakespearean Alchemy: Themes and Variations in Literary Criticism.* Ann Arbor: Q.E.D. Press, 1985. xvii, 83 pp.
"Ode to Tragic Joy," 53-59; on this poem and "Sailing to Byzantium."

319. JEFFARES, A. NORMAN: "Notes on Yeats's 'Lapis Lazuli,'" *MLN,* 65:7 (Nov 1950), 488-91.

320. KING, S. K.: "Eliot, Yeats, and Shakespeare," *Theoria,* 5 (1953), 113-19.
"The endurance of virtue" in "Marina," *The Winter's Tale,* and this poem.

321. LABISTOUR, MARION: "'Lapis Lazuli,'" *Critical Survey,* 3:1 (Winter 1966), 13-16.

322. MENDEL, SYDNEY: "Yeats' 'Lapis Lazuli,'" *Expl,* 19:9 (June 1961), no. 64.

323. MIHĂILĂ, RODICA: "William Butler Yeats: 'Lapis Lazuli.' Note de analiză," *Limbile moderne în şcoală,* 2 (1973), 107-10.

324. NATH, RAJ, and WILLIAM I. ELLIOT[T] (eds): *Essays in Modern Criticism.* Allahabad: Kitab Mahal, 1976. vii, 176 pp.
P. S. Sastri: "The Poetics of the Lyric: An Examination of Elder Olson's Analysis of 'Sailing to Byzantium,'" 138-56; reprinted from *LCrit,* 9:1 (Winter 1969), 70-77 (see DD540); William I. Elliott: "A Reading of Yeats's 'Lapis Lazuli,'" 157-67.

325. O'DONNELL, WILLIAM H.: "The Art of Yeats's 'Lapis Lazuli,'" *MR,* 23:2 (Summer 1982), 353-67.

326. PARKER, DAVID: "Yeats's 'Lapis Lazuli,'" *N&Q,* os 222 / ns 24:5 (Oct 1977), 452-54.
The iconographic significance of the lapis lazuli, given to Yeats by Harry Clifton.

327. SANESI, ROBERTO: "'Lapis Lazuli,'" *Osservatore politico letterario,* 7:10 (Oct 1961), 81-91.
Reprinted in *Poesia e critica,* 1:2 [Dec 1961], 5-18.

328. SNIPES, KATHERINE: "The Artistic Imagination in Action: Yeats's 'Lapis Lazuli,'" *CEA*, 39:1 (Nov 1976), 15-16.

329. WARNER, JOHN M.: "'Lapis Lazuli': Structure through Analogy," *CP*, 3:2 (Fall 1970), 41-48.

See also CA4, 12, 26, 27, 56, 61, 91, 92, 103, 128, 168, CB135, 371, CC31, 182, 226, 250, CD224, 813, 886, 1175, 1179, 1261, DA18, 26, 30, 34, 45, 49, 53, DB70, 75, 156, 173, 178, 203, DC34, 109, 188, 240, 406a, DD332, 337, 439, EE292, FC64, FD73, FE55.

Last Poems
Last Poems and (Two) Plays

329a. BILLIGHEIMER, RACHEL V.: "Tragic Joy: Art and Violence in Yeats's Last Poems," *USF Language Q*, 26:1-2 (Fall-Winter 1987), 31-35.

330. BRADFORD, CURTIS: *Yeats's "Last Poems" Again*. No. 8 of *DPYCP* (1966, CA20), 257-88.

Includes "The Order of Yeats's *Last Poems*," *MLN*, 76:6 (June 1961), 515-16. Argues for the validity of Yeats's arrangement of his poems in *Last Poems and Two Plays*, which is obscured in *Collected Poems*.

331. GRIFFIN, JON NELSON: "Profane Perfection: Yeats' *Last Poems* ," °Ph.D. thesis, U of Rochester, 1986. 171 pp. (*DAI*, 47:4 [Oct 1986], 1318A)

332. HAHN, CLAIRE: "The Moral Center of Yeats's *Last Poems*," *Thought*, 50:198 (Sept 1976), 301-11.

Mainly on "The Gyres," "Lapis Lazuli," "The Circus Animals' Desertion," and "Under Ben Bulben"; the moral center is "truth."

333. HENN, T. R.: "The Accent of Yeats' *Last Poems*," *E&S*, 9 (1956), 56-72.

The theme of sexuality is less prevalent than Vivienne Koch (DA28) thinks.

334. HOFFMAN, BRYANT E.: "Myself Must I Remake: Yeats's *Last Poems* (1936-1939)," *LitR*, 20:4 (Summer 1977), 401-28.

335. HOLLAND, PATRICK: "Yeats and the Musician's Art in *Last Poems*," *Eire*, 6:4 (Winter 1971), 49-64.

The music/song/ballad motif in *Last Poems and Two Plays* and *New Poems*.

336. MARCUS, PHILLIP L.: "Yeats's *Last Poems:* A Reconsideration," *YeA*, 5 (1987), 3-14.

Reopens the question of the contents and order of this group of poems.

337. SHIMA, HIROYUKI: "Yeats's Janus-Faced Sincerity in *Last Poems*," *SELit*, 62:2 (Dec 1985), 293-308.

Mainly on "The Gyres," "The Statues," "Lapis Lazuli," "A Bronze Head," "The Circus Animals' Desertion," "News for the Delphic Oracle," and "The Man and the Echo."

338. STALLWORTHY, JON (ed): *Yeats: "Last Poems." A Casebook*. Lon-

don: Macmillan, 1968. 280 pp.
Contains "Introduction" (pp. 11-22), 20 previously published pieces, a set of "Questions," and an insufficient bibliography. The selection is rather one-sided. Not analyzed in this bibliography.
Reviews:
- [G. S. Fraser]: "Devoted to Yeats," *TLS*, 20 June 1968, 641.
- J. B. G[oedhals], *UES*, 6:4 (Nov 1968), 103-4.

339. SULTAN, STANLEY: *Yeats at His Last*. Dublin: Dolmen Press, 1975. 48 pp. (New Yeats Papers. 11.)
A discussion of the coherence and integrity of *Last Poems and Two Plays*.
Reviews:
- Warwick Gould: "Symbols and Systems," *TLS*, 25 Feb 1977, 218.
- F. S. L. Lyons: "Keeping Up with Yeats Studies," *IrT*, 19 Aug 1975, 8.
- Timothy Webb, *RES*, 28:112 (Nov 1977), 499-503.

340. WILSON, F. A. C.: "Yeats's Last Poems," *MSpr*, 54:1 (1960), 10-19.

See also AE21, CA4, 22, CD2, 1179, DB210, DD438, G828, 837-44, 848-83 and note.

"The Leaders of the Crowd"

341. UTLEY, FRANCIS LEE: "Three Kinds of Honesty," *JAF*, 66:261 (July-Sept 1953), 189-99.
Note on this poem and on "The Scholars," pp. 192-93.

"Leda and the Swan"

342. ADAMS, JOHN F.: "'Leda and the Swan': The Aesthetics of Rape," *BuR*, 12:3 (Dec 1964), 47-58.
An analysis of the poem as an expression of "the sexual dream-myth."

343. ALTIERI, CHARLES: "Rhetorics, Rhetoricity, and the Sonnet as Performance," *Tennessee Studies in Literature*, 25 (1980), 1-23.
See pp. 18-21.

344. BARNWELL, W. C.: "The Rapist in 'Leda and the Swan,'" *SAB*, 42:1 (Jan 1977), 62-68.

345. BARRICELLI, JEAN-PIERRE, and JOSEPH GIBALDI (eds): *Interrelations of Literature*. NY: MLA, 1982. vi, 339 pp.
Jonathan Culler: "Literature and Linguistics," 1-24, comments on Halliday's interpretation of "Leda and the Swan" (DD354).
Ulrich Weisstein: "Literature and the Visual Arts," 251-77, includes a note on "Sailing to Byzantium."

346. BERKELMAN, ROBERT: "The Poet, the Swan, and the Woman," *UKCR*, 28:3 (Mar 1962), 229-30.

347. BRENNAN, MATTHEW: "Yeats's Revisions of 'Leda and the Swan,'" *NConL*, 13:3 (May 1983), 5-7.

348. BRONZWAER, W. J. M.: *Tense in the Novel: An Investigation of Some Potentialities of Linguistic Criticism*. Groningen: Wolters Noordhoff, 1970. ix, 160 pp.
Includes a discussion of Halliday's analysis of this poem, pp. 117-22 (see DD354).

349. BUTLER, GERALD J.: "Latent Content in 'Leda and the Swan' by W. B. Yeats," *Recovering Literature*, 9 (1981), 30-41.
A psychoanalytic interpretation of the rape motif.

350. CAWS, MARY ANN: "Winging It, or Catching Up with Kierkegaard and Some Swans," *Yale French Studies*, 66 (1984), 83-90.
Compares the poem with its French translation by Yves Bonnefoy (in *CRB*, 37 [1962], 68).

351. COLE, E. R.: "Three Cycle Poems of Yeats and His Mystico-Historical Thought," *Personalist*, 46:1 (Winter 1965), 73-80.
The other poems are "The Mother of God" and "The Magi."

352. COOK, ALBERT: "Language and Myth," *Boundary 2*, 5:3 (Spring 1977), 653-78.
See pp. 656-58.

353. DEMETILLO, RICAREDO: *The Authentic Voice of Poetry*. Diliman, Quezon City: U of the Philippines, 1962. ix, 337 pp.
On this poem, pp. 7-9; on "Sailing to Byzantium," pp. 10-11.

354. DUTHIE, GEORGE IAN (ed): *English Studies Today*. 3rd series. Lectures and papers read at the fifth conference of the International Association of Professors of English held at Edinburgh and Glasgow, August 1962. Edinburgh: UP, 1964. 256 pp.
M. A. K. Halliday: "Descriptive Linguistics in Literary Studies," 25-39; reprinted in Angus McIntosh and Michael Alexander Kirkwood Halliday: *Patterns of Language: Papers in General, Descriptive and Applied Linguistics*. London: Longmans, 1966. xi, 199 pp. (pp. 56-69).
See also "The Linguistic Study of Literary Texts" in Horace G. Lunt (ed): *Proceedings of the Ninth International Congress of Linguistics*. Cambridge, Mass., August 27-31, 1962. The Hague: Mouton, 1964. xxii, 1174 pp. (Janua Linguarum. Series Maior. 12.), pp. 302-7.
A revised version of Halliday's article was published as "The Linguistic Study of Literary Texts" in: Seymour Chatman and Samuel R. Levin (eds): *Essays on the Language of Literature*. Boston: Houghton Mifflin, 1967. ix, 450 pp. (pp. 217-23).
For comments on Halliday's interpretation see DD345, 348.

355. DUVALL, CECIL H., and JOHN B. HUMMA: "The Opening Phrase of Yeats' 'Leda and the Swan,'" *RS*, 40:2 (June 1972), 131-32.
The sexual connotations of the word "blow."

356. GIBBONS, TOM: *Literature and Awareness: An Introduction to the Close Reading of Prose and Verse*. London: Arnold, 1979. ix, 134 pp.
See pp. 5-7.

357. GREENFIELD, STANLEY B.: "Grammar and Meaning in Poetry," *PMLA*, 82:5 (Oct 1967), 377-87.

358. HARGROVE, NANCY D.: "Esthetic Distance in Yeats's 'Leda and the Swan,'" *ArQ*, 39:3 (Autumn 1983), 235-45.

358a. HOFFMANN, PAUL: *Symbolismus*. München: Fink, 1987. 242 pp. (Deutsche Literatur im 20. Jahrhundert. 2. / UTB. 526.)
"William Butler Yeats: 'Leda and the Swan,'" 222-28.

359. HOLLANDER, JOHN: "Poems That Talk to Themselves: Some Figurations of Modes of Discourse," *Shenandoah*, 34:3 (1983), 3-83.
On this poem and "Among School Children," pp. 25-27, "A Stick of Incense," pp. 40-42, "The Song of the Happy Shepherd," pp. 51-52.

360. HOPE, ALEC DERWENT: *The New Cratylus: Notes on the Craft of Poetry*. Melbourne: Oxford UP, 1979. xi, 179 pp.
See pp. 94-95, 112-15.

361. JOHNSON, ANTHONY L.: "Sound and Sense in W. B. Yeats's 'Leda and the Swan' and 'The Second Coming,'" *Istituto universitario orientale: Annali. Anglistica*, 21:1-2 (1978), 139-58, and 2 tables.
An exercise in "phonostylistics."

362. KOCH, WALTER A.: "Einige Probleme der Textanalyse," *Lingua*, 16:4 (1966), 383-98.
Contains a linguistic analysis of the poem.

363. LIND, L. R.: "Leda and the Swan: Yeats and Rilke," *ChiR*, 7:2 (Spring 1953), 13-17.
Compares Yeats's poem with Rilke's "Leda."

364. MADGE, CHARLES: "Leda and the Swan," *TLS*, 20 July 1962, 532.
Yeats's source may have been a bas-relief in the British Museum rather than a Michelangelo painting (illustrated). Correspondence by Giorgio Melchiori, 3 Aug 1962, 557, supporting Madge's thesis; by Hugh Ross Williamson, 31 Aug 1962, 657, asking for a pictorial source of "On a Picture of a Black Centaur by Edmund Dulac." See also the article by Charles B. Gullans, 9 Nov 1962, 864, who finds the source for "Leda" in a woodcut by T. Sturge Moore (illustrated), and a letter by Charles Madge, 16 Nov 1962, 873.

365. MARGOLIS, JOSEPH: "Yeats' 'Leda and the Swan,'" *Expl*, 13:6 (Apr 1955), no. 34.

366. MEDLICOTT, R. W.: "Leda and the Swan: An Analysis of the Theme in Myth and Art," *Australian and New Zealand J of Psychiatry*, 4:1 (Mar 1970), 15-23.

367. O'HARA, DANIEL T.: *The Romance of Interpretation: Visionary Criticism from Pater to de Man*. New York: Columbia UP, 1985. xi, 255 pp.
Discusses Geoffrey H. Hartman's reading of this poem (CB191), pp. 125-29.

368. PRATT, JOHN CLARK: *The Meaning of Modern Poetry*. NY: Doubleday, 1962. xi, 400 pp.
This is a weird anthology. The index lists a Yeats reference on p. 375; there one finds the text of the poem plus some comment, as well as a note to continue on p. 376. On p. 376 Pratt gives further comments and refers you to p. 369 (and then to pp. 361, 377 ["When you have followed my suggestions and are either informed or thoroughly disgusted, return to page 369 and try again"], 380, and 382). Or you might continue from 376 to 371

and to 390 (where he refers you back to 369); 382 (remember that?) continues into 383 and then to 370 (and then to 381, 384, and 386), also to 378 (cf. 385, 387, 391, 392) and 388 (from there to 389 [and from there to 381, 384, and 386]). Help!

369. RADER, RALPH W.: "Notes on Some Structural Varieties and Variations in Dramatic 'I' Poems and Their Theoretical Implications," *VP*, 22:2 (Summer 1984), 103-20.
Contains a note on this poem.

370. REID, JANE DAVIDSON: "Leda, Twice Assaulted," *JAAC*, 11:4 (June 1953), 378-89.
A comparison with Rilke's "Leda."

371. ROSENTHAL, MACHA LOUIS, and ARTHUR JAMES MARSHALL SMITH (eds): *Exploring Poetry*. NY: Macmillan, 1967 [1955]. xli, 758 pp.
On this poem and "Sailing to Byzantium," pp. 576-82; a comparison of "A Dialogue of Self and Soul" with Eliot's "Little Gidding," 702-3.

372. SCOTT, CLIVE: "A Theme and a Form: Leda and the Swan and the Sonnet," *MLR*, 74:1 (Jan 1979), 1-11.
See pp. 9-11.

373. SEYMOUR, THOM: "Yeats's 'Leda and the Swan,'" *Expl*, 39:1 (Fall 1980), 22-23.
The use of "knowledge" and "power" in Yeats and De Quincey.

374. SKELTON, ROBIN: *Poetry*. London: English Universities Press, 1963. vii, 179 pp. (Teach Yourself Books.)
See pp. 137-39.

375. STEIN, ARNOLD: "Milton and Metaphysical Art: An Exploration," *ELH*, 16:2 (June 1949), 120-34.
See pp. 129-30.

376. STOCK, A. G.: "The Swan and the Dove: A Note on Two Poems of Yeats," *JJCL*, 16-17 (1978-79), 67-70.
This poem and "The Mother of God."

377. SUŠKO, MARIO: "Neki aspekti Yeatsove pjesme 'Leda i labud'" [Some aspects of Yeats's poem "Leda and the Swan"], *Republika*, 25:9 (Sept 1969), 494-95.

378. TROWBRIDGE, HOYT: "'Leda and the Swan': A Longinian Analysis," *MP*, 51:2 (Nov 1953), 118-29.
Reply by Leo Spitzer: "On Yeats's Poem 'Leda and the Swan,'" :4 (May 1954), 271-76; reprinted in Spitzer's *Essays on English and American Literature*. Edited by Anna Hatcher. Princeton: Princeton UP, 1962. xvii, 290 pp. (pp. 3-13).

379. VERNON, JOHN: *Poetry and the Body*. Urbana: U of Illinois Press, 1979. x, 155 pp.
See pp. 50-52.

380. VICKERY, JOHN B.: *Myths and Texts: Strategies of Incorporation and Displacement*. Baton Rouge: Louisiana State UP, 1983. xv, 214 pp.
Includes "Three Modes and a Myth," *WHR*, 12:4 (Autumn 1958), 371-78. Discusses the handling of the Leda myth by Yeats, Aldous Huxley, and Robert Graves, pp. 28-37.

381. WIDDOWSON, HENRY GEORGE: *Stylistics and the Teaching of Literature*. London: Longman, 1975. ix, 128 pp.
On this poem, pp. 7-14; "An Irish Airman Foresees His Death," pp. 40-41.

382. WIND, EDGAR: *Pagan Mysteries in the Renaissance*. New and enlarged edition. London: Faber & Faber, 1968. xiii, 345 pp.
See p. 167.

383. WIRRER, JAN: *Literatursoziologie, linguistische Poetik: Zur Diskussion zwischen Linguistik und Literaturwissenschaft anhand zweier Texte von W. B. Yeats*. München: Bayerischer Schulbuchverlag, 1975. 299 pp. (Grundfragen der Literaturwissenschaft. 9.)
Originally a Dr.phil. thesis, U of Tübingen, 1972. The texts, this poem and *The Countess Cathleen,* are virtually smothered by an ambitious attempt to construct a theory of literature on the premises of linguistics and Marxism. Discusses Yeats's political convictions rather crudely along the lines of George Orwell and Conor Cruise O'Brien.

See also BA3, CA4, 12, 26, 66, 73, 91, 100, 103, 125, 128, CB160, 191, 290, 371, CC44, 99, 131, 132, 312, 341, CD55, 224, 536, 749, 1432, 1438, CE42, DA4, 14, 30, 34, 35(II), 36, 38, 49, DB64, 70, 218, 280, DC2, 61, 102, 114, 189, 190, 269, 312, DD20, 157, 281, 435, 578, 592, 620, 657, 680, FD19, HD35, 183, HF52.

"Lines Written in Dejection"

See CD458, DA35(II).

"The Living Beauty"

384. STORHOFF, GARY, and LINDA STORHOFF: "'A Mind of Winter': Yeats's Early Vision of Old Age," *CLAJ,* 21:1 (Sept 1977), 90-97.
An analysis of this poem and of "The Cold Heaven."

See also DA38.

"Long-legged Fly"

385. ALTIERI, CHARLES: "Abstraction as Act: Modernist Poetry in Relation to Painting," *Dada/Surrealism,* 10-11 (1982), 106-34.
Contains a note on this poem.

385a. ———: "Contemporary Philosophy and Modernist Writing: Or How to Take Seriously the Unmaking of Empiricism," *CEA,* 50:2-4 (Winter 1987--Summer 1988), 2-18.
This poem as an example of impersonality and a "modernist version of Hegel's dialectic between substance and subject."

386. CROSS, KENNETH GUSTAV WALTER, and DERICK R. C. MARSH (eds): *Poetry: Reading and Understanding. An Anthology with Commentaries and Questions*. Wellington, N.Z.: Reed, 1966. xvi, 245 pp.
See pp. 171-75.

387. D'AVANZO, MARIO L.: "Yeats' 'Long-legged Fly,'" *Expl,* 34:3 (Nov 1975), no. 23.

The indebtedness to Coleridge's *Biographia Literaria.*

388. DYSON, A. E.: "An Analysis of Yeats's 'Long-legged Fly,'" *Critical Survey,* 2:2 (Summer 1965), 101-3.

389. GHISELIN, BREWSTER: "The Tree of Knowledge, the Tree of Life," *WHR,* 35:4 (Winter 1981), 297-303.
Contains a note on this poem.

390. GILLHAM, D. G.: "Five Studies in Metaphor," *ESA,* 22:2 (Sept 1979), 57-69.

391. HODGES, ROBERT R.: "The Irony of Yeats's 'Long-legged Fly,'" *TCL,* 12:1 (Apr 1966), 27-30.

392. NEWCOMB, JOHN TIMBERMAN: "'There on That Scaffolding': Yeats's Objectification of the Artist in 'Long-Legged [sic] Fly,'" *CLQ,* 23:3 (Dec 1987), 173-85.

393. ROGERS, WILLIAM ELFORD: "Yeat[s]'s 'Long-legged Fly' and Coleridge's *Biographia Literaria,*" *CP,* 8:1 (Spring 1975), 11-21.
The source of the refrain is in chapter VII of *B.L.*

394. SOUTHAM, B. C.: "Yeats: Life and the Creator in 'The Long Legged Fly [sic],'" *TCL,* 6:4 (Jan 1961), 175-79.
See James L. Allen: "Yeats' 'Long-legged Fly,'" *Expl,* 21:6 (Feb 1963), no. 51; B. C. Southam, 22:9 (May 1964), no. 73.

See also CA12, 56, 103, 128, CC31, 226, DA34, 38, 45, 49, DB23, 53, 70, 244, DC153, 240.

"A Love Song"

See CD92.

"The Lover Asks Forgiveness because of His Many Moods"

See CA14, CC260.

"The Lover Mourns for the Loss of Love"

395. KLINKENBORG, VERLYN, and HERBERT CAHOON: *British Literary Manuscripts.* NY: Pierpont Morgan Library in association with Dover Publications, 1981. 2 vols.
Autograph manuscript of "Aodh to Dectora" and note in vol. 2, item 115; see also the index to vol. 2 for Yeats MSS. in the library.

"The Lover Pleads with His Friends for Old Friends"

See HF42.

"The Lover Speaks to Hearers of His Songs in Coming Days"

See CC260.

"The Lover Tells of the Rose in His Heart"

See CC260, DC275.

"The Lover's Song"

See DA36, 45.

"Lullaby"

See CA14.

"Mad as the Mist and Snow"

See DB160.

"The Madness of King Goll"

396. FOLEY, BRIAN: "Yeats's 'King Goll': Sources, Revision, and Revisions," *Yeats,* 4 (1986), 17-32.

397. KINAHAN, FRANK: "A Source Note on 'The Madness of King Goll,'" *YeA,* 4 (1986), 189-94.

See also DA11, DC275, FD19.

"The Magi"

398. JOHNSON, ANTHONY L.: "W. B. Yeats's 'The Magi,'" *Analysis: Quaderni di anglistica,* 3 (1985), 5-22.
A predominantly linguistic analysis.

399. JOSELYN, SISTER M.: "Twelfth Night Quartet: Four Magi Poems," *Renascence,* 16:2 (Winter 1964), 92-94.
By Eliot, John Peale Bishop, Edgar Bowers, and Yeats.

400. MCGINNIS, WAYNE D.: "Giotto and Yeats' 'The Magi,'" *RS,* 42:3 (Sept 1974), 182-85.

401. SANDERS, PAUL: "Yeats' 'The Magi,'" *Expl,* 25:7 (Mar 1967), no. 53.

402. SCHLEGEL, KEITH W.: "Yeats' 'The Magi' and Eliot's 'The Journey of the Magi': The Failure of Epiphany," *Cithara,* 16:1 (Nov 1976), 49-56.

403. SOUSA, R.: "Concrete Poetry: A Contrastive Approach," *Kentucky Romance Q,* 23:2 (1976), 199-221.

404. TULLY, ROSEMARY FRANKLIN: "A Pictorial Source for Yeats's 'The Magi,'" *Eire,* 8:4 (Winter 1973), 84-90.
Benozzo Gozzoli's "The Journey of the Magi" (1469), a fresco in the Medici-Riccardi Chapel, Florence.

405. WELSH, ANDREW: *Roots of Lyric: Primitive Poetry and Modern Po-*

ets. Princeton: Princeton UP, 1978. xi, 276 pp.
See pp. 94-97.

See also CA128, CC31, 312, 341, CD454a, 1123, DB28, DC275, DD351, FC49.

"Maid Quiet"

406. ALSPACH, RUSSELL K.: "Yeats's 'Maid Quiet,'" *MLN*, 65:4 (Apr 1950), 252-53.
A bibliographical note.

See also CC1.

"The Man and the Echo"

See CA12, 128, 150, 169, CC99, 226, DA26, 28, 34, 35(II), 45, 49, DB35, DC267, DD337.

"The Man Who Dreamed of Faeryland"

407. BRODER, PEGGY F.: "Irish Soil, Irish Spirit, Irish Themes: An Introduction to the Poetry of W. B. Yeats," *Iowa English Bulletin,* 30:1 (Fall 1980), 12-13.

See also CD43, DA35(I), DB28, 156, HF30, 55.

"A Man Young and Old"

408. FUJIMOTO, REIJI: "W. B. Yeats's 'A Man Young and Old': The Wild Regrets for Youth and Love," *HSELL,* 26 (1981), 46-58.

409. KEITH, W. J.: "Yeats's 'The Empty Cup,'" *ELN,* 4:3 (Mar 1967), 206-10.

410. SOMER, JOHN: "Unageing Monuments: A Study of W. B. Yeats' Poetry Sequence, 'A Man Young and Old,'" *BSUF,* 12:4 (Autumn 1971), 28-36.

See also DA4, 6, 20, 26, 49, DB70, 127, 210, DC133, 141, DD680.

"Margot"

See CA150.

"The Mask"

See CD1214, EB147.

"A Meditation in Time of War"

411. JEFFARES, A. NORMAN: "The Source of Yeats's 'A Meditation in Time of War,'" *N&Q,* 193:24 (27 Nov 1948), 522.

Blake's poem "Time."

"Meditations in Time of Civil War"

412. CULLINGFORD, ELIZABETH: "How Jacques Molay Got Up the Tower: Yeats and the Irish Civil War," *ELH,* 50:4 (Winter 1983), 763-89.
The significance of Freemasonry in this poem.

413. CURTIS, PENELOPE: "Yeats: The Tower in Time of Civil War," *Melbourne Critical R,* 6 (1963), 69-82.

414. DAVIS, RACHEL JEAN: "Speaking of Places: Poetry on Location," °Ph.D. thesis, Cornell U, 1982. 290 pp. (*DAI,* 43:10 [Apr 1983], 3323A)
Discusses this poem and "The Tower."

415. GLEN, HEATHER: "The Greatness of Yeats's 'Meditations,'" *Critical R,* 12 (1969), 29-44.

416. GREER, SAMMYE CRAWFORD: "The Poet's Role in an Age of Emptiness and Chaos: A Reading of Yeats's 'Meditations in Time of Civil War,'" *Eire,* 7:3 (Autumn 1972), 82-92.

417. HENN, THOMAS RICE: *The Apple and the Spectroscope: Being Lectures on Poetry Designed (in the Main) for Science Students.* London: Methuen, 1951. xix, 166 pp.
"Two Poems by Yeats: 'The Stare's Nest by My Window' and 'Before the World Was Made,'" 49-58.

418. MCFARLANE, BRIAN (ed): *Viewpoints 80: H.S.C. English Literature.* Malvern, Australia: Sorrett, 1980. 223 pp.
Vincent Buckley: "Yeats and Meditations," 59-64.

419. NORTH, MICHAEL: "Symbolism and Obscurity in 'Meditations in Time of Civil War,'" *CritQ,* 19:1 (Spring 1977), 5-18.

420. PLATER, ORMONDE: "Water Imagery in Yeats' 'Meditations in Time of Civil War,'" *Style,* 2:1 (Winter 1968), 59-72.

421. SEYBOLT, STEPHEN: "A Reading of 'Meditations in Time of Civil War,'" *MSE,* 2:4 (Fall 1970), 107-16.

422. THWAITE, ANTHONY: "Yeats and 'Sato's Ancient Blade,'" *Adam,* 25:261 (1957), 9.
Montashigi is Yeats's version of Motoshige, who lived ca. 1330.

423. *Viewpoints 84.* Melbourne: Longman Sorrett, [1984]. ix, 258 pp.
Beverly Hahn: "Yeats's 'Mysterious Wisdom': 'Meditations in Time of Civil War,'" 245-56.

424. WHITEHEAD, LEE M.: "The Honey-Bees of W. B. Yeats' 'The Stare's Nest at [sic] My Window': Echoes of Orpheus," *CJIS,* 5:2 (Dec 1979), 55-59.

See also CA4, 12, 112, 128, CC31, 130, 274, CD458, 794, 1164, DA14, 20, 22, 30, 49, 53, DB70, 127, 209, 210, 233, DC114, 133, 267, DD443, 446, 666, 680, FD46, HB6.

"Meeting" (part 10 of "A Woman Young and Old")

See DD780.

"Memory"

425. PURDY, DWIGHT H.: "Singing amid Uncertainty: Image and Idea in Yeats's 'Memory,'" *ELN*, 15:4 (June 1978), 295-302.
The poem is "an exemplary philosophical lyric on two of Yeats's favorite themes, the ambiguity of idealism and the inherent contradictions in a Romantic theory of poetic remembering."

426. ZITNER, SHELDON PAUL, JAMES D. KISSANE, and MYRON M. LIBERMAN: *A Preface to Literary Analysis*. Chicago: Scott, Foresman, 1964, iv, 140 pp.
See pp. 28-31.

See also CA154, DA36, 38, 44, DB160.

"A Memory of Youth"

See DC281a.

"Men Improve with the Years"

See CA53a, CD721, DB70.

"Meru" (part 12 of "Supernatural Songs")

See CA12, 126, CC31, CD139, 1168, DA49, DC189, 267.

"Michael Robartes and the Dancer"

426a. ARKINS, BRIAN: "Yeats and Tertullian," *N&Q*, os 233 / ns 35:3 (Sept 1988), 341.
"This Latin text" refers to Tertullian's *De anima*.

See also CC132, DA6, 49, DD427.

Michael Robartes and the Dancer

427. CULLINGFORD, ELIZABETH: "Yeats and Women: *Michael Robartes and the Dancer*," *YeA*, 4 (1986), 29-52.
On Yeats's treatment of Maud and Iseult Gonne, Constance Markievicz, and of his own marriage in "Michael Robartes and the Dancer," "Easter 1916," "Solomon and the Witch," "A Prayer for My Daughter," and other poems.

428. O'BRIEN, JAMES H.: "Overshadowers and Ideal Forms in Yeats's *Michael Robartes and the Dancer*," *Descant*, 11:4 (Summer 1967), 37-47.

See also CA22.

"Mohini Chatterjee"

429. WITT, MARION: "Yeats' 'Mohini Chatterjee,'" *Expl,* 4:8 (June 1946), no. 60.
Compared with "Kanva on Himself."

See also CA26, 103, 130, DA35(I&II), 49, DC267.

"The Moods"

430. WITT, MARION: "Yeats' 'The Moods,'" *Expl,* 6:3 (Dec 1947), no. 15.

See also CC260, DA49, DD461.

"The Mother of God"

431. ALBU, RODICA: "Reading a Poem by Yeats," *ASUI,* 31 (1985), 43-45.

432. BROOKS, CLEANTH: "Religion and Literature," *SR,* 82:1 (Winter 1974), 93-107.
On this poem, "Wisdom," and "A Prayer for My Son."

433. JENNINGS, MARGARET M.: "'The Mother of God': William Butler Yeats," *Spirit,* 38:4 (Winter 1972), 34-38.

434. KELLIHER, HILTON, and SALLY BROWN: *English Literary Manuscripts.* London: British Library, 1986. 80 pp.
Includes a reproduction of a corrected and annotated proof version of this poem, p. 67.

See also CA14, CC44, CD224, DC267, 337, DD351, 376.

"The Mountain Tomb"

See CA26, DA36, 49.

"The Municipal Gallery Revisited"

435. ABSE, DANNIE, and JOAN ABSE (eds): *Voices in the Gallery: Poems & Pictures Chosen by Dannie & Joan Abse.* London: Tate Gallery, 1986. 212 pp.
Prints this poem together with the Mancini portrait of Lady Gregory, and "Leda and the Swan" together with the British Museum marble relief (pp. 139-41, 186-87, 204).

435a. FALLON, BRIAN: "Gallery Pays Yeats Tribute," *IrT,* 1 Aug 1988, 12.
A tribute to Yeats's poem by bringing it "to life pictorially."

436. *Yeats at the Municipal Gallery.* Dublin: Claremont House, 1959. [8 pp.]
Contains an essay by Arland Ussher: "Yeats at the Municipal Gallery," [1-2], with comments on the paintings mentioned in the poem; the text of the poem; and black-and-white reproduc-

tions of the paintings.

See also BF190, CA4, 92, 103, 112, 118, DA18, 34, 35(II), 49, DB70, 90, 223, DC295, DD214, EE12.

"Never Give All the Heart"

See CD880.

"The New Faces"

437. JEFFARES, A. NORMAN: "'The New Faces': A New Explanation," *RES*, 23:92 (Oct 1947), 349-53.
The reference to Lady Gregory.

See also CC130, DA38.

New Poems

438. DEVINE, EVERETT DEWEY: "What Rough Beast: The Late Poems of William Butler Yeats," °Ph.D. thesis, Miama U, 1979. 191 pp. (*DAI*, 40:3 [Sept 1979], 1458A)
Discusses the last two volumes of verse, *New Poems* and *Last Poems and Two Plays*.

See also DD335, G826-28.

"News for the Delphic Oracle"

439. FRIAR, KIMON, and JOHN MALCOLM BRINNIN (eds): *Modern Poetry: American and British*. NY: Appleton-Century-Crofts, 1951. xix, 580 pp.
Notes on this poem, "Lapis Lazuli," "Byzantium," "Two Songs from a Play," "The Tower," "Nineteen Hundred and Nineteen," and *A Vision*, pp. 546-60.

440. OWER, JOHN: "Yeats' 'News for the Delphic Oracle,'" *Expl*, 28:1 (Sept 1969), no. 7.

441. WIND, EDGAR: *The Eloquence of Symbols: Studies in Humanist Art*. Edited by Jaynie Anderson. Oxford: Clarendon Press, 1983. xxxvi, 135 pp.
"Yeats and Raphael: The Dead Child on a Dolphin," 103-5; reprinted from *TLS*, 25 Oct 1963, 874. The statue that served as a pictorial source for the poem.

See also CA12, 26, 53a, 61, 90, 92, 103, 128, 129, DA1, 49, DB70, DC71, 267, DD337, FD73.

"Nineteen Hundred and Nineteen"

442. FOSHAY, TOBY A.: "Yeats's 'Nineteen Hundred and Nineteen': Chronology, Chronography, and Chronic Misreading," *JNT*, 13:2 (Spring 1983), 100-108.

443. GRAHAM, DESMOND: *Introduction to Poetry*. London: Oxford UP, 1968. vii, 168 pp.
See pp. 80-85, 123-24; on "Meditations in Time of Civil War," part 6 ("The Stare's Nest by My Window"), pp. 111-18.

444. MCWHIRTER, DAVID B.: "The Rhythm of the Body in Yeats's 'Nineteen Hundred and Nineteen,'" *CollL*, 13:1 (Winter 1986), 44-54.

445. OPPEL, HORST (ed): *Die moderne englische Lyrik: Interpretationen*. Berlin: Schmidt, 1967. 342 pp.
Willi Erzgräber on this poem, pp. 96-116; on "A Dialogue of Self and Soul," 164-84; Arno Esch on "Among School Children," 137-49.

446. THIESMEYER, LYNN: "Meditations against Chaos: Yeats's War of Irish Independence," *Perspectives on Contemporary Literature*, 10 (1984), 23-32.
On Yeats's war poetry, especially this poem and "Meditations in Time of Civil War."

See also CA4, 12, 14, 53a, 56, 73, 91, 92, 103, 112, 118, 128, CB274, 360, CC99, 130, 312, 341, DA14, 20, 26, 35(II), 49, 53, DB70, 127, 146, 161, 196, 209, 210, DC259, 267, 270a, 369, DD203, 439, 569, 680, FD19, 46.

"The Nineteenth Century and After"

447. BELL, IAN F. A.: "Oblique Contexts in Yeats: The Homer of 'The Nineteenth Century and After,'" *PQ*, 65:3 (Summer 1986), 335-44.
The Homeric imagery was suggested by Pound's "Hugh Selwyn Mauberley."

See also DA44.

"No Second Troy"

448. FRÉCHET, RENÉ: "Sur trois poèmes de Yeats," in Genet: *William Butler Yeats* (1981, CA32), 39-43.
Short notes on this poem, "The People," and "Demon and Beast."

449. HARTMAN, CHARLES OSSIAN: "Principles of Free Verse," Ph.D. thesis, Washington U (St. Louis), 1976. ii, 271 pp. (*DAI*, 37:4 [Oct 1976], 2174A)
Contains a metrical analysis of this poem, pp. 142-53.

See also CA26, 91, CB504, CD408, DA26, 34, 36, 38, DB28, 104, DD612.

"The Old Age of Queen Maeve"

See CC183.

"The Old Men Admiring Themselves in the Water"

450. CHATMAN, SEYMOUR (ed): *Literary Style: A Symposium*. London: Oxford UP, 1971. xv, 427 pp.
Ruqaiya Hasan: "Rime and Reason in Literature," 299-329, contains a stylistic analysis of the poem.

451. HARTMAN, CHARLES: "At the Border," *OhR,* 28 [1982], 81-92.
Contains a note on the prosody of this poem.

See also DA34, DC275.

"An Old Song Resung"

452. DŁUSKA, MARIA: *Studia i rozprawy*. Kraków: Wydawnictwo literackie, 1970. 2 vols.
Analyzes the prosody of the English original and of the Polish translation by Jan Kasprowicz, 1:429-30.

"The Old Stone Cross"

453. PERRINE, LAURENCE: "Yeats and Shakespeare: 'The Old Stone Cross,'" *MBL,* 3:2 (Fall 1978), 159-60.

See also DC267, FD73.

"Old Tom Again"

See CA103.

"On a Child's Death"

454. SCHUCHARD, RONALD: "Yeats's 'On a Child's Death': A Critical Note," *YeA,* 3 (1985), 190-92.
The relationship with Maud Gonne and her two children.

"On a Picture of a Black Centaur by Edmund Dulac"

455. FLANIGAN, BEVERLY OLSON: "Nominal Groups in the Poetry of Yeats and Auden: Notes on the Function of Deixis in Literature," *Style,* 18:1 (Winter 1984), 98-105.
Analyzes this poem and Auden's "Musée des Beaux Arts."

456. NIELSEN, MARGARET E.: "A Reading of W. B. Yeats's Poem 'On a Picture of a Black Centaur by Edmund Dulac,'" *Thoth,* 4:2 (Spring 1963), 67-73.

See also CA12, 26, 61, CB68, CC99, DA14, 49, DB100, 199, 233, DC267, DD364, 680, FC64.

"On a Political Prisoner"

457. PERRINE, LAURENCE: "Yeats' 'On a Political Prisoner,' 19-24," *Expl,* 32:8 (Apr 1974), no. 64.

See also CA118, 122, DC359, DD266.

"On Mr. Nettleship's Picture in the Royal Hibernian Academy"

See CA61, DA11.

"On Those That Hated the Playboy of the Western World, 1907"

See DA49.

"On Woman"

See DA4, 22, DC275.

"Owen Aherne and His Dancers"

See DD680.

"Pardon, Old Fathers. . . ."

See CA128, CC130, DA26.

"Parnell's Funeral"

458. HOLLAND, PATRICK: "From Parnell to O'Duffy: The Composition of Yeats's 'Parnell's Funeral,'" *CJIS*, 2:1 (May 1976), 15-20.

459. WILSON, F. A. C.: "Yeats' 'Parnell's Funeral,' II," *Expl*, 27:9 (May 1969), no. 72.
A source in Sordello.

See also CA112, 118, 124, 128, CC99, CD458, DA49, 53, DC8, FD46.

"Parting"
(part 7 of "A Woman Young and Old")

460. KOSSICK, SHIRLEY G.: "*Troilus and Criseyde:* The Aubades," *UES*, 9:1 (Mar 1971), 11-13.
A comparison with this poem.

See also DA44.

"Paudeen"

460a. PAULIN, TOM: *Thomas Hardy: The Poetry of Perception*. London: Macmillan, 1975. x, 225 pp.
Contains a note on this poem, pp. 9-10.

See also DA35(I), DB233, DD465a.

"The Peacock"

See DA36.

"The People"

461. ROSENTHAL, M. L.: "The 'Actaeon-Principle': Political Aesthetic of Joyce and the Poets," *SoR*, 23:3 (July 1987), 541-56.

Contains notes on "The People" as a political love poem and on "The Moods" as echoed in Pound's Canto 80.

See also CA128, DA26, DB210a, DD448.

"The Phases of the Moon"

462. ASSOCIATION INTERNATIONALE DE LITTÉRATURE COMPARÉE / INTERNATIONAL COMPARATIVE LITERATURE ASSOCIATION: *Littérature de diverses cultures au vingtième siècle / Twentieth Century Literatures Originating in Different Cultures*. Edited by Béla Köpeczi and György M. Vajda. Stuttgart: Bieber, 1980. 1006 pp. (Actes du VIIIe congrès / Proceedings of the 8th Congress: Vol. 2.)

Suzanne Nalbantian: "The Stylistic Alchemy from Metaphor to Metonymy and Its Concordance with Changes in Aesthetics," 869-77; contains a short note on this poem.

463. KENNER, HUGH: "A Possible Source in Coleridge for 'The Phases of the Moon,'" *Yeats*, 3 (1985), 174-75.

See also BA3, CA91, 100, 126, CC99, 130, CD224, DA22, 49, DC186, 267, 275.

"The Pilgrim"

464. JEFFARES, A. N.: "A Great Black Ragged Bird," *Hermathena*, 118 (Winter 1974), 69-81.

Yeats's interest, as shown in this poem, in the Lough Derg pilgrimage, and its sources; among them St. John Seymour's *St. Patrick's Purgatory: A Medieval Pilgrimage in Ireland* (1919).

"The Pity of Love"

465. WALSH, CHAD: *Doors into Poetry*. Englewood Cliffs: Prentice-Hall, 1962. xxvii, 292 pp.

Note on this poem, pp. 32-33; on "Sailing to Byzantium," 54-56.

See also CD471, DA35(I).

"The Players Ask for a Blessing. . . ."

See CA66.

Poems Written in Discouragement

465a. KEEN, WILLIAM P.: "Yeats' *Poems Written in Discouragement, 1912-1913:* An Earlier Modern Poetic Sequence," *JIL*, 17:1 (Jan 1988), 37-45.

Especially on "Paudeen" as the central poem of the sequence.

See also CA112.

"The Poet Pleads with the Elemental Powers"

See CC260, DC62.

"A Poet to His Beloved"

See CC260.

"Politics"

466. FELVER, CHARLES STANLEY, and MARTIN K. NURMI (eds): *Poetry: An Introduction and Anthology*. Columbus, Ohio: Merrill, 1967. vii, 504 pp.
Contains notes on this poem (pp. 8-10) and "The Black Tower" (pp. 111-14).

See also DA34, 36, DB58.

"A Prayer for My Daughter"

467. BECK, WARREN: "Boundaries of Poetry," *CE*, 4:6 (Mar 1943), 342-50.

468. BIVENS, WILLIAM P.: "Noun Phrase Case Schemes in the Deep Structure of Poems," *Style*, 8:2 (Spring 1974), 305-21.

469. BROOKS, CLEANTH: "Yeats: His Poetry and Prose," *English*, 15:89 (Summer 1965), 177-80.
An extract from a lecture, made by a rather incompetent editor. The surviving snippet concerns itself largely with this poem.

470. ———: "Metaphor, Paradox and Stereotype," *BJA*, 5:4 (Oct 1965), 315-28.
A note on metaphor and cliché in the poem, pp. 324-25.

471. CLOTHIER, CAL: "Some Observations on Yeats' 'A Prayer for My Daughter,'" *Agenda*, 9:4--10:1 (Autumn-Winter 1971/72), 39-45.

472. GILL, BRENDAN: "The Good Magic of Household Gods," *Architectural Digest*, 37:3 (Apr 1980), 30.

473. GOSHI, KEIGO: [In Japanese] "On 'A Prayer for My Daughter' by W. B. Yeats," *Humanities*, 7 (Sept 1958), 20-29.
Includes a summary in English.

474. HARDY, JOHN EDWARD: *The Curious Frame: Seven Poems in Text and Context*. Notre Dame: U of Notre Dame Press, 1962. xiv, 196 pp.
Based on "Some Problems in the Explication of Poetry," Ph.D. thesis, Johns Hopkins U, 1955. iii, 180 pp. "Yeats' 'A Prayer for My Daughter': The Dimensions of the Nursery," 116-50.

475. MARTIN, C. G.: "A Coleridge Reminiscence in Yeats's 'A Prayer for My Daughter,'" *N&Q*, os 210 / ns 12:7 (July 1965), 258-60.
The image of the tree in Coleridge's "Ver Perpetuum."

476. OATES, JOYCE CAROL: *The Profane Art: Essays and Reviews*. NY: Dutton, 1983. ix, 212 pp.

"'At Least I Have Made a Woman of Her': Images of Women in Yeats, Lawrence, Faulkner," 35-62; reprinted from *GaR*, 37:1 (Spring 1983), 7-30. The Yeats section is largely on this poem.

477. ROWLAND, BERYL: "The Other Father in Yeats's 'A Prayer for My Daughter,'" *OL*, 26:4 (1971), 284-90.
The other father is Coleridge.

See also CA4, 12, 53a, 60, 118, CB70, CC31, 130, 132, 155, CD458, DA4, 34, 36, 44, 49, DB8, 70, 203, DC14, 102, DD427, 569, 748, FC64, HA8, HD30.

"A Prayer for My Son"

See CA100, CC155, DA49, DC42, 267, 307a, DD432, 680, HF49.

"A Prayer for Old Age"

See DC247a.

"A Prayer on Going into My House"

See CC130, DA49.

"Presences"

See DA35(II).

"The Priest and the Fairy"

See CD713.

"The Protestants' Leap"

See CB242.

"Quarrel in Old Age"

See DC297.

"The Realists"

See CC99.

"Red Hanrahan's Song about Ireland"

478. ALSPACH, RUSSELL K.: "Two Songs of Yeats's," *MLN*, 61:6 (June 1946), 395-400.
Bibliographical note on this poem and on "The Song of Wandering Aengus."

479. BALLIET, CONRAD A.: "Maud Gonne's Favorite Poem," *AN&Q,* 21: 1&2 (Sept/Oct 1982), 14-16.
The poem is "Red Hanrahan's Song about Ireland" and not "The Two Trees." This note was published earlier in the same periodical, 17:7 (Mar 1979), 102-3.

480. MUNCH-PEDERSEN, OLE: "Some Aspects of the Rewriting of W. B. Yeats's 'Red Hanrahan's Song about Ireland,'" *OL,* 36:2 (1981), 155-72.

481. QUINN, SISTER M. BERNETTA: "Yeats and Ireland," *EJ,* 54:5 (May 1965), 449-50.

See also CC164, DA26.

"Remembrance"

482. JOCHUM, K. P. S.: "An Unknown Variant of an Early Yeats Poem," *N&Q,* os 216 / ns 18:11 (Nov 1971), 420-21.
A revised version of this poem, entitled "To---," in the *New York Evening Post* of 31 Jan 1921, 6. Its authenticity is unclear.

"Reprisals"

483. [EDWARDS, OLIVER]: "Note on the Publication of 'Reprisals,'" *Rann,* 2 (Autumn 1948), 1.

484. FINNERAN, RICHARD J.: "The Manuscript of W. B. Yeats's 'Reprisals,'" *Text,* 2 (1985), 269-77.
The version commonly accepted as definitive is only a working draft. The best text is the original corrected typescript in the National Library of Ireland (MS. 13,583). The various texts (here reprinted) "help us to understand the complex and ambivalent attitudes which Yeats had towards Robert Gregory."

See also CA53a, CC130, FD46.

Responsibilities

485. O'BRIEN, JAMES H.: "Yeats and the Sources of Morality," *UR,* 3:10 [1966?], 48-60.
In the poems of this volume.

See also BB104, CA22, CC290, CD618, DC335, G322, 345-53 and note.

"The Results of Thought"

See DA44, DC267, 297.

"Ribh at the Tomb of Baile and Aillinn" (part 1 of "Supernatural Songs")

See CA26, CD224, DA49, DC267, DD53.

"Ribh Considers Christian Love Insufficient" (part 5 of "Supernatural Songs")

See CA12, 14, 26, 126, DA49, DC247a, 267.

"Ribh Denounces Patrick" (part 2 of "Supernatural Songs")

See CA12, 26, 126, CD224, DA49, DC267.

"Ribh in Ecstasy" (part 3 of "Supernatural Songs")

See CA12, DC267.

"Roger Casement"

486. ANON.: "Poet Yeats and Poet Noyes," *Catholic Bulletin,* 27:3 (Mar 1937), 171-72.

"His bumptious and blundering parade of his bockety ballad . . . this rheumatic rhapsody from the Pretentious Pensionary of Bull."

487. NOYES, ALFRED: *Two Worlds for Memory*. London: Sheed & Ward, 1953, xi, 339 pp.

"Sir Roger Casement," 123-37.

488. YEATS, W. B.: "Irish Poet's Striking Challenge: Roger Casement (After Reading *The Forged Casement Diaries* by Dr. Maloney)," *IrP,* 2 Feb 1937, 6.

The poem plus a short note by Yeats. See "Vindication of Casement," 3 Feb 1937, 9; tributes by Sean T. O'Kelly, Eoin MacNeill, and Liam Grogan in praise of Yeats's poem. Also the editorial, "A Poet's Vindication," ibid., p. 8.

Muiris O Catháin: "Buidheachas," 4 Feb 1937, 4, a poem on Yeats in Gaelic.

"Alfred Noyes Replies to W. B. Yeats," 12 Feb 1937, 8-9; editorial, ibid., p. 8.

W. B. Yeats: "Mr. Noyes' 'Noble Letter': Mr. Yeats Revises Song," 13 Feb 1937, 8.

See also FD46.

The Rose

489. SCHLEIFER, RONALD: "The Pathway of *The Rose:* Yeats, the Lyric, and the Syntax of Symbolism," *Genre,* 18:4 (Winter 1985), 375-96.

Examines the relationship between "Yeats's early poetry and the symbolist movement in literature" and discusses "his conception of lyric poetry at the beginning of his career." Uses syntactic models derived from Derrida and concentrates on "When You Are Old" and "The Rose of Battle."

See also CB185, DD160.

"The Rose of Battle"

See CC171a, DB136, DC275, DD489.

"The Rose of Peace"

See DC275.

"The Rose of the World"

See CC171a, CD745, 1154.

"The Rose Tree"

490. BROWN, T. J.: "English Literary Autographs XLIX: William Butler Yeats, 1865-1939," *BC,* 13:1 (Spring 1964), 53 (and illustration facing p. 53).

491. SHUMAKER, WAYNE: *An Approach to Poetry*. Englewood Cliffs: Prentice-Hall, 1965. xxviii, 443 pp.
See pp. 49-52.

See also FD46, HD126.

"The Rose upon the Rood of Time"

492. ELLIS D'ALESSANDRO, JEAN MAY: "W. B. Yeats (1865-1939): Early Influences at Work in the Imagery and Language of 'The Rose on [sic] the Rood of Time,'" *Lingue del mondo,* 43:3 (May/June 1978), 219-27.

See also CC171a.

"Running to Paradise"

See CC1, 141, CD92.

"The Sad Shepherd"

See CA7, CD224, DA35(I), 36, DB196, DC150, 275, DD616.

"Sailing to Byzantium"

493. ABAD, GÉMINO H.: *A Formal Approach to Lyric Poetry*. Quezon City: U of the Philippines Press, 1978. xix, 437 pp.
Numerous references to the poem (see index).

494. ALLEN, JAMES LOVIC: "Yeats's Byzantium Poems and the Critics, Reconsidered," *CLQ,* 10:2 (June 1973), 57-71.
A classified evaluation, especially of criticism after 1962.

495. ———: "From Traditional to Personal Myth: Yeats's Prototypes and Anologues [sic] for the Golden Bird of Byzantium," *CJIS,* 5:2

(Dec 1979), 1-30.
The main analogues are the bird-soul symbolism, the symbols of the tree of life and of paradise, and the staring eye image.

496. ARNHEIM, RUDOLF, W. H. AUDEN, KARL SHAPIRO, and DONALD A. STAUFFER: *Poets at Work: Essays Based on the Modern Poetry Collection at the Lockwood Memorial Library, University of Buffalo*. Introduction by Charles D. Abbott. NY: Harcourt, Brace, 1948. x, 186 pp.
D. A. Stauffer: "Genesis, or The Poet as Maker," 37-82; notes allusions to "Sailing to Byzantium" in a poem by R. P. Blackmur, p. 47.

497. BAKER, HOWARD: "Domes of Byzantium," *SoR,* 7:3 (Winter 1941/42), 639-52.

498. BARBER, CHARLES: *Poetry in English: An Introduction*. London: Macmillan, 1983. xi, 220 pp.
On this poem, pp. 63-69; "He Tells of the Perfect Beauty," 98-101.

499. BEJA, MORRIS: "*2001:* Odyssey to Byzantium," *Extrapolation,* 10:2 (May 1969), 67-68.
Yeats's journey to Byzantium is analogous to the one undertaken by the astronaut in Stanley Kubrick's film *2001*.

500. BOGOEVA, LJILJANA: "Traženje smisla i puta: 'Putovanje u Vizant' Vilijama Batlera Jejtsa," *Gradina,* 18:3 (Mar 1983), 90-97.
"The search for meaning and the way: 'Sailing to Byzantium' by WBY."

501. BONNEFOY, YVES: *Entretiens sur la poésie*. Neuchatel: Baconnière, 1981. 170 pp.
"La traduction de la poésie (1976)," 95-102; on the problems confronting the translator of this poem. Bonnefoy's translation was published together with a note "On Translating Yeats" in *Modern Poetry in Translation,* 16 (Spring 1973), 11-12.
An English version of the essay was published as "Translating Poetry." Translated by John Alexander and Clive Wilmer, *PNR,* 46 (1985), 5-7. See also DD549.

502. BRADFORD, CURTIS: "Yeats's Byzantium Poems: A Study of Their Development," *PMLA,* 75:1 (Mar 1960), 110-25.
Revised version in CA121. Discusses the MS. drafts.

503. BURKE, KENNETH: *A Grammar of Motives and A Rhetoric of Motives*. Cleveland: World, 1962 [1945, 1950]. xxv, 868 pp.
"Symbolic Action in a Poem by Keats," 459-61, refers to this poem and "Among School Children." "The Problem of the Intrinsic," 465-84, discusses Olson's article on "Sailing to Byzantium" (see DD540). Further note on both Byzantium poems, pp. 840-41.

504. CAMPBELL, HARRY MODEAN: "Yeats's 'Sailing to Byzantium,'" *MLN,* 70:8 (Dec 1955), 585-89.

505. CRUMP, GEOFFREY: *Speaking Poetry*. London: Dobson, 1968 [1953]. viii, 231 pp.
Note on this poem, pp. 41-42; on some other Yeats poems, passim (see index).

506. DAALDER, JOOST: "Some Possible Sources for Yeats's 'Sailing to

Byzantium': A Reconsideration," *YER,* 9:1 (Fall 1987), 1-16.
Gibbon's *Decline and Fall,* Andersen, Keats, and Marvell.

507. DONALDSON, ALLAN: "A Note on W. B. Yeats's 'Sailing to Byzantium,'" *N&Q,* os 199 / ns 1:1 (Jan 1954), 34-35.
A source in Madame Blavatsky and theosophy.

508. DOUGLAS, WALLACE, ROY LAMSON, and HALLETT SMITH (eds): *The Critical Reader: Poems, Stories, Essays.* NY: Norton, 1949. xiv, 785 pp.
See pp. 115-18.

509. DUME, THOMAS L.: "Yeats' Golden Tree and Birds in the Byzantium Poems," *MLN,* 67:6 (June 1952), 404-7.

510. EGGENSCHWILER, DAVID: "Nightingales and Byzantine Birds, Something Less than Kind," *ELN,* 8:3 (Mar 1971), 186-91.
Keats's nightingale and Yeats's golden bird represent two "radically different ideals of art."

511. ERZGRÄBER, WILLI: "Interpretation and Kritik moderner englischer Lyrik," *Neusprachliche Mitteilungen,* 24:1 (1971), 9-18.

512. FINNERAN, RICHARD J. (ed): *William Butler Yeats: The Byzantium Poems.* Columbus, Ohio: Merrill, 1970. v, 160 pp. (Merrill Literary Casebook Series.)
Contains an introduction (pp. 1-10), the text of the two poems, other relevant passages from Yeats's poetry and prose, and 17 items of previously published criticism. Not analyzed in this bibliography.

513. FRASER, JOHN: "Playing for Real: Discourse and Authority," *UTQ,* 56:3 (Spring 1987), 416-34.
Contains a short discourse analysis of this poem, pp. 424-25.

514. FRÉCHET, RENÉ: "Yeats's 'Sailing to Byzantium' and Keats's 'Ode to a Nightingale,'" in Maxwell and Bushrui: *W. B. Yeats, 1865-1965* (1965, CA71), 217-19.

515. °GOEDHALS, BARRIE: "'The Return to Imagination': A Brief Study of W. B. Yeats's 'Sailing to Byzantium' and 'Byzantium,'" *UES,* 1:3 (Sept 1963), 1-9.

516. GWYNN, FREDERICK L.: "Yeats's Byzantium and Its Sources," *PQ,* 32:1 (Jan 1953), 9-21.
Some of the sources are Shakespeare's *King Lear,* Lamb's essays on Shakespeare's tragedies, and Gibbon's *Decline and Fall of the Roman Empire.* See D. J. Greene: "Yeats's Byzantium and Johnson's Lichfield," 33:4 (Oct 1954), 433-35.

517. HAGOPIAN, JOHN V.: "Thirteen Ways of Looking at a Blackbird," *AN&Q,* 1:6 (Feb 1963), 84-85.
Wallace Stevens's poem is indebted to Yeats's.

518. HAWTHORN, JEREMY: *Identity and Relationship: A Contribution to Marxist Theory of Literary Criticism.* London: Lawrence & Wishart, 1973. xi, 195 pp.
Notes on this poem, "The Second Coming," and "Easter 1916," pp. 50-54, 173-75.

519. HILL, ARCHIBALD A.: "Method in Source Study: Yeats' Golden Bird of Byzantium as a Test Case," *TSLL*, 17:2 (Summer 1975), 525-38.

520. HOLBERG, STANLEY M.: "'Sailing to Byzantium': A New Source and a New Reading," *ELN*, 12:2 (Dec 1974), 111-16.
The source is "The Story of Conn-eda" in Yeats's *Fairy and Folk Tales of the Irish Peasantry*.

521. HOLLOWAY, JOHN: *Widening Horizons in English Verse*. Evanston: Northwestern UP, 1967. ix, 115 pp.
Some notes on Yeats, the Nō, the 18th-century Irish "aisling," *Purgatory*, and this poem, pp. 92-102.

522. JOHNSON, ANTHONY L.: "Sign, Structure and Self-Reference in W. B. Yeats's 'Sailing to Byzantium,'" *Annali della Scuola normale superiore di Pisa: Classe di lettere e filosofia*, 8 (1978), 213-47.

523. KENNER, HUGH: "Reflections on the Status of the Text," *Cumberland Poetry R*, 1:1 (Winter 1981), 64-71.
Contains a note on textual problems in this poem.

524. KLEINSTÜCK, JOHANNES: "W. B. Yeats: 'Sailing to Byzantium,'" *NS*, 9:11 (Nov 1960), 527-39.

525. KLIEWER, WARREN: "The Bruised Body," *Cresset*, 32:10 (Oct 1969), 8-12.
Stanislavskiĭ's method of beginning in the body and moving out into the region of the soul resembles the plot of the poem.

526. KOCH, WALTER A.: *Taxologie des Englischen: Versuch einer einheitlichen Beschreibung der englischen Grammatik und englischer Texte*. München: Fink, 1971. 434 pp. (Internationale Bibliothek für allgegemeine Linguistik / International Library of General Linguistics. 5.)
See pp. 387-95 for an interpretation on the basis of information theory and advanced linguistics.

527. LENSE, EDWARD: "Sailing the Seas to Nowhere: Inversions of Yeats's Symbolism in 'Sailing to Byzantium,'" *Yeats*, 5 (1987), 95-106.
An "analysis of the poem's context," i.e., its images and ideas as reflected in some of Yeats's other works.

528. LESSER, SIMON O.: "'Sailing to Byzantium'--Another Voyage, Another Reading," *CE*, 28:4 (Jan 1967), 291-310.
Against Olson's interpretation (DD540). Correspondence by D. C. Fowler: "Lesser on Yeats's 'Sailing to Byzantium,'" :8 (May 1967), 614; Frederic I. Carpenter: "A Lesser Byzantium," ibid., 614-15; and Lesser's reply, ibid., 615-17.
Lesser's article (minus the correspondence) is reprinted in his *The Whispered Meanings: Selected Essays*. Edited by Richard Sprich and Richard W. Noland. Amherst: U of Massachusetts Press, 1977. ix, 238 pp. (pp. 128-48).

529. MCFARLANE, BRIAN (ed): *Viewpoints 78: H.S.C. English Literature*. Malvern, Australia: Sorrett, 1978. vii, 256 pp.
Elisabeth Grove: "Yeats and the Artist: 'Sailing to Byzantium,'" 69-75.

530. ——— (ed): *Viewpoints 81: H.S.C. English Literature*. Malvern, Australia: Sorrett, 1981. 240 pp.

Graham Burns: "Yeats's City of Unageing Intellect: 'Sailing to Byzantium,'" 62-68.

531. ——— (ed): *Viewpoints 82: H.S.C. English Literature*. Malvern, Australia: Sorrett, 1982. 264 pp.
Jennifer Wightman: "Rough Passage to Byzantium," 46-50.

532. MALAGI, R. A.: "The Artifice of Eternity: Yeats's 'Sailing to Byzantium' and Keats's 'Ode on a Grecian Urn,'" *J of Karnatak U (Humanities)*, 19 (1975), 84-91.
A comparison.

533. MARTIN, W. R.: "A Possible Source for Yeats's 'Sailing to Byzantium,'" *CJIS*, 3:2 [i.e., 3:1] (June 1977), 83-86.
A source in Castiglione.

534. MASON, HAROLD ANDREW: *The Tragic Plane*. Oxford: Clarendon Press, 1985. vii, 197 pp.
See pp. 84-85.

534a. MEIHUIZEN, N[ICHOLAS]: "Birds and Bird-Song in Wordsworth, Shelley and Yeats: The Study of a Relationship between Three Poems," *ESA*, 31:1 (1988), 51-63.
"The Solitary Reaper," "To a Skylark," and this poem.

535. MELLER, HORST (ed): *Zeitgenössische englische Dichtung: Einführung in die englische Literaturbetrachtung mit Interpretationen*. I: Lyrik. Frankfurt/Main: Hirschgraben, 1966. 148 pp.
Siegbert S. Prawer: "'Sailing to Byzantium': W. B. Yeats," 72-79.

536. MURPHY, GWENDOLEN (ed): *The Modern Poet*. London: Sidgwick & Jackson, 1951 [1938]. xx, 208 pp.
Note on both Byzantium poems, pp. 152-54.

537. MURRAY, PATRICK: *Herbert to Yeats*. Dublin: Educational Company, 1972. 64 pp. (Inscapes. 1.)
"This series is designed specifically to meet the needs of students in Irish post-primary schools" (back cover). Contains a note on this poem, pp. 57-60, and on "Among School Children," 61-64.

538. NOTOPOULOS, JAMES A.: "Sailing to Byzantium," *CJ*, 41:2 (Nov 1945), 78-79.
The possible Byzantine sources of the golden bird image.

539. ———: "Byzantine Platonism in Yeats," *CJ*, 54:7 (Apr 1959), 315-21.
Platonic philosophy and Byzantine art in the poem.

540. OLSON, ELDER: "'Sailing to Byzantium': Prolegomena to a Poetics of the Lyric," *UKCR*, 8:3 (Spring 1942), 209-19.
Reprinted in CA36, DD569, and in Olson's *On Value Judgements in the Arts and Other Essays*. Chicago: U of Chicago Press, 1976. ix, 365 pp. (pp. 3-14). See DD324, 503, 528, 569, and W. K. Wimsatt: "Comment on 'Two Essays in Practical Criticism,'" *UKCR*, 9:2 (Winter 1942), 139-43.

541. PARKS, L. C.: "The Hidden Aspect of 'Sailing to Byzantium,'" *EA*, 16:4 (Oct-Dec 1963), 333-44.
Rosicrucian influences.

542. PECKHAM, MORSE, and SEYMOUR CHATMAN (eds): *Words, Meaning, Poem*. NY: Crowell, 1961. xx, 683 pp.
See pp. 274-85.

543. PHILLIPS, ROBERT S.: "Yeats' 'Sailing to Byzantium,' 25-32," *Expl*, 22:2 (Oct 1963), no. 11.
Andersen's "The Emperor and the Nightingale" as source for the golden bird. Phillips does not seem to have noted Schanzer's earlier article on the same subject (DD554).

544. PHILLIPS, STEVEN R.: "The Monomyth and Literary Criticism," *CollL*, 2:1 (Winter 1975), 1-16.
The "usefulness as an approach to literature of the monomyth as developed by Joseph Campbell" in Conrad's "The Secret Sharer," Lawrence's "The Horse Dealer's Daughter," and this poem.

545. PIGGOTT, JAN RICHARD: "The Context of Yeats's 'Sailing to Byzantium,'" °Ph.D. thesis, U of California (Davis), 1971. 350 pp. (*DAI*, 32:7 [Jan 1972], 3692A)
A source study.

546. *Profession 83*. Selected articles from the Bulletin of the Association of Departments of English and the Association of Departments of Foreign Languages. NY: Modern Language Association, 1983. iv, 52 pp.
Lawrence I. Lipking: "The Practice of Theory," 21-28; reprinted from °*ADE Bulletin*, 76 (Winter 1983), 22-29; discusses the question whether this poem makes sense as a "piece of language."

547. RAY, WILLIAM ERNEST: "The Education of Prometheus," *Interpretations*, 5 (1973), 33-43.
Also on the influence of Blake and Shelley.

548. RAYMOND, WILLIAM O.: "'The Mind's Internal Heaven' in Poetry," *UTQ*, 20:3 (Apr 1951), 215-32.

549. *Le romantisme anglo-américaine: Mélanges offerts à Louis Bonnerot*. Paris: Didier, 1971. 421 pp. (Études anglaises. 39.)
Yves Bonnefoy: "Sailing to Byzantium," 307-16; a translation and a note. See also DD501.
René Fréchet: "Trois poèmes de W. B. Yeats: 'Easter 1916,' 'Coole Park and Ballylee 1931,' 'The Circus Animals' Desertion,'" 317-30; translations and notes.

550. ROSS, DONALD: "Stylistic Contrasts in Yeats's Byzantium Poems," *Lang&S*, 8:4 (Fall 1975), 293-305.

551. ROSS, RALPH, JOHN BERRYMAN, and ALLEN TATE (eds): *The Arts of Reading*. NY: Crowell, 1960. xv, 488 pp.
See pp. 352-54.

552. RÜDIGER, HORST (ed): *Komparatistik: Aufgaben und Methoden*. Stuttgart: Kohlhammer, 1973. 165 pp. (Sprache und Literatur. 85.)
Ulrich Weisstein: "Zur wechselseitigen Erhellung der Künste," 152-65; contains a note on this poem, pp. 157-59.

553. SAN JUAN, EPIFANIO: *Poetics: The Imitation of Action. Essays in Interpretation*. Rutherford, N.J.: Fairleigh Dickinson UP, 1979. 134 pp.
"William Butler Yeats: 'Sailing to Byzantium,'" 56-77; revised

version of "Yeats's 'Sailing to Byzantium' and the Limits of Modern Literary Criticism," *RLV*, 38:5 (1972), 492-507.

554. SCHANZER, ERNEST: "'Sailing to Byzantium,' Keats, and Andersen," *ES*, 41:6 (Dec 1960), 376-80.
The "Ode to a Nightingale" and the Emperor's nightingale as influences.

555. SCHMIDT-HIDDING, WOLFGANG: *Learning English: Book of English Verse. Interpretations*. Stuttgart: Klett, 1966. 96 pp.
Notes on this poem and "The Second Coming" (in German), passim.

556. °SEN, S. C.: "'Her Vision in the Wood' and 'Sailing to Byzantium,'" *BDE*, 2:3&4 (1961).

557. SRIVASTAVA, KAMTA C.: "'Sailing to Byzantium': A Note in Dissent," in Srivastava and Dutta: *Unaging Intellect* (1983, CA108), 188-93.
The poem is an artistic and emotional failure.

558. STAGEBERG, NORMAN C.: "Yeats' 'Sailing to Byzantium,'" *Expl*, 6:2 (Nov 1947), no. 14.
Explains "perne."

559. STUDING, RICHARD: "'That Is No Country for Old Men'--A Yeatsian Ambiguity?" *RS*, 41:1 (Mar 1973), 60-61.
"That" could be Byzantium itself.

560. SULLIVAN, RUTH ELIZABETH: "Backward to Byzantium," *L&P*, 17:1 (1967), 13-18.
Beneath the poem's "conscious level, beneath the intellectual, spiritual, and aesthetic values . . . lies an unconscious wishful fantasy that moves . . . not forward toward some higher and superhuman state . . . but backward toward very early infancy."
See comments by Aileen Ward, ibid., pp. 30-33; Clare M. Murphy, 38-40; and Mrs. Sullivan, 43-46.

561. THOMAS, WRIGHT, and STUART GERRY BROWN (eds): *Reading Poems: An Introduction to Critical Study*. NY: Oxford UP, 1941. xiv, 781 pp.
On this poem, "Byzantium," and "The Second Coming," pp. 712-16.

562. TRILLING, LIONEL (ed): *The Experience of Literature: A Reader with Commentaries*. NY: Holt, Rinehart & Winston, 1967. xxiv, 1320 pp.
Note on this poem, pp. 921-23; on *Purgatory*, 369-71. Reprinted in Trilling's *Prefaces to The Experience of Literature*. NY: Harcourt Brace Jovanovich, 1979. xvi, 302 pp. (pp. 269-73, 51-55).

563. TRUCHLAR, LEO: *Zum Symbol des Schiffes in der englischsprachigen Lyrik*. Wien: Verband der österreichischen Neuphilologen, 1968. 31 pp. (Moderne Sprachen. Schriftenreihe. 12.)
Note on the ship symbol, pp. 27-29.

564. VENTER, J. A.: "Phonic Patterning in 'Sailing to Byzantium,'" *ESA*, 10:1 (Mar 1967), 40-46.

565. WALTON, GEOFFREY: "Yeats's 'Perne': Bobbin or Bird?" *EIC*, 16:2 (Apr 1966), 255-58.

566. WEBB, EUGENE: "Criticism and the Creative Process," *WCR,* 2:2 (Fall 1967), 13-20.
Contains a note on the revisions of the poem.

567. WERLICH, EGON: *Poetry Analysis: Great English Poems Interpreted.* With additional notes on the biographical, historical, and literary background. Dortmund: Lensing, 1967. 238 pp.
"William Butler Yeats: 'Sailing to Byzantium,'" 161-88.

568. WHEELOCK, JOHN HALL: *What Is Poetry.* NY: Scribner's, 1963. 128 pp.
See pp. 81-86.

569. WILLIAMS, OSCAR (ed): *Master Poems of the English Language: Over One Hundred Poems Together with Introductions by Leading Poets and Critics of the English-Speaking World.* NY: Washington Square Press, 1967 [1966]. xxiii, 1093 pp.
Elder Olson on this poem, pp. 875-80 (reprinted from DD540); Sarah Youngblood on "A Prayer for My Daughter," 883-87; Richard P. Blackmur on "The Second Coming," 888-92 (reprinted from DB21); Robin Skelton on "Nineteen Hundred and Nineteen," 896-900; Reed Whittemore on "A Dialogue of Self and Soul," 903-6.

570. WILLIAMS, RAYMOND: *Reading and Criticism.* London: Muller, 1950. x, 142 pp.
See pp. 53-55.

571. °YEATS, W. B.: *Sailing to Byzantium (with Discussion).* Kent, Ohio: Kent State U, National Tape Repository, [19--].
Two reels, nos. L79-80; listed in AE41. No further details available.

See also BA3, CA4, 12, 37, 56, 73, 91, 92, 100, 122, 123, 126, 151, CB290, 370, 384, 503, CC31, 58, 155, 178, 291, 327, CD99, 203, 204, 224, 289, 395, 457, 458, 554, 705, 861, 1009, 1081, 1081a, 1187, 1214, 1224, 1447, CE272, DA12, 14, 24, 26, 34, 35(II), 36, 44, 49, DB13, 28, 30, 35, 50, 64, 70, 75, 90, 95, 104, 119, 127, 141, 156, 183, 199, 203, 232, 252, 255, DC8, 42, 44, 49, 102, 114, 173, 267, 270a, 295, 312, 327, 387, DD19, 52, 67, 70, 71, 73, 76, 77, 80, 82, 83, 84a, 88-91, 93-95, 97, 98, 102, 104, 110, 111, 113, 115, 116, 294, 314, 318, 324, 345, 353, 371, 465, 657, 664, 680, 689, 741, 753, FC137, FD19, FE55, 59, 80, G1571, HE11, HF45.

"The Saint and the Hunchback"

See CA73.

"The Scholars"

572. BURROWS, LEONARD: *Browning the Poet: An Introductory Study.* Nedlands: U of Western Australia Press, 1969. ix, 305 pp.
See pp. 129-30.

573. INGLIS, FRED: *An Essential Discipline: An Introduction to Literary Criticism.* London: Methuen, 1968. xiv, 272 pp.
See pp. 90-92: The poem is bad, both in style and content.

See also DD341.

"The Second Coming"

574. ALLAN, GEORGE: "Ceremony of Innocence," *Encounter* [Indianapolis], 34:1 (Winter 1973), 44-51.
A religious meditation on contemporary issues and problems prompted by a reading of this poem.

575. ALLEN, JAMES LOVIC: "What Rough Beast? Yeats's 'The Second Coming' and *A Vision*," *REAL*, 3 (1985), 223-63.
Discusses, among other things, the system of history underlying Yeats's thought, the origin and meaning of "beast," and the importance of the sphinx image and its source in the tarot deck.

576. BLOOM, EDWARD A.: "Yeats' 'Second Coming': An Experiment in Analysis," *UKCR*, 21:2 (Winter 1954), 103-10.
See also Edward Alan Bloom, Charles H. Philbrick, and Elmer M. Blistein: *The Order of Poetry: An Introduction*. NY: Odyssey Press, 1961. xv, 172 pp. (pp. 43-52).

577. BROOKER, JEWEL SPEARS: "'The Second Coming' and 'The Waste Land': Capstones of the Western Civilization Course," *CollL*, 13:3 (Autumn 1986), 240-53.

578. CAPPUZZO, MARCELLO: "W. B. Yeats: 'The Second Coming' e 'Leda and the Swan,'" *Teoria e critica*, 1:1 (Sept-Dec 1972), 155-70.

579. CHADHA, RAMESH: "Yeats's Symbolism in 'The Second Coming,'" *Indian Scholar*, 2:1 (Jan 1980), 27-34.

580. DAVIS, WILLIAM A.: "Tennyson's 'Merlin and Vivien' and Yeats's 'The Second Coming,'" *CLQ*, 20:4 (Dec 1984), 212-16.

581. DAVY, CHARLES: "Yeats and the Desert Titan," *TLS*, 2 Sept 1960, 561.
Letters by A. Norman Jeffares and Rupert and Helen Gleadow, 16 Sept 1960, 593.

582. EVANS, WALTER: "From Wordsworth's *The Prelude* to Yeats's 'The Second Coming,'" *YER*, 6:1 (1979), 31-37.
Parallels between Yeats's poem and *The Prelude*, X, 78-93.

583. FAN, ANDREW: "Yeats's 'Second Coming': A Stylistic View," *Waiguoyu*, 4 (38) (July 1985), 37-39.

584. *A Festschrift for Edgar Ronald Seary: Essays in English Language and Literature Presented by Colleagues and Former Students*. St. John's: Memorial U of Newfoundland, 1975. vii, 224 pp.
Robert O'Driscoll: "'The Second Coming' and Yeats's Vision of History," 170-81.

585. FINDLAY, L. M.: "W. E. H. Lecky and 'The Second Coming,'" *YER*, 5:2 (1978), 3-4.
An echo from Lecky's *The Rise and Influence of Rationalism in Europe*.

586. FISCH, HAROLD: *A Remembered Future: A Study in Literary Mythology*. Bloomington: Indiana UP, 1984. xi, 194 pp.
See pp. 146-47.

587. FLEISSNER, R. F.: "The Second Coming of Guess Who? The 'Rough

Beast' as Africa in 'The Second Coming,'" *NConL,* 6:5 (Nov 1976), 7-9.
Connects the poem with the Lion of Judah and the Harlem Renaissance.

588. FOWLER, ROGER (ed): *Style and Structure in Literature: Essays in the New Stylistics*. Oxford: Blackwell, 1975. viii, 262 pp.
E. L. Epstein: "The Self-Reflexive Artefact: The Function of Mimesis in an Approach to a Theory of Value for Literature," 40-78; contains a note on this poem and Blake's "The Tyger."

589. GARAB, ARRA M.: "Two American Sources of W. B. Yeats's 'The Second Coming,'" *YER,* 7:1&2 (June 1982), 117-19.
A sonnet by Percy MacKaye, entitled "Christmas 1915," and a fable by Edward J. O'Brien, entitled "The Fool," both published in the Jan 1916 issue of *The Forum*.

590. GIBBS, A. M.: "The Rough Beasts of Yeats and Shakespeare," *N&Q,* os 215 / ns 17:2 (Feb 1970), 48-49.
A source in *The Rape of Lucrece*.

591. HORRELL, JOE: "Some Notes on Conversion in Poetry," *SoR,* 7:1 (Summer 1941), 117-31.
Analyzes the meaning of "beast," pp. 123-26.

592. JEROME, JUDSON: *The Poet and the Poem*. Cincinnati: Writer's Digest, 1963. 227 pp.
"Six Senses of the Poet," 20-33; reprinted from *Colorado Q,* 10:3 (Winter 1962), 225-40; discusses this poem.
"Man Bites Dog," 137-43; on "Leda and the Swan": "What is going on here? Just what the poem says--a girl is being raped by a bird. That, surely, is bigger news than that of man biting dog."

593. ———: *Poetry: Premeditated Art*. Boston: Houghton Mifflin, 1968. xxxiv, 542 pp.
Note on the meter of the poem, pp. 100-103.

594. KLEINSTÜCK, JOHANNES: "W. B. Yeats: 'The Second Coming.' Eine Studie zur Interpretation und Kritik," *NS,* 10:7 (July 1961), 301-13.

595. MARTIN, GRAHAM DUNSTAN: "The Bridge and the River: Or the Ironies of Communication," *PoT,* 4:3 (1983), 415-35.
Includes a note on two French translations of the poem.

596. MAZZARO, JEROME L.: "Yeats' 'The Second Coming,'" *Expl,* 16:1 (Oct 1957), no. 6.
The falcon as related to the sphinx.

597. MORGAN, KEITH: "Yeats and Thompson," *New Society,* 25 Nov 1982, 359.
Criticizes E. P. Thompson who said that this poem is "one of the most necessary, and full-throated political statements of this century" (ibid., 11 Nov 1982, 244).

598. MURPHY, RUSSELL E.: "The 'Rough Beast' and Historical Necessity: A New Consideration of Yeats's 'The Second Coming,'" *SLitI,* 14:1 (Spring 1981), 101-10.
The "rough beast" has to be seen in a positive light.

599. PITTOCK, MURRAY: "Falcon and Falconer: 'The Second Coming'

and Marvell's *'Horatian* Ode,'" *IUR,* 16:2 (Autumn 1986), 175-79.
Marvell's "Horatian Ode upon Cromwell's Return from Ireland" is the "basis for an ironic reading by Yeats of Cromwell's achievement."

600. SAVAGE, D. S.: "Two Prophetic Poems," *Adelphi,* 22:1 (Oct-Dec 1945), 25-32.
On Yeats's poem and Wilfred Owen's "Strange Meeting." Contends that Yeats foresaw the advent of fascism and became a victim of his own prophecy in later life. Refers to Owen's exclusion from the *Oxford Book of Modern Verse.*

601. SPENDER, STEPHEN: *Life and the Poet.* London: Secker & Warburg, 1942. 128 pp. (Searchlight Books. 18.)
Note on the poem, pp. 96-102, involving a comparison with the poetry of T. S. Eliot and D. H. Lawrence.

602. ———: "La crise des symboles," *France libre,* 7:39 (15 Jan 1944), 206-10.
English version published as "The Crisis of Symbols," *Penguin New Writing,* 19 (1944), 129-35.

603. STALLWORTHY, JON: "'The Second Coming,'" *Agenda,* 9:4--10:1 (Autumn-Winter 1971/72), 24-33.
A second attempt to decipher the MS. versions (for the first attempt see DA44), plus an interpretation.

604. TENNENHOUSE, LEONARD (ed): *The Practice of Psychoanalytic Criticism.* Detroit: Wayne State UP, 1976. 280 pp.
Richard P. Wheeler: "Yeats's 'Second Coming': What Rough Beast?" 152-70; reprinted from *AI,* 31:3 (Fall 1974), 233-51. The poem is "grounded in the core situation of infantile helplessness and separation overcome by a fantasy of omnipotent rage."

605. UNGER, LEONARD, and WILLIAM VAN O'CONNOR: *Poems for Study.* NY: Rinehart, 1953. xxi, 743 pp.
See pp. 582-86.

606. VAN DOREN, MARK: *Introduction to Poetry.* NY: Sloane, 1951. xxix, 568 pp.
Interpretation of this poem, pp. 80-85; of "The Cat and the Moon," 85-89; of "The Ballad of Father Gilligan," 130-33.

607. WALSH, JOHN HERBERT: *Presenting Poetry: An Account of the Discussion Method with Twenty-two Examples.* London: Heinemann, 1973. viii, 112 pp.
See pp. 107-11.

608. WEEKS, DONALD: "Image and Idea in Yeats' 'The Second Coming,'" *PMLA,* 63:1 (Mar 1948), 281-92.
Comments on the influence of Shelley and the relationship with *A Vision.*

609. YEATS, MICHAEL: "The Abortion Referendum," *IrT,* 5 May 1983, 11.
Letter to the editor, protesting against the unauthorized use of quotations from this poem in a pamphlet on the abortion issue.

See also BA3, 20, CA4, 12, 26, 53a, 56, 63, 73, 91, 92, 100, 103, 118, 125, 128, 149, CB290, 371, 453, CC29, 31, 95, 341, CD224, 367,

418, 749, 760, 817, 1000, 1214, CE458, DA26, 30, 34, 35(I), 36, 44, 49, DB8, 28, 53, 70, 90, 156, 228, DC34, 42, 49, 170, 219, 259, 267, 269, 295, 312, 406a, DD52, 146, 299, 361, 518, 555, 561, 569, 624, FC49, 56a, 64, FD46, FE80.

"The Secret Rose"

See CA12, CC1, 31, 260, CD224, DA26.

"September 1913"

610. ANON.: "The Art Gallery," *IrT,* 8 Sept 1913, 6.
Editorial on the poem that appears on p. 7 as "Romance in Ireland." See also Lady Gregory's letter, p. 7.

611. DALSIMER, ADELE M.: "By Memory Inspired: W. B. Yeats's 'September 1913' and the Irish Political Ballad," *CLQ,* 12:1 (Mar 1976), 38-49.
The indebtedness of the poem to the street song "By Memory Inspired," published as a Cuala Press broadside in 1909.

612. DUCKE, JOSEPH: *Poetry 3: Shorter Poems for the Leaving Certificate*. Dublin: Educational Company, 1981. iii, 51 pp. (Inscapes. 18.)
Note on this poem and on "No Second Troy," pp. 38-42.

See also BB116, CA4, 112, CB439, CC341, DA26, 34, 35(I), DB104, HD89.

"The Seven Sages"

See CA118, 128, DA14.

"Shepherd and Goatherd"

613. MCGUINN, REX ALEXANDER: "Discourtesy of Death: The Elegy in the Twentieth Century," °Ph.D. thesis, U of North Carolina at Chapel Hill, 1980. 311 pp. (*DAI,* 42:2 [Aug 1981], 714A)
Discusses this poem and "In Memory of Major Robert Gregory."

See also CA60, 92, 129, CC130, 271, CD247, 1214, 1239, DC267.

"Sixteen Dead Men"

See FD46.

"Solomon and the Witch"

614. MEIHUIZEN, NICHOLAS: "Yeats, Frye, and the Meeting of Saint and Poet," *Theoria,* 67 (Oct 1986), 53-60.
The meeting of saint and poet in this poem, explained by references to Northrop Frye's essay on *A Vision* (CA22).

See also CA60, 91, 92, 122, 130, DA4, 30, DB203, DC275, DD427.

"Solomon to Sheba"

See DA30, 34.

"A Song"

See DB70.

"Song of Spanish Insurgents"

615. KELLY, JOHN S.: "'Song of Spanish Insurgents': A Newly Discovered Poem by Yeats," *YeA,* 3 (1985), 179-81.
Published in *North & South,* 5 Mar 1887. See James Loughlin: "A Long-Lost Poem by W. B. Yeats," *IrT,* 22 July 1986, 10.

"The Song of the Happy Shepherd"

616. AHRENDS, GÜNTER, and HANS ULRICH SEEBER (eds): *Englische und amerikanische Naturdichtung im 20. Jahrhundert.* Tübingen: Narr, 1985. 456 pp.
H. U. Seeber: "Selbstdarstellung von Dichtung in moderner englischer Lyrik und die Tradition der Pastoraldichtung," 31-49; has a note on this poem and "The Sad Shepherd," pp. 38-40.

617. STEMMLER, THEO: "W. B. Yeats' 'Song of the Happy Shepherd' and Shelley's *Defense of Poetry,*" *Neophilologus,* 47:3 (July 1963), 221-25.

618. WITT, MARION: "Yeats's 'The Song of the Happy Shepherd,'" *PQ,* 32:1 (Jan 1953), 1-8.
The early MS. version compared with the printed version.

See also CA7, CD224, 886, DA35(I), DB28, 196, DC150, 275, DD359.

"The Song of the Old Mother"

See CC260, DD127, HA2, 3.

"The Song of Wandering Aengus"

619. GOLDZUNG, VALERIE J.: "Yeats's Tradition and 'The Song of Wandering Aengus,'" *MSE,* 1:1 (Spring 1967), 8-16.
Tradition is the union of literature, philosophy, and nationality.

620. HALL, ROBERT: "Aengus and Leda," *LIT,* 2 (1958), 42-46.
The union of God and man, not possible in "The Song of Wandering Aengus," is achieved in "Leda and the Swan."

621. MAZZARO, JEROME L.: "Apple Imagery in Yeats' 'The Song of Wandering Aengus,'" *MLN,* 72:5 (May 1957), 342-43.

622. ROSENBERG, BRUCE A.: "Irish Folklore and 'The Song of Wandering Aengus,'" *PQ,* 46:4 (Oct 1967), 527-35.

See also CA61, CC31, 260, CD92, 1429, 1431-32, DA35(II), 38, 49,

DC62, 270a, DD138, 294, 478, 770, HF68.

"The Sorrow of Love"

623. ANON.: "A Literary Foundling," *Douglas Library Notes,* 11:3 (Summer 1962), 13-16.
The history of the first printing of the poem, which involved the assistance of Bliss Carman and Louise Imogen Guiney.

624. D'ÎAKONOVA, NINA ÎAKOVLEVNA: *Analiticheskoe chtenie (Angliĭskaîa poeziîa XVIII-XX vekov): Posobie dlîa studentov pedagogicheskikh institutov i filologicheskikh fakul'tetov universitetov.* Leningrad: Izdatel'stvo "Prosveshchenie," 1967. 267 pp.
Title on cover: *Three Centuries of English Poetry.* An anthology with comments and questions. See "William Butler Yeats (Born 1965--Died 1939)," 242-50; on this poem and "The Second Coming."

625. GENIUŠIENĖ, IZOLDA: "W. B. Yeats's Simplification of His Poetic Diction," *Literatūra,* 18:3 (1976), 64-70.
Analyzes the two versions of the poem.

626. JAKOBSON, ROMAN: *Selected Writings. III: Poetry of Grammar and Grammar of Poetry.* Edited with a preface by Stephen Rudy. The Hague: Mouton, 1981. xviii, 814 pp.
Jakobson & Rudy: "Yeats' 'Sorrow of Love' through the Years," 601-38. Reprint of a pamphlet with the same title, first published Lisse (Holland): Peter de Ridder Press, 1977. 55 pp. (PdR Press Publications on William Butler Yeats. 1.)
Also reprinted in *PoT,* 2:1a (Autumn 1980), 97-125. The same issue contains Jakobson's "On Poetic Intentions and Linguistic Devices in Poetry: A Discussion with Professors and Students at the University of Cologne," 87-96, in which he comments on his linguistic analysis of the poem and its sources. The discussion was originally published in German in *Arbeitspapier (Institut für Sprachwissenschaft, Universität Köln),* 32 (Dec 1976), 1-18.
Both items are reprinted in Jakobson's *Verbal Art, Verbal Sign, Verbal Time.* Edited by Krystyna Pomorska and Stephen Rudy. Oxford: Blackwell, 1985. xiv, 209 pp. (pp. 69-107).
Reviews of the pamphlet:
- Morton W. Bloomfield, *PoT,* 1:1-2 (Autumn 1979), 409-10.
- Ronald Schleifer: "The Rhetoric of Passivity," *MLN,* 92:5 (Dec 1977), 1106-16.

627. MONTEIRO, GEORGE: "Unrecorded Variants in Two Yeats Poems," *PBSA,* 60:3 (1966), 367-68.
In this poem and in "When You Are Old."

628. NÉMETH, ANDOR: "Az 'újraköltött' vers" [The "repoeticized" poem], *Nyugat,* 28:1 (Jan 1935), 63-64.
Compares the early and late versions of the poem.

629. PORTER, JAMES E.: "Yeats's 'The Sorrow of Love,'" *Expl,* 38:1 (Fall 1979), 43-44.
The revisions of the poem. See also Charles C. Walcutt: "Yeats's 'The Sorrow of Love,'" *Expl,* 39:1 (Fall 1980), 12.

630. STAMM, RUDOLF: *The Shaping Powers at Work: Fifteen Essays on Poetic Transmutation.* Heidelberg: Winter, 1967. 320 pp.
"'The Sorrow of Love': A Poem by William Butler Yeats Revised

by Himself," 198-209; reprinted from *ES,* 29:3 (June 1948), 79-87. "William Butler Yeats and 'The Ballad of Reading Gaol' by Oscar Wilde," 210-19; translation of the article in CD1145.

See also CA26, 27, DA35(I), 44, 49, DB203, DC295, G626.

"Speech after Long Silence"

631. BROWN, WALLACE CABLE: "A Poem Should Not Mean But Be," *UKCR,* 15:1 (Autumn 1948), 57-64.
Contains a note on this poem.

"The Spirit Medium"

See DA22, FC49.

"The Spur"

632. HENDERSON, HANFORD: "Yeats' 'The Spur,'" *Expl,* 15:6 (Mar 1957), no. 41.

See also DA45, DB70.

"The Stare's Nest by My Window" (part 6 of "Meditations in Time of Civil War")

See DA36, DD417, 424, 443.

"The Statesman's Holiday"

See CA92, 118.

"The Statues"

633. ARCHIBALD, DOUGLAS: "'The Statues' and Yeats's Idea of History," *Gaéliana,* 6 (1984), 165-76.
Comments on the relationship between this poem and *A Vision.*

634. BAGCHEE, SHYAMAL: "Sexual Passion and Nationalism *in extremis* in Yeats's 'The Statues,'" *CJIS,* 6:2 (Dec 1980), 18-33.

635. BARNWELL, WILLIAM C.: "A Possible Italian Influence on Yeats's 'Statues,'" *PQ,* 56:1 (Winter 1977), 140-43.
Tullio Lombardo's effigy of Guidarello Guidarelli.

636. GRIFFIN, JON: "Profane Perfection: 'The Statues,'" *CollL,* 13:1 (Winter 1986), 21-28.

637. MARTIN, W. R.: "Possible Sources for Yeats's 'The Statues,'" *CJIS,* 3:2 (Nov 1977), 43-48.
Wyndham Lewis, Spengler, and Edith Hamilton's *The Greek Way* (1930).

See also CA12, 26, 27, 61, 91, 100, 103, 124, 128, 130, 157, CB332,

CC226, CD139, 1173, DA28, 35(II), 45, 49, DB8, DC1, 267, 416, 424, DD63, 181, 337, FC64.

"A Stick of Incense"

638. ROGERS, ROBERT: *Metaphor: A Psychoanalytic View*. Berkeley: U of California Press, 1978. xi, 148 pp.
See pp. 73-76.

See also DD359.

"The Stolen Child"

639. CASWELL, ROBERT W.: "Yeats' 'The Stolen Child,'" *Expl*, 25:8 (Apr 1967), no. 64.

640. LAGAN, PATRICK: "Was Yeats Referring to Donegal or Sligo Rosses?" *IrP*, 14 May 1962, 8.

See also DC62, HD32.

"Stream and Sun at Glendalough"

See DB70.

"Supernatural Songs"

641. BOULGER, JAMES D.: "Moral and Structural Aspects in W. B. Yeats's Supernatural Songs," *Renascence*, 27:2 (Winter 1975), 57-70.

642. GREEN, BRIAN (ed): *Generous Converse: English Essays in Memory of Edward Davis*. Cape Town: Oxford UP, 1980. 160 pp.
Jacques Berthoud: "The Originality of Yeats's 'Supernatural Songs,'" 145-59.

See also CA12, 77, 91, 124, 126, CC178, CD2, 1010, 1077, DA20, 49, DB210, DC77, 133, 185, DD53, 233, 246, 725.

"Sweet Dancer"

See CA150, DA36.

"Symbols"

See DD740.

"That the Night Come"

643. DEAN, H. L.: "Yeats' 'That the Night Come,'" *Expl*, 31:6 (Feb 1973), no. 44.
The function of Maud Gonne in the poem.

See also CD1181, DA35(I), DD748.

"There" (part 4 of "Supernatural Songs")

See DC267.

"These Are the Clouds"

See DB233, DC295, DD240.

"Those Dancing Days Are Gone"

644. BORNSTEIN, GEORGE: "Yeats's 'Those Dancing Days Are Gone' and Pound's 'Canto 23,'" *YeA*, 2 (1983), 93-95.

645. PRUITT, VIRGINIA: "Yeats: A Major Theme in a 'Minor' Poem," *CLQ*, 17:4 (Dec 1981), 197-200.
The unity of the physical and the spiritual or of the finite and the infinite.

See also DC247a.

"Those Images"

See CD224.

"A Thought from Propertius"

646. SULLIVAN, JOHN PATRICK: *Ezra Pound and Sextus Propertius: A Study in Creative Translation*. Austin: U of Texas Press, 1964. xi, 192 pp.
See pp. 178-80.

See also CD1075, DA36.

"The Three Bushes"

647. PARTRIDGE, EDWARD B.: "Yeats's 'The Three Bushes'--Genesis and Structure," *Accent*, 17:2 (Spring 1957), 67-80.

See also CA66, DA4, 18, 20, 28, 45, 49, DC133, DD135, EE292.

"The Three Hermits"

See DA34, DC275.

"Three Marching Songs"

See DD142.

"The Three Monuments"

See DD680.

"Three Songs to the One Burden"

See CA112, 128, DA18, 49, DB223, DD722, FD46, 73.

"Three Songs to the Same Tune"

648. O'SHEA, EDWARD: "'An Old Bullet Imbedded in the Flesh': The Migration of Yeats's 'Three Songs to the Same Tune,'" *Yeats,* 4 (1986), 121-42.
Yeats's politics as reflected in the revisions of this poem.

"Three Things"

649. HENRY, NAT: "Yeats' 'Three Things,'" *Expl,* 33:5 (Jan 1975), no. 38.

650. PERRINE, LAURENCE: "Yeats' 'Three Things,'" *Expl,* 32:1 (Sept 1973), no. 4.

651. WERTENBAKER, THOMAS J.: "Yeats' 'Three Things,'" *Expl,* 34:9 (May 1976), no. 67.

See also DA6.

"To---"

See DD482.

"To a Friend Whose Work Has Come to Nothing"

See CA128, DA36, DC275.

"To a Poet Who Would Have Me Praise Certain Bad Poets. . . ."

652. POUND, EZRA: "Un inedito Poundiano: A un poeta che voleva indurmi a dir bene di certi cattive poeti, emuli suoi e miei," *Almanacco del Pesce d'oro,* [1] (1960), 16.
Italian translation plus note.

See also HD139.

"To a Shade"

See CA112, DB53, FC49.

"To a Wealthy Man Who Promised a Second Subscription. . . ."

653. ANON.: "A Pensioner on Paudeen," *Sinn Féin,* 18 Jan 1913, 1. Attacks the poem ("this rhymed schoolboy's prose"). Correspondence by Padraic Colum: "Mistaken Identity," 25 Jan 1913, 1; and editor's comment, ibid.

654. [HONE, JOSEPH]: "Art and Aristocracy," *IrT,* 11 Jan 1913, 6.

See also p. 7 of the same issue. Correspondence by "Val d'Arno," 13 Jan 1913, 6; "Paudeen," ibid.; William M. Murphy, 18 Jan 1913, 8.

See also CC130, 341, DA26, 36, 49.

"To a Young Beauty"

655. PERRINE, LAURENCE: "Yeats and Landor: 'To a Young Beauty,'" *N&Q,* os 217 / ns 19:9 (Sept 1972), 330.
A source in Landor's *Imaginary Conversations*.

See also DB70.

"To an Isle in the Water"

See HF30.

"To Be Carved on a Stone at Thoor Ballylee"

See CC130, DB70, DC275.

"To Dorothy Wellesley"

See CA12.

"To His Heart, Bidding It Have No Fear"

656. WITT, MARION: "Yeats' 'To His Heart, Bidding It Have No Fear,'" *Expl,* 9:5 (Mar 1951), no. 32.

See also BA3, CC1, 260.

"To Ireland in the Coming Times"

See CA112, CC141, CD660, DC62, 369.

"To Maurice Bowra"

See BB21.

"To the Rose upon the Rood of Time"

657. LAWRENCE, KAREN, BETSY SEIFTER, and LOIS RATNER: *The McGraw-Hill Guide to English Literature*. NY: McGraw-Hill, 1985. 2 vols.
K. L.: "W. B. Yeats," 2:303-16; notes on this poem, "Leda and the Swan," "Sailing to Byzantium," "Among School Children," and "The Circus Animals' Desertion."

See also CA66, 112, CC31, CD1214, DA34, 35(I), 49, DC275.

"Tom O'Roughley"

See DA30, DC275.

"Tom the Lunatic"

See CA103, DA36.

"Towards Break of Day"

658. KEITH, W. J.: "Yeats's Double Dream," *MLN,* 76:8 (Dec 1961), 710-15.

See also DA49, DD51, 729.

"The Tower"

659. BROOKS, HAROLD F.: "W. B. Yeats: 'The Tower,'" *DUJ,* os 73 / ns 42:1 (Dec 1980), 9-21.

660. °CHATTERJI, B.: "'The Tower,'" *BDE,* 1:2 (1960).

661. GEIGER, DON: *The Age of the Splendid Machine.* Tokyo: Hokusei-do Press, 1961. xiii, 178 pp.
"The Cry in 'The Tower,'" 51-73.

662. KLUG, M. A.: "Pursuit of Confusion in 'The Tower,'" *CollL,* 13:1 (Winter 1986), 29-35.

663. MARCUS, PHILLIP L.: "'I Declare My Faith': Eliot's 'Gerontion' and Yeats's 'The Tower,'" *PLL,* 14:1 (Winter 1978), 74-82.
Yeats's poem is an answer to Eliot's.

663a. MIŁOSZ, CZESŁAW: *Ogród nauk.* Paryż [Paris]: Instytut literacki, 1981. 256 pp. (Dzieła zbiorewe. 10. / Biblioteka kultury. 332.)
"William Butler Yeats: Wieża,'" 195-201, a translation of "The Tower" and note.

664. PRUITT, VIRGINIA: "Return from Byzantium: W. B. Yeats and 'The Tower,'" *ELH,* 47:1 (Spring 1980), 149-57.
"The Tower" proposes an alternative answer to the questions asked and answered in "Sailing to Byzantium."

665. SETURAMAN, V. S.: "'The Tower' by Yeats," *Mother India,* 17:10&11 (5 Dec 1965), 97-100.

666. SMITH, STAN: "Writing a Will: Yeats's Ancestral Voices in 'The Tower' and 'Meditations in Time of Civil War,'" *IUR,* 13:1 (Spring 1983), 14-37.

667. SPINALBELLI, ROSALBA: "W. B. Yeats: 'The Tower,'" *Spicilegio moderno,* 8 (1977), 124-42.
In Italian; English summary on p. 248: "In this semantic and stylistic analysis . . . particular attention is given to the poet's notion of 'unity of being,' and to its quest and attainment through the poetic form."

668. THIESMEYER, LYNN: "Excluded Myths: Vision and Disguise in Yeats's 'The Tower,'" *YER*, 8:1&2 (1986), 50-63.

669. YOUNGBLOOD, SARAH: "A Reading of 'The Tower,'" *TCL*, 5:2 (July 1959), 74-84.

See also CA4, 12, 14, 26, 63, 92, 100, 112, 118, 128, CC53, 130, 131, 182, CD198, 442, 1437, DA1, 14, 26, 22, 34, 35(II), 43, 49, 53, DB70, 127, DC327, DD414, 680, FB30, FE80.

The Tower

670. GENIUŠIENĖ, IZOLDA: "William Butler Yeats's Poetic Collection *Tower*," *Literatūra*, 22:3 (1980), 28-36.

671. GRENNAN, EAMON: "Mastery and Beyond: Speech and Silence in *The Tower*," *EI*, 7 (Dec 1982), 55-70.

672. JEWETT, ROBERT M.: *Artistic Tension in the Poetry of W. B. Yeats: An Introduction*. Trieste: Università degli studi di Trieste, 1980. 82 pp. (Università degli studi di Trieste. Scuola superiore di lingue moderne per interpreti e traduttori: Pubblicazioni. 1.)

Based on a °Ph.D. thesis, George Peabody College for Teachers, 1975. 117 pp. (*DAI*, 36:8 [Feb 1976], 5281A). On the poems in *The Tower*, which show Yeats's quest for Unity of Being through communication with Anima Mundi.

673. O'BRIEN, JAMES H.: "Yeats' Dark Night of Self and *The Tower*," *BuR*, 15:2 (May 1967), 10-25.

674. O'CASEY, SEAN: "Four Letters: Sean O'Casey to Oliver St. John Gogarty." Edited by James F. Carens, *JJQ*, 8:1 (Fall 1970), 111-18.

In two of the letters O'Casey ridicules *The Tower*.

675. RAU-GUNTERMANN, MECHTHILD: "Die Einheit von W. B. Yeats' *The Tower* (1928): Zu einer Poetik des lyrischen Zyklus im Symbolismus," Dr.phil. thesis, U of Köln, 1974. ii, 133, 5 pp.

Includes a summary in English, reprinted in *EASG*, 1974, 110-11. Discusses this volume of poems as a lyric cycle, its symbolism, and its dependence on *A Vision*.

676. SULLIVAN, JAMES T.: "A Gay Goodnight: A Study of Irish Tragedy," Ph.D. thesis, Brandeis U, 1973. v, 234 pp. (*DAI*, 35:6 [Dec 1974], 3773A)

"W. B. Yeats," 50-109; on *The Tower*.

677. Jejts, Viljem Batler [YEATS, W. B.]: *Kula* [The Tower]. Izbor iz celokupnog pesničkog dela, predgovor, beleške i prevod sa engleskog Milovan Danojlić. Beograd: Beogradskii izdavačko-grafički zavod, 1978. 248 pp.

M. Danojlić: "Jejtsovi koreni" [Yeats's roots], 7-53; reprinted from *Letopis matice srpske*, year 153 / 419:6 (June 1977), 778-808. See also by Danojlić: "Kako sam prevodio Jejtsa" [How I translated Yeats], *Rukovet*, year 25 / 49:3-4 (Mar-Apr 1979), 225-26.

"Beleške," 221-35; explanatory notes.

Jovan Janićijević: "Viljem Batler Jejts na srpskohrvatskom," 239-47; Yeats in Serbo-Croatian translation and Serbo-Croatian criticism of Yeats (a bibliography). For reviews see G1539-1540.

678. ———: *Ballylee: The Tower.* Selections from the *Tower* poems, and a letter describing Ballylee by his wife, George. With an introduction by Mary Chenoweth and wood engravings by John DePol. Lewisburg, Pa.: Press of Appletree Alley, 1983. 45 pp.
"Introduction," 7-10; "Letter to Dr. Oliver Gogarty from Mrs. W. B. Yeats," 44-45. See also G1570.

679. ———: *La torre.* Introduzione e commento di Anthony L. Johnson, traduzione de Ariodanti Marianni. Testa inglese a fronte. Milano: Rizzoli, 1984. 299 pp.
"Una vita di Yeats," 5-45; "Giudici critici," 47-55; "Nota su *La Torre* ," 56-57; "Bibliografia essenziale su *La torre*," 58-62; "Commento," 195-290; "Glossario," 291-96.

679a. ———: *The Tower.* With an introduction by Bel Mooney. London: Folio Press, 1987. 63 pp.
"Introduction," 9-12.

680. YOUNG, DAVID: *Troubled Mirror: A Study of Yeats's "The Tower."* Iowa City: U of Iowa Press, 1987. xiv, 153 pp.
Discusses the 1928 volume as a coherent book of poetry, as an equivalent of the long poem, and hence as proof that Yeats is a major modern poet. Analyzed in section DD.

See also CA22, CD48, DA14, DB209, G517-46 and note, 1539-40, 1570.

"The Travail of Passion"

See CA26, CC1, 260, DA30, DC167, DD770.

"The Two Kings"

See CC1, 173, DA4.

"Two Songs from a Play"

681. ARKINS, BRIAN: "Yeats and the Prophecy of Eunapius," *N&Q,* os 230 / ns 32:3 (Sept 1985), 378-79.
The phrase "a fabulous, formless darkness" comes from Eunapius via E. R. Dodds.

682. BRILLI, ATTILIO: "Dioniso, Cristo e il 'Fascio degli anni' in Yeats," *Studi urbinati di storia, filosofia e letteratura,* ns B / 43:2 (1969), 269-76.

683. BROWER, REUBEN ARTHUR: *The Fields of Light: An Experiment in Critical Reading.* NY: Oxford UP, 1951. xii, 218 pp.
See pp. 83-88.

683a. DILLON, GEORGE L.: *Introduction to Contemporary Linguistic Semantics.* Englewood Cliffs: Prentice-Hall, 1977. xix, 150 pp.
Contains a note on the semantics of "heart" in this poem, p. 41.

683b. HOHULIN, RICHARD: "Beyond Relations between Propositions," *Notes on Translation,* 122 (Nov 1987), 44-55.
On the problems involved in translating parts of the poem into Antipolo Ifugao, a language in the Philippines.

684. LYNEN, JOHN F.: "Forms of Time in Modern Poetry," *QQ*, 82:3 (Autumn 1975), 344-64.
Comments on this poem and on *A Vision*.

685. MARSH, DERICK RUPERT CLEMENT: *Creativity and Control*. Bundoora, Victoria: La Trobe U, 1970. 19 pp. (La Trobe U Inaugural Lecture. 12.)
See p. 18.

686. [POGER, SIDNEY]: "A Note on Yeats' 'Two Songs from a Play,'" *Eire*, 6:1 (Spring 1971), 143-44.
The crow is traditionally associated with Apollo, the god of poetry.

687. RAYAN, KRISHNA: *Suggestion and Statement in Poetry*. London: Athlone Press, 1972. ix, 182 pp.
See pp. 91-93.

688. RINGBOM, HÅKAN (ed): *Style and Text. Studies Presented to Nils Erik Enkvist*. Stockholm: Skriptor, 1975. 441 pp.
E. L. Epstein: "Syntactic Laws and Detemporalized Expression in Modern Literature," 305-16; on the first of the two songs.

689. TOLIVER, HAROLD: *Animate Illusions: Explorations of Narrative Structure*. Lincoln: U of Nebraska Press, 1974. ix, 412 pp.
Note on this poem and "Sailing to Byzantium," pp. 179-84.

690. URE, PETER: "Yeats and the Prophecy of Eunapius," *N&Q*, os 199 / ns 1:8 (Aug 1954), 358-59.
Neo-Platonic sources.

See also CA26, 53a, 66, 92, 128, CC99, 341, CD384, 1214, DA49, DB70, 90, 127, 199, DC61, 114, 267, DD168, 439, 680.

"Two Songs of a Fool"

691. JEFFARES, A. NORMAN: "'Two Songs of a Fool' and Their Explanation," *ES*, 26:6 (Dec 1945), 169-71.
Biographical explanation.

See also DD132.

"The Two Titans"

See BA3, 20, CD1218, EE389.

"The Two Trees"

692. MORTENSEN, ROBERT: "Yeats's *Vision* and 'The Two Trees,'" *SB*, 17 (1964), 200-22.
Yeats revised the poem "with *A Vision* in mind."

693. NILSEN, HELGE NORMANN: "'The Two Trees' by William Butler Yeats: The Symbolism of the Poem and Its Relation to Northrop Frye's Theory of Apocalyptic and Demonic Imagery," *OL*, 24:1 (1969), 72-76.

694. POPOT, RAYMONDE: "Lectures d'un poème de Yeats: 'The Two

Trees,'" *EI,* 4 (Dec 1979), 67-88.

See also CA12, 130, 150, CC46, CD258, DA30, 35(I), 49, DB50, 203, DC247, 275, DD479.

"The Unappeasable Host"

See CC1, DD770.

"Under Ben Bulben"

695. ALLEN, JAMES LOVIC: "'Horseman, Pass By!': Metaphor and Meaning in Yeats's Epitaph," *CP,* 10:1 (Spring 1977), 17-22.

696. COFFEY, BRIAN: "A Note on Rat Island," *UR,* 3:8 [1966?], 25-28.
Actually a note on the word "trade" in this poem and its implications for the writing of poetry, including some remarks on "The Lake Isle of Innisfree."

697. COMPRONE, JOSEPH J.: "Unity of Being and W. B. Yeats' 'Under Ben Bulben,'" *BSUF,* 11:3 (Summer 1970), 41-49.

698. CRONE, G. R.: "Horseman, Pass By," *N&Q,* os 214 / ns 16:7 (July 1969), 256-57.
The epitaph may derive from vignettes on the *Mappa mundi* in Hereford Cathedral.

699. FRÉCHET, RENÉ: "Aristocratiques désirs," *Artus,* 15 (Winter 1983-84), 26.

700. HASSETT, JOSEPH M.: "The Meaning of the 'Cold Eye' in Yeats's Epitaph," *Eire,* 18:1 (Spring 1983), 61-79.

701. HIRSCH, EDWARD: "Yeats's 'Under Ben Bulben," *Expl,* 39:4 (Summer 1981), 21.
The identity of the horseman in the epitaph.

702. HIRSCHBERG, STUART: "Art as the Looking Glass of Civilization in W. B. Yeats's 'Under Ben Bulben,'" *Studies,* 71:284 (Winter 1982), 399-404.

703. HÖLTGEN, KARL JOSEF, LOTHAR HÖNNIGHAUSEN, EBERHARD KREUTZER, and GÖTZ SCHMITZ (eds): *Tradition und Innovation in der englischen und amerikanischen Lyrik des 20. Jahrhunderts: Arno Esch zum 75. Geburtstag.* Tübingen: Niemeyer, 1986. xii, 271 pp.
E. Kreutzer: "W. B. Yeats und sein testamentarisches Credo in 'Under Ben Bulben,'" 95-110.

704. SHAKESPEARE, WILLIAM: *Timon of Athens.* Edited by H. J. Oliver. London: Methuen, 1959. lii, 155 pp. (Arden Edition of the Works of William Shakespeare.)
See p. 140 for the editor's suggestion that Yeats's epitaph is indebted to Timon's.

705. SWAMINATHAN, S. R.: "Shakespeare's *Hamlet* and Yeats's 'Under Ben Bulben,'" *LCrit,* 10:3 (Winter 1972), 35-46.

See also CA2, 7, 12, 63, 66, 91, 103, 112, 128, CB5, 234, CC51, 178,

CD92, 110, 561, 886, DA22, 34, 35(II), 45, 49, DC114, 267, 304a, 416, DD332, FC64, FE80, HD200, HF43.

"Under Saturn"

See CA112, DA38.

"Under the Moon"

See CC1, CD92.

"Under the Round Tower"

See CC130, 183, DD749.

"Upon a Dying Lady"

706. FREEMAN, JOHN: "Decadence," *Root and Branch,* 2:3 (Mar 1918), 55-58.
Criticizes section 2 as "decadent" and "rigidly conventional."

707. J.: "Yeats's 'Upon a Dying Lady,'" *Little R,* 4:5 (Sept 1917), 30-31.

See also AE104a, CA4, DA20, 49, DB210, DC133, DD250.

"Upon a House Shaken by the Land Agitation"

708. YOSHINO, MASAAKI: "Yeats's Logic of Death: The Fairy Poems and the Gregory Poems," *SELit,* English Number, 1985, 37-51.
Mainly a discussion of this poem, *On Baile's Strand,* and "An Irish Airman Foresees His Death."

See also CC130.

"Vacillation"

See CA4, 12, 14, 26, 53a, 91, 92, CB176, CC31, 44, 99, 231, CD458, 711, 887, 1010, DA14, 20, 35(II), 49, DB23, 50, 70, DC267, FC64.

"The Valley of the Black Pig"

See CA128, CC1, 260, 261, 341, DA11, DD770.

"Veronica's Napkin"

709. MURPHY, RUSSELL: "A New Source for 'Veronica's Napkin,'" *ELN,* 23:4 (June 1986), 42-49.
The source is Mrs. Arthur (Eugénie) Strong's *Apotheosis and After Life: Three Lectures on Certain Phases of Art and Religion in the Roman Empire* (1915), which also influenced "Byzantium." Both poems are concerned with the fate of the soul after death.

See also CA103, 128, DA36, DC267.

"The Wanderings of Oisin"

710. ALSPACH, RUSSELL K.: "Some Sources of Yeats's "'The Wanderings of Oisin,'" *PMLA*, 58:3 (Sept 1943), 849-66.
Michael Comyn's "The Lay of Oisin on the Land of Youth," other Ossianic material, Kickham's *Knocknagow*, Ferguson, and others.

711. BLAKE, JAMES JOSEPH: "William Butler Yeats's 'The Wanderings of Oisin' in Relation to Irish-Gaelic Ossianic Literature, English Translations and Adaptations of Ossianic Texts, and Nineteenth-Century Editorial Commentary about Them," Ph.D. thesis, New York U, 1979. iii, 406 pp. (*DAI*, 40:11 [May 1980], 5871A; reprinted *YeA*, 1 [1982], 214)

712. CLANCY, CHARLES J.: "Yeats's 'Oisin,'" *Eire 19*, 1 (3 Aug 1977), 17-24.

713. COSMAN, MADELEINE PELNER: "Mannered Passion: W. B. Yeats and the Ossianic Myths," *WHR*, 14:2 (Spring 1960), 163-71.
Purports to be a source study, but does not quote a single source as evidence. Besides that, rather weak on facts.

714. DALSIMER, ADELE M.: "W. B. Yeats' 'The Wanderings of Oisin': Blueprint for a Renaissance," *Eire*, 11:2 (Summer 1976), 56-76.
The poem as Yeats's model for the Irish writers of the 1890's.

715. FASS, BARBARA FRANCES: *La Belle Dame sans Merci & the Aesthetics of Romanticism*. Detroit: Wayne State UP, 1974. 312 pp.
"Artist and Philistine," 224-46, a discussion of the influence of Keats and Swinburne on the poem.

716. JOSEPH, CHRISTIANE: "Les voyages d'Usheen," in Genet: *William Butler Yeats* (1981, CA32), 129-45.

717. MARSHALL, KATHLEEN ENGEL: "Modern Irish Poets and Dramatists and the Fenian Circle," Ph.D. thesis, Trinity College Dublin, 1973. iii, 292 pp.
Discusses this poem on pp. 39-68; *Diarmuid and Grania* on pp. 156-93.

718. OSAKA, OSAMU: "A Note on W. B. Yeats's 'The Wanderings of Oisin,'" *Studies in English Language and Literature* [Fukuoka], 16 (June 1966), 107-56.

719. REED, JOHN ROBERT: *Decadent Style*. Athens: Ohio UP, 1985. xiv, 274 pp.
See pp. 92-94 for a discussion as a decadent poem.

720. SIDNELL, MICHAEL J.: "The Allegory of Yeats's 'The Wanderings of Oisin,'" *CLQ*, 15:2 (June 1979), 137-51.

721. TAKADA, ERIKO: "Yeatsian Myth as Seen in 'The Wanderings of Oisin,'" *Bulletin of Seisen Women's College*, 28 (1980), 46-65.

722. TANNEN, DEBORAH: "Celtic Elements in Three Works by William Butler Yeats," *Folklore and Mythology Studies*, 2 (1978), 30-35.
This poem, *The Shadowy Waters,* and "Three Songs to the One

Burden."

See also BA3, CA4, 7, 12, 26, 61, 63, 69, 91, 112, 114, 123, 126, 128, CB440, CC54, 55, 61, 167, 171a, 309, 345, CD622, 713, 1214, DA1, 11, 49, DC62, 188, 342, 383, DD770, EE219, 499, FE80.

"The Watch-Fire"

723. MAHONY, CHRISTINA HUNT, and EDWARD O'SHEA: "A Note on 'The Watch-Fire,'" *Poetry,* 135:4 (Jan 1980), 224-26.

"What Is the Explanation of It All?"

724. GOULD, WARWICK: "'What Is the Explanation of It All?': Yeats's 'Little Poem about Nothing,'" *YeA,* 5 (1987), 212-13.
A poem written by Yeats for Edith Shackleton Heald in 1938.

See also AE21.

"What Magic Drum" (part 7 of "Supernatural Songs")

725. SMITH, DENIS E., and F. A. C. WILSON: "The Source of Yeats's 'What Magic Drum?'" *PLL,* 9:2 (Spring 1973), 197-201.
Bhagwan Shri Hamsa's *The Holy Mountain*.

See also CA126, DC267.

"What Then?"

726. SKELTON, ROBIN: "The First Printing of W. B. Yeats's 'What Then?'" *IrB,* 2:3/4 (Autumn 1963), 129-30.
Includes some variants not recorded in the *Variorum Edition*.

727. SWAMINATHAN, S. R.: "Bhartrihari, Yeats and Tagore: History of a Poem," *VQ,* 38:1-2 (1972-73), 72-75.
The poem is probably derived from some lines in the work of the legendary Sanskrit poet Bhartrihari whom Yeats may have read in Tagore's translation.

See also CA53a, CD876, DA34, DB70, 223, DC153.

"The Wheel"

728. SALERNO, NICHOLAS A.: "A Note on Yeats and Leonardo da Vinci," *TCL,* 5:4 (Jan 1960), 197-98.
The poem echoes a passage from Leonardo's notebooks.

729. SAUL, GEORGE BRANDON: "Yeatsian Brevities," *N&Q,* os 199 / ns 1:12 (Dec 1954), 535-36.
A note on this poem and on "Towards Break of Day."

See also CA130.

"When You Are Old"

730. BERGGREN, KERSTIN: Note on the poem in Swedish, *Studiekamraten,* 48:8 (1966), 150.

731. BLUMENTHAL, MARIE LUISE: "Über zwei Gedichte von Ronsard und von W. B. Yeats," *Neuphilologische Zeitschrift,* 3:1 (1951), 11-15.
A comparison with Ronsard's "Quand vous serez bien vieille."

732. CALLAN, NORMAN: *Poetry in Practice.* London: Drummond, 1938. xii, 189 pp.
The poems of Yeats and Ronsard, pp. 174-76.

733. JEUNE, SIMON: *Littérature générale et littérature comparée: Essai d'orientation.* Paris: Minard, 1968. 147 pp. (Situation. 17.)
"Yeats, imitateur de Ronsard," 111-18.

734. MACKEY, WILLIAM F.: "Yeats's Debt to Ronsard on a *Carpe Diem* Theme," *Comparative Literature Studies,* 5:19 (1946), 4-7.

735. MACMANUS, FRANCIS: "Adventures of a Sonnet," *IrM,* 69:812 (Feb 1941), 85-90.
Yeats and Ronsard.

736. MINTON, ARTHUR: "Yeats' 'When You Are Old,'" *Expl,* 5:7 (May 1947), no. 49.
See also Marion Witt, 6:1 (Oct 1947), no. 6; and Elisabeth Schneider, :7 (May 1948), no. 50.

737. RYDING, ERIC S.: "Yeats's 'When You Are Old,'" *Expl,* 38:1 (Fall 1979), 21-22.

738. SNOW, WILBERT: "A Yeats-Longfellow Parallel," *MLN,* 74:4 (Apr 1959), 302-3.
Yeats's poem and Longfellow's *Outre-Mer.*

See also CB363, DC49, 295, DD489, 627, HD104, HF36.

"Whence Had They Come?" (part 8 of "Supernatural Songs")

See CA126, DD246.

"Where My Books Go"

739. BERG, VIOLA JACOBSON: *Pathways for the Poet: Poetry Patterns Explained and Illustrated.* Milford, Minn.: Mott Media, 1977. 235 pp.
Invents a stanzaic form called "The Yeats," of which this poem is the original pattern (pp. 201-2).

"While I, from That Reed-throated Whisperer. . . ."

See CA128, CC130, DB233.

"The White Birds"

740. DAICHES, DAVID: *The Place of Meaning in Poetry.* Edinburgh:

Oliver & Boyd, 1935. v, 80 pp.
On the symbolism of this poem and of "Symbols," pp. 42-44.

See also DB252.

"Who Goes with Fergus?"

741. BRYSON, LYMAN, and others (eds): *Symbols and Society*. NY: Cooper Square, 1964 [1955]. xi, 611 pp. (Symposium of the Conference on Science, Philosophy, and Religion. 14.)
William Y. Tindall: "The Literary Symbol," 337-67; contains a note on this poem, pp. 364-65.
William F. Lynch: "The Evocative Symbol," 427-52; contains a note on "Sailing to Byzantium," pp. 431-32.

742. EMPSON, WILLIAM: *Seven Types of Ambiguity*. Harmondsworth: Penguin Books, 1965 [1930]. xiv, 256 pp. (Peregrine Book. Y2.)
Note on the poem, pp. 187-91. See criticism by Andrew Rutherford: "Yeats' 'Who Goes with Fergus?'" *Expl*, 13:7 (May 1955), no. 41.

743. GARAB, ARRA M.: "The Judeo-Christian Background of W. B. Yeats's 'Who Goes with Fergus?'" *ArQ*, 39:3 (Autumn 1983), 215-22.

744. GREENBAUM, SIDNEY, GEOFFREY LEECH, and JAN SVARTVIK (eds): *Studies in English Linguistics for Randolph Quirk*. London: Longman, 1980. xvi, 304 pp.
Edmund L. Epstein: "Non-Restrictive Modifiers: Poetic Features of Language," 221-34.

745. NEWELL, KENNETH B.: "Yeats's Fergus as a Sun God," *Eire*, 13:1 (Spring 1978), 76-86.
The poem is best explained by taking Fergus's nature to be that of a sun god. Includes comments on *The Countess Cathleen*.

See also DA36, DC62, 109.

"Why Should Not Old Man Be Mad?"

746. WHEALE, JOHN: *N&Q*, os 225 / ns 27:6 (Dec 1980), 537-38.
Query concerning the identity of the girl; thinks that she cannot have been Iseult Gonne.

"The Wild Old Wicked Man"

747. GARDNER, C. O.: "An Analysis of Yeats's 'Wild Old Wicked Man,'" *Critical Survey*, 2:2 (Summer 1965), 104-8.

See also DA4, 28, DB70.

"The Wild Swans at Coole"

748. BROOKS, CLEANTH, JOHN THIBAUT PURSER, and ROBERT PENN WARREN (eds): *An Approach to Literature: A Collection of Prose and Verse with Analyses and Discussions*. Alternate 4th edition. NY: Appleton-Century-Crofts, 1967 [1935]. xvii, 888 pp.

Note on this poem, pp. 311-12; on "That the Night Come," 317-19; on "A Prayer for My Daughter," 359-63.

749. C., R. J.: "Yeats' 'The Wild Swans at Coole,'" *Expl,* 2:4 (Jan 1944), Q20.
Asks for Yeats's pronunciation of rhyme words in this poem and in "Under the Round Tower." Answer by T. O. Mabbott, 3:1 (Oct 1944), no. 5; by Marion Witt, :2 (Nov 1944), no. 17.

750. CASWELL, ROBERT W.: "Yeats's Odd Swan at Coole," *Eire,* 4:2 (Summer 1969), 81-86.
There is a discrepancy between the 59 swans at the beginning of the poem and the pairs of swans at the end. The odd swan is related to the solitary poet on the shore.

751. CROFT, P. J. (ed): *Autograph Poetry in the English Language: Facsimiles of Original Manuscripts from the Fourteenth to the Twentieth Century.* Compiled and edited with an introduction, commentary and transcripts by P. J. Croft. London: Cassell, 1973. 2 vols.
Facsimile and transcript of a late draft of the poem together with note, 2:152-53.

752. DESAI, RUPIN W.: "Yeats's Swans and Andersen's Ugly Duckling," *CLQ,* 9:6 (June 1971), 330-35.

752a. FOX, LINDA L.: "Nine and Fifty as Symbol in Yeats's 'The Wild Swans at Coole,'" *ELN,* 26:1 (Sept 1988), 54-58.
This particular number refers to "Yeats's view of the cyclicity of history," because it "signals the beginning of an hour's last minute."

753. GÖLLER, KARL HEINZ (ed): *Die englische Lyrik: Von der Renaissance bis zur Gegenwart.* Düsseldorf: Bagel, 1968. 2 vols.
Gisela and Gerhard Hoffmann: "William Butler Yeats: 'The Wild Swans at Coole,'" 2:299-308. Gisela Hoffmann: "William Butler Yeats: 'Sailing to Byzantium,'" 2:309-20.

754. HAHN, SISTER M. NORMA: "Yeats' 'The Wild Swans at Coole': Meaning and Structure," *CE,* 22:6 (Mar 1961), 419-21.

755. MCFARLAND, THOMAS: *Romanticism and the Forms of Ruin: Wordsworth, Coleridge, and Modalities of Fragmentation.* Princeton: Princeton UP, 1981. xxxiv, 433 pp.
See pp. 282-84.

756. *National Poetry Festival Held in the Library of Congress October 22-24, 1962: Proceedings.* Washington, D.C.: Library of Congress, General Reference and Bibliography Division, 1964. ii, 367 pp.
Léonie Adams: "The Problem of Form," 275-80; refers to this poem, pp. 278-80.

757. PUHVEL, MARTIN: "Yeats's 'The Wild Swans at Coole,'" *Expl,* 45:1 (Autumn 1986), 29-30.
The 59 swans, hard to count in reality, come from the 59 silver bells in "Thomas Rymer."

758. SHANLEY, J. LINDON: "Thoreau's Geese and Yeats's Swans," *AL,* 30:3 (Nov 1958), 361-64.
The poem echoes the "Spring" chapter in *Walden.*

759. SHAPIRO, KARL: "Prosody as the Meaning," *Poetry*, 73:6 (Mar 1949), 336-51.
Note on this poem, pp. 340-41.

760. VOGEL, JOSEPH F.: "Yeats's 'Nine-and-Fifty' Swans," *ELN*, 5:4 (June 1968), 297-300.
The probable source for this unusual number is "Thomas Rymer."

761. YOUNIS, RAYMOND AARON: "Yeats's 'The Wild Swans at Coole,'" *Expl*, 46:4 (Summer 1988), 25-26.

See also BB97, CA12, 14, 60, 91, 110, DA34, 35(II), 36, 43, 49, DB28, 70, 90, 203, 242, DC49, 275, DD41.

The Wild Swans at Coole

762. DEELY, JOHN (ed): *Semiotics 1984*. Lanham, Md.: UP of America, 1984. xii, 739 pp. (Proceedings of the 9th Annual Meeting of the Semiotic Society of America.)
Len Hatfield: "Signs of Authority in Yeats' *The Wild Swans at Coole*," 13-22.

763. GORDAN, JOHN D. "An Anniversary Exhibition: The Henry W. and Albert A. Berg Collection, 1940-1965. Part II," *BNYPL*, 69:9 (Nov 1965), 597-608.
"William Butler Yeats: The Holograph of *The Wild Swans at Coole*," 605.

764. HATFIELD, LEONARD L.: "Speaking with Authority: Credibility and Authenticity in Browning's *Men and Women* and Yeats' *The Wild Swans at Coole*," °Ph.D. thesis, Indiana U, 1986. 232 pp. (*DAI*, 47:8 [Feb 1987], 3047A)

765. MARTZ, LOUIS LOHR, and AUBREY WILLIAMS (eds): *The Author in His Work: Essays on a Problem in Criticism*. New Haven: Yale UP, 1978. xix, 407 pp.
David Young: "'The Living World for Text': Life and Art in *The Wild Swans at Coole*," 143-60. On the "effective ways" in which Yeats uses "his own life and self as a key to the order and meaning" of the poems in this volume.

766. O'BRIEN, JAMES H.: "Yeats's Discoveries of Self in *The Wild Swans at Coole*," *CLQ*, 8:1 (Mar 1968), 1-13.

767. ROSENTHAL, M. L.: "Notes on the 'Memory'-Sequence in Yeats's *The Wild Swans at Coole*," *Yeats*, 5 (1987), 133-41.

768. YOSHINO, MASAAKI: [In Japanese] "William B. Yeats and Maud Gonne: Revision of *The Wild Swans at Coole*," *Studies in English Language and Literature*, 33 (Jan 1983), 15-39.
English summary, pp. 122-23.

See also CA22, 170, CB129, G373-86 and note.

The Wind among the Reeds

769. DAYAN, JOAN: "The Love Poems of *The Wind among the Reeds:* A Circle Drawn around the Absolute," *CLS*, 16:1 (Mar 1979), 79-87.

770. GROSSMAN, ALLEN RICHARD: *Poetic Knowledge in the Early Yeats: A Study of "The Wind among the Reeds."* Charlottesville: UP of Virginia, 1969. xxv, 240 pp.

Based on °"The Last Judgment of the Imagination: A Study of Yeats' *The Wind among the Reeds*," Ph.D. thesis, Brandeis U, 1960. An analysis more of the sources and the background than of the poems themselves, with particular emphasis on the occult tradition. Analyzed in sections DD and FA.

Reviews:

- Arra M. Garab: "The Legacy of Yeats," *JML*, 1:1 (1970), 137-40.
- Giles Gunn, *MP*, 69:1 (Aug 1971), 87-91.
- Edwin Honig: "On Knowing Yeats," *VQR*, 45:4 (Autumn 1969), 700-704.
- J. R. Mulryne, *MLR*, 66:3 (July 1971), 680-81.
- Patrick Murray, *Studies*, 59:234 (Summer 1970), 215-18.
- Marjorie Perloff: "Yeats as Gnostic," *ConL*, 12:4 (Autumn 1971), 554-61.

771. HOLDSWORTH, CAROLYN ANNE: "'The Book of My Numberless Dreams': A Manuscript Study of Yeats's *The Wind among the Reeds*," Ph.D. thesis, Tulane U, 1983. x, 309 pp. (*DAI*, 44:9 [Mar 1984], 2763A-64A; reprinted *Yeats*, 3 [1985], 207-8, and *YeA*, 4 [1986], 312)

Contains chapters on the early reviews of the book, the writing and publishing history, Yeats's habits of composition and revision, and an analysis of "He Tells of the Perfect Beauty," followed by transcriptions of the MS. versions of the poems and various appendices.

772. PRUITT, VIRGINIA D.: "Yeats' *The Wind among the Reeds*," *Expl*, 35:4 (Summer 1977), 19-20.

The symbolism of wind and reed in the poems of this volume.

773. SCHLEIFER, RONALD: "Principles, Proper Names, and the Personae of Yeats's *The Wind among the Reeds* ," *Eire*, 16:1 (Spring 1981), 71-89.

See also CB29, 185, CC1, 239, 290, DB231, FA26, G147-62 and note, 1356.

The Winding Stair

774. ACKLEY, RANDALL WILLIAM: "*The Winding Stair:* Variations on a Theme," *RS*, 37:4 (Dec 1969), 313-19.

The theme of "life."

775. LEMIEUX, SISTER M. ST. AUGUSTINE: "Modes of the 'I': Yeats's Selves in *The Winding Stair and Other Poems*," Ph.D. thesis, U of Notre Dame, 1966. vii, 278 pp. (*DAI*, 27:4 [Oct 1966], 1059A-60A)

776. O'BRIEN, JAMES H.: "Self vs. Soul in Yeats's *The Winding Stair*," *Eire*, 3:1 (Spring 1968), 23-39.

See also CA22, CB131, CC222, CD1019, DA14, G537, 554-55, 567-604.

"Wisdom"

See CA128, DA49, DD432, 680.

"The Withering of the Boughs"

See CC1, CD1063, DA35(II).

"A Woman Homer Sung"

777. JEFFARES, A. NORMAN: "A Source for 'A Woman Homer Sung,'" *N&Q,* 195:5 (4 May 1950), 104.
In Shelley's *Hellas.*

See also DA36.

"A Woman Young and Old"

778. ALLEN, JAMES L.: "Yeats's 'Her Vision in the Wood,'" *Expl,* 18:8 (May 1960), no. 45.

779. CURTLER, ELIZABETH SEAVER: "'A Woman Young and Old': Love in Yeats's Vision," °Ph.D. thesis, Duke U, 1977. 232 pp. (*DAI,* 38:8 [Feb 1978], 4840A)
Includes a discussion of the sequence's relation to *A Vision.*

780. FARREN, ROBERT: *Towards an Appreciation of Poetry.* Dublin: Metropolitan Publishing Co., 1947. 76 pp.
Note on "Meeting," pp. 54-55.

781. JUMPER, WILL C.: "Form *versus* Structure in a Poem of W. B. Yeats," *Iowa English Yearbook,* 7 (Fall 1962), 41-44.
On "From the *Antigone.*"

782. NEILL, JEFFREY P.: "The Study of Literature: An Introductory Method," *CE,* 31:5 (Feb 1970), 450-62.
Contains an interpretation of "Father and Child."

See also CA20, 53a, 66, CD1010, DA4, 14, DB127, 210, DC77, 133, 141, DD56, 417, 460, DE33.

"Words"

See CA14, CD1214, DA30.

Words for Music Perhaps

783. DONOGHUE, DENIS: "The Vigour of Its Blood: Yeats's *Words for Music Perhaps,*" *KR,* 21:3 (Summer 1959), 376-87.

See also CC141, CD1010, DA20, 49, DB70, 210, DC77, 178, G565-66 and note.

DE Less Substantial Material

1. ANON.: "Living English Poets: William Butler Yeats," *Current Literature,* 31:2 (Aug 1901), 244-45.

2. ANON.: "The Poetry of W. B. Yeats (1865-1939)," *English,* 15:89 (Summer 1965), 167-69.

3. ANON.: "Irish Poetry," *SatRL,* 2 Feb 1901, 144-45.

4. ANON.: "Poetry Album: William Butler Yeats," *Scholastic,* 8-13 Dec 1941, 21.

5. ANON.: "Poetry: The Quality of Recent Verse. Mr. Yeats as a Prophet," *Times,* 4 Nov 1919, 45.

6. ARNS, KARL (ed): *Jüngstes England: Anthologie und Einführung.* Leipzig: Kuner, 1925. vii, 322 pp.

"Die Iren," 275-87; on Yeats, pp. 278-81.

7. BACONSKY, ANATOL E.: *Panorama poeziei universale contemporane.* Bucureşti: Albatros, 1972. 911 pp.

"William Butler Yeats," 806-13; a short introduction and translations of seven poems.

8. BARNARD, ROBERT: *A Short History of English Literature.* Oxford: Blackwell / Oslo: Universitetsforlaget, 1984. vii, 218 pp.

Note on Yeats's poetry, pp. 145-48.

9. BEACH, JOSEPH WARREN: *The Concept of Nature in Nineteenth-Century English Poetry.* NY: Macmillan, 1936. xii, 618 pp.

"Yeats and AE," 535-38.

10. BECKETT, SAMUEL: *Disjecta: Miscellaneous Writings and a Dramatic Fragment.* Edited with a foreword by Ruby Cohn. London: Calder, 1983. 178 pp.

"Recent Irish Poetry," 70-76; reprinted from *BmL,* 86:515 (Aug 1934), 235-36 (where it was published under the pseudonym Andrew Belis); and from *Lace Curtain,* 4 (Summer 1971), 58-63. Contains a few notes on Yeats's poetry.

11. BHAWANI SHANKAR: *Studies in Modern English Poetry.* Allahabad: Students' Friends, 1936. xi, 279 pp.

On Yeats's poetry, pp. 46-50 and passim (see index).

12. BICKLEY, FRANCIS: "The Tendency of Modern Poetry," *Oxford and Cambridge R,* 3 (Lent Term 1908), 105-20.

See pp. 115-16.

13. BIRÓ, LAJOS PÁL: *A modern angol irodalom törtênete 1890-1941.* Budapest: Hungária Kiadás, [1942]. 287 pp.

See pp. 139-45.

14. BLUMENFELD, JACOB P.: "Convention and Modern Poetry: A Study in the Development of Period Mannerisms," Ph.D. thesis, U of Tennessee, 1957. vii, 214 pp. (*DAI,* 18:4 [Apr 1958], 1427)

Refers to some Yeats poems, passim, but does not expand.

15. BOURNIQUEL, CAMILLE: *Irlande.* Paris: Editions du Seuil, 1955. 192 pp. (Collection Petite Planète. 5.)

English edition: *Ireland.* Translated by John Fisher. London: Vista Books, 1960. 192 pp. (Vista Books. W8.). "Abbey Street," 157-63; on the Irish theater. "La mort d'Ossian," 165-69; on Yeats's poetry.

16. BOYD, JOHN D.: *A College Poetics*. Lanham, Md.: UP of America, 1983. xv, 332 pp.
See index for some notes on Yeats's poetry.

17. BROWN, HARRY, and JOHN MILSTEAD: *What the Poem Means: Summaries of 1000 Poems*. Glenview, Ill.: Scott, Foresman, 1970. v, 314 pp.
See pp. 296-304 for short synopses of 25 Yeats poems.

18. BUNNELL, WILLIAM STANLEY: *Ten Twentieth-Century Poets*. Bath: Brodie, [1963]. 89 pp.
See pp. 64-74 for an introduction to Yeats's poetry on the freshman level.

19. BURNSHAW, STANLEY: *The Seamless Web: Language-Thinking, Creature-Knowledge, Art-Experience*. NY: Braziller, 1970. xv, 320 pp.
Scattered notes on Yeats's poetry, passim (see index).

20. CECIL, LORD DAVID: *Library Looking-Glass: A Personal Anthology*. London: Constable, 1975. xi, 299 pp.
Contains a few notes on some of Yeats's poems (see index).

21. CHAKRAVARTY, AMIYA: *Modern Tendencies in English Literature*. Calcutta: Book Exchange, [1945?]. x, 74 pp. (Greater India Series. 5.)
"Yeats and the Moderns," 1-9. When Yeats climbed the winding stair of his tower, he became a modern poet.

22. CHILDS, KENNETH W.: "The Orphic Style," °Ph.D. thesis, U of Utah, 1972. 88 pp. (*DAI*, 33:6 [Dec 1972], 2886A)
On some Yeats poems, according to abstract.

23. CHILMAN, ERIC: "W. B. Yeats," *Poetry R*, 4:2 (Feb 1914), 70-72.

24. CLAUSEN, CHRISTOPHER: *The Place of Poetry: Two Centuries of an Art in Crisis*. Lexington: UP of Kentucky, 1981. ix, 145 pp.
Scattered remarks on Yeats (see index).

25. COLERIDGE, STEPHEN: *An Evening in My Library among the English Poets*. London: Lane, 1916. ix, 217 pp.
See pp. 188-90; finds deficiencies of "natural justification" in Yeats's poetry.

26. COLLINS, H. P.: *Modern Poetry*. London: Cape, 1925. 224 pp.
"Where We Stand," pp. 9-18; notes that Yeats is outside the tradition of English poetry.

27. COUSINS, JAMES H.: "William Butler Yeats: The Celtic Lyrist," *Poetry R*, 1:4 (Apr 1912), 156-58.
"Yeats' poetry will long outlive the poet, though at present the poet has outlived his poetry."

28. COWELL, RAYMOND: *The Critical Enterprise: English Studies in Higher Education*. London: Allen & Unwin, 1975. 156 pp.
Some notes on Yeats's poetry, passim (see index).

29. DAVISON, EDWARD: *Some Modern Poets and Other Critical Essays*. Freeport, N.Y.: Books for Libraries Press, 1968 [1928]. ix, 255 pp.
"Three Irish Poets," 175-96; reprinted from *EJ*, 15:5 (May 1926), 327-36. AE, Yeats, and James Stephens.

30. DOBRÉE, BONAMY: *The Broken Cistern*. London: Cohen & West, 1954. ix, 158 pp. (Clark Lectures. 1952-53.)
Some notes on Yeats's poetry, passim (see index). The original title of the lectures was "Public Themes in English Poetry."

31. DOORN, WILLEM VAN: "How It Strikes a Contemporary: A Pageant with Comments," *ES*, 5:6 (Dec 1923), 193-207.

32. DOUGLAS, ALFRED, LORD: *The Principles of Poetry: An Address Delivered before the Royal Society of Literature on December 2nd, 1943*. [London: Richards Press, 1943]. 27 pp.
Some disparaging remarks, pp. 22-23.

33. DUNNING, JENNIFER: "Dances Made from Poems on Two Stages," *NYT*, 6 Mar 1981, C1, C11.
Preview of a performance of a dance cycle based on the Crazy Jane poems and "A Woman Young and Old" by the American Theater Laboratory, NY, directed by Ara Fitzgerald, composer Wall Matthews; perhaps identical with the show listed under HE33. See also Jennifer Dunning: "Dance: Ara Fitzgerald and 2 by Yeats," *NYT*, 8 Mar 1981, section 1, 48.

34. DYSON, A. E. (ed): *Poetry Criticism & Practice: Developments since the Symbolists. A Casebook*. London: Macmillan, 1986. 217 pp.
Reprinted pieces, numerous references to Yeats (see index).

35. EDFELT, JOHANNES: *Strövtåg*. Stockholm: Bonniers, 1941. 179 pp.
"En lyrikers väg" [A poet's way], 94-101.

36. EDGAR, PELHAM: "The Poetry of William Butler Yeats," *Globe*, 24 Dec 1904, Magazine section, 5.

37. ELLIOTT, GEORGE P.: *A Piece of Lettuce: Personal Essays on Books, Beliefs, American Places, and Growing Up in a Strange Country*. NY: Random House, 1964. xi, 217 pp.
See pp. 36-42 for Elliott's struggles whether or not to like Yeats's poetry.

38. ERSKINE, JOHN: *The Delight of Great Books*. London: Nash & Grayson, 1928. 312 pp.
"Modern Irish Poetry," 295-312; on Yeats, pp. 303-5.

39. FREER, ALLEN, and JOHN ANDREW (eds): *Cambridge Book of English Verse, 1900-1939*. Cambridge: UP, 1970. xi, 205 pp.
"W. B. Yeats," 24-26; notes on several poems, 150-66.

40. GIFFORD, HENRY: *Comparative Literature*. London: Routledge & Kegan Paul, 1969. xii, 99 pp.
On Yeats as a writer of Irish poetry in the English language, pp. 21-24.

41. GÖLLER, KARL HEINZ (ed): *Epochen der englischen Lyrik*. Düsseldorf: Bagel, 1970. 278 pp.
Rudolf Haas: "Die moderne englische Lyrik," 209-35; on Yeats, pp. 220-22 and passim.

42. GRIERSON, HERBERT JOHN CLIFFORD, and J. C. SMITH: *A Critical History of English Poetry*. Revised edition. London: Chatto & Windus, 1950 [1944]. viii, 539 pp.
See pp. 476-79.

43. GRIGORESCU, DAN: *Direcţii în poezia secolului XX.* Bucureşti: Editura Eminescu, 1975. 336 pp.
See index for some notes on Yeats's poetry.

44. GRIGSON, GEOFFREY: *The Private Art: A Poetry Notebook.* London: Allison & Busby, 1982. iv, 231 pp.
Short references to Yeats (see index).

45. GUPTA, N. DAS: *Literature of the Twentieth Century.* Gwalior: Kitab Ghar, 1967. 225, vii pp.
"W. B. Yeats," 30-38; a survey of his poetry. On the Irish theater, pp. 104-8, 110-14.

46. GUTNER, M. (ed): *Antologii͡a novoĭ angliĭskoĭ poezii.* Leningrad: Gosudarstvennoe izdatel'stvo "Khudozhestvennai͡a literatura," 1937. 455 pp.
"Uil'i͡am Betler Eĭts," 245-54, 14 poems translated into Russian; note on the poems, pp. 437-38.

47. GWYNN, STEPHEN: "Irish Nationalist Poetry," *Literature,* 23 Sept 1899, 298-300.

48. HALDAR, S.: "The Poetry of William Butler Yeats," *Modern R,* 101:602 (Feb 1957), 139-47.

49. HART, JEFFREY: "Yeats: No Rootless Flower," *Triumph,* 5:3 (Mar 1970), 28-30.

50. HILLYER, ROBERT: *In Pursuit of Poetry.* NY: McGraw-Hill, 1960. xiii, 231 pp.
Criticizes the obscurity of Yeats's poetry, pp. 178-81.

51. HOAGLAND, KATHLEEN (ed): *1000 Years of Irish Poetry: The Gaelic and Anglo-Irish Poets from Pagan Times to the Present.* NY: Devin-Adair, 1947. liv, 830 pp.
"Anglo-Irish Poetry," xli-liv. Patrick MacDonough: "Bring Home the Poet," 629; a poem on Yeats.

52. HOBSBAUM, PHILIP: *Tradition and Experiment in English Poetry.* London: Macmillan, 1979. xiii, 343 pp.
See pp. 230-31.

53. HODGSON, GERALDINE EMMA: "Some Irish Poetry," *ContempR,* 98:537 (Sept 1910), 323-40.
Reprinted in *Living Age,* 29 Oct 1910, 282-93. On Yeats's poetry, passim; on *The Countess Cathleen,* pp. 332-37.

54. ———: *Criticism at a Venture.* London: Macdonald, 1919. vii, 215 pp.
Scattered remarks, passim (see index).

55. ———: "Three Candles: III. Ireland," *Quest* [London], 19:4 (July 1928), 400-413.
Dream, vision, and escape in modern Anglo-Irish poetry, including Yeats's.

56. HOGGART, RICHARD: "An Approach to Yeats," *School Librarian,* 7:3 (Dec 1954), 173-74, 177-80.
An overview of the poetry for "senior forms of grammar schools."

57. HOLLOWAY, JOHN: "How Goes the Weather?" in Jeffares: *Yeats, Sligo and Ireland* (1980, CA51), 89-97.
The West of Ireland weather, especially the wind and the rain, and its occasional appearances in Yeats's poetry.

58. HUNGERLAND, ISABEL C.: *Poetic Discourse*. Berkeley: U of California Press, 1958. v, 177 pp. (California U Publications in Philosophy. 33.)
References to Yeats's poetry on pp. 8-9, 12, 22, 25-26, 41, 92, 117-18, 129, 134.

59. HUNTER, JIM (ed): *Modern Poets*. London: Faber & Faber, 1968. 4 vols.
Notes on Yeats's poetry, 1:13-14, 44-50.

60. JAKOBITZ, ELLY: *Der Ausdruck des poetischen Empfindens in der modernen englischen Poesie*. Greifswald: Adler, 1935. 111 pp.
A Dr.phil. thesis, U of Greifswald, 1935. On symbols in Yeats's poetry, pp. 88-96. Negligible.

61. JOHNSON, LIONEL: "On Irish Poets Writing English Verse," *CathW*, 92:552 (Mar 1911), 858-61.

62. JUMPER, WILL C., LILLIAN SARA ROBINSON, and ELAINE SHOWALTER: Correspondence concerning an issue on "Women and the Profession" with supporting arguments taken from Yeats's poetry, *CE*, 33:2 (Nov 1971), 247-50.

63. JURAK, MIRKO (ed): *English Poetry: An Anthology with a Critical and Historical Introduction for Foreign Students*. Ljubljana: Državna Založba Slovenije, 1972. 239 pp.
"William Butler Yeats," 204-12; texts of five poems with notes and questions.

64. KAPOOR, A. N.: *Modern English Poetry (1900-1920): The Decline and Fall of the Naturalistic Tradition*. Allahabad: Kitab Mahal, 1962. vi, 169 pp. (Masters of English Literature Series. 8.)
"William Butler Yeats," 112-24.

64a. KAVANAGH, PAUL, and PETER KUCH: "Scored for the Voice: An Interview with Vincent Buckley," *Southerly*, 47:3 (Sept 1987), 249-66.
Includes some comments on Yeats's poetry.

65. K[ELLER], T. G.: "The Poet of the Abbey Theatre: Evolution of Mr. W. B. Yeats," *Northern Whig*, 3 Nov 1908, 5.
Surveys the poetical work and concludes: "The boughs of his lyrical impulse have indeed withered."

66. KELLY, T. J.: *The Focal Word: An Introduction to Poetry*. Brisbane: Jacaranda Press, 1965. x, 317 pp.
Notes on some Yeats poems, pp. 261-68.

67. KING, RICHARD ASHE: "Mr. W. B. Yeats," *BmL*, 12:72 (Sept 1897), 142-43.
Yeats is a "distinctively Irish" poet.

68. KING, S. K.: "W. B. Yeats: Six Poems," *Crux*, 6:2 (Apr-June 1972), 25-28.

69. KINSELLA, THOMAS (ed): *The New Oxford Book of Irish Verse*. Ox-

ford: Oxford UP, 1986. xxx, 423 pp.
The "Introduction," xxiii-xxx, includes some comments on Yeats. A selection of seven poems appears on pp. 309-16.

70. KOCH, KENNETH, and KATE FARRELL: *Sleeping on the Wing: An Anthology of Modern Poetry with Essays on Reading and Writing*. NY: Random House, 1981. xvii, 315 pp.
"William Butler Yeats," 77-81.

71. KOPCEWICZ, ANDRZEJ: *Funkcja obrazu w strukturze wiersza: Na podstawie wczesnej poezji anglo-amerykańskiej XX w*. Poznań: Uniwersytet im. Adama Mickiewicza, 1969. 132 pp. (Uniwersytet im. Adama Mickiewicza w Poznaniu. Prace wydziału filologicznogo. Seria Filologia angielska. 2.)
Contains a few notes on the imagery of Yeats's poems.

72. KORAB, KARL: *Irland*. Mit 102 Farbabbildungen nach Photographien und 20 Reproduktionen nach Zeichnungen von Karl Korab. Gedichte von W. B. Yeats. Wien: Brandstätter, 1982. 128 pp.
A book of color photographs and drawings with extracts from Yeats's poetry in German translation.

73. KRUZHKOV, GRIGORIĬ: "'Zhizn' rozhdaet literatury, kak strast' rozhdaet cheloveka'--U. B. Ĭeĭts," *Poeziia*, 36 (1983), 177-80.
"Life produces literature as passion produces people"; note on Yeats and translations of four poems.

74. LALOU, RENÉ: *Panorama de la littérature anglaise contemporaine*. Paris: Kra, 1927. 251 pp.
"Yeats et la poésie," 182-89.

75. LANGBAUM, ROBERT: *The Poetry of Experience: The Dramatic Monologue in Modern Literary Tradition*. London: Chatto & Windus, 1957. 246 pp.
Some notes, passim (see index).

76. LAWLER, JUSTUS GEORGE: *Celestial Pantomime: Poetic Structures of Transcendence*. New Haven: Yale UP, 1979. xi, 270 pp.
See index for some notes.

77. LEGRAS, CHARLES: *Chez nos contemporains d'Angleterre*. Paris: Ollendorff, 1901. iii, 332 pp.
"W. B. Yeats & William Watson," 207-19.

78. LESLIE, SHANE: "Wiliam [sic] Yeats." Translated into French by Georgette Camille, *Echanges*, 5 (Dec 1931), 86-91.

79. LEVAL, ROGER DE: *5 essais sur la poésie anglaise contemporaine*. Préface de Brand Whitlock. Paris: Editions gauloises, [1924]. 55 pp.
"W.-B. Yeats: Prix Nobel 1923," 25-33. Probably identical with the same author's °"W. B. Yeats," *Vie intellectuelle*, 10:11 (1 Jan 1924), 190-91.

80. LORENZ, LINCOLN: *Fall of Apollo: The Lost Art and Wisdom of Poetry*. Published by subscription. [Greensboro, N.C., 1972]. xvi, 3-450 pp.
See index for some remarks on Yeats's poetry.

81. MACBETH, GEORGE (ed): *Poetry 1900 to 1975*. A revised and updated edition of *Poetry 1900-1965* [1967]. London: Longman / Faber &

Faber, 1979. xviii, 348 pp.
See pp. 20-21, 41-45.

82. MACDONAGH, THOMAS: *Thomas Campion and the Art of English Poetry*. NY: Russell & Russell, 1973 [1913]. ix, 129 pp.
See pp. 52-55 for notes on the "chanting quality" of Yeats's verse.

83. MACDONOUGH, PATRICK J.: "The Poet of the Gael," *Notre Dame Scholastic*, 37:15 (Jan 1904), 249-52.
Includes a poem entitled "William Butler Yeats."

84. MCGILL, ANNA BLANCHE: "Concerning a Few Anglo-Celtic Poets," *CathW*, 75:450 (Sept 1902), 775-85.
Naively enthusiastic about Yeats's poetry.

85. MACKENNA, AILEEN (ed): *Ring of Verse*. Dublin: Fallon, 1968. 175 pp.
A few negligible notes, pp. 11, 13, 15, 18, 20-21.

86. MACLEOD, FIONA: "The Irish Muse," *NAR*, 179:576 (Nov 1904), 685-97; :577 (Dec 1904), 900-912.
Contains some remarks on Yeats's poetry.

87. MACWEENEY, ALEN: "Yeats--MacWeeney--Ireland: Conjuring the Magic in a Great Bardic Vision." A photographic essay by Alen MacWeeney, text by Artelia Court, *American Photographer*, 6:3 (Mar 1981), 56-67.
Photographs with captions from Yeats's poetry.

88. MARSHALL, JOHN: "Some Aspects of Mr. Yeats' Lyric Poetry," *QQ*, 13:3 (Jan-Feb-Mar 1906), 241-45.

89. [MAXWELL, IAN R.]: *Three Modern Poets: Selections from Gerard Manley Hopkins, William Butler Yeats, Thomas Stearns Eliot*. Melbourne: Department of English, U of Melbourne, 1947. 92 pp.
"Introduction," 9-25; "William Butler Yeats," 47-49.

90. MAYNARD, THEODORE: "The Poems of William Butler Yeats," *America*, 6 Nov 1920, 65-66.
Qualified praise of the early poetry, crushing criticism of the later poetry ("he has not worn well . . . hopelessly lost his way," etc.).

91. MÉGROZ, RODOLPHE LOUIS: *Modern English Poetry, 1882-1932*. London: Nicholson & Watson, 1933. ix, 267 pp.
See pp. 87-91, 120-23, and passim (see index).

92. MICKOSKA AČESKA, OLGA: "Vilijam Batler Jejts: Pretstavnik na angliskata moderna poezija" [WBY: A representative of modern English poetry], *Mlad borec*, 7 Mar 1979, 19.

93. MILLS, JOHN GASCOIGNE: "Some Aspects of Poetic Creation," *Ochanomizu Joshi Daigaku Jimbun Kagaku Kiyō*, 10 (1957), 1-16.

94. MONRO, HAROLD: *Some Contemporary Poets*. London: Parsons, 1920. 224 pp.
Some scattered remarks, passim (see index).

95. MORRIS, HELEN: *The New Where's That Poem: An Index of Poems*

for Children. Arranged by subject, with a bibliography of books of poetry. Oxford: Blackwell, 1985. vii, 264 pp.
See index for some Yeats references under such headings as cats, changelings, dancing, fiddler, ghosts, etc.

96. MORTON, DAVID: *The Renaissance of Irish Poetry, 1880-1930*. NY: Washburn, 1929. 256 pp.
Contains only a few scattered remarks on Yeats's poetry.

97. NASSAR, EUGENE PAUL: *Essays Critical and Metacritical*. Rutherford, N.J.: Fairleigh Dickinson UP, 1983. 204 pp.
Notes on Yeats's poetry, pp. 29-32 and passim (see index).

98. NICOLL, W. ROBERTSON: "London Letter: The Young Poets of Ireland," *BmNY*, 1:5 (June 1895), 328-30.
Yeats is "the most genuinely poetical of our young minstrels."

99. NIMS, JOHN FREDERICK: *Western Wind: An Introduction to Poetry*. NY: Random House, 1974. xxxvi, 468 pp.
See index for some notes on Yeats's poems.

100. O'CONNOR, WILLIAM VAN: *Sense and Sensibility in Modern Poetry*. Chicago: U of Chicago Press, 1948. xii, 279 pp.
Scattered remarks on Yeats's poetry (see index).

101. Ó HUANACHÁIN, MÍCHEÁL: "An snáthaid & an taipéis" [The needle and the carpet], *Comhar*, 24:7 (July 1965), 9-11.

102. ORSZÁGH, LÁSZLÓ: "A legújabb angol líra," *Magyar szemle*, 34:1 (Sept 1938), 45-53.
"The newest English poetry"; short note on Yeats, p. 48.

103. PESCHMANN, HERMANN: "Yeats and His English Contemporaries," *English*, 9:51 (Autumn 1952), 88-93.
Misnomer; a sketch of the development of Yeats's poetry with occasional glimpses of his contemporaries.

104. PETERKIEWICZ, JERZY: *The Other Side of Silence: The Poet at the Limits of Language*. London: Oxford UP, 1970. viii, 128 pp.
See pp. 39-40.

105. PORTER, PETER, and ANTHONY THWAITE: *The English Poets from Chaucer to Edward Thomas*. London: Secker & Warburg, 1974. ix, 320 pp.
See pp. 310-12.

106. PUJALS, ESTEBAN: *La poesía inglesa del siglo XX*. Barcelona: Editorial Planeta, 1973. 254 pp. (Ensayos Planeta de linguística y critica literaria. 23.)
"La poesía de Yeats, Lawrence y de la Mare," 31-37; on Yeats, pp. 31-34.

107. RABONI, GIOVANNI: "Omaggio a Yeats: Variazioni su 'esperienza e astrazione,'" *Aut aut*, 12:68 (Mar 1962), 172-76.
Not so much on Yeats but rather a general essay on experience and abstraction in 20th-century English poetry.

108. RODMAN, SELDEN: "Poetry between the Wars," *CE*, 5:1 (Oct 1943), 1-8.

109. RUSSELL, FRANCIS: "The Archpoet," *Horizon*, 3:2 (Nov 1960), 66-69.

"As a young man, Yeats made old men's verses--he said so himself--but when he grew old, his verse became young."

110. RYAN, W. P.: "Poetry in 1895," *Weekly Sun*, 1 Dec 1895, Literary Supplement, 12.

111. SANESI, ROBERTO (ed): *Poeti inglesi del 900*. Testi, traduzioni e introduzioni a cura di Roberto Sanesi. Milano: Bompiani, 1960. 564 pp.

See pp. 25-34.

112. SCHELLING, FELIX EMMANUEL: *The English Lyric*. Port Washington, N.Y.: Kennikat Press, 1967 [1913]. xi, 335 pp.

Some notes (see index).

113. SEN, MIHIR KUMAR: *Inter-war English Poetry with Special Reference to Eliot's "Objective Correlative" Theory*. Burdwan: U of Burdwan, 1967. xxiv, 216 pp.

Contains a few notes on Yeats.

114. SHAHANI, RANJEE G.: "Some Recent English Poets," *Asiatic R*, ns 31:106 (Apr 1935), 379-89.

115. "SHELMALIER": "Plea for 'Bad Popular Poetry,'" *Phoblacht*, 14 July 1934, 2, 7.

Yeats should also write it.

116. SHRIBMAN, DAVID: "Jefferson, Yeats and Tolstoy Offer Hints to Hart's Thinking," *NYT*, 5 Apr 1984, 12.

Presidential hopeful Gary Hart confesses to be influenced by Yeats's poetry.

117. SMITH, MICHAEL: *Anglo-Irish Poetry for the Leaving Certificate*. Dublin: Gill & Macmillan, 1975. 31 pp.

See pp. 7-12.

118. STEIN, FRANCIS PATIKY: "'And Time Runs On,' Cried She. 'Come Out of Charity, Come Dance with Me in Ireland,'" *Glamour*, 58:2 (Oct 1967), 144-57.

Perhaps the strangest thing that has ever happened to Yeats's poetry: quotations from his verse are used as caption titles for fashion photographs. Also honored are Joyce and MacNeice.

119. STEPHEN, MARTIN: *English Literature*. London: Longman, 1986. ix, 246 pp. (Longman Exam Guides.)

See pp. 214-15 for "Examination Topics in Yeats' Poetry."

120. TAUFER, VENO: Note on Yeats's poetry, following translations of eight poems, *Nova revija*, 5-6 (1982/83), 535-36.

121. [TEASDALE, SARA]: "The Later Yeats," *Poetry*, 15:5 (Feb 1920), 288-89.

Note on the excellence of Yeats's later poetic work.

122. UNTERMEYER, LOUIS (ed): *Modern American Poetry--Modern British Poetry*. NY: Harcourt, Brace & World, 1962. xxvi, 701; xxiii, 541 pp.

"William Butler Yeats," [2]:104-7.

123. WALTON, JACOB: "The Poems of W. B. Yeats," *Primitive Methodist QR,* os 45 / ns 25:3 (July 1903), 472-80.

124. WARNER, FRANCIS: "Explorations in Poetic Growth," *Western Mail,* 16 Jan 1965, 5.

125. WARNER, REX: "Modern English Poetry," *International Literature,* 7 (July 1939), 80-85.
"One might demand from [Yeats] more political understanding: one cannot demand finer poetry."

126. WARREN, CLARENCE HENRY: "William Butler Yeats," *BmL,* 82:492 (Sept 1932), 284-86.

127. ———: *Wise Reading.* London: Newnes, [1936]. 160 pp.
Yeats's poems are included in the list of the world's best books, pp. 90-93.

128. W[HITE], H. O.: "Mr. W. B. Yeats: A Brief Study of His Poetry," *Sheffield Daily Telegraph,* 23 Nov 1922, 3.
See also BF156.

129. WHITELEY, ISABEL: "The Poetry of William Butler Yeats," *Catholic Reading Circle R,* 9:1 (Oct 1896), 12-15.

130. WILBUR, RICHARD: *Responses: Prose Pieces 1953-1976.* NY: Harcourt Brace Jovanovich, 1976. xii, 238 pp.
"Poetry and Happiness," 91-114; contains some notes on Yeats.

131. WILD, FRIEDRICH: *Die englische Literatur der Gegenwart seit 1870: Versdichtungen.* Leipzig: Dioskuren Verlag, 1931. 299 pp.
"Keltische Renaissance und Mystik," 155-67; on Yeats, pp. 157-60.

132. WOLLMAN, MAURICE (ed): *Ten Twentieth-Century Poets.* London: Harrap, 1957. 224 pp.
Notes on Yeats and some of his poems, pp. 145-47, 205-16. See also Graham Handley: *Brodie's Notes on Ten Twentieth-Century Poets.* London: Pan Educational, 1978. 108 pp., which contains an article on Yeats's poetry (pp. 87-95) based on Wollman's notes.

133. WOODHEAD, CHRIS (ed): *Nineteenth and Twentieth Century Verse: An Anthology of Sixteen Poets.* Oxford: Oxford UP, 1984. 239 pp.
Notes on Yeats's poetry, pp. 82-83, 204-7.

134. YEATS, W. B.: *W. B. Yeats.* London: Benn, [1927]. 31 pp. (The Augustan Book of English Poetry. Second series. 4.)
Humbert Wolfe: "Introductory Note," iii [i.e., 3].

135. ———: *Poèmes.* Traduits par Alliette Audra, préface de Edmond Jaloux. Paris: Colombe, 1956. 95 pp.
"Préface," 9-13; reprinted from *Temps,* 23 Apr 1939, 5.

136. ———: *Poems / Poesie.* Traduzione di Leone Traverso. Nota di Margherita Guidacci. Milano: Cederna, 1949. 218 pp.
"Nota," 201-6.

137. ———: *A Selection of Poetry by W. B. Yeats (1865-1939).* Cambridge: Metcalfe, 1951. 16 pp. (*Oasis,* no. 4 [Nov 1951].)

Anon.: "Yeats, a Sketch," 4. Presumably printed as a program for a poetry reading by Siobhan McKenna on 25 Nov 1951.

138. ———: *Slova snad pro hudbu: Výbor z poesie*. Translated by Jiří Valja, with preface and explanatory notes by Jiří Levý. Praha: SNKLU, 1961. 144 pp. (Světová četba. 265.)
"Poezie Williama Butlera Yeatse," 7-16.

139. ———: *Running to Paradise*. An introductory selection by Kevin Crossley-Holland, illustrated by Judith Valpy. NY: Macmillan, 1968. 94 pp.
"Introduction," 9-24; for juvenile readers. See also G1385.

140. [———]: *Viljem Batler Jejts*. Translation and introduction by Ranka Kuić. Beograd: Mlado pokolenje, 1971. 66 pp. (Ljubav i poezija. 9.)
Introduction, pp. 5-8.

141. ———: *Poesie*. Translated by Leone Traverso. Firenze: Vallecchi, 1973. viii, 180 pp. (Tascabili Vallecchi. 40.)
Margherita Guidacci: "Notizia introduttiva," v-viii.

142. ———: "Ljubavne pjesme" [Love poems]. Translated by Slobodan Blagojević and Hamdija Demirović, *Stvaranje*, 32:4 (Apr 1977), 647-51.
Followed by a short note on Yeats, pp. 651-52.

143. ———: [In Japanese] *The Collected Poems of W. B. Yeats*. Translated by Hiroshi Suzuki. Tokyo: Hokuseido Press, 1982. xi, 332, 20 pp.
Includes notes and a bibliography.

144. ———: *Geef nooit het hele hart*. Translated by A. Roland Holst and Jan Eijkelboom. Vianen: Kwadraat, 1982. 55 pp.
Dutch translations of 13 poems facing the English originals, and an "Inleiding" by Eijkelboom, pp. 7-11.

145. ———: *Trenta-quatre poemes*. Traducció i nota preliminar de M. Villangómez Llobert. Barcelona: Edicions dels Quaderns Crema, 1983. 95 pp. (Poesia dels Quaderns Crema. 8.)
"Nota preliminar," 7-14.

146. ———: *A Poet to His Beloved: The Early Love Poems of W. B. Yeats*. Introduction by Richard Eberhart. NY: St. Martin's Press, 1985. xiii, 66 pp.
"Introduction," ix-xi.

E THE PLAYS

EA Books and Pamphlets Exclusively on Yeats

1. BECKER, ARTHUR WILLIAM JOHN: "Yeats as a Playwright," D.Phil. thesis, Oxford U, 1953. viii, 538 pp.

A detailed analysis of Yeats's dramatic theories and of the individual plays. The chapter on *The Player Queen* has been published separately (see EE425).

2. BELL, GLORIA JEAN: "Imitation, Freedom, and the Triadic Model in the Early Dramatic and Narrative Works of W. B. Yeats," Ph.D. thesis, U of Colorado at Boulder, 1982. vii, 251 pp. (*DAI*, 43:4 [Oct 1982], 1149A; reprinted *Yeats*, 1 [1983], 184-85, and *YeA*, 4 [1986], 302)

2a. BERTHA, CSILLA: *A drámaíró Yeats*. Budapest: Akadémiai kiadó, 1988. 236 pp. (Modern filológiai füzetek. 43.)

"Yeats the playwright"; with a summary in English, pp. 235-36. An introduction for Hungarian readers.

3. BLOCH, DONALD ALAN: "The Reciprocal Relationship between W. B. Yeats's Plays and His Poems," Ph.D. thesis, Harvard U, 1970. i, 280 pp.

Discusses *Deirdre, The Player Queen,* and *The King of the Great Clock Tower,* including the MS. versions, and the poems written at the same time.

4. BRADLEY, ANTHONY: *William Butler Yeats*. NY: Ungar, 1979. x, 306 pp. (World Dramatists.)

A play-by-play analysis with references to actual performances. Includes a chapter on "Yeats and the Abbey Theatre" and photographs of recent productions. Analyzed in section EE.

Reviews:

- Richard Bonaccorso, *Eire,* 16:4 (Winter 1981), 131-32.
- Patricia McFate, *YeA,* 1 (1982), 223-24.
- Maureen Murphy, *CollL,* 8:1 (Winter 1981), 104-5.
- Natalie Crohn Schmitt, *MD,* 24:1 (Mar 1981), 107-8.

5. BÜLOW, ISOLDE VON: *Der Tanz im Drama: Untersuchungen zu W. B. Yeats' dramatischer Theorie und Praxis*. Bonn: Bouvier, 1969. x, 205 pp. (Studien zur englischen Literatur. 1.)

Originally a Dr.phil. thesis, U of Hamburg, 1968. Generally on Yeats's dramatic theories and on the theory and practice of the dance in his plays; includes a discussion of the influence of the Nō. Besides numerous small inaccuracies, the thesis suffers from the author's lack of acquaintance with actual productions.

Reviews:

- Gerhard Hoffmann, *Anglia,* 90:1/2 (1972), 266-70.
- H[orst] O[ppel], *NS,* 19:8 (Aug 1970), 421.

6. BURGHARDT, LORRAINE HALL: "The Snake and the Eagle: Modern Criticism and the Drama of W. B. Yeats. A Historical and Analytical Study of Modern Theory and a Dramatic Form," Ph.D. thesis, U of Chicago, 1968. ii, 366 pp.

7. BUSHRUI, SUHEIL BADI: *Yeats's Verse Plays: The Revisions, 1900-1910*. Oxford: Clarendon Press, 1965. xv, 240 pp.

Based on °"Adam's Curse: A Study of Yeats's Revisions of His

Verse Plays, 1900-1910," Ph.D. thesis, U of Southampton, 1962. Discusses *The Shadowy Waters, On Baile's Strand, The King's Threshold, Deirdre,* and *The Green Helmet.*
Reviews:
- Curtis Bradford: "A Yeats Gathering," *MLQ,* 28:1 (Mar 1967), 96-101.
- Denis Donoghue: "Between the Lines," *Guardian,* 25 Mar 1966, 8.
- [G. S. Fraser]: "Yeats's Variations," *TLS,* 9 Mar 1967, 187.
- T. R. Henn: "New Angle on Yeats," *IrT,* 16 Oct 1965, 8.
- K. P. S. Jochum, *Anglia,* 84:3/4 (1966), 494-97.
- Peter Elvet Lewis, *DUJ,* os 58 / ns 27:3 (June 1966), 167-68.
- Sean Lucy: "Yeatsiana: A Voice for the Stage," *IrI,* 26 Feb 1966, 10.
- Thomas MacIntyre: "Joyce for the Multitude," *IrP,* 6 Nov 1965, 6.
- Donald T. Torchiana: "Three Books on Yeats," *PQ,* 46:4 (Oct 1967), 536-56.
- Peter Ure, *ES,* 48:3 (June 1967), 264-68.
- Marion Witt, *MP,* 64:4 (May 1967), 377-79.

8. CLARK, DAVID RIDGLEY: *W. B. Yeats and the Theatre of Desolate Reality.* Dublin: Dolmen Press, 1965. 125 pp.

Incorporates: "W. B. Yeats's *Deirdre:* The Rigour of Logic," *DM,* 33:1 (Jan-Mar 1958), 13-21; "Yeats and the Modern Theatre," *Threshold,* 4:2 (Autumn-Winter 1960), 35-56; "W. B. Yeats and the Drama of Vision," *ArQ,* 20:2 (Summer 1964), 127-41; "*Nishikigi* and Yeats's *The Dreaming of the Bones,*" *MD,* 7:2 (Sept 1964), 111-25. Besides the two plays mentioned, the book also discusses *The Words upon the Window-Pane* and *Purgatory.*

The book is an abridgment of "The Theatre of Desolate Reality: W. B. Yeats's Development as a Dramatist," Ph.D. thesis, Yale U, 1955. ii, 279 pp., which is also concerned with *The Countess Cathleen,* all the plays from *Four Plays for Dancers* to *The Words upon the Window-Pane,* and *The Death of Cuchulain.*
Reviews:
- Eavan Boland, *DM,* 4:1 (Spring 1965), 71-72.
- [Austin Clarke]: "The Tragedy of Trust," *TLS,* 1 July 1965, 552.
- [John Jordan]: "Yeats and the Theatre," *Hibernia,* 29:3 (Mar 1965), 27.
- Thomas Kilroy, *Studies,* 55:220 (Winter 1966), 441-43.
- Vivian Mercier, *MD,* 7:3 (Dec 1964), 357-58.
- Hermann Peschmann, *English,* 16:92 (Summer 1966), 67-69.
- John Unterecker: "Yeats as Dramatist," *MR,* 6:2 (Winter-Spring 1965), 433-34.

9. °COOKE, VIRGINIA BETH BELL: "Yeats's Drama in Continental Context: From Drama to Dream Play," Ph.D. thesis, Queen's U (Kingston, Ont.), 1975. iv, 356 pp.

10. DORN, KAREN: *Players and Painted Stage: The Theatre of W. B. Yeats.* Brighton: Harvester / Totowa, N.J.: Barnes & Noble, 1984. xiv, 143 pp. plus 32 illustrations.

Based on "Play, Set and Performance in the Theatre of W. B. Yeats," Ph.D. thesis, U of Cambridge, 1973. vi, 212 pp. Incorporates "Dialogue into Movement: W. B. Yeats's Theatre Collaboration with Gordon Craig," in O'Driscoll and Reynolds: *Yeats and the Theatre* (1975, CA81), 109-36; "Stage Production and the Greek Theatre Movement: W. B. Yeats's Play *The Resurrection* and His Versions of *King Oedipus* and *Oedipus at Colonus*," *ThR*, 1:3 (May 1976), 182-204.

On the interaction between dramatic form and stage performance; with chapters on the collaboration with E. G. Craig, the influence of the Nō on the dance plays, *Deirdre*, and the plays mentioned above.

Reviews:
- David R. Clark, *YeA*, 4 (1986), 231-35.
- Eric Domville, *MD*, 30:3 (Sept 1987), 432-34.
- Mari Kathleen Fielder, *TJ*, 37:3 (Sept 1985), 394-95.
- Emelie FitzGibbon: "The Tradition of Naturalism," *BooksI*, 82 [i.e., 84] (June 1984), 107-8.
- James W. Flannery: "Yeats on the Aisle," *ILS*, 4:2 (Fall 1985), 34.
- ———, *CJIS*, 14:1 (July 1988), 74-79.
- Nicholas Grene, *ThR*, 10:2 (Summer 1985), 185-86.
- Peter van de Kamp, *IUR*, 5:1 (Spring 1985), 108-11.
- David Krause, *Yeats*, 3 (1985), 225-29.
- George O'Brien, *MLR*, 83:2 (Apr 1988), 430-32.
- Micheál O hAodha: "The Old Lady Says 'Noh,'" *IrT*, 6 Oct 1984, 13.

11. EREMINA, I. K.: *Dramaturgii͡a U. B. Eĭtsa (Dramy ob Irlandii)*. Avtoreferat dissertat͡siĭ na soiskanie uchenoĭ stepeni kandidata filologicheskikh nauk. Moskva: Moskovskiĭ oblastnoĭ pedagogicheskiĭ institut imeni N. K. Krupskoĭ, 1970. ii, 25 pp.

A dissertation abstract; I have not seen the thesis itself.

12. FLANNERY, JAMES WILLIAM: *W. B. Yeats and the Idea of a Theatre: The Early Abbey Theatre in Theory and Practice*. New Haven: Yale UP, 1976. xxi, 404 pp.

Based on a Ph.D. thesis with the same title, Trinity College Dublin, 1970. xi, 572 pp. Incorporates "W. B. Yeats and the Abbey Theatre Company," *ETJ*, 27:2 (May 1975), 179-96; "W. B. Yeats, Gordon Craig, and the Visual Arts of the Theatre," in O'Driscoll and Reynolds: *Yeats and the Theatre* (1975, CA81), 82-108.

Flannery's thesis is that "Yeats's dramatic theories are more important than his actual practices" (p. xii), although the plays themselves are far from negligible, as he found when he directed some of them in production. Discusses the development of Yeats's ideas of drama, the theater, and acting, Anima Mundi, Unity of Being and of Culture, the heroic ideal, the cult of the Irish peasant, Irish folklore, and the Sinn Fein ideology. Also on the cooperation with Craig, the Fay brothers, Maud Gonne, Lady Gregory, Miss Horniman, Martyn, Moore, Synge, and the involvement in the Irish Literary Theatre, the Abbey Theatre and the Irish National Theatre Society, as well as on the influence of Ibsen, Symons, Villiers de l'Isle Adam, Lugné-Poe, Maeterlinck, Wagner, Wilde, and John O'Leary. Includes a discussion of *A Vision*, analyzed in section EE.

Reviews:
- Ronald Ayling, *DR*, 57:4 (Winter 1977-78), 788-91.
- John Coleby, *Gambit*, 8:30 (1977), 108-9.
- John D. Conway, *Eire*, 12:4 (Winter 1977), 144-46.
- Gary T. Davenport: "Yeats in the Theater," *SR*, 85:4 (Fall 1977), 671-74.
- Denis Donoghue: "The Hard Case of Yeats," *NYRB*, 26 May 1977, 3-4, 6, 8.
- Philip Edwards: "Golden Dawn and Golden Sunset," *THES*, 4 Mar 1977, 23.

- Edward Engelberg: "Perspectives on Yeats," *New Boston R,* 3:2 (Fall 1977), 14-15.
- Richard J. Finneran, *JML,* 6:4 (1977), 738-43.
- Christopher Fitz-Simon: "The Foundations Laid," *Drama,* 125 (Summer 1977), 74-75.
- René Fréchet, *EA,* 32:4 (Oct-Dec 1979), 491-92.
- A. Norman Jeffares, *ThR,* 4:1 (Oct 1978), 68-69.
- Brian John, *Four Decades,* 2:2 (July 1978), 118-20.
- Elizabeth Mackenzie, *N&Q,* os 225 / ns 27:5 (Oct 1980), 471-74.
- Phillip L. Marcus, *JEGP,* 76:2 (Apr 1977), 265-68.
- Augustine Martin, *Studies,* 70:227 [i.e., 70:277] (Spring 1981), 99-101.
- D. E. S. Maxwell: "Yeats and the Theatre," *UTQ,* 47:1 (Fall 1977), 92-94.
- Julian Moynahan: "The Poet, His Love, and His Plays," *NYTBR,* 27 Feb 1977, 8, 10.
- Robert O'Driscoll, *ETJ,* 29:4 (Dec 1977), 571-72.
- Andrew Parkin, *CJIS,* 3:2 (Nov 1977), 49-50.
- Hilary Pyle, *RES,* 29:114 (May 1978), 241-42.
- Lorna Reynolds: "A Dancing Dog," *Hibernia,* 4 Feb 1977, 25.
- Eric Salmon, *QQ,* 85:1 (Spring 1978), 146-48.
- Ronald Schleifer, *WLT,* 51:2 (Spring 1977), 283-84.
- ———, *GaR,* 31:3 (Fall 1977), 736-39.
- Ian Shaw, *Humanities Association R,* 28:2 (Spring 1977), 209-12.
- Arvid F. Sponberg, *ACIS Newsletter,* 7:3 (Oct 1977), 5-6.
- Roy E. Teele, *Literature East & West,* 19:1-4 (Jan-Dec 1975), 269-71.
- Georges-Denis Zimmermann, *ES,* 60:4 (Aug 1979), 526-28.

13. GIDMARK, JOHN HENRY: "'And Yet But Six-and-Twenty': Yeats's *Collected Plays* as a Reflection of His Moon," Ph.D. thesis, U of North Dakota, 1978. x, 305 pp. (*DAI,* 39:9 [Mar 1979], 5524A-25A)

Relates the 26 plays to the 26 phases of the Great Wheel; "the correlations between the Great Wheel of *A Vision* and the structure of *The Collected Plays* were . . . keenly intuited by Yeats himself" (abstract).

14. GOOD, MAEVE P.: *W. B. Yeats and the Creation of a Tragic Universe*. London: Macmillan, 1987. ix, 176 pp.

Based on a Ph.D. thesis with the same title, Trinity College Dublin, 1984. iv, 384 pp. Contains chapters on Cuchulain as an archetypal hero, *A Vision,* and the following plays: *At the Hawk's Well, The Only Jealousy of Emer, The Dreaming of the Bones, Calvary, The Resurrection, The Words upon the Window-Pane, Purgatory,* and *The Death of Cuchulain.*

15. HAERDTER, MICHAEL: "William Butler Yeats--Das theatralische Werk," Dr.phil. thesis, U of Wien, 1964. xiv, 443 pp.

Explores the connections between Yeats the poet-dramatist and Yeats the man of the theater.

16. HARRISON, DOROTHY GULBENKIAN: "W. B. Yeats's Plays: The Ritual of a Lost Faith," °Ph.D. thesis, State U of New York at Albany, 1971. 250 pp. (*DAI,* 32:4 [Oct 1971], 2091A)

17. JEFFARES, ALEXANDER NORMAN and ANTHONY STEPHEN KNOWLAND: *A Commentary on the Collected Plays of W. B. Yeats*. London: Macmillan, 1975. xxvi, 313 pp.

The authors give the publishing histories, the sources, the facts of composition, and the dates of first performance of all plays and gloss difficult passages. There are only occasional references to previous criticism and there is no bibliography and no index.

Reviews:
- Denis Donoghue: "Yeatsiana," *Spect,* 19 July 1975, 84-85.
- Edward Engelberg: "Yeats on Stage," *SR,* 84:1 (Jan-Mar 1976), 167-74.
- William R. Evans, *Eire,* 13:2 (Summer 1978), 153.
- Anthony Farrow, *Cithara,* 16:1 (Nov 1976), 76-79.
- George Mills Harper: "'Always . . . Verify Your References, Sir!'" *CEA,* 38:3 (Mar 1976), 34-37.
- Priscilla Johnston, *JML,* 5:4 (1976), 849-51.
- F. S. L. Lyons: "Keeping Up with Yeats Studies," *IrT,* 19 Aug 1975, 8.
- ———: "Plays for Aristocrats," *TLS,* 10 Oct 1975, 1187.
- Sean McMahon: "The Painted Stage," *Hibernia,* 3 Oct 1975, 14.
- J. R. Mulryne, *MLR,* 72:3 (July 1977), 669-70.
- Johann A. Norstedt, *CollL,* 3:2 (Spring 1976), 152-53.
- Andrew Parkin, *NCTR,* 5:2 (Autumn 1977), 120-22.
- A. V. C. Schmidt, *N&Q,* os 225 / ns 27:4 (Aug 1980), 380-81.

18. JOCHUM, KLAUS PETER: *Die dramatische Struktur der Spiele von W. B. Yeats.* Frankfurt/Main: Athenäum, 1971. vii, 260 pp. (Frankfurter Beiträge zur Anglistik und Amerikanistik. 2.)

Originally a Dr.phil. thesis, U of Frankfurt, 1968. Contains an English summary, pp. 255-56; reprinted in *EASG,* 1971, 139-41. A play-by-play analysis, including a chapter on the influence of the Nō. Analyzed in section EE.

Reviews:
- Anne Dedio, *ES,* 55:4 (Oct 1974), 484.
- Rudolf Halbritter, *Anglia,* 90:4 (1972), 548-50.
- R[üdiger] Krohn, *Wissenschaftlicher Literaturanzeiger,* 11:4 (Sept 1972), 125.
- Klaus Peter Steiger, *NS,* 22:10 (Oct 1974), 484.

19. JONES, DAVID R.: "W. B. Yeats: The Poet in the Theatre," Ph.D. thesis, Princeton U, 1968. viii, 275 pp. (*DAI,* 29:12 [June 1969], 4489A-90A)

20. KEYES, EVELYN CAMPBELL VINCENT: "A Theatre for Ideals: Yeats's Stagecraft in Context from *The Countess Kathleen* (1892) to *Cathleen ni Houlihan* (1902)," °Ph.D. thesis, U of Texas at Austin, 1972. 260 pp. (*DAI,* 33:7 [Jan 1973], 3651A)

Discusses *The Countess Cathleen, The Land of Heart's Desire, The Shadowy Waters, Cathleen ni Houlihan,* and *Diarmuid and Grania.*

21. KHAĬCHENKO, ELENA GRIGOR'EVNA: *Poeticheskiĭ teatr Uil'i͡ama Batlera Ĭitsa.* Avtoreferat dissertat͡siĭ. Moskva: Gosudarstvennyĭ ordena trudovogo krasnogo znameni institut teatral'nogo iskusstva imeni A. V. Lunacharskogo, 1977. 16 pp.

A dissertation abstract.

22. KNOWLAND, ANTHONY STEPHEN: *W. B. Yeats: Dramatist of Vision.* With a preface by Cyril Cusack. Gerrards Cross: Smythe / Totowa, N.J.: Barnes & Noble, 1983. xvi, 256 pp. (Irish Literary Studies. 17.)

A chronological play-by-play analysis "of the plays' meaning related to their effect in performance" (p. xv). Unfortunately, no actual performances are analyzed or even referred to. Analyzed in section EE.

Reviews:

- Andrew Carpenter: "At the Abbey," *TLS,* 29 June 1984, 733.
- Richard Allen Cave, *YeA,* 4 (1986), 239-41.
- Emelie Fitzgibbon: "Nobody Gets Old," *BooksI,* 81 (Mar 1984), 38-39.
- James W. Flannery: "Yeats on the Aisle," *ILS,* 4:2 (Fall 1985), 34.
- ———, *CJIS,* 14:1 (July 1988), 74-79.
- Jacqueline Genet, *EI,* 9 (Dec 1984), 341-42.
- Augustine Martin: "Tireless and Vivid Experimenter," *IrI,* 26 May 1984, 11.
- Micheal O hAodha: "The Cuchulain Quintet," *IrT,* 31 Dec 1983, 13.
- Andrew Parkin: "Drama East and West," *CJIS,* 12:1 (June 1986), 79-84.
- Katharine Worth, *RES,* 37:145 (Feb 1986), 139-40.

23. Entry canceled.

24. MARTIN, HEATHER CARMEN: *W. B. Yeats: Metaphysician as Dramatist.* Gerrards Cross: Smythe, 1986. xiv, 153 pp.

Based on "Metaphysician as Dramatist: The Struggle of the Spirit in the Drama of W. B. Yeats," °Ph.D. thesis, U of British Columbia, 1980. (*DAI,* 41:11 [May 1981], 4722A; reprinted *YeA,* 2 [1983], 101-2). Incorporates "Of Flood and Fire: A Study of *The Player Queen,*" *CJIS,* 7:1 (June 1981), 49-60; "W. B. Yeats: More Realist than Idealist," *CJIS,* 9:2 (Dec 1983), 77-80.

Argues that Yeats's metaphysics, the result of his magical, mystical, and philosophical studies, finds its most elaborate expression in the plays. Analyzed in section EE.

Reviews:

- John Hanratty: "Singing-Masters of the Soul," *BooksI,* 118 (Nov 1987), 218-19.
- Bruce Henderson: "Yeats and Drama," *ELT,* 31:2 (1988), 226-29.

25. MILLER, LIAM: *The Noble Drama of W. B. Yeats.* Dublin: Dolmen Press, 1977. xv, 365 pp. (New Yeats Papers. 13.)

An illustrated "biography" of the plays (their creation, background, and production) and of the contemporary Irish theater. Discusses the influence of, and collaboration with, E. G. Craig, the Fay brothers, Edmund Dulac, Lady Gregory, Miss Horniman, Edward Martyn, George Moore, T. Sturge Moore, and Ezra Pound, also the importance of the Nō. Analyzed in section EE.

Reviews:

- Kane Archer: "Grandeur like That of Babylon," *BooksI,* 16 (Sept 1977), 162-64.
- David R. Clark, *Malahat R,* 46 (Apr 1978), 151-52.
- Gary T. Davenport: "Yeats in the Theater," *SR,* 85:4 (Fall 1977), 671-74.
- Denis Donoghue: "Players and Painted Stage," *Hibernia,* 28 Oct 1977, 24.
- Edward Hirsch, *WLT,* 52:2 (Spring 1978), 290.
- David Krause, *Eire,* 13:1 (Spring 1978), 150-58.
- Roger McHugh: "Artificial Flowers," *TLS,* 23 Dec 1977, 1509.
- Christopher Murray, *IUR,* 8:1 (Spring 1978), 122-26.
- Andrew Parkin, *CJIS,* 4:1 (June 1978), 77-78.
- Kathleen Raine: "Plays in a Taxi," *List,* 1 Sept 1977, 284.
- Christiane Thilliez, *EI,* 2 (Dec 1977), 282-85.
- Jack W. Weaver, *CollL,* 6:2 (Spring 1979), 158-59.

26. MOORE, JOHN REES: *Masks of Love and Death: Yeats as Dramatist*. Ithaca: Cornell UP, 1971. xiv, 362 pp.

Based on "Evolution of Myth in the Plays of W. B. Yeats," Ph.D. thesis, Columbia U, 1957. viii, 252 pp. (*DAI*, 17:7 [July 1957], 1556-57). Incorporates "Cold Passion: A Study of *The Herne's Egg*," *MD*, 7:3 (Dec 1964), 287-98; "The Janus Face: Yeats's *The Player Queen*," *SR*, 76:4 (Oct-Dec 1968), 608-30.

Three introductory chapters on the concept of the mask, the characteristics of Yeats's drama, and the Cuchulain myth; followed by play-by-play analyses. Analyzed in section EE.

Reviews:
- Anon., *YR*, 61:1 (Autumn 1971), xii, xiv.
- [Austin Clarke]: "Yeats's Attempts at Poetic Drama," *TLS*, 27 Aug 1971, 1020.
- Anthony Cronin: "Yeats Seminar," *IrP*, 26 June 1971, 12.
- Anne Dedio, *ES*, 55:1 (Feb 1974), 90.
- George M. Harper, *ELN*, 9:4 (June 1972), 316-17.
- D. E. S. Maxwell, *DR*, 51:2 (Summer 1971), 290-91.
- Andrew Parkin, *MD*, 15:2 (Sept 1972), 211-12.
- Hilary Pyle, *RES*, 23:90 (May 1972), 249-50.
- August W. Staub, *QJS*, 58:4 (Dec 1972), 480-81.
- Donald T. Torchiana: "Some Recent Books on W. B. Yeats," *JIL*, 5:2 (May 1976), 60-81.
- Harold H. Watts, *JML*, 3:3 (Feb 1974), 838-39.
- Stanley Weintraub, *BA*, 46:2 (Spring 1972), 307-8.

27. MYLES, ASHLEY E.: *Theatre of Aristocracy: A Study of W. B. Yeats as a Dramatist*. Salzburg: Institut für Anglistik und Amerikanistik, Universität Salzburg, 1981. vi, 124 pp. (Salzburg Studies in English Literature: Poetic Drama & Poetic Theory. 52.)

Based on a °Ph.D. thesis, Kashi Vidyapith, Varanasi, India (1976). Attempts to discuss Yeats as a successful writer of *poetic* dramas against the background of the abortive verse dramas of the 19th century. The interpretations are of little value. Ignores almost all previous Yeats criticism.

Reviews:
- Brian John: "Yeats the Dramatist," *ILS*, 2:2 (Oct 1983), 19.
- Andrew Parkin, *CJIS*, 10:1 (June 1984), 147-51.

28. NATHAN, LEONARD EDWARD: *The Tragic Drama of William Butler Yeats: Figures in a Dance*. NY: Columbia UP, 1965. xii, 307 pp.

Based on °"W. B. Yeats' Development as a Tragic Dramatist, 1884-1939," Ph.D. thesis, U of California (Berkeley), 1961. iii, 471 pp. Includes discussions of the influence of Maeterlinck, Pater, Shakespeare, Villiers de l'Isle Adam, and of the Nō. Analyzed in section EE.

Reviews:
- [Austin Clarke]: "Yeats as Dramatist," *TLS*, 25 Nov 1965, 1071.
- Anne Dedio, *Anglia*, 85:3/4 (1967), 509-10.
- D. J. Gordon, *MLR*, 63:3 (July 1968), 693-94.
- T. R. Henn, *RES*, 17:68 (Nov 1966), 444-47.
- Brian John: "Hurt into Poetry," *JGE*, 18:4 (Jan 1967), 299-306.
- Giorgio Melchiori, *N&Q*, os 211 / ns 13:11 (Nov 1966), 430-31.
- M. K. Naik, *IJES*, 7 (1966), 125-28.
- B. Rajan: "Conflict, More Conflict!" *UTQ*, 35:3 (Apr 1966), 315-20.
- Ann Saddlemyer, *QQ*, 73:2 (Summer 1966), 296-97.
- Priscilla Washburn Shaw: "The Yeats Centenary: Part of the Harvest," *VQR*, 42:1 (Winter 1966), 173-76.
- Peter Ure, *ES*, 48:3 (June 1967), 264-68.

29. PARKIN, ANDREW [TERENCE LEONARD]: *The Dramatic Imagination of W. B. Yeats*. Dublin: Gill & Macmillan / NY: Barnes & Noble, 1978. xi, 208 pp.

Based on "The Importance of Yeats's Drama," Ph.D. thesis, Bristol U, 1969. ix, 638 pp. Incorporates "Dramatic Elements in the Poetry of W. B. Yeats," *Anglo-Irish Studies,* 2 (1976), 109-27.

Although mainly concerned with the plays, Parkin also discusses Yeats's theory of the imagination and its working in the poetry and prose. Includes a chapter on the influence of the Nō. Analyzed in section EE.

Reviews:
- Richard J. Finneran, *ACIS Newsletter,* 11:[1] (Feb 1981), 3-4.
- James W. Flannery, *CJIS,* 5:2 (Dec 1979), 64-69.
- Warwick Gould: "W. B. Yeats's Dramatic Imagination: A Review Article," *Themes in Drama,* 3 (1981), 203-21.
- Phillip L. Marcus, *YER,* 6:2 (1979), 56-57.
- Santosh Pall, *Studies,* 70:227 [i.e., 70:277] (Spring 1981), 101; revised in 71:281 (Spring 1982), 94-95.
- Joseph Ronsley: "Yeats's Dramatic Imagination," *Mosaic,* 12:3 (Spring 1979), 177-80.
- R. P. Ryan, *UES,* 17:2 (Sept 1979), 63.

30. POLI͡UDOVA, TAT'I͡ANA MIKHAĬLOVNA: *Dramaturgii͡a U. B. Ĭetsa kont͡sa XIX--nachala XX vekov. (Teorii͡a poeticheskoĭ dramy. Masterstvo dramaturga)*. Avtoreferat dissertat͡siĭ. Moskva: Moskovskiĭ ordena Lenina i ordena trudovogo krasnogo znameni gosudarstvennyĭ pedagogicheskiĭ institut imeni V. I. Lenina, 1978. ii, 16 pp.

"Yeats's playwriting at the end of the 19th and the beginning of the 20th century: The theory of poetic drama; the craft of the playwright"; a dissertation abstract.

31. SCHMITT, NATALIE SUE CROHN: "The Ritual of a Lost Faith: The Drama of William Butler Yeats," Ph.D. thesis, Stanford U, 1968. iv, 473 pp. (*DAI,* 29:7 [Jan 1969], 2281A)

32. SCHNEIDER, JOSEPH LEONDAR: *Unity of Culture in Yeats's Drama*. Seoul: Seoul National UP, 1980. vii, 158 pp.

Based on "W. B. Yeats and the Theatre of Intellectual Reformation," Ph.D. thesis, Duke U, 1972. x, 266 pp. (*DAI,* 33:11 [May 1973], 6374A). Mainly on *The King's Threshold, The Dreaming of the Bones, Purgatory, Deirdre,* and the Cuchulain plays.

Reviewed by Ronald Schuchard, *YeA,* 1 (1982), 248-51.

33. SIEGEL, SANDRA F.: "Play of the Mind: The Theater of W. B. Yeats," Ph.D. thesis, U of Chicago, 1968. iv, 115 pp.

34. STRABEL, AUDREY LEE ELISE: "Yeats' Development of a Symbolic Drama," Ph.D. thesis, U of Wisconsin, 1953. vi, 409 pp.

35. TAYLOR, RICHARD: *The Drama of W. B. Yeats: Irish Myth and the Japanese Nō*. New Haven: Yale UP, 1976. xiii, 247 pp.

More on the Nō than on Irish myth. "In the final analysis, Nō was not so much a direct influence on Yeats as the source of a new point of departure for continued experimentation with established themes and aesthetic concerns" (p. 161). Analyzed in section EE.

Reviews:
- T. J. Cribb, *Anglo-Irish Studies,* 3 (1977), 123-25.
- Gary T. Davenport: "Yeats in the Theater," *SR,* 85:4 (Fall 1977), 671-74.

- Kathleen Draycott, *Asian Affairs,* os 65 / ns 9:2 (June 1978), 216-18.
- Richard J. Finneran, *JML,* 6:4 (1977), 738-43.
- Christopher Fitz-Simon: "The Foundations Laid," *Drama,* 125 (Summer 1977), 74-75.
- René Fréchet, *EA,* 32:4 (Oct-Dec 1979), 490-91.
- William Gordon, *DR,* 57:2 (Summer 1977), 393-95.
- Toshimitsu Hasegawa, *SELit,* 55:English Number (1980), 80-87.
- Eileen Katō, *MN,* 32:3 (Autumn 1977), 397-99.
- John Kwan-Terry, *WLT,* 51:3 (Summer 1977), 508.
- Elizabeth Mackenzie, *N&Q,* os 225 / ns 27:5 (Oct 1980), 471-74.
- Vincent Mahon, *RES,* 29:114 (May 1978), 239-41.
- Phillip L. Marcus, *JEGP,* 76:2 (Apr 1977), 265-68.
- Earl Milner [i.e., Miner]: "The Need for Nō," *TLS,* 25 Aug 1978, 948.
- P. G. O'Neill, *Bulletin of the School of Oriental and African Studies,* 40:2 (1977), 452.
- Andrew Parkin, *NCTR,* 6:2 (Autumn 1978), 119-20.
- Ronald Schleifer, *GaR,* 31:3 (Fall 1977), 736-39.
- A. G. Stock, *IUR,* 7:1 (Spring 1977), 131-33.
- Roy E. Teele, *Literature East & West,* 19:1-4 (Jan-Dec 1975), 267-69.
- Reiko Tsukimura, *Arcadia,* 13:2 (1978), 211-15.
- Georges-Denis Zimmermann, *ES,* 60:4 (Aug 1979), 526-28.

36. ———: *A Reader's Guide to the Plays of W. B. Yeats.* London: Macmillan, 1984. ix, 197 pp.

A play-by-play analysis; the introduction outlines Yeats's theory of drama. Analyzed in section EE.

Reviews:
- Andrew Carpenter: "At the Abbey," *TLS,* 29 June 1984, 733.
- Eric Domville, *MD,* 30:3 (Sept 1987), 432-34.
- E. J. Dumay, *EI,* 10 (Dec 1985), 307-8.
- James W. Flannery: "Yeats on the Aisle," *ILS,* 4:2 (Fall 1985), 34.
- ———, *CJIS,* 14:1 (July 1988), 74-79.
- Rory Ryan, *UES,* 23:1 (Apr 1985), 52-53.
- Katharine Worth, *YeA,* 4 (1986), 238.

37. URE, PETER: *Yeats the Playwright: A Commentary on Character and Design in the Major Plays.* London: Routledge & Kegan Paul, 1963. vii, 182 pp.

Incorporates: "Yeats's Christian Mystery Plays," *RES,* 11:42 (May 1960), 171-82; "Yeats's Hero-Fool in *The Herne's Egg,*" *HLQ,* 24:2 (Feb 1961), 125-36; "Yeats's *Deirdre,*" *ES,* 42:4 (Aug 1961), 218-30; "The Evolution of Yeats's *The Countess Cathleen,*" *MLR,* 57:1 (Jan 1962), 12-24.

The pioneer study. Discusses most of the plays under various aspects (revisions and rewriting, dramatic theory and practice, irony, myth, realism). Analyzed in section EE.

Reviews:
- [Austin Clarke]: "Dramatic Treatment," *TLS,* 1 Feb 1963, 78.
- Denis Donoghue: "Countries of the Mind," *Guardian,* 11 Jan 1963, 5.
- Padraic Fallon: "Yeats and the Stage," *IrT,* 26 Jan 1963, 8.
- G. S. Fraser, *List,* 16 May 1963, 843.
- René Fréchet, *EA,* 18:4 (Oct-Dec 1965), 425-26.
- Donna Gerstenberger, *MD,* 6:4 (Feb 1964), 463-64.
- Keith Harrison: "Delicate Raddle," *Spect,* 22 Feb 1963, 237.
- Robert Hethmon, *ETJ,* 16:4 (Dec 1964), 381-82.

- K. P. S. Jochum, *NS*, 14:6 (June 1965), 297-99.
- Rolf Lass, *Kilkenny Magazine*, 10 (Autumn-Winter 1963), 103-6.
- Andrew Mathieson: "The Indomitable Irishry," *Drama*, 95 (Winter 1969), 82, 84.
- Patrick Murray: "Yeats on Stage," *IrP*, 30 Aug 1969, 10.
- Richard M. Ohmann, *Wisconsin Studies in Contemporary Literature*, 5:3 (Autumn 1964), 276-77.
- V. de S. Pinto, *CritQ*, 6:2 (Summer 1964), 186-87.
- J. V. Ramamrutham, *LHY*, 5:1 (Jan 1964), 78-80.
- Jon Stallworthy, *RES*, 15:58 (May 1964), 215-17.
- Rudolf Stamm, *ES*, 50:2 (Apr 1969), 218-21.
- Sarah Youngblood, *Drama Survey*, 3:2 (Oct 1963), 319-20.

38. WALKER, ROBERT LESLIE: "W. B. Yeats's Plays and the Modern Theater," Ph.D. thesis, U of Connecticut, 1975. vi, 198 pp. (*DAI*, 36:2 [Aug 1975], 913A)

"Yeats is a far more important playwright than either the performance record of his plays or the critical reaction to them would indicate." "His work . . . directly anticipated the plays of Samuel Beckett and his fellow absurdists" (abstract).

39. WIEDNER, ELSIE MARGARET: "The Use of the Theater for the Presentation of Metaphysical Ideas: A Comparative Study of W. B. Yeats and Paul Claudel," Ph.D. thesis, Radcliffe College, 1961. iv, 301 pp.

Describes Yeats's theater as one of "epiphany" and concentrates on *The Countess Cathleen, The Shadowy Waters, At the Hawk's Well, The Cat and the Moon, The Player Queen, The Resurrection, The Herne's Egg, Purgatory*, and *The Death of Cuchulain*. Finds that the theater of Yeats and Claudel remained "unique" and exerted no influence on later playwrights.

40. WORTH, KATHARINE: *The Irish Drama of Europe from Yeats to Beckett*. London: Athlone Press, 1978. ix, 276 pp.

Yeats's plays figure prominently in most chapters. Discusses the relationship with Maeterlinck, Symons, Craig, Wilde, Synge, O'Casey, and Beckett; also Yeats's influence on modern English theater and some recent productions. Analyzed in section EE.

Reviews:

- Kane Archer: "Unlimited by Locale," *BooksI*, 27 (Oct 1978), 163-64.
- Peter Faulkner, *DUJ*, 74:2 (June 1982), 316-17.
- Christopher Fitz-Simon: "Ireland through European Eyes," *Drama*, 130 (Autumn 1978), 76.
- Nicholas Grene, *MLR*, 76:1 (Jan 1981), 173-75.
- Declan Kiberd: "Synge, Yeats, Marx, and the European Perspective," *Literary R*, 12 (21 Mar--3 Apr 1980), 9-13.
- G. Lernout, *RBPH*, 63:3 (1985), 629-33.
- Milton Levin, *Eire*, 14:4 (Winter 1979), 149-52.
- Christopher Murray, *IUR*, 9:2 (Autumn 1979), 362-64.
- George E. Nichols, *TJ*, 31:4 (Dec 1979), 558.
- Lorna Reynolds: "Into Europe," *Hibernia*, 5 Oct 1978, 15.
- Ronald Schuchard, *RES*, 30:120 (Nov 1979), 494-95.
- Kurt Tetzeli von Rosador, *Archiv*, year 135 / 220:1 (1983), 177-81.

41. YEATS, W. B.: *The Variorum Edition of the Plays*. Edited by Russell K. Alspach, assisted by Catharine C. Alspach. London: Macmillan, 1966. xxv, 1136 pp.

Alspach's introduction, pp. xi-xvi, describes the editorial principles and difficulties; it is partly based on "The Variorum Edition of Yeats's Plays," in Jeffares and Cross: *In Excited Reverie* (1965, CA48), 194-206; and "It Is Myself That I Remake," *JJQ*, 3:2 (Winter 1966), 95-108. Includes a list of first performances, an index of characters, a general index, and William Becker's introduction to *Diarmuid and Grania*, pp. 1169-71; reprinted from *DM*, 26:2 (Apr-June 1951), 2-4. For reviews see G1147-1148.

See also AA11, AB7, AF3, CA33, 57, 81, 95, 117, 123, 125, CD25, 348, 984, 1369, 1410, FG9.

EB Substantial Articles and Parts of Books

1. AAS, L.: "William Butler Yeats og hans verker dramatikeren: Yeats og det irske teater," *Ord och bild*, 36:8 (Aug 1927), 461-68.
Discusses only the pre-1910 plays.

2. ANNIAH GOWDA, H. H.: *The Revival of English Poetic Drama (in the Edwardian & Georgian Periods)*. [Bangalore: Government Press], 1963. xvii, 322 pp.
"The Influence of the Noh on Verse Drama," 221-55 (on Yeats, 225-36); "Yeats's Verse Plays," 283-309. An enlarged edition was published in °Bombay: Orient Longman, 1972. xiii, 366 pp.

3. ———: *Dramatic Poetry from Mediaeval to Modern Times: A Philosophic Enquiry into the Nature of Poetic Drama in England, Ireland and the United States of America*. Madras: Macmillan, 1972. xiv, 406 pp.
See pp. 272-93 and passim.

4. AUGHTRY, CHARLES EDWARD (ed): *Landmarks in Modern Drama from Ibsen to Ionesco*. Boston: Houghton Mifflin, 1963. ix, 726 pp.
"William Butler Yeats (1865-1939)," 386-89; a note on Yeats's place in the tradition of verse drama and on *On Baile's Strand*.

5. BACKER, FRANZ DE: "William Butler Yeats," *Vandaag*, 1:1 (15 Feb 1929), [8-10].
A survey of the dramatic work.

6. BEERS, HENRY A.: "The English Drama of To-day," *NAR*, 180:582 (May 1905), 746-57.
Contains a note on Yeats, especially on *The Land of Heart's Desire*, pp. 753-55.

7. BELL, SAM HANNA: *The Theatre in Ulster: A Survey of the Dramatic Movement in Ulster from 1902 until the Present Day*. Dublin: Gill & Macmillan, 1972. xi, 147 pp.
Notes on Yeats's plays, passim, especially in "The Lyric Players Theatre," 114-24. See also EB90.

8. BENNETT, JAMES O'DONNELL: "Mr. Yeats as Missionary," *Chicago Record-Herald*, 27 Jan 1904, 6.
Saw some performances of Yeats's plays (unspecified) and liked them, but was annoyed by Yeats's introductory speeches: "Mr. Yeats is the type of propagandist which [sic], possessing tremendous zeal in a good cause, seems determined to go the hardest way about forwarding that cause. Why not work from within and with the theater as it exists today rather than against it and aloof from it?"

9. BENTLEY, ERIC: *The Playwright as Thinker: A Study of Drama in Modern Times*. NY: Reynal & Hitchcock, 1946. x, 382 pp.

The English edition was published as *The Modern Theatre: A Study of Dramatists and the Drama*. London: Hale, 1950. xxv, 290 pp. On Yeats, passim (see index), especially pp. 222-26 (English edition, pp. 159-61); he was a "dramatist manqué," because the wrong kind of people sat in his theater.

10. ———: *In Search of Theater*. NY: Knopf, 1953. xxiii, 411, ix pp.

"Yeats's Plays," 315-26; reprinted from *KR*, 10:2 (Spring 1948), 196-208; also in CA36. See also EB64.

"Heroic Wantonness," 327-41; reprint of "Irish Theatre: Splendeurs et Misères," *Poetry*, 79:4 (Jan 1952), 216-32; a review of EF52.

11. BERNARD, JEAN JACQUES, and others: *Le théâtre anglais d'hier et d'aujourd'hui*. Avec des textes de [. . .] W.-B. Yeats [. . .]. Paris: Pavois, 1945. 228 pp. (Théâtre. 2.)

"William-Butler Yeats," 136-42; largely translated excerpts from *The Pot of Broth* and *The Land of Heart's Desire*.

12. BERTHA, CSILLA: "Yeats nó drámái: Nemzeti gondolat és egyetemes jelentés," *Hevesi szemle*, 9:2 (June 1981), 45-50.

"Yeats's Nō plays: The national idea and the general meaning"; mainly on *At the Hawk's Well, The Only Jealousy of Emer*, and *Calvary*.

13. ———: "W. B. Yeats drámaírói útkeresése," *Egri Ho Si Minh Tanárképző Főiskola Tudományos Közleményei*, 16 (1982), 299-311.

"Yeats's early experiments as a dramatist"; with an English summary.

14. BLAU, HERBERT: "Windlasses and Assays of Bias," *Encore*, 9:5 (Sept-Oct 1962), 24-40.

See pp. 33-35.

15. BLOCK, HASKELL MAYER, and ROBERT GORDON SHEDD (eds): *Masters of Modern Drama*. With introductions and notes. NY: Random House, 1962. xii, 1199 pp.

"William Butler Yeats (1865-1939)," 427-28; an introduction to Yeats's plays and to *At the Hawk's Well*.

16. BOGARD, TRAVIS, and WILLIAM I. OLIVER (eds): *Modern Drama: Essays in Criticism*. NY: Oxford UP, 1965. vi, 393 pp. (Galaxy Books. 138.)

Thomas Parkinson: "The Later Plays of W. B. Yeats," 385-93. Stresses the influence of the Nō and emphasizes the theatricality of the plays, but does not go very deep into the possibilities of an actual performance.

17. BOYD, ERNEST AUGUSTUS: *The Contemporary Drama of Ireland*. Dublin: Talbot Press / London: Unwin, 1918. vii, 228 pp.

See pp. 47-87. "Yeats imposed a new standard which was at once literary and national, and out of its adoption there grew that poetic flowering which constituted the chief distinction of the Celtic Renaissance" (pp. 48-49). Discusses the plays to 1910 and concludes that he "is an isolated figure in the repertory of the Abbey Theatre." His plays, however, put him among "the first of the poetic dramatists of to-day" in western Europe (p. 86).

Reviews:
- Anon.: "The Irish Stage," *Nation* [London], 31 Aug 1918, 576, 578.
- [Harold Child]: "The Irish Drama," *TLS,* 20 June 1918, 287.
- John Louis Haney, *MLN,* 32:8 (Dec 1917), 494-96.
- [F. C. Moore]: "The Irish Theatre," *Spect,* 14 Dec 1918, 697-98; reprinted in *Living Age,* 11 Jan 1919, 119-21.
- R. H. C. [i.e., A. R. Orage]: "Readers and Writers," *New Age,* 25 July 1918, 201.
- J. Ranken Towse: "The Drama of Ireland," *Nation,* 15 Nov 1917, 546-47.
- Katharine Tynan: "The Irish Theatre," *BmL,* 54:324 (Sept 1918), 184-85.

18. ———: "Making the Drama Safe from Democracy," *Irish Commonwealth,* 1:2 (Apr 1919), 66-72.
Deplores Yeats's withdrawal from the popular theater: "Does he think that, in so doing, he escapes the duty which his genius owes to the contemporary theatre?"

19. BRADBROOK, MURIEL CLARA: *English Dramatic Form: A History of Its Development.* London: Chatto & Windus, 1965. 205 pp.
"Yeats and the Revival," 123-42. The revival of imagination in Yeats's plays.

20. BULLOUGH, GEOFFREY: "Poetry in Modern English Drama," *Cairo Studies in English,* 1959, 26-42.
See pp. 26-28.

21. CAMPBELL, JOHN: "The Rise of the Drama in Ireland," *New Liberal R,* 7:39 (Apr 1904), 291-307.
Especially on *The Countess Cathleen.*

22. CHAMBERS, E. K.: "The Experiments of Mr. Yeats," *Academy,* 9 May 1903, 465-66.
Especially on *Cathleen ni Houlihan,* Yeats's dramatic theories, and his Speaking-to-the-Psaltery experiments.

23. CHANDLER, FRANK WADLEIGH: *Aspects of Modern Drama.* NY: Macmillan, 1939 [1914]. ix, 494 pp.
On Yeats's pre-1910 plays, pp. 239-47 and passim (see index).

24. CHATURVEDI, B. N.: *English Poetic Drama of the Twentieth Century.* Gwalior: Kitab Ghar, 1967. x, 115 pp.
"Revival of Poetic Drama and the Plays of W. B. Yeats," 7-30.

25. CHIARI, JOSEPH: *Landmarks of Contemporary Drama.* London: Jenkins, 1965. 223 pp.
See pp. 83-85 and passim (see index).

26. CLARKE, AUSTIN: "W. B. Yeats and Verse Drama," *Threshold,* 19 (Autumn 1965), 14-29.
This is a disappointing article, especially because it starts so well. Clarke argues that poetry today is largely a silent art and that this curtails the possibilities of a successful verse drama. He does not, however, pursue his argument in his discussion of Yeats's plays and does not show whether or why their poetry can be spoken and communicated.

27. CLARKE, BRENNA KATZ: *The Emergence of the Irish Peasant Play*

at the Abbey Theatre. Ann Arbor: UMI Research Press, 1982. xii, 223 pp. (Theater and Dramatic Studies. 12.)
Frequent references to Yeats (see index).

28. COLUM, PADRAIC: "Poet's Progress: W. B. Yeats in the Theatre," *TAM*, 19:12 (Dec 1935), 936-43.
Reprinted in Rosamond Gilder and others (eds): *Theatre Arts Anthology: A Record and a Prophecy*. NY: Theatre Arts Books, [1950]. xvi, 687 pp. (pp. 143-51). A somewhat longer version of the article appeared as "A Poet's Progress in the Theatre," *DM*, 11:2 (Apr-June 1936), 10-23.

29. CRAIG, EDWARD GORDON: *The Theatre Advancing*. Boston: Little, Brown, 1920 [i.e., 1919]. vii, 298 pp.
"The Poet and Motion Pictures," 266-68: "His plays as they were at first are as well fitted for the modern stage as are Shakespeare's plays--that is to say, not at all."

30. DALGARD, OLAV: *Teatret i det 20. hundreåret*. New revised edition. Oslo: Norske Samlaget, 1976 [1955]. 345 pp. (Orion-bokene. 192.)
"Yeats--Synge," 35-40.

31. DASGUPTA, PRANABENDU: "The 'Subjective' Tradition: A Comparative Analysis of the Dramatic Motives in the Plays of W. B. Yeats and Rabindranath Tagore," Ph.D. thesis, U of Minnesota, 1963. ii, 65 pp. (*DAI*, 27:12 [June 1967], 4245A)

32. DAVIDSON, CLIFFORD, C. J. GIANAKARIS, and JOHN H. STROUPE (eds): *Drama in the Twentieth Century: Comparative and Critical Essays*. NY: AMS Press, 1984. xii, 387 pp. (AMS Studies in Modern Literature. 11.)
F. C. McGrath: "Paterian Aesthetics in Yeats' Drama," 125-40; reprinted from *CompD*, 13:1 (Spring 1979), 33-48. Discusses Pater's influence on Yeats's dramatic theories and on his view of Shakespeare, as well as *The Shadowy Waters* and *On Baile's Strand*.
Murray Baumgarten: "'Body's Image': *Yerma, The Player Queen,* and the Upright Posture," 141-50; reprinted from *CompD*, 8:3 (Fall 1974), 290-99. "Yeats and Lorca celebrate the body by articulating and enacting its image."

33. DONOGHUE, DENIS: *The Third Voice: Modern British and American Verse Drama*. Princeton: Princeton UP, 1959. vi, 286 pp.
"Yeats and the Clean Outline," 32-61; reprinted from *SR*, 65:2 (Apr-June 1957), 202-25. Yeats's development as a verse dramatist, especially in *The Shadowy Waters, The Hour-Glass, At the Hawk's Well,* and *A Full Moon in March*. See index for further references.

34. D[RINKWATER], J[OHN]: "Notes," *Scallop-Shell*, 2 (Apr 1911), 2-4.

35. DRIVER, TOM FAW: *Romantic Quest and Modern Query: A History of the Modern Theatre*. NY: Delacorte Press, 1970. xviii, 493 pp.
On Yeats, passim (see index), especially pp. 131-36. Disappointing, because Yeats's plays are not related to the problem reflected in the book's title, and somewhat uninformed.

36. EDWARDS, HILTON: *The Mantle of Harlequin*. Dublin: Progress House, 1958. xvi, 127 pp.
On Yeats's plays, the Abbey, and the Gate Theatre, pp. 1-6.

Photographs of Gate productions of *The King of the Great Clock Tower* and *The Countess Cathleen* between pp. 16-17, 80-81.

37. EGRI, PÉTER: *Törésvonalak: Drámai irányok az európai századfordulón (1871-1917)*. Budapest: Gondolat, 1983. 448 pp.
"Broken lines: Dramatic trends in Europe at the turn of the century." See "William Butler Yeats," 138-61, discussed as a representative of symbolist drama. The greater part of this essay was published as "A lehetőség drámája: W. B. Yeats költői színpadáról" [The drama of possibility: WBY's poetic theater], *FK*, 23:1 (1977), 40-46.

38. ELLIS-FERMOR, UNA: *The Irish Dramatic Movement*. London: Methuen, 1964 [1939]. xvii, 241 pp.
Still a very good book. Contains the following chapters: "The Origins and Significance of the Irish Dramatic Movement," "The English Theatre in the Nineties," "The Early History of the Movement," "Ideals in the Workshop," and individual chapters on various playwrights. On Yeats see pp. 91-116, and passim.
Reviews:
- Anon.: "The Rise of the Irish Drama," *IrT*, 23 Dec 1939, 5.
- F. S. Boas, *English*, 3:14 (Summer 1940), 86-87.
- [Harold Child]: "Ireland's Dramatic Renaissance: Poetic Faith and Works," *TLS*, 9 Dec 1939, 714.
- Austin Clarke, *DM*, 15:2 (Apr-June 1940), 70-71.
- Denis Donoghue, *Studies*, 44:[] (Spring 1955), 121-22.
- Gabriel Fallon: "Amazing Theatres," *IrM*, 68:799 (Jan 1940), 30-37.
- J. J. H[ogan], *Studies*, 28:112 (Dec 1939), 692-94.

39. ENGELKING, LESZEK: "Yeats sztuka dla tancerzy" [Yeats's plays for dancers], *Literatura na świecie*, 124 (Aug 1981), 208-19.

40. EREMINA, I. K.: "Ranniaia dramaturgiia Uil'iama Batlera Eĭtsa" [The early drama of WBY], *Moskovskiĭ oblastnoĭ pedagogicheskiĭ institut imeni N. K. Krupskoĭ: Uchenye zapiski*, 175:10 (1967), 113-27.

41. EVANS, GARETH LLOYD: *The Language of Modern Drama*. London: Dent, 1977. xx, 252 pp.
"W. B. Yeats--The Poet in the Theatre," 114-28.

42. EYLER, AUDREY S.: "His Hour Come Round at Last?--W. B. Yeats, Playwright," *Eire*, 13:4 (Winter 1978), 52-64.
Mainly an analysis of the July 1976 Dublin production of *The Hour-Glass*, *The Words upon the Window-Pane*, and *The Cat and the Moon*. See also EE306.

43. FARAG, F. F.: "The Unpopular Theatre of W. B. Yeats," *Cairo Studies in English*, 1963/66, 97-108.
Particularly on *The Shadowy Waters*, *The Unicorn from the Stars*, and the influence of the Nō.

44. FAY, WILLIAM GEORGE, and CATHERINE CARSWELL: *The Fays of the Abbey Theatre: An Autobiographical Record*. With a foreword by James Bridie. NY: Harcourt, Brace, 1935. xv, 314 pp.
In Fay's view, the Abbey "was first and foremost a theatrical, not a literary movement" (p. 106). Contains scattered comments on Yeats's plays, especially *Deirdre* (pp. 207-10). The Fays found that Yeats's dramatic verse was "as easy to speak as any play of Shakespeare's" (p. 112).

45. FEICHTNER, WALTER: "Das Wiederaufleben des englischen Versdramas im zwanzigsten Jahrhundert," Dr.phil. thesis, U of Wien, 1951. ii, 133 pp.
On Yeats's theory of verse drama, pp. 16-18; on his plays, 33-37.

46. FLANNERY, JAMES W.: "The Abbey Theatre: Dublin, Summer 1970," *ETJ,* 22:4 (Dec 1970), 414-15.
The public may yet come around to see the importance and quality of Yeats's plays.

47. ———: "Poetry and Politics in Revolutionary Belfast," *George Spelvin's Theatre Book,* 4:3 (Fall 1982), 69-78.
Reprinted in *Threshold,* 33 (Winter 1983), 27-33. On staging *Cathleen ni Houlihan* and *The Unicorn from the Stars* and generally on Yeats's "dramatic legacy."

48. FOX, R. M.: "Yeats and Social Drama," *IrW,* 9 (Oct 1949), 62-67.
Yeats's dislike of social drama was a mistake. There is enough social life in Ireland to provide subject matter for drama.

49. [FRASER, G. S.]: "Ideas into Drama," *TLS,* 19 Aug 1960, 529.
The problematic relationship between ideas and dramatic effectiveness in Yeats's plays.

50. FRICKER, ROBERT: *Das historische Drama in England von der Romantik bis zur Gegenwart.* Bern: Francke, 1940. vi, 363 pp. (Schweizer anglistische Arbeiten / Swiss Studies in English. [8].)
See pp. 287-95, 312-15.

51. ———: *Das moderne englische Drama.* 2nd edition, revised. Göttingen: Vandenhoeck & Ruprecht, 1974 [1964]. 239 pp. (Kleine Vandenhoeck-Reihe. 1172.)
"William Butler Yeats," 32-45, and passim (see index).

52. GAD, CARL: *Omkring kulturkrisen: Strejftog i moderne litteratur.* København: Schultz, 1929. 203 pp.
"W. B. Yeats og den keltiske renaissance," 71-86. An extended version was published as "Moderne irsk theater," *Ugens tilskuer,* 6:299 (23 June 1916), 313-15; :301 (7 July 1916), 329-31; :309 (1 Sept 1916), 391-94. See especially the third installment.

53. GAMACHE, LAWRENCE B., and IAN S. MACNIVEN (eds): *The Modernists: Studies in a Literary Phenomenon. Essays in Honor of Harry T. Moore.* Rutherford, N.J.: Fairleigh Dickinson UP, 1987. 303 pp.
James Flannery: "In Search of a Poetic Drama for the Post-Modernist Age," 75-91; discusses Yeats's dramas briefly.

54. GAMBERINI, SPARTACO: "Il teatro di William Butler Yeats: L'Abbey Théâtre, Ezra Pound e i nô, le ultimo opere," *Rivista di studi teatrali,* 1:11-12 (July-Dec 1954), 47-89.

55. GASKELL, RONALD: *Drama and Reality: The European Theatre since Ibsen.* London: Routledge & Kegan Paul, 1972. x, 171 pp.
Notes on Yeats's plays, passim (see index).

56. GASSNER, JOHN: *The Theatre in Our Times: A Survey of the Men, Materials and Movements in the Modern Theatre.* NY: Crown, 1963 [1954]. xiii, 609 pp.
"Yeats: The Limits of Drama," 226-33.

57. ———: *Directions in Modern Theatre and Drama.* An expanded version of *Form and Idea in Modern Theatre.* NY: Holt, Rinehart & Winston, 1965 [1956]. xvi, 457 pp.
Scattered notes on Yeats's plays, especially on *A Full Moon in March* (see index).

58. ———, and RALPH GILMORE ALLEN (eds): *Theatre and Drama in the Making.* Boston: Houghton Mifflin, 1964. 2 vols.
Scattered references to Yeats, passim, especially 2:784-86.

59. GASSNER, JOHN: *Dramatic Soundings: Evaluations and Retractions Culled from 30 Years of Dramatic Criticism.* Introduction and posthumous editing by Glenn Loney. NY: Crown, 1968. xx, 716 pp.
See index for some notes on the plays.

60. GERSTENBERGER, DONNA LORINE: *The Complex Configuration: Modern Verse Drama.* Salzburg: Institut für Englische Sprache und Literatur, Universität Salzburg, 1973. vi, 178 pp. (Salzburg Studies in English Literature: Poetic Drama. 5.)
Based on "Formal Eperiments in Modern Verse Drama," Ph.D. thesis, U of Oklahoma, 1958. v, 195 pp. (*DAI,* 19:7 [Jan 1959], 1757-58). "W. B. Yeats: 'Everything Sublunary Must Change,'" 10-40; especially on *The Shadowy Waters, At the Hawk's Well, Calvary,* and *Purgatory.*

61. GOGARTY, OLIVER: "The Irish Literary Revival: Present Poetry and Drama in Dublin," *Dublin Evening Mail,* 4 Mar 1905, 2.
Criticizes Yeats's plays, particularly *On Baile's Strand,* because they tend "to lilliputianise our legends."

62. GONZALEZ PADILLA, MARÍA ENRIQUETA: "El teatro de W. B. Yeats," *Anglia: Anuario de estudios angloamericanos,* 2 (1969), 105-21.

63. GOSSE, EDMUND: "The Revival of Poetic Drama," *Atlantic Monthly,* 90:538 (Aug 1902), 156-66.
Notes that Yeats "obtains new effects by plunging deeper than the dramatist has hitherto been expected to plunge into the agitations and exigencies of the soul." Unlike Stephen Phillips, however, he "separates himself from the common observation of mankind."

64. GRIFFIN, CHRISTOPHER: "Visions and Revisions," *Theatre Ireland,* 9/10 (Spring/Summer 1985), 145-51.
Interview with Eric Bentley who comments on Yeats's plays. See also EB9-10.

65. GUERRERO ZAMORA, JUAN: *Historia de teatro contemporáneo.* Barcelona: Flors, 1961. 4 vols.
"William Butler Yeats," 2:243-55.

66. GWYNN, STEPHEN: "Poetry and the Stage," *FortnR,* os 91 / ns 85:506 (Feb 1909), 337-51.
Reprinted in *Living Age,* 3 Apr 1909, 3-14.

67. HABART, MICHEL: "Le théâtre irlandais," *Théâtre populaire,* 9 (Sept-Oct 1954), 24-43.
On Yeats's plays, passim.

68. HAERDTER, MICHAEL: "William Butler Yeats--Irisches Theater zwischen Symbolismus und Expressionismus," *Maske und Kothurn,* 11:1 (1965), 30-42.

Mainly on *Deirdre, The Words upon the Window-Pane* and the influence of the Nō.

69. HALBRITTER, RUDOLF: *Konzeptionsformen des modernen anglo-amerikanischen Kurzdramas: Dargestellt an Stücken von W. B. Yeats, Th. Wilder and* [sic] *H. Pinter*. Göttingen: Vandenhoeck & Ruprecht, 1975. 250 pp. (Palaestra. 263.)

English summary in *EASG*, 1975, 126-29. "Yeats' Symbolauffassung," 41-48 (Yeats's concept of the symbol); "William Butler Yeats' symbolistische Kurzdramen," 48-101, on *The Shadowy Waters, On Baile's Strand, At the Hawk's Well, The Only Jealousy of Emer*, and *Calvary*.

Reviews:

- Rüdiger Imhof, *MD*, 20:1 (Mar 1977), 101-4.
- Heinz Kosok, *GRM*, 28:3 (1978), 373-75.
- Kurt Tetzeli von Rosador, *Archiv*, year 130 / 215:1 (1978), 191-94.

70. HENDERSON, W. A.: "The Abbey Theatre: Mr. Yeats's Innings," *Sunday Independent*, 1 Oct 1922, 4.

On the unpopularity of Yeats's "beautiful poetic plays."

71. HENSEL, GEORG: *Spielplan: Schauspielführer von der Antike bis zur Gegenwart*. Berlin: Propyläen, 1966. 2 vols.

"Das Sprechzimmer der Seelenkenner oder: Dramatiker, die man Naturalisten nennt" [The consultation room of those who know the soul, or: Dramatists who are called naturalists], 2, xii; contains an Irish section (pp. 786-804) with notes, somewhat incongruously, on Yeats's plays, especially *The Countess Cathleen* and *The Unicorn from the Stars* (pp. 789-92). Second edition: 1975. 1459 pp. (on Yeats, pp. 815-18).

72. HINCHLIFFE, ARNOLD P.: *Modern Verse Drama*. London: Methuen, 1977. xiii, 80 pp. (Critical Idiom. 32.)

Passim; considers *Purgatory* to be Yeats's "finest verse drama."

73. HOGAN, ROBERT: *After the Irish Renaissance: A Critical History of the Irish Drama since "The Plough and the Stars."* Minneapolis: U of Minnesota Press, 1967. xii, 282 pp.

On Yeats, passim (see index), especially pp. 147-51. Maintains that his later plays are private statements, that most of the plays are undramatic, and that he was never interested in the theater and knew little about it.

74. HOUGHTON, NORRIS: *The Exploding Stage: An Introduction to Twentieth Century Drama*. NY: Weybright & Talley, 1971. xv, 269 pp.

On Yeats ("a sort of fin-de-siècle hippie"), pp. 110-12 and passim (see index).

75. HUNT, HUGH, KENNETH RICHARDS and JOHN RUSSELL TAYLOR: *1880 to the Present*. London: Methuen, 1978. xlv, 298 pp. (Revels History of Drama in English. 7.)

See index for references to Yeats.

76. IREMONGER, VALENTIN: "Yeats as a Playwright," *IrW*, 31 (Summer 1955), 51-56.

Yeats had no interest in the theater "as we know it. . . . All his plays are, in fact, poems--or what poems also are, meditations--but, within his self-imposed limits, they are highly dramatic."

77. *Istoriîa zapadnoevropeĭskogo teatra. Tom* 6. Moskva: Iskusstvo, 1974. 656 pp.
E. V. Kornilova: "Irlandskiĭ teatr," 125-58; on Yeats's early plays.

78. JAMESON, STORM: *Modern Drama in Europe*. London: Collins, 1920. xxvi, 280 pp.
Yeats "represents the last state in symbolic imbecility"; his worst play is *The Land of Heart's Desire*. Yeats is defended by B[rinsley] M[acNamara]: "Books and Their Writers," *Gael* [Dublin], 14 Nov 1921, 18-19.

79. KHAĬCHENKO, E.: "Poeticheskiĭ teatr U.-B. Ĭitsa" [WBY's poetic theater], *Teatr*, 6 (June 1977), 127-35.

80. KHAN, B. A.: *The English Poetic Drama*. Aligarh: Muslim U, 1962. xiv, 79 pp. (Faculty of Arts Publication Series. 8.)
See pp. 28-32.

81. KNIGHT, GEORGE WILSON: *The Golden Labyrinth: A Study of British Drama*. London: Phoenix House, 1962. xiv, 402 pp.
See pp. 322-28 and passim.

82. KRAUSE, DAVID: *The Profane Book of Irish Comedy*. Ithaca: Cornell UP, 1982. 341 pp.
Incorporates "The Ironic Victory of Defeat in Irish Comedy," *OCA*, 1 (1982), 33-63; and other previously published articles. On Yeats passim (see index).

83. LAMM, MARTIN: *Det moderna dramat*. Stockholm: Bonnier, 1948. v, 363 pp.
"Irländskt drama," 299-319. English edition: *Modern Drama*. Translated by Karin Elliott. Oxford: Blackwell, 1952. xx, 359 pp. "Irish Drama," 293-314; on Yeats, pp. 295-302 (prefers the pre-1910 plays).

84. LEAMON, WARREN: "Shaw, Yeats and the Modern Theatre," Ph.D. thesis, University College Dublin, 1973. ii, 261 pp.
Compares the achievements of Yeats and Shaw as dramatists and critics.

85. ———: "The Romantic as Playwright," *WHR*, 36:2 (Summer 1982), 97-108.

86. LENSON, DAVID: *Achilles' Choice: Examples of Modern Tragedy*. Princeton: Princeton UP, 1975. xi, 178 pp.
"Toward Lyric Tragedy: W. B. Yeats," 65-97. Mainly on *The Unicorn from the Stars*, *King Oedipus*, and Yeats's "tragic" poems.

87. LUCAS, FRANK LAURENCE: *The Drama of Chekhov, Synge, Yeats, and Pirandello*. London: Cassell, 1963. xii, 452 pp.
"William Butler Yeats," 239-355; discusses *A Vision*, and, somewhat superficially, most of the plays.

88. LUNARI, GIGI: *Il movimento drammatico irlandese (1899-1922)*. Bologna: Cappelli, 1960. 175 pp. (Documenti di teatro. 13.)
See especially "William B. Yeats e l'idea di un teatro," 41-62; "Il Teatro Letterario Irlandese e la prima fase sperimentale (1899-1901)," 63-79, with notes on *The Countess Cathleen* and *Diarmuid and Grania*, and passim (no index).

89. ——— (ed): *Teatro irlandese.* Milano: Nuova Accademia, 1961. 320 pp. (Thesaurus Litterarum, sezione terza: Teatro di tutto il mondo. 29.)

See "Panorama del teatro irlandese," 9-36.

90. LYRIC PLAYERS THEATRE, BELFAST: *A Needle's Eye.* [Edited by Mary O'Malley and John Boyd]. Belfast: Lyric Players Theatre, [1980?]. 112 pp.

See particularly John W. Boyle: "The Making of a Theatre, 1951-68," 7, 9-10; on the Yeats productions put on by the theater. See also EB7, 121.

Denis Donoghue: "The Politics of Yeats's Theatre," 13, 15, 17; see FG17.

Seamus Deane: "Synge's Western Worlds," 19-25.

John Hewitt: "In Recollection of Drumcliffe, September, 1948," 47; a poem.

W. R. Rodgers: "Prologue to *The Countess Cathleen*," 48-49; a poem.

Sam McCready: "Imperceptibly into Song," 51-54; on Yeats's views concerning dramatic speech, recitation, and the speaking to the psaltery experiments.

Conor O'Malley: "The Plays of W. B. Yeats--A Time of Reassessment," 64-70; argues that the plays are "thoroughly theatrical in conception," but have had only few successful performances because they are very demanding.

Raymond Warren: "An Idea of Music," 79-83; see also EC116.

"Lyric Theatre Productions 1969-1979," 95, 99, 101, 103; the productions include most of Yeats's plays. Numerous photographs throughout the book of productions of Yeats's plays.

91. MCBRIEN, PETER: "Dramatic Ideals of To-day," *Studies,* 11:42 (June 1922), 235-42.

"Mr. Yeats's drama is not great art, for great art is always humanly alive."

92. *McGraw-Hill Encyclopedia of World Drama.* [Revised edition]. NY: McGraw-Hill, 1984. 5 vols.

Carol Gelderman: "Irish Drama," 3:65-75; "Yeats, William Butler (1865-1939)," 5:184-87.

93. MCGREEVY, THOMAS: "Mr. W. B. Yeats as a Dramatist," *Revue anglo-américaine,* 7:1 (Oct 1929), 19-36.

94. MCHUGH, ROGER: "The Plays of W. B. Yeats," *Threshold,* 19 (Autumn 1965), 3-13.

95. MCLEOD, STUART RAMSAY: *Modern Verse Drama.* Salzburg: Institut für Englische Sprache und Literatur, Universität Salzburg, 1972. iv, 345 pp. (Salzburg Studies in English Literature: Poetic Drama. 2.)

Based on "Problems of Poetry and Dramaturgy in Modern Verse Drama," Ph.D. thesis, U of Florida, 1961. iv, 364 pp. (*DAI,* 29:3 [Sept 1968], 904A). See passim; discusses *The Herne's Egg, The Dreaming of the Bones,* and *A Full Moon in March.*

96. MACNEICE, LOUIS: "Some Notes on Mr. Yeats' Plays," *New Verse,* 18 (Dec 1935), 7-9.

97. MAGILL, FRANK N. (ed): *Critical Survey of Drama: English Language Series.* Englewood Cliffs, N.J.: Salem Press, 1985. 6 vols.

Cóilín D. Owens: "William Butler Yeats," 5:2115-22.

98. MALONE, ANDREW E.: *The Irish Drama*. NY: Blom, 1965 [1929]. vii, 351 pp.

See pp. 42-52, 129-46, and passim. Malone was a regular theatergoer and critic whose taste was essentially conservative. Yeats's later plays are beyond his comprehension, of the earlier ones he says: "Two or three of his plays are dramatic in the ordinary meaning of the word, but all the others depend upon something which is strictly not necessary to the theatre. . . . He is not the greatest of the symbolists, in fact it is doubtful if he be a profound thinker at all. Surfaces and emotions have attracted him more than logic and thought" (p. 145).

Reviews:
- Anon., *DM*, 4:3 (July-Sept 1929), 73-75.
- Anon.: "Irish Drama," *SatRL*, 15 June 1929, 802.
- Anon., *TAM*, 14:3 (Mar 1930), 269-70.
- Ralph Sargent Bailey, *Theatre*, 50:343 (Oct 1929), 6.
- [Harold Child]: "The Irish Drama," *TLS*, 23 May 1929, 417.
- W[illiam] D[awson], *Studies*, 18:70 (June 1929), 353-54.
- M. R. N., *IrSt*, 29 June 1929, 333-34.
- M. P.: "'Irlandskaia' dramaturgiia," *Vestnik inostrannoĭ literatury*, 5 (1930), 175-76.
- [Geoffrey Phibbs]: "The Theatre in Dublin," *Nation & Athenaeum*, 15 June 1929, 369-70.
- [V. S. Pritchett]: "The Irishman's Stage," *Spect*, 17 Aug 1929, 226.
- W. P. Ryan: "Drama and Democracy," *BmL*, 76:455 (Aug 1929), 271.

99. MANDELBAUM, ALLEN: "Stasis and Dynamis: Two Modes of the Literary Imagination," Ph.D. thesis, Columbia U, [1951]. v, 276 pp. (*DAI*, 12:4 [1952], 426)

Note on Yeats as a "static dramatist," pp. 203-9.

100. MARTINEC, DOMINIK: "Dramatik W. B. Yeats: Čiže tiene nad írskym symbolizmom. (Niekol'ko informácií o jeho názorach a diele)," *Slovenské divadlo*, 16:3 (1968), 351-76.

"The dramatist W. B. Yeats: Shadows over Irish symbolism; some informations on his opinions and his work"; on the plays and the dramatic theories.

101. MAXWELL, DESMOND ERNEST STEWART: *A Critical History of Modern Irish Drama, 1891-1980*. Cambridge: Cambridge UP, 1984. xvii, 250 pp.

Many references to Yeats's plays and his work for the Irish theater (see index).

Reviews:
- Ronald Ayling, *Essays in Theatre*, 5:2 (May 1987), 139-44.
- Seamus Deane, *CJIS*, 12:1 (June 1986), 95-97.
- James F. Kilroy, *Yeats*, 4 (1986), 209-13.

102. MEACHAEN, PATRICK: "Two Irish Dramatists," *Library Assistant*, 20:341 (June 1927), 123-34.

Yeats and O'Casey; *The Countess Cathleen*, *The Land of Heart's Desire*, and *Cathleen ni Houlihan* are Yeats's best plays. "The remainder . . . are in reality beautiful dramatic poems."

103. MERCIER, VIVIAN: "In Defense of Yeats as a Dramatist," *MD*, 8:2 (Sept 1965), 161-66.

Mainly on *The Player Queen*, *Purgatory*, and *The Resurrection*.

104. MISRA, K. S.: *Twentieth Century English Poetic Drama: A Revaluation*. New Delhi: Vikas, 1981. vii, 367 pp.
"Poetic Drama before T. S. Eliot: The Irish Phase," 16-49, and passim on Yeats's plays (see index).

105. MOONEY, DONAL: "W. B. Yeats: No Dramatist He," *Hibernia*, 24 Aug 1973, 19.
Refers to a London-based "Yeats Repertory Theatre Company" directed by Niema Ash, on which see also EC3a, 109.

106. MOORE, JOHN REES: "Cuchulain, Christ, and the Queen of Love: Aspects of Yeatsian Drama," *TDR*, 6:3 (Mar 1962), 150-59.

107. ———: "The Idea of a Yeats Play," in Maxwell and Bushrui: *W. B. Yeats 1865-1965* (1965, CA71), 154-66.
"The plays . . . are for our time whether we will or no."

108. NICOLL, ALLARDYCE: *British Drama: An Historical Survey from the Beginnings to the Present Time*. 4th edition revised. London: Harrap, 1951 [1925]. vii, 533 pp.
"Irish Dramatists," 391-99. On Yeats's early plays, pp. 405-10.

109. ———: *World Drama from Aeschylus to Anouilh*. London: Harrap, 1951 [1949]. iv, 1000 pp.
"The Irish School," 689-98; on Yeats, pp. 729-31 and passim (see index).

110. ———: *English Drama, 1900-1930: The Beginnings of the Modern Period*. Cambridge: UP, 1973. x, 1083 pp.
Notes on Yeats's plays, passim (see index).

111. NÜNNING, JOSEFA (ed): *Das englische Drama*. Darmstadt: Wissenschaftliche Buchgesellschaft, 1973. xiv, 538 pp.
Paul Goetsch: "Yeats and Synge," 492-97; mainly on *The Dreaming of the Bones* and *Purgatory*.

112. OBERG, ARTHUR KENNETH: "Contemporary Verse and Poetic Drama," Ph.D. thesis, Harvard U, 1965. iii, 303 pp.
"Yeats as Poetic Dramatist," 158-218.

113. O'CONNOR, FRANK, STEPHEN SPENDER, and EDITH EVANS: "Verse and Prose in Drama: A Discussion," *List*, 13 Feb 1941, 239-40.
Yeats is mentioned passim.

114. O'CONNOR, FRANK: *The Art of the Theatre*. Dublin: Fridberg, 1947. 50 pp.
See pp. 24-26.

115. O'DRISCOLL, ROBERT (ed): *Theatre and Nationalism in Twentieth-Century Ireland*. Toronto: U of Toronto Press, 1971. 216 pp.
See especially Ann Saddlemyer: "Stars of the Abbey Ascendancy," 21-39; on the foundations and early history.

George Mills Harper: "'Intellectual Hatred' and 'Intellectual Nationalism': The Paradox of Passionate Politics," 40-65.

W. B. Yeats: "Two Lectures on the Irish Theatre." Edited by Robert O'Driscoll, 66-88. First printing of a lecture written in 1913 and reprint of "The Irish Dramatic Movement" from *The Voice of Ireland* (Wade 314A).

David R. Clark: "Yeats, Theatre, and Nationalism," 134-55; on *The Death of Cuchulain* and *The Dreaming of the Bones*.

M. J. Sidnell: "Hic and Ille: Shaw and Yeats," 156-78; includes seven previously unpublished letters from WBY to GBS, 1901-32.

Four photographs from a performance of *The Death of Cuchulain*.

Reviews:
- [Austin Clarke]: "Abbey Ascendant," *TLS*, 28 Jan 1972, 100.
- Gabriel Fallon: "Soul and Soil," *IrP*, 16 Oct 1971, 12.
- T. R. Henn, *MLR*, 67:4 (Oct 1972), 879-80.
- Denis Johnston: "National Theatre," *Hibernia*, 3 Mar 1972, 11.
- Tomas MacAnna: "An Irish Theatre?" *IrT*, 6 Nov 1971, 9.
- Norman H. MacKenzie, *DR*, 51:3 (Autumn 1971), 433-35.
- Brian F. Tyson, *MD*, 14:4 (Feb 1972), 480-81.

116. Ó HAODHA, MICHEÁL: *Theatre in Ireland*. Oxford: Blackwell, 1974. xiv, 160 pp.

Includes chapters on "The Founders of the National Theatre" (among them Yeats) and "Poetry on the Fringe" (Yeats's plays and their influence).

117. Ó h-É[igeartaigh] [O'HEGARTY], P. S.: "W. B. Yeats, Dramatist?" *Inis Fáil*, 30 (Mar 1907), 4-5.

"Mr. Yeats' genius is essentially lyrical, not dramatic."

118. ———: "Irish Dramatic Impressions," *Irish Nation*, 16 July 1910, 1.

Continued in the following issues; see particularly "V.--Poetical Drama and the Pilgrim Players," 13 Aug 1910, 1; "VII.--Yeats," 24 Sept 1910, 1.

119. OLSSON, JAN OLOF, and MARGARETA SJÖGREN: *Plogen och stjärnorna: Irländsk dramatik i verkligheten och på scenen. En krönika skriven för Radioteaterns huvudserie 1968/69 "Det irländska dramat."* Stockholm: Sverige's Radios Förlag, 1968. 208 pp.

"The plough and the stars: Irish drama in reality and on the stage." Yeats is discussed on pp. 62-102 and passim (see index). In the course of the program, *Cathleen ni Houlihan* and *The Unicorn from the Stars* were broadcast. See also the review by Clas Zilliacus, *Eire*, 4:2 (Summer 1969), 150-52.

120. O'MAHONY, MATHEW: *Progress Guide to Anglo-Irish Plays*. Dublin: Progress House, 1960. xx, 182 pp.

Author and title indexes, as well as plot outlines. Yeats's plays are annotated passim.

121. O'MALLEY, MARY: "The Dream Itself," *Threshold*, 19 (Autumn 1965), 58-63.

The Yeats productions of the Lyric Players Theatre, Belfast. See also *Lyric Theatre, 1951-1968*. [Belfast, 1968. 69 pp.] (a souvenir of the opening of the new theater); Mary O'Malley: "Theatre in Belfast," *Iris Hibernia*, 4:3 (1960), 55-57; "Irish Theatre Letter," *MR*, 6:1 (Autumn-Winter 1964-65), 181-86; and EB90. The company specializes in the production of Yeats's plays.

122. ORR, JOHN: *Tragic Drama and Modern Society: Studies in the Social and Literary Theory of Drama from 1870 to the Present*. London: Macmillan, 1981. xix, 280 pp.

"The Irish Renaissance," 117-62; discusses *On Baile's Strand* and *The Death of Cuchulain*. Reviewed by David Krause, *Yeats*, 1 (1983), 209-15.

123. PAINTER, SUSAN GAY: "'Drama within the Limitations of Art': A Study of Some Plays by Maeterlinck, Yeats, Beckett, and Pinter," Ph. D. thesis, U of London, 1978. 2 vols.
"W. B. Yeats," 1:146-231, includes sections on Yeats and Maeterlinck, *The Shadowy Waters, The Hour-Glass, The Cat and the Moon,* and Yeats in relation to Shaw and Eliot. See also "Beckett and Yeats," 2:58-64.

123a. PARKIN, ANDREW: "Escaping the Press and People Digesting Their Dinners with Particular Reference to *The Herne's Egg* ," *EI,* 13:1 (June 1988), 81-93.
A defense of Yeats's plays (they are "tougher than was at one time thought possible").

124. PATTERSON, GERTRUDE: "W. B. Yeats in the Theatre: The Challenge of the Poetic Play," *YER,* 6:2 (1979), 29-40.
Reprinted in *Threshold,* 31 (Autumn/Winter 1980), 17-30. Compares the plays of Yeats and Eliot.

125. PEACOCK, RONALD: *The Poet in the Theatre*. NY: Hill & Wang, 1960 [1946]. xiii, 198 pp. (Dramabook. D23.)
"Yeats," 117-28 (one of the ablest defenses of Yeats the dramatist).

126. ———: *The Art of Drama*. London: Routledge & Kegan Paul, 1960 [1957]. vi, 263 pp.
Some scattered notes (see index).

127. PELLIZZI, CAMILLO: *Il teatro inglese*. Milano: Treves, 1934. v, 434 pp. (Il teatro del novecento. 3.)
See pp. 234-42. English edition: *English Drama: The Last Great Phase*. Translated by Rowan Williams. London: Macmillan, 1935. ix, 306 pp. (pp. 176-83).

128. PETER, JOHN: *Vladimir's Carrot: Modern Drama and the Modern Imagination*. London: Deutsch, 1987. xi, 372 pp.
See index for some notes on Yeats's plays, particularly *At the Hawk's Well*.

129. PINE, RICHARD (ed): *All for Hecuba*. An exhibition to mark the Golden Jubilee of the Edwards-MacLiammóir partnership and of the Gate Theatre 1928-1978. [Dublin: Hugh Lane Gallery of Modern Art, 1978]. Unpaged.
Frequent references to performances of Yeats's plays; his involvement in the Irish theater is also discussed in Pine's article "The Gate Theatre 1928-1978."

130. POEL, WILLIAM: "Poetry in Drama," *ContempR,* 104:575 (Nov 1913), 699-707.
Yeats's plays are too theoretical in nature.

131. POPKIN, HENRY: "Yeats as Dramatist," *TDR,* 3:3 (Mar 1959), 73-82.

132. PRIOR, MOODY ERASMUS: *The Language of Tragedy*. Bloomington: Indiana UP, 1966 [1947]. xi, 430 pp. (Midland Book. MB86.)
The second edition incorporates "Poetic Drama: An Analysis and a Suggestion," *EIE,* 1949, 3-32. On Yeats's dramatic theory and practice, especially *Calvary* and *Purgatory,* pp. 326-40, and passim (see index).

133. *Problemy metoda i poetiki v zarubezhnykh literaturakh XIX–XX vekov: Mezhvuzovskiĭ sbornik nauchnykh trudov.* Perm': Permskiĭ ordena trudovogo krasnogo znameni gosudarstvennyĭ universitet im. A. M. Gor'kogo, 1985. 168 pp.

T. M. Polîudova: "Svoeobrazie zhanrovoĭ struktury poeticheskoĭ dramy U. B. Ĭetsa" [The originality of the genre structures of WBY's poetic drama], 75–84; discusses Yeats's dramatic theories and *Cathleen ni Houlihan*.

134. PROTOPOPESCU, DRAGOŞ: *Fenomenul englez: Studii si interpretări.* Bucureşti: Fundaţia pentru literatură şi artă "Regele Carol II," 1936. 472 pp.

"Lirism englez contemporan, sau spre o substanţializare a poeziei," 362–437; on Yeats's plays, pp. 378–87.

135. RAFROIDI, PATRICK, RAYMONDE POPOT, and WILLIAM PARKER (eds): *Aspects of the Irish Theatre.* Lille: P.U.L. / Paris: Editions universitaires, [1972]. 300 pp. (Cahiers irlandais. 1.)

On Yeats see especially Pascale Mathelin: "Irish Myths in the Theatre of W. B. Yeats," 163–71.

Raymonde Popot: "The Hero's Light," 173–212; discusses the Cuchulain myth.

Mireille Schodet: "The Theme of Diarmuid and Grainne," 213–23.

Christiane Thilliez: "From One Theatrical Reformer to Another: W. B. Yeats's Unpublished Letters to Gordon Craig," 275–86; includes quotations from the letters that are now in the Bibliothèque Nationale, Paris. The most interesting article of the collection.

See also the review by Andrew T. L. Parkin, *Eire,* 8:2 (Summer 1973), 137–44.

136. REISS, TIMOTHY J.: "The Golden Cradle and the Beggar-Man: Problems of Yeats's Poetics," *CRCL,* 3:1 (Winter 1976), 75–93.

Uses Bakhtin's distinction between monological discourse and dialogical intercourse in an interpretation of the plays, particularly *The King's Threshold* and *The Unicorn from the Stars.*

137. REXROTH, KENNETH: *Bird in the Bush: Obvious Essays.* NY: New Directions, 1959. x, 246 pp.

"The Plays of Yeats," 235–41.

138. ROBINSON, LENNOX: "Recipe for a National Theatre," *Realist,* 1:3 (June 1929), 130–41.

On Yeats's plays, passim.

139. ——— (ed): *The Irish Theatre.* Lectures delivered during the Abbey Theatre Festival held in Dublin in August 1938. London: Macmillan, 1939. xiii, 229 pp.

See especially Andrew E. Malone: "The Early History of the Abbey Theatre," 1–28.

F. R. Higgins: "Yeats and Poetic Drama in Ireland," 65–88. Yeats is the only poetic dramatist in Ireland; he has no predecessors and no successors.

Michael MacLiammoir: "Problem Plays," 199–227; i.e. plays that deal with Irish problems, among them *The Countess Cathleen* and *The Land of Heart's Desire.*

Reviews:

- Anon.: "Irish Poetry and Plays," *Scotsman,* 29 Feb 1940, 9.
- Anon., *TAM,* 24:4 (Apr 1940), 299–300.

- Benjamin Gilbert Brooks: "The Irish Theatre," *Nineteenth Century and After*, 128:762 (Aug 1940), 196-200.
- Ivor Brown: "The Irish Motley," *Obs*, 25 Feb 1940, 4.
- [Harold Child]: "Forty Years of Irish Drama," *TLS*, 13 Apr 1940, 182, 186.
- [———]: "Vital Drama," *TLS*, 13 Apr 1940, 183.
- Austin Clarke: "The Abbey," *NSt*, 6 Apr 1940, 472, 474.
- Norah Hoult: "The Irish Theatre," *LLT*, 25:33 (May 1940), 158-62.
- L. A. G. Strong: "The Eagle Mind," *Time and Tide*, 9 Mar 1940, 251-52.

140. ROLL-HANSEN, DIDERIK: "W. B. Yeats som dramatiker," *Edda*, year 52 / 65:3 (1965), 153-64.
Yeats's reaction to the plays of Ibsen and Shaw.

141. ROY, EMIL: *British Drama since Shaw*. With a preface by Harry T. Moore. Carbondale: Southern Illinois UP, 1972. xv, 143 pp.
On Yeats, passim (see index), particularly pp. 36-53 on *The Player Queen*, *The Words upon the Window-Pane*, and *Purgatory*.

142. RUYSSEN, HENRI: "Le théâtre irlandais," *Vie des peuples*, 6:23 (10 Mar 1922), 554-70.

143. SADDLEMYER, ANN: "'The Heroic Discipline of the Looking Glass': W. B. Yeats's Search for Dramatic Design," in Skelton and Saddlemyer: *The World of W. B. Yeats* (1967, CA102), 57-73.
Mostly on *The Player Queen* and the influence of Gordon Craig and Ricketts.

144. SANDBERG, ANNA: "The Anti-Theater of W. B. Yeats," *MD*, 4:2 (Sept 1961), 131-37.
Mainly on *At the Hawk's Well*. Uninformed.

145. SARCAR, SUBHAS: "Modern Poetic Drama," *BDE*, 4:3&4 (1963), 38-48.
"Yeats's greatest contribution to modern drama was that by upholding the urgency of passion and its articulation in beautiful words he paved the way for poetic drama."

146. SCHILLER, SISTER MARY BEATRICE: "Trends in Modern Poetic Drama in English, 1900-1938," Ph.D. thesis, U of Illinois, 1939. xii, 416 pp.
On Yeats's plays, pp. 102-10, 267-74, and passim (see index).

147. SEKINE, MASARU (ed): *Irish Writers and the Theatre*. Gerrards Cross: Smythe / Totowa, N.J.: Barnes & Noble, 1986. viii, 246 pp. (Irish Literary Studies. 23. / IASAIL-Japan Series. 2.)
Richard Allen Cave: "Dramatising the Life of Swift," 17-32; on *The Words upon the Window-Pane*.
Christopher Murray: "Lennox Robinson: The Abbey's Anti-Hero," 114-34; contains some notes on Yeats.
M. Sekine: "Yeats and the Noh," 151-66; on *At the Hawk's Well*, *The Only Jealousy of Emer*, *The Dreaming of the Bones*, and *Deirdre*.
Sumiko Sugiyama: "What's *The Player Queen* All About?" 179-207; also on the poem "The Mask."
Robert Welch: "The Emergence of Modern Anglo-Irish Drama: Yeats and Synge," 208-17; asks "What was Yeats's idea of drama?"; analyzes *Cathleen ni Houlihan*.

Katharine Worth: "Scenic Imagery in the Plays of Yeats and Beckett," 218-32.

148. °SENA, VINOD: "W. B. Yeats and English Poetic Drama," *English Miscellany* [Delhi], 2 (1963), 23-36.

149. SHARP, WILLIAM L.: "W. B. Yeats: A Poet Not in the Theatre," *TDR*, 4:2 (Dec 1959), 67-82.
The plays, especially *At the Hawk's Well* and *Calvary*, fail because they lack "individual speech."

150. SINKO, GRZEGORZ, and TADEUSZ GRZEBIENIOWSKI: *Teatr krajów zachodniej Europy XIX i początku XX wieku* [The theater of the west European countries in the 19th and early 20th centuries]. Vol. 1: *Kraje anglosakie*. Warszawa: Państwowe Wydawnictwo Naukowe, 1954. 210 pp. (Skrypty dla szkół wyższych państwowy instytut sztuki. Materiały do nauki historii teatru. 11.)
"Teatr i dramat irlandzki na przelomie XIX i XX wieku" [Irish theater and drama at the turn of the 19th and 20th century], 126-43.

151. SPENDER, STEPHEN: "The Poetic Drama Today," *List*, 30 Jan 1936, 224-26.
Yeats "has been defeated by blank verse."

152. STAMM, RUDOLF: "Von Theaterkrisen und ihrer Überwindung: Der Beitrag eines Anglisten zur deutsch-schweizerischen Berufsbühnenfrage," *Jahrbuch der Gesellschaft für schweizerische Theaterkultur*, 16 (1946), 1-102.
See "Neues poetisches Drama," 51-70.

153. ———: *Geschichte des englischen Theaters*. Bern: Francke, 1951. 484 pp.
See pp. 388-93, 404-9.

154. ———: *Zwischen Vision und Wirklichkeit: Zehn Essays*. Bern: Francke, 1964. 204 pp.
"William Butler Yeats als Theaterdichter," 140-62; reprint of "William Butler Yeats und das Theater," *NZZ*, 11 May 1963, 22rv; 12 May 1963, 4rv. Discusses *The Land of Heart's Desire*, *Deirdre*, and *Purgatory* as specimens of highly successful drama.

155. STAUB, AUGUST W.: "The 'Unpopular Theatre' of W. B. Yeats," *QJS*, 47:4 (Dec 1961), 363-71.
Yeats's dramas fail because he had the wrong models: Maeterlinck, Gordon Craig and the Nō.

156. STOKES, JOHN ALEC ANTHONY: "The Non-Commercial Theatres in London and Paris in the Late Nineteenth Century and the Origins of the Irish Literary Theatre and Its Successors," Ph.D. thesis, U of Reading, 1968. xii, 578 pp.
See particularly "W. B. Yeats and an Irish Theatre," 119-35; "W. B. Yeats and Bedford Park," 213-21; "Mise-en-scène in Theory and Practice," 276-96; "Yeats and the Actor 1899," 299-304; "The Psaltery," 305-15; "Correspondence between F. J. Fay and W. B. Yeats," 393-485.

157. STORER, EDWARD: "Dramatists of To-day. VIII.--W. B. Yeats," *British R*, 5:3 (Mar 1914), 415-22.
Reprinted in *Living Age*, 9 May 1914, 329-32.

158. STYAN, JOHN LOUIS: *Modern Drama in Theory and Practice*. Cambridge: Cambridge UP, 1981. 3 vols.
See vol. 1: *Realism and Naturalism*. xiii, 208 pp. ("Conflicts in Dublin: The Irish Dramatic Movement," 91-108); vol. 2: *Symbolism, Surrealism, and the Absurd*. xi, 224 pp. ("Symbolist Drama in English: Yeats and the Japanese *Noh* Drama," 61-69, mainly on *At the Hawk's Well*.

158a. TAYLOR, RICHARD: "Lyric Drama from Yeats and Eliot to Beckett and Pinter: Modernist Method and Technique," *Forum Modernes Theater*, 3:2 (1988), 124-41.
Yeats's dramatic method and technique constitute "an important step in the development of twentieth-century theatre."

159. THOULESS, PRISCILLA: *Modern Poetic Drama*. Oxford: Blackwell, 1934. vii, 204 pp.
"W. B. Yeats," 136-62.

160. TISHUNINA, N. V.: *Tema nat͡sional'no-osvoboditel'noĭ bor'by v irlandskom teatre XX veka*. Leningrad: Leningradskiĭ gosudarstvennyĭ institut teatra, muzyki i kinematografii, 1977. 71 pp.
"The theme of the struggle for national independence in the Irish theater of the 20th century." See "Poeticheskai͡a drama V. B. Ĭetsa," 15-45, and passim.

161. TOMLINSON, ALAN: "W. B. Yeats the Playwright," *Gambit*, 4:15 (1970), 98-101.
Yeats's plays now get the attention they deserve; it is hoped that this will lead to more performances.

162. TOWNSHEND, GEORGE: "Yeats's Dramatic Poems," *Drama*, [2]:5 (Feb 1912), 192-208.
"Aesthetic idealism" is the most powerful motive behind the plays, particularly in *The Countess Cathleen, The Shadowy Waters, The Land of Heart's Desire*, and *Where There Is Nothing*.

163. TUNBERG, JACQUELINE DUFFIÉ: "British and American Verse Drama, 1900-1965: A Survey of Style, Subject Matter, and Technique," Ph.D. thesis, U of Southern California, 1965. vi, 657 pp. (*DAI*, 26:4 [Oct 1965], 2226-27)
"William Butler Yeats," 133-77.

164. ULANOV, BARRY (ed): *Makers of the Modern Theater*. NY: McGraw-Hill, 1961. viii, 743 pp.
"William Butler Yeats, 1865-1939," 213-15; includes comments on *On Baile's Strand* and *Purgatory*.

165. UNTERECKER, JOHN: "The Shaping Force in Yeats's Plays," *MD*, 7:3 (Dec 1964), 345-56.
It would appear from this rather rambling essay that "action" is the shaping force, but no satisfactory definition of the term is provided. Mostly on *Purgatory*.

166. USANDIZAGA, ARANZAZU: *Teatro y política: El movimiento dramático irlandés*. Bellaterra: Universidad autónoma de Barcelona, 1985. 182 pp.
On Yeats passim, especially in "Formación del movimiento dramático," 57-71; "El teatro de Yeats," 73-115.

167. VÖLKER, KLAUS: *Irisches Theater I: William Butler Yeats, John*

Millington Synge. Velber: Friedrich, 1967. 109 pp. (Friedrichs Dramatiker des Welttheaters. 29.)

Totally inadequate.

168. WARNER, FRANCIS (ed): *Studies in the Arts: Proceedings of the St. Peter's College Literary Society*. Oxford: Blackwell, 1968. viii, 180 pp.

T. R. Henn: "Yeats and the Theatre," 62-81.

169. WEIAND, HERMANN J. (ed): *Insight IV: Analyses of Modern British and American Drama*. Frankfurt: Hirschgraben, 1975. 275 pp.

John A. M. Rillie: "Preface," 7-12; "William Butler Yeats," 173-81, a short introduction and an analysis of *Purgatory*.

170. WEINTRAUB, STANLEY (ed): *Modern British Dramatists, 1900-1945*. Detroit: Gale, 1982. 2 vols. (Dictionary of Literary Biography. 10.)

See Stanley Weintraub: "William Butler Yeats," 2:227-37; William H. O'Donnell: "The Abbey Theatre and Irish Drama, 1900-1945," 2:309-18.

171. WEST, WILLIAM CHANNING: "Concepts of Reality in the Poetic Drama of W. B. Yeats, W. H. Auden, and T. S. Eliot," Ph.D. thesis, Stanford U, 1964. iv, 244 pp. (*DAI*, 25:10 [Apr 1965], 6120-21)

"William Butler Yeats," 8-81; on Yeats's dramatic theories, *Where There Is Nothing, The Unicorn from the Stars, The Hour-Glass, The Player Queen,* and *Purgatory*.

172. WEYGANDT, CORNELIUS: *Irish Plays and Playwrights*. Port Washington: Kennikat Press, 1966 [1913]. xi, 314 pp.

On Yeats, pp. 37-71.

Reviews:

- F. L. B.: "The Celtic Renaissance," *CambR*, 34:859 (22 May 1913), 479-81. Criticizes Yeats because he has led the movement astray into mysticism.
- Warren Barton Blake: "Irish Plays and Players," *Independent*, 6 Mar 1913, 515-19.
- Edith Kellogg Dunton: "Irish Plays and Players," *Dial*, 54:644 (16 Apr 1913), 335-37.
- Frank Swinnerton: "General Literature," *Blue R*, 1:3 (July 1913), 194-99.
- [John Ranken Towse], *Nation*, 17 Apr 1913, 398-99.

173. WILDE, PERCIVAL: *The Craftsmanship of the One-Act Play*. Boston: Little, Brown, 1923. xiv, 396 pp.

Scattered notes (see index), particularly on *Cathleen ni Houlihan* (p. 65).

174. WILLIAMS, RAYMOND: *Drama from Ibsen to Brecht*. London: Chatto & Windus, 1968. 352 pp.

Revised version of *Drama from Ibsen to Eliot*. London: Chatto & Windus, 1954. 283 pp. Part of the Yeats material was first published in "Criticism into Drama, 1898-1950," *EIC*, 1:2 (Apr 1951), 120-38.

"The Irish Dramatists," 113-53, contains a section on Yeats. Connects his dramatic theories, especially their escapist character, with his dramatic output.

175. WORTH, KATHARINE J.: "Yeats and the French Drama," *MD*, 8:4 (Feb 1966), 382-91.

Yeats as a precursor of Samuel Beckett.

176. YEATS, W. B.: *Drammi celtici*. Introduzione di Roberto Sanesi, traduzione di Francesco Vizioli. Parma: Guanda, 1963. xxxiii, 325 pp. (Fenice. NS. Sezione Poeti. 2.)
"Introduzione," i-xxx; contains "Cuchulain nella terra desolata," reprinted from *Osservatore politico letterario,* 8:9 (Sept 1962), 93-102, on *At the Hawk's Well* and *The Green Helmet;* "Oltre il Calvario," reprinted from EE41.

177. ———: *Selected Plays*. Edited with an introduction and notes by A. Norman Jeffares. London: Macmillan, 1964. v, 276 pp.
"Introduction," 1-15; "Notes," 257-64. Reprinted with minor alterations as *Eleven Plays of William Butler Yeats*. NY: Collier Books, 1973. v, 250 pp. See also G1146.

See also AB2, AC2, 9, 13, 14, 19, 20, 22, 34, 59, 61, 63, 67, 71, 84, AE37, BB115, 207, BE140, CA22, 35, 37, 38, 41, 43, 61, 65, 93, 97, 100, 109, 124, 150, 151, 168, CB58, 89, 122, 179, 183, 196, 233, 255, 258, 344, 371, 403, 464, 540, 546, CC37, 49, 155, 155a, 168, 174, 181, 190, 332, 351, CD7, 8, 58, 68, 138, 139, 187, 194, 262, 334, 349, 350, 426, 435, 500, 503, 504, 550, 562, 782, 919, 943, 1161, 1173, 1192, 1252, 1296, 1353, 1356, 1375-75a, DA2, DB51, 54, 72, 82, 102, 105, 166, 175, 177, 181, 206, DC55, 103, 124, 223, 227, 265, 292, 301, 310, 334a, DD205, EF39, 54, 86, FC74, FE16, FF12, FG3, 26, 40, 50, G276-77, 290, 302-8, 442-53 and note, 653-95 and note, 772-73, 806-25, 920-39 and note, 1146-48, 1351, 1355, 1365-68, 1370, 1375, 1514, HA10.

EC Themes and Types

1. ABOOD, EDWARD F.: "The Reception of the Abbey Theatre in America, 1911-1914," Ph.D. thesis, U of Chicago, 1962. ii, 218 pp.
Presents a wealth of material, taken mostly from newspaper reviews of the performances. For the reception of Yeats's plays, see pp. 49-57 and 133-42. I have not included these reviews in my bibliography.

2. ALLEN, JAMES L.: "Yeats's Bird-Soul Symbolism," *TCL,* 6:3 (Oct 1960), 117-22.

3. *Angol-amerikai filológiai-módszertani ülésszak 1980*. Edited by Miklós Trócsányi and A. C. Rouse. Pécs: Pécsi Tanárképző Főiskola, 1981. vi, 209 pp.
Csilla Bertha: "The Patriotic and Universal Concerns of W. B. Yeats as Demonstrated in His 'Dance Plays,'" 136-47. On *The Only Jealousy of Emer, The Dreaming of the Bones,* and *Calvary*.

3a. ASH, NIEMA: "The Importance of Dance in Yeats's Theatre," *Celtic Dawn,* 1 (Spring 1988), 4-11. (Illustrated)

4. BACKÈS, JEAN-LOUIS: "Aspects du drame poétique dans le symbolisme européen (Blok, Yeats, Claudel, Hofmannsthal)," Thèse complémentaire, Doctorat ès-lettres, U of Paris IV, [1972]. i, 239, x pp.
Chapter I, "Le drame historique," contains interpretations of *Cathleen ni Houlihan* and *The Unicorn from the Stars,* pp. 64-75. Yeats is also referred to passim.

5. BAUŽYTĖ, GALINA: "William Butler Yeats and Symbolism," *Literatūra,* 18:3 (1976), 45-63.
Yeats's theory of symbolism as practiced in the plays.

6. BENTLEY, ERIC: *What Is Theatre? Incorporating "The Dramatic Event" and Other Reviews, 1944-1967.* London: Methuen, 1969. xvi, 491 pp.

"On Staging Yeats," 94-97; reprinted from *NewRep,* 15 June 1953, 17-18. Thoughts on staging *The Player Queen* and *The Words upon the Window-Pane.*

7. BERTHA, CSILLA: "Történelem- és világkép Yeats kései drámáiban," *FK,* 29:3-4 (1983), 441-46.

"Historical and world view in Y's later plays."

8. ———: "The Natural and the Supernatural in the Plays of W. B. Yeats," *Studies in English and American,* 6 (1986), 14-22.

9. BHATNAGAR, K. C.: *The Symbolic Tendency in Irish Renaissance.* Chandigarh: Panjab U, 1962. 18 pp. (Research Bulletin [Arts] of the U of the Panjab. 37.)

Symbolic imagery in the plays of Yeats and others.

10. BLOCK, HASKELL M.: "Symbolist Drama: Villiers de l'Isle-Adam, Strindberg, and Yeats," *NY Literary Forum,* 4 (1980), 43-46, 48.

11. BRADBROOK, M. C.: "The Good Pagan's Achievement: The Religious Writing of W. B. Yeats," *Christian Drama,* 1:6 (June 1948), 1-6.

"In those plays where he states more directly the problems of his own inner life, Yeats turned to the Christian stories and characters. . . . The good pagan runs no risk of handling such stories too lightly or easily. Precisely because they are so difficult for him to use, they are, when employed by a writer as powerful and scrupulous as Yeats, the only adequate vehicle of his deepest experiences."

12. BRAMSBÄCK, BIRGIT: *Folklore and W. B. Yeats: The Function of Folklore Elements in Three Early Plays.* Stockholm: Almqvist & Wiksell, 1984. xi, 178 pp. (Acta Universitatis Upsaliensis: Studia Anglistica Upsaliensia. 51.)

Incorporates "William Butler Yeats and Folklore Material," *Béaloideas,* 39-41 (1971-73), 56-68 (see also CD92). On *The Countess Cathleen, The Land of Heart's Desire,* and *The Shadowy Waters.*

Reviews:

- Genevieve Brennan, *YeA,* 4 (1986), 247-48.
- Eric Domville, *MD,* 30:3 (Sept 1987), 432-34.
- René Fréchet, *EA,* 39:4 (Oct-Dec 1986), 473.
- G. Lernout, *RBPH,* 63:3 (1985), 629-33.
- Janet Madden-Simpson: "All Arts and Parts," *BooksI,* 91 (Mar 1985), 36-37.
- Maureen Murphy, *ILS,* 6:1 (Spring 1987), 25.
- Christopher Murray, *CompD,* 21:1 (Spring 1987), 91-93.
- George O'Brien, *MLR,* 83:2 (Apr 1988), 430-43.
- Dáithí Ó hÓgáin, *IUR,* 16:1 (Spring 1986), 93-94.
- Mary Helen Thuente, *Yeats,* 4 (1986), 189-92.

13. BROGUNIER, JOSEPH: "Expiation in Yeats's Late Plays," *Drama Survey,* 5:1 (Spring 1966), 24-38.

In *The Dreaming of the Bones, The Words upon the Window-Pane,* and *Purgatory* the dead *and* the living expiate their sins.

14. BROOKS, JEAN R.: "'The Half-Read Wisdom of Daemonic Images' in the Cuchulain Plays of W. B. Yeats," in Srivastava und Dutta: *Unaging Intellect* (1983, CA108), 132-75.

15. BURROWS, RACHEL: "The Yeats Theatre," *IrT,* 10 June 1965, vii.
How to stage the later plays. Emphasizes that actors should know in detail the meaning of the plays and their symbolism.

16. BYARS, JOHN A.: "Yeats's Introduction of the Heroic Type," *MD,* 8:4 (Feb 1966), 409-18.
In *The King's Threshold* and *On Baile's Strand.*

17. CARDEW, A. L.: "Symbolist Drama and the Problem of Symbolism," Ph.D. thesis, U of Essex, 1980. iv, 334 pp.
"W. B. Yeats and the Drama of Myth and the Ideal," 189-282. Traces the symbolist drama from its roots in German romanticism through Wagner, Nietzsche, Villiers de l'Isle Adam and Mallarmé to Yeats and discusses the romantic and mythic aspects of his plays. Also on the influence of Blake and Boehme.

18. CAVE, RICHARD ALLEN: "Yeats's Late Plays: 'A High Grave Dignity and Strangeness,'" *PBA,* 68 (1982), 299-327.
Mainly on *The Herne's Egg, Purgatory,* and *The Death of Cuchulain.*

19. CHIPASULA, FRANK MKALAWILE: "Epiphany Blazing into the Head: The Quest for Inner Truth and Transcendence in W. B. Yeats's Verse Drama," °Ph.D. thesis, Brown U, 1987. 203 pp. (*DAI,* 48:4 [Oct 1987], 927A)
Thematic and structural epiphanies in Yeats's plays.

20. CLEMENTS, WILLIAM M.: "Pious and Impious Peasants: Popular Religion in the Comedies of Lady Gregory and John M. Synge," *CLQ,* 14:2 (Mar 1978), 42-48.
Includes notes on the stage Irishman in Yeats's plays.

21. COHN, RUBY: *ETJ,* 21:2 (May 1969), 227.
Review of a performance of *Cuchulain,* a conflation of *At the Hawk's Well, On Baile's Strand, The Only Jealousy of Emer,* and *The Death of Cuchulain,* which was performed at the Little Theater, Stanford U, March 1969.

22. COLTRANE, ROBERT: "From Legend to Literature: W. B. Yeats and the Cuchulain Cycle," *Lock Haven R,* 12 (1971), 24-46.

23. CONNORS, IRENE, and MARSHALL LEVIJOKI: "Yeats: A New Momentum," *Theatre News,* 11:8 (May 1979), 18-19.
On the Yeats Theatre Festival at the U of Michigan, Ann Arbor, March 1978 and the question of how to perform the Cuchulain plays. According to a flyer sent to me by George Bornstein, another such festival took place on 19-22 Mar 1980.

24. Entry canceled.

25. EDINBURGH FESTIVAL: IRISH FESTIVAL PLAYERS: *Cuchulain by W. B. Yeats.* [Edinburgh, 1958. 7 pp.]
Program of a performance of the five Cuchulain plays in the chronological order of Cuchulain's life. Program note by Meryl Gourley, pp. [6-7].

26. *Edinstvo i. nat͡sional'noe svoeobrazie v mirovom literaturnom prot͡sesse: Sbornik nauchnykh rabot.* Vol. 2. Leningrad: Leningradskiĭ gosudarstvennyĭ pedagogicheskiĭ institut imeni A. I. Gert͡sena, 1977. 136 pp.

T. M. Krivina: "Metaforicheskiĭ obraz Irlandii v dramaturgii Vil'i͡ama Batlera Ĭeĭtsa," 114-20. "The metaphorical picture of Ireland in the plays of WBY."

27. ENO, R. D.: "Yeats' Theatre," *DM,* 10:1 (Winter/Spring 1973), 9-17.
The difficulties of staging Yeats's plays, particularly with regard to his stage directions, the dance, the music, the language, and the use of the open stage.

28. EYLER, AUDREY STOCKIN: "William Butler Yeats, Folklorist to Dramatist: The Gaelic Heritage of the Dramatic Fool," Ph.D. thesis, U of Minnesota, 1978. 180 pp. (*DAI,* 39:12 [June 1979], 7055A)
Discusses *The Countess Cathleen, The Hour-Glass, On Baile's Strand,* and *The Herne's Egg.*

29. FARRELLY, JAMES P.: "Cuchulain: Yeats's 'Mental Traveller,'" *Husson R,* 4:1 (Dec 1970), 32-41.
Analyzes *At the Hawk's Well, The Only Jealousy of Emer,* and *The Death of Cuchulain* as related to *A Vision.*

30. FARRINGTON, ROBERT MARTIN: "European Lyric Folkdrama: Toward a Definition," Ph.D. thesis, New York U, 1979. iv, 319 pp. (*DAI,* 40:11 [May 1980], 5852A)
"The Use of Natural Symbol in Yeats' Cuchulain Cycle," 283-98.

31. FRIEDMAN, BARTON ROBERT: *Adventures in the Deeps of the Mind: The Cuchulain Cycle of W. B. Yeats.* Princeton: Princeton UP, 1977. xiii, 152 pp.
Includes "Reflections of a Son of Talma: A Reading of *The Death of Cuchulain* ," *ArQ,* 27:4 (Winter 1971), 308-20; "*On Baile's Strand* to *At the Hawk's Well:* Staging the Deeps of the Mind," *JML,* 4:3 (Feb 1975), 625-50. Discusses, not very convincingly, the five Cuchulain plays and *Deirdre.*
Reviews:
- James Lovic Allen, *YER,* 5:2 (1978), 62-64.
- Gary T. Davenport: "Yeats in the Theater," *SR,* 85:4 (Fall 1977), 671-74.
- Phillip L. Marcus, *JEGP,* 77:1 (Jan 1978), 148-50.
- Lawrence Millman, *Kritikon Litterarum,* 7:3/4 (1978), 209-10.
- Christopher Murray, *IUR,* 7:2 (Autumn 1977), 280-82.
- David C. Nimmo, *Four Decades,* Special Review Supplement (Jan 1979), 16-18.
- Kathleen Raine: "Facts of the Irish Mind," *TLS,* 27 Jan 1978, 94.
- B[ernard] S[hare]: "Goodbye Byzantium," *BooksI,* 23 (May 1978), 77.

31a. FUCHS, ELINOR: "Yeats Fever," *Soho Weekly News,* 19 Mar 1980, 55.
A survey of recent productions of Yeats plays in New York (Jean Erdman: *Moon Mysteries,* see EE43; Christopher Martin: *Cuchulain the Warrior King,* see EE26; James Flannery: Open Space productions, see EE239).

32. GALLAGHER, SEAN FINBARR (ed): *Woman in Irish Legend, Life, and Literature.* Gerrards Cross: Smythe, 1983. 157 pp. (Irish Literary Studies. 14.)
The book is identical with *CJIS,* 8:2 (Dec 1982). See Andrew Parkin: "Women in the Plays of W. B. Yeats," 38-57, and passim.

33. GENET, JACQUELINE: "Rituel païen et rituel chrêtien dans le drame poétique: Yeats et Eliot," *Gaéliana*, 6 (1984), 179-201.

34. GILL, STEPHEN M.: *Six Symbolist Plays of Yeats*. New Delhi: Chand, [1971]. ix, 94 pp.

The plays are *The Countess Cathleen*, *On Baile's Strand*, *The Green Helmet*, *At the Hawk's Well*, *The Only Jealousy of Emer*, and *The Death of Cuchulain*. The discussion of their symbolism is inadequate; as a whole the book is rather naive.

35. GOEKE, DIETER, and JOACHIM KORNELIUS: "On Measuring Irishisms," *FJS*, 9 (1976), 45-59.

The frequency of Irishisms per hundred words in selected plays by Yeats and others.

36. GOLDMAN, MICHAEL PAUL: "The Point of Drama: The Concept of Reverie in the Plays of W. B. Yeats," Ph.D. thesis, Princeton U, 1962. vi, 196 pp. (*DAI*, 23:9 [Mar 1963], 3373-74)

37. GOODMAN, HENRY: "The Plays of William Butler Yeats as Myth and Ritual," Ph.D. thesis, U of Minnesota, 1952. x, 542 pp. (*DAI*, 13:6 [1953], 1193-94)

38. GORSKY, SUSAN R.: "A Ritual Drama: Yeats's Plays for Dancers," *MD*, 17:2 (June 1974), 165-78.

39. HAYES, J. J.: "Mr. Yeats Plans an Experiment," *NYT*, 25 Aug 1929, section VIII, 2.

Dance and music in the plays for dancers, especially in *Fighting the Waves*. See also a review of a performance by M. G. Palmer in the same issue, section III, 3.

40. HENN, THOMAS RICE: *The Harvest of Tragedy*. London: Methuen, 1966 [1956]. xvi, 304 pp. (University Paperbacks. UP177.)

"The Irish Tragedy (Synge, Yeats, O'Casey)," 197-216. Discusses *The Countess Cathleen*, *On Baile's Strand*, *The Player Queen*, *Calvary*, *Purgatory*, and *The Death of Cuchulain*, pp. 205-12. See also passim.

41. HETHMON, ROBERT HENRY: "The Theatre's Anti-Self: A Study of the Symbolism of Yeats' Unpopular Plays," Ph.D. thesis, Stanford U, 1957. iv, 515 pp. (*DAI*, 17:4 [1957], 917)

42. HOFFMANN, GERHARD: "Die Funktion der Lieder in Yeats' Dramen," *Anglia*, 89:1 (1971), 87-116.

The function of the songs in *The Countess Cathleen*, *The Land of Heart's Desire*, *Cathleen ni Houlihan*, *Deirdre*, *The Player Queen*, *At the Hawk's Well*, *The Only Jealousy of Emer*, *A Full Moon in March*, and *The Death of Cuchulain*.

43. JACQUET, KATHERINE MCGINN: "Greek Aspects of W. B. Yeats' Plays of the Irish Heroic Age," Ph.D. thesis, Arizona State U, 1967. v, 106 pp. (*DAI*, 28:4 [Oct 1967], 1397A-98A)

Discusses *On Baile's Strand*, *The Only Jealousy of Emer*, *The Death of Cuchulain*, *Deirdre*, and Yeats's use of the mask.

44. JAECKLE, ERWIN: *Bürgen des Menschlichen*. Zürich: Atlantis, 1945. 224 pp.

"Yeats," 31-54; slightly extended version of "Yeats zum Gedächtnis," *Mass und Wert*, 2:5 (May-June 1939), 658-76. Discusses Celtic myths, sagas, and fairy tales and, to a much lesser degree, their use in Yeats's plays.

45. JAY, JOHN: "What Stood in the Post Office?" *Threshold,* 19 (Autumn 1965), 30-40.
The staging of the Cuchulain plays.

46. JOHNSON, JOSEPHINE: "Yeats: What Methods? An Approach to the Performance of the Plays," *Carrell,* 10:2 (1969), 19-32.
Reprinted in *QJS,* 57:1 (Feb 1971), 68-74. Includes a discussion of the influence of the Nō, a comparison with Brecht, and an interpretation of *Calvary*.

46a. KELLY, JOHN: "Cut to a Pattern," *TLS,* 7-13 Oct 1988, 1113.
A performance of *Under the Moon* at the ICA Theatre, London, a synopsis of the Cuchulain plays made by John Martin.

47. KENNELLY, BRENDAN: "The Heroic Ideal in Yeats's Cuchulain Plays," *Hermathena,* 101 (Autumn 1965), 13-21.

48. KENT, CONSTANCE KEMLER: "Stasis and Silence: A Study of Certain Symbolist Tendencies in the Modern Theatre," °Ph.D. thesis, Columbia U, 1973. 282 pp. (*DAI,* 34:6 [Dec 1973], 3404A-05A)
Includes a chapter on *Four Plays for Dancers, The Cat and the Moon,* and *Purgatory*.

49. KERSNOWSKI, FRANK LOUIS: "The Irish Scene in Yeats's Drama," Ph.D. thesis, U of Kansas, 1963. iii, 162 pp. (*DAI,* 24:12 [June 1964], 5409)

50. ———: "Portrayal of the Hero in Yeats' Poetic Drama," *Renascence,* 18:1 (Autumn 1965), 9-15.
Discusses *The Shadowy Waters, On Baile's Strand, Deirdre,* and *The Green Helmet*.

51. KHAĬCHENKO, E.: "Prints͡ip maski v dramaturgii U. B. Ĭetsa," *Teatr i dramaturgii͡a,* 6 (1976), 249-56.
On the use of masks in the plays.

52. KIM, MYUNG WHAN: "Mythopoetic Elements in the Later Plays of W. B. Yeats and the Noh," °Ph.D. thesis, Indiana U, 1969. 237 pp. (*DAI,* 30:11 [May 1970], 4949A)

53. ———: "Dance and Rhythm: Their Meaning in Yeats and the Noh," *MD,* 15:2 (Sept 1972), 195-208.
Mainly on *The Cat and the Moon* and *The King of the Great Clock Tower*.

54. KNAPP, JULIET LEE: "Symbolistic Drama of To-day," *Poet Lore,* 32:2 (Summer 1921), 201-33.
Mentions Yeats passim, especially *The Land of Heart's Desire*.

55. KNOX, DAVID BLAKE: "Ideological Factors in Yeats' Early Drama," *Anglo-Irish Studies,* 1 (1975), 83-96.
Topicality and non-topicality in *The Countess Cathleen, Cathleen ni Houlihan, The King's Threshold,* and *On Baile's Strand.*

56. KOLB, EDUARD, and JÖRG HASLER (eds): *Festschrift Rudolf Stamm zu seinem sechzigsten Geburtstag am 12. April 1969*. Bern: Francke, 1969. 291 pp.

Robert Fricker: "Das Kathedralenmotiv in der modernen englischen Dichtung," 225-38. *The King's Threshold, Calvary,* and *The Resurrection* are seen as examples of the "revival of the verse drama of Christian character," pp. 227-28.

57. KORNELIUS, JOACHIM: "Stilstatistische Untersuchungen zum Drama der 'Irish Renaissance' unter besonderer Berücksichtigung des Dramenwerks J. M. Synges: Ein Beitrag zur mathematisch-stilistischen Analyse der Formalstruktur dramatischer Werke," Dr.phil. thesis, U of Giessen, 1974. 227 pp.

English summary in *EASG,* 1975, 124-26. Includes statistical analyses of *Cathleen ni Houlihan, On Baile's Strand, The Death of Cuchulain,* and *Deirdre*. For an extract see "Authorspecific and Groupspecific Variation of Style-Markers in Irish Renaissance Drama," *FJS,* 8 (1975), 33-46.

58. KRAJEWSKA, WANDA: "Dramat narodowy W. B. Yeatsa i Stanisława Wyspiańskiego," *Acta Philologica,* 9 (1977), 91-114.

"The national drama of WBY and Stanisław Wyspiański."

59. KRIVINA, TEREZA MENAKHIMOVNA: *Poeticheskai͡a drama Vil'i͡ama Batlera Ĭeĭtsa. (K probleme interpretat͡sii nat͡sional'noĭ mifologii i fol'klora)*. Avtoreferat dissertat͡siĭ. Leningrad: Leningradskiĭ ordena trudovogo krasnogo znameni gosudarstvennyĭ pedagogicheskiĭ institut imeni A. I. Gert͡sena, 1978. 19 pp.

"The poetic drama of WBY: On the problem of interpretation of national mythology and folklore."

60. LEAMON, WARREN: "The Tragedy of Dogmatism: Yeats's Later Plays," *SWR,* 62:2 (Spring 1977), 169-81.

Mainly on *At the Hawk's Well, Calvary, The Resurrection,* and *Purgatory*.

61. ———: "Theatre as Dream: Yeats's Stagecraft," *MD,* 20:2 (June 1977), 145-56.

On stage directions and stage effects.

62. ———: "Yeats: Skeptic on Stage," *Eire,* 21:1 (Spring 1986), 129-35.

On the realistic elements in the plays.

63. LEDERMAN, MARIE JEAN: "The Myth of the Dead and Resurrected God in Seven Plays of W. B. Yeats: A Psychoanalytic Interpretation," Ph.D. thesis, New York U, 1966. ix, 182 pp. (*DAI,* 27:4 [Oct 1966], 1059A)

At the Hawk's Well, The Green Helmet, On Baile's Strand, The Only Jealousy of Emer, The Death of Cuchulain, Calvary, and *The Resurrection*.

64. LELAND, BRUCE HARRISON: "The Mask of Farce: The Farces of W. B. Yeats," Ph.D. thesis, Rutgers U, 1976. viii, 193 pp. (*DAI,* 37:6 [Dec 1976], 3613A)

Discusses *The Pot of Broth, The Green Helmet, The Player Queen,* and *The Herne's Egg*.

65. LILJEGREN, STEN BODVAR: *Irish Studies in Sweden*. Upsala: Lundequist, 1961. 40 pp. (Irish Essays and Studies. 6.)

A highly personal and undocumented record of Liljegren's attempts to promote the study of Irish language and literature in Sweden and elsewhere. Contains an abstract of an unpublished essay on the Irish background of Yeats's plays, pp. 22-24.

66. LINKE, HANSJÜRGEN: "Das Los des Menschen in den Cuchulain-Dramen: Zum 100. Geburtstag von W. B. Yeats" [The fate of man in the Cuchulain plays], *NS*, 14:6 (June 1965), 253-68.

67. LONDRAVILLE, RICHARD: "I Have Longed for Such a Country: The Cuchulain Cycle as Peking Opera," *Yeats*, 2 (1984), 165-94. (Illustrated)

Describes his own production of the cycle at Fu-Hsing dramatic academy near Taipei, Taiwan. The preparations for this production are described in Londraville's "W. B. Yeats's Anti-Theatre and Its Analogs in Chinese Drama: The Staging of the Cuchulain Cycle," *Asian Culture Q*, 11:3 (Autumn 1983), 23-31.

68. LYNCH, WILLIAM JARLATH: "W. B. Yeats' Edwardian Poetic Drama: Studies in Literary Growth," Ph.D. thesis, U of California, San Diego, 1975. xvii, 242 pp. (*DAI*, 36:6 [Dec 1975], 3733A)

Discusses *The Shadowy Waters, The King's Threshold, On Baile's Strand,* and *Deirdre*.

69. MCCORMICK, JANE L.: "Drive That Man Away: The Theme of the Artist in Society in Celtic Drama, 1890-1950," *Susquehanna U Studies*, 8:3 (June 1969), 213-29.

In *The Countess Cathleen, The King's Threshold,* and *The Words upon the Window-Pane*.

70. MACDONALD, EILEEN MARIE: "The Mask of Landscape: A Study of Inner Landscape in the Plays and Poetry of W. B. Yeats," Ph.D. thesis, Bryn Mawr College, 1972. v, 239 pp. (*DAI*, 33:9 [Mar 1973], 5185A)

The Shadowy Waters, The Dreaming of the Bones, Purgatory, At the Hawk's Well, and "Byzantium."

71. MAINS, MELINDA POOLE: "Staging Myth: Dramatic Techniques of Yeats and Lorca," Ph.D. thesis, U of Washington, 1980. ii, 219 pp. (*DAI*, 41:5 [Nov 1980], 2098A; reprinted *YeA*, 1 [1982], 217)

On *The Countess Cathleen, On Baile's Strand, The Green Helmet, At the Hawk's Well, The Only Jealousy of Emer,* and *The Death of Cuchulain*.

72. MANNING, DALE: "Beyond Colonus: Tragic Vision and the Transfigured Imagination in the Late Works of Henry James, William Butler Yeats, and T. S. Eliot," Ph.D. thesis, George Peabody College for Teachers of Vanderbilt U, 1982. vii, 240 pp. (*DAI*, 43:6 [Dec 1982], 1968A; reprinted *Yeats*, 1 [1983], 186-87, and *YeA*, 4 [1986], 315-16)

"William Butler Yeats," 142-79; mainly on *Purgatory, The Death of Cuchulain* and the translation of *Oedipus of Colonus*.

73. MEIR, COLIN: "Yeats and the Language of Drama," *Gaéliana*, 3 (1981), 101-15.

74. MILLER, LIAM: "Notes on Designing a Screen for Certain Plays of William Butler Yeats," *Era*, 5 (1980), 43-44.

75. °O'GRADY, ANNE FRANCIS: "Patterns of Mythology in Modern Irish Drama," Ph.D. thesis, U of Alberta, 1974. ix, 346 pp.

Chapters 2 and 3 deal specifically with Yeats's attitude to and interpretation of Irish myths (information kindly supplied by the U of Alberta Library).

76. [O'GRADY, STANDISH]: "Notes and Comments," *All Ireland R,* 12 Apr 1902, 83-84.

Advises Yeats not to dramatize the heroic cycles, "they are too great."

77. ORR, KARIN KATHLEEN: "Ironic Themes and Techniques in the Drama of William Butler Yeats and Their Relationship to the Use of Irony in the Modern Theater," Ph.D. thesis, Wayne State U, 1976. v, 322 pp. (*DAI,* 37:11 [May 1977], 7146A)

78. PARKIN, ANDREW: "Singular Voices: Monologue and Monodrama in the Plays of W. B. Yeats," *MD,* 18:2 (June 1975), 141-52.

79. PERL, JEFFREY MICHAEL: *The Tradition of Return: The Implicit History of Modern Literature.* Princeton: Princeton UP, 1984. xii, 327 pp.

On Yeats's tragic dramas, pp. 121-43, and passim (see index).

80. PINCISS, G. M.: "A Dancer for Mr. Yeats," *ETJ,* 21:4 (Dec 1969), 386-91.

The function of the dance in Yeats's plays and its performance by the dancer Ninette de Valois.

81. PITKIN, WILLIAM: "Stage Designs, Masks & Costumes for Plays by W. B. Yeats." With introductory notes by Sherman Conrad, *Bard R,* 3:2 (Apr 1949), 93-110.

The Herne's Egg, The King of the Great Clock Tower, The Only Jealousy of Emer, At the Hawk's Well, and *The Player Queen.*

82. *Problemy zhanra literatur stran Zapadnoĭ Evropy i SZhA (XIX-pervai͡a polovina XX vv.): Mezhvuzovskiĭ sbornik nauchnykh trudov.* Leningrad: Leningradskiĭ ordena trudovogo krasnogo znameni gosudarstvennyĭ pedagogicheskiĭ institut imeni A. I. Gert͡sena, 1983. 156 pp.

N. V. Tishunina: "Zhanrovoe svoeobrazie 'teatra masok' U. B. Ĭetsa," 39-56. "The originality as genre of Yeats's theater of masks." Discusses Yeats's views on the use of masks in drama, the influence of the Nō and *At the Hawk's Well.*

83. QUINN, KATHLEEN ANNE: "Mothers, Heroes, and Hearts Turned to Stone: Mythologizing and Demythologizing in Irish Drama," Ph.D. thesis, Washington State U, 1986. vii, 289 pp. (*DAI,* 47:10 [Apr 1987], 3755A)

Discusses Irish mythological themes in Yeats's plays; especially *Cathleen ni Houlihan, Deirdre, The Dreaming of the Bones,* and *The Green Helmet.*

84. QURESHI, ZAHID JAMIL: "The Forming of Yeatsian Drama: A Study of the Manuscripts 1915-1939," D.Phil. thesis, U of Oxford, 1976. ii, 9, vii, 542 pp.

"This thesis consists of more or less separate studies of the composition of nine of Yeats's later plays," i.e., *At the Hawk's Well, The Only Jealousy of Emer, The Dreaming of the Bones, Calvary, Fighting the Waves, The Words upon the Window-Pane, The Resurrection, Purgatory, The Death of Cuchulain.* Quotes from the unpublished drafts and manuscripts.

85. REEVES, HALBERT ADAIR: "The Dramatic Effectiveness of Yeats's Imagery in the Later Plays," Ph.D. thesis, U of North Carolina at Chapel Hill, 1968. ii, 210 pp. (*DAI,* 29:12 [June 1969], 4467A)

86. REIS, DAVID STEPHEN: "The Opposition of Antithetical and Primary in the Plays of W. B. Yeats," Ph.D. thesis, State U of New York at Stony Brook, 1980. vi, 235 pp. (*DAI*, 41:6 [Dec 1980], 2602A; reprinted *YeA*, 1 [1982], 219-20)

"Despite great differences in subject matter and technique, Yeats' plays consistently dramatize an opposition between passion, intuition, heroism and self-assertion, on the one hand, and reason, prudence, convention, community and self-submission, on the other hand" (abstract). On *The Countess Cathleen, The Shadowy Waters, Where There Is Nothing, The Hour-Glass, The King's Threshold, On Baile's Strand, Deirdre, Calvary, The Resurrection, The King of the Great Clock Tower, The Herne's Egg,* and *Purgatory*.

87. RICHMAN, LARRY KERMIT: "The Theme of Self-Sacrifice in Yeats's Drama," °Ph.D. thesis, Duke U, 1970. 229 pp. (*DAI*, 31:10 [Apr 1971] 5422A)

88. ROUYER, ANDRÉ: "In Quest of W. B. Yeats: Notes on the French Production of Three Plays." Translated by John Boyle, *Threshold*, 1:1 (Feb 1957), 22-30.

The Land of Heart's Desire, The Shadowy Waters, and *The Only Jealousy of Emer*. See also EE388.

89. ROWE, GABRIELLE: "Structural and Dramatic Functions of the Face Mask in the Development of Modern Drama," Ph.D. thesis, U of Michigan, 1974. iii, 215 pp. (*DAI*, 35:11 [May 1975], 7325A-26A)

"Mask in the Drama of William Butler Yeats," 62-103; in theory and practice, also on the influence of the Nō.

90. RUSSELL, BRENDA LEE: "The Influence of the Saga Tradition on the Irish Drama: 1900-1920," °Ph.D. thesis, U of Oregon, 1971. 248 pp. (*DAI*, 32:6 [Dec 1971], 3328A-29A)

On the Cuchulain plays.

91. RYAN, SISTER M. ROSALIE: "Symbolic Elements in the Plays of William Butler Yeats, 1892-1921," Ph.D. thesis, Catholic U of America, 1952. xxii, 203 pp.

92. SALVATI, JULIANNE MIA: "W. B. Yeats and His 'Sweet Dancer,'" °Ph.D. thesis, U of Rhode Island, 1981. 158 pp. (*DAI*, 43:2 [Aug 1982], 307A-8A; reprinted *Yeats*, 1 [1983], 183-184, and *YeA*, 4 [1986], 317)

Explores the dancer's impact on the dance plays.

93. *Sbornik trudov k problemam romantizma i realizma v zarubezhnoĭ literature kon͡tsa XIX i XX veka*. Moskva: Moskovskiĭ oblastnoĭ pedagogicheskiĭ institut imeni N. K. Krupskoĭ, 1973. 364 pp.

I. K. Eremina: "P'esy o Kukhuline V. B. Eĭtsa," 254-66. "WBY's Cuchulain plays."

94. SCHNEIDER, JOSEPH L.: "Yeats and the Common Man," *Studies*, 73:289 (Spring 1984), 37-46.

Mainly on the plays.

95. SEKI, MASAKO: "Dance in the Plays of W. B. Yeats," *Essays and Studies in British & American Literature*, 16:1 (Summer 1968), 1-34.

In the early plays and in those influenced by the Nō.

96. SKENE, REG: *The Cuchulain Plays by W. B. Yeats: A Study*. London: Macmillan, 1974. xiii, 278 pp.

Argues that each of the five plays corresponds to "an important phase on the great wheel of symbolic moon phases which is at the heart of the system of *A Vision*" and that "each play may be seen as a crisis point in the life of a single man" (p. 15). The plays are thus seen in the wider context of Yeats's life and thought. One of the general chapters deals with Yeats's concept of drama and staging. Unfortunately, Skene does not discuss the principles of staging that underlay his own productions of 1969, and he neglects much previous criticism.

Reviews:
- Anne Clissmann, *RES*, 27:108 (Nov 1976), 504-5.
- Denis Donoghue: "That Anglo-Irish Man," *THES*, 18 Apr 1975, 17.
- ———: "The Hard Case of Yeats," *NYRB*, 26 May 1977, 3-4, 6, 8.
- Edward Engelberg: "Yeats on Stage," *SR*, 84:1 (Jan-Mar 1976), 167-74.
- Serge Fauchereau: "Multiple Yeats," *Quinzaine littéraire*, 208 (16-30 Apr 1975), 13-14.
- Richard J. Finneran: "W. B. Yeats," *ConL*, 17:1 (Winter 1976), 142-47.
- James W. Flannery, *ETJ*, 28:2 (May 1976), 276-78.
- Maurice Harmon, *IUR*, 5:1 (Spring 1975), 189-91.
- Maurice Hennessy, *TES*, 8 Aug 1975, 15.
- Graham Hough: "Yeats and the Magic of Power," *TLS*, 14 Feb 1975, 160.
- Brendan Kennelly: "The Ritual of a Lost Faith," *IrT*, 30 Nov 1974, iv.
- Norman H. MacKenzie, *Humanities Association R*, 27:2 (Spring 1976), 221-23.
- Gerard O'Flaherty: "Burning Wheel of Love," *Hibernia*, 10 Jan 1975, 32.
- Andrew Parkin, *CJIS*, 1:1 (June 1975), 62-64.
- Linda Ray Pratt: "Yeats as Dramatist," *PrS*, 50:2 (Summer 1976), 177-78.
- John Stokes, *MLR*, 72:2 (Apr 1977), 422-24.
- Eugene Watters: "DEDI-cation," *IrP*, 28 Dec 1974, 8.
- Harold H. Watts, *JML*, 4:5 (1975), 147-48.
- Georges-Denis Zimmermann, *ES*, 57:5 (Oct 1976), 464-68.

97. SMITH, SUSAN VALERIA HARRIS: *Masks in Modern Drama*. Berkeley: U of California Press, 1984. xi, 237 pp.

On masks in Yeats's plays, pp. 53-60, 160-64, and passim (see index).

98. SOCIÉTÉ DES ANGLICISTES DE L'ENSEIGNEMENT SUPÉRIEUR: *La raison et l'imaginaire*. Actes du Congrès de Rennes (1970). Paris: Didier, [1973], 223 pp. (Études anglaises. 45.)

André Chapoy: "Note sur l'imaginaire dans le théâtre du Yeats," 213-22; on occultism in Yeats's plays, especially in *The Shadowy Waters* and *The Dreaming of the Bones*.

99. SORELL, WALTER: *Facets of Comedy*. NY: Grosset & Dunlap, 1972. viii, 340 pp.

"Irish Humor and Eloquence," 114-25.

100. ———: *The Other Face: The Mask in the Arts*. Indianapolis: Bobbs-Merrill, 1973. 240 pp.

Note on masks in Yeats's plays, pp. 68-70.

101. SPANOS, WILLIAM VAIOS: *The Christian Tradition in Modern British Verse Drama: The Poetics of Sacramental Time.* New Brunswick: Rutgers UP, 1967. xvi, 400 pp.
Contains a few references to Yeats's plays (see index).

102. *Stage Design at the Abbey Theatre: An Exhibition of Drawings and Models.* Dublin: Peacock Theatre, 1967. 22 pp.
Includes the settings for some of Yeats's plays.

103. STEINER, GEORGE: *The Death of Tragedy.* London: Faber & Faber, 1961. viii, 355, xii pp.
Note on Yeats's dramatic verse, pp. 316-18; also passim (see index).

104. SULLIVAN, JAMES PATRICK: "The Genesis of Hiberno-English: A Socio-Historical Account," Ph.D. thesis, Yeshiva U, 1976. vi, 177 pp. (*DAI*, 37:3 [Dec 1976], 1520A)
Some examples are taken from plays by Yeats.

105. SUSS, IRVING DAVID: "Yeatsian Drama and the Dying Hero," *SAQ*, 54:3 (July 1955), 369-80.

106. TETZELI VON ROSADOR, KURT: *Das englische Geschichtsdrama seit Shaw.* Heidelberg: Winter, 1976. 356 pp. (Anglistische Forschungen. 112.)
"Lady Gregory und William Butler Yeats," 179-216; discusses Yeats's view of history and the following "historical" plays: *Calvary, The Dreaming of the Bones, The Resurrection,* and *The Words upon the Window-Pane.*

107. TIMM, NEIL HERMAN: "A Comparative Study of Pirandello, Yeats, and Brecht: The Mask as Paradigm for Modern Theater," Ph.D. thesis, Columbia U, 1973. vii, 303 pp. (*DAI*, 37:7 [Jan 1977], 4340A)
"Yeats: The Truth of Art," 95-175; on the Cuchulain plays, *The Player Queen,* and *The Words upon the Window-Pane.*

108. TIPPETT, SIR MICHAEL: *Moving into Aquarius.* Expanded edition. St. Albans: Paladin Books, 1974 [1959]. 172 pp.
"Drum, Flute and Zither," 67-84; on music in drama, including Yeats's later plays. See index for further Yeats references.

109. °UNIVERSITY OF LONDON. AUDIO-VISUAL CENTRE: *The Yeats Dance Plays: A Discussion.* London: U of London, 1973. Videotape, 42 minutes.
A discussion between Katharine Worth, Niema Ash (choreographer and director of the Yeats Theatre Company), and Cedric Smith (composer and assistant director).

The Audio-Visual Centre possesses videotapes of two productions of the Yeats Theatre Company: *The Cat and the Moon* and *At the Hawk's Well* (1973, 24 and 34 minutes); also videotapes of four productions made by Richard Cave and Katharine Worth and a student company: *Calvary, The King of the Great Clock Tower, The Dreaming of the Bones* (1977, 24, 30, 23 minutes), and *Deirdre* (1978, 65 minutes); see also EE142. I owe this information to Ms. Patricia Gulliford of the Audio-Visual Centre.

110. VALOIS, NINETTE DE: *Step by Step: The Formation of an Establishment.* London: Allen, 1977. x, 204 pp.
"William Butler Yeats," 179-86. The dance plays and reminiscences. See also EC115.

111. VENDLER, HELEN HENNESSY: "Yeats's Changing Metaphors for the Otherworld," *MD*, 7:3 (Dec 1964), 308-21.

The relation otherworld-world suggests the relations art-life and imagination-experience.

112. VERHULST, MARGARET MERCHANT: "Myth and Symbol in the Plays of William Butler Yeats," Ph.D. thesis, U of Texas at Austin, 1969. iii, 174 pp. (*DAI*, 30:7 [Jan 1970], 3028A)

113. VIGL, HARALD: "Studien zur Syntax der dramatischen Werke von Lady Gregory, W. B. Yeats and J. M. Synge," Dr.phil. thesis, U of Innsbruck, 1954. iv, 149 pp.

See pp. 106-21 for a discussion of Anglo-Irish syntax ("Kiltartanese") in Yeats's plays.

114. VOGT, KATHLEEN MARILYN: "Chance and Choice in the Drama of W. B. Yeats," °Ph.D. thesis, U of Massachusetts, 1970. 190 pp. (*DAI*, 31:5 [Nov 1970], 2406A)

115. WALKER, KATHRINE SORLEY: *Ninette de Valois: Idealist without Illusions*. With contributions by Dame Ninette. London: Hamilton, 1987. x, 373 pp.

Incorporates "The Festival and the Abbey: Ninette de Valois' Early Choreography, 1925-1934," *Dance Chronicle*, 7:4 (1985), 379-412; 8:1&2 (1985), 51-100.

See index for notes on the staging of some of Yeats's dance plays, particularly *On Baile's Strand* at the Cambridge Festival Theatre (see EE401), and *Fighting the Waves*, *The Dreaming of the Bones*, *At the Hawk's Well*, and *The King of the Great Clock Tower* at the Abbey. See also EC110.

116. WARREN, RAYMOND: "An Idea of Music," *Threshold*, 19 (Autumn 1965), 64-73.

Revised as "Music in the Plays of W. B. Yeats," *Composer*, 20 (Summer 1966), 18-19, 21, 23-24 (see also EB90). "A composer who has written incidental music for a number of the plays of W. B. Yeats, reflects on the role of music in these plays, and on some of the problems he had to face." For the incidental music see HC308.

117. WEDWICK, CATHERINE COWEN: "The Treatment of Women in the Plays of William Butler Yeats," Ph.D. thesis, Bowling Green State U, 1975. v, 147 pp. (*DAI*, 36:11 [May 1976], 7057A)

118. WENNEKER, JEROME SIDNEY: "The Chorus in Contemporary Drama," D.F.A. thesis, Yale U, 1961. iii, 439 pp.

See pp. 244-49.

119. WHITE, BEATRICE: "A Persistent Paradox," *Folklore*, 83:2 (Summer 1972), 122-31.

The motif of the severed head; on Yeats's plays, pp. 130-31.

120. WHITE, JUDITH SIMPSON: "William Yeats and the Dancer: A History of Yeats's Work with Dance Theatre," Ph.D. thesis, U of Virginia, 1979. viii, 147 pp. (*DAI*, 40:9 [Mar 1980], 5051A; reprinted *YeA*, 1 [1982], 209-10)

Consists of two parts, a history of dance and the symbolist theater in Yeats's time and the development of Yeats's drama.

121. WORTH, KATHARINE JOYCE: "Symbolism in Modern English Drama,"

Ph.D. thesis, U of London, 1953. iii, 350 pp.
"Symbolism in Irish Drama," 149-212; on Yeats, pp. 149-80.

ED Yeats and the Nō

1. ALBRIGHT, DANIEL: "Pound, Yeats, and the Noh Theater," *Iowa R,* 15:2 (Spring-Summer 1985), 34-50.
Also on some of Pound's references to Yeats in his cantos.

2. ARCAIS, GISELLA: "W. B. Yeats e il teatro No," *Annali della Facoltà di lettere e filosofia dell'Università di Cagliari,* 36 (1973), 437-53.
Particularly on *The Only Jealousy of Emer.*

3. ARNOTT, PETER: *The Theatres of Japan.* London: Macmillan, 1969. 319 pp.
"Some English Imitations," 291-302; on Yeats, 291-98: "The Yeats adaptations remain one of the happiest instances of the transposition of styles: perhaps because of the striking similarities between the Japanese and Celtic temperaments; perhaps because, in Yeats, they found the rare combination of the mystic and practising dramatic poet."

4. BAKSI, PRONOTI: "The Noh and the Yeatsian Synthesis," *REL,* 6:3 (July 1965), 34-43.
The Nō "embodied much of what had already found expression in different strands of his own work."

5. BAUŽYTĖ, GALINA: "Japonu teatras no ir V. B. Jeitso dramaturgija," *Literatūra,* 29:3 (1987), 35-41.
"The Japanese Nō theater and the plays of WBY," with an English summary; discusses the plays in the context of Yeats's idea of Unity of Being.

6. BERTHA, CSILLA: "Egy különös drámai kísérlet a század elején," *Hevesi szemle,* 7:4 (Dec 1979), 17-21.
"An extraordinary dramatic experiment in the early 20th century"; i.e., Yeats's interest in the Nō.

7. BOTTOMLEY, GORDON: *Scenes and Plays.* London: Constable, 1929. vii, 123 pp.
"Note," 120-23; on Yeats and the Nō, Bottomley's models.

8. BROWN, RICHARD P.: "Some Notes on Yeats and the Noh," *Southern Theatre,* 23:3 (Summer 1980), 15-21.

9. ERNST, EARLE: "The Influence of Japanese Theatrical Style on Western Theatre," *ETJ,* 21:2 (May 1969), 127-38.

10. FRANCHI, FLORENCE: "Ulick O'Connor, W. B. Yeats et le nô japonais," *CCEI,* 7 (1982), 43-53.

11. ———: "Les *Four Plays for Dancers* de W. B. Yeats et l'influence du No japonais," thesis, Doctorat de spécialité de 3ème cycle, Université Paul Valéry, Montpellier III, 1982. vii, 392 pp.

12. ———: "L'influence des *Four Plays for Dancers* de W. B. Yeats et le théâtre européen contemporain," *Gaéliana,* 5 (1983), 101-8.
The use of Nō conventions by Yeats and other dramatists.

13. GHOSH, PRABODH CHANDRA: *Poetry and Religion as Drama.* Calcutta: World Press, 1965. xiii, 213 pp.

"Yeats and the Nō," 124-43, and passim (see index). Includes "Poetic Drama and W. B. Yeats," *Calcutta R,* series 3 / 170:1 (Jan 1964), 41-65.

14. GUTIERREZ, DONALD: *The Maze in the Mind and the World: Labyrinths in Modern Literature.* Troy, N.Y.: Whitston, 1985. xv, 197 pp.

"Yeats and the Noh Theatre," 38-54; incorporates "Ghosts Benefic and Malign: The Influence of the Noh Theatre on Three Dance Plays of Yeats," *Forum* [Houston], 9:2 (Summer 1971), 42-48. On *At the Hawk's Well, The Dreaming of the Bones,* and *Purgatory.*

15. HASEGAWA, TOSHIMITSU: "Yeats and the Noh: The Supernatural in Drama," *Review of English Literature / Eibungaku hyōron,* 42 (Feb 1980), 25-56.

16. HUBBELL, LINDLEY WILLIAMS: *Miscellany.* Tokyo: Nan'un-do, 1972. 125 pp.

"Yeats, Pound, and Nō Drama," 103-11; reprinted from *East-West R,* 1:1 (Spring 1964), 70-78. Yeats "fell between the stools" of an aristocratic art for the few (the Nō) and a communal theater (the Sophocles translations).

17. ISHIBASHI, HIRO: *Yeats and the Noh: Types of Japanese Beauty and Their Reflection in Yeats's Plays.* Edited by Anthony Kerrigan. No. 6 of *DPYCP* (1966, CA20), 125-96. (Illustrated)

Includes an appendix, "Yeats and Zen."

18. JACQUOT, JEAN (ed): *Les théâtres d'Asie.* Paris: Editions du Centre national de la Recherche Scientifique, 1961, 308 pp. (Conférences du Théâtre des Nations [1958-59]. Journées d'Études de Royaumont [28 May--1 June 1959].)

J. Jacquot: "Craig, Yeats et le théâtre d'Orient," 271-83. Yeats's knowledge of Craig's ideas prepared him for the influence of the Nō.

19. KAMP, PETER VAN DE: "Yeats's Noh-Noh Drama," *ILS,* 5:1 (Spring 1986), 16.

A review of Masaru Sekine: *Ze-Ami and His Theories of Noh Drama* (1985); the book itself contains only a passing reference to Yeats.

20. °KIM, MYUNG WHAN: "The Vision of the Spiritual World in Yeats's Plays and the Noh," *Phoenix,* 14 (1970), 39-79.

21. LAI, STANLEY SHENG-CHUAN: "Oriental Crosscurrents in Modern Western Theater," °Ph.D. thesis, U of California, Berkeley, 1983. 489 pp. (*DAI,* 45:3 [Sept 1984], 684A-85A)

22. LEE, SANG-KYONG: *Nô und europäisches Theater: Eine Untersuchung der Auswirkungen des Nô auf Gestaltung und Inszenierung des zeitgenössischen europäischen Dramas.* Frankfurt/Main: Lang, 1983. 272 pp. (Europäische Hochschulschriften. Reihe 18: Vergleichende Literaturwissenschaft. 32.)

Incorporates "Auswirkungen des Nō auf das europäische Theater," *Maske und Kothurn,* 22:3/4 (1976), 269-96. See "Versuche einer Nô-Adaptation durch William Butler Yeats," 161-87; mainly on *At the Hawk's Well, The Dreaming of the Bones,* and *The Only Jealousy of Emer.*

23. LONDRAVILLE, RICHARD JOHN: "To Asia for a Stage Convention: W. B. Yeats and the *Noh*," °Ph.D. thesis, State U of New York at Albany, 1970. 244 pp. (*DAI*, 31:6 [Dec 1970], 2925A-26A)

24. MILLS, JOHN GASCOIGNE: "W. B. Yeats and Noh," *Japan Q*, 2:4 (Oct 1955), 496-500.

25. MOORE, GERALD: "The *Nō* and the Dance Plays of W. B. Yeats," *Japan Q*, 7:2 (Apr-June 1960), 177-87.

26. MURRAY, PETER: "Noh: The Japanese Theatre of Silence," *Icarus*, 4:15 (Feb 1955), 102-7.

27. PRASAD, R. C., and A. K. SHARMA (eds): *Modern Studies and Other Essays: In Honour of Dr R. K. Sinha*. New Delhi: Vikas Publishing House, 1987. xiv, 304 pp.
B. N. Prasad: "Yeats and the Noh Plays of Japan," 167-81.

28. PRONKO, LEONARD CABELL: *Theater East and West: Perspectives toward a Total Theater*. Berkeley: U of California Press, 1967. x, 230 pp.
See pp. 71-73: Yeats did not understand the Nō.

29. QAMBER, AKHTAR: *Yeats and the Noh: With Two Plays for Dancers by Yeats and Two Noh Plays*. NY: Weatherhill, 1974. 161 pp.
Discusses *At the Hawk's Well* and *The Only Jealousy of Emer;* a somewhat superficial and naive study.
Reviews:
- N. M. Beerbohm, *LCrit*, 12:4 (1977), 85-87.
- James W. Flannery, *ETJ*, 28:2 (May 1976), 276-78.
- Masoodul Hasan, *AJES*, 1:1 (1976), 148-51.
- Hiro Ishibashi, *MN*, 30:3 (Autumn 1975), 345-46.
- F. S. L. Lyons: "Keeping Up with Yeats Studies," *IrT*, 19 Aug 1975, 8.
- Derek Mahon: "A Few Images," *NSt*, 6 June 1975, 758-59.
- Richard Taylor, *Literature East & West*, 18:2-4 (Mar 1974), 390-91.
- Roy E. Teele, *J of Asian Studies*, 35:4 (Aug 1976), 697-99.
- Anthony Thwaite: "Help from Japan," *TLS*, 25 July 1975, 837.

30. RAZ, YA'ACOV: [In Hebrew] "Will East and West Meet? Yeats's Experiences with the Japanese Nō Theater," *Bamah*, 79-80 (1978-79), 100-18.

31. THOMPSON, FRANCIS J.: "Ezra in Dublin," *UTQ*, 21:1 (Oct 1951), 64-77.
A survey of the plays written under the influence of the Nō and Ezra Pound. Includes a somewhat overingenious interpretation of the political implications of *At the Hawk's Well*.

32. THWAITE, ANTHONY: "A Talk with Ito," *Truth*, 3 Aug 1956, 899.
The Japanese dancer who took part in the first performance of *At the Hawk's Well*.

33. ———: "Yeats and the Noh," *Twentieth Century*, 162:967 (Sept 1957), 235-42.
The Nō, only imperfectly understood by Yeats, "did not act as his model but his justification."

34. WELLS, HENRY WILLIS: *The Classical Drama of the Orient*. Lon-

don: Asia Publishing House, 1965. viii, 348 pp.
See pp. 307-20 and passim. On *At the Hawk's Well,* which bears the closest resemblance to the Nō; also on *The Only Jealousy of Emer, The Dreaming of the Bones, The Resurrection, The King of the Great Clock Tower,* and *A Full Moon in March.*

35. YUN, CHANG SIK: "The Tragic Theatre: The Nō and Yeats's Dance Plays," Ph.D. thesis, Princeton U, 1972. iv, 318 pp. (*DAI,* 33:7 [Jan 1973], 3608A-9A)

See also CA61, 147, 151, 156, 161, 165, CB58, 59, 375, 403, CC350, CD137-39, 291, 588-89, 1024, 1025, 1048b, 1093, DA22, DD23, EA5, 8, 10, 18, 25, 28, 29, 35, EB2, 12, 16, 43, 54, 68, 147, 155, 158, EC46, 52, 53, 82, 89, 95, EE2, 4, 7, 10, 13, 16, 18, 19, 235a, 251, 457, FE48, FG4, 11, 43, 54, 58, G399, 1265.

EE Single Plays

This section is arranged alphabetically by individual plays and collections of plays. Together with the cross references, it serves as a complete index to all the interpretations of plays listed in this bibliography. Cross references are made to analyzed books and articles. These items have been analyzed whenever they contain coherent interpretations of plays and, in the case of books, reliable indexes; they are marked accordingly. I have not analyzed EA17, which is an obvious starting point for any study of the plays. This section includes Yeats's early dramatic attempts *Mosada, The Island of Statues, Time and the Witch Vivien,* and *The Seeker.* No cross references have been made to musical renderings in section HC.

There are subdivisions for most plays into parts I and II; part I comprises general criticism, whereas part II lists selected reviews of performances, preferably first nights.

Whatever incredulous academics may think, several of Yeats's plays are still performed successfully, and not just in Ireland. Some reviews of more recent productions are also included.

At the Hawk's Well I

1. BABLER, OTTO F.: "A Speckled Shin," *N&Q,* 154:26 (30 June 1928), 461.
Asks for the origin of the phrase; answers by Paul McPharlin, 155:5 (4 Aug 1928), 87; F. William Cock, :7 (18 Aug 1928), 122.

2. BERTHA, CSILLA: "A Nó dráma Yeatsi változata," *Egri Ho Si Minh Tanárképző Főiskola Tudományos Közleményei,* 15 (1979), 153-61.
"Yeats's version of the Nō drama"; with an English summary.

3. FLANAGAN, HALLIE: *Dynamo.* NY: Duell, Sloan and Pearce, 1943. x, 176 pp.
Quotes T. S. Eliot's letter of 18 Mar 1933, in which he suggests a production of *Sweeney Agonistes* along the lines of Yeats's preface and notes to *At the Hawk's Well* (pp. 82-84).

4. GENET, JACQUELINE: "Yeats et le Nô: *Au puits de l'épervier,*" in Genet: *William Butler Yeats* (1981, CA32), 336-53.

5. JOCHUM, K. P. S.: "W. B. Yeats's *At the Hawk's Well* and the Dialectic of Tragedy," *VQ,* 31:1 (1965-66), 21-28.
An interpretation based on Kenneth Burke's theory of tragedy.

6. KNAPP, BETTINA LIEBOWITZ: *A Jungian Approach to Literature.* Carbondale: Southern Illinois UP, 1984. xvi, 403 pp.

"4. Yeats (1865-1939): *At the Hawk's Well*--An Unintegrated Anima Shapes a Hero's Destiny," 227-64; reprinted from *EI*, 8 (Dec 1983), 121-38. Reviewed by Barbara J. Frieling, *Yeats*, 4 (1986), 204-6.

7. KOMESU, OKIFUMI: "*At the Hawk's Well* and *Taka No Izumi* in a 'Creative Circle,'" *YeA*, 5 (1987), 103-13.

Taka No Izumi is a retranslation of Yeats's play into a Japanese Nō play by Mario Yokomichi.

8. KURDYS, DOUGLAS BELLAMY: *Form in the Modern Verse Drama.* Salzburg: Institut für Englische Sprache und Literatur, Universität Salzburg, 1972. iii, 419 pp. (Salzburg Studies in English Literature: Poetic Drama. 17.)

Originally a Ph.D. thesis, Stanford U, 1968. iv, 419 pp. (*DAI*, 30:3 [Sept 1969], 1139A). See "The Dance Plays and *Purgatory*, by W. B. Yeats," 18-70; also on *At the Hawk's Well, The Dreaming of the Bones,* and *A Full Moon in March.*

9. MCGRATH, F. C.: "*At the Hawk's Well:* Unified Form in Yeats's Drama," *CJIS*, 3:2 [i.e., 3:1] (June 1977), 59-71.

10. MENON, K. P. K., M. MANUEL, and K. AYYAPPA PANIKER (eds): *Literary Studies: Homage to Dr. A. Sivaramasubramonia Aiyer.* Trivandrum: St. Joseph's Press for the Dr. A. Sivaramasubramonia Aiyer Memorial Committee, 1973. vi, 258 pp.

S. Ramaswamy: "*At the Hawk's Well* and the Noh," 211-15.

11. NICOLL, ALLARDYCE: *Readings from British Drama: Extracts from British and Irish Plays.* London: Harrap, 1928. 446 pp.

See pp. 384-87 for an extract from the play and a note.

12. °OPEN UNIVERSITY: FACULTY OF ARTS: *Twentieth-Century Poetry (A 306).* Milton Keynes: Open University, [197-]. Videocassettes.

No. 8: *At the Hawk's Well.* A color-film performance, produced by Paul Kafno. No. 9: *W. B. Yeats: To Write for My Own Race.* Graham Martin discusses "Easter 1916" and "The Municipal Gallery Revisited."

13. PLOWRIGHT, POH SIM: "The Influence of Oriental Theatrical Techniques on the Theory and Practice of Western Drama," Ph.D. thesis, U of London, 1976. 542 pp.

"Yeats, *At the Hawk's Well,* and the Myth of Nō as an Aristocratic Art," 76-128. Reprints the program of a Japanese production of the play and of Mario Yokomichi's *Takahime* (which is based on *At the Hawk's Well*), pp. 514-20, as well as Yokomichi's text in an English translation by Don Kenny, pp. 521-29.

14. REEVES, HALBERT A.: "Dramatic Effectiveness of the Imagery in Yeats's *At the Hawk's Well,*" *McNR*, 19 (1968), 27-35.

15. SCHMITT, NATALIE CROHN: "Intimations of Immortality: W. B. Yeats's *At the Hawk's Well,*" *TJ*, 31:4 (Dec 1979), 501-10.

16. SHARONI, EDNA G.: "*At the Hawk's Well:* Yeats's Unresolved Conflict between Language and Silence," *CompD*, 7:2 (Summer 1973), 150-73.

Also on the influence of the Nō and Zen Buddhism.

17. SPRINCHORN, EVERT (ed): *20th-Century Plays in Synopsis*. NY: Crowell, 1966. xii, 493 pp.
See pp. 457-61 for synopses of this play, *The Only Jealousy of Emer, The Dreaming of the Bones, Calvary,* and *The Words upon the Window-Pane.*

18. TAYLOR, RICHARD: "Assimilation and Accomplishment: Nō Drama and an Unpublished Source for *At the Hawk's Well*," in O'Driscoll and Reynolds: *Yeats and the Theatre* (1975, CA81), 137-58.
The source is Zeami's play *Yoro*, here reprinted in Fenollosa's translation as transcribed by Dorothy Pound.

19. TSUKIMURA, REIKO: "A Comparison of Yeats's *At the Hawk's Well* and Its Noh Version *Taka no izumi*," *Literature East & West*, 11:4 (Dec 1967), 385-97.
Yeats's play, itself modeled on the Nō in a general way, was transformed into a Nō play by Mario Yokomichi. In the process, its meaning changed considerably.

20. VLASOPOLOS, ANCA: "Thematic Contexts in Four of Yeats's Plays," *MD*, 24:1 (Mar 1981), 67-72.
On this play, *The Cat and the Moon, A Full Moon in March,* and *Purgatory.*

21. VOGT, KATHLEEN M.: "Counter-Components in Yeats's *At the Hawk's Well*," *MD*, 17:3 (Sept 1974), 319-28.

22. WORTHEN, WILLIAM B.: "The Discipline of the Theatrical Sense: *At the Hawk's Well* and the Rhetoric of the Stage," *MD*, 30:1 (Mar 1987), 90-103.

23. YAMAGUCHI, KIMIHO: [In Japanese] "W. B. Yeats: Two Combustions of Life Energy. A Study of *At the Hawk's Well* ," *Memoirs of the Osaka Institute of Technology*, series B / 27:2 (1983), 269-83.
Includes an abstract in English.

See also BA3, 20, BB170, BG44, CA10, 12, 14, 28a, 60, 63, 91, 122, 125, 130, 149, 156, 170, CC141, 167, CD137, 389, 428, 588, 589, 984, 1048b, EA4, 8, 14, 18, 22, 24, 25, 26, 28, 29, 32, 35, 36, 37, 39, 40, EB12, 15, 33, 60, 69, 128, 144, 147, 149, 158, 176, EC14, 29, 31, 34, 42, 60, 63, 70, 71, 81, 82, 84, 96, 107, 109, 115, ED14, 22, 29, 31, 32, 34, EE47, 123, 337, 361, 503, FE48, HA16, HB9, HF26.

At the Hawk's Well II

24. ANON.: "Court and Society," *Obs*, 9 Apr 1916, 5.
Report of the first performance at Lady Cunard's House. The report is not concerned with the play whose author is not mentioned by name, but with the social occasion. See also the announcement in the issue of 2 Apr, p. 5.

25. ANON.: "Are You in the Nō? The Symbolic Drama of Japan, Ages Old, Mystic, Aristocratic, Has Made Fashionable London Its Own," *Vogue*, 1 July 1916, 69.

26. CROSSETTE, BARBARA: "Off Broadway Offers Yeats and Beckett," *NYT*, 12 Oct 1979, C1, C6.
Performances of *Cuchulain the Warrior King* (the five Cuchulain plays) at the CSC Repertory Theatre, New York. See also James

W. Flannery (who was dramaturgical consultant): "A Rare Look at the Mythic Plays of Yeats," *NYT*, 14 Oct 1979, section II, D1, D4; Mel Gussow: "All 5 Yeats 'Cuchulain' Plays: The Stuff of Legend," *NYT*, 23 Oct 1979, C24. See also EC31a.

27. GUBERNATIS, RAPHAËL DE: "Irish Saké," *Nouvel observateur*, 11-17 Nov 1983, 11.
Review of a performance of *Au puits de l'épervier* (the French title), produced by Hideyuki Yano.

28. JONES, DAVID R.: *ETJ*, 23:1 (Mar 1971), 90-91.
Review of a performance of this play, *Purgatory*, *Calvary*, and *A Full Moon in March* by the Chicago Circle Players, U of Illinois at Chicago Circle, November 1970.

29. LEVETT, KARL: "New York: Jungles and Buried Treasure," *Drama*, 154 (1984), 46-47.
Note on the Quaigh Theatre production of *Yeats*, consisting of *At the Hawk's Well*, *The Dreaming of the Bones*, and *The King's Threshold*, directed by Sam McCready.

30. M[ITCHELL], S[USAN] L.: "*At the Hawk's Well*--An Impression," *IrSt*, 12 Apr 1924, 142.
A performance in Yeats's drawing room.

31. NOWLAN, DAVID: "Four Plays by W. B. Yeats," *IrT*, 20 June 1984, 10.
Performances of this play, *The Cat and the Moon*, *The Dreaming of the Bones*, and *Cathleen ni Houlihan* at the Peacock Theatre. See "The Fascination of What's Difficult," *IrT*, 23 June 1984, 10 ("Charles Hunter examines the dramatic fortunes of W. B. Yeats and discusses the playwright with Ray Yeates, the director of the '4 Yeats Plays,' now running at the Peacock").
Further reviews: Richard Allen Cave, *YeA*, 4 (1986), 242-46; David Krause, *Yeats*, 3 (1985), 225-29.

32. RONSLEY, JOSEPH: Review of a performance of *At the Hawk's Well*, *A Full Moon in March*, and *The Cat and the Moon* by the English Theatre Company, U of Ottawa, directed by James Flannery, *ETJ*, 24:2 (May 1972), 199-200.

See also BB86, CE212, EC21, EE420, 556.

The Bridegroom

See CA130, EA35.

Calvary I

33. GERSTENBERGER, DONNA: "The Saint and the Circle: The Dramatic Potential of an Image," *Criticism*, 2:4 (Fall 1960), 336-41.
Compares the use in this drama, Eliot's *Murder in the Cathedral*, and Spender's *Trial of a Judge*.

34. GOSE, ELLIOTT B.: "The Lyric and the Philosophic in Yeats's *Calvary* ," *MD*, 2:4 (Feb 1960), 370-76.

35. GUERRERO ZAMORA, JUAN: *Uno de vosotros: Auto sacramental. Ju-*

das: Ensayos. Barcelona: Flors, 1957. 224 pp.
See pp. 187-89.

36. HIRSCHBERG, S[TUART]: "Yeats and the Grand Inquisitor in *Calvary*," *Theatre Annual*, 30 (1974), 14-17.

37. PEARCE, HOWARD D.: "Artist of Bones: Yeats's *Calvary* as Poem and Play," *Modernist Studies*, 3:1 (1979), 19-34.

38. ROSTON, MURRAY: *Biblical Drama in England: From the Middle Ages to the Present Day*. London: Faber & Faber, 1968. 335 pp.
"W. B. Yeats and D. H. Lawrence," 264-79; on this play and on *The Resurrection*.

39. THOMPSON, LESLIE M.: "Spender's 'Judas Iscariot,'" *ELN*, 8:2 (Dec 1970), 126-30.
Compares Spender's poem with Yeats's play.

40. ———: "The Multiple Uses of the Lazarus Motif in Modern Literature," *Christian Scholar's R*, 7:4 (1978), 306-29.

41. YEATS, W. B.: *Calvario*. A cura di Roberto Sanesi. Varese: Editrice Magenta, 1960. 55 pp. (Oggetti e simbolo. 8.)
"Prefazione," 7-22, incorporates "Scheda al teatro di William Butler Yeats," *Aut aut*, 5:26 (Mar 1955), 130-39. Reprinted in EB176.

See also CA12, 60, 73, 91, 125, 130, CC10, 44, 196, CD428, DA35(II), DC18, EA4, 8, 14, 18, 22, 24, 25, 26, 28, 29, 35, 36, 37, 40, EB12, 60, 69, 132, 149, 176, EC3, 40, 46, 56, 60, 63, 84, 86, 106, 109, EE17, 415, FC121, FE48.

Calvary II

42. FLANNERY, JAMES W.: "Action and Reaction at the Dublin Theatre Festival," *DM*, 5:3&4 (Autumn/Winter 1966), 26-36.
Reprinted in *ETJ*, 19:1 (Mar 1967), 72-80. Reviews his own productions of this play and of *The Resurrection* at Trinity College Dublin during the 1965 Theatre Festival and the discussions after the performances.

43. GUSSOW, MEL: "Theater: 3 'Visionary' Plays by Yeats: Jean Erdman Interprets His *Moon Mysteries*. Dances, Music and Noh Blended with Mime," *NYT*, 18 Jan 1973, 47.
A performance of this play, *The Cat and the Moon*, and *A Full Moon in March* by Jean Erdman and Company at the Theater St. Clements, New York. See also the review by Jerry Tallmer: "Miss Erdman, Mr. Yeats," *NY Post*, 25 Nov 1972, 20. For a different production under the title *Moon Mysteries* see EC31a.
A videotape of a performance of 15 Dec 1974 is in the Dance Collection of the New York Public Library, Lincoln Center for the Performing Arts.

44. HUNTER, CHARLES: "*Calvary* and *Resurrection* at the Peacock," *IrT*, 17 Sept 1986, 12.

45. JORDAN, JOHN: "Dublin Theatre Festival," *Hibernia*, 29:11 (Nov 1965), 17.
Performances of this play, *The Resurrection*, and *Deirdre*.

See also EE28, 485, 497.

The Cat and the Moon I

46. GENET, JACQUELINE: "*Le chat et la lune:* Kyogen philosophique," in Genet: *William Butler Yeats* (1981, CA32), 365-74.

47. *Kindlers Literaturlexikon*. Zürich: Kindler, 1965-74. 8 vols.
Contains notes by E[ckart] St[ein] on this play, 1:2239; *Cathleen ni Houlihan,* 1:2250-51; *The Countess Cathleen,* 2:298; *The Death of Cuchulain,* 2:631; *Deirdre,* 2:762; *The Hour-Glass,* 3: 2175-76; and *The Land of Heart's Desire,* 4:983-84; by W[alter] K[luge] on *The Shadowy Waters,* 6:1262-63; and *The Unicorn from the Stars,* 7:156-58; by J[ohann] N. S[chmidt] on *At the Hawk's Well,* 8:107-8.

47a. *"Moralité" medioevale. "Jeu" simbolista. Materiali e testi per una messa in scena*. Pisa: Servizio editoriale universitario, 1986. iii, 110 pp. (Quaderni di Baubo. 1.)
Contains *Il gatto e la luna,* translated by Edoardo Carlotti, pp. 25-40; two essays by the translator: "Lettura storico-critica del 'Play for dancers' di W. B. Yeats," 41-66, and "Ipotesi di una messa in scena originale di *The Cat and the Moon*," 67-71; and Massimo Lenzi: "Tracce per un regista assente," 75-85, followed by diagrams for a possible production. The other play is La Vigné's *Moralité de l'aveugle et de boiteux*.

See also CA60, 130, CD572, DD123-24a and note, EA4, 8, 18, 22, 25, 26, 35, 36, 39, 40, EB123, EC48, 53, 109, EE20, EG32, HA15, 16.

The Cat and the Moon II

48. ANON.: "A Play by W. B. Yeats at the Abbey Theatre," *IrT,* 22 Sept 1931, 4.

49. ANON.: "Abbey Theatre Dublin: New Play by W. B. Yeats," *Times,* 24 Sept 1931, 10.

50. DAVIE, DONALD: "The Dublin Theatre Festival," *Twentieth Century,* 162:965 (July 1957), 71-73.

51. M., M.: "New Play by Mr. W. B. Yeats," *IrI,* 22 Sept 1931, 8.

See also EB42, EE31, 32, 239, 306, 330, 420.

Cathleen ni Houlihan I

52. ANON.: *Theatre,* 3:29 (July 1903), 158-59.

53. BACKÈS, JEAN-LOUIS: "L'allégorie de l'Irlande dans *Cathleen ni Houlihan*," *Gaéliana,* 8 (1986), 151-60.

54. BESSAI, DIANE E.: "Who Was Cathleen ni Houlihan?" *Malahat R,* 42 (Apr 1977), 114-29.
The literary sources of this character and her treatment in Yeats's play.

55. BRENNAN, ROBERT: *Allegiance*. Dublin: Browne & Nolan, 1950. x, 373 pp.

The last line of the play was suggested by Arthur Griffith (pp. 202-3). See also EF40.

56. BRYANT, SOPHIE: *The Genius of the Gael: A Study of Celtic Psychology and Its Manifestations*. London: Unwin, 1913. 292 pp.

"The Gael in Literature," 183-218; contains high praise of this play.

57. BYARS, JOHN A.: "The Brief and Troublesome Reign of Cathleen ni Houlihan (1902-1907)," *SAB*, 40:2 (May 1975), 40-46.

58. CHADWICK, JOSEPH: "Family Romance as National Allegory in Yeats's *Cathleen ni Houlihan* and *The Dreaming of the Bones*," *TCL*, 32:2 (Summer 1986), 155-68.

59. COLBY, ELBRIDGE: "Some Irish Plays and Social Sketches," *SAQ*, 13:3 (July 1914), 248-59.

Mainly on Seamus MacManus, who is considered to be a better writer and truer representative of the Irish people than Yeats. Proves his point by misreading *Cathleen ni Houlihan*.

60. COLEMAN, ANTONY: "A Calendar for the Production and Reception of *Cathleen ni Houlihan*," *MD*, 18:2 (June 1975), 127-40.

Quotes from the prompt book and the newspaper reviews of the first performance.

61. COUNTRYMAN, JOHN CODDINGTON: "Life Imitates Art: The Drama of the 1916 Easter Uprising in Ireland," °Ph.D. thesis, Bowling Green State U, 1977. 462 pp. (*DAI*, 38:11 [May 1978], 6404A)

According to information supplied by the Bowling Green State University Libraries, the author discusses *Cathleen ni Houlihan* and *The Dreaming of the Bones*.

62. DALTON, G. F.: "The Tradition of Blood Sacrifice to the Goddess Eire," *Studies*, 63:252 (Winter 1974), 343-54.

63. DANIEL, WALTER C.: "Public vs. Private Commitment in Two Plays of W. B. Yeats and Sean O'Casey," *CLAJ*, 23:2 (Dec 1979), 213-19.

This play and O'Casey's *The Plough and the Stars*.

64. GILL, W. W.: "Kathleen ni-Hoolihan," *N&Q*, 174:4 (2 Apr 1938), 248.

Answers a query by John Libis, :11 (12 Mar 1938), 188, concerning the meaning and origin of the name.

65. GWYNN, STEPHEN: "An Uncommercial Theatre," *FortnR*, os 78 / ns 72:432 (1 Dec 1902), 1044-54.

66. HAMEL, A. G. VAN: "On Anglo-Irish Syntax," *Englische Studien*, 45:2 (Sept 1912), 272-92.

Most of the examples are drawn from this play and from *The Unicorn from the Stars*.

67. HOLT, EDGAR: *Protest in Arms: The Irish Troubles 1916-1923*. London: Putnam, 1960. 328 pp.

The play was probably the most effective propaganda piece of the Irish literary revival (pp. 21-22).

68. MARKIEVICZ, CONSTANCE GORE-BOOTH: *Prison Letters of Countess Markievicz (Constance Gore-Booth)*. Also poems and articles relating to Easter Week by Eva Gore-Booth and a biographical sketch by Esther Roper. London: Longmans Green, 1934. xix, 315 pp.
The play was for both sisters "a sort of gospel" (pp. 63-64, 155).

69. MARTIN, AUGUSTINE: "Kinesis[,] Stasis, Revolution in Yeatsean Drama," *Gaéliana*, 6 (1984), 155-62.
Comments on this play, *The Dreaming of the Bones*, and *The Death of Cuchulain*. See also CA168.

70. MILLETT, FRED BENJAMIN, and GERALD EADES BENTLEY: *The Art of the Drama*. NY: Appleton-Century, 1935. viii, 253 pp.
Note on the play, pp. 163-64.

71. MILLETT, FRED BENJAMIN: *Reading Drama: A Method of Analysis with Selections for Study*. NY: Harper, 1950. x, 252 pp.
See pp. 115-17 and passim (see index).

72. "NÉALL": "The Irish Literary Movement," *IrM*, 48:566 (Aug 1920), 397-402; :567 (Sept 1920), 453-61; :568 (Oct 1920), 524-32.
Includes a discussion of the play, pp. 457-61.

73. O NÉILL, SÉAMUS: "Did Yeats' Poem [sic] Inspire Easter Rising?" *IrP*, 11 Oct 1967, 9.
Perhaps, but it wasn't a good play. Correspondence by L[iam] S. Cogan, 17 Oct 1967, 9; O Néill: "Did Yeats Send Them Out to Die?" 20 Oct 1967, 11.

74. RAMASWAMY, S.: "Two Faces of Cathleen," *IJES*, 10 (1969), 40-46.
Compares the play with Lady Gregory's *The Rising of the Moon*.

75. WEISWEILER, JOSEF: *Heimat und Herrschaft: Wirkung und Ursprung eines irischen Mythos*. Halle: Niemeyer, 1943. 149 pp. (Schriftenreihe der deutschen Gesellschaft für keltische Studien. 11.)
See pp. 25-27 and 86-89 for notes on the origin of the allegorical protagonist.

See also BA20, BG110, CA145, CB194, 371, CC10, 61, 341, CD92, 113, 444, 632, 1321, CE406, DD190, EA4, 18, 20, 22, 25, 26, 29, 36, EB22, 47, 102, 119, 133, 147, 173, EC4, 42, 55, 57, 83, EE47, 289, 359, 365, 368, EF2, 40, 95, 106, EG33, FD60, G224-35 and note.

Cathleen ni Houlihan II

76. ANON.: "The Irish Players," *Academy*, 8 June 1912, 727-28.

77. ANON.: "Two Irish Plays by Mr. W. B. Yeats and A. E.: The Performance Last Night," *FrJ*, 3 Apr 1902, 5.

78. ANON.: "New Irish Plays Produced," *Gael*, 21:5 (May 1902), 166-67.
Includes a photograph of Maud Gonne.

79. ANON.: "Maxine Elliott's--Irish Players," *NY Dramatic Mirror*, 6 Dec 1911, 6.

80. ANON.: "Mr. Yeats's New Play," *United Irishman*, 5 Apr 1902, 5.

81. FIRKINS, OSCAR W.: "Cathleen Ni Hoolihan at the Bramhall Playhouse," *Weekly R,* 21 July 1920, 76.
"A divine play perfectly acted."

82. GUEST, L. HADEN: "The Irish Theatre," *New Age,* 20 June 1907, 124-25.
Reviews performances of this play and of *The Shadowy Waters.*

83. IMLAH, MICK: "Unprepared to Be Shot," *TLS,* 15 July 1983, 753.
Review of a performance at the Lyric Studio, Hammersmith; apparently a failure.

84. M., D. L.: "In Aid of the Abbey Theatre," *Nation & Athenaeum,* 16 Apr 1921, 104, 106.
Includes a review of a performance of this play.

85. MARTYN, EDWARD: Letter concerning the production of the play, *United Irishman,* 19 Apr 1902, [1].
Editor's reply, ibid.

86. [MASSINGHAM, HAROLD]: "The Irish Players," *Athenaeum,* 8 June 1912, 663-64.

87. NEUNER, HEINRICH LUDWIG: "Giessener Stadttheater: *Die Tochter von Houlihan,*" *Giessener Anzeiger,* 16 Oct 1939, [5].
For another review see Ludwig Weber: "Butler Yeats: *Tochter von Houlihan,*" *Oberhessische Tageszeitung,* 16 Oct 1939, [5].

88. Y[OUNG], E[LLA]: "The Irish Plays," *All Ireland R,* 19 Apr 1902, 101.

See also BB104, 155, EE31, 60, 302, 310, 381, 382, 400, EF77.

The Countess Cathleen I

89. ANON.: Note on *The Countess Cathleen* as an "un-Irish" play, *Claidheamh Soluis,* 6 May 1899, 121.
See further notes in 13 May 1899, 137; 20 May 1899, 153 (on the un-Irishness of the Irish literary movement); and a letter by P. H. Pearse, 157: "Against Mr. Yeats personally we have nothing to object. He is a mere English poet of the third or fourth rank, and as such he is harmless. But when he attempts to run an 'Irish' Literary Theatre it is time for him to be crushed."

90. ANON.: Leader on *The Countess Cathleen, Daily Express,* 8 May 1899, 4.

91. ANON.: "Irish Literary Theatre," *Daily Express,* 12 May 1899, 5-6.
Long summary of a speech by T. P. Gill on this play, Yeats's answer, plus related speeches by George Moore, J. F. Taylor, Standish O'Grady, and others.

92. ANON.: "*The Countess Cathleen,*" *Daily Nation,* 6 May 1899, 4.
An editorial protesting against the proposed performance "in the names of morality and religion." See "Irish Literary Theatre," 8 May 1899, 4; letters by "Spectator," M. G. C., and "A Catholic Irishman," ibid., 5; and a report of Yeats's speech, 5-6.
Further letters by "An Irish Catholic," 9 May 1899, 3; a re-

view of the performance, 5-6; an editorial, "Cardinal Logue's Letter," 10 May 1899, 4; the letter itself, 5; more letters by "Catholic Students of the Royal University" (T. M. Kettle and others), Myles O'Shea, and "L.," and a telegram from F. Hugh O'Donnell, ibid.

See also 12 May 1899, 5-6, for letters by T. W. Rolleston and F. Hugh O'Donnell and a report of T. P. Gill's and the *Daily Express*'s banquet for Yeats and of Yeats's speech, plus an editorial on p. 4. See also EE116.

93. ANON.: "The Irish Literary Theatre," *Gael,* 18:3 (June 1899), 78-79.
Endorses F. Hugh O'Donnell (EE120).

94. ANON.: "All Ireland," *United Irishman,* 29 Apr 1899, 1.
Defends Yeats against O'Donnell. See 13 May 1899, 1; and Frank Ryan's letter: "Mr. Yeats and His Critics," 20 May 1899, 4.

95. ARCHER, WILLIAM: "Mr. George Moore as a Dramatic Critic," *Daily Chronicle,* 20 Jan 1899, 3.
Actually a review of Moore's introduction to Martyn's *The Heather Field and Maeve* (EE118), in which Archer defends his view of Yeats's plays, especially *The Countess Cathleen,* as beautiful poems but difficult to stage. See Moore's reply, 25 Jan 1899, 3: Archer's reservations against a staging of *The Countess Cathleen* are unfounded. See Archer, 26 Jan 1899, 3, and finally Yeats's letter: "Mr. Moore, Mr. Archer and the Literary Theatre," 30 Jan 1899, 3 (reprinted in *Letters,* 308-11).

96. ARMSTRONG, WILLIAM ARTHUR (ed): *Classic Irish Drama.* Harmondsworth: Penguin, 1964. 224 pp. (Penguin Play. PL54.)
See "Introduction: The Irish Dramatic Movement," 7-15. "*The Countess Cathleen,*" 17-19.

97. ASSOCIATION INTERNATIONALE DE LITTÉRATURE COMPARÉE/ INTERNATIONAL COMPARATIVE LITERATURE ASSOCIATION: *Literature and the Other Arts.* Edited by Zoran Konstantinović and others. Innsbruck: Verlag des Instituts für Sprachwissenschaft der Universität Innsbruck, 1981. 354 pp. (Actes du IXe Congrès / Proceedings of the 9th Congress. Part 3. / Innsbrucker Beiträge zur Literaturwissenschaft. Sonderheft 51.)
Sylvia M. Patsch: "*The Countess Cathleen:* The Irish Legend of Sin, Redemption, and Vicarious Self-Sacrifice as Interpreted by William Butler Yeats, Werner Egk, and Oskar Kokoschka," 269-72. See also EE98, 108, 124, and HC108.

98. BAUER, GERO, FRANZ K. STANZEL, and FRANZ ZAIC (eds): *Festschrift Prof. Dr. Herbert Koziol zum siebzigsten Geburtstag.* Wien: Braumüller, 1973. xi, 338 pp. (Wiener Beiträge zur englischen Philologie. 75.)
Harro Heinz Kühnelt: "Oskar Kokoschka, Werner Egk und die *Irische Legende* nach William Butler Yeats," 169-87. See also EE97, 108, 124, and HC108.

99. CARDULLO, BERT: "Notes toward a Production of W. B. Yeats's *The Countess Cathleen*," *CJIS,* 11:2 (Dec 1985), 49-67.

100. CLARK, BARRETT HARPER: *The British and American Drama of Today: Outlines for Their Study.* Suggestions, questions, biographies and bibliographies for use in connection with the study of the more

important plays. Cincinnati: Stewart & Kidd, 1921 [1915]. xiii, 317 pp.
"The Irish Drama," 179-90; notes on this play, pp. 181-87.

101. ———: *A Study of the Modern Drama*. A handbook for the study and appreciation of typical plays, European, English, and American, of the last three-quarters of a century. NY: Appleton-Century, 1938 [1925]. xv, 534 pp.
"The Irish Drama," 331-57; the Yeats section (pp. 331-36) is again concerned with *The Countess Cathleen*.

102. CLARK, DAVID R.: "Vision and Revision: Yeats's *The Countess Cathleen*," in Skelton and Saddlemyer: *The World of W. B. Yeats* (1967, CA102), 140-58.
The revisions in the published versions.

103. CLARKE, AUSTIN: "The Cardinal and the Countess," *Ariel*, 3:3 (July 1972), 58-65.
Comments on the opposition to the play by F. Hugh O'Donnell and Cardinal Logue.

104. CLERY, ARTHUR E.: "A Roman Catholic Student on *Countess Cathleen*," *Daily Express*, 11 May 1899, 5.
Letter to the editor. The same page contains Cardinal Logue's letter. Further correspondence by "Observer," 12 May 1899, 6; L. M. Little, 13 May 1899, 3.

105. *La comtesse Cathleen de William Butler Yeats*. [Paris]: Comédie de Provence, [1961?]. [16 pp.]
A theater program with notes by Madeleine Gibert [p. 1] and Michèle Dalmasso [pp. 2-6].

106. CRIBB, J. J. LL.: "Yeats, Blake, and *The Countess Cathleen*," *IUR*, 11:2 (Autumn 1981), 165-78.
The two years' break (1889-1891) in the composition of the play was filled by Yeats's Blake studies which in turn influenced the play's conclusion.

107. EBBUTT, MAUDE ISABEL: *Hero-Myths & Legends of the British Race*. London: Harrap, 1916 [1910]. xxix, 374 pp.
"The Countess Cathleen," 156-83; a retelling based explicitly on Yeats's play.

108. EGK, WERNER: "Irische Legende," *Österreichische Musikzeitschrift*, 10:4 (Apr 1955), 125-30.
Archetypal characters and situations in Yeats's play prompted Egk to write his opera, *Irische Legende* (HC108). See also EE97, 98, and 124.

109. ENGEL, EDUARD: Preface to his German translation of the play, *Bühne und Welt*, 6:2 (15 Oct 1903), 45.

110. FRAZIER, ADRIAN: "The Making of Meaning: Yeats and *The Countess Cathleen*," *SR*, 95:3 (Summer 1987), 451-69.
The play, although insignificant as a piece of drama, is a "fundamentally significant document in the coming to consciousness of the Irish nation."

111. GILKES, MARTIN: "*Countess Cathleen* by the Avon," *English*, 3:16 (Spring 1941), 159-64.

Introduction to a performance by Randle Ayrton's Dramatic School at Stratford-upon-Avon.

112. HADDON, ELIZABETH (ed): *Three Dramatic Legends*. London: Heinemann, 1964. ix, 196 pp.
See pp. 131-38.

113. HERLITSCHKA, HERBERTH E.: "Zur *Gräfin Katlin* und über ihren Dichter," *Bühnen der Stadt Köln: Programmblätter der Kammerspiele*, 7 Mar 1962, 2-4, 8-12.
Includes four photographs of the performance. For reviews see EE159.

114. H[EYNEN], H. G.: Note to his translation of the play, *Roeping*, 8:10 (July 1930), 489.

115. JOHNSON, LIONEL: "*The Countess Cathleen*," *Beltaine*, 1 (May 1899), 10-11.

116. KETTLE, T. M., and others: "Mr. Yeats's *Countess Cathleen:* Letter from University Students," *FrJ*, 10 May 1899, 6.
The same page contains a letter from T. W. Rolleston. See EE92.

117. LINDEMANN, REINHOLD: "Das Religiöse bei W. B. Yeats," *Blätter der Städtischen Bühnen Frankfurt am Main*, 6:19 (1939), 225-28.
Mostly on religious themes in *The Countess Cathleen*.

118. MARTYN, EDWARD: *The Heather Field and Maeve*. With an introduction by George Moore. London: Duckworth, 1899. xxviii, 129 pp.
Moore's introduction contains praise of Yeats's play, pp. xx-xxii. See also EE95.

119. MEHL, DIETER (ed): *Das englische Drama: Vom Mittelalter bis zur Gegenwart*. Düsseldorf: Bagel, 1970. 2 vols.
Heinz Bergner: "Yeats: *The Countess Cathleen*," 2:173-85, 369-71.

120. [O'DONNELL, FRANK HUGH]: *Souls for Gold! Pseudo Celtic Drama in Dublin*. London: Nassau Press, 1899. 14 pp.
Two vitriolic letters. The first, "Faith for Gold," was published as "Celtic Drama in Dublin: Mr. Frank Hugh O'Donnell Asks--Is This Celtic?" *FrJ*, 1 Apr 1899, 6. The second letter, "Blasphemy and Degradation," was refused publication in *FrJ*. Both are reprinted in EF39.

121. OHDEDAR, ADITY KUMAR: "*The Countess Cathleen:* A Fine Poetic Drama," *Calcutta R*, 3rd series / 132:3 (Sept 1954), 213-20.

122. O'NEILL, GEORGE: "The Inauguration of the Irish Literary Theatre," *New Ireland R*, 11:4 (June 1899), 246-52.

123. OPPEL, HORST (ed): *Das moderne englische Drama: Interpretationen*. Berlin: Schmidt, 1966 [1963]. 382 pp.
Gerhard Stebner on this play, pp. 26-41; Rudolf Stamm on *Deirdre*, 60-84; Johannes Kleinstück on *At the Hawk's Well*, 149-65.

124. PATSCH, SYLVIA: *"The Countess Cathleen": Sage--Drama--Oper--Illustration*. Innsbruck: Kommissionsverlag der österreichischen Kommissionsbuchhandlung, 1974. vii, 193 pp. (Veröffentlichungen der Universität Innsbruck. 88.)
Based on a Dr.phil. thesis, U of Innsbruck, 1973. vi, 341 pp.

English summary in *EASG*, 1974, 112-13. Discusses the play and its sources, Henry von Heiseler's German translation, the operatic version by Werner Egk (see HC108), and Oskar Kokoschka's illustrations to Egk's opera. See also EF97-98.

125. REISCHLE, HELMUT: "Die sieben Fassungen des Dramas *The Countess Cathleen* von W. B. Yeats: Ein Vergleich," Dr.phil. thesis, U of Tübingen, 1961. xvii, 325 pp.
Maintains that Yeats's six major revisions improve the play step by step.

126. REYNOLDS, CORINA J. (ed): *Teatro irlandés*. Madrid: Editora nacional, 1983. 399 pp. (Biblioteca de la literatura y el pensamiento universales. 52.)
"El Abbey Theatre y tres piezas irlandesas de teatro," 9-36, comments on this play, translated as *La condesa Catalina,* pp. 39-107. Colin Smythe informs me that the compiler was Lorna Reynolds whose first name was mangled by the printer.

127. SIDNELL, MICHAEL JOHN: "A Critical Study of the Evolution of W. B. Yeats's Play *The Countess Cathleen,* from Its Source to the Version of 1899," M.A. thesis, U of London, 1961. 266 pp.

128. ———: "Manuscript Versions of Yeats's *The Countess Cathleen,*" *PBSA*, 56:1 (1962), 79-103.
A description and chronological account of the MSS. relating to this play, deposited in the National Library of Ireland.

129. ———: "Yeats's First Work for the Stage: The Earliest Versions of *The Countess Cathleen*," in Maxwell and Bushrui: *W. B. Yeats 1865-1965* (1965, CA71), 167-88.
A discussion of the pre-1892 MS. versions.

130. SMYTHE, COLIN: "*The Countess Cathleen:* A Note," *YeA*, 3 (1985), 193-97.
Bibliographical and biographical note on the production of copies.

131. SYMONS, ARTHUR: "A New Art of the Stage," *Monthly R*, 7:21 (June 1902), 157-62.
Contains a note on this play, pp. 161-62.

132. THORPE, JAMES: "Writers at Work: The Creative Process and Our View of Art," *HLQ*, 30:3 (May 1967), 195-206.
On the revisions of this play, pp. 202-5.

133. VINCIGUERRA, MARIO: *Romantici e decadenti inglesi*. Foligno: Campitelli, 1926. 208 pp.
"Il teatro irlandese," 179-98; contains notes on this play and *The Land of a Heart's Desire*.

134. Entry canceled.

See also BA20, BB155, BC6, CA61, 82, 91, 111, 123, 126, CB29, 70, 185, 241, CC1, 290, 341, CD447, 661, 1370, 1414, DD383, 745, DE53, EA4, 8, 12, 18, 20, 22, 24, 25, 26, 28, 29, 36, 37, 39, EB21, 36, 71, 88, 90, 102, 139, 162, EC12, 28, 34, 40, 42, 55, 69, 71, 86, EE47, 365, EF39, 46, 66, FA29, FD57, 60, G42-60, 118, 1358, 1363, HA10, 14, HD83, HF50.

The Countess Cathleen II

135. ANON.: "Piękne słuchowisko o dobrej księżniczce" [Beautiful radio play on a good countess], *Antena*, 2:5 (1957), 30-31.
Review of a Polish radio version of the play.

136. ANON.: "Irish Literary Theatre: First Night of the *Countess Cathleen*," *Daily Express*, 9 May 1899, 5.
Positive reaction. See the leader in the same issue, pp. 4-5.

137. ANON.: "Irish Literary Theatre: *The Countess Cathleen*. Production Last Night," *FrJ*, 9 May 1899, 5.

138. ANON.: "W. B. Yeats: *Gospa Cathleena* ," *Gled. list Narodnega gledališča--Drama*, 13 (1932/33), 2-4.
This is a program for a performance in Ljubljana (Yugoslavia). For reviews of the performance see Fr[an] G[ovekar], *Slovenski narod*, 11 Feb 1933, 4; F[rance] K[oblar], *Slovenec*, 9 Feb 1933, 4; J[uš] K[ozak], *Jutro*, 8 Feb 1933, 3-4. See also CB546.

139. ANON.: "*The Countess Cathleen* at the Court," *ILN*, 20 July 1912, 88.

140. ANON.: "Irish Literary Theatre: *The Countess Cathleen* ," *Irish Daily Independent*, 9 May 1899, 4.

141. ANON.: "Irish Literary Theatre," *IrT*, 9 May 1899, 5.
Short extract reprinted in CA50, pp. 113-14.

142. ANON.: "*The Countess Cathleen*," *IrT*, 19 July 1944, 3.
Review of a radio production.

143. ANON.: "The Irish Players," *NY Dramatic Mirror*, 26 Feb 1913, 7.

144. ANON.: "Billy Kelly and the Irish Literary Theatre," *Outlook* [London], 20 May 1899, 519-20.
"How things wint . . . whin Misther Yeats brought the fairies to the footlights."

145. ANON.: Note on a "copyright performance" of the play, *United Ireland*, 14 May 1892, 1.
The "performance" (actually a recital) took place at the Athenaeum, Shepherds Bush, London, on 6 May 1892.

146. BAUMGARTEN, L. VON: Review of a German production in Frankfurt/Main, *Neue Literatur*, 35:5 (May 1934), 313.
See reviews by [Rudolf Ge]ck: "Frankfurter Schauspielhaus: Uraufführung von *Gräfin Chatleen* [sic], Drama von W. B. Yeats," *Frankfurter Zeitung*, 16 Feb 1934, 1-2; and, by the same critic, in *Literatur*, 36:8 (May 1934), 463-64.

147. BEERBOHM, MAX: *More Theatres: 1898-1903*. With an introduction by Rupert Hart-Davis. London: Hart-Davis, 1969. 624 pp.
"In Dublin," 141-44; reprinted from *SatRL*, 13 May 1899, 586-88, where it was signed "Max."

148. CLARKE, AUSTIN: "*The Countess Cathleen*," *IrT*, 27 May 1944, 2.
Preview of a production by the Lyric Theatre; see also the review in *IrT*, 5 June 1944, 3.

149. COOPER, BRYAN: "Two Plays: A Criticism," *Irish R,* 1:11 (Jan 1912), 571-72.

150. FINGALL, ELIZABETH MARY MARGARET BURKE PLUNKETT, COUNTESS OF: *Seventy Years Young: Memories Told to Pamela Hinkson.* London: Collins, 1937. 441 pp.
Reminiscences of a tableau of the play, directed by Yeats, in which the countess made a lovely corpse, pp. 234-35.

151. HAMILTON, CLAYTON: "New Irish Plays," *Everybody's Magazine,* 28:5 (May 1913), 678-80.

152. H[AYES], J. J.: "Poetry at Lyric, Prose at the Abbey," *CSM,* 18 Mar 1950, Magazine section, 5.

153. HOGAN, THOMAS: "Theatre," *Envoy,* 2:4 [i.e., 2:5] (Apr 1950), 72-77.

154. [JOHNSON, LIONEL]: "Irish Literary Theatre: First Night of the *Countess Cathleen,*" *Dublin Evening Mail,* 9 May 1899, 1.

155. LORENTOWICZ, JAN: *Dwadzieścialat teatru.* Warszawa: Hoesick, 1929-30. 2 vols.
"William Butler Yeats: *Księżniczka Kasia,*" 2:192-95; a review of a Polish performance in the Teatr Rozmaitości, 19 Dec 1914.

156. [MASSINGHAM, HAROLD]: "The Close of the Irish Season," *Athenaeum,* 20 July 1912, 71-72.

157. MOORE, GEORGE: "The Irish Literary Theatre," *Samhain,* [1] (Oct 1901), 11-13.
Contains some carefully worded criticism of a performance of the play and of its author's dramatic theories.

158. O., S.: "Yeats and the Irish Theatre," *English R,* 12:1 (Aug 1912), 146-48.
"The Abbey Theatre of Yeats and Lady Gregory must now be pronounced to be not only the most interesting, but the best theatrical model in these islands."

159. RISCHBIETER, HENNING: "Yeats *Gräfin Katlin* in Köln," *Theater heute,* 3:4 (Apr 1962), 27.
See also Albert Schulze Vellinghausen: "Fern und schwierig--eine Verslegende: William Butler Yeats *Die Gräfin Cathleen* in Köln," *FAZ,* 14 Mar 1962, 20; Heinz Stephan: "Zwischen Gut und Böse: *Die Gräfin Katlin* von W. B. Yeats in Köln erstaufgeführt," *Kölnische Rundschau,* 9 Mar 1962, 5; and Wilhelm Unger: "Beweggrund oder Tat: W. B. Yeats' *Die Gräfin Katlin* in den Kammerspielen," *Kölner Stadtanzeiger,* 9 Mar 1962, 4. See also EE113.

160. T[RAVERS], P[AMELA]: "The Ellen Terry Barn Theatre," *New English Weekly and New Age,* 13 July 1939, 207-8.
Performances of this play, *Purgatory,* and *The Resurrection.*

See also AE96, BB50, CB546, EE92, EF46.

Country of the Young

161. ADAMS, HAZARD: "Yeats' *Country of the Young,*" *PMLA,* 72:3

(June 1957), 510-19.
An unpublished play, a variant of Lady Gregory's *The Travelling Man*. Adams examines both texts and discusses parallels and differences.

The Death of Cuchulain I

162. FRIEDMAN, BARTON R.: "Reflections of a Son of Talma: A Reading of *The Death of Cuchulain*," *ArQ*, 27:4 (Winter 1971), 308-20.
The Old Man as mouthpiece and image of the dying Yeats.

163. JOCHUM, K. P. S.: "Yeats's Last Play," *JEGP*, 70:2 (Apr 1971), 220-29.

164. JORDAN, CARMEL: "The Harlot in Yeats' *The Death of Cuchulain*," *ELN*, 24:4 (June 1987), 61-65.
The harlot represents "the tendency of modern Ireland to prostitute herself."

165. KIM, HWAJA: "The Self and the Antiself in *Samson Agonistes* and *The Death of Cuchulain*," Ph.D. thesis, U of Iowa, 1976. iii,121 pp. (*DAI*, 37:5 [Nov 1976], 2896A)
"The Antiself and *The Death of Cuchulain*," 61-105.

166. MARCUS, PHILLIP L.: "Myth and Meaning in Yeats's *The Death of Cuchulain*," *IUR*, 2:2 (Autumn 1972), 133-48.

167. ———: "'I Make the Truth': Vision and Revision in Yeats's *The Death of Cuchulain*," *CLQ*, 12:2 (June 1976), 57-64.

168. ———: "'Remembered Tragedies': The Evolution of the Lyric in Yeats's *The Death of Cuchulain*," *IUR*, 6:2 (Autumn 1976), 190-202.
On the MS. versions of the concluding song and on Yeats's view of Irish politics as evident from the play drafts.

169. RAMSEY, WARREN: "Some Twentieth Century Ideas of the Verse Theatre," *CLS*, Special Advance Issue (1963), 43-50.
Note on this play, pp. 48-49.

170. SHARTAR, I. MARTIN: "The Theater of the Mind: An Analysis of Works by Mallarmé, Yeats, Eliot, and Beckett," Ph.D. thesis, Emory U, 1966. vii, 216 pp. (*DAI*, 27:7 [Jan 1967], 2161A)
"Yeats's *The Death of Cuchulain:* Blackout--Heaven's Blaze in the Theater of the Mind," 64-103.

171. YEATS, W. B.: *The Death of Cuchulain*. Manuscript materials including the author's final text. Edited by Phillip L. Marcus. Ithaca: Cornell UP, 1982. x, 182 pp. (The Cornell Yeats.)
Photographic facsimiles of the MS. and a late typescript version (the latter including corrections in Yeats's handwriting), facing the editor's transcriptions. The introduction (pp. 3-16) traces the evolution of the play and evaluates the changes made by Yeats while he composed it. For reviews see G1563-1567.

See also CA10, 12, 63, 90, 91, 122, 123, 125, 129, CC14a, 61, 141, 182, 274, EA4, 8, 14, 18, 22, 24, 25, 26, 28, 29, 32, 35, 36, 37, 39, 40, EB115, 122, EC14, 18, 29, 31, 34, 40, 42, 43, 57, 63, 71, 72, 84, 96, 107, EE47, 69, 257, 281, 469, G828, 837-44, 848-83 and note, 1563-67.

The Death of Cuchulain II

172. T., W.: "Theatre," *IrP,* 3 Dec 1945, 7.
The performance by Austin Clarke's Lyric Theatre. There are no extensive reviews in the other Dublin papers.

See also EC21, EE26, 266, 404, 420.

Deirdre I

173. ANON.: "Experiments: *Deirdre* ," *Festival Theatre (New Lease) Programme,* 13 (12 Feb 1934), 1-2.

174. BAKER, RONALD L.: "The Deirdre Legend in Three Irish Plays," *Indiana English J,* 9:2 (Winter 1974/75), 16-20.
The Deirdre plays by AE, Yeats, and Synge.

175. BICKLEY, FRANCIS: "Deirdre," *Irish R,* 2:17 (July 1912), 252-54.
Yeats's *Deirdre* is too beautiful for the stage.

176. BRAMSBÄCK, BIRGIT: "The Musician's Knife in Yeats's *Deirdre*," *SN,* 41:2 (1969), 359-66.

177. BYRNE, CYRIL J., and MARGARET HARRY (eds): *Talamh an Eisc: Canadian and Irish Essays.* Halifax, N.S.: Nimbus, 1986. viii, 255 pp.
Identical with *CJIS,* 12:2 (June 1986). See Robert O'Driscoll: "Foundations of the Literary and Musical Revival," 48-70, which contains a note on this play.

178. COTTER, EILEEN MARY: "The Deirdre Theme in Anglo-Irish Literature," Ph.D. thesis, U of California (Los Angeles), 1967. x, 259 pp. (*DAI,* 28:5 [Nov 1967], 1815A)
"W. B. Yeats's *Deirdre* ," 150-73.

179. FACKLER, HERBERT VERN: *That Tragic Queen: The Deirdre Legend in Anglo-Irish Literature.* Salzburg: Institut für englische Sprache und Literatur, Universität Salzburg, 1978. xii, 161 pp. (Salzburg Studies in English Literature. Poetic Drama & Poetic Theory. 39.)
"W. B. Yeats's *Deirdre* (1906)," 104-13; revised version of "W. B. Yeat[s]'s *Deirdre:* Intensity by Condensation," *Forum* [Houston], 6:3 (Summer 1968), 43-46.

180. GUTIÉRREZ DE LA SOLANA, ALBERTO, and ELIO ALBA-BUFFILL (eds): *Festschrift José Cid Pérez.* NY: Senda Nueva de Ediciones, 1981. 369 pp.
William J. Duffy: "Deirdre, Yeats and Synge," 181-84.

181. KALDECK, WILHELM: "Die Deirdre-Sage und ihre Bearbeitungen," Dr.phil. thesis, U of Wien, 1924. iii, 124 pp.
"William Butler Yeats," 76-87. Negligible.

182. MAANEN, W. VAN: "Voorwoord [to his translation of the play]," *Onze eeuw,* 24 / part 3:3 (Sept 1924), 193-95.

183. MCHUGH, ROGER: "Írskar sögur og ensk-írskar bókmenntir," *Skírnir,* 126 (1952), 14-42.
The Deirdre saga and its treatment by Irish writers.

184. ———: "Literary Treatment of the Deirdre Story," *Threshold,* 1:1 (Feb 1957), 36-49.

184a. MAES-JELINEK, HENA, PIERRE MICHEL, and PAULETTE MICHEL-MICHOT (eds): *Multiple Worlds, Multiple Words: Essays in Honour of Irène Simon.* Liège: English Department, U of Liège, 1988. xv, 322 pp.
Jacqueline Genet: "Yeats's *Deirdre* as a Chess-game and a Poet's Game," 123-38.

185. MERCIER, VIVIAN: "The Morals of Deirdre," *YeA,* 5 (1987), 224-31.
The versions written by modern playwrights (including Yeats) are characterized by "puritanical habits of behaviour" and do no justice to the original.

186. MILLER, MARCIA SCHUYLER KELLEY. "The Deirdre Legend in English Literature," Ph.D. thesis, U of Pennsylvania, 1950. iii, 293 pp. (*DAI,* 13:5 [1953], 798)
"Yeats and Synge," 205-59.

187. NEUFELD, JAMES EDWARD: "The Art of Imitation: Classical Dramaturgical Techniques on the Twentieth-Century Stage," Ph.D. thesis, U of Chicago, 1974. ii, 232 pp.
Discusses this play as "a drama along Greek lines without using Greek plot material," pp. 205-11.

188. PEAUX, JOHA. R.: "Deirdre," *Nieuwe Rotterdamsche Courant,* 26 Jan 1924, Avondblad A, gewijd aan de letterkunde, 4-5.

189. RAJAN, BALACHANDRA: "Yeats, Synge and the Tragic Understanding," *YeSt,* 2 (Bealtaine 1972), 66-79.
A comparison of the Deirdre plays of AE, Yeats, and Synge.

190. ROBERTS, ETHEL TERESA: "The Greek Tragic Chorus and Adaptations of It in Modern Drama in English," Ph.D. thesis, Arizona State U, 1969 [i.e., 1968?]. iv, 231 pp. (*DAI,* 29:7 [Jan 1969], 2276A-77A)
See pp. 104-22.

191. ROHAN, VIRGINIA BARTHOLOME: "The Writing of W. B. Yeats' *Deirdre:* A Study of the Manuscripts," Ph.D. thesis, U of Massachusetts, 1974. xvi, 895 pp. (*DAI,* 36:10 [Apr 1976], 6713A-14A)

192. RUYSSEN, HENRI: "Le théâtre irlandais," *Revue germanique,* 5:1 (Jan-Feb 1909), 123-25.

193. SALERNO, HENRY F. (ed): *English Drama in Transition, 1880-1920.* NY: Pegasus, 1968. 544 pp.
See pp. 387-90.

194. SLATTERY, SISTER MARGARET PATRICE: "*Deirdre:* The 'Mingling of Contraries' in Plot and Symbolism," *MD,* 11:4 (Feb 1969), 400-403.

195. STAMM, RUDOLF (ed): *Three Anglo-Irish Plays.* Bern: Francke, 1943. iii, 114 pp. (Bibliotheca Anglicana. 5.)
"Introduction," 3-18; with notes on this play.

196. STEWART, JAMES: "A Yeats Allusion," *Neuphilologische Mitteilungen,* 82:2 (1981), 214-16.
A source in the Middle Irish *An Tenga Bithnua* via Lady Gregory's *Book of Saints and Wonders.*

197. *Tragicheskoe i komicheskoe v zarubezhnoĭ literature: Mezhvuzovskiĭ sbornik nauchnykh trudov.* Perm': Permskiĭ gosudarstvennyĭ pedagogicheskiĭ institut, 1986. 111 pp.
T. M. Poliudova: "Svoeobrazie dramaticheskoĭ struktury tragedii V. B. Ĭetsa *Deĭrdre*" [The originality of the dramatic structure of Yeats's tragedy *Deirdre*], 46-59.

198. VINALL, SHIRLEY W.: "Some Lines by W. B. Yeats in an Italian Magazine," *N&Q*, os 218 / ns 20:9 (Sept 1973), 327-29.
Reprints Yeats's "A Dirge over Dierdre e Naisi," *Poesia* [Milano], 2:9-10-11-12 (Oct 1906--Jan 1907), 12, and comments on it.

199. WICKSTROM, GORDON MINTON: "The Deirdre Plays of AE, Yeats, and Synge: Patterns of Irish Exile," Ph.D. thesis, Stanford U, 1968. vi, 310 pp. (*DAI*, 29:11 [May 1969], 4027A)

200. ————: "Legend Focusing Legend in Yeats's *Deirdre*," *ETJ*, 30:4 (Dec 1978), 466-74.

See also BB25, CA12, 91, 123, CB152a, 149, 233, 280, CC49, 167, 180, CD55, 313, 519, 717, 859, 880, 1105, 1154, 1161, 1173, 1297, 1308, DB82, EA3, 4, 7, 8, 10, 12, 18, 22, 25, 26, 28, 29, 32, 35, 36, 37, EB44, 68, 147, 154, EC31, 42, 43, 50, 57, 68, 83, 109, EE47, 123, 337, FG18, G264-68, HA10.

Deirdre II

201. ANON.: "The Court Theatre: The Irish Players," *Academy*, 17 June 1911, 746-47.

202. ANON.: "The Abbey Theatre: Production of a New Play," *Daily Express*, 26 Nov 1906, 7.

203. ANON.: "The Abbey Theatre: Mr. Yeats's New Play, *Deirdre*," *IrT*, 26 Nov 1906, 7.

204. ANON.: "Abbey Theatre: Mrs. Patrick Campbell as Deirdre," *IrT*, 10 Nov 1908, 7.

205. B.: "The Irish Players," *T.P.'s Weekly*, 16 June 1911, 744.

206. [BETTANY, FREDERICK GEORGE]: Note on Mrs. Patrick Campbell's performance, *Athenaeum*, 5 Dec 1908, 729-30.

207. [————]: "Irish Drama," *Athenaeum*, 26 June 1909, 767-68.

208. DONAGHY, LYLE: "The Staging of a Play," *IrSt*, 27 Mar 1926, 70-71.
Reviews a "bad" production. Correspondence by Geoffrey Phibbs and C. H. Whitton, 3 Apr 1926, 97; by Donaghy, 10 Apr 1926, 125-26.

209. O'B., K. M.: "Mrs. Patrick Campbell and the Abbey Theatre: Interesting Announcement," *Dublin Evening Mail*, 11 Nov 1908, 2.
An interview about the play. A review of the performance by M. O'D. appears on the same page.

210. O'CONAIRE, MICHEÁL: "The Death of Deirdre," *Sinn Féin*, 1 Dec 1906, 3.

211. TITTERTON, W. R.: "Drama," *New Age*, 10 Dec 1908, 142-43.

See also BF74, EE45.

Diarmuid and Grania I

212. CANDON, THOMAS HENRY: "The Legend of Diarmuid and Grania: Its History and Treatment by Modern Writers," Ph.D. thesis, Boston U, 1954. ii, 154 pp.
"George Moore and William Butler Yeats," 83-90.

213. FREEMAN, JOHN: *A Portrait of George Moore in a Study of His Work*. London: Laurie, 1922. xi, 283 pp.
On the making of this play, pp. 141-45.

214. GREGORY, LADY ISABELLA AUGUSTA (ed): *Ideals in Ireland*. London: At the Unicorn, 1901. 107 pp.
George Moore: "Literature and the Irish Language," 45-51; reprint of "The Irish Literary Renaissance and the Irish Language: An Address [delivered at the meeting of the promoters of the Irish Literary Theatre]," *New Ireland R*, 13:2 (Apr 1900), 65-72. Contains some remarks on this play.

215. GWYNN, STEPHEN: "The Irish Literary Theatre and Its Affinities," *FortnR*, os 76 / ns 70:420 (1 Dec 1901), 1050-62.

216. KENNEDY, EILEEN: "George Moore to Edward Elgar: Eighteen Letters on *Diarmuid and Grania* and Operatic Dreams," *ELT*, 21:3 (1978), 168-87.

217. LANG, MATHESON: *Mr. Wu Looks Back: Thoughts and Memories*. London: Stanley Paul, 1941. 224 pp.
Yeats and Moore at the rehearsal of the play, pp. 48-49.

218. MACCOLGAN, SHAN: "*Diarmuid and Grania*--Another View," *United Irishman*, 2 Nov 1901, 5.
Correspondence by a disgusted Catholic "Parent," who believes everything the *Leader* tells him, 30 Nov 1901, 6; by "Parent of Ten," 7 Dec 1901, 3; and by "Willoughby Wallaby Wobbles," 14 Dec 1901, 7, where the whole thing becomes rather ridiculous.

219. MACKILLOP, JAMES: *Fionn Mac Cumhaill: Celtic Myth in English Literature*. Syracuse: Syracuse UP, 1986. xvii, 227 pp.
See index for notes on Yeats's use of the myth, especially in this play and "The Wanderings of Oisin." See also CC53.

220. MITCHELL, SUSAN LANGSTAFF: *George Moore*. Dublin: Maunsel, 1916. 149 pp. ([Irishmen of To-day. 4.])
On Yeats, passim, especially pp. 100-103 on the genesis of this play.

221. MOORE, GEORGE: *George Moore in Transition: Letters to T. Fisher Unwin and Lena Milman, 1894-1910*. Edited with a commentary by Helmut E. Gerber. Detroit: Wayne State UP, 1968. 343 pp.
On Yeats, passim (see index); on *Diarmuid and Grania*, pp. 224-26.

222. ———, and W. B. YEATS: *Diarmuid and Grania: A Three Act Tragedy*. Introduction by Anthony Farrow. Chicago: De Paul U, 1974.

i, 59 pp. (Irish Drama Series. 10.)
"Introduction," 1-18, comments on the Yeats-Moore collaboration.

223. NEWLIN, PAUL A.: "The Artful Failure of George Moore's Plays," *Eire,* 8:1 (Spring 1973), 62-84.

224. NOËL, JEAN C.: *George Moore: L'homme et l'oeuvre (1852-1933).* Paris: Didier, 1966. xiv, 706 pp. (Études anglaises. 24.)
Numerous references to Yeats, especially in "Pour le Théâtre littéraire irlandais: *Diarmuid and Grania* (1901)," 304-10.

225. WEAVER, JACK WAYNE: "Some Notes on George Moore and Professor Watson," *ELT,* 6:3 (1963), 147-50.
On Yeats, Moore, and the composition of the play.

226. YEATS, W. B., and GEORGE MOORE: "A Critical Edition of *Diarmuid and Grania* by William Butler Yeats and George Moore." Edited by Ray Small. Editor's Ph.D. thesis, U of Texas, 1958. vi, 324 pp. (*DAI,* 19:5 [Nov 1958], 1073-74)
Contains an earlier typescript 1 and a later typescript 2 (the text used in the *Variorum Edition of the Plays*), an account of the Yeats-Moore collaboration, a critical analysis of the play, the sources of the legend, and a glossary.

See also BB155, BC6, BG144, CB447, CD206, 394, 838, 846, 963, 1154, DD717, EA4, 12, 20, 25, 26, 41, EB88, 135, EF24, 46, G1516, HE26.

Diarmuid and Grania II

227. ANON.: "The Irish Literary Theatre: *Diarm[u]id and Grania*," *Daily Express,* 22 Oct 1901, 5-6.

228. ANON.: "The Irish Literary Theatre: Successful Performances Last Night. A Crowded and Enthusiastic Audience," *FrJ,* 22 Oct 1901, 4.
See also "By the Way," *FrJ,* 24 Oct 1901, 4.

229. ANON.: "The Irish Theatre: *Diarmuid and Grania* ," *Irish Daily Independent and Daily Nation,* 22 Oct 1901, 5.

229a. ANON.: "Gaiety Theatre: The Irish Literary Theatre," *IrT,* 22 Oct 1901, 4.
"Although the play was in prose, Mr. Yeats's rare poetic gift and perfect mastery of his craft were never more finely demonstrated."

230. ANON.: "An Irish Play and an English Afterpiece," *Leader,* 2 Nov 1901, 155-56.
Correpondence by Mac an Chuill: "Diarmuid and Grainne," ibid., 157-58; and Moore's defense: "On the Thoughtlessness of Critics," 9 Nov 1901, 174-76, plus editorial, 176-77.

231. M., A. M.: "Too Much Grania," *Evening Herald,* 22 Oct 1901, 2.
"To be perfectly frank, this work of Messrs. Yeats and Moore is a bit of a disappointment. It is very dreary at times, there is a wearisome repetition of sentiment in long dialogues and irritating speeches, and a startling absence of any Celtic atmosphere."

232. SAMPSON, MARTIN W.: "The Irish Literary Theatre," *Nation,* 21 Nov 1901, 395-96.

See also BG41, EF46.

The Dreaming of the Bones I

233. FRIEDMAN, BARTON R.: "How the Bones Dream: Yeats's Nightmare of History," in Srivastava and Dutta: *Unaging Intellect* (1983, CA108), 107-21.

234. LEWIS, SAUNDERS: "Recent Anglo-Celtic Drama," *Welsh Outlook,* 9:99 (Mar 1922), 63-65.

235. Q., J.: "Note on *The Dreaming of the Bones,*" *Little R,* 5:9 (Jan 1919), 61-63.

235a. VUKMIROVICH, JOHN: "Politics of the Heart: W. B. Yeats' *The Dreaming of the Bones* and *Nishikigi* ," *JIL,* 17:1 (Jan 1988), 45-54.

236. WARSCHAUSKY, SIDNEY: "Yeats's Purgatorial Plays," *MD,* 7:3 (Dec 1964), 278-86.
On this play, *The Words upon the Window-Pane,* and *Purgatory.*

See also BG178, CA12, 60, 91, 122, 125, 130, 161, CC38, 350, CD137, EA4, 8, 14, 18, 22, 24, 25, 26, 28, 29, 32, 35, 36, 37, 40, EB95, 111, 115, 147, EC3, 13, 70, 83, 84, 98, 106, 109, 115, ED14, 22, 34, EE8, 17, 58, 61, 69, 443, FD46, FE48, HA16.

The Dreaming of the Bones II

237. ANON.: "Abbey Theatre Ballet: *The Dreaming of the Bones,*" *IrT,* 7 Dec 1931, 5.

238. ANON.: "The Abbey Theatre Dublin: A New Play by Mr. W. B. Yeats," *Times,* 9 Dec 1931, 10.

239. LASK, THOMAS: "Theater: 3 Yeats One-Acters at Open Space," *NYT,* 9 Feb 1980, 12.
Review of James W. Flannery's production of this play, *The King of the Great Clock Tower,* and *The Cat and the Moon* at the Open Space Theater Experiment, New York. See also EC31a.

240. S., D.: "*The Dreaming of the Bones:* Mr. Yeats's Dance Play," *IrI,* 7 Dec 1931, 11.

See also EE29, 31, 382, 497.

Fighting the Waves I

See BB7, CA10, CD148, 963, EA25, 35, EC39, 84, 115, EE418.

Fighting the Waves II

241. ANON.: "*Fighting the Waves:* Mr. Yeats's New Ballet Play," *IrT,* 14 Aug 1929, 6.

242. ANON.: "*Fighting the Waves:* Mr. Yeats's New Ballet in Dublin," *Times,* 15 Aug 1929, 8.

243. BELFOE, A.-E.: "*En combattant les vagues* par le sénateur W. B. Yeats: Matinée spéciale au Lyric Theatre Hammersmith," *Figaro,* 22 June 1930, 5.

244. BROSNAN, GERALD: "Dublin's Abbey--The Immortal Theatre," *TAM,* 35:10 (Oct 1951), 36-37.
Anecdotes, including one of a typical Dubliner's reaction to a performance of this play.

245. C[URRAN], C. P.: "*Fighting the Waves,*" *IrSt,* 17 Aug 1929, 475-76.
Correspondence by "Stall," 24 Aug 1929, 489-90.

246. DE B[LACAM], A[ODH]: "The Theatre," *Spect,* 24 Aug 1929, 243.

247. G[OOD], J. W.: "Ballet Play by Mr. Yeats: New Experiment at the Abbey," *IrI,* 14 Aug 1929, 6.

248. HAYES, J. J.: "A Ballet at the Abbey," *NYT,* 22 Sept 1929, section IX, 4.

249. MORTON, DAVID: "A Letter from Dublin: Immediate and Retrospective," *Drama* [Chicago], 20:4 (Jan 1930), 106, 108.

250. PAGE, TIM: "Music: Antheil and Yeats," *NYT,* 12 July 1983, C11.
Review of a production of this play by the Castle Hill Theater Company, musical score by George Antheil. The music was "an unwelcome intrusion."

See also EC39.

Four Plays for Dancers

251. BERTHA, CSILLA: "Spiritual Realities and National Concerns in Yeats's Noh Plays," *Angol filológiai tanulmányok,* 16 (1983), 51-61.

252. MURPHY, GEORGE M.: "Yeats's *Four Plays for Dancers:* The Quest for Individuality," *Eire,* 12:4 (Winter 1977), 86-96.
The plays follow a thematic development towards Unity of Being.

253. SMITH, BOBBY L.: "The Dimensions of Quest in *Four Plays for Dancers*," *ArQ,* 22:3 (Autumn 1966), 197-208.

See also BC6, CA60, EC38, 48, ED11, 12, G369-72 and note, 395-416 and note.

A Full Moon in March I

254. BENSTON, ALICE NAOMI: "Theatricality in Contemporary Drama," Ph.D. thesis, Emory U, 1962. vii, 254 pp. (*DAI,* 24:5 [Nov 1963], 2026-27)
Note on this play and on *Purgatory,* pp. 205-11.

255. BENTLEY, ERIC (ed): *From the Modern Repertoire.* Series one. Bloomington: Indiana UP, 1958 [1949]. 406 pp.

Sees Kenneth Burke's tragic rhythm in the play and suggests that it is a "dramatic meditation," pp. 404-6.

256. BURZYŃSKA, JOANNA: "Yeatsian Methods of Expressing an Archetypal Situation in *A Full Moon in March*," *Linguistica et Anglica Gedaniensia*, 2 (1981), 109-24.

257. HAIMS, LYNN: "Apocalyptic Vision in Three Late Plays by Yeats," *SoR*, 14:1 (Jan 1978), 46-65.
This play, *The Death of Cuchulain*, and *Purgatory*.

258. KELLOGG, PATRICIA ROSSWORM: "The Myth of Salome in Symbolist Literature and Art," Ph.D. thesis, New York U, 1975. ii, 173 pp. (*DAI*, 36:11 [May 1976], 7410A)
See pp. 151-55.

259. KNAPP, BETTINA L.: *Archetype, Dance, and the Writer*. Troy, N.Y.: Bethel Publishing Co., 1983, viii, 176 pp.
"Yeats: The Archetypal *Vagina Dentata* Dances," 111-27.

260. NASSAAR, CHRISTOPHER S.: "Vision of Evil: The Influence of Wilde's *Salome* on *Heart of Darkness* and *A Full Moon in March*," *VN*, 53 (Spring 1978), 23-27.

261. ROSE, MARILYN GADDIS: "The Daughters of Herodias in *Hérodiade, Salomé,* and *A Full Moon in March*," *CompD*, 1:3 (Fall 1967), 172-81.

262. SCHMITT, NATALIE CROHN: "Dramatic Multitude and Mystical Experience: W. B. Yeats," *ETJ*, 24:2 (May 1972), 149-58.
"Emotion of multitude" in this play and the dramatic structure that makes it possible.

See also CA12, 14, 125, 126, 128, 129, 165, CB194, CC14a, 183, 211, CD231, 247, 791, 1214, DC180, EA4, 18, 22, 25, 26, 28, 29, 35, 36, 37, 40, EB33, 57, 95, EC42, ED34, EE8, 20, 500, G707-24, HE35.

A Full Moon in March II

263. FUNKE, LEWIS: "3 Plays by Yeats at the Living Theatre," *NYT*, 20 Sept 1960, 48.
This play, *Purgatory*, and *The Herne's Egg*.

See also EE28, 32.

The Green Helmet (The Golden Helmet) I

See CA10, 63, CB93, CC49, 141, 167, EA4, 7, 18, 22, 25, 26, 32, 35, 36, 37, 40, EB176, EC14, 31, 34, 50, 63, 64, 71, 83, 96, 107.

The Green Helmet (The Golden Helmet) II

264. ANON.: "Three New Plays at the Abbey Theatre," *FrJ*, 20 Mar 1908, 10.

265. ANON.: "Court Theatre," *Times*, 23 June 1910, 12.

266. BOLLERY, JEAN, and JOSÉ QUIROGA: "Le Théâtre Oblique," *Clivages,* 2 (June 1974), 93-98.
Interview about the Yeats production by the Théâtre Oblique d'Henri Ronse. The production, entitled *Le cycle de Cuchulain,* included this play, *On Baile's Strand, The Only Jealousy of Emer,* and *The Death of Cuchulain.* The translation by Yves de Bayser was published in *Obliques.* Collection Théâtre Oblique: Numéro spécial, 1973, 95 pp.
For reviews of the performance see Michel Cournot: "Le cycle de Cuchulain," *Monde,* 15 Dec 1973, 31; Robert Kanters, *Express,* 24-30 Dec 1973, 5; and G1514.

267. "CNO CÚIL": "More New Plays at the 'Abbey,'" *Peasant and Irish Ireland,* 28 Mar 1908, [5].
"As a satire on our national propensity to contention it is excellent."

268. COLUM, PADRAIC: "A Topical Play by Mr. W. B. Yeats," *MGuard,* 14 Feb 1910, 12.

269. COX, J. H.: "A Whole Range of History: New Plays at the Abbey," *IrI,* 20 Mar 1908, 5.

270. ———: "The Story of a Helmet: Mr. Yeats's Versified Play," *IrI,* 11 Feb 1910, 8.

271. H[OWE], P. P.: "At the Theatre," *Justice,* 2 July 1910, 12.

272. R.: "Court: *The Green Helmet.* A Play in Ballad Metre by W. B. Yeats," *SunT,* 26 June 1910, 6.

273. TRENCH, HERBERT: "Dramatic Values and a Suggested Solution," *SatRL,* 25 June 1910, 815-16.

274. UAP., S.: "*The Green Helmet* ," *Irish Nation,* 19 Feb 1910, 5.

See also EE26.

Heads or Harps

See CD508.

The Herne's Egg I

275. ARMSTRONG, ALISON: "Prosecutors Will Be Violated: Sexuality and Heroism in *The Herne's Egg* ," *CJIS,* 9:2 (Dec 1983), 43-56.

276. COLLINS, JAMES A.: "'Where All the Ladders Start'. (The Dramatic Verse of W. B. Yeats's *The Herne's Egg*)," *LHY,* 9:2 (1968), 105-14.

277. GUHA, NARESH: "A New Interpretation of Yeats's *The Herne's Egg,*" *JJCL,* 5 (1965), 105-16.
Discusses the influence of Shri Purohit Swami and Tagore.

278. MURSHID, K. S.: "Yeats, Woman and God," *Venture,* 1:2 (June 1960), 166-77.
Sex, religion, and Indian influences.

279. NEVO, RUTH: "Yeats's Passage to India," *YeA*, 4 (1986), 13-28.
Discusses the play's indebtedness to the Upanishads.

280. PARKIN, ANDREW: "The Case of the Eighth Rapist," *CJIS*, 10:1 (June 1984), 127-31.
A textual problem.

281. PEARCE, DONALD R.: "Yeats' Last Plays: An Interpretation," *ELH*, 18:1 (Mar 1951), 67-76.
A political interpretation of this play, *Purgatory*, and *The Death of Cuchulain*.

282. POGER, SIDNEY: "Ritual and Parody in *The Herne's Egg*," *CJIS*, 4:1 (June 1978), 37-44.

See also BB174, CA12, 73, 91, 122, 123, 125, 126, 129, CB403, CC17, 182, 183, 250, CD1, 78, 89, 1077, 1173, EA4, 18, 22, 25, 26, 35, 36, 37, 39, 40, EB95, 123a, EC16, 28, 64, 81, 86, EE362, FD46, G806-25 and note.

The Herne's Egg II

283. K.: "Two Lyric Plays in Abbey Theatre," *IrT*, 30 Oct 1950, 7.

284. LEVENTHAL, A. J.: "Dramatic Commentary," *DM*, 26:1 (Jan-Mar 1951), 49-51.
"The audience appeared somewhat disturbed by the unusual theme and the Apuleian approach."

285. QUILLIGAN, PATRICK: "*The Herne's Egg* at the Damer," *IrT*, 10 July 1986, 10.
Review of a performance by the Renaissance Theatre Company at Damer Hall.

See also EE263.

The Hour-Glass I

286. BARLEY, JOSEPH WAYNE: *The Morality Motive in Contemporary English Drama*. Mexico, Mo.: Missouri Printing and Publishing Co., 1912. 124 pp. (Ph.D. thesis, U of Pennsylvania, 1911)
On this play, pp. 22-25; on *Where There Is Nothing*, 36-37.

287. BUSHRUI, S. B.: "*The Hour-Glass:* Yeats's Revisions, 1903-1922," in Maxwell and Bushrui: *W. B. Yeats, 1865-1965* (1965, CA71), 189-216.

288. ELCHEN, SILVIA VERA: "Costume in the Theatre of Edward Gordon Craig," °Ph.D. thesis, U of Toronto, 1977. (*DAI*, 39:7 [Jan 1979], 3924A)
Includes "A Note on Craig and Yeats," dealing with Craig's costume design for the Fool.

289. FILON, AUGUSTIN: "Le réveil de l'âme celtique," *Journal des débats politiques et littéraires*, 19 Apr 1905, 1.
In this play, *The King's Threshold*, and *Cathleen ni Houlihan*.

290. JOHN, BRIAN: "Yeats's Butterflies," *CJIS*, 2:1 (May 1976), 51-53.
The indebtedness of the play to Blake.

291. LEEPER, JANET: *Edward Gordon Craig: Designs for the Theatre*. Harmondsworth: Penguin Books, 1948. 48 pp. and 40 illustrations. (King Penguin Books. 40.)

Designs for this play (stage set and mask of the Fool) and for *On Baile's Strand* (mask of the Blind Man), illustrations 22-24; notes, pp. 46-47.

292. MUNCH-PEDERSEN, OLE: "Yeats's Synge-Song," *IUR*, 6:2 (Autumn 1976), 204-13.

A folksong, "The Noble Enchanter," collected on Tory Island by Edmund Edward Fournier d'Albe and translated by Lady Gregory, has some similarities of theme with Synge's *The Shadow of the Glen* and is the source of the song in Yeats's *The Hour-Glass*. It also appears in "The Three Bushes" and in an early version of "Lapis Lazuli."

293. MURRAY, CHRISTOPHER: "Three Sketches by Jack B. Yeats of the Camden Theatre, 1902," *YeA*, 3 (1985), 125-32.

Revised version of an article with the same title published in *Prompts*, 4 (Nov 1982), 3-7. Includes a sketch for a production of this play.

294. PARKER, J. STEWART: "Yeats's *The Hour Glass*," *MD*, 10:4 (Feb 1968), 356-63.

295. PHILLIPS, C. L.: "The Writing and Performance of *The Hour-Glass*," *YeA*, 5 (1987), 83-102.

296. PHILLIPS, STEVEN R.: "W. B. Yeats' *The Hour-Glass* and the Faust Legend," *RS*, 38:3 (Sept 1970), 240-41.

297. POTTER, ROBERT: *The English Morality Play: Origins, History and Influence of a Dramatic Tradition*. London: Routledge & Kegan Paul, 1975, ix, 286 pp.

On this play and *Everyman*, pp. 228-30.

298. REINERT, OTTO (ed): *Modern Drama: Alternate Edition*. Boston: Little, Brown, 1966. xxxvii, 630 pp.

See pp. 351-54 for an expanded version of "Yeats' *The Hour-Glass*," *Expl*, 15:3 (Dec 1956), no. 19.

See also BB18, 214, CC250, CD519, 1154, 1173, CE181, EA4, 12, 18, 22, 25, 26, 35, 36, EB33, 123, 171, EC28, 86, EE47, 360, 365, 369, FE73, G224-35 and note.

The Hour-Glass II

299. ANON.: "Abbey Theatre: New Scenery System," *IrT*, 13 Jan 1911, 8.

The Craig screens.

300. ANON.: "The Morality Play Society: Mr. Yeats's *Hour Glass*," *Times*, 10 Feb 1912, 10.

301. ANON.: "The Wise Fool: A Yeats Morality Broadcast," *Times*, 23 Aug 1954, 10.

302. ARCHER, WILLIAM: "Irish Plays," *World*, 12 May 1903, 784-85.

This play and *Cathleen ni Houlihan*.

303. F., C.: "3. Kammerspiel-Abend: Irische Einakter," *Arbeiterzeitung*, 20 Feb 1935, 3.
A performance in Basel, Switzerland. Further reviews by K.: "Stadttheater: Irische Einakter im Kammerspielzyklus," *Basler Nachrichten*, 20 Feb 1935, 1. Beilage, [3]; kl.: "Stadttheater in Basel: Irische Einakter von J. M. Synge and W. B. Yeats," *National-Zeitung*, 20 Feb 1935, 6; and S[iegfried] S[treicher]: "Basler Stadttheater," *Basler Volksblatt*, 20 Feb 1935, [3].

304. GODING, LOLA: "A Play Producer's Notebook," *EJ*, 12:3 (Mar 1923), 207-8.
"The *Hour Glass* by Samuel Butler Yeats, provides one of the best plays that I have ever tried for high-school production."

305. H., W.: "Verträumte Spiele: Einakter aus Japan und Irland im Studio der Städtischen Bühnen Essen," *Essener Woche*, 23-31 May 1959, 13.
Further reviews by H. S.: "Premiere war schwach besucht: Einakterabend im Bühnenstudio," *Neue Ruhrzeitung*, 14 May 1959, 10; Gerhard Schön: "Lyrische Legende: Essen erinnert an William Butler Yeats," *Rheinische Post*, 20 May 1959, 2; Werner H. Schröter: "Frömmigkeit gegen No-Artistik: Essener Studio," *Mittag*, 3 June 1959, 4; and Werner Tamms: "Die Szene als poetisches Gleichnis," *Westdeutsche Allgemeine Zeitung*, 15 May 1959, 10.

306. KENNEDY, MAEV: "Three Yeats Plays at the Project," *IrT*, 14 July 1976, 9.
This play, *The Words upon the Window-Pane*, and *The Cat and the Moon* at the Project Arts Theatre, Dublin, directed by James W. Flannery. See also "Elgy Gillespie Talks to a Visiting American Director and Academic, Jim Flannery, about Staging Yeats," 13 July 1976, 8, and EB42.

307. M'C., F.: "The Irish National Theatre Society," *Daily Express*, 16 Mar 1903, 6.

308. ROBERTS, R. ELLIS: "W. B. Yeats, Dramatist," *NSt*, 2 Nov 1935, 636-37.
Also performances of *The Pot of Broth* and *The Player Queen*.

309. S., R. H.: "The New Irish Plays," *United Irishman*, 21 Mar 1903, 3.

310. WALKLEY, ARTHUR BINGHAM: *Drama and Life*. London: Methuen, 1907. viii, 331 pp.
"The Irish National Theatre (May, 1903)," 309-15; reprinted from *TLS*, 8 May 1903, 146, where it was published anonymously. Reviews this play and *Cathleen ni Houlihan*.

See also BE36, CD741, EB42, EE433, EF77.

The Island of Statues

311. ALSPACH, RUSSELL K.: "Yeats's First Two Published Poems," *MLN*, 58:7 (Nov 1943), 55-57.
A bibliographical note.

See also BA3, CA7, 12, 61, 126, CC92, CD1214, 1218, 1241, DA11, DC62, 90, EA4, 18, 28, 29, EE390, G1656.

King Oedipus I

312. ANON.: "Sophocles, Yeats and Dr. Gogarty," *NYHT*, 15 Jan 1933, section VII, 4.
Report of a Gogarty lecture on Yeats's translation.

313. CLARK, DAVID R. and JAMES B. MCGUIRE: "Yeats's Versions of Sophocles: Two Typescripts," in O'Driscoll and Reynolds: *Yeats and the Theatre* (1975, CA81), 215-77.
Editions of early versions of this play and of *Oedipus at Colonus*.

314. ———: "The Writing of *Sophocles' King Oedipus*," *Yeats*, 2 (1984), 30-74.
A chronicle of Yeats' growing interest in Sophocles and of the genesis of his own version; numerous quotations from unpublished material.

315. GRAB, FREDERIC D.: "Yeats's *King Oedipus*," *JEGP*, 71:3 (July 1972), 336-54.
Also generally on Yeats and Sophocles and on Yeats's dramatic theory.

316. SCHULL, REBECCA: "The Preparation of King Oedipus," *Arts in Ireland*, 2:1 (1973), 15-21. (Illustrated)
The preparations for the performance of Yeats's version on 4 Apr 1973, with Richard Murphy's additions. See also "Rebecca Schull Talks to the Poet Richard Murphy about His Recently Completed Additions to the W. B. Yeats Version of Sophocles' *King Oedipus* for the Abbey Theatre and about His Own Background," *IrT*, 17 May 1973, 12, and EE327.

317. "ULSTERMAN": "Farewell Broadcast by the Abbey Players," *Radio Times*, 4 Sept 1931, 537.
King Oedipus, broadcast from Belfast on 14 Sept 1931.

318. YEATS, W. B.: "W. B. Yeats's Unpublished Talk on His Version of *King Oedipus* Broadcast from the BBC Belfast Studio on 8 September 1931." Introductory note by Karen Dorn, *YeA*, 5 (1987), 195-99.
N.B.: The talk was published in the *Irish Weekly and Ulster Examiner*, 12 Sept 1931, 9.

See also BE118, BF184, CA67, CC250, CD1236, EA4, 10, 25, EB86, G547-49, HA9, 11.

King Oedipus II

319. ARKINS, BRIAN: "A Classical Perspective," *Theatre Ireland*, 14 (Feb/Mar/Apr 1988), 22-23.
A production by the Druid Theatre Company.

320. BENÉT, WILLIAM ROSE: "The Theatre," *SatR*, 28 Jan 1933, 402.

321. C[URRAN], C. P.: "Oedipus at the Abbey," *IrSt*, 11 Dec 1926, 326.

322. DE CASSERES, BENJAMIN: "Yeats' *King Oedipus*," *Arts & Decoration*, 38:5 (Mar 1933), 58, 63.

323. GARLAND, ROBERT: "W. B. Yeats Tells All as Dublin Thespians Give *King Oedipus:* Translation and Adaptation of Sophocles' Melodrama More Lively in Its Pace Than Might Have Been Expected," *NY World Telegram,* 16 Jan 1933, 10.
"All" means how and why he wrote the translation.

324. G[OOD], J. W.: "*Oedipus the King* Staged: Enthusiasm at Abbey," *IrI,* 8 Dec 1926, 6.

325. HAYES, J. J.: "Sophocles and Yeats Win Dublin," *NYT,* 26 Dec 1926, section VII, 4.

326. ———: "Oedipus in Dublin: The Theatre Rediscovers a Popular Success," *BET,* 22 Jan 1927, part 3, 6-7.

327. QUIDNUNC: "An Irishman's Diary," *IrT,* 4 Apr 1973, 11.
On the Abbey production by Michael Cacoyannis, who had asked Richard Murphy to complete Yeats's "defective" text.

The King of the Great Clock Tower I

See CA12, 91, 125, 126, 128, 129, 165, CC14a, 211, CD213, 791, CE102, DA1, DC180, EA3, 4, 18, 22, 25, 26, 28, 35, 36, 37, 40, EB36, EC53, 81, 86, 109, 115, ED34, EE412, FD46, G696-724.

The King of the Great Clock Tower II

328. ANON.: "Memorable 'First Night,'" *SunT,* 5 Aug 1934, 5.
This play and *The Resurrection.* N.B.: There are no reviews in the Irish papers because of a strike.

329. DAVRAY, HENRY D.: Note on the performance of this play and *The Resurrection, MercF,* year 45 / 255:871 (1 Oct 1934), 197-98.

330. WORTH, KATHARINE: "A Meeting Place of Arts," *TLS,* 23 Oct 1981, 1235.
Reviews performances of this play and *The Cat and the Moon* at the Cottesloe Theatre.

See also EE239, 493, 494.

The King's Threshold I

331. BLOCK, HASKELL M.: "Yeats's *The King's Threshold:* The Poet and Society," *PQ,* 34:2 (Apr 1955), 206-18.

332. BORNSTEIN, GEORGE: "A Borrowing from Wilde in Yeats's *The King's Threshold,*" *N&Q,* os 216 / ns 18:11 (Nov 1971), 421-22.
A borrowing from *The Decay of Lying.*

333. BUSHRUI, S. B.: "*The King's Threshold:* A Defence of Poetry," *REL,* 4:3 (July 1963), 81-94.

334. ———: "Yeats: The Poet as Hero," *E&S,* 35 (1982), 101-23.
A revised version of "Le poète comme héros," in Genet: *William Butler Yeats* (1981, CA32), 318-35. The theme of the poet's responsibility to society.

335. FALLON, GABRIEL: "A Forgotten Prologue: When Did Yeats Write It?" *IrT,* 13 Sept 1960, 5.
Correspondence by Micheál O hAodha, 14 Sept 1960, 7; Corinna Salvadori, 16 Sept 1960, 7; Austin Clarke, 17 Sept 1960, 9; Gabriel Fallon, 20 Sept 1960, 7.

336. FRIEDMAN, BARTON R.: "Under a Leprous Moon: Action and Image in *The King's Threshold,*" *ArQ,* 26:1 (Spring 1970), 39-53.

337. MASON, RUPERT: *Robes of Thespis: Costume Design by Modern Artists.* Edited for Rupert Mason by George Sheringham and R. Boyd Morrison. London: Benn, 1928. xv, 143 pp., 109 plates.
"Irish Dramatic Costume," 33-62; contains plates with costumes by Charles Ricketts for this play, Norah MacGuinness for *Deirdre,* and Laurence Bradshaw for *At the Hawk's Well.*

338. O'GRADY, STANDISH: "On *The King's Threshold,*" *All Ireland R,* 24 Oct 1903, 340.
A letter to Yeats expressing dissatisfaction with the play because it is "unreal," "unnatural," and "unhuman." See the defense of the play by T. W. Rolleston: "Mr. Yeats' Play," 31 Oct 1903, 351-52, and O'Grady's reply, 352.

339. OHDEDAR, ADITYA KUMAR: "*The King's Threshold:* A Significant Modern Poetic Drama," *LCrit,* 3:2 (Summer 1957), 21-28.

340. PYLE, HILARY: *Jack B. Yeats in the National Gallery of Ireland.* Dublin: National Gallery of Ireland, 1986. xviii, 94 pp.
A design for a mountain backcloth for this play is reproduced and discussed on pp. 34-35. Other references to WBY, passim.

341. SUBOCZEWSKI, IRENE: "The Figure of the Artist in Modern Drama from Ibsen to Pirandello," Ph.D. thesis, U of Maryland, 1970. viii, 314 pp. (*DAI,* 31:11 [May 1971], 6074A)
"Yeats's *The King's Threshold,*" 224-34.

See also AE102, BB60, CA12, 91, 123, 126, CB447, CC49, CD446, 713, 880, 1103, 1105, 1173, 1214, EA4, 7, 12, 18, 22, 25, 26, 29, 32, 35, 36, 37, EB136, EC16, 55, 56, 68, 69, 86, EE289, EG31, FD46, 73, FG61, G236-37 and note, HD6, HF35, 54, 64.

The King's Threshold II

342. ANON.: "Irish National Theatre Society: Production of Two New Plays," *FrJ,* 9 Oct 1903, 5-6.
Includes an account of Yeats's speech at the conclusion of the performance.

343. ANON.: "Two New Plays--Irish National Theatre," *Irish Daily Independent and Daily Nation,* 9 Oct 1903, 6.

344. ANON.: "Irish National Theatre," *IrT,* 9 Oct 1903, 8.

345. ANON.: "*The King's Threshold,*" *Sinn Féin,* 8 Nov 1913, 1.

346. ANON.: "All Ireland," *United Irishman,* 17 Oct 1903, 1.
Reviews a performance of the play and comments generally on Yeats's work for the Irish National Theatre Society.

347. ARCHER, WILLIAM: "Irish Plays at the Royalty," *World,* 29 Mar 1904, 551.

348. BEERBOHM, MAX: *Around Theatres.* London: Hart-Davis, 1953 [1924]. xvi, 583 pp.
"Some Irish Plays and Players," 314-19; reprinted from *SatRL,* 9 Apr 1904, 455-57. The Irish theater is an oasis in the sandy desert of contemporary English drama. Reviews a performance of this play. Reprinted in CA50, pp. 141-50.

349. "Chanel" [i.e., CLERY, ARTHUR EDWARD]: "Plays with Meanings," *Leader,* 17 Oct 1903, 124-25.

350. H., E.: "The Irish National Theatre," *Pilot,* 2 Apr 1904, 309.
Review of this play and of *The Pot of Broth.*

351. "IGNOTUS": "*The King's Threshold,*" *United Irishman,* 24 Oct 1903, 3.

352. K[ETTLE], T. M.: "The Irish National Theatre Society," *New Ireland,* 17 Oct 1903, 5.
Includes a note on *Samhain* (Wade 229).

353. L[YND], R[OBERT] W[ILSON]: "Ireland and the Play," *To-day,* 6 Apr 1904, 264.

354. RYAN, HUBERT S.: "Some Irish Plays," *Outlook* [London], 2 Apr 1904, 233-34.

355. [WALKLEY, A. B.]: "The Irish National Theatre," *TLS,* 1 Apr 1904, 102.

See also BE74, EE29, EF77, G114.

The Land of Heart's Desire I

356. ANON.: *Bibelot,* 9:6 (June 1903), 4 unnumbered pages preceding p. 183.
Note on this play, "an outbreathing of that Celtic sorrowfulness over bright things faded. . . ."

357. FARRELL, MICHAEL: "Plays for the Country Theatre," *Bell,* 2:1 (Apr 1941), 78-84.
See pp. 80-81.

358. GENET, JACQUELINE: "De l'utilisation du folklore: *The Land of Heart's Desire* de W. B. Yeats," *Gaéliana,* 8 (1986), 133-50.

359. GUNNELL, DORIS: "Le nouveau théâtre irlandais," *Revue,* series 6 / year 23 / 94:1 (1 Jan 1912), 91-106.
Comments on this play, *The Hour-Glass,* and *Cathleen ni Houlihan.*

360. HILLS, S. J.: "Frieda Lawrence," *TLS,* 6 Sept 1985, 975.
Letter to the editor asking for information about Frieda Weekley, the co-translator of the German version of the play, entitled *Das Land der Sehnsucht* (Wade, p. 406). See also letter by John Worthen, 11 Oct 1985, 1139.

361. HIRSCH, FOSTER: "The Hearth and the Journey: The Mingling of Orders in the Drama of Yeats and Eliot," *ArQ,* 27:4 (Winter 1971), 293-307.

Discusses this play and *At the Hawk's Well.*

362. JEFFARES, A. NORMAN: "Three Plays by W. B. Yeats: *The Land of Heart's Desire* (1894), *The Words upon the Window-Pane* (1930), *The Herne's Egg* (1938)," *Gaéliana,* 4 (1982), 57-74.

363. KOSOK, HEINZ (ed): *Das englische Drama im 18. und 19. Jahrhundert.* Berlin: Schmidt, 1976. 379 pp.

Klaus Peter Jochum: "William Butler Yeats: *The Land of Heart's Desire*," 308-17.

364. *Literatura i mifologii͡a: Sbornik nauchnykh trudov.* Leningrad: Leningradskiĭ ordena trudovogo krasnogo znameni gosudarstvennyĭ pedagogicheskiĭ institut imeni A. I. Gert͡sena, 1975. 144 pp.

T. M. Krivina: "Nat͡sional'nai͡a mifologii͡a v dramaturgii V. B. Ieĭtsa (P'esy *Zemli͡a serdechnykh zhelaniĭ* i *Na meli Baĭli*," 79-99. "National mythology" in this play and *On Baile's Strand.*

365. LYMAN, KENNETH COX: "Critical Reaction to Irish Drama on the New York Stage: 1900-1958," Ph.D. thesis, U of Wisconsin, 1960. ix, 834 pp. (*DAI,* 21:3 [Sept 1960], 699)

Includes discussions of this play, *Cathleen ni Houlihan, The Hour-Glass, The Pot of Broth, The Countess Cathleen,* and *The Words upon the Window-Pane.*

366. MILLER, NELLIE BURGET: *The Living Drama: Historical Development and Modern Movements Visualized. A Drama of the Drama.* NY: Century, 1924. xx, 437 pp.

"The New Theater of Ireland," 330-53; on Yeats's plays, pp. 331-35. Discusses this play "as an example of the best of Mr. Yeats's works, with its mysticism, its twilight moods, and its formless yearning."

367. REES, LESLIE (ed): *Modern Short Plays.* Sydney: Angus & Robertson, 1951. 276 pp.

See pp. 259-60.

368. SADDLEMYER, ANN: "The 'Dwarf-Dramas' of the Early Abbey Theatre," in Jeffares: *Yeats, Sligo and Ireland* (1980, CA51), 197-215.

Includes notes on *The Land of Heart's Desire, Cathleen ni Houlihan,* and *The Pot of Broth.*

369. SHIPLEY, JOSEPH TWADELL: *Guide to Great Plays.* Washington: Public Affairs Press, 1956. xi, 867 pp.

This play and *The Hour-Glass* are Yeats's "great plays," pp. 837-39.

370. SMYTHE, COLIN: "A Note on Some of Yeats's Revisions for *The Land of Heart's Desire*," in O'Driscoll and Reynolds: *Yeats and the Theatre* (1975, CA81), 285-86.

Unpublished MS. revisions made in 1911.

371. YEATS, W. B.: *The Land of Heart's Desire.* With a foreword by James S. Johnson. San Francisco: Windsor Press, 1926. vii, 29 pp.

"Foreword," v-vii: The play is the essence of the genuinely Irish and national sentiment.

See also AE100, BE18, CA91, 111, CC1, 309, CD444, 1193, 1205, 1318, EA18, 20, 22, 24, 25, 26, 28, 29, 36, EB6, 11, 78, 102, 139, 154, 162, EC12, 42, 54, 88, EE47, 133, 406, 443, EF24, 106, FA29, G77-84, 309-11, 1348-50, 1357, 1364, HF31.

The Land of Heart's Desire II

372. ANON.: "Dr. Todhunter's New Play," *Daily Chronicle*, 30 Mar 1894, 6.

373. ANON.: "Abbey Theatre: Mr. Yeats's *Land of Heart's Desire*," *IrT*, 17 Feb 1911, 5.
"In the days when he was still a true and natural poet, and a seer without affectation, Mr. W. B. Yeats wrote a little play called *The Land of Heart's Desire*."

374. ANON.: "Irish Plays in London," *Irish Weekly Independent*, 7 Apr 1894, 5.

375. ANON.: "A Special Double Bill," *NY Dramatic Mirror*, 3 Nov 1900, 16.
First American performance at Wallack's, New York: "Tedious in the extreme."

376. ANON.: "Some of the Folk in *The Land of Heart's Desire*," *Sketch*, 25 Apr 1894, 669.
Four photographs (reprinted in *Collected Letters*, 1: opposite p. 406); see also the short review on p. 714.

377. ANON.: "Theatrical Literature," *Sun*, 28 Oct 1900, part 2, 8.

378. A[RCHER], W[ILLIAM]: "The Theatre," *World*, 4 Apr 1894, 26-28.

379. Dbd. [i.e., DIEBOLD, BERNHARD]: "Irische Einakter," *Frankfurter Zeitung*, 12 Mar 1919, 1.
A performance in the Frankfurter Schauspielhaus.

380. DITHMAR, EDWARD A.: "At the Theatres," *NYT*, 28 Oct 1900, 22.

381. GILMAN, LAWRENCE: "The Neo-Celtic Drama in America," *Lamp*, 27:3 (Oct 1903), 231-33.
Performances of this play, *The Pot of Broth*, and *Cathleen ni Houlihan*.

382. MCAVOCK, DESMOND: "Abbey Theatre: The Early Plays of Yeats," *Hibernia*, 29:3 (Mar 1965), 27-28.
Performances of this play, *Cathleen ni Houlihan*, and *The Dreaming of the Bones*. See also Patrick O'Connor: "Theatre," *Furrow*, 16:6 (June 1965), 374-76.

383. O'DONOGHUE, D. J.: "Cockneys Enraged: A Notable Experiment," *IrI*, 9 Mar 1908, 4.
Reminiscences of the first performance.

384. Ö[STERLING], A[NDERS]: "Irländskt program på Klubbteatern," *Svenska dagbladet*, 27 Nov 1927, 6.
Performance of the Swedish translation, *Längtans land*.

385. R.: "Two Irish Dramatists," *United Ireland*, 21 Apr 1894, 1.

386. S., W. T.: "The Past and the Future of Our Drama--VII.," *Academy,* 3 Sept 1904, 168-69.

Praises the work of the Irish National Theatre Society with specific reference to this play. Correspondence by "Dublin": "The Irish National Theatre Society," 17 Sept 1904, 202: The society does not deserve the name Irish because Yeats has a "peculiarly un-Irish imagination."

387. SULLIVAN, MARGARET F.: "Triumph of the 'Literary Play,'" *Dial,* 30:360 (16 June 1901), 391-93.

A performance at the Chicago Grand Opera House.

388. ZERAFFA, MICHEL: "Drames et poésie," *Europe,* 34:131-32 (Nov-Dec 1956), 225-29.

Contains a short note on André Rouyer's production of this play, *The Only Jealousy of Emer,* and *The Shadowy Waters.* See EC88.

See also BB52.

Mosada

389. HOPKINS, GERARD MANLEY: *Further Letters of Gerard Manley Hopkins Including His Correspondence with Coventry Patmore.* Edited with notes and an introduction by Claude Colleer Abbott. London: Oxford UP, 1956 [1938]. xliii, 465 pp.

In a letter to Patmore of 7 Nov 1886, Hopkins expresses his opinion of *Mosada,* which he hasn't read, and of "The Two Titans," which he has and doesn't like (pp. 373-74). Extract reprinted in CA50, pp. 64-65.

390. YEATS, W. B.: *The Early Poetry. Volume I: "Mosada" and "The Island of Statues."* Manuscript materials by W. B. Yeats, edited by George Bornstein. Ithaca: Cornell UP, 1987. xii, 442 pp. (The Cornell Yeats.)

Contains transcriptions of the MSS. with prefaces and annotations, also facsimiles of the entire *Mosada* material, of the first draft of *The Island of Statues,* and of 17 pages of later versions. The "Introduction," 3-16, discusses the composition of the two plays. For a review see G1656.

See also CC46, CD1218, DA11, EA4, 18, 28, G1, 1656.

Oedipus at Colonus I

See CC250, EA10, 25, EC72, EE313.

Oedipus at Colonus II

391. G[OOD], J. W.: "At the Abbey Theatre: Mr. Yeats's *Oedipus at Colonus,*" *IrI,* 13 Sept 1927, 10.

392. STARKIE, WALTER: "*Oedipus at Colonus* at the Abbey Theatre," *IrSt,* 17 Sept 1927, 40-41.

Correspondence by T. G. Keller and "Arcos," 24 Sept 1927, 60: "What has come to Mr. Yeats that he permitted such demonstration of inartistry on the Abbey stage?"

On Baile's Strand I

393. BARNET, SYLVAN, MORTON BERMAN, and WILLIAM BURTO (eds): *Eight Great Tragedies*. NY: New American Library, 1957. 443 pp. (Mentor Book. MQ461.)
See pp. 324-27.

394. CANFIELD, CURTIS (ed): *Plays of the Irish Renaissance, 1880-1930*. With an introduction and notes. NY: Washburn, 1938 [1929]. 436 pp.
"Plays Based on Ancient Gaelic Legends and Mythology," 15-26; includes notes on this play and *The Only Jealousy of Emer*.

395. COLCORD, LINCOLN: "Imagined Drama," *NewRep*, 11 Sept 1915, 157.

395a. *Landmarks of Irish Drama*. With an introduction by Brendan Kennelly. London: Methuen, 1988. xlvi, 539 pp.
Contains this play together with an analysis by Kennelly (pp. xix-xxiv).

396. MCCARTHY, PATRICK A.: "Talent and Tradition in Yeats' *On Baile's Strand*," *Eire*, 11:1 (Spring 1976), 45-62.
Discusses the Irish mythological sources.

397. POLI͡UDOVA, T. M.: "Drama Ĭetsa *Na otmeli Baĭl:* Analiz dramaticheskoĭ struktury i zhanrovoĭ spet͡sifiki p'esy," *Problemy metoda i zhanra v zarubezhnoĭ literature: Sbornik trudov*, 2 (1978), 54-70.
"Yeats's drama *On Baile's Strand:* Analysis of the play's dramatic structure and of the genre specifics."

398. SCHROETER, JAMES: "Yeats and the Tragic Tradition," *SoR*, 1:4 (Oct 1965), 835-46.
On this play's paradoxical use of Greek tragedy and mythology: Although the pattern of action seems to conform to those of Sophocles and Aeschylus, Yeats manages to steer the play's meaning into the opposite direction. Sophocles would not have consented to Yeats's contention that Cuchulain's mistake was his momentary surrender to reason and order.

399. SOMERS, JOHN WILMOT: "The Sources and Aesthetics of Modern Drama," Ph.D. thesis, U of Missouri, Columbia, 1973. iv, 257 pp. (*DAI*, 35:2 [Aug 1974], 1287A-88A)
See pp. 157-65.

See also BA3, CA10, 12, 60, 63, 91, 122, 123, 126, CB274, CC49, 141, 167, 250, 318, 351, 428, CD519, 880, 984, 987, 1103, 1105, 1173, 1214, DA35(I), DD708, EA4, 7, 12, 18, 22, 24, 25, 26, 28, 29, 32, 35, 36, 37, EB4, 32, 61, 69, 122, 164, EC14, 16, 28, 31, 34, 40, 43, 50, 55, 57, 63, 68, 71, 86, 96, 107, 115, EE291, 364, 394, 428, FD73, FG10, G236-37 and note, HA8, HD164.

On Baile's Strand II

400. ANON.: "The New Abbey Theatre: Opening Performance," *Daily Express*, 28 Dec 1904, 5.
This play and *Cathleen ni Houlihan*.

401. ANON.: "A Mixed Programme," *Festival Theatre R*, [1]:6 (Jan 1927), 2-4.

A photograph of the performance appears in 3:47 (17 Nov 1928), 5. See also also EC115 and Richard Cave: *Terence Gray and the Cambridge Festival Theatre*. Cambridge: Chadwyck-Healey, 1980. 97 pp. plus 50 slides. (Theatre in Focus.). Slides 31-32 are from the 1927 performance of this play; see description in the booklet, pp. 54-56.

402. ANON.: "Irish National Theatre: Opening Night. New Play by Mr. Yeats," *FrJ*, 28 Dec 1904, 5-6.
Includes a report of a short speech by Yeats.

403. ANON.: "National Drama: The Abbey Theatre. Auspicious Inauguration," *Irish Daily Independent and Daily Nation*, 28 Dec 1904, 6.
See also the editorial, "Abbey Theatre," p. 4.

404. CALTA, LOUIS: "Theatre: Yeats Cycle. Two Celtic Plays in One-Night Stand," *NYT*, 13 Apr 1959, 34.
Performances of this play and *The Death of Cuchulain* by the New York Theatre Society at the Beekman Tower Hotel Theatre.

405. Chanel [i.e., CLERY, ARTHUR EDWARD]: "The Deserted Abbey," *Leader*, 28 Apr 1906, 151-52.

406. D., A.: "The Irish Players Again," *Academy*, 22 June 1907, 610-11.
The reviewer thinks this play inferior to *The Land of Heart's Desire*.

407. GREIN, J. T.: "Two Irish Plays," *SunT*, 10 Dec 1905, 13.
"We are spellbound by the poet, but we are not held by the dramatist."

408. JOY, MAURICE: "The Irish National Theatre," *Speaker*, 24 Dec 1904, 309-11.

409. ———: "Mr. Yeats's New Play," *Speaker*, 7 Jan 1905, 353.

410. [MASEFIELD, JOHN]: "The Irish National Theatre," *MGuard*, 29 Dec 1904, 4.

411. ———: "Irish Plays in Dublin: *On Baile's Strand* at the Abbey Theatre," *Daily News*, 4 Jan 1905, 6.

See also BE28, EC21, EE26, 266, EF77.

The Only Jealousy of Emer I

412. CAVE, RICHARD ALLEN: "A Style for Yeats's Dance Plays: 'The More Passionate Is the Art the More Marked Is the Selection,'" *YES*, 9 (1979), 135-53; 3 illustrations between pp. 134-35.
"This article is a record of productions of three of Yeats's plays for dancers (*The Only Jealousy of Emer*, *Calvary*, and *The King of the Great Clock Tower*) which I worked on with a group of student actors." See also EC109.

413. COHN, RUBY, and BERNARD FRANK DUKORE (eds): *Twentieth Century Drama: England, Ireland, the United States*. NY: Random House, 1966. ix, 692 pp.
See pp. 147-50.

414. KNAPP, BETTINA LIEBOWITZ: *Theatre and Alchemy*. Detroit: Wayne State UP, 1980. xiii, 284 pp.

"*The Only Jealousy of Emer:* Recycling the Elements," 89-110; revised version of "An Alchemical Brew: From *Separatio* to *Coagulatio* in Yeats's *The Only Jealousy of Emer*," *ETJ*, 30:4 (Dec 1978), 447-65.

415. SCANLON, SISTER ALOYSE: "The Sustained Metaphor in *The Only Jealousy of Emer*," *MD*, 7:3 (Dec 1964), 273-77.

416. SHAUGHNESSY, EDWARD L.: "Masks in the Dramaturgy of Yeats and O'Neill," *IUR*, 14:2 (Autumn 1984), 205-20.

Discusses this play and *The Player Queen*.

417. WILSON, F. A. C.: "Yeats and Gerhart Hauptmann," *SoRA*, [1]:1 (1963), 69-73.

Suggests that this play was influenced by Hauptmann's *Die versunkene Glocke*.

418. WINNETT, STEPHEN R.: "An Edition of the Manuscripts of Two Plays by W. B. Yeats, *The Only Jealousy of Emer* and *Fighting the Waves*," D.phil. thesis, Oxford U, 1978. iii, 315 pp.

Contains chapters on the publishing and performing history of the plays and the sources, on the evolutions of the texts from earliest draft to first printing, critical analyses of the revisions, and full transcriptions of all extant MSS.

See also BB146, CA10, 12, 28a, 63, 91, 122, 123, 125, 130, CB528, CC61, 141, 167, DC180, EA4, 8, 12, 14, 18, 22, 24, 25, 26, 28, 29, 32, 35, 36, 37, 40, EB12, 69, 147, EC3, 14, 28, 31, 34, 42, 43, 63, 71, 81, 84, 88, 96, 107, ED2, 22, 29, 34, EE17, 500, EG32, FC121, FE48, HA15, 17, HE20.

The Only Jealousy of Emer II

419. ANON.: "Maskerspel en maskerdans," *Nieuwe Rotterdamsche Courant*, 28 Nov 1926, C1.

Review of the Dutch performance: translation by Helene Swarth, production and leading part by Albert van Dalsum, masks by Hildo Krop. See also Anon.: "Stadsschouwburg te Amsterdam," 29 Nov 1926, C1; W. L. Thieme: "Het maskerspel van Vrouwe Emer," ibid., trying to make sense of the play.

This was the second Dutch performance; the first took place in 1922. For reviews see Cornelis Veth: "Tooneel," *Nieuws van den dag*, 4 Apr 1922, Tweede blad, 5; Ks.: "Maskerspel: Vrouwe Emer's groote strijd," *Algemeen handelsblad*, 3 Apr 1922, 9 ("The audience . . . , although mostly an artistic audience, did not take to the play").

See also Hildo Krop: Photographs of the masks for Cuchulain, Eithne Inguba, Emer, Bricriu, and the Woman of the Sea, *Wendingen*, 7:2 (1925), 14-15.

420. ANON.: "Students Revive Plays by Yeats," *Times*, 1 Dec 1965, 15.

The Bristol University Drama Studio productions of this play, *At the Hawk's Well, The Death of Cuchulain,* and *The Cat and the Moon*.

421. BARNES, CLIVE: "Stage: Bright Twin Bill," *NYT*, 25 Mar 1970, 36.

Performance by the La Mama Repertory Company at the Performing Garage. Music by Barbara Benary. See also Mel Gussow: "*Jealousy of Emer*," 25 Jan 1972, 26, for a review of another performance by the La Mama group; Walter Kerr: "Drama, Not Long Out of the Womb," *NYT*, 26 Apr 1970, section II, 1, 5 (illustrated); Arthur Sainer: "Peering Down the Tunnel," *Village Voice*, 12 Feb 1970, 49.

422. DUNNING, JENNIFER: "Open Eye Stages *Jealousy of Emer, Play for Dancers*," *NYT*, 30 Dec 1973, 20.
The Open Eye Theatre Co., NY.

423. LEVENTHAL, A. J.: "Dramatic Commentary," *DM*, 24:1 (Jan-Mar 1949), 38-41.

See also EC21, EE26, 266, 388.

The Player Queen I

424. ANON.: "Mr. Yeats and His New Play," *Irish Nation*, 16 July 1910, 8.
Interview about the play.

425. BECKER, WILLIAM: "The Mask Mocked: Or, Farce and the Dialectic of the Self. (Notes on Yeats's *The Player Queen*)," *SR*, 61:1 (Jan-Mar 1953), 82-108.
An extract from EA1.

426. HINDEN, MICHAEL: "Yeats's Symbolic Farce: *The Player Queen*," *MD*, 14:4 (Feb 1972), 441-48.

427. NEWTON, NORMAN: "Yeats as a Dramatist: *The Player Queen*," *EIC*, 8:3 (July 1958), 269-84.
A defense of Yeats's dramatic intelligence.

428. S[ADDLEMYER], A[NN]: "Notes on the Plays," *Beltaine* [Victoria, B.C.], 1 (Mar 1965), [6-8].
Notes on this play and *On Baile's Strand*.

429. YEATS, W. B.: *The Writing of "The Player Queen."* Manuscripts of W. B. Yeats transcribed, edited & with a commentary by Curtis Baker Bradford. DeKalb: Northern Illinois UP, 1977. xxv, 483 pp. (Manuscripts of W. B. Yeats.)
The book has to be used with some care because the publisher failed to include corrections made by the general editor of the series, David R. Clark; see Clark's note in *Year's Work in English Studies*, 58 (1977), 416. For reviews see G1525-1530.

See also BA3, CA7, 12, 73, 125, 126, 129, 167, CC180, 182, 183, 290, CD313, 880, 1173, EA3, 4, 8, 18, 22, 24, 25, 26, 29, 35, 36, 37, 39, EB32, 103, 141, 143, 147, 171, EC6, 40, 42, 64, 81, 107, EE416, FC121, G1525-30.

The Player Queen II

430. ANON.: "A Yeats Satire: First Production in the Abbey of *The Player Queen*," *FrJ*, 10 Dec 1919, 2.

431. ANON.: "The Abbey Theatre: New Play by Mr. W. B. Yeats," *IrT,* 10 Dec 1919, 6.

432. ANON.: "The Stage Society," *Times,* 28 May 1919, 15.
". . . revealing a new gift in Mr. Yeats, the gift of writing thoroughly enjoyable nonsense."

433. COOKMAN, A. V.: "The Theatre," *LMerc,* 33:194 (Dec 1935), 191-92.
Performances of this play, *The Hour-Glass,* and *The Pot of Broth.*

434. HORN, EFFI: "Büchner-Theater: Partiegefühle beim Sandkasten," *Münchner Merkur,* 23 May 1966, 4.
A performance in München; see also G. J.: "Dilettanten-Mühen: Premiere im Büchner-Theater," *Süddeutsche Zeitung,* 23 May 1966, 12; Kth.: "Von bösen Weibern," *Abendzeitung,* 23 May 1966, 13.

435. LEWISOHN, LUDWIG: "Drama: Importations," *Nation,* 31 Oct 1923, 495-96.
"Terribly overwritten and therefore terribly dull."

436. P[OWER], J[OSEPH] A.: "Villon at the Abbey: Mr. W. B: Yeats Out with Muck Rake. New Play's Tepid Welcome," *Evening Telegraph,* 10 Dec 1919, 2.

437. "PRIOR": "*The Player Queen,*" *IrSt,* 13 Dec 1919, 608-9.
"Most of the audience went to be mystified, and they came away disappointed, because they were not quite sure what they ought to be mystified about."

438. SMITH, HESTER TRAVERS: "Drama in Ireland, 1919-1920," *Drama* [Chicago], 10:9 (June 1920), 308-9.
"Perhaps the most important dramatic event . . . was the production of *The Player Queen.*"

439. S[TRACHEY], J[AMES]: "Swinburne and Mr. Yeats," *Athenaeum,* 6 June 1919, 438.
"The audience gasped. . . ."

440. YOUNG, STARK: "At the Neighborhood," *NewRep,* 31 Oct 1923, 257.
A performance at the Neighborhood Playhouse.

See also EE308.

The Pot of Broth I

441. Blaghd, Earnán de [i.e., BLYTHE, ERNEST]: *Slán le hUltaibh: Imleabhar II de Chuimhní Cinn.* Baile Átha Cliath: Sáirséal agus Dill, 1971. 200 pp.
See pp. 53-55.

442. DRAVAINE, CLAUDE: Note on his translation of the play, *Jeux, tréteaux et personnages,* 15:112 (Nov-Dec 1946), 276-78.

443. GOURLEY, MERYL: "Four Plays by W. B. Yeats," *Icarus,* 5:17 (Nov 1955), 27-31.
This play, *The Land of Heart's Desire, The Dreaming of the Bones,* and *Purgatory.*

444. MÜLLER, MAX (ed): *Two English One-Act Plays by Modern Irish Authors.* Mit Einleitung und Anmerkungen herausgegeben von Max Müller. Frankfurt/Main: Diesterweg, 1928. iv, 47 pp. (Diesterwegs Neusprachliche Schulausgaben mit deutschen Anmerkungen. 15.)
See pp. 6-9, 35-41.

445. Ó MUIRITHE, DIARMAID: "'There's Broth in the Pot,'" *Éigse,* 18:2 (1981), 305-8.
The source of the song.

446. YEATS, W. B.: *A húsleves.* Budapest: Gondolat, 1961. 95 pp. (Játékszín. 32.)
Contains a producer's postscript, pp. 7-8.

See also CD572, EA4, 18, 22, 25, 26, 36, EB11, EC64, EE365, 368, G224-35 and note, HA15.

The Pot of Broth II

447. ANON.: "The Samhain Festival," *FrJ,* 31 Oct 1902, 4.

448. MACCARTHY, DESMOND: *The Court Theatre, 1904-1907: A Commentary and Criticism.* Edited with a foreword and additional material by Stanley Weintraub. Coral Gables: U of Miami Press, 1966 [1907]. xxvi, 182 pp. (Books of the Theatre Series. 6.)
See p. 116 for a list of performances of this play.

See also EE308, 350, 381, 433.

Purgatory I

449. ALCORN, MARSHALL WISE: "'Still Razor-Keen, Still like a Looking-Glass': Literary Studies in Narcissistic Sublimation and Lyric Volition," °Ph.D. thesis, U of Texas at Austin, 1981. 338 pp. (*DAI,* 42:11 [May 1981], 4829A)
On this play, according to abstract.

450. ANON.: "Mr. Yeats Explains Play: Plot of *Purgatory* Is Its Meaning. Dramatist's Answer to U.S. Priest's Query," *IrI,* 13 Aug 1938, 9.
Interview with Yeats about the Rev. Terence L. Connolly's question; reprinted in BA13, 2:231-32. See also EE476.

451. BADAL, JAMES JESSEN: "Studies in the Tragic Altitude," Ph.D. thesis, Case Western Reserve U, 1975. vi, 269 pp. (*DAI,* 37:2 [Aug 1976], 961A-62A)
"The Old Man: The Contemporary Hero," 219-45.

452. BARNET, SYLVAN, MORTON BERMAN, and WILLIAM BURTO (eds): *An Introduction to Literature: Fiction--Poetry--Drama.* 2nd edition. Boston: Little, Brown, 1963 [1961]. 611 pp.
See pp. 453-57.

453. BHOWANI-SETHI, UMA, and LEWIS T. CETTA: "The Theme of Reincarnation in Yeats's *Purgatory,*" *Theatre Annual,* 30 (1974), 7-13.
The use of Hindu and theosophical ideas of reincarnation.

454. BROWNE, ELLIOTT MARTIN: *Verse in Modern English Theatre.* The

W. D. Thomas Memorial Lecture delivered at the University College at Swansea on 28 February, 1963. Cardiff: U of Wales Press, 1963. 32 pp.
See pp. 31-32.

455. BURZYŃSKA, JOANNA: "Evocation of the Creative Consciousness: W. B. Yeats's *Purgatory*," *Uniwersytet Gdański: Zeszyty naukowe wydziału humanistycznego. Filologia angielska,* 4 (1984), 95-109.

456. CALDERWOOD, JAMES L., and HAROLD E. TOLIVER (eds): *Forms of Drama*. Englewood Cliffs: Prentice-Hall, 1969, v, 601 pp.
See pp. 192-93.

457. CIUK, ANDRZEJ: "The Analysis of Application of the Noh Technique in W. B. Yeats's *Purgatory*," *Zeszyty naukowe Wyższej Szkoły Pedagogicznej im. Powstańców Śląskich w Opolu. Filologia angielska,* 1 (1986), 87-94.
The indebtedness to the Nō and Yeats's view of history.

458. COLLINS, JAMES A.: "The Dramatic Verse of W. B. Yeats in *Purgatory*," *LHY,* 9:1 (Jan 1969), 91-98.

459. FREDRICKS, MARY VIRGINIA: "An Approach to the Teaching of Oral Interpretation in Terms of Dramatic Action," Ph.D. thesis, U of Minnesota, 1961. iii, 356 pp. (*DAI,* 22:4 [Oct 1961], 1300-1301)
Analysis of the play as a scene-role-gesture relationship, pp. 266-81.

460. GASKELL, RONALD: "*Purgatory*," *MD,* 4:4 (Feb 1962), 397-401.

461. GINER, OSCAR: "Exorcisms," *Theater,* 9:3 (Summer 1978), 75-81.
Purgatory is one of those plays that "serve as means for cleansing away, as rituals of exorcism for the knowledge of the corruption that has tainted the soul of the nation, that has eaten away at the integrity of its tradition."

462. GORE, JEANNE GUERRERO: "William Butler Yeats's *Purgatory:* Tragedy or Its Mirror-Image?" °Ph.D. thesis, George Peabody College for Teachers at Vanderbilt U, 1981. 96 pp. (*DAI,* 42:11 [May 1982], 4832A; reprinted *Yeats,* 1 [1983], 182-83, and *YeA,* 4 [1986], 310-11)

463. KAWIN, BRUCE FREDERICK: *Telling It Again and Again: Repetition in Literature and Film*. Ithaca: Cornell UP, 1972. ix, 197 pp.
See pp. 72-84.

464. LAPISARDI, FREDERICK S.: "A Most Conscious Craftsman: A Study of Yeat[s]'s *Purgatory* as the Culmination of His Expressed Dramatic Theories," *Eire,* 2:4 (Winter 1967), 87-99.
"If Yeats is ever generally accepted as a playwright, *Purgatory* will stand as his greatest dramatic achievement, for it is in this play that most of his expressed theories reach fruition." Most of the preceding plays are failures of one sort or another.

465. LIGHTFOOT, MARJORIE J.: "*Purgatory* and *The Family Reunion:* In Pursuit of Prosodic Description," *MD,* 7:3 (Dec 1964), 256-66.

466. LINEBARGER, JAMES MORRIS: "Yeats' Symbolist Method and the Play *Purgatory*," Ph.D. thesis, Emory U, 1963. viii, 172 pp. (*DAI,* 24:9 [Mar 1964], 3750-51)

467. MACLEISH, ARCHIBALD: "The Poet as Playwright," *Atlantic Monthly*, 195:2 (Feb 1955), 49-52.
Contains a note on this play.

468. MOORE, JOHN REES: "An Old Man's Tragedy--Yeats' *Purgatory*," *MD*, 5:4 (Feb 1963), 440-50.

469. REEVES, HALBERT A.: "Dramatic Economy of Imagery in Two of Yeats's Later Plays," *McNR*, 23 (1976-77), 44-49.
This play and *The Death of Cuchulain*.

470. REINERT, OTTO (ed): *Drama: An Introductory Anthology*. Boston: Little, Brown, 1961. xi, 652 pp.
Note on this play, pp. 473-75; reprinted in Reinert's *Modern Drama: Nine Plays*. Boston: Little, Brown, 1962. xxvii, 491 pp. (pp. 311-13).

471. RUBINSTEIN, HAROLD FREDERICK, and JOHN COURTENAY TREWIN (eds): *The Drama Bedside Book*. London: Gollancz, 1966. 544 pp.
The section "Darkest Hour" contains a complete reprint of the play plus an introductory note, pp. 395-403.

472. SCHMITT, NATALIE CROHN: "Curing Oneself of the Work of Time: W. B. Yeats's *Purgatory*," *CompD*, 7:4 (Winter 1973/74), 310-33.
Discusses the play as religious drama and concentrates on rituals of rebirth and renewal.

473. SOCIÉTÉ DES ANGLICISTES DE L'ENSEIGNEMENT SUPÉRIEUR: *Poétique(s): Domaine anglais*. Actes du Congrès de Lyon, 1981. Lyon: Presses unversitaires de Lyon, 1983. 423 pp.
Jacqueline Genet: "W. B. Yeats: *Purgatory*," 169-84.

474. VANDERWERKEN, DAVID L.: "*Purgatory:* Yeats's Modern Tragedy," *CLQ*, 10:5 (Mar 1974), 259-69.

475. YEATS, W. B.: *Purgatory: Manuscript Materials Including the Author's Final Text*. Edited by Sandra F. Siegel. Ithaca: Cornell UP, 1986. xi, 222 pp. (The Cornell Yeats.)
The "Introduction," 3-26, discusses the manuscripts, the "Patterns of Revision" of the play, the publication of *On the Boiler*, and the arguments advanced in both the play and the essay. This is followed by facsimile reprints and transcriptions of various versions of the play. For reviews see G1654-1655.

See also BB250, CA4, 12, 14, 90, 91, 118, 122, 123, 125, 126, 128, 129, 170, CB194, 274, 280, CC14a, 38, 112, 350, CD149, 196, 197, 400, 428, 572, 695, 901, 987, 1173, 1386, 1433, CE37, 153, DA17, 53, DB50, 72, 175, DD521, 562, EA4, 8, 14, 18, 22, 24, 25, 26, 28, 29, 32, 35, 36, 37, 39, 40, EB60, 72, 103, 111, 132, 141, 154, 164, 165, 169, 171, EC13, 16, 40, 48, 60, 70, 72, 84, 86, ED14, EE8, 20, 236, 254, 257, 281, 443, 497, 554, FA63, 64, FD46, 73, G828, 837-44, 848-83 and note, 1654-55, HA15, HE31.

Purgatory II

476. ANON.: "Mr. W. B. Yeats's New Play: Theatre Festival Production. 'His Own Beliefs,'" *Evening Mail*, 11 Aug 1938, 8.
See also in the same issue "Yeats Play 'Not Understood': Enquirers Are 'Left Guessing,'" p. 9. The following issue contains

an interview with Yeats, in which some of the problems are explained: "Puzzle of the New Play: Explanations by Mr. Yeats. 'The Dead Suffer,'" 12 Aug 1938, 12. See also EE450.

477. ANON.: "Abbey Theatre Festival: Mr. Yeats's New Play," *Times*, 16 Aug 1938, 10.

478. ANON.: "Poetic Play of Great Power: Yeats's *Purgatory*," *Times*, 30 Aug 1955, 5.
A performance in Edinburgh.

479. ANON.: "Irish Plays in Edinburgh: *Purgatory* Revived," *Times*, 29 Aug 1957, 3.

480. C., L.: "New Yeats Play Given at Abbey," *IrP*, 11 Aug 1938, 7.

481. CAVE, RICHARD: "Two Views of Purgatory: Beckett and Yeats at the Edinburgh Festival, 1977," *JBeckS*, 3 (Summer 1978), 121-27.
Performances of this play and Beckett's *Embers*.

481a. D[URAND], G[UY]: "Suite ternaire," *Esprit*, 8-9 (Aug-Sept 1987), 79-80.
Review of *Suite irlandaise*, a production by La Compagnie Jean Bollery at the Théâtre de Poche Montparnasse, which included *Purgatory* in the translation by Pierre Leyris.

482. ELLIS-FERMOR, UNA: "The Abbey Theatre Festival (7-20 Aug 1938)," *English*, 2:9 (1938), 174-77.

483. M[ALONE], A[NDREW] E.: "Abbey Theatre Festival: A New Yeats Play," *IrT*, 11 Aug 1938, 6.
Correspondence by John Lucy, 15 Aug 1938, 5; Frank O'Connor, 16 Aug 1938, 8; Diarmuid Brennan, Mary Manning, and others, 17 Aug 1938, 5; and continued in subsequent issues.

484. O'FAOLAIN, SEAN: "The Abbey Festival," *NSt*, 20 Aug 1938, 281-82.

485. ROSENFIELD, RAY: "Yeats Plays at Lyric, Belfast," *IrT*, 1 July 1983, 10.
Sam McCready's production of *Purgatory*, *Calvary*, and *The Resurrection* as a single drama.

486. S., D.: "Great Poet Has Warm Reception: New Yeats Play at the Abbey," *IrI*, 11 Aug 1938, 10.

See also EE28, 160, 263.

The Resurrection I

487. BABU, M. SATHYA: "Treatment of Christianity in W. B. Yeats' *The Resurrection*," *Wisconsin Studies in Literature*, 5 (1968), 53-63.
Reprinted in *LCrit*, 11:2 (Summer 1974), 32-42. "The theme of the play has little to do with Christianity as an institutional religion."

488. BAIRD, SISTER MARY JULIAN: "A Play on the Death of God: The Irony of Yeats's *The Resurrection*," *MD*, 10:1 (May 1967), 79-86.
Written from an orthodox Catholic point of view.

489. BAUSKA, BARRY: "Yeats: A Case for Resurrection," *CJIS*, 5:1 (June 1979), 52-68.

490. GOULD, WARWICK: "The 'Myth [in] . . . Reply to a Myth': Yeats, Balzac, and Joachim of Fiore," *YeA*, 5 (1987), 238-51.
Explanation of a textual puzzle in Yeats's introduction to this play with reference to "The Adoration of the Magi," "The Tables of the Law," "Rosa Alchemica," and Yeats's cyclical view of history.

491. MORGAN, MARGERY M.: "Shaw, Yeats, Nietzsche, and the Religion of Art," *Komos*, 1:1 (Mar 1967), 24-34.
The influence of Nietzsche and Shaw's *Major Barbara* on this play.

492. SPALTRO, KATHLEEN AGNES: "As Though God's Death Were But a Play: Literature and Dogma in Crisis," °Ph.D. thesis, Northwestern U, 1981. 209 pp. (*DAI*, 42:9 [Mar 1982], 3689A)
Includes a discussion of this play.

See also CA7, 12, 14, 53a, 91, 122, 123, 125, CC10, 44, 196, 293, CD247, 428, 1214, 1406, DC18, DD681-90 and note, EA4, 8, 10, 14, 18, 22, 25, 26, 28, 35, 36, 37, 39, EB103, EC56, 60, 63, 84, 86, 106, ED34, EE38, FC142, HA16.

The Resurrection II

493. ANON.: "Dublin Stage Survey: Two New Plays by Mr. Yeats," *IrI*, 4 Oct 1934, 6.
This play and *The King of the Great Clock Tower*. There are no other reviews in the Irish papers because of a strike.

494. ANON.: "The Abbey Theatre: Two New Plays by W. B. Yeats," *Times*, 31 July 1934, 12.
This play and *The King of the Great Clock Tower*.

495. ANON.: "Dublin Festival Play on the Genesis of a Bully," *Times*, 23 Sept 1965, 8.

496. ATKINSON, BROOKS: "Abbey Odds and Ends," *NYT*, 20 Nov 1934, 24.

497. ROSENFIELD, RAY: "Four Plays of Yeats at the Lyric," *IrT*, 27 & 28 Mar 1970, 8.
This play, *Calvary*, *Purgatory*, and *The Dreaming of the Bones*.

See also EE42, 44, 45, 160, 328, 329, 485.

The Seeker

See CA126, CC46, CD1214, 1218, DA11, DC62, EA4, 18.

The Shadowy Waters I

498. GOLDGAR, HARRY: "Axël de Villiers de l'Isle Adam et *The Shadowy Waters* de W. B. Yeats," *RLC*, 24:4 (Oct-Dec 1950), 563-74.

499. OLIVERO, FEDERICO: *Studi su poeti e prosatori inglesi.* Torino: Bocca, 1925. vi, 394 pp.

"La leggenda di Ulisse nel Tennyson e in alcuni poeti irlandesi," 212-32; contains a paraphrase of this play and "The Wanderings of Oisin."

500. PARKIN, ANDREW: "Yeats's Orphic Voice," *CJIS,* 2:1 (May 1976), 44-50.

The Orpheus myth in this play, *The Only Jealousy of Emer, The Words upon the Window-Pane,* and *A Full Moon in March.* Reprinted in Srivastava and Dutta: *Unaging Intellect* (1983, CA108), 122-31.

501. SIDNELL, MICHAEL JOHN: "A Critical Examination of W. B. Yeats's *The Shadowy Waters* with a Transcription and Collation of the Manuscript Versions," Ph.D. thesis, U of London, 1967. v, 548 pp.

See also EE505.

502. ———: "Manuscript Versions of Yeats's *The Shadowy Waters:* An Abbreviated Description and Chronology of the Papers Relating to the Play in the National Library of Ireland," *PBSA,* 62:1 (1968), 39-57.

See also Lola L. Szladits: "Addenda to Sidnell: Yeats's *The Shadowy Waters,*" :4 (1968), 614-17 (additional material from the Lady Gregory Collection in the Berg Collection); and EE505.

503. WORTH, KATHARINE: "Evolution of the European 'Drama of the Interior': Maeterlinck, Wilde, and Yeats," *Maske und Kothurn,* 25:1-2 (1979), 161-70.

Discusses this play and *At the Hawk's Well.*

504. YEATS, W. B.: *A Tower of Polished Black Stones: Early Versions of "The Shadowy Waters."* Arranged and edited by David Ridgley Clark and George Mayhew with five illustrations by Leonard Baskin and drawings by the poet. Dublin: Dolmen Press, 1971. xvi, 71 pp. (Dolmen Editions. 11.)

"Introduction," vii-xvi, comments on the early versions, which differ greatly from the published texts. Further commentary, passim. See also next item; for reviews see G1473-1475.

505. ———: *Druid Craft: The Writing of "The Shadowy Waters."* Manuscripts of W. B. Yeats transcribed, edited, and with a commentary by Michael J. Sidnell, George P. Mayhew, David R. Clark. Amherst: U of Massachusetts Press, 1971. xxiii, 349 pp. (Manuscripts of W. B. Yeats. 1.)

This edition of MS. versions supersedes all previous editions, i.e., Clark's "Aubrey Beardsley's Drawing of the 'Shadows' in W. B. Yeats's *The Shadowy Waters,*" *MD,* 7:3 (Dec 1964), 267-72; CB443, EE501, 502, and 504.

Contains the transcriptions, chapters on structure, plot, symbols, mythical allusions, visions, and the published versions. For reviews see G1464-1472.

See also BA3, BB155, CA12, 17, 26, 91, 126, 160, CB83, 443, CC1, 147, 180, 284, CD55, 78, 428, 791, 880, 987, 1136, 1154, 1214, CE212, DA11, 30, 30, 35(I), DC62, 180, DD722, EA4, 7, 12, 18, 20, 22, 24, 25, 26, 28, 29, 35, 36, 39, 40, EB32, 33, 43, 60, 69, 123, 162, EC12, 50, 68, 70, 86, 88, 98, EE47, FE73, G163-79 and note, 1464-75.

The Shadowy Waters II

506. ANON.: "The Abbey Theatre: Production of New Plays," *Daily Express,* 10 Dec 1906, 6.

507. ANON.: "Irish National Theatre Society: Plays at the Molesworth Hall," *FrJ,* 15 Jan 1904, 6.

508. ANON.: Two photographs of, and some comments on, a performance of the play, *ILN,* 24 Aug 1929, 336.

509. ANON.: "*The Shadowy Waters:* Theosophists and Mr. Yeats's Play," *Inis Fáil,* 11 (Aug 1905), 3.

510. ANON.: "Irish National Theatre," *IrT,* 15 Jan 1904, 8.

511. ANON.: "Abbey Theatre," *IrT,* 10 Dec 1906, 8.

512. "Chanel" [i.e., CLERY, ARTHUR EDWARD]: "Plays That Are Not Plays," *Leader,* 30 Jan 1904, 379-81.

See also EE82, 388, EF77.

Time and the Witch Vivien

513. CLARK, DAVID R., and ROSALIND E. CLARK: "Sailing from Avalon: Yeats's First Play, *Vivien and Time,*" *Yeats,* 5 (1987), 1-86.
Yeats's first poetic work, a MS. version of this play. The Clarks print the text and discuss the play's place in Yeats's poetical development as well as his use of the Arthurian tradition and of pictorial sources.

514. YEATS, W. B.: "Le temps et la sorcière Vivien." Translated by Alain de Gourcuff, *Alphée,* 10 (1983), 5-10.
French translation plus translator's note on p. 11.

See also BA3, CC46, EA4, 18.

The Unicorn from the Stars I

515. BRYAN, ROBERT A., and others (eds): *. . . All These to Teach: Essays in Honor of C. A. Robertson.* Gainesville: U of Florida Press, 1965. x, 248 pp.
George M. Harper: "The Reconciliation of Paganism & Christianity in Yeats' *Unicorn from the Stars,*" 224-36.

516. HERING, GERHARD FRIEDRICH: *Der Ruf zur Leidenschaft: Improvisationen über das Theater.* Köln: Kiepenheuer & Witsch, 1959. 358 pp.
"William Butler Yeats: *Das Einhorn von den Sternen,*" 165-71.

517. KENTER, HEINZ DIETRICH: "Irland und sein Dichter W. B. Yeats," *Landestheater Württemberg-Hohenzollern, Programm,* series 7 (1959/60), 50-53.

518. MERCIER, VIVIAN: "Douglas Hyde's 'Share' in *The Unicorn from the Stars,*" *MD,* 7:4 (Feb 1965), 463-65.
Besides being responsible for some material in *Where There Is Nothing,* Hyde may or may not have had a hand in this play.

519. NEWLIN, NICHOLAS: "The Language of Synge's Plays: The Irish Element," Ph.D. thesis, U of Pennsylvania, 1949. xii, 187 pp.
Includes a discussion of the play.

520. YEATS, W. B.: *Das Einhorn von den Sternen: Ein tragisches Spiel in drei Akten.* Deutsch von Herberth E. Herlitschka. Emsdetten: Lechte, 1956. 89 pp. (Dramen der Zeit. 14.)
Artur Müller: "Vorwort," 5-10.

See also CA12, 73, 126, CC239, 290, CD500, 508, 604, DA35(II), EA4, 18, 22, 24, 25, 26, 28, 35, 36, 37, EB43, 47, 71, 86, 119, 136, 171, EC4, EE47, 66, 536-38, FA57, FE73, G1657.

The Unicorn from the Stars II

521. ANON.: "New Play at the Abbey Theatre: *The Unicorn from the Stars*," *Daily Express*, 22 Nov 1907, 6.
Quotes Yeats's explanations of the play and compares its action to "the ravings of a maniac." Yeats should try to write "screaming farces."

522. ANON.: "*The Unicorn from the Stars* at the Chanticleer," *NSt*, 9 Dec 1939, 821.
For another review see "Chanticleer Theatre: *The Unicorn from the Stars*," *Times*, 6 Dec 1939, 6.

523. A[TKINSON ?], F. M.: "The Abbey Theatre: *The Unicorn from the Stars*," *Dublin Evening Mail*, 22 Nov 1907, 2.
"There is neither incident nor character in the play. Not a vestige of drama."

524. BAUKLOH, FRIEDHELM: "W. B. Yeats: *Das Einhorn von den Sternen*," *Echo der Zeit*, 9 Sept 1956, 15.
The performance in Köln. See also Ludwig Gatter: "Irischer Narr in Christo: Yeats-Premiere in Köln," *FAZ*, 19 Jan 1956, 8; Brigitte Jeremias: "Auch eine irische Legende: *Das Einhorn von den Sternen* von Yeats in den Kölner Kammerspielen," *Mittag*, 17 Jan 1956, unpaged; Werner Koch: "Das Jenseits ist in uns: Anmerkung zu Yeats' tragischem Spiel *Das Einhorn von den Sternen*," *Tribüne: Halbmonatsschrift der Bühnen der Stadt Köln*, 25:9 (1955/56), 80-82 (a sketch of the stage setting and a photograph of the performance are printed in 25:10, before p. 97).

525. BAYER, HANS: "Theater-Archäologie in Tübingen: Das Einhorn erwies sich als ziemlich versteinerter Fund," *Abendpost*, 13 Jan 1960, [6].
The Tübingen performance. See also Jürgen Buschkiel: "Von den Nazis einst verboten: *Das Einhorn von den Sternen* von William Butler Yeats wieder aufgeführt," *Welt*, 14 Jan 1960, 5.; -f.: "*Das Einhorn von den Sternen:* Tragisches Spiel von William Butler Yeats," *Reutlinger Generalanzeiger*, 7 Jan 1960, unpaged; gzm.: "Rauchwolken über Irland: W. B. Yeats: *Das Einhorn von den Sternen* im Landestheater," *Reutlinger Nachrichten*, 8 Jan 1960, unpaged; R. M.: "Irische Vision: Yeats' *Das Einhorn von den Sternen* in Tübingen," *Stuttgarter Zeitung*, 12 Jan 1960, 11; W. Q.: "Heimatkunst aus Irland: Yeats-Premiere in Tübingen," *Stuttgarter Nachrichten*, 30 Dec 1959, 6; tg.: "Alles vergehe, die Seele bestehe! W. B. Yeats's *Einhorn von den Sternen* im Landestheater," *Schwäbisches Tagblatt*, 28 Dec 1959, unpaged.

526. COX, J. H.: "Unicorns and Much Mysticism at the Abbey Theatre," *IrI,* 22 Nov 1907, 4.

527. EWAN: "The Unicorn and the Bard," *Sinn Féin,* 30 Nov 1907, 3.
"It won't do, Mr. Yeats!"

528. KIN.: "Gedenkfeier für W. B. Yeats im Stadttheater: *Das Einhorn von den Sternen* in der Sonntagsmatinee," *Basler Nachrichten,* 2 May 1939, 2. Beilage, [10].
A performance in Basel. See also -r-f.: "Die Verzückung, die zur Vernichtung führt," *Neue Basler Zeitung,* 2 May 1939, 7; S[iegfried] S[treicher]: "Stadttheater Basel," *Basler Volksblatt,* 2 May 1939, 1; R. Wst.: "Stadttheater: *Das Einhorn von den Sternen* von Butler Yeats," *National-Zeitung,* 2 May 1939, [5].

529. P., H. T.: "A Strange Irish Play," *BET,* 17 Apr 1913, part 2, 13.

Where There Is Nothing I

530. BEWLEY, CHARLES: "The Irish National Theatre," *Dublin R,* 152: 304 (Jan 1913), 132-44.
Reprinted in *Living Age,* 15 Feb 1913, 410-18. Criticizes the "paganism" of this play and of "The Crucifixion of the Outcast."

531. BORSA, MARIO: *The English Stage of To-day.* Translated from the original Italian and edited with a prefatory note by Selwyn Brinton. London: Lane, 1908. xi, 317 pp.
Originally °*Il teatro inglese contemporaneo.* Milano: Treves, 1906. See pp. 301-14 on this play.

532. BULFIN, WILLIAM: *Rambles in Erinn.* Dublin: Gill, 1925 [1907]. xxiii, 456 pp.
On the impression the play made on a real (?) tinker: "It's all wrong" (pp. 296-98).

533. GOLDMAN, EMMA: *The Social Significance of the Modern Drama.* Boston: Badger, 1914. 315 pp.
"The Irish Drama: William Butler Yeats," 250-60; enthusiastic praise of the anarchism preached in this play.

534. HARPER, GEORGE MILLS: "The Creator as Destroyer: Nietzschean Morality in Yeats's *Where There Is Nothing,*" *CLQ,* 15:2 (June 1979), 114-25.
"Nietzsche was the impetus and *Where There Is Nothing* the most significant vehicle for conveying the Romantic paradox that the highest and keenest creative joy can be realized only in destruction."

535. MCFATE, PATRICIA ANN, and WILLIAM E. DOHERTY: "W. B. Yeats's *Where There Is Nothing:* Theme and Symbolism," *IUR,* 2:2 (Autumn 1972), 149-61.

536. THATCHER, DAVID S.: "Yeats's *Where There Is Nothing:* A Critical Study," M.A. thesis, McMaster U, 1964. viii, 130 pp.
Compares this play with *The Unicorn from the Stars* and discusses the influence of Nietzsche.

537. ———: "Yeats's Repudiation of *Where There Is Nothing,*" *MD,*

14:2 (Sept 1971), 127-36.
He repudiated the play and preferred the biographically less interesting *The Unicorn from the Stars* for moral reasons because it might offend George Moore.

538. YEATS, W. B.: *Where There Is Nothing by W. B. Yeats. The Unicorn from the Stars by W. B. Yeats and Lady Gregory*. Edited with an introduction and notes by Katharine Worth. Washington, D.C.: Catholic U of America Press / Gerrards Cross: Smythe, 1987. ix, 166 pp. (Irish Dramatic Texts.)
Includes a long introduction and annotations to the texts. The introduction is concerned with background, composition and publication, sources (occultism, Blake, Spenser, Nietzsche, Tolstoy, Vedantism, Ibsen), analyses of the plays, production and critical reception, and the reworking of the one play into the other. See also G1656.

See also BA3, BC6, CA12, 73, 126, CC46, 49, 239, 290, CD149, 604, 841, 846, 880, 1154, EA12, 18, 22, 24, 25, 28, 37, EB162, 171, EC86, EE286, 518, FE73, G187-95 and note, 1657.

Where There Is Nothing II

539. A., L. F.: "Mr. Yeats' New Play: *Where There Is Nothing* by the Stage Society," *Daily Chronicle*, 28 June 1904, 3.
"An exhilarating afternoon with five acts of pure hallucination."

540. ANON.: "The Drama," *Academy*, 2 July 1904, 19-20.

541. ANON.: *Era*, 2 July 1904, 13.

542. ANON.: "The Court," *Stage*, 30 June 1904, 13.
A play with an "elaborate but rather futile symbolism" by "that original Irish bard" who, "as an authority on social and ethical questions, is as little to be depended on as his queer creation, Paul Ruttledge."

543. ANON.: "Court Theatre: *Where There Is Nothing*," *Times*, 28 June 1904, 11.

544. ARCHER, WILLIAM: "The Theatre," *World*, 5 July 1904, 28-29.

545. CHESTERTON, G. K.: "Nothing," *Daily News*, 2 July 1904, 6.
A good play with a detestable philosophy.

546. G[REIN], J. T.: "The Stage Society: *Where There Is Nothing*," *SunT*, 3 July 1904, 4.
". . . misty, . . . weird, and . . . indistinct."

547. S., E. F.: "The Stage from the Stalls," *Sketch*, 6 July 1904, 412.
"It is a pity that an author with such ability as Mr. Yeats, with intense interest in ideas and a noble control of language, should show so little balance and sense of proportion."

The Words upon the Window-Pane I

548. ARCHIBALD, DOUGLAS N.: "*The Words upon the Window-Pane* and Yeats's Encounter with Jonathan Swift," in O'Driscoll and Reynolds:

Yeats and the Theatre (1975, CA81), 176-214.

549. BARNET, SYLVAN, MORTON BERMAN, and WILLIAM BURTO (eds): *The Genius of the Irish Theater*. NY: New American Library, 1960. 366 pp. (Mentor Book. MT315.)
See pp. 194-97.

550. CANFIELD, CURTIS (ed): *Plays of Changing Ireland*. With introductions and notes. NY: Macmillan, 1936. xv, 481 pp.
"Note on *The Words upon the Window-Pane*," 3-7.

551. FITZGERALD, MARY: "'Out of a Medium's Mouth': The Writing of *The Words upon the Window-Pane*," *CLQ*, 17:2 (June 1981), 61-72.
Yeats is obviously indebted to *Swift and Stella* (1926), a rather bad play by Charles Edward Lawrence.

552. FLANAGAN, THOMAS: "A Discourse by Swift, a Play by Yeats," *UR*, 5:1 (Spring 1968), 9-22.
The influence of Swift's *Discourse of the Contests and Dissensions between the Nobles and the Commons in Athens and Rome*.

553. MINER, EARL ROY: "A Poem by Swift and W. B. Yeats's *The Words upon the Window-Pane*," *MLN*, 72:4 (Apr 1957), 273-75.
Swift's "Written upon Windows at Inns, in England," no. 6.

554. PETELER, PATRICIA MARJORIE: "The Social and Symbolic Drama of the English-Language Theatre, 1929-1949," Ph.D. thesis, U of Utah, 1961. iv, 356 pp. (*DAI*, 22:12 [June 1962], 4441-42)
On this play and *Purgatory*, passim.

555. ROGAL, SAMUEL J.: "Keble's Hymn and Yeats's *The Words upon the Window-Pane*," *MD*, 16:1 (June 1973), 87-89.

See also CA14, 118, 122, 169, CC38, CD963, 1267, 1270, DC143, EA4, 8, 14, 18, 22, 25, 26, 28, 29, 35, 36, 37, EB68, 141, 147, EC6, 13, 69, 84, 106, 107, EE17, 236, 362, 365, 500, FC18, 49, 95, FG44, HA15, HE31.

The Words upon the Window-Pane II

556. ANON.: "A Contrast in Moods: Two Yeats Plays in Dublin," *IrT*, 18 Nov 1930, 4.
This play and *At the Hawk's Well*.

557. ANON.: "No Bricks for Irish Players This Time," *Literary Digest*, 19 Nov 1932, 17-18.
"Only by stretching a point can it be called a play at all."

558. ANON.: "Mr. W. B. Yeats's Play," *Times*, 24 Nov 1937, 20.
A broadcast version. For another review see Grace Wyndham Goldie: "Blow, Ye Trumpets!" *List*, 1 Dec 1937, 1206.

559. ANON.: "Swift in Dublin," *Week-end R*, 29 Nov 1930, 793-94.

560. ATKINSON, BROOKS: "W. B. Yeats and J. Swift," *NYT*, 29 Oct 1932, 18.
"Since it is a mad little play altogether, it stimulates the imagination enormously. Only a poet would attempt anything so rash, and succeed so well."

561. BROWN, JOHN MASON: "The Play: William Butler Yeats Speaks after the Irish Players Perform *The Words upon the Window-Pane*," *NY Evening Post*, 29 Oct 1932, section III, 4.
"His words of explanation were sadly needed."

562. HOGAN, ROBERT: "Dublin: The Summer Season and the Theatre Festival, 1967," *Drama Survey*, 6:3 (Spring 1968), 315-23.

563. MALONE, ANDREW E.: "The Irish Theatre in 1930," *DM*, 6:2 (Apr-June 1931), 1-11.
Includes a review of a performance of this play, pp. 6-7.

564. S., D.: "*The Words upon the Window-Pane:* New Yeats Play at the Abbey," *IrI*, 18 Nov 1930, 12.

See also EB42, EE306.

EF Yeats's Theatrical Activities

1. A.: "The King of England as a Patron of Art," *Sinn Féin*, 23 Feb 1907, 3.
On Miss Horniman's subsidizing the Abbey, with some swipes at Yeats.

2. ANON.: "New Dublin Theatre: Application of Letters Patent. Wealthy English Lady's Help for Irish Drama. The Future of the National Drama," *FrJ*, 5 Aug 1904, 2.
Long report of the legal proceedings of Miss Horniman's application, including Yeats's evidence with reference to *Cathleen ni Houlihan*. See also the issue of 9 Aug, p. 2.
For another report see "Proposed Irish Literary Theatre: Application for a Patent. Interesting Evidence," *IrT*, 5 Aug 1904, 3; editorial on p. 4; see also 9 Aug 1904, 7; 10 Aug 1904, 3.

3. ANON.: "The Abbey Theatre," *IrT*, 1 Apr 1919, 4.
Praise of its work but criticism of the directors' reluctance to test the public's opinion as to what they want to see. Yeats is not "a sound judge of the Irish public's taste in drama."

4. ANON.: "De Valera as Play Censor," *MGuard Weekly*, 13 Apr 1934, 296.
The attempts of the De Valera government to prevent the Abbey company from performing *The Playboy* and *The Plough and the Stars* in the United States and Yeats's views on this interference. Reprinted in BA13, 2:224-26.

5. ANON.: "The Abbey Theatre: What Is Wrong with the Drama," *MGuard Weekly*, 19 Apr 1935, 318.
On Yeats's plans to produce more foreign plays because there are not enough Irish ones of quality.

6. BELL, SAM HANNA, NESCA ADELINE ROBB, and JOHN HEWITT (eds): *The Arts in Ulster: A Symposium*. London: Harrap, 1951. 173 pp.
David Kennedy: "The Drama in Ulster," 47-68; contains notes on Yeats and the Abbey's influence on the Ulster theater.

7. BLYTHE, ERNEST: *The Abbey Theatre*. Dublin: National Theatre Society, [1963?]. [32 pp.]
A history and a commentary.

8. BRODZKY, LEON: "The Lesson of the Irish Theatre: A Movement Full of Valuable Suggestions for the Creation of an Australian Drama," *British Australasian*, 9 Aug 1906, 20.
Says that he talked to Yeats and Synge.

9. CLARKE, BRENNA KATZ, and HAROLD FERRAR: *The Dublin Drama League 1918-1941*. Dublin: Dolmen Press, 1979. 40 pp. (Irish Theatre Series. 9.)
On the cover the dates are 1919-1941. Includes a discussion of Yeats's involvement and a list of productions, including some of his plays.

10. COLLIJN, GUSTAF: "Yeats et son théâtre," *Gil Blas*, 4 Jan 1912, 5.

11. COLUM, PADRAIC: "Early Days of the Irish Theatre," *DM*, 24:4 (Oct-Dec 1949), 11-17; 25:5 [i.e., 25:1] (Jan-Mar 1950), 18-25.

12. CONOLLY, LEONARD W. (ed): *Theatrical Touring and Founding in North America*. Westport, Ct.: Greenwood Press, 1982, xiv, 245 pp. (Contributions in Drama and Theatre Studies. 5.)
Ann Saddlemyer: "Thoughts on National Drama and the Founding of Theatres," 193-211. "I would like to suggest . . . some tentative, exploratory comparisons between Canadian and Irish theatre." On Yeats passim.

13. Lee [i.e., CORKERY, DANIEL]: "Mr. Yeats in Cork," *Leader*, 30 Dec 1905, 313-14.
Summarizes and criticizes a talk by Yeats on "What Is a National Theatre." See "Cork Literary and Scientific Society: Lecture by Mr. W. B. Yeats," *Cork Examiner*, 15 Dec 1905, 7.

14. CRONIN, T. B.: "Drama as a Nationalising Force," *Sinn Féin*, 24 Nov 1906, 3.
Yeats's work for the Irish drama and theater.

15. DALSIMER, ADELE M.: "Players in the Western World: The Abbey Theatre's American Tours," *Eire*, 16:4 (Winter 1981), 75-93.
Describes and documents the tours 1911-12, 1912-13, 1914, 1931-32, 1932-33, and 1934-35.

16. D'AMICO, MASOLINI: *Dieci secoli di teatro inglese 970-1980*. Milano: Mondadori, 1981. x, 462 pp.
Some notes on Yeats's theatrical activities, pp. 318-21, 346-48.

17. DRIMBA, OVIDIU: *Teatrul de la origini și pînă azi*. București: Albatros, 1973. vii, 431 pp.
"Yeats și dramaturgia irlandeză," 246-52.

18. DUKES, ASHLEY: "The British Isles," *TAM*, 23:4 (Apr 1939), 252-56.
Contains a note on Yeats and the Abbey Theatre, pp. 252-53.

19. DUNCAN, GEORGE A.: *The Abbey Theatre in Pictures*. Dublin: National Press Service of Ireland, 1962. 47 pp.

20. EDWARDS, PHILIP: *Threshold of a Nation: A Study in English and Irish Drama*. Cambridge: Cambridge UP, 1979. xiii, 264 pp.
Includes *Nationalist Theatre: Shakespeare and Yeats*. An inaugural lecture delivered 4 December 1975. Liverpool: Liverpool UP, 1976. 23 pp. Describes Yeats's theatrical activities, pp. 1-14,

191-211, and passim (see index).

Reviews:

- Rupin W. Desai, *YER*, 8:1&2 (1986), 128-30.
- Denis Donoghue, *Renaissance Q*, 34:2 (Summer 1981), 279-82.
- Michael Hattaway, *RES*, 33:130 (May 1982), 240-41.
- Declan Kiberd: "Synge, Yeats, Marx, and the European Perspective," *Literary R*, 12 (21 Mar--3 Apr 1980), 9-13.
- Edward Partridge, *YeA*, 1 (1982), 225-34.
- Katharine Worth: "Elizabethan Sunrise, Irish Sunset," *TLS*, 29 Feb 1980, 242.

21. FALLON, GABRIEL: "Drama of Lost Leaders," *IrM*, 65:773 (Nov 1937), 769-76.

Strong criticism of a dictatorial "Director Yeats."

22. ———: "Words on a National Theatre," *IrM*, 66:783 (Sept 1938), 631-38.

Yeats is not the founder of Ireland's national theater; in fact, there is no Irish national theater. "An Irish National Theatre will come in time, despite Abbey Theatre Festivals and the 'perverseness' of Mr. Yeats. But that time will be Ireland's time. And not before."

23. ———: *The Abbey and the Actor*. Dublin: National Theatre Society, 1969. 59 pp.

On the acting tradition of the Abbey. See "Yeats and the Actor," 39-46, and passim.

24. FAY, FRANK J.: *Towards a National Theatre: The Dramatic Criticism*. Edited and with an introduction by Robert Hogan. Dublin: Dolmen Press, 1970. 111 pp. (Irish Theatre Series. 1.)

Reprints, mostly from *United Irishman* between 1 July 1899 and 15 Nov 1902, i.e., the period in which the Irish National Theatre grew from idea to reality. Of particular interest: "Introduction," 7-12.

"Mr. Yeats and the Stage," 50-53 (*United Irishman*, 4 May 1901, 6); exhorts Yeats to be less polished, less oratorical, and more vigorous: "The plays which Mr. Yeats wishes to see on the stage . . . remind me of exquisitely beautiful corpses."

"*The Land of Heart's Desire*," 69-71 (27 July 1901, 3); on the success of the play in America.

"The Irish Literary Theatre," 71-73 (26 Oct 1901, 2); discusses *Diarmuid and Grania*.

"*Samhain*," 74-77 (26 Oct 1901, 2); on Yeats's periodical (Wade 227).

"The Irish Literary Theatre," 77-79 (2 Nov 1901, 2); again on *Diarmuid and Grania*.

"Mr. Yeats' Lecture on the Psaltery," 95-97 (8 Nov 1902, 3). Correspondence by X. Y. Z. (22 Nov 1902, 3); not reprinted.

25. FAY, GERARD: *The Abbey Theatre: Cradle of Genius*. Dublin: Clonmore & Reynolds, 1958. 190 pp.

A personal and selective rather than comprehensive history of the Abbey. Quotes much unpublished material, but documentation is virtually nonexistent. On Yeats, passim.

26. FAY, W. G.: "Yeats and the Irish Drama: Part of a Broadcast," *List*, 2 Mar 1939, 484.

More on the Irish drama than on Yeats.

27. FEENEY, WILLIAM J.: *Drama in Hardwicke Street: A History of the Irish Theatre Company*. Rutherford, N.J.: Fairleigh Dickinson UP, 1984. 319 pp.

Frequent references to Yeats's theatrical activities, especially on pp. 21-34 and 293-95; also on the Martyn-Yeats relationship (see index).

28. FITZGERALD, WILLIAM GEORGE (ed): *The Voice of Ireland (Glór na h-Éireann): A Survey of the Race and Nation from All Angles by the Foremost Leaders at Home and Abroad*. [Revised edition]. Dublin: Virtue, [1924] [1923]. xx, 612 pp.

T. C. Murray: "Church and Stage in the New Day: A Defence and a Plea for Co-operation," 278-81: "These writers [among them Yeats] are what they are not because of their Protestantism, but in spite of it. In studying the work of W. B. Yeats, whether in verse or in prose drama, the most casual student will observe that he reaches his highest moments only when his mind is absorbed in Catholic ways of thought."

See also William J. Flynn: "The Irish Literary Theatre," 466-70.

29. FITZ-SIMON, CHRISTOPHER: *Irish Theatre*. Dublin: Eason, 1979 [24 pp.]. (Irish Heritage Series. 26.)

Illustrated pamphlet, includes some notes on Yeats.

30. ———: *The Irish Theatre*. London: Thames & Hudson, 1983. 208 pp.

See especially "An Ancient Idealism," 133-49.

31. FLANNERY, JAMES W.: "High Ideals and the Reality of the Marketplace: A Financial Record of the Early Abbey Theatre," *Studies*, 71:283 (Autumn 1982), 246-69.

32. FLINN, PATRICIA ELLEN: "The People behind the Early Irish National Theatre: A Study of Their Personalities, Ideas and Politics and How They Affected the Growth and Development of the Abbey Theatre," Ph.D. thesis, New York U, 1978, ix, 215 pp.

The title appears somewhat differently in *DAI*, 39:6 (Dec 1978), 3229A. Contains chapters on the Irish Literary Theatre, Yeats and the Fays, Yeats and Miss Horniman, Yeats as a director together with Lady Gregory and Synge, the *Playboy* controversy, and the break-up of the original concept after the death of Synge.

33. Hueffer, Ford Madox [later FORD, FORD MADOX]: "The Irish Theatre," *Daily News*, 20 June 1910, 10.

Letter to the editor supporting Lady Gregory and Yeats's appeal on behalf of the Irish National Theatre.

34. FUJIWARA, HIROSHI: [In Japanese] "W. B. Yeats and the Irish Dramatic Movement," *SELit*, 26:2 (Nov 1949), 239-60.

English summary, pp. 359-60.

35. FULLER, EUNICE: "The Abbey Theatre: Lady Gregory on Its Ways and Methods," *BET*, 7 Oct 1911, last edition, part 3, 4.

Interview with Lady Gregory with frequent references to Yeats.

36. GHEORGHIU, MIHNEA: *Modalitatea conformistă a dramei: Orientări în teatrul contemporană. John Millington Synge, Sean O'Casey, Eugene O'Neill, Jean Anouilh, Thornton Wilder, Federico Garcia Lorca.*

București: Cartea Românească, 1948. 161 pp.
"Currentul irlandez: John Millington Synge, Sean O'Casey, Eugene O'Neill," 45-89; refers to Yeats passim.

37. GILL, MICHAEL J.: "Neo-Paganism and the Stage," *New Ireland R*, 27:3 (May 1907), 179-87.
Anti-Synge, anti-Yeats.

38. GONNE MACBRIDE, MAUD: "A National Theatre," *United Irishman*, 24 Oct 1903, 2-3.
See correspondence by J. B. Yeats and editor's comment, 31 Oct 1903, 7. About Synge's *In the Shadow of the Glen;* refers to WBY passim.

39. GREGORY, LADY ISABELLA AUGUSTA: *Our Irish Theatre: A Chapter of Autobiography*. With a foreword by Roger McHugh. Gerrards Cross: Smythe, 1972. 279 pp. (Illustrated) (Coole Edition of the Works of Lady Gregory. 4.)
The first edition was published in 1913; there is also an edition with an introduction by Daniel J. Murphy, NY: Capricorn Books, 1965. xxi, 319 pp. (Capricorn Books. CAP114.)

A personal rather than an objective history. Includes letters to Yeats, Lionel Johnson's prologue to *The Countess Cathleen* (see HD83), and notes on Yeats's plays; also two chapters on the *Playboy* riots in Ireland and America, one chapter on the controversy over Shaw's *The Shewing-Up of Blanco Posnet*, a list of "Plays Produced by the Abbey Theatre Co.," and several appendices; of which the following are relevant to this bibliography:

"The Irish Theatre and the Irish People," reprinted from *YR*, 1:2 (Jan 1912), 188-91.

"The Coming of the Irish Players," reprinted from *Collier's*, 21 Oct 1911, 15, 24.

Interviews with Lady Gregory on the Abbey's American tours, reprinted from various newspapers.

"Last Year," reprinted from *Beltaine*, 2 (Feb 1900), 25-28; a sampling of press reactions to performances of *The Countess Cathleen*.

F. Hugh O'Donnell's *Souls for Gold* (see EE120).

See also CE394.

Reviews of the 1913 and 1972 editions:
- Anon.: "The Modern Irish Theater," *Independent*, 20 Apr 1914, 140.
- Anon.: "Mr. Yeats's Theatre," *Nation* [London], 7 Feb 1914, 799-800.
- Anon.: "The Irish Theatre," *NSt*, 14 Feb 1914, 601.
- Anon.: "Lady Gregory's Irish Theatre," *Outlook* [London], 28 Mar 1914, 425.
- Anon.: "In the Abbey," *TLS*, 30 Mar 1973, 354; comments on *The Countess Cathleen*.
- Padraic Colum: "Irish Plays and Irish Poets," *New Witness*, 19 Mar 1914, 632-33.
- [A. P. Graves], *Athenaeum*, 28 Feb 1914, 324.
- Hildegarde Hawthorne: "Lady Gregory: Her Account of the Irish Theatre Movement," *NYTBR*, 28 Dec 1913, 765.
- W. P. R[yan]: "The Irish Theatre," *BmL*, 45:269 (Feb 1914), 269-70.
- [John Ranken Towse], *Nation*, 5 Feb 1914, 140-41.
- James W. Tupper: "Synge and the Irish Theatre," *Dial*, 56:665 (1 Mar 1914), 177-79.

- Sir Frederick Wedmore: *Certain Comments*. London: Selwyn & Blount, 1925. 95 pp. (pp. 61-65; reprinted from an unidentified periodical).

40. [GRIFFITH, ARTHUR]: "The Origin of the Abbey Theatre," *Sinn Féin*, 14 Feb 1914, 1.
Yeats did not build the National Theatre; he ruined it. Says that he suggested the end to *Cathleen ni Houlihan*.

41. GVOZDEV, A.: "Irlandskiĭ teatr," *Iskusstvo i zhizn*, 6 (June 1940), 10-13.

42. HARTNOLL, PHYLLIS (ed): *The Oxford Companion to the Theatre*. Fourth edition. Oxford: Oxford UP, 1983 [1951]. x, 934 pp.
"Abbey Theatre," 1-2; "Ireland," 418-29; "Yeats," 907. The third edition (1967. xv, 1088 pp.) contains a Yeats entry by Una Ellis-Fermor (pp. 1021-22).

43. HICKEY, DES, and GUS SMITH: *A Paler Shade of Green*. London: Frewin, 1972. 253 pp.
American edition: °*Flight from the Celtic Twilight*. Indianapolis: Bobbs-Merrill, 1973. Interviews with Irish dramatists and actors. Yeats and the Abbey are mentioned passim.

44. HILDY, FRANKLIN JOSEPH: "Reviving Shakespeare's Stagecraft: Nugent Monck and the Maddermarket Theatre, Norwich, England," °Ph. D. thesis, Northwestern U, 1980. 517 pp. (*DAI*, 41:9 [Mar 1981], 3781A-82A)
The abstract refers to Yeats who invited Monck to work at the Abbey Theatre.

45. HOGAN, ROBERT (ed): *Seven Irish Plays 1946-1964*. Minneapolis: U of Minnesota Press, 1967. v, 472 pp.
"Pull Back the Green Curtains," 3-27; "No, the Irish dramatic renaissance is definitely not with Yeats in his grave. Indeed, perhaps it was never with Yeats at all."

46. ———, and JAMES KILROY: *The Modern Irish Drama: A Documentary History*. Dublin: Dolmen Press, 1975--. 6 vols.
Vol. 4 written by Hogan, Richard Burnham and Daniel P. Poteet; vol. 5 written by Hogan and Burnham.
1.: *The Irish Literary Theatre 1899-1901*. 1975. 164 pp. (Irish Theatre Series. 6.). Includes discussions of *The Countess Cathleen* and *Diarmuid and Grania* (production and first performances with extensive quotations from newspaper reviews).
2.: *Laying the Foundations 1902-1904*. 1976. 164 pp. (Irish Theatre Series. 7.). On Yeats passim, including letters to and from him.
3.: *The Abbey Theatre: The Years of Synge 1905-1909*. 1978. 385 pp. (Irish Theatre Series. 8.). On Yeats passim, including letters to and from him.
4.: *The Rise of the Realists 1910-1915*. 1979. 532 pp. (Irish Theatre Series. 10.). On Yeats passim, including letters and statements, also letters to Yeats from various persons, including two from G. B. Shaw.
5.: *The Art of the Amateur 1916-1920*. 1984. 368 pp. (Irish Theatre Series. 12.). Numerous references to Yeats, including lengthy quotations from unpublished letters.
6.: Not yet published.

47. HUNT, HUGH: *The Theatre and Nationalism in Ireland.* Swansea: University College of Swansea, 1974. 21 pp. (W. D. Thomas Memorial Lecture. 1974.)

Includes notes on Yeats's involvement.

48. ———: *The Abbey: Ireland's National Theatre 1904-1978.* Dublin: Gill & Macmillan, 1979. xiii, 306 pp.

An erratum slip states that the correct title should include the years *1904-1979.* A semi-official history, written at the request of the directors of the National Theatre Society. See index for the many references to Yeats.

49. HUNTER, CHARLES: "A Tale of Two Theatres," *IrT,* 28 Mar 1987, Weekend, 1-2.

The Abbey and the Gate, with some references to Yeats.

50. IRISH TIMES: "The New Abbey Theatre: A Supplement to the *Irish Times,*" *IrT,* 18 July 1966, i-iv.

51. JOY, MAURICE: "The Irish Literary Revival: Some Limitations and Possibilities," *New Ireland R,* 23:5 (July 1905), 257-66.

"I do not understand what conception of honesty justifies Mr. Yeats in assuming the greatest Irish name it could bear [Irish National Theatre] for a theatre which is, at present, obnoxious to all but a handful of the Irish people."

52. KAVANAGH, PETER: *The Story of the Abbey Theatre: From Its Origins in 1899 to the Present.* NY: Devin-Adair, 1950. xi, 243 pp.

Reprinted: Orono, Maine: National Poetry Foundation, 1984. Concentrates on the share Yeats had in the creation of the theater. Emphasizes the many quarrels between the directors, the actors, and the audience, and claims that Yeats and Lady Gregory's role was dictatorial and that Yeats annoyed everybody until the theater was solely his. The book is rather superficial at times, lacks adequate documentation at various places, and contains several errors.

Reviews:

- Eric Bentley: "Irish Theatre: Splendeurs et Misères," *Poetry,* 79:4 (Jan 1952), 216-32; reprinted as "Heroic Wantonness" in EB10.
- Walter Prichard Eaton: "Drama Born of Tensions," *NYHTB,* 12 Nov 1950, 32.
- Gabriel Fallon: "Dr. Kavanagh's 'Abbey Theatre,'" *IrM,* 79:935 (May 1950), 208-12, 240.
- Thomas Hogan: "The Abbey," *IrT,* 7 Apr 1951, 6.
- Roger McHugh, *Envoy,* 4:16 (Mar 1951), 74-77.
- Sean O'Casey: "The Tumult and the Pathos," *NYTBR,* 15 Oct 1950, 6, 30.
- E. B. P[ettet], *ETJ,* 3:4 (Dec 1951), 356-58.
- Henry Popkin, *TAM,* 34:12 (Dec 1950), 5-6, 90.
- Francis J. Thompson: "Yeats' Theatre," *Hopkins R,* 4:2 (Winter 1951), 73-75.
- Allys Dwyer Vergara, *Renascence,* 3:2 (Spring 1951), 168-70.

53. ———: *Beyond Affection: An Autobiography.* NY: Peter Kavanagh Hand Press, 1977. v, 201 pp.

Quotes a letter from Frank O'Connor discussing Yeats's Abbey policies, pp. 124-26.

54. KEELER, CHESTER WILLIAM: "The Abbey Theatre and the Brothers

Fay: An Examination and Assessment of the Influence of the Theatrical Practice of the Irish National Theatre Society and National Theatre Society, Limited, upon the Irish Dramatic Movement, 1902-1908," Ph.D. thesis, U of California, Santa Barbara, 1973. xv, 648 pp. (*DAI*, 34:9 [Mar 1979], 6163A-64A)

Quotes and discusses a wealth of unpublished material such as promptbooks, minutes, memoranda (some of them by Yeats), Holloway's notes, letters (including some to and from Yeats), etc. Quotes or lists reviews of productions. On Yeats's plays, passim, also on the relationship between the Abbey directors and the brothers Fay (with a heavy pro-Fay and anti-Yeats bias).

55. KELSALL, MALCOLM: "Makers of a Modern Theatre: Frank and William Fay," *ThR*, 3:3 (May 1978), 188-99.

Contains some notes on Yeats.

56. KELSON, JOHN HOFSTAD: "Nationalism in the Theater: The Ole Bull Theater in Norway and the Abbey Theater in Ireland: A Comparative Study," Ph.D. thesis, U of Kansas, 1963. xiii, 288 pp. (*DAI*, 24:12 [June 1964], 5387)

57. KOVALEV, I.: "Irlandskiĭ teatr: Ėkho krizisa i tragedii," *Teatr*, 11 (Nov 1972), 162-68.

"Irish theatre: Echo of crisis and tragedy."

58. KULLMAN, COLBY H., and WILLIAM C. YOUNG (eds): *Theatre Companies of the World*. Westport, Ct.: Greenwood Press, 1986. 2 vols.

Laura H. Weaver: "Abbey Theatre Company," 2:664-71.

59. LAGO, MARY M.: "Irish Poetic Drama in St. Louis," *TCL*, 23:2 (May 1977), 180-94.

T. W. Rolleston's rather difficult job of organizing an Irish cultural show and performances of Irish plays at the St. Louis World Fair, 1904. Contains notes on Yeats's non-involvement.

60. W. [i.e., LAWRENCE, W. J.]: "Abbey Theatre: Serious Rupture. Resignation of the Brothers Fay. The Policy of Present Management," *Dublin Evening Mail*, 13 Jan 1908, 3.

This is continued in subsequent issues by anonymous articles and letters from "W." and Yeats as well as from others. The Yeats letters are reprinted in *Uncollected Prose*, 2:357-61.

61. LEVENTHAL, A. J.: "Yeats and the Abbey Theatre," *IrT*, 10 June 1965, vii.

62. LUKE, PETER (ed): *Enter Certain Players: Edwards-MacLiammóir and the Gate 1928-1978*. Dublin: Dolmen Press, 1978. 104 pp.

Reminiscences and appreciations by playwrights, critics and actors, with some references to Yeats.

63. L[YND], R[OBERT] W[ILSON]: "The Inspiration of Dublin," *Today*, 4 Jan 1905, 275-76.

Mostly on the Abbey and Yeats's work for it.

64. MAC ANNA, TOMAS: "The Abbey: The First 75 Years," *IrT*, 19 Jan 1980, 11.

65. ———: "The Abbey's First Night," *IrT*, 25-27 Dec 1984, 10.

"Secondhand reminiscences" of the opening of the theater on 27 Dec 1904.

66. MCCANN, SEAN (ed): *The Story of the Abbey Theatre*. London: New English Library, 1967. 157 pp. (Four Square Books. 1774.)

Contents: Sean McCann, "The Beginnings," 7-17.

Anthony Butler: "The Guardians," 18-52; curious, gossipy, and sometimes revolting, up-valuing Moore, Martyn, AE, Lady Gregory, and the Fays, and debunking Yeats, whom Butler prefers to call "Wobbly Wily Willie the Wonder Wire Walker." Although Butler may be right in insisting that Yeats's adulators have glossed over the less admirable aspects of his character and actions, many of his own statements are plainly wrong, malicious, or lacking documentary proof.

Sean McCann: "The Theatre Itself," 53-68; on the old Abbey buildings, its anecdotes, and its ghosts.

Catherine Rynne: "The Playwrights," 69-100; a chronicle, 1904-66.

Gabriel Fallon: "The Abbey Theatre Acting Tradition," 101-25. Contains a section on "Yeats and the Actor."

Donal Dorcey: "The Big Occasions," 126-57; the performances of controversial plays and the reactions of press and public. Particularly on the rows about *The Countess Cathleen, The Shadow of the Glen, The Playboy of the Western World, The Shewing-Up of Blanco Posnet, The Plough and the Stars,* and *The Silver Tassie*.

67. MACDONAGH, DONAGH: "The Death-Watch Beetle," *Drama,* 12 (Feb 1949), 4-7.

"The Abbey was Yeats. When he lived it lived, too, and when he died it died with him."

68. MACLIAMMÓIR, MICHEÁL: *Theatre in Ireland*. Dublin: At the Three Candles for the Cultural Relations Committee of Ireland, 1964 [1950]. 83 pp. (Irish Life and Culture. 1.)

69. MACNAMARA, BRINSLEY: *Abbey Plays 1899-1948: Including the Productions of the Irish Literary Theatre. With a Commentary and an Index of Playwrights*. Dublin: At the Sign of the Three Candles, [1949]. 84 pp.

69a. MIKHAIL, EDWARD HALIM (ed): *The Abbey Theatre: Interviews and Recollections*. London: Macmillan, 1988. xxx, 251 pp.

Reprinted pieces (not analyzed in this bibliography), with numerous references to Yeats (see index).

70. M[ITCHELL], S[USAN] L.: "Dramatic Rivalry," *Sinn Féin,* 8 May 1909, 1.

Berates Yeats for letting go Maire Nic Shiubhlaigh.

71. MOORE, GEORGE: "George Moore on the Irish Theatre: The Intimate and Reminiscent Impressions of the Noted Writer," *BET,* 23 Sept 1911, part 3, 8.

72. MORLEY, SHERIDAN (ed): *Theatre 72: Plays, Players, Playwrights, Theatres, Opera, Ballet*. London: Hutchinson, 1972. 288 pp.

Michael MacLiammoir: "Dramatic Accidents," 37-49. "The Irish Theatre in the twentieth century, viewed by its most distinguished actor-manager," includes notes on Yeats.

73. MURRAY, CHRISTOPHER: "Early Shakespearean Productions by the Abbey Theatre," *TN,* 33:2 (1979), 66-79.

Comments on Yeats's theater policy and his views on Shakespeare.

74. MURRAY, T. C.: "Whither the National Theatre?" *Guth na nGaedheal,* 1936, 28-29.
Criticizes Yeats for following international rather than national ideals in the Abbey Theatre.

75. NATIONAL GALLERY OF IRELAND: *The Abbey Theatre 1904/1979.* Dublin: National Gallery of Ireland, 1980. 48 pp.
Catalog of an exhibition, 27 Dec 1979--11 Feb 1980. Introduction by James White.

76. NESBITT, CATHLEEN: *A Little Love and Good Company.* London: Faber & Faber, 1975. 263 pp.
"The Irish Players, 1910-1911," 51-56.

77. NIC SHIUBHLAIGH, MAIRE: *The Splendid Years: Recollections as Told to Edward Kenny.* With appendices and lists of Irish theatre plays, 1899-1916. Foreword by Padraic Colum. Dublin: Duffy, 1955. xix, 207 pp.
On the early years of the Abbey, which the author left in 1905, and the Theatre of Ireland, which she joined in 1906. She returned to the Abbey for a brief spell and for the American tour of 1911/12 (described in some detail). On Yeats see pp. 14-16, 19-20, 33-34, 49-50, 52-53, and 59-60; discusses first performances of *Cathleen ni Houlihan, The Hour-Glass, The King's Threshold, The Shadowy Waters,* and *On Baile's Strand.*

78. O'BRIEN, JOSEPH VALENTINE: *"Dear Dirty Dublin": A City in Distress, 1899-1916.* Berkeley: U of California Press, 1982. xiv, 338 pp.
Notes on Yeats and the Abbey Theatre, pp. 50-53, 56.

79. O HAODHA, MÍCHEÁL: *The Abbey--Then and Now.* Dublin: Abbey Theatre, 1969. 98 pp.
A short illustrated history of the theater.

80. ————: *Pictures at the Abbey: The Collections of the Irish National Theatre with a "Conversation Piece" by Lennox Robinson and Sixty-Four Illustrations, Twenty-Eight in Colour.* Mountrath, Portlaoise: Dolmen Press in association with The Irish National Theatre Society Limited, 1983. 64 pp.
Includes Robinson's *Pictures in a Theatre* (EF86).

81. O'MAHONY, T. P.: "Theatre in Ireland," *Eire,* 4:2 (Summer 1969), 93-100.
The Abbey is now recovering from the stifling Yeats influence.

82. O'NEILL, GEORGE: "Irish Drama and Irish Views," *American Catholic QR,* 37:146 (Apr 1912), 322-32.
Reprinted as "Abbey Theatre Libels," *Irish Catholic,* 31 Aug 1912, 6; 7 Sept 1912, 6. Attacks Yeats, passim.

83. PAUL-DUBOIS, LOUIS: "Le théâtre irlandais," *Revue des deux mondes,* period 8 / year 105 / 27:3 (1 June 1935), 631-57.

84. PHILLIPS, GARY JAMES: "The Dublin Drama League: 1918-1942," Ph.D. thesis, Southern Illinois U at Carbondale, 1980. iv, 266 pp. plus photocopies of programs etc. (*DAI,* 41:2 [Aug 1980], 682A)
Yeats is referred to passim.

85. RAFROIDI, PATRICK: "Tragédie rurale et tragédie urbaine au Théâtre de l'Abbaye," *Traveaux et mémoires,* [1] (Sept 1974), 97-108.

86. ROBINSON, LENNOX: *Ireland's Abbey Theatre: A History, 1899-1951*. Port Washington: Kennikat Press, 1968 [1951]. xiv, 224 pp.

Includes *Pictures in a Theatre: A Conversation Piece*. Dublin: Abbey Theatre, [1947]. 24 pp.; conversations on the paintings hanging in the Abbey Theatre, compiled from a series of articles published in the *Leader*, also in EF80.

According to the author, the book is neither an "appreciation" nor a "criticism," but a "history," i.e., a compilation of the bare facts. Reminiscences of Yeats and comments on his plays, passim (see index).

Reviews:
- William Becker: "Shades of the Abbey," *NewRep*, 21 July 1952, 22.
- John Bryson: "The Abbey," *NSt*, 15 Mar 1952, 316.
- Joseph Carroll: "The Abbey Theatre: A Riotous History Tamely Told," *TAM*, 36:10 (Oct 1952), 6-7.
- Austin Clarke: "The Truth about the Abbey Theatre," *John o' London's Weekly*, 25 Jan 1952, 75.
- René Fréchet, *EA*, 6:1 (Feb 1953), 78-79.
- K[enneth] H[opkins], *Spect*, 8 Feb 1952, 188.
- Desmond MacCarthy: "At the Abbey," *SunT*, 30 Dec 1951, 3.
- Roger MacHugh: "Yeats, Synge and the Abbey Theatre," *Studies*, 41:163-64 (Sept-Dec 1952), 333-40.
- Edith Shackleton: "The Abbey Theatre," *Britain To-day*, 192 (Apr 1952), 42-43.
- T[erence] S[mith], *IrW*, 18 (Mar 1952), 53-54.

87. ROWELL, GEORGE, and ANTHONY JACKSON: *The Repertory Movement: A History of Regional Theatre in Britain*. Cambridge: Cambridge UP, 1984. ix, 230 pp.

"The Abbey Theatre, Dublin," 31-34, and passim (see index).

88. S.: "Mr. Yeats and the British Association," *Sinn Féin*, 19 Sept 1908, unpaged.

Criticizes what he sees as Yeats's attempts to monopolize the Abbey Theatre. Correspondence by P. S. O hEigeartaigh, 26 Sept 1908, 1.

89. SADDLEMYER, ANN: "'Worn Out with Dreams': Dublin's Abbey Theatre," in Skelton and Saddlemyer: *The World of W. B. Yeats* (1967, CA102), 74-102.

90. SCHUCHARD, RONALD: "W. B. Yeats and the London Theatre Societies, 1901-1904," *RES*, 29:116 (Nov 1978), 415-46.

On Yeats's dramatic activities in London and his involvement with the Literary Theatre Club, the Stage Society, and the Masquer's Society, also his dealings with Florence Farr, T. Sturge Moore, Laurence Binyon, Charles Ricketts, Pamela Colman Smith, Arnold Dolmetsch, Gordon Craig, Gilbert Murray, Arthur Symons, Edith Craig, and others. Draws on unpublished material.

91. SIDNELL, MICHAEL J.: *Dances of Death: The Group Theatre of London in the Thirties*. London: Faber & Faber, 1984. 368 pp.

See pp. 114-16 and 266-69 on Yeats's involvement with the Group Theatre and the Poets' Theatre.

92. SOCIÉTÉ DES ANGLICISTES DE L'ENSEIGNEMENT SUPÉRIEUR: *Tradition et innovation: Littérature et paralittérature*. Actes du Congrès de Nancy (1972). Paris: Didier, 1975. 470 pp. (Congrès de la S.A.E.S. 12.)

Gérard Leblanc: "L'Abbey Theatre: Une difficile naissance," 291-305.

93. STARKIE, WALTER: "Den irländska nationalteatern." Translated from the author's MS. by A. L. W., *Ord och bild,* 38:10 (Oct 1929), 529-48; :11 (Nov 1929), 593-608.

94. ———: "Ireland To-day," *Quarterly R,* 271:538 (Oct 1938), 343-60.

On the Abbey Theatre and Yeats, passim.

95. ———: *Shaw & Yeats: Dr. Walter Starkie Discusses the Irish Theatre*. North Hollywood: Center for Cassette Studies, 1973. 2 cassettes, nos. 33783-84, 43 and 42 minutes.

Discusses, among others, the following questions: What were the maxims that guided Yeats in founding the Abbey Theatre? Why did Yeats view Shaw's works with both hatred and admiration? What influence did women have on the creative life of Yeats? Why was *Cathleen ni Houlihan* significant to the Irish people?

96. SUSS, IRVING DAVID: "The Decline and Fall of Irish Drama," Ph.D. thesis, Columbia U, 1951. vi, 207 pp. (*Microfilm Abstracts,* 11:4 [1951], 841-42)

97. SYNGE, JOHN MILLINGTON, LADY ISABELLA AUGUSTA GREGORY and W. B. YEATS: *Theatre Business: The Correspondence of the First Abbey Theatre Directors: William Butler Yeats, Lady Gregory, and J. M. Synge*. Selected and edited by Ann Saddlemyer. Gerrards Cross: Smythe, 1982. 330 pp.

Incorporates *Some Letters of John M. Synge to Lady Gregory and W. B. Yeats*. Selected by Ann Saddlemyer. Dublin: Cuala Press, 1971. vii, 87 pp. Reviewed by [Austin Clarke]: "The Angel of the Abbey," *TLS,* 8 Oct 1971, 1222.

Includes 42 letters etc. from Yeats to Synge, 54 from Lady Gregory to Synge, 75 from Synge to Lady Gregory, 23 from Synge to Yeats, and one from Lady Gregory to Yeats on Synge's death, plus associated material, and a chronology of events, pronouncements and productions. The editor (who has done a thorough job) also provides an introduction (pp. 9-18). Some of the letters are reprinted in CD1349.

Reviews:

- Richard Allen Cave, *YeA,* 3 (1985), 249-54.
- Mary FitzGerald, *Yeats,* 1 (1983), 218-21.
- James W. Flannery, *Theatre Survey,* 24:1-2 (May-Nov 1983), 141-45.
- Grattan Freyer: "The Poet and the Intriguers," *BooksI,* 69 (Dec 1982), 217, 219.
- Nicholas Grene, *Hermathena,* 133 (Winter 1982), 74-76.
- Brian John, *UTQ,* 52:4 (Summer 1983), 434-35.
- Carl Markgraf: "At the Abbey Theatre," *ELT,* 26:4 (1983), 324-26.
- Micheal O hAodha: "Plays and Controversies," *IrT,* 5 June 1982, 12.
- Andrew Parkin, *CJIS,* 10:1 (June 1984), 147-51.
- Ronald Schuchard: "Synge as Triumvir," *ILS,* 3:1 (Spring 1984), 39.
- Brian Tyson, *ESC,* 11:1 (Mar 1985), 99-102.
- Katharine Worth: "Manoeuvres of Management," *TLS,* 22 Oct 1982, 1158.

98. "TAXPAYER": "A National Theatre: Does 'The Abbey' Need Reform to Merit This Description? 'The Irish' and 'The Natives.' Plea for New Directorate and Larger State Subsidy," *Star* [Dublin], 2 Feb 1929, 2.

Yeats, described as "fitted . . . with the natural attributes of an Armenian colporteur of Persian carpets," would not qualify for the new directorate.

99. TENNYSON, CHARLES: "The Rise of the Irish Theatre," *ContempR*, 100:548 (Aug 1911), 240-47.

Yeats's "scheme" has developed away from him.

100. TISHUNINA, NATALII͡A VIKTOROVNA: *U. B. Ĭets i stanovlenie teatral'noĭ kul'tury v Irlandii*. Avtoreferat dissertat͡siĭ. Leningrad: Leningradskiĭ gosudarstvennyĭ institut teatra, muzyki i kinematografii, 1978. 25 pp.

"WBY and the creation of a theatrical culture in Ireland," a dissertation abstract.

101. TREWIN, JOHN COURTENAY: *The Theatre since 1900*. London: Dakers, 1951. 339 pp.

"The Abbey," 46-48; "Yeats and Synge," 48-52.

102. VALOIS, NINETTE DE: Talk about the Abbey Theatre and W. B. Yeats, *Trinity News,* 11:10 (13 Feb 1964), 5.

103. YEATS, W. B.: "Seven Letters of W. B. Yeats." Edited by Ronald Ayling, *Theoria,* 20 (15 June 1963), 60-70.

On Abbey affairs.

104. ———: "'Theatre Business, Management of Men': Six Letters by W. B. Yeats." Edited by Ronald Ayling, *Threshold,* 19 (Autumn 1965), 48-57.

Letters 1-3 and 5-7 from the preceding item.

105. ———: "W. B. Yeats on Plays and Players." Edited by Ronald Ayling, *MD,* 9:1 (May 1966), 1-10.

Again includes letters 5-7.

106. ———: *Dous dramas populares*. Translated by Plácido R. Castro and the brothers Vilar Ponte. Vigo: Castrelos, 1977. 70 pp. (O moucho. 53.)

"Nota dos editores," 7-8; Anton Vilar Ponte und Plácido R. Castro: "Liñas de abrente," 11-21 (on Yeats and the Irish theatre). The plays are *Cathleen ni Houlihan* and *The Land of Heart's Desire*.

See also AC8, 70, AE1, 43-46, 48-50, 70, 82, 85, BA10, BB98, 115, 116, 119, 128, 155, 174, 182, 206, 207, 251, BE26, 27, 33a, 34, 35, 38, 47, 50, 51, 59, 60, 66, 68, 124, 129, 137, BF13, 18, 19, 58, 66-68, 78, 80, 84, 86, 89, 90, 91, 94, 95, 97, 128, 133, 135, 137, 140, 142, 143, 144, 145, 149, 151, 154, 155, 162, 167, 170, 171, 178, 187, BG24, CA6, 35, 41, 43, 69, 95, 109, 112, 165, CB12, 241, 270, 337, 357, 382, 415, 501, 512, 532, CC276, 336, CD103, 340, 503, 504, 506, 519, 571, 573, 616, 741-42, 767, 800, 841, 919, 930, 1154, 1291-93, 1300, 1309, 1321, 1332, 1350, DC278, DE15, 45, EA4, 12, 15, 25, EB10, 38, 44, 101, 129, 139, 156, 170, EE346, FE109, FG19, 32, 38, HF10.

EG Less Substantial Material

1. ANON.: "Dramatic Movement in Ireland: Paper by Mr. Sheehy-Skeffington, M.A.; Speeches of Mr. T. M. Kettle, M.P., and Others," *FrJ*, 25 Mar 1907, 5.
On Yeats's plays, passim.

2. ANON.: "Mr. Yeat[s]'s Irish Plays Charmingly Acted at the Carnegie Lyceum, New York," *Gael*, 22:7 (July 1903), 237-38.

3. ANON.: "The New Irish Peasant," *Gentleman's Magazine*, 300:2103 (Mar 1906), 143-50.
Reprinted in *Living Age*, 5 May 1906, 301-5. Reminiscences of the lovable Irish peasant of old, who has disappeared from the Abbey plays but is still to be found in Yeats's plays and stories.

4. BERGHOLZ, HARRY: *Die Neugestaltung des modernen englischen Theaters, 1870-1930*. Berlin: Bergholz, 1933. xv, 314 pp.
Contains a list of productions of English repertory theaters, some of which performed plays by Yeats (see index).

5. BERTIN, MICHAEL (ed): *The Play and Its Critic: Essays for Eric Bentley*. Lanham, Md.: UP of America, 1986. xxvii, 349 pp.
Herbert Blau: "The Myth of Ritual in the Marketplace of Signs," 305-39; contains some remarks on Yeats.

6. BRENNAN, SISTER MARY JEANNETTE: "Irish Folk History Drama," Ph.D. thesis, Niagara U, 1946. xxiv, 280 pp.
"William Butler Yeats," 16-38. Negligible.

7. BROCKETT, OSCAR GROSS, and ROBERT R. FINDLAY: *Century of Innovation: A History of European and American Theatre and Drama since 1870*. Englewood Cliffs: Prentice-Hall, 1973. xv, 826 pp.
On Yeats's plays, pp. 161-65.

8. BRODZKY, LEON: "The Irish National Theatre," *Lone Hand*, 1 May 1908, 105-10.

9. BURTON, ERNEST JAMES: *A Student's Guide to British Theatre and Drama*. London: Jenkins, 1963. 191 pp.
See pp. 155-56.

10. CHESTERTON, GILBERT KEITH: *G. F. Watts*. London: Duckworth, 1906 [1904]. viii, 174 pp.
"In Mr. Yeats' plays there is only one character: the hero who rules and kills all the others, and his name is Atmosphere" (see pp. 28-29).

11. *Contemporary Theatre*. London: Arnold, 1962. 208 pp. (Stratford-upon-Avon Studies. 4.)
Kenneth Muir: "Verse and Prose," 97-115.

12. CORRIGAN, ROBERT WILLOUGHBY (ed): *The Modern Theatre*. NY: Macmillan, 1964. xxii, 1287 pp.
See pp. 877-78.

13. COULTER, CAROL: "An Irishwoman's Diary," *IrT*, 8 Sept 1986, 11.
On James W. Flannery and his interest in Yeats's plays.

14. COURTNEY, RICHARD: *Outline History of British Drama*. Totowa,

N.J.: Littlefield, Adams, 1982. ix, 336 pp.
"William Butler Yeats (1865-1939)," 196-99.

15. DELALLE, ANTE: "Moderna irska drama i tragedija: William B. Yeats," *Renesansa*, 1:8 (1921), 7.

16. DIETRICH, MARGARET: *Das moderne Drama: Strömungen, Gestalten, Motive*. Stuttgart: Kröner, 1963 [1961]. 714 pp. (Kröner Taschenausgabe. 220.)
Contains some notes on Yeats's plays (see index). Unreliable.

17. DOBRÉE, BONAMY: "Poetic Drama in England Today," *SoR*, 4:3 (Winter 1938/39), 581-99.
Dismisses Yeats's plays as not being "solidly in the theatre."

18. DOWNER, ALAN SEYMOUR: *The British Drama: A Handbook and Brief Chronicle*. NY: Appleton-Century-Crofts, 1950. xi, 397 pp.
Note on Yeats's plays, pp. 326-28.

19. ELLEHAUGE, MARTIN: "Nogle hovedtyper indenfor det moderne irske drama," *Edda*, year 16 / 29:4 (1929), 456-64.
"Some principal types of modern Irish drama."

20. *Enciclopedia dello spettacolo*. Roma: Casa Editrice le Maschere, 1954-66. 10 vols.
S[ybil] Ro[senfeld]: "Dublino," 4:1041-47; M[alcolm] Mo[rley]: "Irlanda," 6:606-12; W[illiam] A. Ar[mstrong]: "Yeats," 9:2045-48.

21. ENRIGHT, D. J.: "A Note on Irish Literature and the Irish Tradition," *Scrutiny*, 10:3 (Jan 1942), 247-55.
The problem of writing Irish literature in the English language, with some disparaging remarks on Yeats's plays.

22. EREMINA, I. K.: "Irlandskaîa dramaturgiîa konîsa XIX--nachala XX vv.," *Moskovskiĭ oblastnoĭ pedagogicheskiĭ institut imeni N. K. Krupskoĭ. Uchenye zapiski*, 152:9-10 (1964), 81-100.
Contains a short section on Yeats (pp. 83-85).

23. FECHTER, PAUL: *Das europäische Drama: Geist und Kultur im Spiegel des Theaters*. Mannheim: Bibliographisches Institut, 1956-58. 3 vols.
On Yeats's plays, 2:169-79. Many names and dates are wrong.

24. FOX, RICHARD MICHAEL: *Green Banners: The Story of the Irish Struggle*. London: Secker & Warburg, 1938. 352 pp.
"Emerging Ireland," 16-24; "Celtic Renaissance," 25-32.

25. GIROUX, ROGER: "William Butler Yeats (1865-1939)," *CRB*, 37 (1962), 69-70.

26. GRZEBIENIOWSKI, TADEUSZ: "Teatr i dramat w Irlandii jako czynniki odradzającej sie kultury narodowej" [Theater and drama in Ireland as an element of revival of its national culture], *Kultura i społeczeństwo*, 2:4 (1958), 190-200.
On Yeats's plays, passim.

27. HARTMANN, ALFONS: *Der moderne englische Einakter*. Leipzig: Noske, 1936. 181 pp. (Aus Schrifttum und Sprache der Angelsachsen. 6.)
"Der irische Einakter," 36-67; refers to Yeats's one-act plays.

28. HEISELER, HENRY VON: *Sämtliche Werke*. Heidelberg: Schneider, 1965. 799 pp.
Note on Yeats's plays and his own translations of them, pp. 211-13 (see also CD550 and EG72).

29. JANKOVIĆ, MIRA: "Engleska poetska drama dvadesetog stoljeća" [English poetic drama of the 20th century], *Umjetnost riječi*, 1:2 (1957), 143-55.

30. KINDERMANN, HEINZ: *Theatergeschichte Europas*. Salzburg: Müller, 1959-74. 10 vols.
"Die Sonderentwicklung des irischen Theaters," 9:491-514; on Yeats's plays, passim.

31. KREYMBORG, ALFRED (ed): *Poetic Drama: An Anthology of Plays in Verse from the Ancient Greek to the Modern American*. NY: Modern Age Books, 1941. viii, 855 pp.
On Yeats, pp. 33-34; on *The King's Threshold*, pp. 726-27.

32. KVAM, KELA (ed): *Europeisk avantgarde teater 1896-1930: Irland / Tyskland. Tekster, kommentarer*. Odense: Odense Universitetsforlag, 1976. 483 pp.
Contains translations of *The Only Jealousy of Emer, The Cat and the Moon,* the introduction to *Certain Noble Plays of Japan* and extracts from "A People's Theatre"; also a short biography and bibliography and a few notes, pp. 11-55.

33. LEAL, RINE (ed): *Teatro irlandès*. Selección, prólogo y notas de Rine Leal. Habana: Consejo Nacional de Cultura, 1966. 479 pp.
"A manera de homenaje," 7-24; note on Yeats, pp. 25-26. Includes a translation of *Cathleen ni Houlihan*.

34. LÉOPOLD-LACOUR, [ ]: "Le théâtre en Irlande," *Comoedia*, 10 Nov 1924, 2.
An interview with Maurice Bourgeois, mostly on Yeats and Synge. Although this is marked "à suivre," I have not been able to find any continuation.

35. LEWISOHN, LUDWIG: *The Modern Drama: An Essay in Interpretation*. NY: Viking Press, 1928 [1915]. xii, 340 pp.
On the Irish "neo-romantic drama," pp. 267-74. Yeats's "art is based upon a vision of things which is not only unreal but, if one must be frank, puerile." Does not consider any of Yeats's plays written after 1903.

36. MCBRIEN, PETER F.: *Higher English Drama: How to Know Good Drama, and to Say Why It Is Good.* A textbook of literary appreciation and an anthology from the best plays in English, including Anglo-Irish drama, for intermediate, civil service, university, and other students. Dublin: Intermediate & University College, [1931]. 269 pp.
Some of the examples are taken from Yeats.

37. MACKAY, CONSTANCE D'ARCY: *The Little Theatre in the United States*. NY: Holt, 1917. viii, 277 pp.
Lists Yeats's plays performed by American little theaters.

38. MCKENNA, DAVID: "The Word and the Flesh--A View of Theatre as Performance," *Crane Bag*, 6:1 (1982), 90-91.
Contains some deprecatory remarks on Yeats.

39. MADELIN, [ ]: "William Butler Yeats," *Oeuvre*, époque 3 / fascicle 70 / no. 2 (Feb 1924), 50-53.

40. MATLAW, MYRON: *Modern World Drama: An Encyclopedia*. London: Secker & Warburg, 1972. xxiii, 960 pp.
On Yeats see pp. 842-44. Plays cited by Matlaw in small caps are summarized in alphabetical order, passim.

41. MATTHEWS, BACHE: *A History of the Birmingham Repertory Theatre*. London: Chatto & Windus, 1924. xv, 250 pp.
Some references to Yeats (see index). The appendices give the dates of performances of Yeats plays by the Pilgrim Players and the Birmingham Repertory Theatre.

42. MELCHINGER, SIEGFRIED, and HENNING RISCHBIETER (eds): *Welttheater: Bühnen, Autoren, Inszenierungen*. Braunschweig: Westermann, 1962. 596 pp.
H. Rischbieter: "Die irischen Dramatiker," 427-32.

43. MENNLOCH, WALTER: "Dramatic Values," *Irish R*, 1:7 (Sept 1911), 325-29.
The Abbey Theatre has become a fixture; its playwrights develop mannerisms. Yeats's plays do not seem capable of further development.

44. MERRILL, JOHN, and MARTHA FLEMING: *Play-Making and Plays: The Dramatic Impulse and Its Educative Use in the Elementary and Secondary School*. NY: Macmillan, 1930. xix, 579 pp.
Contains synopses of several Yeats plays, pp. 541-42.

45. MORGAN, ARTHUR EUSTACE: *Tendencies of Modern English Drama*. London: Constable, 1924. vii, 320 pp.
"The Irish Pioneers," 139-57.

46. MOSES, MONTROSE JONAS (ed): *Representative British Dramas Victorian and Modern*. Revised edition with introductions and bibliographies. Boston: Heath, 1931 [1918]. xvi, 996 pp.
"William Butler Yeats," 901-5.

47. MROCZKOWSKI, PRZEMYSŁAW: *Dżentelmeni i poeci: Eseje z literatury angielskiej*. Kraków: Wydawnictwo literackie, 1975. 308 pp.
"Nurty wczorajszego dramatu," 254-77. "The wake of the drama of yesterday," contains a note on the early plays of Yeats, pp. 266-68.

48. [O'BRIEN, MAURICE NEILL]: *Irish Plays*. NY: National Service Bureau, Federal Theatre Project, 1938. xii, 110 pp. (Publication 47-L.)
Includes synopses of several Yeats plays.

49. Entry canceled.

50. O'CONNOR, FRANK: "The Unicorn from the Stars," *IrT*, 21 Dec 1939, 2.
Complains that the Abbey does not produce Yeats's plays or a Yeats memorial program.

51. Ó DROIGHNEÁIN, MUIRIS: *Taighde i gComhair stair litridheachta na nua-Ghaedhilge ó 1882 annas*. Baile Átha Cliath: Oifig díolta foillseacháin rialtais, 1936. 266 pp.

A history of the literature of the Gaelic literary revival; see "An 'Irish Literary Theatre,'" 94-97, and index for remarks on Yeats.

52. O'NEILL, GEORGE: "Recent Irish Drama and Its Critics," *New Ireland R,* 25:1 (Mar 1906), 29-36.
Detects a certain "mystico-pagan cant" in Yeats's plays and does not like it.

53. O'RYAN, AGNES: "The Drama of the Abbey Theatre," *Irish Educational R,* 6:3 (Dec 1912), 154-63.

54. PEYTON, ANN: "Yeats, Zen, and the Theatre of Enlightenment," *South Asian R,* 3 (July 1979), 54-59.
Somewhat vague and poorly organized.

55. R.: "William Butler Yeats," *Dramma,* 22:10 (1 Apr 1946), 46-47.

56. R., B., and E. R.: "Some Plays of W. B. Yeats," *Festival Theatre R,* 5:86 (28 Nov 1931), 1-3.

57. REST, JAIME: *El teatro inglés.* Buenos Aires: Centro Editor de América Latina, 1968. 104 pp. (Enciclopedia de teatro historia. 7.)
"El teatro irlandés," 72-82; on Yeats's plays, pp. 74-76.

58. REYNOLDS, ERNEST: *Modern English Drama: A Survey of the Theatre from 1900.* With a foreword by Allardyce Nicoll. Norman: U of Oklahoma Press, 1951 [1949]. 240 pp.
"Yeats, Synge, and the Irish School," 87-97.

59. RUBERTI, GUIDO: *Storia del teatro contemporaneo.* 2nd edition. Bologna: Cappelli, 1928 [1920-21]. 3 vols.
"B. W. Yeats [sic]," 3:895-96.

60. SALGĀDO, GĀMINI: *English Drama: A Critical Introduction.* London: Arnold, 1980. vi, 234 pp.
"The Irish Theatre: Yeats, Synge and O'Casey," 183-86. Worthless.

61. SAUL, GEORGE BRANDON: "Yeats's Dramatic Accomplishment," in Maxwell and Bushrui: *W. B. Yeats 1865-1965* (1965, CA71), 137-53.
Prejudiced (against Yeats) and useless.

62. SCHMITZ-MAYR-HARTING, ELISABETH: "The Irish National Theatre: From Edward Martyn to Sean O'Casey," Dr.phil. thesis, U of Wien, 1956 [i.e., 1961]. ii, 296 pp.
On Yeats pp. 149-203. Not very illuminating.

63. SELENIĆ, SLOBODAN: *Dramski pravci XX veka.* Beograd: Umetnička akademija u Beogradu, 1971. 241 pp.
See pp. 142-44.

64. SIMONS, LEO: *Het drama en het tooneel in hun ontwikkeling.* [Amsterdam]: Wereldbibliotheek, 1932. 699 pp. (Nederlandsche Bibliotheek. [585.])
"De vlucht uit de werkelijkheid . . . in Engeland en Ierland" [The flight from reality in England and Ireland], 551-69; on Yeats, passim.

65. STEIN, RITA, and FRIEDHELM RICKERT (eds): *Major Modern Dram-*

atists. Volume 1: American, British, Irish, German, Austrian and Swiss Dramatists. NY: Ungar, 1984. xv, 570 pp.
See pp. 315-33 for 24 short extracts from longer works of criticism.

66. *Teatral'nai͡a ént͡siklopedii͡a.* Moskva: Gosudarstvennoe nauchnoe izdatel'stvo "Sovetskai͡a ént͡siklopedii͡a," 1961-67. 6 vols.
El[ena Vi͡acheslavovna] K[ornilova]: "Irlandskiĭ literaturnyĭ teatr," 2:903; "Irlandskiĭ teatr i dramaturgii͡a," 2:903-4; "Ĭits, Eĭts," 2:1013.

67. TOBIN, MICHAEL: "The Ponderings of a Playgoer," *Iris Hibernia,* 4:3 (1960), 27-39.
Includes a note on Yeats's plays, pp. 32-35.

68. TÖREL, SEDAT: *Essays in English Literature.* Ankara: Hacettepe & Taş, 1980. xi, 180 pp.
"The Plays of Synge and Yeats as Contribution to the Irish Freedom Movement," 149-52; negligible.

69. WILD, FRIEDRICH: *Die englische Literatur der Gegenwart seit 1870: Drama und Roman.* Wiesbaden: Dioskuren-Verlag, 1928. iv, 403 pp.
"Anglo-irisches Drama," 82-106; on Yeats's plays, pp. 83-89 and passim (see index).

70. WOOD, J. BERTRAM: "The Irish Drama," *Humberside,* 6:2 (Oct 1938), 99-116.

71. YEATS, W. B.: *Tři hry. (Temné vody. Na Bailové břehu. Deirdre).* Translated by Jaroslav Skalický, preface by Eva Jurčinová. Praha: Otto, 1928. 103 pp. (Sborník světové poesie. 155.)
"Předmluva" [Preface], 5-7. See also G1375.

72. ———: *Irische Schaubühne.* Deutsch von Henry von Heiseler. [München: Schmidberger], 1933. vi, 289 pp.
The "Vorbemerkung des Herausgebers," [v-vi], quotes von Heiseler's reasons for translating the plays (see also EG28). For reviews see G1365-1368.

73. Z[ABEL], M. D.: "Poetry for the Theatre," *Poetry,* 45:3 (Dec 1934), 152-56.
Contains a few notes on Yeats's plays.

F THE PROSE

FA Prose Fiction and Prose in General

Part 1: General Studies

1. ALLEN, JAMES LOVIC, and M. M. LIBERMAN: "Transcriptions of Yeats's Unpublished Prose in the Bradford Papers at Grinnell College," *Serif,* 10:1 (Spring 1973), 13-27.

A description of Bradford's transcriptions of "what he considered to be the major items of Yeats's unpublished prose." They include (1) *The Speckled Bird,* (2) first drafts of *Autobiographies,* (3) journals, (4) works completed but never published, (5) extracts from the manuscript books, and (6) addresses. The article concentrates on the last three groups, which include items belonging to Yeats's political, occult, and literary interests.

See also Allen's "Yeats's Unpublished Prose in the Bradford Papers: Errata and Addenda," *Serif,* 11:4 (Winter 1975), 50-52.

2. AVERILL, DEBORAH M.: *The Irish Short Story from George Moore to Frank O'Connor*. Washington, D.C.: UP of America, 1982. x, 328 pp.

Yeats is referred to passim (see index).

3. BEEBE, MAURICE: *Ivory Towers and Sacred Founts: The Artist as Hero in Fiction from Goethe to Joyce*. NY: New York UP, 1964. xi, 323 pp.

Art as religion in the early stories, pp. 153-58.

4. BROWN, STEPHEN JAMES: *Ireland in Fiction: A Guide to Irish Novels, Tales, Romances, and Folk-lore*. Volume one, introduction by Desmond J. Clarke. NY: Barnes & Noble, 1969 [1915]. xxviii, 362 pp.

See pp. 312-13. First published as °*Reader's Guide to Irish Fiction* (1910). Vol. 2 (1985) is not relevant to this bibliography.

5. CALLAN, EDWARD: *Yeats on Yeats: The Last Introductions and the "Dublin" Edition*. Dublin: Dolmen Press, 1981. 112 pp. (New Yeats Papers. 20.)

An edition of Yeats's "A General Introduction for My Work," "Introduction" to *Essays and Introductions,* and "An Introduction for My Plays." The texts are "edited from the manuscripts" (not from the published versions), but the editorial principles are not clear. Includes copious annotations, an essay "Yeats on Yeats," pp. 13-36, and letters by publishers' agents related to the proposed "Dublin" edition which never materialized.

Reviews:

- Richard J. Finneran, *ILS,* 1:1 (Spring 1982), 13.
- Jacqueline Genet, *EI,* 7 (Dec 1982), 269-71.
- Janet Madden-Simpson: "Tools of the Trade," *BooksI,* 59 (Dec 1981), 237-38.
- William H. O'Donnell, *YeA,* 2 (1983), 109-11.
- Andrew Parkin, *CJIS,* 10:1 (June 1984), 147-51.

6. CROWLEY, MARY: "The Norman Tradition in Anglo-Irish Literature," *IrSt,* 4 Jan 1930, 354-56.

Especially in the prose style, including Yeats's.

7. FARROW, ANTHONY: "Yeats and the Irish Short Story," *AntigR,* 17 (Spring 1974), 35-42.

The influence of Yeats's short stories on Moore and Joyce.

8. FINNERAN, RICHARD J.: *The Prose Fiction of W. B. Yeats: The Search for "Those Simple Forms."* Dublin: Dolmen Press, 1973. 42 pp. (New Yeats Papers. 4.)

Traces "the development and basic themes of Yeats's prose fiction"; includes a bibliographical note on the texts.

Reviews:

- Dean Doner, *MFS*, 20:2 (Summer 1974), 247-51.
- Graham Hough: "Yeats and the Magic of Power," *TLS*, 14 Feb 1975, 160.
- Elizabeth Mackenzie, *N&Q*, os 221 / ns 23:7 (July 1976), 314-15.

9. FOLEY, T. P., and MAUD ELLMAN[N]: "A Yeats and George Moore Identification," *N&Q*, os 223 / ns 25:4 (Aug 1978), 326-27.

The novelist Jeremiah O'Donovan (1873-1942), mentioned in "Emmet the Apostle of Irish Liberty" (see *Uncollected Prose*, 2:325).

10. FORKNER, BEN (ed): *Modern Irish Short Stories*. Preface by Anthony Burgess. Harmondsworth: Penguin, 1980. 557 pp.

See Burgess's "Preface" (pp. 15-19) and Forkner's introduction (pp. 21-42), especially pp. 25-27. Reprints "The Twisting of the Rope."

11. FOSTER, JOHN WILSON: *Fictions of the Irish Literary Revival: A Changeling Art*. Syracuse: Syracuse UP / Dublin: Gill & Macmillan, 1987. xxi, 409 pp.

See especially "The Path of the Chameleon: The Symbolist Strategy--W. B. Yeats," 73-93; "Visions and Vanities: Yeats, Lady Gregory, and Folklore," 203-18; "The Mount of Transfiguration: The Writer as Fabulist--W. B. Yeats, James Stephens," 236-72. Analyzed in part 2 of this section.

12. GARVEY, JAMES JOSEPH: "W. B. Yeats's Prose: A Linguistic Description of 'Stylistic Competence,'" Ph.D. thesis, U of Michigan, 1972. xii, 262 pp. (*DAI*, 33:5 [Nov 1972], 2372A)

Analyzes 20 short passages from *Uncollected Prose, Autobiographies, Essays and Introductions*, and *A Vision*.

13. GOULD, WARWICK: "'Lionel Johnson Comes the First to Mind': Sources for Owen Aherne," in Harper: *Yeats and the Occult* (1975, FC40), 255-84.

14. GRANTHAM, SHELBY SMITH: "The Prose Fiction of William Butler Yeats," Ph.D. thesis, U of Virginia, 1973. iii, 349 pp. (*DAI*, 34:4 [Oct 1973], 1910A)

Discusses *John Sherman and Dhoya, The Celtic Twilight, The Secret Rose, The Speckled Bird, A Vision,* and *Stories of Michael Robartes and His Friends*.

15. HARRIS, WENDELL V.: "English Short Fiction in the 19th Century," *SSF*, 6:1 (Fall 1968), 1-93.

See pp. 41-44, 77, 79, 81-82.

16. ———: *British Short Fiction in the Nineteenth Century: A Literary and Bibliographic Guide*. Detroit: Wayne State UP, 1979. 211 pp.

See pp. 141-43 and index.

17. HIRSCH, EDWARD: "'Contention Is Better than Loneliness': The Poet as Folklorist," *Genre*, 12:4 (Winter 1979), 423-37.

On Yeats's folklore collections. See also CB172.

18. ———: "A War between the Orders: Yeats's Fiction and Transcendental Moment," *Novel,* 17:1 (Autumn 1983), 52-66.
The war between realistic narrative and visionary poetics.

19. JEFFARES, A. NORMAN: "Prose Fed by Experience," *Western Mail,* 16 Jan 1965, 5.
Mainly on the style of Yeats's prose.

20. KEARNEY, RAYMOND WILLIAM: "Yeats, the Man of Letters," Ph.D. thesis, Pennsylvania State U, 1972. iii, 113 pp. (*DAI,* 33:12 [June 1973], 6915A-16A)
Discusses *Autobiographies, Explorations, Mythologies* and *Essays and Introductions.*

21. KELLY, JOHN S.: "Yeatsian Magic and Rational Magic: An Uncollected Review of W. B. Yeats," *YeA,* 3 (1985), 182-89.
An anonymous review of G. C. Leland's *Gypsy Sorcery* in the *National Observer,* 18 Apr 1891.

22. KING, BRUCE A.: "Yeats's Irishry Prose," in Maxwell and Bushrui: *W. B. Yeats 1865-1965* (1965, CA71), 127-35.
Irish elements in Yeats's prose.

23. LESTER, JOHN A.: "Joyce, Yeats, and the Short Story," *ELT,* 15:4 (1972), 305-14.

24. °MCLEAN, WINIFRED ISABELLA ANNE: "*The Savoy* (1896): Its Genesis and History, and Its Significance as an Organ of the Celtic Revival," Ph.D. thesis, U of Hull, 1971. vii, 368 pp.
"Yeats' Role in the *Savoy,* and His Contributions apart from the Three Narratives," 143-88; "Yeats' Three *Savoy* Narratives: 'The Binding of the Hair,' 'Rosa Alchemica,' and 'The Tables of the Law,'" 189-237. Also chapters on Arthur Symons, Olivia Shakespear, Lionel Johnson, Ernest Rhys, and Fiona Macleod. (Information kindly supplied by the U of Hull Library)

25. O'DONNELL, WILLIAM HUGH: *A Guide to the Prose Fiction of W. B. Yeats.* Ann Arbor: UMI Research Press, 1983. vii, 182 pp. (Studies in Modern Literature. 12.)
Based on "The Prose Fiction of W. B. Yeats: 1887-1905," °Ph.D. thesis, Princeton U, 1971. 344 pp. (*DAI,* 33:1 [July 1972], 321A).
The standard monograph on its subject. "This study identifies the factors that led the young poet into prose fiction and then provides detailed introductions to each of his stories and novels. Two major elements are prominent in his prose fiction. Most of the stories make use of Irish folklore, and many of them reflect his continuing debate on the attractions and liabilities of the traditional quest of occult magic." Includes a discussion of the collaboration with Lady Gregory.
Reviews:
- Peter van de Kamp, *IUR,* 15:1 (Apr 1986), 108-11.
- Mary Helen Thuente, *Yeats,* 2 (1984), 305-9.

26. ———: "Yeats as Adept and Artist: *The Speckled Bird, The Secret Rose,* and *The Wind among the Reeds,*" in Harper: *Yeats and the Occult* (1975, FC40), 55-79.
Yeats's way to the higher level of Adeptship in the Golden Dawn as reflected in his narrative prose works and some poems.

27. RANKINE-GALLOWAY, H. M. F.: "Mythologies," in Genet: *William*

Butler Yeats (1981, CA32), 383-94. (In French)

28. SAUL, GEORGE BRANDON: *Rushlight Heritage: Reflections on Selected Irish Short-Story Writers of the Yeatsian Era*. Philadelphia: Walton Press, 1969. vi, 140 pp.

On Yeats's short stories see pp. 9-13; reprint of "The Short Stories of William Butler Yeats," *Poet Lore*, 57:3 (July 1962), 371-74; also in DC334.

29. SCARBOROUGH, DOROTHY: *The Supernatural in Modern English Fiction*. NY: Octagon Books, 1967 [1917]. vii, 329 pp.

Notes on the supernatural in Yeats's prose fiction and in *The Countess Cathleen* and *The Land of Heart's Desire*, passim.

30. SHERESHEVSKAI͡A, MIRRA, and L. POLI͡AKOVA (comps): *Probuzhdenie: Rasskazy irlandskikh pisateleĭ*. Leningrad: Khudozhestvennai͡a literatura, 1975. 480 pp.

"Awakening: Stories of Irish writers." See pp. 5-6 of the preface for a note on Yeats; the anthology includes "Ryzhii Khanrakhan" ("Red Hanrahan"), pp. 23-31.

31. WRIGHT, DAVID: "Not for Publication: The Correspondence of Yeats and Joyce," *CJIS*, 10:1 (June 1984), 113-26.

The differences between Yeats's and Joyce's epistolary personae.

32. YEATS, W. B.: *Opowiadania o Hanrahanie rudym. Tajemnicza róża. Rosa alchemica*. Translated by Józef Birkenmajer. Lwów: Nakładem Wydawnictwa Polskiego, 1925. xx, 222 pp. (Bibljoteka Laureatów Nobla. 41.)

"Słowo wstępne" [Foreword], ix-xx.

33. ———: *Selected Prose*. Edited with an introduction and notes by A. Norman Jeffares. London: Macmillan, 1964. 286 pp.

"Introduction," 9-18; "Notes," 263-86. The edition contains extracts from the autobiographical writings, some letters, essays, stories, and introductions.

34. ———: "W. B. Yeats's Prose Contributions to Periodicals: 1900-1939." Edited by Charles Colton Johnson. Editor's Ph.D. thesis, Northwestern U, 1968. xxi, 622 pp. (*DAI*, 29:9 [Mar 1969], 3141A)

The editor provides a skimpy introduction (pp. v-xix) and some annotations.

35. ———: *Uncollected Prose*. Collected and edited by John P. Frayne and Colton Johnson. NY: Columbia UP / London: Macmillan, 1970-75. 2 vols.

Volume 1: *First Reviews and Articles, 1886-1896*. 437 pp. Based on "The Early Critical Prose of W. B. Yeats: Forty-one Reviews." Edited with an introduction and notes by John Patrick Frayne. Editor's °Ph.D. thesis, Columbia U, 1967. 440 pp. (*DAI*, 30:10 [Apr 1970], 4449A-50A).

Frayne provides head- and footnotes as well as a useful three-part introduction: "Innisfree and Grub Street," 20-34, supplies the biographical background; "Twilight Propaganda," 35-59, discusses Yeats's relationship with the Irish writers of the 1880s and 1890s (particularly Davis, Mangan, and Ferguson), his preoccupation with Irish subject matter, and his efforts to create the Irish literary revival; "Yeats as Critic-Reviewer," 60-77, explains the principles of literary criticism underlying the early prose.

Volume 2: *Reviews, Articles and Other Miscellaneous Prose, 1897-1939*. 543 pp. "Introduction," 19-32; also head- and footnotes; appendix to volume 1, index to both volumes. For reviews see G1417-1448.

36. ———: *Mitologías: El crepúsculo celta. La rosa secreta. Leyendas de Hanrajan el Rojo. La rosa alquímica. Las tablas de la ley. La adoración de los magos. Per amica silentia lunae*. Traducción, prólogo y notas: Fernando Robles. Madrid: Ediciones Felmar, [1977]. 440 pp. (Fontana mayor. 11.)
"Prólogo," 13-21; also several notes.

37. ———: *Hanrahan Rudy i inne opowiadania*. Translated by Jadwiga Piątkowska. Kraków: Wydawnictwo Literackie, 1978. 127 pp.
Krystyna Stamirowska: "Polowie" [Afterword], 119-25. For reviews see G1537-1538.

See also AC10, CA7, 65, 69, 93, 99, CB58, 185, 430, 443, CC49, 54, 104, 105, 183, 190, 239, 324, CD42, 136, 817, 849, DC75, 252, 334, DD313, EA2, 29, FB41, FC115, 143, FE55, 115, G269-75, 318-20, 469-77, 514-16, 884-88, 1060-75 and note, 1352-54, 1373, 1417-48 and note, 1537-38, 1546-47.

Part 2: Single Works

Part 2 serves as an index of all interpretations of narrative works listed in this bibliography or taken from analyzed monographs (with the exception of FA25, which is required reading for a study of this subject). This part includes studies of *On the Boiler*. Interpretations of *Per Amica Silentia Lunae* and *A Vision* will be found in section FC, part 2.

"The Adoration of the Magi"

38. FIXLER, MICHAEL: "The Affinities between J.-K. Huysmans and the 'Rosicrucian' Stories of W. B. Yeats," *PMLA*, 74:4 (Sept 1959), 464-69.
On this story, "The Tables of the Law," and "Rosa Alchemica."

See also BG102, CA73, 126, 128, CC182, 260, CD625, 664, 684, EE490, FA11, G145-46.

"The Binding of the Hair"

39. BRENNAN, GENEVIEVE: "'The Binding of the Hair' and Yeats's Reading of Eugene O'Curry," *YeA*, 5 (1987), 214-23.
The source of the story in O'Curry's *On the Manners and Customs of the Ancient Irish* and the singing head motif.

See also CC211, 260, FA24.

"The Book of the Great Dhoul and Hanrahan the Red"

See CA63, CC260.

The Celtic Twilight

40. BENNETT, ARNOLD: *Letters*. Edited by James Hepburn. London: Oxford UP, 1966-87. 4 vols.
See letter of 7 Feb 1899 (2:119-20), in which Bennett praises *The Celtic Twilight*.

41. FINNERAN, RICHARD J.: "Yeats's Revisions of *The Celtic Twilight*," *Tulane Studies in English*, 20 (1972), 97-105.
Important revisions that have been frequently overlooked.

42. HIRSCH, EDWARD: "Coming Out into the Light: W. B. Yeats's *The Celtic Twilight* (1893, 1902)," *J of the Folklore Institute*, 18:1 (Jan-Apr 1981), 1-22.

43. KINAHAN, FRANK: "Hour of Dawn: The Unity of Yeats's *The Celtic Twilight* (1893, 1902)," *IUR*, 13:2 (Autumn 1983), 189-205.

44. MCHUGH, ROGER: "Yeats's Kind of Twilight," *TriQ*, 4 [Fall 1965], 126-29.
Discusses the stories in this collection and in *The Secret Rose*.

45. RAINE, KATHLEEN: "Ben Bulben fixe le décor," in Genet: *William Butler Yeats* (1981, CA32), 44-59.
Mainly on the Irish material in this collection.

46. YEATS, W. B.: *The Celtic Twilight*. With an introduction by Kathleen Raine, illustrated by Jean Townsend. Gerrards Cross: Smythe, 1981. 160 pp.
"Introduction," 7-29.

47. ———: *Le crépuscule celtique*. Traduction du Centre de littérature, linguistique et civilisation des pays de langue anglaise de l'Université de Caen sous la direction de Jacqueline Genet. Lille: Presses universitaires de Lille, 1982. 131 pp. (Traduit de l'irlandais. 8.)
J. Genet: "Introduction," 9-26.

48. ———: *El crepúsculo celta*. Translated by Javier Marías. Madrid: Ediciones Alfaguara, 1985. 195 pp. (Literatura Alfaguara. 162.)
"Nota sobre el texto," 13-14; "Notas," 189-91.

See also CA14, 90, CC324, 354, FA14, 17, FE25, G61-76, 180-86, 1560.

"The Cradles of Gold"

See DD770.

"The Crucifixion of the Outcast"

49. ANDREWS, C. E.: "One of W. B. Yeats's Sources," *MLN*, 28:3 (Mar 1913), 94-95.
The story is indebted to *The Vision of Mac Conglinne*.

50. BECKSON, KARL: "A Mythology of Aestheticism," *ELT*, 17:4 (1974), 233-49.

51. MARCUS, PHILLIP L.: "A Fenian Allusion in Yeats," *UR*, 4:3 (Win-

ter 1967), 282.
A quotation from John O'Leary.

See also CC260, EE530.

"The Curse of Hanrahan the Red"

See CC260.

"The Curse of the Fires and of the Shadows"

See CC260.

"The Death of Hanrahan the Red"

See CC260, FA65.

"Dhoya"

52. MARCUS, PHILLIP L.: "Possible Sources for Yeats's 'Dhoya,'" *N&Q,* os 212 / ns 14:10 (Oct 1967), 383-84.
The sources are in *Leabhar na h-Uidhri* (Book of Dun Cow).

See also CA126, FA14, 61, 62, G31-41, 1386-89, 1568-68a.

Fairy and Folk Tales of Ireland

See CA90, CC356, FA17, G1489, 1515.

Fairy and Folk Tales of the Irish Peasantry

53. KINAHAN, F[RANK]: "Armchair Folklore: Yeats and the Textual Sources of *Fairy and Folk Tales of the Irish Peasantry,*" *Proceedings of the Royal Irish Academy: Section C,* 83:10 (1983), 255-67.

54. YEATS, W. B. (ed): *Fairy and Folk Tales of Ireland.* Edited by W. B. Yeats with a foreword by Kathleen Raine. Gerrards Cross: Smythe, 1973. xix, 389 pp.
The book combines *Fairy and Folk Tales of the Irish Peasantry* (1888) and *Irish Fairy Tales* (1892). "Foreword," v-xvi, comments on Yeats's belief in fairies and psychic phenomena; reprinted in the next item and in CA90. See also G1515.

55. ——— (ed): *Fairy and Folk Tales of Ireland.* With a foreword by Kathleen Raine and a list of sources by Mary Helen Thuente. Gerrards Cross: Smythe, 1977. xxvi, 389 pp.
Also published London: Pan Books, 1979. "Foreword," v-xvi, reprinted from the preceding item; "A List of Sources," xvii-xxi.
This list appeared in a somewhat different form as "A Bibliography of W. B. Yeats's Sources for *Fairy and Folk Tales of the Irish Peasantry* and *Irish Fairy Tales,*" *Irish Booklore,* 3:1 (1977), 43-49.

See also CC247, 324, DD520, FA11, 17, G30, 1149-54.

John Sherman

56. BALK, MARY MCARDLE: "Yeats's *John Sherman:* An Early Attempt to Reconcile Opposites," *YER,* 6:1 (1979), 45-50.
Discusses the role of self and anti-self.

57. HARMON, MAURICE (ed): *Image & Illusion: Anglo-Irish Literature and Its Contexts. A Festschrift for Roger McHugh.* Portmarnock: Wolfhound Press, 1979. 174 pp.
This is largely identical with *IUR,* 9:1 (Spring 1979). See William M. Murphy: "William Butler Yeats's *John Sherman:* An Irish Poet's Declaration of Independence," 92-111. Identifies the real-life models for this novel and discusses it as a guide to Yeats's psychological development.
James Stewart: "Three That Are Watching My Time to Run," 112-18. The source of the song in *The Unicorn from the Stars,* perhaps written by Hyde and not by Yeats, is an anonymous Irish poem of the 17th century.

58. HENKE, SUZETTE A.: "Yeats's *John Sherman:* A Portal of Discovery," *CJIS,* 8:1 (June 1982), 25-35.

59. MULRYNE, J. R.: "Printer's Copy for Part of Volume Seven of the W. B. Yeats *Collected Works in Verse and Prose* (1908)," *SB,* 30 (1977), 235-40.
Yeats's revisions of *John Sherman.*

60. OSAKA, OSAMU: [In Japanese] "Yeats: *John Sherman* Reconsidered," *Studies in English Language and Literature,* 28 (1978), 73-93 (English summary, 167-72); 33 (Jan 1983), 41-63 (English summary, 124-25).

61. YEATS, W. B.: *John Sherman & Dhoya.* Edited with an introduction, collation of the texts, and notes by Richard J. Finneran. Detroit: Wayne State UP, 1969. 137 pp.
Based on "A Critical Edition of William Butler Yeats's *John Sherman and Dhoya.*" Editor's °Ph.D. thesis, U of North Carolina at Chapel Hill, 1968. 159 pp. (*DAI,* 30:1 [July 1969], 318A).
"Introduction," 9-36; a commentary on composition and publication history, the sources, and the importance of the two stories for Yeats's later work, plus a short interpretation. "Explanatory Notes," 133-37. For reviews see G1386-1389.

62. ———: *John Sherman. Dhoya.* Introduzione de Pietro de Logu; traduzione e note di Dario Calimani. Torino: Einaudi, 1982. xxx, 119 pp. (Centopagine. 70.)
"Introduzione," v-xxvi; "Nota biografica," xxvii-xxx; "Note," 103-15. For reviews see G1568-68a.

See also AE24, BA3, CA7, 69, 126, CC220, CD146, FA14, 76, G31-41, 1386-89.

"Kathleen the Daughter of Hoolihan and Hanrahan the Red"

See CC260.

"The Last Gleeman"

See CD945.

"Of Costello the Proud. . ."

See CC260, FA71.

"The Old Men of the Twilight"

See CC260.

On the Boiler

63. SCHNEIDER, JOSEPH LEONDAR: "Yeats's Unreconciled Opposites," *CLQ,* 11:3 (Sept 1975), 179-86.
Mainly in *On the Boiler* and *Purgatory*.

64. SIEGEL, SANDRA F.: "Yeats's Quarrel with Himself: The Design and Argument of *On the Boiler*," *BRH,* 81:3 (Autumn 1978), 349-68.
"The history of the composition and publication of the text reveals a design and argument of greater complexity, one that unsettles the identification of Yeats with his fictional surrogates." Includes a discussion of *Purgatory*.

See also CA14, 118, EE475, FB24, FD22, 46, 73.

"Out of the Rose"

See CC260.

"Red Hanrahan"

65. ACKERMAN, CARA: "Yeats' Revisions of the Hanrahan Stories, 1897 and 1904," *TSLL,* 17:2 (Summer 1975), 505-24.
Narrative alterations and occult meaning in this story and "The Death of Hanrahan the Red."

66. ALDERSON SMITH, PETER: "Nugent the Magician," *N&Q,* os 227 / ns 29:4 (Aug 1982), 352.
Request for the source of a story which in turn is the source of "Red Hanrahan."

See also CA63, CC141, FA30.

"The Religion of a Sailor"

See CA14.

Representative Irish Tales

See CC247, 324, FA17, G1156-60, 1542-45.

Rosa Alchemica

67. SCHULER, ROBERT M.: "W. B. Yeats: Artist or Alchemist?" *RES,* 22:85 (Feb 1971), 37-53.

On Yeats's use of the symbols and doctrines of mystical alchemy in this story and some poems.

68. YEATS, W. B.: *Rosa alchemica*. Nota introduttiva e traduzione di Renato Oliva. Torino: Einaudi, 1976. xxx, 61 pp. (Centopagine. 45.)
"Nota introduttiva," v-xxvii; "Nota bio-bibliografica," xxix-xxx.

See also CA56, 73, 126, 128, CC28, 182, 260, CD224, 809, 984, 986, 1154, DD770, EE490, FA11, 24, 38, FE73, G1359-62.

"The Rose of Shadow"

See CA14, CC260.

The Secret Rose

69. DUFOUR, MICHEL: "Le symbole de la rose dans *La rose secrète* de W. B. Yeats," *Gaëliana*, 3 (1981), 25-44.

70. GUTIN, STANLEY SAMUEL: "*The Secret Rose:* A Study in the Early Prose Fiction of William Butler Yeats," Ph.D. thesis, U of Pennsylvania, 1971. xvii, 333 pp. (*DAI*, 32:4 [Oct 1971], 2090A)

71. MCCARTHY, WILLIAM PAUL: "Part I. *The Lives of the Poets:* Johnson's Essay on Man. Part II. Stories from *The Secret Rose* by W. B. Yeats: A Critical Variorum Text. [. . .]," Ph.D. thesis, Rutgers U, 1974. iv, 196 pp. (*DAI*, 35:6 [Dec 1974], 3692A)
See pp. 71-161 (introduction on textual problems, pp. 72-98; texts, pp. 99-161). The stories are "The Wisdom of the King," "Proud Costello, MacDermot's Daughter, and the Bitter Tongue," and "Where There Is Nothing, There Is God."

72. MARTIN, THOMAS AUGUSTINE: "Versions of Form in the Irish Short Story: An Exploration of Narrative Technique and the Relation between Volume and Story in the Work of Four Irish Short Story Writers," Ph.D. thesis, University College Dublin, 1972. vi, 259 pp.
"'Apocalyptic Structure' in *The Secret Rose*," 1-59. See also Martin's "*The Secret Rose* and Yeats's Dialogue with History," *Ariel*, 3:3 (July 1972), 91-103; "Apocalyptic Structure in Yeats's *The Secret Rose*," *Studies*, 64:253 (Spring 1975), 24-34.

73. °WINNETT, STEPHEN RICHARD: "*The Secret Rose* by W. B. Yeats: A Variorum Edition Based on the 1927 Text, with Facing Commentary and Textual and Critical Introductions," M.A. thesis, Queen's U (Kingston, Ont.), 1974. xlvi, 305 pp.

74. YEATS, W. B.: *The Secret Rose: Stories by W. B. Yeats. A Variorum Edition*. Edited by Phillip L. Marcus, Warwick Gould, and Michael J. Sidnell. Ithaca: Cornell UP, 1981. xxxiv, 275 pp.
"Introduction," xiii-xxxiv; explains the history of textual transmission and editorial principles. "Census of Other Manuscript and Proof Materials," 261-63. "Bibliography," 265-71.
See also Richard J. Finneran: "An Omission in *The Secret Rose, Stories by W. B. Yeats: A Variorum Edition*," *Yeats*, 1 (1983), 154; Warwick Gould : "Two Omissions from *The Secret Rose, Stories by W. B. Yeats: A Variorum Edition*," *YeA*, 3 (1985), 198. For reviews see G1549-1562.

75. ———: *Les histoires de la rose secrète*. Traduction du Centre de littérature, linguistique et civilisation des pays de langue anglaise de l'Université de Caen sous la direction de Jacqueline Genet. Lille: Presses universitaires de Lille, 1984. 169 pp.

J. Genet: "Introduction," 9-27. There are also some explanatory footnotes in the text.

See also CA14, CB134, CC182, 324, FA14, 26, 44, FB22, G130-44, 1549-62, 1569, 1598-99.

The Speckled Bird

76. FALLON, ANN CONNERTON: "Toward the Internalization of the Myth: Three Studies of W. B. Yeats's Revisions of His Unpublished Novel *The Speckled Bird*," Ph.D. thesis, Brandeis U, 1980. vi, 216 pp. (*DAI*, 40:12 [June 1980], 6289A; reprinted *YeA*, 1 [1982], 214-15)

Discusses the father figure, the motif of the divided self including a comparison with *John Sherman*, and the symbol of the Blessed Mother in the context of the revisions of the novel.

77. O'DONNELL, WILLIAM H.: "Yeats's Fictional Fathers in *The Speckled Bird*," *Eire*, 15:2 (Summer 1980), 7-17.

The portrayal of the fathers in the four versions of the novel provides "some interesting new evidence about the complex relationship between Yeats and his father."

78. YEATS, W. B.: "*The Speckled Bird*," *Bell*, 1:6 (Mar 1941), 23-30.

An extract from the concluding chapter of Book I, plus introductory remarks and a short summary of the remainder of the novel by J. M. Hone.

79. ———: "*The Speckled Bird:* A Novel by W. B.Yeats." A section from the novel with a note by Curtis Bradford, *IrW*, 31 (Summer 1955), 9-18.

80. ———: *The Speckled Bird*. Edited by William H. O'Donnell. Dublin: Cuala Press, 1973-74. 2 vols.

Volume I: 1973. xi, 88 pp.; contains a "Preface" by the editor, pp. v-x, and Book I. Volume II: 1974. iii, 100 pp.; contains Books II-IV and some notes.

81. ———: *Literatim Transcription of the Manuscripts of William Butler Yeats's "The Speckled Bird."* Edited by William H. O'Donnell. Delmar, N.Y.: Scholars' Facsimiles & Reprints, 1976. 486 pp.

"Introduction," 5-15; on the problems of transcription. Includes conversion tables to the edited version (see next item).

82. ———: *The Speckled Bird: With Variant Versions*. Annotated and edited by William H. O'Donnell. Toronto: McClelland & Stewart, 1976. lix, 275 pp. (Yeats Studies Series.)

Lorna Reynolds and Robert O'Driscoll: "General Editors' Introduction," xv-xix. "Editor's Introduction," xxiii-lix; critical and editorial. There are also copious footnotes. For reviews see G1521-1524.

See also BA20, CD2, 146, 809, FA1, 14, 26, FB40, G1380, 1521-24.

Stories of Michael Robartes and His Friends

See CC17, FA14, FD46.

Stories of Red Hanrahan

83. FINNERAN, RICHARD J.: "'Old Lecher with a Love on Every Wind': A Study of Yeats' *Stories of Red Hanrahan*," *TSLL,* 14:2 (Summer 1972), 347-58.

The sources and revisions and the meaning of the stories.

84. HIRSCH, EDWARD: "'And I Myself Created Hanrahan': Yeats, Folklore, and Fiction," *ELH,* 48:4 (Winter 1981), 880-93.

"That the modern poet could dismantle his own subversive isolation by rooting his work in a communal poetics is an idea that informs Yeats's major work of prose fiction, *Stories of Red Hanrahan*."

85. YEATS, W. B.: "Versions of the Stories of Red Hanrahan." Edited by Michael J. Sidnell, *YeSt,* 1 (Bealtaine 1971), 119-74.

Reprints the early versions and collates their revisions in *The Secret Rose* (1897). Lists the variants of the post-1903 versions, which were written with the help of Lady Gregory. Editor's comments on pp. 119-22 and 166-68.

86. ———: "A Variorum Edition of W. B. Yeats's Stories of Red Hanrahan." Edited by Richard Louis Bonaccorso. Editor's Ph.D. thesis, U of Connecticut, 1972. iii, 219 pp. (*DAI,* 33:6 [Dec 1972], 2922A)

"Introduction," 1-41; includes a discussion of the collaboration with Lady Gregory.

87. ———: *Geschichten von Rot-Hanrahan*. Leipzig: Insel, 1978. 68 pp. (Insel Bücherei. 628.)

Karl Heinz Berger: "Nachwort," 57-67.

See also CC1, FA11, G238-40.

The Tables of the Law

88. YEATS, W. B.: "*The Tables of the Law:* A Critical Text." Edited by Robert O'Driscoll, *YeSt,* 1 (Bealtaine 1971), 87-118.

Reprints the text and the variants, prefaced by a lengthy interpretation (pp. 87-101).

See also CA126, 128, CC182, 260, CD224, 604, 637, 664, 693, EE490, FA11, 24, 38, G145-46.

"The Twisting of the Rope and Hanrahan the Red"

See CC260, FA10.

"A Very Pretty Little Story"

See CC211.

"The Vision of Hanrahan the Red"

See CC260.

"Where There Is Nothing There Is God"

See CC260, DC62, FA71.

"The Wisdom of the King"

See CC260, FA71.

FB The Autobiography

1. ADAMS, HAZARD: "Some Yeatsian Versions of Comedy," in Jeffares and Cross: *In Excited Reverie* (1965, CA48), 152-70.
Comedy in *Autobiographies* and *A Vision*.

2. ARCHIBALD, DOUGLAS: "On Editing Yeats's *Autobiographies*," *Gaéliana*, 8 (1986), 161-73.
Discusses textual problems and Yeats's relationship with Aubrey and Mabel Beardsley.

3. B[ABLER], O[TTO] F.: "Queries from W. B. Yeats's Autobiographies" *N&Q*, 171:24 (12 Dec 1936), 421-22.
Answers by W. W. G[ill], 172:8 (20 Feb 1937), 142.

4. BUCKLEY, VINCENT: "Yeats: The Great Comedian," *Malahat R*, 5 (Jan 1968), 77-89.
Humor and lack of humor in *Autobiographies*.

5. CARY, MEREDITH RAY: "Novelistic Autobiography: A Special Genre," °Ph.D. thesis, U of Washington, 1968. 184 pp. (*DAI*, 29:7 [Jan 1969], 2207A-8A)
Includes a discussion of Moore's *Hail and Farewell* and Yeats's counterattack in *Autobiographies*.

6. ———: "Yeats and Moore--An Autobiographical Conflict," *Eire*, 4:3 (Autumn 1969), 94-109.
Moore's description of Yeats in *Hail and Farewell* is more successful than Yeats's description of Moore in *Dramatis Personae*, which is, in fact, an altogether inferior book.

7. COE, RICHARD N.: *When the Grass Was Taller: Autobiography and the Experience of Childhood*. New Haven: Yale UP, 1984. xvi, 315 pp.
Note on *Reveries over Childhood and Youth*, pp. 284-85.

8. CULBERTSON, DIANA: "Twentieth Century Autobiography: Yeats, Sartre, Nabokov. Studies in Structure and Form," °Ph.D. thesis, U of North Carolina at Chapel Hill, 1971. 257 pp. (*DAI*, 32:12 [June 1972], 6968A)

9. DAVIES, JOAN MARY: "The Prose Style of W. B. Yeats' *Autobiography*," °Ph.D. thesis, U of Maryland, 1981. 170 pp. (*DAI*, 42:8 [Feb 1982], 3609A; reprinted *Yeats*, 1 [1983], 180-81, and *YeA*, 4 [1986], 304-5)

10. DONOGHUE, DENIS, and FRANK KERMODE: "Jongsen," *TLS,* 11 Feb 1972, 157.

Letter to the editor explaining that the mysterious painter Jongsen, mentioned in "The Tragic Generation," does not exist and may really be Cornelius van Ceulen Janssen.

11. FINNEY, BRIAN: *The Inner I: British Literary Autobiography of the Twentieth Century.* London: Faber & Faber, 1985. 286 pp.

"W. B. Yeats: *Reveries over Childhood and Youth,*" 150-57, and passim (see index). See also review by P. N. Furbank: "Early Lives," *LRB,* 5 June 1986, 11-12.

12. FIRTH, JOHN MIRKIL: "O'Casey and Autobiography," Ph.D. thesis, U of Virginia, 1965. v, 165 pp. (*DAI,* 26:10 [Apr 1966], 6039)

Contains some remarks on Yeats's *Autobiographies,* pp. 119-24.

13. FLEISHMAN, AVROM: *Figures of Autobiography: The Language of Self-Writing in Victorian and Modern England.* Berkeley: U of California Press, 1983. xiv, 486 pp.

"The Autobiography of William Butler Yeats: Perfection of the Life," 319-36.

14. GIANNOTTI, THOMAS JOHN: "A Language of Silence: Writing the Self in Yeats and Synge, Joyce and Beckett," Ph.D. thesis, U of California, Riverside, 1985. viii, 225 pp. (*DAI,* 46:12 [June 1986], 3725A; reprinted *Yeats,* 5 [1987], 203-4)

"Abolishing and Re-Creating Language: Synge and Yeats," 53-110; on *Memoirs* and *Autobiographies.*

15. GORLIER, CLAUDIO: "Maschera e confessione: Da Yeats a Spender," *Paragone,* 7:76 (Apr 1956), 10-24.

Compares the autobiographies of Yeats and Spender.

16. JACOBS, MARGARET ELIZABETH GUERNSEY: "Swordsman, Saint, or Prophet--'Is That, Perhaps, the Sole Theme?': Yeats's Shaping of Autobiography into Prophecy through Creation of a Personal Myth," Ph.D. thesis, Emory U, 1985. xi, 403 pp. (*DAI,* 46:6 [Dec 1985], 1634A; reprinted *Yeats,* 4 [1986], 183-84)

On Yeats's "conception of the poet's role in society and its foundation in his belief in the importance of poetry as a metaphysical force" (p. 1).

17. JOHNSTON, DILLON: "The Perpetual Self of Yeats's *Autobiographies,*" *Eire,* 9:4 (Winter 1974), 69-85.

18. JOHNSTON, WALTER D.: "The Integral Self in Post-Romantic Autobiography," °Ph.D. thesis, U of Virginia, 1969. 209 pp. (*DAI,* 31:1 [July 1970], 391A-92A)

19. KÜNNE, WULF: *Konzeption und Stil von Yeats' "Autobiographies."* Bonn: Bouvier, 1972. 247 pp. (Studien zur englischen Literatur. 9.)

Originally a Dr.phil. thesis, U of Hamburg, 1971; contains an English summary, reprinted in *EASG,* 1972, 89-92. A thorough analysis of *Autobiographies* as an example of a literary genre as well as of its language and style, including a general discussion of Yeats's prose style.

20. LEVIN, GERALD: "The Yeats of the Autobiographies: A Man of Phase 17," *TSLL,* 6:3 (Autumn 1964), 398-405.

The connections between *Autobiographies* and *A Vision.*

21. MCVEIGH, PAUL JOSEPH: "Mirror and Mask: A Study of the Major Autobiographical Prose of William Butler Yeats," Ph.D. thesis, Trinity College Dublin, 1983. vi, 445 pp. (*DAI*, 46:4 [Dec 1985], 859, item 4130C; reprinted *Yeats*, 4 [1986], 185-86)

22. MARTIN, AUGUSTINE (ed): *The Genius of Irish Prose*. Dublin: Mercier Press, 1985. 174 pp. (Thomas Davis Lectures.)

Terence Brown: "Literary Autobiography in Twentieth-Century Ireland," 89-98; on Yeats's autobiography and his presence in other writers' autobiographies.

A. Martin: "Fable and Fantasy," 110-20; contains a note on the stories in *The Secret Rose*.

Maurice Harmon: "Literary Biography in Twentieth Century Ireland," 155-64; on Hone's Yeats biography (BA8).

23. MORAN, GERARD PAUL: "W. B. Yeats's *Autobiographies* in the Context of Other Irish Autobiographical Writings," Ph.D. thesis, U of London, 1984. i, 333 pp.

A book-by-book analysis of *Autobiographies* and comparisons with the autobiographies of Sir Jonah Barrington, Carleton, John Mitchel, George Moore, Maud Gonne, James Stephens, Ernie O'Malley, Tom Barry, O'Casey, Gogarty, O'Faolain, O'Connor, and Austin Clarke.

24. NEUMAN, SHIRLEY C.: *Some One Myth: Yeats's Autobiographical Prose*. Mountrath, Portlaoise: Dolmen Press, 1982. 160 pp. (New Yeats Papers. 19.)

Discusses the individual books of *Autobiographies* as well as *A Vision* and *On the Boiler*, and "demonstrates and attempts to evaluate Yeats's exploitation of the possibilities of autobiography in the service of his conviction that biography is but the dramatic embodiment of myth." Emphasizes "Yeats's attempt to create a biographical equivalent of myth through his manipulation of the autobiographical form and through the implications of his style" (back cover).

Reviews:

- James Lovic Allen, *YER*, 8:1&2 (1986), 134-35.
- Steve Connelly, *Eire*, 18:4 (Winter 1983), 152-58.
- Julian Moynahan: "The Best Book on Yeats's Autobiographies," *ILS*, 3:1 (Spring 1984), 51.
- James Olney, *Yeats*, 2 (1984), 300-5.

25. O'BRIEN, KEVIN PATRICK: "Will and Reverie: The Personae of W. B. Yeats' Autobiography," °Ph.D. thesis, Fordham U, 1972. 202 pp. (*DAI*, 33:7 [Jan 1973], 3662A)

Includes a comparison with Moore's *Hail and Farewell*.

26. O'HARA, DANIEL THOMAS: *Tragic Knowledge: Yeats's Autobiography and Hermeneutics*. NY: Columbia UP, 1981. xii, 192 pp.

Based on "Under the Watch-Mender's Eye: The Simplifying Image of the Creator in *The Autobiography of William Butler Yeats*," °Ph.D. thesis, Temple U, 1976. 220 pp. (*DAI*, 36:12 [June 1976], 8049A). Incorporates "The Irony of Tradition in W. B. Yeats's *Autobiography:* An Essay in Dialectical Hermeneutics," *Boundary 2*, 5:3 (Spring 1977), 679-709.

An analysis on the basis of Paul Ricoeur's dialectical hermeneutics; interprets the autobiography as proceeding from ironical perception to tragic self-knowledge.

Reviews:

- Hazard Adams, *JAAC*, 40:4 (Summer 1982), 434.

- James Lovic Allen: "A Tragic Book," *ILS*, 2:2 (Oct 1983), 18.
- Ed Block, *WHR*, 37:1 (Spring 1983), 86-90.
- Richard Brown: "Confronting the Anti-Self," *TLS*, 2 Oct 1981, 1125.
- Seamus Deane, *YES*, 15 (1985), 330-31.
- George Mills Harper, *MP*, 81:4 (May 1984), 435-40.
- Lawrence Kramer, *YER*, 8:1&2 (1986), 142-44.
- Elizabeth Mackenzie, *N&Q*, os 229 / ns 31:4 (Dec 1984), 542-44.
- Wallace Martin: "William Butler Yeats," *ConL*, 23:2 (Spring 1982), 239-43.
- Shirley Neuman, *PSt*, 7:2 (Sept 1984), 196-99.
- James Olney, *YeA*, 2 (1983), 112-25.
- Robert C. Petersen: "Yeats the Autobiographer: A Dialogue of Self and Soul," *ELT*, 26:2 (1983), 143-44.

27. OLNEY, JAMES (ed): *Autobiography: Essays Theoretical and Critical*. Princeton: Princeton UP, 1980. xi, 361 pp.

Yeats is referred to or discussed passim, especially in the following: William L. Howarth: "Some Principles of Autobiography," 84-114; reprinted from *NLH*, 5:2 (Winter 1974), 363-81; see the section "Autobiography as Poetry," pp. 104-14.

J. Olney: "Some Versions of Memory / Some Versions of *Bios:* The Ontology of Autobiography," 236-67; includes "W. B. Yeats's Daimonic Memory," *SR*, 85:4 (Fall 1977), 583-603. See also FC64.

28. ———: "The Uses of Comedy and Irony in *Autobiographies* and Autobiography," *Yeats*, 2 (1984), 195-208.

29. PASCAL, ROY: *Design and Truth in Autobiography*. Cambridge, Mass.: Harvard UP, 1960. ix, 202 pp.

Passim (see index), especially pp. 136-39. In Yeats, the elements of dream and reality "are curiously combined and curiously dissociated."

30. PERLOFF, MARJORIE: "'The Tradition of Myself': The Autobiographical Mode in Yeats," *JML*, 4:3 (Feb 1975), 529-73.

Yeats's views of the autobiographer, his own autobiography, and autobiographical poems, particularly "The Tower."

31. PILLING, JOHN: *Autobiography and Imagination: Studies in Self-Scrutiny*. London: Routledge & Kegan Paul, 1981. ix, 178 pp.

"W. B. Yeats: *Reveries over Childhood and Youth*," 36-49, 150-54. See the review by James Olney, *YeA*, 2 (1983), 112-25.

32. PIRRI, JOHN JOSEPH: "William Butler Yeats and Symbolic Autobiography," Ph.D. thesis, U of Wisconsin, 1972. v, 274 pp. (*DAI*, 33:9 [Mar 1973], 5137A)

Includes comparisons with Augustine's *Confessions*, Wordsworth's *Prelude*, Carlyle's *Sartor Resartus*, J. S. Mill's *Autobiography*, and Gosse's *Father and Son*.

33. REILLY, KEVIN PATRICK: "Irish Literary Autobiography: The Goddesses Poets Dream Of," Ph.D. thesis, U of Minnesota, 1979. v, 259 pp. (*DAI*, 40:6 [Dec 1979], 3322A)

See also "Irish Literary Autobiography: The Goddesses That Poets Dream Of," *Eire*, 16:3 (Fall 1981), 57-80.

34. RONSLEY, JOSEPH: *Yeats's Autobiography: Life as Symbolic Pattern*. Cambridge, Mass.: Harvard UP, 1968. xii, 172 pp.

Based on "The Design of *The Autobiography* of W. B. Yeats,"

°Ph.D. thesis, Northwestern U, 1966. 184 pp. (*DAI*, 28:1 [July 1967], 241A). An attempt to discover "the design underlying Yeats's presentation of events, people, and ideas" (p. 1), i.e., the fusion of life and art, the establishment of Unity of Culture and Unity of Being, and the blending of personal and Irish history. Contains numerous remarks on *A Vision*.

Reviews:
- [G. S. Fraser]: "Single-Minded," *TLS*, 7 Nov 1968, 1249.
- T. R. Henn, *RES*, 20:79 (Aug 1969), 373-75.
- Richard Howard: "Masters and Friends," *Poetry*, 113:5 (Feb 1969), 338-60 (pp. 356-58).
- Brendan Kennelly: "Yeats and Blake," *Hibernia*, 29 Nov--12 Dec 1968, 14.
- Augustine Martin, *Studies*, 60:237 (Spring 1971), 98-102.
- J. R. Mulryne, *MLR*, 66:3 (July 1971), 680-81.
- Hermann Peschmann, *English*, 19:103 (Spring 1970), 28-29.
- August W. Staub, *QJS*, 55:1 (Feb 1969), 98-99.
- Alex Zwerdling, *ELN*, 7:3 (Mar 1970), 236-38.

35. *Schrijvers in eigen spiegel: Autobiografie, dagboek, brieven*. Zes belichtigen door J. M. M. Aler [etc.]. Lezingen gehouden gedurende het cursusjaar 1959/60 voor de School voor Taal- en Letterkunde to 's-Gravenhage. Den Haag: Servire, 1960. 152 pp. (Servire Luxe-pockets. 36.)

M. D. E. de Leve: "Yeats," 107-22.

36. Entry canceled.

37. SCHWENKER, GRETCHEN L.: "A Commentary on the Autobiographies of W. B. Yeats," Ph.D. thesis, U of Stirling, 1980. iii, 545 pp.

Annotations geared to the London 1955 edition (Wade 211L).

38. °SWARTZ, SHIRLEY CAROL: "The Impersonal Self in Modern Autobiography: [Gertrude] Stein, [Wyndham] Lewis, and Yeats," Ph.D. thesis, U of Alberta, 1976. vii, 365 pp.

39. THORBURN, DAVID, and GEOFFREY HARTMAN (eds): *Romanticism: Vistas, Instances, Continuities*. Ithaca: Cornell UP, 1973. 284 pp.

Yeats's autobiography is referred to in Michael G. Cooke: "Modern Black Autobiography in the Tradition," 255-80 (pp. 267-70). See also passim.

40. WEINTRAUB, STANLEY: "Autobiography and Authenticity: Memoir Writing among Some Late Victorians," *CVE*, 7 (Nov 1978), 1-20.

On some of the factual discrepancies between *Memoirs*, *Autobiographies*, and *The Speckled Bird*. Also published in *Sources for Reinterpretation: The Use of Nineteenth-Century Literary Documents. Essays in Honor of C. L. Cline*. Austin: Department of English and Humanities Research Center, U of Texas, 1975. ix, 101 pp. (pp. 1-21).

41. WRIGHT, DAVID GRAHAM: *Yeats's Myth of Self: The Autobiographical Prose*. Dublin: Gill & Macmillan / Totowa, N.J.: Barnes & Noble, 1987. xi, 127 pp.

Based on "Autobiographical Expression in Yeats and Joyce," °Ph. D. thesis, U of Toronto, 1978. (*DAI*, 40:1 [July 1979], 254A). Incorporates "Behind the Lines: Strategies of Self-Portraiture in Yeats and Joyce," *CLQ*, 16:3 (Sept 1980), 148-57; "Yeats as a Novelist," *JML*, 12:2 (July 1985), 261-76.

"I am interested in the rhetorical strategies which [Yeats]

uses in his autobiographical prose to draw us towards particular impressions of his life--even while we may imagine that he is simply and objectively narrating events which had once occurred in the real world" (p. ix). Includes a "Writing and Publication History of *Autobiographies* and Related Texts," 115-19.
Reviews:
- Brendan Duddy, *Studies,* 77:308 (Winter 1988), 487-89.
- Lucy Ingrams: "The Mask Slips," *Literary R,* 115 (Jan 1988), 51.

42. ———: "The Elusive Self: Yeats's Autobiographical Prose," *CJIS,* 4:2 (Dec 1978), 41-55.
Includes a comparison with Joyce.

43. YEATS, W. B.: *Reflections*. Transcribed and edited by Curtis Bradford from the Journals. Dublin: Cuala Press, 1970. iii, 63 pp.
"Notes," 59-63. For reviews see G1414-1416.

44. ———: *Le frémissement du voile*. Préface et traduction de Pierre Leyris. Paris: Mercure de France, 1970. 301 pp.
"Préface du traducteur," 7-13. See G1412.

45. ———: *Memoirs: Autobiography--First Draft. Journal*. Transcribed and edited by Denis Donoghue. London: Macmillan, 1972. 318 pp.
"Introduction," 9-15. For reviews see G1476-1511.

46. ———: *Dramatis Personae suivi de Aliénation et de La mort de Synge*. Translated by Pierre Leyris, preface by Robert Maguire. Paris: Mercure de France, 1974. 199 pp.
"Préface," 7-10.

46a. ———: *Autobiographien*. Translated by Susanne Schaup, edited by Wolfgang Wicht. Leipzig: Insel, 1984. 472 pp.
W. Wicht: "Nachwort," 411-28; sees the autobiographies as a unique and authentic document of a poet's personality, of the Irish struggle for political and cultural independence, and of international artistic developments. "Anmerkungen," 429-60.

47. ———: *Autobiografieen*. Translated by Sjaak Commandeur, Rien Verhoef, and Jan Eijkelboom. Amsterdam: Arbeiderspers, 1985. 544 pp. in 2 vols. (Privé-domein. 111.)
"Aantekeningen," 2:517-44, comprises a short textual note, a chronology, biographical notes on the most important persons, and an index.

48. ZABEL, MORTON DAUWEN: "The Thinking of the Body: Yeats in the Autobiographies," *SoR,* 7:3 (Winter 1941/42), 562-90.
Interpretation of *Autobiographies* along the lines of Yeats's poetic development.

See also BB33, 52, BG2, CA14, 22, 99, CB160, 440a, 540, CC25, 104, 107, 244, CD379, 395, 500, 830, DB8, 134, FA1, 12, 20, 33, FD46, G323-44, 417-27, 466-68, 483-510, 536, 550, 725-71 and note, 829-36 and note, 940-45, 1008-34 and note, 1379-80, 1412, 1414-16, 1476-1511.

FC Mystical, Occult, Religious, and Philosophical Writings and Activities

Part 1: General Studies

1. ADAMS, STEVE LAMAR: "A Critical Edition of the First Two Months of W. B. Yeats's Automatic Script," °Ph.D. thesis, Florida State U, 1982. 278 pp. (*DAI,* 45:8 [Feb 1985], 2522A; reprinted *Yeats,* 4 [1985], 179-80)

2. ALLEN, JAMES LOVIC: "Belief versus Faith in the Credo of Yeats," *JML,* 4:3 (Feb 1975), 692-716.
Provides "evidence . . . that Yeats did believe with deep conviction a number of basic propositions derived from his lifelong preoccupation with the occult." Quotes from the exchange of letters between Yeats and his "daimon" Leo Africanus.

3. ———: "Life as Art: Yeats and the Alchemical Quest," *SLitI,* 14:1 (Spring 1981), 17-42.
Yeats's interest in spiritual alchemy as related to his view of life as art.

4. ANON.: "Mr. W. B. Yeats," *Light,* 49:2538 (31 Aug 1929), 413.
Praises Yeats as a "mystic" and "psychical researcher."

5. *Approaches to the Study of Twentieth-Century Literature*. Proceedings of the Conference in the Study of Twentieth-Century Literature. First session, May 2-4, 1961. East Lansing: Michigan State U, [1962?]. vi, 169 pp.
Quotes an unidentified query whether Yeats's view of history was diachronic or synchronic. Answer by Walter J. Ong: It was a modified synchronism (pp. 97-98).

6. AYTON, WILLIAM ALEXANDER: *The Alchemist of the Golden Dawn: The Letters of the Revd W. A. Ayton to F. L. Gardner and Others 1886-1905*. Edited with an introduction by Ellic Howe. Wellingborough: Aquarian Press, 1985. 112 pp.
See index for some references to Yeats.

7. BELL, CHARLES G.: "Modern Poetry and the Pursuit of Sense," *Diogenes,* 10 (1955), 57-65.
Contains notes on Yeats's difficult position "with regard to philosophic sense."

8. BRYSON, MARY E.: "Metaphors for Freedom: Theosophy and the Irish Literary Revival," *CJIS,* 3:2 [i.e., 3:1] (July 1977), 32-40.
The influence of theosophy on Yeats and others.

9. CAMPBELL, BRUCE F.: *Ancient Wisdom Revived: A History of the Theosophical Movement*. Berkeley: U of California Press, 1980. x, 249 pp.
Note on the influence of the Theosophical Movement on the Irish literary revival and on Yeats, pp. 165-69.

10. CAVENDISH, RICHARD (ed): *Encyclopedia of the Unexplained: Magic, Occultism and Parapsychology*. London: Routledge & Kegan Paul, 1974. 304 pp.
See E[llic] H[owe]: "Golden Dawn," 99-106; C[hristopher] M[cIntosh]: "William Butler Yeats," 279.

11. CAVENDISH, RICHARD: *The Tarot*. London: Joseph, 1975. 191 pp.
See pp. 33, 37, 40, 45 for notes on Yeats's use of the Tarot.

12. ———: *A History of Magic*. London: Weidenfeld & Nicholson, 1977. v, 180 pp.
Contains a few notes on Yeats (see index).

13. CHABRIA, R. G.: "Yeats and Theosophy," *Theosophist*, 92:11 (Aug 1971), 313-25.

14. CHESTERTON, GILBERT KEITH: *Sidelights on New London and Newer York and Other Essays*. London: Sheed & Ward, 1932. 235 pp.
"Magic and Fantasy in Fiction," 228-35, refers to Yeats's "cabalistic games and cryptograms," which Chesterton does not approve of (pp. 233-34).

15. CLARK, DAVID R.: "'Metaphors for Poetry': W. B. Yeats and the Occult," in Skelton and Saddlemyer: *The World of W. B. Yeats* (1967, CA102), 38-50.
Mainly a discussion of "A General Introduction for My Work."

16. COPE, JACKSON I.: *Joyce's Cities: Archaeologies of the Soul*. Baltimore: Johns Hopkins UP, 1981. xii, 144 pp.
On Yeats cabalistic interests, pp. 74-78.

17. [CROWLEY, ALEISTER]: "The Temple of Solomon the King," *Equinox*, 1:3 (Mar 1910), 133-280.
Contains an account of the revolt against MacGregor Mathers (D. D. C. F.) with references to Yeats (D. E. D. I.) and Florence Farr (S. S. D. D.), pp. 253-54.

18. CUMMINS, GERALDINE: "W. B. Yeats and Psychical Research," *Occult R*, 66:2 (Apr 1939), 132-33, 135, 137, 139.
Contains some reminiscences of Yeats at séances and a note on *The Words upon the Window-Pane*.

19. ———: *Unseen Adventures: An Autobiography Covering Thirty-four Years of Work in Psychical Research*. London: Rider, 1951. 183 pp.
Recalls some psychical experiments with Yeats, pp. 25, 32-33, 79, 85-89.

20. DALSIMER, ADELE M.: "'Intellect and Imagination Stand Face to Face': Yeats's Correspondence with T. Sturge Moore," *ArQ*, 32:2 (Summer 1976), 101-24.
Discusses the vacillations in Yeats's philosophical arguments and his misreadings of other philosophers.

21. DAVIDSON, CLIFFORD: "Yeats: The Active and Contemplative Modes of Life," *Renascence*, 23:4 (Summer 1971), 192-97.
Yeats's "religious quest" through occult studies and the Tarot.

22. Deletić [i.e., DETELIĆ], MIRJANA: "Magijsko i okultno u teorijskim radovima i poeziji V. B. Jejtsa," *Književnost*, year 37 / 73:1-2 (1982), 210-29.
"Magic and occultism in the theoretical works and the poetry of WBY."

23. *Directions: Theology in a Changing Church*. Dublin: APCK, 1970. viii, 255 pp.

Cosslett Quin: "A Pragmatic Consideration of Some Irish Traditions, and Their Relationship to the Tradition of the Faith and the Scriptural Revelation," 1-40; contains a section on "W. B. Yeats and the Recovery of Tradition," 34-40 (Yeats and the Church of Ireland).

24. DOBSON, ROGER: "Yeats and the Golden Dawn," *Antiquarian Book Monthly R,* 14:4 (Apr 1987), 136-39.

25. DOWNES, GWLADYS V.: "W. B. Yeats and the Tarot," in Skelton and Saddlemyer: *The World of W. B. Yeats* (1967, CA102), 51-53.

26. EBON, MARTIN: *They Knew the Unknown.* NY: World Publishing Co., 1971. xiii, 285 pp.
"Yeats: A Poet's Lifetime Vision," 176-95; a retelling of Yeats's preoccupation with supernatural and psychic phenomena.

27. FARAG, FAHMY FAWZY: "W. B. Yeats's Daimon," *Cairo Studies in English,* 1961/62, 135-44.
Also on the concept of the mask.

28. FITZROY, CHRISTOPHER: "The Cult of Yeats," *Ireland's Catholic Standard,* 2 Oct 1964, 5.
A polemic against Yeats's "cabalistic" beliefs. Letters by John O'Riordan and K. McD., 30 Oct 1964, 5; R. Donnellan, 6 Nov 1964, 5; FitzRoy and J. P. B., 13 Nov 1964, 5; O'Riordan and Thomas O'Donnell, 20 Nov 1964, 5; "Ben Bulben," 27 Nov 1964, 5.

29. FRASER, G. S.: "Yeats as a Philosopher," *Phoenix* [Seoul], 10 (Summer 1965), 46-59.
On the correspondence with T. Sturge Moore and the relevance of Yeats's philosophy to his poetry.

30. FRICK, KARL R. H.: *Licht und Finsternis: Gnostisch-theosophische und freimaurerisch-okkulte Geheimgesellschaften bis an die Wende zum 20. Jahrhundert.* Graz: Akademische Druck- und Verlagsgesellschaft, 1973-78. 2 vols. in 3 parts.
Some notes on Yeats's occult interests in vol. 2, part 2:377-87.

31. FULLER, JEAN OVERTON: *The Magical Dilemma of Victor Neuburg.* London: Allen, 1965. xv, 295 pp.
On Yeats's association with the Golden Dawn, pp. 120-23, 126.

31a. GIBBONS, TOM: "Yeats, Joyce, Eliot and the Contemporary Revival of Cyclical Theories of History," *AUMLA,* 69 (May 1988), 151-63.

32. GILBERT, ROBERT A.: *The Golden Dawn: Twilight of the Magicians.* Wellingborough: Aquarian Press, 1983. 144 pp.
Several references to Yeats (see index).

33. ————: *The Golden Dawn Companion: A Guide to the History, Structure, and Workings of the Hermetic Order of the Golden Dawn.* Wellingborough: Aquarian Press, 1986. xi, 209 pp.
See index for some notes on Yeats.

34. ————: "Magical Manuscripts: An Introduction to the Archives of the Hermetic Order of the Golden Dawn," *YeA,* 5 (1987), 163-77.
Descriptions of the various collections and of the material referring to or written by Yeats; reprints some of this material, including letters by Yeats.

35. GOLDMAN, ARNOLD: "Yeats, Spiritualism, and Psychical Research," in Harper: *Yeats and the Occult* (1975, FC40), 108-29.
On Yeats's involvement with mediums and with Leo Africanus.

35a. GRUBB, H. T. HUNT: "Yeats as an Occultist," *Occult R,* 67:4 (Oct 1940), 191-95.

36. HARPER, GEORGE MILLS: "From Zelator to Theoricus: Yeats's Link with the Invisible Degrees,'" *YeSt,* 1 (Bealtaine 1971), 80-86.
Yeats's promotion from Zelator Adeptus Minor to Theoricus Adeptus Minor in the Golden Dawn.

37. ———: "'Meditations upon Unknown Thought': Yeats's Break with MacGregor Mathers," *YeSt,* 1 (Bealtaine 1971), 175-202.
A long introduction to Yeats's Golden Dawn activities at the time of the break with Mathers, pp. 175-82, and the relevant documents prepared by Yeats and Florence Farr.

38. ———: "Yeats on the Occult," *PMLA,* 86:3 (May 1971), 490.
Announces the following projects: "(1) a critical and historical study of Yeats's religion, (2) a critical edition with an extended introduction of *A Vision* (1925), and (3) an edition of selected letters to Yeats." See BC1, FC39, and 149.

39. ———: *Yeats's Golden Dawn.* London: Macmillan, 1974. x, 322 pp.
An extensively documented history of Yeats's involvement in the Order with special attention given to the critical years 1900-1901, and of the impact on Yeats's work of this period. Discusses the relationships between Yeats and Florence Farr, Miss Horniman, MacGregor Mathers, Mrs. Moina Mathers, Christina Mary Stoddart, and other members of the Order. See also FC89.
Reviews:
- James Lovic Allen, *JML,* 5:4 (1976), 845-46.
- Mary E. Bryson, *CJIS,* 3:2 [i.e., 3:1] (June 1977), 94-97.
- Denis Donoghue, *MLR,* 71:1 (Jan 1976), 151-52.
- Serge Fauchereau: "Multiple Yeats," *Quinzaine littéraire,* 16-30 Apr 1975, 13-14.
- Monk Gibbon: "Search for the Holy Grail," *Hibernia,* 24 Jan 1975, 18.
- Maurice Harmon, *IUR,* 5:1 (Spring 1975), 189-91.
- Maurice Hennessy: "Yeats: Playwright and Rosicrucian," *TES,* 8 Aug 1975, 15.
- John Holloway: "Golden Dawn, Angry Light," *THES,* 17 Jan 1975, III.
- Graham Hough: "Yeats and the Magic of Power," *TLS,* 14 Feb 1975, 160.
- Elizabeth Mackenzie, *N&Q,* os 221 / ns 23:1 (Jan 1976), 34-36.
- Antoine Ó Ceallaigh, *Eire,* 11:2 (Summer 1976), 149-51.
- Robert M. Schuler, *RES,* 27:107 (Aug 1976), 359-61.
- Eugene Watters: "DEDI-cation," *IrP,* 28 Dec 1974, 8.
- Georges-Denis Zimmermann, *ES,* 57:5 (Oct 1976), 464-68.

40. ——— (ed): *Yeats and the Occult.* Toronto: Macmillan, 1975. xxi, 322 pp. (Yeats Studies Series.)
Contains a short introduction by Lorna Reynolds and Robert O'Driscoll; for individual entries see BB254, BD15, CA90, CD574, 698, 810, DA22, DC347, FA13, 26, FC35, 41-43, 46, and 117.
Reviews:
- Stephen J. Adams, *Four Decades,* 1:4 (July 1977), 311-13.

- Douglas Archibald, *ACIS Newsletter*, 8:3 (Oct 1978), 3.
- J. S. Atherton: "The Golden Dawn and the Great Memory," *TLS*, 10 Sept 1976, 1104.
- William C. Barnwell, *SAB*, 43:4 (Nov 1978), 171-74.
- Terence Brown, *IUR*, 6:2 (Autumn 1976), 256-59.
- John Bryson: "The Golden Dawn," *Books and Bookmen*, 21:250 (July 1976), 50-51.
- Mary E. Bryson, *CJIS*, 3:2 [i.e., 3:1] (June 1977), 94-97.
- Leo Daly: "Elder Faiths," *BooksI*, 10 (Jan/Feb 1977), 19-21.
- Denis Donoghue, *MLR*, 73:3 (July 1978), 628-30.
- Doug Fetherling, *Quill & Quire*, 42:2 (Feb 1976), 37.
- Olwen Francis, *Theosophical J*, 18:3 (May/June 1977), 31-32.
- Daniel A. Harris, *JML*, 5:4 (1976), 846-48.
- Eileen Kennedy, *Eire*, 12:4 (Winter 1977), 146-47.
- Elizabeth Mackenzie, *N&Q*, os 225 / ns 27:5 (Oct 1980), 471-74.
- Derek Mahon: "Pern in a Gyre," *NSt*, 13 Aug 1976, 215-16.
- Vincent Mahon, *RES*, 29:114 (May 1978), 239-41.
- Augustine Martin, *Anglo-Irish Studies*, 4 (1979), 119-21.
- John B. Mays: "Opening a Dozen Doors to a Long Shuttered House of Yeats," *Globe and Mail*, 20 Dec 1975, 35.
- Christopher Ricks: "The Poet among the Shades," *SunT*, 15 Aug 1976, 31.
- G. B. Tennyson, *Christian Scholar's R*, 7:2-3 (1977), 268-70.
- Mervyn Wall: "The Trembling of the Veil," *Hibernia*, 16 July 1976, 27.
- R. G. Yeed: "Yeats Studies Series," *JIL*, 5:2 (May 1976), 86-90.
- Lorna Young: "A Scholarly Look at Poet-Dramatist," *Citizen*, 28 Feb 1976, 74.

41. HARPER, GEORGE MILLS: "Yeats's Occult Papers," in Harper: *Yeats and the Occult*, (1975, FC40), 1-10.
A survey of the papers in the possession of Michael Yeats.

42. ———, and JOHN S. KELLY: "Preliminary Examination of the Script of E[lizabeth] R[adcliffe]," in Harper: *Yeats and the Occult* (1975, FC40), 130-71.
An annotated edition of Yeats's essay of that title, with an introduction on E. R. and automatic writing.

43. HARPER, GEORGE MILLS: "'A Subject of Investigation': Miracle at Mirebeau," in Harper: *Yeats and the Occult* (1975, FC40), 172-89.
An annotated edition of Yeats's account of a visit to Mirebeau, France, in May 1914, together with Maud Gonne and Everard Feilding, to investigate bleeding oleographs of the sacred heart.

44. ———: "'Unbelievers in the House': Yeats's Automatic Script," *SLitI*, 14:1 (Spring 1981), 1-15.
Describes the sequence of "some 450 sessions" between 1917 and 1921 with more than 8600 recorded questions and 3600 answers. Numerous short quotations from unpublished material.

44a. ———: "'An Old Man's Frenzy': Editing Yeats's Occult Papers," *SoAR*, 53:2 (May 1988), 3-10.

45. HEINE, ELIZABETH: "'W. B. Yeats' Map in His Own Hand,'" *Biography*, 1:3 (Summer 1978), 37-50.
Analyzes Yeats's horoscope.

45a. HIRST, DESIREE: "The Theosophical Preoccupations of Blake and Yeats," *AJES*, 11:2 (Oct 1986), 209-31.

46. HOOD, WALTER KELLY: "Michael Robartes: Two Manuscripts," in Harper: *Yeats and the Occult* (1975, FC40), 204-24.
An edition of "Appendix by Michael Robartes" and "Michael Robartes Foretells," intended as part of *A Vision* but not included.

47. HOUGH, GRAHAM: *The Mystery Religion of W. B. Yeats*. Brighton: Harvester Press / Totowa, N.J.: Barnes & Noble, 1984. xi, 129 pp.
An extract was published as "*A Vision:* Some Notes and Queries," *YeA*, 3 (1985), 213-21. On Yeats's religious and occult preoccupations and beliefs, his relationship with Madame Blavatsky, the Golden Dawn, theosophy, psychical phenomena, *A Vision*, and some related poems.
Reviews:
- James Lovic Allen, *YeA*, 4 (1986), 265-67.
- Seamus Deane: "Yeats and the Occult," *LRB*, 18-31 Oct 1984, 27.
- Jacqueline Genet, *EI*, 9 (Dec 1984), 344.
- George Mills Harper, *Yeats*, 4 (1986), 199-202.
- Peter van de Kamp, *IUR*, 15:1 (Spring 1985), 108-11.
- Johannes Kleinstück, *Anglia*, 104:1/2 (1986), 262-63.
- Peter Redgrove: "Tapping the Great Mind," *TLS*, 30 Nov 1984, 1366.

48. HOWE, ELLIC: *The Magicians of the Golden Dawn: A Documentary History of a Magical Order, 1887-1923*. With a foreword by Gerald Yorke. London: Routledge & Kegan Paul, 1972. xxviii, 306 pp.
On Yeats's Golden Dawn activities, passim (see index).

49. ILIOPOULOS, SPYRIDON: "'Out of a Medium's Mouth': Yeats's Art in Relation to Mediumship, Spiritualism and Psychical Research," Ph.D. thesis, U of Warwick, 1985. xi, 360 pp.
Abstract in *Index to Theses*, 36:2 (1988), 473. Discusses Yeats's "involvement with mediums, 'controls,' and 'spirit-visitors,'" as well as the pertinent MSS., especially those dealing with Leo Africanus. A major part of the thesis is concerned with "spiritistic" works such as "To a Shade," "The Cold Heaven," "The Magi," "In Memory of Major Robert Gregory," "An Image from a Past Life," "The Second Coming," "All Souls' Night," "The Spirit Medium," "The Apparitions," *The Words upon the Window-Pane*, and others. The appendixes contain transcriptions of "Records of Seances," 1912-16; a Leo Africanus MS. (ca. 1915); extracts from "The Poet and the Actress," "Clairvoyant Search for Will" (Hugh Lane's will), and from the notebook of William Stainton Moses (a MS. in Yeats's possession which "may be related to the spiritualistic sources of some of his major poems").

50. INGLIS, BRIAN: *Science and Parascience: A History of the Paranormal, 1914-1939*. London: Hodder & Stoughton, 1984. 382 pp.
For some remarks on Yeats and the paranormal see especially pp. 33-34 (Yeats and "Eva C.," i. e. Marthe Béraud).

50a. IVENS, MICHAEL: "Yeats: The Faustian Quest," *Books and Bookmen*, 17:195 (Dec 1971), 20-22.
Yeats's occult interests.

51. JACKSON, P. E.: "Recollections of the Old Dublin Lodge, Ely Place, in the Years 1891-2-3-4," *Theosophy in Ireland*, 17:3 (July-Sept 1938), 22-25; :4 (Oct-Dec 1938), 21-25; 19:1 (Jan-Mar 1940), 15-18; :2 (Mar-June 1940), 20-24.
Yeats is mentioned passim.

52. JENNRICH, PETER: *Die Okkupation des Willens: Macht und Methoden der neuen Kultbewegungen.* Hamburg: Hoffmann & Campe, 1985. 254 pp.

See pp. 156-66 for some rather perfunctory notes on Yeats's occult interests.

53. JOHN, BRIAN: "The Philosophical Ideas of W. B. Yeats," M.A. thesis, U of Wales, 1959. vi, 501 pp.

Author's summary of contents: (1) A review of the various aesthetic alternatives open to the young poet at the end of the 19th century together with a brief introduction to and elucidation of Yeats's major philosophical terms. . . . (2) An analysis and evaluation of Yeats's poetry through the expression and interaction of his various poetic masks. (3) An examination of Yeats's philosophical ideas and their expression in the system, as appearing in the two editions of *A Vision,* in relation to his poetic achievement.

54. KALOGERA, LUCY SHEPARD: "Yeats's Celtic Mysteries," Ph.D. thesis, Florida State U, 1977. v, 311 pp. (*DAI,* 38:4 [Oct 1977], 2140A-41A)

On Yeats's attempts "to create a specifically Irish esoteric-visionary society in which he and Maud [Gonne] would be united in a mystical marriage of mage and sibyl" (p. 5), a project known as "Celtic Mysteries" or "Castle of Heroes." Includes transcripts of MSS. dated 1897-1899 and later undated ones by Yeats and others, concerned with mystical activities; discusses the Golden Dawn and Yeats's relationships with George Pollexfen, Maud Gonne, McGregor Mathers, Moina Mathers, Miss Horniman, Florence Farr, William Sharp/Fiona Macleod, AE, and others.

55. KERMODE, FRANK: *The Sense of an Ending: Studies in the Theory of Fiction.* NY: Oxford UP, 1967. xi, 187 pp. (Mary Flexner Lectures. 1965.)

"The Modern Apocalypse," 93-124; first published as "The New Apocalyptists," *PR,* 33:3 (Summer 1966), 339-61. Comments on Yeats's historical dialectics, passim.

56. KING, FRANCIS: *Ritual Magic in England: 1887 to the Present Day.* London: Spearman, 1970. 224 pp.

Notes on Yeats's involvement in the Golden Dawn, pp. 73-78, 202, and passim (see index).

56a. KUCH, PETER: "Yeats and the Occult," *Prudentia: A Journal Devoted to the Intellectual History of the Ancient World,* 1985, supplement, 199-218.

Argues that Yeats used the occult in order "to secure access to a personality that was the opposite of that he believed himself to be" and "to command a spiritual power without incurring a commitment to any set . . . of beliefs or doctrines." Discusses "The Second Coming" and "The Apparitions."

57. LENOSKI, DANIEL S.: "The Metaphysics behind Yeats's Aesthetics," *Anglo-Irish Studies,* 3 (1977), 19-34.

58. MCCORMICK, JANE L.: "A Poet, Playwright, Essayist & Nobel Prize Winner Who Mixed in the *Para*normal: William Butler Yeats & Psychic Phenomena," *Psychic,* 1:6 (May-June 1970), 19-23.

See also the same author's "Psychic Phenomena in Literature," 3:4 (Jan-Feb 1972), 40, 42-44.

59. *Man, Myth, and Magic: An Encyclopedia of the Supernatural.* [Edited by Richard Cavendish]. [London:] Purnell, [1970-72]. 7 vols.

Kathleen Raine: "Golden Dawn" 3:1131-34; and "W. B. Yeats," 7:3066-68.

60. MANN, A. T.: *The Round Art: The Astrology of Time and Space.* [Limpsfield, England]: Paper Tiger, 1979. 299 pp.

For Yeats's horoscope see pp. 193, 198-99, 251.

61. MARTINICH, ROBERT ANTHONY: "W. B. Yeats's *Sleep and Dream Notebooks*," °Ph.D. thesis, Florida State U, 1982. 263 pp. (*DAI*, 45:4 [Oct 1984], 1123A; reprinted *Yeats*, 3 [1985], 216)

An edition of the notebooks, written by Yeats and Mrs. Yeats, 1920-23.

62. MERCIER, ALAIN: *Les sources ésotériques et occultes de la poésie symboliste (1870-1914).* Paris: Nizet, 1969-74. 2 vols.

See 2:25-34 and passim.

63. NETHERCOT, ARTHUR HOBART: *The First Five Lives of Annie Besant.* Chicago: U of Chicago Press, 1960. xii, 419 pp.

Note on Yeats, Madame Blavatsky, Annie Besant, and theosophy, pp. 300-304.

64. OLNEY, JAMES: *The Rhizome and the Flower: The Perennial Philosophy--Yeats and Jung.* Berkeley: U of California Press, 1980. xv, 379 pp.

Incorporates "W. B. Yeats's Daimonic Memory" (see FB27). An essay in the history of ideas: Develops Yeats's philosophical poetics in relation to archetypes and the perennial philosophy, and in comparison with Jung's thoughts. (Yeats and Jung knew nothing or very little of each other and direct influence is impossible.) Analyzed in section DD.

Reviews:
- James Lovic Allen, *SHR*, 16:1 (Winter 1982), 86-87.
- Cleanth Brooks, *YeA*, 1 (1982), 244-47.
- Gary Davenport: "Yeats and Belief," *SR*, 89:3 (Summer 1981), 469-73.
- Robertson Davies: "Jung, Yeats and the Inner Journey," *QQ*, 89:3 (Autumn 1982), 471-77.
- Paul John Eakin, *Criticism*, 22:4 (Fall 1980), 394-96.
- Harry Goldgar: "Philosophy of Yeats, Jung Clarified," *Times-Picayune*, 26 June 1980, section 6, 4.
- George Mills Harper, *SAQ*, 80:2 (Spring 1981), 233-34.
- G. Lernout, *RBPH*, 63:3 (1985), 629-33.
- Herbert J. Levine: "Explorers of the Human Psyche," *VQR*, 57:3 (Summer 1981), 554-57.
- Colin McDowell, *AUMLA*, 55 (May 1981), 111-13.
- Elizabeth Mackenzie, *N&Q*, os 228 / ns 30:1 (Feb 1983), 90-92.
- Shirley Neuman, *PSt*, 7:2 (Sept 1984), 196-99.
- Corinna Peterson, *J of Analytical Psychology*, 27:4 (1982), 391-92.
- Michael Sprinker, *Philosophy & Literature*, 5:2 (Autumn 1981), 243-44.

65. O'RAHILLY, ALFRED: "Mr. Yeats as Theologian," *Irish Tribune*, 23 Apr 1926, 9-10.

Criticizes Yeats's "Our Need for Religious Sincerity," first published as "The Need for Audacity of Thought" (*Uncollected Prose*,

2:461-65). Correspondence by Donald Attwater, 14 May 1926, 16; O'Rahilly, 4 June 1926, 19.

66. PEARCE, DONALD: "Unfashionable Gyre: A Plea for Magic," *Twentieth Century* [Melbourne], 11:1 (Spring 1956), 60-68.
Yeats's kind of magic.

67. *Poetry and Prophecy*. West Stockbridge, Mass.: Lindisfarne Press, 1979. 80 pp. (Lindisfarne Letter. 9.)
William Irwin Thompson and Kathleen Raine: "Poetry and Prophecy," 7-15; subtitled "Remarks on the esoteric tradition in a symposium on W. B. Yeats, at Lindisfarne in Manhattan 9 November 1978." The same volume contains K. Raine's "Waste Land, Holy Land," 16-28 (see CB384).

68. RAJAN, B.: "W. B. Yeats and the Unity of Being," *Nineteenth Century and After*, 146:871 (Sept 1949), 150-61.

69. ———: "Yeats and the Renaissance," *Mosaic*, 5:4 (Summer 1972), 109-18.
Again on the concept of Unity of Being.

70. REGARDIE, ISRAEL: *My Rosicrucian Adventure: A Contribution to a Recent Phase of the History of Magic, and a Study in the Technique of Theurgy*. Chicago: Engelke, 1936. 145 pp.
Mentions Yeats twice (under his own name und under his pseudonym D. E. D. I.) in connection with the Golden Dawn, pp. 52-53.

71. RIBSTEIN, FLORENCE: "La tradition mystique et occulte dans la formation et l'oeuvre de William Butler Yeats," thesis, Doctorat de 3e cycle, Université de Paris III--Sorbonne Nouvelle, 1985. v, 328 pp.

72. ROBERTS, MARIE: *British Poets and Secret Societies*. London: Croom Helm, 1986. xv, 181 pp.
"William Butler Yeats," 126-58; on Yeats's preoccupation with the Golden Dawn and with Rosicrucianism.

73. ROBERTSON, LINDA K.: "Irish Ghosts: The Haunting of William Butler Yeats," *Publications of the Missouri Philological Association*, 10 (1985), 44-49.
Discusses Yeats's belief in ghosts.

74. SCHMITT, NATALIE CROHN: "Ecstasy and Insight in Yeats," *BJA*, 11:3 (Summer 1971), 257-67.
Yeats's faith postulated the unity of experience and the experienced, perception and creation, ecstasy and insight. Truth is therefore "an aesthetic matter." These observations are applied to a discussion of the plays.

75. SCHUCHARD, MARSHA KEITH MANATT: "Freemasonry, Secret Societies, and the Continuity of the Occult Traditions in English Literature," Ph.D. thesis, U of Texas at Austin, 1975. vii, 698 pp. (*DAI*, 36:5 [Nov 1975], 2792A-93A)
"W. B. Yeats and Fin de Siècle Occultism," 619-70, and passim.

76. SENIOR, JOHN: *The Way Down and Out: The Occult in Symbolist Literature*. Ithaca: Cornell UP, 1959. xxvii, 217 pp.
"The Artifice of Eternity: Yeats," 145-69. Yeats's occult and visionary preoccupations are rather "empty" compared to those of Blake and AE. Nevertheless, he wrote good poetry.

77. SHERRARD, PHILIP: *W. B. Yeats & the Search for Tradition*. Ipswich: Golgonooza Press, 1975. 21 pp. (Sir Maurice Bowra Lecture, U of Oxford. 1975.)

The metaphysical tradition behind Yeats's poetic philosophy.
Reviews:
- Warwick Gould, *Four Decades*, 1:4 (July 1977), 288-90.
- Desiree Hirst, *AWR*, 25:55 (Autumn 1975), 167-69.

78. SPENCE, LEWIS (ed): *An Encyclopaedia of Occultism: A Compendium of Information on the Occult Sciences, Occult Personalities, Psychic Science, Magic, Demonology, Spiritism, and Mysticism*. London: Routledge, 1920. xiv, 451 pp.

W. G. B[laikie] M[urdoch]: "Yeats," 438.

79. SPIVEY, TED R.: "W. B. Yeats and the 'Children of the Fire': Science, Poetry, and Visions of the New Age," *SLitI*, 14:1 (Spring 1981), 123-34.

Yeats as a forerunner of modern occult, paranormal, and psychic thinking and writing.

80. STUDIES IN THE LITERARY IMAGINATION: "W. B. Yeats: The Occult and Philosophical Backgrounds," *SLitI*, 14:1 (Spring 1981).

Ted R. Spivey: "Editor's Comment," v-vii; for individual entries see CA60, CC189, 217, 245, DD598, FC3, 44, 79, and 84. Reviewed by Donald T. Torchiana, *Yeats*, 1 (1983), 221-26.

81. SULLIVAN, JACK (ed): *The Penguin Encyclopedia of Horror and the Supernatural*. NY: Viking, 1986. xxx, 482 pp.

Note on Yeats, pp. 475-77.

82. SYMONDS, JOHN: *The Great Beast: The Life of Aleister Crowley*. London: Rider, 1951. 316 pp.

Note on Yeats's role in the Golden Dawn schism, pp. 32-33.

83. THOMPSON, VANCE: "The Tame Ghosts of Yeats and the Sar Peladan," *Criterion* [NY], 13 Jan 1900, 9-10.

Account of a séance with Yeats and Sâr Péladan in Paris.

84. THORNTON, WELDON: "Between Circle and Straight Line: A Pragmatic View of W. B. Yeats and the Occult," *SLitI*, 14:1 (Spring 1981), 61-75.

85. UNDERWOOD, PETER: *A Gazetteer of Scottish and Irish Ghosts*. London: Souvenir Press, 1973. 252 pp.

Note on the ghost at Renvyle House in Connemara in which Yeats was interested, pp. 194-96.

86. ———: *No Common Task: The Autobiography of a Ghost-Hunter*. London: Harrap, 1983. 239 pp.

Note on Yeats as a "typical Ghost Club member," pp. 148-49.

87. [UPWARD, ALLEN]: *Some Personalities*. By 20/1631. Boston: Cornhill Publication Co., 1922. xiii, 302 pp.

Tried, sometime in the 1880s, to get into "telepathic communication" with Yeats. The experiment failed (pp. 57-58).

88. VICTOR, PIERRE: "Magie et sociétés secrètes: L'ordre hermétique de la Golden Dawn," *Tour Saint-Jacques*, 2 (Jan-Feb 1956), 46-55; 3 (Mar-Apr 1956), 39-47.

Notes on Yeats in 3, pp. 42-43, 45-46.

89. WATKINS, STEVE: "A Yeats Man: George Harper Unlocks the Secrets of the Great Irish Poet and His Mysterious Scripts," *Florida State U Bulletin: Research in Review,* 81:2 (Spring 1987), 14-17.
On Harper's studies in Yeats's occult writings.

90. WEBB, JAMES: *The Flight from Reason.* Volume 1 of *The Age of the Irrational.* London: Macdonald, 1971. xiv, 305 pp.
On Yeats's occult interests, pp. 208-13 and passim (see index). Revised and republished as *The Occult Underground.* LaSalle, Ill.: Open Court, 1974. vii, 387 pp. (On Yeats, pp. 321-27.)

91. WESTON, JESSIE LAIDLAY: *From Ritual to Romance.* Garden City: Doubleday, 1957 [1920]. xvii, 217 pp. (Doubleday Anchor Book. A125.)
Quotes from a letter by Yeats in which he comments on the Tarot symbols, p. 79.

92. WILSON, COLIN: *The Occult.* London: Hodder & Stoughton, 1971. 601 pp.
On Yeats, pp. 102-9 and passim (see index).

93. ———: *Mysteries: An Investigation into the Occult, the Paranormal and the Supernatural.* London: Hodder & Stoughton, 1978. 667 pp.
See index for references to Yeats.

94. YEATS, W. B.: "The Manuscript of 'Leo Africanus.'" Edited by Steve L. Adams and George Mills Harper, *YeA,* 1 (1982), 3-47.
The "Editorial Introduction" (pp. 3-17) surveys Yeats's involvement with Leo Africanus and his psychical experiments from 1909 to 1919.

95. YELLEN, SHERMAN: "The Psychic World of W. B. Yeats," *Tomorrow,* 10:1 (Winter 1962), 99-106.
A defense of Yeats, "the staunch advocate of psychic research," and a note on *The Words upon the Window-Pane* (the play is reprinted on pp. 107-22).

See also AE28, BA3, 14, 18, 49, 52, 58, 63, 70, 78, 93, 155, 163, 224, BE1, 108, BF3, 98, 106, 107, 126, 130, 132, CA4, 31, 40, 49, 53a, 73, 90, 99, 103, 128, 129, 130, 147, 148, 151, CB41, 103, 147, 233, 371, 404, 498, CC41, 46, 48, 104, 116, 146, 171a, 189, 194, 203, 245, 252, 253, 332, 343, CD1, 6, 14, 23, 139, 174, 175a, 224, 268, 278-80, 323, 352, 434, 527, 576, 627, 688, 698, 699, 708, 807-10, 872, 876, 1048, 1049, 1070, 1109, 1149, 1151, 1154, 1160, 1258, 1410, 1418, DA3, 11, 38, DC18, 277, 284, 300, DD51, 752a, 770, EA12, 14, 98, EE490, FA1, 21, 25, 26, G1060-75 and note, 1487.

Part 2: Individual Works

This part serves as an index to all substantial listings of *Per Amica Silentia Lunae* and *A Vision* in this bibliography and to interpretations in analyzed monographs.

Per Amica Silentia Lunae

96. HOFFMAN, BRYANT E.: "All Imaginable Things: Yeats's *Per Amica Silentia Lunae,*" *IRA,* 1 (1980), 56-72.
Also on "Ego Dominus Tuus."

97. LICKINDORF, ELIZABETH T.: "W. B. Yeats's *Per Amica Silentia Lunae*," *ESA*, 25:1 (1982), 39-53.
Includes a discussion of related poems.

98. LOFARO, MICHAEL A.: "The Mask with No Eyes: Yeats's Vision in *Per Amica Silentia Lunae*," *Style*, 10:1 (Winter 1976), 51-66.
"Yeats's rhetorical techniques function as protective devices which in turn mirror his inability to delineate a tenable aesthetic creed."

98a. °SHIMA, HIROYUKI: "W. B. Yeats's *Per Amica Silentia Lunae:* Somnambulistic Vision and Anima Mundi," *Sophia English Studies*, 6 (1981), 43-61.

99. YEATS, W. B.: *Per Amica Silentia Lunae*. French translation by Georges Garnier, Jacqueline Genet, and Pamela Zeini; introduction by Jacqueline Genet. Villeneuve-d'Ascq: Presses universitaires de Lille, 1979. 69 pp. (Traduit de l'irlandais. 4.)
"Introduction," 7-23. See also G1541.

See also CA4, 12, 60, 92, 100, CC107, 132, 182, 146, CD2, 353, 1011, 1048b, CE320, DA22, DC281a, DD220, FC108, FE56, G354-68 and note, 1374, 1541.

A Vision

100. ADAMS, HAZARD: "Symbolism and Yeats's *A Vision*," *JAAC*, 22:4 (Summer 1964), 425-36.
Discusses the book as "a grammar of poetic symbolism" and as "a work of literary art of a kind for which we have had . . . no critical terminology." Stresses the various uses of irony in the book.

101. ———: *Philosophy of the Literary Symbolic*. Tallahassee: University Presses of Florida, 1983. xiv, 466 pp.
"The Early Yeats," 140-50; "Stylistic Arrangements of Experience," 287-324; and passim (see index). On *A Vision*, some poems, and Yeats's indebtedness to Blake. Reviewed by Edward Engelberg, *Yeats*, 3 (1985), 217-24.

102. ALLEN, JAMES LOVIC: "Yeats's Phase in the System of *A Vision*," *Eire*, 8:4 (Winter 1973), 91-117.
Yeats's phase was 13, not 17 as is commonly believed.

103. ———: "'The Red and the Black': Understanding 'The Historical Cones,'" *YeA*, 3 (1985), 209-12.
The importance of the red and black parts of the diagram.

104. ARGÜELLES, JOSE A.: *The Transformative Vision: Reflections on the Nature and History of Human Expression*. Berkeley/London: Shambala, 1975. viii, 364 pp.
On *A Vision* and the Great Wheel, pp. 223-27.

105. ARKINS, BRIAN: "Yeats and Bishop Xenaias," *N&Q*, os 232 / ns 34:1 (Mar 1987), 56-57.
The identity of Xenaias, referred to in section IV of "Dove or Swan."

106. ARONSON, ALEX: "Myth and Modern Poetry. I: W. B. Yeats," *VQ*,

17:1 (May-July 1951), 35-43.

The "myth" of *A Vision* replaces the Celtic mythology of Yeats's earlier phase. Without it, some of his poems cannot be understood. Eventually, however, "the myth, and the twenty-eight phases of the moon leave us cold, [and] we are persuaded by the poetry."

107. BARROW, CRAIG WALLACE: "Comprehensive Index to William Butler Yeats's *A Vision*," *BNYPL*, 77:1 (Autumn 1973), 51-62.

A subject and name index to the 2nd edition (NY, 1938; Wade 192); also applicable to Wade 191 and subsequent reprints.

108. BENSON, CARL FREDERICK: "A Study of Yeats' *A Vision*," Ph.D. thesis, U of Illinois, 1948. iv, 257 pp.

An analysis of both versions, of *Per Amica Silentia Lunae*, of their sources, and of their effect on Yeats's poetry.

109. BROWN, P. L. R.: "Psychological Aspects of Some Yeatsian Concepts," *Mosaic*, 11:1 (Fall 1977), 21-35.

Finds some of the concepts developed in *A Vision* to be psychologically credible; indicates parallels with Jungian ideas.

110. BUSTEED, MARILYN, RICHARD TIFFANY, and DOROTHY WERGIN: *Phases of the Moon: A Guide to Evolving Human Nature*. Berkeley: Shambala, 1974. 224 pp.

Based throughout on Yeats's "system"; *A Vision* is referred to passim.

111. BUTLER, CHRISTOPHER: *Number Symbolism*. London: Routledge & Kegan Paul, 1970. xiii, 186 pp.

See pp. 162-64.

112. CALLAN, EDWARD: "Huddon and Duddon in Yeats's *A Vision:* The Folk Tale as Gateway to the Universal Mind," *Michigan Academician*, 6:1 (Summer 1973), 5-16.

112a. CARACCIOLO, PETER L. (ed): *The "Arabian Nights" in English Literature: Studies in the Reception of "The Thousand and One Nights" into British Culture*. London: Macmillan, 1988. xxix, 330 pp.

Warwick Gould: "'A Lesson for the Circumspect': W. B. Yeats's Two Versions of *A Vision* and the *Arabian Nights*," 244-80.

113. CARBERG, JOAN S.: "*A Vision* by William Butler Yeats," *Daedalus*, 103:1 (Winter 1974), 141-56.

Also on related poems. (N.B.: This issue of *Daedalus* was entitled "Twentieth-Century Classics Revisited.")

113a. CHATTERJEE, VISVANATH (ed): *The Romantic Tradition*. Calcutta: Department of English, Jadavpur U, 1984. vii, 158 pp. (Jadavpur U Essays and Studies. 4.)

Arup Rudra: "*A Vision:* Between Romantic and Modern," 116-20. The book is an expression of both romanticism and modernism.

114. COMFORT, ALEX: *Darwin and the Naked Lady: Discursive Essays on Biology and Art*. NY: Braziller, 1962. xiii, 174 pp.

Sees *A Vision* as an example of the "soft-centred approach" to generalization, pp. 13-21: "The soft-centred approach is to state the regularity [in an observed sequence of events], call it a law, a truth, or a spiritual reality, and treat these names as if they were explanations" (p. 4).

115. CROFT, BARBARA LEA: *"Stylistic Arrangements": A Study of William Butler Yeats's "A Vision."* Lewisburg, Pa.: Bucknell UP, 1987. 196 pp.

Based on "'Stylistic Arrangements': A Comparative Study of the Two Versions of W. B. Yeats's *A Vision*," Ph.D. thesis, U of Toronto, 1977. x, 269 pp. (*DAI*, 39:3 [Sept 1978], 1545A-46A). Includes discussions of the early occult writings, of the stories contained in *A Vision*, and of its prose style, also a comparison of the two versions.

116. DECKER, M. B.: "A Correction in Yeats's *A Vision*," *N&Q*, os 218 / ns 20:9 (Sept 1973), 329-30.

117. FINNERAN, RICHARD J.: "On Editing Yeats: The Text of *A Vision* (1937)," *TSLL*, 19:1 (Spring 1977), 119-34.

Supersedes "A Preliminary Note on the Text of *A Vision* (1937)," in Harper: *Yeats and the Occult* (FC40), 317-20; on the publishing history, includes comments on the problem of editing the poems. It would seem that a final authentic text of *A Vision* is not likely to be realized.

118. FISHWICK, MARSHALL: "Yeats and Cyclical History," *Shenandoah*, 1:2 (Summer 1950), 52-56.

119. FLETCHER, IAN: "History and Vision in the Work of W. B. Yeats," *SoR*, 4:1 (Winter 1968), 105-26.

An omnibus review, discussing the problems of history in Yeats's work, the reception and interpretation of *A Vision*, and generally the state of Yeats scholarship.

119a. FRIAR, KIMON: "*A Vision* of William Butler Yeats," *Expansional R* [Wilmington, Ohio], 1:1 (May 1953), 6-11.

A short exposition of its contents. My thanks to Wilmington College Library for providing a copy.

120. FRYE, NORTHROP: *Spiritus Mundi: Essays on Literature, Myth, and Society*. Bloomington: Indiana UP, 1976. xvii, 296 pp.

"The Rising of the Moon," 245-74; reprinted from Donoghue and Mulryne: *An Honoured Guest* (1965, CA22), 8-33. On *A Vision*.

121. HARPER, GEORGE MILLS: *The Making of Yeats's "A Vision": A Study of the Automatic Script*. London: Macmillan, 1986. 2 vols. (xvi, 301, xvii, 463 pp.)

A chronological study with copious quotations from the script, made by Yeats and Mrs. Yeats between 5 Nov 1917 and 22 Apr 1925. Includes references to various poems and plays indebted to *A Vision*, especially *Calvary*, *The Only Jealousy of Emer*, and *The Player Queen*. See also FC89.

Reviews:

- Warwick Gould: "Gratitude to the Unknown Instructors," *THES*, 15 Jan 1988, 13.
- Steven Helmling: "Yeats Early and Late," *SR*, 95:3 (Summer 1987), 490-94.
- Elizabeth Bergmann Loizeaux: "On Yeats and His Scholars," *MQR*, 27:4 (Autumn 1988), 657-64.
- Claude Rawson: "A Question of Potency," *TLS*, 24 July 1987, 783-85.

122. HELMLING, STEVEN: "Esoteric Comedies: Proto-Modern Strategies of Imagination in Carlyle, Newman, and Yeats," Ph.D. thesis, Rutgers U,

1983. vi, 299 pp. (*DAI*, 44:12 [June 1984], 3695A; reprinted *Yeats*, 3 [1985], 210-11, and *YeA*, 4 [1986], 311-12)

"'Because There is Safety in Derision': Yeats's *Vision*," 198-283, and passim. An earlier version of the Yeats chapter appeared as "Yeats's Esoteric Comedy," *HudR*, 30:2 (Summer 1977), 230-46. On the book's comic aspects.

123. HOOD, CONNIE KELLY: "A Search for Authority: Prolegomena to a Definitive Critical Edition of W. B. Yeats's *A Vision* (1937)," Ph.D. thesis, U of Tennessee, 1983. iii, 276 pp. (*DAI*, 44:4 [Oct 1983], 1082A-83A; reprinted *Yeats*, 2 [1984], 263, and *YeA*, 4 [1986], 312-13)

Contains chapters on the origins and composition of the book, its reception and publishing history, a list of emendations, a textual commentary, notes on the manuscripts, etc. Uses much unpublished material.

124. ———: "The Remaking of *A Vision*," *Yeats*, 1 (1983), 33-67.

A survey of the textual changes made by Yeats after the first edition as well as those made by Mrs. Yeats and Thomas Mark after his death.

125. HOOD, WALTER KELLY: "A Study of *A Vision* by W. B. Yeats," Ph.D. thesis, U of North Carolina at Chapel Hill, 1968. iv, 245 pp. (*DAI*, 29:7 [Jan 1969], 2264A)

A book-by-book analysis, conceived by its author as "a philosophical study from a literary point of view" (p. iii).

126. KAPPLER, KEVIN ANDREW: "A Multi-Dimensional Evaluation of Therapeutic Process: The Psychological Application of W. B. Yeats' *A Vision*," °Ph.D. thesis, California School of Professional Psychology, Berkeley, 1981. 146 pp. (*DAI*, 42:10 [Apr 1982], 4173B; reprinted *YeA*, 4 [1986], 314)

"This dissertation makes W. B. Yeats' *A Vision* more accessible to psychologists through comparing it with the theories of Freud and Jung" (abstract).

127. KIM, TAI YUL: "Three Aesthetics of the Mask: Nietzsche, Yeats and Pirandello," Ph.D. thesis, Indiana U, 1974. iii, 151 pp. (*DAI*, 34:12 [June 1974], 7709A)

128. KORKOWSKI, EUGENE: "Yeats' *Vision* as Philosophic *Satura*," *Eire*, 12:3 (Fall 1977), 62-70.

Yeats's elaborate fictions in the introduction suggest that he modeled the book on Menippean satire.

129. LASSETER, ROLLIN AMOS: "A Powerful Emblem: Epistemology in Yeats's Poetic Vision," °Ph.D. thesis, Yale U, 1970. 235 pp. (*DAI*, 31:6 [Dec 1970], 2924A)

130. LEMONNIER, LEON: "Le symbolisme mystique de Yeats," *Nouvelle revue critique*, 22:4 (Summer 1938), 227-35.

131. °MCDOWELL, COLIN: "W. B. Yeats's *A Vision:* A Study of Its Meaning," M.A. thesis, Monash U, 1982. 229 pp.

132. ———: "The 'Opening of the *Tinctures*' in Yeats's *A Vision*," *Eire*, 20:3 (Fall 1985), 71-92.

133. ———: "The Six Discarnate States of *A Vision* (1937)," *Yeats*, 4 (1986), 87-98.

134. ———: "To 'Beat upon the Wall': Reading *A Vision*," *YeA*, 4 (1986), 219-27.

135. MARKOVIĆ, VIDA E.: "Jejtsova vizija," *Gradina*, 15:1 (Jan 1980), 19-28.

136. MULLER, HERBERT J.: "The New Criticism in Poetry," *SoR*, 6:4 (Spring 1941), 811-39.
Criticizes Cleanth Brooks's treatment of *A Vision* (CB68). See J. V. Healy: "Scientific and Intuitable Language," 7:1 (Summer 1941), 214-16, who defends *A Vision* against Muller's critique.

137. MURPHY, RUSSELL: "Yeats's Christ Pantokrator and the Image of Edessa: Some New Observations on the Significance of Byzantium in Yeats's Historical System," *YER*, 8:1&2 (1986), 41-49.
The image of Christ Pantokrator as appropriated by Yeats from Byzantine art and used in the historical system of *A Vision*.

138. PARKINSON, THOMAS: "This Extraordinary Book," *YeA*, 1 (1982), 195-206.
A Vision (1925).

139. PEARCE, DONALD: "Philosophy and Phantasy: Notes on the Growth of Yeats's 'System,'" *UKCR*, 18:3 (Spring 1952), 169-80.
A defense of *A Vision* as a book in its own right and as a dictionary of Yeats's symbols.

140. POWELL, GROSVENOR E.: "Yeats's Second *Vision:* Berkeley, Coleridge, and the Correspondence with Sturge Moore," *MLR*, 76:2 (Apr 1981), 273-90.
Only after the publication of *A Vision* (1925) did Yeats begin to read philosophy seriously. The influence of Berkeley and Coleridge and of the correspondence with T. Sturge Moore is apparent in the 1937 version of the book, which gains thereby in philosophical clarity.

141. RAI, RAMA NAND: "A Study of W. B. Yeats's *A Vision*," *J of the School of Languages*, 6:1&2 (Monsoon 1978 & Winter 1978-79), 34-41.

142. SETHI, UMA K. BHOWANI: "W. B. Yeats and Reincarnation: A Study of Yeats's Use of the Hindu and Theosophical Concept of Reincarnation in His Works," Ph.D. thesis, U of Colorado, 1973. vii, 163 pp. (*DAI*, 34:12 [June 1974], 7782A)
Mainly on *A Vision*, some related poems, and *The Resurrection*.

143. SPIVAK, GAYATRI CHAKRAVORTY: "Some Theoretical Aspects of Yeats's Prose," *JML*, 4:3 (Feb 1975), 677-91.
Historiography and archetypism in *A Vision* and *Ideas of Good and Evil*.

144. STOCK, A. G.: "*A Vision* (1925 and 1937)," *IJES*, 1:1 (1960), 38-47.

145. SUTHERLAND, ALEXANDER CHARLES: "Yeats's Revisions of *A Vision:* A Study of the Text, with Appendices of Textual Variants and Annotations," Ph.D. thesis, New York U, 1978. v, 1243 pp. (*DAI*, 39:12 [June 1979], 7364A)
The annotations are valuable.

146. TEGTMEIER, RALPH: *Okkultismus und Erotik in der Literatur des*

Fin de Siècle. Königswinter: Tegtmeier, 1983. 140 pp.
"William Butler Yeats," 68-73; a note on hermaphroditism in *A Vision*.

147. THOMPSON, WILLIAM IRWIN: *At the Edge of History*. NY: Harper & Row, 1971. xi, 180 pp.
Notes on Yeats's view of history, especially in *A Vision*, pp. 76-78, 166-67, and passim.

148. YEATS, W. B.: *A Critical Edition of Yeats's "A Vision" (1925)*. Edited by George Mills Harper and Walter Kelly Hood. London: Macmillan, 1978. l, xxiii, 256, 108 pp.
"Editorial Introduction," xi-l (on the genesis of the book); explanatory "Notes," 1-108. For reviews see G1531-1536.

149. YEOMANS, EDWARD: "W. B. Yeats and the 'Electric Motor Vision,'" *Alphabet*, 7 (Dec 1963), 44-48.
On *A Vision*. Once Yeats had started the motor that drives the great wheel, he was unable to switch it off.

See also BA3, 14, BB138, 240, BG133, 218, CA4, 7, 10, 12, 17, 22, 26, 49, 53a, 60, 61, 66, 73, 77, 90, 91, 92, 99, 100, 103, 110, 111, 122, 125, 126, 128, 129, 130, CB5, 68, 152a, 371, 374, 527, CC5, 14a, 17, 29, 38, 91, 99, 107, 146, 181, 182, 190, 230, 290, 308, 311, 348, CD2, 3, 8, 22, 77, 78, 136, 143, 174, 224, 301, 322, 353, 358, 395, 604, 624, 628, 631, 643, 654, 658, 675, 720, 760, 809, 861, 880, 984, 1010-13, 1019, 1030, 1037, 1077, 1168, 1173, 1214, 1239, 1253, DA3, 16, 17, 22, 26, 42, 43, DB2, 10, 50, 136, 144, 172, 196, DC1, 15, 50, 59, 114, 145, 148, 188, 275, 300, 347, 387, DD15, 84a, 118, 124, 439, 575, 608, 614, 633, 675, 684, 692, 779, EA12, 13, 14, 24, EB87, EC29, 96, FA12, 14, FB1, 20, 24, 34, FC46, 47, 53, FD27, FE46, 48, G478-82, 551-53, 774-803, 1035-38 and note, 1531-36.

FD Political Writings and Activities

1. ADAMS, HAZARD: "Criticism, Politics, and History: The Matter of Yeats," *GaR*, 24:2 (Summer 1970), 158-82.
A discussion of sociopolitical interpretations in general, their applicability to Yeats, and a review of previously published criticism of his politics.

2. ANON.: "The Irish Literary Theatre: Interview with Mr. George Moore. He Wants the Censorship of the Church," *FrJ*, 13 Nov 1901, 5-6.
Yeats is mentioned passim. See his letter: "Mr. W. B. Yeats on the Value of Discussion: The Proposed Censorship," 15 Nov 1901, 4 (reprinted in *Letters*, pp. 356-57), and editorial commentary on the same page on Yeats's view of censorship.

3. ANON.: "Problem of Divorce: Dr. W. B. Yeats Replies to Bishops," *IrT*, 12 June 1925, 7.
See also the editorial on p. 6: "Divorce in the Free State."

4. ANON.: "Lively Exchanges," *IrT*, 8 Feb 1926, 6.
Patrick McCartan states that Yeats went to London to negotiate the abolition of the oath of allegiance. This is denied by Yeats and by President Cosgraves's office: "Letter from Senator Yeats," 9 Feb 1926, 5 (not in Wade).

5. ANON.: "The Bergin Trial [. . .]: Dr. Yeats and His Claims," *Phoblacht,* 20 June 1925, 3.
Condemns Yeats's views on divorce and his claim that he belongs to the tradition of Burke and Swift.

6. ANON.: "Thanks, Mr. Yeats," *Phoblacht,* 30 July 1926, 1.
"In Mr. Yeats's own words, the horrors of the civil war were inflicted upon the Irish people so that Mr. Cosgrave and his friends might 'remain on the friendliest of terms with royalty.'"

7. ANON.: "The Irish Scene 1925," *Round Table,* 15:60 (Sept 1925), 749-68.
Comments on Yeats's divorce speech, pp. 756-57.

8. ANON.: "Mr. Yeats and St. Thomas," *Standard* [Dublin], 29 Sept 1928, 12.
Criticizes Yeats's stand on the censorship bill.

9. ARNOLD, CARROLL C.: "Oral Rhetoric, Rhetoric, and Literature," *Philosophy & Rhetoric,* 1:4 (Fall 1968), 191-210.
Discusses Yeats's undelivered speech on divorce as an example of oral rhetoric (as opposed to literary rhetoric).
Reprinted in Eugene Edmond White (ed): *Rhetoric in Transition: Studies in the Nature and Uses of Rhetoric.* University Park: Pennsylvania State UP, 1980. x, 181 pp. (pp. 175-73).

10. AUDEN, W. H.: *The English Auden: Poems, Essays, and Dramatic Writings 1927-1939.* Edited by Edward Mendelson. London: Faber & Faber, 1977. xxv, 469 pp.
"The Public v. the Late Mr. William Butler Yeats," 389-93; reprinted from *PR,* 6:3 (Spring 1939), 46-51. The public prosecutor: Yeats did not care for the social problems of his time. The council for the defense: "However false or undemocratic his ideas, his diction shows a continuous evolution towards what one might call the true poetic style." No verdict is given.
"In Memory of W. B. Yeats," 241-43. The *LMerc* version of Auden's elegy (see HD5).

11. AUSUBEL, HERMAN: *In Hard Times: Reformers among the Late Victorians.* NY: Columbia UP, 1960. xi, 403 pp.
Some notes on Yeats's involvement in late 19th-century politics, passim (see index).

12. BLANSHARD, PAUL: *The Irish and Catholic Power: An American Interpretation.* Boston: Beacon Press, 1953. viii, 375 pp.
On Yeats's views of the relationship between the state and the Catholic church, pp. 25, 72-73, 89, 160-62. Written from an anti-Catholic point of view.

13. BODKIN, THOMAS: *Hugh Lane and His Pictures.* Dublin: Stationery Office for An Chomhairle Ealaion (The Arts Council), 1956 [1932]. xv, 96 pp. and 51 plates.
Refers to Yeats's defense of Lane's unwitnessed codicil.

14. BRADY, L. W.: "'The Beggars Have Changed Places': Revolution in Ireland," *Historical News,* 24 (May 1972), 9-13.
Comments on Yeats's political views.

15. BRATT, EYVIND: "Var Yeats fascist?" [Was Yeats a fascist?], *Göteborgs-posten,* 7 July 1984, page number not available.

16. BROWN, MALCOLM: *The Politics of Irish Literature: From Thomas Davis to W. B. Yeats*. London: Allen & Unwin, 1972. xii, 431 pp.

On Yeats, passim. See particularly "Enter: W. B. Yeats," 311-25, on his attitude toward the Irish/English problem and his connection with John O'Leary.

"Poetry Defends the Gap: Yeats and Hyde," 348-70 (the quarrel with Sir Charles Gavan Duffy and Yeats's nationalism, which Brown mistakenly considers to be "noteworthy for his laughable alienation from the Irish nation, past or present").

"Literary Parnellism," 371-90. Again the Yeats picture is distorted: Brown sees an undue selfdramatization whenever Yeats speaks of Parnell and concludes: "Yeats's practice demonstrated with resounding finality the untruth of his theory that whatever is well said must be so."

I have two main objections to this book: (1) its sloppy style substitutes for precise argument at crucial places; (2) the documentation is poor, especially that of the early Irish opposition to Yeats.

Reviews:

- Betty Abel: "Ireland in Literature," *ContempR*, 221:1280 (Sept 1972), 164-65.
- Anon.: "Political Characters and Literary Characters," *TLS*, 7 July 1972, 764.
- S. H. B., *Irish Booklore*, 2:2 (1976), 312-14.
- J. C. Beckett, *English Historical R*, 88:347 (Apr 1973), 398-99.
- Richard J. Finneran, *SHR*, 8:2 (Spring 1974), 257-59.
- Ian Fletcher, *N&Q*, os 219 / ns 21:1 (Jan 1974), 37-39.
- John Frayne, *JEGP*, 73:1 (Jan 1974), 141-44.
- Thomas Kinsella: "Literature and Politics in Ireland," *JML*, 3:1 (Feb 1973), 115-19.
- M. A. Klug, *DR*, 52:3 (Autumn 1972), 498-501.
- James J. McAuley, *Malahat R*, 28 (Oct 1973), 143-45.
- Donal McCartney: "Politics Their Fuel. . . ?" *IrI*, 13 May 1972, 8.
- Roger McHugh, *RES*, 25:97 (Feb 1974), 104-5.
- Norman H. MacKenzie, *QQ*, 80:3 (Autumn 1973), 481-82.
- John Mulcahy: "Romantic Ireland?" *Hibernia*, 14 Apr 1972, 12.
- Sean O'Faolain: "Genteel Dastards, Bellowing Slaves," *Guardian*, 25 May 1972, 16.
- Frances S. Smith, *Canadian J of Political Science*, 8:4 (Dec 1975), 593.
- Robert W. Uphaus, *Eire*, 8:3 (Autumn 1973), 151-53.

17. BYRNE, JOSEPH: Rejoinder to Yeats's speech on divorce, *Catholic Bulletin*, 15:7 (July 1925), 685.

17a. CAIRNS, DAVID, and SHAUN RICHARDS: *Writing Ireland: Colonialism, Nationalism and Culture*. Manchester: Manchester UP, 1988. x, 178 pp.

Extended discussion of Yeats's cultural nationalism and politics (see index).

18. CARDEN, MARY: "The Few and the Many: An Examination of W. B. Yeats's Politics," *Studies*, 58:229 (Spring 1969), 51-62.

18a. CHADWICK, JOSEPH: "Violence in Yeats's Later Politics and Poetry," *ELH*, 55:4 (Winter 1988), 869-93.

Asks "how and to what degree his work is involved with fascism."

19. CRAIG, ROBERT CAIRNS: *Yeats, Eliot, Pound, and the Politics of Poetry: Richest to the Richest*. London: Croom Helm, 1982. ix, 323 pp.
Based on °"W. B. Yeats, T. S. Eliot, and the Associationist Aesthetic," Ph.D. thesis, U of Edinburgh, 1978. Includes "The Continuity of Associationist Aesthetic: From Archibald Alison to T. S. Eliot (and Beyond)," *DR*, 60:1 (Spring 1980), 20-37.

Analyzes "the dynamics of the process that led Yeats, Eliot and Pound from a 'pure' poetry to a poetry of social involvement." This is done with the help of associationist psychology which "is entirely dependent on the power of memory" (p. 24). The reification of memory leads the three poets to a "justification for repressive political doctrines" (p. 289). Refers specifically to the Byzantium poems, "Easter 1916," "In Memory of Major Robert Gregory," "Leda and the Swan," "The Madness of King Goll," and "Nineteen Hundred and Nineteen."

Reviews:
- Bernard Bergonzi: "Modern Metamorphoses: From Ovid to Ezra Pound," *Encounter*, 61:1 (July-Aug 1983), 79-82.
- Haskell M. Block, *WHR*, 38:2 (Summer 1984), 186-89.
- Richard Burton, *YeA*, 3 (1985), 264-70.
- Seamus Deane: "Yeats and the Occult," *LRB*, 18-31 Oct 1984, 27.
- F. Farag, *CJIS*, 11:2 (Dec 1985), 87-88.
- Edward Hirsch, *Criticism*, 24:4 (Fall 1982), 398-400.
- Laurence Lerner: "The Illiberal Imagination," *NSt*, 5 Mar 1982, 23-24.
- Edward Neill: "Open Poem, Closed Society," *TES*, 21 Jan 1983, 31.
- James Olney: "Modernism, Yeats, and Eliot," *SR*, 92:3 (Summer 1984), 451-66.
- Marjorie Perloff: "The Politics of Modern Poetry," *ConL*, 25:1 (Spring 1984), 88-92.
- Allan Rodway, *N&Q*, os 228 / ns 30:6 (Dec 1983), 558-59.
- Hugh Witemeyer, *Yeats*, 1 (1983), 191-96.

20. CROSS, GUSTAV: "'My Hundredth Year Is at an End': Reflections on the Yeats Centenary," *Quadrant*, 10:39 (Jan-Feb 1966), 62-69.
Yeats and fascism.

21. CUANA: "Doctors Bodkin and Yeats in Their Animal Coinage Book," *Catholic Bulletin*, 21:4 (Apr 1931), 348-52.
Abusive.

22. CULLINGFORD, ELIZABETH M. S.: *Yeats, Ireland, and Fascism*. London: Macmillan, 1981. viii, 251 pp.
Based on "The Politics of W. B. Yeats," D.Phil. thesis, Oxford U, 1977. vi, 370 pp. Essentially a rebuttal of Conor Cruise O'Brien's charge that Yeats's political thinking was fascist from the beginning (see FD59). Actually, Yeats was always an ardent Irish nationalist who insisted on a close connection between his political thinking and his poetry. Describes the evolution of his political thought from the influence of O'Leary and Morris to the involvement with fascism and the late anarchy of *On the Boiler* as a consistent development. A good book, although occasionally onesided. See also FD30.

Reviews:
- Bernard Benstock: "The Soul of Yeats under Fascism," *ILS*, 2:1 (Spring 1983), 24.
- Reed Way Dasenbrock, *MLN*, 97:5 (Dec 1982), 1262-65.
- Gary Davenport: "Yeats and Belief," *SR*, 89:3 (Summer 1981), 469-73.

- Seamus Deane: "Blueshirt," *LRB*, 4-17 June 1981, 23-24.
- Richard J. Finneran: "Yeats's Politics," *Review*, 5 (1983), 59-68.
- Graham Good: "The Politics of Yeats and Joyce," *CJIS*, 9:1 (June 1983), 81-88.
- Brian John: "Yeats's Politics," *UTQ*, 51:3 (Spring 1982), 303-6.
- Declan Kiberd, *IUR*, 12:1 (Spring 1982), 122-23.
- F. S. L. Lyons: "The Poet as Politician," *TLS*, 15 May 1981, 550.
- ———, *YeA*, 2 (1983), 144-53.
- Conor Cruise O'Brien: "What Rough Beast?" *Obs*, 19 July 1981, 28.
- Maurice R. O'Connell, *Clio*, 13:3 (Spring 1984), 303-5.
- Brian Tippett, *L&H*, 9:1 (Spring 1983), 127-28.

23. DANGERFIELD, GEORGE: *The Damnable Question: A Study in Anglo-Irish Relations*. London: Constable, 1977. xvi, 400 pp.
On Yeats's nationalism, pp. 32-35, 107-8, 219-20, and passim (see index).

24. DAVIS, RICHARD P.: *Arthur Griffith and Non-Violent Sinn Fein*. Dublin: Anvil Books, 1974. xxi, 232 pp.
Yeats is mentioned passim (see index).

25. DONOGHUE, DENIS: "The Problem of Being Irish," *TLS*, 17 Mar 1972, 291-92.
Yeats's relationship with Irish literature and politics.

26. [ELIOT, T. S.]: "The Censorship: And Ireland," *Criterion*, 8:31 (Dec 1928), 185-87.
Comments on Yeats's article "The Irish Censorship" (see *Uncollected Prose*, 2:480-85 and FD83).

27. FARAG, FAHMY: *The Opposing Virtues: Two Essays. "Needless Horror or Terrible Beauty: Yeats's Ideas of Hatred, War and Violence" & "W. B. Yeats and the Politics of 'A Vision.'"* Dublin: Dolmen Press, 1978. 56 pp. (New Yeats Papers. 15.)
Incorporates "W. B. Yeats and the Politics of *A Vision*," *CJIS*, 1:1 (June 1975), 9-26; "The Poet as the Nation's Daimon: The Cabbalistic Politics of W. B. Yeats," *CJIS*, 2:2 (Dec 1976), 32-46; "W. B. Yeats's Politics in the Thirties," *ESC*, 2:4 (Winter 1976), 452-70 (partly reprinted as "The Staring Fury and the Blind Lush Leaf: Yeats and the Antinomial Nature of Energy," *J of English: Sana'a U*, 6 [Sept 1979], 1-21).
Reviews:
- Patrick Holland, *Mosaic*, 12:3 (Spring 1979), 171-75.
- Norman H. MacKenzie, *CJIS*, 4:2 (Dec 1978), 64-68.
- Patrick Rafroidi, *EI*, 3 (Dec 1978), 114-17.
- B[ernard] S[hare]: "Goodbye Byzantium," *BooksI*, 23 (May 1978), 77.

28. FITZPATRICK, DAVID: "Yeats in the Senate," *Studia Hibernica*, 12 (1972), 7-26.
A shortened and revised version appears in O'Driscoll and Reynolds: *Yeats and the Theatre*, (1975, CA81), 159-75.

28a. FOSTER, ROBERT FITZROY: *Modern Ireland 1600-1972*. London: Lane / Penguin Press, 1988. xiii, 688 pp.
Some references to Yeats (see index).

29. FREYER, GRATTAN: "The Politics of W. B. Yeats," *Politics and Letters*, 1:1 (Summer 1947), 13-20.
Especially on Yeats's fascist leanings and some relevant poems.

30. ———: *W. B. Yeats and the Anti-Democratic Tradition*. Dublin: Gill & Macmillan / Totowa, N.J.: Barnes & Noble, 1981. x, 143 pp.
The aim of the book "is to trace . . . the evolution of Yeats's political ideas and their interplay in the intellectual climate of his age." The last chapter reviews previous assessments of Yeats's political thought, notably those by Conor Cruise O'Brien (FD59) and Elizabeth Cullingford (FD22). A general rather than a scholarly, thesis-oriented book.
Reviews:
- Eavan Boland: "Last Romantic," *IrT*, 13 Feb 1982, 12.
- Richard J. Finneran: "Yeats's Politics," *Review*, 5 (1983), 59-68.
- David Fitzgerald: "Off Centre," *IrP*, 25 Feb 1982, 6.
- Wayne E. Hall, *VS*, 28:1 (Autumn 1984), 191-92.
- George Mills Harper, *MP*, 81:4 (May 1984), 435-40.
- F. S. L. Lyons, *Yeats*, 1 (1983), 196-98.
- Lucy McDiarmid: "Yeats and Democracy," *ILS*, 2:1 (Spring 1983), 23.
- Janet Madden-Simpson: "That Man's Scope," *BooksI*, 62 (Apr 1982), 59-60.
- Brian Martin: "Madly Elitist," *TLS*, 6 Aug 1982, 867.
- Tom Paulin, *NSt*, 5 Feb 1982, 24.
- Hilary Pyle, *RES*, 35:140 (Nov 1984), 576-77.
- Brian Tippett, *L&H*, 9:1 (Spring 1983), 127-28.

31. FRIAR, KIMON: "Politics and Some Poets," *NewRep*, 7 July 1952, 17-18.
Yeats and fascism.

32. GENET, JACQUELINE: "Yeats et la révolution," in Genet: *William Butler Yeats* (1981, CA32), 159-73.
Yeats's Irish nationalism and its reflection in his poetry.

33. GOETSCH, PAUL, and HEINZ-JOACHIM MÜLLENBROCK (eds): *Englische Literatur und Politik im 20. Jahrhundert*. Wiesbaden: Athenaion, 1981. vii, 196 pp. (Athenaion Literaturwissenschaft. 17.)
Lothar Hönnighausen: "Konservative Kulturkritik und Literaturtheorie zwischen den Weltkriegen: Yeats und Eliot," 95-110. On Yeats's right-wing cultural politics.

34. GOULD, WARWICK: "'Sordid' View of Yeats," *Obs*, 5 Feb 1984, 14.
Refers to Conor Cruise O'Brien's criticism of Yeats's alleged fascism in an article entitled "Why Machiavelli and I Are 'Sordid,'" 29 Jan 1984, 9.

35. GRAVES, ALFRED PERCEVAL: "The State and the Child," *IrSt*, 26 Dec 1925, 491-92.
Comments on Yeats's article "The Child and the State" (see *Uncollected Prose*, 2:454-61).

36. HAMILTON, ALASTAIR: *The Appeal of Fascism: A Study of Intellectuals and Fascism, 1919-1945*. Foreword by Stephen Spender. London: Blond, 1971. xxiii, 312 pp.
See pp. 278-80 and passim (see index).

37. HARPER, GEORGE MILLS: "Yeats's Intellectual Nationalism," *DM*,

4:2 (Summer 1965), 8-26.

Part of the article appeared as "Art and Propaganda in the Nationalism of William Butler Yeats" in Association internationale de littérature comparée / International Comparative Literature Association: *Actes du IVe Congrès / Proceedings of the IVth Congress*. Fribourg, 1964. Edited by François Jost. The Hague: Mouton, 1966. 2 vols. (1:245-53).

38. HARVIE, CHRISTOPHER: "Yeats and Irish Politics," *Feedback*, 1:1 (May 1966), 41-46.

"The most dangerous part of Yeats' political thought in his last years was not his 'elegant fascism' but his reawakening of interest in violent nationalism."

39. HASSAN, IHAB (ed): *Liberations: New Essays on the Humanities in the Revolution*. Middletown, Ct.: Wesleyan UP, 1971. xvi, 216 pp.

David Daiches: "Politics and the Literary Imagination," 100-116; contains some notes on Yeats.

40. HONE, J. M.: "Yeats as Political Philosopher," *LMerc*, 39:233 (Mar 1939), 492-96.

41. HORSLEY, LEE SONSTENG: "Song and Fatherland: W. B. Yeats and the Tradition of Thomas Davis 1886-1905," M.Phil. thesis, U of Reading, 1967. iv, 233 pp.

42. HOWLEY, JOHN: "Censorship and St. Thomas Aquinas," *IrSt*, 6 Oct 1928, 92-93.

Criticizes Yeats's article of that title (see *Uncollected Prose*, 2:477-80). Correspondence by A. E. F. Horniman, ibid., 93; by Yeats: "Wagner and the Chapel of the Grail," 13 Oct 1928, 112 (ibid., 2:485-86).

43. "IRIAL" [i.e. Frederick Ryan]: "Censorship and Independence," *United Irishman*, 23 Nov 1901, 3.

Criticizes Yeats's views as expressed in "The Proposed Censorship." See Yeats's answer: "Literature and the Conscience," 7 Dec 1901, 3 (in *Uncollected Prose*, 2:262-64); and again "Irial," 14 Dec 1901, 5.

43a. JOANNON, PIERRE: *Le rêve irlandais: Thèmes et figures du nationalisme irlandais*. La Gacilly: Artus, 1988. 212 pp.

This constitutes nos. 29-30 of the periodical *Artus*. See "Le rêve anglo-irlandais," 59-80, which is partly concerned with Yeats's Anglo-Irish nationalism.

44. JORDAN, JOHN: "Senator Yeats and Civil Rights," *Hibernia*, 14 Dec 1973, 16.

Yeats's defense of civil liberties was far ahead of his time, and it is only now that we begin to appreciate it. Correspondence by Maureen Ahern: "Silly Willy," 4 Jan 1974, 2.

45. KAIN, RICHARD M.: "Yeats and Irish Nationalism," in Maxwell and Bushrui: *W. B. Yeats 1865-1965* (1965, CA71), 54-61.

46. KRIMM, BERNARD G.: *W. B. Yeats and the Emergence of the Irish Free State 1918-1939: Living in the Explosion*. Troy, N.Y.: Whitston, 1981. xvii, 305 pp.

Based on a Ph.D. thesis with the same title, Northwestern U, 1974. ix, 379 pp. (*DAI*, 35:10 [Apr 1975], 6720A).

Discusses Yeats as political poet-counsellor to the Irish nation; analyzes "Nineteen Hundred and Nineteen," *The Dreaming of the Bones, The King's Threshold,* "Easter 1916," "The Rose Tree," "Sixteen Dead Men," "The Second Coming," "Reprisals," "Meditations in Time of Civil War," *The Trembling of the Veil, Stories of Michael Robartes and His Friends, Purgatory,* "Three Songs to the Same Tune," "Parnell's Funeral," *The Herne's Egg* (as an anti-De Valera play), *On the Boiler, The King of the Great Clock Tower,* "Roger Casement," "The Curse of Cromwell," and associated works in their political contexts. Also on the public function of the Abbey Theatre, the censorship question, the Irish Academy of Letters, and Yeats's alleged fascist leanings. Valuable, but no index.

Reviews:
- Craig Wallace Barrow, *Eire,* 18:3 (Fall 1983), 147-49.
- Seamus Deane, *YES,* 15 (1985), 330-31.
- Richard J. Finneran: "Yeats's Politics," *Review,* 5 (1983), 59-68.
- George Mills Harper, *MP,* 81:4 (May 1984), 435-40.
- Declan Kiberd, *IUR,* 12:1 (Spring 1982), 122-23.
- F. S. L. Lyons, *YeA,* 2 (1983), 144-53.
- Janet Madden-Simpson: "That Man's Scope," *BooksI,* 62 (Apr 1982), 59-60.
- Hilary Pyle, *RES,* 35:139 (Aug 1984), 411-12.

47. LYND, ROBERT: "Poets as Patriots," *British R,* 6:2 (May 1914), 264-80.
An article based on Yeats's contention in *Ideas of Good and Evil* (in "What Is 'Popular Poetry'?") that patriotism is something like "an impure desire in an artist."

48. LYONS, FRANCIS STEWART LELAND: *Ireland since the Famine: 1850 to the Present.* London: Weidenfeld and Nicolson, 1971. xiii, 852 pp.
"The Battle of Two Civilisations," 219-42; on Yeats's role in Irish politics, pp. 229-42, and passim (see index).

49. MCCARTAN, PATRICK: "William Butler Yeats--the Fenian," *Ireland-American R,* 1:3 [1940?], 412-20.
An expanded version of "Yeats--the Patriot," *National Student,* 29:5 (Mar 1939), 8-10. Reprinted in CD763. Yeats was never a sworn member of the Irish Republican Brotherhood, but he regarded himself as one. He was introduced into the IRB by John O'Leary, who had also entered it without being sworn in. The Fenians, in turn, always supported Yeats.

50. MACCOLL, D. S.: "The National Gallery Bill, and Sir Hugh Lane's Bequest," *Nineteenth Century and After,* 81:480 (Feb 1917), 383-98.
Refutes Yeats's views about Lane's codicil.

51. MALINS, EDWARD: *Yeats and the Easter Rising.* No. 1 of *DPYCP* (1965, CA20), 1-28. (Illustrated)
Reprinted in *MR,* 7:2 (Spring 1966), 271-84. Discusses the effect of the Easter Rising on Yeats's political convictions and his poetry.

52. MARLOWE, N.: "The Silence of Mr. Yeats," *New Ireland,* 31 July 1915, 187-89.
In political matters.

53. METSCHER, PRISCILLA: *Republicanism and Socialism in Ireland: A*

Study in the Relationship of Politics and Ideology from the United Irishmen to James Connolly. Frankfurt/Main: Lang, 1986. vii, 617 pp. (Bremer Beiträge zur Literatur- und Ideologiegeschichte. 2.)
Contains a section on the "Irish language and literary renaissance," pp. 260-68, which includes some comments on Yeats.

54. MOHR, MARTIN ALFRED: "The Political and Social Thought of William Butler Yeats," Ph.D. thesis, State U of Iowa, 1964. iii, 302 pp. (*DAI*, 25:4 [Oct 1964], 2497-98)

55. MOORE, WILLIAM: Letter to the editor, *IrSt*, 9 Aug 1924, 690.
On Yeats's dialogue "Compulsory Gaelic" (in *Uncollected Prose*, 2:439-49). Correspondence by Hewson Cowen, 16 Aug 1924, 724.

56. MORRIS, JOHN A.: "Fascist Ideas in English Literature," *Patterns of Prejudice*, 13:4 (July/Aug 1979), 22-31; 13:5 (Sept/Oct 1979), 25-34, 36.
On Yeats in 13:4.

57. NAG, GOURIE: "W. B. Yeats and Politics: Some Approaches," Ph. D. thesis, U of Edinburgh, 1969 [i.e., 1970]. xv, 413 pp.
Contains chapters on Yeats's relationship with his father, the Fenian identity (John O'Leary), aristocratic socialism (William Morris), Maud Gonne (including notes on *The Countess Cathleen* and the love poems), Parnell (with notes on relevant poems), and the fascist phase (Yeats and Kevin O'Higgins); also "Reference Outline of W. B. Yeats's Political Activities and Interests, 1885-1939."

58. NORMAN, EDWARD: *A History of Modern Ireland*. London: Allen Lane / Penguin Press, 1971. 330 pp.
See index for a few deprecatory notes on Yeats's political views.

59. O'BRIEN, CONOR CRUISE: "Passion and Cunning: An Essay on the Politics of W. B. Yeats," in Jeffares and Cross: *In Excited Reverie* (1965, CA48), 207-78.
Incorporates "Yeats and Fascism: What Rough Beast," *NSt*, 26 Feb 1965, 319-22; "Passion and Cunning," *IrT*, 10 June 1965, iv; "Yeats and Irish Politics," *TriQ*, 4 [Fall 1965], 91-98. Reprinted in *TriQ*, 23/24 (Winter/Spring 1972), 142-203.
A highly controversial piece; O'Brien argues that there is no break between Yeats's poetry and politics, which became increasingly authoritarian and fascist in later years. Many reviews of CA48 take issue with O'Brien's analysis; see especially those by Cosgrave, Donoghue, Empson, Fraser, and Kramer. See also FD22, 30, and 72.

60. ———: *States of Ireland*. London: Hutchinson, 1972. 336 pp.
"Songs of the Irish Race," 48-64; on Yeats's early political involvement and the reception of *The Countess Cathleen*. See also pp. 69-71 on *Cathleen ni Houlihan* and passim (see index).

61. Ó BROIN, LEON: *Revolutionary Underground: The Story of the Irish Republican Brotherhood 1858-1924*. Dublin: Gill & Macmillan, 1976. x, 245 pp.
See index for notes on Yeats's involvement.

62. ———: "Cúlra réabhlóideach W. B. Yeats," *Galvia*, 11 (1977), 32-53.
"WBY's revolutionary background."

63. O'CONNOR, ULICK: *A Terrible Beauty Is Born: The Irish Troubles 1912-1922*. London: Granada, 1981 [1975]. 192 pp.
On Yeats's political activities, passim (the index is unreliable).

64. O'REILLY, JAMES P.: "A Reply to Mr. Yeats," *IrSt,* 28 Mar 1925, 73-74.
Criticizes Yeats's "An Undelivered Speech," on divorce (in *Uncollected Prose,* 2:449-52).

65. O'SULLIVAN, DONAL: *The Irish Free State and Its Senate: A Study in Contemporary Politics*. London: Faber & Faber, 1940. xxxi, 666 pp.
On Yeats's Senate activities, passim (see index), especially on his speech on divorce (pp. 167-68): "This extraordinary speech was happily unique in the history of the senate . . . it poisoned the atmosphere that surrounded the question of divorce."

66. PRESS, JOHN: *The Lengthening Shadows*. London: Oxford UP, 1971. ix, 191 pp.
Defends Yeats against those critics who find his attitude toward 20th-century politics and social issues reactionary and pernicious, passim (see index).

67. QUINN, PETER A.: "Yeats and Revolutionary Nationalism: The Centenary of '98," *Eire,* 15:3 (Fall 1980), 47-64.
Yeats's involvement in the Irish Republican Brotherhood and the Irish National Brotherhood.

68. RUTHVEN, K. K.: "On the So-Called Fascism of Some Modernist Writers," *SoRA,* 5:3 (Sept 1972), 225-30.
Includes Yeats.

69. SADDLEMYER, ANN: "'The Noble and the Beggarman': Yeats and Literary Nationalism," in Skelton and Saddlemyer: *The World of W. B. Yeats* (1967, CA102), 6-23.
Particularly in the 1880s and 1890s.

70. SHEEHY, MICHAEL: *Is Ireland Dying? Culture and the Church in Modern Ireland*. NY: Taplinger Publishing Co., 1968. 256 pp.
On Yeats, passim (see index), especially pp. 120-28: Yeats's view of "paganism as earthy, potent, creative, and Christianity as lofty, transcendental but humanly negative" originated in the "anti-human policy" of the Irish Catholic church, which "specially contributed to Yeats's failure to achieve a unified system, since it was on Ireland his hopes were specially centred."

71. SHEERAN, P. F.: "Colonists and Colonized: Some Aspects of Anglo-Irish Literature from Swift to Joyce," *YES,* 13 (1983), 97-115.
Notes Yeats's ambiguous reaction to the colonizer-colonized dilemma of the Anglo-Irish.

72. SPENDER, STEPHEN: *The Thirties and After: Poetry, Politics, People (1933-75)*. London: Macmillan, 1978. 286 pp.
"W. B. Yeats: *A Vision*," 34-36; reprint of G799. "Notes on Revolutionaries and Reactionaries," 186-208; reprinted from *PR,* 34:3 (Summer 1967), 359-81; criticizes Harrison (CB190) and O'Brien (FD59).

73. STANFIELD, PAUL SCOTT: *Yeats and Politics in the 1930s*. London: Macmillan, 1988. x, 227 pp.
Based on "W. B. Yeats and Politics in the 1930s," °Ph.D. thesis,

Northwestern U, 1984. 469 pp. (*DAI*, 45:12 [June 1985], 3648A-49A; reprinted *Yeats*, 4 [1986], 181-82). Contains chapters on Yeats and de Valera, the Blueshirt episode, "Yeats, Socialism and Tragedy" (O'Casey, the *Oxford Book of Modern Verse*, and war poetry), "Yeats and Balzac," and "Yeats and Eugenics," including a discussion of *On the Boiler*. Analyzed in sections DD and EE.

74. STANFORD, W. B.: "Yeats in the Irish Senate," *REL*, 4:3 (July 1963), 71-80.
Criticizes Pearce's edition of *Senate Speeches* (W211R/S) and adds some thoughts on Yeats's politics.

75. STENFERT KROESE, W. H.: "Yeats en het fascisme," *Litterair paspoort*, 6:52 (Dec 1951), 225-26.

76. THOMPSON, FRANCIS JOHN: "Fenianism and the Celtic Renaissance," Ph.D. thesis, New York U, 1940 (for 1941). xxxv, 1281 pp.
On Yeats, passim.

77. TIERNEY, MICHAEL (ed): *Daniel O'Connell: Nine Centenary Essays*. Dublin: Browne & Nolan, 1949. vii, 306 pp.
John J. Horgan criticizes Yeats's view of O'Connell as expressed in the Senate speech of 11 June 1925 (pp. 275-76).

78. TIERNEY, WILLIAM: "Irish Writers and the Spanish Civil War," *Eire*, 7:3 (Autumn 1972), 36-55.
Contains a note on Yeats's attitude, pp. 50-51.

79. WHITE, TERENCE DE VERE: "The Social Mask of the Poet," *IrT*, 10 June 1965, iii-iv.
Yeats's aristocratic ideals and political vagaries.

80. WITT, MARION: "'Great Art Beaten Down': Yeats on Censorship," *CE*, 13:5 (Feb 1952), 248-58.

81. WOODMAN, KIERAN: *Media Control in Ireland 1923-1983*. Carbondale: Southern Illinois UP, 1985. viii, 248 pp.
See index for some notes on Yeats's views on censorship.

82. YEATS, MICHAEL: "Yeats: The Public Man," *SoR*, 5:3 (July 1969), 872-85.
More precisely, Yeats as an Irish nationalist.

83. YEATS, W. B.: "The Irish Censorship," *Spect*, 29 Sept 1928, 391-92.
Correspondence by William McCarthy, 6 Oct 1928, 435-36; Padraig Ua h'Eichthighearnan and H. Strachey, 13 Oct 1928, 488; Areopagitica, 20 Oct 1928, 528; Ezra Pound, 1 Dec 1928, 819. Yeats's article is reprinted in *Uncollected Prose*, 2:480-85; see FD26.

84. ———: *The Senate Speeches*. Edited by Donald R. Pearce. Bloomington: Indiana UP, 1960. 183 pp.
"Introduction," 11-26, comments on Yeats's political career and discusses the relationship of imagination and politics in Yeats's speeches. The book also contains the congratulations for the Nobel Prize award, mainly by Oliver St. John Gogarty, pp. 153-55. For reviews see G1076-1092 and FD74.

85. ———: *W. B. Yeats and the Designing of Ireland's Coinage*.

Texts by W. B. Yeats and others, edited with an introduction by Brian Cleeve. Dublin: Dolmen Press, 1972. 76 pp. (New Yeats Papers. 3.)

Contents: Brian Cleeve: "The Yeats Coinage," 5-8.

WBY: "What We Did or Tried to Do," 9-20.

J. J. McElligott: "Irish Coinage Past and Present," 21-24.

Leo T. McCauley: "From the Summary of the Proceedings of the Committee," 25-39.

Thomas Bodkin: "The Irish Coinage Designers. A lecture delivered at the Metropolitan School of Art, Dublin, 30th November, 1928," 40-54.

Thomas Bodkin: "Postscript to *Coinage of Saorstat Eireann,* 1928," 55-60.

Arthur E. J. Went: "The Coinage of Ireland, 1000 A.D. to the Present Day," 61-67.

Brian Cleeve: "Afterword," 68-75; short biographies of the competitors.

Items 2-4 and 6 are reprinted from *Coinage of Saorstat Eireann* (Wade 317). For the Yeats scholar the book is of little interest, since Cleeve's introduction fails to discuss Yeats's work on the coinage committee in the context of his life and work.

For reviews see G1512-1513. N.B.: Yeats's portrait now graces the £20 note of the Central Bank of Ireland.

See also BA10, BB66, 170, 217, BE4, 34, 35, 40, 54, 61, 68, 76, 82, 85, 99, 102, 111, 113, 114, 120, 124-26, 130, 134, BF56, 78, 100, 102, 105, 127, 131, 138, 153, 159, 168, 179, BG89, CA38, 40, 48, 49, 53a, 55, 65, 74, 77, 118, 151, 154, 156, 161, CB100, 114, 122, 135, 149a, 168, 185, 190, 194, 231, 258, 276, 325, 439, 440, 498, 507, CC21, 26, 42, 46, 71, 85, 86, 104, 109, 116, 120, 149, 152, 155a, 160a, 183, 191, 192, 198, 199, 201, 221, 232-34, 236, 241, 274, 322, 340, CD40, 668, 763, 773, 876, 879, 919, 958, 962, 973-76, 1029, 1041, 1045, 1428, CE26, DA13, 22, 46, DB252, DC64, 116, 127, 158, 163, 170, 230, 239, 248, 258, 271, 349, DD198, 199, 210a, 383, 597, 600, 648, EB90, 115, EE168, 281, FA1, 63, 64, FG42, G971, 1076-92, 1512-13, 1642.

FE Theory and Criticism of Poetry and Literature

1. ACHARYA, PRADIP: "Some Observations on Yeats as a Critic," *Dibrugarh UJ of English Studies,* 2 (1978), 112-24.

2. ADAMS, HAZARD: "Yeats, Dialectic, and Criticism," *Criticism,* 10:3 (Summer 1968), 185-99.

The dialectic of subjectivity and objectivity in Yeats's thought and his ideas about the dichotomy of literature and science.

3. ADAMS, J. DONALD: "Speaking of Books," *NYTBR,* 13 Feb 1944, 2.

Discusses Yeats's views of art and the artist.

4. ———: "Speaking of Books," *NYTBR,* 9 June 1946, 2.

Discusses Yeats's ideas on the moral element in literature.

5. AGARWALA, D. C.: "Yeats's Concept of Image," *Triveni,* 36:2 (July 1967), 23-35.

On Yeats's use of the term in his prose and poetry. For Yeats, images "form the content of which symbols are the only fitting and successful medium of communication." His "images" have little in common with Imagism.

6. ANON.: Critical note on Yeats's articles on "Irish National Literature," *FrJ,* 5 Aug 1895, 4.
The *Bookman* articles (see *Uncollected Prose,* 1:359-64).

7. ANON.: "At the 'Historical': An Outsider on Professor Dowden," *Saturday Herald,* 2 Mar 1895, 4.
Dowden's and the reporter's opinion of Yeats's list of the thirty best Irish books (see *Uncollected Prose,* 1:351).

8. BALFOUR, BARBARA LOUISE: "The Poetic Theory of W. B. Yeats, 1885-1939," Ph.D. thesis, U of Kansas, 1977. iv, 168 pp. (*DAI,* 38:7 [Jan 1978], 4154A)

9. BARTLETT, DONALD RADFORD: "William Butler Yeats as a Literary Critic," Ph.D. thesis, Memorial U of Newfoundland, 1972. vii, 266 pp. (*DAI,* 34:11 [May 1974], 7219A)

10. BEDIENT, CALVIN: "A New Anthology of Old-Fashioned Modern Poetry," *NYTBR,* 17 June 1973, 4-5.
A review of Philip Larkin's *Oxford Book of Twentieth-Century English Verse,* including frequent comparisons with Yeats's anthology.

11. BERWIND, SANDRA MURRAY: "The Origin of a Poet: A Study of the Critical Prose of W. B. Yeats, 1887-1907," Ph.D. thesis, Bryn Mawr College, 1968. iv, 247 pp. (*DAI,* 29:11 [May 1969], 3998A-99A)

12. BEYETTE, THOMAS KENT: "Symbolism and Victorian Literature," °Ph.D. thesis, U of Texas at Austin, 1969. 197 pp. (*DAI,* 30:12 [June 1970], 5440A)
Includes a discussion of Yeats's symbolist theories.

13. BLOCK, HASKELL M.: "Some Concepts of the Literary Elite at the Turn of the Century," *Mosaic,* 5:2 (Winter 1971/72), 57-64.
Compares Yeats's concept of the literary elite with that of Mallarmé and George.

14. BRATER, ENOCH: "W. B. Yeats: The Poet as Critic," *JML,* 4:3 (Fall 1975), 651-76.

15. BROOKS, CLEANTH: *The Language of the American South.* Athens: U of Georgia Press, 1986. xi, 58 pp. (Mercer U Lamar Memorial Lectures. 28.)
Concludes with a note on Yeats's view of the oral tradition, pp. 53-54.

16. BRUCH, HERMANN: *W. B. Yeats: Dichterische Theorie zwischen Isolation und Integration.* Bern: Lang, 1975. viii, 228 pp. (Europäische Hochschulschriften. Reihe XIV: Angelsächsische Sprache und Literatur. 31.)
Based on a Dr.phil. thesis, U of Marburg, 1974. Discusses the question whether Yeats's development is characterized by continuity or ruptures; looks primarily at his critical writings, but also at some poems and plays. Reviewed by R. Breugelmans, *RBPH,* 60:3 (1982), 760-63 (in English).

17. CHRIST, CAROL T.: *Victorian and Modern Poetics.* Chicago: U of Chicago Press, 1984. ix, 178 pp.
The moderns are Eliot, Pound, and Yeats. Discusses Yeats's indebtedness to A. H. Hallam and his views on history, the mask,

and the image. Reviewed by Daniel A. Harris, *Yeats,* 4 (1986), 192-99.

18. COSGROVE, BRIAN: "Arnold, Mangan, Blake, Yeats and the Vindication of the Subjective Inspiration," *Gaéliana,* 8 (1986), 63-73.

19. CRONIN, JOHN: *The Anglo-Irish Novel. Volume One: The Nineteenth Century.* Belfast: Appletree Press, 1980. 197 pp.

Volume two not yet published. Contains some remarks on Yeats's views of the Irish novelists (see index).

20. DAVIS, ROBERT BERNARD: "The Shaping of an Agate: A Study of the Development of the Literary Theory of W. B. Yeats from 1885 to 1910," Ph.D. thesis, U of Chicago, 1956. iii, 239 pp.

Yeats's literary theory is based on the "belief that literature is the expression of the moods, or the emotional states which constitute reality, through symbols" (p. 6). Discusses among others this basic theory, the Irish element (folklore, legend, the literary revival, the Irish theater), aestheticism and symbolism (the importance of Blake, the Rhymers' Club, Pater, and French symbolism, as well as the fin de siècle element), Yeats's dramatic theories, and his defense of Synge.

21. DETELIĆ, MIRJANA: "Simbolistički koreni jejtsove književne teorije" [The symbolist roots of Y's literary theory], *Književna reč,* 29 (1974), 19.

22. DION, SISTER CLARICE DE SAINTE MARIE: *The Idea of "Pure Poetry" in English Criticism, 1900-1945.* Washington, D.C.: Catholic U of America, 1948. iv, 137 pp.

On Yeats's criticism of "impurities" ("curiosities about politics, about science, about history, about religion") in relation to A. C. Bradley's idea of poetry for poetry's sake, pp. 15-16 and passim (see index).

23. EGLINTON, JOHN, W. B. YEATS, A. E., and WILLIAM LARMINIE: *Literary Ideals in Ireland.* London: Unwin, [1899]. i, 88 pp.

Reprinted NY: Lemma, 1973. Reprint of a controversy on Irish national literature published in the *Daily Express* [Dublin]:

Eglinton: "What Should Be the Subjects of a National Drama?" 9-13 (10 Sept 1898, 3).

Yeats: "A Note on National Drama," 17-20 (24 Sept 1898, 3).

Eglinton: "National Drama and Contemporary Life?" 23-27 (8 Oct 1898, 3).

Yeats: "John Eglinton and Spiritual Art," 31-37 (29 Oct 1898, 3).

Eglinton: "Mr. Yeats and Popular Poetry," 41-46 (5 Nov 1898, 3).

A. E.: "Literary Ideals in Ireland," 49-54 (12 Nov 1898, 3).

Larminie: "Legends as Material for Literature," 57-65 (19 Nov 1898, 3).

Yeats: "The Autumn of the Flesh," 69-75 (3 Dec 1898, 3).

A. E.: "Nationality and Cosmopolitanism in Literature," 79-88 (10 Dec 1898, 3); reprinted in DB211.

For reviews see G1273-1280.

24. *Englische und amerikanische Lyrik des 20. Jahrhunderts im weltliterarischen Kontext.* Beiträge der Arbeitsberatung vom 28. bis 30. April 1980 in Ahrenshoop zur Bestimmung von Ziel und Methode des Forschungsprojekts. Rostock: Wilhelm-Pieck-Universität, Sektion Sprach-

und Literaturwissenschaft, 1981. 128 pp.
Wolfgang Wicht: "William Butler Yeats und das widerspruchsvolle Gegenbild der Kunst" [WBY and the contradictory counterpart of art], 46-56; on Yeats's views of the social function of art.

25. ERZGRÄBER, WILLI, and PAUL GOETSCH (eds): *Mündliches Erzählen im Alltag, fingiertes mündliches Erzählen in der Literatur*. Tübingen: Narr, 1987. 206 pp. (ScriptOralia. 1.)
K. P. S. Jochum: "W. B. Yeats und die mündliche irische Überlieferung," 136-53; discusses Yeats's preoccupation with the oral Irish tradition in theory and practice, especially in *The Celtic Twilight*.

26. FALLIS, RICHARD CARTER: "The Poet as Critic: The Literary Criticism of W. B. Yeats," Ph.D. thesis, Princeton U, 1972. x, 497 pp. (*DAI*, 33:8 [Feb 1973], 4410A-11A)
Includes chapters on Yeats's career as literary critic, the style and structure of his critical prose, his theory of literature, the relationship to English literature past and contemporary (especially Blake and Shelley), and to Irish literature and culture; also a "Selective Index to Yeats's Criticism."

27. ———: "'I Seek an Image': The Method of Yeats's Criticism," *MLQ*, 37:1 (Mar 1976), 68-81.
Yeats's method "of criticism via portraiture or image-making" is indebted to his father and to Pater.

28. FARAG, FAHMY: "Forcing Reading and Writing on Those Who Want Neither: W. B. Yeats and the Irish Oral Tradition," *CJIS*, 11:2 (Dec 1985), 7-15.

29. FAULKNER, PETER: "The Sources of the Literary Criticism of W. B. Yeats," [M.A. thesis, U of Birmingham, 1960?]. vi, 192, iv pp.
The sources are J. B. Yeats, the Romantic tradition, Irish nationalism, Blake, Arthur Hallam, Arthur Symons, Villiers de l'Isle Adam, Synge, Nietzsche, Lady Gregory, Pound, Wyndham Lewis, the Irish 18th century, and Indian mysticism.

30. ———: "Yeats as Critic," *Criticism*, 4:4 (Fall 1962), 328-39.
A survey of Yeats's criticism from the earliest reviews to 1934. Maintains that Yeats contradicted himself considerably at different times, but that there is always "the continuity of his concern with unity."

31. ———: "Yeats as a Reviewer: *The Bookman*, 1892-1899," *IrB*, 2:3/4 (Autumn 1963), 115-21.

32. FINNERAN, RICHARD J.: "Yeats and the *Bookman* Review of *The Chain of Gold*," *PLL*, 9:2 (Spring 1973), 194-97.
Prints and discusses the anonymous review of Standish O'Grady's book, attributed to Yeats (reprinted in *Uncollected Prose*, 2:515).

33. FOSTER, JOHN WILSON: "Yeats and the Folklore of the Irish Revival," *Eire*, 17:2 (Summer 1982), 6-18.
Cultural nationalists such as Yeats believed that "Irish folklore could be reborn as literature," but this is questionable.

34. FURBANK, PHILIP NICHOLAS: *Reflections on the Word "Image."* London: Secker & Warburg, 1970. vii, 160 pp.
Note on Yeats's use of the word "image," pp. 32-33.

35. GLASSIE, HENRY (ed): *Irish Folktales*. NY: Pantheon, 1985. xvii, 357 pp.

The "Introduction," 3-29, includes a discussion of Yeats's interest in Irish folktales. See also "Notes," 337-53.

36. GRIFFITHS, ERIC: "Writing and Speaking: The Work of Eliot, Yeats and Pound," Ph.D. thesis, Cambridge U, 1980. v, 234 pp.

The attitudes of these poets "to the voicing of their poems" (abstract). See especially "Yeats's Performance," 47-85.

37. HANSON, CLARE: *Short Stories and Short Fictions, 1880-1980*. London: Macmillan, 1985. viii, 189 pp.

Contains some notes on the importance of Yeats's theory of the imagination, especially on pp. 83-85. Does not discuss Yeats's own fiction.

38. °HASKELL, DENNIS: "The Poetic Theory and Practice of W. B. Yeats," Ph.D. thesis, U of Sydney (Australia), 1982.

39. HILL, JOHN EDWARD: "Dialectical Aestheticism: Essay on the Criticism of Swinburne, Pater, Wilde, James, Shaw, and Yeats," °Ph.D. thesis, U of Virginia, 1972. 147 pp. (*DAI*, 33:7 [Jan 1973], 3648A-49A)

40. HOFFMAN, DANIEL G., and SAMUEL HYNES (eds): *English Literary Criticism: Romantic and Victorian*. London: Owen, 1968 [1963]. xi, 322 pp.

Note on Yeats and symbolism, pp. 312-13.

41. HÜTTEMANN, GERTA: "Wesen der Dichtung und Aufgabe des Dichters bei William Butler Yeats," Dr.phil. thesis, U of Bonn, 1929. 88 pp.

"WBY's views of the concept of poetry and the function of the poet." Discusses the influence of the French symbolists and of Henry More.

Reviews:

- Karl Arns, *NS*, 40:7 (Oct 1932), 441.
- C. Garnier, *Revue anglo-amèricaine*, 7:3 (Feb 1930), 271-72.
- Helene Richter, *Beiblatt zur Anglia*, 42:2 (Feb 1931), 52-54.
- Jakob Walter, *Deutsche Literaturzeitung*, 23 Aug 1930, 1600-1602.

42. INNES, C. L.: "Language in Black and Irish Nationalist Literature: The Media versus the Message," *MR*, 16:1 (Winter 1975), 77-91.

Discusses Yeats's views on the use of the English language by Irish writers.

43. JACKSON, THOMAS H.: "Herder, Pound, and the Concept of Expressionism," *MLQ*, 44:4 (Dec 1983), 374-93.

Includes comments on Yeats's symbolist theories.

44. JAGGI, SATYA DEV: *Coleridge's and Yeats' Theory of Poetry*. Delhi: Cosla, 1967. vi, 109 pp.

Not a comparison of both critics, but a collection of independent essays. The Yeats section (pp. 73-106) is subheaded "Poetry as Personal Utterance," "Poetry and the Buried Self," "Unity of Being and the Poet's World," "Art and Impersonality," "Poetry and Truth," "Theory of Symbolism," and "Poetry and Morality."

45. JAIN, VIRENDRA VIJAI: *W. B. Yeats as Literary Critic*. Delhi: Atma Ram, 1980. vi, 322 pp.

Incorporates "Yeats's Contributions to Blake Criticism," *IJES*, 15 (1974), 54-62; includes chapters on Yeats's view of symbolism, the dramatic theories, and the *Oxford Book of Modern Verse*. A somewhat unfocused and unattractive study; see also the review by Edward Engelberg, *YeA*, 2 (1983), 154-58.

46. KHAN, JALILUDDIN AHMAD: "The Role of Intellect in Yeats's Imagination," *Venture*, 1:1 (Mar 1960), 58-69.
Includes a discussion of *A Vision* and of the Yeats--Sturge Moore correspondence.

47. KIRKHAM, MICHAEL: "The Edwardian Critical Opposition," *UTQ*, 45:1 (Fall 1975), 19-34.
Contains notes on Yeats's literary criticism.

48. KOMESU, OKIFUMI: *The Double Perspective of Yeats's Aesthetic*. Gerrards Cross: Smythe / Totowa, N.J.: Barnes & Noble, 1984. 200 pp. (Irish Literary Studies. 20.)
Based on "W. B. Yeats: Vision and Experience," Ph.D. thesis, Michigan State U, 1968. vii, 216 pp. (*DAI*, 29:6 [Dec 1968], 1900A). Maintains that Yeats was a "dualist" in his philosophy, aesthetic theory, and creative work. His involvement in Hindu thought and the Nō are part of this dualism. Discusses *A Vision*, "Certain Noble Plays of Japan," *At the Hawk's Well, Calvary, The Dreaming of the Bones, The Only Jealousy of Emer*, and, briefly, several poems.
Reviews:
- Hazard Adams, *Yeats*, 4 (1986), 206-9.
- Edward Engelberg, *YeA*, 5 (1987), 267-70.
- Jacqueline Genet, *EI*, 11 (1986), 244.
- Justine Johnstone, *Hermathena*, 138 (Summer 1985), 82-83.
- Peter van de Kamp, *IUR*, 15:1 (Spring 1985), 108-11.
- Declan Kiberd: "Taking Stock of Yeats," *TLS*, 13 Feb 1987, 166.
- Janet Madden-Simpson: "All Arts and Parts," *BooksI*, 91 (Mar 1985), 36-37.
- Andrew Parkin: "Drama East and West," *CJIS*, 12:1 (June 1986), 79-84.
- Anthony Roche, *SHR*, 20:3 (Summer 1986), 271-73.

49. LANHAM, JON: "Some Further Textual Problems in Yeats: *Ideas of Good and Evil*," *PBSA*, 71:4 (Oct-Dec 1977), 453-72.
Discusses the publication history and the authority (some of it questionable) for the changes that the text underwent in the process.

50. LEHMANN, ANDREW GEORGE: *The Symbolist Aesthetic in France, 1885-1895*. Oxford: Blackwell, 1950. viii, 328 pp.
Yeats on symbolism, pp. 281-85 and passim.

51. °LENOSKI, DANIEL STANLEY: "The Poet as Priest: Some Aspects of Yeats's Aesthetics 1885-1910," Ph.D. thesis, Queens U (Kingston, Ont.), 1974. xi, 365 pp.

52. ———: "The Descent from the Mountain: A Study of the Relationship between the Aesthetic Theory of W. B. Yeats and His Post-1900 Change in Poetic Style," *CJIS*, 2:1 (May 1976), 21-31.

53. ———: "The Symbolism of Rhythm in W. B. Yeats," *IUR*, 7:2 (Autumn 1977), 201-12.

54. ———: "The Symbolism of Sound in W. B. Yeats: An Explanation," *EI*, (Dec 1978), 47-55.

55. LENTRICCHIA, FRANK RICHARD: *The Gaiety of Language: An Essay on the Radical Poetics of W. B. Yeats and Wallace Stevens*. Berkeley: U of California Press, 1968. x, 213 pp. (Perspectives in Criticism. 19.)

Based on "The Poetics of Will: Wallace Stevens, W. B. Yeats, and the Theoretic Inheritance," °Ph.D. thesis, Duke U, 1966. 225 pp. (*DAI*, 27:5 [Nov 1966], 1373A). Yeats rejected the romantic and symbolist theories of poetry and created a "poetics of will and impersonation" that is "framed in tragic awareness" (p. 62) and that prescribes the making of poetry as the poet's assertion of freedom. Comments on the early stories and several poems, particularly the Byzantium poems and "Lapis Lazuli."

Reviews:
- Robert J. Bertholf, *SoRA*, 3:4 (1969), 378-80.
- Philip Le Brun, *RES*, 21:82 (May 1970), 239-40.
- Laurence Lieberman: "Poet-Critics and Scholar-Critics," *Poetry*, 115:5 (Feb 1970), 346-52 (pp. 350-51).
- Joseph N. Riddel, *JEGP*, 68:4 (Oct 1969), 718-23.

56. LIPKING, LAWRENCE I.: *The Life of the Poet: Beginning and Ending Poetic Careers*. Chicago: U of Chicago Press, 1981. xvi, 243 pp.

"Per Amica Silentia Lunae," 47-64; on Yeats's version of the life of the poet in *Per Amica Silentia Lunae*. See also "Auden on Yeats," 151-60; and passim (see index). Reviewed by E. P. Bollier, *Yeats*, 1 (1983), 202-6.

57. LOMAS, HERBERT: "The Critic as Anti-Hero: War Poetry," *HudR*, 38:3 (Autumn 1985), 376-89.

Includes notes on Yeats's view of war poetry.

58. LUCAS, JOHN: *Romantic to Modern Literature: Essays and Ideas of Culture 1750-1900*. Brighton: Harvester Press, 1982. vii, 231 pp.

"From Naturalism to Symbolism," 188-205; first published in *Renaissance and Modern Studies*, 21 (1977), 124-39; see also CB127. Includes notes on Yeats's view of symbolism.

59. LUDOWYK, EVELYN FREDERICK CHARLES: *Marginal Comments*. Colombo: Ola Book Co., 1945. viii, 148, xxii pp.

Comments on Yeats's theory of the symbol and the two Byzantium poems, pp. 58-69.

60. LUNDGAARD, LYNN: "The Importance of the Visual Arts in the Esthetic of W. B. Yeats," Ph.D. thesis, U of Oklahoma, 1980. iii, 281 pp. (*DAI*, 41:5 [Nov 1980], 2104A; reprinted *YeA*, 1 [1982], 217-18)

Discusses the influence of Blake, Pater, and the Pre-Raphaelites.

61. MCBRIDE, JOHN DENNIS: "Primal and Bardic: The Role of Ireland in Yeats' Early Aesthetics," Ph.D. thesis, U of Illinois, 1967. v, 236 pp. (*DAI*, 28:12 [June 1968], 5062A)

Claims that the struggle between permanence and flux, apparent in the later Yeats, is also important in the early work, where the retreat into the Irish fairyland signifies the futile search for permanence. Mainly on the early criticism and poetry.

62. MACDONOGH, CAROLINE: "La notion de chant chez Yeats," in Genet: *William Butler Yeats* (1981, CA32), 275-80.

Yeats's interest in song structures.

63. [M'GRATH, JOHN]: "North and South," *United Ireland,* 18 Aug 1894, 1.
Re Yeats's "Some Irish National Books." See his letter, 1 Sept 1894, 1; reprinted in *Uncollected Prose,* 1:339-40 (together with a note by M'Grath), and in *Collected Letters,* 1:397-98.

64. MADDEN, REGINA DOROTHY: "The Literary Criticism of the Irish Renaissance," Ph.D. thesis, Boston U, 1938. ii, 297 pp.
See pp. 44-79.

65. MADDEN, WILLIAM A.: "The Divided Tradition in English Criticism," *PMLA,* 73:1 (Mar 1958), 69-80.
Notes on Yeats and the relationship between poetry and religion, passim.

66. MAN, PAUL DE: "Lyric and Modernity," *Selected Papers from the English Institute,* 1969, 151-76.
On the preface to the *Oxford Book of Modern Verse,* pp. 155-58.

67. [MATHER, FRANK JEWETT]: "Mute, Inglorious Literature," *Nation,* 25 Oct 1906, 344.
On Yeats's essay "Literature and the Living Voice."

68. MEIR, COLIN: "A la recherche d'un language naturel," in Genet: *William Butler Yeats* (1981, CA32), 262-74.
Natural language in Yeats's poetry theory and practice.

69. ———: "Yeats's Early Nationalism," *Gaéliana,* 8 (1986), 75-90.
In the early critical prose, especially that on Allingham, Ferguson, and Katharine Tynan.

70. Olkyrn, I. [i.e., MILLIGAN, ALICE]: "Literature and Politics," *United Ireland,* 16 Dec 1893, 1.
Letter about a National Literary Society meeting; refers to Yeats's views about Irish literature. Correspondence by Yeats, 23 Dec 1893, 5; 30 Dec 1893, 1; reprinted in *Uncollected Prose,* 1:305-10, and in *Collected Letters,* 1:369-74.

71. MONK, DONALD EDWARD: "Symbolist Tendencies in English Poetics (1885-1930)," Ph.D. thesis, U of Manchester, 1966. 466 pp.
"W. B. Yeats," 190-250.

72. MÜLLER, JOACHIM (ed): *Gestaltung Umgestaltung: Festschrift zum 75. Geburtstag von Hermann August Korff.* Leipzig: Koehler & Amelang, 1957. 291 pp.
Wolfgang Kayser: "W. B. Yeats: 'Der dichterische Symbolismus,' übersetzt und erläutert von Wolfgang Kayser," 239-48. A translation of "The Symbolism of Poetry," together with some explanatory notes.

73. NIMMO, DAVID CLARENCE: "Yeats's Metaphors of the Mind," Ph.D. thesis, U of Newcastle, 1977. x, 352 pp.
Mirror and lamp as metaphors of the mind in Yeats's assessment of literary history in the introduction to the *Oxford Book of Modern Verse,* as well as in the poetry, "Rosa Alchemica," *The Shadowy Waters, The Hour-Glass,* and *Where There Is Nothing / The Unicorn from the Stars.*

74. ORR, LEONARD: "Yeats's Theories of Fiction," *Eire,* 21:2 (Summer 1986), 152-58.

75. PARRINDER, PATRICK: *Authors and Authority: A Study of English Literary Criticism and Its Relation to Culture 1750-1900*. London: Routledge & Kegan Paul, 1977. viii, 199 pp.
Note on Yeats's place in 19th-century literary criticism, pp. 168-72.

76. POLLETTA, GREGORY THOMAS: "The Progress in W. B. Yeats's Theories on Poetry," Ph.D. thesis, Princeton U, 1961. vii, 576 pp. (*DAI*, 22:7 [Jan 1962], 2399-400)

77. PRASAD, BAIDYA NATH: "Letters of W. B. Yeats to Katharine Tynan--A Study," *IJES*, 11 (1970) 87-98.
Mostly on Yeats's ideas about literature as expressed in these letters.

78. ———: *The Literary Criticism of W. B. Yeats*. New Delhi: Classical Publishing Company, 1985. xiii, 257 pp.
Includes chapters on the Romantic and the Victorian background, the influence of John Butler Yeats, O'Leary, Pater, Wilde, and Nietzsche, Yeats's idea of symbolism, and his theory of drama.

79. PUTZEL, STEVEN D.: "Towards an Aesthetic of Folklore and Mythology: W. B. Yeats, 1888-1895," *SFQ*, 44 (1980), 105-30.

80. RAI, RAMA NAND: *W. B. Yeats: Poetic Theory and Practice*. Salzburg: Institut für Anglistik und Amerikanistik, Universität Salzburg, 1983. v, 210 pp. (Salzburg Studies in English Literature: Poetic Drama and Poetic Theory. 54.)
Contains chapters on Yeats's "thematic concept of poetry," his "concept of style and technique," and on his poetic theory as applied to selected poems, particularly "Among School Children," "Byzantium," "Cuchulain Comforted," "Sailing to Byzantium," "The Second Coming," "The Tower," "Under Ben Bulben," and "The Wanderings of Oisin."
Reviews:
- E. P. Bollier, *Yeats*, 3 (1985), 249-52.
- Andrew Parkin, *CJIS*, 10:1 (June 1984), 147-51.

81. ROSENBLATT, LOUISE: *L'idée de l'art pour l'art dans la littérature anglaise pendant la période victorienne*. Paris: Champion, 1931. 328 pp. (Bibliothèque de littérature comparée. 70.)
Some references to Yeats, pp. 291-93 and passim (see index).

82. RUBIN, MARTIN HEYMAN: "Yeats's Critical Viewpoint in His Last Decade," Ph.D. thesis, U of Virginia, 1976. i, 144 pp. (*DAI*, 37:5 [Nov 1976], 2901A)
Mainly on Yeats's introduction to the *Oxford Book of Modern Verse*, his treatment of Pater, Wilde, and the "central tradition of English poetry" in his anthology, and his refusal to include the war poets.

83. RUDRA, A.: "Imagination, Symbol and Magic: A Note on Yeats's Early Essays," *IJES*, 15 (1974), 63-69.

84. SENA, VINOD: *The Poet as Critic: W. B. Yeats on Poetry, Drama and Tradition*. Delhi: Macmillan of India, 1980. xv, 232 pp.
Also published as *W. B. Yeats: The Poet as Critic*. London: Macmillan, 1981. Based on "The Poet as Critic: W. B. Yeats on Poetry, Drama, and Tradition," Ph.D. thesis, Cambridge U, 1970. xi, 406 pp.

Incorporates: "Yeats on the Possibility of an English Poetic Drama," *MD,* 9:2 (Sept 1966), 195-205; a plea for Yeats as dramatic theorist. See also note by Rupin W. Desai, *MD,* 11:4 (Feb 1969), 396-99.

"W. B. Yeats & the Indian Way of Wisdom," *Quest* [Bombay], 62 (July-Sept 1969), 76-77; on the influence of Mohini Chatterjee.

"W. B. Yeats and the Storm-Beaten Threshold," *DM,* 8:4&5 (Summer/Autumn 1970), 56-75; discusses Yeats's view of war poetry, the influence of Arnold, and his theory of tragedy.

"Catharsis or Ecstasy: W. B. Yeats on Tragedy," *LCrit,* 11:3 (Winter 1974), 17-28; based in part on the preceding item.

"The Poet as Critic: The Relevance of Yeats's Literary Criticism," *LCrit,* 12:4 (1977), 18-32.

"W. B. Yeats and the Victorians: Two Case Studies," *LCrit,* 14:2 (1979), 9-25; the influence of Browning and A. H. Hallam.

"W. B. Yeats, Matthew Arnold and the Critical Imperative," *VN,* 56 (Fall 1979), 10-14. Also in Srivastava and Dutta: *Unaging Intellect* (1983, CA108), 176-87.

"W. B. Yeats, Personality and Tradition," *Humanities R,* 2:1 (Jan-Mar 1980), 24-28.

"W. B. Yeats on the Critic in the Poet," *J of Literary Studies,* 3:2 (Dec 1980), 25-33.

Reviews:

- Eavan Boland: "Yeats as a Critic," *IrT,* 8 May 1982, 12.
- Maureen Corrigan: "Yeats as Critic," *ILS,* 2:1 (Spring 1983), 21.
- Edward Engelberg, *YeA,* 2 (1983), 154-58.
- D. G. Gillham, *U of Cape Town Studies in English,* 13 (Nov 1983), 72-74.
- Ragini Ramachandra, *LCrit,* 16:2 (1981), 90-93.
- Rajiva Verma: "Yeats as a Critic," *Humanities R,* 3:1 (Jan-June 1981), 38-40.

85. SHAW, IAN CHARLES: "W. B. Yeats and the Quest for the Iconic Mode," Ph.D. thesis, U of Toronto, 1973. x, 287 pp. (*DAI,* 35:9 [Mar 1975], 6110A-11A)

A study of Yeats's aesthetic ideas.

86. SHERMAN, DEBORAH ANNE: "Yeatsian Talk: The Critical Theory of W. B. Yeats and the Victorian Background," Ph.D. thesis, Brown U, 1982. vi, 424 pp. (*DAI,* 43:11 [May 1983], 3606A; reprinted *Yeats,* 2 [1984], 262, and *YeA,* 4 [1986], 318-19)

Discusses the concepts of "reverie," "mood," and "emotion of multitude."

87. SHMIEFSKY, MARVEL: *Sense at War with Soul: English Poetics (1865-1900).* The Hague: Mouton, 1972. 172 pp. (De Proprietatibus Litterarum. Series Maior. 13.)

Based on "English Poetic Theory: 1864-1900," Ph.D. thesis, New York U, 1964. iii, 235 pp. (*DAI,* 27:5 [Nov 1966], 1345A-46A). "W. B. Yeats: Ideas of Good and Evil (1896-1903)," 131-44, and passim (see index).

88. SINGH, BHIM: "W. B. Yeats on Modern Poetry," *Kurukshetra U Research J,* 2:1 (Dec 1967--Jan 1968), 23-29.

Particularly on Eliot.

89. SINGH, BRIJRAJ: *The Development of a Critical Tradition from Pater to Yeats.* New Delhi: Macmillan, 1978. vii, 147 pp.

Based on "A Study of the Concepts of Art, Life, and Morality in

the Criticism of Five Writers from Pater to Yeats," °Ph.D. thesis, Yale U, 1971. 242 pp. (*DAI*, 32:6 [Dec 1971], 3331A-32A). Discusses Yeats's influence on Symons's view of symbolism, pp. 59-80; Yeats's poetics, pp. 104-41.
See review by Ragini Ramachandra, *LCrit*, 16:3 (1981), 70-74.

90. SLOAN, BARRY: *The Pioneers of Anglo-Irish Fiction 1800-1850*. Gerrards Cross: Smythe / Totowa, N.J.: Barnes & Noble, 1986. xxxvii, 277 pp. (Irish Literary Studies. 21.)
See index for some references to Yeats's comments on the early Anglo-Irish novelists.

91. SMALL, IAN C.: "Yeats and Johnson on the Limitations of Patriotic Art," *Studies*, 63:252 (Winter 1974), 379-88.
Lionel Johnson's essay "Poetry and Patriotism" influenced Yeats, who wrote an essay with the same title and published both in *Poetry and Ireland* (Wade 242).

92. SO, SUSAN SUK-NING: "Modern Verse Defined by W. B. Yeats: A Comparative Study of Romance, Tragedy, and the Lyric, with an Introduction to Tu Fu and His Antithetical Tradition," °Ph.D. thesis, Princeton U, 1982. 493 pp. (*DAI*, 43:8 [Feb 1983], 2660A; reprinted *Yeats*, 2 [1984], 258-59, and *YeA*, 4 [1986], 319-20)

93. STALLWORTHY, JON: "Yeats as Anthologist," in Jeffares and Cross: *In Excited Reverie* (1965, CA48), 171-92.
The making of the *Oxford Book of Modern Verse*, including previously unpublished memos from the publisher's files and Yeats letters.

94. STANFORD, DEREK (ed): *Critics of the 'Nineties*. London: Baker, 1970. 244 pp.
"W. B. Yeats, 1865-1939," 120-26: "Yeats's achievement, as a critic of the 'nineties, lies in two fields: his attempt to provide the Celtic Renaissance with a rough and ready working-body of ideas, as bearing on contemporary Irish letters, and his formulation of Symbolism--a French and Continental poetic--largely in terms of the Irish background and his occult studies."

94a. STOREY, MARK (ed): *Poetry and Ireland since 1800: A Source Book*. London: Routledge, 1988. viii, 221 pp.
See "Introduction," 5-31, on Yeats's place in Irish literature; the book contains six extracts from his early critical prose.

95. SULLIVAN, CHARLES WILLIAM: "The Influence of Celtic Myth and Legend on Modern Imaginative Fiction," Ph.D. thesis, U of Oregon, 1976. vi, 206 pp. (*DAI*, 37:9 [Mar 1977], 5979A-80A)
The first chapter (pp. 1-21) comments on Yeats's essay "The Celtic Element in Literature."

96. TAKAMATSU, YUICHI: [In Japanese] "The Situation of Yeats in 1906," *SELit*, 43:2 (Mar 1967), 197-213.
English summary, pp. 295-96. Discusses the concept of "oratory."

97. TAYLOR, ESTELLA RUTH: *The Modern Irish Writers: Cross Currents of Criticism*. NY: Greenwood Press, 1969 [1954]. ix, 176 pp.
Based on °"Mutual Criticism in the Modern Irish School of Literature," Ph.D. thesis, Northwestern U, 1946. A study of the literary criticism that the poets and writers of the revival (including Yeats) wrote about their colleagues and about themselves,

arranged thematically (e.g., "The Expatriate Considered," "The Irish Mind and Character," "The Attitude toward the English," "The Language Problem").

98. THEALL, DONALD F.: "Communication Theories in Modern Poetry: Yeats, Pound, Eliot, and Joyce," Ph.D. thesis, U of Toronto, 1954. iii, 429 pp.

"W. B. Yeats: Magic, Communication, and the *Anima Mundi*," 1-73.

99. TURNER, W. J.: "Yeats and Song-Writing," *NSt,* 22 Apr 1939, 606-7.

100. TUVESON, ERNEST LEE: *The Imagination as a Means of Grace: Locke and the Aesthetics of Romanticism.* Berkeley: U of California Press, 1960. v, 218 pp.

Note on Yeats's concept of symbolism and aestheticism, pp. 194-98.

101. UEDA, MAKOTO: *Zeami, Bashō, Yeats, Pound: A Study in Japanese and English Poetics.* The Hague: Mouton, 1965. 165 pp. (Studies in General and Comparative Literature. 1.)

Based on a °Ph.D. thesis, U of Washington, 1961. 179 pp. (*DAI,* 22:11 [May 1962], 4007-8). "W. B. Yeats: Imagination, Symbol, and the Mingling of Contraries," 65-89; an exposition of Yeats's thought that does not venture very far beyond paraphrase. The final chapter, "Toward a Definition of Poetry," 124-56, compares the four writers' theories. Reviewed by Earl Miner, *CL,* 18:2 (Spring 1966), 176-77.

102. WARNER, ERIC, and GRAHAM HOUGH (eds): *Strangeness and Beauty: An Anthology of Aesthetic Criticism 1840-1910.* Cambridge: Cambridge UP, 1983. 2 vols.

"William Butler Yeats (1865-1939)," 2:158-209, 288-91; an introduction (pp. 158-62) and annotated extracts from Yeats's critical writings. Includes an extract from Symons's "Mr. W. B. Yeats" (CB474), 2:240-42.

103. WARSCHAUSKY, SIDNEY: "W. B. Yeats as Literary Critic," Ph.D. thesis, Columbia U, 1957. x, 314 pp. (*DAI,* 17:7 [1957], 1559-60)

Includes a discussion of Yeats's theory of tragedy.

104. WELLEK, RENÉ: *A History of Modern Criticism: 1750-1950. Volume 5: English Criticism, 1900-1950.* New Haven: Yale UP, 1986. xxiv, 343 pp.

"W. B. Yeats," 1-13 (part of a chapter "Symbolism in English") and passim (see index). For further Yeats references see index to *Volume 6: American Criticism, 1900-1950.* New Haven: Yale UP, 1986. viii, 345 pp.

105. WIEGNER, KATHLEEN KNAPP: "W. B. Yeats and the Ritual Imagination," Ph.D. thesis, U of Wisconsin, 1967. vi, 244 pp. (*DAI,* 28:12 [June 1968], 5077A-78A)

106. WIMSATT, WILLIAM KURTZ, and CLEANTH BROOKS: *Literary Criticism: A Short History.* London: Routledge & Kegan Paul, 1965 [1957]. xviii, 755, xxii pp.

On Yeats, passim (see index), especially pp. 597-606. The discussion centers on the concepts of imagination and knowledge in Yeats's literary criticism, philosophy, and poetry.

107. WITT, MARION: "Yeats on the Poet Laureateship," *MLN*, 66:6 (June 1951), 385-88.
On the unsigned "The Question of the Laureateship" (in *Collected Letters*, 1:324-26).

108. WOODCOCK, GEORGE: "Old and New Oxford Books: The Idea of an Anthology," *SR*, 82:1 (Winter 1974), 119-30.
Notes on Yeats's *Oxford Book of Modern Verse*, passim.

108a. ———: "Kinds of Combat: Notes on Writers and the War," *Event*, 15:2 (1986), 5-18.
Contains some notes on Yeats's view of war poetry.

109. YEATS, W. B.: *Letters to the New Island*. Edited with an introduction by Horace Reynolds. London: Oxford UP, 1970 [1934]. xii, 222 pp.
"Introduction," 3-66. Discusses Yeats's early preoccupation with Irish literature and theater and the relationship with and influence of John O'Leary, Blake, Hyde, Todhunter, the Rhymers' Club, Florence Farr, Maud Gonne, and others, and his role in the Irish literary revival. For reviews see G633-652.

110. ———: *Selected Criticism*. Edited with an introduction and notes by A. Norman Jeffares. London: Macmillan, 1970 [1964]. 295 pp.
"Introduction," 7-16; "Notes," 273-92.

111. ———: "Language and Rhythm in Poetry: A Previously Unpublished Essay by W. B. Yeats," *Shenandoah*, 26:4 (Summer 1975), 77-79.
Introductory note by Richard Fallis.

112. ———: "A Critical Edition of *Ideas of Good and Evil* by W. B. Yeats, with Complete Collation, Notes and Commentary." Edited by Jon Alan Lanham. Editor's Ph.D. thesis, U of Toronto, 1976. x, 582 pp. (*DAI*, 39:3 [Sept 1978], 1551A-52A)
"Introduction," 1-71; "Textual History," 72-120; "Bibliographical Description of the Texts," 121-39; also textual and explanatory notes and an index.

113. ——— (ed): *Representative Irish Tales*. Compiled, with an introduction and notes by W. B. Yeats and a foreword by Mary Helen Thuente. Gerrards Cross: Smythe, 1979. 364 pp.
"Foreword," 7-20, revised in CC324. Discusses the criteria underlying Yeats's selection, especially his view of the Irish peasant. See also "A List of Sources," 21-23. For reviews see G1542-1545.

114. ———: *Funde: Ausgewählte Essays*. Auswahl, Nachwort und Anmerkungen von Wolfgang Wicht. Leipzig: Kiepenheuer, 1980. 279 pp.
"Nachwort," 198-221 (on Yeats's literary theories); "Anmerkungen," 222-76 (detailed notes).

115. ———: *Selected Criticism and Prose*. Edited with an introduction and notes by A. Norman Jeffares. London: Pan Books, 1980. xx, 15-554 pp.
The book is a conflation of *Selected Criticism* (W211DD) and *Selected Prose* (W211CC); the introduction (pp. ix-xx) is new.

116. ———: *Explorations*. Textes choisis par Mrs. W. B. Yeats. Traduction du Centre de littérature, linguistique et civilisation des pays de langue anglaise de l'Université de Caen sous la direction de

Jacqueline Genet. Lille: Presses universitaires de Lille, 1981. iv, xix, 427 pp. (Traduit de l'irlandais. 5.)

J. Genet: "Introduction," iii-xiv. See also G1546.

117. ———: *La taille d'une agate et autres essais.* Présentation par Pierre Chabert, traduction du Centre de littérature, linguistique et civilisation des pays de langue anglaise de l'Université de Caen sous la direction de Jacqueline Genet. Paris: Klincksieck, 1984. 290 pp.

P. Chabert: "Présentation," 7-22; on Yeats's literary theories. P. Chabert and Sandra Solov: "Glossaire," 241-87; a glossary of names.

118. ———: *Essais et introductions.* Traduction du Centre de littérature, linguistique et civilisation des pays de langue anglaise de l'Université de Caen sous la direction de Jacqueline Genet. Lille: Presses universitaires de Lille, 1985. 257 pp.

J. Genet: "Introduction," 9-28. Most of the essays are followed by explanatory notes. See also G1653.

119. ———: "Uil'i͡am Batler Ĭeĭts ob iskusstve," *Voprosy literatury,* 1 (Jan 1987), 174-204.

"WBY on art"; a collection of extracts from Yeats's prose, selected, translated, and introduced (pp. 174-80) by A. Livergant.

See also BB170, BE37, 62, 72, 104, 116, BF3, 22, 35, 44, 53, 59-62, 71, 77a, 79, 81, 88, 113, 121, 123, 139, 146, 152, 174, 186, CA14, 27, 31, 49, 57, 61, 69, 88, 92, 110, CB41, 70, 80, 160, 194, 202, 242, 295, 332, 467, CC28, 45, 55, 58, 63, 165, 168, 173, 182, 185, 187, 203, 208, 212, 232, 233, 239, 247, 250, 274, 285, 324, 341, CD7, 14, 37, 57, 58, 96, 110, 138, 224, 239, 240, 249, 250, 254, 266, 268, 320, 386, 529, 647, 653a, 707, 712, 758, 772, 817, 872, 876, 885, 970, 980, 992, 1015, 1048, 1077, 1138, 1154, 1173, 1214, 1220, 1222, 1223, 1238, 1240, 1241, 1285, 1302, 1325, 1405, 1415, 1428, 1441, 1448, 1454, 1455, DA10, 19, 21, 30, 35, 42, DB24, 28, 32, 46, 51, 80, 94, 166, 253, DC2, 13, 16, 68, 140, 251, 398, 420, DD199, 489, EA29, EB69, EC5, FA1, 17, 18, 20, 35, FB16, 30, FC53, 64, 100, 101, 143, FD17a, 19, 33, 37, 69, 73, FF3, G196-221 and note, 315-17, 387-90, 454-65 and note, 633-52 and note, 804-5, 1093-1129 and note, 1136-45, 1176-92, 1198-1242 and note, 1290-1319 and note, 1405-11 and note, 1417-48 and note, 1653.

FF "Speaking to the Psaltery"

1. ANON.: "Samhain Festival," *FrJ,* 28 Oct 1902, 6.

A Speaking to the Psaltery performance.

2. ANON.: "Samhain," *FrJ,* 3 Nov 1902, 6.

A review of a performance by Florence Farr and a report of a speech by Yeats.

3. ANON.: "'Speaking to the Psaltery': Mr. W. B. Yeats in Manchester," *MGuard,* 19 May 1903, 7.

A summary of Yeats's speech and a review of Florence Farr's performance, followed by a favorable comment of the paper's music critic on Yeats's conception of the relation between music and poetry.

4. ANON: "Words and Music," *Musical News,* 11 Feb 1905, 129-30.

Criticizes Yeats's efforts as "archaic."

5. ANON.: "Mr. Yeats's Method of Reciting," *Sphere*, 21 June 1902, 278.

6. ARCHER, WILLIAM: "Sing-Songing and Song-Singing," *Morning Leader*, 7 June 1902, 4.

7. BAUGHAN, E. A.: "The Chanting of Poems," *Outlook* [London], 21 Jan 1905, 89-90.
Yeats's theory is shaky, Florence Farr's performance childish.

8. CHESTERTON, G. K.: "Mr. Yeats and Popularity," *Daily News*, 16 May 1903, 8.
Yeats's speaking to the psaltery, which purports to revive a "popular art," isn't popular at all but a "modern paradox of eccentric sanity."

9. FARR, FLORENCE: *The Music of Speech, Containing the Words of Some Poets, Thinkers and Music-Makers Regarding the Practice of the Bardic Art Together with Fragments of Verse Set to Its Own Melody.* London: Mathews, 1909. ii, 27 pp.
Dedicated to Yeats. Contains quotations from various articles and reviews about herself, Yeats, and the recitals, extracts from her own writings on the subject, and fragments of poems set to musical notes (no Yeats poem included). See also HC334.

10. HERFORD, C. H.: "Speaking to the Psaltery," *MGuard*, 9 May 1903, 8.

11. JOHNSON, JOSEPHINE A.: "The Music of Speech: Florence Farr and W. B. Yeats," *LPer*, 2:1 (Nov 1981), 56-65.

12. MALINS, EDWARD: *Yeats and Music*. No. 12 of *DPYCP* (1968, CA20), 481-508.
Incorporates "Yeats and the Bell-Branch," *Consort*, 21 (Summer 1964), 287-98. On Florence Farr's "Speaking to the Psaltery" experiments and on the music in Yeats's plays, particularly that specifically written for them.

13. [NEVINSON, H. W.]: "Daily Chronicle Office," *Daily Chronicle*, 18 Feb 1901, 5.

14. R[UNCIMAN], J. F.: "At the Alhambra and Elsewhere," *SatRL*, 23 Feb 1901, 236-37.
Includes an account of Yeats's "cantilating" recitals.

15. S., H. A.: "The Art of the Chaunt," *Westminster Gazette*, 18 Jan 1905, 2.
The theory is "plausible enough," but the result was "sadly disappointing."

16. SCHUCHARD, RONALD: "The Minstrel in the Theatre: Arnold, Chaucer, and Yeats's New Spiritual Democracy," *YeA*, 2 (1983), 3-24.
Yeats's dreams of a theater of speech and a revived oral culture were conceived in opposition to Arnold and prompted by his reading of Chaucer in 1905. Quotes from newspaper reports of Yeats speeches and "Speaking to the Psaltery" performances.

17. ———: "'As Regarding Rhythm': Yeats and the Imagists," *Yeats*, 2 (1984), 209-26.
Florence Farr and her Speaking to the Psaltery experiment is a

connecting link between Yeats and the Imagists. Refers frequently to Ezra Pound and T. E. Hulme.

18. SYMONS, ARTHUR: *Plays, Acting and Music: A Book of Theory.* London: Constable, 1909 [1903]. xii, 323 pp.
"The Speaking of Verse," 173-81, not contained in the 1903 edition, reprinted from *Academy,* 31 May 1902, 559. Maintains that Yeats's theory differs greatly from Florence Farr's performance. See Yeats's reply, 7 June 1902, 590-91 (reprinted in *Letters,* pp. 373-74).

See also BE5, BF25, 65, BG73, CD434, DB46, 47, DC420, EB22, 90, 156, EF24, FE36, FG24, HC334, HD3.

FG Theory of Drama and Tragedy

1. *Academy Papers.* Addresses on the Evangeline Wilbour Blashfield Foundation of the American Academy of Arts and Letters. NY: Scribner's, 1925-51. 2 vols.
George Pierce Baker: "Speech in Drama," 2:19-38; on Yeats, pp. 34-35.

2. ARCHER, WILLIAM: "Study and Stage: 'Words That Sing and Shine,'" *Morning Leader,* 7 Jan 1905, 4.
Takes exception to Yeats's criticism in "The Play, the Player, and the Scene," that Ibsen has no "words that sing and shine" but agrees that more plays should be written that qualify in this respect.

3. ARRELL, DOUGLAS HARRISON: "The Old Drama and the New: Conceptions of the Nature of Theatrical Experience in the Work of William Archer, G. B. Shaw, W. B. Yeats, E. G. Craig, and H. Granville Barker," Ph.D. thesis, U of London, 1976. 544 pp.
"The Poetic Theatre of W. B. Yeats," 197-285; on Yeats's dramatic theory, some plays, and the problems of their production.

4. BAIRD, JAMES: *Ishmael.* Baltimore: Johns Hopkins Press, 1956. xxviii, 446 pp.
Note on Yeats's thoughts about the Nō, pp. 70-71.

5. BAKER, GEORGE PIERCE: "Rhythm in Recent Dramatic Dialogue," *YR,* 19:1 (Sept 1929), 116-33.
Contains notes on how Yeats wished a dialogue to be spoken.

6. BAKSI, PRONOTI: "Yeats and Eliot as Theorists of Contemporary Drama: A Comparative Study," M.A. thesis, U of London, 1965 [i.e., 1966]. 286 pp.

7. BARNES, T. R.: "Yeats, Synge, Ibsen, and Strindberg," *Scrutiny,* 5:3 (Dec 1936), 257-62.
Yeats's dramatic ideals compared with those of Synge, Ibsen, and Strindberg.

8. BLAKE, WARREN BARTON: "The Theater and Beauty," *Independent,* 23 Feb 1914, 271.
On Yeats's lecture "The Theatre of Beauty."

9. BLAU, HERBERT: "W. B. Yeats and T. S. Eliot: Poetic Drama and Modern Poetry," Ph.D. thesis, Stanford U, 1954. vi, 671 pp. (*DAI,*

14:3 [1954], 523-24)
Discusses Yeats's dramatic theories (which he finds similar to Eliot's) and his plays, pp. 174-429.

10. *Cahiers d'Aran,* 1 (Spring 1969), [17 pp.].
A periodical issued by the Théâtre d'Aran (1, square Rocamadour, Paris 16e), directed by Isabelle Garma. The theater expressly derives its principles of staging and acting from Yeats and intends to produce several Yeats plays, among others *On Baile's Strand,* which is discussed on [p. 9]. No other issue of the periodical seems to have been published.

11. CALENDOLI, GIOVANNI: "La polemica teatrale di W. Buttler [sic] Yeats: I limiti del realismo nell'arte dell'attore," *Fiera letteraria,* 11 Nov 1962, 5.
Yeats's dramatic theory as influenced by the Nō.

12. CARLSON, MARVIN: *Theories of the Theatre: A Historical and Critical Survey, from the Greeks to the Present.* Ithaca: Cornell UP, 1984. 529 pp.
Note on Yeats as a theorist of symbolist drama, pp. 304-6.

13. CHADWICK, JOSEPH KEENE: "Yeats: The Politics and Aesthetics of Tragedy," °Ph.D. thesis, U of California, Berkeley, 1983. 358 pp. (*DAI,* 45:3 [Sept 1984], 848A; reprinted *Yeats,* 3 [1985], 214-15)

14. CHENEY, SHELDON: *The Art Theater: Its Character as Differentiated from the Commercial Theater; Its Ideals and Organization; and a Record of Certain European and American Examples.* NY: Knopf, 1925 [1917]. ix, 281 pp.
Scattered references to Yeats's dramatic theories (see index).

15. "Chanel" [i.e., CLERY, ARTHUR EDWARD]: "Mr. Yeats and Theatre Reform," *Leader,* 28 Mar 1903, 72.

16. ———: "The Philosophy of an Irish Theatre," *Leader,* 31 Oct 1903, 154-55.

17. DONOGHUE, DENIS: "The Politics of Yeats's Theatre," *Threshold,* 25 (Summer 1974), 27-33.
On Yeats's ideas of the function of theater and drama. Also in EB90.

18. DRAPER, R. P.: *Lyric Tragedy.* London: Macmillan, 1985. vii, 231 pp.
See index for some notes on *Deirdre* and on Yeats's views on lyric tragedy.

19. EGLINTON, JOHN: "Life and Letters," *IrSt,* 12 June 1920, 566.
A causerie on Yeats's theatrical aspirations.

20. FALLETTI, CLELIA: "Yeats e l'attore di cultura poetica," *Quaderni di teatro,* 4:16 (May 1982), 92-101.
Discusses Yeats's dramatic theories and his ideas on actors and acting.

21. FALLON, GABRIEL: "Theatre," *Month,* 17:3 (Mar 1957), 206-8.
Argues for the necessity of sticking to Yeats's principles in order to restore a genuine Irish theater of quality.

22. ———: "The Abbey Tradition of Acting," *IrT,* 22 July 1966, 12; 23 July 1966, 10.

Includes remarks on Yeats's ideas of acting.

23. FAULK, CAROLYN SUE: "The Apollonian and Dionysian Modes in Lyric Poetry and Their Development in the Poetry of W. B. Yeats and Dylan Thomas," Ph.D. thesis, U of Illinois, 1963. iv, 372 pp. (*DAI,* 24:10 [Apr 1964], 4173-74)

On Yeats's theory of tragedy and its indebtedness to Nietzsche, and on some related poems.

24. FLANNERY, JAMES W.: "W. B. Yeats and the Actor," *Studies,* 62: 245 (Spring 1973), 1-17.

A "conspectus on Yeats's view of acting," with notes on the Speaking to the Psaltery experiments.

25. ———: "W. B. Yeats, Gordon Craig and the Visual Arts of the Theatre," in O'Driscoll and Reynolds: *Yeats and the Theatre* (1975, CA81), 82-108.

On staging problems.

26. GRAVETT, ALBERT KENT: "The Use of Myth in the Performance Theories of Richard Wagner, Friedrich Nietzsche, and William Butler Yeats," Ph.D. thesis, New York U, 1976. vii, 183 pp. (*DAI,* 37:9 [Mar 1977], 5442A)

"Nietzsche and Yeats," 98-108; "William Butler Yeats: Myth for a Literary Theatre," 109-59, discusses the Cuchulain plays.

27. GUPTA, ALKA: "W. B. Yeats on Poetic Drama," *IJES,* 20 (1980), 145-57.

28. HARPER, GEORGE MILLS: *The Mingling of Heaven and Earth: Yeats's Theory of Theatre.* Dublin: Dolmen Press, 1975. 48 pp. (New Yeats Papers. 10.)

Demonstrates that Yeats had "a complete and consistent aesthetic of the theatre founded upon a romantic faith in symbolic art" (p. 37).

Reviews:

- Edward Engelberg: "Yeats on Stage," *SR,* 84:1 (Jan-Mar 1976), 167-74.
- Warwick Gould: "Symbols and Systems," *TLS,* 25 Feb 1977, 218.
- F. S. L. Lyons: "Keeping Up with Yeats Studies," *IrT,* 19 Aug 1975, 8.
- ———: "Plays for Aristocrats," *TLS,* 10 Oct 1975, 1187.
- Sean McMahon: "The Painted Stage," *Hibernia,* 3 Oct 1975, 14.
- St. John Sweeney, *JIL,* 5:2 (May 1976), 84-85.
- Timothy Webb, *RES,* 28:112 (Nov 1977), 499-503.

29. HASAN, MASSODUL: "Yeats's Theory of Drama," *IJES,* 24 (1984), 43-52.

30. HETHMON, ROBERT H.: "Total Theatre and Yeats," *Colorado Q,* 15:4 (Spring 1967), 361-77.

Yeats's dramatic theories and the modern world.

31. HUGHES, GLENN: "Concerning a Theatre of the People," *Drama,* [Chicago], 11:2 (Nov 1920), 45-46.

On Yeats's lecture of that title.

32. JEFFARES, ALEXANDER NORMAN: *A Poet and a Theatre.* Inaugural

lecture, May 21st, 1946. Groningen: Wolters, 1946. 20 pp.
Answers the questions how the Abbey Theatre was created and why Yeats wanted a theatre. See review by R[udolf] St[amm], *ES*, 27:4 (Aug 1946), 128.

33. KENNEDY, ALAN: *The Protean Self: Dramatic Action in Contemporary Fiction*. NY: Columbia UP, 1974. xi, 304 pp.
Borrows his concept of "dramatic action" from Yeats's writings (pp. 36-39, 51-60, and passim).

34. KERMODE, FRANK: "Players and Painted Stage," in Donoghue: *The Integrity of Yeats* (1964, CA21), 47-57.

35. KETTLE, THOMAS: "Mr. Yeats and the Freedom of the Theatre," *United Irishman*, 15 Nov 1902, 3.
On Yeats's article "The Freedom of the Theatre" (see *Uncollected Prose*, 2:295-99). Correspondence by Fred Ryan: "The Artist as Teacher," 22 Nov 1902, 3; M. C. Joy: "Mr. Yeats and the Freedom of the Theatre," 29 Nov 1902, 3.

36. KIBERD, DECLAN: "The Fall of the Stage Irishman," *Genre*, 12:4 (Winter 1979), 451-72.
Includes comments on Yeats.

37. *Literaturnai͡a teorii͡a i khudozhestvennoe tvorchestvo: Sbornik nauchnykh trudov*. Moskva: Moskovskiĭ ordena Lenina i ordena trudovogo krasnogo znameni gosudarstvennyĭ pedagogicheskiĭ institut imeni V. I. Lenina, 1979. 148 pp.
T. M. Poli͡udova: "Kont͡sept͡sii͡a poeticheskoĭ dramy u Uil'i͡ama Batlera Ĭetsa" [WBY's concept of poetic drama], 117-34.

38. MENGEL, HAGAL: *Sam Thompson and Modern Drama in Ulster*. Frankfurt/Main: Lang, 1986. xxiii, 603 pp. (Bremer Beiträge zur Literatur- und Ideologiegeschichte. 3.)
"The Origins of Modern Drama in Ulster," 1-164, contains notes on Yeats's dramatic theories and theatrical activities.

39. MILLER, LIAM: "W. B. Yeats and Stage Design at the Abbey Theatre," *Malahat R*, 16 (Oct 1970), 50-64.
Includes 20 illustrations between pp. 64-85. On Yeats's ideas about stage design and how they worked in the Abbey Theatre.

40. ———: "The Eye of the Mind: Yeats and the Theatre of the Imagination," *Temenos*, 7 (1986), 29-69.

41. MÜNCH, WILHELM: "Gedanken eines Poeten in Shakespeares Stadt," *Shakespeare Jahrbuch*, 40 (1904), 204-12.
Discusses the dramatic theory expounded in "At Stratford-on-Avon" and Yeats's view of Shakespeare.

42. MURRAY, CHRISTOPHER: "Yeats's Political Theatre," *Gaéliana*, 8 (1986), 103-16.
"The story of Yeats's political theatre is really the story of a modern quarrel between aesthetics and politics." Discusses the dramatic criticism in *Uncollected Prose*.

43. NARANG, G. L.: "The Influences behind Yeats's Dramatic Theory," *Kurukshetra U Research J*, 1:2 (June-July 1967), 283-89.
The influences are Irish Nationalism, his own subjective nature, and the Nō.

44. NYSZKIEWICZ, HEINZ (ed): *Zeitgenössische englische Dichtung: Einführung in die englische Literaturbetrachtung mit Interpretationen. III. Drama.* Frankfurt/Main: Hirschgraben, 1968. 233 pp.

The Editor: "Zielsetzungen des modernen englischen Dramas: George Bernard Shaw und William Butler Yeats," 15-27; on their dramatic theories (see also pp. 27-74, passim).

Wolfgang Schlegelmilch: "*The Words upon the Window-Pane:* W. B. Yeats," 99-115.

45. O HAODHA, MICHEÁL: "Yeats and *The Voice of Ireland*," *Yeats Association Bulletin,* 2 (Spring 1968), [1-2].

On Yeats's article "The Irish Dramatic Movement" in W314A.

46. OREL, HAROLD: "Yeats as a Young Man," *Books and Libraries at the U of Kansas,* 25 (Feb 1961), 1-5.

Yeats's contributions to *Samhain* on drama and theater.

47. PARKER, STEWART: "State of Play," *CJIS,* 7:1 (June 1981), 5-11.

"Yeats's writings on the theatre are the only substantial body of theory we have," but they did not produce a national dramatic tradition.

48. [PEARSE, P. H. ?]: "Mr. Yeats on the Drama," *Claidheamh Soluis,* 28 Jan 1905, 7.

49. PEYTON, ANN COLEMAN: "Unseen Reality: A Study of the Significance of the Dramatic Theories of William Butler Yeats," °Ph.D. thesis, Florida State U, 1973. 253 pp. (*DAI,* 34:6 [Dec 1973], 3427A)

50. PRIOR, MOODY E.: "Yeats's Search for a Dramatic Form," *TriQ,* 4 [Fall 1965], 112-14.

Why the early Yeats turned away from the drama of his time and began to write plays himself.

51. SADDLEMYER, ELEANOR ANN: "A Study of the Dramatic Theory Developed by the Founders of the Irish Literary Theatre and the Attempt to Apply This Theory in the Abbey Theatre, with Particular Reference to the Achievements of the Major Figures during the First Two Decades of the Movement," Ph.D. thesis, U of London, 1961. 661 pp. (Illustrated)

Especially on Yeats, Lady Gregory, and Synge.

52. SALMON, ERIC (ed): *Bernhardt and the Theatre of Her Time.* Westport, Ct.: Greenwood Press, 1984. xi, 289 pp. (Contributions in Drama and Theatre Studies. 6.)

S. Beynon John: "Actor as Puppet: Variations on a Nineteenth-Century Theatrical Idea," 243-68; comments on Yeats's view of the actor as puppet and on the influence of Gordon Craig.

53. SCHLEIFER, RONALD: "The Civility of Sorrow: Yeats's Daimonic Tragedy," *PQ,* 58:2 (Spring 1979), 219-35.

Yeats's concept of tragedy in his prose and poetry.

54. SELLIN, ERIC: "The Oriental Influence in Modern Western Drama," *France-Asie/Asia,* 21:1 (1966), 85-93.

Discusses the influence of the Nō on Yeats's dramatic theory.

55. SEN GUPTA, D. P.: "Yeats's Views on the Drama and the Stage," *VQ,* 30:3 (1964-65), 205-18.

56. SNODDY, OLIVER: "Yeats and Irish in the Theatre," *Eire,* 4:1 (Spring 1969), 39-45.

Collects some of Yeats's opinions on Gaelic plays and the necessity of having good texts.

57. STOLL, ELMAR EDGAR: *From Shakespeare to Joyce: Authors and Critics; Literature and Life.* NY: Doubleday, Doran, 1944. xxi, 442 pp.

"Poetry and the Passions: An Aftermath," 163-83; reprinted from *PMLA,* 55:5 (Dec 1940), 979-92. On Yeats's dramatic theories.

58. STUCKI, YASUKO: "Yeats's Drama and the Nō: A Comparative Study in Dramatic Theories," *MD,* 9:1 (May 1966), 101-22.

59. TISHUNINA, N.: "Teatral'nai͡a ėstetika rannego U. B. Ĭetsa," *Teatr i dramaturgii͡a,* 6 (1976), 239-48.

"The aesthetics of theater of the early WBY."

60. TODHUNTER, JOHN: "Blank Verse on the Stage," *FortnR,* os 78 / ns 71:422 (Feb 1902), 346-60.

Contains a short note on Yeats's dramatic theories, pp. 359-60.

61. *Tragicheskoe i komicheskoe v zarubezhnoĭ drame: Sbornik nauchnykh trudov.* Perm': Permskiĭ gosudarstvennyĭ pedagogicheskiĭ institut, 1979. 64 pp.

T. M. Poli͡udova: "Kont͡sept͡sii͡a tragedii u U. B. Ĭetsa," 14-32; mostly on *The King's Threshold.*

See also BE10, 28, 39, 67, 117, BF11, 12, 24, 33, 37, 40, 42, 46, 48, 51, 71, 77, 82, 85, 86, 90, 92, 96, 97, 101, 109-12, 115, 116, 118, 124, 134, 135, CA57, 88, 92, 124, CD25, 26, 112a, 139, 304, 334, 349, 350, 916, 987, 1154, 1173, 1177, 1180, 1252, 1405, DA35, DB166, 202, DC418, EA1, 5, 30, 36, 37, EB22, 32, 45, 84, 90, 100, 132, 133, 147, 156, 171, 174, EC82, 89, 96, EE157, 315, 352, 464, EF24, FE20, 45, 78, 84, 92, 103, FF16, G122, 444-53, 653-83 and note, 1136-45 and note, 1193, 1195-96, 1403-4.

G REVIEWS OF BOOKS BY YEATS

The arrangement of the entries in Part 1 of this section is geared to Wade's bibliography, third edition (1968). Each group of reviews of an individual volume is headed by a W number, a short title, and the year of publication. It will be found that some publications received very few or no reviews at all. I am also aware of the fact that more reviews are hidden in the daily and weekly press of Great Britain, Ireland, the United States, and other countries. Very short notices as well as reviews that I have not been able to inspect personally have been excluded. Reviews of items such as W252/253 have been included only when they are concerned with Yeats's contribution to the book in question.

Reviews of books not in Wade are listed in Part 2 of this section. They are arranged chronologically and then alphabetically by title of the book reviewed. Each group of reviews of an individual volume is headed by a short bibliographical description. Further details can be found in the forthcoming fourth edition of Wade's bibliography, compiled by Colin Smythe.

Part 1

W1: *Mosada* (1886)

1. T[YNAN], K[ATHARINE]: "Three Young Poets," *IrM,* 15:165 (Mar 1887), 166-68.

Extract reprinted in CA50, pp. 66-67. "We are glad to welcome a new singer in Erin, one who will take high place among the world's future singers. . . ."

W2: *The Wanderings of Oisin* (1889)

2. ACOE: *Clonmel Chronicle,* 23 Feb 1889, [4].

3. ANON.: "Notes on Books," *Atalanta,* 2:8 (May 1889), 551-52.

Detects "an element of absolute genius in this poem."

4. ANON.: "Literary Bric-a-Brac," *Boston Evening Traveller,* 17 Aug 1889, 2.

Probably written by Lilian Whiting (see *Collected Letters,* 1:134).

5. ANON.: *Daily Free Press* [Aberdeen], 18 Feb 1889, 3.

6. ANON.: *Dublin Evening Mail,* 13 Feb 1889, [4].

7. ANON.: "Some Recent Poetry," *FrJ,* 1 Feb 1889, 2.

"Mr. Yeats has yet to rid his mind of the delusion that obscurity is an acceptable substitute for strenuous thought and sound judgment." This was probably written by John F. Taylor (see *Collected Letters,* 1:139).

8. ANON.: "Literature of the Day," *Glasgow Evening News,* 14 Mar 1889, 2.

"Mr. Yeats is no ordinary writer. He has the poetic instinct strongly, and the power to give it delightful expression."

9. ANON.: "Poetry and Verse," *Glasgow Herald,* 12 Mar 1889, 4.

10. ANON.: *IrT,* 4 Mar 1889, 6.

11. ANON.: *MGuard,* 28 Jan 1889, 6
Detects much promise but also a certain roughness in the poetry. Yeats's music is not so much that of the "true lyre" as that of the "barrel organ."

12. ANON.: "Literary Extracts," *North Wales Observer and Express,* 31 May 1889, [6].
Yeats is "a prodigy, a second Keats."

13. ANON.: "Recent Verse by Minor Poets," *St. James Budget,* 16 Feb 1889, 15.

14. ANON.: "Recent Verse," *SatRL,* 9 Mar 1889, 292-93.

15. ANON.: "Recent Verse," *Scottish Leader,* 20 June 1889, 2.
"Full of the characteristic defects of Irish poetry--the apparently incurable carelessness, the inveterate laxity of hold and looseness of structure, the somewhat ramshackle motion of the verse, and the want of taste and judgment in imagery and epithet."

16. ANON.: *Spect,* 27 July 1889, 122.
"His volume is a refreshing change from the commonplace of much modern verse." See Yeats's letter, 3 Aug 1889, 143; reprinted in *Collected Letters,* 1:176-77.

17. ANON.: "New Poetry and Prose," *United Ireland,* 23 Mar 1889, 6.

18. [BLAKE, CARTER]: *Lucifer,* 4:19 (15 Mar 1889), 84-86.

19. [COFFEY, GEORGE]: "Books," *Evening Telegraph,* 6 Feb 1889, 4.
"With pleasure we recognise . . . the work of a young Irish writer, which unmistakably oversteps the borders of verse, and claims companionship in the larger domains of poetry."

20. [DONOVAN, ROBERT]: "A New Irish Poet," *Nation* [Dublin], 25 May 1889, 3.
"His book, for a first book, is one of great power and maturity, but, we cannot add, of much promise of better things. . . . The poets's imagination has been . . . indulged at the expense of his other faculties. And we think his imagination will never be brighter or more active in the future. That is why we have not much expectation that Mr. Yeats will surpass these first efforts."

21. [HENLEY, W. E.]: "A New Irish Poet," *Scots Observer,* 9 Mar 1889, 446-47.

22. M., R.: "A Volume of Poems," *Inquirer,* 14 Sept 1889, 586-87.
The poetry "proceeds purely and truly from the reawakened harp."

23. ROLLESTON, T. W.: "Irish Literature: A Criticism in Dialogue," *Pilot* [Boston], 4 May 1889, 2.

24. [RUSSELL, MATTHEW]: *IrM,* 17:188 (Feb 1889), 109-10.

25. SMITH, DEXTER: "Literary London," *BET,* 30 July 1889, 6.

26. THOMPSON, FRANCIS: *The Real Robert Louis Stevenson and Other*

Critical Essays. Identified and edited by Terence L. Connolly, with a complete bibliography. NY: University Publishers, 1959. xiii, 409 pp.
"W. B. Yeats," 201-203; reprint of an anonymous untitled review of W2 in *Weekly Register*, 27 Sept 1890, 407-8. Reprinted in CA50, pp. 73-75.
"Mr. Yeats's Poems," 203-9; reprint of an anonymous review of W17 and W27 in *Academy*, 6 May 1899, 501-2 (reprinted in CA50, pp. 104-8). See "Mr. W. B. Yeats and *The Wind among the Reeds*," 20 Jan 1900, 63, an announcement of the award of 25 guineas, quoting extracts from the review.
"The Irish Literary Movement: Mr. Yeats as Shepherd," 210-15; reprint of an anonymous review of W225 in *Academy*, 17 Mar 1900, 235-36.

27. TODHUNTER, JOHN: *Academy*, 30 Mar 1889, 216-17.

28. TYNAN, KATHARINE: "Mr. W. B. Yeats's Poetry," *Weekly Freeman and Irish Agriculturist*, 9 Mar 1889, 11.

29. ———: "Yeats's Poems," *Providence Sunday J*, 12 May 1889, 2.

30. WILDE, OSCAR: *The Artist as Critic: Critical Writings*. Edited by Richard Ellmann. London: Allen, 1970. xviii, 446 pp.
"[Yeats's *Fairy and Folk Tales*]," 130-35; reprint of The Editor: "Some Literary Notes," *Woman's World*, 2:16 (Feb 1889), 221-24, a review of W212 (221-22).
"Yeats's *The Wanderings of Oisin*," 150-51; reprinted from an anonymous review, "Three New Poets," *Pall Mall Gazette*, 12 July 1889, 3; extract reprinted in CA50, pp. 72-73. "Mr. Yeats does not try to 'out-baby' Wordsworth. . . , but he occasionally succeeds in 'out-glittering' Keats."
See also *A Critic in Pall Mall: Being Extracts from Reviews and Miscellanies*. Selected by E. V. Lucas. London: Methuen, 1919. vii, 218 pp. This contains both of the above reviews (pp. 152-57, 160-62) and "Mr. W. B. Yeats," 158-60; a reprint of a different review of W2, first published in "Some Literary Notes," *Woman's World*, 2:17 (Mar 1889), 277-80.
The first item and extracts from the second item are also contained in *Literary Criticism of Oscar Wilde*. Edited by Stanley Weintraub. Lincoln: U of Nebraska Press, 1968. xxxvi, 253 pp. (pp. 92-98).

N.B.: Yeats collected more than 25 reviews of his first substantial book of poetry and pasted them in a notebook, now in the National Library of Ireland, MS. 31,087.

W4/5: *John Sherman and Dhoya* (1891)

31. A., L. F.: "A Causerie," *ILN*, 21 Nov 1891, 667.
"The author . . . is evidently a lady who does not believe in the 'mystery of the sex.'"

32. ANON.: "Novels of the Week," *Athenaeum*, 26 Dec 1891, 858-59.
The author "has a certain grace of style which atones in part for the extreme thinness of his matter."

33. ANON.: "Six New Novels," *Black and White*, 2 Jan 1892, 18.

34. ANON.: "New Novels," *Daily Chronicle*, 30 Nov 1891, 3.

35. ANON.: "Books of the Week," *MGuard,* 24 Nov 1891, 7.
A section in the middle of column 4 is on this book; it may have been written by John F. Taylor (see *Collected Letters,* 1:272). "The story is nothing, the telling is a good deal."

36. ANON.: "Notes on Books," *News of the World,* 29 Nov 1891, 3.

37. ANON.: "New Books and Reprints," *SatRL,* 5 Dec 1891, 650.

38. ANON.: "Two New Irish Books," *United Ireland,* 28 Nov 1891, 5.

39. ANON.: "Belles Lettres," *Westminster R,* year 69 / 137:2 (Feb 1892), 221-27.
See pp. 224-25.

40. [RUSSELL, MATTHEW]: "Notes on New Books," *IrM,* 19:222 (Dec 1891), 662-63.

41. [TYNAN, KATHARINE]: "Books and Their Authors," *Evening Telegraph,* 29 Dec 1891, 2.
Obviously written by an insider who knows the identity of the author, as many British reviewers did not. KT is identified in *Collected Letters,* 1:275. She wrote another anonymous review: "Our Reviewer's Table," *Irish Daily Independent,* 4 Jan 1892, 7.

W6/7: *The Countess Kathleen and Various Legends and Lyrics* (1892)

42. ANON.: "Recent Verse," *Athenaeum,* 7 Jan 1893, 14-16.

43. ANON.: "Ireland in London: Irish Literature," *Irish Catholic and Nation,* 3 Sept 1892, 4.

44. ANON.: "Our Reviewer's Table," *Irish Daily Independent,* 2 Sept 1892, 2.

45. ANON.: *IrM,* 20:232 (Oct 1892), 557-58.

46. ANON.: "Verse and Poetry," *National Observer,* 3 Sept 1892, 408-9.

47. ANON.: "Lines Based on Irish Lore," *NYT,* 8 Oct 1893, 23.

48. ANON.: "Recent Verse," *SatRL,* 22 Oct 1892, 484-86.

49. ANON.: "Dramatic and Other Verse," *Speaker,* 12 Nov 1892, 598.

50. [DAVIDSON, JOHN]: "A Minor," *Daily Chronicle,* 1 Sept 1892, 3.
On the play: "The morality is excellent, but as an artistic achievement the drama has much to lack." On the poems: "The verses have not enough beauty of diction or true lyrical quality to make up for their want of any other attraction."

51. GUINEY, LOUISE IMOGEN: "Enter William Butler Yeats," *Independent,* 28 Dec 1893, 4.
"The essence of literary perfection."

52. [HIGGINSON, THOMAS WENTWORTH]: "Recent Poetry," *Nation,* 15 Dec 1892, 452-54.
"One of the most original and powerful of recent poetic volumes."

53. JOHNSON, LIONEL: *Academy,* 1 Oct 1892, 278-79.
Reprinted in CA50, pp. 78-82.

54. LE GALLIENNE, RICHARD: *Retrospective Reviews: A Literary Log.* London: Lane / NY: Dodd, Mead, 1896. 2 vols.
"W. B. Yeats: *The Countess Cathleen,*" 1:168-73; a reprint of the anonymous "Logroller's Literary Notes of the Week," *Star,* 1 Sept 1892, 2. Correspondence by John Augustus O'Shea, 3 Sept 1892, 4, pointing out that he supplied the source for the play.
"*William Blake:* Edited by Ellis and Yeats," 1:245-51; a review of W218; reprinted from *Star,* 25 Mar 1893, 2.

55. [MCCARTHY, JUSTIN HUNTLEY]: "Books and Book Gossip," *Sunday Sun,* 28 Aug 1892, 3.

56. TRAILL, H. D.: *New R,* 7:43 (Dec 1892), 747-49.
"No instance of such successful treatment of supernatural legend in poetic or dramatic form has come in my way for a long time past." But: "The general scheme of Mr. Yeats's blank verse leaves much to be desired. It is, to say the least of it, unfortunate that the very first line of the drama should be short by a foot."

57. TYNAN, KATHARINE: "Mr. Yeats' New Book," *United Ireland,* 3 Sept 1892, 5.
See editorial note [by John M'Grath ?]: "North and South," 10 Sept 1892, 1, commenting on Yeats's book and on his quarrel with Charles Gavan Duffy and including a letter by Yeats (see *Collected Letters,* 1:315).

58. VICTORY, LOUIS H.: "Mr W. B. Yeats's Recent Poems," *Irish Society,* 22 Oct 1892, 1008-9.
"As an Irish poet of abnormal powers, Mr. Yeats stands alone to-day."

59. W., C.: "Mr. Yeats's New Book," *BmL,* 3:13 (Oct 1892), 25-26.

60. WATSON, WILLIAM: "The Countess Kathleen," *ILN,* 10 Sept 1892, 334.
Reprinted in CA50, pp. 76-77. "Mr. Yeats's artistic means are ambitious; he fails to produce any kind of effect, and the disaster is accordingly considerable."

W8/9: *The Celtic Twilight* (1893/1894)

61. ANON.: *Critic,* 8 Sept 1894, 156.

62. ANON.: "The Glamour of the Celt," *Daily Chronicle,* 15 Jan 1894, 3.
"It is a contribution, by means of art, to the study of the ancient Irish question and the problem of race."

63. ANON.: "Lights and Shadows of a Celtic Twilight," *Dial,* 17:195 (1 Aug 1894), 69-70.

64. ANON.: *Guardian,* 20 June 1894, 954.

65. ANON.: "Books of the Week," *MGuard,* 23 Jan 1894, 9.

66. ANON.: *National Observer*, 3 Mar 1894, 403-4.

67. ANON.: *SatRL*, 6 Jan 1894, 27.

68. ANON.: "Two Aspects of 'Paganism,'" *Speaker*, 19 May 1894, 562-63.

69. ANON.: *Spect*, 28 Apr 1894, 565.

70. G-Y.: *BmL*, 5:29 (Feb 1894), 157-58.
Sees in the book the signs for a new Celtic revival of English literature.

71. JONES, DORA M.: "*The Celtic Twilight:* The Poems of W. B. Yeats," *London QR*, os 94 / ns 4:1 (July 1900), 61-70.
Enthusiastic review of W8, 17, and 27.

72. LANG, ANDREW: "Irish Fairies," *ILN*, 23 Dec 1893, 802.
Reprinted in CA50, pp. 82-85.

73. M'GRATH, J.: *United Ireland*, 23 Dec 1893, 5.

74. RHYS, ERNEST: *Academy*, 24 Mar 1894, 244.

75. E. Y. [i.e., RUSSELL, GEORGE WILLIAM]: "Books Old and New," *Irish Homestead*, 8 Sept 1900, 588-89.

76. [SYMONS, ARTHUR]: *Athenaeum*, 10 Feb 1894, 173-74.
"It reasserts the eternal reality of romance. . . ."

W10/11: *The Land of Heart's Desire* (1894)

77. ANON.: "Poems by Irish Writers," *Critic*, 7 July 1894, 3-4.

78. ANON.: "In Old, Old Ireland," *Daily Chronicle*, 24 Apr 1894, 3.
"The quintessence of Celtic folk-lore."

79. ANON.: "Poetry, Verse, and Drama," *Glasgow Herald*, 26 Apr 1894, 10.

80. ANON.: "Recent English Poetry," *Nation*, 22 Nov 1894, 388-89.
"Although disfigured and blighted in the publishing by one of Mr. Beardsley's ugliest and most meaningless frontispieces, the poem itself is as rare and unique as witch-hazel blossom."

81. ANON.: "Recent Verse," *National Observer*, 16 June 1894, 128.

82. ANON.: "Lines to Thank Ibsen For," *NYT*, 28 Oct 1894, 27.
"At the best a childish groping after effects which are of no value when attained. . . . As long as we have Stevenson, Kipling, Conan Doyle, Stanley Weyman, William Morris, and a few minor writers like Bliss Carman, we need not fear that the epidemic will spread."

83. G-Y.: *BmL*, 6:33 (June 1894), 87.

84. J., R. B.: *CambR*, 15:384 (31 May 1894), 373.

W15/16: *Poems* (1895)

85. ANON.: "Comment on New Books," *Atlantic Monthly,* 78:467 (Sept 1896), 425.

86. ANON.: *CathW,* 62:370 (Jan 1896), 565.

87. ANON.: "Verse," *Daily News,* 6 Dec 1895, 7.

88. ANON.: "Poetry, Verse, and Drama," *Glasgow Herald,* 24 Oct 1895, 8.

89. ANON.: *Guardian,* 18 Dec 1895, 1977.
A "book of capital importance. . . . But Mr. Yeats's range is strictly limited. . . , it remains to be seen whether he is capable of anything more."

90. ANON.: "Books of the Week," *MGuard,* 11 Nov 1895, 4.

91. ANON.: "Two Voices of Today," *National Observer,* 14 Dec 1895, 141-42.
This review may be by W. E. Henley; see BD24, p. 28.

92. ANON.: "Taste and Fancy in Them," *NYT,* 1 Mar 1896, 31.

93. ANON.: "Recent Poetry and Verse," *Speaker,* 4 Jan 1896, 22-23.

94. DAVRAY, HENRI-D.: *MercF,* 19:1 (July 1896), 181-82.

95. GARNETT, RICHARD: "Mr. Yeats's Poems," *ILN,* 21 Dec 1895, 766.

96. *Good Reading about Many Books Mostly by Their Authors.* London: Unwin, 1894-95. 264 pp.
Anon.: "Under the Moon," 197-98. Note about Yeats's forthcoming volume of poetry, to be entitled thus (published eventually as *Poems,* 1895). This note could be by Yeats himself.

97. [HIGGINSON, THOMAS WENTWORTH]: "Recent Poetry," *Nation,* 12 Dec 1895, 429-31.

98. [JOHNSON, LIONEL]: "A Poet," *Daily Chronicle,* 8 Nov 1895, 3.

99. M[ACDONELL], A[NNIE]: "Mr. Yeats's Poems," *BmL,* 9:51 (Dec 1895), 94-95.
Reprinted in *BmNY,* 2:5 (Jan 1896), 423-24; extract reprinted in CA50, pp. 89-91. See also Macdonell's "Some Books of the Season," *English Illustrated Magazine,* 14:147 (Dec 1895), 374-78.

100. M'G[RATH], J[OHN]: "The Changing of 'Oisin,'" *United Ireland,* 14 Dec 1895, 5.
Suggests that Ireland has at long last found a "national poet."

101. [MILLAR, JOHN HEPBURN]: "Recent Celtic Experiments in English Literature," *Blackwood's Edinburgh Magazine,* 159:967 (May 1896), 716-29.
See pp. 719-20.

102. PAYNE, WILLIAM MORTON: "Recent Books of English Poetry," *Dial,* 20:235 (1 Apr 1896), 205-11.
See p. 207.

103. P[ORTER, CHARLOTTE ?]: "Recent British Verse," *Poet-Lore,* 8:1 ([Spring] 1896), 38-41.
See pp. 39-40.

104. RHYS, ERNEST: *Academy,* 22 Feb 1896, 151-52.
Extract reprinted in CA50, pp. 91-94.

105. [ROSCOE, ELIZABETH MARY]: "Mr. Yeats's Poems," *Spect,* 25 Jan 1896, 136-37.

106. AE [i.e., RUSSELL, GEORGE WILLIAM]: "The Poetry of William B. Yeats," *Irish Weekly Independent,* 26 Oct 1895, 9.

107. WAUGH, ARTHUR: "London Letter," *Critic,* 2 Nov 1895, 184-85.
See also the anonymous notice, 21 Dec 1895, 426.

See also BF6.

W17: *Poems* (1899)

108. ANON.: "Reviews of Books," *Irish Daily Independent,* 8 May 1899, 8.
"His besetting sin is his affection for symbolism and his keen desire to find some strange significance in confused or unintelligible phrases of old tradition."

109. ANON.: "Three Noteworthy Poets," *Literature,* 3 June 1899, 565-66.

110. ANON.: "A Revised Yeats," *Outlook* [London], 22 July 1899, 810-11.
". . . poems to which we understand the final touches have yet to be given."

111. ANON.: "The Magic Muse of Mr. W. B. Yeats," *Sketch,* 5 July 1899, 460.
"Among living English poets his is the clearest individuality, and . . . the most authentic."

112. [CHAMBERS, E. K.]: *Athenaeum,* 17 June 1899, 747-48.
Compares Yeats and Mallarmé.

113. FOWLER, J. H.: "Mr. Yeats's Poems," *Morning Leader,* 10 June 1899, Literary Supplement, 1.

114. NEVINSON, HENRY WOODD: *Books and Personalities.* London: Lane, 1905. xiii, 317 pp.
Reprinted reviews: "The Poet of the Sidhe," 218-25; reprint of "Yeats," *Daily Chronicle,* 26 May 1899, 3; a review of W17.
"The Latter Oisin," 226-32; reprinted from *Daily Chronicle,* 3 Jan 1901, 3; a review of W30.
"Irish Plays of 1904," 245-50, reprint of "The Irish Plays," *Speaker,* 2 Apr 1904, 12-13; reviews a performance of *The King's Threshold.*

115. [THOMPSON, FRANCIS]: "Yeats," *Daily Chronicle,* 26 May 1899, 3.

See also CB474, G26, 71, 154.

W18: *Poems* (1901)

116. ANON.: *CambR*, 22:564 (5 June 1901), 360.

117. ANON.: "Poetry, Verse, and Drama," *Glasgow Herald*, 18 Apr 1901, 10.

118. ANON.: "The Revised Poetry of Mr. Yeats," *Literature*, 25 May 1901, 439-41.
Contains a long note on the revisions and sources of *The Countess Cathleen*.

119. ANON.: "Mr. Yeats's Poems," *Spect*, 25 May 1901, 773-74.

120. B., J. C.: *Guardian*, 17 July 1901, 990-91.

121. [DOUGLAS, JAMES]: *Athenaeum*, 8 Mar 1902, 298-300.

122. E., F. Y.: "Plays and Lyrics of W. B. Yeats," *Speaker*, 11 May 1901, 168-69.

123. GWYNN, STEPHEN: *To-day and To-morrow in Ireland: Essays on Irish Subjects*. Dublin: Hodges Figgis / London: Macmillan, 1903. xix, 223 pp.
"The Gaelic Revival in Literature," 1-37; includes a review of W18 and 227. First published anonymously in *Quarterly R*, 195: 390 (Apr 1902), 423-49.
"Celtic Sagas Retold," 38-58; reprint of "Celtic Sagas," *Macmillan's Magazine*, 87:517 (Nov 1902), 95-104. A review of W256.

124. [THOMPSON, FRANCIS]: "A Poet's Poet," *Daily Chronicle*, 16 Apr 1901, 3.

125. [———]: "The Poet as Tinkerer," *Academy*, 11 May 1901, 409-10.
Not all the revisions are to the better.

126. T[HOMPSON], F[RANCIS]: "A Poet of the Inexpressible," *ILN*, 7 Sept 1901, 331.

W20: *Poems* (1908)

127. ANON.: "A School of Irish Poetry," *Edinburgh R*, 209:427 (Jan 1909), 94-118.
Reviews W20 and 64.

128. FLINT, F. S.: "Recent Verse," *New Age*, 29 Aug 1908, 352-53.
"This volume . . . is a source of pure joy."

129. [O'CONNOR, T. P.]: "Mr. W. B. Yeats's Lyrics," *T.P.'s Weekly*, 10 July 1908, 40.

W21-23: *The Secret Rose* (1897/1905)

130. ANON.: *Critic*, 27 Nov 1897, 320.

131. ANON.: "Mysteries of the Neo-Celtic Movement," *Dial*, 24:284 (16 Apr 1898), 266-67.

132. ANON.: "Novels and Stories," *Glasgow Herald,* 15 Apr 1897, 9.

133. ANON.: "Visions and Dreams," *Librarian and Current Literature,* 15 May 1897, 6-7.

134. ANON.: "The Secret Rose," *Literary World* [London], 18 June 1897, 582.
Also in *Literary World* [Boston], 13 Nov 1897, 399.

135. ANON.: *SatRL,* 10 Apr 1897, 365.

136. ANON.: "A Poet's Prose," *Speaker,* 8 May 1897, 524-25.
"Few will deny to Mr. Yeats the possession of genius, yet it were well that he should strive a little to make himself intelligible to the plain people." Correspondence by Yeats, 22 May 1897; reprinted in *Letters,* p. 285.

137. ANON.: "Mr. Yeats's New Book," *United Ireland,* 1 May 1897, 3.

138. C., C.: *Nationist,* 16 Nov 1905, 145.
"We confess we are far from wholly understanding the drift of Mr. Yeats's stories, and we are equally uncertain whether it is worth our while to make the attempt. . . . After all, Mr. Yeats is over forty, and we are entitled to look for a little maturity and fullness in his thought."

139. [CHRISTIE, MARY ELIZABETH]: *Spect,* 17 July 1897, 82-83.

140. M[ACDONELL], A[NNIE]: *BmL,* 12:68 (May 1897), 36-37.
Reprinted in *BmNY,* 6:2 (Oct 1897), 152-54.

141. MOORE, GEORGE: "Mr. Yeats's New Book," *Daily Chronicle,* 24 Apr 1897, 3.
Compares Yeats and Stevenson and finds the former far better and the latter trivial. Correspondence by Vernon Blackburn: "Mr. George Moore on Stevenson," *Academy,* 1 May 1897, 476.
See Richard Le Gallienne: *Sleeping Beauty and Other Prose Fancies.* London: Lane, 1900. viii, 211 pp. ("The Dethroning of Stevenson," 151-60).

142. [SEAMAN, OWEN]: *Athenaeum,* 22 May 1897, 671.
Discusses Yeats's stylistic anachronisms. Reprinted in CA50, pp. 97-100, where the author is not identified.

143. S[HORTER], C. K.: "Notes on New Books," *ILN,* 24 Apr 1897, 569.

144. THOMPSON, FRANCIS: *Literary Criticisms.* Newly discovered and collected by Terence L. Connolly. NY: Dutton, 1948. xv, 617 pp.
"A Schism in the Celtic Movement," 326-32. Reprint of an anonymous review of W297, *Academy,* 1 July 1899, 8-10.
"William Butler Yeats," 370-73. Reprint of an anonymous review of W21, *Academy,* 1 May 1897, 467. Reprinted in CA50, pp. 95-97, where the author is not identified.
"Fiona Macleod on Mr. W. B. Yeats," 373-76. See CB285.

W25: *The Tables of the Law and The Adoration of the Magi* (1904)

145. THOMAS, EDWARD: "As the Wings of a Dove," *Week's Survey,* 13

Aug 1904, 544-45.

146. [———]: "Back into Other Years," *Daily Chronicle*, 15 Aug 1904, 3.
Both reviews are reprinted in CA50, pp. 145-51.

W27/28: *The Wind among the Reeds* (1899)

147. ANON.: "A Garland of Poets," *Critic*, os 35 / ns 32:867 (Sept 1899), 847-52.
See pp. 850-51.

148. ANON.: "Poetry, Verse, and Drama," *Glasgow Herald*, 3 May 1899, 11.

149. ANON.: "Notes on Books," *ILN*, 22 July 1899, 104.

150. ANON.: "Reviews of Books," *Irish Daily Independent*, 1 May 1899, 6.

151. ANON.: "The Gaelic Melancholy," *Literature*, 29 Apr 1899, 439.

152. ANON.: "Yeats's *Wind among the Reeds* ," *NYTBR*, 17 June 1899, 399.

153. ANON.: "The Muse of Mr. Yeats," *Outlook* [London], 29 Apr 1899, 423.

154. ANON.: "Books of the Week," *Times*, 8 July 1899, 6.
Includes a review of W17.

155. DAVIDSON, JOHN: "A Spirit," *Speaker*, 29 Apr 1899, 499.

156. DAVRAY, HENRI-D.: *MercF*, 31:115 (July 1899), 267-68.

157. [GWYNN, STEPHEN]: "Two Poets," *Spect*, 8 July 1899, 54-55.
Appreciates the beauty of the poems, but deplores the lack of "masterful and far-reaching ideas."

158. [HIGGINSON, THOMAS WENTWORTH]: "Recent Poetry," *Nation*, 22 June 1899, 479-81.

159. LE GALLIENNE, RICHARD: "Mr. W. B. Yeats's New Poems," *Star*, 19 May 1899, 1.

160. M[ACDONELL], A[NNIE]: *BmL*, 16:92 (May 1899), 45-46.
Reprinted in *BmNY*, 9:6 (Aug 1899), 555.

161. MACLEOD, FIONA: "Mr. Yeats' New Book," *Daily Express*, 22 Apr 1899, 3.

162. [Bland, Mrs. (NESBIT, E.)]: *Athenaeum*, 15 July 1899, 88.
"Mrs. Bland" is the attribution made in the marked copy; Edith Nesbit (Mrs. Hubert Bland) is known to have contributed poetry criticism to the *Athenaeum*.

See also CB474, G26, 71.

W30/31: *The Shadowy Waters* (1900/1901)

163. ANON.: "Mr. Yeats's New Play," *Academy,* 26 Jan 1901, 81-82.

164. ANON.: *BmL,* 19:114 (Mar 1901), 196.

165. ANON.: "Poetry, Verse, and Drama," *Glasgow Herald,* 27 Dec 1900, 3.
"The chief characters . . . talk in a mystic jargon that is enough to make a saint swear."

166. ANON.: *Guardian,* 13 Mar 1901, 359.

167. ANON.: "An Irish Symbolist," *Independent,* 22 Aug 1901, 1988-90.

168. ANON.: *Literature,* 12 Jan 1901, 34.

169. ANON.: "A Great Poem," *MGuard,* 4 Mar 1901, 6.

170. ANON.: *Monthly R,* 3:7 (Apr 1901), 17-18.

171. ANON.: "Poets from Ireland," *Outlook* [London], 12 Jan 1901, 760-61.
It is neither drama, nor Celtic, nor Irish but "pretty English."

172. ANON.: *Pilot,* 13 July 1901, 46-47.

173. ANON.: "Books of Verse," *Standard* [London], 13 Aug 1901, 6.

174. [CHAMBERS, E. K.]: "Two Celtic Poets," *Athenaeum,* 12 Jan 1901, 39-40.

175. C[HESTERTON], G. K.: "The Shadowy Poet," *Speaker,* 19 Jan 1901, 437-39.

176. [GATES, LEWIS EDWARDS]: "Recent Verse," *Nation,* 22 Aug 1901, 152-55.

177. GUTHRIE, WILLIAM NORMAN: "W. B. Yeats," *SR,* 9:3 (July 1901), 328-31.

178. PAYNE, WILLIAM MORTON: "Recent Poetry," *Dial,* 31:367 (1 Oct 1901), 238-45.
See pp. 238-39.

179. [THOMPSON, FRANCIS]: "The Literary Week," *Academy,* 26 May 1900, 439-40.
Reviews the *North American Review* version (Wade, p. 359).

See also CB474, G114.

W35/36: *The Celtic Twilight* (1902)

180. ANON.: "Literature," *ILN,* 20 Sept 1902, supplement, iv.

181. ANON.: "Mr. Yeats's Recent Writings," *Independent,* 12 Nov 1903, 2691-92.
Also a review of W47. Both works, and the Irish literary revival, are "nothing after all but another form of decadence, no

spontaneous movement but an abuse of spirit, like mysticism and symbolism. . . ."

182. BOYNTON, H. W.: "Air and Earth," *Atlantic Monthly,* 92:552 (Oct 1903), 565-72.
See pp. 565-69; also a review of W44/45, 46/47.

183. [CHRISTIE, MARY ELIZABETH]: "A Book of Irish Folk-Lore," *Spect,* 20 Sept 1902, 405-6.

184. C[HUBB, PERCIVAL ?]: "A Celtic Writer and the Celtic Movement: A Suggestion for Summer Reading," *Ethical Record,* 4:5 (June-July 1903), 208-9.

185. DALBY, W. BURKITT: "The New Mysticism," *London QR,* 100:2 (Oct 1903), 239-60.
See pp. 250, 255-56, 258.

186. [THOMAS, EDWARD]: "The Charm of Mr. Yeats," *Daily Chronicle,* 12 July 1902, 3.
Extract reprinted in CB482.

W41: *Where There Is Nothing* (1902)

187. ANON.: *Academy,* 13 Dec 1902, 661-62.
"Subversive and revolutionary enough to please the most advanced."

188. [NEVINSON, H. W.]: "Last Week in Ireland: Mr. W. B. Yeats's Latest Play," *Daily Chronicle,* 10 Nov 1902, 9.

W44/45: *Where There Is Nothing: Plays for an Irish Theatre I* (1903)

189. ANON.: *MGuard,* 11 June 1903, 12.

190. ANON.: "The Celtic Spirit," *Pilot,* 19 Sept 1903, 289.
"Hardly anything published by him at any time has pleased us so ill."

191. [KNIGHT, J.]: "Drama," *Athenaeum,* 21 May 1904, 665-66.
Also a review of W53 and 56.

192. LYND, ROBERT: "Ibsenising Ireland," *To-day,* 24 June 1903, 276-77.

193. [THOMPSON, FRANCIS]: "A Drama of Revolt," *Academy,* 4 July 1903, 10.
Reprinted in CA50, pp. 138-40, where the reviewer is not identified.

194. [WALKLEY, ARTHUR BINGHAM]: *TLS,* 26 June 1903, 201-2.

195. [WRIGHT, WILMER CAVE FRANCE]: *Nation,* 16 July 1903, 53.

See also G182, 213.

W46/47: *Ideas of Good and Evil* (1903)

196. ANON.: "The Cave and the Tower," *British Weekly*, 21 May 1903, 137-38.
Less a review than a discussion of the symbols of cave and tower in Christian tradition, prompted by Yeats's discussion of Shelley.

197. ANON.: "'That Other Beauty,'" *Daily News*, 19 May 1903, 8.
"Sincere and delicate and very beautiful prose."

198. ANON.: "Essays and Plays by an Irish Mystic," *Dial*, 36:430 (16 May 1904), 331-32.

199. ANON.: "Miscellaneous," *Glasgow Herald*, 8 June 1903, 12.
A detailed critique of Yeats's theories; "the general impression is one of exaggeration and unreality."

200. ANON.: "Notes on New Books," *ILN*, 13 June 1903, 900.

201. ANON.: "Ideas of Good and Evil," *IrT*, 22 May 1903, 7.

202. ANON.: "The Celtic Revival: Mr. Yeats on His Artistic Creed," *MGuard*, 12 June 1903, 12.
Jeffares (CA50, pp. 133-35, where the review is reprinted) says that the reviewer may have been George Saintsbury.

203. ANON.: *Monthly R*, 13:37 (Oct 1903), 95-96.

204. ANON.: "Yeats on Art," *NYT*, 17 Jan 1903, supplement, 48.

205. ANON.: "The Ideas of Mr. Yeats," *Pilot*, 29 Aug 1903, 205-6.

206. ANON.: "On the Heels of the Symbol," *SatRL*, 12 Sept 1903, 334-35.
Yeats fails to define the term "symbol."

207. ANON.: "The Hidden Beauty," *Speaker*, 30 May 1903, 213.

208. BENNETT, EDWARD: "The Passing Hour," *English Illustrated Magazine*, 29:5 (Aug 1903), 549-53.
See pp. 552-53.

209. CARY, ELISABETH LUTHER: "Ideas of Mr. Yeats: A New Volume of Striking Prose Essays by the Irish Poet," *NYTBR*, 11 July 1903, 477-78.

210. [CHILD, HAROLD]: "The Essays of a Symbolist," *TLS*, 12 June 1903, 184-85.

211. EGLINTON, JOHN: *Anglo-Irish Essays*. Dublin: Talbot Press / London: Unwin, 1917. vi, 129 pp.
"The Philosophy of the Celtic Movement," 41-46; a review of W46/47. "Irish Books," 79-89; a complaint that the Irish literary revival has not yet produced "the Irish Book."

212. HELM, W. H.: "The Coming of the Fairies," *Morning Post*, 4 June 1903, 2.
"Mr. Yeats and his friends know well that the folk are still in the land, and if mystical prose and symbolical poetry can draw them out into the open they will soon be visible again."

213. L[OCKWOOD], L[OUISE] B.: *Ethical Record,* 4:5 (June-July 1903), 209.
Also a review of W42/44.

214. [NEVINSON, H. W.]: "A Poet's Criticism," *Daily Chronicle,* 23 May 1903, 3.

215. P AND Q: "Pages in Waiting," *World,* 2 June 1903, 936-38.

216. REYNOLDS, STEPHEN: *Weekly Critical R,* 16 July 1903, 11; 23 July 1903, 17-18.

217. S[HORTER], C. K.: "A Literary Letter," *Sphere,* 6 June 1903, 220.

218. Entry canceled.

219. [VENGEROVA, Z.]: *Vestnik Evropy,* 38:8 (Aug 1903), 830-36.

220. [WALKLEY, A. B.]: "The State Called Reverie," *Academy,* 13 June 1903, 589-90.
Correspondence by Arthur Clutton-Brock, 20 June 1903, 617-19.

221. [WRIGHT, WILMER CAVE FRANCE]: *Nation,* 16 July 1903, 52-53.

See also CD1287a, G181, 182.

W49: *In the Seven Woods* (1903)

222. BOYNTON, H. W.: "Books Old and New: Stops of Various Quills," *Atlantic Monthly,* 93:555 (Jan 1904), 119-27.
See pp. 120-21.

223. [NEVINSON, H. W.]: "Across the Irish Sea," *Daily Chronicle,* 1 Sept 1903, 3.

W52/54: *The Hour-Glass and Other Plays: Plays for an Irish Theatre II* (1904/1905)

224. ANON.: "Dramatic Notes," *Academy,* 2 Apr 1904, 383-84.
Also a review of W56; reprinted in CA50, pp. 140-41. "If Mr. Yeats and his fellow workers desire to found a living Irish drama they must look to the life of to-day, not of yesterday, and must take for their characters human beings, not abstractions."

225. ANON.: "Ireland in Drama," *Daily Chronicle,* 8 June 1904, 3.
Also a review of W56.

226. ANON.: "Three Fascinating Plays," *Daily News,* 29 Apr 1904, 4.

227. ANON.: "Poetry, Verse, and Drama," *Glasgow Herald,* 2 Apr 1904, 8.
Deplores the "treatment of Irish romance in a Maeterlinckian fashion," which is "solely concerned with the magic of old names, catch-words, and unabiding dreams." Also a review of W56.

228. ANON.: "Books of the Week," *MGuard,* 12 Apr 1904, 5.
Also a review of W56.

229. ANON.: "A Live Dramatic Poet," *SatRL*, 28 May 1904, 688.
Also a review of W56.

230. ANON.: "Mr. Yeats's Plays," *Spect*, 25 June 1904, 989.
Also a review of W56.

231. ANON.: "Recent Books of Verse," *Standard*, 13 Apr 1904, 8.

232. [BOYNTON, H. W.]: "Three Dramatic Studies," *Atlantic Monthly*, 93:559 (May 1904), 712-14.

233. P AND Q: *World*, 24 May 1904, 904.
Also a review of W56.

234. THOMAS, EDWARD: "The Music of Mr. Yeats," *Week's Survey*, 18 June 1904, 449.
Also a review of W56; extract reprinted in CB482.

235. [WRIGHT, WILMER CAVE FRANCE]: *Nation*, 18 Aug 1904, 144.

See also G191.

W56: *The King's Threshold and On Baile's Strand: Plays for an Irish Theatre III* (1904)

236. ANON.: "Two Beautiful Plays," *Daily News*, 26 Mar 1904, 4.

237. ANON.: *Monthly R*, 17:50 (Nov 1904), 157-60.

See also CB474, G191, 224, 225, 227-30, 233, 234.

W59: *Stories of Red Hanrahan* (1904)

238. L[YND], R[OBERT] W[ILSON]: "The Book World," *Black and White*, 10 June 1905, 801.

239. [STEELE, ROBERT]: *Athenaeum*, 2 June 1906, 667.
"If Mr. Yeats had never published a line of verse, he might rest a claim of immortality on these *Stories*. . . ."

240. [THOMAS, EDWARD]: *Academy*, 22 July 1905, 759.
Reprinted in CA50, pp. 160-61, where the reviewer is not identified.

W64: *Poems, 1899-1905* (1906)

241. ANON.: "Poetry, Verse, and Drama," *Glasgow Herald*, 20 Nov 1906, 9.
Praises the lucidity of the verse but concludes: "We begin to fear that we must study Lady Gregory's books on Ireland or remain for ever in the outer dark."

242. ANON.: "Verse and Its Public," *SatRL*, 16 Feb 1907, 206-7.

243. ANON.: "Mr. W. B. Yeats's Poems," *T.P.'s Weekly*, 2 Nov 1906, 556.

244. B., M.: "Mr. Yeats's Poems," *Morning Post,* 19 Nov 1906, 2.

245. BEECHING, H. C.: "Mr. Yeats's New Poems," *BmL,* 31:182 (Nov 1906), 74-75.

246. [BROCK, ARTHUR CLUTTON]: "The Celtic Movement," *TLS,* 14 Dec 1906, 414.

247. [BUCHAN, JOHN]: "Recent Verse," *Spect,* 8 Dec 1906, 930-31.

248. DAVRAY, HENRY-D.: *MercF,* 65:230 (15 Jan 1907), 364-65.

249. [PICKTHALL, R. G.]: *Athenaeum,* 15 Dec 1906, 770.
"The book suffers from its obvious connexion with the movement which is seeking--not always judiciously--to force a Gaelic literature into existence."

250. SCRUTATOR: "Yeats of the Dramas," *Sinn Féin,* 24 Nov 1906, 3.
"Viewing the work of the National Theatre Society in the light of, and as expounded by, this book, one stands well-nigh aghast at its ineffectualness and its almost hopeless aloofness from humanity." See T. B. Cronin: "Drama as a Nationalising Force," ibid.

251. T[HOMAS], E[DWARD]: "Mr. Yeats Revises," *Daily Chronicle,* 1 Jan 1907, 3.
Extract reprinted in CB482.

See also G127.

W65/71/98: *The Poetical Works I-II* (1906/1907/1912)

252. ANON.: "New Poems and Plays," *American R of Reviews,* 46:6 (Dec 1912), 750-52.

253. ANON.: "Recent Verse," *Nation,* 10 Jan 1907, 34-35.

254. ANON.: "Revised Yeats Plays," *NYTBR,* 6 Apr 1913, 196.

255. ANON.: "Idle Notes by an Idle Reader," *Putnam's Monthly,* 2:12 (Apr 1907), 118-21.

256. CARMAN, BLISS: "William Yeats and Alfred Noyes," *NYT Saturday R,* 2 Feb 1907, 68.
"You may read many of Mr. Yeats's poems only to be borne away by a sense of rapt elation without exact meaning and without any definite ideas of what he is trying to say. . . . With Mr. Noyes . . . the case is different. You will never be in any doubt about his meaning, but neither will you be carried out of yourself by any exaltation of words, any intensity of passion, any abandon of beauty."

257. GREENSLET, FERRIS: "The Year on Parnassus," *Atlantic Monthly,* 100:6 (Dec 1907), 843-51.

258. JOHNSTON, CHARLES: "The Poems of W. B. Yeats," *NAR,* 187:629 (Apr 1908), 614-18.

259. LUHRS, MARIE: "Gentle Poet," *Poetry,* 30:6 (Sept 1927), 346-49.

260. RITTENHOUSE, JESSIE B.: "A Glance at Recent Poetry," *Putnam's Monthly,* 3:3 (Dec 1907), 362-67.
See pp. 363-64.

261. [TOWSE, JOHN RANKEN]: *Nation,* 17 Oct 1912, 365.

262. WADDELL, ELIZABETH: "Yeats," *Mirror,* 9 Jan 1913, 5-6.
Includes a review of W101.

263. WILLCOX, LOUISE COLLIER: "The Poetic Drama," *NAR,* 186:622 (Sept 1907), 91-97.
See pp. 92-94.

W69: *Deirdre: Plays for an Irish Theatre V* (1907)

264. ANON.: "Some Poetical Plays," *Guardian,* 1 Jan 1908, 18-19.

265. ANON.: "New Books," *MGuard,* 3 Sept 1907, 5.

266. [BETTANY, FREDERICK GEORGE]: "Two Irish Plays," *Athenaeum,* 5 Oct 1907, 415-16.
Discusses the influence of Maeterlinck.

267. [THOMAS, EDWARD]: "A Poet and Others," *Daily Chronicle,* 28 Sept 1907, 3.

268. T[HOMAS], E[DWARD]: *BmL,* 33:193 (Oct 1907), 47.

W72: *Discoveries* (1907)

269. ANON.: *Academy,* 28 Mar 1908, 621.

270. ANON.: *BmL,* 33:197 (Feb 1908), 216-17.

271. ANON.: "A Poet's Confidences," *MGuard,* 20 Jan 1908, 5.

272. ELTON, OLIVER: "Mr. W. B. Yeats's New Book," *Tribune,* 7 Jan 1908, 2.

273. Ó CONGHAILE, SEUMAS: "The Poet at the Looking Glass," *Sinn Féin,* 22 Feb 1908, [3].
"His affectations of style, once so charming and impulsive and individual, are becoming stereotyped."

274. [STEELE, ROBERT]: *Athenaeum,* 11 Jan 1908, 41.

275. THOMAS, EDWARD: "An Irish Poet," *Daily Chronicle,* 18 May 1908, 3.
Extract reprinted in CB482.

W73: *The Unicorn from the Stars and Other Plays* (1908)

276. ANON.: "More of the Irish Literary Drama," *Dial,* 45:536 (16 Oct 1908), 255-56.

277. ANON.: *Nation,* 11 June 1908, 540.

W75-82: *The Collected Works in Verse and Prose* (1908)

278. ANON.: "Poetry, Verse, and Drama," *Glasgow Herald,* 8 Oct 1908, 11.

279. ANON.: "New Books," *MGuard,* 16 Oct 1908, 5.

280. ANON.: "New Books," *MGuard,* 24 Dec 1908, 3.

281. Entry canceled.

282. ANON.: "Poetry and Neo-Kelticism," *SatRL,* 7 Nov 1908, 577-78.

283. ANON.: *SatRL,* 27 Feb 1909, 280.

284. BARING, MAURICE: *Punch and Judy & Other Essays.* London: Heinemann, 1924. x, 370 pp.
"Mr. Yeats's Poems," 228-32; reprinted from an unidentified periodical.

285. DE LA MARE, WALTER: "The Works of Mr. Yeats," *BmL,* 35:208 (Jan 1909), 191-92.

286. GARNETT, EDWARD: "The Work of W. B. Yeats," *English R,* 2:1 (Apr 1909), 148-52.

287. HUNEKER, JAMES GIBBONS: *The Pathos of Distance: A Book of a Thousand and One Moments.* NY: Scribner's, 1913. viii, 394 pp.
"The Celtic Awakening," 219-44; a rapturous praise, includes "A Poet of Visions," published anonymously as "Yeats, the Poet of Vision," *NY Sun,* 25 July 1909, section III, 2 (review of W75-82).

288. [NEVINSON, H. W.]: "By the Waters of Babylon," *Nation* [London], 17 Oct 1908, 122.

289. [STRACHEY, LYTTON]: "Mr. Yeats's Poetry," *Spect,* 17 Oct 1908, 588-89.
Reprinted in CA50, pp. 164-68.

290. TENNYSON, CHARLES: "Irish Plays and Playwrights," *Quarterly R,* 215:428 (July 1911), 219-43.

291. [THOMAS, EDWARD]: "Celtic Natural Magic," *Morning Post,* 17 Dec 1908, 2.

291a. ———: "An Irish Poet," *Daily Chronicle,* 6 Mar 1909, 3.
Extracts from both reviews are reprinted in CB482.

W84: *The Green Helmet and Other Poems* (1910)

292. ANON.: "Mr. Yeats's New Book," *Academy,* 6 May 1911, 547.

293. ANON.: *English R,* 8:1 (Apr 1911), 181-82.

294. ANON.: "The Later Yeats," *Irish R,* 1:2 (Apr 1911), 100-101.
Notes an increasingly aristocratic and isolated attitude.

295. ANON.: "Mr. Yeats's New Play," *Nation* [London], 31 Dec 1910, 578, 580.

296. DELATTRE, FLORIS: *Revue germanique*, 7:4 (July-Aug 1911), 449-50.

297. [PICKTHALL, R. G.]: "Verse," *Athenaeum*, 18 Feb 1911, 186.

W88: *Synge and the Ireland of His Time* (1911)

298. ANON.: *Academy*, 14 Oct 1911, 485-86.
Correspondence by M. P.: "W. B. Yeats and J. M. Synge," 21 Oct 1911, 522-23.

299. ANON.: *Athenaeum*, 26 Aug 1911, 240-41.

300. ANON.: *English R*, 9:4 (Nov 1911), 719-20.

301. ANON.: "An Irishman's Ireland," *NYTBR*, 17 Sept 1911, 556.

W92: *Plays for an Irish Theatre* (1911)

302. ANON.: *English R*, 11:2 (May 1912), 330-31.

303. [BETTANY, FREDERICK GEORGE]: *Athenaeum*, 13 Jan 1912, 51-52.

304. [CHILD, HAROLD]: "Mr. Yeats's Plays," *TLS*, 28 Dec 1911, 540.
Partly reprinted as "Seventy-Five Years On," *TLS*, 26 Dec 1986, 1449.

305. [CRAIG, GORDON ?]: *Mask*, 4:4 (Apr 1912), 342-43.

306. FIGGIS, DARRELL: "The Theatre," *BmL*, 41:246 (Mar 1912), 304-5.

307. PALMER, JOHN: "Footlights and the Super-Doll," *SatRL*, 20 Jan 1912, 74-76.

308. T[ENNYSON], C[HARLES ?]: "Mr. W. B. Yeats's Plays," *ContempR*, 101:558 (June 1912), 902-3.

W94: *The Land of Heart's Desire* (1912)

309. ANON.: "Present-Day Criticism," *New Age*, 2 May 1912, 10-11.
"This vague, pale, gaping drama. . . ." Correspondence by James Stephens, 9 May 1912, 46-47; reprinted in BC14.

310. CHESTERTON, G. K.: "Efficiency in Elfland," *Eye-Witness*, 20 June 1912, 21-22.
Reprinted in *Living Age*, 3 Aug 1912, 317-19. This is a veritable Chestertonian paradox that nevertheless makes some sense. He argues that the play's vague fairyland world is really a fake. The play was written by an efficient, almost heartless poet. "There is only one thing wanting, one little flaw in the Land of Heart's Desire. The heart does not desire it."

311. RUYSSEN, HENRI: *Revue germanique*, 9:3 (May-June 1913), 358-59.

W95: *The Land of Heart's Desire. The Countess Cathleen* (1925)

312. [THOMSON, GEORGE]: "Four Plays," *Nation & Athenaeum*, 13 June 1925, 345-46.
". . . strangely out of date nowadays."

W99: *Poems* (1912)

313. ANON.: "Mr. Yeats' Poems," *Academy*, 4 Jan 1913, 6-7.
"It is discomforting to see a poet, having won his way to a distinguished position, occupying his middle years with not much more than a careful revision of his early poems, just when we should expect him to display the maturity and strength of his powers."

314. THOMAS, EDWARD: *Poetry and Drama*, 1:1 (Mar 1913), 53-56.
Praises the revisions. But: "He seems to have been revising in cold blood what was written in a mood now inaccessible. I cannot but be surprised that he has made the attempt, since it is one which he might find it necessary to renew indefinitely at intervals, should his energy remain unclaimed by creation."

W101: *The Green Helmet and Other Poems* (1912)

315. ANON.: "Yeats and His Red Man," *American R of Reviews*, 47:3 (Mar 1913), 371-72.
Also a review of W102.

See also G262.

W102: *The Cutting of an Agate* (1912)

316. SHERMAN, STUART P.: "John Synge," *Nation*, 26 Dec 1912, 608-11.

317. TUPPER, JAMES W.: "J. M. Synge and His Work," *Dial*, 54:642 (16 Mar 1913), 233-35.

See also G315.

W104/105: *Stories of Red Hanrahan. The Secret Rose. Rosa Alchemica* (1913/1914)

318. ANON.: "Five Fiction Books of Quality," *American R of Reviews*, 50:1 (July 1914), 121-22.

319. ANON.: "A Book of Celtic Tales by Mr. Yeats," *Dial*, 57:676 (16 Aug 1914), 110-11.

320. [NEVINS, ALLAN]: *Nation*, 30 Apr 1914, 501-2.

W106: *A Selection from the Love Poetry* (1913)

321. ANON.: "Mr. Yeats and Some Others," *Academy*, 30 Aug 1913, 262-63.

W110: *Responsibilities: Poems and a Play* (1914)

322. POUND, EZRA: *Literary Essays.* Edited with an introduction by T. S. Eliot. London: Faber & Faber, 1954. 464 pp.
"The Later Yeats," 378-81; reprinted from *Poetry,* 4:2 (May 1914), 64-69; reprinted in CA50, pp. 186-89. A French version appears in CA32, 408-11.

See also DB89.

W111-113: *Reveries over Childhood and Youth* (1915/1916)

323. ANON.: "Irish Memories," *American R of Reviews,* 53:6 (June 1916), 764-65.

324. ANON.: "A Book of Memories and Musings," *Dial,* 61:722 (15 July 1916), 68.

325. ANON.: "Mr. Yeats's Youth," *Independent,* 24 July 1916, 130.

326. ANON.: *Irish Book Lover,* 8:5&6 (Dec & Jan 1916-17), 59-61.
Also a review of W115.

327. ANON.: "Mr. Yeats's Childhood and Youth," *Literary Digest,* 9 Sept 1916, 621.

328. ANON.: "Mr. Yeats on Himself," *Nation* [London], 28 Oct 1916, 150, 152.
Also a review of W115.

329. ANON.: *Nation,* 4 Jan 1917, 28.

330. ANON.: "Looking Backward," *NSt,* 11 Nov 1916, 139-40.
Also a review of W115.

331. ANON.: "William Butler Yeats," *NYTBR,* 20 Aug 1916, 328.

332. ANON.: "Something That Never Happens," *SatRL,* 4 Nov 1916, supplement, v.

333. BLAKE, BARTON: "Yeats and Youth," *YR,* 6:2 (Jan 1917), 410-12.

334. C., P.: "A Poet's Upbringing," *Poetry,* 11:1 (Oct 1917), 51-54.

335. [CHILD, HAROLD]: "Mr. Yeats in Middle Age," *TLS,* 19 Oct 1916, 499.
Also a review of W115. "It is . . . improbable that he will 'wither into the truth.' He has more leaves and flowers yet to sway in the sun; and we, who have the earlier leaves and flowers to enjoy, need not be perturbed by any phrases about the 'lying days of my youth.'"

336. DAVRAY, HENRY-D.: *MercF,* 118:444 (16 Dec 1916), 719-20.
Also a review of W115.

337. GILTINAN, CAROLINE: "William Butler Yeats," *Poetry R of America,* 1:3 (July 1916), 45-46.

338. H., A. J.: *America,* 24 June 1916, 263.

339. L[ESLIE], S[HANE]: "The Making of an Irish Poet: Mr. Yeats Looks Back on Childhood and Youth," *Ireland,* 17 June 1916, 15-16.

340. L[ITTELL], P[HILIP]: "Books and Things," *NewRep,* 24 June 1916, 202.

341. C., R. H. [i.e., ORAGE, A. R.]: "Readers and Writers," *New Age,* 2 Nov 1916, 15-16.

342. ROBINSON, LENNOX: "Memory Harbour," *NSt,* 16 Sept 1916, 567-68.

343. A. E. [i.e., RUSSELL, GEORGE WILLIAM]: *Imaginations and Reveries*. Dublin: Maunsel, 1921 [1915]. ix, 316 pp.
"A Poet of Shadows," 34-38; reprinted from DB211. "The Boyhood of a Poet," 39-42; reprinted from *New Ireland,* 16 Dec 1916, 88-89 (a review of W111).

344. [WRIGHT, F. H.]: "An English Parnassian--and Some Others," *Athenaeum,* Nov 1916, 527-29.
Also a review of W115.

W115/116: *Responsibilities and Other Poems* (1916)

345. ANON.: "Verse and Verse-Makers," *American R of Reviews,* 54:6 (Dec 1916), 674-76.

346. ANON.: "The Poetry of Mr. Yeats," *SatRL,* 11 Nov 1916, 460-61.

347. B., W. S.: "The Fragile Poetic Art of Mr. Yeats: His Latest Volume Reveals a Slackening of Poet's Energies during the Rapid Passing of the Years," *BET,* 6 Dec 1916, part 3, 4.

347a. H. D. [DOOLITTLE, HILDA]: "Responsibilities," *Agenda,* 25:3-4 (Autumn/Winter 1987/88), 51-54.
A previously unpublished review. See also Gary Burnett: "A Poetics out of War: H. D.'s Responses to the First World War," 54-63, for some notes on H. D.'s view of Yeats.

348. FIRKINS, O. W.: "The Lyre in Britain," *Nation,* 19 July 1917, 6-7.

349. L[ESLIE], S[HANE]: "Two Poets of the Time," *Ireland,* 23 Dec 1916, 6-7.

350. MAYNARD, THEODORE: "The Metamorphosis of Mr. Yeats," *Poetry R,* 10:4 (July-Aug 1919), 169-75.
Also a review of W120, 123, and 124.

351. O'B., C.: "Poetry," *Studies,* 6:21 (Mar 1917), 154-57.
Compares Yeats and Thomas MacDonagh.

352. P[OUND], E[ZRA]: "Mr. Yeats' New Book," *Poetry,* 9:3 (Dec 1916), 150-51.

353. ROBINSON, LENNOX: "Beauty Like a Tightened Bow," *New Ireland,* 16 Dec 1916, 90-91.

See also G326, 328, 330, 335, 336, 344.

W118: *The Wild Swans at Coole, Other Verses and a Play in Verse* (1917)

See CC222.

W120/121: *Per Amica Silentia Lunae* (1918)

354. ANON.: "Ireland in Poetry," *American R of Reviews,* 57:5 (May 1918), 554-55.

355. ANON.: "Black Magic," *Athenaeum,* Apr 1918, 196-97.

356. ANON.: "Yeats's Justification of the 'Dual Personality' of Artists: An Argument That Some of His Friends Regard as Subversive of Everything Good," *Current Opinion,* 64:5 (May 1918), 345-46.

357. ANON.: "Mr. Yeats Theorizes," *Nation* [London], 16 Feb 1918, 628, 630.

358. ANON.: *Nation,* 21 Mar 1918, 326.

359. ANON.: "Some Recent Books of Poetry," *NYTBR,* 19 May 1918, 236.

360. ANON.: *Quest* [London], 9:3 (Apr 1918), 522-24.

361. ANON.: "Poems [sic] by Yeats," *Springfield Sunday Republican,* 2 June 1918, 15A.

362. BICKLEY, FRANCIS: "Anima Poetae," *BmL,* 54:320 (May 1918), 74.

363. [BROCK, ARTHUR CLUTTON]: "Reality by Moonlight," *TLS,* 7 Feb 1918, 66.
"Into that 'Celtic Twilight' we cannot follow him. . . . And yet, with it all, Mr. Yeats is a poet, as moonlight is beautiful. The beauty that we see is the only thing common between his mind and ours." Reprinted in CA50, pp. 206-10, where the reviewer is not identified.

364. [CRAIG, GORDON ?]: *Mask,* 8:10 (Nov 1918), 39-40.
"It is one of those profound little works which yawn before us like an abyss as we trip or stumble along our little path . . . and no amount of ribaldry can bring us to the brink."

365. [ELIOT, T. S.]: *Egoist,* 5:6 (June-July 1918), 87.
Admits that he understands only half of the book.

366. F[AUSSET], H. I'A.: *CambR,* 39:980 (6 June 1918), 444.

367. SHANKS, EDWARD: "Our London Letter," *Dial,* 64:763 (28 Mar 1918), 286-88.

368. TYNAN, KATHARINE: *Studies,* 7:25 (Mar 1918), 188-89.
"This book is but a new stage on the road of mystery and magic which has slowly but surely taken away the poet from his poetry . . . it is painfully unlike the Yeats one remembers."

See also G350.

W123: *Two Plays for Dancers* (1919)

369. ANON.: "Mr. Yeats," *Nation* [London], 5 Apr 1919, 20, 22.
Also a review of W124.

370. BOYD, ERNEST: "The Irish Renaissance--Renascent," *Dial*, 67:795 (26 July 1919), 53-55.

371. C[LARKE], A[USTIN]: "The World Lost for Love," *IrSt*, 25 Oct 1919, 438-39.

372. SHANKS, EDWARD: *First Essays on Literature*. Freeport, N.Y.: Books for Libraries Press, 1968 [1923]. ix, 267 pp.
"The Later Poetry of Mr. W. B. Yeats," 238-44; reprint of an anonymous review of W123 and 124, *NSt*, 29 Mar 1919, 582.

See also G350.

W124/125: *The Wild Swans at Coole* (1919)

373. ANON.: "Criticisms of Modern Poetry: Yeats [. . .]," *American R of Reviews*, 59:5 (May 1919), 556-57.

374. ANON.: *Dial*, 67:795 (26 July 1919), 72.
"The Wild Swans at Coole beat upon the fancy with ineffectual wings."

375. ANON.: "Recent Books of Poetry," *Nation*, 7 June 1919, 917-19.

376. ANON.: "With Irish Bards Old and New," *NYTBR*, 21 Sept 1919, 477.

377. ANON.: "The New W. B. Yeats and Others," *Poetry R*, 10:3 (May-June 1919), 152-53.

378. ANON.: "Mr. Yeats," *SatRL*, 12 Apr 1919, 353-54.

379. ANON.: "New Yeats Volume: Disillusionment Uppermost," *Springfield Daily Republican*, 6 May 1919, 8.

380. B., W. S.: "The Poetry of William Butler Yeats: A New Book of His Verse Which Maintains His Qualities of Subtle Workmanship and Symbolic Imagery," *BET*, 12 Apr 1919, part 3, 9.

381. [BROCK, ARTHUR CLUTTON]: "Tunes Old and New," *TLS*, 20 Mar 1919, 149.
Reprinted in CA50, pp. 213-15, where the reviewer is not identified.

382. FIRKINS, O. W.: "Mr. Yeats and Others," *Review* [NY], 28 June 1919, 151-53.

383. MACNAMARA, BRINSLEY: "Macnamara on Yeats," *Irish Commonwealth*, 1:3 (May 1919), 172-73.

384. MURRY, JOHN MIDDLETON: *Aspects of Literature*. NY: Knopf, 1920. ix, 204 pp.
"Mr. Yeats's Swan Song," 39-45; reprint of an anonymous review, *Athenaeum*, 4 Apr 1919, 136-37, and *Living Age*, 10 May 1919,

342-45. Reprinted in CA36 and 50 (pp. 216-20); see also DB129.

385. TOWNE, CHARLES HANSON: "The Vanished Yeats, the Never Vanishing Kipling, and Some Others," *BmNY*, 49:5 (July 1919), 617-22.
"Yeats has died, artistically."

386. TYNAN, KATHARINE: "A Strayed Poet," *BmL*, 56:332 (May 1919), 78-79.
"A plague upon what led him to those fountains of a fantastic and muddling philosophy."

See also G350, 369, 372.

W126: *The Cutting of an Agate* (1919)

387. ANON.: "Mr. Yeats in Prose," *Nation* [London], 28 June 1919, 395-96.

388. BICKLEY, FRANCIS: "Mr. Yeats's Odyssey," *BmL*, 56:335 (Aug 1919), 174.

389. DE LA MARE, WALTER: *Private View*. With an introduction by Lord David Cecil. London: Faber & Faber, 1953. xvi, 256 pp.
"A Lapidary," 90-94; reprint of an anonymous review, *TLS*, 1 May 1919, 235; also in CA50, pp. 226-30.

390. E[LIOT], T. S.: "A Foreign Mind," *Athenaeum*, 4 July 1919, 552-53.
"Mr. Yeats on any subject is a cause of bewilderment and distress." Reprinted in CA50, pp. 230-32.

W128: *Selected Poems* (1921)

391. ANON.: *NAR*, 215:796 (Mar 1922), 426-27.

392. COLUM, PADRAIC: "Mr. Yeats's Selected Poems," *Dial*, 71:4 (Oct 1921), 464-68.
Extract reprinted in CA50, pp. 245-50.

393. GORMAN, HERBERT S.: "The Later Mr. Yeats," *Outlook*, 19 Apr 1922, 655-56.
Also a review of W129.

394. WILKINSON, MARGUERITE: "The Lonely Poetry of Mr. Yeats," *NYTBR*, 14 Aug 1921, 14.

W129/130: *Four Plays for Dancers* (1921)

395. ANON.: *CambR*, 43:1059 (2 Dec 1921), 147.

396. ANON.: "Poetic Drama," *Nation & Athenaeum*, 11 Feb 1922, 730-32.
Correspondence by Robert N. D. Wilson, 25 Feb 1922, 793.

397. ANON.: "Moonlight Visions," *Obs*, 20 Nov 1921, 4.

398. ANON.: "Plays in Verse," *Outlook* [London], 31 Dec 1921, 557-58.

399. ANON.: "The Wizardry of Mr. Yeats," *SatRL*, 3 Dec 1921, 643.
Yeats's plays "would have developed in precisely the same direction had not the Noh plays been discovered to the Occident."

400. ANON.: "Plays for Dancers: Mr. Yeats Employs a Japanese Model," *Springfield Daily Republican*, 8 Mar 1922, 12.

401. BISHOP, JOHN PEALE: "Decorative Plays," *Literary R*, 4 Mar 1922, 465.

402. BURROW, C. KENNETT: "Four Real Poets," *John o' London's Weekly*, 7 Jan 1922, 461.

403. [CHILD, HAROLD]: "Plays for Dancers," *TLS*, 15 Dec 1921, 840.
"This sort of drama is in the straight line of descent from Mr. Yeats's previous plays." N.B.: In *YES*, 16 (1986), 142, Virginia Woolf is wrongly identified as the reviewer. I owe this correction to Andrew McNeillie.

404. COLUM, PADRAIC: "A New Dramatic Art," *Dial*, 72:3 (Mar 1922), 302-4.
In these plays, "Mr. Yeats makes a dramatic structure that admirably fits his art; in them he can be abstract and circumstantial, dramatic and lyrical, expressionistic and traditional. Above all, he can be ritualistic."

405. D., B. H., and L. E. B.: *Quest* [London], 13:3 (Apr 1922), 422-24.

406. FIRKINS, O. W.: "The Old Time in the New Drama," *YR*, 12:1 (Oct 1922), 193-94.

407. GOSSE, EDMUND: "Plays in Verse," *SunT*, 11 Dec 1921, 6.
The plays are "childish" and devoid of meaning.

408. HEAD, CLOYD: "Mr. W. B. Yeats' Plays," *Poetry*, 19:5 (Feb 1922), 288-92.

409. LYND, ROBERT: "Mr. W. B. Yeats's Experiments," *Daily News*, 2 Dec 1921, 8.
"Yeats's ideal spectators would be a queer sort of men and women, with uncivilised imaginations and civilised minds--let us say neo-Platonist South Sea Islanders."

410. M[ACNAMARA], B[RINSLEY]: "Books and Their Writers," *Gael*, 26 Dec 1921, 6-7.
"It is rather startling to realise suddenly that no one in Ireland nowadays thinks of attacking W. B. Yeats. . . . It should remain eternally as a reproach to us if other peoples were to exhibit a deeper acquaintance with his work than we ourselves."

411. MOULT, THOMAS: "Poets and the Play," *Time and Tide*, 10 Mar 1922, 226-27.

412. OULD, HERMON: "Caviare," *English R*, 34:5 (May 1922), 447-53.

413. R., W. L.: *BmL*, 61:363 (Dec 1921), Christmas Supplement, 38, 40.

414. WILSON, EDMUND: "The Poetry of Mr. W. B. Yeats," *Freeman*, 29 Mar 1922, 68-69.

415. [YOUNG, STARK]: *TAM,* 6:1 (Jan 1922), 79.

416. Y[OUNG], S[TARK]: "Five Books of Plays," *NewRep,* 15 Mar 1922, 83-84.

See also G393.

W131: *Four Years* (1921)

417. ANON.: "Two Victorians at Close Range," *NYTBR,* 29 May 1921, 5.
On Yeats and Oscar Wilde.

418. LE GALLIENNE, RICHARD: "A Moonbeam's Autobiography," *NYTBR,* 28 Aug 1921, 3, 24.
Reviews the *Dial* version (Wade, p. 381).

W133: *The Trembling of the Veil* (1922)

419. ANON.: "Mr. Yeats Explains Himself," *Nation & Athenaeum,* 30 Dec 1922, 520-22.
Also a review of W134 and 136.

420. ANON.: "Memoirs of a Poet," *Morning Post,* 10 Nov 1922, 4.

421. ANON.: "Mr. Yeats and the Nineties," *Obs,* 12 Nov 1922, 4.

422. ANON.: "Mr. Yeats's Youth: Poet and Mystic," *Times,* 19 Dec 1922, 15.

423. BINYON, LAURENCE: "William Butler Yeats," *BmL,* 63:376 (Jan 1923), 196-99.

424. [BROCK, ARTHUR CLUTTON]: "The Memories of Mr. Yeats," *TLS,* 23 Nov 1922, 761.

425. DE B[LACAM], A[ODH]: "Memoirs of W. B. Yeats: Genesis of the Celtic Movement Described," *IrI,* 13 Nov 1922, 8.

426. ELLIS, STEWART MARSH: *Mainly Victorian.* London: Hutchinson, [1925]. 403 pp.
"W. B. Yeats," 280-86; reprinted in part from "Current Literature," *FortnR,* os 119 / ns 113:676 (1 Apr 1923), 690-702. Correspondence by D. L. Todhunter, os 120 / ns 114:629 (July 1923), 163, on Yeats's share in the production of John Todhunter's *Sicilian Idyll.*

427. O'H[EGARTY], P. S.: *Irish R,* 1:6 (6 Jan 1923), 7

W134/135: *Later Poems* (1922/1924)

428. ANON.: "William Butler Yeats," *BET,* 17 May 1924, part 6, 3.

429. ANON.: *Outlook,* 6 Aug 1924, 549.

430. ANON.: "The Real Mr. Yeats," *SatRL,* 20 Jan 1923, 82.
Also a review of W136.

431. AUSLANDER, JOSEPH: *Atlantic Monthly,* 134:2 (Aug 1924), Atlantic's Bookshelf section, 8.

432. BOYD, ERNEST: "From the Yellow Nineties to the Nobel Prize," *Literary Digest International Book R,* 3:26 (Jan 1925), 88-89.
Also a review of W137.

433. [CHILD, HAROLD]: "Mr. Yeats's Dreams," *TLS,* 28 Dec 1922, 871.
Also a review of W136; reprinted in CA50, pp. 251-56, where the reviewer is not identified.

434. COLUM, PADRAIC: "Mr. Yeats's Plays and Later Poems," *YR,* 14:2 (Jan 1925), 381-85.
Also a review of W137; reprinted in CA50, pp. 256-59.

435. FRENCH, CECIL: *Golden Hind,* 1:3 (Apr 1923), 28.
"Mr. Yeats might be described as the spoiled child of letters. He does outrageous things; he affronts his readers, bewilders, exasperates them; but he is greatly loved."

436. HELLMAN, GEORGE S.: "Exquisite Lyricism," *Voices,* 3:5 (Sept-Oct 1924), 143-46.

437. KOSZUL, A.: *LanM,* 22:1 (Jan-Feb 1924), 81-82.

438. Affable Hawk [i.e., MACCARTHY, DESMOND]: "Books in General," *NSt,* 6 Jan 1923, 407.

439. ———: "Books in General," *NSt,* 24 Nov 1923, 212.
Discusses Yeats as a love poet.

440. O'CONOR, NORREYS JEPHSON: "A New Yeats Collection," *BmNY,* 60:1 (Sept 1924), 91.
Also a review of W137.

441. SQUIRE, JOHN COLLINGS: *Essays on Poetry.* Freeport, N.Y.: Books for Libraries Press, 1967 [1923]. viii, 228 pp.
"Mr. Yeats's Later Verse," 160-70; reprint of "Poetry," *LMerc,* 7:40 (Feb 1923), 431-32. See also "Mr. Yeats's Later Verse," *Obs,* 26 Nov 1922, 4.

See also G419.

W136/137: *Plays in Prose and Verse* (1922/1924)

442. LEPPER, JOHN HERON: *New Witness,* 16 Feb 1923, 109-10.

443. MEREDITH, H. O.: "The Plays of W. B. Yeats," *NSt,* 27 Jan 1923, 481-83.

See also G419, 430, 432-34, 440.

W139/140: *Plays and Controversies* (1923/1924)

444. [FAUSSET, HUGH I'ANSON]: "Mr. Yeats and His Theatre," *Spect,* 8 Mar 1924, 373.

445. GARNIER, CHARLES M.: *Revue anglo-américaine,* 1:6 (Aug 1924),

549-50.

446. GIBBS, SIR PHILIP: "The Chance of a People's Theatre: W. B. Yeats and the Irish Drama," *John o' London's Weekly,* 5 Jan 1924, 508.

447. LUCAS, FRANK LAURENCE: *Authors Dead & Living.* NY: Macmillan, 1926. x, 297 pp.
"Sense and Sensibility," 241-44, reprinted from *NSt,* 8 Mar 1924, 634-35.

448. O'CONOR, NORREYS JEPHSON: "A Pioneer in Retrospect," *SatR,* 9 May 1925, 738.
Also a review of W142.

449. RIVOALLAN, A.: *LanM,* 23:3 (Apr 1925), 214-15.
Also a review of W141.

450. A. E. [i.e. RUSSELL, GEORGE WILLIAM]: *IrSt,* 5 Jan 1924, 534.

451. RYAN, W. P.: *BmL,* 65:390 (Mar 1924), 310.

452. [SHANKS, EDWARD]: "Mr. Yeats's Theatre," *TLS,* 10 Jan 1924, 20.
"Certainly one of the best books on the theatre published for several years." About the "No" plays: "Some day an influence from them will enter the modern, the popular theatre and be powerful there; but they themselves never will." Reprinted in CA50, pp. 259-62, where the reviewer is not identified.

453. WINDER, BLANCHE: "Modern Poetic Drama," *Poetry R,* 15:2 (Mar-Apr 1924), 69-84.
See pp. 74-77.

W141/142: *Essays* (1924)

454. ANON.: "Mr. Yeats's Essays," *SatRL,* 5 July 1924, 15.

455. C[OUSINS], J. H.: "Yeats as a Proseman," *Madras Mail,* 12 Sept 1924, 10.

456. [FAUSSET, HUGH I'ANSON]: "Mr. Yeats's Prose," *TLS,* 22 May 1924, 318.
Reprinted in CA50, pp. 262-65. The prose has developed less radically than his verse. Correspondence by Henry Festing Jones, 29 May 1924, 340.

457. ———: "Mr. Yeats and the 'Nineties,'" *Spect,* 24 May 1924, 844-45.

458. GARNIER, CH. M.: *Revue anglo-américaine,* 2:5 (June 1925), 448-51.

459. H[OLMES], J. F.: "Yeats's Essays," *NSt,* 12 July 1924, 414, 416.

460. HOOPS, J[OHANNES]: *Englische Studien,* 58:3 (1924), 454-55.

461. KENDON, FRANK: "Belles Lettres," *LMerc,* 11:64 (Feb 1925), 432-34.

462. AE [i.e. RUSSELL, GEORGE WILLIAM]: "The Essays of W. B. Yeats," *IrSt,* 7 June 1924, 397-98.

463. SAMPSON, GEORGE: "Two Ways of Criticism," *BmL,* 66:394 (July 1924), 201-2.

464. SONNENSCHEIN, HUGO: "In Quest of Poesy," *Literary R,* 6 Dec 1924, 4.

465. [THOMAS, GILBERT]: "Poet's Prose," *Nation & Athenaeum,* 28 June 1924, 416, 418.

See also G448, 449.

W146: *The Bounty of Sweden* (1925)

466. GOSSE, EDMUND: "A Poet's Thanks," *SunT,* 26 July 1925, 6.
Regards Yeats as an English poet and criticizes his insistence on Irish allegiances and unorthodox lore: "Will he never learn that he knows all there is to know about fairies and mahatmas, and nothing whatever about international polemics?" See the anonymous reply (presumably by AE) in *IrSt,* 1 Aug 1925, 645.

467. Grieve, C. M. [real name of MACDIARMID, HUGH]: "Mannigfaltig: *The Dial,* Yeats, Strindberg, and Modern Swedish Literature," *New Age,* 25 Sept 1924, 260-61.
Review of the *Dial* version (Wade, p. 382).

468. M[ITCHELL], S[USAN] L.: *IrSt,* 1 Aug 1925, 658, 660.

W147/148: *Early Poems and Stories* (1925)

469. ANON.: *CambR,* 47:1150 (6 Nov 1925), 74-75.

470. ANON.: *Quarterly R,* 246:487 (Jan 1926), 217-18.
Never in his later work has Yeats "excelled those products of his unspoiled youth."

471. [FAUSSET, HUGH I'ANSON]: "Mr. Yeats in Transition," *TLS,* 8 Oct 1925, 652.
Reprinted in CA50, pp. 266-68.

472. GARNIER, CHARLES M.: *Revue anglo-américaine,* 3:5 (June 1926), 454-56.

473. H[IGGINS], B[ERTRAM]: *Calendar of Modern Letters,* 2:9 (Nov 1925), 210-11.

474. PRIESTLEY, J. B.: "The First Celt," *SatRL,* 3 Oct 1925, 374.

475. A. E. [i.e., RUSSELL, GEORGE WILLIAM]: "The Youth of a Poet," *IrSt,* 17 Oct 1925, 176-77.
Reprinted as "Yeats's Early Poems," *Living Age,* 28 Nov 1925, 464-66. This review elicited a voluminous correspondence in the *Irish Statesman* on the question of whether Yeats is an Irish or an English poet, which ran until 16 Jan 1926. Among the contributors were Frank O'Connor and Sean O'Faolain.

476. RYAN, W. P.: "The Youth of Mr. Yeats," *BmL*, 69:414 (Mar 1926), 323-24.

477. [THOMSON, GEORGE]: "Celtic Twilight," *Nation & Athenaeum*, 24 Oct 1925, 156.

W149: *A Vision* (1925)

478. ANON.: *Adelphi*, 4:4 (Oct 1926), 266.

479. ANON.: "The Visionary Yeats," *NSt*, 27 Mar 1926, 749-50.

480. ANON.: *Quest* [London], 18:1 (Oct 1926), 96-98.

481. [DE SELINCOURT, BASIL]: "Mr. Yeats's Occultism," *TLS*, 22 Apr 1926, 296.

"His book, with its accomplishment, its genius of intuition, its fleeting beauty, is tiresome because of the conviction it leaves with us that he knows this as well as anyone and yet cannot detach himself from the delights of dalliance."

482. AE [i.e. RUSSELL, GEORGE WILLIAM]: *IrSt*, 13 Feb 1926, 714-16.

"Here I fall away from a mind I have followed, I think, with understanding, since I was a boy, and as he becomes remote in his thought I wonder whether he has forgotten his own early wisdom." Reprinted in CA50, pp. 269-73.

See also CB527.

W150: *Estrangement* (1926)

483. ANON.: *DM*, ns 2:2 (Apr-June 1927), 72-73.

484. AE [i.e., RUSSELL, GEORGE WILLIAM]: *IrSt*, 4 Sept 1926, 713-14.

W151/152: *Autobiographies* (1926/1927)

485. ANON.: "The Tragic Generation: W. B. Yeats's Memories of the 'Eighties' and 'Nineties,'" *John o' London's Weekly*, 22 Jan 1927, 544-45.

486. ANON.: *Outlook*, 23 Mar 1927, 376-77.

487. ANON.: *Quarterly R*, 248:492 (Apr 1927), 427.

488. BICKLEY, FRANCIS: "Mr. Yeats and Himself," *BmL*, 71:425 (Feb 1927), 282-83.

489. CHURCH, RICHARD: "The Lifting of the Veil," *Spect*, 20 Nov 1926, 912, 914.

490. ———: "W. B. Yeats and the Creative Mask," *Calendar of Modern Letters*, 3:4 (Jan 1927), 316-19.

Reprinted in CA50, pp. 274-79.

491. DAVIDSON, DONALD: *Nashville Tennessean*, 27 Mar 1927, Magazine section, 7.

492. DEUTSCH, BABETTE: "The Autobiographies of Yeats: This Eminent Poet, If Mystic and Magician, Has Grappled Reality," *Literary R,* 7 May 1927, 5.

493. E[DSALL], R[ICHARD] L[INN]: *CathW,* 125:748 (July 1927), 566-67.

494. EGLINTON, JOHN: "Mr. Yeats's Autobiographies," *Dial,* 83:2 (Aug 1927), 94-97.

495. FORMAN, HENRY JAMES: "Yeats's Memories of His Youth: *Autobiographies* Is the Story of a Poet's Development," *NYTBR,* 15 May 1927, 13.

496. GARNIER, C.: *Revue anglo-américaine,* 7:3 (Feb 1930), 270-71.

497. K[ELLER], T. G.: *DM,* ns 2:2 (Apr-June 1927), 70.

498. LUHRS, MARIE: "Gentle Poet," *Poetry,* 30:5 (Aug 1927), 279-83.

499. LYND, ROBERT: "Men of Letters," *Obs,* 19 Dec 1926, 6.

500. M[ACNEICE], F[REDERICK] L[OUIS]: *Cherwell,* 19:1 (29 Jan 1927), 28.

"When the rest of the world is sublimely vegetable, it is very illbred in Mr. Yeats still to be spiritual."

501. MILES, HAMISH: *Monthly Criterion,* 5:3 (June 1927), 353-56.

502. MINCHIN, H. C.: "Memory Harbour," *SunT,* 21 Nov 1926, 8.

503. PAYNE, L. W.: "The Inner Life of a Poet," *SWR,* 13:1 (Oct 1927), 123-25.

504. RIVOALLAN, A.: "Quelques livres sur l'Irlande," *LanM,* 26:8 (Nov-Dec 1928), 501-11.

See pp. 505-8; also a review of W158.

505. AE [i.e., RUSSELL, GEORGE WILLIAM]: "The Memories of a Poet," *IrSt,* 4 Dec 1926, 302-3.

506. VAN DOREN, MARK: "First Glance," *Nation,* 16 Mar 1927, 291.

507. WALSH, THOMAS: *Commonweal,* 27 Apr 1927, 696-97.

508. WILSON, EDMUND: "Yeats's Memoirs," *NewRep,* 23 Feb 1927, 22-23.

509. WOOLF, LEONARD: "Life That Is a Vision," *Nation & Athenaeum,* 1 Jan 1927, 482.

510. WYLIE, ELINOR: "Path of the Chameleon," *NYHTB,* 13 Feb 1927, 1, 6.

Includes a reproduction of Yeats's drawing of Maud Gonne.

W153: *Poems* (1927)

511. ANON.: "Mr. Yeats's Afterthoughts," *NSt,* 16 Apr 1927, 17.

512. SEYMOUR, WILLIAM KEAN: "Mr. Yeats's Poetry," *G.K.'s Weekly,* 12 Mar 1927, 289.

"It is . . . for the evocative phrase and music--not for profundity, that we turn to Mr. Yeats."

W156: *October Blast* (1927)

513. AE [i.e., RUSSELL, GEORGE WILLIAM]: *IrSt,* 27 Aug 1927, 597-98.

W157: *Stories of Red Hanrahan and The Secret Rose* (1927)

514. [CLARKE, AUSTIN]: "Red Hanrahan," *TLS,* 8 Dec 1927, 929.

515. L[OBO], G[EORGE] E[DMUND]: "W. B. Yeats Illustrated," *Dublin Art Monthly,* 1:4 (Jan 1928), 20-21.
Praises Norah McGuinness's illustrations.

516. Y. O. [i.e., RUSSELL, GEORGE WILLIAM]: *IrSt,* 17 Dec 1927, 354.
Actually on Norah McGuinness's illustrations, which are considered to be superfluous.

W158/159: *The Tower* (1928)

517. ANON.: *Annual Register,* 170 (1928), II, 30.

518. ANON.: *Living Age,* 15 Apr 1928, 747-48.
Reprinted from an unspecified issue of the *Morning Post.*

519. ANON.: "Mr. W. B. Yeats," *NSt,* 7 Apr 1928, 829-30.

520. B., A. F.: *CambR,* 50:1220 (19 Oct 1928), 41.

521. BENNETT, ARNOLD: "Books and Persons: The 'Monstrous Conceit' of Some Modernists," *Evening Standard,* 1 Mar 1928, 5.

522. BRULÉ, A.: *Revue anglo-américaine,* 5:6 (Aug 1928), 570-71.

523. CHURCH, RICHARD: "W. B. Yeats," *Spect,* 3 Mar 1928, 324.

524. [CLARKE, AUSTIN]: "Mr. Yeats's New Poems," *TLS,* 1 Mar 1928, 146.
Reprinted in CA50, pp. 282-85.

525. DAVIDSON, DONALD: *Nashville Tennessean,* 15 July 1928, Magazine section, 7.
Deplores the disappearance of Yeats's romanticism.

526. DEM., S.: "Poems of Pessimism," *ContempR,* 134:755 (Nov 1928), 671-73.

527. DEUTSCH, BABETTE: "The Making of a Soul," *NYHTB,* 5 Aug 1928, 1-2.

528. DRINKWATER, JOHN: *Daily Telegraph,* 28 Feb 1928, 17.

529. EGLINTON, JOHN: "Mr. Yeats's Tower," *Dial,* 86:1 (Jan 1929), 62-65.

530. FLETCHER, JOHN GOULD: *Criterion,* 8:30 (Sept 1928), 131-32.

Reprinted in CA50, pp. 286-87.

531. GREGORY, HORACE: "After a Half-Century," *Poetry,* 33:1 (Oct 1928), 41-44.

532. GWYNN, STEPHEN: *FortnR,* os 129 / ns 123:736 (Apr 1928), 561-63.

533. H[IGGINS], F. R.: *IrSt,* 14 Apr 1928, 112-13.

534. HILLYER, ROBERT: "A Poet Young and Old," *New Adelphi,* 3:1 (Sept-Nov 1929), 78-80.

535. MCB., P.: "An Intellect Unaging: Latest Poems of W. B. Yeats," *IrI,* 27 Feb 1928, 4.

536. O'FAOLAIN, SEAN: "Four Irish Generations," *Commonweal,* 1 May 1929, 751.
Also a review of W162.

537. ÖSTERLING, ANDERS: *Horisonter.* Stockholm: Bonnier, 1939. 256 pp. "Den unge Yeats och den gamle," 205-21. Reprint of "Den unge Yeats," *Svenska dagbladet,* 7 July 1934, 7 (a review of W173), and "W. B. Yeats," *Svenska dagbladet,* 13 Jan 1934, 9-10 (a review of W158 and 169).

538. R[ITCHIE], E[LIZA]: *DR,* 8:4 (Jan 1929), 572.

539. ROBERTS, R. ELLIS: *BmL,* 74:439 (Apr 1928), 42-43.

540. SPENCER, THEODORE: *NewRep,* 10 Oct 1928, 219-20.
Extract reprinted in CA50, pp. 287-90.

541. STEWART, GEORGE R.: *U of California Chronicle,* 30:4 (Oct 1928), 484-85.

542. TASKER, J. DANA: "A Philosophy of Faith," *Outlook,* 19 Sept 1928, 831, 840.

543. TWITCHETT, E. G.: "Poetry," *LMerc,* 18:106 (Aug 1928), 433-36.

544. WOLFE, HUMBERT: "The Tower," *Obs,* 19 Feb 1928, 9.

545. ———: *SatRL,* 25 Feb 1928, 225-26.

546. [WOOLF, VIRGINIA]: "Mr. Yeats," *Nation & Athenaeum,* 21 Apr 1928, 81.
"Mr. Yeats has never written more exactly and more passionately."

See also G504.

W160/61: *Sophocles' King Oedipus* (1928)

547. ANON.: *ContempR,* 133:749 (May 1928), 673-75.
". . . very Irish, very effective, and, indeed, very Greek."

548. GLOVER, M. R.: "Some Verse Translations," *Classical R,* 43:1 (Feb 1929), 16-18.

549. [SMYTH, A. E.]: "Four Greek Poets," *TLS*, 22 Nov 1928, 876. Extract reprinted in CA50, pp. 290-91.

W162: *The Death of Synge* (1928)

550. O'FAOLAIN, SEAN: "Yeats on Synge," *IrSt*, 29 Sept 1928, 71-72. "The fact is that Synge was by nature what Yeats has never been, and has always been trying to become by way of romance or mask or discipline." Correspondence by Arthur Lynch, 20 Oct 1928, 131; Stephen MacKenna, 3 Nov 1928, 169-70.

See also G536.

W163: *A Packet for Ezra Pound* (1929)

551. O'FAOLAIN, SEAN: "Mr. Yeats's Trivia," *Commonweal*, 18 Sept 1929, 512-13.
"This somewhat artificial connection with spirituality has not benefited Mr. Yeats's work, whether in prose or verse."

552. ———: "Mr. Yeats's Kubla Khan," *Nation*, 4 Dec 1929, 681-82.

553. AE [i.e., RUSSELL, GEORGE WILLIAM]: *IrSt*, 7 Sept 1929, 11-12. Reprinted in *Living Age*, 1 Oct 1929, 186-88.

W164: *The Winding Stair* (1929)

554. [BROCK, ALAN CLUTTON]: *TLS*, 6 Nov 1930, 910.
Reprinted in CA50, pp. 299-301, where the reviewer is not identified.

555. AE [i.e., RUSSELL, GEORGE WILLIAM]: *IrSt*, 1 Feb 1930, 436-37.

See also CC222.

W165: *Selected Poems Lyrical and Narrative* (1929)

556. BRULÉ, A.: *Revue anglo-américaine*, 8:3 (Feb 1931), 265-66.

557. DAVRAY, HENRY D.: *MercF*, year 41 / 218:760 (15 Feb 1930), 227-28.

558. GIBSON, WILFRID: "W. B. Yeats," *BmL*, 77:460 (Jan 1930), 227-28.

559. MACCARTHY, DESMOND: "The Poetry of Mr. Yeats," *SunT*, 24 Nov 1929, 8.
Discusses Yeats as a love poet.

560. O'FAOLAIN, SEAN: *Criterion*, 9:36 (Apr 1930), 523-28.
Criticizes Yeats's revisions and his preoccupation with occultism.

561. Y. O. [i.e., RUSSELL, GEORGE WILLIAM]: "The Reading of Poetry," *IrSt*, 9 Nov 1929, 191-92.

562. S., B.: *MGuard*, 27 Nov 1929, 7.

W167: *Stories of Michael Robartes and His Friends* (1931)

563. [CLARKE, AUSTIN]: *TLS,* 24 Mar 1932, 214.

564. P[OWELL], C[HARLES]: "Mr. W. B. Yeats," *MGuard,* 2 May 1932, 5.

W168: *Words for Music Perhaps and Other Poems* (1932)

565. BRADBROOK, M. C.: "Songs of Experience," *Scrutiny,* 2:1 (June 1933), 77-78.

566. COLUM, PADRAIC: "Sailing to Byzantium," *Spect,* 9 June 1933, 841.

See also CC222, CD383.

W169/170: *The Winding Stair and Other Poems* (1933)

567. ANON.: *Church of Ireland Gazette,* 10 Nov 1933, 648.

568. ANON.: "W. B. Yeats," *Church Times,* 29 Sept 1933, 361.

569. ANON.: "Mr. Yeats's Poems," *IrT,* 14 Oct 1933, 4.

570. ANON.: *LLT,* 9:51 (Dec 1933), 486-90.

571. ANON.: "The New Poetry--and Poetry," *Modern Scot,* 4:3 (Oct 1933), 250-53.
Compares Yeats and Pound and finds the latter lacking in universality.

572. ANON.: "Donne and the Moderns: A New Volume by W. B. Yeats," *Scotsman,* 28 Sept 1933, 2.

573. ARNS, KARL: *Englische Studien,* 69:1 (July 1934), 145-46.

574. BÄNNINGER, KONRAD: "W. B. Yeats' neue Gedichte," *NZZ,* 15 Apr 1934, Literarische Beilage, [8].

575. BLUNDEN, EDMUND: *Book Society News,* 5:10 (Oct 1933), 19.
This item and item G688 are listed in B. J. Kirkpatrick's *A Bibliography of Edmund Blunden* (Oxford: Clarendon Press, 1979). The *Book Society News* were issued to members only. There are no files listed in BUCOP and ULS. Typewritten copies were kindly provided by Miss Kirkpatrick.

576. BROWNE, WYNYARD: "Poetry," *LMerc,* 28:168 (Oct 1933), 549-51.

577. BRULÉ, A.: *Revue anglo-américaine,* 11:4 (Apr 1934), 360-61.

578. [BUCHANAN, GEORGE]: "Mr. Yeats's New Poems," *TLS,* 5 Oct 1933, 666.
Reprinted as "Fifty Years On: *The Winding Stair*," *TLS,* 7 Oct 1983, 1087; also in CA50, pp. 327-31; in both cases the reviewer is not identified.

579. CHURCH, RICHARD: "Yeats Re-Emerges," *NSt,* 14 Oct 1933, Supplement, vi, viii.

580. ———: *FortnR,* os 140 / ns 134:803 (Nov 1933), 629-30.

581. ———: "The Secret of Youth," *CSM,* 23 Dec 1933, 9.

582. E., C.: "Mr. Yeats's Latest 'Message,'" *Irish News,* 23 Sept 1933, 3.

583. FALLON, PADRAIC: *DM,* 9:2 (Apr-June 1934), 58-65.

584. FAUSSET, HUGH I'ANSON: "Mr. Yeats and His Dark Tower: Poems of Protest and Regret," *Yorkshire Post,* 25 Oct 1933, 6.

585. GREGORY, HORACE: "Yeats: Envoy of Two Worlds," *NewRep,* 13 Dec 1933, 134-35.
Also a review of W171.

586. GRIGSON, GEOFFREY: "Is Ezra Pound a Great Poet? The Testimony of Yeats," *Morning Post,* 15 Sept 1933, 4.

587. ———: "A Fanatic Heart," *New Verse,* 6 (Dec 1933), 24, 26.

588. HONE, J. M.: "Mr. Yeats's Poems," *Week-end R,* 21 Oct 1933, 414.

589. ———: "Letter from Ireland," *Poetry,* 43:5 (Feb 1934), 274-79.
Includes a note on the Irish Academy of Letters.

590. HUTCHINSON, PERCY: "The Poems of William Butler Yeats," *NYTBR,* 24 Dec 1933, 2, 10.
Also a review of W171.

591. LEAVIS, F. R.: "The Latest Yeats," *Scrutiny,* 2:3 (Dec 1933), 293-95.
The collection is not as good as *The Tower;* "the proud sardonic tension . . . is slackened."

592. PARSONS, I. M.: "Port after Storm," *Spect,* 6 Oct 1933, 452.

593. PORTEUS, HUGH GORDON: *Criterion,* 13:51 (Jan 1934), 313-15.
Reprinted in CA50, pp. 331-34.

594. P[OWELL], C[HARLES]: "W. B. Yeats," *MGuard,* 2 Oct 1933, 5.

595. POWELL, DILYS: "Mr. Yeats's New Poems: A Mind in Conflict," *SunT,* 19 Nov 1933, 10.

596. RIVOALLAN, A.: *LanM,* 32:4 (June 1934), 308-9.

597. SPENDER, STEPHEN: "Honour to Yeats," *List,* 11 Oct 1933, Supplement, xi.

598. STUART, FRANCIS: "Mr. Yeats's New Poems," *IrP,* 3 Oct 1933, 6.

599. SUNNE, RICHARD: "Men and Books," *Time and Tide,* 30 Sept 1933, 1151-52.

600. T., P. C.: *Irish Book Lover,* 22:3 (May-June 1934), 72-73.

601. WALTON, EDA LOU: "Cast Out Remorse," *Nation,* 13 Dec 1933, 684-86.
Also a review of W171.

602. WARREN, C. HENRY: "The New Yeats," *BmL,* 85:507 (Dec 1933), 230.

603. WOLFE, HUMBERT: "Windy Halls of Heaven," *Obs,* 1 Oct 1933, 5.

604. Z[ABEL], M. D.: "The Summers of Hesperides," *Poetry,* 43:5 (Feb 1934), 279-87.
Also a review of W171.

See also G537.

W171/172: *The Collected Poems* (1933)

605. ANON.: *Annual Register,* 175 (1933), II, 29-30.

606. ANON.: *DM,* 9:3 (July-Sept 1934), 63-66.

607. ANON.: *List,* 31 Jan 1934, 213.

608. ANON.: *List,* 17 June 1936, 1175.

609. ANON.: "Yeats's Collected Poems," *NSt,* 3 Feb 1934, 160, 162.

610. ARMSTRONG, MARTIN: "Daemonic Images," *Weekend R,* 6 Jan 1934, 729-30.

611. BENÉT, WILLIAM ROSE: "This Virtue," *SatR,* 16 Dec 1933, 349-50.

612. BLACKMUR, R. P.: "Under a Major Poet," *American Mercury,* 31: 122 (Feb 1934), 244-46.

613. B[RÉGY], K[ATHERINE]: *CathW,* 140:836 (Nov 1934), 241-42.

614. COLUM, PADRAIC: "On Yeats," *Commonweal,* 18 May 1934, 70-71.

615. DEUTSCH, BABETTE: "Certain Good," *VQR,* 10:2 (Apr 1934), 298-302.
"Hostile to the intellect, although marked by an acute and nimble intelligence, Yeats's genius is incapable of interpreting this age to itself."

616. E., C.: "The Poems of Yeats: Little in Common with Ireland," *Irish News,* 23 Dec 1933, 3.

617. FOX, ARTHUR W.: "Collected Poems of William Butler Yeats," *Papers of the Manchester Literary Club,* 61 (1935), 62-80.

618. HAWKINS, DESMOND: "Recent Verse," *New English Weekly,* 22 Feb 1934, 448-49.

619. K[UNITZ], S. J.: "The Roving Eye: The Collected Poems of Yeats," *Wilson Bulletin for Librarians,* 8:6 (Feb 1934), 350-51.

620. LAWRENCE, C. E.: "Poetry and Verse and Worse," *Quarterly R,* 262:520 (Apr 1934), 299-314.

621. MACCARTHY, DESMOND: "A Note on the Poems of Yeats: The Forerunner," *SunT,* 4 Feb 1934, 8.
Reprinted in CA50, pp. 317-22.

622. M[ACDONAGH], D[ONAGH]: "Re-Written Poems: Yeats' Collected Work," *IrP,* 1 Jan 1934, 10.

623. MATTHIESSEN, F. O.: "Yeats and Four American Poets," *YR,* 23:3 (Mar 1934), 611-17.

624. PATERSON, ISABEL: "The Pure Flame of W. B. Yeats's Poetry: Such Sustained Intensity Suggests Stepping Out of Time into Eternity," *NYHTB,* 3 Dec 1933, 9.

625. P[OWELL], C[HARLES]: "The Collected Yeats," *MGuard,* 5 Feb 1934, 5.

626. READ, HERBERT: *A Coat of Many Colours.* London: Routledge & Kegan Paul, 1956 [1945]. x, 352 pp.

"The Later Yeats," 208-12; reprinted from *Criterion,* 13:52 (Apr 1934), 468-72; reprinted in CA50, pp. 322-26. Discusses the revisions of "The Sorrow of Love."

627. ROBERTS, R. ELLIS: "The Greatest Living Master in English," *News Chronicle,* 24 Jan 1934, 4.

628. SCOVELL, E. J.: "W. B. Yeats," *Time and Tide,* 10 Mar 1934, 322-23.

629. SHANKS, EDWARD: "Prince of Our Poets," *John o' London's Weekly,* 10 Feb 1934, 721.

630. SPENDER, STEPHEN: "Hammered Gold," *Spect,* 23 Feb 1934, 284, 286.

Criticizes Yeats's "incomplete approach to humanity."

631. T., A. B.: "Collected Poems of William Butler Yeats: He Is Revealed as Distinctly More a Pagan Than He Was Twenty-five Years Ago," *BET,* 6 Jan 1934, Book section, 1.

632. WEST, GEOFFREY: *Adelphi,* ns 8:3 (June 1934), 227-31.

See also G585, 590, 601, 604.

W173: *Letters to the New Island* (1934)

633. ANON.: "Literature and Nationality: Early Letters by Mr. Yeats," *IrT,* 23 June 1934, 5.

634. ANON.: "W. B. Yeats and Ireland," *Springfield Daily Republican,* 3 Feb 1934, 8.

635. ANON.: "Letters to America: Mr. Yeats as a Young Journalist," *Times,* 6 Apr 1934, 7.

636. BOLAND, EAVAN: "Letters and Men of Letters," *IrT,* 1 Aug 1970, 10.

637. CHURCH, RICHARD: "Yeats Forty Years Ago," *NSt,* 4 Aug 1934, 157-58.

638. [CLARKE, AUSTIN]: "A Celt in London," *TLS,* 12 Apr 1934, 259.

639. COGHLAN, JOHN: *BmL,* 86:515 (Aug 1934), 251.

640. COLUM, PADRAIC: "The Man in the Youth," *SatR,* 2 June 1934, 722-23.
Reprinted anonymously in *DM,* 9:3 (July-Sept 1934), 66-68.

641. DEUTSCH, BABETTE: "The Poet as a Young Man," *Nation,* 14 Mar 1934, 309-10.

642. G[REGORY], H[ORACE]: *NewRep,* 13 June 1934, 136.

643. HERSEY, F. W. C.: *MLN,* 50:6 (June 1935), 411-12.

644. MACCARTHY, DESMOND: "William Butler Yeats: The Journalism of a Poet," *SunT,* 17 June 1934, 8.

645. MONKHOUSE, ALLAN: "A Bookman's Notes: A Great Irishman," *MGuard,* 8 June 1934, 7.

646. MURRAY, PATRICK: "What the Young Man Wrote," *IrI,* 6 June 1970, 10.

647. P., R.: "Irish Renaissance Rehearsal," *CSM,* 27 June 1934, Weekly Magazine section, 10.
Yeats's major theme is "the importance of nationalism to an author." "Such an intense aesthetic nationalism is all the easier for a poet when the country of his devotion is not a political reality, and indeed it is in the desire to develop the cultural unity of a people that we find the expression of a true national spirit as opposed to the blind, selfish nationalism so evident in the world today."

648. QUINN, KERKER: "Memories Differ," *YR,* 26:1 (Sept 1936), 208-10.
Also a review of W186.

649. R., G. R. B.: "Letters from W. B. Yeats during His Earlier Years: He Was Even Then on His Way as the Guiding Spirit of the Irish Renaissance," *BET,* 17 Mar 1934, Book section, 1.

650. STRONG, L. A. G.: "Letters to America," *Obs,* 15 July 1934, 5.

651. SUNNE, RICHARD: "Men and Books," *Time and Tide,* 2 June 1934, 702-3.

652. WALTON, EDA LOU: "When William Butler Yeats Was Twenty-six," *NYTBR,* 8 Apr 1934, 4.

See also G537.

W175/176: *Wheels and Butterflies* (1934/1935)

653. ANON.: *DM,* 11:1 (Jan-Mar 1936), 70-72.
Also a review of W177 and 179.

654. ANON.: *Evening Mail,* 22 Nov 1934, 7.

655. ANON.: "Mr. Yeats as Playwright," *Glasgow Herald,* 27 Dec 1934, 2.
Also a review of W177.

656. ANON.: "Experiments in Dramatic Art: New Plays from Mr. Yeats," *IrI,* 4 Dec 1934, 5.

657. ANON.: *LLT,* 11:61 (Jan 1935), 483-86.
Also a review of W177.

658. ANON.: *List,* 30 Jan 1935, 209.
Also a review of W177.

659. ANON.: "Yeats as a Dramatist," *Scotsman,* 17 Dec 1934, 15.
Also a review of W177.

660. ANON.: *TAM,* 19:8 (Aug 1935), 647.
"The introductions . . . provide the richest fodder."

661. BOGAN, LOUISE: "For Garrets and Cellars," *Poetry,* 46:2 (May 1935), 100-104.

662. [BUCHANAN, GEORGE]: "New Poetic Drama," *TLS,* 24 Jan 1935, 37-38.
Also a review of W177 and 179.

663. C., F.: *Granta,* 44:996 (23 Jan 1935), 198.

664. CAZAMIAN, M.-L.: *Revue anglo-américaine,* 12:5 (June 1935), 450-51.

665. CLARKE, AUSTIN: "The Poetic Drama of Mr. Yeats," *LMerc,* 31:184 (Feb 1935), 391-92.
Also a review of W177.

666. F., E.: "Recent Plays," *Oxford Magazine,* 53:17 (2 May 1935), 536-37.
Also a review of W177.

667. FLETCHER, JOHN GOULD: *SoR,* 1:1 (Summer 1935), 199-203.

668. FREEMAN, E. L.: "Dreamers, Thinkers, and a Lecturer," *Frontier & Midland,* 16:1 (Autumn 1935), 70-72.

669. GARRETT, JOHN: *Criterion,* 14:56 (Apr 1935), 488-91.
Also a review of W177.

670. GOLDRING, DOUGLAS: "Celtic Mists," *Liverpool Post and Mercury,* 15 Jan 1935, 5.

671. GREGORY, HORACE: "Yeats: Last Spokesman," *NewRep,* 18 Sept 1935, 164-65.
Also a review of W177 and 179.

672. JOHNSTON, DENIS: "Mr. Yeats as Dramatist," *Spect,* 30 Nov 1934, 843.
Reprinted in CA50, pp. 349-52.

673. MACCARTHY, DESMOND: "New Plays by W. B. Yeats: A Poet's Butterflies," *SunT,* 13 Jan 1935, 8.

674. M[ACDONAGH], D[ONAGH]: "Mr. Yeats' Symbolism," *IrP,* 18 Dec 1934, 10.

675. ÖSTERLING, ANDERS: "Små dramer av Yeats," *Svenska dagbladet,* 9 Feb 1935, 7.

676. POORE, C. G.: "The Savor, the Splendor and the Eloquence of Yeats," *NYTBR,* 24 Feb 1935, 3, 15.

677. P[OWELL], C[HARLES]: "Plays by Mr. Yeats," *MGuard,* 20 Dec 1934, 5.

678. REYNOLDS, HORACE: "Supernatural Plays," *SatR,* 9 Mar 1935, 535.

679. RICE, PHILIP BLAIR: "A Bell with Many Echoes," *Nation,* 3 Apr 1935, 397-98.

680. RIVOALLAN, A.: *LanM,* 34:3 (Mar 1936), 187-88.

681. TAGGARD, GENEVIEVE: "The Mysteries of W. B. Yeats: Another Stage in the Irishman's Poetic Pilgrimage Finds Him in a Not Quite Mystic Reverie," *NYHTB,* 12 May 1935, 2.

682. WOLFE, HUMBERT: "Poets for All," *Obs,* 2 Dec 1934, 19.

683. W[YATT], E[UPHEMIA] V[AN] R[ENSSELAER]: *CathW,* 141:846 (Sept 1935), 755.

See also G696.

W177/178: *The Collected Plays* (1934/1935)

684. ANON.: "W. B. Yeats and Dramatic Expression," *CSM,* 28 Aug 1935, Weekly Magazine section, 11.

685. B[ABITS], M[IHALY]: "Költo, forradalom és heroizmus" [Poet, revolution, and heroism], *Nyugat,* 28:3 (Mar 1935), 259-60.

686. BALL, ARTHUR: *FortnR,* os 143 / ns 137:819 (Mar 1935), 380-81.

687. BERRYMAN, JOHN: *The Freedom of the Poet.* NY: Farrar, Straus & Giroux, 1976. x, 390 pp.

"The Ritual of W. B. Yeats," 245-52; reprinted from *Columbia R,* 17:4&5 (May-June 1936), 26-32, where the author's name appears as John McAlpin Berryman.

688. BLUNDEN, EDMUND: *Book Society News,* 6:2 (Dec 1934), 12.

See G575.

689. COLM: *Irish Book Lover,* 23:2 (Mar-Apr 1935), 54.

690. COLUM, MARY M.: "Worker in Dreams," *Forum and Century,* 94:5 (Nov 1935), 278-79.

691. DEUTSCH, BABETTE: "Plays in a Living Language: The Dramatic Genius of W. B. Yeats Voiced in Symbolism, Folklore and Beauty," *NYHTB,* 1 Sept 1935, 2.

692. GREGORY, HORACE: "Poets in the Theatre," *Poetry,* 48:4 (July 1936), 221-28.

See pp. 226-27.

693. REYNOLDS, HORACE: "That Dream-Made World of Yeats the Dramatist: In His *Collected Plays* We Have the Fruits of a Flaming Effort to Restore a Nation's Consciousness," *NYTBR,* 1 Sept 1935, 2, 8.

694. STRONG, L. A. G.: "The Plays of W. B. Yeats," *John o' London's Weekly,* 5 Jan 1935, 550.

695. VALLETTE, J.: *LanM,* 33:7 (Dec 1935), 650-51.

See also G653, 655, 657-59, 662, 665, 666, 669, 671, 696.

W179/A: *The King of the Great Clock Tower, Commentaries and Poems* (1934/1935)

696. ANON.: "Poetry's Return to Theatre: Three Books by W. B. Yeats," *IrT,* 5 Jan 1935, 7.
Also a review of W175 and 177.

697. B., E.: "Return of Yeats: The Prose Dialogue of a Dance Play," *BET,* 8 June 1935, Book section, 4.

698. BAKER, HOWARD: "Wallace Stevens and Other Poets," *SoR,* 1:2 (Autumn 1935), 373-96.
See pp. 391-93: "Refusing to formulate experience, Yeats has really no means of telling the natural from the supernatural."

699. BENÉT, WILLIAM ROSE: "Contemporary Poetry," *SatR,* 18 May 1935, 20-21.

700. DEUTSCH, BABETTE: "Yeats Is Not Too Old for Poetry: Nearing Seventy, He Wondered; But He Still Has the Power of Words," *NYHTB,* 11 Aug 1935, 6.

701. LYND, ROBERT: "A Great Poet Condemned," *News Chronicle,* 1 Feb 1935, 4.
The reference is to Pound's condemnation as recorded in Yeats's preface to his book.

702. M[AYNARD], T[HEODORE]: *CathW,* 142:848 (Nov 1935), 254-55.

703. PARSONS, I. M.: "The Winding Stair," *Spect,* 11 Jan 1935, 57.

704. P[OORE], C. G.: "Five-Finger Exercises of a Genius," *NYTBR,* 2 June 1935, 2.

705. REYNOLDS, HORACE: "New Poems by Yeats," *CSM,* 17 July 1935, Weekly Magazine section, 11.

706. Z[ABEL], M. D.: "For Saints and Patriots," *Poetry,* 46:2 (May 1935), 104-8.

See also G653, 662, 671.

W182: *A Full Moon in March* (1935)

707. ANON.: "New Poetry," *DM,* 11:1 (Jan-Mar 1936), 72-75.

708. ANON.: "*A Full Moon in March:* Mr. Yeats's New Book of Poems,"

IrT, 14 Dec 1935, 7.

709. ANON.: *List,* 1 Jan 1936, 41.

710. ANON.: "Recent Poetry," *Scotsman,* 23 Dec 1935, 13.

711. [BUCHANAN, GEORGE]: "The Mind of Mr. Yeats in Verse," *TLS,* 7 Dec 1935, 833.
Reprinted in CA50, pp. 358-60, where the reviewer is not identified.

712. C[AZAMIAN], M. L.: *Revue anglo-amèricaine,* 13:5 (June 1936), 445-46.

713. CLARKE, AUSTIN: "Mr. Yeats--Contrasts in Verse and Prose," *LMerc* 33:195 (Jan 1936), 341-42.
"Mr. Yeats proves himself master of that eloquence which he spent half a lifetime eradicating from his own literary movement." Reprinted in CA50, pp. 362-64.

714. FAUSSET, HUGH I'A.: "Time and Mr. Yeats," *Yorkshire Post,* 19 Feb 1936, 6.

715. GRIGSON, GEOFFREY: "W. B. Yeats in His Green Old Age: The Poet and His Emblems," *Morning Post,* 18 Feb 1936, 16.

716. GRUBB, H. T. HUNT: *Poetry R,* 27:1 (Jan-Feb 1936), 62-63.

717. M[ACDONAGH], D[ONAGH]: "Mr. Yeats's New Poems," *IrP,* 10 Dec 1935, 11.

718. POWELL, CHARLES: "Recent Poetry," *MGuard,* 30 Dec 1935, 5.

719. RIVOALLAN, A.: *LanM,* 34:10 (Dec 1936), 643.

720. ROBERTS, MICHAEL: "The Moon and the Savage, Sunlit Heart," *Spect,* 27 Dec 1935, 1078-79.
Reprinted in CA50, pp. 360-62.

721. S., D.: "A Variety of Plays: Two Poetic Versions of a Yeats Drama," *IrI,* 28 Jan 1936, 4.

722. SMITH, JANET ADAM: *Criterion,* 15:60 (Apr 1936), 521-22.

723. W., G.: *Granta,* 45:1023 (12 Feb 1936), 237.

724. WAINEWRIGHT, RUTH M. D.: *English,* 1:3 (1936), 259-60.

W183: *Dramatis Personae* (1935)

725. ANON.: *DM,* 11:2 (Apr-June 1936), 67-68.

726. CHURCH, RICHARD: "A Portrait in Vitriol," *NSt,* 14 Mar 1936, 398.

W186/187: *Dramatis Personae* (1936)

727. ANON.: "Yeatsian Memories," *Commonweal,* 24 July 1936, 332.

728. ANON.: *Evening Mail,* 22 May 1936, 5.
See also "Jottings by a Man about Town," 5 June 1936, 6.

729. ANON.: "The Irish Revival," *Outlook* [Glasgow], 1:4 (July 1936), 84-86.

730. ANON.: *Quarterly R,* 267:529 (July 1936), 185.

731. ANON.: "Prize Poet's Progress," *Time,* 18 May 1936, 83.

732. ANON.: "Mr. W. B. Yeats Looks Back: Varied Reminiscences," *Times,* 22 May 1936, 19.

733. ATKINSON, BROOKS: "W. B. Yeats, Man of Letters," *NYT,* 7 June 1936, section IX, 1.

734. B., C. E.: "Books of the Day," *ILN,* 20 June 1936, 1126.

735. BOSANQUET, THEODORA: "Men and Books," *Time and Tide,* 13 June 1936, 849.

736. BUCKRAM, ELIOT: "An Irish Poet," *Church of England Newspaper,* 5 June 1936, 5.

737. BURDETT, OSBERT: "W. B. Yeats's Memories: Stories of George Moore and a Visit to the Swedish Court," *John o' London's Weekly,* 20 June 1936, 421.

738. C.: "Yeats and His Literary Friends," *Irish News,* 17 June 1936, 4.

739. [CLARKE, AUSTIN]: "Mr. Yeats's Reminiscences: Years of Peace and the Age of Disillusion," *TLS,* 23 May 1936, 434.

740. ———: "Mr. Yeats and His Contemporaries," *LMerc,* 34:200 (June 1936), 169-70.

741. COLUM, PADRAIC: "Yeats Looks Back," *SatR,* 16 May 1936, 7.

742. CONLAY, IRIS: "Mirror to Man," *Catholic Herald,* 7 Aug 1936, 4.

743. DAVRAY, HENRY D.: *MercF,* 271:919 (1 Oct 1936), 184.

744. DEUTSCH, BABETTE: "The Aristocratic Ideal Voiced by W. B. Yeats," *NYHTB,* 17 May 1936, 6.

745. EVANS, B. IFOR: "Mr. Yeats Looks Back," *MGuard,* 12 June 1936, 9.

746. FLACCUS, KIMBALL: "Yeats as Dictator, the Man to Whom Pose Has Become a Second Self," *NY Sun,* 15 June 1936, 24.

747. GANNETT, LEWIS: "Books and Things," *NYHT,* 12 May 1936, 19.

748. GILMORE, WILLIAM: "Yeats: Patriarch of the Irish Renaissance. He Stands as an Apostle of Aristocratic Values in a Democratized World," *Brooklyn Daily Eagle,* 19 July 1936, Books, unpaged.

749. GRIGSON, GEOFFREY: "Wisdom from Yeats," *Morning Post,* 26 May 1936, 16.

750. GRUBB, H. T. HUNT: "A Poet's Friends," *Poetry R*, 27:4 (July-Aug 1936), 317-22.

751. JEFFERS, UNA: "A Poet Remembers," *Pacific Weekly*, 20 July 1936, 45.

752. JENCKEN, EDWARD N.: "Yeats and Ireland," *Springfield Daily Republican*, 16 May 1936, 6.

753. MACDONAGH, DONAGH: "Yeats Never Forgets," *Ireland To-day*, 1:2 (July 1936), 75, 77.

754. MCM[ANUS], M. J.: "W. B. Yeats Looks Back," *IrP*, 2 June 1936, 6.

755. MACNEICE, LOUIS: *Criterion*, 16:62 (Oct 1936), 120-22.

756. M[ARTIN], C[HRISTOPHER]: *CathW*, 143:857 (Aug 1936), 626-27.

757. MASON, H. A.: "Yeats and the Irish Movement," *Scrutiny*, 5:3 (Dec 1936), 330-32.

758. MORTIMER, RAYMOND: "Books in General," *NSt*, 30 May 1936, 861.
Discusses the Yeats-Moore relationship.

759. MUIR, EDWIN: "A High Monologue: Autobiographical Papers by Mr. W. B. Yeats," *Scotsman*, 28 May 1936, 15.

760. ÖSTERLING, ANDERS: "W. B. Yeats berättar bl. a. om Stockholmsbesöket 1923 da han hämtade Nobelpriset," *Stockholmstidningen*, 24 Aug 1936, 6.
"WBY tells among other things of his visit to Stockholm in 1923 when he received the Nobel Prize."

761. PRITCHETT, V. S.: "W. B. Yeats Speaking," *CSM*, 1 July 1936, Weekly Magazine, 11.

762. RASCOE, BURTON: *Esquire*, 6:2 (Aug 1936), 184-85.

763. REYNOLDS, HORACE: "Yeats Continues His Memoirs: One of the Great Intellectual Autobiographies of Our Time," *NYTBR*, 17 May 1936, 1.

764. SCHNELL, JONATHAN: "From a Poet's Notebook," *Forum and Century*, 95:6 (June 1936), v.

765. STARKIE, WALTER: "A Great Irish Poet Looks Back: Mr. Yeats Gives Us a Book of Memories," *IrI*, 14 July 1936, 6.

766. STRONG, L. A. G.: "The Aristocratic Ideal," *Spect*, 29 May 1936, 988.

767. TROY, WILLIAM: "The Lesson of the Master," *Nation*, 17 June 1936, 780.

768. VINES, SHERARD: "Mr. Yeats and the Irish Revival," *List*, 1 July 1936, 43.

769. W., G.: *Granta*, 45:1034 (3 June 1936), 437-38.

770. WOLFE, HUMBERT: "Yeats and George Moore: Great Writers at Cross Purposes," *Obs,* 14 June 1936, 8.

771. YOUNG, GEORGE MALCOLM: *Daylight and Champaign: Essays.* London: Hart-Davis, 1948 [1937]. 296 pp.

"Magic and Mudlarks," 169-75; reprinted from *SunT,* 31 May 1936, 8. A review of W186.

"Forty Years of Verse," 176-91; reprinted from *LMerc,* 35:206 (Dec 1936), 112-22. A review of W250. Correspondence by A. C. Boyd, :207 (Jan 1937), 314 (not reprinted).

See also G648.

W190: *Nine One-Act Plays* (1937)

772. CAZAMIAN, M. L.: *EA,* 2:1 (Jan-Mar 1938), 65-66.

773. M[URRAY], T. C.: "Yeats the Dramatist," *IrP,* 13 July 1937, 8.

W191/192: *A Vision* (1937/1938)

774. ANON.: *Church of Ireland Gazette,* 4 Feb 1938, 77.

775. ANON.: *List,* 8 Dec 1937, 1271.

776. ANON.: *New English Weekly,* 20 Jan 1938, 291-92.

777. ANON.: *NSt,* 22 Jan 1938, 140.

778. B., C. E.: "Books of the Day," *ILN,* 22 Jan 1938, 126.

779. BALD, R. C.: *Philosophical R,* 48:284 (Mar 1939), 239.

780. BENÉT, WILLIAM ROSE: "Speculations of a Poet," *SatR,* 12 Mar 1938, 19.

781. BRONOWSKI, J.: "Yeats's Mysticism," *CambR,* 59:1440 (19 Nov 1937), 113.

782. CAZAMIAN, M. L.: *EA,* 2:3 (July-Sept 1938), 315.

783. COLUM, MARY M.: "A Poet's Philosophy," *Forum and Century,* 99:4 (Apr 1938), 213-15.

784. DEUTSCH, BABETTE: "Bones of a Poet's Vision," *NYHTB,* 8 May 1938, 16.

785. E., C.: "Mr. W. B. Yeats's Latest Book: 'The Shoemaker Should Stick to His Last,'" *Irish News,* 8 Nov 1937, 3.

786. E[DWARDS], O[LIVER]: "Beyond the Normal," *Liverpool Daily Post,* 9 Nov 1937, 4.

787. O F[aracháin], R[oibeárd] [FARREN, ROBERT]: "Invisible Beings Communicated with Mr. Yeats, He Says," *IrI,* 2 Nov 1937, 4.

". . . trivial and unprofitable."

788. G[RIGSON], G[EOFFREY] E[DWARD]: "Thy Chase Had a Beast in

View," *New Verse*, 29 (Mar 1938), 20-22.
Yeats is a quack and his chase after beauty is repulsive.

789. GRUBB, H. T. HUNT: "A Poet's Dream," *Poetry R*, 29:2 (Mar-Apr 1938), 123-41.

790. HOLMES, JOHN: "Poetry Now," *BET*, 23 Apr 1938, part 3, 2.

791. MUIR, EDWIN: "Mr. Yeats's Vision: Messages of the 'Communicators,'" *Scotsman*, 18 Oct 1937, 13.

792. O'FAOLAIN, SEAN: "Mr. Yeats's Metaphysical Man," *LMerc*, 37: 217 (Nov 1937), 69-70.

793. PANHUYSEN, JOS[EPH]: "Het visioen van William Butler Yeats," *Boekenschouw*, 31:7 (15 Nov 1937), 315-20.

794. QUINN, KERKER: "Through Frenzy to Truth," *YR*, 27:4 (Summer 1938), 834-36.
Also a review of W196.

795. REYNOLDS, HORACE: "W. B. Yeats Expounds His 'Heavenly Geometry': In *A Vision* He Sets Forth a System of Enormous Complexity and Range," *NYTBR*, 13 Mar 1938, 2.
"It is possible that it [the book] may some day be regarded as one of the great milestones of discovery on man's journey of exploration of the spirit world. . . . It reveals much of the man, among other things that either Yeats hasn't a stime of a sense of humor, or--a Gargantuan one."

796. RIVOALLAN, A.: *LanM*, 36:4 (May-June 1938), 384-85.

797. ROBERTS, MICHAEL: "The Source of Poetry," *Spect*, 19 Nov 1937, Supplement, 14, 16.
"Mr. Yeats has written one of the simplest accounts of poetic composition that has ever appeared, but he has written it in his own language."

798. SALKELD, CECIL FFRENCH: "Mummy Is Become Merchandise," *Ireland To-day*, 2:11 (Nov 1937), 77-79.

799. SPENDER, STEPHEN: *Criterion*, 17:68 (Apr 1938), 536-37.
Reprinted in CA50, pp. 400-3, and in FD72.

800. WALTON, EDA LOU: "Lend a Myth to God," *Nation*, 9 July 1938, 51-52.
Also a review of W196.

801. WILLIAMS, CHARLES: "Staring at Miracle," *Time and Tide*, 4 Dec 1937, 1674, 1676.

802. WILLIAMS, MICHAEL: "Doom," *Commonweal*, 25 Mar 1938, 611.

803. WILSON, EDMUND: "Yeats's Vision," *NewRep*, 20 Apr 1938, 339.

W194: *Essays 1931 to 1936* (1937)

804. [CLARKE, AUSTIN]: "Yeatsian Fantasy," *TLS*, 22 Jan 1938, 56.
Also a review of W195; reprinted in CA50, pp. 394-96, where the

reviewer is not identified.

805. O'FAOLAIN, SEAN: "More Ideas of Good and Evil," *LMerc,* 37:220 (Feb 1938), 454-55.

W195/196: *The Herne's Egg: A Stage Play / The Herne's Egg and Other Plays* (1938)

806. ANON.: "The Latest Egg of the Academy Auk," *Catholic Bulletin,* 28:3 (Mar 1938), 185-86.

807. ANON.: *List,* 23 Feb 1938, 431.

808. ANON.: "Drama in Verse: A Yeats Fantasy," *Scotsman,* 28 Feb 1938, 13.

809. BARKER, GEORGE: *LLT,* 18:11 (Spring 1938), 173.

810. C., W. R.: *Dublin R,* 202:405 (Apr-June 1938), 387.

811. C[AZAMIAN], M. L.: *EA,* 3:1 (Jan-Mar 1939), 66-67.

812. CLARKE, AUSTIN: "Irish Poets," *NSt,* 29 Jan 1938, 178, 180.
"Mists of his own past have defeated Mr. Yeats at last." Reprinted in CA50, pp. 397-98.

813. ———: "A Stage Fantasy," *LMerc,* 37:221 (Mar 1938), 551-52.

814. DEUTSCH, BABETTE: "Three New Gaelic Plays," *NYHTB,* 29 May 1938, 9.

815. FLETCHER, HELEN: "Leda in Eire," *Time and Tide,* 12 Mar 1938, 355.

816. GRUBB, H. T. HUNT: "A Rabelaisian Yeats," *Poetry R,* 29:4 (July-Aug 1938), 327-30.

817. LAWRENCE, C. E.: "Poetry and Otherwise," *Quarterly R,* 271:537 (July 1938), 153-73.
See pp. 163-64.

818. Ó MEÁDHRA, SEÁN: *Ireland To-day,* 3:2 (Feb 1938), 183.

819. POWELL, CHARLES: "Recent Verse," *MGuard,* 1 Mar 1938, 7.

820. REYNOLDS, HORACE: "Three New Plays in Verse by Yeats," *NYTBR,* 29 May 1938, 8.

821. ———: "Short Plays by Yeats," *CSM,* 14 June 1938, 8.

822. SMITH, JANET ADAM: "Recent Verse," *Criterion,* 17:68 (Apr 1938), 520-23.
Reprinted in CA50, pp. 398-400.

823. STRONG, L. A. G.: "A Violent Fable," *Spect,* 25 Feb 1938, 330.

824. WILSON, EDMUND: *NewRep,* 29 June 1938, 226.

825. WYATT, EUPHEMIA VAN RENSSELAER: *Commonweal,* 3 June 1938, 164.

See also G794, 800, 804.

W197: *New Poems* (1938)

826. BARNES, T. R.: "Yeats' New Poems," *Townsman,* 2:5 (Jan 1939), 25-26.

827. SCOTT, WINFIELD TOWNLEY: "Yeats at 73," *Poetry,* 53:2 (Nov 1938), 84-88.

828. ZABEL, MORTON DAUWEN: "Two Years of Poetry, 1937-1939," *SoR,* 5:3 (Winter 1939/40), 568-608.
See pp. 605-8. Also a review of W200; compares Yeats and Rilke.

W198: *The Autobiography* (1938)

829. ANON.: "Autobiography of William Butler Yeats," *Sign,* 18:3 (Oct 1938), 187-88.
"One closes the book toying with the intriguing speculation--what would Yeats not have become had he received the Faith!"

830. C., R. J.: "William Butler Yeats Reviews 75 Years," *Springfield Sunday Union and Republican,* 18 Sept 1938, 7E.

831. "AN CHRUIMH LEABHAR": *Celtic Digest,* 1:5 (Nov 1938), 27.

832. COLUM, MARY M.: "The Conqueror Artist," *Forum and Century,* 100:5 (Nov 1938), 226-27.

833. D., A. C., *Magnificat,* 63:1 (Nov 1938), 51-52.

834. GREGORY, HORACE: "Personae and Masks," *Nation,* 4 Feb 1939, 152-54.

835. HOLMES, JOHN: "An Anglo-Irish Poet Looks into All His Years," *BET,* 17 Sept 1938, section 3, 1.

836. TINKER, EDWARD LAROCQUE: "New Editions, Fine & Otherwise," *NYTBR,* 4 Sept 1938, 12.

See also CB105.

W200: *Last Poems and Two Plays* (1939)

837. ANON.: "The Last Work of W. B. Yeats: Much-Discussed Play Included in Notable Volume," *IrT,* 5 Aug 1939, 7.

838. ANON.: *List,* 24 Aug 1939, 394-95.

839. [CLARKE, AUSTIN]: "W. B. Yeats: The Last Poems," *TLS,* 22 July 1939, 438.

840. GWYNN, STEPHEN: "W. B. Yeats," *FortnR,* os 152 / ns 146:874 (Oct 1939), 457-58.

841. LEAVIS, F. R.: "The Great Yeats, and the Latest," *Scrutiny,* 8:4 (Mar 1940), 437-40.
Finds the poems lacking in quality and inferior to those in *The Tower* because they do not possess "complex tension."

842. MACCARTHY, DESMOND: "The Last Poems of Yeats," *SunT,* 13 Aug 1939, 6.

843. PROKOSCH, FREDERIC: "W. B. Yeats," *Spect,* 4 Aug 1939, 190.

844. ———: "Yeats's Testament," *Poetry,* 54:7 [i.e., 54:6] (Sept 1939), 338-42.
"Spasmodic, fragmentary, horrible."

See also G828.

W202: *On the Boiler* (1939)

845. ANON.: *New Alliance,* 1:1 (Autumn 1939), 106.

846. [CLARKE, AUSTIN]: "Yeats's 'Patter,'" *TLS,* 21 Oct 1939, 612.

847. SPENDER, STEPHEN: "Honey-Bubblings of the Boilers," *NSt,* 11 Nov 1939, 686-87.

W203/204: *Last Poems & Plays* (1940)

848. AARONSON, L.: *Nineteenth Century and After,* 127:759 (May 1940), 634-36.

849. ANON.: *Atlantic Monthly,* 166:2 (Aug 1940), Bookshelf.

850. ANON.: "The Last of Yeats," *Bulletin* [Sydney], 10 July 1940, Red Page, 2.

851. ANON.: "The Last Poems and Plays of W. B. Yeats," *IrT,* 9 Mar 1940, 5.

852. ANON.: *List,* 31 Mar 1940, 593-94.

853. ANON.: "Irish Poetry and Plays: W. B. Yeats's Posthumous Collection," *Scotsman,* 29 Feb 1940, 9.

854. ANON.: *TCD,* 46:806 (15 Feb 1940), 97-98.

855. ANON.: "Shaw and Yeats," *TAM,* 24:8 (Aug 1940), 613.

856. ANON.: "Poetry," *Time,* 3 June 1940, 76, 78-79.
"The life of . . . Yeats . . . was a wild-goose chase after poetical wisdom--a chase that did not end before the goose was caught, cooked and eaten. How Yeats swallowed his bird--beak, bones and feathers--he has told in detail in his classic *Autobiography*. How the meal sat on his stomach is made plain in his motley, fearful, sometimes scabrous, more often superb *Last Poems & Plays*."

857. AUDEN, W. H.: "Yeats: Master of Diction," *SatR,* 8 June 1940, 14.

858. BLUNDEN, EDMUND: *Book Society News*, Mar 1940, 19.

859. BROWN, IVOR: "The Irish Motley," *Obs*, 25 Feb 1940, 4.

860. [CHILD, HAROLD]: "Forty Years of Irish Drama: Yeats, Synge and Lady Gregory. From the Visionaries to the Realists," *TLS*, 13 Apr 1940, 182, 186.

861. COLUM, MARY M.: "An Old Man's Eagle Mind," *YR*, 29:4 (Summer 1940), 806-8.

862. ———: "Poets and Psychologists," *Forum*, 103:6 (June 1940), 322-24.
Compares Housman and Yeats.

863. DEUTSCH, BABETTE: "Sad, Proud and Tender Poems: W. B. Yeats, Facing Death, Wrote with Amazing Vitality," *NYHTB*, 2 June 1940, 4.

864. DUPEE, F. W.: "The Book of the Day: Last Poems of Yeats, Who Lived to Witness the Chaos of Post-War Europe," *NY Sun*, 30 May 1940, 12.

865. FORBES-BOYD, ERIC: "The Last Poems and Plays of W. B. Yeats," *CSM*, 13 Apr 1940, Weekly Magazine, 13.

866. GRUBB, H. T. HUNT: "The Curtain Falls," *Poetry R*, 31:3 (May-June 1940), 217-26.

867. HEALY, J. V.: "The Final Poems of Yeats: His Last Collection Recapitulates All He Accomplished with His Art," *NYTBR*, 19 May 1940, 1, 16.

868. H[OGAN], J. J.: *Studies*, 29:116 (Dec 1940), 650-53.

869. HOLMES, JOHN: "Poems and Things," *BET*, 24 June 1940, 11.

870. HOULT, NORAH: "The Irish Theatre," *LLT*, 25:33 (May 1940), 158-62.

871. K[NICKERBOCKER], F. W.: "Where Ladders Start," *SR*, 49:4 (Oct-Dec 1941), 568-69.

872. KREYMBORG, ALFRED: "Hands Across the Sea," *Living Age*, 358: 4485 (June 1940), 394-96.

873. LEE, LAWRENCE: "The Extension of Poetry in Time," *VQR*, 16:3 (Summer 1940), 481-84.

874. MACCARTHY, DESMOND: "W. B. Yeats on Poetry," *SunT*, 16 June 1940, 4.
Also a review of W325.

875. MACMANUS, FRANCIS: "Mr. Yeats' Last Poems," *IrP*, 5 Mar 1940, 6.

876. R[ANSOM], J. C.: "Old Age of a Poet," *KR*, 2:3 (Summer 1940), 345-47.

877. ROSENBERGER, COLEMAN: "Consuming Its Rag and Bone," *Accent*, 1:1 (Autumn 1940), 56-57.

878. SHANKS, EDWARD: "Yeats the Symbolist: Why He Discarded His Romantic Epithets," *John o' London's Weekly,* 5 Apr 1940, 14.

879. STRONG, L. A. G.: "The Eagle Mind," *Time and Tide,* 9 Mar 1940, 251-52.

880. T., P. C.: *Irish Book Lover,* 27:4 (July 1940), 238-39.

881. WANNING, ANDREWS: "Criticism and Principles: Poetry of the Quarter," *SoR,* 6:4 (Spring 1941), 792-810.
See pp. 798-800.

882. WILDER, AMOS N.: "Yeats' Final Flight," *Christian Century,* 10 July 1940, 878.

883. ZABEL, MORTON DAUWEN: "The Last of Yeats," *Nation,* 12 Oct 1940, 333-35.
Also a review of W325; reprinted with revisions in CA36.

See also CB53, 288.

W205: *If I Were Four-and-Twenty* (1940)

884. ANON.: *List,* 13 Feb 1941, 242.

885. [CLARKE, AUSTIN]: "W. B. Yeats," *TLS,* 16 Nov 1940, 580.

886. ————: *DM,* 16:1 (Jan-Mar 1941), 64.

887. GIBBON, MONK: *Bell,* 1:2 (Nov 1940), 91, 93.

888. SCOTT-JAMES, R. A.: "When Yeats Was Fifty-four," *Spect,* 18 Oct 1940, 392, 394.

W211/A: *The Collected Poems* (1950/1951)

889. ANON.: *Adelphi,* 27:1 (Nov 1950), 80-81.

890. ANON.: "The Finest of Modern Poets? . . . Bid for Yeats," *Newsweek,* 9 Apr 1956, 120-22.
Also a review of W211M.

891. ANON.: "Lasting Songs," *Time,* 21 May 1951, 128, 130.

892. AVISON, M.: *Canadian Forum,* 30:361 (Feb 1951), 261.

893. BRÉGY, KATHERINE: *CathW,* 173:1036 (July 1951), 316-17.

894. BREIT, HARVEY: "Repeat Performances," *NYTBR,* 3 June 1951, 23.

895. BRYSON, JOHN: "An Old Man's Eagle Mind," *Time and Tide,* 7 Oct 1950, 998-99.

896. [CLARKE, AUSTIN]: "Yeats and His Critics," *TLS,* 25 Aug 1950, 525-26.

897. COLE, THOMAS: "W. B. Yeats's Complete Poems," *Voices,* 146 (Sept-Dec 1951), 48-50.

898. DARRAS, JACQUES: "Mesures de Yeats," *Critique*, 31:338 (July 1975), 696-706.

899. DERLETH, AUGUST: "Clear Voices," *Voices*, 161 (Sept-Dec 1956), 44-46.

900. DORN, NORMAN K.: "The Myriad World of Yeats," *SF Chronicle*, 10 May 1959, This World section, 27.

901. [EDWARDS, OLIVER]: *Rann*, 9 (Summer 1950), 1-3.

902. ELLMANN, RICHARD: "The Identity of Yeats," *KR*, 13:3 (Summer 1951), 512-15.

903. FERLING, LAWRENCE: "The Second Volume of Poems by William Butler Yeats," *SF Chronicle*, 25 Nov 1951, Christmas Book section, 15.

904. GALLAGHER, JAMES: "Yeats Collective But Not Definitive," *Spirit*, 18:3 (July 1951), 92-93.

905. GILLETT, ERIC: "Yeats Collected," *National and English R*, 135: 811 (Sept 1950), 292-94.

906. GUY, EARL F.: *DR*, 30:4 (Jan 1951), 428-30.

907. MCE[LDERRY], B. R.: *Personalist*, 38:3 (Summer 1957), 314-15.

908. MURPHY, RICHARD: "Books and Writers," *Spect*, 11 Aug 1950, 183.

909. POORE, CHARLES: "Books of the Times," *NYT*, 10 May 1951, 29.

910. REMÉNYI, JÓZSEF: "Két költö" [Two poets], *Látóhatár*, 5:5 (1954), 305-7.

911. ROSENTHAL, M. L.: "Sources in Myth and Magic," *Nation*, 23 June 1956, 533-35.
Also a review of W211M.

912. STAUFFER, DONALD A.: "A Half Century of the High Poetic Art of William Butler Yeats: Here Are the Lyrics and Dramatic Poems of the Great Irishman, That 'One-Man Renaissance,' Most Wanted to Endure," *NYHTB*, 6 May 1951, 3.

913. TINDALL, W. Y.: "Art Whose End Is Peace," *ASch*, 20:4 (Autumn 1951), 482, 484, 486.

914. UNGER, LEONARD: "The New Collected Yeats," *Poetry*, 80:1 (Apr 1952), 43-51.

915. VERY, ALICE: *Poet Lore*, 56:3 (Autumn 1951), 277-82.

916. VIERECK, PETER: "Technique and Inspiration: A Year of Poetry," *Atlantic Monthly*, 189:1 (Jan 1952), 81-83.

917. WARD, A. C.: *Litterair paspoort*, [5]:42 (Dec 1950), 236-37.

918. WARNER, REX: "Books in General," *NSt*, 23 Sept 1950, 300-301.

919. W[ATT], I[AN] P.: *CambR*, 72:1747 (28 Oct 1950), 82.

See also CB53, 288.

W211D/E: *The Collected Plays* (1952/1953)

920. ANON.: "Master of Poetic Drama," *Church Times*, 12 Dec 1952, 900.

921. ANON.: *List*, 5 Mar 1953, 397, 399.

922. ANON.: "Yeats's Second String," *Nation*, 4 July 1953, 16.

923. BERTRAM, ANTHONY: "Reflection of Sunset," *Tablet*, 27 Dec 1952, 530-31.

924. BUDDINGH', C[ORNELIS]: "Drama's van een dichter," *Critisch Bulletin*, 20:3 (Mar 1953), 135-38.

925. CLARKE, AUSTIN: "Plays in Search of a Theatre," *IrT*, 18 Oct 1952, 8.

926. DAVIES, ROBERTSON: "Observations on Yeats' Plays," *Saturday Night*, 31 Jan 1953, 22.

927. EATON, WALTER PRICHARD: "Great Lyric Poet's Plays," *NYHTB*, 14 June 1953, 6.

928. F[ERLING], L[AWRENCE]: *SF Chronicle*, 13 Sept 1953, This World section, 16.

929. HABART, MICHEL: "W. B. Yeats et le théâtre aristocratique," *Critique*, 10:88 (Sept 1954), 739-53.

930. MACDONAGH, DONAGH:: "Folding and Unfolding of a Cloth," *IrP*, 18 Nov 1952, 6.

931. MCELDERRY, B. R.: *Personalist*, 35:4 (Autumn 1954), 427-28.

932. MULKERNS, VAL: "Will Managers Please Take Note?" *Bell*, 18:7 (Dec 1952), 444, 446, 448.

933. O'CONNOR, FRANK: "A Lyric Voice in the Irish Theatre: Yeats, the Poet, Says Frank O'Connor, Was the Magnificent Master of the One-Act Drama," *NYTBR*, 31 May 1953, 1, 16.

Reprinted on pp. 130-34 of Francis Brown (ed): *Highlights of Modern Literature: A Permanent Collection of Memorable Essays from the New York Times Book Review*. NY: New American Library, 1954. 240 pp. (Mentor Book. M104.). Includes personal reminiscences.

934. [PRYCE-JONES, ALAN]: "Yeats as Dramatist," *TLS*, 21 Nov 1952, 760.

Reprinted in *Griffin*, 2:5 (1953), 23-28.

935. REYNOLDS, HORACE: "Yeats' Poetic Drama," *CSM*, 30 July 1953, 11.

936. RIDLER, ANNE: "The Passion in Drama," *Drama*, 37 (Summer 1955), 37-38.

937. SALINGAR, LEO: "Yeats the Dramatist," *Highway*, 44 (Mar 1953), 222-25.

938. WHITE, MARIE A. UPDIKE: *SAQ,* 53:1 (Jan 1954), 153-54.

939. WOODCOCK, GEORGE: *Northern R,* 7:1 (Oct 1954), 43-46.

See also CB288.

W211G: *The Autobiography* (1953)

940. BEVINGTON, HELEN: *SAQ,* 53:2 (Apr 1954), 300-301.

941. GREGORY, HORACE: "Yeats Revisited," *Poetry,* 84:3 (June 1954), 153-57.

942. JACKINSON, ALEX: *American Poetry Magazine,* 34:4 (1953), 8-9.

943. PERRINE, CATHERINE: "Yeats and the Nineties," *SWR,* 39:1 (Winter 1954), 96.

944. POORE, CHARLES: "Books of the Times," *NYT,* 12 Dec 1953, 17.

945. STAUB, AUGUST W.: "Yeats: The Hundredth Year," *QJS,* 52:1 (Feb 1966), 81-85.

W211H/I: *Letters to Katharine Tynan* (1953)

946. ANON.: *List,* 20 Aug 1953, 312.

947. ANON.: *Quarterly R,* 291:598 (Oct 1953), 550-51.

948. ANON.: "Letters of the Younger Yeats," *Sunday Independent,* 3 Jan 1954, 6.
Correspondence by Pamela Hinkson, 7 Feb 1954, 6.

949. BERRIGAN, DANIEL: *Thought,* 29:112 (Spring 1954), 143-44.

950. BRÉGY, KATHERINE: *CathW,* 178:1063 (Oct 1953), 76.

951. CLARKE, AUSTIN: "Between Friends," *IrT,* 11 July 1953, 6.

952. CONNOLLY, TERENCE L.: "The Grass Is Greener," *Renascence,* 8:3 (Spring 1956), 167-68.

953. DEUTSCH, BABETTE: "Yeats as a Correspondent, in His Lonely Youth and His Rich Maturity," *NYHTB,* 13 Dec 1953, 8.
Also a review of W340.

954. FAY, GERARD: "Yeats's Letters," *MGuard,* 19 June 1953, 4.

955. H., L.: *DM,* 30 [i.e., 29]:1 (Jan-Mar 1954), 48-49.

956. [HONE, J. M.]: "Yeats When Young," *TLS,* 17 July 1953, 462.

957. KIELY, BENEDICT: "Letters from Yeats to a Flamingo," *IrP,* 20 June 1953, 4.
Flamingo was Francis Thompson's description of KT.

958. MACNEICE, LOUIS: "A Poet's Progress," *Obs,* 12 July 1953, 7.

959. O'DONOGHUE, FLORENCE: "Letters of Yeats," *Dublin R*, 228:436 (1954), 102-4.
Also a review of W340.

960. O'H., T.: "Yeats's Letters to Katharine Tynan," *IrI*, 15 Aug 1953, 4.

961. REYNOLDS, HORACE: "Absorbed in Poetry, Race and Vision," *NYTBR*, 27 Dec 1953, 4, 11.
Also a review of W340. Correspondence by R. L. Wilbur: "Letters and Discoveries," 24 Jan 1954, 24.

962. RODGERS, W. R.: "By the Waters of Babylon," *NSt*, 18 July 1953, 78, 80.

963. SHACKLETON, EDITH: "Yeats as a Young Man," *Britain To-day*, 210 (Oct 1953), 44-45.

964. V., J.: *SF Chronicle*, 23 Aug 1953, This World section, 15.

965. WARNER, REX: "Yeats in His Youth," *Spect*, 24 July 1953, 108.

966. WHITE, TERENCE DE VERE: *Studies*, 42:[] (Winter 1953), 474-76.
Also a review of W340.

W211J/K: *The Letters* (1954/1955)

967. ADAMS, HAZARD: "Yeats the Stylist and Yeats the Irishman," *Accent*, 15:3 (Summer 1955), 234-37.

968. ANON.: *CE*, 16:7 (Apr 1955), 466.

969. ANON.: "Yeats in His Letters," *Nation*, 9 July 1955, 29.

970. ANON.: *Quarterly R*, 293:604 (Apr 1955), 279-80.

971. AUDEN, W. H.: "I Am of Ireland," *New Yorker*, 19 Mar 1955, 142-46, 149-50.
Includes lengthy comments on Yeats's poetry and on his political views.

972. BRADFORD, CURTIS B.: "Yeats's Letters," *VQR*, 32:1 (Winter 1956), 157-60.

973. BROOKS, CLEANTH: "Yeats's Letters," *YR*, 44:4 (June 1955), 618-20.

974. CAZAMIAN, MADELEINE-L.: "La correspondence de W. B. Yeats," *EA*, 8:1 (Jan-Mar 1955), 50-60.

975. CLARKE, AUSTIN: "Catching the Post," *IrT*, 30 Oct 1954, 6.

976. COLUM, MARY: "In a Lifetime of Letters Yeats Spelled Out His Own Genius," *NYTBR*, 20 Feb 1955, 7.

977. CONNOLLY, CYRIL: *Previous Convictions*. London: Hamilton, 1963. xv, 414 pp.
"Yeats's Crucial Year," 252-54; reprinted from *SunT*, 9 Jan 1955, 5.

978. DAY LEWIS, C.: *LMag,* 1:10 (Nov 1954), 85-88.

979. DEUTSCH, BABETTE: "W. B. Yeats' Letters Are a Self-Portrait: They Reveal the Poet in All His Complexity and Grandeur," *NYHTB,* 6 Mar 1955, 3.

980. DOLBIER, MAURICE: "Letters of a Poet," *Harper's Magazine,* 210: 1259 (Apr 1955), 98.

981. DUPEE, FREDERICK WILCOX: *"The King of Cats" and Other Remarks on Writers and Writing.* Second edition. Chicago: U of Chicago Press, 1984 [1965]. xxi, 363 pp.

"The King of Cats," 36-42; reprint of "The Deeds and Dreams of Yeats," *PR,* 23:1 (Winter 1956), 108-11.

982. EDEL, LEON: "No More Opinions . . . No More Politics," *NewRep,* 14 Mar 1955, 21-22.

983. ELLMANN, RICHARD: "Yeats without Panoply," *SR,* 64:1 (Jan-Mar 1956), 145-51.

984. EVANS, ILLTUD: "A Poet to His Friends," *Tablet,* 19 Mar 1955, 279-80.

985. FAY, GERARD: "Yeats in His Letters: Passion, Literary and Political," *MGuard,* 24 Sept 1954, 8-9.

986. FERGUSON, DELANCEY: "Dreamer with His Dander Up," *SatR,* 14 May 1955, 12, 44.

987. HÄUSERMANN, H. W.: *ES,* 36:5 (Oct 1955), 284-86.

988. HAMILTON, IAIN: "Truth Embodied," *Spect,* 1 Oct 1954, 416, 418.

989. [HONE, J. M.]: "Yeats as Letter Writer," *TLS,* 15 Oct 1954, 656.

990. JEFFARES, A. N.: "William Butler Yeats: A Mind Michael Angelo Knew," *Meanjin,* 14:4 (Summer 1955), 565-68.

Also a review of W211L.

991. KENNER, HUGH: "Unpurged Images," *HudR,* 8:4 (Winter 1956), 609-17.

992. LERMAN, LEO: "Collected Poets," *Mademoiselle,* 41:1 (May 1955), 125.

993. M., W. P.: *DM,* 31 [i.e., 30]:1 (Jan-Mar 1955), 52-53.

994. MACKENZIE, COMPTON: "Sidelight," *Spect,* 1 Oct 1954, 395.

An extract is reprinted in BA13, 1:140-42.

995. MCLUHAN, H. MARSHALL: "Yeats and Zane Grey," *Renascence,* 11:3 (Spring 1959), 166-68.

996. MANLEY, SEON: "The Yeats Letters: Cold Light on the Celtic Twilight," *New Leader,* 16 May 1955, 21-22.

997. MERCIER, VIVIEN: "Yeats' Lifelong Immersion in the Spirit of Ireland," *Commonweal,* 25 Mar 1955, 660-61.

998. MOORE, HARRY T.: "Rich, Intimate View of Poet W. B. Yeats," *Boston Sunday Herald,* 27 Feb 1955, 48.

999. O'NEILL, MICHAEL J.: *Thought,* 30:119 (Winter 1955/56), 618-19.

1000. P., P.: "Yeats as Seen in His Letters," *IrI,* 2 Oct 1954, 6.

1001. PHELPS, ROBERT: "Walking Naked," *KR,* 17:3 (Summer 1955), 495-500.

1002. READ, HERBERT: "W. B. Yeats," *List,* 7 Oct 1954, 582, 585.

1003. REYNOLDS, HORACE: "The Poet's Life in His Letters," *CSM,* 24 Feb 1955, 11.

1004. ROBINSON, LENNOX: *I Sometimes Think.* Dublin: Talbot Press, 1956. 166 pp.
"W. B. Yeats," 101-4; reprint of "I Sometimes Think . . . Pity Poor Yeats," *IrP,* 13 Nov 1954, 8.

1005. RODGERS, W. R.: "Facets of Yeats," *Obs,* 6 Feb 1955, 9.

1006. S[MITH], T[ERENCE]: *IrW,* 28 (Sept 1954), 67-68.

1007. VOGLER, LEWIS: "Yeats's Letters Uncover the Roles He Played," *SF Chronicle,* 10 Apr 1955, This World section, 21.

See also CB288, DB132, DD75, G1025.

W211L: *Autobiographies* (1955)

1008. ADAMS, HAZARD: "Where All Ladders Start," *Western R,* 19:3 (Winter 1955), 229-34.
Also a review of W340.

1009. ANON.: "Voices of a Poet," *Church Times,* 29 Apr 1955, 4.

1010. ANON.: "Poet's Self-Portrait," *Economist,* 30 Apr 1955, Spring Books, 9.

1011. ANON.: *Quarterly R,* 293:606 (Oct 1955), 558.

1012. ANON.: "Yeats's Story: A Modern Fable," *Scotsman,* 31 Mar 1955, 11.

1013. ANON.: "Portrait of the Artist as a Young Man," *Times,* 17 Mar 1955, 9.

1014. BAILEY, ANTHONY: "The Close Companions," *Isis,* 27 Apr 1955, 24.

1015. BODKIN, THOMAS: "A Poet's Memories," *Birmingham Post,* 22 Mar 1955, 3.

1016. BRAYBROOKE, NEVILLE: "Poetry, Magic, Mysticism," *Catholic Herald,* 5 Aug 1955, 3.

1017. CLARKE, AUSTIN: "Cast a Cold Eye," *IrT,* 2 Apr 1955, 8.

1018. FALLON, GABRIEL: "A Handful of Sligo Soil," *Books of the Month,* 70:5 (Mar 1955), 15, 24.

1019. FAY, GERARD: "The Poet," *MGuard,* 25 Mar 1955, 10.

1020. [FRASER, G. S.]: "Heroic Profiles," *TLS,* 29 Apr 1955, 201.

1021. ———: "Platonic Tolerance," *NSt,* 21 May 1955, 723-24.

1022. MANGANELLI, GIORGIO: "Yeats autobiografo," *Mulino,* 4:10 (Oct 1955), 956-58.

1023. PAUL, DAVID: "Yeats and the Irish Mind," *Twentieth Century,* 158:941 (July 1955), 66-75.

1024. PHILLIPSON, WULSTAN: "W. B. Yeats," *Month,* 14:5 (Nov 1955), 309-10.

1025. POWELL, ANTHONY: "Celtic Mist," *Punch,* 18 May 1955, 620.
Also a review of W211J.

1026. RAINE, KATHLEEN: "The Discipline of the Symbol," *List,* 24 Mar 1955, 540.
Correspondence by Henry Lamb, 31 Mar 1955, 577.

1027. ROBINSON, LENNOX: "On *Autobiographies* by W. B. Yeats," *Library R,* 115 (Autumn 1955), 162, 164.

1028. SEYMOUR, WILLIAM KEAN: *St. Martin's R,* 770 (May 1955), 174.

1029. STRONG, L. A. G.: *LMag,* 2:6 (June 1955), 83-86.

1030. TOYNBEE, PHILIP: "Good Books and Bad," *Obs,* 24 Apr 1955, 13.

1031. VALLETTE, JACQUES: "Souvenirs d'écrivains," *MercF,* 325:1105 (Sept 1955), 141-44.

1032. WADE, ALLAN: "A Poet Young and Old," *Time and Tide,* 26 Mar 1955, 402-3.

1033. [WHITE, SEAN J.]: "Foreword" [to the Yeats issue], *IrW,* 31 (Summer 1955), 7-8.

1034. WRIGHT, DAVID: "New Blood, Old Emotions," *TES,* 28 Nov 1980, 24.
Also a review of W211DD.

See also G990.

W211M: *A Vision* (1956)

1035. DAVENPORT, WILLIAM H.: *Personalist,* 38:3 (Summer 1957), 315.

1036. DONOGHUE, DENIS: "Countries of the Mind," *Guardian,* 11 Jan 1963, 5.

1037. GALLAGHER, JAMES: "A Precis of a Myth," *Spirit,* 23:5 (Nov 1956), 154-55.

1038. WEBER, RICHARD: *Dubliner*, 6 (Jan-Feb 1963), 69-70.

See also G890, 911.

W211N: *The Variorum Edition of the Poems* (1957)

1039. BRADFORD, CURTIS: "The Variorum Edition of Yeats's Poems," *SR*, 66:4 (Oct-Dec 1958), 668-78.

1040. CLARKE, AUSTIN: "The Perfectionist," *IrT*, 22 Mar 1958, 6.

1041. FLETCHER, IAIN: *VS*, 2:1 (Sept 1958), 72-75.

1042. GREGORY, HORACE: "Like a Chambered Nautilus," *NYTBR*, 22 Dec 1957, 5, 18.

Includes reminiscences of a meeting with Yeats in 1934. Correspondence by Karl Beckson, 26 Jan 1958, 24. The review is reprinted in DC143.

1043. HARVEY, W. J.: "Visions and Revisions: The Variorum Edition of Yeats," *EIC*, 9:3 (July 1959), 287-99.

1044. [HONE, J. M.]: "Yeats in Youth and Maturity," *TLS*, 7 Mar 1958, 126.

See correspondence by R. W. Chapman, 28 Mar 1958, 169; J. W. Bryce, 18 Apr 1958, 209; Katherine Haynes Gatch, 23 May 1958, 283.

1045. HOOVER, ANDREW G.: *QJS*, 44:1 (Feb 1958), 90-91.

1046. JOHNSTON, GEORGE: "The Variorum Yeats," *Tamarack R*, 11 (Spring 1959), 97-102.

1047. KERMODE, FRANK: "Adam's Curse," *Encounter*, 10:6 (June 1958), 76-78.

1048. MENON, NARAYANA: "The Poems of W. B. Yeats," *Cultural Forum*, 6:1 (Sept-Oct 1963), 37-43.

1049. MUIR, EDWIN: "Changing the Style," *Obs*, 30 Mar 1958, 16.

1050. PARKINSON, THOMAS: "Contesting a Will," *KR*, 20:1 (Winter 1958), 154-59.

1051. REANEY, JAMES: "The Variorum Yeats," *UTQ*, 28:2 (Jan 1959), 203-204.

1052. REEVE, F. D.: "The Variorum Yeats," *Voices*, 166 (May-Aug 1958), 35-37.

1053. REYNOLDS, HORACE: "How Yeats Wrote and Wrote Again," *CSM*, 31 Oct 1957, 11.

1054. ROSENTHAL, M. L.: "Metamorphoses of Yeats," *Nation*, 5 Apr 1958, 298-99.

1055. SAUL, GEORGE BRANDON: *ArQ*, 13:4 (Winter 1957), 373.

1056. SCHOECK, R. J.: "A Poet's Craft," *Spirit*, 25:2 (May 1958),

56-58.

1057. SCOTT, WINFIELD TOWNLEY: "The Remaking of an Artist," *SatR,* 7 Dec 1957, 47-50.

1058. URE, PETER: *ES,* 41:4 (Aug 1960), 281-83.

1059. WITT, MARION: *Assembly,* 17:2 (Summer 1958), 23.

See also CB288.

W211P/Q: *Mythologies* (1959)

1060. ANGOFF, ALLAN: "Yeats' Poetic Sources," *Tomorrow,* 7:4 (Autumn 1959), 87-93.
Discusses Yeats's "mystical life."

1061. ANON.: "Yeats," *Scotsman,* 25 Apr 1959, 13.

1062. BUCKLEY, VINCENT: *Quadrant,* 4:15 (Winter 1960), 90-91.

1063. COLUM, PADRAIC: "A Passion That Became Poetry," *SatR,* 1 Aug 1959, 16-17.
Includes some reminiscences.

1064. DEUTSCH, BABETTE: "W. B. Yeats," *NYHTB,* 23 Aug 1959, 8.

1065. ELLMANN, RICHARD: "Imagination versus Reality," *Chicago Sunday Tribune,* 2 Aug 1959, part 4, 2.

1066. HENN, T. R.: "A Look into Darkness," *NSt,* 11 Apr 1959, 518-19.

1067. HEPPENSTALL, RAYNER: "The Alchemist," *Obs,* 15 Mar 1959, 22.

1068. HOFFMAN, DANIEL G.: *JAF,* 76:299 (Jan-Mar 1963), 83-86.

1069. HOGAN, WILLIAM: "The Celtic Myths of William Butler Yeats," *SF Chronicle,* 30 July 1959, 33.

1070. MERCIER, VIVIAN: "The Making of a Poet," *NYTBR,* 2 Apr 1959, 4.
". . . more pose than prose."

1071. O'BRIEN, CONOR CRUISE: *Writers and Politics.* NY: Pantheon Books, 1965. xxii, 259 pp.
"The Great Conger," 119-20; reprinted from *Spect,* 22 May 1959, 736 (written under the pseudonym Donat O'Donnell).

1072. READY, WILLIAM B.: *Critic,* 18:2 (Oct-Nov 1959), 50-51.

1073. REANEY, JAMES: *Canadian Forum,* 39:461 (June 1959), 64-65.

1074. REEVES, JAMES: "Verbal Toughness," *Time and Tide,* 2 May 1959, 508.

1075. SAUL, GEORGE BRANDON: *ArQ,* 16:1 (Spring 1960), 90-93.

See also CB35.

W211R/S: *The Senate Speeches* (1960/1961)

1076. ANON.: "Senator Yeats," *Times*, 4 Jan 1962, 11.

1077. CLARKE, AUSTIN: "The Irish Liberal," *IrT*, 16 Dec 1961, 10.

1078. DAICHES, DAVID: "The Practical Visionary," *Encounter*, 19:3 (Sept 1962), 71-74.
Also a review of W211T/U.

1079. DAVIE, DONALD: "Poet in the Forum," *Guardian*, 22 Dec 1961, 8.

1080. DOBBS, KILDARE: "No Petty People," *Saturday Night*, 17 Mar 1962, 35-36.

1081. ELLMANN, RICHARD: "Heard and Seen," *NSt*, 8 Dec 1961, 887-88.
Correspondence by William Empson: "A Question of Stock," 29 Dec 1961, 989; E. MacLysaght and Ellmann: "Taking Stock," 19 Jan 1962, 85.

1082. G[RAHOR], O[LGA]: "Govori W. B. Yeatsa v senatu," *Naši razgledi*, 24 Feb 1962, 79.

1083. HENN, T. R.: *List*, 21 Dec 1961, 1084.

1084. MERCIER, VIVIAN: "To Pierce the Dark Mind," *Nation*, 10 Dec 1960, 460-61.

1085. O'CONNOR, FRANK: "This Side of Innisfree," *Reporter*, 22 Dec 1960, 44-45.

1086. Ó GLAISNE, RISTEÁRD: *Focus* [Dublin], 5:1 (Jan 1962), 17-18.

1087. O'ROURKE, JOSEPH: *QJS*, 47:3 (Oct 1961), 318.

1088. [PAUL, DAVID]: "Poet as Senator," *TLS*, 22 Dec 1961, 916.
"It is a triumphant irony that a man so often viewed by his contemporaries . . . as the weirdest of dreamers should have proved so splendidly the reverse when called upon to act as one of his country's statesmen."

1089. SANESI, ROBERTO: "William Butler Yeats uomo pubblico," *Aut aut*, 12:67 (Jan 1962), 69-71.
Reprinted in *Poesia e critica*, 1:3 [Dec 1962], 172-75.

1090. SPEAIGHT, ROBERT: "Poet and Prophet," *Tablet*, 9 Dec 1961, 1176, 1178.

1091. T., A.: ". . . But Not Yeats," *IrI*, 3 Feb 1962, 10.

1092. URE, PETER: *RES*, 14:54 (May 1963), 220-21.

See also CA49, FD74.

W211T/U: *Essays and Introductions* (1961)

1093. ANON.: "Irish Genius," *Church Times*, 21 Apr 1961, 4.

1094. ANON.: "The Poet's 'Powerful and Passionate Syntax,'" *Scots-*

man, 25 Feb 1961, Weekend Magazine, 2.

1095. ANON.: "Odd & Haunting Master," *Time,* 16 June 1961, 88-90.

1096. BROADBENT, JOHN: "Speaking with His Own Tongue," *Time and Tide,* 2 Mar 1961, 335.

1097. CHURCH, RICHARD: "The Consistency of Genius," *John o' London's,* 16 Feb 1961, 176.

1098. CLARKE, AUSTIN: "The Prose of Yeats," *IrT,* 25 Feb 1961, 8.

1099. DEUTSCH, BABETTE: "A Poet's Credo Set Down in His Prose," *NYHTB,* 6 Aug 1961, 4.

1100. DICKINSON, PETER: "The Magic of Criticism," *Punch,* 26 Apr 1961, 663.

1101. ELLMANN, RICHARD: "Three Ages of Yeats," *NSt,* 23 June 1961, 1011-12.

1102. GASKELL, RONALD: *LMag,* 1:3 (June 1961), 89, 91, 93.

1103. HEALY, CAHIR: "Yeats in Many Moods," *Irish News,* 8 Apr 1961, 2.

1104. [HEPPENSTALL, RAYNER]: "Tame Swan at Coole," *TLS,* 17 Feb 1961, 97-98.

1105. HOLLOWAY, DAVID: "Yeats on Poetry," *Daily Telegraph,* 17 Feb 1961, 19.

1106. IGOE, W. J.: "A Great Writer's Only Real Apologia: His Work," *Chicago Sunday Tribune,* 9 July 1961, part 4, 2.

1107. IREMONGER, VALENTINE: "The Remarkable Lady Gregory," *Catholic Herald,* 30 June 1961, 3.

1108. JEFFARES, A. NORMAN: *Stand,* 5:2 [1961?], 55-57.

1109. K., F. J.: "Yeats as Critic," *IrI,* 22 Apr 1961, 10.

1110. KAIN, RICHARD M.: "The Bold Voice of Ireland," *Louisville Times,* 6 June 1961, section 1, 9.

1111. KENNER, HUGH: "Yeats's Essays," *Jubilee,* 9:10 (Feb 1962), 39-43.

1112. KERMODE, FRANK: "The Spider and the Bee," *Spect,* 31 Mar 1961, 448-49.

1113. LANGBAUM, ROBERT: "The Symbolic Mode of Thought," *ASch,* 31:3 (Summer 1962), 454, 456, 458, 460.

1114. LID, RICHARD W.: "Nathanael West Reconsidered and Another Helping of Yeats," *SF Chronicle,* 23 July 1961, This World section, 20.

1115. MACCALLUM, H. R.: "W. B. Yeats: The Shape Changer and His Critics," *UTQ,* 32:3 (Apr 1963), 307-13.
Also a review of W211Y/Z.

1116. MCCARTHY, PATRICK J.: *ArQ,* 19:3 (Autumn 1963), 277-79.

1117. MCHUGH, ROGER: "Yeats's Plenty," *Kilkenny Magazine,* 4 (Summer 1961), 24-30.

1118. MORTIMER, RAYMOND: "Yeats on Himself and Others," *SunT,* 19 Feb 1961, 26.

1119. MORTON, J. B.: "Yeats under the Microscope," *Tablet,* 8 Apr 1961, 330-31.

1120. NORMAN, SYLVA: *Aryan Path,* 32:7 (July 1961), 326-27.

1121. O'CONNOR, FRANK: "Conclusions Were Right," *NYTBR,* 2 July 1961, 4-5.

"Information usually wrong, arguments always wrong, Yeats still had the fairy gift of making his conclusions right."

1122. READ, HERBERT: "What Yeats Believed," *List,* 9 Mar 1961, 459.

1123. REYNOLDS, HORACE: "Yeats in His Collected Essays: A Poet's 'Structure of Thought,'" *CSM,* 22 June 1961, 7.

1124. STEWART, J. I. M.: "Hankering after Magic," *Sunday Telegraph,* 5 Mar 1961, 7.

1125. TOMLINSON, CHARLES: "Pull Down Thy Vanity," *Poetry,* 98:4 (July 1961), 263-66.

1126. TRILLING, LIONEL: *Speaking of Literature and Society.* Edited by Diana Trilling. Oxford: Oxford UP, 1982. xv, 429 pp. (Works of Lionel Trilling: Uniform Edition.)

"Yeats as Critic," 381-86; reprinted from *Mid-Century,* 27 (Summer 1961), 3-8.

1127. UNTERECKER, JOHN: *MD,* 5:2 (Sept 1962), 249-50.

1128. WAIN, JOHN: "Poetry and the Past," *Obs,* 5 Mar 1961, 31.

1129. WATSON, GEORGE: "The Essays of Yeats," *Oxford Magazine,* ns 1:18 (4 May 1961), 324.

"To re-read these essays is to realize afresh how preposterously Yeats's own works are a mixture of feelings from everywhere under the sun, how uncritical and syncretic the whole caste [sic] of his intelligence was."

See also G1078.

W211W: *Selected Poems* (1962)

1130. GALLAGHER, JAMES: "A Valuable Paperback," *Spirit,* 29:2 (May 1962), 62-63.

1131. MOORE, JOHN R.: "Swan or Goose," *SR,* 71:1 (Jan-Mar 1963), 123-33.

1132. WELLS, HENRY W.: "Two Poets," *Voices,* 179 (Sept-Dec 1962), 54-56.

Compares Yeats and Hugh MacDiarmid.

W211X: *Selected Poetry* (1962)

1133. BOSE, AMALENDU: "W. B. Yeats: His Poetry and Thought," *IJES*, 3 (1962), 158-67.

1134. HENN, T. R.: "Yeats Revisited," *RLV*, 31:4 (1965), 404-5.
Also a review of W211BB, 211CC, and 211DD.

1135. WHITE, SEAN J.: "More to Yeats than Innisfree," *IrP*, 25 Aug 1962, 6.

W211Y/Z: *Explorations* (1962/1963)

1136. ANON.: "Collecting Yeats," *Times*, 23 Aug 1962, 11.

1137. CONNOLLY, CYRIL: "Solitary Outlaw," *SunT*, 26 Aug 1962, 21.

1138. CROSS, GUSTAV: "Yeats: Angry Old Poet," *Sydney Morning Herald*, 17 Nov 1962, 16.

1139. D[ELEHANTY], J[AMES]: *Kilkenny Magazine*, 8 (Autumn-Winter 1962), 56-58.

1140. KERMODE, FRANK: "Dublin 1904," *NSt*, 21 Sept 1962, 366.

1141. MACALERNON, DON: "On the Yeats Shelf," *Focus* [Dublin], 6:1 (Jan 1963), 24.

1142. MACLIAMMÓIR, MICHEÁL: "Merlin in the Market-place," *Spect*, 21 Sept 1962, 403-4.

1143. MURPHY, RICHARD: "The Empty Tower at Ballylee," *Obs*, 7 Oct 1962, 29.

1144. REANEY, JAMES: "Yeats Unconquered," *Canadian Forum*, 42:504 (Jan 1963), 235-36.

1145. [WARNER, FRANCIS]: "A Poet's Prose," *TLS*, 5 Oct 1962, 778.
Criticizes the unexplained and unjustified omission of important paragraphs.

See also G1115.

W211BB: *Selected Plays* (1964)

1146. ANDREW, M. G.: *UES*, 14:2&3 (Sept 1976), 99-100.

See also G1134.

W211CC: *Selected Prose* (1964)

See G1134.

W211DD: *Selected Criticism* (1964)

See G1034, 1134.

W211EE/FF: *The Variorum Edition of the Plays* (1966)

1147. DONOGHUE, DENIS: "Between the Lines," *Guardian*, 25 Mar 1966, 8.

1148. [FRASER, G. S.]: "Yeats's Variations," *TLS*, 9 Mar 1967, 187.

W212: *Fairy and Folk Tales of the Irish Peasantry* (1888)

1149. ANON.: *IrM*, 16:185 (Nov 1888), 687-88.

1150. ANON.: "Irish Folk Lore," *Nation* [Dublin], 27 Oct 1888, 4.

1151. ANON.: "Irish Fairy Stories," *Pilot* [Boston], 17 Nov 1888, 4.

1152. ANON.: "Publications Received," *Sligo Chronicle*, 13 Oct 1888, 3.

1153. ANON.: *Sligo Independent*, 13 Oct 1888, 4.

1154. [NUTT, ALFRED]: *Athenaeum*, 9 Feb 1889, 174-75.

See also G30.

W214: *Stories from Carleton* (1889)

1155. ANON.: *Nation* [Dublin], 28 Dec 1889, 4.
Correspondence by Yeats: "Carleton as an Irish Historian," 11 Jan 1890, 5 (reprinted in *Uncollected Prose*, 1:166-69, and in *Collected Letters*, 1:205-7), and editor's reply, ibid.

W215: *Representative Irish Tales* (1891)

1156. ANON.: *IrM*, 19:217 (July 1891), 378-79.

1157. ANON.: *NYT*, 12 Apr 1891, 19.

1158. ANON.: *SatRL*, 30 May 1891, 664-65.
Very critical of Yeats's preface.

1159. ANON.: "Irish Stories," *United Ireland*, 16 May 1891, 5.
See also "Irish Literary Notes," 30 May 1891, 5.

1160. ROLLESTON, T. W.: *Academy*, 10 Oct 1891, 306-7.
"The selection and editing of these tales could hardly have been put into better hands than those of Mr. Yeats. . . ."

W216: *Irish Fairy Tales* (1892)

1161. ANON.: *SatRL*, 7 May 1892, 551.

1162. Logroller [i.e., LE GALLIENNE, RICHARD]: "'Logroller's' Literary Notes of the Week," *Star*, 28 Apr 1892, 2.

1163. ROLLESTON, T. W.: "The Fairy Tales of Ireland," *Library R*, 1:6 (Aug 1892), 342-45.

W218: *The Works of William Blake* (1893)

1164. ANON.: *SatRL*, 4 Feb 1893, 126-27.

1165. ANON.: "Two Mystics on Blake," *Speaker*, 15 Apr 1893, 429-30.

1166. [JOHNSON, LIONEL]: "A Guide to Blake," *Westminster Gazette*, 16 Feb 1893, 3.

1167. ———: *Post Liminium: Essays and Critical Papers*. Edited by Thomas Whittemore. London: Mathews, 1911. xiv, 307 pp.
"William Blake," 81-90; reprinted from *Academy*, 26 Aug 1893, 163-65.

1168. M'G[RATH], J[OHN]: "North and South," *United Ireland*, 22 Apr 1893, 1.

1169. OLD, W. R.: *Theosophist*, 14:11 (Aug 1893), 697-99.

1170. [STEPHENS, FREDERICK GEORGE]: *Athenaeum*, 30 Dec 1893, 920-21.

See also CD1350, G54.

W219: *The Poems of William Blake* (1893)

1171. ANON.: "A New Blake," *BmL*, 6:31 (Apr 1894), 22-23.

1172. ANON.: "An Impatient Muse," *Daily Chronicle*, 4 Jan 1894, 3.

1173. ANON.: *Nation*, 15 Feb 1894, 123.

1174. ANON.: *SatRL*, 3 Mar 1894, 239-40.

W221: *Poems of William Blake* (1905; reprinted 1969)

1175. JORDAN, JOHN: "William on William," *IrI*, 16 Aug 1969, 6.

W225: *A Book of Irish Verse* (1895)

1176. ANON.: "Four Irish Books," *Athenaeum*, 6 Apr 1895, 434-35.
Extract reprinted in CA50, pp. 86-88.

1177. ANON.: "The Bookshelf," *Black and White*, 13 Apr 1895, 504.
"The fact is that the earlier Irish poets were incomplete Saxons. It is only since Mr. Yeats and Miss Tynan took the matter in hand and began to write in English after the ancient modes that the principle of nationality became efficient in poetry."

1178. ANON.: *Daily Express*, 21 Mar 1895, 7.

1179. ANON.: *Guardian*, 24 July 1895, 1110.
"Mr. Yeats's Preface and notes are disfigured by a good deal of captious and inept criticism."

1180. ANON.: "A Garland of Irish Poetry," *Leeds Mercury*, 14 Apr 1900, Weekly Supplement, 4.

1181. ANON.: "Irish Verse," *SatRL,* 23 Mar 1895, 384-85.

1182. ANON.: "Some Recent Books of Verse," *Speaker,* 20 Apr 1895, 443-44.

1183. ANON.: *United Ireland,* 23 Mar 1895, 1.
Correspondence by Hester Sigerson, 30 Mar 1895, 5.

1184. ANON.: *United Irishman,* 10 Mar 1900, 5.

1185. E., F. Y.: "The Prospects of Anglo-Irish Poetry," *Speaker,* 28 Apr 1900, 111-12.

1186. ESTERRE-KEELING, ELSA D': "Four Irish Books," *Academy,* 27 Apr 1895, 349-51.

1187. JOHNSON, LIONEL: "Ireland in Verse," *Daily Chronicle,* 11 May 1900, 3.

1188. QUILL: "Books to Read," *ILN,* 17 Mar 1900, 372.

1189. [RYAN, W. P. ?]: "With the Irish in Great Britain," *New Ireland R,* 3:3 (May 1895), 184.

1190. [STRACHEY, JOHN ST. LOE]: "Irish Verse," *Spect,* 13 Apr 1895, 502-503.

1191. [TYNAN, KATHARINE]: Long untitled review as part of the editorial, *Irish Daily Independent,* 19 Mar 1895, 4.
Author identified in *Collected Letters,* 1:454.

See also G26.

W226: *Beltaine* (1899 ff.)

1192. ANON.: "The Younger Generation," *Pilot,* 11 Aug 1900, 185-86.
Includes a review of *Dome,* 6 (Apr 1900), which contains Yeats's "The Symbolism of Poetry." "We listen with pleasure, though with imperfect comprehension" to Yeats's discussion of symbolism. But: "There is a good deal of nonsense mixed up with the Irish literary movement."

W227: *Samhain* (no. 1, 1901)

See EF24, G123.

W229: *Samhain* (no. 3, 1903)

See EE352.

W230: *Samhain* (no. 4, 1904)

1193. [WALKLEY, A. B.]: "The Drama: Mr. Yeats on the Irish Theatre," *TLS,* 6 Jan 1905, 5.

W235: *Poems of Spenser* (1906)

1194. BAILEY, JOHN CANN: *Poets and Poetry: Being Articles Reprinted from the Literary Supplement of "The Times."* Oxford: Clarendon Press, 1911. 217 pp.
"Spenser," 45-54; reprinted from *TLS,* 2 Nov 1906, 365-66. Contains an extensive discussion of Yeats's introduction.

W241: *Samhain* (no. 7, 1908)

1195. ANON.: "Books and Bookmen," *MGuard,* 14 Nov 1908, 7.

1196. Tonson, Jacob [i.e., BENNETT, ARNOLD]: "Books and Persons," *New Age,* 3 Dec 1908, 112-13.

W242: *Poetry and Ireland: Essays by W. B. Yeats and Lionel Johnson* (1908)

1197. ANON.: "Poetry and Patriotism," *MGuard,* 29 Dec 1908, 4.

W250/251: *The Oxford Book of Modern Verse* (1936)

1198. ANON.: "A New Oxford Book of Verse," *National R,* 108:684 (Feb 1937), 261-62.

1199. ANON.: *N&Q,* 172:1 (2 Jan 1937), 16.

1200. ANON.: "Yeats's 'Modern' Anthology Keyed to Disillusionment," *Springfield Sunday Republican,* 17 Jan 1937, 7E.

1201. ANON.: "Modern Verse: Mr. Yeats's Anthology," *Times,* 20 Nov 1936, 10.

1202. ARNS, KARL: *Englische Studien,* 72:1 (Oct 1937), 136-38.

1203. BENÉT, WILLIAM ROSE: "Contemporary Poetry," *SatR,* 21 Nov 1936, 22.

1204. BINYON, LAURENCE: *English,* 1:4 (1937), 339-40.

1205. BORGES, JORGE-LUIS: *Textos cautivos: Ensayos y reseñas en "El hogar."* Edited by Enrique Sacerio-Garí and Emir Rodríguez Monegal. Barcelona: Tusquets Editores, 1986. 345 pp. (Marginales. 92.)
See pp. 135-36 for a short review of the anthology, reprinted from °*El hogar* [Buenos Aires], 28 May 1937.

1206. BULLETT, GERALD: "Poetry in Our Time: Mr. Yeats's Personal Anthology," *John o' London's Weekly,* 27 Nov 1936, 357.

1207. CROWLEY, PAUL: "Mr. Yeats Selects," *Commonweal,* 4 Dec 1936, 163-64.

1208. DAVRAY, HENRY D.: *MercF,* 277:938 (15 July 1937), 420-21.

1209. DAY LEWIS, C.: "Poetry To-day," *Left R,* 2:16 (Jan 1937), 899-901.

1210. DE SELINCOURT, BASIL: "Bare Bones: Mr. Yeats and the Modern Poets," *Obs,* 22 Nov 1936, 5.

1211. ———: "Modern Verse," *MGuard,* 27 Nov 1936, 7.
Introduction and selection are "whimsical"; too many poems are concerned with defeat, gloom, and the grave. Good as the selection sometimes is, a better one might have been made with poems not in Yeats's anthology.

1212. DEUTSCH, BABETTE: "The Personal Poetic Tastes of W. B. Yeats: His Choices for This Anthology Are Surprising, He Likes the Irish and Omits America," *NYHTB,* 13 Dec 1936, 9.

1213. G., R.: "Moderner and Moderner," *CambR,* 58:1420 (22 Jan 1937), 192-93.

1214. GWYNN, STEPHEN: "The Yeats Anthology: Some Omissions," *FortnR,* os 147 / ns 141:842 (Feb 1937), 237-39.

1215. H[AMPSHIRE], S[TUART] N.: *Oxford Magazine,* 4 Feb 1937, 343.

1216. HAWKINS, A. DESMOND: "Yeats as Anthologist," *New English Weekly,* 11 Mar 1937, 431-32.

1217. HAYWARD, JOHN: "Mr. Yeats's Book of Modern Verse," *Spect,* 20 Nov 1936, Supplement, 3.
Reprinted in CA50, pp. 378-81. Criticizes the choice of poets, the introduction ("fragmentary . . . tantalising and unintegrated"), and the "slovenly proof-reading." Correspondence by W. J. Turner: "Mr. Yeats's Anthology," 27 Nov 1936, 950; by Yeats and I. M. Parsons, 4 Dec 1936, 995.

1218. HILLYER, ROBERT: *Atlantic Monthly,* 159:3 (Mar 1937), Bookshelf.

1219. ———: *MLN,* 52:8 (Dec 1937), 618-19.
"An amazingly bad compilation. . . ."

1220. HOGAN, J. J.: *Ireland To-day,* 2:1 (Jan 1937), 82-83.

1221. HOLMES, JOHN: "Modern Verse Selected by William Butler Yeats," *BET,* 26 Dec 1936, part 6, 2.
An anthology "of first rank."

1222. HONE, JOSEPH: "A Letter from Ireland," *Poetry,* 49:6 (Mar 1937), 332-36.

1223. JAMES, TREVOR: "The Nineteenth Century and After," *LLT,* 16:7 (Spring 1937), 165-67.

1224. KEVIN, NEIL: "Modern and 'Modern' Poets (1892-1935)," *Irish Ecclesiastical Record,* series 5 / 49:3 (Mar 1937), 242-51.

1224a. LUNDQVIST, ARTUR: "Engelsk lyrik," *Bonniers litterära magasin,* 6:[] (May 1937), 371-83.
See pp. 373-75.

1225. LYND, ROBERT: "Not a Subject for Poetry," *John o' London's Weekly,* 18 Dec 1936, 508.
Criticizes the exclusion of the war poets.

1226. MACM[ANUS], M. J.: "Modern Poetry: Mr. Yeats's Choice," *IrP*, 1 Dec 1936, 6.

1227. MASON, H. A.: "Yeats and the English Tradition," *Scrutiny*, 5:4 (Mar 1937), 449-52.
Yeats's taste in the selection is "merely eccentric," and the introduction is "perverse." Reprinted in CA50, pp. 385-87.

1228. MATTHIESSEN, F. O.: "W. B. Yeats and Others," *SoR*, 2:4 (Spring 1937), 815-34.
See pp. 815-27.

1229. NICHOLS, ROBERT: "Weimar and Wasteland," *Time and Tide*, 12 Dec 1936, 1785-86.

1230. ÖSTERLING, ANDERS: "Poesi med nyckel" [Poetry with key], *Stockholmstidningen*, 4 Sept 1937, 6.

1231. PRESS, JOHN: "Anthologies," *REL*, 1:1 (Jan 1960), 62-70.
See pp. 65-66.

1232. R[EILLY], J[OSEPH] J.: *CathW*, 145:865 (Apr 1937), 113-14.

1233. REYNOLDS, HORACE: "Yeats Assays a Poetic Era: The Oxford Book of Modern Verse Is 'More a Yeats Item Than an Anthology of Modern British and Irish Poetry' But It Reflects a Distinguished Literary Taste," *CSM*, 10 Feb 1937, Weekly Magazine, 6.

1234. [SPARROW, JOHN]: "Mr. Yeats Selects the Modern Poets: A Time of Literary Confusion," *TLS*, 21 Nov 1936, 957.
An almost enthusiastic review that praises the eccentricity of the selection as an original judgment. Reprinted in CA50, pp. 381-85.

1235. SPENDER, STEPHEN: "Modern Verse--Minus the Best of It," *Daily Worker*, 16 Dec 1936, 7.
Complains that the war poets were omitted. Correspondence by R. B. Marriott, 19 Dec 1936, 4; W. J. Turner, 29 Dec 1936, 4. This is presumably the review referred to in Yeats's letter to Dorothy Wellesley, dated 23 Dec [1936] (see *Letters*, p. 875).

1236. ———: "Notes on the Way," *Time and Tide*, 19 Dec 1936, 1802-4.

1237. STONIER, G. W.: "Mr. Yeats Fumbles," *NSt*, 5 Dec 1936, 940, 942.
"What the book suffers from most is not so much bad taste as an incoherent tactlessness. . . . The Introduction does not help. Apart from its inadequacy as a historical sketch, it contains strange critical blunders."

1237a. TIERNEY, MICHAEL: "Poems of To-day and Yesterday: Selection by Dr. W. B. Yeats," *IrI*, 15 Dec 1936, 4.

1238. VINES, SHERARD: "Mr. Yeats and Modern Poetry," *List*, 2 Dec 1936, Supplement, iv.

1239. WALTON, EDA LOU: "From Stars to Bones," *Nation*, 5 Dec 1936, 663, 665.

1240. WIDDEMER, MARGARET: "The Yeats Book of Modern Verse," *NYTBR*,

13 Dec 1936, 2.

1241. WOOD, FREDERICK T.: *ES,* 19:4 (Aug 1937), 187-88.

1242. Z[ABEL], M. D.: "Poet as Anthologist," *Poetry,* 49:5 (Feb 1937), 273-78.

See also CB105, 374, G771.

W252/253: *The Ten Principal Upanishads* (1937)

1243. ANON.: "Poetry of Ancient India," *Church Times,* 16 Apr 1937, 472.

1244. [BROCK, ALAN CLUTTON]: "Myths for the Poets," *TLS,* 22 May 1937, 393.
Reprinted in CA50, pp. 388-89, where the reviewer is not identified.

1245. D., M.: "The Hindu Search for God and Truth," *IrI,* 20 Apr 1937, 4.

1246. DE SELINCOURT, BASIL: "Interior Heaven: The Teaching of the Upanishads," *Obs,* 25 Apr 1937, 5.

1247. KUNITZ, STANLEY J.: "May I Never Be Born Again," *Poetry,* 51:4 (Jan 1938), 216-18.

1248. M[AIRET], P[HILIP]: "Views and Reviews," *New English Weekly,* 17 June 1937, 191-92.

1249. NICHOLS, ROBERT: "Upanishads for Everyman," *LMerc,* 36:211 (May 1937), 76-77.

1250. REYNOLDS, HORACE: "The Upanishads and William B. Yeats," *NYTBR,* 30 Jan 1938, 3, 20.

1251. THOMAS, E. J.: "Old Light from the East," *CambR,* 59:1437 (29 Oct 1937), 55.

1252. YEATS-BROWN, F.: "At the Feet of the Masters," *List,* 28 Apr 1937, Supplement, vii.

W255: W. T. Horton: *A Book of Images* (1898)

1253. ANON.: "Books with Pictures," *Literature,* 20 Aug 1898, 150-51.
The book "has to be taken very, very seriously or it cannot be taken at all, and Mr. Yeats, with his well-developed sense of Celtic glamour and deficiency in Celtic humour, is just the man to do this in a fine, confused way."

W256/257: Lady Gregory: *Cuchulain of Muirthemne* (1902/1903)

1254. ANON.: *Guardian,* 15 Oct 1902, 1461.

1255. ANON.: *New Ireland R,* 17:4 (June 1902), 253-54.

1256. BOLAND, EAVAN: "Lady Gregory and the Anglo-Irish," *IrT,* 16 May 1970, 9.
Also a review of W258.

1257. [CRAIGIE, W. A.]: *Athenaeum,* 2 Aug 1902, 146-47.

1258. GARNETT, EDWARD: "Books Too Little Known: The Cuchullin Saga," *Academy,* 14 Feb 1903, 156-58.

1259. MACLEOD, FIONA: "The Four Winds of Eirinn," *FortnR,* os 79 / ns 73:434 (1 Feb 1903), 340-54.

1260. [ROBINSON, FRED NORRIS]: "Lady Gregory's Cuchulain," *Nation,* 28 Apr 1904, 334-35.

See also CD1344, G123.

W258/259: Lady Gregory: *Gods and Fighting Men* (1904)

1261. BLUNT, WILFRID SCAWEN: *Speaker,* 6 Feb 1904, 450-52.

See also G1256.

W263/266: Rabindranath Tagore: *Gitanjali* (1912/1919)

1262. ANON.: "East and West," *Westminster Gazette,* 7 Dec 1912, 5.

1263. [MORE, PAUL ELMER]: "Romance from Bengal," *Nation,* 15 May 1913, 500.

1264. ROLLESTON, T. W.: *Hibbert J,* 11:3 (Apr 1913), 692-94.

W269: Ernest Fenollosa and Ezra Pound: *Certain Noble Plays of Japan* (1916)

1265. ANON.: "The Japanese Masque," *Nation* [London], 14 Oct 1916, 87.
"We confess to preferring Mr. Yeats's highly-trained and eloquent introduction to all the material which has provoked it."

W289: *Poems and Ballads of Young Ireland* (1888)

1266. S[IGERSON], H[ESTER]: "Recent Publications," *Providence Sunday Journal,* 26 Aug 1888, 2.
"There is a ring of ease and music of true poetry about Mr. W. B. Yeats which cannot fail to charm when he lays aside that obscurity, which disfigures so many of his poems."

W291: *The Book of the Rhymers' Club* (1892)

1267. [DAY, FRED HOLLAND], *Mahogany Tree,* 1:20 (14 May 1892), 317-18.

1268. DOD: "The Book of the Rhymers' Club," *United Ireland,* 5 Mar 1892, 5-6.

1269. TOMSON, GRAHAM R.: *Academy,* 26 Mar 1892, 294-95.

1270. [TYNAN, KATHARINE]: "Our Reviewer's Table," *Irish Daily Independent,* 25 Feb 1892, 6-7.
Author identified in *Collected Letters,* 1:278.

1271. W., H.: *IrM,* 20:226 (Apr 1892), 212-16.

W294: *The Second Book of the Rhymers' Club* (1894)

1272. N., M. P.: "With the Irish in Britain," *New Ireland R,* 1:6 (Aug 1894), 390-96.
See p. 392.

W297: John Eglinton, W. B. Yeats, AE, William Larminie: *Literary Ideals in Ireland* (1899)

1273. ANON.: "For Irish Poets," *Daily Chronicle,* 29 July 1899, 3.

1274. ANON.: *Guardian,* 23 Aug 1899, 1150.
". . . a long dissertation by Mr. Yeats on the spirit of decadence . . . which contains a great deal of eloquence and a great deal of nonsense."

1275. ANON.: "The Irish Literary Movement," *Literature,* 8 July 1899, 9.

1276. ANON.: "Irish Literary Ideals," *SatRL,* 30 Sept 1899, 427.

1277. GIBBON, MONK: "*Literary Ideals in Ireland:* A Comparison," *IrSt,* 5 Dec 1925, 399-400.

1278. JERROLD, LAURENCE: *Humanité nouvelle,* year 4 / 6:35 (1900), 620-22.

1279. MACLEOD, FIONA: *BmL,* 16:95 (Aug 1899), 136-37.

1280. Q[UILLER-] C[OUCH], A[RTHUR] T[HOMAS]: "A Literary Causerie: Irish Literary Ideals," *Speaker,* 17 June 1899, 690-92.

See also G144.

W300: Lady Gregory (ed): *Ideals in Ireland* (1901)

1281. Lugh [i.e., PYPER, W. J. STANTON]: "Ideals in Ireland," *United Irishman,* 23 Feb 1901, 2.

W312: Lady Gregory: *Visions and Beliefs in the West of Ireland* (1920)

1282. ANON.: "A Happy Collaboration," *NSt,* 2 Oct 1920, 712.

1283. ANON.: "Spoof from Ireland," *SatRL,* 2 Oct 1920, 280-81.

1284. [BROCK, ARTHUR CLUTTON]: "Fairies and Discoveries," *TLS,* 23 Sept 1920, 613.

1285. COLUM, PADRAIC: "Folk Seers," *Dial,* 69:3 (Sept 1920), 300-302.

1286. DE CASSERES, BENJAMIN: "West of Ireland in Vision and Belief," *NYTBR,* 23 May 1920, 270.

1287. MORRIS, LLOYD R.: "The Mood of the Irish Mind," *Outlook,* 2 June 1920, 222-23.

1288. REID, FORREST: *Retrospective Adventures.* London: Faber & Faber, 1941. 286 pp.
"The Host of the Air," 156-60; reprinted from *Athenaeum,* 22 Oct 1920, 550.

1289. STEWART, HERBERT L.: "A Treasury of Folklore," *Weekly R* [NY], 13 Oct 1920, 320-21.

See also CB342.

W325/A: *Letters on Poetry from W. B. Yeats to Dorothy Wellesley* (1940)

1290. ANON.: *Atlantic Monthly,* 166:6 (Dec 1940), Bookshelf.

1291. ANON.: *List,* 4 July 1940, 29.

1292. BLACKMUR, RICHARD P.: "W. B. Yeats' Letters on Poetry," *Decision,* 1:2 (Feb 1941), 63-65.

1293. BOGAN, LOUISE: "Verse," *New Yorker,* 19 Oct 1940, 87-89.

1294. BROOKS, CLEANTH: *MLN,* 57:4 (Apr 1942), 312-13.

1295. BROWNLOW, TIMOTHY: *DM,* 4:1 (Spring 1965), 78-81.

1296. CERVIN, GERT: "Poeten och ladyn," *Sydsvenska dagbladet snällposten,* 28 July 1964, 6.

1297. [CHILD, HAROLD]: "Wise and Gay," *TLS,* 8 June 1940, 279.

1298. [———]: "Hatred, Pity and Love: W. B. Yeats's Last Thoughts on His Vision," *TLS,* 8 June 1940, 282.

1299. CLARKE, AUSTIN: *DM,* 16:1 (Jan-Mar 1941), 65-66.

1300. CLAYBOROUGH, ARTHUR: *MSpr,* 59:4 (1965), 442.

1301. DAVIES, ROBERTSON: "Testament for Poets from W. B. Yeats," *Saturday Night,* 18 Jan 1941, 20.

1302. DE SELINCOURT, BASIL: "Letters from Yeats," *Obs,* 9 June 1940, 4.

1303. ———: "Letters on Poetry," *MGuard,* 24 June 1940, 7.

1304. DEUTSCH, BABETTE: "As One Poet to Another," *NYHTB,* 13 Oct 1940, 20.

1305. FITTS, DUDLEY: "Yeats to Wellesley," *SatR,* 21 Dec 1940, 20.

1306. Sister Mariella [GABLE, MARIELLA]: *Commonweal,* 18 Oct 1940, 532-33.

1307. HOLMES, JOHN: "Poems and Things," *BET,* 11 Nov 1940, 9.

1308. JACK, PETER MONRO: "Mr. Yeats on Poetry," *NYTBR,* 1 Dec 1940, 20.

1309. JENCKES, EDWARD N.: "Poets' Letters," *Springfield Republican,* 21 Sept 1940, 6.

1310. LYND, SYLVIA: *Book Society News,* June 1940, 16.

1311. MELLERS, W. H.: "Petulant Peacock," *Scrutiny,* 9:2 (Sept 1940), 197-99.

1312. MEYERSTEIN, E. H. W.: *English,* 3:15 (Autumn 1940), 136-38.

1313. POWELL, LAWRENCE CLARK: "Speaking of Books: Yeats-Wellesley Letters," *NYTBR,* 28 Mar 1965, 2.

1314. R[EYNOLDS], H[ORACE]: "Yeats Portrayed by Himself," *CSM,* 2 Nov 1940, Weekly Magazine, 12.

1315. S., W.: *Clergy R,* ns 20:3 (Mar 1941), 273-75.

> "Yeats throughout all his periods appears chiefly as a literary man who always contrived to miss the truth about the things which most excited his interest--ballads, English prosody, Eastern thought, and so forth."

1316. SCOTT, WINFIELD TOWNLEY: "The Foolish, Passionate Man," *Accent,* 1:4 (Summer 1941), 247-50.

1317. SIMON, IRÈNE: *RLV,* 31:4 (1965), 410-13.

1318. TATE, ALLEN: *The Poetry Reviews of Allen Tate 1924-1944.* Edited with an introduction by Ashley Brown and Frances Neel Cheney. Baton Rouge: Louisiana State UP, 1983. xiii, 214 pp.

> "Yeats's Last Friendship," 195-96; reprinted from *NewRep,* 25 Nov 1940, 730, 732.

1319. UNTERMEYER, LOUIS: "Yeats and Others," *YR,* 30:2 (Dec 1940), 378-85.

> See pp. 378-80.

See also G874, 883.

W327/329: Florence Farr, Bernard Shaw, W. B. Yeats: *Letters* (1941/1946)

1320. ANON.: *NSt,* 17 Jan 1942, 47.

1321. [CHILD, HAROLD]: "Florence Farr and Her Friends," *TLS,* 7 Mar 1942, 118.

1322. CLARKE, AUSTIN: "Private File," *IrT,* 14 Sept 1946, 4.

1323. EVANS, B. IFOR: "Letters from Shaw and Yeats," *MGuard,* 3 Feb 1942, 3.

1324. FAUSSET, H. I'A.: *Aryan Path,* 17:10 (Oct 1946), 395.

1325. GWYNN, STEPHEN: "Shaw, Yeats, and a Lady," *Obs,* 11 Jan 1942, 3.

1326. HONE, JOSEPH: "Shaw, Yeats and Florence Farr," *Bell,* 13:1 (Oct 1946), 80.

1327. JOHN, GWEN: *DM,* 17:2 (Apr-June 1942), 53-54.

1328. REYNOLDS, HORACE: "Farr to Yeats to Shaw," *CSM,* 2 May 1942, Weekly Magazine, 12.

1329. REYNOLDS, LORNA: *DM,* 22:1 (Jan-Mar 1947), 52-53.

1330. ROBINSON, LENNOX: "Letters to an Amateur," *IrT,* 10 Jan 1942, 5.

1331. SMITH, STEVIE: "Shaw and Yeats," *John o' London's Weekly,* 28 June 1946, 137.

"Shaw is by far the more sensitive, truly imaginative, passionate and intuitive person; in fact, the better man of the two."

1332. TURNER, W. J.: "Lively Letters," *Spect,* 21 June 1946, 642.

W340/341: W. B. Yeats and T. Sturge Moore: *Their Correspondence* (1953)

1333. ANON.: *Adelphi,* 30:2 (1954), 198-200.

1334. ANON.: "Collision of Ideas," *Nation,* 5 Dec 1953, 472-73.

1335. ANON.: "Poets in Argument," *Times,* 26 Sept 1953, 9.

1336. ASKEW, MELVIN W.: *BA,* 28:3 (Summer 1954), 357.

1337. CLARKE, AUSTIN: "Give and Take," *IrT,* 3 Oct 1953, 6.

1338. C[OHEN], J. M.: "Poets' Letters," *Obs,* 11 Oct 1953, 11.

1339. COLLINS, CLIFFORD: "Philosophy between Poets," *Spect,* 20 Nov 1953, 598.

1340. C[ORMAN], C[ID]: *Black Mountain R,* 1 (Spring 1954), 48-51.

1341. HAWARD, LAWRENCE: "Two Poets," *MGuard,* 9 Oct 1953, 4.

1342. HENN, T. R.: "The Cat and the Moon," *NSt,* 3 Oct 1953, 386, 388.

1343. [HONE, J. M.]: "Yeats and Sturge Moore," *TLS,* 23 Oct 1953, 681.

1344. JONES, T. H.: "Letters of W. B. Yeats," *Month,* 11:3 (Mar 1954), 187-88.

1345. KENNER, HUGH: "Some Elders," *Poetry,* 83:6 (Mar 1954), 357-63, 366.

1346. SPENDER, STEPHEN: "Misery and Grandeur of Poets," *List,* 8 Oct 1953, 608.

1347. TAYLOR, GEOFFREY: "Letters between Yeats and Sturge Moore," *Time and Tide,* 17 Oct 1953, 1352.

See also G953, 959, 961, 966, 1008.

Wade, p. 406: *Das Land der Sehnsucht* (1911)

1348. BRIE, FRIEDRICH: *Schöne Literatur,* 13:11 (18 May 1912), 201-2.

1349. HAEBLER, ROLF GUSTAF: *Schöne Literatur,* 13:14 (29 June 1912), 249-50.
Yeats's name is consistently misspelled as Seats.

1350. NOLL, GUSTAV: *Beiblatt zur Anglia,* 22:12 (Dec 1911), 370-71.

Wade, p. 407: *Tragedie irlandesi* (1914)

1351. VINCIGUERRA, MARIO: "Rassegna inglese," *Conciliatore,* 2:2 (31 July 1915), 216-33.
See pp. 216-29.

Wade, p. 408: *Erzählungen und Essays* (1916)

1352. EICHLER, ALBERT: *Beiblatt zur Anglia,* 28:10 (Oct 1917), 298-302.

1353. FRANCK, HANS: "William Butler Yeats: Der Gründer der 'Sinn-fein'-Bewegung," *Tägliche Rundschau,* 2 Nov 1916, Unterhaltungsbeilage, 1030-31.
The strange title ("Yeats, the founder of Sinn Fein") has its origin in the assumption that "Samhain" is pronounced "Sinn Fein."

1354. STRUNZ, FRANZ: *Literarisches Zentralblatt für Deutschland,* 69:1 (5 Jan 1918), 38.

Wade, p. 409: *Irländska dramer* (1923)

1355. B--n, B. [BERGMAN, BO]: "Nobelpristagarens dramatik," *Dagens nyheter,* 26 Nov 1923, 5.

Wade, p. 410: *Blaesten mellem sivene* (1924)

1356. KRISTENSEN, TOM: *Den evige uro.* København: Gyldendal, 1958. 161 pp.
"W. B. Yeats: *Blaesten mellem sivene*," 26-28; reprinted from *Tilskueren,* 42:3 (Mar 1925) 230-31.

Wade, p. 411: *Längtans land* (1924)

1357. ÖSTERLING, ANDERS: "Keltiska dramer," *Svenska dagbladet,* 28 Mar 1924, 9.

Wade, p. 412: *Gräfin Cathleen* (1925)

1358. LOERKE, OSKAR: *Der Bücherkarren: Besprechungen im "Berliner Börsen-Courier," 1920-1928.* Edited by Hermann Kasack and Reinhard Tgahrt. Heidelberg: Schneider, 1965. 447 pp. (Veröffentlichungen der Deutschen Akademie für Sprache und Dichtung Darmstadt. 34.)

Review of *Gräfin Cathleen,* pp. 336-37; reprinted from °*Berliner Börsen-Courier,* 9 May 1926.

Review of *Die chymische Rose,* pp. 392-93; reprinted from °*Berliner Börsen-Courier,* 25 Sept 1927.

Wade, p. 412: *Die chymische Rose* (1927)

1359. ARNS, KARL: *Gral,* 22:7 (Apr 1928), 467.

1360. BEHLER-HAGEN, MALLY: *Schöne Literatur,* 29:2 (Feb 1928), 86.

1361. FRANZEN, ERICH: *Literarische Welt,* 27 Jan 1928, 6.

1362. KREUDER, ERNST: *Simplicissimus,* 14 Aug 1932, 234.

See also G1358.

Wade, p. 413: *Hraběnka Cathleenová* (1929)

1363. VANĚK, F.: *Lidové noviny,* 8 June 1929, 15.

Wade, p. 414: *Země touhy* (1929)

1364. VANĚK, F.: "Tři překlady z W. B. Yeatse," *Lidové noviny,* 20 Apr 1929, 19.

Wade, p. 414: *Irische Schaubühne* (1933)

1365. ARNS, KARL: *Neue Literatur,* 36:2 (Feb 1935), 94.

1366. BÄNNINGER, KONRAD: "Heiselers Yeats-Übertragung," *Neue Schweizer Rundschau,* ns 3:6 (Oct 1935), 382-84.

1367. BRAUN, HANNS: "William Butler Yeats: Irische Schaubühne," *Deutsche Zeitschrift,* 47:9 (June 1934), 576-78.

1368. DRAWS-TYCHSEN, HELLMUT: "Die Dramen von William Butler Yeats," *Berliner Tageblatt,* 11 Feb 1934, 1.

Wade, p. 415: *Poesie* (1939)

1369. ALTICHIERI, GILBERTO: *Letteratura,* 4:1 (Jan 1940), 154-55.

Wade, p. 422: *Théâtre* (1954)

1370. HABART, MICHEL: *Théâtre populaire,* 7 (May-June 1954), 93-94.

Wade, p. 422: *Poèmes choisis* (1954)

1371. FRÉCHET, RENÉ: *EA,* 9:2 (Apr-June 1956), 180-82.

Wade, p. 424: *Verzen in vertaling* (1955)

1372. RENS, LIEVEN: "Poeziekroniek," *Nieuwe stemmen,* 11:7 (May 1955), 247-48.

Part 2
(Books Not in Wade)

***Objevy: Essaye* (Praha, 1920)**

1373. Nk. [NOVÁK, BOHUMIL]: "Zapomenutá kniha" [A forgotten book], *Rozhledy,* 7 Jan 1935, 247.

***Per Amica Silentia Lunae* (Brno, 1925)**

1374. SKOUMAL, A.: *Tvar,* 3 (1929), 308-11.

***Tři hry* [Three plays] (Praha, 1928)**

1375. -PA.-: *Zvon,* 29:3 (27 Oct 1928), 42-43.

***Gedichte* (Zürich, 1958)**

1376. DRAWS-TYCHSEN, HELLMUT: "Bemühungen um Yeats," *Welt und Wort,* 14:6 (June 1959), 171-72.

***Versek* (Budapest, 1960)**

1377. RONAY, GYÖRGY: "Yeats versei," *Élet és irodalom,* 21 Oct 1960, 6.

***Poesie* (Milano, 1961)**

1378. PEROSA, SERGIO: *Verri,* 7:3 (Aug 1962), 90-93.

***Enfance et jeunesse resongées* (Paris, 1965)**

1379. JUIN, HUBERT: "Yeats, poète de la confession feutrée," *Magazine littéraire,* 103-104 (Sept 1975), 96-98.
Also a review of *Le frémissement du voile* (1970) and *Dramatis personae* (1974).

1380. MARGERIE, DIANE DE: "Yeats: Les autobiographies," *Quinzaine littéraire,* 16-30 Apr 1975, 14-16.
Includes reviews of *Le frémissement du voile* (1970), *Dramatis personae* (1974), and *The Speckled Bird* (1973-74).

Quaranta poesie (Torino, 1965)

1381. BALDI, SERGIO: "Poesie di Yeats," *Approdo letterario,* 11:32 (Oct-Dec 1965), 108-9.

1382. SERPIERI, ALESSANDRO: "Poesia anglo-americana," *Ponte,* 21:10 (Oct 1965), 1316-24.
See pp. 1322-23.

1383. ZOLLA, ELÉMIRE: "Traduzione di Yeats," *Corriere della sera,* 4 Aug 1965, 3.

Runoja [Poems] (Helsinki, 1966)

1384. TUURNA, MARJA-LEENA: "Irlannin suuri runoilija" [Ireland's great poet], *Valvoja,* 87:1 (1967), 42-44.

Running to Paradise (London, 1967)

1385. [GRIGSON, GEOFFREY]: "Words," *TLS,* 30 Nov 1967, 1146.

John Sherman & Dhoya (Detroit, 1969)

1386. ALLEN, JAMES L.: "Recent Yeatsiana: The Failed Quest for Unity of Being," *JML,* 2:1 (Sept 1971), 148-54.

1387. FLETCHER, IAN: *N&Q,* os 216 / ns 18:7 (July 1971), 275-76.

1388. HENN, T. R.: *MLR,* 65:4 (Oct 1970), 891-93.

1389. SAUL, GEORGE BRANDON: *ArQ,* 26:2 (Summer 1970), 191-92.

W. B. Yeats and Margot Ruddock: *Ah, Sweet Dancer* (London, 1970)

1390. ANDERSON, PATRICK: "Dance to Madness," *Sunday Telegraph,* 16 Aug 1970, 8.

1391. BRONZWAER, W.: *DQR,* 1:1 (1971), 42-43.

1392. FLANAGAN, THOMAS: "W. B. Yeats: The Opportunity to Love," *Hibernia,* 7 Aug 1970, 10.

1393. [FRASER, G. S.]: "Saving Yeats from the Critics," *TLS,* 12 Mar 1971, 292.

1394. KAIN, RICHARD M.: *Eire,* 6:2 (Summer 1971), 171-74.

1395. MARTIN, AUGUSTINE: *Studies,* 60:237 (Spring 1971), 98-102.

1396. MILLAR, DAVID: "Late Love," *IrP,* 5 Sept 1970, 12.

1397. ÖSTERLING, ANDERS: "Yeats skyddsling" [Yeats's protégée], *Sydsvenska dagbladet snällposten,* 3 Oct 1970, 4.

1398. RAYMOND, JOHN: "In Yeats' Shadow," *SunT,* 23 Aug 1970, 26.

1399. SCOTT, PAUL: "Poet and Disciple," *Country Life*, 6 Aug 1970, 369.

1400. SIMON, JOHN: "A Muse Driven Mad," *New Leader*, 26 July 1971, 18-19.

1401. SNOW, C. P.: "Poet's Last Dance," *Financial Times*, 23 July 1970, 22.

1402. WHITE, TERENCE DE VERE: "St. Martin's Summer," *IrT*, 1 Aug 1970, 10.

See also G1424.

Beltaine/Samhain (Reprint, London, 1970)

1403. CLARKE, AUSTIN: "The Bad Fairy of Abbey Street," *IrT*, 2 Jan 1971, 8.
The bad fairy is the "rural playwright," who destroyed Yeats's dreams of a poetic theater.

1404. SHARE, BERNARD: "First Principles," *Hibernia*, 5 Mar 1971, 20.

W. B. Yeats and Thomas Kinsella: *Davis, Mangan, Ferguson?* (Dublin, 1970)

1405. CORRADINI FAVATI, GABRIELLA: "Tradizione e letteratura in Irlanda: Dal mito alla realtà," *RLMC*, 25:4 (Dec 1972), 273-78.

1406. [FRASER, G. S.]: "Saving Yeats from the Critics," *TLS*, 12 Mar 1971, 292.

1407. GIBBON, MONK: "The Critical Balance," *IrI*, 14 Mar 1970, 10.

1408. HEDBERG, JOHANNES: *MSpr*, 67:3 (1973), 266-68.

1409. MAXTON, HUGH: "Investigating Loss," *Hibernia*, 17 Apr 1970, 23.

1410. O HUANACHÁIN, MICHEÁL: "Follow an Antique Drum," *DM*, 8:6 (Winter 1970/71), 70-74.

1411. WATTERS, EUGENE: "Link-Men," *IrP*, 27 & 28 Mar 1970, 12.

See also G1440.

Le frémissement du voile (Paris, 1970)

1412. FAUCHEREAU, SERGE: "Le testament de Yeats," *Quinzaine littéraire*, 16-31 Oct 1970, 5-6.
Also a review of *Uncollected Prose*, vol. 1.

See also G1379, 1380.

The Poems (NY: Limited Editions Club, 1970)

1413. DREYFUS, JOHN: "Ten British Poets for the Limited Editions

Club," *PrL,* 9:2 (Summer 1976), 51-67.
See pp. 59-60.

Reflections (Dublin, 1970)

1414. CRONIN, ANTHONY: "Poet above All," *IrP,* 6 Mar 1971, 12.

1415. JORDAN, JOHN: "From Yeats's Journal," *IrI,* 6 Mar 1971, 6.

1416. WHITE, TERENCE DE VERE: "Inside the Factory of the Muse," *IrT,* 27 Feb 1971, 10.

Uncollected Prose, I-II (London, NY, 1970-1975)

1417. ALLEN, JAMES LOVIC: "Recent Yeatsiana: The Failed Quest for Unity of Being," *JML,* 2:1 (Sept 1971), 148-54.

1418. ———: *JEGP,* 76:1 (Jan 1977), 148-49.

1419. BERGSTEN, STAFFAN: *Samlaren,* 93 (1972), 280.

1420. BRUNS, GERALD L.: *Spirit,* 38:4 (Winter 1972), 41-45.

1421. CAREW, RIVERS: "Marginalia," *IrP,* 1 Aug 1970, 10.

1422. CHAPOY, ANDRÉ: "*Proses éparses* de Yeats. (Recherches pour un article)," *CCEI,* 2 (1977), 7-16.
A fragmentary review, left unfinished when Chapoy died in 1977.

1423. COLEMAN, ALEXANDER: *NYTBR,* 25 Oct 1970, 40.

1424. DONOGHUE, DENIS: "Golden Dawn," *List,* 1 Oct 1970, 457.
Also a review of *Ah Sweet Dancer* (1970).

1425. FARROW, ANTHONY: *Cithara,* 16:1 (Nov 1976), 76-79.

1426. FINNERAN, RICHARD J.: *JML,* 6:4 (1977), 738-43.
Points out defects and omissions.

1427. [FRASER, G. S.]: "Saving Yeats from the Critics," *TLS,* 12 Mar 1971, 292.

1428. FUROMOTO, TAKETOSHI: *SELit,* 54:English Number (1978), 140-46.

1429. GELPI, BARBARA: "Misty Foreshadowings of W. B. Yeats," *CSM,* 27 Aug 1970, 11.

1430. HOGAN, ROBERT: *JIL,* 5:2 (May 1976), 90-92.
Lists several additions.

1431. JEFFARES, A. NORMAN: *RES,* 22:87 (Aug 1971), 375-76.

1432. ———: *RES,* 28:109 (Feb 1977), 114.

1433. JORDAN, JOHN: "Early Nobility," *Hibernia,* 12 June 1970, 12.

1434. KAIN, RICHARD M.: *Eire,* 6:1 (Spring 1971), 133-36.

1435. LANGBAUM, ROBERT: "Growth of a Great Critic," *ASch*, 41:3 (Summer 1972), 460, 462, 464, 466.

1436. MACKENZIE, ELIZABETH: *N&Q*, os 225 / ns 27:5 (Oct 1980), 471-74.

1437. MACKENZIE, NORMAN H.: "The Yeats Canon and Recent Scholarship," *QQ*, 78:3 (Autumn 1971), 462-64.

1438. MAYHEW, GEORGE P.: *BA*, 45:3 (Summer 1971), 523.

1439. MOLESWORTH, CHARLES: "He Kept a Sword Upstairs," *Nation*, 11 Jan 1971, 58, 60.

1440. MONTAGUE, JOHN: "The Young and the Old Campaigner," *Guardian*, 3 Sept 1970, 7.
Also a review of *Davis, Mangan, Ferguson* (1970).

1441. MOORE, HARRY T.: *SatR*, 20 June 1970, 37-39.

1442. PERLOFF, MARJORIE: *MLR*, 73:4 (Oct 1978), 896-99.

1443. SADDLEMYER, ANN: *JEGP*, 70:3 (July 1971), 567-69.

1444. SCHLEIFER, RONALD: *WLT*, 51:2 (Spring 1977), 287.

1445. STUART, FRANCIS: "The Public Man," *Hibernia*, 31 Oct 1975, 14.

1446. VENDLER, HELEN: "In Praise of Impulse," *TLS*, 14 Jan 1977, 28-29.

1447. WEBB, TIMOTHY: *SN*, 43:2 (1971), 594-96.

1448. WORDSWORTH, ANN: "Art Itself," *Spect*, 13 June 1970, 790-92.

See also G1412.

Werke (Neuwied, 1970-1973)

1449. BLÖCKER, GÜNTER: "Die Maske eines anderen Lebens anlegen!" *FAZ*, 18 Sept 1971, Literaturblatt, unpaged.

1450. ————: "Irrlichterndes Spiel mit vielen Masken: Die deutsche Ausgabe von William Butler Yeats ist mit seiner Autobiographie abgeschlossen," *FAZ*, 11 May 1974, Bilder und Zeiten, [5].

1451. HELWIG, WERNER: "Yeats auf Deutsch," *Darmstädter Echo*, 10 Jan 1972, 22.

1452. ————: "William Butler Yeats--Mystiker und Senator," *Merkur*, 26:5 (May 1972), 490-93.

1453. KLEINSTÜCK, JOHANNES: "W. B. Yeats, der letzte Romantiker," *Welt der Literatur*, 3 Sept 1971, 5.

1454. ————: "W. B. Yeats: Ein Poet macht Maske," *Welt*, 17 Jan 1974, Welt des Buches, I.

1455. KRAMBERG, K. H.: "Wie eine langbeinige Fliege: Ausgewählte

Gedichte als Auftakt zur deutschen Yeats-Ausgabe," *Süddeutsche Zeitung,* 17/18 July 1971, [117].

1456. ———: "Wovon träumen die Toten? Vision und Maske in Yeats' erzählender Prosa," *Süddeutsche Zeitung,* 17 Nov 1971, Weihnachts-Literatur-Beilage, 5.

1457. ———: "Nach uns der wüste Gott. Abschlussband der grossen Yeats-Ausgabe: Die Autobiographie," *Süddeutsche Zeitung,* 9 Mar 1974, 100.

1458. KROHN, R[ÜDIGER]: *Wissenschaftlicher Literaturanzeiger,* 11:3 (June 1972), 84.

1459. LICHTWITZ, MANUEL: "Eine Chance für Yeats," *Frankfurter Rundschau,* 3 July 1971, Zeit und Bild, VI.

1460. UTZ, JOACHIM: *Archiv,* year 126 / 211:1 (July 1974), 142-47.
Detailed criticism of the inadequacies of both preface and translations in the poetry volume.

1461. WALLMANN, JÜRGEN P.: "Von der Stimmung zur Rechenschaft," *Tat,* 3 July 1971, 33.

1462. ———: "Yeats wird entdeckt," *Darmstädter Echo,* 2 Oct 1971, 55.

1463. ———: "William Butler Yeats' Werke: 'Ich weiss sehr wenig von mir.' Zur Autobiographie des irischen Dichters," *Deutsche Zeitung,* 30 Nov 1973, 12.

See also CB203.

Druid Craft: The Writing of "The Shadowy Waters" (Amherst, 1971)

1464. ANON.: *Eire,* 7:3 (Autumn 1972), 144-45.

1465. CLARKE, AUSTIN: "Deep Waters," *IrT,* 27 Mar 1972, 10.

1466. LEAMON, WARREN: "Wasteland of the Imagination," *Hibernia,* 31 Mar 1972, 10.

1467. MARSH, D. R. C.: *AUMLA,* 41 (May 1974), 95-96.

1468. PARKIN, ANDREW: *UTQ,* 41:4 (Summer 1972), 388-90.

1469. ———: *NCTR,* 1:1 (Spring 1973), 70-72.

1470. SAUL, GEORGE BRANDON: *MD,* 15:3 (Dec 1972), 343-44.

1471. SPIVAK, GAYATRI CHAKRAVORTY: *PQ,* 51:2 (Apr 1972), 493-95.

1472. WEBB, TIMOTHY: *RES,* 25:98 (May 1974), 239-42.

See also G1474.

A Tower of Polished Black Stones (Dublin, 1971)

1473. [CLARKE, AUSTIN]: "Yeats as an Adolescent Dreamer," *TLS*, 17 Mar 1972, 311.

1474. FINNERAN, RICHARD J.: "Progress Report on the Yeats Industry," *JML*, 3:1 (Feb 1973), 129-33.
Also a review of *Druid Craft* (1971).

1475. ZIMMERMANN, GEORGES-DENIS: *ES*, 55:6 (Dec 1974), 568.

Memoirs (London, 1972)

1476. BOLAND, JOHN: "Poet's Self-Portrait," *Hibernia*, 16 Feb 1973, 14.

1477. BRIDGES, L.: *National R*, 17 Apr 1973, 906.

1478. BRYSON, JOHN: "Unexpurgated Yeats," *Books and Bookmen*, 18: 210 (Mar 1973), 52-53.

1479. BURGHARDT, LORI HALL: *Masterplots*, 1974, 264-68.
Reprinted in Frank N. Magill (ed): *Survey of Contemporary Literature*. Revised edition. Updated reprints of 2,300 essay-reviews from *Masterplots* annuals, 1954-1976, and *Survey of Contemporary Literature Supplement*. Englewood Cliffs: Salem Press, 1977. 12 vols. (7:4921-25).

1480. BUTLER, ANTHONY: "Our Willie," *Reality*, 37:4 (Apr 1973), 28-31.
"Splendid rubbish."

1481. ELLMANN, RICHARD: "The Confessions of W. B. Yeats," *Guardian*, 11 Jan 1973, 9.
See also "Portrait of the Artist," *Guardian Weekly*, 27 Jan 1973, 27.

1482. FARROW, ANTHONY: *Cithara*, 14:1 (Dec 1974), 126-30.

1483. GREEN, MARTIN: "Experience and Strategy," *Tablet*, 20 Jan 1973, 58.

1484. GRIGSON, GEOFFREY: "The Bubblings of a Poet's Mind," *Country Life*, 1 Mar 1973, 552-53.

1485. HAMBURGER, MICHAEL: *Art as Second Nature: Occasional Pieces 1950-1974*. Cheadle: Carcanet New Press, 1975. vii, 156 pp.
"Yeats's *Memoirs*," 70-72; reprinted from *Poetry Nation*, 1 (1973), 130-32.

1486. HARDY, BARBARA: "The Memoirs of W. B. Yeats," *Spect*, 13 Jan 1973, 42-43.

1487. HARPER, GEORGE MILLS: "'Passion and Precision': Some Observations on Editing Yeats," *SoR*, 11:2 (Apr 1975), 452-63.
Ostensibly a review of *Memoirs*, actually an essay on the difficulties awaiting a future editor of Yeats's unpublished occult writings.

1488. HOWES, VICTOR: "Portrait of the Artist as a Young Mind," *CSM*, 9 May 1973, 13.

1489. JEFFARES, A. NORMAN: "The Great Purple Butterfly," *SR,* 82:1 (Winter 1974), 108-18.
Also a review of *Fairy and Folk Tales of Ireland* (1973).

1490. KERMODE, FRANK: "Scribbles and Revelations," *NSt,* 12 Jan 1973, 54-55.

1491. LEHMANN-HAUPT, CHRISTOPHER: "Fragments of Yeats's Mask," *NYT,* 2 Apr 1973, 33.

1492. [MCSWEENEY, KERRY]: "Perfection of the Life or of the Work," *QQ,* 80:3 (Autumn 1973), 497-98.

1493. MARCUS, PHILLIP L.: "Memoir and Myth," *IrP,* 20 Jan 1973, 10.

1494. MAYHEW, GEORGE P.: *BA,* 48:2 (Spring 1974), 377.

1495. MENON, NARAYANA: "A Personal Document," *Illustrated Weekly of India,* 26 Aug 1973, 43.

1496. MONSMAN, GERALD: *SAQ,* 73:3 (Summer 1974), 407-8.

1497. MUGGERIDGE, MALCOLM: "Books," *Esquire,* 80:478 (Sept 1973), 16, 18.

1498. MURRAY, MICHELE: "Sure, Yeats Was a Crackpot--But Also a Great Poet," *National Observer,* 14 Apr 1973, 23.

1499. NYE, ROBERT: "Yeats as Bardic Poet," *Times,* 11 Jan 1973, 10.

1500. O'HARA, J. D.: "Before the Peacock Screamed," *WashP,* 22 Apr 1973, Book World, 13.

1501. O'RIORDAN, JOHN: "The Mask of Yeats," *Library R,* 24:1 (Spring 1973), 34-36.

1502. PARKINSON, THOMAS: "Yeats Writing about Himself to Himself," *NYTBR,* 29 Apr 1973, 2-3.

1503. PESCHMANN, HERMANN: *English,* 22:113 (Summer 1973), 83-84.

1504. POPE, JOHN: "New Yeats Material Released," *Times-Picayune,* 3 June 1973, section 2, 12.

1505. RAINE, KATHLEEN: "Man behind the Magic," *Sunday Telegraph,* 14 Jan 1973, 12.

1506. SCHNACK, ELISABETH: "Memoiren von William Butler Yeats," *NZZ,* 19 May 1973, 37.

1507. SNOW, C. P.: "Come into the Garden, Maud," *Financial Times,* 11 Jan 1973, 10.

1508. STALLWORTHY, JON: "An Irish Window: Remaking W. B. Yeats," *Encounter,* 43:2 (Aug 1974), 59-65.

1509. TOYNBEE, PHILIP: "Behind the Yeats Mask," *Obs,* 14 Jan 1973, 34.

1510. WHITE, TERENCE DE VERE: "Closer to Yeats," *IrT*, 6 Jan 1973, 10.

1511. ŻYCIEŃSKA, EWA: "Anglia," *Poezja*, 9:7 (July 1973), 97-98.

See also CB149a, 160.

W. B. Yeats and the Designing of Ireland's Coinage (Dublin, 1972)

1512. LAPPIN, MARY: "Ritual and Magic," *Hibernia*, 22 Sept 1972, 10.

1513. SUTHERLAND, C. H. V.: *N&Q*, os 220 / ns 22:5 (May 1975), 228.

"Le cycle de Cuchulain" (*Obliques*, 1973)

1514. NORES, DOMINIQUES: "Une méditation sur l'écriture scénique," *Quinzaine littéraire*, 178 (1-15 Jan 1974), 36.
A review of the book as well as of the production; see EE266.

Fairy and Folk Tales of Ireland (Gerrards Cross, 1973)

1515. [FLETCHER, IAN]: "Leprechaunucopia," *TLS*, 22 June 1973, 726.

See also G1489.

The Speckled Bird (Dublin, 1973-74)

See G1380.

Diarmuid and Grania (Chicago, 1974)

1516. MACKILLOP, JAMES: *ACIS Newsletter*, 8:4 (Dec 1978), 5-6.

Dramatis Personae (Paris, 1974)

See G1379, 1380.

Poesie (Milano, 1974)

1517. MOROSI, NADIR: "Poesie di William," *Italia che scrive*, 57:9-10 (Sept-Oct 1974), 37.

Choix des poèmes (Paris, 1975)

1518. GUILLOT, CLAUDE: "Yeats en français," *LanM*, 72:1 (1978), 92-95.

1519. LABRIOLLE, J[ACQUELINE] DE: *RLC*, 50:3 (July-Sept 1976), 331-32.

1520. MARTIN, GRAHAM DUNSTAN: *EA,* 32:2 (Apr-June 1979), 239-40.

The Speckled Bird (Toronto, 1976)

1521. FINNERAN, RICHARD J.: *JML,* 7:4 (1979), 849-51.

1522. LEGATE, DAVID M.: "Fiction by Yeats," *Montreal Star,* 25 Mar 1978, D3.

1523. PUTZEL, STEPHEN D.: *Four Decades,* 2:4 (July 1979), 229-31.

1524. WEINTRAUB, STANLEY: "Three Views of the Nineties," *Review,* 1 (1979), 301-8.

The Writing of "The Player Queen" (DeKalb, 1977)

1525. BONACCORSO, RICHARD: *Eire,* 14:3 (Fall 1979), 157-60.

1526. DISKIN, PATRICK: *N&Q,* os 224 / ns 26:4 (Aug 1979), 368-69.

1527. FINNERAN, RICHARD J.: "W. B. Yeats: Some Recent Bibliographical and Editorial Work," *Review,* 1 (1979), 233-48.

1528. HARPER, GEORGE MILLS: *JEGP,* 78:3 (July 1978), 467-68.

1529. KAIN, RICHARD M.: *JIL,* 7:2 (May 1978), 176-77.

1530. ROHAN, VIRGINIA BARTHOLOME: *CompD,* 15:1 (Spring 1981), 76-80.

A Critical Edition of Yeats's "A Vision" (1925) (London, 1978)

1531. DODSWORTH, MARTIN: *English,* 28:130 (Spring 1979), 104-6.

1532. ELLMANN, RICHARD: "A Vision before Revision," *Books and Bookmen,* 24:7 (Apr 1979), 52.

1533. GOULD, WARWICK: *N&Q,* os 226 / ns 28:5 (Oct 1981), 458-60.

1534. ———: "W. B. Yeats's Dramatic Imagination: A Review Article," *Themes in Drama,* 3 (1981), 203-21.

1535. RONSLEY, JOSEPH: *IUR,* 9:2 (Autumn 1979), 352-55.

1536. RYAN, R. P.: *UES,* 17:2 (Sept 1979), 63-64.

Hanrahan rudy (Kraków, 1978)

1537. KONKOWSKI, ANDRZEJ: "Rycerz rubinowej róży" [Knight of the red rose], *Nowe książki,* 30 Apr 1979, 24-26.

1538. KRAJEWSKA, WANDA: "Pierwszy Yeats po wojnie" [First Yeats after the war], *Literatura na świecie,* 97 (May 1979), 338-42.

Kula (Beograd, 1978)

1539. JEKNIĆ, DRAGOLJUB: "Romantik iz charobne kule," *Stvaranje,* 34:2 (Feb 1979), 322-24.

"The Romantic from the magic tower"; an almost identical review appeared as "Pesme V. B. Jejtsa" [The poems of WBY], *Letopis matice srpske,* year 155 / 424:1-2 (July-Aug 1979), 431-34.

1540. KUKIĆ, BRANKO: *Gradac,* 6:22-23 (1978), 90-91.

Per Amica Silentia Lunae (Villeneuve-d'Ascq, 1979)

1541. FRÉCHET, RENÉ: *EA,* 35:1 (Jan-Mar 1982), 99.

Representative Irish Tales (Gerrards Cross, 1979)

1542. ARGOFF, N. JEANNE: *CJIS,* 6:2 (Dec 1980), 68-71.

1543. CAVE, RICHARD ALLEN: *RES,* 32:128 (Nov 1981), 501-2.

1544. GREACEN, ROBERT: "Yeats's Image of Ireland," *Literary R,* 4 (16-29 Nov 1979), 19.

1545. MADDEN-SIMPSON, JANET: "The Specificity of Experience," *BooksI,* 37 (Oct 1979), 161.

The Celtic Twilight (Gerrards Cross, 1981)

See G1560.

Explorations (Lille, 1981)

1546. JEFFARES, A. NORMAN: *IUR,* 12:1 (Spring 1982), 121-22.

Fiabe irlandesi (Torino, 1981)

1547. CITATI, PIETRO: "Come vivere allegri insieme ai folletti," *Corriere della sera,* 10 Mar 1982, 3.

Ich hatte die Weisheit, die Liebe uns gibt (Berlin, 1981)

1548. WICHT, WOLFGANG: *ZAA,* 31:1 (1983), 73-74.

The Secret Rose (Ithaca, 1981)

1549. BONACCORSO, RICHARD: *Eire,* 17:2 (Summer 1982), 155-56.

1550. BORNSTEIN, GEORGE: *YeA,* 2 (1983), 126-28.

1551. CAVE, RICHARD ALLEN: "Vision and Revision," *THES,* 6 Nov 1981, 14.

1552. CLARK, DAVID: "The Secrets of the Rose," *ILS,* 1:1 (Spring

1982), 13.

1553. FRAYNE, JOHN P.: *JEGP,* 82:3 (July 1983), 459-62.

1554. GENET, JACQUELINE: *EI,* 7 (Dec 1982), 268-69.

1555. ———: *EA,* 37:1 (Jan-Mar 1984), 110-11.

1556. HARPER, GEORGE MILLS: *MP,* 81:4 (May 1984), 435-40.

1557. LITZ, A. WALTON: "The Tone of the Nineties," *TLS,* 23 Oct 1981, 1240.

1558. MACKENZIE, ELIZABETH: *N&Q,* os 229 / ns 31:4 (Dec 1984), 542-44.

1559. MADDEN-SIMPSON, JANET: "Tools of the Trade," *BooksI,* 59 (Dec 1981), 237-38.

1560. MARTIN, AUGUSTINE: *IUR,* 12:1 (Spring 1982), 113-16.
Also a review of *The Celtic Twilight* (1981).

1561. O'HARA, DANIEL T.: *VS,* 26:1 (Autumn 1982), 99-101.

1562. STANFORD, DEREK: *J of the Eighteen Nineties Society,* 14 (1983-84), 28.

The Death of Cuchulain (Ithaca, 1982)

1563. BORNSTEIN, GEORGE: *Yeats,* 1 (1983), 206-9.

1564. CAVE, RICHARD ALLEN: *YeA,* 3 (1985), 244-48.

1565. FLANNERY, JAMES W.: "Yeats's Cuchulain," *ILS,* 1:2 (Fall 1982), 20.

1566. FREYER, GRATTAN: "The Poet and the Intriguers," *BooksI,* 69 (Dec 1982), 217, 219.

1567. LOIZEAUX, ELIZABETH BERGMANN: *AEB,* 7:1&2 (1983), 48-53.

John Sherman. Dhoya (Torino, 1982)

1568. CITATI, PIETRO: "Restare in Irlanda a vivere le fiabe," *Corriere della sera,* 26 Sept 1982, 3.

1568a. FERRARA, F[ERNANDO]: *Istituto universitario orientale: Annali. Anglistica,* 25:1 (1982), 167-69.

The Secret Rose (London, 1982)

1569. BOLAND, EAVAN: "Yeats as a Critic," *IrT,* 8 May 1982, 12.

Ballylee: The Tower (Lewisburg, Pa., 1983)

1570. SELUZICKI, CHARLES: *Fine Print,* 10:4 (Oct 1984), 141.

Byzantium (Redding Ridge, Ct., 1983)

1571. B[AGCHEE], S[HYAMAL], *YER,* 8:1&2 (1986), 147-48.

The Poems: A New Edition (NY, 1983; Dublin, London, 1984)

1572. ALBRIGHT, DANIEL: "The Magician," *NYRB,* 31 Jan 1985, 29-32.

1573. BORNSTEIN, GEORGE: "Yeats's Texts and Contexts," *MLS,* 16:2 (Spring 1986), 82-87.

1574. DOAR, HARRIET: "The Definitive Yeats: New Collection Captures the Poet's Depth and Passion," *Charlotte Observer,* 29 July 1984, 9F.

1575. DONOGHUE, DENIS: "Textual Choices," *THES,* 8 June 1984, 20.
Correspondence by Richard J. Finneran: "Yeats Errors," 22 June 1984, 2.

1576. FRAYNE, JOHN P.: *JEGP,* 86:1 (Jan 1987), 139-44.

1577. GARDNER, ANTHONY: *Harpers and Queen,* May 1984, 204.

1578. GARRATT, ROBERT F.: "The Poetic State of Ireland," *CP,* 20 (1987), 158-64.

1579. GOLDGAR, HARRY: "A Scholarly Task: The Great Yeats Event," *Times-Picayune,* 11 Dec 1983, section 3, 12.

1580. GOULD, WARWICK: "The Editor Takes Possession," *TLS,* 29 June 1984, 731-33.
Correspondence by Denis Donoghue, 20 July 1984, 811; by Mary FitzGerald, 20 July 1984, 811 (also on Yeats's poem "Friends"); Richard J. Finneran, 3 Aug 1984, 868-69; A. Norman Jeffares and W. Gould, 10 Aug 1984, 893; R. J. Finneran, 31 Aug 1984, 969; W. Gould, 21 Sept 1984, 1055.

1581. HEANEY, SEAMUS: "A New and Surprising Yeats," *NYTBR,* 18 Mar 1984, 1, 35-36.
Correspondence by Michael Scholnick: "Notable Changes," 22 Apr 1984, 23. Heaney's review is reprinted in *Yeats,* 3 (1985), 260-66.

1582. [HOGAN, ROBERT]: *JIL,* 13:1&2 (Jan-May 1984), 142-43.

1583. JENNINGS, ELIZABETH: "How Yeats's Work Unfolded," *Daily Telegraph,* 31 Aug 1984, 6.

1584. JOHNSTON, JUDITH L.: *Magill's Literary Annual,* 1985, 692-96.

1585. KREUTZER, EBERHARD: *Archiv,* year 139 / 224:1 (1987), 171-75.

1586. MCCORMACK, W. J.: "Extrapolated Felines," *BooksI,* 85 (July-Aug 1984), 125-26.

1587. MARTIN, AUGUSTINE: "Yeats: Vision and Revision," *IrT,* 16 June 1984, 12.

1588. MAYS, JAMES: *IUR,* 14:2 (Autumn 1984), 303-4.

1589. MONTAGUE, JOHN: "What to Make of W. B. Yeats," *Guardian*, 14 June 1984, 21.

1590. O'HARA, DANIEL T.: "The Specialty of Self-Victimization in Recent Yeats Studies," *ConL*, 27:2 (Summer 1986), 285-89.

1591. OWENS, CÓILÍN: "The Poems of W. B. Yeats," *ILS*, 3:2 (Fall 1984), 28.

1592. PAULIN, TOM: *Ireland & the English Crisis*. Newcastle upon Tyne: Bloodaxe Books, 1984. 222 pp.
"Shadow of the Gunmen," 202-4; reprinted from *Obs*, 10 June 1984, 22.

1593. PETTINGELL, PHOEBE: "Different Revelations," *New Leader*, 12 Dec 1983, 10-11.

1594. RICKS, CHRISTOPHER: "A Trick of the Voice," *SunT*, 20 May 1984, 43.

1595. RUBIN, MERLE: "Solipsism and Beyond--The Poetry of W. B. Yeats," *CSM*, 2 Mar 1984, B3, B8.
See also by the same reviewer: "New Edition Gives Us Yeats's Poems as the Poet Himself Intended," *CSM*, 19 Apr 1984, 22-23.

1596. SIDNELL, MICHAEL J.: "Unacceptable Hypotheses: The New Edition of Yeats's Poems and Its Making," *YeA*, 3 (1985), 225-43.

1597. SPENDER, STEPHEN: "Revisiting W. B. Yeats, in Youth and Age," *USA Today*, 23 Dec 1983, 3D.

Les histoires de la rose secrète (Lille, 1984)

1598. FRÉCHET, RENÉ: *EA*, 38:4 (Oct-Dec 1985), 486.

1599. GAUTIER, JEAN-LUC: *Nouvelle revue française*, 390-391 (July-Aug 1985), 171-72.

Poems of W. B. Yeats: A New Selection (London, 1984)

1600. FRAYNE, JOHN P.: *JEGP*, 86:1 (Jan 1987), 139-44.

1601. FRÉCHET, RENÉ: *EA*, 39:2 (Apr-June 1986), 235-36.

1602. SIMMONS, JAMES: *N&Q*, os 231 / ns 33:2 (June 1986), 267-68.

1603. WORTH, KATHARINE: *RES*, 37:146 (May 1986), 287-88.

The Collected Letters. Volume One (Oxford, 1985)

1604. ABLEY, MARK: "A Magician of Verse," *Maclean's*, 9 June 1986, 58.

1605. ANON.: "Poet Off Parade," *Economist*, 15 Mar 1986, 104.

1605a. ANON. [H. H. Anniah Gowda?]: "Yeats's Epistles," *LHY*, 27:2 (July 1986), 124-28.

1605b. BARROW, CRAIG: *Eire,* 22:4 (Winter 1987), 155-57.

1606. BLYTHE, RONALD: "Almost Instant Maturity," *Country Life,* 20 Feb 1986, 458.

1607. BROWN, TERENCE: "The Music of Time," *Irish R,* 1 (1986), 93-95.

1608. CAREY, JOHN: "Every Last Scrawl," *SunT,* 9 Feb 1986, 43.

1609. CURTIS, ANTHONY: "Irish Poet's Eyes," *Financial Times,* 15 Feb 1986, Weekend FT section, XIV.

1610. DEANE, SEAMUS: "The Poet's Dream of an Audience," *TLS,* 7 Mar 1986, 235-36.

1611. DONOGHUE, DENIS: "The Young Yeats," *NYRB,* 14 Aug 1986, 14-16.

1612. DOWLING, LINDA: *MLR,* 83:1 (Jan 1988), 174-75.

1613. ELLMANN, RICHARD: "Yeats in Love," *NewRep,* 12 May 1986, 33-35.

1614. FENTON, JAMES: "Irish Bard Head and Mumbo-Jumbo," *Times,* 6 Feb 1986, 11.

1615. FINNERAN, RICHARD J.: "W. B. Yeats: Early Letters and His Library," *Review,* 9 (1987), 205-14.

1616. FLETCHER, IAN: "Yeats: Letters and the Visual Arts," *ELT,* 30:4 (1987), 475-81.

1617. FRAYNE, JOHN P.: *JEGP,* 86:3 (July 1987), 464-66.

1618. FRÉCHET, RENÉ: *EA,* 39:4 (Oct-Dec 1986), 474-75.

1619. FULLER, ROY: "Log-Rolling," *LMag,* 26:1&2 (Apr-May 1986), 145-46, 148.

1620. GENET, JACQUELINE: "Yeats Revisited," *EI,* 11 (1986), 241-44.
In French.

1621. GÖRNER, RÜDIGER: "Vom Werden eines Dichters: Über die Briefe des jungen Yeats," *NZZ,* 8 Nov 1986, 70.

1622. GRENE, NICHOLAS: *N&Q,* os 232 / ns 34:4 (Dec 1987), 565-67.

1623. GROSS, JOHN: "Books of the Times," *NYT,* 22 Apr 1986, 23.

1624. HANRATTY, JOHN: "The Reality of Fairies," *BooksI,* 103 (May 1986), 99-100.

1625. HARDY, BARBARA: "Cry of the Heart," *Books and Bookmen,* 365 (Mar 1986), 18.

1626. HARMON, MAURICE: *IUR,* 16:1 (Spring 1986), 101-2.

1627. HEANEY, SEAMUS: "Genius on Stilts," *Obs,* 23 Feb 1986, 28.
See also *Obs,* 30 Nov 1986, 21, where Heaney selects the book as one of the most important publications of the year.

1628. HELMLING, STEVEN: "Yeats Early and Late," *SR,* 95:3 (Summer 1987), 490-94.

1629. HOLLOWAY, DAVID: "Yeats on the Way Up," *Daily Telegraph,* 7 Feb 1986, 16.

1630. JEFFARES, A. N.: "Practical Romantic," *Yorkshire Post,* 1 May 1986, 14.

1631. JENKINS, NICHOLAS: "Retrospective Intimacy," *Literary R,* 97 (July 1986), 52.

1632. KENNELLY, BRENDAN: "Passions of a Shy Warrior," *NYTBR,* 29 June 1986, 14.

1633. KREUTZER, EBERHARD: *Archiv,* year 139 / 224:1 (1987), 171-75.

1634. LOIZEAUX, ELIZABETH BERGMANN: *Yeats,* 5 (1987), 230-35.

1635. MEIR, COLIN: "Literature," *Linen Hall R,* 3:3 (Summer 1986), 30-31.

1636. MEYERS, JEFFREY: "Fairies and Peahens," *National R,* 15 Aug 1986, 43-44.

1637. MONTAGUE, JOHN: "Full of Mysticism and Magic," *Guardian,* 30 Jan 1986, 20.

1638. MOYNAHAN, JULIAN: "The Letters of W. B. Yeats," *ILS,* 5:2 (Fall 1986), 24.

1639. NYE, ROBERT: "Early Thoughts of the Gland Old Man," *Scotsman,* 5 Apr 1986, Weekend Scotsman, 3.

1640. O'BRIEN, CONOR CRUISE: "Yeats's Letters: 'Was Irish National Feeling Not Noble and Enlightened by Definition, Then?'" *List,* 20 Mar 1986, 24-25.

1641. ORMROD, RICHARD: "A Flight into Faeryland," *Spect,* 8 Feb 1986, 27.

1642. PAULIN, TOM: "Dreadful Sentiments," *LRB,* 3 Apr 1986, 9-10.
Discusses Yeats's early nationalist politics.

1643. PETTINGELL, PHOEBE: "Young Yeats," *New Leader,* 22 Sept 1986, 14-15.

1644. ROBERTS, DIANE: *WHR,* 41:1 (Spring 1987), 88-91.

1645. ROBINSON, ALAN: *RES,* 38:150 (May 1987), 271-72.

1646. RUSSELL, NOEL: "Revising the Batty Image," *Irish News,* 3 Apr 1986, 6.

1647. SMYTHE, COLIN: "Yours, W B," *London Standard,* 26 Feb 1986, 19.

1648. STACK, FRANK: "Lyricism and Life," *THES,* 21 Mar 1986, 23.

1649. TAYLOR, DANIEL: *Magill's Literary Annual,* 1987, 142-45.

1650. VENDLER, HELEN: *New Yorker,* 16 Mar 1987, 96, 100-104.

1651. WAUGH, AUBERON: "Voice from Innisfree," *Sunday Telegraph,* 2 Feb 1986, 12.

1652. WHITE, TERENCE DE VERE: "Yeats in His Letters," *IrT,* 1 Feb 1986, 12.

Essais et introductions (Lille, 1985)

1653. FRÉCHET, RENÉ: *EA,* 39:4 (Oct-Dec 1986), 473-74.

Purgatory (Ithaca, 1986)

1654. FLANNERY, JAMES W.: "No Racist Apologia for Yeats," *ILS,* 6:1 (Spring 1987), 24.

1655. WORTH, KATHARINE J.: *RES,* 39:153 (Feb 1988), 141-42.

The Early Poetry. Volume I: Mosada and The Island of Statues (Ithaca, 1987)

1656. LOIZEAUX, ELIZABETH BERGMANN: "On Yeats and His Scholars," *MQR,* 27:4 (Autumn 1988), 657-64.

Where There Is Nothing . . . The Unicorn from the Stars (Washington, D.C., 1987)

1657. RICHARDSON, ALAN: "Grand Talk, Indeed," *ILS,* 7:2 (Fall 1988), 12.

H RECORDINGS AND IMAGINATIVE RENDERINGS

HA Recordings

1. *The Abbey Reads*. Dublin: National Theatre Society / Paycock Publications, 1986.

A collection of cassette recordings. The following include selections from Yeats: ABB 004: Four poems read by Donal McCann, Philip O'Sullivan, and Desmond Cave.

ABB 006: One poem read by Donal McCann.

ABB 007: 22 poems read by Barry McGovern, Clive Geraghty, Cyril Cusack, Donal McCann, Desmond McCann, Patrick Laffan, and Siobhan McKenna.

ABB 012: Two poems read by Barry McGovern and Patrick Laffan.

2. AUDIO ARTS: [W. B. Yeats], *Audio Arts,* 1:4 (1975). Tape recording (cassette).

Contents: Yeats reads "The Song of the Old Mother" and a comment on "A Faery Song" (recorded 1934), "Coole Park and Ballylee," III and IV, and "The Lake Isle of Innisfree" (recorded 1937). Mrs. Yeats reads "The Poet's Children" from W. R. Rodgers's BBC program, 1949 (see also BB209). Oliver St. John Gogarty reads "Yeats and George Moore" from the same program. Anne Yeats, interviewed by William Furlong in 1974, reminisces about her father. Ulick O'Connor talks about Yeats and Gogarty. Robert Vahey and Jane Morant read several Yeats texts.

3. *The Caedmon Treasury of Modern Poets Reading Their Own Poetry*. Caedmon, TC 2006, [195-]. 2 12" long-play records.

Yeats reads "The Song of the Old Mother," "The Lake Isle of Innisfree," and extracts from "Coole Park and Ballylee" (side 2).

4. °DE MOTT, BENJAMIN: *Beyond Dailiness: Yeats*. NY: McGraw-Hill, 1968. 45 minutes.

A tape recording made live at the Poetry Center of the Young Men's and Young Women's Hebrew Association, New York.

5. MCKENNA, SIOBHAN: *Siobhan McKenna Reading Irish Poetry*. Spoken Arts, 707, [1956]. 12" long-play record.

Includes 16 Yeats poems; cover note by Padraic Colum.

6. °MACLIAMMOIR, MICHAEL: *Michael MacLiammoir in Revolutionary Speeches and Poems of Ireland*. Spoken Arts, 749, [1959]. 12" long-play record.

Includes a Yeats selection.

7. °MASSEY, RAYMOND (ed): *Helen Hayes, Raymond Massey, Thomas Mitchell*. RCA Victor, LM 1812-13, [1955]. 2 12" long-play records.

Includes some Yeats poems.

8. O'CONNOR, FRANK: *The Irish Tradition*. Folkways, FL 9825, 1958. 12" long-play record.

O'Connor lectures on Irish literature, with special emphasis on the revival period, and reads and comments upon the recognition scene in *On Baile's Strand* and "A Prayer for My Daughter." The text of the lecture accompanies the record. See also HA26.

9. PARTCH, HARRY: *Sophocles' King Oedipus*. Based on the version by William Butler Yeats. San Francisco: Wolfe, [1952?]. 16" record.

A musical drama performed at Mills College, Oakland, California, in Mar 1952; the record is in the Mills College Library. I have been unable to locate a printed score. Reviewed by Wilford Leach: "Music for Words Perhaps," *TAM,* 37:1 (Jan 1953), 65-68.

In 1985, the Library of Congress produced a film of this "Music-Dance-Drama" for 4 intoner-actors, other actors, singing voices, dancers and 11 musicians; there is a copy in the Music Library of the U of Illinois, Urbana.

10. ROBINSON, LENNOX: *Lennox Robinson Presents William Butler Yeats.* Spoken Arts, 751-52, [1958?]. 2 12" long-play records.

On the first record Robinson reads his reminiscences of Yeats, together with some poems; on the second record he reads an essay on Yeats as a playwright and passages from *The Countess Cathleen* and *Deirdre*. See also HA25 and 26.

This recording may be identical with °*W. B. Yeats: Poems and Memories*. Read by Lennox Robinson. HEAR (Home Educational Art Records, Ltd.), 751.

11. SOPHOCLES: *Oedipus Rex*. The William Butler Yeats translation, chorus and music by Thorpe Davies, additional dialogue by E. V. Watling, directed by Tyrone Guthrie. Caedmon, TC 2012, [1957]. 2 12" long-play records.

From the sound track of the motion picture starring Douglas Campbell with the members of the Stratford, Ontario, Shakespearean Festival Players.

See also °*Oedipus Rex*. In a version by W. B. Yeats. A Stratford Shakespearean Festival Foundation of Canada production, directed by Tyrone Guthrie, produced by Leonid Kipnis. S.l.: Corinth Video, [1985?]. Videocassette (VHS), 90 minutes. (The 1956 production)

12. THOMAS, DYLAN: *An Evening with Dylan Thomas Reading His Own Poetry and Other Poems*. Caedmon, TC 1157, 1963. 12" long-play record.

Reads three Yeats poems: "In Tara's Halls," "The Three Bushes," and "Lapis Lazuli." Recorded at the U of California, 10 Apr 1950.

13. °———: *Dylan Thomas Reads the Poetry of William Butler Yeats and Others*. Caedmon, TC 1353, [1971]. 12" long-play record.

14. YEATS, W. B.: *The Countess Cathleen*. Incidental music composed by Robert M. Abramson, performed by Siobhán McKenna, John Neville, and others, directed by Tom Clancy. Tradition Recording, TLP 501, [1957?]. 12" long-play record.

Notes on slipcase by Padraic Colum.

15. ———: *Five One Act Plays*. Caedmon, TRS 315, [1966]. 3 12" long-play records.

Contains *The Cat and the Moon, The Only Jealousy of Emer, The Pot of Broth, Purgatory,* and *The Words upon the Window-Pane;* directed by Howard Sackler. A 31-page booklet is included, containing the texts and an article by Walter Starkie: "The Irish Dramatic Movement," 3-4, and by Cyril Cusack: "From Behind the Mask," 5-6.

16. ———: *Noh Plays*. Directed by Barry Cassin and Noel MacMahon, music composed and directed by Gerard Victory. Argo, RG 468-69, 1965. 2 12" long-play records.

Contains *At the Hawk's Well, The Dreaming of the Bones, The Cat and the Moon,* and *The Resurrection;* cover note by Noel MacMahon. Reviewed by Charles Acton: "Four Plays by Yeats," *IrT,* 16 Feb 1966, 10.

17. ———: *The Only Jealousy of Emer.* Counterpoint/Esoteric, 5506, [195-]. 12" long-play record.
Directed by Bonnie Bird, music by Lou Harrison, cover note by Barry Ulanov. The recording is based on a performance "given by students and instructors in the Summer Workshop in Dance and Drama at Reed College in Oregon in the summer of 1949."

18. °———: *Poems.* Read by Mary O'Farrell and C. Day Lewis. Columbia [London], DX 1637-38, [19--]. 2 78 rpm records.

19. °———: *Poems.* Read by Robert Speaight. Harvard Vocarium Records, L 1012-13, 1941. 78 rpm record (12").

20. °———: *Poems.* Spoken according to his own directions by V. C. Clinton-Baddeley, Marjorie Westbury, and Jill Balcon. Jupiter, jur OOB2, [1958]. 10" long-play record.
See also HA26. This recording seems to be identical with °*Poems by W. B. Yeats Spoken According to His Own Directions.* Folkways Records, FL 9864, 1973. 1 side of 12" long-play record.

21. ———: *The Poems of William Butler Yeats.* Read by Yeats, Siobhan McKenna, and Michael MacLiammoir. Spoken Arts, 753, [1959?]. 12" long-play record.
Also on °Argo, R 182, [19--]. See HA25-27.

22. ———: *The Poetry of Yeats.* Read by Siobhan McKenna and Cyril Cusack. Caedmon, TC 1081, 1958. 12" long-play record.
See also HA26 and 27.

23. °———: *W. B. Yeats, June 13, 1865: A Centenary Record.* Jupiter, JEP OC38, [1965]. 7" record.
Read by Gabriel Woolf, V. C. Clinton-Baddeley, and Michael Gwynn.

24. ———: *Yeats.* Read by Chris Curran, Jim Norton, Arthur O'Sullivan, Sheila Manahan. Argo, RG 449, [1966]. 12" long-play record.
Thirty-five poems from all periods.

Appendix to Section HA: Reviews

25. GREENE, DAVID: "Recordings of William Butler Yeats," *Evergreen R,* 2:8 (Spring 1959), 200-201.
Review of HA10 and 21.

26. ROACH, HELEN: *Spoken Records.* NY: Scarecrow Press, 1963. 213 pp.
Reviews of HA21 (pp. 46-47), 22 (pp. 69-70), 20 (pp. 127-28), 8 (pp. 150-51), and 10 (pp. 155-56).

27. [SINGER, BURNS]: "Verse on the Record," *TLS,* 14 July 1961, 434.
Review of HA21 and 22.

See also AC42, 43, AE41, 112, CD400, DA17, DB75, HB11, HC2, 18, 42, 80, 125, 143, 197, 204, 248, 302, 305.

HB Films

1. BRITISH BROADCASTING CORPORATION: *Horseman, Pass By! The Story of a Poet: W. B. Yeats (1865-1939)*. Film script. [London]: B.B.C. Television, [1965?]. ii, 25 pp.

Narrated by Frank O'Connor and Brendan Kennelly, music composed by Gerard Victory, directed and produced by Malcolm Brown. Broadcast on 23 Jan 1966. (I have not seen the film; the script is in the National Library of Ireland, P2478.)

For a review of the film see "Notes on Broadcasting," *Times*, 29 Jan 1966, 5. An edited version of Frank O'Connor's contribution was published as "'A Gambler's Throw': On W. B. Yeats," *List*, 17 Feb 1966, 237-39.

2. °———: *Horseman, Pass By*. London: BBC-TV, 1967.

Motion picture, 59 mins., black and white; released in the US by Time-Life Films. Presents a biography of W. B. Yeats; includes scenes of Ireland and England and footage of Yeats reading his poetry; narrated by Frank O'Connor. See entry in the National Union Catalog: Audiovisual Materials, a-412-594.

3. °———: *W. B. Yeats and the Coming Times*. TV program, BBC 1, 2 June 1974.

Participants: Michael Yeats, Anne Yeats, Micheál MacLiammóir, Ninette de Valois, Kathleen Raine, George Steiner, John Kelly, Geoffrey Watkins, Dermott MacManus, Ted Brown, T. R. Henn. See *Radio Times*, 30 May 1974, 23; and a letter by Melanie M. Worrall and Colin Radford: "W. B. Yeats, Prophet," *List*, 20 June 1974, 798.

4. ———: *Poems in Their Place: The Poet W. B. Yeats*. Introduced by Seamus Heaney, photography by Russ Walker, produced by John Ormond. London: BBC, 1981.

A video cassette produced by BBC Wales, length about 15 minutes. Concentrates on Coole Park and Thoor Ballylee with citations of appropriate poems.

5. °*Cradle of Genius*. Dublin: Plough Productions, 1961. 16mm black and white film, 33 minutes.

Director: Paul Rotha; commentary: Frank O'Connor; music: Gerard Victory; cast: Siobhan McKenna, Sean Barlow, Maureen Delaney, May Craig, Cyril Cusack.

Summary: A tribute to the poets, playwrights, and actors who contributed to the fame of the Abbey Theatre from 1930 to 1950. Presents dialogues and soliloquies performed by well-known Irish actors who reminisce about Yeats and others. Filmed in the ruins of the old Abbey Theatre (description adapted from the entry in the National Union Catalog of Motion Pictures and Film Strips, 1963-67). See also "Au Revoir to the Abbey Theatre," *SunT*, 25 Jan 1959, 9.

6. IRISH TIMES: *Meditations in Time of Civil War*. Dublin: Irish Times, 1984. Videocassette.

Directed by Lelia Doolan, produced by Maeve Donelan. The poem is read by Richard Murphy and discussed by Augustine Martin. See review by Deaglán de Bréadún: "Sligo School Shows Video Film Based on Yeats Poem," *IrT*, 18 Aug 1984, 16.

7. °*W. B. Yeats--A Tribute*. Dublin: National Film Institute, 1950. 16mm black and white film, 23 minutes.

Directed and written by John D. Sheridan, narrated by Cyril Cusack, poetry reading by Siobhan McKenna und Michael MacLiammoir, music by Eamonn Gallchobhair. Traces the career of the poet Yeats by combining scenes of places that played an important part in his life--Sligo County, Dublin, and London. Relevant quotations from his poems are read to create an impression of the man and his work. (Description adapted from the entry in the National Union Catalog, 1953-57, 28:905)

8. °YEATS, W. B.: *To Write for My Own Race & The Second Coming.* Milton Keynes: Open University, 1975-78. 1 videocassette. (Open University Videocassette A 306.09/10.)

9. °———: *At the Hawk's Well.* Milton Keynes: Open University Educational Enterprises, 1977. Film, black-and-white, 24 mins.

Produced by Open University for BBC; producer Paul Kafno, music by Judith Bignum, choreography by Gillian Lynne. Broadcast on BBC 2, 22 May 1976. See *Radio Times,* 22-28 May 1976, 19.

10. *Yeats Country.* Dublin: Department of External Affairs of Ireland, 1965. 16mm color film, 18 minutes.

Producers: Joe Mendoza, Patrick Carey; director and photographer: Patrick Carey; literary advisers: T. R. Henn, Liam Miller; commentator: Tom St. John Berry; music: Brian Boydell; editor: Ann Chegwidden. The film re-creates the moods and impressions of the poetry of Yeats with scenes of mountains, lakes, rivers, and buildings of Ireland. Recounts some of the legends from which Yeats drew his material. Discusses his poetry in relation to his life and social environment and the literary movement of the early 20th century. (Description adapted from the National Union Catalog of Motion Pictures and Film Strips)

Reviewed by Liam Miller: "Patrick Carey and the Making of *Yeats Country*," *Ireland of the Welcomes,* 17:3 (Sept-Oct 1968), 19-30; Quidnunc: "An Irishman's Diary," *IrT,* 9 Apr 1965, 11. See also HD166.

11. °*Yeats Remembered.* S.l.: Guidance Associates, 1975. 2 filmstrips and 2 discs (12").

Made by Brian and Sheila Seed; includes a discussion guide. Explores the life and poetry of W. B. Yeats; includes exclusive interviews with the poet's children and excerpts from interviews with the poet which were broadcast by BBC; see Library of Congress Catalogs: Films, 1976, and National Union Catalog: Audiovisual Materials, a-431-312.

12. °*Young Cassidy.* London: Sextant Films, released in the US by Metro-Goldwin-Mayer, 1965. Color film, 108 minutes.

Producers: Robert D. Graff, Robert Emmett Ginna; director: Jack Cardiff; screenplay: John Whiting; music: Sean O Riada; director of photography: Ted Sciafe; editor: Anne V. Coates; cast: Rod Taylor, Julie Christie, Michael Redgrave, Edith Evans, Flora Robson, Maggie Smith. Based on O'Casey's autobiography. A biographical drama about the literary rebel Sean O'Casey and his life in Dublin in 1911, during the troubled times of opposition to the British. (Description adapted from the National Union Catalog of Motion Pictures and Film Strips, 1963-67)

According to Eileen O'Casey, one of the characters in the film is Yeats; see CD928, pp. 283, 287.

See also CD938, DC272, EC109, EE12, 43, HA9, 11.

HC Musical Renderings

This section is most certainly incomplete. It is amazing, however, to see how many Yeats poems and plays have been set to music. Yeats himself was less than happy with the compositions; Robert Frost relates that Yeats once "said that nothing he hated more than having his poems set to music--it stole the show" (see Cleanth Brooks and Robert Penn Warren: *Conversations on the Craft of Poetry*. NY: Holt, Rinehart & Winston, 1961, p. 13). Ethel Mannin reports a similar opinion (see BB149). The composer John Foulds notes: "W. B. Yeats and I discussed this question of music to poems more than once, some years ago, and I sympathized quite sincerely with the poet's conclusion that no musician of all those who had made the attempt had been able to enhance his poems; but that in every case . . . the effect of the songs was appreciably less than would have been the case had the poems been declaimed without music" (see *Music Today: Its Heritage from the Past, and Legacy to the Future*. London: Nicholson & Watson, 1934, p. 69).

Entries are arranged alphabetically by composer with the exception of the music contained in Yeats's own books, which are listed under Yeats. The entries are not cross-referenced to sections DD and EE and they are not listed in the index of chronology. For literature on Yeats and music the reader is referred to the subject index IE; the literature on the "Reading to the Psaltery" experiments will be found in section FF.

A great many compositions are unpublished; for these I cite my sources by using the following abbreviations:

Banfield: See DC25
CCE: Catalog of Copyright Entries (United States Copyright Office)
Deale: See AC26
DLC: Library of Congress
G&T: Gooch and Thatcher (see AC36)
Grove: See AC37
ICN: Newberry Library, Chicago
IU: University of Illinois Library
LU: University of London Library
NIC: Cornell University Library
NLI: National Library of Ireland
NN: New York Public Library

1. °ADLER, SAMUEL: *Three Songs*. For medium voice and piano. Chapel Hill, N.C.: Hinshaw Music, 1978.
One of them on a text by Yeats; details not available.

2. °AHROLD, FRANK: "Second Coming." [MS., ca. 1978?].
I do not know whether the score has been published. Recorded: Composers Recordings, CRI SD389, 1978. 12" long-play record. Performed by Philip Langridge, tenor, and the London Symphony Orchestra, conducted by Harold Farberman. Notes on jacket in part by the composer. Based on three poems by Yeats: "The Gyres," "The Tower," and "The Second Coming."

3. °ALTER, MARTHA: "A Prayer for My Daughter." MS., 1962. (CCE)

4. °AMBROS, VLADIMÍR: "The Cap and Bells." Song for alto solo and piano, MS., 1949. (G&T)

5. °ANDREWS, MARK: "The Fiddler of Dooney: Song." MS., pre-1939. (G&T)

6. ANTHEIL, GEORGE: "Fighting the Waves." Copyist's MS., 1929 [?]. In DLC, accompanied by holograph letter from author to composer, dated 16 Aug [1929?]. See also HC337.

7. °———: "Six Songs." For female voice and piano, MS., 1933. (DLC: Antheil Collection).
Source: Whitesitt (CD148), p. 212. Includes "Down by the Salley Gardens" and "The Sorrow of Love."

8. °ASHFORTH, ALDEN: "Byzantia: Two Journeys after Yeats." MS., n.d. (G&T)
Composition for quadrophonic tape, including "Byzantium" and "Sailing to Byzantium."

9. ASTON, PETER: *Five Songs of Crazy Jane*. For unaccompanied soprano. London: Novello, 1964.
These songs are "I Am of Ireland," "Crazy Jane Grown Old Looks at the Dancers," "Those Dancing Days Are Gone," "Crazy Jane Talks with the Bishop," and "Three Things."

10. °AUSTIN, FREDERIC: *Love's Pilgrimage*. Three songs for medium voice and piano forte. London: Enoch, 1920.
Contains "He Wishes for the Cloths of Heaven."

11. °AVNI, TZVI: "Leda and the Swan." [MS., 1983?].
See Margaret Ipsen: "Misleading Note," *Times*, 12 Apr 1983, 13.

12. °BACKER-GRÖNDAHL, FRIDTJOF: "Down by the Salley Gardens." Autograph score, May 1936. (NLI)

13. °BANTOCK, GRANVILLE: *The Hosting of the Sidhe*. Part-song for unaccompanied double chorus of mixed voices. London: Williams, 1930.

14. °BARASH, MICHAEL: "Stolen Child." Words by W. B. Yeats, MS., 1975. (CCE)

15. BARBER, SAMUEL: *Collected Songs for High Voice*. NY: Schirmer, 1955.
"The Secrets of the Old, op. 13, no. 2," 34-37. Composed in 1941.

16. °BARON, STEVE: "Her Anxiety." MS., 1966. (CCE)

17. °BAX, SIR ARNOLD: "The Fiddler of Dooney." Song for solo voice and piano, MS., 1907. (G&T, Banfield)
Banfield also lists "To an Isle in the Water" (pre-1924, lost).

18. ———: *Tone Poems 2*. Bryden Thomson conducts the Ulster Orchestra. Chandos Records, ABRD 1133, 1985. 12" long-play record.
This includes *Into the Twilight* (1908) and *In the Faery Hills* (1909); the sleeve note by Lewis Foreman comments on Bax's interest in Yeats. The score (apparently not published) of *Into the Twilight* is prefaced by Yeats's poem of that title. *In the Faery Hills* has a middle section based to some extent on a passage from "The Wanderings of Oisin"; published London: Murdoch, 1926. See also CD179-180.

19. °BEATSON, THOMAS JEFFERSON: *Down by the Salley Gardens*. For male chorus a cappella. NY: Flammer, 1951.

20. °BEDFORD, HERBERT: *Unaccompanied Songs*. London: Goodwin & Tabb, 1922.
"Aedh Wishes for the Cloths of Heaven," no. 8.

21. °BEESON, JACK: "Lullaby." Song for alto solo and piano, MS., n.d. (G&T)

22. °———: "Three Love Songs." For low female voice and piano, MS., n.d. (G&T)
"Crazy Jane on God," "Crazy Jane Reproved," and "Her Anxiety."

23. °BENNETT, RICHARD R.: "Crazy Jane." For soprano solo and chamber ensemble, MS., 1968-69. (G&T)

24. BENTON, DANIEL: *Studies on Yeats' "A Crazed Girl."* Pianoforte or electric piano (1976). NY: Seesaw Music Corp., 1977.

25. BERGER, ARTHUR VICTOR: *Three Poems of Yeats from "Words for Music, Perhaps."* NY: New Music, 1950 / *New Music: A Quarterly*, 24:1 (Oct 1950).
"Crazy Jane on the Day of Judgment," "His Confidence," and "Girl's Song."

26. BERKELEY, LENNOX: *Colonus' Praise*. For chorus and orchestra, op. 31. [London, before 1951]. (IU)

27. °———: "Lullaby." For medium voice and piano, MS., 1943. (Banfield)

28. BESLEY, MAURICE: *The Angels Are Stooping: Song*. London: Enoch, 1923.
"A Cradle Song."

29. °BISHOP, THOMAS BURKE, FRED KOLLER, and MEGAN MCDONOUGH: "Songs for Seymour." Words by Fred Rubin and W. B. Yeats, MS., 1977. (CCE)

30. °BISSELL, KEITH: *Four Songs for High Voice and Harp*. Poems by W. B. Yeats. Waterloo, Ont.: Waterloo Music, 1977.
"A Cradle Song," "To a Child Dancing in the Wind," "O Do Not Love Too Long," "When You Are Old."

31. °———: *The Old Men Admiring Themselves in the Water*. For mixed chorus and piano. Toronto: Caveat Music, distributed by Kerby, 1980.

32. BLANK, ALLAN: "Eight Songs for Voice and Piano." MS., 1957. (CCE)
Contains "Down by the Salley Gardens," "To an Isle in the Water," "The Falling of the Leaves," and "Brown Penny."

33. °BODLEY, SEOIRSE: "A Drinking Song." For baritone solo and piano, MS., 1953. (G&T)

34. °———: "Never to Have Lived Is Best." Song cycle for soprano and orchestra, MS., 1965. (G&T)
This was commissioned for the Yeats centenary; see *Eire*, 5:3 (Autumn 1970), 133.

35. °BOOTH, THOMAS: "When You Are Old." MS., 1968. (CCE)

36. °BOUGHTON, RUTLAND: "The Wind. Into the Twilight." MS., 1916–17. (Banfield)

37. ———: *Celtic Prelude: The Land of Heart's Desire.* For piano, violin, and violoncello. London: Augener, 1923.
I do not know whether this was intended for Yeats's play; see G&T, p. 855, item 7565.

38. °BOURGEOIS, DEREK: "Six Songs of Wandering." For baritone solo and piano, MS., 1962. (G&T)
Includes "A Mad Song," i.e., "The Song of Wandering Aengus."

39. °BOYDELL, BRIAN: "A Terrible Beauty Is Born." Cantata, MS., 1965. (G&T, Deale)
For soloists, narrator, choir, and orchestra; commissioned for the 1916 commemoration. First performance 1966; texts by Yeats and others. Includes "Red Hanrahan's Song about Ireland" and "Easter 1916."

40. °———: "Four Yeats Poems." For soprano solo and orchestra, MS., 1965. (G&T, Deale)
First performance 1968; includes "The Cloths of Heaven," Musician's song from *Deirdre,* "Drinking Song," and "Red Hanrahan's Song."

41. °BOYLE, INA: "The Stolen Child: Song." MS., 1926/27. (Deale)

42. BRANDUARDI, ANGELO: *Branduardi canta Yeats: Dieci ballate su liriche di William Butler Yeats.* Ariola Eurodisc, 207783, 1986. 12" long-play record.
Recording of Italian versions of "The Wild Swans at Coole," "The Cap and Bells," "The Song of Wandering Aengus," "The Cloak, the Boat and the Shoes," "To a Child Dancing in the Wind," "The Fiddler of Dooney," "When You Are Old," "An Irish Airman Foresees His Death," "Down by the Salley Gardens," and "The Lake Isle of Innisfree." The translations or adaptations by Luisa Zappa Branduardi are printed on the inside of the jacket. The music is by Branduardi, except for "The Song of Wandering Aengus," which is by Donovan Leitch (see HC197). The scores seem to be unpublished.
Reviews:
- Marion-Elizabeth Hawkes, *Celtic Dawn,* 1 (Spring 1988), 44.
- Ugo Volli: "E Angelo incontrò un poeta," *Grazia,* 13 Apr 1986, 84-86.

43. °BRASH, JAMES: *Down by the Salley Gardens.* Song for solo voice and piano. London: Curwen, 1945.

44. BRAUN, RUTH FISHER: "The Lake Isle of Innisfree." MS., n.d. (NN)

45. BRETTINGHAM SMITH, JOLYON: *The Death of Cuchulain / Cuchulains Tod.* From the play of the same name by William Butler Yeats / Nach dem gleichnamigen Bühnenstück von William Butler Yeats in der deutschen Übersetzung von Ursula Clemen. Vocal score / Klavierauszug. Berlin: Bote & Bock, 1975.
Marked as op. 5 (1973). An opera with a short prefatory note.

46. °———: *Dancing Days: 1975.* Based on the poem "Those Dancing Days Are Gone" from the collection *Words for Music Perhaps* by W. B.

Yeats, for soprano with tambourine and instrumental ensemble. Berlin: Bote & Bock, 1976.

47. °BRIAN, HAVERGAL: "A Faery Song, op. 13c." For mezzo soprano, MS., 1906. (Banfield, G&T)

48. °———: *To an Isle in the Water*. Song. London: Chester, [pre-1940].

49. °BRIDGE, FRANK: *When You Are Old*. London: Chappell, 1920.

50. °BRIGGS, ALICE: "Down by the Salley Gardens." MS., 1961. (CCE)

51. BRITTEN, BENJAMIN: *Folk-Song Arrangements for Voice and Piano*. London: Boosey & Hawkes, 1943-61. 6 vols.
"The Salley Gardens," 1:1-3.

52. °BROWN, JAMES: "The Song of Wandering Aengus." For baritone or bass solo and piano, MS., n.d. (G&T)

53. °BROWNE, WILLIAM DENIS: "Had I the Heavens' Embroidered Cloths. The Fiddler of Dooney." MS., 1909. (Banfield)

54. °BRUMBY, COLIN: *The Cloths of Heaven*. Song for female voices. London: Boosey, 1961.

55. °BRYSON, ERNEST: "The Cloak, the Boat, and the Shoes." For chorus and orchestra, MS., pre-1927. (G&T)

56. °BUCK, WILLIAM A.: "Six Yeats Songs." MS., 1981. (CCE)

57. °BURROWS, BENJAMIN: "Innisfree." MS., 1928. (Banfield)

58. °BURTCH, MERVYN: "Anashuya and Vijaya." Chamber opera, MS., n.d. (G&T)

59. °———: "The Island Dream." Song for alto solo, flute, piano, MS., n.d. (G&T)
"The Indian to His Love."

60. °BUSH, ALAN: "The Lake Isle of Innisfree." For tenor and piano, MS., 1926. (Banfield)

61. °BUTLER, WALTER: *Four Irish Lyrics*. London: Boosey, 1918.
Includes "The Lake Isle of Innisfree," "The Cloak, the Boat, and the Shoes," and "The Fiddler of Dooney."

62. °BYERS, DAVID: "The Wind among the Reeds." Choral, MS., 1969. (Deale)

63. °CAHN, RICHARD: "Down by the Salley Gardens." MS., 1970 (CCE)

64. °———: "Two Songs for Voice and Piano." MS., 1976. (CCE)
Texts by W. B. Yeats, details not available.

65. CAMPBELL-TIPTON, [LOUIS]: *All the Words That I Gather*. Song with piano accompaniment. NY: Schirmer, 1911.
"Where My Books Go."

66. CARPENTER, JOHN ALDEN: *The Player Queen*. Song from an unfinished play by W. B. Yeats. NY: Schirmer, 1915.

67. °CARTER, JOHN: *The Cloths of Heaven*. Song for chorus a cappella. Boston: Frank Music Co., 1968.

68. CAVE, LAWRENCE HAROLD: "Purgatory: A Chamber Opera in One Act after Yeats," °Ph.D. thesis, Harvard U, 1986. 135 pp. (*DAI*, 47:7 [Jan 1987], 2359A)

69. °CAVIANI, RON: *When You Are Old*. Song, a cappella. Champaign, Ill.: Fostco Music Press, 1980.

70. CHANDLER, LEN H.: "I Made My Song a Coat," *Broadside*, 65 (15 Dec 1965), [8].

71. °CLARK, ROSEMARY: "The Cat and the Moon: Opera." MS., n.d. (G&T)

72. °CLARKE, DOUGLAS: "The Countess Cathleen." Incidental music, MS., pre-1952. (G&T)

73. CLARKE, REBECCA: *Songs*. London: Rogers, 1928.
Includes "The Cloths of Heaven," "Down by the Salley Gardens," "Shy One" ("To an Isle in the Water"), "A Dream [of Death]."

74. COERNE, LOUIS ADOLPHE: *Three Songs for High Voice with Piano Accompaniment*. NY: Schirmer, 1919.
No. 1: "Into the Twilight."

75. °COHN, JAMES MYRON: "Music for *The Only Jealousy of Emer*." MS., 1955. (CCE)

76. °COLLINS, FLETCHER: "Words for Music Perhaps." MS., 1972. (CCE)

77. °COLLINS, J. H.: *Two Songs*. London: Oxford UP, 1929.
Includes "Down by the Salley Gardens" (G&T).

78. °COUCH, JANETTE: "The Lake Isle of Innisfree." Song for low voice and piano, MS., 1955. (G&T)

79. °COX, SIDNEY: "The Falling of the Leaves." For mezzo-soprano and piano, MS., 1948. (NIC)

80. CROSSE, GORDON: *Purgatory*. Opera in 1 act, op. 18. German translation by Ernst Roth. London: Oxford UP, 1968.
Commissioned by B.B.C. 2 Television and first performed at the Cheltenham Festival, 7 July 1966. Reviewed by Elliott Schwartz, *Musical Q*, 63:4 (Oct 1977), 972-78.
Recorded: °Argo, ZRG 810, 1975. 12" long-play record. Performed by Peter Bodenham, tenor; Glenville Hargreaves, baritone, Orchestra and Chorus of the Royal Northern College of Music, conducted by Michael Lankaster. Program notes by the composer and by S. Walsh on container; libretto, from the play, 1 leaf, inserted.

81. ———: *Ceremony, Op. 19*. For orchestra with solo cello. London: Oxford UP, 1972.
In a short prefatory note, Crosse states: "This piece was composed soon after I completed my opera *Purgatory*. It shares some

musical material with the opera, and also the connection with Yeats. The title, *Ceremony,* is intended to reflect Yeats's frequent use of this word."

82. °CROSSLEY-HOLLAND, PETER: "Two Mystical Songs." For baritone and orchestra, MS., 1945. (G&T)
One of the songs is "Into the Twilight."

83. °CUMMINS, FRED JAY: "The Wild Old Wicked Man." MS., 1976. (CCE)

84. CURRY, ARTHUR MANSFIELD: *The Fiddler of Dooney*. Song for bass or baritone. Boston: Thompson, 1909.

85. °DALBY, MARTIN: "Yellow Hair." Song for soprano solo and piano, MS., n.d. (G&T)
"For Anne Gregory."

86. °DAMON, JULIA: *The Valley of Lovers*. Song. Newton Center: Wa-Wan Press, 1906.

87. °DEALE, EDGAR MARTIN: "The Cloths of Heaven." MS., 1967. (Deale)

88. °———: *Down by the Salley Gardens*. Part-song. London: Elkin, 1957.

89. °DE BEER, ALAN: *Down by the Salley Gardens*. Song. London: Chester, 1935.

90. °DECEVEE, ALICE: *Down by the Salley Gardens*. Song. NY, [pre-1940]. (G&T)

91. °DELIUS, FREDERICK: "The Lake Isle of Innisfree." MS., ca. 1913. (Banfield)

92. DEL RIEGO, TERESA: *How Shall I Miss You (Cradle Song)*. NY: Chappell, 1914.

93. °DONOVAN, RICHARD: *Down by the Salley Gardens*. Air: The Maids of Mourne Shore, arranged for soprano 1 and 2 and alto. NY: Galaxy Music, 1931.

94. DOUTY, NICHOLAS: *Two Songs for a Medium Voice with Piano Accompaniment*. NY: Schirmer, 1913.
No. 1: "A Cradle Song."

95. °DROSTE, DOREEN: *Red Hanrahan's Song about Ireland*. For four-part chorus of mixed voices with piano accompaniment. NY: Associated Music Publishers, 1966.

96. °———: *The Song of Wandering Aengus*. A cappella. NY: Galaxy / London: Galliard, 1973.

97. °———: *When You Are Old*. Song. NY: Associated Music Publishers, 1968.

98. DUKE, JOHN WOODS: *Yellow Hair*. Song for medium voice and piano accompaniment. Boston: Row Music Co., 1953.
"For Anne Gregory."

99. °———: *Brown Penny*. Vocal solo. NY: Fischer, 1976.

100. °———: *The Song of Wandering Aengus*. Vocal solo, medium voice. NY: Fischer, 1976.

101. °DUNCAN, CHESTER: "Girl's Song." MS., 1966. (G&T)

102. °———: *Then and Now: Songs*. Waterloo, Ont.: Waterloo Music, 1974.
Includes "A Cradle Song" and "A Nativity" (G&T).

103. DUNHILL, THOMAS FREDERICK: *The Wind among the Reeds*. A cycle of four songs for tenor voice and orchestra, op. 30. London: Stainer & Bell, 1911.
"To Dectora" (i.e., "He Thinks of Those Who Have Spoken Evil of His Beloved"), "The Host of the Air," "The Cloths of Heaven," and "The Fiddler of Dooney."

104. DUNN, JAMES PHILIP: *Album of New Songs*. Volume one for high voice. NY: Fischer, 1917.
"A Faery Song" (no. 5)

105. °DYER-BENNET, RICHARD: "The Salley Gardens." MS., 1966. (CCE)

106. °EATON, JOHN: "Three Yeats Songs: For soprano solo and piano." MS., n.d. (G&T)
"Girl's Song," "Lullaby," "Irish Poets, Learn Your Trade" (from "Under Ben Bulben").

107. EDMUNDS, JOHN: *Byzantium: Ten Songs to Texts by W. B. Yeats*. S.l.: Privately printed, [1976?]. (LU)
Actually eleven songs: "Wisdom," "Crazy Jane and the Bishop," "Death," "The Squirrel," "Leda and the Swan," "The Mother of God," "The Second Coming," "The Hazel Wood," "The Delphic Oracle upon Plotinus," "Sailing to Byzantium," and "Byzantium."

108. EGK, WERNER: *Musik--Wort--Bild: Texte und Anmerkungen, Betrachtungen und Gedanken*. München: Langen-Müller, 1960. 314 pp.
"Irische Legende: Oper in fünf Bildern," 113-82. Reprint of *Irische Legende: Text zu einer Oper*. Freiburg i.B.: Klemm-Seemann, [1955]. 48 pp. An opera based on *The Countess Cathleen*.
"Ausbruch aus der Hoffnungslosigkeit: Ein Briefwechsel zur Oper *Irische Legende* anlässlich der Uraufführung bei den Salzburger Festspielen 1955," 183-96; reprinted from *Frankfurter Hefte*, 10:5 (May 1955), 318-25. An exchange of letters between Egk und Reinhold Kreile.
"Rundfunkeinrichtung zur *Irischen Legende*," 197-200. The changes made for the radio version.
See also EE108 and 124.

109. EICHHEIM, HENRY: *Seven Songs*. Boston: Boston Music Co., 1910.
"The Heart of the Woman" (no. 1) and "Aedh Wishes His Beloved Were Dead" ["He Wishes His Beloved Were Dead"] (no. 7).

110. ELGAR, SIR EDWARD: *Incidental Music and Funeral March, "Grania and Diarmid" [sic] (George Moore and W. B. Yeats)* [op. 42]. London: Novello, 1902.
Includes a rendering of "There Are Seven That Pull the Thread." See also CD394.

111. °ERICKSON, ELAINE M.: *Down by the Salley Gardens*. For soprano or tenor solo and string orchestra. NY, n.d. (G&T)

112. FAIRCHILD, BLAIR: *Three Songs with Pianoforte Accompaniment*. Boston: Thompson, 1909.
No. 1: "The Lake Isle of Innisfree."

113. °FAY, VERNON: *The Song of the Old Mother*. For male voices. Charlotte, N.C.: Brodt Music Co., 1966.

114. °FEARING, JOHN: *When You Are Old*. Song for medium voice and piano forte. Vancouver: Western Canada Music Co., 1968.

115. °FIELD, COREY: "Yeats Song." [MS., 1979?].
Performed at the Guildhall School of Music and Drama, London, 13 Nov 1979; see Albert Alan Owen: "First Performances, Commissions," *Composer*, 69 (Spring 1980), 36.

116. FIELDEN, THOMAS PERCEVAL: *The Lake Isle of Innisfree*. London: Breitkopf & Härtel, 1911.

117. °FLANAGAN, WILLIAM: "After Long Silence." For voice and piano, MS., 1946. (NN)

118. FLORES, BERNAL: "The Land of Heart's Desire (A Chamber Opera)," °Ph.D. thesis, U of Rochester, 1964. 226 pp. (*DAI*, 28:2 [Aug 1967], 707A)
"The whole play, word by word, is used as a libretto in the opera. . . . The style of the music is atonal" (abstract).

119. FOGEL, CLYDE VAN NUYS: *Two Poems by William Butler Yeats*. For solo voice with piano accompaniment. NY: Schirmer, 1911.
"He Wishes for the Cloths of Heaven" and "He Wishes His Beloved Were Dead."

120. FOOTE, ARTHUR: *The Lake Isle of Innisfree*. For soprano or tenor. Boston: Schmidt, 1921.

121. FORREST, OSWALD: *The Wind among the Reeds*. Song for solo voice. London: Chappell, 1902.
The text is "The Heart of the Woman."

122. ————: *The Lake Isle of Innisfree*. Song. London: Weekes, 1903.

123. °FRANK, FRANCIS: *The Fiddler of Dooney*. Song. London: Novello, [pre-1940]. (G&T)

124. GANZ, RUDOLPH: *The Angels Are Stooping*. A song with piano accompaniment. NY: Schirmer, 1917.
"A Cradle Song."

125. °GERBER, STEVEN R.: "Songs from *The Wild Swans at Coole* (Yeats)." [MS., 1982?].
I do not know whether this has been published. Recorded: Opus One Records, 86. [1982?]. 12" long-play record. Performed by Joanna Arnold, soprano, assisted by a small ensemble, including the composer. Jacket notes by the composer. The songs include "A Song," "To a Young Girl," "The Dawn," "A Deep-Sworn Vow," and "An Irish Airman Foresees His Death."

126. °GIBBS, GEOFFREY D.: "The Lake Isle of Innisfree." Song for medium-low voice and piano, MS., n.d. (G&T)

127. GILBERT, HENRY F.: *Faery Song*. Newton Center, Mass.: Wa-Wan Press, 1905.

"The wind blows out of the gates of the day" from *The Land of Heart's Desire*.

128. GILMAN, LAWRENCE: "The Heart of the Woman (For Contralto Voice)," *Wa-Wan Series of American Compositions,* 2:1 (Sept 1903), 12-14.

129. ———: "A Dream of Death: Recitation with Piano Accompaniment," *Wa-Wan Series of American Compositions,* 2:2 (Sept 1903), 1-3.

130. ———: "The Curlew: Recitation with Piano Accompaniment," *Wa-Wan Series of American Compositions,* 3:1 (July 1904), 1-2.

131. °GINSBURG, GERALD M.: "When You Are Old." MS., 1985. (CCE)

132. °GOW, DAVID: *To an Isle in the Water*. Part-song for unaccompanied voice. Sevenoaks: Novello, 1977.

133. °GRANT, PARKS: "The Wild Swans at Coole, op. 12, no. 4." Song for mezzo-soprano or baritone solo und piano, MS., 1941. (G&T, NN)

134. GRAVES, ALFRED PERCEVAL (ed): *The Irish Song Book with Original Irish Airs*. London: Unwin, 1895 [1894]. xxiv, 188 pp.

"Down by the Salley Gardens." Air--The Maids of Mourne Shore, p. 55.

135. °GRIFFES, CHARLES T.: *Three Tone-Pictures*. For piano solo or chamber ensemble. NY: Schirmer, 1915.

One of them, "The Lake at Evening," was inspired by "The Lake Isle of Innisfree" (G&T).

136. GURNEY, IVOR: *Twenty [i.e., Forty] Songs*. London: Oxford UP, 1938-59. 4 vols.

"Down by the Salley Gardens" and "Cathleen ni Houlihan" (°vol. 1), "The Folly of Being Comforted" (°vol. 2), "A Cradle Song" and "The Fiddler of Dooney" (vol. 4).

G&T and Banfield also list the following songs by Gurney (all in MS.): "All the Words That I Utter (Song in the Night)." Song for solo voice and piano, 1925 ("Where My Books Go"). "The Cloths of Heaven," 1920. "A Faery Song," 1920. "The Happy Townland," 1920. "The Lake Isle of Innisfree," 1918. "Maid Quiet," ca. 1922. "A Visit from the Sea," 1909 (I do not know what this refers to). "When You Are Old," ca. 1909. "The Wind Blows Out of the Gates of the Day," ca. 1921; from *The Land of Heart's Desire*. See also CD526.

137. °HADLEY, PATRICK: "Crazy Jane." Seven songs for soprano and harp, MS., 1958. (Banfield)

138. °———: "Ephemera." For soprano or tenor, flute, oboe, clarinet, five strings or string orchestra, and piano, MS., 1924. (Banfield)

139. ———: *A Faery Song Sung by the People of Faery over Diarmuid and Grania, in Their Bridal Sleep under a Cromlech*. For female chorus and orchestra. London: Oxford UP, 1927.

140. °HAENSELMAN, CARL FERDINAND: "Three Chamber Orchestra Scores for Modern Dance," M.A. thesis, U of Colorado, 1950.

One of them is based on *The King of the Great Clock Tower.*

141. °HAGEMAN, RICHARD: *The Fiddler of Dooney*. Song. NY: Schirmer, 1946.

142. °HALL, ARTHUR E.: *Down by the Salley Gardens*. Arranged for male chorus unaccompanied. Air: The Maids of Mourne Shore. NY: Galaxy Music, 1933.

143. HARBISON, JOHN: *A Full Moon in March*. Opera in one act. Adapted from W. B. Yeats's play; vocal score by Randall Hodgkinson. NY: Associated Music Publishers, 1983.

This was performed by the Boston Musica Viva in 1979; see Andrew Porter: "Words for Music Perhaps," *New Yorker,* 28 May 1979, 111-12, 115-17. Another performance was reviewed by Stephanie Von Buchau: "San Francisco / Bay Area," *Opera News,* 47:1 (July 1982), 34-35 ("in many ways typical of modern opera--emotionally dry, philosophically pretentious, physically static").

Recorded: Composers Recordings, CRI SD454H, 1983, 12" long-play record. Performed by the Boston Musica Viva, jacket notes by an anonymous author.

144. °HARRIS, DOROTHY STEPHENSON: "When You Are Old." Song, MS., 1958. (CCE)

145. °HARRIS, EDWARD: *Cloths of Dreams*. Words by W. B. Yeats. NY: Boosey & Hawkes, 1950.

Presumably "He Wishes for the Cloths of Heaven."

146. °HARRIS, RUSSELL G.: *The Only Jealousy of Emer*. Op. 18. NY: American Composers Alliance, 1943.

For solo voices, five speakers, and instrumental ensemble (violin, clarinet, cornet, bassoon, trombone, double bass, and percussion).

147. °HARRISON, LOU: "The Only Jealousy of Emer: Opera," 1949. (Grove, 4:116: "after a story of W. B. Yeats")

See also HA17.

148. °HART, FRITZ: "A Cradle Song." Song for voice and piano, MS., 1913 (G&T, Banfield)

149. °———: "The Land of Heart's Desire." Opera in one act, op. 18, 1914. (G&T)

150. °HARTY, HAMILTON: *The Fiddler of Dooney: Song*. London: Boosey, 1938.

151. HARVEY, JONATHAN: *Cantata I*. For soprano and baritone soli, chorus, small string orchestra, and organ. Borough Green: Novello, 1968.

Section 2 is a song, "The Mother of God"; section 4 is a melodrama, "The Second Coming."

152. ———: *Four Images after Yeats*. For piano solo. Borough

Green: Novello, 1984.
First performance in 1969. The first three Images are accompanied by extracts from "The Statues," "Vacillation," and "The Phases of the Moon." The last Image, "Purgatory," is prefaced by an extract from *A Vision*. Reviewed by Peter Evans: "Jonathan Harvey's Recent Works," *Musical Times,* 116:1589 (July 1975), 616-19.

153. °———: "Four Songs of Yeats." For bass solo and piano, MS., 1965. (G&T)
"He Wishes for the Cloths of Heaven," "A Drunken Man's Praise of Sobriety," "The Four Ages of Man," and "Sweet Dancer."

154. °———: "A Full Moon in March: Opera." [MS., 1967?].
I do not know whether this has been published. There is an announcement in the *Times,* 8 Feb 1967, 6, that the opera would be performed at the Southampton University Arts Festival.

155. °HAUFRECHT, HERBERT: *A Pot of Broth: One Act Opera*. NY: American Composers Alliance, 1965.
Produced in 1964 on WNYC radio, New York, according to G&T.

156. °HAWKINS, JOHN: *Three Cavatinas*. Text on fragments from W. B. Yeats and others. Toronto: Berandel, 1969.
For soprano solo, violin, violoncello, celesta, and percussion. Includes fragments from *The Winding Stair* (G&T; CCE lists the publication date as Don Mills, Ont.: BMI Canada, 1967).

157. °HAYES, MALCOLM: "Into the Night." [MS., 1985?].
A choral cycle, comprising "What Was Lost," "The Black Tower," and "The Man and the Echo"; broadcast by BBC Radio 3, 18 Oct 1985; reviewed by Calum MacDonald, *Tempo,* 160 (Mar 1986), 58.

158. °HEALEY, DEREK: "Six Irish Songs." For solo voice and piano, MS., 1962. (G&T)
Includes "A Cradle Song" and "A Drinking Song."

159. °HEININEN, PAAVO: "Love's Philosophy." MS., 1968. (G&T)
Includes "The Cloths of Heaven."

160. °HENDERSON, RAY: *Down by the Salley Gardens*. Arranged on an Irish folk tune. S.l.: Kjos, 1957.

161. HERBERT, MURIEL: *The Lake Isle of Innisfree*. Song for soprano, alto, and piano, arranged by Basil Ramsey. London: Elkin, 1963.

162. °HILL, MABEL WOOD: "To the Poet Who Claims That His Rhythms Are Lost in Song--Quintette of Oboe, Violin, Viola, Piano, and Voice Reciting with Rhythms and Meaning of the Poems of W. B. Yeats." MS., before 1941. (DLC)
Contains "Be You Still" (i.e., "To His Heart, Bidding It Have No Fear"), "Cloths of Heaven," "Innisfree," and "The Curlew" ("He Reproves the Curlew").

163. °HINCHCLIFFE, IRVIN: *Down by the Salley Gardens*. In G. London: Murdoch, 1931.

164. HOMER, SIDNEY: *Four Songs with Piano Accompaniment, op. 17*. NY: Schirmer, 1906.
No. 3: "Michael Robartes Bids His Beloved Be at Peace."

165. ———: *The Fiddler of Dooney*. Song with piano accompaniment, op. 20. NY: Schirmer, 1909.

166. °HOUSMAN, ROSALIE: "The Angels Are Stooping." MS., 1935. (NN)
"A Cradle Song."

167. °———: "[The] Song of the Old Mother." MS., n.d. (NN)

168. °HOWE, MARY: *Songs*. Volume 3: Baritone songs. NY: Galaxy Music, 1959.
Includes "The Lake Isle of Innisfree."

169. °HUGGLES, JOHN: "Those Dancing Days Are Gone." For coloratura, clarinet, viola, and cello, MS., 1958. (G&T)

170. HUGHES, HERBERT: *Irish Country Songs*. Edited, arranged, and for the most part collected by Herbert Hughes. London: Boosey, 1909-36. 4 vols.
"Down by the Salley Gardens," 1:37-39. Set to the air of The Maids of Mourne Shore, for voice and piano.

171. °HUGHES, SPIKE: "Incidental Music for *The Player Queen*," 1927. (Grove, 4:400)

172. °HUSS, HENRY HOLDEN: "Irish Faery Song: The Wind Blows out of the Gate of the Sky [sic]." For soprano and piano, MS., [1921?]. (NN)

173. °HYWEL, JOHN: "The Only Jealousy of Emer: Incidental Music." MS., n.d. (G&T)

174. IRELAND, JOHN: *Songs Sacred and Profane*. With piano accompaniment. London: Schott, 1934.
"The Salley Gardens," no. 4.

175. °JENSEN, JAMES ALBERT: "Songs of Age: Original Compositions." Texts from the collected poems of W. B. Yeats, MS., 1975. (CCE)

176. °JOHNSON, PHOEBE: *To an Isle in the Water*. Song for solo voice and piano. London: Curwen, 1921.

177. °JOHNSON, REGINALD THOMAS: *Down by the Salley Gardens*. Part-song for men's voices, unaccompanied. London: Curwen, 1952.

178. °JONES, ROBERT W.: *The Coming of Wisdom with Time*. Motet, a cappella. Bryn Mawr: Elkan-Vogel, 1973.

179. °JOUBERT, JOHN: *Incantation*. For unaccompanied chorus and soprano solo. Words from the play *The Resurrection* by W. B. Yeats. London: Novello, 1957.

180. ———: "On Setting Yeats's 'Byzantium,'" *Musical Times*, 123: 1670 (Apr 1982), 249-50.
Describes his composition "Gong-Tormented Sea," first performed on 29 Apr 1982 at Birmingham Town Hall, a work for symphony orchestra and chorus, based on "Byzantium."

181. °KAHN, RACHAEL: "A Collection of English, American, and Irish Verse Set to Music." Arranged by Murray Ross, MS., 1961. (CCE)
Vol. 2 contains one or more Yeats poems; details not available.

182. KALOMIRIS, MANOLIS: *The Shadowy Waters*. London: British Broadcasting Corporation, [1953].

"A musical dramatic poem in one Act with a Prologue based on the poem of W. B. Yeats translated into Greek by Veta Pezopoulos. Retranslated into English by Geoffrey Dunn who has used, wherever possible, Yeats's own wording" ([1]). Performed on the B.B.C. Third Programme, 23 and 26 Oct 1953.

183. °KASTLE, LEONARD: "Two Songs of Love." MS., 1957. (CCE)

One of them with words by Yeats; details not available.

184. KAUDER, HUGO: *The Fiddler of Dooney*. Song for voice and violin (1940). NY: Seesaw Music, 1974.

185. ———: *Song from "Deirdre."* Voice with flute and harp (1933). NY: Seesaw Music, 1974.

186. °KEATS, DONALD: *A Drinking Song*. For four-part chorus of men's voices a cappella. NY: Schirmer, 1965.

187. °KELLY, THOMAS: "The Everlasting Voices." Song a cappella, MS., 1959. (G&T, Deale)

188. °———: "Innisfree." Song for solo voice and piano, MS., 1949. (G&T)

189. °KENNEDY, JOHN BRODBIN: *Down by the Salley Gardens*. For male voice with piano. NY: Boosey & Hawkes, 1973.

190. °———: *The Falling of the Leaves*. Song. NY: Boosey & Hawkes, 1973.

191. °LANGERT, JULES: "Leda and the Swan." Song for baritone solo and piano, MS., n.d. (G&T)

192. °LARCHET, JOHN F.: "The Land of Heart's Desire." Incidental music, n.d. (Deale)

193. °LEE, LORRAINE A.: "Cap and Bells." Words by W. B. Yeats, MS., 1979. (CCE)

194. °———: "Colonel Martin." Words by W. B. Yeats, MS., 1979. (CCE)

195. °LE FLEMING, CHRISTOPHER: *To an Isle in the Water*. London: Chester, 1931.

196. LEHMANN, LIZA: *The Lake Isle of Innisfree*. Song. NY: Boosey, 1911.

197. °LEITCH, DONOVAN: *Song of Wandering Aengus*. London: Donovan, n.d. (G&T)

Recorded by Donovan Leitch: *H.M.S. Donovan*. Dawn Records, DNLD.4001, 1971. 2 12" long-play records. See also HC42.

CCE lists this as °*The Song of Wandering Aengus / La belle chanson d'été*. Paroles françaises de Alvys [i.e., Albrecht Marcuse], musique de Donovan Leitch, sur un poème de W. B. Yeats. S.l.: Société d'Editions musicales internationales, 1971.

198. °LEONI, FRANCO: "The Land of Heart's Desire." Opera, [MS.,

1921?].

In a letter to Allan Wade of 18 Oct 1921 Yeats refers to a performance in Milano, Italy (see *Letters*, p. 674).

199. °LEROUX, ALAIN: *The Ballad of Father Gilligan*. Piano et chant. S.l.: Editions musicales Alpha, 1973.

200. °LEVY, RON: "Five Songs after Yeats." For soprano, MS., 1979. (CCE)

201. °LEY, HENRY G.: "Album of Songs, op. 8." For solo voice and piano, MS., n.d. (G&T)

Includes "A Cradle Song," "The Lake Isle of Innisfree."

202. °LIDOV, DAVID: "Crazy Jane's Songs." For solo voice and piano, MS., 1967, revised 1970. (G&T)

"Crazy Jane and Jack the Journeyman," "Crazy Jane and the Bishop," "Crazy Jane Grown Old Looks at the Dancers," "Crazy Jane on God," "Crazy Jane on the Day of Judgment," "Crazy Jane Reproved," "Crazy Jane Talks with the Bishop."

203. °LINDROTH, SCOTT: "The Folly of Being Comforted." For baritone voice and four trombones, MS., 1980. (CCE)

204. LOEFFLER, CHARLES MARTIN: *Five Irish Fantasies for Voice and Orchestra or Piano*. NY: Schirmer, 1934 [1908]. 5 vols.

Contains "The Hosting of the Sidhe," "The Host of the Air," "The Fiddler of Dooney," and "The Ballad of the Foxhunter."

Recorded: *La mort de Tintagiles: Five Irish Fantasies*. New World Records, NW 332, 1985. 12" long-play record. Performed by Neil Rosenshein, tenor, and the Indianapolis Symphony Orchestra, conducted by John Nelson.

205. °LUCIFER, ALVIN: *That the Night Come*. Song for soprano. Don Mills, Ont.: BMI, 1962.

206. °MACONCHY, ELIZABETH: "Six Settings of Yeats Poems for Three-Part Woman's Chorus, with Harp, Clarinet and 2 Horns." MS., 1951 [?]. (Grove, 5:483)

Further details not available. According to Deale, this was first performed in 1952.

207. °MALLINSON, ALBERT: *Dream of a Blessed Spirit*. Song for soprano or tenor solo and piano. Oakville, Ont.: Harris, 1907.

"All the Heavy Days Are Over" from *The Countess Cathleen*.

208. °———: *To an Isle in the Water*. Song for soprano or tenor solo and piano. Oakville, Ont.: Harris, 1907.

209. °MANHEIM, ERNEST: "Down by the Salley Gardens." MS., 1948. (CCE)

210. °MANSON, GLORIA E.: "The Stolen Child." Song for solo voice, choir, and piano, MS., 1956. (G&T)

211. °MARSHALL, NICHOLAS: "Five Winter Songs." For medium voice and piano, MS., n.d. (G&T)

Includes "The Cat Went Here and There" from *The Cat and the Moon*.

212. °———: "The Falling of the Leaves." Songs for high voice and instruments, MS., n.d. (G&T)
Includes "He Wishes for the Cloths of Heaven," "The Falling of the Leaves," "The Fiddler of Dooney," "The Lover Tells of the Rose in His Heart," "The Host of the Air," "The White Birds."

213. °MARTIN, PHILIP: "Innisfree." For high voice and piano, MS., 1969/71. (Deale)
Deale also lists "The Voice," song, words by W. B. Yeats (first performance 1973); I do not know which poem was set to music.

214. °MERINO, JOHN C.: "Words." Music with words by W. B. Yeats, sound cassette, 1983. (CCE)

215. °MERVYN, EDWARD: *The Land of Heart's Desire*. Musical setting.
Edward Malins writes that this musical setting "is still being issued by a leading firm of London dramatic music publishers" (see FF12, p. 498), but he gives no details and I have not been able to find it. It is not listed by Banfield and G&T.

216. °METHOLD, DIANA: *Down by the Salley Gardens*. Song. London: Cramer, 1937.

217. °MILFORD, ROBIN: *A Dream of Death*. Song for bass solo and piano. London: Oxford UP, [pre-1958]. (G&T)

218. °———: *The Fiddler of Dooney*. London: Oxford UP, 1925.
Also in *A Book of Songs*. London: Oxford UP, 1942.

219. °MISHKIN, HENRY GEORGE: *Down by the Salley Gardens*. For four-part chorus of men's voices, a cappella. Old Irish air from The Maids of Mourne Shore. Boston: Schirmer, 1951.

220. °MITCHELL, HELEN I.: *Down by the Salley Gardens*. Waterloo, Ont.: Waterloo Music, 1957.

221. °MOERAN, ERNEST JOHN: *A Dream of Death*. London: Oxford UP, 1925.

222. MOFFAT, ALFRED: *The Minstrelsy of Ireland: 200 Songs Adapted to Their Traditional Airs*. London: Augener, 1897. x, 346 pp.
"Down by the Salley Gardens," 47. For voice and piano, adapted from the air Far beyond Yon Mountains.

223. °MOORE, EDWARD C.: *The Land of Heart's Desire*. Song, words by W. B. Yeats. Chicago: Gamble Hinged Music, 1913.

224. °MOORE, FREDERICK B.: "To an Isle in the Water." MS., 1975. (CCE)

225. °MORRIS, JOHN LEONARD: "A Cradle Song." MS., 1981. (CCE)
CCE also lists the following MSS.: "To an Isle in the Water," "The Song of the Old Mother," "The Fiddler of Dooney," "When You Are Old," and "The Lover Pleads" (all 1981).

226. °MORRISON, ANGUS: *The Lake Isle of Innisfree*. Song. London: Boosey, 1917.

227. °MOURANT, WALTER: *When You Are Old*. Song for medium voice and piano. NY: American Composers Alliance, 1971.

228. °MULHOLLAND, JAMES: *Love Songs of the Irish.* For four-part chorus of mixed voices and piano. Totowa, N.J.: European American Music Corporation, 1981.
No. 1: "Down by the Salley Gardens."

229. °NABOKOV, NICOLAS: *Brown Penny.* For women's voices. NY: Associated Music Publishers, 1957.

230. °NAN, SHELI: "The Cuchulain Cycle." MS., 1979. (CCE)
Details not available.

231. °NELSON, HAVELOCK: *The Lonely of Heart (Land of Heart's Desire).* London: Curwen, 1968.

232. °———: "The Countess Cathleen." Incidental music for a radio version, MS., n.d. (G&T, Deale)
G&T and Deale also list incidental music for *The King's Threshold,* Deale adds incidental music for *On Baile's Strand.*

233. °———: "Suite: The Land of Heart's Desire." For soprano and orchestra, MS., 1959. (Deale)

234. °———: "W. B. Yeats." Incidental music for a TV documentary, MS., n.d. (G&T)

235. °O'GALLAGHER, EAMONN: "The Countess Cathleen. The King's Threshold." Incidental music, MS., n.d. (Deale)

236. °OWENS, SUSAN ELIZABETH: "Innisfree: From the Lake Isle of Innisfree." For soprano and chamber group (flute, viola, bassoon, cello), MS., 1981. (CCE)

237. °PALMER, JOHN: *The Everlasting Voices.* Chicago: Summy, 1915.

238. °———: *The Lake Isle of Innisfree.* Song. Chicago: Summy, 1915.

239. °———: *The Old Men Admiring Themselves in the Water.* London: Novello, 1913.

240. °PARKE, DOROTHY: "The Falling of the Leaves." Song for solo voice and piano, MS., 1963. (G&T, Deale)

241. °PARKER, ALICE, and ROBERT SHAW: *Down by the Salley Gardens.* For four-part chorus of men's voices a cappella, set on a traditional Irish air. [NY]: Lawson-Gould Music, 1961.

242. °PASATIERI, THOMAS: *Calvary: A Religious Musical Drama in One Act to the Text of the Play by William Butler Yeats.* NY: Belwin-Mills, 1972.

243. °PAVIOUR, PAUL: "Crazy Jane." For soprano solo and piano, MS., 1969. (G&T)
Includes: "Crazy Jane and Jack the Journeyman," "Crazy Jane and the Bishop," "Crazy Jane Grown Old Looks at the Dancers," "Crazy Jane on the Day of Judgment," "Crazy Jane Reproved," and "Crazy Jane Talks with the Bishop."

244. °PEEL, GERALD GRAHAM: *The Country Lover: Album of Five Songs.* London: Chappell, 1910.

No. 3: "The Lake Isle of Innisfree."

245. °PLUMSTEAD, MARY: *Down by the Salley Gardens*. London: Curwen, 1951.

246. °POSTON, ELIZABETH: *The Lake Isle of Innisfree*. Song. London: Rogers, 1926.

247. °———: *Maid Quiet*. Song. London: Rogers, 1926.

248. °PUTSCHÉ, THOMAS: *The Cat and the Moon*. An opera in one act. NY: Seesaw Music, 1974.
Recorded: *The Cat and the Moon*. Opera in one act, based on a play by W. B. Yeats. Composers Recordings, CRI SD 245, [196-]. 12" long-play record. Composed in 1957; performed by the Contemporary Chamber Players, U of Chicago (three singers), conducted by Ralph Shapey. According to G&T (p. 837), the first performance took place in Hartford, Ct., in 1960.

249. RICCI, VITTORIO: *Three Musical Ideas*. London: Williams, 1909.
Contains "A Cradle Song" for voice and piano.

250. °RIES, LAWRENCE E.: "Five Midsummer Songs." MS., 1985. (CCE)
Includes musical settings of Yeats poems, details not available.

251. RIETI, VITTORIO: *Two Songs between Two Waltzes*. NY: General Music / London: Novello, 1964.
"The Fiddler of Dooney (A Waltz)," "When You Are Old (A Barcarolle)," "Maid Quiet (A Madrigal)," and "Brown Penny (Another Waltz)."

252. °RITCHIE, TOM VERNON: "The Lake Isle of Innisfree." Song for solo voice and piano, MS., 1972. (G&T, CCE)
G&T and CCE also list "When Your Are Old and Gray." Song for high or low voice and piano, MS., 1969.

253. °ROBBINS, REGINALD C.: *When You Are Old*. Songs for bass or baritone, no. 74. Paris: Senart, 1929.

254. °ROBERT, MAX: "Crowd of Stars: A Scenario for an Operatic Play in Two Acts." Based upon and featuring 41 poems by W. B. Yeats, MS., 1983. (CCE)

255. ROBERTON, HUGH STEVENSON: *The Cloths of Heaven*. Part song for men's voices (unaccompanied). London: Curwen, 1944.

256. °RODERICK-JONES, RICHARD: "The Wind among the Reeds." For soprano solo and piano, MS., 1966. (G&T)
"He Wishes for the Cloths of Heaven," "The Everlasting Voices," "He Reproves the Curlew," "To His Heart Bidding It Have No Fear," and "The Valley of the Black Pig."

257. °ROLLIN, ROBERT LEON: "Brown Penny." For mezzo-soprano, baritone, flute, oboe, violin, viola, cello, and piano, M.F.A. thesis, Cornell U, 1971.
See also next item.

258. °———: "Four Songs of Dreams and Love." MS., n.d. (G&T)
The songs are "The Cat Went Here and There" from *The Cat and the Moon*, "The Old Men Admiring Themselves in the Water,"

"Down by the Salley Gardens," and "Brown Penny." G&T also list an undated MS., "The Only Jealousy of Emer," incidental music.

259. °RONALD, LANDON: "Had I the Heavens' Embroidered Cloths." Song for solo voice and piano, MS., pre-1924. (G&T)

260. °ROOTHAM, CYRIL BRADLEY: *The Stolen Child.* Four-part song. London: Stainer & Bell, 1911.

261. °ROREM, NED: *To a Young Girl.* Song. NY: Boosey & Hawkes, 1972.

262. °ROUTH, FRANCIS: *A Woman Young and Old.* Poems by W. B. Yeats set for high voice and piano. London: Redcliffe Editions, 1976.

263. °RUDOLPH, ROBIN: "The Lake Isle of Innisfree." MS., 1976. (CCE)

264. SCHÖNTHAL, RUTH: "Works." MS., 1949-52. (ICN)

Contains "9 Lyric-Dramatic Songs for Mezzo Soprano & Piano by D. B. Yeats [sic]": "The Lake Isle of Innisfree," "The Pity of Love," "The Everlasting Voices," "To a Child in the Wind," "He Tells of a Valley Full of Lovers," "A Coat," "The Travail of Passion," "That the Night Come," and "The Second Coming."

265. °SCHWARTZ, FRANCIS: "Wisdom." Song for voice and tape, MS., n.d. (G&T)

"The Coming of Wisdom with Time."

266. °SCHWARTZ, PAUL: "A Poet to His Beloved." For high or medium voice and piano, MS., 1945. (G&T)

"He Hears the Cry of the Sedge," "He Tells of the Perfect Beauty," "He Thinks of Those Who Have Spoken Evil of His Beloved," "To His Heart Bidding It Have No Fear," "A Poet to His Beloved," "The Lover Pleads with His Friends for Old Friends."

267. °SCOTT, FRANCIS GEORGE: "Sixteen Dead Men." MS., 1933. (Banfield)

268. SHAW, MARTIN: *The Land of Heart's Desire.* London: Curwen, 1917.

Musical rendering of "The wind blows out of the gates of the day."

269. ———: *Down by the Salley Gardens.* London: Curwen, 1919.

270. °SHIFRIN, SEYMOUR: "The Cat Went Here and There." Song for soprano solo and piano, MS., n.d. (G&T)

G&T also list an undated song "No Second Troy." G&T and CCE list a "Lament for Oedipus: What Can the Shadow-Like Generations of Man Attain" from *Sophocles' King Oedipus.* Cantata for female chorus and string quartet or string orchestra and piano, MS., 1976.

271. SIRIUS: *Running to Paradise.* Brutkasten Records, 85 R 030, 1982. 12" long-play record.

The group Sirius consists of four German musicians who play various kinds of mostly electrical instruments. The compositions are by Stefan Neubauer who also sings the lyrics. The following Yeats poems are included: "The Sad Shepherd," "The Fiddler of

Dooney," "Why Should Not Old Men Be Mad?" "Running to Paradise," "September 1913," "Three Songs to the One Burden, III," and "The Happy Townland." The score seems to be unpublished.

272. °SKUTA, RONALD GEORGE: "The Cloak, the Boat and the Shoes." MS., 1970. (CCE)

273. °———: "I Call to the Eye of the Mind." MS., 1972. (CCE)
Obviously from *At the Hawk's Well.*

274. °———: "Mad as the Mist and Snow." MS., 1970. (CCE)

275. °SMITH, LEONARD B.: *Down by the Salley Gardens*. Irish tune, poem by W. B. Yeats, arranged for band. Grosse Point Woods, Mich.: Accompaniments Unlimited, 1976.

276. °SMOOT, RICHARD JORDAN: "Collected Opuses 1, 2, 3." MS., 1979. (CCE)
Incorporates poetry by Yeats, details not available.

277. °SOMERS, HARRY STUART: *Zen, Yeats and Emily Dickinson*. Toronto: Canadian Music Centre, 1975.
For two narrators, soprano, flute, piano, and tape. Performed by CBC in April 1975. The text includes words, phrases, and stanzas from Yeats's works.

278. °STAINBROOK, LISA: "Salley Gardens." MS., 1985. (CCE)

279. °STEIN, LEON: *Deirdre: An Opera*. NY: Composer's Facsimile Edition, 1956.

280. °STEVENS, BERNARD: *Running to Paradise*. London: Novello, 1968.

281. °STEWART, DOUGLAS MACDONALD: *Had I the Heaven's Embroidered Cloths*. Song. London: Novello, 1918.

282. °STILMAN, JULIA: "Rituals, 1975: Magic Rituals of the Golden Dawn." Cantata no. 4, MS., 1976. (NN)
The text is "A Deep-Sworn Vow." For chorus and orchestra (timpani, percussion, harp, guitar or piano, celesta, harmonium, strings).

283. °STOKES, ERIK: *Wondrous World: Elegy on Our Threatened Home*. Minneapolis: Horspfal Music Concern, 1984.
For solo voices and 4-channel electronic tape, with words from Yeats's poetry and other sources.

284. °SWAIN, FREDA: "Operatic Setting for *The Shadowy Waters*." MS., n.d. / "The Harp of Aengus after W. B. Yeats." For violin and orchestra, 1924. (Grove, 8:199; G&T list a MS., 1922)

285. °TANENBAUM, ELIAS: "Cygnology (Three Songs on Leda and the Swan)." For soprano solo and orchestra, MS., 1958. (G&T)

286. TAYLOR, STANLEY: *Down by the Salley Gardens*. Set for voice and piano (or harp) with ad lib recorder. London: Curwen, 1963.

287. °THATCHER, GER A.: "Golden Apples." MS., 1986. (CCE)
Based on "The Song of Wandering Aengus."

288. °TIPPETT, SIR MICHAEL: *Lullaby*. For six voices, words by W. B. Yeats. London: Schott, 1960.

289. °———: "The Mask of Time." [MS., 1984?].
A choral symphony with quotations from Yeats's poems. See Paul Driver: "First Performances: *The Mask of Time*," *Tempo*, 149 (June 1984), 39-44.

290. °———: "Words for Music Perhaps." MS., ca. 1960. (G&T)
Incidental music for speaking voices and chamber ensemble; text made up of a sequence of poems by Yeats. For a review of a performance see Andrew Clements: "Senior Citizen," *NSt*, 18 Jan 1980, 98-99. Performed on BBC Radio 4, 26 Oct 1985; see *Radio Times*, 26 Oct--1 Nov 1985, 28.

291. °TOBIN, JOHN: *Down by the Salley Gardens*. Song for voice and piano. London: Elkins, 1938.

292. VACCHI, FABIO: *Ballade: Per soprano e orchestra da camera*. Milano: Ricordi, 1981.
A musical setting of "The Three Bushes" (English text; an Italian version is also provided, translator's name not given).

293. °VERRALL, JOHN: *The Rose of the World*. Song for soprano solo, flute, and piano. NY: American Composers Alliance, [19--]. (G&T, NN)

294. VICTORY, GERARD: "The Dreaming of the Bones." Incidental music, MS., 1968. (Deale, G&T)
Deale also lists incidental music for *The Resurrection*, *The Cat and the Moon*, and *At the Hawk's Well*.

295. °———: "The Land of Heart's Desire: Opera." MS., 1965.
Not in Deale, not in G&T; see *RTV Guide*, 1 Jan 1965, 19.

296. °VINE, JOHN: *Down by the Salley Gardens*. Arranged on an Irish air for tenor solo and male voices. London: Oxford UP, 1948.

297. VOORMOLEN, ALEXANDER: *La sirène*. Romance pour orchestre et chant (ou saxophone alto). Poème de Jules van der Becke d'après W. B. Yeats. Amsterdam: Donemus, [1949].
"The Mermaid" from "A Man Young and Old."

298. °WALKER, GWYNETH: "Three Songs for Tres Voces." MS. and sound cassette, 1983. (CCE)
"After poems of W. B. Yeats."

299. °WALLACH, JOELLE: "Yeatsongs of a Fool." MS., 1984. (CCE)
Two songs, incorporating poems by Yeats.

300. °WALTER, DAVID: "Song of Wandering Aengus." MS., 1969. (CCE)

301. °WALTERS, TIM: "Tim Walters Music." Sound cassette, 1985. (CCE)
Includes a musical rendering of "The Hosting of the Sidhe."

302. WALTON, JAKE (ed): *Keltische Folksongs: Texte und Noten mit Begleit-Akkorden*. Frankfurt/Main: Fischer, 1983. 175 pp.
Jake Walton: "Innisfree," 32-33 (recorded: °Jake Walton: *The Gloaming Grey*. Folk Freak, FF 4001).
Ciaran Brennan: "Down by the Sall[e]y Gardens," 80-81 (recorded: °*Clannad in Concert*. Intercord, INT 160.124).

Richard Dyer-Bennet: "The Song of Wandering Aengus," 91-92 (recorded: °Roger Nicholson / Jake Walton / Andrew Cronshaw: *Times & Tradition for the Dulcimer*. Trailer, CER 2094).

303. WARD, DAVID: "A Full Moon in March: Opera." [MS., 1962-68?]. See Peter Cudmore: "First Performances: *The Snow Queen*," *Tempo*, 150 (Sept 1984), 40-42.

304. °WARLOCK, PETER: "The Cloths of Heaven: Song." MS., 1920-22. (G&T)
According to Banfield, this was published in 1982 (no details given). G&T and Banfield also list "A Drinking Song." MS., 1920-22; "The Everlasting Voices." Song for solo voice and piano, MS., 1915, and several lost songs. See next item.

305. ———: *The Curlew*. For tenor voice, flute, English horn, and string quartet. London: Stainer & Bell, 1924.
Contains the following poems: "He Reproves the Curlew," "The Lover Mourns for the Loss of Love," "The Withering of the Boughs," and "He Hears the Cry of the Sedge." Yeats did not like the music; see BB149.
In 1973, the same publisher issued a facsimile reprint with an introductory note by Fred Tomlinson, commenting on Yeats's view of Warlock's music.
For one of several recordings see Arabesque Recordings, 8018, 1980. 12" long-play record. Performed by Ian Partridge and the Music Group of London, program notes by Ward Botsford.

306. ———: *The Everlasting Voices*. Poem by W. B. Yeats. London: Thames Publishing, 1975.
The last four bars are by Anthony Ingle. The last page contains a note by Fred Tomlinson: "Yeats and Warlock." See also CD1419-1420.

307. ———: "Mr. Yeats and a Musical Censorship," *Musical Times*, 63:948 (Feb 1922), 123-24.
Letter to the editor complaining about the difficulties of obtaining permission to set Yeats's poems to music.

308. °WARREN, RAYMOND: "At the Hawk's Well." Incidental music, MS., 1968. (G&T)
G&T also list MSS. of incidental music for *Calvary* (1966), *The Cat and the Moon* (1965), *The Death of Cuchulain* (1968), *Deirdre* (1966), *A Full Moon in March* (1961), *The Hour-Glass* (1962), *On Baile's Strand* (1968), *The Only Jealousy of Emer* (1968), *The Player Queen* (1964), and *Purgatory* (1962). See also EC116.

309. °———: *Elegy: The Lover Mourns for the Loss of Love*. Part-song, unaccompanied. London: Novello, 1964.

310. °———: "Irish Madrigals: Cantata." MS., 1959. (G&T)
Includes "A Faery Song," "The Moods," and "The Cloak, the Boat, and the Shoes."

311. °———: "Motionless under the Moon-Beam from *Calvary*." For mixed chorus a cappella, MS., 1962. (G&T)

312. °———: "The Pity of Love." For tenor solo and guitar, MS., 1965. (G&T)
Includes "O Do Not Love Too Long," "For Anne Gregory," "The

Mask," "The Pity of Love," "When Your Are Old," and "Brown Penny."

313. ———: *Songs of Old Age*. A song cycle for voice and piano, words by W. B. Yeats. Sevenoaks: Novello, 1971.

"Men Improve with the Years," "The Old Men Admiring Themselves in the Water," "O Do Not Love Too Long," "A Song," "From Oedipus at Colonus," "After Long Silence," "Those Dancing Days Are Gone," and "Sailing to Byzantium."

314. °WEBBER, LLOYD: *The Fiddler of Dooney*. Two-part song. London: Ascherberg, Hopwood & Crew, 1964.

315. WEIGEL, EUGENE: *Four Songs for Women's Voices*. South Hadley, Mass.: Valley Music Press, 1950.

"To an Isle in the Water," "A Drinking Song," "A Cradle Song," and "To a Squirrel at Kyle-na-no."

316. WEISGALL, HUGO: *Purgatory*. Opera in one act. Bryn Mawr, Pa.: Merion Music, 1959.

317. °WERTHER, R. T.: *The Lake Isle of Innisfree*. Sydney: Chappell, 1966.

318. °WESTERGAARD, PETER: "Cantata III (Leda and the Swan)." MS., 1961. (G&T)

319. °WHETTAM, GRAHAM: "Three Songs from 'The Rose' for High Voice and Piano." MS., n.d. (G&T).

Performed London 1967; revised in 1973 as "Three Songs to Poems by Yeats" (G&T). Includes "A Cradle Song," "A Dream of Death," and "When You Are Old."

320. WHITHORNE, EMERSON: *Shy One*. A song for medium voice with piano accompaniment, op. 31, no. 2. NY: Schirmer, 1916.

"To an Isle in the Water."

321. °WHITLOW, CHARLES: "Three Songs on Yeats." MS., 1986. (CCE)

322. °WICKENS, DENNIS: "The Everlasting Voices." Song cycle for high voice and piano, MS., n.d. (G&T)

323. °WIENIAWSKI, IRÈNE: *Two Songs*. London: Chappell, 1900.

No. 2: "Down by the Salley Gardens."

324. °WILLAN, HEALEY: *Healey Willan Song Albums*. No. 2. Oakville, Ont.: Frederick Harris, 1926.

Contains "The Lake Isle of Innisfree" and "To an Isle in the Water." According to G&T (p. 855), Willan also composed "Poem (or Celtic Sketch No. 1)" (1903-5, revised 1930) for string quartet (revised for string orchestra, 1950), and a "Sonata for Violin and Piano No. 3 in B Minor" (1922), both of which were inspired by Yeats's poems.

325. °———: "The Shadowy Waters." Incidental music for radio, MS., 1960. (G&T)

326. °WILLIAMSON, MALCOLM: "The Death of Cuchulain." For five male voices and percussion instruments, MS., 1974. (CCE)

327. °WILSON, JAMES: "A Woman Young and Old." For soprano and Irish harp, MS., 1966. (Deale, G&T)

Deale also lists "Three Yeats Songs." MS., 1970. G&T list "Yeats Songs, op. 39." For soprano solo and piano, n.d., including "The Cat Went Here and There" from *The Cat and the Moon*, "Lullaby," and "Sweet Dancer."

328. °———: "Upon Silence, op. 54." For soprano solo, unaccompanied, MS., n.d. (G&T)

Includes "A Coat" and "Long-legged Fly."

329. °WOOD, HUGH: *To a Child Dancing in the Wind*. Part song, unaccompanied; no. 1 of *Two Choruses, op. 16*. Borough Green: Novello, 1974.

330. °———: "To a Friend Whose Work Has Come to Nothing." For chorus a cappella, MS., 1973. (G&T)

331. °WOODGATE, LESLIE: *Down by the Salley Gardens*. Irish air for two treble voices and piano. London: Oxford UP, 1950.

332. WORDEN, MAGDALEN: *Cradle-Song*. Song for solo voice with piano accompaniment. NY: Schirmer, 1912.

333. WYNER, YEHUDI: *Psalms and Early Songs*. NY: Associated Music Publishers, 1973.

Includes "When You Are Old."

334. YEATS, W. B.: *The Collected Works in Verse and Prose*. Stratford-on-Avon: Shakespeare Head Press, 1908. 8 vols.

Volume 3 contains music by Florence Farr for *The King's Threshold, On Baile's Strand,* and *Deirdre* (pp. 225-30); by Sara Allgood for *Deirdre* (p. 230); by Arthur Darley for *The Shadowy Waters* (p. 231); traditional Irish airs for *The Unicorn from the Stars* and *The Hour-Glass* (p. 232); by Florence Farr for *Cathleen ni Houlihan* (p. 233); and a note by Florence Farr on the speaking to the psaltery together with her notations for the following poems: Song from *The Land of Heart's Desire*, "The Happy Townland," and "He Thinks of His Past Greatness When a Part of the Constellations of Heaven." Also notations by Yeats for "The Song of Wandering Aengus" and "The Song of the Old Mother" and by A. H. Bullen for "The Host of the Air" (pp. 235-39).

Volume 8 contains "A Bibliography of the Writings of William Butler Yeats" by Allan Wade and John Quinn (pp. 197-287; see also AA15).

335. ———: *Four Plays for Dancers*. London: Macmillan, 1921. xi, 138 pp.

Edmond [sic] Dulac: "Music for *At the Hawk's Well*," 89-101; includes a note on the instruments.

Walter Morse Rummel: "Music for *The Dreaming of the Bones*," 107-25; includes notes on instruments and performance.

336. ———: *Sophocles' King Oedipus: A Version for the Modern Stage*. London: Macmillan, 1928. vi, 61 pp.

Music for the chorus and a note by L[ennox] R[obinson], 55-61.

337. ———: *Wheels and Butterflies*. NY: Macmillan, 1935. ix, 163 pp.
George Antheil: "Music for *Fighting the Waves*," 141-63. See also CD148 and HC6.

338. ———: *New Poems*. Dublin: Cuala Press, 1938. iv, 47 pp.
See pp. 41-45 for Edmund Dulac's music for "The Three Bushes," traditional Irish airs for "The Curse of Cromwell," "Come Gather round Me Parnellites," "The Pilgrim," and "Colonel Martin."

339. °YINGLING, DOUGLAS ALAN: "The Blue Denim Song Book." MS. and sound cassette, 1979. (CCE)
Includes "Her Anxiety."

340. °YOUNG, DOUGLAS: *Four Nature Songs*. London: Faber Music, 1964-77.
No. 3: *The Cat and the Moon* (1977); no. 4: *The Wild Swans at Coole* (1976).

341. °———: "Realities." For soprano, tenor and instruments, MS., 1970-73. (G&T)
Includes "Crazy Jane Grown Old Looks at the Dancers," "Crazy Jane Talks with the Bishop," "Her Dream," "Those Dancing Days Are Gone," "Three Things."

342. °ZAHLER, NOEL BARRY: "Three Songs." For mezzo soprano and chamber orchestra, MS., 1974. (NN)
"The Moods," "The Dawn," "He and She."

343. °ZANDERS, DOUGLAS: "The Lake Isle of Innisfree." Song for solo voice and piano, MS., 1952. (G&T)

See also CD148, DC25, DD182, 186, HA9, 14, 16, 17, HB10, HE27, 35, 36.

HD Poems on Yeats

Some of the most dreary or most exhilarating Yeatsiana (depending on the reader's attitude) may be found among the poems written about Yeats, many of which are, regrettably, quite worthless. The subject proves to be an irresistible attraction, not only among Irish poets from the 1940s onward who try to digest their literary past. Easily the best poem among the lot is Auden's elegy; three quotations from others may serve to illustrate my point (authors will remain mercifully unidentified):

> And, through the mists of Innisfree
> in undiluted glory--See!
> The feckless fairies of the isles are dancing round his tomb.
>
> Yeats would have it so;
> Truth without device,
> Every word a blow,
> None struck twice.
> Yet the magic is
> That the music sings:
> A naked Goddess his,
> But sheathed in wings.
>
> A son of Sligo now careers sublime,
> The truest, sweltest poet of our time,
> Whose fame in every cultured nation rings,
> In cots of peasants, palaces of kings,
> Whose mystic call allures us to explore

Enchanting fields we never saw before.
Immortal Yeats! long may thy course aspire;
Long may thy adept fingers tune the lyre;
Long may the lustre of thy mind aspire,
The brightest flame cast from the muse's fire.

Because there are no adequate bibliographies, I may not have picked up all the relevant material; many items in this section (as well as in section HF) were found accidentally.

1. ADAMS, HAZARD: "At Yeats's Grave: Drumcliff," *SR,* 84:1 (Jan-Mar 1976), 119.

2. ALLOTT, KENNETH: *Collected Poems.* Foreword by Roy Fuller. London: Secker & Warburg, 1975. 110 pp.
"The Memory of Yeats," 76-78; reprinted from *Poetry London,* 2:8 (Nov-Dec 1942), 66-67.

3. ANON.: "Tramping Troubadours," *Truth,* 3 July 1902, 6.
A poem prefaced by the following remark: "Mr. Yeats (according to 'The By-Stander' in the *Graphic* [14 June 1902, 794]) is of opinion that poets should no longer print their effusions, but should go about the country instead, reciting them to the accompaniment of a psaltery."

4. AUDEN, WYSTAN HUGH, and LOUIS MACNEICE: *Letters from Iceland.* London: Faber & Faber, 1937. 268 pp.
See p. 242.

5. AUDEN, W. H.: "In Memory of W. B. Yeats," *NewRep,* 8 Mar 1939, 123.
This version does not include the section beginning "You were silly like us." See the version published in *LMerc,* 39:234 (Apr 1939), 578-80, which includes the omitted section but lacks line 30 of the *NewRep* version. Both versions have been reprinted in various collections. See CC127, 201, CD156-170, DC162, and FD10.

5a. ———: *Homage to Clio.* NY: Random House, 1960. viii, 93 pp.
Contains a limerick on Yeats, p. 90.

6. B., B.: "To Eithne Magee in *The King's Threshold,*" *T.C.D.,* 20: 364 (16 Dec 1914), 183.

7. BAIRD, ANDREW: "Yeats in Criticism," *SoR,* 14:4 (Oct 1978), 757.

8. BAKER, PETER: "W. B. Yeats," *Poetry Q,* 2:4 (Winter 1940), 100.

9. BARKER, GEORGE: *Collected Poems.* Edited by Robert Fraser. London: Faber & Faber, 1987. xxi, 838 pp.
"The Death of Yeats," 53-54; reprinted from *Poetry London,* 1:2 (Apr 1939), [1].

10. ———: "More News for the Delphic Oracle," *Texas Q,* 8:4 (Winter 1965), 149.

11. ———: *The Golden Chains.* London: Faber & Faber, 1968. 60 pp.
Poem no. 67 (p. 42) is on Yeats.

12. ———: "Ben Bulben Revisited," *PNR,* 32 (9:6) (1983), 39.
Also in *YeA,* 3 (1985), 149-50.

13. "BATES, WILLIAM CUTLER": "On Seeing a Man Get Ill in the Abbey Theatre on Thursday Last," *Sinn Féin,* 25 Jan 1913, 7.

14. BERRYMAN, JOHN: *His Toy, His Dream, His Rest: 308 Dream Songs.* NY: Farrar, Straus & Giroux, 1969. xxi, 317 pp.
Several songs are concerned with Yeats, particularly nos. 312, 313, 331, and 334. See also CD212-218.

15. BIRAM, JOHN: "W. B. Yeats," *Cornhill,* 177:1057/1058 (Autumn/Winter 1968/69), 147-48.

16. BOLAND, EAVAN: "Yeats in Civil War," *DM,* 5:2 (Summer 1966), 26.

17. BOLD, ALAN: *Society Inebrious.* With an introduction by Hugh Macdiarmid. Edinburgh: Hamilton, 1965. 43 pp.
"Epitaph for W. B. Yeats," 29.

18. BOTTOMLEY, GORDON: *Lyric Plays.* London: Constable, 1932. xii, 166 pp.
Dedicatory poem, "To W. B. Yeats," v-vi.

19. BOTTRALL, RONALD: "Remembering William Butler Yeats," *Landfall,* 31:3 (Sept 1977), 266.

20. BRIGGS, ERNEST: *The Merciless Beauty: A Poetry Sequence.* Brisbane: Meanjin Press, 1943. i, 29 pp. (Folios of Australian Poetry. [1.])
"William Butler Yeats," 21-27.

21. BROWN, HARRY: *The End of a Decade.* Norfolk, Ct.: New Directions, 1940. [32 pp.] (Poet of the Month. 1:2.)
"On the Death of Yeats," [12]; reprint of "Elegy on the Death of Yeats," *Twentieth Century Verse,* 17 (Apr/May 1939), 12.

22. BROWNLOW, TIMOTHY: *The Hurdle Ford.* Dublin: New Square Publications, 1964. 28 pp.
"Dublin," 7-10.

23. ———, and RIVERS CAREW: *Figures Out of Mist.* Dublin: New Square Publications, 1966. 47 pp.
Rivers Carew: "Sligo 1965 (In Memory of W. B. Yeats)," 44-45; reprinted from *DM,* 4:2 (Summer 1965), 27.

24. BURNETT, DAVID: *Diversities.* London: Magpie Press, 1968. 35 pp.
"On Reading Yeats," 22.

25. ———: *Jackdaw.* With engravings by Kirill Sokolov. Edinburgh: Tragara Press, 1980. 69 pp.
"Yeats," 55. Also published: Durham: Black Cygnet Press, 1980. 64 pp. (p. 52).

26. BURNS, RICHARD: "Three Verse Pieces for W. B. Yeats," *UR,* 3:8 [1966?], 72.

27. BYRNE, J. PATRICK: "Yeats," *UKCR,* 9:3 (Spring 1943), 204.

28. BYRNE-SUTTON, GEOFFREY: "To William Butler Yeats," *JIL,* 10:1 (Jan 1981), 87.

29. CAMPBELL, ROY: *The Collected Poems.* London: Bodley Head, 1949-

57. 2 vols.

"Félibre (To Frédéric Mistral, Neveu)," 2:111-12, contains the following lines on Yeats:

Yeats on his intellect could pull the blinds
Rapping up spooks. He fell for freaks and phoneys.
Weird blue-stockings with damp, flatfooted minds,
Theosophists and fakirs, were his cronies.

30. CARRUTH, HAYDEN: *Nothing for Tigers: Poems, 1959-1964*. NY: Macmillan, 1965. viii, 85 pp.

"A Pseudo-Prayer," 44-47. According to Carruth, this is modeled on "A Prayer for My Daughter"; see "How Not to Rate a Poet," *SatR*, 12 Feb 1966, 21, 43-44. This essay was reprinted in *Effluences from the Sacred Caves: More Selected Essays and Reviews*. Ann Arbor: U of Michigan Press, 1983. vii, 286 pp. (pp. 11-16).

31. CASEY, JUANITA: "To the Reel 'Homo the Sap': Post-Yeats Songs of Lunacy My Mother Hadn't Time to Teach Me," *JIL*, 10:2 (May 1981), 27-29.

A poem or rather a collage of Yeats quotations. See also "Write One Who Loved Horses," 35.

32. CIOSMAH, MARY: "A New England Woods," *Stuffed Crocodile*, 2:8 (Nov 1975), 140-41.

A poem on Yeats's "The Stolen Child."

33. CLARKE, AUSTIN: *Flight to Africa and Other Poems*. Dublin: Dolmen Press, 1963. 128 pp.

"The Abbey Theatre Fire," 16-17. Another poem, "Abbey Theatre Fire," appears on p. 8 of Clarke's *Too Great a Vine: Poems and Satires. Second Series*. Templeogue, County Dublin: Bridge Press, 1957. 29 pp.

34. ———: *The Echo at Coole & Other Poems*. Dublin: Dolmen Press, 1968. 78 pp.

"A Centenary Tribute: W. B. Yeats," 9-10. "In the Savile Club," 11-13. "The Echo at Coole," 13-14.

35. CLIFFORD, GAY: "Against Yeats," *Encounter*, 56:4 (Apr 1981), 39.

Poem on "Leda and the Swan."

36. CLUER, ELISABETH: "Homage to Yeats," *IrT*, 7 Aug 1948, 4.

37. COATES, FLORENCE EARLE: *Mine and Thine*. Boston: Houghton, Mifflin, 1904. xv, 175 pp.

"To William Butler Yeats," 52-53.

38. COLUM, PADRAIC: *Irish Elegies*. Fourth edition. Dublin: Dolmen Press, 1976. 32 pp.

"The Arch-Poet: William Butler Yeats 1865-1939," 26-27; reprinted from BB44.

39. CRONIN, ANTHONY: "The Great Poetry Boom, 1970's," *DM*, 8:8 (Summer 1971), 116-17.

Partly concerned with Yeats. Contains the remarkable lines "Yeats, Yeats, Yeats, Yeats, / Fart, fart, fart, fart."

40. CUMBERLEGE, MARCUS: "Coole Park and Ballylee, Winter: For Michael Mulkhere," *DM*, 8:8 (Summer 1971), 8-9.

41. CURLE, J. J.: "Homage to Yeats," *Poetry R*, 42:6 (Nov-Dec 1952), 328.

42. DANIELS, EARL: "On a Line of William Butler Yeats," *Spirit*, 7:3 (July 1940), 81.
A line from "Easter 1916."

43. DOLLARD, JAMES BERNARD: *Irish Lyrics and Ballads*. Toronto: McClelland, Goodchild & Stewart, 1917. viii, 131 pp.
"To William Butler Yeats," 40; reprinted from *Ireland* [NY], 24 June 1916, 6. "William Butler Yeats," 51.

44. DONALD, ANDREW: "Yeats," *PoetryA*, 100 (Mar 1985), 86.

45. DOYLE, LIAM: "W. B. Yeats," *Leader*, 4 Feb 1939, 572.

45a. DUHIG, IAN: "Nineteen Hundred and Nineteen," *Irish R*, 3 (1988), 91.
Partly on Yeats.

46. DURYEE, MARY BALLARD: *Words Alone Are Certain Good: William Butler Yeats. Himself, the Poet, His Ghost*. Dublin: Dolmen Press, 1961. 45 pp.
Fourteen poems plus annotations indicating their relation to Yeats's life and work.
Reviews:
- John Hewitt: "Three Americans," *Threshold*, 5:2 (Autumn-Winter 1961/62), 81-84.
- [A. N. Jeffares], *TLS*, 5 July 1963, 498-99. Detects "a touch of banality."

47. EAGLETON, TERRY: "The Ballad of Willie Yeats," *ILS*, 6:1 (Spring 1987), 3.
Extract from a nine-verse affair, printed under the heading "Poets at Sligo." The same issue contains a pastiche of Yeats phrases in an untitled poem by an anonymous author, presented by Ruth H. Bauerle (p. 24).

48. EGAN, DESMOND: *Collected Poems*. Orono, Maine: National Poetry Foundation, 1983. 224 pp.
See "In Francis Ledwidge's Cottage," 210-12, and "Non Symbolist," 216-17, where Egan declares his aversion to Yeats. The first poem is also included in Egan's *Seeing Double*. Newbridge: Goldsmith Press, [1983]. 47 pp. (pp. 31-33).

49. EMANS, ELAINE V.: "For William Butler Yeats," *CentR*, 25:2 (Spring 1981), 162.
A poem on the nine bean rows in "The Lake Isle of Innisfree."

50. FALLON, PADRAIC: *Poems*. Dublin: Dolmen Press, 1974. 190 pp.
"Yeats at Athenry Perhaps," 53-55; reprinted from *IrT*, 10 June 1965, viii. "On the Tower Stairs," 58-60. "Stop on the Road to Ballylee," 61-63. "Yeats's Tower at Ballylee," 64-68; reprinted from *DM*, 26:4 (Oct-Dec 1951), 1-5. See also CD430.

51. FARRAGHER, SHAUN: "At Yeats's Grave," *Sword of Light*, [1:1] (Spring 1974), 47.

52. FERLINGHETTI, LAWRENCE: *A Coney Island of the Mind: Poems*. NY: New Directions, 1958. 93 pp. (New Directions Paperbook. 74.)

"Reading Yeats I Do Not Think," 90-91; reprinted from °*Pictures of the Gone World*. San Francisco: City Lights Pocket Bookshop, 1955. [42 pp.].

53. FITZPATRICK, W. P.: "Among Schoolchildren," *SHR,* 13:1 (Winter 1979), 83.

54. FLINT, ERIC: "On Reading Yeats' 'A Deep Sworn Vow,'" *WHR,* 21:2 (Spring 1967), 163.

55. FORSSELL, LARS: *Ändå: Dikter*. Stockholm: Bonnier, 1968. 126 pp.
"Tolv variationer till minne av W. B. Yeats," 27-56.

56. FRASER, GEORGE SUTHERLAND: *Poems of G. S. Fraser*. Edited by Ian Fletcher and John Lucas. Leicester: Leicester UP, 1981. 209 pp.
"For Yeats," 34-35; "Elegy for Freud and Yeats," 44-45; "Home Thoughts on Ireland," 174-76. The first two poems are reprinted from *Home Town Elegies*. London: Poetry London, 1944. 44 pp. (pp. 18-20, 30).

57. GAWSWORTH, JOHN: "The Return (W. B. Y. Reinterred)," *Literary Digest,* 3:4 (Winter 1948), 30.

58. GIBBON, MONK: *This Insubstantial Pageant*. NY: Devin-Adair, 1951. 190 pp.
"Yeats's Earlier Poems," 24; reprinted from *IrSt,* 29 Mar 1930, 67; reprinted in CA50, 298. "The Heroic Mind," 105.

59. ———: *The Velvet Bow and Other Poems*. London: Hutchinson, 1972. 94 pp.
"Yeats's Earlier Poems," 52; "On Re-reading Yeats," 89. See also BA4.

60. GIBSON, WILFRID: *Solway Ford and Other Poems*. A selection made by Charles Williams. London: Faber & Faber, 1945. 74 pp.
"The Three Poets," 73-74; first published as "The Three Poets: A Reminiscence," *English,* 5:27 (Autumn 1944), 81-82. On T. Sturge Moore, Laurence Binyon, and Yeats.

61. GINSBERG, ALLEN: *Planet News 1961-1967*. San Francisco: City Lights, 1974 [1968]. 144 pp.
"After Yeats," 74 (written in 1964).

62. GODDEN, RICHARD: "Yeats and the Surfer. A Fragment for Yeats," *Samphire,* 2:4 (Spring/Summer 1974), 2.

63. GOGARTY, OLIVER ST. JOHN: *The Collected Poems*. London: Constable, 1951. xxvii, 212 pp.
Horace Reynolds: "Gogarty in the Flesh," xv-xxvii; contains some Yeats anecdotes.
"To the Lady--," 24-25 (the poet referred to is Yeats).
"To W. B. Yeats Who Says That His Castle of Ballylee Is His Monument," 25.
"To the Poet W. B. Yeats, Winner of the Nobel Prize 1924 [sic]. (To Build a Fountain to Commemorate His Victory)," 30-31; reprinted from *IrSt,* 15 Dec 1923, 427.
"Elegy on the Archpoet William Butler Yeats Lately Dead," 200-6; reprinted from *Contemporary Poetry,* [1:3] (Autumn 1941), 3-7.

64. GRIGSON, GEOFFREY: *The Collected Poems of Geoffrey Grigson 1924-1962*. London: Phoenix House, 1963. 268 pp.
"Committed, or Mr Yeats and Mr Logue," 234-35.

65. ———: *The Fiesta and Other Poems*. London: Secker & Warburg, 1978. 91 pp.
"Was Yeats a Fascist?" 25.

66. H., E.: "To a Celtic Poet," *Outlook* [London], 6 Oct 1900, 304.
Presumably addressed to Yeats, since it repeats many of his early poetic clichés.

67. HALL, JOHN CLIVE: *The Burning Hare*. London: Chatto & Windus / Hogarth Press, 1966. 50 pp.
"The Wood," 12. "The Vigil," 17.

68. HAMMOND, MAC: "Of What Is Past or Passing or to Come: A Mosaic for W. B. Yeats," *Audience*, 4:2 [Oct? 1956], 10.

69. HARGADON, MICHAEL A.: *A Lovely Home*. Dublin: Maunsel, 1915. viii, 75 pp.
"William Butler Yeats," 7.

70. HARRIS, MICHAEL: *Poems*. With an introduction by Sir Compton Mackenzie. Dublin: Dolmen Press, 1965. 28 pp.
"Coole 1960: In Memoriam Yeats, Lady Gregory, Synge, Douglas Hyde," 9.

71. HARTNETT, MICHAEL: *A Farewell to English and Other Poems*. Dublin: Gallery Press, 1975. 35 pp.
"A Farewell to English," 30-35; a farewell "to all the Poets I have loved," including Yeats, who is nevertheless criticized as "our bugbear Mr. Yeats / who forced us into exile / on islands of bad verse." Reprinted on pp. 56-62 of *Poems in English*. Dublin: Dolmen Press, 1977. 80 pp.; and on pp. 157-59 of *Collected Poems*. Volume 1. Dublin: Raven Arts Press / Manchester: Carcanet Press, 1985. 168 pp.

72. HAYES, JOAN: "Sligo Holy Well: Tribute to W. B. Yeats," *Everyman*, 2 (1969), 109.

73. HOFFMAN, DANIEL: "Instructions to a Medium to Be Transmitted to the Shade of W. B. Yeats, the Latter Having Responded in a Seance Held on 13 June 1965, Its Hundredth Birthday," *Shenandoah*, 16:4 (Summer 1965), 5-6.
Reprinted: *Shenandoah*, 35:2-3 (1984), 176-77.

74. HOFFMANN, DIETER (ed): *Personen: Lyrische Portraits von der Jahrhundertwende bis zur Gegenwart*. Frankfurt/Main: Societäts-Verlag, 1966. 288 pp.
Karl Alfred Wolken: "Yeats, nach einem späten Bild" [Yeats, after a late portrait], 244-45.

75. HOPE, ALEC DERWENT: *The Wandering Islands*. Sydney: Edwards & Shaw, 1955. 74 pp.
"William Butler Yeats," 43; revised version of "On the Death of William Butler Yeats," *Direction* [Melbourne], 1:4 (Winter 1948), 48. Reprinted in Jeffares and Cross: *In Excited Reverie* (CA48), HD77, and elsewhere.

76. ———: *A Late Picking: Poems 1965-1974*. Sydney: Angus & Robertson, 1975. viii, 94 pp.

"A Letter to David Campbell on the Birthday of W. B. Yeats, 1965," 3-5. See note on p. 88. Part III of the poem was first published in °*Australian*, 12 June 1965, 9.

77. ———: *Collected Poems 1930-1970*. Sydney: Angus & Robertson, 1972. xxii, 300 pp.

"William Butler Yeats," 72 (see HD75); "The Apotelesm of W. B. Yeats," 227-228; first published in *Poetry*, 114:3 (June 1969), 174, and *Quadrant*, 13:60 (July-Aug 1969), 9.

N.B.: All of Hope's Yeats poems are included in CD563.

78. HORDER, JOHN: "Crazy Jane and Yeats," *Transatlantic R*, 22 (Autumn 1966), 70-71.

79. HOUSTON, RALPH: "On First Reading W. B. Yeats," *Poetry Ireland*, 14 (July 1951), 17-18.

80. HURLEY, DORAN: "For Maud Conne [sic] MacBride and William Butler Yeats: A Literary Romance of Modern Ireland. And God Stands Winding His Lonely Horn," *Ireland-American R*, [1]:4 [1940?], 73-74.

81. HUTCHISON, JOE: "Sonnet for W. B. Yeats," *Prism International*, 12:3 (Spring 1973), 106.

82. An Craoibhin Aoibhinn [i.e., HYDE, DOUGLAS]: "An Answer to Mr. Yeats' Poem 'In [sic] the Abbey Theatre,'" *Irish R*, 2:23 (Jan 1913), 561.

In reply to Yeats's "At the Abbey Theatre," :22 (Dec 1912), 505.

83. JOHNSON, LIONEL: *The Complete Poems*. Edited by Iain Fletcher. London: Unicorn Press, 1953. xlviii, 395 pp.

"A Cornish Night: To William Butler Yeats," 25-29. Written in 1888.

"To Samuel Smith with a Copy of W. B. Yeats' *The Celtic Twilight*," 251-52. Written in 1895.

"Prologue," 259-60; reprinted from *Beltaine*, 1 (May 1899), 5. According to a note on p. 1 of the same issue, the prologue was spoken at the first performance of *The Countess Cathleen*. Reprinted in EF39.

"In a Copy of Yeats's Poems. To Edmund Gosse," 273. Written in 1895.

Fletcher mentions Yeats passim in "Introduction," xi-xliv, and in "Textual Notes," 325-95.

Reissued as *The Collected Poems of Lionel Johnson*. Second and revised edition, edited by Ian Fletcher. NY: Garland, 1982. lxxvi, 381 pp. (Garland English Texts. 3.). The first, third and fourth poem appear on pp. 21-24, 218-19 and 212. For the second poem see note on p. 347. See also "To Edmund Gosse. With a Copy of W. B. Yeats' *The Celtic Twilight*" (1893), 210.

84. KENNEDY, M. J.: "At Drumcliffe (For the Birthday of W. B. Yeats)," *IrI*, 5 June 1965, 12.

85. KENNELLY, BRENDAN: "Yeats," *Icarus*, 31 (June 1960), 2.

86. ———: "Yeats," *Acorn*, 10 (Spring 1966), 4.

Also in Jeffares and Cross: *In Excited Reverie* (1965, CA48), 193.

87. KERNAN, PLOWDEN: *Hawthorn Time in Ireland and Other Poems*. Los Angeles: Ward Ritchie Press, 1939. xii, 81 pp.
"W. B. Yeats," 49.

88. KEYES, SIDNEY: *The Collected Poems*. Edited with a memoir and notes by Michael Meyer. London: Routledge, 1945. xxiv, 124 pp.
"William Yeats in Limbo," 17; written in 1940 (see note on p. 118). "The Island City," 55-56; written in 1941 (see note on p. 121).

89. KILMER, JOYCE: *Main Street and Other Poems*. NY: Doran, 1917. 78 pp.
"Easter Week," 66-67; an answer to Yeats's "September 1913."

90. KINSELLA, THOMAS: "Tara: A Poem for Yeats," *Guardian*, 12 June 1965, 7.

91. ———: *Nightwalker and Other Poems*. Dublin: Dolmen Press, 1968. 86 pp.
"Death in Ilium (In Yeats's Centenary Year)," 50; reprinted in *Poems 1956-1973*. Mountrath, Portlaoise: Dolmen Press, 1980. 192 pp. (p. 98).

92. KRAUSE, DAVID: "Antiphonies: Twelve Poems and a Tilly," *IUR*, 10:1 (Spring 1980), 98-102.
One poem is entitled "Yeats," another ("Sweet Lion") deals with Yeats's hero-worship.

93. KROLL, ERNEST: "Spirits at Coole," *ArQ*, 30:4 (Winter 1974), 342.

94. LAVELLE, TOM: "William Butler Yeats and the Dishes," *Gorey Detail*, 6 (Summer 1982), [29].

95. LERNER, LAURENCE: "Yeats I Brought to You. . . ," *CritQ*, 3:3 (Autumn 1961), 238.

96. ———: "The Shirt," in Maxwell and Bushrui: *W. B. Yeats, 1865-1965* (1965, CA71), xvi.

97. LESLIE, SHANE: "In Memoriam--W. B. Yeats," *Irish Library Bulletin*, 9:[10] (Oct 1948), 159-60.

98. ———: "The Wake of Willie Yeats," *Irish Library Bulletin*, 9:[10] (Oct 1948), 166.

99. LOGAN, JOHN: "At Drumcliffe Churchyard, County Sligo," *Threshold*, 34 (Winter 1983/84), 54-55.

100. LOWELL, AMY: *The Complete Poetical Works*. With an introduction by Louis Untermeyer. Boston: Houghton Mifflin, 1955. xxxi, 607 pp.
"On 'The Cutting of an Agate' (By W. B. Yeats)," 591; first published in *Poetry and Drama*, 2:7 (Sept 1914), 291.

101. LOWRY, MALCOLM: *Selected Poems of Malcolm Lowry*. Edited by Earle Birney with the assistence of Margerie Lowry. San Francisco: City Lights Books, 1962. 81 pp. (Pocket Poets Series. 17.)
"Rilke and Yeats," 72; reprinted from °*Evidence*, 4 (Winter 1962), 83.

102. LYNCH, BRIAN: "West from Ballylee," *UR*, 3:8 [1966?], 72.

103. "MAC": "To Certain Anglo-Irish Writers," *Phoblacht,* 18 Mar 1927, 2.

"For what ye are we know you all, / With words so big and minds so small."

104. MCAULEY, JAMES J.: "After Yeats, after Ronsard. . . ," *IrT,* 6 Dec 1980, 12.

Poem on the theme of "When You Are Old."

105. MCCRACKEN, D. J.: "After Re-Reading Yeats," *Acorn,* 4 (Spring 1963), 7.

106. MACDIARMID, HUGH: *Poetry Like the Hawthorn from "In Memoriam James Joyce."* Hemel Hempstead: Glen, 1962. 7 pp.

A poem on the death of Yeats, reprinted from *Wales,* 11 (Winter 1939-40), 296-97. Also in *In Memoriam James Joyce: From a Vision of World Language.* Glasgow: MacLellan, 1955. 150 pp. (pp. 35-36).

107. ———: "Ingenium Omnia Vincit," in Jeffares and Cross: *In Excited Reverie* (1965, CA48), 88.

108. MACDONNELL, RANDAL: "'Abbey' Epitaphs," *Leader,* 12 Sept 1908, 81.

The customary *Leader* sneers.

109. MCFADDEN, ROY: *The Garryowen.* London: Chatto & Windus / Hogarth Press, 1971. 40 pp.

"In Drumcliffe Churchyard," 39; reprinted from *IrW,* 8 (July 1949), 57.

110. MACGILL-EAIN, SOMHAIRLE / MACLEAN, SORLEY: *Reothairt is Contraigh: Taghadh de Dhàin 1932-72 / Spring Tide and Neap Tide: Selected Poems 1932-72.* Edinburgh: Canongate, 1977. ix, 182 pp.

"At Yeats's Grave," 162, 164 / "Aig Uaigh Yeats," 163, 165.

111. MCGLAUN, RITHIA: "Safe in Byzantium," *Contempora,* 1:1 (Mar 1970), 5.

112. MACGLOIN, TOMMY: "Yeats," *Icarus,* 5:16 (May 1955), 26.

113. MACKEY, THOMASINA: "Centenary," *IrI,* 14 Oct 1965, 13.

114. MACKINLAY, JAMES: "Thoughts on Yeats," *Lagan,* [2 (1944)], 79.

115. MACLEISH, ARCHIBALD: *"The Wild Old Wicked Man" & Other Poems.* London: Allen, 1969. ix, 45 pp.

"The Wild Old Wicked Man," 44-45.

116. MANDER, JOHN: "William Morris and William Yeats," *Delta,* [1 (1953), 11].

117. MANSFIELD, RICHARD: "Yeat[s]'s Grave," *Focus,* 5:6 (June 1962), 134.

118. MARSZAŁEK, JAN: *Nad ranem.* Warszawa: Ludowa Spółdzielnia Wydawnicza, 1970. 60 pp.

"Spotkanie z W. B. Yeatsem," 13. "A meeting with WBY," reprinted from *Odra,* 10:3 (1970), 75-76.

119. ———: *Zajastrzębienie*. Warszawa: Krajowa Agencja Wydawnicza, 1978. 220 pp.
"William Butler Yeats," 87.

120. MASEFIELD, JOHN: "Old 18, Woburn Buildings, or The Generosities of Life." MS., Bodleian Library, Oxford (Ms. Eng. Poet. d. 195, fol. 117).
A poem "Remembering November the 5th, 1900." I do not know whether it is identical with one of the poems contained in BA12.

121. MEDDAUGH, DAVID H.: "To William B. Yeats," *Four Winds*, 1:1 (Summer 1952), 28-29.

122. MEREDITH, WILLIAM: *Ships and Other Figures*. Princeton: Princeton UP, 1948. vii, 40 pp.
"In a Copy of Yeats' Poems," 24. First published in *Poetry*, 70:2 (May 1947), 68; also in *Earth Walk: New and Selected Poems*. NY: Knopf, 1970. x, 99 pp. (p. 38).

123. MERRILL, JAMES: *From the First Nine: Poems 1946-1976*. NY: Atheneum, 1982. xii, 365 pp.
"Flying from Byzantium," 192-94; reprinted from *Salmagundi*, 1:3 (1966), 61.

124. MEYER, BILL: "Yeats' Last Eyes. Yeats Jogs on the Cliff Paths," *Gorey Detail*, 7 (1983), [28].

125. MILNE, EWART: *Boding Day: Poems*. London: Muller, 1947. 32 pp.
"Christmas Eve, 1945," 24.

126. ———: "Water for the Rose," *Irish Democrat*, ns 56 (Aug 1949), 6.
Poem on the line "O words are lightly spoken" from "The Rose Tree."

127. ———: *Diamond Cut Diamond: Selected Poems*. London: Bodley Head, 1950. 64 pp.
"Oboe for Yeats," 10.

128. MONTAGUE, JOHN: *Patriotic Suite*. Dublin: Dolmen Press, 1966. 16 pp.
The sections "Wanderings of Oisin," "Abbey Theatre," and "Take Your Stand" are concerned with Yeats. The poem was extensively revised and included in *The Rough Field*. Dublin: Dolmen Press, 1979. 83 pp. "Wanderings of Oisin" is now simply "3"; "Abbey Theatre" has been eliminated; "Take Your Stand" has been retained (pp. 63-70). See also the new section "9."

129. MOORE, MARIANNE: *Poems*. London: Egoist Press, 1921. 24 pp.
"To William Butler Yeats on Tagore," 8; reprinted from *Egoist*, 2:5 (1 May 1915), 77.

130. MURPHY, DOROTHY S. (ed): *Pine's the Canadian Tree: An Anthology*. Hamilton, Ont.: Power Poetry Society Press, 1975. vii, 192 pp.
Ken Gibson: "William Butler Yeats," 45.

131. NELSON, LAWRENCE G.: "Two Sonnets: Requiem for a Keltic Gyravague," *CEA*, 33:3 (Mar 1971), 28.

132. O'BROIN, PADRAIG: "Yeats," *Laurel R*, 5:2 (Fall 1965), 2.

133. O'CONNOR, FRANK: "Directions for *My* Funeral (Written after the Burial of W. B. Yeats)," *Atlantic Monthly,* 223:2 (Feb 1969), 120.

134. ———: "On a House Shaken by the Land Agitation (With Apologies to W. B. Yeats)," *JIL,* 4:1 (Jan 1975), 24-25.
Written about 1926.

135. O'DOWDA, TIM: "Maud Gonne to W. B. Yeats," *Spect,* 28 June 1980, 27.
Entry for a competition "to write a poem in which the poet's mistress, reversing the traditional roles, urges him *not* to propose."

136. Ó FARACHÁIN, ROIBEÁRD [Robert Farren]: *Time's Wall Asunder.* NY: Sheed & Ward, 1939. viii, 86 pp.
"Yeats," 61.

137. OKIGBO, CHRISTOPHER: "Lament for the Masks. For W. B. Yeats: 1865-1939," in Maxwell and Bushrui: *W. B. Yeats 1865-1965* (1965, CA71), xiii-xiv.

138. OSHIMA, SHOTARO: *Poems.* Tokyo: Hokuseido Press, 1973. x, 109 pp.
"Thoor Ballylee: On Its Being Repaired on the Centenary of Yeats 1965," 51.
"To the Land of the Ever-Living: A Tribute to W. B. Yeats," 59-60. Also in *Poems: Journeys and Scenes.* Tokyo: Hokuseido Press, 1968. 16 pp. (pp. 1-2).

139. O'SULLIVAN, SEUMAS: *Collected Poems.* Dublin: Orwell Press, 1940. 226 pp.
"To a Poet," 58; reprinted from *Sinn Féin,* 30 June 1906, 3. The answer to Yeats's "To a Poet, Who Would Have Me Praise Certain Bad Poets, Imitators of His and Mine."

140. PAYNE, BASIL: "Remembering Yeats," *Kilkenny Magazine,* 15 (Spring-Summer 1967), 135.

141. PAYNE, ELIZABETH: "W. B. Yeats," *Circle,* [1:1] (Dec 1941), 35.

142. PIĄTKOWSKI, JERZY: "Gwiazda która krzyk zostawia (Motyw z W. B. Yeatsa)," *Życie literackie,* 26:20 (16 May 1976), 5.
"The star that stops the cry"; a poem on Yeats's "Leda and the Swan." Reprinted in *Gwiazda wędrowna.* Kraków: Wydawnictwo literackie, 1978. 68 pp. (p. 8).

143. PITTOCK, MURRAY: "Thoor Ballylee," *Cumberland Poetry R,* 6:2 (Spring 1987), 89.

144. PLATTHY, JENŐ: *Summer Flowers.* NY/Tokyo: Information Publishing, 1960. 372 pp.
"Yeats," 354.

145. *Poets of Tomorrow: Second Selection. Cambridge Poetry 1940.* London: Hogarth Press, 1940. 87 pp.
Maurice James Craig: "In Memory of William Butler Yeats," 30-31.

146. POLITE, FRANK: "Shade of Yeats," *December,* 11:1-2 (1969), 164.

147. POLLARD, MARGUERITE: "In Memoriam: W. B. Yeats," *Poetry R,* 30:3 (Mar-Apr 1939), 151.

148. POTTS, PAUL: "William Butler Yeats, 1865-1939," *Poetry Q,* 8:1 (Spring 1946), 38.

149. POULIN, A.: "Sailing from Byzantium," *CP,* 5:1 (Spring 1972), 24.

150. POUND, EZRA: *The Cantos.* NY: New Directions, 1970. v, 802 pp.
References to Yeats are contained in cantos 41 (p. 205), 74 (433), 76 (453), 77 (473), 79 (487), 80 (496, 504, 505, 507, 508, 511), 82 (524-25), 83 (528, 529, 533-34). See John Hamilton Edwards and William W. Vasse: *Annotated Index to the Cantos of Ezra Pound: Cantos I-LXXXIV.* Berkeley: U of California Press, 1959. xvii, 332 pp.
Further Yeats references in cantos 93 (p. 632), 95 (645), 96 (661), 97 (676), 98 (685, 686), 101 (725), 102 (728, 729), 113 (789), 114 (793).
For discussions of these references see CD1023, 1069, 1074.

151. POWYS, JOHN COWPER: *Odes and Other Poems.* London: Rider, 1896. vi, 54 pp.
"To W. B. Yeats," 15.

152. PURDY, ALFRED: *The Cariboo Horses.* Toronto: McClelland & Stewart, 1965, 112 pp.
"Malachi Stilt-Jack Am I," 51-52.

153. REILLY, ROBERT: "To William B. Yeats, Author of 'The Wanderings of Oisin,'" *IrM,* 17:191 (May 1889), 277.

154. REYNOLDS, LORNA: "Thoor Ballylee, June 1965," *UR,* 3:8 [1966?], 101.

155. ROETHKE, THEODORE: *The Collected Verse: Words for the Wind.* Garden City: Doubleday, 1958. 212 pp.
Part 1 of "Four for Sir John Davies," entitled "The Dance" (p. 120), is expressly indebted to Yeats ("I take this cadence from a man named Yeats"). See also "The Dying Man: In Memoriam W. B. Yeats," 185-90.
For discussions of these poems and of Roethke's indebtedness to Yeats see CD1118-25.

156. ROSEN, STANLEY: "Yeats I. Yeats II," *SR,* 82:1 (Winter 1974), 79-80.

157. SACKETT, S. J.: "An Open Letter to W. B. Yeats," *AR,* 20:3 (Fall 1966), 293.

158. SALOMON, I. L.: "Thoor Ballylee," *DM,* 8:4&5 (Summer/Autumn 1970), 81.

159. SCHEVILL, JAMES: *Ambiguous Dancers of Fame: Collected Poems 1945-1985.* Athens: Swallow Press / Ohio UP, 1987. xiv, 278 pp.
"For the Old Yeats," 92; reprinted from *ASch,* 33:2 (Spring 1964), 236. "Yeats, Riveted to Revisions," 261-62.

160. SCHWARTZ, LLOYD: "Yeats' Prayer," *MR,* 20:2 (Summer 1979), 260.
A poem composed of "(in reverse order of frequency) all the words Yeats used in his poems a hundred times or more."

161. SHAPIRO, KARL: *Essay on Rime*. NY: Random House, 1945. vii, 72 pp.
A long poem. The following lines pertain to Yeats: 493-504, 1393-401, 1788-93.

162. SIMMONS, JAMES: "A Famous Poet," in Maxwell and Bushrui: *W. B. Yeats 1865-1965* (1965, CA71), 226.

163. ———: *Energy to Burn: Poems*. London: Bodley Head, 1971. 63 pp.
"For the Centenary," 55. Reprinted in *Judy Garland and the Cold War*. Belfast: Blackstaff Press, 1976. iv, 59 pp. (on pp. 4-5; see also "J. M. Synge," 6.)

164. ———: *From the Irish*. Belfast: Blackstaff Press, 1985. xi, 78 pp.
"On Baile Strand," 29; reprinted from *IrT*, 10 Mar 1984, 13. Refers to *On Baile's Strand* and "The Circus Animals' Desertion."
"Beautiful Lofty Things," 31-32; a parody of Yeats's poem.
"The Busker," reprinted from *IrT*, 1 Dec 1984, 12.

165. SMITH, ARTHUR JAMES MARSHALL: *Collected Poems*. Toronto: Oxford UP, 1962. Unpaged.
"Ode: On the Death of William Butler Yeats," no. 9.

166. SMYTHE, COLIN: "Yeats Country," *EI*, 2 (Dec 1977), 18.
Poem written after having seen Patrick Carey's film (HB10).

167. SPARROW, JOHN: "W. B. Yeats," *Oxford Magazine*, ns 3:18 (9 May 1963), 274.

168. STALLWORTHY, JON: "From W. B. Yeats to His Friend Maud Gonne," *REL*, 4:3 (July 1963), 70.

169. ———: "On Being Asked for a Centenary Poem," *English*, 15:89 (Summer 1965), 169.

170. STEEN, SHIELA: *The Honeysuckle Hedge*. London: Oxford UP, 1943. v, 48 pp.
"W. B. Yeats, Died Roquebrune, Cap Martin, 28 Jan. 1939," 18-19; first published under the name S. M. Tusting, *English*, 2:10 (1939), 228-29.

171. STOW, RANDOLPH: "Anarchy: For W. B. Yeats in Mid-Winter," in Jeffares and Cross: *In Excited Reverie* (1965, CA48), 279.

172. STUART, FRANCIS: "Remembering Yeats," *IrT*, 12 June 1982, 12.

173. SULLIVAN, NANCY: "For W. B. Yeats From One Who Never Made Young Men Catch Their Breath When She Was Passing," *Shenandoah*, 15:1 (Autumn 1963), 43.

174. SWAN, JON C.: "Sonnet to W. B. Yeats," *Personalist*, 39:4 (Autumn 1958), 372.

175. TATE, ALLEN: *Poems*. NY: Scribner's, 1960. xii, 224 pp.
"Winter Mask: To the Memory of W. B. Yeats," 62-65; first published in *Chimera*, 1:4 (Spring 1943), 2-3.

176. TATE, JAMES: "The Whole World's Sadly Talking to Itself--W. B.

Yeats," *Poetry,* 110:4 (July 1967), 239.

177. TETEL, MARCEL (ed): *Symbolism and Modern Literature: Studies in Honor of Wallace Fowlie.* Durham, N.C.: Duke UP, 1978. vii, 299 pp.
Karl Shapiro: "W. B. Y.," 173.

178. THOMAS, PETER: "The Debtors: Tribute to Yeats," *Ibadan,* 21 (Oct 1965), 52.

179. THOMAS, RONALD STUART: *The Stones of the Field.* Carmarthen: Druid Press, 1946. 49 pp.
"Memories of Yeats Whilst Travelling to Holyhead," 22; reprinted from *Poetry London,* 2:10 (Dec 1944), 176.

180. TOMLINSON, CHARLES: *Relations and Contraries.* Aldington, Kent: Hand and Flower Press, 1951. pp. 261-292. (Poems in Pamphlet. 9 [1951].)
"Monuments. (Variations on a Theme of Yeats)," 275-78.

181. TURNER, WALTER JAMES: *Fossils of a Future Time?* London: Oxford UP, 1946. xiii, 143 pp.
"W. B. Yeats," 24-26; first published as "Ode (In Memory of W. B. Yeats)," *NSt,* 18 Feb 1939, 243.

182. UNTERECKER, JOHN: "Abelard Perhaps and Perhaps Heloise--Variations on a Theme by W. B. Yeats," *Poetry Ireland,* 7&8 (Spring 1968), 94-95.

183. VAN DUYN, MONA: *To See, to Take: Poems.* NY: Atheneum, 1970. viii, 97 pp.
"Leda," 12; reprinted from *QR of Literature,* 14:1 (1966), 212. An answer to "Leda and the Swan"; see also "Leda Reconsidered," which is not directly concerned with Yeats's poem.

184. W., A. M.: "The Ideal Beauty Show," *Leader,* 29 Mar 1913, 153. Poem, scene: "A hall filled with long-haired bards, bounders and other intensely cultured persons. Pensioner Yeats comes forward to chant, and is received with a tremulous outburst of rhymthical [sic] cheering, followed by an opal hush." See by the same versifier: "The Opal Hush Bungery," 5 Apr 1913, 177.

185. W., B.: "William Butler Yeats," *IrT,* 18 Sept 1948, 6.

186. WAKE, GABRIEL: *Earthquake: A Vision of Ireland.* S.l., 1924. [4 pp.]
A satiric poem with a section on Yeats.

187. WATKINS, VERNON: *Selected Poems.* Norfolk, Conn.: New Directions, 1948. vii, 92 pp.
"Yeats' Tower," 24; reprinted from *Wales,* 3 (Autumn 1937), 86-87.

188. ———: *The Lamp and the Veil: Poems.* London: Faber & Faber, 1945. 61 pp.
"Yeats in Dublin," 7-19; first published in *LLT,* 21:20 (Apr 1939), 67-78; also in *New Directions,* 10 (1948), 172-82; *Poetry Ireland,* 11 (Oct 1950), 3-12; and *DM,* 6:1 (Spring 1967), 19-29.

189. ———: "The Last Poems of Yeats," *LLT,* 23:28 (Nov 1939), 312-13.

190. ———: *The Collected Poems*. Ipswich: Golgonooza Press, 1986. xvii, 495 pp.

Reprints the poems listed in the three preceding items, pp. 13-14, 59-68, 480-82. For another poem on Yeats see DB251. See also CA162 and CD1421-1425.

191. WATSON, WILLIAM: *The Muse in Exile: Poems*. London: Jenkins, 1913. 116 pp.

"A Chance Meeting," 95. This epigram is quoted, or rather misquoted, by Gogarty (BA5, p. 21), who says that Watson alluded to Yeats.

192. WEBER, RICHARD: *Lady & Gentleman*. Dublin: Dolmen Press, 1963. 30 pp.

"Yeats in London," 23; reprinted from *TLS*, 13 July 1962, 508.

193. WEISS, NEIL: "W. B. Yeats," *Chelsea*, 7 (May 1960), 73-74.

194. WELLESLEY, DOROTHY: *Early Light: The Collected Poems*. London: Hart-Davis, 1955. 255 pp.

"To Yeats," 253.

195. WHEATCROFT, JOHN: "Reading Yeats on the Beach," *DR*, 46:3 (Autumn 1966), 318.

196. WHITE, GAIL: "For Yeats & the Rhymers [sic] Club," *SCR*, 6:2 (Apr 1974), 69.

197. WILKINSON, MARGUERITE O. B.: "To William Butler Yeats," *Little R*, 1:4 (Apr 1914), 52.

198. WILSON, GRAEME: "Yeats," *DQ*, 6:4 (Winter 1972), 33-34.

199. WILSON, PATRICK: *Staying at Ballisodare*. Northwood, Middlesex: Scorpion Press, 1960. 23 pp.

A long poem concerned with Yeats passim.

200. WILSON, R. N. D.: "Postcript to an Epitaph," *DM*, 24:3 (July-Sept 1949), 1-2.

Yeats's epitaph in "Under Ben Bulben."

201. WINN, G. HOWARD: "Thoor Ballylee 1969," *Barat R*, 5:2 (Autumn 1970), 104.

202. WRIGHT, CAROLYNE: "In the Yeats Class," *Fiddlehead*, 117 (Spring 1978), 64.

203. WYMAN, LINDA: "Concerning the Relevance of Falconers," *CEA*, 33:3 (Mar 1971), 35.

204. ZINCKE, JOAN: "Yeats' Message to Ireland," *Colorado Q*, 23:1 (Summer 1974), 28.

See also BA12, 22, BB153, CA53, 148, CB90, 99, 199, 235, 509, CD102, 218, 563, 751, 752, DA48, DB251, 256, DD72, 488, DE51, 83, EB90.

HE Novels, Stories, Plays, and Ballets on or Using Material by Yeats

This section is incomplete; in some cases it has not been possible to obtain more detailed information. I do not include items where the allusions to Yeats are tenuous or slight or unclear. For abbreviations of sources see headnote to section HC.

1. AUDEN, WYSTAN HUGH, and CHESTER KALLMAN: *Elegy for Young Lovers: Opera in Three Acts*. Music by Hans Werner Henze. Mainz: Schott, 1961.

Vocal score in English and German, *Textbuch* in German, translated by Ludwig Landgraf [i.e., Ludwig Landgraf von Hessen].

According to Callan (CD157) and others, the main character, the poet Gregor Mittenhofer, is modelled on Yeats. The *Textbuch* contains a note by Auden and Kallman indicating that some parts of Mittenhofer's character reflect the life of a poet who wrote in English; but the poet is not named (p. 64).

2. °BARRETT, GLENN EDWARD: "The King of the Cats: A Play with Music." MS., 1986. (CCE)

Based on Yeats's poems.

3. °BUFANO, ROCCO, and JOHN DUFFY: "Horseman, Pass By: Musical," 1969.

I do not know whether this has been published. The musical was performed at the Fortune Theater, 62 East 4th Street, New York (see "A Yeats Musical: *Horseman, Pass By* Bows off Broadway," *NYT*, 16 Jan 1969, 46). It was based on the writings of Yeats and had the following characters: Intellect, Political Man, Imagination, Spirit, Sensuality, Vanity, Timidity, and The Voice; a sort of morality, it appears.

4. °CALLAN, EDWARD T.: "Come, Dance with Me in Ireland: A Performance of W. B. Yeats." A monologue, incorporating verse and prose by Yeats, MS., 1985. (CCE)

This may be identical with *I Am of Ireland: An Entertainment of W. B. Yeats*, performed at the Peacock Theatre, Dublin, with music by Grainne Yeats and Bosco Hogan as Yeats. See note in *IrT*, 1 Aug 1988, 12; review by David Nowlan, ibid., 4 Aug 1988, 12. Another performance took place at the Yeats Summer School; see *IrT*, 8 Aug 1988, 9.

5. CLARK, TOM: "The Gang of Eight," *Exquisite Corpse*, 2:5-7 (May-July 1984), 12-13.

A short prose sketch (if this is the word) of a robbery featuring characters called Yeats, Hemingway, Pound, Joyce, Ford, Hulme, Wyndham Lewis, and Dillinger. Yeats drives the getaway car.

6. CRANDALL, DAVID: *Crazy Jane: A Dance-Drama in One Act*. Tokyo: Clearwater, 1983. i, 14 pp.

In English, together with a Japanese translation by Noriko Komatsu; title on cover. A play on motifs derived from Yeats, first performed in Sept 1983 at the Tokyo Union Church.

7. [CROWLEY, ALEISTER]: "At the Fork of the Road," *Equinox*, 1:1 (Mar 1909), 101-8.

A short story. According to Crowley, it is a "true account of an episode of [the late 1890s]." He identifies some of its characters: Will Bute = Yeats; Hypatia Gay = Althea Gyles; Publisher = Leonard Smithers; and adds: "The identification is conjectural, depending solely on the admission of Miss Gyles" (see BB49, 1: 259)--which is quite probably an infernal lie. Virginia Moore (BA14, p. 210) identifies the main character, Count Swanoff, as Crowley himself. The sickening story deals with the hellish machinations of Will Bute, who sends Hypatia Gay to seduce Swanoff. After a near success, Hypatia is punished severely through counter-magic. See BB70.

8. ———: *Moonchild: A Prologue*. London: Mandrake Press, 1929. 335 pp.

A novel in which Yeats appears as Gates (see FC56). The first appearance is on p. 152.

9. D'ARCY, MARGARETTA, and JOHN ARDEN: *The Non-Stop Connolly Show: A Dramatic Cycle of Continuous Struggle in Six Parts*. London: Pluto Press, 1977-78. 6 vols.

Maud Gonne and Yeats appear in part 3. See also Arden's *To Present the Pretence: Essays on the Theatre and Its Public (Including Two Essays Written in Collaboration with Margaretta D'Arcy)*. London: Eyre Methuen, 1977. 216 pp. Arden and D'Arcy's essay "A Socialist Hero on the Stage: Dramatising the Life and Work of James Connolly," 92-138, contains notes on Yeats.

10. DAVENPORT, GUY: *Da Vinci's Bicycle: Ten Stories*. Baltimore: Johns Hopkins UP, 1979. xiii, 165 pp.

"Ithaka," 114-20, contains Pound's story that Yeats is not buried in Drumcliffe Churchyard but lies at the bottom of the Mediterranean.

11. DUNNING, JENNIFER: "Paul Taylor Creates a Dark New Work," *NYT*, 18 Mar 1984, part 2, 22.

A ballet based on "Sailing to Byzantium," set to music by Edgar Varèse, and performed by the Paul Taylor Dance Company at the City Center Theater, New York. See also the reviews by Anna Kisselgoff: "The Dance: A Paul Taylor Premiere," 21 Mar 1984, section C, 14; Howard Moss: "Real Guys," *NYRB*, 31 May 1984, 31-33.

11a. EAGLETON, TERRY: *Saints and Scholars*. London: Verso, 1987. vii, 145 pp.

A novel whose main characters are James Connolly and Ludwig Wittgenstein, with occasional references to Yeats.

12. [GALE, NORMAN ROWLAND]: *All Expenses Paid*. Westminster: Constable, 1895. vi, 113 pp.

A short comic novel describing the journey to Parnassus of a couple of "minor poets," headed by Yeats. The journey has been paid by one Mr. Patterson, formerly a pork butcher, now a modern Maecenas.

13. °GOLDSTONE, PATRICIA: "The Circus Animals' Desertion." MS., 1975.

The dramatis personae of this play include Yeats, Maud Gonne, Lady Gregory and Mrs. Yeats (played by the same actress), and Iseult Gonne. First performance at the Focus Theatre, Dublin, 9 Dec 1975. See review by Seamus Kelly, *IrT*, 10 Dec 1975, 9.

14. GOOD, MAURICE: *John Synge Comes Next*. Dublin: Dolmen Press,

1973. 88 pp.

A one-man show, "fashioned out of Synge's own works." Contains some references to Yeats.

15. HIBBIN, NINA: "Chatter-Box," *NSt*, 14 Aug 1981, 22-23.

A review of various B.B.C. radio programs, including "Frank Delaney's hagiography of W. B. Yeats, *Something to Perfection Brought* (Radio 4)." Details not available since the *Radio Times* was not published because of a strike.

16. JAMES, CLIVE: *Brilliant Creatures: A First Novel*. London: Cape, 1983. 317 pp.

The title is taken from "The Wild Swans at Coole"; the notes appended to the novel refer to "Yeatsian adductions" (pp. 282-84).

17. JAMES, ROBERT [i.e., Robert Hogan and James Douglas]: "The Writer's Trilogy I: There Are Joys. A Play in Two Acts," *JIL*, 10:1 (Jan 1981), 3-60.

A play about the uproars accompanying the first performance of a play called *Love in a Glen* "in the first decade of this century." The characters are thinly disguised notables of the early days of the Irish National Theatre, including a "Walter Bayard Slate." See also parts II and III: "What Is the Stars: A Play in Two Acts," :2 (May 1981), 59-124; "Cast a Cold Eye: A Play in Three Acts," :3 (Sept 1981), 3-74.

18. KISSELGOFF, ANNA: "Dance: 'Lunar Parables' by Pearson Company," *NYT*, 1 June 1985, 31.

Review of a performance of a work "keyed to fragments of text by W. B. Yeats" by the Jerry Pearson Dance Company.

There was also a performance by the Dublin Contemporary Dance Theatre at Project Arts Centre, Dublin, on 19 Mar 1985. See program reprinted in FC71; the "dance/theatre piece" was "inspired by one of Yeats's primary interests--the power of symbols to evoke indefinable and yet precise emotions.'"

19. °LLOYD, PETER: "Dreams That Have No Moral: W. B. Yeats." An adaptation for the stage, MS., 1982. (CCE)

Listed as a "play in 6 scenes."

20. °MCGEHEE, HELEN: "The Only Jealousy of Emer." Choreography and costumes: Helen McGehee. Music: Benjamin Britten (Cello Sonata in C). Libretto: After the play by W. B. Yeats. 1967.

First performance at Marygorve College, Detroit, Mich., 12 Oct 1967. Further performances at Kaufmann Concert Hall, NY, 7 Dec 1967 and 19 Mar 1969. See review by Clive Barnes: "Dance: Helen McGehee. Graham Disciple Gives Premiere of *The Only Jealousy of Emer*," *NYT*, 9 Dec 1967, 62.

21. °MACKEN, WALTER: "Recall the Years." 1966.

A revue staged to celebrate the opening of the new Abbey Theatre. See the following reviews: Anon.: "Ireland's Most Famous Theatre Reopens," *Times*, 19 July 1966, 14; Gerard Fay: "Theatre Built on Sand," *Hibernia*, 30:8 (Aug 1966), 9; Madeline Winkler-Betzendahl: "Gedenkt der Jahre: Das neue Abbey Theatre rekapituliert seine Geschichte," *Theater heute*, 7:11 (Nov 1966), 36.

22. °MACLIAMMÓIR, MICHEÁL: "Talking about Yeats," 1965 [?].

MacLiammóir's one-man Yeats show. See reviews by Michael Billington: "Welcome Partiality: Talking about Yeats," *Times*, 30

Sept 1970, 13; Charles Lewsen: "Talking about Yeats," *Times,* 14 Oct 1971, 13; Terence Tobin: "MacLiammoir vs. Yeats," *Drama Critique,* 9:1 (Winter 1966), 35-36.

23. MARTYN, EDWARD: "Romulus & Remus: Or, The Makers of Delights. A Symbolist Extravaganza in One Act," *Irish People,* 21 Dec 1907, Supplement, 1-2.

A satire on Yeats, who appears as Remus Delaney, hairdresser, and on Moore, Lady Gregory, and Martyn himself. Somewhat dull, but contains one really good line: "As for living Miss Hoolihan at least can do that for me." Reprinted in *George Spelvin's Theatre Book,* 2:3 (Fall 1979), 87-106.

24. ———: *The Dream Physician: Play in Five Acts.* Dublin: Talbot Press / London: Unwin, [1917?]. vi, 87 pp.

George Augustus Moon = George Moore; Beau Brummell = Yeats (he appears with a banjo; presumably a comment on the "Speaking to the Psaltery" experiments); Otho = James Joyce (he says to Brummell: "I see you are too old to influence me," p. 67).

For reprint see Seumas MacManus: *The Townland of Tamney: A One Act Comedy* [and] Edward Martyn: *The Dream Physician: A Comedy.* Introduction by Patricia McFate. Chicago: De Paul U, 1972. i, 73 pp. (Irish Drama Series. 7.)

25. MOORE, GEORGE: *Evelyn Innes.* London: Unwin, 1898. v, 480 pp.

A novel in which the character of Ulick Dean is modeled on Yeats. See his description in chapter 14 (p. 182).

26. °OLCSAN, LOIS J.: "Tara: A Play." MS., 1981. (CCE)

Based in part on *Diarmuid and Grania.*

27. PUSBACH, JUNELLA MARIE: "I Am of Ireland: A Play with Music." Lyrics by W. B. Yeats, music by Stephen R. Scott, MS., 1982. (CCE)

28. ROSMAN, ELEANOR M.: "'A Vision': A Dance Based on Two Symbols from the Poetry of W. B. Yeats," M.A. thesis, New York U, 1970. iv, 75 pp.

The two symbols are "Gyre" and "Golden Bird." Performed on 19 and 20 Dec 1969 at New York Unversity; the author was the choreographer.

29. RYAN, WILLIAM PATRICK: *Daisy Darley or The Fairy Gold of Fleet Street.* London: Dent, 1913. vi, 398 pp.

A novel; see pp. 165-67 for a satiric portrait of Yeats, here simply called "a poet."

30. °SHEA, JOHN ERNEST: "With a Faery, Hand in Hand." MS., 1980. (CCE)

Listed as "New script & compilation," includes 12 Yeats poems.

31. SHYRE, PAUL: *Yeats and Company.* Adapted by Paul Shyre. [Los Angeles, 1965]. Typescript, 1 vol., various pagings. (NN)

Produced by The Theatre Group at the U of Southern California, Los Angeles, on 23 Oct 1965. Among the characters are Yeats, Maud Gonne, Oscar Wilde, Lady Gregory, T. S. Eliot, Sean O'Casey, and John Butler Yeats. Includes performances of *Purgatory* and *The Words upon the Window Pane.*

32. STUART, FRANCIS: *Black List / Section H.* With a preface and postscript by Harry T. Moore. Carbondale: Southern Illinois UP,

1971. ix, 442 pp.
A largely autobiographical novel in which Yeats, Maud and Iseult Gonne, and other figures of the time appear under their own names.

33. °*Sweet Dancer: Motion Picture*. [1964?]. 58 minutes, black-and-white.
This is the Ballet Rambert production, filmed onstage by Edmée Wood. See *Dictionary Catalog of the Dance Collection, New York Public Library*. Boston: Hall, 1974 (10:6850).
The production opened at the Sadler's Wells Theatre, London, on 20 July 1964. Choreography by Walter Gore, music by Frank Martin (Eight Preludes for Piano), libretto after W. B. Yeats (same source, 9:6196).
Reviews:
- Clive Barnes, Noel Goodwin, and Peter Williams: "Sweet Dancer," *Dance and Dancers*, 15:9 (Sept 1964), 12-15.
- Fernau Hall: "Ballet Rambert at Sadler's Wells: Sweet Dancer," *Ballet Today*, 14:16 (Oct 1964), 6.
- Oleg Kerensky: "Sweet Dancer and the Rest of the Rambert Season," *Dancing Times*, 54:648 (Sept 1964), 627.

34. WILSON, ROBERT ANTON: *Masks of the Illuminati*. London: Sphere Books, 1981. vii, 294 pp.
A kind of fantastic novel, partly on the Golden Dawn. Characters include Yeats, Joyce, Pound, Einstein, and others. The Yeats references start on p. 67.

35. °YEATS, W. B.: "A Full Moon in March." Ballet libretto, 1951.
Based on this play; choreography by Gertrude Lippincott, music by Henry Cowell, hand masks by Robert Moulton. First performance at the YWCA Benton Hall, Minneapolis, 18 Oct 1951. See *Bibliographic Guide to Dance*, 1981.

36. °———: *Words for Music Perhaps*. NY: American Theater Lab for Dance Theater Workshop's The Winter Events, 1981. Videotape, 55 mins.
An evening of music and dance/theater, based on Yeats's poetry. Music written and performed by Wall Matthews. Choreographed and performed by Ara Fitzgerald. There is a copy in NN. See also DE33.

See also BB204, CB212, CC146, CD200, 444, 1148, 1155-56, 1438a, DE33.

HF Parodies

1. *The Abbey Row NOT Edited by W. B. Yeats*. Dublin: Maunsel, 1907. 12 pp.
The authors of this skit on the first production of Synge's *The Playboy of the Western World* are thought to have been Page Lawrence Dickinson, Frank Sparrow, Richard Caulfield Orpen, William Orpen, Joseph Hone, and Susan L. Mitchell. Yeats is mentioned passim.

1a. ALLEN, WOODY: *Without Feathers*. London: Elm Tree Books, 1976. ix, 211 pp.
"The Irish Genius," 117-22; a note on *The Annotated Poems of Sean O'Shawn*, "the Great Irish poet, considered by many to be the most incomprehensible and hence the finest poet of his time."

(N.B.: The parody is a little lame because the target, obviously Yeats, is only imperfectly realized.)

2. ANON.: "Competition No. 573," *Spect,* 25 Oct 1969, 574.
Conditions: To write two stanzas of a poem modeled on "The Lake Isle of Innisfree," "celebrating the attractions of a dream island for hippies, Liberal MPs or any other minority groups." Five parodies are printed.

3. ANON.: "Next Week's Programme at the Abbey Theatre: *The College Playboy*. A Tragedy in Two Acts by Post and Neo Synge," *T.C.D.*, 22:386 (8 Mar 1916), 226-28.

4. B.: "Cap and Bells Up-to-Date," *T.C.D.*, 23:398 (28 Feb 1917), 97.

5. BRADBY, GODFREY FOX: *Parody and Dust-Shot*. London: Oxford UP, 1931. viii, 42 pp.
"What Really Happens (After W. B. Yeats)," 18; a parody of "The Lake Isle of Innisfree." See also DD284.

6. BRAHMS, CARYL: "A Parody: The Lamentable Effect of a Sea-Fever upon the Muse of Mr. Yeats," *Time and Tide,* 14 Oct 1927, 903.
A parody of "The Lake Isle of Innisfree."

7. BRETT, SIMON (ed): *The Faber Book of Parodies*. London: Faber & Faber, 1984. 383 pp.
G. K. Chesterton: "Variations on an Air Composed on Having to Appear in a Pageant as Old King Cole," 275-78 ("after W. B. Yeats," 276-77); reprint of HF9.
Peter Titheradge: "Teatime Variations," 279-82 ("after W. B. Yeats," 281).
Roger Woddis: "The Hero: On the Birmingham Pub Bombings of 21 November 1974," 369-70; reprint of HF68.
Ezra Pound: "The Lake Isle," 370; reprint of part of HF42.

8. BROOKS, SYDNEY: "Sydney Brooks's Selection of the Best Thirty Irish Books a la 'Yeats,'" *Irish Figaro,* 16 Mar 1895, 169-70.
A parody of Yeats's "The Thirty Best Irish Books" (see *Collected Letters,* 1:140-45).

9. CHESTERTON, GILBERT KEITH: *Collected Poems*. NY: Dodd, Mead, 1966. vii, 391 pp.
"Variations on an Air: Composed on Having to Appear in a Pageant as Old King Cole," 43-46; includes a variation "After W. B. Yeats." See also HF7 and 71.

10. Chanel [i.e., CLERY, ARTHUR EDWARD]: *The Idea of a Nation*. Dublin: Duffy, 1907. v, 76 pp.
Essays, reprinted mostly from *The Leader*. Of interest: "After the Abbey Is Over," 17-19, a parody of the plays of Yeats and Lady Gregory; "The Philosophy of an Irish Theatre," 48-51, which criticizes Yeats's view that an Abbey dramatist need not be confined to the accepted standards of morality.

11. COMPTON-RICKETT, ARTHUR: *Our Poets at School and Other Fancies in Prose and Verse*. Bournemouth: Cooper, 1921. 72 pp.
Contains a parody of "The Fiddler of Dooney," p. 31.

12. DAY LEWIS, CECIL: *An Italian Visit*. London: Cape, 1953. 77 pp.
"Judith and Holofernes: Donatello (W. B. Y.)," 56-57; a parody

of Yeats's later poetic style. Reprinted on p. 341 of *Collected Poems*. London: Cape / Hogarth Press, 1954. 370 pp.

13. DEANE, ANTHONY CHARLES: *New Rhymes for Old and Other Verses*. London: Lane, 1901. 96 pp.
"The Cult of the Celtic. (An Experiment, Dedicated with Apologies to Fiona Macleod, W. B. Yeats, and Others)," 61-63. Reprinted in HF71.

14. FELTON, JOHN: "Contemporary Caricatures," *Egoist*, 1:15 (1 Aug 1914), 296-97.
No. 2 concerns Mr. W****** B***** Y****.

15. FRENCH, PERCY: *Prose, Poems, and Parodies*. Edited by his sister Mrs. De Burgh Daly with a foreword by Alfred Perceval Graves. Dublin: Talbot Press, [1930]. xix, 204 pp.
"The Queen's After-Dinner Speech," 55-58, alludes to Maud Gonne and Yeats, containing the famous lines

"An' I think there's a slate," sez she,
"Off Willie Yeats," sez she,
"He should be at home," sez she,
"French polishin' a pome," sez she. . . .

16. GOGARTY, OLIVER ST. JOHN: "He Accounts for the Skyscrapers," *American Spectator*, 1:5 (Mar 1933), 2.

17. [GRAVES, CHARLES LARCOM, and EDWARD VERRALL LUCAS]: "The New Battle of Limerick," *Punch*, 13 Nov 1907, 358.
A satirical account of a meeting of various Irish notables which, needless to say, never took place. Yeats airs his views on the limerick and recites his own rather imperfect limerick version of "The Lake Isle of Innisfree."

18. HARRISON, R.: "An Interview with Mr. Y--ts," *New Age*, 18 Jan 1917, 286.

19. HOFFENSTEIN, SAMUEL: *Poems in Praise of Practically Nothing*. NY: Liveright, 1943 [1928]. 217 pp.
"Mr. Yeats Wants a Pot of Gold, All of a Sudden," 145-46.

20. HOLLIS, CHRISTOPHER: "The Innisfree Report," *Spect*, 25 June 1965, 806.

21. HOWE, MARTYN: "The Long Road: A Symbolistic Drama. (This Play May Be Performed at the Abbey Theatre without Fee or Licence)," *T.C.D.*, 21:377 (10 Nov 1915), 127.

22. ———: "Epigrams (In the Style of W. B. Yeats)," *T.C.D.*, 23:397 (21 Feb 1917), 87.

23. "IMAAL": "A Conversation between William Shakespeare and Mr. Yeats (Without Apologies to W. S. Landor)," *Leader*, 5 Dec 1903, 239-41.

24. JOYCE, JAMES: *Ulysses: A Critical and Synoptic Edition*. Prepared by Hans Walter Gabler with Wolfhard Steppe and Claus Melchior. NY: Garland, 1986. 3 vols.
First edition 1922. Buck Mulligan's parody of "Baile and Ailinn," stanza I, appears at the end of the library scene (episode 9, "Scylla and Charybdis"), 1:465. For a complete list of Yeats al-

lusions see CD649 and 686.

25. "Evoe" [KNOX, EDMUND GEORGE VALPY]: *Parodies Regained*. Illustrated by George Morrow. London: Methuen, 1921. x, 114 pp.
"The Deirdrenought. (Mr. W. B. Yeats Presents Dramatically His Views on the Battleship of the Future)," 59-63.

26. LEWIS, DOMINIC BEVAN WYNDHAM: *At the Sign of the Blue Moon*. London: Melrose, 1924. 316 pp.
"Celtic Twilight," 50-56; a parody of *At the Hawk's Well,* here called *At the Pump*.

27. ———: "Synge-Song," *John o' London's Weekly,* 6 Sept 1924, 750.
"Extract from *The Tinker's Aunt,* a one-act peasant play by an unknown author, here printed for the first time, and evidently owing some of its inspiration to the dramatic works of J. M. Synge and the Abbey Theatre, Dublin, generally."

28. MACCULLOCH, CLARE (ed): *Lobsticks. Lobsticks: A Spruce Tree Trimmed of All But the Top Branches*. Guelph: Alive Press, [1974]. 188 pp.
Fred Cogswell: "Spiv's Innisfree," 61.

29. MACMANUS, FRANCIS: "Frivolous Encounters: Signor Alighieri Meets Mr. Yeats," *IrM,* 67:793 (July 1939), 492-97.

30. MACMANUS, MICHAEL JOSEPH: *A Jackdaw in Dublin: A Collection of Parodies and Imitations of Irish Contemporaries*. Dublin: Talbot Press, [1924]. 48 pp.
See "In a Cafe," 9 (parody of "To an Isle in the Water"); "The Dreamer," 10 ("The Man Who Dreamed of Faeryland"); "A Poet's Lament," 11.

31. ———: *A Green Jackdaw: Adventures in Parody*. Dublin: Talbot Press, [1925]. 73 pp.
Contains two Yeats parodies, "The Dreamer" (see preceding item) and "The End of Heart's Desire," 33-34, as well as a play, "Gregorian Chant: A Kiltartanese Comedy (Potted)," 48-52.

32. ———: *So This Is Dublin!* Dublin: Talbot Press, 1927. 123 pp.
"The New Kiltartan History," 77-79, contains a paragraph on "The Poet Yeats."

Professor Jonathan P. Hoggenheim, Lecturer in Poetry and Scientific Salesmanship at Winkinville University, Oskoosh, Massachusetts, rewrites "The Lake Isle of Innisfree" in the American style, pp. 90-91.

"Poets in Collaboration" features "The Lake Isle of Innisfree (Written by Mr. W. B. Y--ts; rewritten by Mr. J--s St--ph--ns)," 120-21.

See also " A Misunderstanding," 123.

33. MACNEICE, LOUIS: *I Crossed the Minch*. London: Longmans, Green, 1938. ix, 248 pp.
Contains a parody of Yeats's prose style, pp. 181-83.

34. Mac [i.e., MACNIE, ISA]: *The Celebrity Zoo (First Visit): Some Desultory Rhymes and Caricatures*. Dublin: Browne & Nolan, 1925. Unpaged.
Yeats is one of the exhibits.

35. MARRIOTT, ERNEST: "The Shadow of the Wind (After W. B. Yeats)," *Manchester Q*, 29:113 (Jan 1910), 87-92.
A parody of *The King's Threshold*.

36. MITCHELL, SUSAN LANGSTAFF: *Aids to the Immortality of Certain Persons in Ireland Charitably Administered*. A new edition with poems added. Dublin: Maunsel, 1913 [1908]. xvii, 89 pp.
Yeats is mentioned or satirized in the following pieces: "Prologue to Some Who Are Mentioned in This Book," xvii (a parody of "When You Are Old").
"George Moore Comes to Ireland," 1-5.
"The Voice of One," 6-15; a play whose dramatis personae are Bates, Barton, and M'Clure (Yeats, Martyn, and Moore).
"The Ballad of Shawe-Taylor and Hugh Lane," 23-26.
"George Moore Becomes High Sheriff of Mayo," 33-35.

37. Moore, Edward [i.e., MUIR, EDWIN]: "Epigrams," *New Age*, 6 Apr 1916, 544.
Contains one "To W. B. Yeats."

38. NASH, OGDEN: *The Face Is Familiar: The Selected Verse of Ogden Nash*. Garden City: Garden City Publishing Co., 1941. xxii, 352 pp.
"The Strange Case of Mr. Fortague's Disappointment," 253-55, a parody of "The Lake Isle of Innisfree."

39. Ó BROIN, PÁDRAIG: *No Casual Trespass*. Toronto: Cló Chluain Tairbh, 1967. ix, 113 pp.
"Railing at Byzantium. (On Reading Certain Anthologized Younger 'Poets')," 4-5.

40. O'CONNOR, BRENDAN: "Le farfadet Mac Phellimey était un nègre!" [The pooka Mac Phellimey was a ghost writer], *Nyx: Dernières lettres avant la nuit*, 1 (First Trimester 1987), 75-79.
Discusses a contribution that Yeats made to a book entitled *James Joyce and the Pooka Mac Phellimey: A Study of a Literary Fabrication* (Dublin: Flaherty, 1923), and in which he proves that Molly Bloom's monolog is actually the work of Mac Phellimey, who lived in the 7th century. . . .

41. O'HIGGINS, BRIAN: *The Voice of Banba: Songs, Ballads and Satires*. Dublin: Hearthstone, [1931]. 114 pp.
"The Isle of Innisfree," 94.

42. POUND, EZRA: *Personae: Collected Shorter Poems*. London: Faber & Faber, 1952. 287 pp.
"Au Jardin," 67; first published as "Und Drang," in *Canzoni*. London: Mathews, 1911. viii, 52 pp. (pp. 51-52). A parody of "The Cap and Bells."
"Amitiés," 110-12; reprinted from *Poetry*, 4:5 (Aug 1914), 173-74. A parody of "The Lover Pleads with His Friends. . . ."
"The Lake Isle," 128; reprinted from *Poetry*, 8:16 (Sept 1916), 277. See also HF7.

43. ———: *Pavannes and Divagations*. Norfolk, Ct.: New Directions, 1958. xi, 243 pp.
"Neath Ben Bulben's Buttoks Lies," 228.

44. POWELL, CHARLES: *The Poets in the Nursery*. With an introduction by John Drinkwater. London: Lane, 1920. 80 pp.
"Little Boy Blue: William Butler Yeats," 35-37.

45. PRESCOTT, PETER S.: *Soundings: Encounters with Contemporary Books*. NY: Coward, McCann & Geoghegan, 1972, 331 pp.
See p. 31 for a parody of "Sailing to Byzantium."

46. PRIESTLEY, JOHN BOYNTON: *Brief Diversions: Being Tales, Travesties, and Epigrams*. Cambridge: Bowes & Bowes, 1922. vii, 60 pp.
"The Later Manner of Mr. W. B. Yeats," 48. "The Poetry of Mr. W. B. Yeats," 57.

47. READ, HERBERT: *Naked Warriors*. London: Arts & Letters, 1919. 60 pp.
"Parody of a Forgotten Beauty," 3; parodies "Into the Twilight."

48. ROSS, ROBERT: *Masques & Phases*. London: Humphreys, 1909. xii, 315 pp.
"Swinblake: A Prophetic Book, with Zarathrusts," 91-102; an imaginary conversation with several poets, among them Yeats.

49. ROWLEY, ROSEMARY: "Prayer for My Son," *Hibernia*, 4 Mar 1977, 25.
Parody of that poem.

50. [RUSSELL, GEORGE WILLIAM]: "Our Cycle Expert and the Literary Drama," *Irish Homestead*, 3 June 1899, 392-93.
The cycle expert is Yeats; extracts from his new drama, *The Countess of the Wheel*, are included.

51. SCHLAU, HANK: "A Coole Evening or The Foundation of the Abbey Theatre," *Gorey Detail*, [1] (1977), 11.

52. SEALY, DOUGLAS: "Aids to Immortality: Seven Parodies," *Dubliner*, 2:2 (Summer 1963), 29-34.
These are parodies on the subject of Leda and the Swan, written in the manner of contemporary Irish poets. A postcript by Rudi Holzapfel (pp. 34-35) answers Yeats's question "Did she put on his knowledge with his power?"

53. SEAMAN, OWEN: *Borrowed Plumes*. Westminster: Constable, 1902. viii, 179 pp.
"Mr. George Moore," 173-75; a parody of a letter from Moore to Yeats.

54. *Secret Springs of Dublin Song*. Dublin: Talbot Press / London: Unwin, 1918. xi, 51 pp.
This collection of anonymous parodies was edited by either Susan L. Mitchell, who signed the preface, or by Ernest A. Boyd, who says so in his own copy, now in the Houghton Library at Harvard. Contains the following Yeats parodies:
Seumas O'Sullivan: "The Wild Dog Compares Himself to a Swan," 14.
AE: "Ideal Poems: (2) Y...s," 26.
Oliver St. John Gogarty: "From *The Queen's Threshold*," 27; "The Old Man Refreshing Himself in the Morning," 29; "A Lament for George Moore," 47-48.

55. SMILES, SAM: Competition No. 814, *NSt*, 22 Sept 1945, 202-3.
Conditions: "The Tate Gallery has reopened. Competitors are invited to write 16 lines, welcoming the pictures back to London, in the style of *Don Juan* or of W. B. Yeats." Answers by Thomas Bodkin ("Down by the Salley Gardens"), Terence Melican (in the

later ballad style), and L. E. J. ("The Man Who Dreamed of Faeryland").

56. SQUIRE, JOHN COLLINGS: *Collected Parodies.* London: Hodder & Stoughton, [1921]. vii, 238 pp.
"How They Do It: No. 6. Numerous Celts," 64; reprinted from *NSt,* 24 May 1913, 212. See also HF71.

57. ——— (ed): *Apes and Parrots: An Anthology of Parodies.* London: Jenkins, 1928. 309 pp.
Harry Graham: "The Cockney of the North," 239-40; a parody of "The Lake Isle of Innisfree."

58. STODART-WALKER, ARCHIBALD: *The Moxford Book of English Verse, 1340-1913.* London: Nash, 1913. 192 pp.
"W. B. Y**ts," 188; a parody of "The Lake Isle of Innisfree."

59. T[HOMAS], D[YLAN] M[ARLAIS]: "In Borrowed Plumes," *Swansea Grammar School Magazine,* 27:1 (Apr 1930), 25-26.
Parody on the theme of Miss Muffett in Yeats's manner.

60. THOMAS, DYLAN, and JOHN DAVENPORT: *The Death of the King's Canary.* With an introduction by Constantine FitzGibbon. London: Hutchinson, 1976. x, 145 pp.
"Elegy. By Fergus O'Hara," 4-5.

61. UNTERMEYER, LOUIS: *Collected Parodies.* NY: Harcourt, Brace, 1926. xiv, 324 pp.
"William Butler Yeats Gives a Symbolically Keltic Version of 'Three Wise Men of Gotham,'" 12; reprinted from *"——— and Other Poets."* NY: Holt, 1916. 121 pp. (pp. 20-21).

62. VILLON, FRANÇOIS: *The Legacy and Other Poems.* Translated by Peter Dale. London: Agenda Editions, 1971. 27 pp. (Agenda Editions. 1.)
"Ballade: A Modern Version," 20, is a pastiche of Yeats phrases.

63. W., A. M.: "Shadows of the Celtic Night (With Apologies to W. B. Mystic Symbol)," *Leader,* 31 Oct 1903, 150-51.

64. ———: "On the King's Threshold," *Leader,* 9 Apr 1904, 102-4.

65. ———: "The Artful Dodger," *Leader,* 9 Dec 1911, 415-16.
A silly attack on Yeats in form of a play scene ("Scene--Outside the Abbey. Time--The Celtic Twilight. Enter Constable Yeats of the Art Division, D.M.P.").

66. ———: "A Talk between Yeats and Goldsmith," *Leader,* 30 Mar 1912, 155.
Satirical skit ("'Tis Bill the Pensioner, I know, / The man who runs the Wild West Show").

67. WILLIAMS, WILLIAM CARLOS: "Lillian," *American Prefaces,* 8:4 (Summer 1943), 296.
A parody of "Down by the Salley Gardens."

68. WODDIS, ROGER: *The Woddis Collection.* London: Barrie & Jenkins, 1979. 96 pp.
"The Hero (After W. B. Yeats): On the Birmingham Pub Bombings of November 21, 1974," 27; a parody of "The Song of Wandering

Aengus." See also HF7.

69. WOLFE, HUMBERT: *Lampoons*. London: Benn, 1925. 109 pp.
"'W. B. Yeats' by W. H. Davies," 89. "'W. H. Davies' by W. B. Yeats," 91.

70. X., O.: "Kleinbier, the Poet: A Literary Portrait," *New Ireland R*, 2:12 (Feb 1895), 803-7.
A satirical sketch of Yeats, who appears as W. B. Kleinbier.

71. ZARANKA, WILLIAM (ed): *Brand-X Poetry: A Parady [sic] Anthology*. London: Picador, 1984. xxviii, 418 pp.
Yeats parodies appear on pp. 294-99: G. K. Chesterton: "Old King Cole" (HF9); Arthur Guiterman: "Mavrone" (not on Yeats at all); J. C. Squire: "The Celtic Lyric" and "Numerous Celts" (HF71); W. Zaranka: "Parachuting Thoor Ballylee"; Anthony C. Deane: "The Cult of the Celtic" (HF13); Robert Peters: "Crazy Bill to the Bishop."

See also BA19, BB116, CA38, CB54, 234, CD471, 660, 818, 1063, 1205, 1321, DB89, HD164.

I INDEXES

IA Index of Names

IB Index of Institutions

IC Index of Collections

This section comprises only books published or edited anonymously, other anonymous texts, as well as anthologies, collections and encyclopedias with or without editor. For reasons of space I do not list the titles of all monographs referred to in this bibliography.

ID Index of Yeats's Works

This index does not list analyses of single poems or of single books of poetry (see section DD), plays (see section EE), fiction and *On the Boiler* (see section FA), as well as of *Per Amica Silentia Lunae* and *A Vision* (see section FC).

IE Index of Selected Subjects

IF Index of Periodicals and Selected Series

IG Index of Chronology

This index of dates of publication does not include the entries in section HC and does not list the reviews of books *on* Yeats.

1882

AA6, 7

1885

BB249

1886

EE389

1887

CB242, CE187, G1

1888

BC19, CD1203, CE12, G1149-53, 1266, HD83

1889

CB489, CD1436, DB170, G2-25, 27-30, 1154-55, HD153

1890

CC225, CE351, G26

1891

CD232, G31, 32, 34-38, 40, 41, 1156-60

1892

AC68, BB27, BC3, 7, BF1, 2, CB354, CD1203, DD55, EE145, G33, 39, 41, 43-46, 48-50, 52-60, 1161-63, 1267-71

1893

BB245, BE1, BF3-5, CB490, CE33, 470, FE70, G42, 47, 51, 54, 72, 73, 1164-70, HD83

1894

BB52, BC3, 15, 17, CB279, 412, 544, CE287, 289, 359, EE372, 374,

1895

1896

1897

1898

1899

1900

1901

1902

1903

1912

1913

1914

1915

1916

1917

1918

1919

1926

BB105, BF170-74, BG154, CB98, 313, 486, 504, CD923, 931, CE167, 250, 275, CF10, DB137, DD298, DE29, EE133, 208, 321, 324, 325, 371, 419, FC65, FD4, 6, G447, 470, 472, 476, 478-82, 484, 489, 499, 502, 505, 1358

1927

BB28, BE112a, CB314, 477, CC301, CD276, 365, 815, 825, 1076, CE214, DB1, DD54, 120, 249, DE74, 134, EB1, 102, EE326, 384, 391-92, 401, G259, 483, 485-88, 490-95, 497-98, 500, 501, 503, 506-14, 516, 1358, HD103, HF6, 32

1928

AC58, BB66, 257, BE113-15, BG47, 133, CB128, 293, 300, 397, 514, CC194, CD498, 656, 891, 929, CE57, 99, 234, 316, CF31, DB12, DC146, 159, 338, DD292, DE29, 38, 55, EE1, 11, 337, 444, EG69, 71, FD8, 26, 42, 83, 85, G504, 515, 517-28, 530-33, 535, 539-47, 549-50, 1359-61, 1375, HF19, 57

1929

BB16, 49, 56, 128, 163, 197, BG65, 144, CB32, 230, 271, 361, 395, 527, CC255, CD139, 1288, CE161, CF28, DB60, 164, DE96, EB5, 52, 93, 98, 138, EC39, ED7, EE155, 241, 242, 245-48, 394, 508, EF93, 98, EG19, FC4, FE41, FG5, G529, 534, 536, 538, 548, 551-53, 559, 561-62, 1363-64, 1374, HE8

193-

BB24

1930

AC24, AE102, BG41, CB94, CD754, 801, 859, 929, CE23, 48, DB238, 256, DC299, DD261, 742, EE114, 243, 249, 556, 559, 564, EG44, FA6, G496, 554-55, 557-58, 560, HD58, HF15, 59

1931

AC78, BB97, 134, 200, 211, BC8, BE116-119, CA34, 70, CB76, 154, 527, CD521, 868, CE36, 127, 371, 436, DC336, DE78, 131, EE48, 49, 51, 237-38, 240, 317, 318, 563, EG36, 46, 56, FD21, FE81, G556, HF5, 41

1932

AC81, BA19, BB34, 60, 166, BE120-33, BF175-82, BG183, 188, CB355, CC284, CD12, 997, CE129, 358, 467, CF16, CG1-7, 9, 11-13, 15, 16, DB140, 150, DD256, DE126, EE557, 560-61, EG64, FC14, FD13, G563-64, 1362, HD18

1933

1934

1935

1936

1937

1938

1939

194–

1940

1941

1942

1943

1944

1945

1946

1947

1948

1949

195–

1950

1951

1952

1953

1954

1955

1956

1957

1958

1959

1960

1961

1962

1963

1964

1965

1966

1967

1968

1969

197–

1970

1971

1972

1973

1974

1975

1976

1977

1978

1979

1980

1981

1982

1983

1984

1985

1986

1987

1988

Darmstadt-Urbana-Freiburg-Bamberg, 1961-1989